PEARSON

COMMON CORE

Literature

THE AMERICAN EXPERIENCE

PEARSON

HOBOKEN, NEW JERSEY • BOSTON, MASSACHUSETTS
CHANDLER, ARIZONA • GLENVIEW, ILLINOIS

Acknowledgments

Grateful acknowledgment is made to the following for copyrighted material:

Advancement Project "10 Things Every Florida Poll Worker Should Know" from http://www. advancementproject.org. Used by permission.

Archaeology Magazine "A Community's Roots" by Samir S. Patel from http://www.archaeology.org. Copyright © 2006 by the Archaeological Institute of America. Used by permission.

Arte Publico Press "The Latin Deli: An Ars Poetica" by Judith Ortiz Cofer from *The Latin Deli.* Used with permission from the publisher of "The Americas Review" (Copyright © 1992 Arte Publico Press-University of Houston).

The James Baldwin Estate "The Rockpile" is collected in *Going to Meet the Man,* © 1965 by James Baldwin. Copyright renewed. Published by Vintage Books. Used by arrangement with the James Baldwin Estate.

Susan Bergholz Literary Services "Antojos" by Julia Alvarez from *Antojos.* Copyright © 1991 by Julia Alvarez. Later published in slightly different form in *How the Garcia Girls Lost Their Accents,* Copyright © 1991 by Julia Alvarez. Published by Plume, an imprint of Dutton Signet, a division of Penguin USA, Inc., and originally in hardcover by Algonquin Books of Chapel Hill. "Straw into Gold: The Metamorphosis of the Everyday" by Sandra Cisneros from *The Texas Observer.* Copyright © 1987 by Sandra Cisneros. First published in *The Texas Observer,* September 1987. Used by permission of Susan Bergholz Literary Services, New York, NY and Lamy, NM. All rights reserved.

BOA Editions Limited "The Gift" by Li-Young Lee from Rose. Copyright © 1986 by Li-Young Lee. All rights reserved. "Study the Masters" by Lucille Clifton from *Blessing the Boats: New and Selected Poems 1988–2000.* Copyright © 2000 by Lucille Clifton. Used with the permission of BOA Editions, Ltd. www.boaeditions.org.

Brooks Permissions "The Explorer" by Gwendolyn Brooks from *Blacks.* Used by permission of Brooks Permissions. Copyright © 1991 by Gwendolyn Brooks, published by Third World Press, Chicago.

The California Council for the Humanities "California Council for the Humanities/Our Mission/ Our History" from http://www.calhum.org. Courtesy of the California Council for the Humanities and its California Stories Initiative. Copyright © 2007 by The California Council for the Humanities. Used by permission.

California Department of Water Resources "California Water Plan Highlights" from *Department of Water Resources Bulletin 160-05.* Copyright © 2005 California Department of Water Resources.

California Secretary of State "Poll Worker Advertisement" from www.sos.ca.gov/elections/outreach/posters/pollworker.pdf. Used by permission.

Sandra Dijkstra Literary Agency "Mother Tongue" by Amy Tan from The Joy Luck Club. Copyright © 1989 by Amy Tan. Used by permission of the author and the Sandra Dijkstra Literary Agency. Copyright © 1989 by Amy -Tan. First appeared in *Threepenny Review.*

Doubleday "Cuttings (later)" by Theodore Roethke from Collected Poems of Theodore Roethke. "Cuttings" by Theodore Roethke from *The Collected Poems of Theodore Roethke. The Collected Poems of Theodore Roethke by Theodore Roethke,* copyright © 1946 by Editorial Publications, Inc. Used by permission of Doubleday, a division of Bantam Doubleday Dell Publishing Group.

Richard Erdoes "When Grizzlies Walked Upright" by Modoc Indians from *American History Customized Reader.* Used by permission.

Faber and Faber Limited "Mirror" by Sylvia Plath from *Crossing the Water.* Copyright © 1963 by Ted Hughes. Used by permission.

Farrar, Straus & Giroux, LLC "Losses" by Randall Jarrell from *The Complete Poems by Randall Jarrell.* Copyright © 1969, renewed 1997 by Mary von S. Jarrell. "The Death of the Ball Turret Gunner" by Randall Jarrell from *The Complete Poems of Randall Jarrell.* Copyright © 1969, renewed 1997 by Mary von S. Jarrell. "The First Seven Years" by Bernard Malamud from *The Magic Barrel.* Copyright © 1950, 1958 and copyright renewed 1977, 1986 by Bernard Malamud. "Coyote v. Acme" by Ian Frazier from *Coyote v. Acme.* Copyright © 1996 by Ian Frazier. "One Art" by Elizabeth Bishop from *Geography III.* Copyright © 1979, 1983 by Alice Helen Methfessel. "Filling Station" by Elizabeth Bishop from *The Complete Poems 1927–1979* by Elizabeth Bishop. Copyright © 1979, 1983 by Alice Helen Methfessel. Used by permission of Farrar, Straus and Giroux, LLC.

Florida Master Site File from http://www.flheritage.com. Used by permission.

Fulcrum Publishing "The Earth on Turtle's Back" by Joseph Bruchac and Michael J. Caduto from *Keepers of the Earth: Native American Stories and Environmental Activities for Children,* © 1998. Used by permission of Fulcrum Publishing, Inc.

Georgia State University "Georgia State University's Web Accessibility Policy," copyright © 2006 is used with permission from the University System of Georgia by and on behalf of Georgia State University.

Graywolf Press "Traveling Through the Dark" by William Stafford from *Stories That Could be True: New and Collected Poems.* Copyright 1962, 1998 by the Estate of William Stafford. Used from *The Way It Is: New and Selected Poems* with the permission of Graywolf Press, Saint Paul, Minnesota.

Harcourt, Inc. "Chicago" by Carl Sandburg from *Chicago Poems,* copyright © 1916 by Holt, Rinehart and Winston and renewed 1944 by Carl Sandburg. "Grass" by Carl Sandburg from *Chicago Poems.* Copyright © 1916 BY Holt, Rinehart and Winston and renewed 1944 by Carl Sandburg. "Everyday Use" by Alice Walker from *In Love & Trouble: Stories of Black Women,* copyright © 1973 by Alice Walker. "The Jilting of Granny Weatherall" by Katherine Anne Porter from *Flowering Judas and Other Stories,* copyright © 1930 and renewed 1958 by Katherine Anne Porter. "The Life You Save May Be Your Own" by Flannery O'Connor from *A Good Man is Hard to Find and Other Stories,* copyright © 1953 by Flannery O'Connor and renewed 1981 by Regina O'Connor. "A Worn Path" by Eudora Welty from *A Curtain of Green and Other Stories,* copyright 1941 and renewed in 1969 by Eudora Welty. Used by permission of Harcourt, Inc. This material may not be reproduced in any form or by any means without the prior written permission of the publisher.

HarperCollins Publishers, Inc. From "Dust Tracks on a Road" by Zora N. Hurston. Copyright © 1942 by Zora Neale Hurston; renewed © 1970 by John C. Hurston. "Mirror" by Sylvia Plath from *Crossing the Water.* Copyright © 1963 by Ted Hughes. Originally appeared in The New Yorker. "Where Is Here?" by Joyce Carol Oates. Copyright © 1992 by The Ontario Review, Inc. Used by permission of HarperCollins Publishers. Excerpt from *Black Boy* by Richard Wright. Copyright © 1944, 1945 by Richard Wright.

Harvard University Press "Because I could not stop for Death (#712)", "I heard a Fly buzz—when I died (#465)", "My life closed twice before its close— (#1732)", "The Soul selects her own Society (#303)", "There's a certain Slant of light (#258)", "There is a solitude of space (#1695)", by Emily Dickinson from *The Poems of Emily Dickinson.* Used by permission of the publishers and the Trustees of Amherst College from *The Poems of Emily Dickinson,* Thomas H. Johnson, ed., Cambridge, Mass.: The Belknap Press of Harvard University Press, Copyright (c) 1951, 1955, 1979 by the Presidents and Fellows of Harvard College.

Acknowledgments continue on page R74, which constitutes an extension of this copyright page.

COVER: Alan Copson/JAI/Corbis

Copyright © 2015 Pearson Education, Inc., or its affiliates. All Rights Reserved. Printed in the United States of America. This publication is protected by copyright, and permission should be obtained from the publisher prior to any prohibited reproduction, storage in a retrieval system, or transmission in any form or by any means, electronic, mechanical, photocopying, recording, or likewise. For information regarding permissions, write to Pearson Curriculum Group Rights & Permissions, 221 River Street, Hoboken, New Jersey 07030.

Pearson, Prentice Hall, and Pearson Prentice Hall are trademarks, in the U.S. and/or other countries, of Pearson Education, Inc., or its affiliates.

SAT is a registred trademark of the College Entrance Examination Board. ACT is a trademark owned by ACT, Inc.

Son of Citation Machine® is a trademark of David Warlick & The Landmark Project.

Wikipedia® is a registered trademark of the Wikimedia Foundation, Inc., ‹http://www.wikimediafoundation.org›

Use of the trademarks implies no relationship, sponsorship, endorsement, sale, or promotion on the part of Pearson Education, Inc., or its affiliates.

Common Core State Standards © Copyright 2010. National Governors Association Center for Best Practices and Council of Chief State School Officers. All rights reserved.

PEARSON

ISBN-13:   978-0-13-326823-2
ISBN-10:   0-13-326823-3

1 2 3 4 5 6 7 8 9 10 11 12 13 V057 18 17 16 15 14

VOLUME TWO

PEARSON

COMMON CORE
Literature

THE AMERICAN EXPERIENCE

PEARSON

HOBOKEN, NEW JERSEY • BOSTON, MASSACHUSETTS
CHANDLER, ARIZONA • GLENVIEW, ILLINOIS

Contributing Authors

The contributing authors guided the direction and philosophy of Pearson Common Core Literature. *They helped to build the pedagogical integrity of the program by contributing content expertise, knowledge of the Common Core State Standards, and support for the shifts in instruction the Common Core will bring. Their knowledge, combined with classroom and professional experience, ensures* Pearson Common Core Literature *is relevant for both teachers and students.*

William G. Brozo, Ph.D., is a Professor of Literacy in the Graduate School of Education at George Mason University in Fairfax, Virginia. He earned his bachelor's degree from the University of North Carolina and his master's and doctorate from the University of South Carolina. He has taught reading and language arts in the Carolinas and is the author of numerous articles on literacy development for children and young adults. His books include *To Be a Boy, To Be a Reader: Engaging Teen and Preteen Boys in Active Literacy; Readers, Teachers, Learners: Expanding Literacy Across the Content Areas; Content Literacy for Today's Adolescents: Honoring Diversity and Building Competence; Supporting Content Area Literacy with Technology* (Pearson); and *Setting the Pace: A Speed, Comprehension, and Study Skills Program.* His newest book is *RTI and the Adolescent Reader: Responsive Literacy Instruction in Secondary Schools.* As an international consultant, Dr. Brozo has provided technical support to teachers from the Balkans to the Middle East, and he is currently a member of a European Union research grant team developing curriculum and providing adolescent literacy professional development for teachers across Europe.

Diane Fettrow spent the majority of her teaching career in Broward County, Florida, teaching high school English courses and serving as department chair. She also worked as an adjunct instructor at Broward College, Nova Southeastern University, and Florida Atlantic University. After she left the classroom, she served as Secondary Language Arts Curriculum Supervisor for several years, working with more than 50 of the district's high schools, centers, and charter schools. During her time as curriculum supervisor, she served on numerous local and state committees; she also served as Florida's K–12 ELA content representative to the PARCC Model Content Frameworks Rapid Response Feedback Group and the PARCC K–12 and Upper Education Engagement Group. Currently she presents workshops on the Common Core State Standards and is working with Pearson on aligning materials to the CCSS.

Kelly Gallagher is a full-time English teacher at Magnolia High School in Anaheim, California, where he has taught for twenty-seven years. He is the former co-director of the South Basin Writing Project at California State University, Long Beach, and the author of *Reading Reasons: Motivational Mini-Lessons for Middle and High School; Deeper Reading: Comprehending Challenging Texts, 4–12; Teaching Adolescent Writers;* and *Readicide: How Schools Are Killing Reading and What You Can Do About It.* He is also a principal author of *Prentice Hall Writing Coach* (Pearson, 2012). Kelly's latest book is *Write Like This* (Stenhouse). Follow Kelly on Twitter @KellyGToGo, and visit him at www.kellygallagher.org.

Elfrieda "Freddy' Hiebert, Ph.D., is President and CEO of TextProject, a nonprofit that provides resources to support higher reading levels. She is also a research associate at the University of California, Santa Cruz. Dr. Hiebert received her Ph.D. in Educational Psychology from the University of Wisconsin-Madison. She has worked in the field of early reading acquisition for 45 years, first as a teacher's aide and teacher of primary-level students in California and, subsequently, as a teacher educator and researcher at the universities of Kentucky, Colorado-Boulder, Michigan, and California-Berkeley. Her research addresses how fluency, vocabulary, and knowledge can be fostered through appropriate texts. Professor Hiebert's research has been published in numerous scholarly journals, and she has authored or edited nine books. Professor Hiebert's model of accessible texts for beginning and struggling readers—TExT—has been used to develop numerous reading programs that are widely used in schools. Dr. Hiebert is the 2008 recipient of the William S. Gray Citation of Merit, awarded by the International Reading Association; is a member of the Reading Hall of Fame; and has chaired a group of experts on early childhood literacy who served in an advisory capacity to the CCSS writers.

 Donald J. Leu, Ph.D., is the John and Maria Neag Endowed Chair in Literacy and Technology and holds a joint appointment in Curriculum and Instruction and Educational Psychology in the Neag School of Education at the University of Connecticut. Don is an international authority on literacy education, especially the new skills and strategies required to read, write, and learn with Internet technologies and the best instructional practices that prepare students for these new literacies. He is a member of the Reading Hall of Fame, a Past President of the National Reading Conference, and a former member of the Board of Directors of the International Reading Association. Don is a Principal Investigator on a number of federal research grants, and his work has been funded by the U.S. Department of Education, the National Science Foundation, and the Bill and Melinda Gates Foundation, among others. He recently edited the *Handbook of Research on New Literacies* (Erlbaum, 2008).

 Ernest Morrell, Ph.D., is a professor of English Education at Teachers College, Columbia University, and the president-elect of the National Council of Teachers of English (NCTE). He is also the Director of Teachers College's Harlem-based Institute for Urban and Minority Education (IUME). Dr. Morrell was an award-winning high school English teacher in California, and he now works with teachers and schools across the country to infuse multicultural literature, youth popular culture, and media production into standards-based literacy curricula and after-school programs. He is the author of nearly 100 articles and book chapters and five books, including *Critical Media Pedagogy: Achievement, Production, and Justice in City Schools* and *Linking Literacy and Popular Culture*. In his spare time he coaches youth sports and writes poems and plays.

 Karen Wixson, Ph.D., is Dean of the School of Education at the University of North Carolina, Greensboro. She has published widely in the areas of literacy curriculum, instruction, and assessment. Dr. Wixson has been an advisor to the National Research Council and helped develop the National Assessment of Educational Progress (NAEP) reading tests. She is a former member of the IRA Board of Directors and co-chair of the IRA Commission on RTI. Recently, Dr. Wixson served on the English Language Arts Work Team that was part of the Common Core State Standards Initiative.

 Grant Wiggins, Ed.D., is the President of Authentic Education in Hopewell, New Jersey. He earned his Ed.D. from Harvard University and his B.A. from St. John's College in Annapolis. Grant consults with schools, districts, and state education departments on a variety of reform matters; organizes conferences and workshops; and develops print materials and Web resources on curricular change. He is perhaps best known for being the co-author, with Jay McTighe, of *Understanding by Design* and *The Understanding by Design Handbook*, the award-winning and highly successful materials on curriculum published by ASCD.

The selections in this book are presented through the lens of three Essential Questions:

What makes American literature American?

What is the relationship between literature and place?

How does literature shape or reflect society?

A Gathering of Voices
Literature of Early America (Beginnings to 1800)

★ INFORMATIONAL TEXT HIGHLIGHTED

PART THREE TEXT SET: **A NATION IS BORN**

DIGITAL ASSETS KEY

These digital resources, as well as audio and the Online Writer's Notebook, can be found at **pearsonrealize.com**.

- Interactive Whiteboard Activities
- Virtual Tour
- Close Reading Notebook
- Video
- Close Reading Tool for Annotating Texts
- Grammar Tutorials

A Growing Nation
Literature of the American Renaissance (1800 to 1870)

PART FOUR TEXT SET: **AMERICAN MASTERS**

DIGITAL ASSETS KEY

These digital resources, as well as audio and the Online Writer's Notebook, can be found at **pearsonrealize.com**.

- Interactive Whiteboard Activities
- Virtual Tour
- Close Reading Notebook
- Video
- Close Reading Tool for Annotating Texts
- Grammar Tutorials

Division, Reconciliation, and Expansion
Literature of the Civil War and the Frontier (1850 to 1914)

DIGITAL ASSETS KEY

These digital resources, as well as audio and the Online Writer's Notebook, can be found at **pearsonrealize.com**.

- Interactive Whiteboard Activities
- Virtual Tour
- Close Reading Notebook
- Video
- Close Reading Tool for Annotating Texts
- G Grammar Tutorials

Disillusion, Defiance, and Discontent
Literature of the Modern Age (1914 to 1945)

PART THREE TEXT SET: **THE HARLEM RENAISSANCE**

DIGITAL ASSETS KEY

These digital resources, as well as audio and the Online Writer's Notebook, can be found at **pearsonrealize.com**.

☐ Interactive Whiteboard Activities

🌐 Virtual Tour

📋 Close Reading Notebook

▶️ Video

🔍 Close Reading Tool for Annotating Texts

Ⓖ Grammar Tutorials

Prosperity and Protest
Literature of the Post-War Era (1945 to 1970)

DIGITAL ASSETS KEY

These digital resources, as well as audio and the Online Writer's Notebook, can be found at **pearsonrealize.com**.

- **Interactive Whiteboard Activities**
- **Virtual Tour**
- **Close Reading Notebook**
- **Video**
- **Close Reading Tool for Annotating Texts**
- **Grammar Tutorials**

New Voices, New Frontiers
Literature of the Contemporary Period (1970 to Present)

PART THREE TEXT SET: **CONTEMPORARY NONFICTION**

DIGITAL ASSETS KEY

These digital resources, as well as audio and the Online Writer's Notebook, can be found at **pearsonrealize.com**.

🖥 **Interactive Whiteboard Activities**

🌐 **Virtual Tour**

📑 **Close Reading Notebook**

▶ **Video**

🔍 **Close Reading Tool for Annotating Texts**

ⓖ **Grammar Tutorials**

Literature

▶ Stories

Adventure Stories

Allegories

Graphic Novels

Humor/Satire

Myths

Realistic Fiction

Science Fiction/Fantasy/Gothic

▶ Drama

Multi-Act Plays

Screenplays

▶ Poetry

Ballads

Informational Text—Literary Nonfiction

▶ Argument

Opinion Pieces

Speeches/Sermons

▶ Exposition

Essays About Art, Literature, and Language

Essays About Ideas

Historical Accounts

Informational Text—Literary Nonfiction

▶ Historical and Literary Background

▶ The American Experience— Reading in the Humanities

▶ Literature in Context—Reading in the Content Areas

▶ World Literature Connections

▶ Literary History

▶ Writing Workshops

▶ Speaking and Listening

▶ Language Study

▶ Text Set Workshops

▶ Test-Taking Practice

The Common Core State Standards will prepare you to succeed in college and your future career. They are separated into four sections—Reading (Literature and Informational Text), Writing, Speaking and Listening, and Language. Beginning each section, the College and Career Readiness Anchor Standards define what you need to achieve by the end of high school. The grade-specific standards that follow define what you need to know by the end of your current grade level.

© Common Core Reading Standards

College and Career Readiness Anchor Standards

Key Ideas and Details

1. Read closely to determine what the text says explicitly and to make logical inferences from it; cite specific textual evidence when writing or speaking to support conclusions drawn from the text.

2. Determine central ideas or themes of a text and analyze their development; summarize the key supporting details and ideas.

3. Analyze how and why individuals, events, and ideas develop and interact over the course of a text.

Craft and Structure

4. Interpret words and phrases as they are used in a text, including determining technical, connotative, and figurative meanings, and analyze how specific word choices shape meaning or tone.

5. Analyze the structure of texts, including how specific sentences, paragraphs, and larger portions of the text (e.g., a section, chapter, scene, or stanza) relate to each other and the whole.

6. Assess how point of view or purpose shapes the content and style of a text.

Integration of Knowledge and Ideas

7. Integrate and evaluate content presented in diverse formats and media, including visually and quantitatively, as well as in words.

8. Delineate and evaluate the argument and specific claims in a text, including the validity of the reasoning as well as the relevance and sufficiency of the evidence.

9. Analyze how two or more texts address similar themes or topics in order to build knowledge or to compare the approaches the authors take.

Range of Reading and Level of Text Complexity

10. Read and comprehend complex literary and informational texts independently and proficiently.

Grade 11 Reading Standards for Literature

Key Ideas and Details

1. Cite strong and thorough textual evidence to support analysis of what the text says explicitly as well as inferences drawn from the text, including determining where the text leaves matters uncertain.

2. Determine two or more themes or central ideas of a text and analyze their development over the course of the text, including how they interact and build on one another to produce a complex account; provide an objective summary of the text.

3. Analyze the impact of the author's choices regarding how to develop and relate elements of a story or drama (e.g., where a story is set, how the action is ordered, how the characters are introduced and developed).

Craft and Structure

4. Determine the meaning of words and phrases as they are used in the text, including figurative and connotative meanings; analyze the impact of specific word choices on meaning and tone, including words with multiple meanings or language that is particularly fresh, engaging, or beautiful. (Include Shakespeare as well as other authors.)

5. Analyze how an author's choices concerning how to structure specific parts of a text (e.g., the choice of where to begin or end a story, the choice to provide a comedic or tragic resolution) contribute to its overall structure and meaning as well as its aesthetic impact.

6. Analyze a case in which grasping point of view requires distinguishing what is directly stated in a text from what is really meant (e.g., satire, sarcasm, irony, or understatement).

Integration of Knowledge and Ideas

7. Analyze multiple interpretations of a story, drama, or poem (e.g., recorded or live production of a play or recorded novel or poetry), evaluating how each version interprets the source text. (Include at least one play by Shakespeare and one play by an American dramatist.)

8. (Not applicable to literature)

9. Demonstrate knowledge of eighteenth-, nineteenth-, and early-twentieth-century foundational works of American literature, including how two or more texts from the same period treat similar themes or topics.

Range of Reading and Level of Text Complexity

10. By the end of grade 11, read and comprehend literature, including stories, dramas, and poems, in the grades 11–CCR text complexity band proficiently, with scaffolding as needed at the high end of the range.

Grade 11 Reading Standards for Informational Text

Key Ideas and Details

1. Cite strong and thorough textual evidence to support analysis of what the text says explicitly as well as inferences drawn from the text, including determining where the text leaves matters uncertain.

2. Determine two or more central ideas of a text and analyze their development over the course of the text, including how they interact and build on one another to provide a complex analysis; provide an objective summary of the text.

3. Analyze a complex set of ideas or sequence of events and explain how specific individuals, ideas, or events interact and develop over the course of the text.

Craft and Structure

4. Determine the meaning of words and phrases as they are used in a text, including figurative, connotative, and technical meanings; analyze how an author uses and refines the meaning of a key term or terms over the course of a text (e.g., how Madison defines *faction* in *Federalist* No. 10).

5. Analyze and evaluate the effectiveness of the structure an author uses in his or her exposition or argument, including whether the structure makes points clear, convincing, and engaging.

6. Determine an author's point of view or purpose in a text in which the rhetoric is particularly effective, analyzing how style and content contribute to the power, persuasiveness, or beauty of the text.

Integration of Knowledge and Ideas

7. Integrate and evaluate multiple sources of information presented in different media or formats (e.g., visually, quantitatively) as well as in words in order to address a question or solve a problem.

8. Delineate and evaluate the reasoning in seminal U.S. texts, including the application of constitutional principles and use of legal reasoning (e.g., in U.S. Supreme Court majority opinions and dissents) and the premises, purposes, and arguments in works of public advocacy (e.g., *The Federalist,* presidential addresses).

9. Analyze seventeenth-, eighteenth-, and nineteenth-century foundational U.S. documents of historical and literary significance (including The Declaration of Independence, the Preamble to the Constitution, the Bill of Rights, and Lincoln's Second Inaugural Address) for their themes, purposes, and rhetorical features.

Range of Reading and Level of Text Complexity

10. By the end of grade 11, read and comprehend literary nonfiction in the grades 11–CCR text complexity band proficiently, with scaffolding as needed at the high end of the range.

© Common Core Writing Standards

College and Career Readiness Anchor Standards

Text Types and Purposes

1. Write arguments to support claims in an analysis of substantive topics or texts, using valid reasoning and relevant and sufficient evidence.

2. Write informative/explanatory texts to examine and convey complex ideas and information clearly and accurately through the effective selection, organization, and analysis of content.

3. Write narratives to develop real or imagined experiences or events using effective technique, well-chosen details, and well-structured event sequences.

Production and Distribution of Writing

4. Produce clear and coherent writing in which the development, organization, and style are appropriate to task, purpose, and audience.

5. Develop and strengthen writing as needed by planning, revising, editing, rewriting, or trying a new approach.

6. Use technology, including the Internet, to produce and publish writing and to interact and collaborate with others.

Research to Build and Present Knowledge

7. Conduct short as well as more sustained research projects based on focused questions, demonstrating understanding of the subject under investigation.

8. Gather relevant information from multiple print and digital sources, assess the credibility and accuracy of each source, and integrate the information while avoiding plagiarism.

9. Draw evidence from literary or informational texts to support analysis, reflection, and research.

Range of Writing

10. Write routinely over extended time frames (time for research, reflection, and revision) and shorter time frames (a single sitting or a day or two) for a range of tasks, purposes, and audiences.

Grade 11 Writing Standards

Text Types and Purposes

1. Write arguments to support claims in an analysis of substantive topics or texts, using valid reasoning and relevant and sufficient evidence.

    a. Introduce precise, knowledgeable claim(s), establish the significance of the claim(s), distinguish the claim(s) from alternate or opposing claims, and create an organization that logically sequences claim(s), counterclaims, reasons, and evidence.

    b. Develop claim(s) and counterclaims fairly and thoroughly, supplying the most relevant evidence for each while pointing out the strengths and limitations of both in a manner that anticipates the audience's knowledge level, concerns, values, and possible biases.

    c. Use words, phrases, and clauses as well as varied syntax to link the major sections of the text, create cohesion, and clarify the relationships between claim(s) and reasons, between reasons and evidence, and between claim(s) and counterclaims.

    d. Establish and maintain a formal style and objective tone while attending to the norms and conventions of the discipline in which they are writing.

    e. Provide a concluding statement or section that follows from and supports the argument presented.

2. Write informative/explanatory texts to examine and convey complex ideas, concepts, and information clearly and accurately through the effective selection, organization, and analysis of content.

    a. Introduce a topic; organize complex ideas, concepts, and information so that each new element builds on that which precedes it to create a unified whole; include formatting (e.g., headings), graphics (e.g., figures, tables), and multimedia when useful to aiding comprehension.

    b. Develop the topic thoroughly by selecting the most significant and relevant facts, extended definitions, concrete details, quotations, or other information and examples appropriate to the audience's knowledge of the topic.

    c. Use appropriate and varied transitions and syntax to link the major sections of the text, create cohesion, and clarify the relationships among complex ideas and concepts.

    d. Use precise language, domain-specific vocabulary, and techniques such as metaphor, simile, and analogy to manage the complexity of the topic.

    e. Establish and maintain a formal style and objective tone while attending to the norms and conventions of the discipline in which they are writing.

    f. Provide a concluding statement or section that follows from and supports the information or explanation presented (e.g., articulating implications or the significance of the topic).

3. Write narratives to develop real or imagined experiences or events using effective technique, well-chosen details, and well-structured event sequences.

    a. Engage and orient the reader by setting out a problem, situation, or observation and its significance, establishing one or multiple point(s) of view, and introducing a narrator and/or characters; create a smooth progression of experiences or events.

b. Use narrative techniques, such as dialogue, pacing, description, reflection, and multiple plot lines, to develop experiences, events, and/or characters.

c. Use a variety of techniques to sequence events so that they build on one another to create a coherent whole and build toward a particular tone and outcome (e.g., a sense of mystery, suspense, growth, or resolution).

d. Use precise words and phrases, telling details, and sensory language to convey a vivid picture of the experiences, events, setting, and/or characters.

e. Provide a conclusion that follows from and reflects on what is experienced, observed, or resolved over the course of the narrative.

Production and Distribution of Writing

4. Produce clear and coherent writing in which the development, organization, and style are appropriate to task, purpose, and audience.

5. Develop and strengthen writing as needed by planning, revising, editing, rewriting, or trying a new approach, focusing on addressing what is most significant for a specific purpose and audience.

6. Use technology, including the Internet, to produce, publish, and update individual or shared writing products in response to ongoing feedback, including new arguments or information.

Research to Build and Present Knowledge

7. Conduct short as well as more sustained research projects to answer a question (including a self-generated question) or solve a problem; narrow or broaden the inquiry when appropriate; synthesize multiple sources on the subject, demonstrating understanding of the subject under investigation.

8. Gather relevant information from multiple authoritative print and digital sources, using advanced searches effectively; assess the strengths and limitations of each source in terms of the task, purpose, and audience; integrate information into the text selectively to maintain the flow of ideas, avoiding plagiarism and overreliance on any one source and following a standard format for citation.

9. Draw evidence from literary or informational texts to support analysis, reflection, and research.

a. Apply *grades 11–12 Reading standards* to literature (e.g., "Demonstrate knowledge of eighteenth-, nineteenth-, and early-twentieth-century foundational works of American literature, including how two or more texts from the same period treat similar themes or topics").

b. Apply *grades 11–12 Reading standards* to literary nonfiction (e.g., "Delineate and evaluate the reasoning in seminal U.S. texts, including the application of constitutional principles and use of legal reasoning [e.g., in U.S. Supreme Court Case majority opinions and dissents] and the premises, purposes, and arguments in works of public advocacy [e.g., *The Federalist*, presidential addresses]").

Range of Writing

10. Write routinely over extended time frames (time for research, reflection, and revision) and shorter time frames (a single sitting or a day or two) for a range of tasks, purposes, and audiences.

© Common Core Speaking and Listening Standards

College and Career Readiness Anchor Standards

Comprehension and Collaboration

1. Prepare for and participate effectively in a range of conversations and collaborations with diverse partners, building on others' ideas and expressing their own clearly and persuasively.

2. Integrate and evaluate information presented in diverse media and formats, including visually, quantitatively, and orally.

3. Evaluate a speaker's point of view, reasoning, and use of evidence and rhetoric.

Presentation of Knowledge and Ideas

4. Present information, findings, and supporting evidence such that listeners can follow the line of reasoning and the organization, development, and style are appropriate to task, purpose, and audience.

5. Make strategic use of digital media and visual displays of data to express information and enhance understanding of presentations.

6. Adapt speech to a variety of contexts and communicative tasks, demonstrating command of formal English when indicated or appropriate.

Grade 11 Speaking and Listening Standards

Comprehension and Collaboration

1. Initiate and participate effectively in a range of collaborative discussions (one-on-one, in groups, and teacher-led) with diverse partners on *grades 11–12 topics, texts, and issues,* building on others' ideas and expressing their own clearly and persuasively.

   a. Come to discussions prepared, having read and researched material under study; explicitly draw on that preparation by referring to evidence from texts and other research on the topic or issue to stimulate a thoughtful, well-reasoned exchange of ideas.

   b. Work with peers to promote civil, democratic discussions and decision-making, set clear goals and deadlines, and establish individual roles as needed.

   c. Propel conversations by posing and responding to questions that probe reasoning and evidence; ensure a hearing for a full range of positions on a topic or issue; clarify, verify, or challenge ideas and conclusions; and promote divergent and creative perspectives.

   d. Respond thoughtfully to diverse perspectives; synthesize comments, claims, and evidence made on all sides of an issue; resolve contradictions when possible; and determine what additional information or research is required to deepen the investigation or complete the task.

2. Integrate multiple sources of information presented in diverse formats and media (e.g., visually, quantitatively, orally) in order to make informed decisions and solve problems, evaluating the credibility and accuracy of each source and noting any discrepancies among the data.

3. Evaluate a speaker's point of view, reasoning, and use of evidence and rhetoric, assessing the stance, premises, links among ideas, word choice, points of emphasis, and tone used.

Presentation of Knowledge and Ideas

4. Present information, findings, and supporting evidence, conveying a clear and distinct perspective, such that listeners can follow the line of reasoning, alternative or opposing perspectives are addressed, and the organization, development, substance, and style are appropriate to purpose, audience, and a range of formal and informal tasks.

5. Make strategic use of digital media (e.g., textual, graphical, audio, visual, and interactive elements) in presentations to enhance understanding of findings, reasoning, and evidence, and to add interest.

6. Adapt speech to a variety of contexts and tasks, demonstrating a command of formal English when indicated or appropriate. (See grades 11–12 Language standards 1 and 3 for specific expectations.)

Common Core Language Standards

College and Career Readiness Anchor Standards

Conventions of Standard English

1. Demonstrate command of the conventions of standard English grammar and usage when writing or speaking.

2. Demonstrate command of the conventions of standard English capitalization, punctuation, and spelling when writing.

Knowledge of Language

3. Apply knowledge of language to understand how language functions in different contexts, to make effective choices for meaning or style, and to comprehend more fully when reading or listening.

Vocabulary Acquisition and Use

4. Determine or clarify the meaning of unknown and multiple-meaning words and phrases by using context clues, analyzing meaningful word parts, and consulting general and specialized reference materials, as appropriate.

5. Demonstrate understanding of figurative language, word relationships, and nuances in word meanings.

6. Acquire and use accurately a range of general academic and domain-specific words and phrases sufficient for reading, writing, speaking, and listening at the college and career readiness level; demonstrate independence in gathering vocabulary knowledge when considering a word or phrase important to comprehension or expression.

Grade 11 Language Standards

Conventions of Standard English

1. Demonstrate command of the conventions of standard English grammar and usage when writing or speaking.
   a. Apply the understanding that usage is a matter of convention, can change over time, and is sometimes contested.
   b. Resolve issues of complex or contested usage, consulting references (e.g., *Merriam-Webster's Dictionary of English Usage, Garner's Modern American Usage*) as needed.

2. Demonstrate command of the conventions of standard English capitalization, punctuation, and spelling when writing.
   a. Observe hyphenation conventions.
   b. Spell correctly.

Knowledge of Language

3. Apply knowledge of language to understand how language functions in different contexts, to make effective choices for meaning or style, and to comprehend more fully when reading or listening.

   a. Vary syntax for effect, consulting references (e.g., Tufte's *Artful Sentences*) for guidance as needed; apply an understanding of syntax to the study of complex texts when reading.

Vocabulary Acquisition and Use

4. Determine or clarify the meaning of unknown and multiple-meaning words and phrases based on *grades 11–12 reading and content*, choosing flexibly from a range of strategies.

   a. Use context (e.g., the overall meaning of a sentence, paragraph, or text; a word's position or function in a sentence) as a clue to the meaning of a word or phrase.

   b. Identify and correctly use patterns of word changes that indicate different meanings or parts of speech (e.g., *conceive, conception, conceivable*).

   c. Consult general and specialized reference materials (e.g., dictionaries, glossaries, thesauruses), both print and digital, to find the pronunciation of a word or determine or clarify its precise meaning, its part of speech, its etymology, or its standard usage.

   d. Verify the preliminary determination of the meaning of a word or phrase (e.g., by checking the inferred meaning in context or in a dictionary).

5. Demonstrate understanding of figurative language, word relationships, and nuances in word meanings.

   a. Interpret figures of speech (e.g., hyperbole, paradox) in context and analyze their role in the text.

   b. Analyze nuances in the meaning of words with similar denotations.

6. Acquire and use accurately general academic and domain-specific words and phrases, sufficient for reading, writing, speaking, and listening at the college and career readiness level; demonstrate independence in gathering vocabulary knowledge when considering a word or phrase important to comprehension or expression.

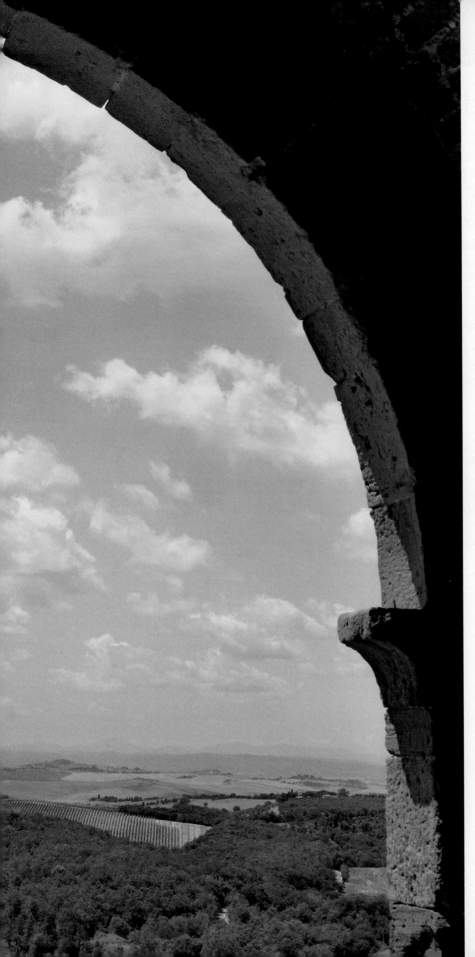

COMMON CORE WORKSHOPS

- BUILDING ACADEMIC VOCABULARY

- WRITING AN OBJECTIVE SUMMARY

- COMPREHENDING COMPLEX TEXTS

- ANALYZING ARGUMENTS

- CONDUCTING RESEARCH

 **Common Core
State Standards**

**Reading Literature 2, 10
Reading Informational Text 2, 4,
5, 6, 8
Writing 1.a, 1.b, 1.e, 7, 8, 9, 9.b
Language 6**

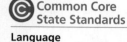

Building Academic Vocabulary

Academic vocabulary is the language used in school, on standardized tests, and—often—in the business world. Academic terms are more formal and specific than the informal vocabulary most people use among friends and family members. Success in school and later in work requires a clear understanding of different types of academic language. The Common Core State Standards require that you acquire and use grade-appropriate academic words and phrases.

Technical Domain-Specific Academic Vocabulary The literary concepts you will learn throughout this book are one type of academic language. These words are specific to the content area—the subject or discipline—of literature. Other disciplines, such as social studies, the sciences, mathematics, and the arts, have their own academic vocabularies. Some content-area words cross disciplines, or have different meanings when applied to different areas of study.

Technical words are an even more specialized type of domain-specific academic vocabulary. These are words and phrases, such as the following, that identify a precise element in the content area and usually do not appear in other disciplines:

Science: pipette; genome
Music: clef; libretto

Critical Reading and Thinking Terms Many academic terms define modes of thinking, discussing, or writing about ideas. In this book, these words appear in the Critical Reading questions at the ends of the selections. Such academic terms also appear in instructions and writing prompts.

A Note on Etymology

Etymology is the branch of linguistics that deals with word origins and the development of languages. Etymologists trace the history of a word in its own language, and then to even earlier sources in other, more ancient languages. Knowledge of a word's etymology will contribute to your understanding of its meaning and help you determine the meaning of other words that share its history. Etymological information for content-area words appears in the charts on the following pages.

Common Core State Standards

Language

6. Acquire and use accurately general academic and domain-specific words and phrases, sufficient for reading, writing, speaking, and listening at the college and career readiness level; demostrate independence in gathering vocabulary knowledge when considering a word or phrase important to comprehension or expression.

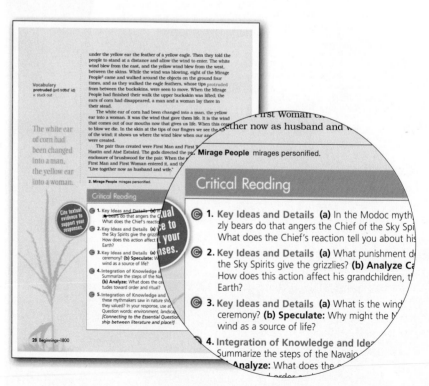

Technical Domain-Specific Academic Vocabulary

Knowledge of technical content-area academic words, and the roots and affixes that compose them, will help you in all of your school courses. As you review the charts below, recognize words that apply to content areas other than those specified here.

Technical Domain-Specific Academic Vocabulary: Science

Term	Meaning	Root/Affix
Accelerate	*v.* increase speed	Latin root -*celer*- = swift Words with the same root: accelerator *n.*; celerity *n.*
Catalyst	*n.* something that acts to bring about a result	Latin root -*cata*- = down; away Words with the same root: cataclysm *n.*; catapult *n.*
Chlorophyll	*n.* green pigment found in plant cells	Greek root -*chloro*- = green Words with the same root: chlorine *n.*; chlorosis *n.*
Chromosome	*n.* strand of proteins that carries the genes of a living creature	Greek prefix *chromo*- = color; pigment Words with the same prefix: chromatic *adj.*; chromate *n.*
Cytoplasm	*n.* colorless substance of a cell; outside the nucleus	Greek suffix -*plasm* = molded; formed Words with the same suffix: bioplasm *n.*; protoplasm *n.*
Entropy	*n.* lack of order that increases over time in a system	Greek root -*tropos*- = turning; deviation Words with the same root: tropical *adj.*; trophy *n.*; heliotrope *n.*
Enzyme	*n.* chemical substance produced by living cells that causes changes in other chemicals	Greek suffix -*zyme* = leavening (an agent that causes fermentation) Words with the same suffix: vitazyme *n.*; microzyme *n.*
Mitosis	*n.* method of cell division	Greek suffix -*osis* = action; process Words with the same suffix: prognosis *n.*; psychosis *n.*
Thermometer	*n.* instrument for measuring temperature	Greek root -*therme*- = hot Words with the same root: thermonuclear *adj.*; thermostat *n.*
Viscous	*adj.* having a thick and sticky fluid consistency	Latin prefix *visco*- = sticky Words with the same prefix: viscometer *n.*; viscosity *n.*

Ordinary Language: Ice cubes placed in water will begin to **break down.**

Academic Language: Ice cubes placed in water will begin the process of **entropy.**

Exploring Academic Vocabulary: Science

The word *thermometer* combines the Greek roots -*therme*-, which means "heat," and -*metr*-, which means "measure." Using this knowledge, determine the meaning of the following words derived from the same roots:

dynameter   odometer   hypothermia   thermography

Then, use a dictionary to confirm the definitions you proposed. If a general dictionary is not sufficient, consult a specialized science dictionary to find the information you need. Explain how the meaning of each word relates to those of its Greek origins.

Technical Domain-Specific Academic Vocabulary: Mathematics

Term	Meaning	Root/Affix
Correlate	*v.* show mutual relationship between items	Latin prefix *cor-* = together; with Words with the same prefix: correspond *v.*; corrosion *n.*
Exponent	*n.* symbol placed above and to the right of a number or letter to show how many times that quantity is to be multiplied by itself	Latin suffix *-ponent* = to put; place; set Words with the same suffix: component *n.*; proponent *n.*
Inflection	*n.* change of a curve or arc from convex to concave or the reverse	Latin root *-flectere-* = to bend Words with the same root: reflection *n.*; deflect *v.*
Logarithm	*n.* power to which a base must be raised to produce a given number	Greek prefix *logos-* = word; speech; reason Words with the same prefix: logic *n.*; logotype *n.*
Statistics	*n.* numerical facts or data	Latin root *-stat-* = condition; position; state Words with the same root: statistical *adj.*; static *adj.*
Permutation	*n.* one of the ways in which a set of things can be arranged or ordered	Latin root *-mutare-* = change Words with the same root: mutable *adj.*; mutation *n.*
Estimate	*v.* calculate approximately	Middle French root *-estimer-* = value; appraise Words with the same root: estimation *n.*; esteem *v.*
Graphic	*adj.* relating to the use of diagrams, graphs, curves	Greek root *-graph-* = writing; drawing Words with the same root: telegraph *n.*; biography *n.*; autograph *n.*
Configure	*v.* construct; arrange	Latin root *-figura-* = shape; form; figure Words with the same root: disfigure *v.*; effigy *n.*

Ordinary Language: We arranged the numerical information in different charts.

Academic Language: We incorporated statistical data into charts.

Exploring Academic Vocabulary: Mathematics

The word *correlate* is built on the Latin prefix *cor-* (also *com-* or *con-*), which means "with" or "together." Using this knowledge, determine the meaning of the following words derived from the same prefix:

correspond   **concert**   **compress**   **congruent**

Then, use an online or print dictionary to confirm the definitions you proposed. Explain how the meaning of each word relates to that of its Latin ancestor.

Technical Domain-Specific Academic Vocabulary: Social Studies

Term	Meaning	Root/Affix
Corporation	*n.* organization of many people authorized to act as a single person	Latin root -*corpus*- = body Words with the same root: corporeal *adj.*; incorporate *v.*
Demography	*n.* study of human populations	Greek prefix *demos*- = people Words with the same prefix: demographic *n.*; democracy *n.*
Economy	*n.* system by which a country's money and goods are used and produced	Greek suffix -*nomy* = law; received knowledge Words with the same suffix: economy *n.*; taxonomy *n.*
Invest	*v.* give money to a company in order to receive a profit	Latin root -*vestire*- = dress; clothe Words with the same root: vestment *n.*; investigation *n.*
Admiral	*n.* high-ranking Naval officer	Arabic root -*amir*- = leader Words with the same root: emirate *n.*; admiralship *n.*
Curfew	*n.* law requiring a population to stay indoors at a stated hour	Old French root -*covrir*- = to cover Words with the same root: covert *adj.*; coverlet *n.*
Lieutenant	*n.* someone who substitutes for another person of greater authority	Old French root -*lieu*- = place Word with the same root: milieu *n.*
Absolutism	*n.* system of government in which a ruler has unlimited power	Latin prefix *ab*- = away; from Words with the same prefix: absolve *v.*
Civic	*adj.* of a city, citizens, or citizenship	Latin root -*civ*- = citizen Words with the same root: civilian *n.*; civilization *n.*

Ordinary Language:
The government urges citizens to **put money into** local businesses.

Academic Language:
The government urges citizens to **invest in** local businesses.

Exploring Academic Vocabulary: Social Studies

The word *economy* is built on the Greek suffix –*nomy*, which means "law; body of received knowledge." Using this knowledge, determine the meaning of the following words derived from the same suffix:

taxonomy   **autonomy**   **astronomy**   **gastronomy**

Then, use an online or print dictionary to confirm the definitions you proposed. Explain how the meaning of each word relates to that of its Greek ancestor.

Technical Domain-Specific Academic Vocabulary: Technology

Term	Meaning	Root/Affix
Gigabyte	*n.* unit of storage capacity in a computer system, equal to 1,073,741,824 bytes	Greek prefix *giga-* = giant Words with the same prefix: gigahertz *n.*; gigantic *adj.*
Macro	*n.* single computer instruction that represents a sequence of operations	Greek prefix *macro-* = long, tall, deep, large Words with the same prefix: macrobiotic *adj.*; macrocosm *n.*
Pixel	*n.* smallest unit of an image on a television or computer screen	Old French suffix *-el* = small one Words with the same suffix: satchel *n.*; model *n.*
Processor	*n.* central part of a computer that does the calculations needed to deal with the information it is given	from Latin root *-cedere-* = to go Words with the same root: proceed *v.*; recede *v.*
Simulation	*n.* situation that produces conditions that are not real but appear real	Latin root *-sim-* = like derived through Indo-European base *sem-/som-* = same; as one Words with the same root: ensemble *v.*; simultaneous *adj.*
Streaming	*n.* method of transmitting data so that it can be delivered and received in a steady stream	German root *-strom-* = current; river Words with the same root: mainstream *n.*; streamline *v.*
Transmitter	*n.* equipment that sends out radio or television signals	Latin prefix *trans-* = across Words with the same prefix: transportation *n.*; transcontinental *adj.*
Debug	*v.* find and correct defects	Latin prefix *de-* = down; from Words with the same prefix: defuse *v.*; defrost *v.*
Export	*v.* in computers, to save data in a format usable by another program	Latin root *-portare-* = to carry Words with the same root: import *v.*; airport *n.*
Binary	*adj.* made up of two parts or things; twofold	Latin root *-bin-* = together; double Words with the same root: binocular *n.*; binomial *n.*

Ordinary Language:
I asked the technician to **remove the defects from** my computer.

Academic Language:
I asked the technician to **debug** my operating system.

Exploring Academic Vocabulary: Technology

The word *simulation* comes from the Latin root *-sim-*, which means "like." This Latin root derives from the Indo-European base *sem-/som-*, which means "same; as one." Using your knowledge of these origins, determine the meaning of the following words derived from the same roots:

resemble   **facsimile**   **verisimilitude**   **semblance**

Then, use a dictionary to confirm the definitions you proposed. Explain how the meaning of each word relates to that of its Indo-European base.

Technical Domain-Specific Academic Vocabulary: The Arts

Term	Meaning	Root/Affix
Allegro	*adv.* faster than allegretto but not so fast as presto	Latin root -*alacer-/-alacris-* = lively; brisk Words with the same root: allegretto *adj.*; *adv.*; alacrity *n.*
Alignment	*n.* arrangement in a straight line	Old French root -*lignier-* = to line Words with the same root: align *v.*; realign *v.*
Craftmanship	*n.* skill used in making handmade objects	Middle English suffix -*schipe*; derived through Anglian suffix -*scip* = state; condition; quality Words with the same suffix: friendship *n.*; dictatorship *n.*
Decrescendo	*n.* gradual decrease in volume	Old French *creissant*; derived through Latin root -*crescere-* = come forth; spring up; grow; thrive Words with the same root: crescent *n.*; increase *v.*
Baritone	*n.* male singing voice lower than a tenor and higher than a bass	Latin root -*tonus-* = sound; tone Words with the same root: monotone *n.*; intonation *n.*
Medium	*n.* material or technique used in art	Latin root -*medius-* = middle Words with the same root: media *n.*; mediate *v.*; median *adj.*
Musicality	*n.* sensitivity to, knowledge of, or talent for music	Latin suffix -*ity* = quality; state; degree Words with the same suffix: normality *n.*; publicity *n.*
Technique	*n.* method or procedure in rendering an artistic work	Indo-European prefix *tek-* = shape; make Words with the same prefix: technical *adj.*; technician *n.*
Tempo	*n.* speed at which a composition is performed	Latin root -*tempus-* = time Words with the same root: temporal *adj.*; temporary *adj.*

> **Ordinary Language:**
> The dancers moved in a perfectly **straight line.**
>
> **Academic Language:**
> The dancers moved in perfect **alignment** on stage.

Exploring Academic Vocabulary: The Arts

The word *craftsmanship* is built on the Anglian suffix -*scip*, which means "state, condition, quality." Using this knowledge, determine the meaning of the following words derived from the same suffix:

musicianship   **readership**   **friendship**   **partnership**

Then, use an online or print dictionary to confirm the definitions you proposed. Explain how the meaning of each word relates to that of its Anglian ancestor.

Vocabulary Across Content Areas

You might recognize words that apply to content areas other than those specified in the charts on the previous pages. For example, notice how the word *accelerator* relates to two different content areas:

Science: accelerator *n.* nerve or muscle that speeds up a body function

Automotive Technology: accelerator *n.* device, such as the foot throttle of an automobile, for increasing the speed of a machine.

While the objects referred to in each definition are different, both of their functions relate to the Latin root *-celer-,* meaning "swift." As you read texts for school, recognize similarities in roots or affixes among words in different content areas. This will help you better understand specific terms and make meaningful connections among topics.

Academic Vocabulary: Critical Thinking Terms

Throughout this book, you will encounter academic vocabulary related to the process of critical thinking. Unlike content-area vocabulary, these words apply equally in all school studies. Being familiar with these academic vocabulary words will be useful as you approach high-stakes standardized tests such as the SAT and ACT. Academic vocabulary will also aid you as you encounter business materials in the workplace.

Term (verb form)	Meaning	Root/Affix
Advocate	Speak or write in support of	Latin root *-voc-* = speak; call Related words: advocate *n.;* advocacy *n.*
Anticipate	Prepare for or signal something	Latin prefix *ante-* = before Related words: anticipatory *adj.;* anticipation *n.*
Arrange	Put into order or sequence	Old French root *-rang-* = rank Related words: arrangement *n.*
Assess	Determine importance, size, or value	Latin root *-sed-/-sess-* = sit Related words: assessment *n.*
Categorize	Place in related groups	Greek prefix *kata-/cata-* = down; against Related words: category *n.;* categorical *adj.*
Compare	Examine in order to discover similarities	Latin root *-par-* = equal Related words: comparison *n.;* comparable *adj.*
Conclude	Determine through logical reasoning	Latin root *-clud-* = shut Related words: conclusion *n.;* conclusive *adj.*
Contrast	Examine in order to discover differences	Latin prefix *con-/com-* = with; together Related words: contrastable *adj.*
Debate	Discuss opposing reasons; argue	French root *-batre-* = to beat Related words: debatable *adj.*
Deduce	Infer from a general principle	Latin root *-duc-* = to lead Related words: deduction *n.;* deductive *adj.*
Defend	Maintain or support in the face of argument	Latin root *-fend-* = to strike; push Related words: defense *n.;* defendant *n.*

Term (verb form)	Meaning	Root/Affix
Describe	Represent in words	Latin root -scrib- = to write Related words: description n.; descriptive adj.
Design	Create; fashion or construct according to plan	Latin root -sign- = to mark Related words: design n.; designer n.
Devise	Form in the mind by new combinations of ideas; invent	Latin root -vid- = to separate Related words: devisable adj.
Differentiate	Recognize a difference	Latin suffix -ate = act Related words: different adj.; differentiation n.
Evaluate	Determine significance, worth, or condition through careful study	Old French root -val- = worth; value Related words: evaluation n.; evaluative adj.
Format	Arrange according to a design or plan	Latin root -form- = form, shape Related words: format n.; formation n.
Generalize	Draw a larger principle from details	Latin root -genus- = stock; kind Related words: generalization n.
Hypothesize	Develop a theory about	Greek prefix hypo- = under, beneath Related words: hypothesis n.; hypothetically adv.
Illustrate	Give examples that support an idea	Latin root -lus- = brighten; illuminate Related words: illustration n.; illustrative adj.
Interpret	Explain the meaning of	Latin root -inter- = between Related words: interpretation n.; interpreter n.
Investigate	Make a systematic examination	French root -vestige- = mark; trace; sign Related words: investigation n.; investigative adj.
Paraphrase	Express in one's own words what another person has said or written	Greek prefix para- = beside Related words: paraphraser n.
Predict	Foretell on the basis of observation, experience, or reason	Latin root -dic- = speak, tell, say Related words: prediction n.; predictable adj.
Refute	Prove an argument or statement false or wrong	Latin root -fut- = beat Related words: refutable adj.; refutably adv.
Sort	Put in place according to kind, class, or nature	Old French root -sortir- = allot; assort Related words: sorter n.
Speculate	Use evidence to guess what might happen	Latin root -spec- = look at; view Related words: speculation n.; speculative adj.
Structure	Create a general plot or outline	Latin root -struct- = to build; assemble Related words: structure n.; structural adj.
Validate	Prove to be factual or effective	Latin root -val- = be strong Related words: valid adj.; validity n.

Ordinary Language: She **explained the meaning of** the story's symbols.

Academic Language: She **interpreted** the meaning of the story's symbols.

Writing an Objective Summary

The ability to write objective summaries is important in college course work and in many careers, such as journalism, business, law, and research work. Writing an effective objective summary involves recording the key ideas of a text as well as demonstrating your understanding.

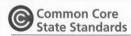

Common Core State Standards

Reading Informational Text
2. Determine two or more central ideas of a text and analyze their development over the course of the text, including how they interact and build on one another to provide a complex analysis; provide an objective summary of the text.

Reading Literature
2. Determine two or more themes or central ideas of a text and analyze their development over the course of the text, including how they interact and build on one another to produce a complex account; provide an objective summary of the text.

Characteristics of an Objective Summary

An effective objective summary is a concise overview of a text. Following are important elements of an objective summary:

- It is **focused,** relaying the main theme or central idea of a text. It includes specific, relevant details that support that theme or central idea, and it leaves out unnecessary supporting details.

- It is **brief,** although the writer must be careful to balance brevity and thoroughness and not misrepresent the text by eliminating important parts.

- It is **accurate** and captures the essence of the longer text it is describing.

- It is **objective.** The writer should refrain from inserting his or her own opinions, reactions, or personal reflections into the summary.

Remember that an objective summary is *not* a collection of sentences or paragraphs copied from the original source. It is *not* a long retelling of every event, detail, or point in the original text. Finally, a good summary does *not* include evaluative comments, such as the reader's overall opinion of or reaction to the selection.

Checklist for Writing an Objective Summary

Before writing an objective summary, be sure you are well acquainted with the text.

- **Understand the entire passage.** You must clearly understand the text's meaning, including any advanced or technical terminology. In your summary, refer to details from the beginning, middle, and end of the text.

- **Prioritize ideas and details.** Determine the main or central ideas of a text and identify the key supporting details. Make sure you recognize which details are less important so that you do not include them in your objective summary.

- **Identify the author's audience and purpose.** Knowing what the author intended to accomplish in the text as well as what audience it was designed to reach will help you summarize accurately.

INFORMATIONAL TEXT

Model Objective Summary

Note the key elements of an effective objective summary, called out in the sidenotes. Then, write an objective summary of a text you have recently read. Review your summary, and delete any unnecessary details, opinions, or evaluations.

Summary of "The Open Window"

"The Open Window," by Saki, ~~the pen name of H.H. Munro~~, is a short story about a nervous man by the name of Framton Nuttel. Set in rural England during the Victorian-Edwardian period, the story tells of a visit that Mr. Nuttel makes to a neighboring estate.

Mr. Framton Nuttel, who has been ordered by his physicians to rest and avoid excitement, has gone to the country for a "nerve cure." His sister has given him letters of introduction to various acquaintances of hers. Framton reluctantly takes his sister's suggestion and calls on the Sappletons.

When Framton arrives at the Sappleton estate, he is met by Mrs. Sappleton's fifteen-year-old niece, Vera. ~~She is quite a character.~~ Vera points to an open window and relates a tragic tale. She tells Framton that exactly three years ago, Mr. Sappleton, Mrs. Sappleton's two younger brothers, and their spaniel went out to hunt, leaving through that very window, and met their death in the bog. Their bodies have never been recovered. The niece explains that her aunt keeps the window open because she expects her husband and brothers to return some day.

Soon thereafter, Mrs. Sappleton enters the room and begins to speak of the hunters. Alarmed, Framton tries to change the topic. He rambles on about his health, noticing that Mrs. Sappleton keeps glancing out of the open window. Suddenly, Mrs. Sappleton exclaims, "Here they are at last!" Framton sees a look of horror in Vera's eyes. Then he turns and sees the figures of three men and a dog approaching. He frantically gathers his belongings and runs away.

As Mr. Sappleton enters through the window, he greets his wife and inquires about the man he spotted running away. Mrs. Sappleton responds that Framton Nuttel was a strange man who dashed off as if he had seen a ghost.

Then Vera mentions that Mr. Nuttel was most likely frightened by the dog. She says that he confided in her that he was once terrified by a pack of wild dogs.

The story ends with this sentence: "Romance at short notice was her specialty."

Eliminate unnecessary details.

A one-sentence synopsis highlighting the theme or central idea of the story can be an effective start to a summary.

This sentence states the writer's opinion and should not be included in an objective summary.

Relating the development of the text in chronological order makes a summary easy to follow.

The writer quotes the final sentence of the story because it is the key to understanding the plot.

Comprehending Complex Texts

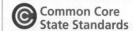
Common Core State Standards

Reading Literature 10. By the end of grade 11, read and comprehend literature, including stories, dramas, and poems, in the grades 11-CCR text complexity band proficiently, with scaffolding as needed at the high end of the range.

During the final years of high school, you will be required to read increasingly complex texts in preparation for college and the workplace. A complex text features one or more of the following qualities:

- challenging vocabulary
- long, complex sentences
- figurative language
- multiple levels of meaning
- unfamiliar settings and situations

The selections in this textbook provide you with a range of readings in many genres. Some of these texts will fall within your comfort zone, but others will be, and should be, more challenging. In order to comprehend and interpret complex texts, practice the reading strategies described here.

Strategy 1: Multidraft Reading

Good readers develop the habit of rereading texts in order to comprehend them completely. To fully understand a text, try this multidraft reading strategy:

1st Reading
The first time you read a text, read to gain its basic meaning. If you are reading a narrative text, look for the basics of the plot: what is happening, and to whom. If the text is nonfiction, look for central ideas and key supporting details. If you are reading poetry, first read to get a sense of who the speaker is. Also take note of the setting and situation.

2nd Reading
During your second reading of a text, focus on the artistry or effectiveness of the writing. Also take note of text structures and organizational patterns. Think about why the author made those choices and what effects they created. Then, examine the author's creative uses of language and the effects of that language. For example, has the author used rhyme, figurative language, or words with negative connotations? If so, to what effect?

3rd Reading
After your third reading, compare and contrast the text with others of its kind you have read. For example, you might compare poems from a certain time period or compare poems written by a single author. Evaluate the text's overall effectiveness and its central idea or theme.

Independent Practice

As you read this sonnet by William Shakespeare, practice the multidraft reading strategy by completing a chart like the one below.

Sonnet 27

Weary with toil, I haste me to my bed,
The dear repose for limbs with travel tired;
But then begins a journey in my head
To work my mind, when body's work's expired:
For then my thoughts—from far where I abide—
Intend a zealous pilgrimage to thee,
And keep my drooping eyelids open wide,
Looking on darkness which the blind do see:
Save that my soul's imaginary sight
Presents thy shadow to my sightless view,
Which, like a jewel hung in ghastly night,
Makes black night beauteous, and her old face new.
   Lo! thus, by day my limbs, by night my mind,
   For thee, and for myself, no quiet find.

Multidraft Reading Chart

	My Understanding
1st Reading Look for key ideas and details that unlock basic meaning.	
2nd Reading Read for deeper meanings. Look for ways in which the author used text structures and language to create effects.	
3rd Reading Read to integrate your knowledge and ideas. Connect the text to others of its kind and to your own experience.	

Strategy 2: Close Read the Text

Complex texts require close reading—a careful analysis of word choices, phrases, and sentences. An awareness of literary techniques and elements, such as allusion, symbolism, analogy, and text structure, contributes to a deep understanding of a complex text. However, a starting point for close reading is comprehension, which is the foundation for interpretation and analysis. Use the following tips to comprehend the text:

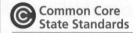

Common Core State Standards

Reading Informational Text
4. Determine the meaning of words and phrases as they are used in a text, including figurative, connotative, and technical meanings; analyze how an author uses and refines the meaning of a key term or terms over the course of a text (e.g., how Madison defines *faction* in *Federalist* No. 10).

Tips for Close Reading

1. **Break down long sentences** into parts. Look for the subject of the sentence and its verb. Then identify which parts of the sentence modify, or give more information about, its subject.

2. **Reread passages.** When reading complex texts, be sure to reread passages to confirm that you understand their meaning.

3. **Look for context clues.** There are several types of context clues, such as the following:

   a. Restatement of an idea. For example, in the sentence below, "to help . . . understand" restates the verb *clarify.*
   The sportscaster tried to **clarify** the offsides violation <u>to help</u> the spectators <u>understand</u> the referee's call.

   b. Definition of sophisticated words. In this sentence, the words *goes beyond* define the verb *transcends.*
   The watercolor painting **transcends,** or <u>goes beyond</u>, the expectations of the viewers.

   c. Examples of concepts and topics.
   The menu listed <u>green beans, corn, and okra</u> as side dishes.

   d. Contrasts of ideas and topics. In the following sentence, the example helps you understand the meaning of *claustrophobia.*
   Adam is **claustrophobic;** he <u>cannot tolerate</u> <u>being cooped up in small spaces.</u>

4. **Identify pronoun antecedents.** If long sentences contain pronouns, reread the text to make sure the pronoun references are clear. The pronoun *its* in the following sentence refers to Yosemite National Park, not to the U.S. government.
   Yosemite National Park was set aside by the U.S. government so people could enjoy **its** natural beauty.

5. **Look for conjunctions,** such as *and, or, yet,* and *however,* to understand relationships between ideas.

6. **Paraphrase,** or restate in your own words, passages of difficult text in order to check your understanding. Remember that a paraphrase is essentially a word-for-word restatement of an original text; it is not a summary.

INFORMATIONAL TEXT

Close-Read Model

As you read this document, take note of the sidenotes that model ways to unlock meaning in the text.

from "The Perils of Indifference" by Elie Weisel

What is indifference? Etymologically, the word means "no difference." A strange and unnatural state in which the lines blur between light and darkness, dusk and dawn, crime and punishment, cruelty and compassion, good and evil.

> This list of contrasts helps you to know that "compassion" is the opposite of "cruelty."

What are its courses and inescapable consequences? Is it a philosophy? Is there a philosophy of indifference conceivable? Can one possibly view indifference as a virtue? Is it necessary at times to practice it simply to keep one's sanity, live normally, enjoy a fine meal and a glass of wine, as the world around us experiences harrowing upheavals?

> Look for antecedents. The abstract noun *indifference* is referred to by the pronouns *its* and *it*.

Of course, indifference can be tempting—more than that, seductive. It is so much easier to look away from victims. It is so much easier to avoid such rude interruptions to our work, our dreams, our hopes. It is, after all, awkward, troublesome, to be involved in another person's pain and despair. Yet, for the person who is indifferent, his or her neighbors are of no consequence. And, therefore, their lives are meaningless. Their hidden or even visible anguish is of no interest. Indifference reduces the other to an abstraction. . . .

> Search for context clues. The words in blue are context clues that help you infer the meaning of the word that appears in yellow.

In a way, to be indifferent to that suffering is what makes the human being inhuman. Indifference, after all, is more dangerous than anger and hatred. Anger can at times be creative. One writes a great poem, a great symphony, one does something special for the sake of humanity because one is angry at the injustice that one witnesses. But indifference is never creative. Even hatred at times may elicit a response. You fight it. You denounce it. You disarm it. Indifference elicits no response. Indifference is not a response.

Indifference is not a beginning, it is an end. And, therefore, indifference is always the friend of the enemy, for it benefits the aggressor—never his victim, whose pain is magnified when he or she feels forgotten. The political prisoner in his cell, the hungry children, the homeless refugees—not to respond to their plight, not to relieve their solitude by offering them a spark of hope is to exile them from human memory. And in denying their humanity we betray our own.

> Break down this long sentence into parts. The text highlighted in yellow conveys the basic meaning of the sentence. The text highlighted in blue provides additional information.

> The examples highlighted in pink help you understand that the word *plight* means "bad situation."

Indifference, then, is not only a sin, it is a punishment. And this is one of the most important lessons of this outgoing century's wide-ranging experiments in good and evil. . . .

Strategy 3: Ask Questions

Be an attentive reader by asking questions as you read. Throughout this text, we have provided questions for you following each selection. Those questions are sorted into three basic categories that build in sophistication and lead you to a deeper understanding of the texts you read. Here is an example from this text:

Some questions are about **Key Ideas and Details** in the text. To answer these questions, you will need to locate and cite explicit information in the text or draw inferences from what you have read.

Some questions are about **Craft and Structure** in the text. To answer these questions, you will need to analyze how the author developed and structured the text. You will also look for ways in which the author artfully used language and how those word choices impacted the meaning and tone of the work.

Critical Reading

1. **Key Ideas and Details (a)** Why does Equiano blame the illness aboard the ship on the "improvident avarice" of the traders? **(b) Infer:** How do the white crewmen view their captives? **(c) Draw Conclusions:** What does the treatment of the slaves reveal about the captors' attitudes toward human life?

2. **Key Ideas and Details (a)** How does Equiano's age affect his experiences during the voyage? **(b) Infer:** How do you think he felt about his experience compared to the fate of other captives on the ship?

3. **Craft and Structure** How does Equiano show his great zest for life despite his assertion that he wants to die? Provide examples from the selection.

4. **Integration of Knowledge and Ideas** What do you think the public of Equiano's day learned about the "accursed trade" of slavery that it may not have known before reading this narrative? In your response, use at least two of these Essential Question vocabulary words: *awareness, compassion, inhumane, avarice.* *[Connecting to the Essential Question: How does literature shape or reflect society?]*

Cite textual evidence to support your responses.

Some questions are about the **Integration of Knowledge and Ideas** in the text. These questions ask you to evaluate a text in many different ways, such as comparing texts, analyzing arguments in the text, and using many other methods of thinking critically about a text's ideas.

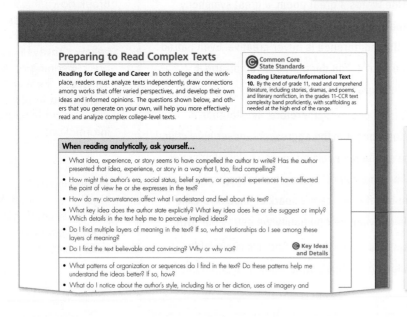

Preparing to Read Complex Texts

Reading for College and Career In both college and the workplace, readers must analyze texts independently, draw connections among works that offer varied perspectives, and develop their own ideas and informed opinions. The questions shown below, and others that you generate on your own, will help you more effectively read and analyze complex college-level texts.

Common Core State Standards

Reading Literature/Informational Text
10. By the end of grade 11, read and comprehend literature, including stories, dramas, and poems, and literary nonfiction, in the grades 11-CCR text complexity band proficiently, with scaffolding as needed at the high end of the range.

When reading analytically, ask yourself...

- What idea, experience, or story seems to have compelled the author to write? Has the author presented that idea, experience, or story in a way that I, too, find compelling?
- How might the author's era, social status, belief system, or personal experiences have affected the point of view he or she expresses in the text?
- How do my circumstances affect what I understand and feel about this text?
- What key idea does the author state explicitly? What key idea does he or she suggest or imply? Which details in the text help me to perceive implied ideas?
- Do I find multiple layers of meaning in the text? If so, what relationships do I see among these layers of meaning?
- Do I find the text believable and convincing? Why or why not?

Key Ideas and Details

- What patterns of organization or sequences do I find in the text? Do these patterns help me understand the ideas better? If so, how?
- What do I notice about the author's style, including his or her diction, uses of imagery and

As you read independently, ask similar types of questions to ensure that you fully enjoy and comprehend texts you read for school and for pleasure. Look for and use the sets of questions provided for Independent Reading at the end of each unit.

EXEMPLAR TEXT

Model

Following is an example of a complex text. The call-out boxes show
sample questions that an attentive reader might ask while reading.

from *1776* by David McCullough

On January 14, two weeks into the new year, George Washington wrote one of the
most forlorn, despairing letters of his life. He had been suffering sleepless nights in
the big house by the Charles. "The reflection upon my situation and that of this
army produces many an uneasy hour when all around me are wrapped in sleep,"
he told the absent Joseph Reed. "Few people know the predicament we are in."

Filling page after page, he enumerated the same troubles and woes he had
been reporting persistently to Congress for so long, and that he would report
still again to John Hancock that same day. There was too little powder, still no
money. . . . So many of the troops who had given up and gone home had, against
orders, carried off muskets that were not their own that the supply of arms was
depleted to the point where there were not enough for the new recruits.

Sample questions:

**Key Ideas and
Details** What central
idea is revealed in this
passage?

Craft and Structure
Why does David
McCullough use a direct
quotation? What image
does Washington create
with the words
"wrapped in sleep"?

**Integration of
Knowledge and
Ideas** What insight
does this passage
give you about
Washington as a
general? What insight
do you gain about the
Revolutionary War?

INFORMATIONAL TEXT

Independent Practice

Write three to five questions you might ask yourself as you read this passage from a
speech delivered by James Bryant Conant, president of Harvard University, in 1940.

from "What Are We Arming to Defend?" by James Bryant Conant

. . . The history of this republic has been unique. And the uniqueness of our way
of life rests not so much on constitutional democracy as on our social
system—a system which is the embodiment of the golden mean of which I
speak. I believe that fundamentally it is this unique form of society that we are
really arming to defend. I believe that the ambition of every thoughtful citizen of
this republic is to assist in keeping inviolate the free way of life which has
developed on this continent in the last two hundred years.

. . . Let me examine for a moment the phrase "social mobility," for this is the
heart of my argument. If large numbers of young people can develop their own
capacities irrespective of the economic status of their parents, then social
mobility is high. . . . Such is the American ideal.

Analyzing Arguments

The ability to evaluate an argument, as well as the ability to make one, are critical skills for success in college and in the workplace.

What Is an Argument?

An *argument* is a presentation of a controversial or debatable issue. In a formal, written argument, the writer logically supports a particular belief, conclusion, or point of view. A good argument is supported with sufficient and valid reasoning and evidence.

Purposes of Argument

There are three main purposes for writing a formal argument:

- to change the reader's mind about an issue
- to convince the reader to accept what is written
- to motivate the reader to take action, based on what is written

Elements of Argument

Claim (assertion)—what the writer is trying to prove
Example: Students should wear uniforms to public high schools.

Grounds (evidence)—the support used to convince the reader
Example: Students will focus less on what they and others are wearing and more on learning.

Justification—the link between the grounds and the claim; why the grounds are credible
Example: The purpose of school is to learn.

Evaluating Claims

When reading or listening to an argument, critically assess the claims that are made. Analyze the argument to identify claims that are based on fact or that can be proved true. Also evaluate evidence that supports the claims. If there is little or no reasoning or evidence provided to support the claims, the argument may not be sound or valid.

Analyzing and Evaluating Structures

As you read an argument, look for ways in which the writer uses structures. For example, the organizational structure, or order in which the writer presents claims and evidence, focuses and shapes the argument. Stylistic structural choices such as repetition and parallel structure can lend emotional power to an argument. Evaluate whether those structures strengthen or detract from the argument's effectiveness.

**Common Core
State Standards**

Language
6. Acquire and use accurately general academic and domain-specific words and phrases, sufficient for reading, writing, speaking, and listening at the college and career readiness level; demonstrate independence in gathering vocabulary knowledge when considering a word or phrase important to comprehension or expression.

Reading Informational Text
5. Analyze and evaluate the effectiveness of the structure an author uses in his or her exposition or argument, including whether the structure makes points clear, convincing, and engaging.
6. Determine an author's point of view or purpose in a text in which the rhetoric is particularly effective, analyzing how style and content contribute to the power, persuasiveness, or beauty of the text.

Model Argument

from *The American Forests* by John Muir

The forests of America, however slighted by man, must have been a great delight to God; for they were the best he ever planted. The whole continent was a garden, and from the beginning it seemed to be favored above all the other wild parks and gardens of the globe . . .

The introduction shows Muir's fondness for the forests of America.

. . . In the settlement and civilization of the country, bread more than timber or beauty was wanted; and in the blindness of hunger, the early settlers . . . regarded God's trees as only a larger kind of pernicious weeds, extremely hard to get rid of. Accordingly, with no eye to the future, these pious destroyers waged interminable forest wars; chips flew thick and fast; trees in their beauty fell crashing by millions, smashed to confusion, and the smoke of their burning has been rising to heaven more than two hundred years. . . . Thence still westward the invading horde of destroyers called settlers made its fiery way over the broad Rocky Mountains, felling and burning more fiercely than ever, until at last it has reached the wild side of the continent, and entered the last of the great aboriginal forests on the shores of the Pacific . . . Clearing has surely now gone far enough; soon timber will be scarce, and not a grove will be left to rest in or pray in. . . .

As evidence, Muir describes the millions of trees that have been destroyed over the past 200 years.

Muir draws the logical conclusion for the audience that the trees will be gone if they continue to be cut down at the current rate.

Every other civilized nation in the world has been compelled to care for its forests, and so must we if waste and destruction are not to go on to the bitter end . . .
[T]he forest plays an important part in human progress, and . . . the advance in civilization only makes it more indispensable. . . . But the state woodlands are not allowed to lie idle. On the contrary, they are made to produce as much timber as is possible without spoiling them. In the administration of its forests, the state righteously considers itself bound to treat them as a trust for the nation as a whole, and to keep in view the common good of the people for all time. . . .

Muir cites other civilized nations' actions as evidence that we must do the same.

Justification: Sustainable and productive forests are a national resource kept for the common good of the people.

Notwithstanding all the waste and use which have been going on unchecked like a storm for more than two centuries, it is not yet too late, though it is high time, for the government to begin a rational administration of its forests. . . .

In their natural condition, or under wise management, keeping out destructive sheep, preventing fires, selecting the trees that should be cut for lumber, and preserving the young ones and the shrubs and sod of herbaceous vegetation, these forests would be a never failing fountain of wealth and beauty. . . .

Claim: It is time for the government to begin a rational administration of the forests.

The outcries we hear against forest reservations come mostly from thieves who are wealthy and steal timber by wholesale. They have so long been allowed to steal and destroy in peace that any impediment to forest robbery is denounced as a cruel and irreligious interference with "vested rights" . . .

The opposition is addressed and refuted.

The Art of Argument: Rhetorical Devices and Persuasive Techniques

Rhetorical Devices

Rhetoric is the art of using language in order to make a point or to persuade listeners. Rhetorical devices such as the ones listed below are accepted elements of argument. Their use does not invalidate or weaken an argument. Rather, the use of rhetorical devices is regarded as a key part of an effective argument.

Examples of Rhetorical Devices	
Repetition The repeated use of certain words, phrases, or sentences	We are compelled to fight the **injustice** of low wages, the **injustice** of long hours, and the **injustice** of child labor.
Parallelism The repeated use of similar grammatical structures	Children should spend their time **playing active games, reading good books,** and **writing imaginative stories.**
Rhetorical Question Calling attention to the issue by implying an obvious answer	Aren't all people created equal?
Sound Devices The use of alliteration, assonance, rhyme, or rhythm	The savage settlers sowed only the seeds of greed to replace the trees they destroyed.
Simile and Metaphor Comparing two seemingly unlike things or asserting that one thing *is* another	Is **America** a **melting pot** or a **tossed salad**?

Persuasive Techniques

Persuasive techniques are often found in advertisements and in other forms of informal persuasion. Although techniques like the ones below are sometimes found in formal arguments, they should not be regarded as valid evidence.

Persuasive Techniques	
Bandwagon Approach/Anti-Bandwagon Approach Appeals to a person's desire to belong; Encourages or celebrates individuality	Our clothes are as unique as you are.
Emotional Appeal Evokes people's fear, anger, or desire	Soon, all you will see will be strip malls and parking lots.
Endorsement/Testimony Employs a well-known person to promote a product or idea	"I support this just cause. You should too!"
Loaded Language The use of words that are charged with emotion	The child laborers are slaves; their childhoods are owned by the factories.
"Plain Folks" Appeal Shows a connection to everyday, ordinary people	"My parents immigrated to this great land and started a new life."
Hyperbole Exaggerates to make a point	All the money in the world wouldn't solve the problem.

INFORMATIONAL TEXT

Model Speech

The excerpted speech below includes examples of rhetorical devices and persuasive techniques.

from *Strike Against War* by Helen Keller

. . . I think the workers are the most unselfish of the children of men; they toil and live and die for other people's country, other people's sentiments, other people's liberties and other people's happiness! The workers have no liberties of their own; they are not free when they are compelled to work twelve or ten or eight hours a day. They are not free when they are ill paid for their exhausting toil. They are not free when their children must labor in mines, mills and factories or starve, and when their women may be driven by poverty to lives of shame. They are not free when they are clubbed and imprisoned because they go on strike for a raise of wages and for the elemental justice that is their right as human beings. . . .

As civilization has grown more complex the workers have become more and more enslaved, until today they are little more than parts of the machines they operate. Daily they face the dangers of railroad, bridge, skyscraper, freight train, stokehold, stockyard, lumber raft and mine. Panting and training at the docks, on the railroads and underground and on the seas, they move the traffic and pass from land to land the precious commodities that make it possible for us to live. And what is their reward? A scanty wage, often poverty, rents, taxes, tributes and war indemnities. . . .

It is your duty to insist upon still more radical measures. It is your business to see that no child is employed in an industrial establishment or mine or store, and that no worker is needlessly exposed to accident or disease. It is your business to make them give you clean cities, free from smoke, dirt and congestion. It is your business to make them pay you a living wage. It is your business to see that this kind of preparedness is carried into every department on the nation, until everyone has a chance to be well born, well nourished, rightly educated, intelligent and serviceable to the country at all times.

Strike against all ordinances and laws and institutions that continue the slaughter of peace and the butcheries of war. Strike against war, for without you no battles can be fought. Strike against manufacturing shrapnel and gas bombs and all other tools of murder. Strike against preparedness that means death and misery to millions of human beings. Be not dumb, obedient slaves in an army of destruction. Be heroes in an army of construction.

Helen Keller uses parallelism to emphasize her point.

The continued use of repetition gives the speech rhythm and emphasizes her points.

The metaphor compares the workers to the machine parts.

The alliteration gives variety to the speech.

Helen Keller answers the rhetorical question to drive home the irony of the word *reward*.

The continued parallelism and repetition show the increasing passion of her argument.

The repetition in the conclusion calls the audience to action; Keller is now using commands.

The emotional appeal and loaded words add intensity to the argument.

Analyzing Legal Meanings and Reasoning

Reading historical and legal texts requires careful analysis of both the vocabulary and the logical flow of ideas that support a conclusion.

Understanding Legal Meanings

The language of historical and legal documents is formal, precise, and technical. Many words in these texts have specific meanings that you need to understand in order to follow the flow of ideas. For example, the first amendment to the U.S. Constitution states that "Congress shall make no law respecting an establishment of religion, or prohibiting the free exercise thereof; or abridging the freedom of speech, or of the press…" To understand this amendment, it is important to know that in this context *exercise* means "practice," *abridging* means "limiting," and *press* means "media." To understand legal meanings:

- Use your knowledge of word roots to help you understand unfamiliar words. Many legal terms have familiar Greek or Latin roots, prefixes, or suffixes.

- Don't assume that you know a word's legal meaning: use a dictionary to check the meanings of key words to ensure that you are applying the correct meaning.

- Replace difficult words with synonyms to help you follow the logic of the argument.

Delineating Legal Reasoning

Works of public advocacy, such as court decisions, political proclamations, proposed laws, and constitutional amendments, use careful reasoning to support conclusions. These strategies can help outline the basic meanings of these texts:

- State the **purpose** of the document in your own words to help you focus on the writer's primary goal.

- Look for the line of reasoning that supports the **arguments** presented. To be valid and persuasive, key arguments should be backed up by clearly stated logical analysis. Be aware of persuasive techniques, such as citing facts and statistics, referring to expert testimonials, and using emotional language with strong connotations.

- Identify the **premises,** or evidence, upon which a decision rests. In legal texts, premises often include **precedents,** which are earlier examples that must be followed or else specifically overturned. Legal reasoning is usually based on the decisions of earlier trials. Be sure you understand precedents in order to identify how the court arrived at the current decision.

Writing About Legal Meanings

After reading the selection on the next page, write a detailed analysis of the meanings of the words *waive* and *waiver* in the *Miranda* v. *Arizona* decision. Explain the definitions of the terms as they are used in this context and provide an example that illustrates a situation in which a suspect "waives effectuation" of the rights outlined by this Supreme Court decision.

Common Core State Standards

Reading Informational Text

4. Determine the meaning of words and phrases as they are used in a text, including figurative, connotative, and technical meanings; analyze how an author uses and refines the meaning of a key term or terms over the course of a text.

8. Delineate and evaluate the reasoning in seminal U.S. texts, including the application of constitutional principles and use of legal reasoning and the premises, purposes, and arguments in works of public advocacy.

Writing

9. Draw evidence from literary or informational texts to support analysis, reflection, and research.

9.b. Apply grades 11–12 Reading standards to literary nonfiction.

INFORMATIONAL TEXT

Model Court Decision

Note the strategies used to evaluate legal meanings and reasoning in this Supreme Court decision from 1966 regarding the rights of criminal suspects. The court addressed the admissibility of information obtained by police.

from *Miranda* v. *Arizona*, Opinion of the Supreme Court

We dealt with certain phases of this problem recently in *Escobedo* v. *Illinois.* There . . . law enforcement officials took the defendant into custody and interrogated him in a police station for the purpose of obtaining a confession. The police did not effectively advise him of his right to remain silent or of his right to consult with his attorney. Rather, they confronted him with an alleged accomplice who accused him of having perpetrated a murder. When the defendant denied the accusation . . . they handcuffed him and took him to an interrogation room. There, while handcuffed and standing, he was questioned for four hours until he confessed. During this interrogation, the police denied his request to speak to his attorney, and they prevented his retained attorney, who had come to the police station, from consulting with him. At his trial, the State, over his objection, introduced the confession against him. We held that the statements thus made were constitutionally inadmissible. . . .

. . . Our holding will be spelled out with some specificity in the pages which follow, but, briefly stated, it is this: the prosecution may not use statements, whether exculpatory or inculpatory, stemming from custodial interrogation of the defendant unless it demonstrates the use of procedural safeguards effective to secure the privilege against self-incrimination. By custodial interrogation, we mean questioning initiated by law enforcement officers after a person has been taken into custody or otherwise deprived of his freedom of action in any significant way. As for the procedural safeguards to be employed, unless other fully effective means are devised to inform accused persons of their right of silence and to assure a continuous opportunity to exercise it, the following measures are required. Prior to any questioning, the person must be warned that he has a right to remain silent, that any statement he does make may be used as evidence against him, and that he has a right to the presence of an attorney, either retained or appointed. The defendant may waive effectuation of these rights, provided the waiver is made voluntarily, knowingly and intelligently. If, however, he indicates in any manner and at any stage of the process that he wishes to consult with an attorney before speaking, there can be no questioning. Likewise, if the individual is alone and indicates in any manner that he does not wish to be interrogated, the police may not question him. The mere fact that he may have answered some questions or volunteered some statements on his own does not deprive him of the right to refrain from answering any further inquiries until he has consulted with an attorney and thereafter consents to be questioned.

The court cites and describes a **precedent**—an earlier court decision in which a suspect's confession was found inadmissible.

The word root *culp-* means "guilt," as in *culpable.* Context and prefixes combine to show that *exculpatory* means "proving innocence" and *inculpatory* means "proving guilt."

The **purpose** of the decision is stated: to guarantee that a suspect's statements are made in accordance with the rights granted by the U.S. Constitution. This **argument** is detailed and supported in the court decision. The context of the argument is the case summarized in the first paragraph.

Composing an Argument

**Common Core
State Standards**

Writing

1.a. Introduce precise, knowledgeable claim(s), establish the significance of the claim(s), distinguish the claim(s) from alternate or opposing claims, and create an organization that logically sequences claim(s), counterclaims, reasons, and evidence.

1.b. Develop claim(s) and counterclaims fairly and thoroughly, supplying the most relevant evidence for each while pointing out the strengths and limitations of both in a manner that anticipates the audience's knowledge level, concerns, values, and possible biases.

1.e. Provide a concluding statement or section that follows from and supports the argument presented.

Choosing a Topic

As you prepare to write an argument, choose a topic that interests you. The topic should be debatable or controversial to some degree.

Then, check to be sure you can make an arguable claim. Ask yourself:

1. What am I trying to prove? What ideas do I need to get across?
2. Are there people who would disagree with my claim? What counterclaims would they make?
3. Do I have evidence to support my claim? Is my evidence sufficient and relevant?

If you are able to put into words what you want to prove and answered "yes" to questions 2 and 3, you have an arguable claim.

Introducing the Claim and Establishing Its Significance

Before you begin writing, determine how much your audience already knows about your chosen topic. Then, provide only as much background information as necessary. If there are issues surrounding your topic, you will need to clarify them for your audience and narrow the focus to your specific claim. Remember that you are not writing a summary of the issue—you are crafting an argument. Once you have provided context for your argument, you should clearly state your claim, or thesis.

Developing Your Claim with Reasoning and Evidence

Now that you have made your claim, support it with evidence, or grounds, and reasons for your claim. A valid argument should have multiple pieces of evidence to support the claim. Evidence can range from personal experience to researched data or expert opinion. Knowing your audience's knowledge level, concerns, values, and possible biases can help you decide what kind of evidence will have the strongest impact. Make sure your evidence is up to date and comes from a credible source. Be sure to credit your sources.

You should also address the opposing counterclaim within the body of your argument. Consider points you have made or evidence you have provided that a person might challenge. Decide how best to refute these counterclaims. One technique for defusing an opponent's claims is to agree with selected parts of them.

Writing a Concluding Statement or Section

Restate your claim in the conclusion of your argument, and summarize your main points. The goal of a concluding section is to provide a sense of closure and completeness to an argument. Make your concluding statement strong enough to be memorable and to leave the reader thinking.

Practice

Exploring both sides of an issue can be a good way to start planning an argument. Complete a chart like the one below to help you plan your own argument.

Topic: **Issue:** _____ _____	
Claim:	**Counterclaim:**
Grounds (Evidence): 1._____ 2._____ 3._____	**Grounds (Evidence):** 1._____ 2._____ 3._____
Justification: 1._____ 2._____ 3._____	**Justification:** 1._____ 2._____ 3._____

When you have completed the chart and developed your own precise claim, consider the following questions:

1. Who is your audience? What type of evidence can you use to best convince those who do not agree with your claim?

2. Is your evidence strong and difficult to dispute? If not, how can you strengthen it or find better evidence?

3. How will you refute the counterclaim? Are there any parts of the counterclaim you agree with?

Conducting Research

Today, information is plentiful. However, not all information is equally useful, or even accurate. Developing strong research skills will help you locate and utilize the valid, relevant, and interesting information you need.

Short-Term Inquiries and Long-Term Investigations

You will conduct many different kinds of research throughout this program, from brief Internet searches to extended, in-depth projects.

- **Short-term research** can help you answer specific questions about a text or extend your understanding of an idea. You will conduct targeted short-term inquiries on a regular basis.

- **Long-term research** allows you to dive into a topic and conduct a detailed, comprehensive investigation. An organized research plan will help you gather and synthesize information from multiple sources.

Research Topics and Questions

Any research project, whether large or small, needs a clear and concise focus in order to avoid wasting your time and energy.

Narrowing Your Focus Before You Begin Research You can avoid many problems by focusing your research before you begin. For example, you might want to learn more about the American wilderness, but that topic is too broad and vague. If you started researching this subject, you could easily end up overwhelmed by the vast amount of information available. Head off trouble before you begin by thinking of a narrower, more manageable topic that interests you.

Narrowing As You Go Preliminary research can help you refine your topic. Your initial findings can help you choose a specific topic to pursue, such as a person, event, or theme.

Formulating a Question A research question can guide your research toward a specific goal and help you gauge when you have gathered sufficient information. Decide on your question, and refer to it regularly to check that your research is on track. Here are three examples of specific questions that could focus an investigation:

- What features of the American wilderness attracted early explorers and settlers?

- Did early settlers view the wilderness as an obstacle to be overcome or as a resource to be appreciated?

- How do first-person accounts of the early-settlement period reflect attitudes toward Native Americans?

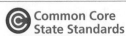

Common Core State Standards

Writing
7. Conduct short as well as more sustained research projects to answer a question (including a self-generated question) or solve a problem; narrow or broaden the inquiry when appropriate; synthesize multiple sources on the subject, demonstrating understanding of the subject under investigation.

8. Gather relevant information from multiple authoritative print and digital sources, using advanced searches effectively; assess the strengths and limitations of each source in terms of the task, purpose, and audience; integrate information into the text selectively to maintain the flow of ideas, avoiding plagiarism and overreliance on any one source and following a standard format for citation.

General Subject

The American Wilderness

Focused Topics

- A writer, journalist, or artist who created works about the American wilderness

- A specific region or geographic feature, such as the Missouri River

- One event, expedition, or law related to the American wilderness

- Depictions of American landscapes in pioneer diaries

Planning Your Research

You will have more success in your longer-term research work if you create and follow a **research plan.** A good plan will include the elements shown in the following chart.

Elements of a Research Plan	
Research Question	Begin with an initial question, but be open to modifying your question as you learn more about your subject.
Source List	Create a list of sources you intend to consult. Plan to use a variety of sources. Add sources to your plan as you discover them. Place a check mark next to sources you have located, and then underline sources you have consulted thoroughly.
Search Terms	Write down terms you plan to investigate using online search engines. Making these decisions before you go online can help you avoid digressions that take you away from your topic.
Deadlines	Break a long-term project into short-term goals in order to avoid stress and achieve success.

Multiple Sources It is important not to rely too heavily on a single source. The creativity and originality of your research depends on how you combine ideas from many places. Plan to include a variety of these resources:

- **Primary and Secondary Resources** Primary resources—including journals, news accounts, autobiographies, pamphlets, documentary footage, and interviews—are texts or media created during the time period you are studying. These first-hand impressions offer authentic perspectives of the time. Secondary resources, such as encyclopedia entries and nonfiction books, interpret and analyze known facts.

- **Print and Digital Resources** The Internet allows fast access to data, but print resources are often edited more carefully. Include both print and digital resources in your research to guarantee that your work is accurate.

- **Media Resources** Documentaries, television programs, podcasts, and museum exhibitions are rich sources of information. Public lectures by people knowledgeable on a topic offer opportunities to hear an expert's thoughts.

- **Original Research** You may wish to conduct original research to include among your sources. For example, you might interview experts or eyewitnesses or conduct a survey.

Online Search Tip Type a word or phrase into a general search engine and you may get thousands of results. Using quotation marks can help you focus a search. Place a phrase in quotation marks to find pages that include exactly that phrase. To limit your search to .edu, .org, or .gov sites, use the search command "site:" followed by the extension. For example, enter "site:.edu" and "Lewis and Clark" and you will get a list of .edu (education) sites that include that phrase.

Finding Authoritative Sources

You need to evaluate your sources to make sure that they will give you information that is both relevant and reliable.

Determining Relevance Not every source you uncover will have information that is related to your investigation. Preview each source to determine its relevance. Scanning a table of contents, a preface, illustration captions, or an index can help you decide whether or not a source will help you answer your research question. When searching for information from magazine or Internet articles, you may come across *abstracts*, which are precise summaries of an article's contents. An abstract is short enough to read carefully and completely. Once you have read it, you can decide whether or not the abstracted article is likely to contain information you can use.

Remember that you do not need to include ideas from every source you consult. Be sure to allow yourself enough time to read and reject information that is not relevant.

Evaluating Reliability You also need to consider whether or not each source provides *accurate* information. Use the following ABC criteria to evaluate any print or digital sources:

- **Authority** Examine the credentials of both the author and the publisher or sponsoring institution. Checking an author's citations in other sources is one way to establish authority. Awards, professional memberships, and other recognitions can also support an author's or a work's credibility. When evaluating Internet sources, prefer those sponsored by educational, nonprofit, or government organizations (which have URLs ending in .edu, .org, or .gov.). Be wary of .com sites, which are commercial or personal.

- **Bias** Most sources strive to be objective, but few are completely without bias. Strong partiality in a source is not always a reason to reject it, though you may want to acknowledge that bias in your analysis. To check for bias, notice sources of funding, including advertising on .com sites. Follow hyperlinks to learn about professional affiliations of writers. These can help you identify possible reasons for biased or selective information.

- **Currency** Use recent sources whenever possible. Outdated content is likely to have been replaced by more recent research. Check the publication date of both print and digital sources. Electronic publications may show that a site has been updated—include both the original date and the most current date in your consideration.

Reliability Checklist

Ask yourself these questions about sources you find.

Authority

- Is the author well-known?
- What are the writer's credentials?
- Does the tone of the writing inspire confidence? Why or why not?

Bias

- Does the author have any obvious biases?
- What is the author's purpose for writing?
- Who is the target audience?

Currency

- When was the work created? Has it been revised?
- Is there more current information available?

Taking Notes

Learning to take complete and thoughtful notes as you research is a key to success. Good notes keep a clear record of your sources and capture ideas and facts. They can also help you summarize.

Notes do not need to be written in complete sentences, but be sure to state your ideas clearly enough so you will understand them when you review and draft.

Index Cards Many researchers find that index cards help them organize information. You will create different types of cards:

Source cards list complete bibliographical information for a source (author, title, place of publication, publisher, date). Create one source card for each source.

Sample Source Card

> **Rhodes, Richard. John James Audubon: The Making of an American.**
> **New York, NY: Alfred A. Knopf, 2004.**

Summary cards provide an overview of main ideas in a section. Write a short form of the source's title and author at the top of the card. Adding a topic can help you organize ideas when you write. Summarize the main idea and significant details of the passage. At the bottom of the card, include the location of the information.

Sample Summary Card

> **Rhodes, Audubon**
>
> **topic: recording nature**
>
> **Chapter 7**
> **Rhodes explains Audubon's big change: He stopped following the tradition of painting birds in stiff poses, started painting them flying.**
>
> **It took him several years to get better at this (not very much formal art training).**
>

pp. 90–106

Quotation cards record an author's exact words. Include the same information as on a summary card, but write down the quotation as it appears. You may note how you might use the quotation in your writing.

Sample Quotation Card

> **Rhodes, Audubon**
>
> **topic: science vs. art**
>
> **Chapter 7**
> **"With his breakthrough to drawing birds in flight, Audubon at twenty-seven abandoned strict illustration and committed himself to expressive art."**
>
> **Use this quote to support the idea that Audubon's bird paintings are not mainly scientific illustrations.**
>

p. 102

Providing Appropriate Citations

To avoid plagiarism, you must give credit for the information and ideas you collect during research. Plagiarism is presenting someone else's words or ideas as your own. Whether plagiarism is intentional or not, it is dishonest and illegal. Avoid it by being careful to cite your sources thoroughly. Follow the format your teacher recommends, such as Modern Language Association (MLA) style.

Deciding What to Cite Common knowledge does not require citation. If a fact appears in three or more sources, it is probably common knowledge. Facts that reflect one person's research or opinion should be cited, as shown in the chart to the right.

Works-Cited List (MLA Style) A works-cited list, or bibliography, must include the following information about each source: the name of the author, editor, and/or translator; title; place and date of publication; publisher.

Model: Works-Cited List

Rhodes, Richard. *John James Audubon: The Making of an American*, New York, NY: Knopf, 2004.

Gebhardt, Kristin, "John James Audubon (1785–1851)," *Museum of Nebraska Art*, 2004. Accessed December 15, 2012.

  http://monet.unk.edu/mona/artexplr/audubon/audubon.html

John James Audubon: Drawn from Nature, Dir. Lawrence R. Hott. Florentine Films/Hott Productions, 2007

Parenthetical Citations (MLA Style) Use parenthetical citations to integrate your research smoothly into your writing. A parenthetical citation appears in the body of your text and briefly identifies the source. The source is fully identified on your works-cited list. You may need to add paraphrases within brackets to place quotations or edited words in context.

Model: Parenthetical Citations

John James Audubon knew that careful observation alone would not be enough to achieve his goal of capturing nature. He needed to find a way "to copy her in her own way, alive and moving!" (Audubon, p. 760) Audubon's early paintings did not satisfy him because he was following the tradition of painting stuffed birds with their wings clamped against their bodies. In May of 1812, he drew a flying whippoorwill. Although it took him many years to perfect his pictures of birds in flight, it was with this "breakthrough [that Audubon]… abandoned strict illustration and committed himself to expressive art." (Rhodes, pp. 101–102)

Common Knowledge

- John James Audubon painted hundreds of birds in their natural habitats.
- Audubon was born in France and moved to the United States when he was 18.
- The first edition of *The Birds of America* was published in 1827.

Facts to be Cited

- Audubon often observed birds in the wild for days before beginning a painting. (Source: Richard Rhodes, *John James Audubon*)
- Audubon used many strategies to sell his work, helping it to reach a wide audience. [Source: Kristin Gebhardt, "John James Audubon (1785–1851)]"

For more information on research and citing sources, see the Writing Workshop on research papers (pp. 664–675) and resource pages on citations (R21–R23).

Practice

Creating a research plan can help you organize a long-term research project. Complete a chart like the one below to plan research and collect details. Begin by choosing a topic that interests you, or use the chart to prepare a research assignment from your classwork. Then, draft a research question that you will answer through investigation.

Topic:

Research Question:

Sources

- Identify sources you will consult for information. Describe the type of source (i.e., encyclopedia, biography, museum Web site, or documentary).
- Tell how you will locate the source. For Internet sites, write the words or phrases you will enter in a search engine.
- Write one or two questions you will ask about each source to determine whether or not it is relevant and reliable.

Print	Digital/Media
Type of source: How you will locate it: Relevance/Reliability:	Type of source: How you will locate it: Relevance/Reliability:
Type of source: How you will locate it: Relevance/Reliability:	Type of source: How you will locate it: Relevance/Reliability:
Type of source: How you will locate it: Relevance/Reliability:	Type of source: How you will locate it: Relevance/Reliability:

Answer these questions before you begin your research:

- How can I be sure that I will not plagiarize any of my sources?
- What deadlines must I meet in order to achieve my goal?
- How will I compile notes so that I can remember and organize the information I find?
- What steps will I take to make sure that my final work reflects my own thoughts and is not overly dependent on one source?

Essential Questions in American Literature

Sometimes, as you read individual stories, poems, or essays, you might feel as if you are acquiring small pieces of a puzzle. Each piece is brightly colored and interesting, but you cannot see how they all fit together. You may wonder, Why does this piece of literature matter? How does it relate to what I already know? You try to fit the new pieces into a bigger picture and give them meaning.

This textbook will help you create that bigger picture. On the following pages, you will find these three Essential Questions, tools for creating meaning from the literature you read:

This symbol will guide you to the Essential Questions in this book.

- **What makes American literature American?**
- **What is the relationship between literature and place?**
- **How does literature shape or reflect society?**

On the next three pages, the Essential Questions are accompanied by descriptions to guide your thinking. These questions re-appear throughout the introductions to units, at the end of every unit, and at the beginning and end of literary selections. You will have opportunities to reconsider them in the light of new information about a literary period or a new experience reading a literary work.

The questions do not have "yes" or "no" answers. They are meant to encourage you to take positions. Different people can answer them in different ways at different times. These large, open-ended questions will

- keep you thinking and making judgments about what you read,
- help you relate literary selections to one another and to larger ideas,
- provide a framework for discussing the selections with your classmates, and
- prompt you to create your own meaningful picture of American literature.

THE ESSENTIAL ? Q

What makes **American** literature *American?*

In one sense, anything written in America is American. But in a deeper way, literature is "American" because it says something fundamental about our identity as Americans. In fact, literature may be the most powerful creative expression of our national and cultural identity.

The selections in this book will spread before you styles, images, expressions, characters, themes, and stories that are uniquely American. By addressing this Essential Question in different ways throughout the book, you will find yourself getting to the heart of American literature.

As you read, keep in mind what it means to be "American." After all, it is American literature that enables us to tell ourselves who we are.

Thematic Vocabulary

To help as you explore this Essential Question, use words like these:

beliefs	**heritage**	**liberty**
diversity	**immigration**	**self-reliance**
freedom	**individualism**	

"What then is the American, this new man?"

—Michel-Guillaume Jean de Crèvecoeur

What is the **relationship** between
literature and *place?*

Europeans imagined America before they knew it. Columbus envisioned a fabled land of gold and spices. Ponce de León dreamt that Florida was the home of a Fountain of Youth. Puritans escaping persecution planned to build a City on a Hill where freedom would reign. Meanwhile, Native Americans told stories inspired by the natural world in which they dwelled.

To dwell in a place is to live in it fully, to merge its real life with the imaginative life you live there. As Emily Dickinson wrote, "I dwell in Possibility." How do Americans shape and reflect all the possibilities of their dwelling place on the earth? How does geography help make literature? Do Americans respond to nature in a unique way?

As you read the selections in this book, consider what it means to live—and to create literature—in a particular place at a particular time.

Thematic Vocabulary
To help as you explore this Essential Question, use words like these:

environment	**natural**	**resources**	**urban**
frontier	**range**	**rural**	**wilderness**
landscape	**region**		

"*...offer thanks to the earth where men dwell...*"

—The Iroquois Constitution

How does **literature** shape or reflect *society?*

Literature is a product of the society from which it springs, reflecting the values, concerns, and spirit of a people. However, literature can be more than a passive mirror. It can act as a force that changes or shapes a society. Novels, stories, plays, poems, and literary nonfiction made by writers can entertain, inform, persuade, challenge, and move readers, both singly and in great numbers. Writers are the entertainers who amuse, the critics who confront, the teachers who share wisdom, and— sometimes—the visionaries who lead the way to the future. Every day, writers celebrate America, define it, defy it, and tell its story. As you read this textbook and keep asking this Essential Question, you will become aware of the defining interactions between American society and its literature.

Thematic Vocabulary

To help as you explore this Essential Question, use words like these:

humorist	regionalism	storytelling
myth	satire	vernacular
persona	social critic	visionary

"In bombers named for girls, we burned The cities we had learned about in school—"

—Randall Jarrell

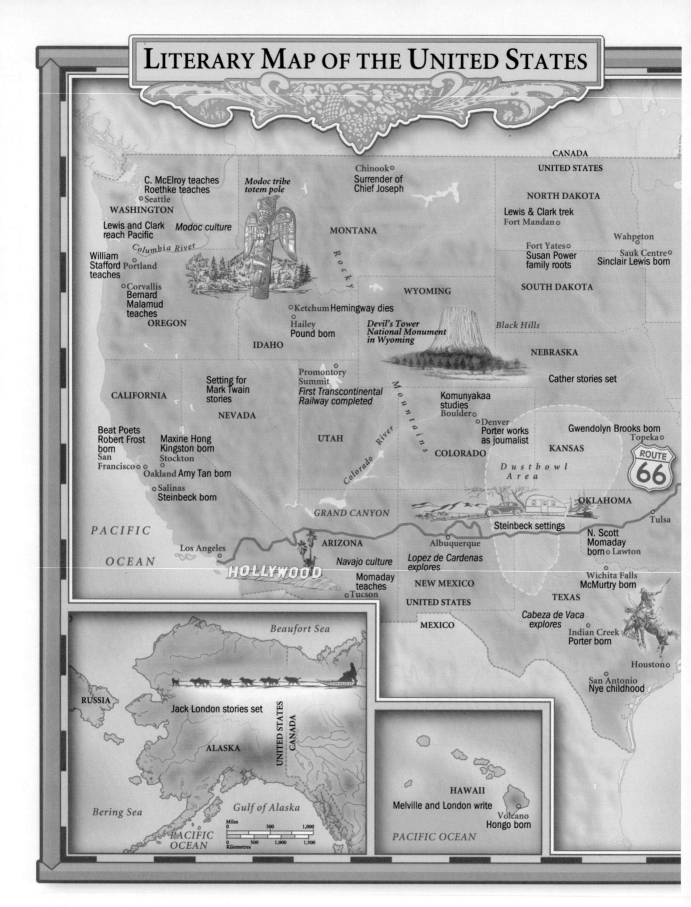

LITERARY MAP OF THE UNITED STATES

CANADA
UNITED STATES

WASHINGTON
C. McElroy teaches
Roethke teaches
○ Seattle

Modoc tribe totem pole

Chinook ○
Surrender of
Chief Joseph

NORTH DAKOTA
Lewis & Clark trek
Fort Mandan ○

Lewis and Clark
reach Pacific

Modoc culture

Wahpeton ○

MONTANA

Fort Yates ○
Susan Power
family roots

Sauk Centre ○
Sinclair Lewis born

Columbia River

William
Stafford
teaches

Portland ○

○ Corvallis
Bernard
Malamud
teaches

OREGON

WYOMING

SOUTH DAKOTA

Rocky

○ Ketchum Hemingway dies

○ Hailey
Pound born

IDAHO

Black Hills

Devil's Tower
National Monument
in Wyoming

NEBRASKA

Cather stories set

CALIFORNIA

Setting for
Mark Twain
stories

Promontory
Summit
*First Transcontinental
Railway completed*

NEVADA

UTAH

Mountains

Komunyakaa
studies
Boulder ○
○ Denver
Porter works
as journalist

COLORADO

*Dustbowl
Area*

KANSAS

Gwendolyn Brooks born
Topeka ○

ROUTE
66

Beat Poets
Robert Frost
born
San
Francisco ○

Maxine Hong
Kingston born
○ Stockton

Oakland Amy Tan born

○ Salinas
Steinbeck born

Colorado River

GRAND CANYON

Steinbeck settings

OKLAHOMA

Tulsa ○

N. Scott
Momaday
born ○ Lawton

Los Angeles ○

ARIZONA

Albuquerque ○

Lopez de Cardenas
explores

Wichita Falls
McMurtry born

PACIFIC

OCEAN

HOLLYWOOD

Navajo culture

Momaday
teaches
○ Tucson

Momaday
teaches

NEW MEXICO

UNITED STATES

MEXICO

TEXAS

Cabeza de Vaca
explores

Indian Creek
Porter born

Houston ○

San Antonio ○
Nye childhood

Beaufort Sea

RUSSIA

Jack London stories set

ALASKA

UNITED STATES
CANADA

Bering Sea

Gulf of Alaska

Miles
0   500   1,000

0   500   1,000   1,500
Kilometres

*PACIFIC
OCEAN*

HAWAII
Melville and London write
Volcano
Hongo born

PACIFIC OCEAN

Literature of the United States: A Continuing Story

This map illustrates the richness and variety of American literature, from Native American creation myths to contemporary fiction. In an important sense, all these varied authors and their works are part of a single ongoing narrative, the story of American literature.

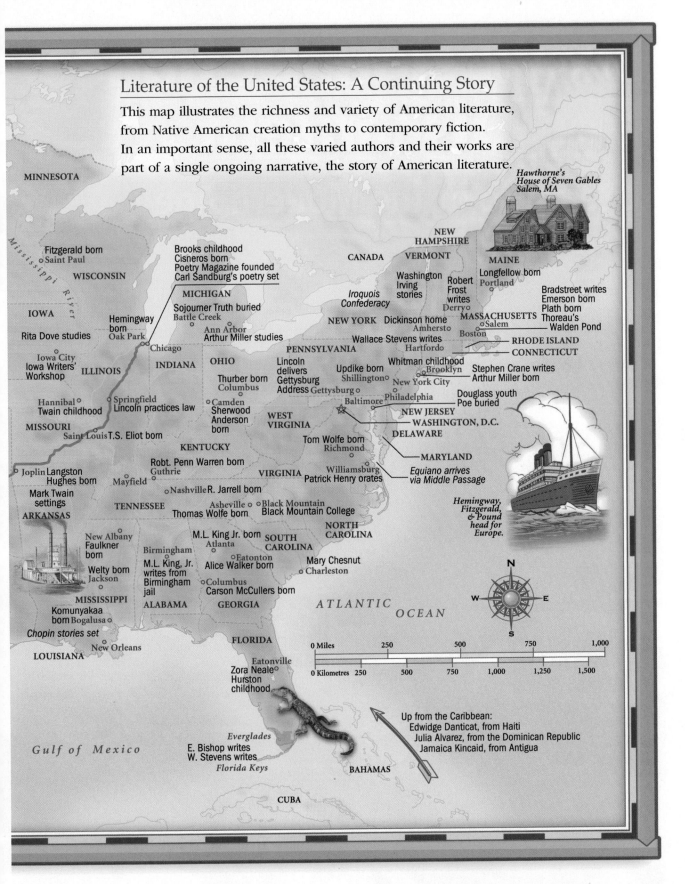

MINNESOTA

Mississippi River

Fitzgerald born
Saint Paul
WISCONSIN

IOWA

Rita Dove studies

Hemingway born
Oak Park

Iowa City
Iowa Writers'
Workshop
ILLINOIS

Chicago

INDIANA

Springfield
Lincoln practices law

Hannibal
Twain childhood
MISSOURI

Saint Louis T.S. Eliot born

Joplin Langston
Hughes born
Mark Twain settings
ARKANSAS

Mayfield

KENTUCKY

Robt. Penn Warren born
Guthrie

Nashville R. Jarrell born

TENNESSEE

New Albany
Faulkner born

Welty born
Jackson

MISSISSIPPI
Komunyakaa born Bogalusa
Chopin stories set

LOUISIANA

New Orleans

Brooks childhood
Cisneros born
Poetry Magazine founded
Carl Sandburg's poetry set

MICHIGAN
Sojourner Truth buried
Battle Creek

Ann Arbor
Arthur Miller studies

OHIO

Thurber born
Columbus

Camden
Sherwood
Anderson
born

WEST
VIRGINIA

CANADA

Iroquois
Confederacy

NEW YORK

Lincoln
delivers
Gettysburg
Address Gettysburg

Updike born
Shillington

Tom Wolfe born
Richmond

VIRGINIA

Williamsburg
Patrick Henry orates

VERMONT

Washington
Irving
stories

Robert
Frost
writes
Derry

Dickinson home
Amherst

Wallace Stevens writes
Hartford

Whitman childhood
Brooklyn
New York City

Baltimore
Philadelphia

NEW JERSEY
WASHINGTON, D.C.
DELAWARE

MARYLAND

NEW
HAMPSHIRE

MAINE
Longfellow born
Portland

MASSACHUSETTS
Salem
Boston

RHODE ISLAND
CONNECTICUT

Stephen Crane writes
Arthur Miller born

Douglass youth
Poe buried

Equiano arrives
via Middle Passage

Hawthorne's
House of Seven Gables
Salem, MA

Bradstreet writes
Emerson born
Plath born
Thoreau's
Walden Pond

Hemingway,
Fitzgerald,
& Pound
head for
Europe.

New Albany
Faulkner born

Birmingham

M.L. King, Jr.
writes from
Birmingham
jail
ALABAMA

Columbus
Carson McCullers born

GEORGIA

M.L. King Jr. born
Atlanta

Eatonton
Alice Walker born

Asheville
Thomas Wolfe born

Black Mountain
Black Mountain College

SOUTH
CAROLINA

NORTH
CAROLINA

Mary Chesnut
Charleston

ATLANTIC OCEAN

FLORIDA

Eatonville
Zora Neale
Hurston
childhood

Everglades
E. Bishop writes
W. Stevens writes
Florida Keys

Gulf of Mexico

BAHAMAS

CUBA

N
W   E
S

0 Miles   250   500   750   1,000

0 Kilometres 250   500   750   1,000   1,250   1,500

Up from the Caribbean:
Edwidge Danticat, from Haiti
Julia Alvarez, from the Dominican Republic
Jamaica Kincaid, from Antigua

Disillusion, Defiance, and Discontent

Literature of the Modern Age
1914–1945

"We asked the cyclone to go around
our barn but it didn't hear us."

— Carl Sandburg, from *The People, Yes*

Alexandre

Unit 4

PART 1 TEXT SET

FACING TROUBLED TIMES

PART 2 TEXT SET

FROM EVERY CORNER OF THE LAND

PART 3 TEXT SET

THE HARLEM RENAISSANCE

CLOSE READING TOOL

Use this tool to practice the close reading strategies you learn.

ONLINE WRITER'S NOTEBOOK

Easily capture notes and complete assignments online.

STUDENT eTEXT

Bring learning to life with audio, video, and interactive tools.

■ Find all Digital Resources at **pearsonrealize.com**.

Snapshot of the Period

The America that entered the twentieth century was a nation achieving world dominance while simultaneously losing some of its youthful innocence. Two world wars, a dizzying decade of prosperity, and a devastating worldwide depression marked this era. With these events came a new age in literature. The upheavals of the early twentieth century ushered in a period of literary boldness and lasting achievement. Many of the monumental figures of American literature, including F. Scott Fitzgerald (shown with his wife, Zelda, at right), William Faulkner, and Ernest Hemingway, rose to prominence during this period. Simultaneously, the movie industry grew from a fledgling experiment into a commercial powerhouse.

In 1919, the 18th Amendment established Prohibition in the United States. The Amendment was repealed in 1933. ▶

Fitzgerald

Hemingway

Faulkner

Porter

Hughes

Hurston

 As you read the selections in this unit, you will be asked to think about them in view of three key questions:

What is the relationship between literature and *place?*

How does literature shape or reflect *society?*

What makes American literature *American?*

World Conflicts

Military Deaths

World War I

CENTRAL POWERS
Austria-Hungary
Germany

ALLIES
United States
British Empire
France
Russia

equals 250,000 military deaths

World War II

AXIS POWERS
Germany
Italy
Japan

ALLIES
United States
USSR
British Empire

equals 500,000 military deaths

The Great Depression

Bank Failures

Unemployment, 1928–1933

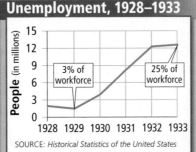

3% of workforce

25% of workforce

SOURCE: *Historical Statistics of the United States*

The Movie Industry

Average Weekly Movie Attendance 1922–1930

People per week (in millions)

SOURCE: *Historical Statistics of the United States*

Integration of Knowledge and Ideas Review the data in the top four graphs against the information on movie attendance in the bottom chart. Based on this combination of data, what inferences can you draw about the role movies play in American society, especially during hard times? **[Connect]**

The Kid – 1921

The Little Princess – 1939

Stagecoach – 1939

The Wizard of Oz – 1939

The Grapes of Wrath – 1940

Mildred Pierce – 1945

Historical Background

The Modern Age (1914–1945)

The years immediately before World War I were marked by practical optimism. Americans believed they had grown up and looked at themselves realistically. Technological know-how made the future look bright. Social problems could be solved. However, World War I shattered American and European values. The war not only remade governments and borders, it made people all over the world rethink what it meant to be a human being.

The Great War World War I was one of the bloodiest and most tragic conflicts ever to occur. The Allies (primarily Britain, France, and Russia) halted the German advances, but both sides dug trenches and brought the war to a standstill. Machine guns made it impossible to overrun the opponent. Almost an entire generation of European men wasted away.

President Woodrow Wilson tried to remain neutral, but that proved impossible. Eventually, unrelenting German submarine attacks swayed public opinion, and in 1917 the United States joined the Allies. American confidence passed quickly. The horrors of combat were unspeakable, intensified by new technology put to wartime use. This was the dark side of the Modern Age: Europeans and Americans had turned the world into a wasteland. As one soldier/poet put it, "I Have a Rendezvous with Death."

The Roaring Twenties The war ended in 1918, but people's minds and hearts were not at peace. Throughout the Twenties, the nation seemed to go on a binge. The economy boomed, and skyscrapers rose. Prohibition made the sale of liquor illegal, leading to bootlegging and the rise of organized crime. Radio arrived, and so did jazz. Movies became big business, and fads abounded: raccoon coats, flagpole sitting, a dance called the Charleston. People let go as prewar values and attitudes were thrown to the winds. The "roar" of the Roaring Twenties tried to drown out the remembered sound of exploding bombs and the horror of death.

TIMELINE

1914: World War I begins.

1915: Olympic track and field champion Jim Thorpe begins his professional football career. ▶

1916: *Chicago Poems* by Carl Sandburg appears.

1914

The New York Times. EXTRA

LUSITANIA SUNK BY A SUBMARINE, PROBABLY 1,260 DEAD;
TWICE TORPEDOED OFF IRISH COAST; SINKS IN 15 MINUTES;
CAPT. TURNER SAVED, FROHMAN AND VANDERBILT MISSING;
WASHINGTON BELIEVES THAT A GRAVE CRISIS IS AT HAND

◀ **1915: England** Because of the war in Europe, travelers are cautioned against transatlantic voyages. The *Lusitania* would be sunk despite these warnings.

1917: Russia Bolsheviks seize control of Russia in October Revolution.

The Great Depression The boom, of course, could not last. In October 1929, the stock market crashed, spurring the Great Depression. By mid-1932, about 12 million Americans—one quarter of the work force—were out of work. Bread lines formed and soup kitchens opened. Depression became more than an economic fact; it became a national state of mind.

The New Deal In the presidential election of 1932, New York's governor Franklin D. Roosevelt defeated president Herbert Hoover. Roosevelt initiated the New Deal, a package of major economic reforms, to strengthen the economy. People found work on huge public projects, such as building dams and bridges. Roosevelt's leadership and policies helped end the Depression and earned him reelection in 1936, 1940, and 1944.

World War II Only twenty years after the end of World War I, the German invasion of Poland ignited World War II. Even after the fall of France in 1940, the dominant mood in the United States was one of isolationism, with most Americans preferring to stay out of the conflict. However, when the Japanese attacked Pearl Harbor, Hawaii, on December 7, 1941, isolationism and neutrality came to a swift end. The United States declared war on the Axis powers—Germany, Japan, and Italy.

After years of bitter fighting in Europe and in the Pacific, the Allies, which included the United States, Great Britain, France, and the Soviet Union, defeated Nazi Germany. Japan surrendered three months later, after the United States dropped atomic bombs on the cities of Hiroshima and Nagasaki. Peace, and the Atomic Age, had arrived.

Key Historical Theme: War and Its Aftermath

- After the shock of World War I, Americans left behind many of the optimistic attitudes and humane values of the prewar world.
- During the Roaring Twenties, Americans gave way to self-indulgence; during the Thirties, they endured intense economic hardship.
- World War II ushered in the Atomic Age.

1918: Worldwide influenza epidemic kills as many as 20 million people.

1919: France Treaty of Versailles ends World War I. ▶

◀ **1918:** President Wilson announces his Fourteen Points in peace plan.

1919: Prohibition becomes law; repealed in 1933.

1921

◀ **1920:** Nineteenth Amendment to Constitution gives American women the right to vote.

Essential Questions Across Time

The Modern Age (1914–1945)

 What is the **relationship** between literature and *place?*

What American places especially affected American life in the first half of the twentieth century?

Cities Immigration, land development, and technological advances in telephones, building materials, power generators, and cars turned towns into cities and cities into metropolises. Big business thrived and the Twenties "roared" on city streets and in downtown hotspots. However, city life also came to mean crowding, poverty, crime, racism, and anonymity.

Towns and Farms Small-town America changed too, especially after World War I. A popular 1919 song asked, "How you gonna keep 'em down on the farm, after they've seen Paree?" Town populations shrank, and many traditions became the subjects of nostalgia. Farmers suffered terribly in the 1930s when severe drought turned the Great Plains into the Dust Bowl.

What non-American places especially affected American life in the first half of the twentieth century?

Battlefields and Boulevards The trenches that scarred Europe's landscape also scarred Americans' minds, undercutting cherished beliefs, such as the nobility of Western culture. On the other hand, the artistic life that flourished in the studios and cafes of Paris pushed Americans into the Modern Age. The battlefields of World War II, including Hiroshima, would leave their indelible marks on both the American psyche and its politics.

> **ESSENTIAL QUESTION VOCABULARY**
>
> These Essential Question words will help you think and write about literature and place.
>
> **development** (di vel´ əp mənt) *n.* building up or expansion
>
> **metropolis** (mə träp´ ə lis) *n.* large city
>
> **anonymity** (an´ ə nim´ ə tē) *n.* condition of lacking individuality or identity

TIMELINE

1921

◄ **1922:** T. S. Eliot publishes *The Waste Land.*

1922: Ireland James Joyce publishes *Ulysses.* ►

1924: The Immigration Act limits the number of immigrants that can enter the United States.

1924: Germany Thomas Mann publishes *The Magic Mountain.*

City became known for crowding, poverty, crime, a racism
severe draught 1930's and many farmers suffered
(Dust bowl)

How did these places show up in the work of modern American writers?

Paris and Modernism After World War I, disenchantment led some American writers to become expatriates, or exiles. Many went to Paris, where they gathered at the home of Gertrude Stein, the writer who dubbed them the "lost generation." Ezra Pound, Ernest Hemingway, F. Scott Fitzgerald, E. E. Cummings, Sherwood Anderson, and other Modernist writers, painters, and musicians created a vibrant cultural life in Paris and gave American writing a dynamic European awareness it had never had before.

Urban Waste Lands T. S. Eliot, born in St. Louis, went to Europe in 1914 and settled in England. Eliot's poem *The Waste Land* (1922), using imagery of a fog-shrouded "Unreal City," summed up the sterility of the postwar world. In a different way, the glittering city-dwellers who populated the fiction of F. Scott Fitzgerald faced their own disillusion and emptiness.

The Harlem Renaissance A new literary age also dawned in northern Manhattan, in Harlem. Countee Cullen, Langston Hughes, Claude McKay, Jean Toomer, Arna Bontemps, and Zora Neale Hurston produced prose and poetry that expressed the African American experience. They also captured the sights, sounds, and emotions of modern urban life.

Towns, Farms, and Plains In sharply satiric novels, Sinclair Lewis took aim at small-town life, particularly in the Midwest. John Steinbeck portrayed the struggles of men and women who work the land, particularly in California and the Southwest. Eudora Welty and William Faulkner used the landscapes of Mississippi in tragicomic tales of family, race, life, and death in the South.

The American EXPERIENCE

CLOSE-UP ON HISTORY

Women Get the Vote

The passage of the Nineteenth Amendment to the Constitution, giving women the right to vote, was a landmark in American social history.

The struggle to grant women the vote, or suffrage, went back many years, but it gathered momentum in the early 1900s. Carrie Chapman Catt organized a state-by-state campaign, and year by year more states in the West and Midwest granted women suffrage, although mostly only in state elections. Gradually, more women called for a voice in national elections, too.

Beginning in 1913, President Woodrow Wilson met with suffragists led by Alice Paul. Wilson, however, did not support a constitutional amendment, and in 1917 suffragists picketed the White House. After several months, police began arresting the protesters. Paul and others went on a hunger strike, but prison officials force-fed them. Upon their release, they resumed picketing.

By early 1918, the tide began to turn. The tireless work of Catt, Paul, and others began to pay off. President Wilson gave his support, and in 1919 Congress passed the Nineteenth Amendment. By August 1920, three fourths of the states had ratified it. The amendment doubled the number of eligible voters in the United States and eliminated a long-standing injustice.

◀ **1925:** Louis Armstrong and his Hot Five become a radio headliner.

1926: Langston Hughes publishes *The Weary Blues*.

1927

1925: F. Scott Fitzgerald publishes *The Great Gatsby*.

◀ **1925: England** Virginia Woolf publishes *Mrs. Dalloway.*

1926: Ernest Hemingway publishes *The Sun Also Rises.*

How does **literature** shape or reflect *society?*

What major social and political events affected American writers in the first half of the twentieth century?

The major events listed below affected how writers thought about themselves and the world, and shaped many of the themes of the age:

- **World War I:** The shock and devastation made it clear that a new world, radically different from the past, would have to be created.

- **The Depression and the New Deal:** Poverty was everywhere, but jobs with the Work Projects Administration (WPA) enabled many writers to survive.

- **World War II, the Atomic Bomb, the Holocaust:** The full effects of these horrors would only become more apparent as the century wore on.

What values, attitudes, and ideas grew from these events?

Disillusion with Old Ideas and Ideals The ideas and ideals of the nineteenth century had failed. They had not prevented the slaughter of World War I, and so new beliefs and attitudes had to take their place.

Wider Cultural Awareness Wars and new technologies made Americans more aware of other cultures and other artistic traditions.

Greater Democratization The middle class continued to expand. Women, African Americans, and immigrants from many countries played increasingly important roles in American cultural life.

Fragmentation of Experience War, the stresses of modern urban life, and the sheer speed of change enmeshed many people in feelings of uncertainty, imbalance, and a sense of discontinuity.

How were these forces expressed in literature?

Out with the Old Above all, Modernism was a desire for the new. Modernist

> ### ESSENTIAL QUESTION VOCABULARY
>
> These Essential Question words will help you think and write about literature and society:
>
> **disillusion** (dis´ i loo´ zhen) *v.* disappoint by taking away ideals or idealism
>
> **awareness** (ə wer´ nis) *n.* state of being conscious, informed
>
> **cultural** (kul´ chər əl) *adj.* relating to a particular society and its way of life

TIMELINE

1927

1927: Charles Lindbergh flies solo and nonstop from New York to Paris. ▶

1928: Germany Kurt Weill and Bertolt Brecht write and produce *The Threepenny Opera.* ▶

1928: China Chiang Kai-shek becomes head of Nationalist government.

1928: Russia Stalin's Five Year Plan is adopted.

writers experimented with new approaches and techniques. They were out to capture the essence of modern life in both the content and form of their work. Modernists looked for new solutions. The old ways of telling stories—in a straight narrative line from beginning to middle to end—were out. The old ways of presenting poetry—in repeating meters and rhyme schemes—were out. In general, the new approaches demanded more from readers than earlier works.

A Global Vision Windows had been opened to the rest of the world. The art of China, Japan, Africa, India, ancient Greece, medieval Italy, Provençal France—all contributed to the mix that became Modernism.

More Writers Women had always played a role in American literary life, but in the twentieth century they became more central than ever. Gertrude Stein shaped Modernist values, and Harriet Monroe, the editor of *Poetry* magazine, championed its verse. With the Harlem Renaissance, African American writers such as Langston Hughes stepped into the limelight, paving the way for generations of African American writers to follow.

Literature in Pieces In previous eras, writers felt obligated to the literary rules and authors who had preceded them. With the onset of Modernism, however, established rules were breakable. Writers and many readers accepted poems and stories in shorter bursts, segments that did not obviously flow from one to the next. Rather than a unified oil painting, a Modernist work was more like a mosaic composed of individual pieces. It required the viewer to organize the pieces into a meaningful picture.

Rise of Popular Culture The paperback revolution was both a cause and an effect of growing democratization in the twentieth century. Beginning in the mid-1930s, books began to be available as paperbacks, which were cheap and portable. This made more literature available to more people more easily. It also led to the merging of "literary" works and "popular" works into one larger cultural stream. Edgar Rice Burroughs' Tarzan adventures, Zane Grey's bestselling westerns, Dashiell Hammett's mysteries—Americans ate them up. Radio also made electronic storytelling enormously popular; many families never missed an episode of *The Shadow* or *Superman*. Movies, too, began to tell stories in more and more spectacular ways. For some, movies even began to replace literature.

1929: Japan Collapse of American silk market hurts workers and farmers.

▶ **1931: Spain** Salvador Dali paints *The Persistence of Memory*.

1933

1929: Stock market crashes in October, followed by the Great Depression of the 1930s. ▼

▲ **1930: India** Mahatma Gandhi leads famous march to the sea to protest British tax on salt.

◀ **1931:** The Empire State Building is completed, becoming the world's tallest building.

BROOKLYN DAILY EAGLE
WALL ST. IN PANIC AS STOCKS CRASH
Attempt Made to Kill Italy's Crown Prince
Hollywood Fire Destroys Films Worth Millions | High Duty Group Gave $700,000 to Coolidge Drive

The American EXPERIENCE

CONTEMPORARY CONNECTION

William Faulkner: Hollywood Script Doctor

William Faulkner's legacy as a Nobel Prize–winning literary giant certainly outshines his lesser-known role as a Hollywood screenwriter.

It was a need for money, not a love of the movies, that drew Faulkner to Hollywood in 1932. In April of that year, he signed a six-week contract with Metro Goldwyn Mayer and began writing a screen adaptation of his own story, "Turn About." Faulkner quickly learned about making artistic concessions—MGM had him write a new character into the film to showcase Joan Crawford, one of their major stars. For the next thirteen years, Faulkner would work intermittently writing screenplays for various studios.

Faulkner did not believe that his screenplays were worthy of any special admiration. However, during his stints in Hollywood, he earned screen credit on films both major and minor, including *To Have and Have Not* (1944), *The Big Sleep* (1946), and *Gunga Din* (1939).

Though Faulkner once said, "Hollywood is a place where a man can get stabbed in the back while climbing a ladder," he did have alliances there. Howard Hawks, one of the foremost directors of the time, was a friend and an ally. Faulkner associated with some actors, as well, and stood up for them, saying, "I know very few actors, but the ones with whom I did come in contact were normal, hard-working people, leading much saner lives than we are led to believe."

TIMELINE

1933: President Roosevelt closes banks; Congress passes New Deal laws.

1933

1933: Germany Adolf Hitler becomes German Chancellor.

▲ **1935:** Alfred Hitchcock's mystery *The 39 Steps* is released in theaters.

1935: Howard Hughes reaches 352 mph in his Hughes Racer, breaking the landplane speed record. ▶

1935: The Social Security Act is passed to provide retirement and unemployment benefits. ▶

A monthly check to you —

INFORMATION may be obtained here

What makes American literature *American?*

What changes in literary elements contributed to American Modernism?

Narrative Conventions Modernist storytellers paid close attention to *how* they told their stories. They often left out transitions between events and omitted the detailed expositions and explanations that readers found in older literature. Sometimes they left plotlines unresolved, refusing to tie up every thread. Readers had to interpret on their own.

Modernists shifted time in their stories, moving among past, present, and future. They also shuttled between inner and outer realities. Influenced by developments in psychology, particularly those of Sigmund Freud and William James, Modernist writers wove characters' dreams and fantasies into their narratives. They tried to create the natural flow of thoughts, memories, and insights—the "stream of consciousness" connected only by associations.

Forms Modernists also broke formal boundaries. Two European giants led the way: Irish writer James Joyce's *Ulysses* (1922) revolutionized the novel with multi-layered chapters based on Homer's *Odyssey*, and French writer Marcel Proust's *In Search of Lost Time* (1913–1927) recaptured his own past in seven free-flowing volumes. Modernists invented new structures, some expansive and encompassing, others compressed. At the small end of the scale, Imagist poets—including Ezra Pound and Hilda Doolittle—created miniatures of hard, clear expression in concrete images.

Themes Most often, works of fiction, poetry, and drama have implied themes. In Modernist works, themes are even more indirect. Readers of modern literature need to pay closer attention, ask more questions, and forge more connections for themselves. In addition, the challenging theme of the nature of art itself often dominated the Modernist imagination.

Tone An overall tone of irony marks many Modernist works. Writers such as Eliot, Hemingway, Fitzgerald, and Faulkner were painfully aware of the gap between the world as it was and the world as it ought to have been.

ESSENTIAL QUESTION VOCABULARY

These Essential Question words will help you think and write about American literature.

consciousness (kän´shəs nis) *n.* totality of one's thoughts, feelings, and impressions

indirect (in´də rekt´) *adj.* suggested, not clearly stated or defined

breadth (bredth) *n.* wide range or variety

1936: Spain Spanish Civil War begins.

1937: Japan invades China, beginning the Second Sino-Japanese War.

1938: The Fair Labor Standards Act establishes a national minimum wage.

1939

1937: Amelia Earhart takes off from Miami for a flight around the world; she disappears over the Pacific Ocean. ▲

1937: Zora Neale Hurston publishes *Their Eyes Were Watching God.* ▶

They were not satirists, mocking the world in order to improve it. They were ironists, dissecting the world simply to make it possible to live in it.

Style In prose, journalism brought a news style into fiction. Most obvious in Hemingway, American style strove for shorter, harder-edged sentences. Snappier dialogue, less flowery descriptions, and everyday American vocabulary gave modern American works a recognizable style. In poetry, free verse enabled such poets as Wallace Stevens, William Carlos Williams, and E. E. Cummings to create new rhythms of variety and surprise.

Imagery High culture and low, domestic and exotic, elegant and vulgar, common and bizarre and everything in between—the twentieth century opened the biggest box of images that writers had ever had. For Ezra Pound, a crowd in a subway could be blossoms on a tree. For F. Scott Fitzgerald, a pair of eyes painted on a billboard could watch a tragedy unfold. For Langston Hughes, a dream could explode. Modernists saw the world with new eyes and helped their readers see it newly too.

Allusion The range of possible allusions grew wider too. T. S.Eliot quoted the Indian Upanishads; Ezra Pound quoted Latin and ancient Greek. Hemingway referred to African tribal customs; Marianne Moore invoked both baseball and basilisks. The reader's familiarity was no longer assumed or even required. The end result was a world-embracing awareness in American literature, a breadth of vision that still amazes us today.

How did the relationship between writers and the public change during the Modernist period?

Modernism began an overall distancing of serious writers from the general reading public. With the rise of mass communication and popular culture, Modernist works were sometimes seen as obscure or elitist. There was no doubt that they made greater demands on readers than Romantic or Realist works. More mental and imaginative effort was required to read Eliot's *The Waste Land* or Stevens's *Harmonium* than to read the Fireside Poets. As a result, some of the literary audience turned away.

TIMELINE

1939

1939: John Steinbeck writes *The Grapes of Wrath* in his California home. ▶

1939: Poland German blitzkrieg invasion of Poland sets off World War II.

1939: *The Wizard of Oz* and *Gone With the Wind* appear in movie theaters. ▶

1940: Civil Aeronautics Board is created to regulate U.S. commercial air traffic.

1940: France French government signs armistice with Germany.

Many writers believe that great literary works teach their readers how to read them. In this sense, Modernist writers also became teachers. In time, people learned how to read Modernist works—how to make the connections, fill in the blanks, listen to new rhythms, and appreciate new images. Modernism gave people new ways to be delighted, and many Modernist devices are now taken for granted in the twenty-first century.

By 1945, what identities had emerged in American literature?

During the Modernist period, the American profile included these varied identities and character types:

- **Denizen of the Waste Land:** wanderer through a war-wearied landscape, spiritually exhausted, in search of new values, defined by T. S. Eliot
- **Member of the Lost Generation:** disillusioned, self-indulgent, escapist, expatriated, embodied by Fitzgerald and Hemingway
- **Triumphant Commoner:** believer in the innate strength of those who remain close to the land, led by Faulkner, Welty, and Steinbeck
- **Poetic Maker:** believer in the saving power of art and imagination, championed by Pound, Stevens, Williams, Cummings, Moore, and Frost
- **African American Artist:** creator of art drawn from the African American experience, represented by Hughes, McKay, Cullen, and Hurston

The American EXPERIENCE

DEVELOPING AMERICAN ENGLISH

Sliding with Slang by Richard Lederer

Slang is hot and slang is cool. Slang is nifty and slang is wicked. Slang is the bee's knees and the cat's meow. Slang is far out, fresh, fly, and phat. Slang is awesome, copacetic, and totally tubular.

Slang is the spice of language. It has added its spice to American literature as American writers, particularly in the Modern Age, have increasingly written in an American voice, using the words and rhythms of everyday American discourse. Listen to the poet Langston Hughes:

Good morning, daddy!

Ain't you heard

The boogie-woogie rumble

Of a dream deferred?

Defining the Lingo The *Dictionary of American Slang* defines slang as "the body of words and expressions frequently used by or intelligible to a rather large portion of the general American public, but not accepted as good, formal usage by the majority." In other words, it is vagabond language that prowls the outskirts of respectable speech, yet few of us can get along without it.

What's in This Name? The word *slang* may have developed from an erroneous past tense (*sling-slang-slung*) or from thieveS' LANGuage or beggarS' LANGuage. Jargon and slang originate with a particular group, but slang gets slung around by the whole population. In fact, slang may now make up a fifth of the American wordscape.

1944: Roosevelt is reelected president for an unprecedented fourth term.

◀ 1945: United Nations Charter signed at end of World War II.

1945

1941: Japanese bomb Pearl Harbor, bringing U.S. into World War II.

◀ 1945: **Germany** Dresden is hit by Allied firebombing raid. Firestorm virtually destroys city.

1945: Atom bombs dropped on Hiroshima and Nagasaki.

Recent Scholarship

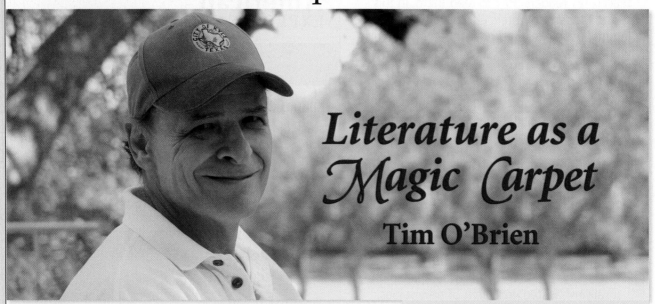

Literature as a Magic Carpet

Tim O'Brien

*A*s a boy of fifteen or sixteen, feeling restless and marooned in a small town on the prairies of southern Minnesota, I began using literature as a kind of magic carpet—a way of flying off to more exciting places on the earth, a way of escaping the brutal Minnesota winters and the dull, drowsy, summertime fields of soybeans and alfalfa and corn. I didn't merely read. I was transported. I *lived* inside stories and novels. Just turn a page—that simple—and I was suddenly a soldier in World War I, or a young man in love during the famous Jazz Age, or a grieving parent, or an aging railroad engineer, or an old African American woman trudging down a path through the frozen woods of Mississippi.

Inventing Stories of My Own

The word "literature," I'll confess, did not mean much to me. It seemed too fancy, too formidable. Even so, by the time I'd graduated from high school, I had read—mostly on my own, mostly for fun—a good many of the stories and poems that appear in this unit. I remember, for instance, my first encounter with Hemingway's "In Another Country" during the summer between my sophomore and junior years. I remember marveling at the water-clear transparency of the prose, the deceptive simplicity of the plot, the quiet, uncomplaining dignity of the characters, those solid nouns, those invigorating verbs, the unspoken and unspeakable emotional pain

About the Author

Tim O'Brien was born in Minnesota. He was drafted after college to fight in the Vietnam War. Although he has written extensively about the war and its aftermath, he resists being labeled a "Vietnam writer." O'Brien's fiction explores the larger themes of betrayal and loss of faith, as well as the tension between truth and fiction. He has been called "the best American writer of his generation."

that hovered like an invisible vapor just above the surface of each page. More than anything, though, I remember thinking: Wow, I want to try this. I want to invent stories of my own. I want to write fiction someday.

Poetry As Explosive As Artillery

Not much later, in the first months of my junior year in high school, these fantasies about becoming a writer were reinforced by the work of two very dissimilar poets, T. S. Eliot and Robert Frost, both of whom are represented in this unit. Until then, I'd stupidly conceived of poetry as something for English teachers and nearsighted librarians. I hadn't realized that a good poem could be as explosive as any artillery round, as powerful as any rocket lifting off for the moon.

Living the Poem

From T. S. Eliot I learned that vivid writing requires vivid imagery, and that vivid imagery requires something unexpected and off the beaten literary path: a patient etherized upon a table; sawdust restaurants; women who come and go, talking of Michelangelo. To this day, Robert Frost's "Stopping by Woods on a Snowy Evening" remains one of my favorite pieces of writing. The words in themselves are ordinary—no need for a dictionary—but the impact of the poem, its pressure on the human spirit, is extraordinary. We feel the cold, snowy dark against our skin. We hear the harness bells, the wind, and the eerie, timeless echo of our own mortality. We don't merely read the poem. We live it. And we come to understand that, one way or another, all of us have promises to keep, and miles to go before we sleep.

Rekindling a Fire

My dream of becoming a writer has come true. And yet rereading these stories and poems has rekindled a fire inside me. I'm a teenager again. I want to write a new novel.

Speaking and Listening: Presentation of Ideas

Tim O'Brien recalls two life-changing effects that literature had on him: It enabled him to escape into other worlds, and it inspired him to write. He remembers the rocket-like effect of reading Hemingway, Eliot, and Frost. While few people go on to become professional writers as O'Brien did, nearly everyone can take off on that literary "magic carpet."

Write a short **testimonial**—a personal statement affirming the value of something— about a literary work you have read. Explain its subject and style and why it is important to you.

▼ **Critical Viewing** In what ways does this young man seem like a reader who uses "literature as a . . . magic carpet," the way Tim O'Brien did? **CONNECT**

Integrate and Evaluate Information

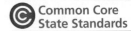 **Common Core State Standards**

1. Use a chart like the one shown to determine the key ideas expressed in the Essential Question essays on pages 694–701. Fill in two ideas related to each Essential Question and note the groups most closely associated with each concept. One example has been done for you.

Essential Question	Key Concept	Key Author
Literature and Place		
American Literature		
Literature and Society	Disillusion with the American Dream	Fitzgerald

2. How do the visual sources in this section (pp. 688–703) add to your understanding of the ideas expressed in words? Cite specific examples.

3. During the Modern era, paperbacks and movies helped to create popular culture. At the same time, the challenging nature of Modernism caused some readers to turn away from serious literature. The effect was a divide between popular and "high" culture. Do you think that divide continues today? Consider the effects of television and the Internet in your response.

4. **Address a Question** Tim O'Brien recalls that as a boy he "lived" inside stories. In today's world, is the experience of playing a video-game avatar or character similar to the transport O'Brien describes? As you explain your thinking, integrate information from this textbook and other sources to support your ideas.

Reading Informational Text
7. Integrate and evaluate multiple sources of information presented in different media or formats as well as in words in order to address a question or solve a problem.

Speaking and Listening
5. Make strategic use of digital media in presentations to enhance understanding of findings, reasoning, and evidence and to add interest.

ESSENTIAL QUESTION VOCABULARY

Use these vocabulary words in your presentations.

Literature and Place
development
metropolis
anonymity

Literature and Society
disillusion
awareness
cultural

American Literature
consciousness
indirect
breadth

Speaking and Listening: Multimedia Presentation

During the Modern Age, popular culture played a growing role in the lives of Americans. Choose one of these popular culture forms and prepare a brief **multimedia presentation** about its significance during the period of 1914–1945:

- jazz and other popular music
- comic strips
- motion pictures
- science fiction

Solve a Research Problem: The topics listed above are very broad. Conduct preliminary research to narrow your focus and then conduct targeted research on that specialized area. Use your research to answer the following questions: Who were some of the outstanding people in this field and what did they do? What characterized works in this field during the time period? What do these works reveal about Americans during this era? Integrate print, visual, and audio examples into your presentation to communicate your points clearly and to add interest to your presentation.

Facing Troubled Times

Connecting to the Essential Question Prufrock, the speaker of this poem, reveals feelings of insecurity and self-consciousness. As you read, notice details that reflect Prufrock's perceptions of other people's opinions. Doing so will help you think about the Essential Question: **How does literature shape or reflect society?**

Close Reading Focus

Dramatic Monologue; Allusion

A troubled J. Alfred Prufrock invites an unidentified companion, perhaps a part of his own personality, to walk with him as he reflects aloud about his bitter realization that life and love are passing him by. His so-called love song is a **dramatic monologue,** a poem or speech in which a character addresses a silent listener. As Prufrock moves through his evening, images, dialogue, and other details reveal his internal conflicts.

Throughout the poem, Prufrock makes **allusions**, or references, to people and historical or literary events that hold meaning for him. For example, in this passage, he alludes to Shakespeare's *Hamlet*:

No! I am not Prince Hamlet, nor was meant to be;
Am an attendant lord, one that will do
To swell a progress, start a scene or two . . .

These allusions form a literary shorthand that paints a portrait of Prufrock and his society. As you read, use footnotes and guided reading questions to understand these allusions and the meanings they hold for Prufrock.

Preparing to Read Complex Texts This poem contains some of the most haunting passages in literature. One of the reasons the poem affects readers so intensely is its musicality—the sweep and fall of the lines, the repetition and rhyme, and the sounds of the words. To fully appreciate the poem, **adjust your reading rate** to *listen* to the poem's rhythms and language. As you read, use a chart like the one shown to note points where you slow down. Record how the music of those moments contributes to the poem's mood and meaning.

Vocabulary

The words below are important to understanding the text that follows. Copy the words into your notebook. Which words end with the same suffix? Which part of speech are they?

tedious	malingers
insidious	meticulous
digress	obtuse

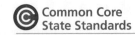

Common Core State Standards

Reading Literature
4. Determine the meaning of words and phrases as they are used in the text, including figurative meanings; analyze the impact of specific word choices on meaning and tone, including language that is particularly fresh, engaging, or beautiful.
5. Analyze how an author's choices concerning how to structure specific parts of a text contribute to its overall structure and meaning as well as its aesthetic impact.

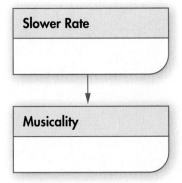

Slower Rate

Musicality

T.S. ELIOT *(1888–1965)*

Author of "The Love Song of J. Alfred Prufrock"

Always well-spoken and somberly attired, Thomas Stearns Eliot was outwardly the model of convention. His work, in contrast, was revolutionary in both form and content.

Beginnings Born into a wealthy family in St. Louis, Eliot grew up in an environment that promoted his intellectual development. He attended Harvard University, where he published a number of poems in the school's literary magazine. In 1910, the year Eliot received his master's degree in philosophy, he completed "The Love Song of J. Alfred Prufrock."

A Literary Sensation Just before the outbreak of World War I, Eliot moved to England where he became acquainted with Ezra Pound, another young American poet. Pound convinced Harriet Monroe, the editor of *Poetry* magazine, to publish "Prufrock." Shortly thereafter, Eliot published a collection entitled *Prufrock and Other Observations* (1917). Eliot's use of innovative poetic techniques and his focus on the despair of modern urban life caused a sensation in the literary world.

Facing a New World Eliot made his literary mark against the backdrop of a rapidly changing society. Disillusioned with the ideologies that produced the devastation of World War I, many people were searching for new ideas and values. Eliot was among a group of such writers and visual artists who called themselves Modernists. Modernist poets believed that poetry had to reflect the genuine, fractured experience of life in the twentieth century, not a romanticized idea of what life was once like.

In 1922, Eliot published *The Waste Land*, a profound critique of the spiritual barrenness of the modern world. Filled with allusions to classical and world literature and to Eastern culture and religion, it was widely read and greatly affected writers and critics.

A Return to Tradition In his search for something beyond the "waste land" of modern society, Eliot became a member of the Church of England in 1927. He began to explore religious themes in poems such as "Ash Wednesday" (1930) and *Four Quartets* (1943)—works that suggest a belief that religion could heal the wounds inflicted by society. In later years, Eliot wrote several plays and a sizable body of literary criticism. In 1948, he received the Nobel Prize for Literature.

Three White Bluebells, 1920, Paul Klee, Artists Rights Society (ARS), New York

THE LOVE SONG OF J. ALFRED PRUFROCK

T. S. Eliot

▲ **Critical Viewing**

How does this painting mirror Modernist ideas about experimenting with artistic forms? **INTERPRET**

BACKGROUND In this poem, J. Alfred Prufrock, a stuffy and inhibited man who is pained by his own passivity, invites the reader, or some unnamed visitor, to join him in a journey. Where Prufrock is and where he is going—to a party, a museum, a tea party, or some other gathering—is open to debate. The most important part of this journey, however, takes place within the inner landscape of Prufrock's emotions, memory, and intellect as he meditates on his life.

S'io credessi che mia risposta fosse
a persona che mai tornasse al mondo,
questa fiamma staria senza più scosse.
Ma per ciò che giammai di questo fondo
non tornò vivo alcun, s'i'odo il vero,
senza tema d'infamia ti rispondo.[1]

---

1. ***S'io credessi . . . ti rispondo*** The epigraph is a passage from Dante's *Inferno*, in which one of the damned, upon being asked to tell his story, says: "If I believed my answer were being given to someone who could ever return to the world, this flame [his voice] would shake no more. But since no one has ever returned alive from this depth, if what I hear is true, I will answer you without fear of disgrace."

Let us go then, you and I,
When the evening is spread out against the sky
Like a patient etherized[2] upon a table;
Let us go, through certain half-deserted streets,
5   The muttering retreats
Of restless nights in one-night cheap hotels
And sawdust restaurants with oyster-shells:
Streets that follow like a tedious argument
Of insidious intent
10 To lead you to an overwhelming question . . .
Oh, do not ask, "What is it?"
Let us go and make our visit.

In the room the women come and go
Talking of Michelangelo.[3]

15 The yellow fog that rubs its back upon the window-panes,
The yellow smoke that rubs its muzzle on the window-panes,
Licked its tongue into the corners of the evening,
Lingered upon the pools that stand in drains,
Let fall upon its back the soot that falls from chimneys,
20 Slipped by the terrace, made a sudden leap,
And seeing that it was a soft October night,
Curled once about the house, and fell asleep.

And indeed there will be time[4]
For the yellow smoke that slides along the street
25 Rubbing its back upon the window-panes;
There will be time, there will be time
To prepare a face to meet the faces that you meet;
There will be time to murder and create,
And time for all the works and days[5] of hands
30 That lift and drop a question on your plate;
Time for you and time for me,
And time yet for a hundred indecisions,
And for a hundred visions and revisions,
Before the taking of a toast and tea.

35 In the room the women come and go
Talking of Michelangelo.

And indeed there will be time
To wonder, "Do I dare?" and, "Do I dare?"
Time to turn back and descend the stair,

Vocabulary

tedious (tēd′ ē əs) *adj.*
boring and wearisome

insidious (in sid′ ē əs)
adj. secretly treacherous

**Dramatic Monologue
and Allusion**

What might the allusion to
Michelangelo suggest about
the women at the party?

Comprehension

At what time of day is
the poem set?

---

2. **etherized** (ē′ thə rīzd) *v.* anesthetized with ether.
3. **Michelangelo** (mī′ kəl an′ jə lō) a famous Italian artist and sculptor (1475–1564).
4. **there will be time** These words echo the speaker's plea in English poet Andrew
   Marvell's "To His Coy Mistress": "Had we but world enough and time . . . "
5. **works and days** Ancient Greek poet Hesiod wrote a poem about farming called
   "Works and Days."

Do I dare Disturb the universe?

40 With a bald spot in the middle of my hair—
    (They will say: "How his hair is growing thin!")
    My morning coat, my collar mounting firmly to the chin,
    My necktie rich and modest, but asserted by a simple pin—
    (They will say: "But how his arms and legs are thin!")
45 Do I dare
    Disturb the universe?
    In a minute there is time
    For decisions and revisions which a minute will reverse.

    For I have known them all already, known them all—
50 Have known the evenings, mornings, afternoons,
    I have measured out my life with coffee spoons;
    I know the voices dying with a dying fall
    Beneath the music from a farther room.
            So how should I presume?

55 And I have known the eyes already, known them all—
    The eyes that fix you in a formulated phrase,
    And when I am formulated, sprawling on a pin,
    When I am pinned and wriggling on the wall,
    Then how should I begin
60 To spit out all the butt-ends of my days and ways?
            And how should I presume?

    And I have known the arms already, known them all—
    Arms that are braceleted and white and bare
    (But in the lamplight, downed with light brown hair!)
65 Is it perfume from a dress
    That makes me so digress?
    Arms that lie along a table, or wrap about a shawl.
            And should I then presume?
            And how should I begin?

        .   .   .   .   .   .

70 Shall I say, I have gone at dusk through narrow streets
    And watched the smoke that rises from the pipes
    Of lonely men in shirt-sleeves, leaning out of windows? . . .

    I should have been a pair of ragged claws
    Scuttling across the floors of silent seas.[6]

        .   .   .   .   .   .

75 And the afternoon, the evening, sleeps so peacefully!

Vocabulary

digress (dī gres′) v. depart temporarily from the main subject

Dramatic Monologue

What do Prufrock's observations of "narrow streets," and "lonely men" suggest he feels about the world?

---

6. I should . . . seas In Shakespeare's *Hamlet,* the hero, Hamlet, mocks the aging Lord Chamberlain, Polonius, saying, "You yourself, sir, should be old as I am, if like a crab you could go backward" (II.ii. 205–206).

Smoothed by long fingers,
Asleep . . . tired . . . or it malingers,
Stretched on the floor, here beside you and me.
Should I, after tea and cakes and ices,
80 Have the strength to force the moment to its crisis?
But though I have wept and fasted, wept and prayed,
Though I have seen my head (grown slightly bald) brought in
    upon a platter,[7]
I am no prophet—and here's no great matter;
I have seen the moment of my greatness flicker,
85 And I have seen the eternal Footman[8] hold my coat, and snicker.
And in short, I was afraid.

And would it have been worth it, after all,
After the cups, the marmalade, the tea,
Among the porcelain, among some talk of you and me,
90 Would it have been worth while,
To have bitten off the matter with a smile,
To have squeezed the universe into a ball
To roll it towards some overwhelming question.
To say: "I am Lazarus,[9] come from the dead,
95 Come back to tell you all. I shall tell you all"—
If one, settling a pillow by her head,
        Should say: "That is not what I meant at all.
        That is not it, at all."

And would it have been worth it, after all,
100 Would it have been worth while,
After the sunsets and the dooryards and the sprinkled streets,
After the novels, after the teacups, after the skirts that trail
    along the floor—
And this, and so much more?—
It is impossible to say just what I mean!
105 But as if a magic lantern[10] threw the nerves in patterns on a
    screen:
Would it have been worth while
If one, settling a pillow or throwing off a shawl,
And turning toward the window, should say:
        " That is not it at all,
110 That is not what I meant, at all."

        .   .   .   .   .   .

No! I am not Prince Hamlet, nor was meant to be;
Am an attendant lord, one that will do

7. **head . . . platter** a reference to the prophet John the Baptist, whose head was delivered on
    a platter to Salome as a reward for her dancing (Matthew 14:1–11).
8. **eternal Footman** death.
9. **Lazarus** (laz´ ə rəs) Lazarus is resurrected from the dead by Jesus in John 11:1–44.
10. **magic lantern** an early device used to project images on a screen.

**Adjusting
Reading Rate**

When you slow down to
read lines 87–98, what do
you notice about Eliot's use
of rhyme?

Comprehension

What questions does
Prufrock repeatedly
ask himself?

To swell a progress,[11] start a scene or two,
Advise the prince; no doubt, an easy tool,
115 Deferential, glad to be of use,
Politic, cautious, and meticulous;
Full of high sentence,[12] but a bit obtuse;
At times, indeed, almost ridiculous—
Almost, at times, the Fool.

120 I grow old . . . I grow old . . .
I shall wear the bottoms of my trousers rolled.

Shall I part my hair behind? Do I dare to eat a peach?
I shall wear white flannel trousers, and walk upon the beach.
I have heard the mermaids singing, each to each.

125 I do not think that they will sing to me.

I have seen them riding seaward on the waves
Combing the white hair of the waves blown back
When the wind blows the water white and black.

We have lingered in the chambers of the sea
130 By sea-girls wreathed with seaweed red and brown
Till human voices wake us, and we drown.

Vocabulary

meticulous (mə tik´ yoo
ləs) *adj.* precise about
details

obtuse (äb toos´)
adj. slow to understand
or perceive

I have heard the mermaids singing, each to each.

---

11. **To swell a progress** to add to the number of people in a parade or scene from a play.
12. **Full of high sentence** speaking in a very ornate manner, often offering advice.

Critical Reading

Cite textual evidence to support your responses.

1. **Key Ideas and Details** **(a) Interpret:** In lines 96–97, how does the woman react to Prufrock? **(b) Describe:** In line 125, how does Prufrock describe the mermaids' reactions to him? **(c) Connect:** How does Prufrock seem to feel about women and their interest in him?

2. **Key Ideas and Details** **(a)** In line 85, who or what does Prufrock see? **(b) Make a Judgment:** Do you think Prufrock is simply afraid of death, or are his fears more complicated? Explain.

3. **Integration of Knowledge and Ideas** Do you think the poem is simply a portrait of one man, or does it represent something deeper in modern society? In your response, use at least two of these Essential Question words: *companionship, reluctance, alienation, self-consciousness. [Connecting to the Essential Question: How does literature shape or reflect society?]*

MODERNISM

Modernism, an artistic movement that rejected traditional forms and emphasized bold new ways of expression, revolutionized arts and audiences worldwide. In 1913, the premiere of the ballet *The Rite of Spring* caused a riot in Paris. Members of the audience were horrified by the dissonant music composed by Igor Stravinsky and the angular movements choreographed by Vaslav Nijinsky. Supporters and detractors shouted and threw punches. Soon, the police arrived to break things up, but many remembered that event as the birth of Modernism.

Artistic movements are not really born in a day, though. They develop slowly. The seeds of Modernism sprouted in the decades before World War I, as many artists came to Paris. The young Spanish painter Pablo Picasso arrived in Paris in 1900 and met writers Guillaume Apollinaire, Max Jacob, and Gertrude Stein. French painters Marcel Duchamp and Fernand Léger were already on the scene. American dancer Isadora Duncan spent time in Paris. So did T. S. Eliot, E. E. Cummings, Edward Munch, Piet Mondrian, and Umberto Boccioni. After the war, Ernest Hemingway, Ezra Pound, James Joyce, and Alexander Calder moved to Paris. The ideas of these Modernist pioneers quickly spread across borders. Modernism had become a truly international movement.

▲ Art in Motion
The son and grandson of Philadelphia sculptors, Alexander Calder moved to Paris in 1926, where he designed toys and a miniature circus. When he created a series of sculptures that moved, Marcel Duchamp dubbed them "mobiles."

HeMobile, 1955, Alexander Calder, CNAC/MNAM/Dist. Réunion des Musées Nationaux / Art Resource, NY

Head of a Woman, 1908, Pablo Picasso, image copyright © The Metropolitan Museum of Art / Art Resource, NY

▲ Cubism Is Born
Picasso was influenced by African art in the development of his Cubist style.

CONNECT TO THE LITERATURE

What evidence of international influences can you find in "The Love Song of J. Alfred Prufrock"?

American Modern
American dancer and choreographer Martha Graham (shown dancing *Letter to the World* in 1940) created the technique and vocabulary for modern dance. In 1944, she choreographed the seminal *Appalachian Spring*, set to music by Aaron Copland. ▶

Literary Analysis

1. **Key Ideas and Details** What do his descriptions of the sky and the city in lines 1–12 suggest about Prufrock's outlook on life?

2. **Key Ideas and Details** **(a)** How can the first line of this **dramatic monologue** be interpreted to suggest that Prufrock sees himself as divided, both seeking and fearing action? **(b)** At what other points does he express a deeply conflicted sense of self?

3. **Craft and Structure** **(a)** At what points in the poem did you **adjust your reading rate** by slowing down to listen for rhyme, repetition, and other sound elements? **(b)** Explain how this strategy helped you better understand the poem.

4. **Craft and Structure** What is the effect of the repetition of "there will be time" in lines 23–34 and again in lines 37–48?

5. **Craft and Structure** Some of Prufrock's **allusions** paint imaginary portraits that reveal his sense of self. Use a chart like the one shown to examine these allusions and what they suggest about Prufrock's self-image.

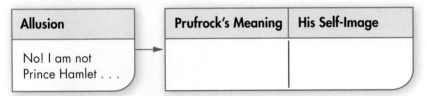

Allusion	Prufrock's Meaning	His Self-Image
No! I am not Prince Hamlet . . .		

6. **Craft and Structure** **(a)** Review the first footnote and explain the meaning of the opening allusion—the passage from Dante's *Inferno*. **(b)** What does this quotation suggest about the content of the poem that follows?

7. **Craft and Structure** **(a)** What is suggested by the repeated reference to Michelangelo? **(b)** In what ways would the portrayal of Prufrock's world be quite different if that reference were to something less refined?

8. **Integration of Knowledge and Ideas** **(a)** In lines 49–54, what image does Prufrock use to describe how he has "measured out" his life? **(b)** In your own words, explain how Prufrock has lived.

9. **Analyzing Visual Information** Explain the humor in this cartoon.

Common Core State Standards

Writing

1. Write arguments to support claims in an analysis of substantive topics or texts, using valid reasoning and relevant and sufficient evidence. *(p. 715)*

4. Produce clear and coherent writing in which the development, organization, and style are appropriate to task, purpose, and audience. *(p. 715)*

Language

3. Apply knowledge of language to understand how language functions in different contexts, to make effective choices for meaning or style, and to comprehend more fully when reading or listening. *(p. 715)*

5.b. Use the relationship between particular words to better understand each of the words. *(p. 715)*

© *The New Yorker* Collection 1994 Bruce Eric Kaplan from cartoonbank.com. All Rights Reserved.

"I have heard the mermaids singing, each to each. I told them to pipe down."

▲ *"I have heard the mermaids singing, each to each. I told them to pipe down."*

Vocabulary Acquistion and Use

Word Analysis: Greek Prefix *di-*

The Greek prefix *di-* (or *dis-*) means "apart" or "away." The word *digress* means "to move away from a subject." Each of the sentences below includes a word containing the prefix *di-* or *dis-*. Indicate whether each sentence is true or false and write a brief explanation of your choice.

1. A path *diverges* if it branches off.
2. If you are *diverted*, your focus is sharp.
3. If a rumor is *dispelled*, people are likely to believe it.
4. If information is *divulged*, many will have access to it.
5. To *dilate* an object will make it more narrow.
6. A *diverse* menu features many similar foods.
7. A *discerning* person can tell truth from lies.

Vocabulary: Synonyms

Review the words from the vocabulary list on page 706. Then, choose the letter of the word that is the best synonym, or word with a similar meaning, for the first word. Explain your thinking.

1. tedious: **(a)** twisted, **(b)** direct, **(c)** humble, **(d)** engaging
2. insidious: **(a)** innocent, **(b)** wealthy, **(c)** dangerous, **(d)** certified
3. digress: **(a)** wander, **(b)** contain, **(c)** hesitate, **(d)** elaborate
4. malingers: **(a)** fakes, **(b)** studies, **(c)** boasts, **(d)** anticipates
5. meticulous: **(a)** messy, **(b)** absurd, **(c)** careful, **(d)** tart
6. obtuse: **(a)** intense, **(b)** stupid, **(c)** friendly, **(d)** prompt

Writing to Sources

Argumentative Text Ever since Eliot's "Love Song" was published in 1915, J. Alfred Prufrock has fascinated readers. For some, Prufrock is merely a man who fails to achieve his dreams. For others, he embodies larger failings of the modern age—an absence of heroism or a general weariness. Write an **essay** presenting and defending your own analysis of this character.

Prewriting Reread the poem, taking notes about Prufrock's character. Pay attention to details that suggest reasons for Prufrock's passivity and fears, and support your viewpoint through detailed references to the text.

Drafting Begin by noting the title and author of the work. Then, state your opinion about Prufrock's character. Use quotes from the poem and precise language to develop your ideas in each body paragraph.

Revising Review your draft. Highlight any words that seem vague or inaccurate. Use a thesaurus to replace them with more specific words.

Model: Revising Word Choice for Accuracy

Prufrock's lament is ~~big~~. sweeping ~~He talks about~~ pines for all that he has lost or that he never had—youth and love. He is keenly aware of, even tormented by, ~~and really upset about~~ the passage of time.

> Replacing vague words with specific ones makes a piece of writing more accurate and powerful.

The Imagist Poets

Background: Imagism

Imagism was a literary movement established in the early 1900s by Ezra Pound and other poets. As the name suggests, the Imagists concentrated on the direct presentation of images, or word pictures. An Imagist poem expressed the essence of an object, person, or incident, without providing explanations. Through the spare, clean presentation of an image, the Imagists hoped to freeze a single moment in time and to capture the emotions of that moment. To accomplish this purpose, the Imagists used the language of everyday speech.

The Imagists were influenced by traditional Chinese and Japanese poetry. Many Imagist poems bear a close resemblance to the Japanese verse forms of *haiku* and *tanka*, which generally evoke an emotional response through the presentation of a single image or a pair of contrasting images.

The Imagist movement was short-lived, lasting only until about 1918. However, for many years that followed, the poems of Pound, Williams, H.D. and other Imagists continued to influence the work of other poets, including Wallace Stevens, T.S. Eliot, and Hart Crane.

Ezra Pound *(1885–1972)*

Author of **"A Few Don'ts"** and **"In a Station of the Metro"**

As both an editor and a poet, Ezra Pound inspired the dramatic changes in American poetry that characterized the Modern Age. His insistence that writers "make it new" led many poets to discard the forms, techniques, and ideas of the past and to experiment with new approaches to poetry.

After college, Pound traveled to Europe, where he spent most of his life. Settling in London and later moving to Paris, he became a vital voice in the growing Modernist movement. Pound influenced the work of the Irish poet William Butler Yeats, as well as that of T. S. Eliot, William Carlos Williams, H. D., Marianne Moore, and Ernest Hemingway—a "who's who" of the literary voices of the age. He is best remembered, however, for his role in the development of Imagism.

Despite his preoccupation with originality and inventiveness, Pound's work often drew upon the poetry of ancient cultures. Many of his poems are filled with literary and historical allusions, requiring that readers apply background knowledge or use reference sources to fully understand his meaning.

William Carlos Williams (1883–1963)

Author of "The Red Wheelbarrow," "This Is Just to Say," and "The Great Figure"

Unlike his fellow Imagists, William Carlos Williams spent most of his life in the United States, where he pursued a double career as a poet and a pediatrician in New Jersey. He felt that his experiences as a doctor provided him with inspiration as a poet, and credited medicine for his ability to "gain entrance to . . . the secret gardens of the self."

The child of immigrants, Williams grew up speaking Spanish, French, and British English. He was enamored of American language and life, and believed that common experience contains the seeds of the extraordinary. In volumes such as *Spring and All* (1923), he focused on capturing the essence of America by depicting ordinary people, objects, and experiences in everyday language.

In his later work, Williams departed from pure Imagism in order to write more expansively. His five-volume poem *Paterson* (1946–1958) explores the idea of a city as a symbol for a man. The poem is based on the real city of Paterson, New Jersey.

Williams continued to write even after his failing health forced him to give up his medical practice. In 1963, he received a Pulitzer Prize for *Pictures from Breughel and Other Poems*, his final volume of poetry.

H.D. (Hilda Doolittle) (1886–1961)

Author of "Pear Tree"

In 1913, Ezra Pound reshaped three of Hilda Doolittle's poems and submitted them to *Poetry* magazine under the name "H. D., Imagiste," thus giving birth to the Imagist movement. The publication of the poems also served to launch the successful career of the young poet, who continued to publish under the name H. D. throughout her life.

Like the Greek lyrics that she admired, H. D.'s early poems were brief, precise, and direct. Often emphasizing light, color, and physical textures, she created vivid, emotive images. In 1925, almost all of H. D.'s early poems were gathered in *Collected Poems*, a book that also contained her translations from the *Odyssey* and from the Greek poet Sappho. She also wrote a play, *Hippolytus Temporizes*, which appeared in 1927, and two prose works, *Palimpsest* (1926) and *Hedylus* (1928). During the later stages of her career, she focused on writing longer works, including an epic poem. H. D. is best remembered, however, for her early Imagist work.

Connecting to the Essential Question Many Imagist poems focus on a single detail of nature or place. As you read, notice how these poems describe ordinary things in extraordinary ways. Doing so will help as you think about the Essential Question: **What is the relationship between literature and place?**

Close Reading Focus

Imagism
Imagism was a literary movement begun in the early 1900s by Ezra Pound and other poets. As the name suggests, Imagist poetry evokes emotion and sparks the imagination through the vivid presentation of a limited number of **images,** or words and phrases that appeal to the senses. The poem "In a Station of the Metro," for example, presents just two images in only two lines and fourteen well-chosen words.

Comparing Literary Works In his essay "A Few Don'ts," Ezra Pound describes the image as more than a simple word-picture:

> An "Image" is that which presents an intellectual and emotional complex in an instant of time.

For Pound, the image brings the reader a new way of seeing—on the physical level through the senses, and on higher levels through the emotions and the intellect. As you read these poems, think about which best achieve the effect of "that sense of sudden growth" that Pound believed was the highest achievement of art.

Preparing to Read Complex Texts When reading Imagist poetry, increase your understanding by **engaging your senses.** As you encounter each image, re-create in your mind the sights, sounds, smells, tastes, and physical sensations it evokes. Note that some images may appeal to more than one sense at a time. For example, in "This Is Just to Say," the image of plums as "delicious / so sweet / and so cold" appeals to both taste *and* touch. Use a chart like the one shown to record how you engage your senses as you read these poems.

Vocabulary

You will encounter the words listed here in the texts that follow. Copy the words into your notebook. Which word is connected to the idea of visibility? How can you tell?

voluminous   **apparition**

dogma

Common Core State Standards

Reading Literature
4. Determine the meaning of words and phrases as they are used in the text, including figurative and connotative meanings; analyze the impact of specific word choices on meaning and tone, including language that is particularly fresh, engaging, or beautiful.
9. Demonstrate knowledge of early-twentieth-century foundational works of American literature, including how two or more texts from the same period treat similar themes or topics.

A Few Don'ts

Ezra Pound

BACKGROUND Ezra Pound was one of the leading figures in the Imagist movement. As the name suggests, Imagists concentrated on the focused presentation of images, or word-pictures. For example, Pound's original draft of "In a Station of the Metro" consisted of 30 lines. Pound whittled away at the poem until he arrived at a work of only 14 words of great precision and power. In this essay, Pound discusses his beliefs about what poetry should and should not be.

An "Image" is that which presents an intellectual and emotional complex in an instant of time. I use the term "complex" rather in the technical sense employed by the newer psychologists, such as Hart, though we might not agree absolutely in our application.

It is the presentation of such a "complex" instantaneously which gives that sense of sudden liberation; that sense of freedom from time limits and space limits; that sense of sudden growth, which we experience in the presence of the greatest works of art.

It is better to present one Image in a lifetime than to produce **voluminous** works.

All this, however, some may consider open to debate. The immediate necessity is to tabulate A LIST OF DON'TS for those beginning to write verses. But I can not put all of them into Mosaic negative.[1]

To begin with, consider the three propositions[2] . . . not as **dogma**—never consider anything as dogma—but as the result of long contemplation, which, even if it is someone else's contemplation, may be worth consideration. . . .

Vocabulary

voluminous (və lo͞om′ ə nəs) *adj.* of enough material to fill volumes

dogma (dôg′ mə) *n.* authoritative doctrines or beliefs

Comprehension

According to Pound, what is an image?

---

1. **Mosaic negative** Pound is referring to the Ten Commandments presented by Moses to the Israelites in the Hebrew Bible. Many of the commandments are in the negative and begin with the words "Thou shalt not . . ."
2. **three propositions** Pound is referring to the three rules that English Imagist poet Frank Stuart Flint formulated for the writing of Imagist poetry:
   1. direct treatment of the "thing" either subjective or objective
   2. to use absolutely no word that does not contribute to the presentation
   3. as regarding rhythm: to compose in sequence of the musical phrase, not in sequence of a metronome

LANGUAGE

Use no superfluous word, no adjective, which does not reveal something.

Don't use such an expression as "dim lands *of peace*." It dulls the image. It mixes an abstraction with the concrete. It comes from the writer's not realizing that the natural object is always the *adequate* symbol.

Go in fear of abstractions. Do not retell in mediocre verse what has already been done in good prose. Don't think any intelligent person is going to be deceived when you try to shirk all the difficulties of the unspeakably difficult art of good prose by chopping your composition into line lengths. . . .

Don't imagine that the art of poetry is any simpler than the art of music, or that you can please the expert before you have spent at least as much effort on the art of verse as the average piano teacher spends on the art of music. . . .

RHYTHM AND RHYME

. . . Don't imagine that a thing will "go" in verse just because it's too dull to go in prose.

Don't be "viewy"—leave that to the writers of pretty little philo-

Imagist Poetry

Why is the rule of avoiding abstractions consistent with the goals of Imagist poetry?

▲ **Critical Viewing** What key details might be emphasized in an Imagist poem about this portrait of Ezra Pound? **SYNTHESIZE**

sophic essays. Don't be descriptive; remember that the painter can describe a landscape much better than you can, and that he has to know a deal more about it.

When Shakespeare talks of the "Dawn in russet mantle clad" he presents something which the painter does not present. There is in this line of his nothing that one can call description; he presents. . . .

Don't chop your stuff into separate *iambs*.[3] Don't make each line stop dead at the end, and then begin every next line with a heave. Let the beginning of the next line catch the rise of the rhythm wave, unless you want a definite longish pause.

In short, behave as a musician, a good musician, when dealing with that phase of your art which has exact parallels in music. The same laws govern, and you are bound by no others. . . .

A rhyme must have in it some slight element of surprise if it is to give pleasure; it need not be bizarre or curious, but it must be well used if used at all. . . .

Don't mess up the perception of one sense by trying to define it in terms of another. This is usually only the result of being too lazy to find the exact word. To this clause there are possibly exceptions.

The first three simple proscriptions[4] will throw out nine-tenths of all the bad poetry now accepted as standard and classic; and will prevent you from many a crime of production. . . .

---

3. **iambs** (ī′ ambz) *n.* metrical feet, each consisting of an unaccented syllable followed by an accented one.
4. **The first three simple proscriptions** reference to Flint's three rules outlined in footnote #2.

Critical Reading

1. **Key Ideas and Details (a)** What three rules does Pound invite readers to consider? **(b) Define:** What is the difference between dogma and the results of "long contemplation"? **(c) Speculate:** Why might Pound prefer a list of "don'ts" to a list of "do's"?

2. **Key Ideas and Details (a)** What does Pound consider preferable to abstractions? **(b) Analyze:** Why would the use of abstractions be offensive to an Imagist poet?

3. **Key Ideas and Details (a)** Does Pound think Shakespeare's image is an example of description or presentation?
   (b) Distinguish: How does presentation differ from description?

4. **Craft and Structure Make a Decision:** Pound says that defining one sense in terms of another is "usually the result of being too lazy to find the exact word." Do you agree with this statement? Explain your position.

5. **Integration of Knowledge and Ideas Evaluate:** Do you think following Pound's "don'ts" would make it easier or more difficult to write poetry? Explain.

Cite textual evidence to support your responses.

IN A STATION OF THE METRO

Ezra Pound

Vocabulary
apparition (ap´ ə rish´ ən) *n.*
act of appearing or
becoming visible

The apparition of these faces in the crowd;
Petals on a wet, black bough.

---

1. **Metro** the Paris subway.

Critical Reading

Cite textual evidence to support your responses.

1. **Key Ideas and Details (a)** What two things does Pound compare in this poem? **(b) Interpret:** In what ways does this poem capture the essence of a single moment?

2. **Key Ideas and Details Analyze:** Given the poem's setting, why is the image of "petals on a wet, black bough" surprising?

3. **Craft and Structure Infer:** Why do you think Pound chose to use the word *apparition* rather than *appearance*?

4. **Integration of Knowledge and Ideas Evaluate:** How well does "In a Station of the Metro" follow the advice given in "A Few Don'ts"? Explain.

The Red Wheelbarrow

William Carlos Williams

so much depends
upon

a red wheel
barrow

5 glazed with rain
water

beside the white
chickens.

Image
What two images dominate this poem?

This Is Just to Say

William Carlos Williams

I have eaten
the plums
that were in
the icebox
5 and which
you were probably
saving
for breakfast

Forgive me
10 they were delicious
so sweet
and so cold

Engaging Your Senses
To what senses does the central image in this poem appeal?

The Great Figure

William Carlos Williams

The Figure 5 in Gold, Charles Demuth, Metropolitan Museum of Art

Among the rain
and lights
I saw the figure 5
in gold
5 on a red
fire truck
moving
tense
unheeded
10 to gong clangs
siren howls
and wheels rumbling
through the dark city.

▲ **Critical Viewing** Artist Charles Demuth created this work of art to accompany his friend Williams's poem. What elements of the painting convey the energy and clamor of the poem? **CONNECT**

Critical Reading

1. **Key Ideas and Details (a)** In "The Red Wheelbarrow," what words does Williams split to run on two lines? **(b) Analyze:** What is the effect? Explain.

2. **Key Ideas and Details (a)** What is the intention of the speaker in "This Is Just to Say"? **(b) Connect:** Which details in the second stanza challenge the speaker's sincerity?

3. **Key Ideas and Details (a)** In "The Great Figure," what detail of the fire truck is the focus of the speaker's experience? **(b) Interpret:** In focusing on this detail, what might Williams be saying about beauty and modern life?

4. **Craft and Structure Evaluate:** Which elements of these poems reflect Williams's interest in portraying and celebrating everyday American life?

Cite textual evidence to support your responses.

PEAR TREE H. D.

Silver dust
lifted from the earth,
higher than my arms reach,
you have mounted,
5   O silver,
higher than my arms reach
you front us with great mass;

no flower ever opened
so staunch a white leaf,
10   no flower ever parted silver
from such rare silver;

O white pear,
your flower-tufts
thick on the branch
15   bring summer and ripe fruits
in their purple hearts.

▲ **Critical Viewing**
Which phrases from the
poem best describe this
image of a pear tree in full
flower? **EVALUATE**

Critical Reading

1. **Key Ideas and Details (a)** What is the "silver dust" referred to
   in the first stanza? **(b) Interpret:** In what sense is the dust "lifted
   from the earth"?

2. **Key Ideas and Details (a)** What does the pear tree's blossom
   anticipate? **(b) Infer:** What time of year is the speaker describing?

3. **Key Ideas and Details Assess:** How would you define the
   speaker's relationship to nature?

4. **Integration of Knowledge and Ideas** What larger portrait of
   the American landscape emerges from the common, everyday
   images in these poems? In your response, use at least two of
   these Essential Question words: *commonplace, medley, essence,
   contemplate.* *[Connecting to the Essential Question: What is
   the relationship between literature and place?]*

*Cite textual
evidence to
support your
responses.*

Literary Analysis

1. **Key Ideas and Details Engage your senses** while rereading "In a Station of the Metro." **(a)** To what senses does the image in this poem appeal? **(b)** How does engaging your senses affect your understanding and appreciation of the poem?

2. **Craft and Structure** Of the fourteen words in "In a Station of the Metro," not one of them is a verb. **(a)** How does this absence reflect the criteria Pound lists in his essay? **(b)** How does it affect the reader's experience of the poem?

3. **Key Ideas and Details** In "The Red Wheelbarrow," what do you think is the "so much" that "depends / upon / a red wheel / barrow"? Apply what you know about **Imagist poetry** to answer this question.

4. **Craft and Structure** In what ways would the meaning of the poem be different if Williams had used "the" instead of "a" to identify the wheelbarrow?

5. **Craft and Structure** Using a chart like the one shown, identify **images** of color in the poems by Williams. Explain the differing emotions these uses of color evoke.

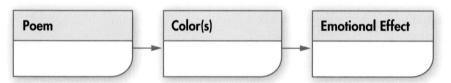

Poem	Color(s)	Emotional Effect

6. **Craft and Structure (a)** To what sense does "Pear Tree" mainly appeal? **(b)** To what sense does "The Red Wheelbarrow" mainly appeal? **(c)** Give two examples of passages from each poem that support your answers.

7. **Integration of Knowledge and Ideas (a)** Which of the five poems engages the sense of hearing most? Explain. **(b)** How do the sounds in that poem help to sharpen the central image?

8. **Integration of Knowledge and Ideas** Although Pound wrote "the painter can describe a landscape much better than you can," in what ways are these poems like paintings?

9. **Comparing Literary Works** In what ways is Pound's advice to **(a)** avoid abstractions and **(b)** avoid superfluous words evident in all of these poems?

10. **Comparing Literary Works (a)** According to Pound, what does a good musician do that a poet should emulate? **(b)** Do H. D. and Williams achieve this skill in their poems? Explain.

11. **Comparing Literary Works** Which of these poems best exemplifies Pound's idea of the image as "that which presents an intellectual and emotional complex in an instant of time"? Explain your choice.

Common Core State Standards

Writing

2. Write explanatory texts to examine and convey complex ideas, concepts, and information clearly and accurately through the effective selection, organization, and analysis of content. *(p. 727)*

2.b. Develop the topic thoroughly by selecting the most significant and relevant facts, extended definitions, concrete details, quotations, or other information and examples appropriate to the audience's knowledge of the topic. *(p. 727)*

2.c Use precise language. *(p. 727)*

Language

4.b. Identify and correctly use patterns of word changes that indicate different meanings or parts of speech. *(p. 727)*

Vocabulary Acquisition and Use

Word Analysis: Forms of *appear*

Several common English words are forms of the verb *appear*, meaning "to come into sight or into being" or "to become understood."

apparent   appearance   apparition

Complete each of the sentences with the correct word from the list above. Explain your choices.

1. He made a brief _____ at the awards dinner, just long enough to pick up his trophy and say a few words.

2. When midnight found the toddlers still running around the house, it became _____ that the babysitter was not in control.

3. The _____ of a face at the window nearly stopped her heart with fear.

Vocabulary: True or False

Decide whether each statement below is true or false. Explain your answers.

1. You should not accept as <u>dogma</u> everything that a two-year-old says.

2. A person who takes <u>voluminous</u> notes can easily store them in a pocket folder.

3. An <u>apparition</u> will go unnoticed by someone wearing a blindfold.

Writing to Sources

Explanatory Text Imagine that you are a magazine editor who has just received a manuscript from an Imagist poet. Write a **letter** to the poet explaining why you will or will not publish his or her poems. Be simple, honest, and kind, and include constructive criticism.

Prewriting Choose a poet and reread the poem or poems. Take notes on the strengths and weaknesses of each poem, citing relevant passages.

Drafting Write a letter that explains why you will or will not publish the poems. Discuss strengths and identify flaws. Support your viewpoint through detailed references to the poet's work.

Revising Review your draft, highlighting any words that are inaccurate or vague. Use a thesaurus to replace these words with more precise choices.

Model: Revising for Clarity

deceptively simple
Your poems are small and ~~not complex~~, but they are rich in imagery

wry
and ideas. I especially enjoyed the ~~incredible~~ tone of "This Is Just
to Say."

Replacing vague words with specific words helps to express ideas exactly.

Connecting to the Essential Question The main character of this story is preoccupied with wealth and all that it brings. As you read, notice Fitzgerald's descriptions of "glittering things." Doing so will help as you think about the Essential Question: **How does literature shape or reflect society?**

Close Reading Focus

Characters; Characterization

All fictional works have **characters,** the personalities represented in a story. Characters fall into two basic categories: **Flat characters** are one-dimensional, with few character traits. Their main role is to advance the action. **Round characters** have many character traits. They are usually the main characters. Authors use these specific strategies to develop characters:

- **Direct characterization:** The narrator simply tells the reader what a character is like. Example: "She is honest."

- **Indirect characterization:** The writer reveals characters through their thoughts, actions, words, and other characters' reactions.

As you read, notice how Fitzgerald brings his characters into sharp focus.

Preparing to Read Complex Texts Fitzgerald often leaves it up to the reader to draw inferences about his characters. To **draw inferences about characters,** combine information from the story with your own knowledge of life. Consider this example:

> *Dexter stood perfectly still . . . if he moved forward a step his stare would be in her line of vision—if he moved backward he would lose his full view of her face.*

If you have ever wanted to hide your interest in someone but could not stop looking, you can draw a strong inference from this scene: Dexter is enthralled by someone. Use a chart like the one shown to draw inferences.

Vocabulary

You will encounter the words listed here in the text that follows. Copy the words into your notebook. Can you infer which two words are nouns? How can you tell?

fallowness	mundane
fortuitous	poignant
sinuous	sediment

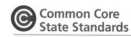
**Common Core
State Standards**

Reading Literature

1. Cite strong and thorough textual evidence to support analysis of what the text says explicitly as well as inferences drawn from the text, including determining where the text leaves matters uncertain.

3. Analyze the impact of the author's choices regarding how to develop and relate elements of a story or drama (e.g., how the characters are introduced and developed).

9. Demonstrate knowledge of early-twentieth-century foundational works of American literature.

F. Scott Fitzgerald *(1896–1940)*

Author of **"Winter Dreams"**

When you open the pages of one of F. Scott Fitzgerald's books, you are transported back in time to the Roaring Twenties, when many Americans lived with reckless abandon, attending wild parties, wearing glamorous clothing, and striving for fulfillment through material wealth. Yet, this quest for pleasure was often accompanied by a sense of inner despair. Fitzgerald was able to capture the paradoxes of this glittering, materialistic lifestyle because he actually lived it.

A Quick Rise to Fame Francis Scott Key Fitzgerald was born in St. Paul, Minnesota, into a family with high social aspirations but little wealth. As a young man, Fitzgerald was eager to improve his social standing. He entered Princeton University in 1913, where he pursued the type of high-profile social life for which he would later become famous. Fitzgerald failed to graduate and soon enlisted in the army.

His first novel, *This Side of Paradise* (1920), published shortly after his discharge from the service, was an instant success. Buoyed by the fame and wealth the book gave him, Fitzgerald courted Zelda Sayre, a southern belle with whom he had fallen in love while in the army. They married in 1920. Together, they blazed an extravagant trail across New York and Europe, mingling with the rich and famous and spending money recklessly.

An American Masterpiece Despite his pleasure-seeking lifestyle, Fitzgerald remained a productive writer. In 1925, he published *The Great Gatsby*, the story of a self-made man whose dreams of love and social acceptance end in tragedy. The book is widely considered to be Fitzgerald's masterpiece and one of the greatest novels in American literature.

Fortunes Turn After the 1929 stock market crash, Fitzgerald's world began to crumble. His wife suffered a series of nervous breakdowns, and financial problems forced him to seek work as a screenwriter. Despite these setbacks, however, he managed to produce many more short stories and a second novel, *Tender Is the Night* (1934). He was in the midst of writing *The Last Tycoon* when he died of a heart attack in 1940. His editor approached the novelist John O'Hara about finishing the book, but O'Hara declined. In a letter O'Hara wrote to author John Steinbeck, he explained his refusal: "Fitzgerald was a better just plain writer than all of us put together. Just words writing."

WINTER DREAMS

F. Scott Fitzgerald

BACKGROUND Written in 1922, this story unfolds against the background of the Jazz Age. Focusing on Dexter Green's obsession with Judy Jones, a beautiful young woman from a prominent wealthy family, Fitzgerald explores the connections between love, money, and social status. Through Dexter, he shows what life was like in the 1920s for an ambitious young man driven by the desire for "glittering things."

◀ **Critical Viewing**
Which details in this illustration demonstrate women's newfound freedoms during the Jazz Age? **DEDUCE**

Some of the caddies were poor as sin and lived in one-room houses with a neurasthenic[1] cow in the front yard, but Dexter Green's father owned the second best grocery store in Black Bear—the best one was "The Hub," patronized by the wealthy people from Sherry Island—and Dexter caddied only for pocket money.

In the fall when the days became crisp and gray, and the long Minnesota winter shut down like the white lid of a box, Dexter's skis moved over the snow that hid the fairways of the golf course. At these times the country gave him a feeling of profound melancholy—it offended him that the links should lie in enforced **fallowness**, haunted by ragged sparrows for the long season. It was dreary, too, that on the tees where the gay colors fluttered in summer there were now only the desolate sandboxes knee deep in crusted ice. When he crossed the hills the wind blew cold as misery, and if the sun was out he tramped with his eyes squinted up against the hard dimensionless glare.

In April the winter ceased abruptly. The snow ran down into Black Bear Lake scarcely tarrying for the early golfers to brave the season with red and black balls. Without elation, without an interval of moist glory, the cold was gone. Dexter knew that there was something dismal about this Northern spring, just as he knew there was something gorgeous about the fall. Fall made him clinch his hands and tremble and repeat idiotic sentences to himself, and make brisk abrupt gestures of command to imaginary audiences and armies. October filled him with hope which November raised to a sort of ecstatic triumph, and in this mood the fleeting brilliant impressions of the summer at Sherry Island were ready grist to his mill. He became a golf champion and defeated Mr. T. A. Hedrick in a marvelous match played a hundred times over the fairways of his imagination, a match each detail of which he changed about untiringly—sometimes he won with almost laughable ease, sometimes he came

Vocabulary
fallowness (fal´ ō nis) *n.* inactivity

Comprehension
What does Dexter do for pocket money?

---

1. **neurasthenic** (no� ́ əs then´ ik) *adj.* here, weak; tired.

up magnificently from behind. Again, stepping from a Pierce-Arrow automobile, like Mr. Mortimer Jones, he strolled frigidly into the lounge of the Sherry Island Golf Club—or perhaps, surrounded by an admiring crowd, he gave an exhibition of fancy diving from the springboard of the club raft. . . . Among those who watched him in open-mouthed wonder was Mr. Mortimer Jones.

And one day it came to pass that Mr. Jones—himself and not his ghost—came up to Dexter with tears in his eyes and said that Dexter was the—best caddy in the club, and wouldn't he decide not to quit if Mr. Jones made it worth his while, because every other—caddy in the club lost one ball a hole for him—regularly—

"No, sir," said Dexter decisively, "I don't want to caddy any more." Then, after a pause: "I'm too old."

"You're not more than fourteen. Why the devil did you decide just this morning that you wanted to quit? You promised that next week you'd go over to the state tournament with me."

"I decided I was too old."

Dexter handed in his "A Class" badge, collected what money was due him from the caddy master, and walked home to Black Bear Village.

"The best—caddy I ever saw," shouted Mr. Mortimer Jones over a drink that afternoon. "Never lost a ball! Willing! Intelligent! Quiet! Honest! Grateful!"

The little girl who had done this was eleven—beautifully ugly as little girls are apt to be who are destined after a few years to be inexpressibly lovely and bring no end of misery to a great number of men. The spark, however, was perceptible. There was a general ungodliness in the way her lips twisted down at the corners when she smiled, and in the—Heaven help us!—in the almost passionate quality of her eyes. Vitality is born early in such women. It was utterly in evidence now, shining through her thin frame in a sort of glow.

She had come eagerly out on to the course at nine o'clock with a white linen nurse and five small new golf clubs in a white canvas bag which the nurse was carrying. When Dexter first saw her she was standing by the caddy house, rather ill at ease and trying to conceal the fact by engaging her nurse in an obviously unnatural conversation graced by startling and irrelevant grimaces from herself.

"Well, it's certainly a nice day, Hilda," Dexter heard her say. She drew down the corners of her mouth, smiled, and glanced furtively around, her eyes in transit falling for an instant on Dexter.

Then to the nurse:

"Well, I guess there aren't very many people out here this morning, are there?"

The smile again—radiant, blatantly artificial—convincing.

Characterization

What methods of characterization does Fitzgerald use in this introduction to Judy Jones?

▲ **Critical Viewing**

How does this painting of two golfers and their caddies compare to your impression of Dexter's experience?
COMPARE AND CONTRAST

"I don't know what we're supposed to do now," said the nurse looking nowhere in particular.

"Oh, that's all right. I'll fix it up."

Dexter stood perfectly still, his mouth slightly ajar. He knew that if he moved forward a step his stare would be in her line of vision—if he moved backward he would lose his full view of her face. For a moment he had not realized how young she was. Now he remembered having seen her several times the year before—in bloomers.

Suddenly, involuntarily, he laughed, a short abrupt laugh—then, startled by himself, he turned and began to walk quickly away.

"Boy!"

Dexter stopped.

"Boy—"

Beyond question he was addressed. Not only that, but he was treated to that absurd smile, that preposterous smile—the memory of which at least a dozen men were to carry into middle age.

"Boy, do you know where the golf teacher is?"

"He's giving a lesson."

"Well, do you know where the caddy master is?"

"He isn't here yet this morning."

Comprehension

What does Dexter suddenly decide one day?

"Oh." For a moment this baffled her. She stood alternately on her right and left foot.

"We'd like to get a caddy," said the nurse. "Mrs. Mortimer Jones sent us out to play golf, and we don't know how without we get a caddy."

Here she was stopped by an ominous glance from Miss Jones, followed immediately by the smile.

"There aren't any caddies here except me," said Dexter to the nurse, "and I got to stay here in charge until the caddy master gets here."

"Oh."

Miss Jones and her retinue now withdrew, and at a proper distance from Dexter became involved in a heated conversation, which was concluded by Miss Jones taking one of the clubs and hitting it on the ground with violence. For further emphasis she raised it again and was about to bring it down smartly upon the nurse's bosom, when the nurse seized the club and twisted it from her hands.

"You little mean old *thing*!" cried Miss Jones wildly.

Another argument ensued. Realizing that the elements of the comedy were implied in the scene, Dexter several times began to laugh, but each time restrained the laugh before it reached audibility. He could not resist the monstrous conviction that the little girl was justified in beating the nurse.

The situation was resolved by the **fortuitous** appearance of the caddy master, who was appealed to immediately by the nurse.

"Miss Jones is to have a little caddy, and this one says he can't go."

"Mr. McKenna said I was to wait here till you came," said Dexter quickly.

"Well, he's here now." Miss Jones smiled cheerfully at the caddy master. Then she dropped her bag and set off at a haughty mince toward the first tee.

"Well?" The caddy master turned to Dexter. "What you standing there like a dummy for? Go pick up the young lady's clubs."

"I don't think I'll go out today," said Dexter.

"You don't—"

"I think I'll quit."

The enormity of his decision frightened him. He was a favorite caddy, and the thirty dollars a month he earned through the summer were not to be made elsewhere around the lake. But he had received a strong emotional shock, and his perturbation required a violent and immediate outlet.

It is not so simple as that, either. As so frequently would be the case in the future, Dexter was unconsciously dictated to by his winter dreams.

Characterization

What does the argument between Judy Jones and her nurse reveal about Judy?

Vocabulary

fortuitous (fôr to͞o′ ə təs) *adj.* fortunate

2

Now, of course, the quality and the seasonability of these winter dreams varied, but the stuff of them remained. They persuaded Dexter several years later to pass up a business course at the State university—his father, prospering now, would have paid his way—for the precarious advantage of attending an older and more famous university in the East, where he was bothered by his scanty funds. But do not get the impression, because his winter dreams happened to be concerned at first with musings on the rich, that there was anything merely snobbish in the boy. He wanted not association with glittering things and glittering people—he wanted the glittering things themselves. Often he reached out for the best without knowing why he wanted it—and sometimes he ran up against the mysterious denials and prohibitions in which life indulges. It is with one of those denials and not with his career as a whole that this story deals.

He made money. It was rather amazing. After college he went to the city from which Black Bear Lake draws its wealthy patrons. When he was only twenty-three and had been there not quite two years, there were already people who liked to say: "Now *there's* a boy—" All about him rich men's sons were peddling bonds precariously, or investing patrimonies precariously, or plodding through the two dozen volumes of the "George Washington Commercial Course," but Dexter borrowed a thousand dollars on his college degree and his confident mouth, and bought a partnership in a laundry.

It was a small laundry when he went into it, but Dexter made a specialty of learning how the English washed fine woolen golf stockings without shrinking them, and within a year he was catering to the trade that wore knickerbockers. Men were insisting that their Shetland hose and sweaters go to his laundry, just as they had insisted on a caddy who could find golf balls. A little later he was doing their wives' lingerie as well—and running five branches in different parts of the city. Before he was twenty-seven he owned the largest string of laundries in his section of the country. It was then that he sold out and went to New York. But the part of his story that concerns us goes back to the days when he was making his first big success.

When he was twenty-three Mr. Hart—one of the gray-haired men who like to say "Now there's a boy"—gave him a guest card to the Sherry Island Golf Club for a weekend. So he signed his name one day on the register, and that afternoon played golf in a foursome with Mr. Hart and Mr. Sandwood and Mr. T. A. Hedrick. He did not consider it necessary to remark that he had once carried Mr. Hart's bag over this same links, and that he knew every trap and gully with his eyes shut—but he found himself glancing at the four caddies who trailed them, trying to catch a gleam or gesture that would remind him of himself, that would lessen the gap which lay between his present and his past.

Comprehension
How does Dexter make money after college?

RB

It was a curious day, slashed abruptly with fleeting, familiar impressions. One minute he had the sense of being a trespasser—in the next he was impressed by the tremendous superiority he felt toward Mr. T. A. Hedrick, who was a bore and not even a good golfer any more.

Then, because of a ball Mr. Hart lost near the fifteenth green, an enormous thing happened. While they were searching the stiff grasses of the rough there was a clear call of "Fore!" from behind a hill in their rear. And as they all turned abruptly from their search a bright new ball sliced abruptly over the hill and caught Mr. T. A. Hedrick in the abdomen.

"By Gad!" cried Mr. T. A. Hedrick, "they ought to put some of these crazy women off the course. It's getting to be outrageous."

A head and a voice came up together over the hill:

"Do you mind if we go through?"

"You hit me in the stomach!" declared Mr. Hedrick wildly.

"Did I?" The girl approached the group of men. "I'm sorry. I yelled 'Fore!'"

Her glance fell casually on each of the men—then scanned the fairway for her ball.

"Did I bounce into the rough?"

It was impossible to determine whether this question was ingenuous or malicious. In a moment, however, she left no doubt, for as her partner came up over the hill she called cheerfully:

"Here I am! I'd have gone on the green except that I hit something."

As she took her stance for a short mashie shot, Dexter looked at her closely. She wore a blue gingham dress, rimmed at throat and shoulders with a white edging that accentuated her tan. The quality of exaggeration, of thinness, which had made her passionate eyes and down-turning mouth absurd at eleven, was gone now. She was arrestingly beautiful. The color in her cheeks was centered like the color in a picture—it was not a "high" color, but a sort of fluctuating and feverish warmth, so shaded that it seemed at any moment it would recede and disappear. This color and the mobility of her mouth gave a continual impression of flux, of intense life, of passionate vitality—balanced only partially by the sad luxury of her eyes.

She swung her mashie impatiently and without interest, pitching the ball into a sand pit on the other side of the green. With a quick, insincere smile and a careless "Thank you!" she went on after it.

"That Judy Jones!" remarked Mr. Hedrick on the next tee, as they waited—some moments—for her to play on ahead. "All she needs is to be turned up and spanked for six months and then to be married off to an old-fashioned cavalry captain."

"My God, she's good looking!" said Mr. Sandwood, who was just over thirty.

"Good looking!" cried Mr. Hedrick contemptuously, "she always

◀ **Critical Viewing**
Golf was once a game reserved for the privileged. How might meeting Judy in a setting like this have affected Dexter's impression of her? **ANALYZE**

Drawing Inferences About Characters
What does Judy's behavior toward the men on the golf course suggest about her character?

Comprehension
What "enormous thing" happens near the fifteenth green?

looks as if she wanted to be kissed! Turning those big coweyes on every calf in town!"

It was doubtful if Mr. Hedrick intended a reference to the maternal instinct.

"She'd play pretty good golf if she'd try," said Mr. Sandwood.

"She has no form," said Mr. Hedrick solemnly.

"She has a nice figure," said Mr. Sandwood.

"Better thank the Lord she doesn't drive a swifter ball," said Mr. Hart, winking at Dexter.

Later in the afternoon the sun went down with a riotous swirl of gold and varying blues and scarlets, and left the dry, rustling night of Western summer. Dexter watched from the veranda of the golf club, watched the even overlap of the waters in the little wind, silver molasses under the harvest moon. Then the moon held a finger to her lips and the lake became a clear pool, pale and quiet. Dexter put on his bathing suit and swam out to the farthest raft, where he stretched dripping on the wet canvas of the springboard.

There was a fish jumping and a star shining and the lights around the lake were gleaming. Over on a dark peninsula a piano was playing the songs of last summer and of summers before that—songs from *Chin-Chin* and *The Count of Luxemburg* and *The Chocolate Soldier*[2]— and because the sound of a piano over a stretch of water had always seemed beautiful to Dexter he lay perfectly quiet and listened.

The tune the piano was playing at that moment had been gay and new five years before when Dexter was a sophomore at college. They had played it at a prom once when he could not afford the luxury of proms, and he had stood outside the gymnasium and listened. The sound of the tune precipitated in him a sort of ecstasy and it was with that ecstasy he viewed what happened to him now. It was a mood of intense appreciation, a sense that, for once, he was magnificently attuned to life and that everything about him was radiating a brightness and a glamor he might never know again.

A low, pale oblong detached itself suddenly from the darkness of the Island, spitting forth the reverberate sound of a racing motorboat. Two white streamers of cleft water rolled themselves out behind it and almost immediately the boat was beside him, drowning out the hot tinkle of the piano in the drone of its

▼ **Critical Viewing**
How does the demeanor of the woman in this drawing compare to your impression of Judy Jones? Explain. **COMPARE AND CONTRAST**

2. *Chin-Chin . . . The Chocolate Soldier* popular operettas of the time.

spray. Dexter raising himself on his arms was aware of a figure standing at the wheel, of two dark eyes regarding him over the lengthening space of water—then the boat had gone by and was sweeping in an immense and purposeless circle of spray round and round in the middle of the lake. With equal eccentricity one of the circles flattened out and headed back toward the raft.

"Who's that?" she called, shutting off her motor. She was so near now that Dexter could see her bathing suit, which consisted apparently of pink rompers.

The nose of the boat bumped the raft, and as the latter tilted rakishly he was precipitated toward her. With different degrees of interest they recognized each other.

"Aren't you one of those men we played through this afternoon?" she demanded.

He was.

"Well, do you know how to drive a motorboat? Because if you do I wish you'd drive this one so I can ride on the surfboard behind. My name is Judy Jones"—she favored him with an absurd smirk—rather, what tried to be a smirk, for, twist her mouth as she might, it was not grotesque, it was merely beautiful—"and I live in a house over there on the Island, and in that house there is a man waiting for me. When he drove up at the door I drove out of the dock because he says I'm his ideal."

There was a fish jumping and a star shining and the lights around the lake were gleaming. Dexter sat beside Judy Jones and she explained how her boat was driven. Then she was in the water, swimming to the floating surfboard with a **sinuous** crawl. Watching her was without effort to the eye, watching a branch waving or a sea gull flying. Her arms, burned to butternut, moved sinuously among the dull platinum ripples, elbow appearing first, casting the forearm back with a cadence of falling water, then reaching out and down, stabbing a path ahead.

They moved out into the lake; turning, Dexter saw that she was kneeling on the low rear of the now uptilted surfboard.

"Go faster," she called, "fast as it'll go."

Obediently he jammed the lever forward and the white spray mounted at the bow. When he looked around again the girl was standing up on the rushing board, her arms spread wide, her eyes lifted toward the moon.

"It's awful cold," she shouted. "What's your name?"

He told her.

"Well, why don't you come to dinner tomorrow night?"

His heart turned over like the flywheel of the boat, and, for the second time, her casual whim gave a new direction to his life.

Drawing Inferences About Characters

What does Judy's reason for leaving the house suggest about her character?

Vocabulary

sinuous (sin´ yōō əs) *adj.* moving in and out; wavy

Comprehension

Where is Dexter when he meets Judy for the third time?

3

Next evening while he waited for her to come downstairs, Dexter peopled the soft deep summer room and the sun porch that opened from it with the men who had already loved Judy Jones. He knew the sort of men they were—the men who when he first went to college had entered from the great prep schools with graceful clothes and the deep tan of healthy summers. He had seen that, in one sense, he was better than these men. He was newer and stronger. Yet in acknowledging to himself that he wished his children to be like them he was admitting that he was but the rough, strong stuff from which they eternally sprang.

When the time had come for him to wear good clothes, he had known who were the best tailors in America, and the best tailors in America had made him the suit he wore this evening. He had acquired that particular reserve peculiar to his university, that set it off from other universities. He recognized the value to him of such a mannerism and he had adopted it; he knew that to be careless in dress and manner required more confidence than to be careful. But carelessness was for his children. His mother's name had been Krimelich. She was a Bohemian of the peasant class and she had talked broken English to the end of her days. Her son must keep to the set patterns.

At a little after seven Judy Jones came downstairs. She wore a blue silk afternoon dress, and he was disappointed at first that she had not put on something more elaborate. This feeling was accentuated when, after a brief greeting, she went to the door of a butler's pantry and pushing it open called: "You can serve dinner, Martha." He had rather expected that a butler would announce dinner, that there would be a cocktail. Then he put these thoughts behind him as they sat down side by side on a lounge and looked at each other.

"Father and mother won't be here," she said thoughtfully.

He remembered the last time he had seen her father, and he was glad the parents were not to be here tonight—they might wonder who he was. He had been born in Keeble, a Minnesota village fifty miles farther north, and he always gave Keeble as his home instead of Black Bear Village. Country towns were well enough to come from if they weren't inconveniently in sight and used as footstools by fashionable lakes.

They talked of his university, which she had visited frequently during the past two years, and of the nearby city which supplied Sherry Island with its patrons, and whither Dexter would return next day to his prospering laundries.

During dinner she slipped into a moody depression which gave Dexter a feeling of uneasiness. Whatever petulance she uttered in her throaty voice worried him. Whatever she smiled at—at him, at a chicken liver, at nothing—it disturbed him that her smile could have no root in mirth, or even in amusement. When the scarlet corners of her lips curved down, it was less a smile than an invitation to a kiss.

Then, after dinner, she led him out on the dark sun porch and deliberately changed the atmosphere.

"Do you mind if I weep a little?" she said.

"I'm afraid I'm boring you," he responded quickly.

"You're not. I like you. But I've just had a terrible afternoon. There was a man I cared about, and this afternoon he told me out of a clear sky that he was poor as a church mouse. He'd never even hinted it before. Does this sound horribly **mundane**?"

"Perhaps he was afraid to tell you."

"Suppose he was," she answered. "He didn't start right. You see, if I'd thought of him as poor—well, I've been mad about loads of poor men, and fully intended to marry them all. But in this case, I hadn't thought of him that way, and my interest in him wasn't strong enough to survive the shock. As if a girl calmly informed her fiancè that she was a widow. He might not object to widows, but—

"Let's start right," she interrupted herself suddenly. "Who are you, anyhow?"

For a moment Dexter hesitated. Then:

"I'm nobody," he announced. "My career is largely a matter of futures."

"Are you poor?"

"No," he said frankly, "I'm probably making more money than any man my age in the Northwest. I know that's an obnoxious remark, but you advised me to start right."

There was a pause. Then she smiled and the corners of her mouth drooped and an almost imperceptible sway brought her closer to him, looking up into his eyes. A lump rose in Dexter's throat, and he waited breathless for the experiment, facing the unpredictable compound that would form mysteriously from the elements of their lips. Then he saw—she communicated her excitement to him, lavishly, deeply, with kisses that were not a promise but a fulfillment. They aroused in him not hunger demanding renewal but surfeit that would demand more surfeit . . . kisses that were like charity, creating want by holding back nothing at all.

It did not take him many hours to decide that he had wanted Judy Jones ever since he was a proud, desirous little boy.

Vocabulary

mundane (mun´ dān´) *adj.* commonplace; ordinary

Characterization

What does this conversation reveal about the characters of Dexter and Judy?

Comprehension

Where do Dexter and Judy have dinner?

Cultural Connection

Fitzgerald's Elusive Women

From Daisy in *The Great Gatsby* to Judy Jones in "Winter Dreams," F. Scott Fitzgerald's fictional landscape is populated by elusive women. This theme mirrors Fitzgerald's life, which was deeply bound up in that of his wife, Zelda. When they first met, Zelda Sayre was a young Southern society girl, the darling of Montgomery, Alabama. Although Fitzgerald believed himself to be socially inferior to Zelda, he finally won her. The marriage that ensued was troubled and stormy, made more so by Zelda's mental illness. In Fitzgerald's fiction, the lovely, elusive woman becomes not only an object of desire in her own right but a symbol of all that is desirable in life.

Connect to the Literature

Do you think Dexter would be so obsessed with Judy if she had not both "beckoned him and yawned at him"? Explain.

4

It began like that—and continued, with varying shades of intensity, on such a note right up to the denouement. Dexter surrendered a part of himself to the most direct and unprincipled personality with which he had ever come in contact. Whatever Judy wanted, she went after with the full pressure of her charm. There was no divergence of method, no jockeying for position or premeditation of effects—there was a very little mental side to any of her affairs. She simply made men conscious to the highest degree of her physical loveliness. Dexter had no desire to change her. Her deficiencies were knit up with a passionate energy that transcended and justified them.

When, as Judy's head lay against his shoulder that first night, she whispered, "I don't know what's the matter with me. Last night I thought I was in love with a man and tonight I think I'm in love with you—" it seemed to him a beautiful and romantic thing to say. It was the exquisite excitability that for the moment he controlled and owned. But a week later he was compelled to view this same quality in a different light. She took him in her roadster to a picnic supper, and after supper she disappeared, likewise in her roadster, with another man. Dexter became enormously upset and was scarcely able to be decently civil to the other people present. When she assured him that she had not kissed the other man, he knew she was lying—yet he was glad that she had taken the trouble to lie to him.

He was, as he found before the summer ended, one of a varying dozen who circulated about her. Each of them had at one time been favored above all others—about half of them still basked in the solace of occasional sentimental revivals. Whenever one showed signs of dropping out through long neglect, she granted him a brief honeyed hour, which encouraged him to tag along for a year or so longer. Judy made these forays upon the helpless and defeated without malice, indeed half unconscious that there was anything mischievous in what she did.

When a new man came to town everyone dropped out—dates were automatically canceled.

The helpless part of trying to do anything about it was that she did it all herself. She was not a girl who could be "won" in the kinetic sense—she was proof against cleverness, she was proof against charm; if any of these assailed her too strongly she would immediately resolve the affair to a physical basis, and under the magic of her physical splendor the strong as well as the brilliant played her game and not their own. She was entertained only by the gratification of her desires and by the direct exercise of her own charm. Perhaps from so much youthful love, so many youthful lovers, she had come, in self-defense, to nourish herself wholly from within.

Succeeding Dexter's first exhilaration came restlessness and dissatisfaction. The helpless ecstasy of losing himself in her was opiate rather than tonic. It was fortunate for his work during the winter that those moments of ecstasy came infrequently. Early in their acquaintance it had seemed for a while that there was a deep and spontaneous mutual attraction—that first August, for example—three days of long evenings on her dusky veranda, of strange wan kisses through the late afternoon, in shadowy alcoves or behind the protecting trellises of the garden arbors, of mornings when she was fresh as a dream and almost shy at meeting him in the clarity of the rising day. There was all the ecstasy of an engagement about it, sharpened by his realization that there was no engagement. It was during those three days that, for the first time, he had asked her to marry him. She said "maybe some day," she said "kiss me," she said, "I'd like to marry you," she said "I love you"—she said—nothing.

The three days were interrupted by the arrival of a New York man who visited at her house for half September. To Dexter's agony, rumor engaged them. The man was the son of the president of a great trust company. But at the end of a month it was reported that Judy was yawning. At a dance one night she sat all evening in a motorboat with a local beau, while the New Yorker searched the club for her frantically. She told the local beau that she was bored with her visitor, and two days later he left. She was seen with him at the station, and it was reported that he looked very mournful indeed.

On this note the summer ended. Dexter was twenty-four, and he found himself increasingly in a position to do as he wished. He joined two clubs in the city and lived at one of them. Though he was by no means an integral part of the stag lines at these clubs, he managed to be on hand at dances where Judy Jones was likely to appear. He could have gone out socially as much as he liked—he was an eligible young man, now, and popular with downtown fathers. His confessed devotion to Judy Jones had rather solidified his position. But he had no social aspirations and rather despised the dancing men who were always on tap for the Thursday or Saturday parties and who filled in at dinners with the younger married set. Already he was playing with the idea of going East to New York. He wanted to take Judy Jones with him. No disillusion as to the world in which she had grown up could cure his illusion as to her desirability.

Remember that—for only in the light of it can what he did for her be understood.

Characterization
What do Judy Jones's varying responses to Dexter's marriage proposals reveal about her feelings for him?

. . . he was glad that she had taken the trouble to lie to him.

Comprehension
What does Dexter learn about the number of Judy's suitors?

Character

Is Irene Scheerer a flat character or a round character? Explain.

Spiral Review

Context Clues Which context clues help you define the word "manifested" in the last sentence of this paragraph?

Eighteen months after he first met Judy Jones he became engaged to another girl. Her name was Irene Scheerer, and her father was one of the men who had always believed in Dexter. Irene was light-haired and sweet and honorable, and a little stout, and she had two suitors whom she pleasantly relinquished when Dexter formally asked her to marry him.

Summer, fall, winter, spring, another summer, another fall—so much he had given of his active life to the incorrigible lips of Judy Jones. She had treated him with interest, with encouragement, with malice, with indifference, with contempt. She had inflicted on him the innumerable little slights and indignities possible in such a case—as if in revenge for having ever cared for him at all. She had beckoned him and yawned at him and beckoned him again and he had responded often with bitterness and narrowed eyes. She had brought him ecstatic happiness and intolerable agony of spirit. She had caused him untold inconvenience and not a little trouble. She had insulted him, and she had ridden over him, and she had played his interest in her against his interest in his work—for fun. She had done everything to him except to criticize him—this she had not done—it seemed to him only because it might have sullied the utter indifference she manifested and sincerely felt toward him.

When autumn had come and gone again it occurred to him that he could not have Judy Jones. He had to beat this into his mind but he convinced himself at last. He lay awake at night for a while and argued it over. He told himself the trouble and the pain she had caused him, he enumerated her glaring deficiencies as a wife. Then he said to himself that he loved her, and after a while he fell asleep. For a week, lest he imagined her husky voice over the telephone or her eyes opposite him at lunch, he worked hard and late, and at night he went to his office and plotted out his years.

At the end of a week he went to a dance and cut in on her once. For almost the first time since they had met he did not ask her to sit out with him or tell her that she was lovely. It hurt him that she did not miss these things—that was all. He was not jealous when he saw that there was a new man tonight. He had been hardened against jealousy long before.

> She had brought him ecstatic happiness and intolerable agony of spirit.

He stayed late at the dance. He sat for an hour with Irene Scheerer and talked about books and about music. He knew very little about either. But he was beginning to be master of his own time now, and he had a rather priggish³ notion that he—the young and already fabulously successful Dexter Green—should know more about such things.

---

3. priggish (prig′ gish) *adj.* excessively proper and smug.

That was in October, when he was twenty-five. In January, Dexter and Irene became engaged. It was to be announced in June, and they were to be married three months later.

The Minnesota winter prolonged itself interminably, and it was almost May when the winds came soft and the snow ran down into Black Bear Lake at last. For the first time in over a year Dexter was enjoying a certain tranquillity of spirit. Judy Jones had been in Florida, and afterward in Hot Springs, and somewhere she had been engaged, and somewhere she had broken it off. At first, when Dexter had definitely given her up, it had made him sad that people still linked them together and asked for news of her, but when he began to be placed at dinner next to Irene Scheerer people didn't ask him about her any more—they told him about her. He ceased to be an authority on her.

May at last. Dexter walked the streets at night when the darkness was damp as rain, wondering that so soon, with so little done, so much of ecstasy had gone from him. May one year back had been marked by Judy's **poignant**, unforgivable, yet forgiven turbulence—it had been one of those rare times when he fancied she had grown to care for him. That old penny's worth of happiness he had spent for this bushel of content. He knew that Irene would be no more than a curtain spread behind him, a hand moving among gleaming teacups, a voice calling to children . . . fire and loveliness were gone, the magic of nights and the wonder of the varying hours and seasons . . . slender lips, down-turning, dropping to his lips and bearing him up into a heaven of eyes . . . The thing was deep in him. He was too strong and alive for it to die lightly.

In the middle of May when the weather balanced for a few days on the thin bridge that led to deep summer he turned in one night at Irene's house. Their engagement was to be announced in a week now—no one would be surprised at it. And tonight they would sit together on the lounge at the University Club and look on for an hour at the dancers. It gave him a sense of solidity to go with her—she was so sturdily popular, so intensely "great."

He mounted the steps of the brownstone house and stepped inside.

"Irene," he called.

Mrs. Scheerer came out of the living room to meet him.

"Dexter," she said, "Irene's gone upstairs with a splitting headache. She wanted to go with you but I made her go to bed."

"Nothing serious, I—"

"Oh, no. She's going to play golf with you in the morning. You can spare her for just one night, can't you, Dexter?"

Her smile was kind. She and Dexter liked each other. In the living room he talked for a moment before he said good night.

Returning to the University Club, where he had rooms, he stood in the doorway for a moment and watched the dancers. He leaned against the doorpost, nodded at a man or two—yawned.

Vocabulary

poignant (poin´ yənt) *adj.* sharply painful to the feelings

Drawing Inferences About Characters

What inferences about Dexter's feelings for Irene can you draw from this description of "a sense of solidity"?

Comprehension

What does Dexter do eighteen months after he meets Judy Jones?

The Jazz Age

When World War I ended in 1918, Americans were desperate for a good time. They roared into the 1920s at breakneck speed, overthrowing rules about clothing, decorum, and personal style. The flapper, with her short dresses, bobbed hair, and complicated social life became a symbol of the times. She rode in sporty automobiles and danced until dawn to the sounds of jazz, a new kind of music critics blamed for a loosening moral code.

F. Scott Fitzgerald's work and life reflected the gaiety of this time, as well as the emptiness many felt when their pleasure seeking did not prove satisfying. Fitzgerald was not only part of the age, he helped to shape it, naming it the Jazz Age. Through both his life and his fiction, he created some of the decade's most enduring images.

Connect to the Literature

How would this story be different if it were *not* set during the Jazz Age?

"Hello, darling."

The familiar voice at his elbow startled him. Judy Jones had left a man and crossed the room to him—Judy Jones, a slender enameled doll in cloth of gold: gold in a band at her head, gold in two slipper points at her dress's hem. The fragile glow of her face seemed to blossom as she smiled at him. A breeze of warmth and light blew through the room. His hands in the pockets of his dinner jacket tightened spasmodically. He was filled with a sudden excitement.

"When did you get back?" he asked casually.

"Come here and I'll tell you about it."

She turned and he followed her. She had been away—he could have wept at the wonder of her return. She had passed through enchanted streets, doing things that were like provocative music. All mysterious happenings, all fresh and quickening hopes, had gone away with her, come back with her now.

She turned in the doorway.

"Have you a car here? If you haven't, I have."

"I have a coupé."

In then, with a rustle of golden cloth. He slammed the door. Into so many cars she had stepped—like this—like that—her back against the leather, so—her elbow resting on the door—waiting. She would have been soiled long since had there been anything to soil her—except herself—but this was her own self outpouring.

With an effort he forced himself to start the car and back into the street. This was nothing, he must remember. She had done this before, and he had put her behind him, as he would have crossed a bad account from his books.

He drove slowly downtown and, affecting abstraction, traversed the deserted streets of the business section, peopled here and there where a movie was giving out its crowd or where consumptive or pugilistic youth lounged in front of pool halls. The clink of glasses and the slap of hands on the bars issued from saloons, cloisters of glazed glass and dirty yellow light.

She was watching him closely and the silence was embarrassing, yet in this crisis he could find no casual word with which to profane the hour. At a convenient turning he began to zigzag back toward the University Club.

"Have you missed me?" she asked suddenly.

"Everybody missed you."

He wondered if she knew of Irene Scheerer. She had been back only a day—her absence had been almost contemporaneous with his engagement.

"What a remark!" Judy laughed sadly—without sadness. She looked at him searchingly. He became absorbed in the dashboard.

"You're handsomer than you used to be," she said thoughtfully. "Dexter, you have the most rememberable eyes."

He could have laughed at this, but he did not laugh. It was the sort of thing that was said to sophomores. Yet it stabbed at him.

"I'm awfully tired of everything, darling." She called everyone darling, endowing the endearment with careless, individual camaraderie.[4] "I wish you'd marry me."

The directness of this confused him. He should have told her now that he was going to marry another girl, but he could not tell her. He could as easily have sworn that he had never loved her.

"I think we'd get along," she continued, on the same note, "unless probably you've forgotten me and fallen in love with another girl."

Her confidence was obviously enormous. She had said, in effect, that she found such a thing impossible to believe, that if it were true he had merely committed a childish indiscretion—and probably to show off. She would forgive him, because it was not a matter of any moment but rather something to be brushed aside lightly.

"Of course you could never love anybody but me," she continued, "I like the way you love me. Oh, Dexter, have you forgotten last year?"

"No, I haven't forgotten."

"Neither have I!"

Was she sincerely moved—or was she carried along by the wave of her own acting?

---

4. **camaraderie** (käm´ ə räd´ ə rē) *n.* warm, friendly feelings.

Drawing Inferences About Characters

Given the information Fitzgerald provides in this conversation, what can you infer about Judy's experiences during her absence?

Comprehension

What does Dexter wonder during his reunion with Judy?

"I wish we could be like that again," she said, and he forced himself to answer:

"I don't think we can."

"I suppose not. . . . I hear you're giving Irene Scheerer a violent rush."

There was not the faintest emphasis on the name, yet Dexter was suddenly ashamed.

"Oh, take me home," cried Judy suddenly; "I don't want to go back to that idiotic dance—with those children."

Then, as he turned up the street that led to the residence district, Judy began to cry quietly to herself. He had never seen her cry before.

The dark street lightened, the dwellings of the rich loomed up around them, he stopped his coupé in front of the great white bulk of the Mortimer Joneses' house, somnolent, gorgeous, drenched with the splendor of the damp moonlight. Its solidity startled him. The strong walls, the steel of the girders, the breadth and beam and pomp of it were there only to bring out the contrast with the young beauty beside him. It was sturdy to accentuate her slightness—as if to show what a breeze could be generated by a butterfly's wing.

He sat perfectly quiet, his nerves in wild clamor, afraid that if he moved he would find her irresistibly in his arms. Two tears had rolled down her wet face and trembled on her upper lip.

"I'm more beautiful than anybody else," she said brokenly, "why can't I be happy?" Her moist eyes tore at his stability—her mouth turned slowly downward with an exquisite sadness: "I'd like to marry you if you'll have me, Dexter. I suppose you think I'm not worth having, but I'll be so beautiful for you, Dexter."

A million phrases of anger, pride, passion, hatred, tenderness fought on his lips. Then a perfect wave of emotion washed over him, carrying off with it a **sediment** of wisdom, of convention, of doubt, of honor. This was his girl who was speaking, his own, his beautiful, his pride.

"Won't you come in?" He heard her draw in her breath sharply.

Waiting.

"All right," his voice was trembling, "I'll come in."

Spiral Review
Setting Identify the analogy Fitzgerald uses in this passage describing the Joneses' house. What does this analogy convey about the setting?

Characterization
What does this wistful remark about her lack of happiness add to Fitzgerald's portrait of Judy's character?

Vocabulary
sediment (sed´ ə mənt) *n.* material that settles to the bottom of a liquid

> Two tears had rolled down her wet face and trembled on her upper lip.

5

It was strange that neither when it was over nor a long time afterward did he regret that night. Looking at it from the perspective of ten years, the fact that Judy's flare for him endured just one month seemed of little importance. Nor did it matter that by his yielding he subjected himself to a deeper agony in the end and gave serious hurt to Irene Scheerer and to Irene's parents, who had befriended him. There was nothing sufficiently pictorial about Irene's grief to stamp itself on his mind.

Dexter was at bottom hard-minded. The attitude of the city on his action was of no importance to him, not because he was going to leave the city, but because any outside attitude on the situation seemed superficial. He was completely indifferent to popular opinion. Nor, when he had seen that it was no use, that he did not possess in himself the power to move fundamentally or to hold Judy Jones, did he bear any malice toward her. He loved her, and he would love her until the day he was too old for loving—but he could not have her. So he tasted the deep pain that is reserved only for the strong, just as he had tasted for a little while the deep happiness.

Even the ultimate falsity of the grounds upon which Judy terminated the engagement that she did not want to "take him away" from Irene—Judy who had wanted nothing else—did not revolt him. He was beyond any revulsion or any amusement.

He went East in February with the intention of selling out his laundries and settling in New York—but the war came to America in March and changed his plans. He returned to the West, handed over the management of the business to his partner, and went into the first officers' training camp in late April. He was one of those young thousands who greeted the war with a certain amount of relief, welcoming the liberation from webs of tangled emotion.

6

This story is not his biography, remember, although things creep into it which have nothing to do with those dreams he had when he was young. We are almost done with them and with him now. There is only one more incident to be related here, and it happens seven years farther on.

It took place in New York, where he had done well—so well that there were no barriers too high for him. He was thirty-two years old, and, except for one flying trip immediately after the war, he had not been West in seven years. A man named Devlin from Detroit came

Characterization
What does Fitzgerald reveal about Dexter's state of mind through direct characterization?

Comprehension
How long does Dexter's renewed romance with Judy last?

into his office to see him in a business way, and then and there this incident occurred, and closed out, so to speak, this particular side of his life.

"So you're from the Middle West," said the man Devlin with careless curiosity. "That's funny—I thought men like you were probably born and raised on Wall Street. You know—wife of one of my best friends in Detroit came from your city. I was an usher at the wedding."

Dexter waited with no apprehension of what was coming.

"Judy Simms," said Devlin with no particular interest; "Judy Jones she was once."

"Yes, I knew her." A dull impatience spread over him. He had heard, of course, that she was married—perhaps deliberately he had heard no more.

"Awfully nice girl," brooded Devlin meaninglessly, "I'm sort of sorry for her."

"Why?" Something in Dexter was alert, receptive, at once.

"Oh, Lud Simms has gone to pieces in a way. I don't mean he ill-uses her, but he drinks and runs around—"

"Doesn't she run around?"

"No. Stays at home with her kids."

"Oh."

"She's a little too old for him," said Devlin.

"Too old!" cried Dexter. "Why, man, she's only twenty-seven."

He was possessed with a wild notion of rushing out into the streets and taking a train to Detroit. He rose to his feet spasmodically.

"I guess you're busy," Devlin apologized quickly. "I didn't realize—"

"No, I'm not busy," said Dexter, steadying his voice. "I'm not busy at all. Not busy at all. Did you say she was—twenty-seven? No, I said she was twenty-seven."

"Yes, you did," agreed Devlin dryly.

"Go on, then. Go on."

"What do you mean?"

"About Judy Jones."

Devlin looked at him helplessly.

"Well, that's—I told you all there is to it. He treats her like the devil. Oh, they're not going to get divorced or anything. When he's particularly outrageous she forgives him. In fact, I'm inclined to think she loves him. She was a pretty girl when she first came to Detroit."

A pretty girl! The phrase struck Dexter as ludicrous.

"Isn't she—a pretty girl, anymore?"

"Oh, she's all right."

"Look here," said Dexter, sitting down suddenly. "I don't understand. You say she was a 'pretty girl' and now you say she's 'all right.' I don't understand what you mean—Judy Jones wasn't a pretty girl, at all. She was a great beauty. Why, I knew her. I knew her. She was—"

Devlin laughed pleasantly.

Drawing Inferences About Characters

What inference about Dexter's feelings for Judy can you draw from his response to Devlin?

"I'm not trying to start a row," he said. "I think Judy's a nice girl and I like her. I can't understand how a man like Lud Simms could fall madly in love with her, but he did." Then he added: "Most of the women like her."

Dexter looked closely at Devlin, thinking wildly that there must be a reason for this, some insensitivity in the man or some private malice.

"Lots of women fade just like *that*," Devlin snapped his fingers. "You must have seen it happen. Perhaps I've forgotten how pretty she was at her wedding. I've seen her so much since then, you see. She has nice eyes."

A sort of dullness settled down upon Dexter. For the first time in his life he felt like getting very drunk. He knew that he was laughing loudly at something Devlin had said, but he did not know what it was or why it was funny. When, in a few minutes, Devlin went he lay down on his lounge and looked out the window at the New York skyline into which the sun was sinking in dull lovely shades of pink and gold.

He had thought that having nothing else to lose he was invulnerable at last—but he knew that he had just lost something more, as surely as if he had married Judy Jones and seen her fade away before his eyes.

Comprehension

How does Devlin describe Judy?

Winter Dreams **751**

The dream was gone. Something had been taken from him. In a sort of panic he pushed the palms of his hands into his eyes and tried to bring up a picture of the waters lapping on Sherry Island and the moonlit veranda, and gingham on the golf links and the dry sun and the gold color of her neck's soft down. And her mouth damp to his kisses and her eyes plaintive with melancholy and her freshness like new fine linen in the morning. Why, these things were no longer in the world! They had existed and they existed no longer.

For the first time in years the tears were streaming down his face. But they were for himself now. He did not care about mouth and eyes and moving hands. He wanted to care, and he could not care. For he had gone away and he could never go back any more. The gates were closed, the sun was gone down, and there was no beauty but the gray beauty of steel that withstands all time. Even the grief he could have borne was left behind in the country of illusion, of youth, of the richness of life, where his winter dreams had flourished.

"Long ago," he said, "long ago, there was something in me, but now that thing is gone. Now that thing is gone, that thing is gone. I cannot cry. I cannot care. That thing will come back no more."

Critical Reading

1. **Key Ideas and Details (a)** At the beginning of Section 2, what does the narrator say Dexter wants? **(b) Interpret:** How does Judy embody his ambitions?

2. **Key Ideas and Details (a)** What actions does Dexter take as a result of his first two meetings with Judy? **(b) Connect:** Find two examples in the story that demonstrate the effects of Judy's casual behavior on Dexter's life.

3. **Key Ideas and Details (a) Interpret:** What is Dexter's response to Judy whenever she reappears in his life? **(b) Analyze:** Why do Dexter's feelings for Judy remain unchanged even after he finally loses her?

4. **Key Ideas and Details Evaluate:** Are Dexter's values and ideas influenced by the times in which he lives, or would his feelings for Judy Jones be the same in any era? Explain.

5. **Integration of Knowledge and Ideas** Explain what material success does for Dexter and what it does not do. Based on this story, what observations can you make about a materialistic culture? Explain. In your response, use at least two of these Essential Question words: *commonplace, disillusioned, criticism, realistic, fortune.* *[Connecting to the Essential Question: How does literature shape or reflect society?]*

Cite textual evidence to support your responses.

Literary Analysis

1. **Craft and Structure** **(a)** Identify two **flat characters** in "Winter Dreams." **(b)** Indicate the most obvious traits of each character. **(c)** Explain how each character helps to advance the story's action.

2. **Craft and Structure** Explain why both Dexter and Judy can be classified as **round characters.**

3. **Craft and Structure** **(a)** What motivates Dexter's drive for success? **(b)** What does Judy want in her life? **(c)** Do their motivations or desires change over the course of the story? Explain.

4. **Integration of Knowledge and Ideas** On the evening of Dexter's first dinner with Judy, she comes downstairs in "a blue silk afternoon dress, and he was disappointed at first that she had not put on something more elaborate." **(a) Draw an inference** to explain Dexter's disappointment. **(b)** How does your own knowledge of life help you draw this inference?

5. **Craft and Structure** **(a)** Use a chart like the one shown to note examples of both **direct characterization** and **indirect characterization** in Fitzgerald's portrayals of Dexter and Judy. **(b)** What do you learn about the characters from each example?

6. **Craft and Structure** **(a)** For both Dexter and Judy, identify an example of direct characterization that Fitzgerald builds on with a specific detail of indirect characterization. **(b)** Based on these examples, summarize the ways in which Fitzgerald uses both types of characterization to create consistent portraits.

7. **Craft and Structure** **(a)** What traits do Dexter and Judy share? **(b)** In what ways are they different? **(c)** Which details of characterization lead you to your answers?

8. **Integration of Knowledge and Ideas** Demonstrate what you have learned about the characters of Dexter and Judy by drawing inferences about their last meeting. What do they say and how do they act as their relationship ends?

9. **Integration of Knowledge and Ideas** Based on this story, what inferences can you draw about Fitzgerald's views of material wealth and social status?

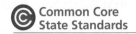

**Common Core
State Standards**

Writing

2. Write informative texts to examine and convey complex ideas, concepts, and information clearly and accurately through the effective selection, organization, and analysis of content. *(p. 754)*

2.b. Develop the topic thoroughly by selecting the most significant and relevant facts, extended definitions, concrete details, quotations, or other information and examples appropriate to the audience's knowledge of the topic. *(p. 754)*

Language

1. Demonstrate command of the conventions of standard English grammar and usage when writing or speaking. *(p. 755)*

Vocabulary Acquisition and Use

Word Analysis: Latin Root -sed-

The word *sediment* means "material that settles to the bottom." It is built on the Latin root -sed-, which means "to sit." This root frequently appears in *words related to the sciences*.

- In geology, *sedimentary* rocks form when sediments build up and are compressed into layers.
- In biology, *sedentary* organisms do not migrate.
- In medical science, *sedation* induces a state of unconsciousness.

For each word below, write a sentence that might be spoken by a scientist, a doctor, or a patient. The sentence should both include the -sed- word and reflect its meaning.

sediment   sedimentary   sedentary   sedate

Vocabulary: Context

Answer each question. Explain your answers.

1. Which is an example of *fallowness:* an empty field or a flourishing vegetable garden?
2. Which is more *fortuitous:* a cancelled test or a difficult test?
3. Which is more *sinuous:* a snake or a ruler?
4. Which is more *mundane:* doing laundry or climbing a mountain?
5. Which is more *poignant:* a wistful memory or a funny joke?
6. Which is more like *sediment:* ocean waves or autumn leaves?

Writing to Sources

Informative Text "Winter Dreams" can be thought of as a commentary on the notion of the American Dream—the idea that a person's success depends more on his or her efforts than on factors such as class or race. In an essay, explore the vision of the American Dream as Dexter experiences it.

Prewriting Scan the story for details relating to Dexter's desire for success. Explain how his desire for "glittering things" motivates his actions, and consider how his pursuit of success relates to his pursuit of Judy. Write a few sentences explaining how these elements of Dexter's life are similar and different.

Drafting In your introduction, name the author and title of the work and clearly state your main idea. In the body of your essay, describe and analyze Dexter's goals. Develop the topic thoroughly by elaborating on your analysis with the most significant and relevant details, quotations, or other information and examples that will help readers understand your ideas.

> **Model: Elaborating for Information**
> Dexter is an outsider looking in on an elegant world. He is so close to it he can almost touch it, and that combination of proximity and distance drives him. As Fitzgerald tells us, "He wanted not association with glittering things and glittering people—he wanted the glittering things themselves."

Direct quotations from the text provide support for the analysis.

Revising Make sure every idea expressed in your essay relates to your main idea. If an idea does not relate, take it out.

Conventions and Style Lesson: Subject-Verb Agreement

Subject-verb agreement requires that a subject and a verb agree in number. Follow this rule even when a phrase or clause comes between the subject and the verb.

Singular noun: *A desire* for luxury *motivates* Dexter.

Plural noun: *Desires* for luxury and success *motivate* Dexter.

Compound subjects make subject-verb agreement more challenging to identify. With *either/or* and *neither/nor*, verbs agree with the closest subject.

Compound subject (singular closest): Neither Judy's *outbursts* nor her *indifference changes* Dexter's feelings.

Compound subject (plural closest): Neither Judy's *indifference* nor her *outbursts change* Dexter's feelings.

When the subject is an indefinite pronoun, the rule may vary. Some indefinite pronouns are always singular, but others are plural.

Indefinite pronoun (singular): *Everyone* here *praises* him.

Indefinite pronoun (plural): *Several* of the golfers *notice* Judy.

Practice Choose the verb in parentheses that agrees with the subject of each sentence.

1. There (was, were) something gloomy and dismal about spring.
2. Mr. Jones, along with the other golfers, (is, are) upset when Dexter decides to quit.
3. Neither several business successes nor money (brings, bring) happiness.
4. Everyone at the parties he attends (stops, stop) asking about Judy.
5. There (is, are) about Dexter something hard-hearted and calculating.
6. One of the reasons that Judy draws attention (is, are) her unpredictability.
7. Either his memories of summer or hope for the future (keeps, keep) Dexter going.
8. Golfers who play at the Sherry Island Golf Club (likes, like) to have Dexter as a caddy.
9. Many of Dexter's admirers (gathers, gather) to see him dive from the raft at the Sherry Island Golf Club.
10. The winter that is long and cold (follows, follow) a glorious fall.

Writing and Speaking

A. Writing Revise each sentence to correct the subject-verb agreement.

Example: After the tears come emptiness.
Revision: After the tears comes emptiness.

1. There was elements of comedy in the fight.
2. A wave of emotions wash over Dexter.
3. Dexter seem callous about his broken engagement to Irene.
4. Either crisp days or snow are a sign of winter's arrival.
5. Each of them are happy in spring and summer.

B. Speaking Compose and present a brief character sketch of Judy. Throughout, maintain correct subject-verb agreement.

Connecting to the Essential Question This selection is part of a novel that changed people's understanding of migrant workers in America. As you read, notice details that portray the turtle's resilience and dignity. Doing so will help as you consider the Essential Question: **How does literature shape or reflect society?**

Close Reading Focus

Allegory; Theme

An **allegory** is a narrative in which every literal element has a symbolic meaning. An allegory does not simply contain symbols, but is a symbol in and of itself. For example, this story is the third chapter of Steinbeck's novel *The Grapes of Wrath*. The novel tells the story of the Joads, a family of farm workers struggling to survive the devastating drought in Oklahoma during the Great Depression. Every element in Steinbeck's description of the turtle and the landscape through which it struggles can be related to the Joads and their struggles.

The allegory of the turtle helps Steinbeck express the novel's **theme**— the message, or comment on life. Novelists rarely state their themes directly. Instead, they reveal themes indirectly through these means:

- Characters' statements, beliefs, and actions
- Events in the plot
- The use of literary devices, such as description and symbol

As you read, consider the deeper meanings of the events in this story.

Preparing to Read Complex Texts To interpret this story as an allegory and better understand the theme, **analyze patterns of symbolism.** Identify individual details and then look at their relationships to each other. For example, Steinbeck includes glancing descriptions of two motorists. Their responses to the turtle create a meaningful pattern that sheds light on the deeper meaning of the story. As you read, look for related details and consider them as part of a larger pattern of meaning. Gather clues in a chart like the one shown.

Vocabulary

You will encounter the words listed here in the the text that follows. Copy the words into your notebook. Which word is a verb? How can you tell?

dispersal   embankment
plodding   frantic

**Common Core
State Standards**

Reading Literature
1. Cite strong and thorough textual evidence to support analysis of what the text says explicitly as well as inferences drawn from the text, including determining where the text leaves matters uncertain.

4. Determine the meaning of words and phrases as they are used in the text, including figurative meanings.

6. Analyze a case in which grasping a point of view requires distinguishing what is directly stated in a text from what is really meant.

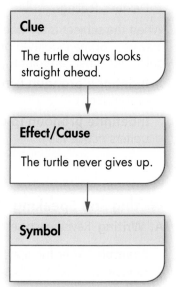

Clue

The turtle always looks straight ahead.

Effect/Cause

The turtle never gives up.

Symbol

JOHN STEINBECK (1902–1968)

Author of "The Turtle" *from The Grapes of Wrath*

No writer portrays more vividly than John Steinbeck what it was like to live through the Great Depression of the 1930s. His stories and novels capture the poverty, desperation, and social injustice experienced by many working-class Americans during this bleak period. As in the works of Naturalist writers like Stephen Crane and Jack London, Steinbeck's characters struggle desperately against forces beyond their understanding or control. While many of his characters suffer tragic fates, they almost always exhibit bravery and dignity in their struggles.

Modest Beginnings Steinbeck was born in Salinas, California. By his late teens, he was supporting himself by working as a laborer. After high school, he enrolled at Stanford University. He left before graduating, however, and spent the next five years drifting across the country, working in a variety of odd jobs, including fish hatcher, fruit picker, laboratory assistant, surveyor, apprentice painter, and journalist.

First Success Steinbeck's first three books received little—or negative— attention from critics. This changed in 1935 when he published *Tortilla Flat*. The book received the California Commonwealth Club's Gold Medal for best novel by a California author. Two years later, the author earned even greater recognition and acclaim with *Of Mice and Men* (1937). The novel became a bestseller and was made into a Broadway play and a movie.

The Great Novel Steinbeck went on to write what is generally regarded as his finest novel. *The Grapes of Wrath* (1939) is the story of the Joad family, Oklahoma farmers dispossessed of their land and forced to become migrant workers in California. The novel won the National Book Award and the Pulitzer Prize and aroused public sympathy for the plight of farm workers.

Steinbeck produced several more successful novels during his later years and in 1962 received the Nobel Prize for Literature. In accepting that award, he noted his belief that literature can sustain people through hard times. He added that it is the writer's responsibility to celebrate the human "capacity for greatness of heart and spirit—for gallantry in defeat, for courage, compassion and love."

THE
TURTLE
from THE GRAPES OF WRATH
JOHN STEINBECK

BACKGROUND The Great Depression of the 1930s was a time of profound economic distress. In 1932, one quarter of all Americans were out of work. One of many factors contributing to the Depression was a drought in Oklahoma. The drought was so severe that farmland literally blew away in massive dust storms. This is the situation faced by the Joad family, whose story Steinbeck tells in his novel *The Grapes of Wrath*. This tale of the turtle is the third chapter of that epic book.

▼ **Critical Viewing**
What challenges would a landscape like this one present? **DEDUCE**

The concrete highway was edged with a mat of tangled, broken, dry grass, and the grass heads were heavy with oat beards to catch on a dog's coat, and foxtails to tangle in a horse's fetlocks, and clover burrs to fasten in sheep's wool: sleeping life waiting to be spread and dispersed, every seed armed with an appliance of dispersal, twisting darts and parachutes for the wind, little spears and balls of tiny thorns, and all waiting for animals and for the wind, for a man's trouser cuff or the hem of a woman's skirt, all passive but armed with appliances of activity, still, but each possessed of the anlage[1] of movement.

The sun lay on the grass and warmed it, and in the shade under the grass the insects moved, ants and ant lions to set traps for them, grasshoppers to jump into the air and flick their yellow wings for a second, sow bugs like little armadillos, plodding restlessly on many tender feet. And over the grass at the roadside a land turtle crawled, turning aside for nothing, dragging his high-domed shell over the grass. His hard legs and yellow-nailed feet threshed slowly through the grass, not really walking, but boosting and dragging his shell along. The barley beards slid off his shell, and the clover burrs fell on him and rolled to the ground. His horny beak was partly opened, and his fierce, humorous eyes, under brows like fingernails, stared straight ahead. He came over the grass leaving a beaten trail behind him, and the hill, which was the highway embankment, reared up ahead of him. For a moment he stopped, his head held high. He blinked and looked up and down. At last he started to climb the embankment. Front clawed feet reached forward but did not touch. The hind feet kicked his shell along, and it scraped on the grass, and on the gravel. As the embankment grew steeper and steeper, the more frantic were the efforts of the land turtle. Pushing hind legs strained

---

1. **anlage** (än′ lä′ gə) *n.* foundation; basis; the initial cell structure from which an embryonic part develops.

Vocabulary

dispersal (di spər′ səl) *n.* distribution

plodding (pläd iŋ) *v.* walking or moving heavily; trudging

embankment (em baŋk′ mənt) *n.* mound of earth or stone built to hold back water or support a roadway

frantic (frant′ ik) *adj.* marked by frenzy

Comprehension
What is the turtle trying to do?

Theme

What does the turtle's reaction to the parapet suggest about the story's theme?

and slipped, boosting the shell along, and the horny head protruded as far as the neck could stretch. Little by little the shell slid up the embankment until at last a parapet[2] cut straight across its line of march, the shoulder of the road, a concrete wall four inches high. As though they worked independently the hind legs pushed the shell against the wall. The head upraised and peered over the wall to the broad smooth plain of cement. Now the hands, braced on top of the wall, strained and lifted, and the shell came slowly up and rested its front end on the wall. For a moment the turtle rested. A red ant ran into the shell, into the soft skin inside the shell, and suddenly head and legs snapped in, and the armored tail clamped in sideways. The red ant was crushed between body and legs. And one head of wild oats was clamped into the shell by a front leg. For a long moment the turtle lay still, and then the neck crept out and the old humorous frowning eyes looked about and the legs and tail came out. The back legs went to work, straining like elephant legs, and the shell tipped to an angle so that the front legs could not reach the level cement plain. But higher and higher the hind legs boosted it, until at last the center of balance was reached, the front tipped down, the front legs scratched at the pavement, and it was up. But the head of wild oats was held by its stem around the front legs.

---

2. parapet (par´ ə pet´) *n.* a low wall or edge of a roof, balcony, or similar structure.

Now the going was easy, and all the legs worked, and the shell boosted along, waggling from side to side. A sedan driven by a forty-year-old woman approached. She saw the turtle and swung to the right, off the highway, the wheels screamed and a cloud of dust boiled up. Two wheels lifted for a moment and then settled. The car skidded back onto the road, and went on, but more slowly. The turtle had jerked into its shell, but now it hurried on, for the highway was burning hot.

And now a light truck approached, and as it came near, the driver saw the turtle and swerved to hit it. His front wheel struck the edge of the shell, flipped the turtle like a tiddly-wink, spun it like a coin, and rolled it off the highway. The truck went back to its course along the right side. Lying on its back, the turtle was tight in its shell for a long time. But at last its legs waved in the air, reaching for something to pull it over. Its front foot caught a piece of quartz and little by little the shell pulled over and flopped upright. The wild oat head fell out and three of the spearhead seeds stuck in the ground. And as the turtle crawled on down the embankment, its shell dragged dirt over the seeds. The turtle entered a dust road and jerked itself along, drawing a wavy shallow trench in the dust with its shell. The old humorous eyes looked ahead, and the horny beak opened a little. His yellow toe nails slipped a fraction in the dust.

Analyzing Patterns of Symbolism
What symbolic meaning might you give to the turtle's actions after it is hit by the truck?

Critical Reading

1. **Key Ideas and Details (a)** What obstacles does the turtle encounter? **(b) Make a Judgment:** Which of these is most dangerous?

2. **Key Ideas and Details (a)** What happens to the turtle in his encounter with the two drivers? **(b) Compare and Contrast:** Based on their actions, what kinds of people do the two drivers seem to be?

3. **Key Ideas and Details (a)** What happens to the red ant that slips inside the turtle's shell? **(b) Distinguish:** What does this event suggest about the turtle's capacity to defend itself?

4. **Key Ideas and Details (a)** What happens to the wild oat head at the end of the story? **(b) Analyze:** What is the author suggesting about the relationships between different forms of life?

5. **Integration of Knowledge and Ideas** What does the portrayal of the turtle lead you to expect about Steinbeck's portrayal of the Joads in *The Grapes of Wrath*? Explain. In your response, use at least two of these Essential Question words: *dignity, resilient, migrant, obstacle.* [*Connecting to the Essential Question:* **How does literature shape or reflect society?**]

Cite textual evidence to support your responses.

Close Reading Activities

The Turtle from *The Grapes of Wrath*

Literary Analysis

1. **Key Ideas and Details** **(a)** Use a chart like the one shown to examine the turtle's actions at each stage of its journey. **(b)** What does the turtle's journey symbolize?

	Obstacles	Turtle's Reactions	Symbolic Meaning
climbs embankment			
crosses road			

2. **Craft and Structure** Steinbeck uses the words *dragging, turning aside for nothing,* and *thrashed slowly* to describe the turtle.
   (a) What effect do these words have on your perception of the turtle?
   (b) In what ways do these words create a **pattern of symbolism**?

3. **Integration of Knowledge and Ideas** Why do you think Steinbeck twice describes the turtle's eyes as "humorous"?

4. **Key Ideas and Details** How would you define the story's **theme**? Defend your answer with details from the selection.

5. **Key Ideas and Details** What connection does the image from the first paragraph of "sleeping life waiting to be spread" have to the story's theme?

6. **Craft and Structure** Notice patterns of symbolism that represent the following ideas:
   (a) people's struggle for survival
   (b) challenges to survival that come from nature
   (c) challenges to survival that come from other people or society

7. **Integration of Knowledge and Ideas** **(a)** Trace the path of the wild oat seeds in this story. **(b)** At the end of *The Grapes of Wrath*, Ma Joad says, "We're the people that live. . . . we're the people—we go on." Explain the ways in which the path of the oat seed expresses similar ideas symbolically.

8. **Craft and Structure** Explain the story of the turtle as an **allegory** for human struggle.

9. **Integration of Knowledge and Ideas** In Chapter 14 of *The Grapes of Wrath*, Steinbeck writes that humanity is defined by the need to struggle toward goals: "Having stepped forward, he may slip back, but only half a step, never the full step back." Explain how the story of the turtle expresses that idea allegorically.

Common Core State Standards

Writing
2. Write informative texts to examine and convey complex ideas, concepts, and information clearly and accurately through the effective selection, organization, and analysis of content. *(p. 763)*
2.b. Develop the topic thoroughly by selecting the most significant and relevant facts, extended definitions, concrete details, quotations, or other information and examples appropriate to the audience's knowledge of the topic. *(p. 763)*
2.c. Use appropriate and varied transitions and syntax to link the major sections of the text, create cohesion, and clarify relationships among complex ideas and concepts.
7. Conduct short as well as more sustained research projects to answer a question; synthesize multiple sources on the subject, demonstrating understanding of the subject under investigation. *(p. 763)*

Language
5. Demonstrate understanding of figurative language, word relationships, and nuances in word meanings. *(p. 763)*

Vocabulary Acquisition and Use

Word Analysis: Latin Prefix *pro-*

In this story, John Steinbeck uses the word *protruded,* which begins with the Latin prefix *pro-,* meaning "forward." Knowing this meaning helps you to define the whole word *protruded,* which means "thrust forward," and other words beginning with the prefix *pro-.*

Add the prefix *pro-* to the word roots below. Then, define each word and use it in a sentence.

1. *-ject*
2. *-ceed*
3. *-gress*
4. *-hibit*
5. *-duce*
6. *-pose*

Vocabulary: Word/Phrase Relationships

Use your knowledge of the words from the vocabulary list on page 756 to determine whether the relationships between the italicized words below and the phrases that follow them are logical. Explain your reasoning.

1. *embankment*	the bottom of a lake
2. *plodding*	tired during a hike
3. *dispersal*	collection of garbage
4. *frantic*	nerves before a test

Writing to Sources

Informative Text "The Turtle" is part of Steinbeck's novel *The Grapes of Wrath,* which portrays the struggles of a Depression-era farm family. Steinbeck intended that readers draw parallels between the turtle and the human characters. Write an **essay** connecting the events described in "The Turtle" to the lives of ordinary people during the Great Depression.

Prewriting Use print and online sources to research the Great Depression to learn how people reacted to adverse economic circumstances. Then, review "The Turtle" and draw parallels.

Drafting First, provide information about the Depression. In your body paragraphs, note facts and data and explain parallels you found to "The Turtle." Use transitional words and phrases that clarify the relationships among ideas. For example, *likewise* and *in the same way* indicate similarity, whereas *to the contrary* and *by contrast* indicate difference. Cite the sources of all facts as you draft.

Model: Providing Internal Documentation

The Oklahoma Dust Bowl heightened the effects of the Great Depression for farmers living in that state. The average rainfall in Oklahoma was under 20 inches a year before the early 1930s, when it suffered a severe drought.
(http://www.britannica.com, Dust Bowl)

Citing sources of facts adds credibility.

Revising Review your essay. Make sure that you have provided enough historical context to support your observations. Add information as needed, and provide correct citations about where you found the material.

Primary Sources

Photographs   **Ballad**
Migrant Mother   **Dust Bowl Blues**

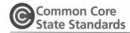 **Common Core State Standards**

About the Text Forms

A **photograph** is a visual image created when light falls on a sensitive surface, such as film or an electronic imager. Photographers use the lens of a camera to admit various degrees of light onto this surface and to focus the image as a human eye would. Timing these tasks to capture a small, meaningful slice of reality is known as the art of photography.

A **ballad** is a song or a song-like poem that tells a story—often, a story about adventure or love. Most ballads use simple language, regular meter, rhyme, and a *refrain*, which is a repeated line or group of lines. Sometimes the refrain varies slightly each time it appears. An ancient form, the ballad experienced new popularity in the mid- to late-twentieth century as folk singers used it to reflect and comment on the social upheavals of the time.

Reading Literature
Reading Informational Text
1. Cite strong and thorough textual evidence to support analysis of what the text says explicitly as well as inferences drawn from the text, including determining where the text leaves matters uncertain.

Preparing to Read Complex Texts

Drawing inferences can enrich your understanding of a document's meaning. When you draw inferences, you make logical guesses about something that is not directly shown or stated. To draw inferences, notice details. Then, apply your own knowledge about people, the world, or life in general to an interpretation of those details. Consider this example:

- **Document:** A historical photograph shows a long line of adults in tattered clothes waiting outside a city building.
- **Details:** tattered clothes, long line
- **Your Knowledge:** Tattered clothes might indicate poverty; long lines suggest people want or need something badly.

By applying your knowledge to the details in the text, you can infer that the people in the photo are seeking help or employment. You can also infer that at the time the photo was taken, many people were in dire need. As you explore the photographs and the ballad, draw inferences to enrich your understanding.

 How does literature shape or reflect *society?*

These documents present powerful testimony to the challenges people faced at a specific historical moment. At the same time, they express universal ideas about human struggle. As you explore these texts, consider what they reveal about their era and about human experience in general.

Note-Taking Guide

Primary-source documents are a rich source of information for researchers. As you read these documents, use a note-taking guide like the one shown to organize relevant and accurate information.

1 Type of Document (check one)

☐ Newspaper ☐ Advertisement ☐ Photograph ☐ Letter
☐ Press Release ☐ Journal ☐ E-mail ☐ Other _____

2 Date(s) of Document _____

3 Maker of Document _____

Maker's Position, Title, or Circumstances _____

4 Purpose and Audience: Why and for whom was the document created or written?
_____

5 Document Information

   a List significant details that you notice about the people and objects included in the document. _____
_____

   b What activities or events are referred to in the document? _____
_____
_____

   c List words or elements that are repeated in the document. _____
_____
_____

   d Based on your notes above, list three inferences you might draw from the photo or ballad. _____
_____

Drawing Inferences
In photos and in song lyrics, every detail counts. Take the time to consider how each object, shadow, or unusual word adds to the work's meaning and significance.

This guide was adapted from the **U.S. National Archives** Photo and Document Analysis worksheets.

Vocabulary

migrant (mī´ grənt) *adj.* moving from place to place (p. 767)

exposures (ek spō´ zhərz) *n.* sections of film on which light falls when a photograph is taken (p. 767)

huddled (hud´ əld) *v.* gathered closely; nestled (p. 767)

stout (stout) *adj.* strong in body; sturdy (p. 769)

THE STORY BEHIND THE DOCUMENTS

Dorothea Lange

Woody Guthrie

A man caught in a dust storm during the Dust Bowl disaster of the 1930s.

On October 29, 1929, or "Black Tuesday," the United States stock market crashed. The prices of stocks, or shares in companies, plummeted. Hundreds of thousands of people who had purchased stock with borrowed money went bankrupt and the economy ground to a virtual halt.

The domino effects of the crash—collectively known as the Great Depression of the 1930s—were far-reaching. Employers who lost money laid off workers. Workers could not pay their bills and lost their homes. Many moved into crowded quarters with relatives, or built makeshift shanty towns. Teenagers wandered the country, looking for work. Children went hungry.

For Americans living on the Great Plains that extend from the Dakotas south to Oklahoma and Texas, these dire circumstances were made catastrophic by a series of dust storms that began in 1933 and continued through the early 1940s. Decades of over-farming had exposed the prairie soil to the scorching sun. When drought set in, the dry soil turned to dust. Sweeping prairie winds carried massive amounts of dirt eastward, devastating homesteads, destroying crops and livestock, and dumping tons of filth on cities as far east as Boston and New York. The drought-stricken area became known as the Dust Bowl. In desperation, more than a half-million people from the Dust Bowl regions migrated to California.

Living and working among the displaced masses were visual artists, such as photographer **Dorothea Lange** (1895–1965), and musician **Woody Guthrie** (1912–1967). These artists became eyewitnesses to the events of history, producing work that documented the times.

Originally from New Jersey, Lange traveled to San Francisco as a young adult. There, she began capturing stark realities on film. Later, she was hired by the government to photograph the country's rural poor. Lange's *Migrant Mother* series of photos are the most famous of these powerful images. It was said of her work that she "photographed the nation's soul."

Another Great Depression-era artist, singer/songwriter Woody Guthrie, once said, "I ain't a writer . . . I'm just a little one-cylinder guitar picker." His songs tell a different story. Born and raised in Oklahoma, Guthrie experienced the Dust Bowl first-hand, finally migrating to California where he wrote and broadcast his first songs. Among these were his Dust Bowl Ballads—tunes that lamented the difficulties of life on the Plains. The songs resonated with the thousands of displaced "Okies" on the west coast, and soon Guthrie's legend was born.

MIGRANT MOTHER

Dorothea Lange

Dorothea Lange took these photographs in February or March of 1936 in Nipomo, California, while she was on assignment photographing **migrant** farm workers. She later gave this account of the experience:

*I saw and approached the hungry and desperate mother, as if drawn by a magnet. I do not remember how I explained my presence or my camera to her, but I do remember she asked me no questions. I made five **exposures**, working closer and closer from the same direction. I did not ask her name or her history. She told me her age, that she was thirty-two. She said that they had been living on frozen vegetables from the surrounding fields, and birds that the children killed. She had just sold the tires from her car to buy food. There she sat in that lean-to tent with her children **huddled** around her, and seemed to know that my pictures might help her, and so she helped me. There was a sort of equality about it.*

Vocabulary

migrant (mī´ grənt) *adj.* moving from place to place

exposures (ek spō´ zhərz) *n.* sections of film on which light falls when a photograph is taken

huddled (hud´ əld) *v.* gathered closely; nestled

DUST BOWL BLUES

Woody Guthrie

Woody Guthrie's first album of original songs, *Dust Bowl Ballads*, was recorded in 1940 in New York City. This album, and those that followed, were celebrated for their "homespun" quality and embraced by Guthrie's fellow artists and musicians. They also opened the door for generations of singer-songwriters who sought to express through their music the social and political ideals of peace, compassion, and equality.

❖◆❖

Primary Sources
Ballad What kind of story do you think this ballad will tell?

I just blowed in, and I got them dust bowl blues,
I just blowed in, and I got them dust bowl blues,
I just blowed in, and I'll blow back out again.
I guess you've heard about ev'ry kind of blues,
I guess you've heard about ev'ry kind of blues,
But when the dust gets high, you can't even see the sky.
I've seen the dust so black that I couldn't see a thing,
I've seen the dust so black that I couldn't see a thing,

▼ Oklahomans head to California, June 1935

And the wind so cold, boy, it nearly cut your water off.
I seen the wind so high that it blowed my fences down,
I've seen the wind so high that it blowed my fences down,
Buried my tractor six feet underground.
Well, it turned my farm into a pile of sand,
Yes, it turned my farm into a pile of sand,
I had to hit that road with a bottle in my hand.
I spent ten years down in that old dust bowl,
I spent ten years down in that old dust bowl,
When you get that dust pneumony, boy, it's time to go.
I had a gal, and she was young and sweet,
I had a gal, and she was young and sweet,
But a dust storm buried her sixteen hundred feet.
She was a good gal, long, tall and **stout**,
Yes, she was a good gal, long, tall and stout,
I had to get a steam shovel just to dig my darlin' out.
These dusty blues are the dustiest ones I know,
These dusty blues are the dustiest ones I know,
Buried head over heels in the black old dust,
I had to pack up and go.
An' I just blowed in, an' I'll soon blow out again.

Drawing Inferences

Where did the speaker once live? Explain how you know.

Vocabulary

stout (stout) *adj.* strong in body; sturdy

Critical Reading

1. **Key Ideas and Details Analyze:** Which aspects of all three of Lange's photographs emphasize the family's isolation and powerlessness?

2. **Key Ideas and Details Evaluate:** Do you think Lange's photographs are more or less powerful because they depict a woman and children but no other adults?

3. **Key Ideas and Details (a)** In "Dust Bowl Blues," what happened to the speaker's farm and his "gal"? **(b) Interpret:** Do you think these things happened in just the way the speaker describes them? Explain. **(c) Deduce:** What larger point about the dust storms is Guthrie making?

4. **Craft and Structure (a) Identify:** What line is repeated in the first and last stanzas of the ballad? **(b) Connect:** Which details in Lange's photographs indicate that this line could also apply to the migrant mother and her family?

5. **Integration of Knowledge and ideas Analyze:** Based on Guthrie's lyrics and Lange's photographs, how did the Dust Bowl affect people's lives?

Photographs • Ballads

Comparing Primary Sources

Refer to your note-taking guide to complete these questions.

1. **(a)** What are your main impressions as you scan the "Migrant Mother" photographs? **(b)** What do you learn about the speaker upon first reading the ballad?

2. **(a)** Using a chart like the one shown, identify one detail from each "Migrant Mother" photograph that you noticed after studying it more closely. **(b)** Do the same for the ballad. **(c)** Write one sentence about life during the Great Depression that incorporates these details.

	Detail	Depression-Era Life
Photo 1		
Photo 2		
Photo 3		
Ballad		

3. **(a)** Describe the tent shown in the lower right "Migrant Mother" photograph. **(b)** Do you think the tent is a sound shelter? Explain.

4. **(a)** In the upper right "Migrant Mother" photograph, what detail is visible on the woman's hand? **(b)** How does this detail shed light on the larger story of this family?

5. **(a)** Compare and contrast what you learn about the Depression from the "Migrant Mother" photographs with what you learn from the ballad. **(b)** Explain the reasons for any similarities and differences.

Vocabulary Acquisition and Use

Use New Words Correctly For each item below, write one sentence in which you use the word correctly.

1. huddled   2. stout

Content-Area Vocabulary Answer each question. Then, explain your answers.

3. Can a *migrant* worker receive regular promotions?

4. Are *exposures* an important part of photography?

Etymology Study The word *migrant* often appears in political science and history texts. The word derives from the Latin word *migrare,* meaning "to move from one place to another." Identify four other words that share this root. Then, use a dictionary to answer these questions:
(a) Which related word can apply to either people or animals? **(b)** Which two related words can apply *only* to people? Explain.

 Common Core State Standards

Writing
7. Conduct short as well as more sustained research projects to answer a question or solve a problem; narrow or broaden the inquiry when appropriate; synthesize multiple sources on the subject, demonstrating understanding of the subject under investigation. *(p. 771)*
8. Gather relevant information from multiple authoritative print and digital sources, using advanced searches effectively. *(p. 771)*
9. Draw evidence from literary or informational texts to support analysis, reflection, and research. *(p. 771)*

Language
6. Acquire and use accurately general academic and domain-specific words and phrases, sufficient for reading, writing, speaking, and listening at the college and career readiness level; demonstrate independence in gathering vocabulary knowledge when considering a word or phrase important to comprehension or expression.

Speaking and Listening
4. Present information, findings, and supporting evidence, conveying a clear and distinct perspective, such that listeners can follow the line of reasoning. *(p. 771)*

Research Task

Topic: The WPA

As the photos of Dorothea Lange and the songs of Woody Guthrie make clear, the Great Depression was a time of crushing poverty. Many Americans survived with the help of the Works Progress Administration (later the Work Projects Administration). Often referred to as the WPA, this federal agency created jobs from writing to road building.

▲ WPA plaque on the Riverwalk in San Antonio, Texas

Assignment: Formulate a research plan related to the WPA. Write a major research question and modify it as necessary to refocus and narrow in on meaningful data. Present an **oral report** in which you discuss the research process itself, as well as your findings on the topic.

Formulate a research plan. Good research begins with a general exploration into a wide area. As you conduct your preliminary research driven by an initial question, you gain perspective on your topic—its outlines, branches, and specific elements that you want to examine in detail. Like an explorer learning a new terrain, you choose one direction rather than another: You revise your research question and refocus your search for useful materials.

RESEARCH TIP

As part of your preliminary research, read the chapter titles of a book or the section headings on a Web site. These concise expressions may give you good leads on how to refocus and refine your research.

Model: Refining a Research Question

Starting Question	Focused Question	Refined Question
What did the WPA do?	What did the WPA do for literature and the arts?	What was the Federal Writers' Project and what did it produce?

Gather sources. Use online and library searches to collect information from a variety of reliable sources. Start with general information, and, as you refine your research question, search more detailed accounts. As you go, critique the research process itself, considering creative steps you might take to acquire more interesting, varied, or reliable information.

Synthesize information. To synthesize is "to bring parts together in order to make a whole." Combine the results of your research to arrive at an idea, a unified whole, that answers your research question.

Organize and present your ideas. For this report, how you proceed is as important as what you find out. Consider presenting your ideas using a cause-and-effect strategy: "Because I found out that . . . , I changed my question to . . . ."

Use a checklist like the one shown to make sure your oral report fulfills the requirements of the assignment.

Research Checklist

☐ Have I refined my main research question so that it is specific and manageable?

☐ Have I answered my main research question?

☐ Does my evidence come from reliable sources?

☐ Have I clearly shown the process of my research?

Connecting to the Essential Question In this poem, Auden refers to official statistics that government and other modern institutions use to define people. As you read, think about the view of modern life portrayed in the poem. Doing so will help you as consider the Essential Question: **How does literature shape or reflect society?**

Close Reading Focus

Satire; Tone

A subgenre found in all forms of literature—poems, essays, novels, plays, and short stories—**satire** is writing that ridicules or exposes the faults of individuals, groups, institutions, or humanity at large. Satirical writings vary in **tone,** or attitude, which may be bitter, harsh, gentle, humorous, sober, or comical. A writer establishes tone through word choice, details, and grammatical structures. For example, in the opening lines of this poem, Auden strings together long, formal phrases full of bureacratic words: *Bureau of Statistics, official complaint, reports, conduct, Greater Community.* These official-sounding words and phrases issue forth from a disembodied speaker to generate a chilling and cynical tone. As you read, identify the object of Auden's satire and note details that add to the speaker's tone.

Preparing to Read Complex Texts Ideas in poetry are not expressed solely in words; often, the structure itself reinforces meaning. Structure includes the following elements:

- *Lines:* Are lines short, long, or varied lengths?
- *Stanzas:* Are stanzas the same length or varied lengths?
- *Grammatical forms:* Does the poet use particular constructions, such as passive voice or collective nouns?

When you **evaluate structure as it relates to meaning,** you understand a poem as a complete whole. As you read, use a chart like the one shown to note structural elements and their relationship to meaning.

Vocabulary

The words below are important to understanding the text that follows. Copy the words into your notebook. What are some other forms of the word *psychology*?

conduct   sensible

psychology

© **Common Core State Standards**

Reading Literature
4. Analyze the impact of specific word choices on meaning and tone.
5. Analyze how an author's choices concerning how to structure specific parts of a text contribute to its overall structure and meaning as well as its aesthetic impact.
6. Analyze a case in which grasping a point of view requires distinguishing what is directly stated in a text from what is really meant.

Structure	Meaning
Variable rhyme	This creates a sense of imbalance, as though something is wrong with "the system."

Wystan Hugh Auden *(1907–1973)*

Author of **"The Unknown Citizen"**

Although he was influenced by the Modernist poets, Wystan Hugh Auden adopted only those aspects of Modernism with which he felt comfortable, choosing to retain many elements of traditional poetry in his work. Throughout his career, he wrote with insight and technical virtuosity about people struggling to preserve their individuality in an increasingly conformist society.

Auden was born in York, England, in 1907, the third of three children. He attended Oxford University, where he made lifelong friendships with two fellow writers, Stephen Spender and Christopher Isherwood. At age twenty-three, Auden published his first volume of poetry, simply titled *Poems*. The book established Auden as the leading voice of a new generation of poets. In the same year, he developed a passionate interest in politics, speaking out against poverty in England and the rise of Nazism in Germany.

A New Country In 1939, just before World War II, Auden moved from England to the United States, where he became a citizen. That move was coincident with his rediscovery of his Christian beliefs. His works *The Double Man* (1941) and *For the Time Being* (1944) depict religion as a way of coping with a disjointed modern society. Despite the comfort he found in religion, Auden became disillusioned with modern life in his later years. He used his poetry to explore the responsibilities of the artist in what he saw as a faithless modern age.

Auden won the Pulitzer Prize in 1948 for his long narrative poem *The Age of Anxiety* (1947), which explores the confusion associated with post–World War II life. He later published several more volumes of poetry and a large body of literary criticism. He also anthologized others' works and coauthored at least one musical composition—a libretto for the opera *The Rake's Progress*. From 1954 to 1973, Auden served as chancellor of the Academy of American Poets. Today, Auden is admired as one of the great poets of the twentieth century.

> **"A poet is, before anything else, a person who is passionately in love with language."**

The Turret Lathe Operator (J. G. Cherry series), Grant Wood, Cedar Rapids Museum of Art, Cedar Rapids, Iowa. © Estate of Grant Wood/Licensed by VAGA, New York, NY

The Unknown Citizen
W.H. Auden

(To JS/07/M/378 This Marble Monument is Erected by the State)

▲ **Critical Viewing**
Does the man in this painting fit Auden's description of "the unknown citizen"? Explain. **EVALUATE**

Vocabulary
conduct (kän′ dukt)
n. behavior

BACKGROUND Auden wrote this poem five years after the passage of the Social Security Act of 1935, which sought to provide workers with pensions after retirement. The system required that each citizen be assigned a unique number. For skeptics like Auden, the system symbolized a frightening new world controlled by bureaucracy.

  He was found by the Bureau of Statistics to be
  One against whom there was no official complaint,
  And all the reports on his conduct agree
  That, in the modern sense of an old-fashioned word, he was a saint,
5 For in everything he did he served the Greater Community.
  Except for the War till the day he retired

He worked in a factory and never got fired,
But satisfied his employers, Fudge Motors Inc.
Yet he wasn't a scab or odd in his views,
10 For his Union reports that he paid his dues,
(Our report on his Union shows it was sound)
And our Social Psychology workers found
That he was popular with his mates and liked a drink.
The Press are convinced that he bought a paper every day
15 And that his reactions to advertisements were normal in every way.
Policies taken out in his name prove that he was fully insured,
And his Health-card shows he was once in hospital but left it cured.
Both Producers Research and High-Grade Living declare
He was fully sensible to the advantages of the Installment Plan
20 And had everything necessary to the Modern Man,
A phonograph, a radio, a car and a frigidaire.
Our researchers into Public Opinion are content
That he held the proper opinions for the time of year;
When there was peace, he was for peace; when there was war,
    he went.
25 He was married and added five children to the population.
Which our Eugenist[1] says was the right number for a parent of
    his generation,
And our teachers report that he never interfered with their
    education.
Was he free? Was he happy? The question is absurd:
Had anything been wrong, we should certainly have heard.

---

1. Eugenist (yo͞o jen´ ist) *n.* a specialist in eugenics, the movement devoted to improving the human species through genetic control.

Vocabulary

psychology (sī käl´ ə jē)
n. science dealing with the human mind

sensible (sen´ sə bəl) *adj.* emotionally or intellectually aware

Critical Reading

1. **Key Ideas and Details (a)** How does the state identify the unknown citizen in the poem's subtitle? **(b) Interpret:** What do these numbers and letters suggest?

2. **Key Ideas and Details (a)** Identify at least three facts the state knows about the citizen. **(b) Interpret:** In what ways is the citizen "unknown"?

3. **Key Ideas and Details (a)** What questions does the speaker refer to as "absurd"? **(b) Make a Judgment:** Are these questions actually absurd? Explain.

4. **Integration of Knowledge and Ideas** What view of individuals in the modern world does Auden express in this poem? In your response, use at least two of these Essential Question words: *alienation, isolated, community, data.* [*Connecting to the Essential Question: How does literature shape or reflect society?*]

Cite textual evidence to support your responses.

Literary Analysis

1. **Key Ideas and Details** Using a chart like the one shown, name four groups that report on the unknown citizen's life and identify the information they have about him.

JS/07/M/378

2. **Craft and Structure (a)** Who is the speaker, or narrator, of this poem? Explain. **(b)** Describe the speaker's **tone. (c)** Cite three examples of word choice in the poem that support your description.

3. **Craft and Structure** Begin to **evaluate structure as it relates to meaning** by identifying three examples of each of the following grammatical structures:
   (a) the use of collective nouns, such as "the Press"
   (b) the use of passive voice, such as "He was found"

4. **Craft and Structure** How does Auden's use of the grammatical structures you identified in question 3 help the poet convey his central idea?

5. **Craft and Structure** How does Auden's use of capitalization add to the poem's meaning?

6. **Craft and Structure (a)** In what ways do the line lengths make the poem look like prose? **(b)** How does this structural quality add to the poem's meaning?

7. **Craft and Structure** In what ways does the tone of the poem add to or support the satire?

8. **Craft and Structure (a)** What societal flaw or folly is the object of Auden's **satire** in this poem? **(b)** Would you characterize this satire as harsh or gentle? Explain.

9. **Integration of Knowledge and Ideas** Do you think this poem implies a call for action or change, or does it simply present a situation? Explain.

10. **Integration of Knowledge and Ideas (a)** In what ways is official knowledge of the unknown citizen limited? **(b)** Do you think deeper knowledge of citizens by government or corporate institutions is either possible or desirable in a modern society? Explain your point of view.

Common Core State Standards

Writing

2. Write informative texts to examine and convey complex ideas, concepts, and information clearly and accurately through the effective selection, organization, and analysis of content. *(p. 777)*

2.b. Develop the topic thoroughly by selecting the most significant and relevant facts, extended definitions, concrete details, quotations, or other information and examples appropriate to the audience's knowledge of the topic. *(p. 777)*

2.f. Provide a concluding statement or section that follows from and supports the information or explanation presented.

Language

4.b. Identify and correctly use patterns of word changes that indicate different meanings or parts of speech. *(p. 777)*

Vocabulary Acquisition and Use

Word Analysis: Greek Root -psych-

In Greek mythology, Psyche was the daughter of a king and was a person of deep emotion. Her name comes from a Greek word meaning "soul," or "mind." The root -psych-, then, means "soul" or "mind" and forms the basis for *psychology* and other English words. Write definitions for the words below. Then, write a sentence in which you use each word correctly.

1. psychiatry
2. psychosomatic
3. psychotic

Vocabulary: Assessing Logic

Decide whether each sentence below is logical. If it is not, rewrite the sentence to fix the logic, but do not replace the italicized word. Explain your answers.

1. Because Mona was interested in sports, she chose to major in *psychology*.
2. Sophia found that her new backpack's *conduct* was bothersome.
3. *Sensible* to the benefits of eating healthfully, Joe ate a candy bar.

Writing to Sources

Informative Text Auden offers a fairly dark vision of modern society. Write an **essay** in which you describe the political nature of the world this poem portrays. Cite specific details from the poem to support your ideas.

Prewriting Reread the poem to address these questions as they apply to the world of the poem: **1.** Do individuals or institutions have power? **2.** How are business and politics connected? **3.** Are individuals able to think for themselves? Record details from the poem that speak to these and other related questions. Then, write a statement summarizing the political nature of the world Auden portrays.

Drafting Include the summary you wrote in your introduction. Then, devote one body paragraph to specific ideas that relate to your summary. Provide quotations from the poem to support your ideas. End with a memorable conclusion in which you restate important ideas from earlier in the essay.

Model: Drafting to Include Quotations

In "The Unknown Citizen," Auden explores the effect of a highly structured society on individuals. In such a society, government policies overwhelm citizens' opinions. The speaker states, "When there was peace, he was for peace; when there was war, he went."

Using direct quotations supports your interpretation of the poem.

Revising Read through your draft to make sure your writing is unified and coherent. Delete stray, unrelated ideas and check that you have supported main points with strong evidence.

Connecting to the Essential Question E. E. Cummings's poetry was radical in his day. While it is celebrated today, it still presents what many see as a radical vision of poetry. As you read, notice elements that distinguish these poems from traditional verse. Doing so will help as you consider the Essential Question: **How does literature shape or reflect society?**

Close Reading Focus

Author's Style

An **author's style** is his or her unique way of writing. Many factors determine style, including word choice, sentence structure, and the arrangement of words on a page. E. E. Cummings's style is among the most distinctive of any American poet. He uses a range of experimental elements and techniques, including the following:

- Unconventional *syntax*, or sentence structure, including the splitting up of words and phrases and the mixing up of parts of speech
- The bending and breaking of grammatical rules
- The unorthodox use of lowercase and uppercase letters
- A minimal or unorthodox use of punctuation
- The elimination of spaces between certain words and characters
- The use of typographical symbols to create visual impact

Cummings's style is not just for show; it is a key part of his meaning and affects how the reader experiences the poems. As you read, think about the effect Cummings's style has on your understanding of each poem.

Preparing to Read Complex Texts The lack of a traditional structure makes the experience of reading an E. E. Cummings poem very different from that of traditional verse. One way to make sure you understand the poet's essential meaning is to **paraphrase,** or restate ideas in your own words. Paraphrasing can help you determine the meaning of passages that may otherwise challenge your comprehension. Use a chart like the one shown to list any unclear phrases or whole passages and paraphrase them.

Vocabulary

The words below are important for understanding the text that follows. Copy the words into your notebook. Are these words nouns or verbs? How can you tell?

sowed   reaped

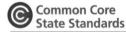

**Common Core
State Standards**

Reading Literature
4. Determine the meaning of words and phrases as they are used in the text, including figurative and connotative meanings; analyze the impact of specific word choices on meaning and tone, including language that is particularly fresh, engaging, or beautiful.
5. Analyze how an author's choices concerning how to structure specific parts of a text contribute to its overall structure and meaning as well as its aesthetic impact.

Language
3.a. Apply an understanding of syntax to the study of complex texts when reading.

Passage
"with up so floating many bells down"

Paraphrase
With the airy sound of ringing bells

E. E. Cummings

(1894–1962)

Author of **"old age sticks"** and **"anyone lived in a pretty how town"**

After working in the French ambulance corps and spending three months behind bars as a political prisoner during World War I, Edward Estlin Cummings studied painting in Paris and subsequently began writing poetry in New York City. A graduate of Harvard University, his first published poems appeared in the *Harvard Monthly*. Though some critics attacked the unconventional style of his poetry, Cummings's work was popular with general readers. People admired his playful use of language, his distinctive use of grammar and punctuation, and his interest in a poem's appearance, a sensitivity that might have stemmed from his talent as a painter. Cummings also became known for his concern for the individual and his discerning eye for life's ironies.

Form vs. Content Although Cummings's poems tend to be unconventional in form and style, they generally express traditional ideas. In his finest poems, Cummings explores the customary poetic terrain of love and nature but makes innovative use of grammar and punctuation to reinforce meaning. Many of his poems also contain comic touches as Cummings addresses the confusing aspects of modern life. Cummings was also a skillful satirist who used his poems to challenge accepted notions and fixed beliefs.

Cummings received a number of awards for his work, including the Boston Fine Arts Poetry Festival Award and the Bollingen Prize in Poetry. In 1968, six years after his death, a volume of his poetry, *The Complete Poems, 1913–1968,* was published. At the time of his death, he was the second most widely read poet in the United States, after Robert Frost.

> **"It takes courage to grow up and become who you really are."**

old age sticks

E. E. Cummings

Remember Now the Days of Thy Youth, 1950, Paul Starrett Sample, Hood
Museum of Art, Dartmouth College, Hanover, NH

old age sticks
up Keep
Off
signs)&

5   youth yanks them
down(old
age
cries No

Tres)&(pas)
10 youth laughs
(sing
old age

scolds Forbid
den Stop
15 Must
n't Don't

&)youth goes
right on
gr
20 owing old

▲ **Critical Viewing** Do the elderly men in this painting belong to a
group similar to the one Cummings describes, or are they a different sort?
On what details do you base your conclusion? **DRAW CONCLUSIONS**

anyone lived in a pretty how town

E. E. Cummings

Background Cummings wrote these poems late in life. After an eventful youth, he settled down to enjoy his family farm in New Hampshire. The poems from this period tend to be gentle and even joyful.

anyone lived in a pretty how town
(with up so floating many bells down)
spring summer autumn winter
he sang his didn't he danced his did.

5 Women and men(both little and small)
cared for anyone not at all
they sowed their isn't they reaped their same
sun moon stars rain

children guessed(but only a few
10 and down they forgot as up they grew
autumn winter spring summer)
that noone loved him more by more

when by now and tree by leaf
she laughed his joy she cried his grief
15 bird by snow and stir by still
anyone's any was all to her

someones married their everyones
laughed their cryings and did their dance
(sleep wake hope and then)they
20 said their nevers they slept their dream

Vocabulary

sowed (sōd) v. scattered; planted

reaped (rēpt) v. gathered; brought in

Paraphrasing

Restate lines 13–14 in your own words.

Comprehension

Which words are repeated in these five stanzas?

Author's Style

How does Cummings's unconventional syntax add to the dream-like quality of the last three stanzas?

stars rain sun moon
(and only the snow can begin to explain
how children are apt to forget to remember
with up so floating many bells down)

25 one day anyone died i guess
(and noone stooped to kiss his face)
busy folk buried them side by side
little by little and was by was

all by all and deep by deep
30 and more by more they dream their sleep
noone and anyone earth by april
wish by spirit and if by yes.

Women and men(both dong and ding)
summer autumn winter spring
35 reaped their sowing and went their came
sun moon stars rain

Critical Reading

1. **Key Ideas and Details (a)** In "old age sticks," what actions do old age and youth take? **(b) Compare and Contrast:** Explain the differences Cummings points out between youth and old age.

2. **Key Ideas and Details (a)** In the final stanza of "old age sticks," what does the poem say is happening to youth? **(b) Interpret:** Explain the irony in this final stanza.

3. **Craft and Structure (a)** In "anyone lived in a pretty how town," what does Cummings name the main male and female characters? **(b) Speculate:** What is the poet suggesting in this choice?

4. **Key Ideas and Details (a)** What does Cummings say the people do with their cryings and their dreams? **(b) Interpret:** What does the poet suggest about the townspeople through these statements?

5. **Key Ideas and Details Evaluate:** What message does the poet convey about the ideas of individuality and conformity?

6. **Integration of Knowledge and Ideas** Do you think the emergence of new approaches to an art form, such as the experimental verse Cummings wrote, reflects larger changes in a society? Explain. In your response, use at least two of these Essential Question words: *innovation, prevail, expertise, enduring, ambiguity. [Connecting to the Essential Question: How does literature shape or reflect society?]*

Literary Analysis

1. **Key Ideas and Details Paraphrase** the following passages: **(a)** lines 5–8 of "old age sticks"; **(b)** lines 13–16 of "anyone lived in a pretty how town."

2. **Integration of Knowledge and Ideas** Explain how the paraphrasing you did in response to question 1 clarified your understanding of each poem.

3. **Craft and Structure (a)** Use a chart like the one shown to identify elements of Cummings's unique **style** as they appear in these two poems. **(b)** Explain how each example adds to the poem's essential meaning.

Element of Style	Example	Meaning
unconventional syntax		
uppercase or lowercase letters		
minimal/unorthodox punctuation		

4. **Craft and Structure (a)** In "anyone lived . . . ," identify two points at which the poet mixes up parts of speech. **(b)** For each one, explain how it adds to the meaning and mood, or feeling, of the poem.

Vocabulary Acquisition and Use

Analogies Analogies show the relationships between pairs of words. Complete each analogy using a word from the vocabulary list on page 778. In each, your choice should create a word pair that matches the relationship between the first two words given. Then, explain your answers.

1. _____ is to *gathered* as *destroyed* is to *constructed*.
2. *Calamity* is to *blessing* as _____ is to *dispersed*.

Writing to Sources

Informative Text Imagine that E. E. Cummings will be giving a poetry reading at a bookstore in your town. As the organizer of the event, write an **introduction** that provides background about the poet and prepares the audience for the poetry they will hear. Select the most relevant and interesting facts about Cummings and include at least one eloquent quotation from the poet. Use a conversational style appropriate to the setting and purpose of the event.

Common Core State Standards

Writing

2. Write informative texts to examine and convey complex ideas, concepts, and information clearly and accurately through the effective selection, organization, and analysis of content.

2.b. Develop the topic thoroughly by selecting the most significant and relevant quotations or other information and examples appropriate to the audience's knowledge of the topic.

Language

5. Demonstrate understanding of word relationships.

Connecting to the Essential Question In these poems, Stevens, MacLeish, and Moore contemplate the art of poetry. As you read, notice details that both suggest and directly state what poetry can and cannot achieve. Your observations will help as you reflect on the Essential Question: **How does literature shape or reflect society?**

Close Reading Focus

Imagery; Personification; Simile

Poets combine rich language with poetic devices to develop a poem's *theme,* or central message. The theme of these three poems is poetry itself: what it is, what it does, and what it means to people and societies. These are abstract ideas. To give them weight and shape, the poets use a variety of literary devices, including the following:

- **Imagery:** word pictures that appeal to the senses
- **Personification:** a figure of speech in which a nonhuman idea or thing is given human qualities
- **Simile:** a figure of speech comparing two seemingly different things and using the words *like* or *as*

Comparing Literary Works As you read, compare how each poet draws on these tools to clothe abstract themes in tangible realities that readers can understand and feel.

Preparing to Read Complex Texts These three poems are about poetry itself; each presents a view of life—an artistic philosophy—in which poetry plays a key role. For example, Stevens holds that the making of a poem is also the making of a self and a world. To understand poems about ideas, read with a different critical lens than you use for poems about more everyday concerns. As you read, **analyze philosophical arguments** that support the poet's message. Note a key idea and then make inferences about a broader philosophy that it implies. Use a chart like the one shown to identify and analyze the philosophical ideas these poems express.

Vocabulary

The words below are important to understanding the texts that follow. Copy the words into your notebook. Write the words you know in one column. What is one similarity that two of the words share?

suffice   palpable

insatiable   derivative

 Common Core State Standards

Reading Literature

1. Cite strong and thorough textual evidence to support inferences drawn from the text, including determining where the text leaves matters uncertain.

4. Determine the meaning of words and phrases as they are used in the text, including figurative meanings; analyze the impact of specific word choices on meaning and tone, including language that is particularly fresh, engaging, or beautiful.

9. Demonstrate knowledge of early-twentieth-century foundational works of American literature, including how two or more texts from the same period treat similar themes or topics.

Language

5.a. Interpret figures of speech in context and analyze their role in the text.

Idea

Supporting Philosophy

Wallace Stevens (1879–1955)

Author of "Of Modern Poetry"

Wallace Stevens believed that the goal of poetry is to capture the interaction between the private, subjective world of the mind and reality. He spent his career writing poems that delve into the imagination and the ways it shapes our perception of the physical world. He uses elaborate imagery and precise language to express his philosophical themes. Stevens depended largely on the natural world for his inspiration because nature, he said, is the only certainty.

Insurance Executive by Day Stevens was born and raised in Reading, Pennsylvania. After completing his education at Harvard University, he took a job at an insurance company in Hartford, Connecticut, and eventually became the company's vice president. He did not publish his first collection of poetry, *Harmonium* (1923), until he was forty-three years old. In *Harmonium* and much of his other work, Stevens uses dazzling imagery to capture the beauty of the physical world while expressing the dependence of that beauty on the perceptions of the observer. Although the book received little public attention, it was praised by critics and launched Stevens's literary career.

Stevens published many volumes of poetry, including *Ideas of Order* (1935), *Parts of a World* (1942), *Transport to Summer* (1947), and *The Auroras of Autumn* (1950). His *Collected Poems* earned him the Pulitzer Prize in 1955. Despite his success as a poet, however, Stevens continued his career in insurance until the end of his life. "It gives a man character as a poet to have this daily contact with a job," he once said. A brilliant and unusual figure, he is now regarded as one of the most important poets of the twentieth century.

Of Modern Poetry

Wallace Stevens

BACKGROUND Wallace Stevens's poetry reflects the influence of the Symbolist literary movement. Originating in the last half of the nineteenth century, Symbolist poets believed that ideas and emotions are difficult to communicate because people perceive the world in such personal ways. These poets tried to convey meaning through symbols—people, places, and objects that represent ideas beyond their concrete meanings. As a result, the work of Symbolist poets like Stevens can often have many interpretations.

Vocabulary
suffice (sə fīs´) v. be adequate; meet the needs of

The poem of the mind in the act of finding
What will suffice. It has not always had
To find: the scene was set; it repeated what
Was in the script.
                              Then the theatre was changed
5 To something else. Its past was a souvenir.

It has to be living, to learn the speech of the place.
It has to face the men of the time and to meet
The women of the time. It has to think about war
And it has to find what will suffice. It has

10 To construct a new stage. It has to be on that stage
And, like an insatiable actor, slowly and
With meditation, speak words that in the ear,
In the delicatest ear of the mind, repeat,
Exactly, that which it wants to hear, at the sound
15 Of which, an invisible audience listens,
Not to the play, but to itself, expressed
In an emotion as of two people, as of two
Emotions becoming one. The actor is
A metaphysician[1] in the dark, twanging
20 An instrument, twanging a wiry string that gives
Sounds passing through sudden rightnesses, wholly
Containing the mind, below which it cannot descend,
Beyond which it has no will to rise.
                                    It must
Be the finding of a satisfaction, and may
25 Be of a man skating, a woman dancing, a woman
Combing. The poem of the act of the mind.

---

1. metaphysician (met´ ə fə zish´ ən) *n.* a person versed in philosophy, especially
those branches that seek to explain the nature of being or of the universe.

Vocabulary

insatiable (in sā´ shə bəl)
adj. constantly wanting more

Critical Reading

1. **Key Ideas and Details (a)** In the first stanza, what does the poet say happened to theater? **(b) Interpret:** What does "the theater" represent?

2. **Key Ideas and Details (a) Interpret:** What does the speaker mean when he says that a poem "has to think about war"? **(b) Analyze:** What does the speaker suggest about the connections poetry must have with its time period?

3. **Key Ideas and Details (a) Summarize:** What topics for poetry does the speaker identify in lines 25–26? **(b) Connect:** How do these topics relate to the conception of poetry presented earlier in the poem?

4. **Craft and Structure (a) Speculate:** The opening and closing lines of the poem are sentence fragments. What verbs might meaningfully complete these lines? Explain your choices.

5. **Integration of Knowledge and Ideas Infer:** Do you think the poet believes the work of poetry to be difficult? Explain.

Cite textual evidence to support your responses.

Archibald MacLeish
(1892–1982)

Author of **"Ars Poetica"**

Archibald MacLeish was born in Glencoe, Illinois. He was trained as a lawyer but, unlike Wallace Stevens, turned his back on his first career to devote himself completely to poetry.

MacLeish's early poems, such as "Ars Poetica," are experimental, reflecting the influence of the Modernists. By contrast, his later poems are more traditional and accessible. As unrest spread throughout the world in the 1930s, MacLeish used poetry to explore political and social issues. Over the course of his career, MacLeish produced more than thirty books and won three Pulitzer Prizes.

Marianne Moore
(1887–1972)

Author of **"Poetry"**

Born in Kirkwood, Missouri, Marianne Moore first gained a footing in the literary world as the editor of *The Dial,* a highly regarded literary journal. In that role, she encouraged many new writers by publishing their work. However, she was hesitant to publish her own work, although many noted poets had admired it. In fact, her first book, *Poems* (1921), was published without her knowledge.

As a Modernist, Moore wrote poems that were inventive, precise, and witty. Unlike other Modernists, however, she chose not to write about the state of modern civilization. Instead, she explored subjects such as animals and nature. "Poetry," one of her best-known poems, explores the subject of poetry itself.

Moore published poems and collections regularly, garnering honors and awards along the way. Her *Collected Poems* (1951) won the Pulitzer Prize and the National Book Award in 1952.

Ars Poetica

Archibald MacLeish

BACKGROUND **Ars Poetica** The title is an allusion to the ancient Roman poet Horace's "Ars Poetica," or "The Art of Poetry," which was composed about 20 B.C. For a contemporary *ars poetica,* see Judith Ortiz Cofer's poem on page 1366.

A poem should be palpable and mute
As a globed fruit.

Dumb
As old medallions to the thumb,

5 Silent as the sleeve-worn stone
Of casement ledges where the moss has grown—

A poem should be wordless
As the flight of birds.

A poem should be motionless in time
10 As the moon climbs,

Leaving, as the moon releases
Twig by twig the night-entangled trees,

Leaving, as the moon behind the winter leaves.
Memory by memory the mind—

Vocabulary
palpable (palʹ pə bəl)
adj. able to be touched, felt, or handled

Comprehension
According to the speaker, how silent should a poem be?

15 A poem should be motionless in time
As the moon climbs.

A poem should be equal to:
Not true.

For all the history of grief
20 An empty doorway and a maple leaf.

For love
The leaning grasses and two lights above the sea—

A poem should not mean
But be.

Critical Reading

Cite textual evidence to support your responses.

1. **Key Ideas and Details (a)** Identify at least three items the speaker compares to poetry. **(b) Analyze:** What do you think the speaker means by saying that a poem should be "palpable and mute," "wordless," and "motionless in time"?

2. **Key Ideas and Details (a)** With what images can a poem show the history of grief, as the speaker states? **(b)** With what images should it show love? **(c) Speculate:** Why do you think MacLeish chooses to focus on these emotions?

3. **Key Ideas and Details (a) Interpret:** What contradiction do you see in lines 7–8? **(b) Analyze:** What do you think this contradiction suggests about the subject, poetry?

4. **Craft and Structure (a) Interpret:** What contrast does the poet make in the final two lines? **(b) Define:** How would you define the difference between *meaning* and *being*?

5. **Integration of Knowledge and Ideas Extend:** In what ways do you think poetry can touch the human spirit? Explain.

Untitled, 1984, Alexander Calder, Solomon R. Guggenheim Museum, New York

Poetry

Marianne Moore

I, too, dislike it: there are things that are important beyond all this
    fiddle.
    Reading it, however, with a perfect contempt for it, one discovers in
it after all, a place for the genuine.
        Hands that can grasp, eyes
5   that can dilate, hair that can rise
            if it must, these things are important not because a

high-sounding interpretation can be put upon them but because
    they are
useful. When they become so derivative as to become
    unintelligible,
the same thing may be said for all of us, that we
    do not admire what
10   we cannot understand: the bat
        holding on upside down or in quest of something to

▲ Critical Viewing
Write a sentence describing this painting "with a perfect contempt for it." Explain what the result shows you about Moore's point in lines 2–3. **CONNECT**

Vocabulary
derivative (də riv′ ə tiv) *adj.* not original; based on something else

Comprehension
Why are the "things" the poet describes in lines 4–5 "important"?

eat, elephants pushing, a wild horse taking a roll, a tireless wolf
    under a tree, the immovable critic twitching his skin like a
        horse that feels a flea, the base-
    ball fan, the statistician—
15   nor is it valid
            to discriminate against "business documents and
    school-books"; all these phenomena are important. One must
        make a distinction
        however: when dragged into prominence by half poets, the result is
            not poetry,
    nor till the poets among us can be
20   "literalists[1] of
            the imagination"—above
                insolence and triviality and can present

    for inspection, "imaginary gardens with real toads in them," shall we
        have
        it. In the meantime, if you demand on the one hand,
25   the raw material of poetry in
            all its rawness and
            that which is on the other hand
                genuine, you are interested in poetry.

1. **literalists** *n.* those who take words at their exact meaning.

Critical Reading

Cite textual evidence to support your responses.

1. **Key Ideas and Details** **(a)** What does the speaker say happens when poems become derivative? **(b) Synthesize:** What qualities does the speaker believe good poetry should possess?

2. **Craft and Structure** **(a) Interpret:** What seeming contradiction exists in the phrase "literalists of the imagination"? **(b) Analyze:** How is the meaning of this phrase extended by the image of "imaginary gardens with real toads"?

3. **Integration of Knowledge and Ideas** Based on the ideas these poets express, do you think poets have a significant role to play in today's world? Defend your opinion, using at least three of these Essential Question words: *contemporary, relevant, expression, communicate, depth.* [*Connecting to the Essential Question: How does literature shape or reflect society?*]

Imagery

What images does the speaker use to describe things that are "genuine"?

Literary Analysis

1. **Craft and Structure (a)** In "Of Modern Poetry," note two examples of **imagery** that relate poetry to a theater performance. **(b)** In line 18, how does Stevens describe the emotional link between actor and audience? **(c)** What does this suggest about the relationship of a reader to a poem?

2. **Craft and Structure (a)** What **simile** does Stevens introduce in line 11? **(b)** How does he develop that simile in the rest of the poem?

3. **Craft and Structure** What example of personification do you find in the first two lines of MacLeish's poem? Explain.

4. **Craft and Structure (a)** In "Ars Poetica," note four images that involve the idea of muteness or silence. **(b)** Which images in the poem suggest ideas of stillness? **(c)** How do these images clarify the poet's meaning in the last two lines?

5. **Craft and Structure (a)** To what senses do Moore's images of animal behavior appeal? **(b)** How do these images help define poetry for Moore?

6. **Craft and Structure (a)** How does Stevens use **personification** to describe the "poem of the act of the mind"? **(b)** How does Moore use it to describe the "genuine"?

7. **Integration of Knowledge and Ideas Analyze the philosophical argument** underpinning Stevens's ideas in "Of Modern Poetry." **(a)** In lines 3–4, how did the "poem of the mind" once find "what will suffice"? **(b)** What change has happened, as noted in lines 4–5? **(c)** What ideas about a new relationship between the modern world and the past is Stevens suggesting?

8. **Integration of Knowledge and Ideas** What philosophical idea about the way people understand reality is suggested in the phrase "the poem of the act of the mind"?

9. **Integration of Knowledge and Ideas (a)** In Moore's poem, what philosophical outlook about the role of art does her discussion of the "genuine" suggest? **(b)** What concept of the "genuine" does the image she quotes in line 23 support?

10. **Comparing Literary Works** Use a chart like the one shown to interpret each poet's use of imagery and simile to advance his or her theme.

 Common Core State Standards

Writing

2. Write informative texts to examine and convey complex ideas, concepts, and information clearly and accurately through the effective selection, organization, and analysis of content. *(p. 794)*

9.a. Apply grades 11–12 Reading standards to literature. *(p. 794)*

Language

4.b. Identify and correctly use patterns of word changes that indicate different meanings or parts of speech. *(p. 794)*

4.d. Verify the preliminary determination of the meaning of a word or phrase. *(p. 794)*

Vocabulary Acquisition and Use

Word Analysis: Latin Root -satis-

The word *insatiable* contains the Latin root -*satis*-, which means "enough." Combined with the prefix *in-*, meaning "not," you can determine that *insatiable* suggests "not enough." Use your knowledge of -*satis*- to define each numbered word. Then, use a dictionary to check your definitions.

1. satisfy
2. dissatisfied
3. satisfactory
4. sate
5. satiate
6. unsatisfactory
7. satiety
8. saturate

Vocabulary: Use New Words

Follow the instructions below to write a sentence for each item, using a word from the vocabulary list on page 784. Use each word only once.

1. Describe the quality of a peach in a beautiful painting.
2. Criticize a musician whose work lacks originality.
3. Explain why a minimal amount of nutritious food is not enough to maintain one's health.
4. Criticize someone who always wants more possessions.

Writing to Sources

Informative Text In these three poems, Stevens, Moore, and MacLeish define poetry by example. Write an **essay** in which you compare and contrast the ideas the poets present in two of these poems. Note the distinct ways each poet explains, above all, why poetry is important.

Prewriting Reread each poem and paraphrase the ideas it presents. Briefly state the poets' philosophies by completing these sentences for each poem:

> Poetry is _____. It is important because _____.

Choose two poets to compare and contrast. After gathering your points of comparison, select a logical organizing principle and main idea to develop in your essay.

Drafting Introduce each poet by providing a general statement about his or her beliefs about poetry. Then, write a brief statement of your main point. Develop your ideas, using quotations from the poem to support your analysis.

Model: Providing Necessary Background

Wallace Stevens believed that human beings perceive the world in an entirely subjective way. For Stevens, reality itself was an expression of the imagination. This view greatly influenced his philosophy of poetry.

The writer begins with general information about Stevens's views to clarify the ideas that will follow.

Revising Review your draft, making sure you have supported your ideas with appropriate quotations. Check that you have clearly stated each poet's basic philosophy of poetry.

From Every Corner of the Land

*I*n a few pages a good story portrays the complexity of a life . . .

— BERNARD MALAMUD

Elements of Short Stories

A **short story** is a brief work of fiction. Short stories have no fixed length, but most can be read in one sitting. A short story includes the key literary elements of fiction.

- **Plot:** the sequence of events that make up the story. A story's plot focuses on a central **conflict,** or struggle that the main character faces. Driven by this conflict, the plot follows a pattern called the "dramatic arc." During the **exposition,** the characters, setting, and conflict are introduced. The conflict intensifies during the **rising action,** reaching its point of highest tension during the **climax.** The intensity of the conflict lessens during the **falling action,** and ends during the **resolution.**
- **Characters:** the personalities who participate in the story. A writer uses techniques of **characterization** to develop and reveal characters.
- **Setting:** the time and place of a story. The setting may serve as the background, or it may play a crucial role in the story.
- **Theme:** the central idea, message, or insight a story explores. The reader may have to piece together different clues to infer the theme.
- **Point of view:** the perspective from which a story is told. With first-person point of view, the narrator is part of the story and refers to himself or herself as *I*. With third-person point of view, the narrator stands outside the story and refers to all the characters as *he* or *she*.

Voice The best short stories do more than simply relate a tale from start to finish. They express an author's distinct voice, or personality on the page. Voice is conveyed through all the elements of the writing, including the author's syntax, tone, characters, plots, and themes. Just as no two singers sound precisely the same, so do author's literary voices differ.

Close Read: Voice in Fiction
These literary elements that contribute to voice appear in the model text at the right.

Description: word portraits of people, places, or things. Descriptive writing uses **images** and may include figurative language. *Example: "She was very old and small and she walked slowly in the dark pine shadows, moving a little from side to side in her steps . . ." (Eudora Welty)*	**Diction/Word Choice:** the writer's use of particular types of words. Diction may be formal, casual, elevated, idiomatic, or any combination thereof. *Example: It was a clear day, and yet there seemed an intangible pall over the face of things . . ." (Jack London)*
Syntax: the length and types of sentences a writer uses *Example: "It was not a matter of live or die. There was no real peril." (Tim O'Brien)*	**Symbolism:** the imbuing of a story element with meaning that is larger than itself. *Example: "Across the street from their house, in an empty lot between two houses, stood the rockpile." (James Baldwin)*

For more practice analyzing short stories, see numerous selections in this book, including those on pages 292, 628, 652, 730, 834, 1011, 1298, 1310, and 1326.

Model

About the Text This classic work by Sarah Orne Jewett (1849–1909) tells the story of Sylvia, a child who lives with her grandmother in rural New England. When a young "sportsman" arrives and offers money for help in finding an elusive white heron, Sylvia's loyalties are tested.

from "A White Heron"
Sarah Orne Jewett

Half a mile from home, at the farther edge of the woods, where the land was highest, a great pine-tree stood, the last of its generation. Whether it was left for a boundary mark, or for what reason, no one could say; the woodchoppers who had felled its mates were dead and gone long ago, and a whole forest of sturdy trees, pines and oaks and maples, had grown again. But the stately head of this old pine towered above them all and made a landmark for sea and shore miles and miles away. Sylvia knew it well. She had always believed that whoever climbed to the top of it could see the ocean; and the little girl had often laid her hand on the great rough trunk and looked up wistfully at those dark boughs that the wind always stirred, no matter how hot and still the air might be below. Now she thought of the tree with a new excitement, for why, if one climbed it at break of day, could not one see all the world, and easily discover from whence the white heron flew, and mark the place, and find the hidden nest? What a spirit of adventure, what wild ambition! What fancied triumph and delight and glory for the later morning when she could make known the secret! It was almost too real and too great for the childish heart to bear.

All night the door of the little house stood open and the whippoorwills came and sang upon the very step. The young sportsman and his old hostess were sound asleep, but Sylvia's great design kept her broad awake and watching.

She forgot to think of sleep. The short summer night seemed as long as the winter darkness, and at last when the whippoorwills ceased, and she was afraid the morning would after all come too soon, she stole out of the house and followed the pasture path through the woods, hastening toward the open ground beyond, listening with a sense of comfort and companionship to the drowsy twitter of a half-awakened bird, whose perch she had jarred in passing. Alas, if the great wave of human interest which flooded for the first time this dull little life should sweep away the satisfactions of an existence heart to heart with nature and the dumb life of the forest!

There was the huge tree asleep yet in the paling moonlight, and small and silly Sylvia began with utmost bravery to mount to the top of it, with tingling, eager blood coursing the channels of her whole frame, with her bare feet and fingers, that pinched and held like bird's claws to the monstrous ladder reaching up, up, almost to the sky itself. First she must mount the white oak tree that grew alongside, where she was almost lost among the dark branches and the green leaves heavy and wet with dew; a bird fluttered off its nest, and a red squirrel ran to and fro and scolded pettishly at the harmless housebreaker.

Description Details paint a word picture of the tree in its setting. They also begin to establish the tree's deeper meaning: it is "the last of its generation," and "a landmark."

Symbol The symbolism of the tree, from where one can "see all the world," intensifies. The tree is also the means by which Sylvia can discover the location of the white heron, yet another of the story's symbols.

Syntax Jewett's long, flowing sentences contribute to her voice. In addition, the piling up of the conjunction *and* in the phrase "triumph and delight and glory" builds a sense of Sylvia's excitement.

Word Choice Jewett's distinctive voice is conveyed in her diction, including the unusual adjective "paling," the reference to Sylvia as "small and silly," and the tree described as a "monstrous ladder."

Building Knowledge and Insight

Connecting to the Essential Question The narrator of this story is given a medal he does not believe he deserves. As you read, look for clues that reveal the author's attitude toward war and the glory that is often associated with it. Doing so will help as you reflect on the Essential Question: **What makes American literature American?**

Close Reading Focus

Style; Theme

Ernest Hemingway's style is among the most influential in American litera-ture. It is characterized by economy and "vigorous English," a phrase he encountered in the style guide of a newspaper for which he once wrote. That style has certain specific ingredients:

- **Syntax:** Hemingway's sentences are short, direct, and forceful.
- **Word Choice:** He uses plain language and few, if any, adjectives.
- **Tone:** He suggests emotions but does not explain them or directly state what characters feel. The reader is left to interpret textual clues.

These elements of Hemingway's style are evident in this description of an Italian army officer's reaction to distressing news: "He looked straight past me and out through the window. Then he began to cry."

Hemingway's style marries perfectly with his **themes**—the messages or insights into life that recur throughout his work. Hemingway's themes address ideals of heroism and courage, relationships between young and old, and the loss of innocence in a disappointing and violent world. As you read "In Another Country," look for trademarks of Hemingway's style and the development of two or more of his significant themes. Notice how these themes interact and add to the richness of the story.

Preparing to Read Complex Texts Even if your life differs entirely from those of characters in a story, you can increase your understanding of fiction by **identifying with characters.** To do so, relate their thoughts and feelings to your own and consider how you would feel in similar circumstances. As you read, use a chart like the one shown to help you identify with a story's characters.

Vocabulary

You will encounter the words listed here in the text that follows. Copy the words into your notebook. What is the prefix in each word?

detached   resign
disgrace

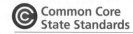 **Common Core State Standards**

Reading Literature

2. Determine two or more themes or central ideas of a text and analyze their development over the course of the text, including how they interact and build on one another to produce a complex account.

4. Determine the meaning of words and phrases as they are used in the text, including figurative and connotative meanings; analyze the impact of specific word choices on meaning and tone, including language that is particularly fresh, engaging, or beautiful.

9. Demonstrate knowledge of early-twentieth-century foundational works of American literature.

Language

3.a. Apply an understanding of syntax to the study of complex texts when reading.

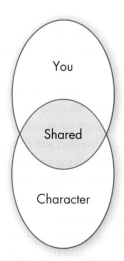

Ernest Hemingway *(1899–1961)*

Author of "In Another Country"

Ernest Hemingway's fiction expressed the sentiments of many members of the post-World War I generation. He wrote about people struggling to maintain a sense of dignity while living in a sometimes hostile world.

The Red Cross Hemingway, the son of a physician, was born and raised in Oak Park, Illinois. In high school, he played football and wrote newspaper columns. Eager to serve in World War I, he tried to join the army but was repeatedly turned away due to an eye defect. He joined the Red Cross ambulance corps instead and, in 1918, was sent to the Italian front. Just before his nineteenth birthday, he was severely wounded and spent several months recovering in a hospital in Milan, Italy. These experiences helped shape his view of the world and provided material for his writing, including the story "In Another Country."

Expatriates After the war, Hemingway had a hard time readjusting to life in the United States. To establish himself as a writer, he went to Paris as a foreign correspondent for the *Toronto Star*. In Paris, he befriended Ezra Pound, Gertrude Stein, F. Scott Fitzgerald, and other American writers and artists living overseas. The literary advice of these friends and his work as a journalist helped him develop his concise, concrete, and highly charged writing style.

In 1925, Hemingway published his first major work, *In Our Time*, a series of loosely connected short stories. A year later he published *The Sun Also Rises*, a novel about a group of British and American expatriates trying to overcome the pain and disillusionment of life in the modern world.

A Famous Life Hemingway eventually became as famous for his lifestyle as he was for his writing. Constantly pursuing adventure, he hunted big game in Africa, attended bullfights in Spain, held records for deep-sea fishing in the Caribbean, and participated in amateur boxing.

The full body of Hemingway's work—including *A Farewell to Arms* (1929), *For Whom the Bell Tolls* (1940), and *The Old Man and the Sea* (1952)—earned him the Nobel Prize in Literature in 1954.

A_{nother} Country

IN

A_{nother} Country

Ernest Hemingway

BACKGROUND World War I, the first truly global war, began in Europe in 1914, sparked by nationalist pride and systems of alliances among nations. The Central Powers (Germany, Austria-Hungary, Turkey) fought the Allies (England, France, Russia) with other nations joining one side or the other. The United States entered the war late, on the side of the Allies. Italy, where this story takes place, was not strategically important, but it helped the Allies by drawing Central Power troops away from other battle areas.

The war lasted four brutal years. Throughout most of the conflict, a stalemate existed. Both sides were dug into trenches, and took turns rushing one another. Each rush was greeted by a barrage of machine-gun fire, with thousands falling dead. Other soldiers fell to new weapons—inventions such as airplanes, long-range artillery, and poison gas. Many of the wounded were saved, however, by advances in medical treatment, such as surgical disinfectants and rehabilitative techniques to strengthen injured limbs.

In the fall the war[1] was always there, but we did not go to it any more. It was cold in the fall in Milan[2] and the dark came very early. Then the electric lights came on, and it was pleasant along the streets looking in the windows. There was much game hanging outside the shops, and the snow powdered in the fur of the foxes and the wind blew their tails. The deer hung stiff and heavy and empty, and small birds blew in the wind and the wind turned their feathers. It was a cold fall and the wind came down from the mountains.

We were all at the hospital every afternoon, and there were different ways of walking across the town through the dusk to the hospital. Two of the ways were alongside canals, but they were long. Always, though, you crossed a bridge across a canal to enter the hospital. There was a choice of three bridges. On one of them a woman sold roasted chestnuts. It was warm, standing in front of her charcoal fire, and the chestnuts were warm afterward in your pocket. The hospital was very old and very beautiful, and you entered through a gate and walked across a courtyard and out a gate on the other side. There were usually funerals starting from the courtyard. Beyond the old hospital were the new brick pavilions, and there we met every afternoon and were all very polite and interested in what was the matter, and sat in the machines that were to make so much difference.

Comprehension
Where do the narrator and his companions go each afternoon?

---

1. the war World War I (1914–1918).
2. Milan (mi lan´) a city in northern Italy.

◀ **Critical Viewing**
Does this painting of a World War I ambulance have the same direct, straightforward quality as Hemingway's prose? Explain. **EVALUATE**

The doctor came up to the machine where I was sitting and said: "What did you like best to do before the war? Did you practice a sport?"

I said: "Yes, football."

"Good," he said. "You will be able to play football again better than ever."

My knee did not bend and the leg dropped straight from the knee to the ankle without a calf, and the machine was to bend the knee and make it move as in riding a tricycle. But it did not bend yet, and instead the machine lurched when it came to the bending part. The doctor said: "That will all pass. You are a fortunate young man. You will play football again like a champion."

In the next machine was a major who had a little hand like a baby's. He winked at me when the doctor examined his hand, which was between two leather straps that bounced up and down and flapped the stiff fingers, and said: "And will I too play football, captain-doctor?" He had been a very great fencer, and before the war the greatest fencer in Italy.

The doctor went to his office in a back room and brought a photograph which showed a hand that had been withered almost as small as the major's, before it had taken a machine course, and after was a little larger. The major held the photograph with his good hand and looked at it very carefully. "A wound?" he asked.

"An industrial accident," the doctor said.

"Very interesting, very interesting," the major said, and handed it back to the doctor.

"You have confidence?"

"No," said the major.

There were three boys who came each day who were about the same age I was. They were all three from Milan, and one of them was to be a lawyer, and one was to be a painter, and one had intended to be a soldier, and after we were finished with the machines, some-times we walked back together to the Café Cova, which was next door to the Scala.[3] We walked the short way through the communist quarter because we were four together. The people hated us because we were officers, and from a wine-shop someone called out, "A basso gli ufficiali!"[4] as we passed. Another boy who walked with us some-times and made us five wore a black silk handkerchief across his face because he had no nose then and his face was to be rebuilt. He had gone out to the front from the military academy and been wounded within an hour after he had gone into the front line for the first time. They rebuilt his face, but he came from a very old family and they could never get the nose exactly right. He went to South America and worked in a bank. But this was a long time ago, and then we did not

---

3. **the Scala** (skä′ lä) an opera house in Milan.
4. **"A basso gli ufficiali!"** (ä bä′ so lye oo fe chä′ le) "Down with officers!" (Italian).

"You are a fortunate young man. You will play football again like a champion."

Identifying With Characters

Have you ever been in a situation like the narrator's in which you did not feel fully accepted or part of a group? How did it make you feel? Explain.

any of us know how it was going to be afterward. We only knew then that there was always the war, but that we were not going to it any more.

We all had the same medals, except the boy with the black silk bandage across his face, and he had not been at the front long enough to get any medals. The tall boy with a very pale face who was to be a lawyer had been a lieutenant of Arditi[5] and had three medals of the sort we each had only one of. He had lived a very long time with death and was a little detached. We were all a little detached, and there was nothing that held us together except that we met every afternoon at the hospital. Although, as we walked to the Cova through the tough part of town, walking in the dark, with light and singing coming out of the wine-shops, and sometimes having to walk into the street when the men and women would crowd together on the sidewalk so that we would have had to jostle them to get by, we felt held together by there being something that had happened that they, the people who disliked us, did not understand.

We ourselves all understood the Cova, where it was rich and warm and not too brightly lighted, and noisy and smoky at certain hours, and there were always girls at the tables and the illustrated papers on a rack on the wall. The girls at the Cova were very patriotic, and I found that the most patriotic people in Italy were the café girls—and I believe they are still patriotic.

The boys at first were very polite about my medals and asked me what I had done to get them. I showed them the papers, which were written in very beautiful language and full of *fratellanza* and *abnegazione*,[6] but which really said, with the adjectives removed, that I had been given the medals because I was an American. After that their manner changed a little toward me, although I was their friend against outsiders. I was a friend, but I was never really one

▲ Wounded Ernest Hemingway (Milan, Italy; 1918)

Vocabulary

detached (di tacht´) *adj.* not emotionally involved

Comprehension

What do the narrator and the "three boys" have in common?

---

5. **Arditi** (är dē´ tē) a select group of soldiers chosen specifically for dangerous campaigns.
6. *fratellanza* (frä tāl än´ tsä) **and** *abnegazione* (äb´ nä gä tzyō´ nā) "brotherhood" and "self-denial" (Italian).

▲ Ernest Hemingway is fourth from the right in this photograph of hospital staff and patients (Milan, Italy; 1918).

Ⓒ
Spiral Review
Characterization
What does the grammar incident reveal about both the narrator's and the major's characters? Explain.

Vocabulary

disgrace (dis grās') *n.* something that brings shame or dishonor

of them after they had read the citations, because it had been different with them and they had done very different things to get their medals. I had been wounded, it was true; but we all knew that being wounded, after all, was really an accident. I was never ashamed of the ribbons, though, and sometimes, after the cocktail hour, I would imagine myself having done all the things they had done to get their medals; but walking home at night through the empty streets with the cold wind and all the shops closed, trying to keep near the street lights, I knew that I would never have done such things, and I was very much afraid to die, and often lay in bed at night by myself, afraid to die and wondering how I would be when I went back to the front again.

The three with the medals were like hunting-hawks; and I was not a hawk, although I might seem a hawk to those who had never hunted; they, the three, knew better and so we drifted apart. But I stayed good friends with the boy who had been wounded his first day at the front, because he would never know now how he would have turned out; so he could never be accepted either, and I liked him because I thought perhaps he would not have turned out to be a hawk either.

The major, who had been the great fencer, did not believe in bravery, and spent much time while we sat in the machines correcting my grammar. He had complimented me on how I spoke Italian, and we talked together very easily. One day I had said that Italian seemed such an easy language to me that I could not take a great interest in it; everything was so easy to say. "Ah yes," the major said. "Why, then, do you not take up the use of grammar?" So we took up the use of grammar, and soon Italian was such a difficult language that I was afraid to talk to him until I had the grammar straight in my mind.

The major came very regularly to the hospital. I do not think he ever missed a day, although I am sure he did not believe in the machines. There was a time when none of us believed in the machines, and one day the major said it was all nonsense. The machines were new then and it was we who were to prove them. It was an idiotic idea, he said, "a theory, like another." I had not learned my grammar, and he said I was a stupid impossible disgrace, and he was a fool to have bothered with me. He was a small man and he sat straight up in his chair with his right hand thrust into the machine and looked straight ahead at the wall while the straps thumped up and down with his fingers in them.

"What will you do when the war is over if it is over?" he asked me.

"Speak grammatically!"

"I will go to the States."

"Are you married?"

"No, but I hope to be."

"The more of a fool you are," he said. He seemed very angry. "A man must not marry."

"Why, Signor Maggiore?"[7]

"Don't call me 'Signor Maggiore.'"

"Why must not a man marry?"

"He cannot marry. He cannot marry," he said angrily. "If he is to lose everything, he should not place himself in a position to lose that. He should not place himself in a position to lose. He should find things he cannot lose."

He spoke very angrily and bitterly, and looked straight ahead while he talked.

"But why should he necessarily lose it?"

"He'll lose it," the major said.

He was looking at the wall. Then he looked down at the machine and jerked his little hand out from between the straps and slapped it hard against his thigh. "He'll lose it," he almost shouted. "Don't argue with me!" Then he called to the attendant who ran the machines. "Come and turn this damned thing off."

He went back into the other room for the light treatment and the massage. Then I heard him ask the doctor if he might use his telephone and he shut the door. When he came back into the room, I was sitting in another machine. He was wearing his cape and had his cap on, and he came directly toward my machine and put his arm on my shoulder.

"I am so sorry," he said, and patted me on the shoulder with his good hand. "I would not be rude. My wife has just died. You must forgive me."

"Oh—" I said, feeling sick for him. "I am so sorry."

He stood there biting his lower lip. "It is very difficult," he said. "I cannot resign myself."

---

7. **Signor Maggiore** (sēn yōr′ mäj jō′ rā) "Mr. Major" (Italian); a respectful way of addressing an officer.

Author's Style

How does Hemingway suggest the major's emotions without explaining them?

▲ **Critical Viewing**

How does this World War I era hospital compare with the one Hemingway describes? **COMPARE AND CONTRAST**

Vocabulary

resign (ri zīn′) v. to accept something as unavoidable; to submit oneself to something negative

Comprehension

Why does the major believe "a man must not marry"?

He looked straight past me and out through the window. Then he began to cry. "I am utterly unable to resign myself," he said and choked. And then crying, his head up looking at nothing, carrying himself straight and soldierly, with tears on both his cheeks and biting his lips, he walked past the machines and out the door.

The doctor told me that the major's wife, who was very young and whom he had not married until he was definitely invalided out of the war, had died of pneumonia. She had been sick only a few days. No one expected her to die. The major did not come to the hospital for three days. Then he came at the usual hour, wearing a black band on the sleeve of his uniform. When he came back, there were large framed photographs around the wall of all sorts of wounds before and after they had been cured by the machines. In front of the machine the major used were three photographs of hands like his that were completely restored. I do not know where the doctor got them. I always understood we were the first to use the machines. The photographs did not make much difference to the major because he only looked out of the window.

Critical Reading

Cite textual evidence to support your responses.

1. **Key Ideas and Details (a)** Why does the narrator go to the hospital every day? **(b) Compare and Contrast:** How do the attitudes of other patients differ from that of the narrator, even though they are facing similar situations? Why?

2. **Key Ideas and Details (a) Infer:** Does the narrator express a pessimistic or optimistic outlook toward the machines at the hospital? **(b) Interpret:** Why do you think he has developed this attitude toward the machines? Explain.

3. **Key Ideas and Details (a)** What happens to the major's wife? **(b)** How does the major react? **(c) Analyze:** What is ironic about the major's situation?

4. **Integration of Knowledge and Ideas Apply:** Do you think this story reflects the sense of disillusionment that arose among writers and artists during World War I? Explain.

5. **Integration of Knowledge and Ideas** Do you think Hemingway presents a typically American view of war in this story? Explain. In your response, use at least three of these Essential Question words: *ideals, exalt, nationality, reflection. [Connecting to the Essential Question: What makes American literature American?]*

Close Reading Activities   *In Another Country*

Literary Analysis

1. Key Ideas and Details Explain how you might **identify with characters** in this story through these details: **(a)** The narrator is a "boy" far from home. **(b)** He feels the Italian boys were "like hunting-hawks; and [he] was not a hawk."

2. Craft and Structure Use a chart like the one shown to identify elements of Hemingway's **style** in this story.

Syntax	Tone	Word Choice

3. Craft and Structure The narrator admits that the papers accompanying his medal inflate his bravery through the use of adjectives. How does this realization connect to Hemingway's sparse use of adjectives in the story?

4. Craft and Structure (a) What are two of the story's **themes**? **(b)** How does Hemingway's style contribute to each theme?

5. Integration of Knowledge and Ideas One theme in Hemingway's writing is the loss of innocence and a shift toward disillusionment. How might you interpret the title of this story as a reflection of that theme?

Vocabulary Acquisition and Use

Use New Words Review the words from the vocabulary list on page 798. Then, answer each question below, using the underlined word in your answer.

1. When might you need to <u>resign</u> yourself to doing something you do not want to do?

2. Is it usually a <u>disgrace</u> to make a mistake? Why or why not?

3. How can you tell if someone is <u>detached</u> during a conversation?

Writing to Sources

Informative Text Hemingway once said, "I always try to write on the principle of the iceberg. There is seven-eighths of it underwater for every part that shows." Reread "In Another Country" with Hemingway's statement in mind. Write an **essay** in which you explore how this "iceberg" approach to writing is evident in the story. Clearly demonstrate your understanding of Hemingway's style and the way he achieves it, citing passages from the story as support.

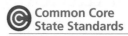
Common Core State Standards

Writing
2. Write informative texts to examine and convey complex ideas, concepts, and information clearly and accurately through the effective selection, organization, and analysis of content.
2.b. Develop the topic thoroughly by selecting the most significant and relevant facts, extended definitions, concrete details, quotations, or other information and examples appropriate to the audience's knowledge of the topic.

Language
4. Determine or clarify the meaning of unknown and multiple-meaning words and phrases based on grades 11–12 reading and content, choosing flexibly from a range of strategies.
4.a. Use context as a clue to the meaning of a word.

Themes Across Time: Author's Insights

Tim O'Brien
Introduces "Ambush"

A Short Story That Is Also Part of a Novel

"Ambush" is part of a larger work of fiction, a novel called *The Things They Carried*, but I must quickly add that the story is also meant to stand entirely on its own. It has a beginning, a middle, and an end. It can be understood and appreciated, I hope, with no additional information.

An Invented Character Who Has My Name Although the main character in the story is named Tim, which is my own name, and although many years ago I did in fact serve as an infantryman in Vietnam, "Ambush" is nonetheless a piece of fiction. The events in this story are largely invented. The characters, too, are invented, including the character named Tim. (I don't have a daughter, for example, and until very recently I had no children at all.) As a novelist and short-story writer, I am not limited by what actually happened. In fiction, I am free to write about what did *not* happen. I can write about what almost happened, or what could've happened, or what should've happened.

Fact Versus Fiction While the story is mostly imagined, it is loosely based on a "real life" ambush during the war. The mosquitoes, the trail junction, the dark night, the tension—all that comes from my own experience. In the actual incident, however, I did not throw a hand grenade that killed the young man. As it truly happened, a group of seven or eight of us simultaneously fired our rifles at three shadowy, barely visible enemy soldiers creeping across a rice paddy. One moment the night was silent, the next moment it exploded— gunfire and screams and yellow-white flashes in the dark. Later, when dawn broke, one of my friends discovered a dead Viet Cong soldier. But I did not inspect the body. I did not so much as glance at it. I certainly did not stand gaping like the character in this story.

Meet the Author

Tim O'Brien is an award-winning fiction writer. His novel *Going After Cacciato* won the National Book Award, *The Things They Carried* was a finalist for a Pulitzer Prize, and *In the Lake of the Woods* was named the best novel of 1994 by *Time* magazine.

Confession and Lament I will never know whether a bullet from my own weapon killed that young man. Perhaps so, perhaps not. But in the end, it doesn't matter. I was there that night. I pulled the trigger. And I am therefore responsible. In my view, that's what "Ambush" is finally about: responsibility. Even now, like the protagonist in this story, I still have trouble forgiving myself. I still hear the gunfire and the screams. I still have the sour, fruity taste of terror in my mouth. I still feel the guilt. And I suppose that's why I sat down one day to write "Ambush"—as a kind of confession, as a lament, as a way of acknowledging my full personal responsibility for the death of a fellow human being.

◀ **Critical Viewing**
This photograph was taken during the Vietnam War. What thoughts and emotions do you imagine these soldiers are experiencing? **SPECULATE**

Critical Reading

1. **Craft and Structure** **(a)** Why did O'Brien choose to write "Ambush" as fiction? **(b) Take a Position:** Do you think fiction is stronger if it is based on real events? Explain.

2. **Key Ideas and Details** **(a)** What does O'Brien say that "Ambush" is finally about? **(b) Infer:** What effect do you think writing "Ambush" has had on O'Brien's memories of his own experience?

As You Read "Ambush" . . .

3. **Craft and Structure** Compare and contrast the events in the story with the real events that O'Brien describes in this commentary.

4. **Integration of Knowledge and Ideas** Think about the ways in which the main character does and does not resemble O'Brien himself.

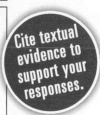
Cite textual evidence to support your responses.

AMBUSH

TIM O'BRIEN

When she was nine, my daughter Kathleen asked if I had ever killed anyone. She knew about the war; she knew I'd been a soldier. "You keep writing these war stories," she said, "so I guess you must've killed somebody." It was a difficult moment, but I did what seemed right, which was to say, "Of course not," and then to take her onto my lap and hold her for a while. Someday, I hope, she'll ask again.

But here I want to pretend she's a grown-up. I want to tell her exactly what happened, or what I remember happening, and then I want to say to her that as a little girl she was absolutely right. This is why I keep writing war stories:

◄ **Critical Viewing**
What does this photograph suggest were some of the physical hardships soldiers experienced in Vietnam? **DEDUCE**

Tim O'Brien
Author's Insight
The character of Kathleen, the narrator's daughter, seemed essential to this story. Adults rarely ask a direct, embarrassing question such as: "Did you ever kill anyone?" But a child of nine might easily ask just such a question.

Comprehension
What question does the narrator's daughter ask?

He was a short, slender young man of about twenty. I was afraid of him—afraid of something—and as he passed me on the trail I threw a grenade that exploded at his feet and killed him.

Or to go back:

Shortly after midnight we moved into the **ambush** site outside My Khe. The whole platoon was there, spread out in the dense brush along the trail, and for five hours nothing at all happened. We were working in two-man teams—one man on guard while the other slept, switching off every two hours—and I remember it was still dark when Kiowa shook me awake for the final watch. The night was foggy and hot. For the first few moments I felt lost, not sure about directions, groping for my helmet and weapon. I reached out and found three grenades and lined them up in front of me; the pins had already been straightened for quick throwing. And then for maybe half an hour I kneeled there and waited. Very gradually, in tiny slivers, dawn began to break through the fog, and from my position in the brush I could see ten or fifteen meters up the trail. The mosquitoes were fierce. I remember slapping at them, wondering if I should wake up Kiowa and ask for some repellent, then thinking it was a bad idea, then looking up and seeing the young man come out of the fog. He wore black clothing and rubber sandals and a gray **ammunition** belt. His shoulders were slightly stooped, his head cocked to the side as if listening for something. He seemed at ease. He carried his weapon in one hand, **muzzle** down, moving without any hurry up the center of the trail. There was no sound at all—none that I can remember. In a way, it seemed, he was part of the morning fog, or my own imagination, but there was also the reality of what was happening in my stomach. I had already pulled the pin on a grenade. I had come up to a crouch. It was entirely automatic. I did not hate the young man; I did not see him as the enemy; I did not ponder issues of morality or politics or military duty. I crouched and kept my head low. I tried to swallow whatever was rising from my stomach, which tasted like lemonade, something fruity and sour. I was terrified. There were no thoughts about killing. The grenade was to make him go away—just evaporate—and I leaned back and felt my mind go empty and then felt it fill up again. I had already thrown the grenade before telling myself to throw it. The brush was thick and I had to lob it high, not aiming, and I remember the grenade seeming to freeze above me for an instant, as if a camera had clicked, and I remember ducking down and holding my breath and seeing little wisps of fog rise from the earth. The grenade bounced once and rolled across the trail. I did not hear it, but there must've been a sound, because the young man dropped his weapon and began to run, just two or three quick steps, then he hesitated, swiveling to

Vocabulary

ambush (am´ bo̅o̅sh´) *n.* lying in wait to attack by surprise

ammunition (am´ yo̅o̅ nish´ ən) *n.* anything hurled by a weapon or exploded as a weapon

muzzle (muz´ əl) *n.* front end of a barrel of a gun

Tim O'Brien
Author's Insight
In these sentences I try to humanize the young enemy soldier—his clothing, his posture, the unhurried and slightly distracted way he walks up the trail.

his right, and he glanced down at the grenade and tried to cover his head but never did. It occurred to me then that he was about to die. I wanted to warn him. The grenade made a popping noise—not soft but not loud either—not what I'd expected—and there was a puff of dust and smoke—a small white puff—and the young man seemed to jerk upward as if pulled by invisible wires. He fell on his back. His rubber sandals had been blown off. There was no wind. He lay at the center of the trail, his right leg bent beneath him, his one eye shut, his other eye a huge star-shaped hole.

It was not a matter of live or die. There was no real peril. Almost certainly the young man would have passed by. And it will always be that way.

Later, I remember, Kiowa tried to tell me that the man would've died anyway. He told me that it was a good kill, that I was a soldier and this was a war, that I should shape up and stop staring and ask myself what the dead man would've done if things were reversed.

None of it mattered. The words seemed far too complicated. All I could do was gape at the fact of the young man's body.

Even now I haven't finished sorting it out. Sometimes I forgive myself, other times I don't. In the ordinary hours of life I try not to dwell on it, but now and then, when I'm reading a newspaper or just sitting alone in a room, I'll look up and see the young man coming out of the morning fog. I'll watch him walk toward me, his shoulders slightly stooped, his head cocked to the side, and he'll pass within a few yards of me and suddenly smile at some secret thought and then continue up the trail to where it bends back into the fog.

Tim O'Brien
Author's Insight
This sentence ("And it will always be that way."), for my money, is among the best I have ever written. Only seven very simple words, yet for me the sentence carries the weight of eternity, the permanent and inescapable horror of war.

Tim O'Brien
Author's Insight
As the narrator imagines the young man continuing up the trail to where it bends back into the fog, he is also imagining that the ambush never occurred, that the dead young man has a long and full life ahead of him in a future that will never be.

Critical Reading

1. **Key Ideas and Details** **(a)** What does the narrator say to describe the degree of danger he faced? **(b) Interpret:** What does he mean when he says "And it will always be that way"?

2. **Key Ideas and Details** **(a) Deduce:** How does the narrator react to the killing? **(b) Interpret:** How does Kiowa respond to the narrator's reaction?

3. **Key Ideas and Details** **(a)** At the end of the story, what does the narrator fantasize? **(b) Interpret:** In what ways does this fantasy contribute to the story's power and meaning?

4. **Craft and Structure** **(a) Compare and Contrast:** The narrator tells his story twice. Compare and contrast the short and long versions. **(b) Speculate:** Why do you think the author chose this narrative device?

5. **Integration of Knowledge and Ideas** **Make a Judgment:** Kiowa uses the expression "a good kill." Is there such a thing? Explain.

Cite textual evidence to support your responses.

Building Knowledge and Insight

A Rose for Emily • Nobel Prize Acceptance Speech

Connecting to the Essential Question In this story, outward appearances conflict in profound ways with the inner world of the main character. As you read, notice details that reveal other people's perceptions of Miss Emily and her family. Doing so will help as you consider the Essential Question: **How does literature shape or reflect society?**

Close Reading Focus

Conflict

A **conflict** is a struggle between opposing forces. It is the engine that drives narrative writing. A conflict achieves **resolution** when the struggle ends and the outcome is revealed. There are two types of literary conflict:

- **Internal conflict** occurs within the mind of a character who is torn by competing values or needs.
- **External conflict** occurs between a character and an outside force, such as another person, society as a whole, nature, or fate.

Internal conflict is at the core of Faulkner's fiction. In his Nobel Prize acceptance speech, he wrote that a writer's responsibility is to address "the problems of the human heart in conflict with itself." As you read "A Rose for Emily," think about its portrayal of a bitterly conflicted human heart. Look beneath the refined surface to find clues about deeper struggles.

Preparing to Read Complex Texts Intentional ambiguity occurs in a literary work when one or more elements can be interpreted in several ways. To **clarify ambiguity,** recognize parts of the action, characterization, or description that the writer may have deliberately left open ended, uncertain, or even inconsistent. Then, look for details or clues in the writing that help you make an interpretation. As you read, use a chart like the one shown to record ambiguous elements. Then, decide which possible interpretation you find most convincing or meaningful.

Vocabulary

You will encounter the words listed here in the texts that follow. Copy the words into your notebook. Which words have more than three syllables?

encroached   circumvent

vanquished   virulent

vindicated   inextricable

Common Core State Standards

Reading Literature

1. Cite strong and thorough textual evidence to support analysis of what the text says explicitly as well as inferences drawn from the text, including determining where the text leaves matters uncertain.

3. Analyze the impact of the author's choices regarding how to develop and relate elements of a story or drama.

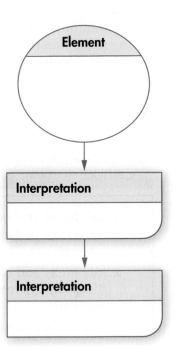

William Faulkner (1897–1962)

Author of "A Rose for Emily" and Nobel Prize Acceptance Speech

For some writers, the place of their roots is a wellspring of story material. Oxford, Mississippi, was such a place for William Faulkner. It became the basis for the imaginary world of Yoknapatawpha County—the setting of many of his novels and stories.

A Writer's Roots Although Faulkner never finished high school, he read a great deal and developed an interest in writing from an early age. In 1925, after an uninspired stint in the British military, Faulkner moved to New Orleans. There he became friends with author Sherwood Anderson, who helped get Faulkner's first novel, *Soldier's Pay*, published. In 1926, Faulkner returned home to Oxford, Mississippi, to devote himself to his writing.

A Gold Mine of Inspiration In what he called his "own little postage stamp of native soil," Faulkner uncovered a "gold mine" of inspiration. So compelling and complex was this source of inspiration that Faulkner decided to create a "cosmos of my own"—the fictional county of Yoknapatawpha. In Oxford, Faulkner wrote a series of novels about the decay of traditional values as small communities became swept up in the changes of the modern age. He used jumbled time sequences, stream-of-consciousness narration, dialect, page-long sentences, and other challenging techniques in his dense and often dark stories.

Experimenting With Narration The novel that first earned him critical acclaim was *The Sound and the Fury* (1929), a complex book exploring the downfall of an old southern family as seen through the eyes of three brothers, one of whom suffers from severe mental retardation. Other innovative works followed, including *As I Lay Dying* (1930), the story of a poor family's six-day journey to bury their mother. Told from fifteen different points of view and exploring people's varying perspectives of death, the novel was a masterpiece of narrative experimentation.

In some of Faulkner's later works, such as *The Unvanquished* (1938) and *The Hamlet* (1940), he returned to a more traditional style. Yet, in these novels, he continued to develop the history of Yoknapatawpha County and its people.

Faulkner was awarded the Nobel Prize for Literature following the publication of *Intruder in the Dust* (1948), a novel in which he confronted the issue of racism. The narrative techniques he pioneered continue to challenge and inspire writers and readers today.

> *"Given the choice between the experience of pain and nothing, I would choose pain."*

A Rose for Emily

William Faulkner

BACKGROUND Like many of William Faulkner's works, this story is set in the fictional town of Jefferson, which is in the fictional county of Yoknapatawpha (ÿuk´ nə pə tô´ fə) in the actual state of Mississippi. Using his real home of Lafayette County, Faulkner created an amazingly detailed world in his fiction, even down to the map of Yoknapatawpha that he included in one novel. "A Rose for Emily" takes place in Jefferson over the course of more than forty years, from around 1875 to 1920, chronicling the life and death of the reclusive Miss Emily Grierson.

I

When Miss Emily Grierson died, our whole town went to her funeral: the men through a sort of respectful affection for a fallen monument, the women mostly out of curiosity to see the inside of her house, which no one save an old manservant—a combined gardener and cook—had seen in at least ten years.

It was a big, squarish frame house that had once been white, decorated with cupolas and spires and scrolled balconies in the heavily lightsome style of the seventies,[1] set on what had once been our most select street. But garages and cotton gins had **encroached** and obliterated even the august[2] names of that neighborhood; only Miss Emily's house was left, lifting its stubborn and coquettish decay above the cotton wagons and the gasoline pumps—an eyesore among eyesores. And now Miss Emily had gone to join the representatives of those august names where they lay in the cedar-bemused cemetery among the ranked and anonymous graves of Union and Confederate soldiers who fell at the battle of Jefferson.

---

1. the seventies the 1870s.
2. august (ô gust ´) *adj.* dignified; inspiring respect.

Vocabulary
encroached (en krōch´ t)
v. intruded

Comprehension
As the story begins, what has happened to Miss Emily?

Alive, Miss Emily had been a tradition, a duty, and a care; a sort of hereditary obligation upon the town, dating from that day in 1894 when Colonel Sartoris, the mayor—he who fathered the edict[3] that no Negro woman should appear on the streets without an apron—remitted her taxes, the dispensation dating from the death of her father on into perpetuity.[4] Not that Miss Emily would have accepted charity. Colonel Sartoris invented an involved tale to the effect that Miss Emily's father had loaned money to the town, which the town, as a matter of business, preferred this way of repaying. Only a man of Colonel Sartoris' generation and thought could have invented it, and only a woman could have believed it.

When the next generation, with its more modern ideas, became mayors and aldermen, this arrangement created some little dissatisfaction. On the first of the year they mailed her a tax notice. February

▼ **Critical Viewing**

How is the house in this photograph similar to and different from Miss Emily's house as described on page 817? **COMPARE AND CONTRAST**

---

3. **edict** (ē′ dikt) *n.* command.

4. **remitted . . . into perpetuity** (pᵿr′ pə tōō′ ə tē) cancelled Emily's taxes forever after her father's death.

San Francisco Museum of Modern Art, Collection of the Sack Photographic Trust (Detail)

came, and there was no reply. They wrote her a formal letter, asking her to call at the sheriff's office at her convenience. A week later the mayor wrote her himself, offering to call or to send his car for her, and received in reply a note on paper of an archaic shape, in a thin, flowing calligraphy in faded ink, to the effect that she no longer went out at all. The tax notice was also enclosed, without comment.

They called a special meeting of the Board of Aldermen. A deputation waited upon her, knocked at the door through which no visitor had passed since she ceased giving china-painting lessons eight or ten years earlier. They were admitted by the old Negro into a dim hall from which a stairway mounted into still more shadow. It smelled of dust and disuse—a close, dank smell. The Negro led them into the parlor. It was furnished in heavy, leather-covered furniture. When the Negro opened the blinds of one window, they could see that the leather was cracked; and when they sat down, a faint dust rose sluggishly about their thighs, spinning with slow motes in the single sun-ray. On a tarnished gilt easel before the fireplace stood a crayon portrait of Miss Emily's father.

They rose when she entered—a small, fat woman in black, with a thin gold chain descending to her waist and vanishing into her belt, leaning on an ebony cane with a tarnished gold head. Her skeleton was small and spare; perhaps that was why what would have been merely plumpness in another was obesity in her. She looked bloated, like a body long submerged in motionless water, and of that pallid[5] hue. Her eyes, lost in the fatty ridges of her face, looked like two small pieces of coal pressed into a lump of dough as they moved from one face to another while the visitors stated their errand.

She did not ask them to sit. She just stood in the door and listened quietly until the spokesman came to a stumbling halt. Then they could hear the invisible watch ticking at the end of the gold chain.

Her voice was dry and cold. "I have no taxes in Jefferson. Colonel Sartoris explained it to me. Perhaps one of you can gain access to the city records and satisfy yourselves."

"But we have. We are the city authorities, Miss Emily. Didn't you get a notice from the sheriff, signed by him?"

"I received a paper, yes," Miss Emily said. "Perhaps he considers himself the sheriff . . . I have no taxes in Jefferson."

"But there is nothing on the books to show that, you see. We must go by the—"

"See Colonel Sartoris. I have no taxes in Jefferson."

"But, Miss Emily—"

"See Colonel Sartoris." (Colonel Sartoris had been dead almost ten years.) "I have no taxes in Jefferson. Tobe!" The Negro appeared. "Show these gentlemen out."

---

5. pallid (pal′ id) *adj.* pale.

Conflict
Which of Miss Emily's conflicts with the townspeople is introduced in this scene?

Spiral Review
Characterization What do the details describing Miss Emily's appearance indicate about her character?

Comprehension
Why do representatives of the town visit Miss Emily?

Vocabulary

vanquished (vaŋʹ kwisht)
v. thoroughly defeated

The American EXPERIENCE

Two Influential Writers

William Faulkner and Ernest Hemingway were probably the two most influential American writers of the twentieth century, even though they were near-opposites. Although Faulkner longed for adventure as a young man, he settled in a tiny corner of rural Mississippi. His prose was dense and complex and featured long, ornate sentences. Hemingway, on the other hand, lived a life of epic adventure, traveling the world and hunting big game. His prose—precise and unadorned—introduced a new way of writing to American literature.

Both men won the Nobel Prize—Faulkner in 1950 and Hemingway in 1954—and though they shared a grudging respect, they also waged a famous war of words. Hemingway said that Faulkner "wrote like an old grandmother," and Faulkner replied that Hemingway was "afraid to use a word of more than five letters."

Connect to the Literature

In "A Rose for Emily," where does Faulkner use dense, complex language, and where does his prose seem more simple and unadorned?

So she **vanquished** them, horse and foot, just as she had vanquished their fathers thirty years before about the smell. That was two years after her father's death and a short time after her sweetheart—the one we believed would marry her—had deserted her. After her father's death she went out very little; after her sweetheart went away, people hardly saw her at all. A few of the ladies had the temerity[6] to call, but were not received, and the only sign of life about the place was the Negro man—a young man then—going in and out with a market basket.

"Just as if a man—any man—could keep a kitchen properly," the ladies said; so they were not surprised when the smell developed. It was another link between the gross, teeming world and the high and mighty Griersons.

A neighbor, a woman, complained to the mayor, Judge Stevens, eighty years old.

"But what will you have me do about it, madam?" he said.

"Why, send her word to stop it," the woman said. "Isn't there a law?"

"I'm sure that won't be necessary," Judge Stevens said. "It's probably just a snake or a rat that nigger of hers killed in the yard. I'll speak to him about it."

The next day he received two more complaints, one from a man who came in diffident deprecation.[7] "We really must do something about it, Judge. I'd be the last one in the world to bother Miss Emily, but we've got to do something." That night the Board of Aldermen met—three graybeards and one younger man, a member of the rising generation.

"It's simple enough," he said. "Send her word to have her place cleaned up. Give her a certain time to do it in, and if she don't . . ."

"Dammit, sir," Judge Stevens said, "will you accuse a lady to her face of smelling bad?"

So the next night, after midnight, four men crossed Miss Emily's lawn and slunk about the house like burglars, sniffing along the base of the brickwork and at the cellar openings while one of them performed a regular sowing motion with his hand out of a sack slung from his shoulder. They broke open the cellar door and sprinkled lime there, and in all the outbuildings. As they recrossed the lawn, a window that had been dark was lighted and Miss Emily sat in it, the light

---

6. **temerity** (tə mərʹ ə tē) *n.* foolish or reckless boldness.
7. **diffident deprecation** (difʹ ə dənt depʹ rə kāʹ shen) timid disapproval.

behind her, and her upright torso motionless as that of an idol. They crept quietly across the lawn and into the shadow of the locusts[8] that lined the street. After a week or two the smell went away.

That was when people had begun to feel really sorry for her. People in our town, remembering how old lady Wyatt, her great-aunt, had gone completely crazy at last, believed that the Griersons held themselves a little too high for what they really were. None of the young men were quite good enough for Miss Emily and such. We had long thought of them as a tableau, Miss Emily a slender figure in white in the background, her father a spraddled[9] silhouette in the foreground, his back to her and clutching a horsewhip, the two of them framed by the back-flung front door. So when she got to be thirty and was still single, we were not pleased exactly, but **vindicated**; even with insanity in the family she wouldn't have turned down all of her chances if they had really materialized.

When her father died, it got about that the house was all that was left to her; and in a way, people were glad. At last they could pity Miss Emily. Being left alone, and a pauper, she had become humanized. Now she too would know the old thrill and the old despair of a penny more or less.

The day after his death all the ladies prepared to call at the house and offer condolence and aid, as is our custom. Miss Emily met them at the door, dressed as usual and with no trace of grief on her face. She told them that her father was not dead. She did that for three days, with the ministers calling on her, and the doctors, trying to persuade her to let them dispose of the body. Just as they were about to resort to law and force, she broke down, and they buried her father quickly.

We did not say she was crazy then. We believed she had to do that. We remembered all the young men her father had driven away, and we knew that with nothing left, she would have to cling to that which had robbed her, as people will.

⇥ III ⇤

She was sick for a long time. When we saw her again, her hair was cut short, making her look like a girl, with a vague resemblance to those angels in colored church windows—sort of tragic and serene.

The town had just let the contracts for paving the sidewalks, and in the summer after her father's death they began the work. The construction company came with niggers and mules and machinery, and a foreman named Homer Barron, a Yankee—a big, dark, ready man, with a big voice and eyes lighter than his face. The little boys would follow in groups to hear him cuss the niggers, and the niggers singing

Vocabulary
vindicated (vin′ də kāt′ əd)
v. cleared from blame

We did not say she was crazy then.

Comprehension
Why do the men break open the cellar door?

"Poor Emily. Her kinsfolk should come to her."

in time to the rise and fall of picks. Pretty soon he knew everybody in town. Whenever you heard a lot of laughing anywhere about the square, Homer Barron would be in the center of the group. Presently we began to see him and Miss Emily on Sunday afternoons driving in the yellow-wheeled buggy and the matched team of bays from the livery stable.

At first we were glad that Miss Emily would have an interest, because the ladies all said, "Of course a Grierson would not think seriously of a Northerner, a day laborer." But there were still others, older people, who said that even grief could not cause a real lady to forget *noblesse oblige*[10]—without calling it *noblesse oblige*. They just said, "Poor Emily. Her kinsfolk should come to her." She had some kin in Alabama; but years ago her father had fallen out with them over the estate of old lady Wyatt, the crazy woman, and there was no communication between the two families. They had not even been represented at the funeral.

And as soon as the old people said, "Poor Emily," the whispering began. "Do you suppose it's really so?" they said to one another. "Of course it is. What else could . . ." This behind their hands; rustling of craned silk and satin behind jalousies[11] closed upon the sun of Sunday afternoon as the thin, swift clop-clop-clop of the matched team passed: "Poor Emily."

She carried her head high enough—even when we believed that she was fallen. It was as if she demanded more than ever the recognition of her dignity as the last Grierson; as if it had wanted that touch of earthiness to reaffirm her imperviousness. Like when she bought the rat poison, the arsenic. That was over a year after they had begun to say "Poor Emily," and while the two female cousins were visiting her.

"I want some poison," she said to the druggist. She was over thirty then, still a slight woman, though thinner than usual, with cold, haughty black eyes in a face the flesh of which was strained across the temples and about the eyesockets as you imagine a lighthouse-keeper's face ought to look. "I want some poison," she said.

"Yes, Miss Emily. What kind? For rats and such? I'd recom—"

"I want the best you have. I don't care what kind."

The druggist named several. "They'll kill anything up to an elephant. But what you want is—"

"Arsenic," Miss Emily said. "Is that a good one?"

"Is . . . arsenic? Yes, ma'am. But what you want—"

"I want arsenic."

The druggist looked down at her. She looked back at him, erect, her face like a strained flag. "Why, of course," the druggist said. "If

---

10. *noblesse oblige* (nō bles′ ō blēzh′) *n.* the presumed duty of the upper classes to behave in a noble and generous way (French).
11. **jalousies** (jal′ ə sēz) *n.* windows or shades with slats that can be adjusted to let in air and light.

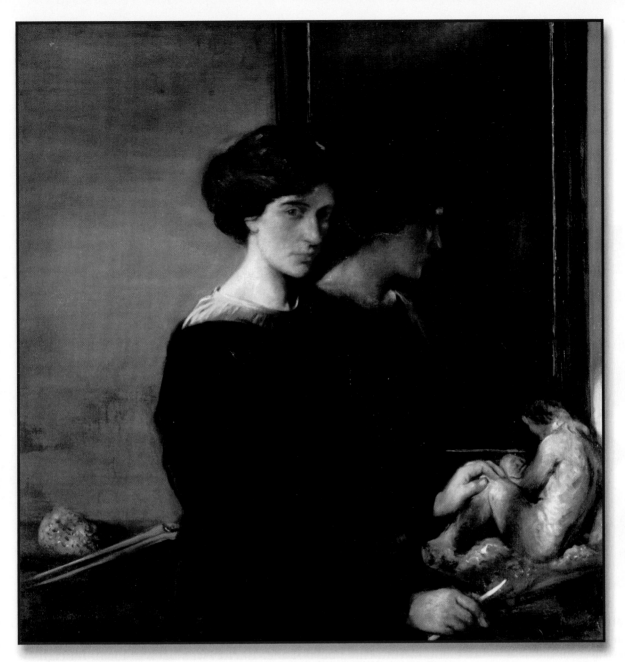

▲ **Critical Viewing** Does this portrait match your mental image of Miss Emily?
Why or why not? **CONNECT**

that's what you want. But the law requires you to tell what you are
going to use it for."

Miss Emily just stared at him, her head tilted back in order to look
him eye for eye, until he looked away and went and got the arsenic
and wrapped it up. The Negro delivery boy brought her the package;
the druggist didn't come back. When she opened the package at home
there was written on the box, under the skull and bones: "For rats."

Comprehension

Why do people begin to
refer to Miss Emily as
"Poor Emily"?

⊰ IV ⊱

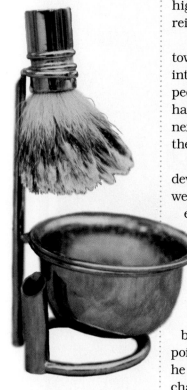

So the next day we all said, "She will kill herself"; and we said it would be the best thing. When she had first begun to be seen with Homer Barron, we had said, "She will marry him." Then we said, "She will persuade him yet," because Homer himself had remarked—he liked men, and it was known that he drank with the younger men in the Elks' Club—that he was not a marrying man. Later we said, "Poor Emily" behind the jalousies as they passed on Sunday afternoon in the glittering buggy, Miss Emily with her head high and Homer Barron with his hat cocked and a cigar in his teeth, reins and whip in a yellow glove.

Then some of the ladies began to say that it was a disgrace to the town and a bad example to the young people. The men did not want to interfere, but at last the ladies forced the Baptist minister—Miss Emily's people were Episcopal—to call upon her. He would never divulge what happened during that interview, but he refused to go back again. The next Sunday they again drove about the streets, and the following day the minister's wife wrote to Miss Emily's relations in Alabama.

So she had blood-kin under her roof again and we sat back to watch developments. At first nothing happened. Then we were sure that they were to be married. We learned that Miss Emily had been to the jeweler's and ordered a man's toilet set in silver, with the letters H. B. on each piece. Two days later we learned that she had bought a complete outfit of men's clothing, including a nightshirt, and we said, "They are married." We were really glad. We were glad because the two female cousins were even more Grierson than Miss Emily had ever been.

So we were not surprised when Homer Barron—the streets had been finished some time since—was gone. We were a little disappointed that there was not a public blowing-off, but we believed that he had gone on to prepare for Miss Emily's coming, or to give her a chance to get rid of the cousins. (By that time it was a cabal[12], and we were all Miss Emily's allies to help **circumvent** the cousins.) Sure enough, after another week they departed. And, as we had expected all along, within three days Homer Barron was back in town. A neighbor saw the Negro man admit him at the kitchen door at dusk one evening.

And that was the last we saw of Homer Barron. And of Miss Emily for some time. The Negro man went in and out with the market basket, but the front door remained closed. Now and then we would see her at a window for a moment, as the men did that night when they sprinkled the lime, but for almost six months she did not appear on the streets. Then we knew that this was to be expected too; as if that quality of her father which had thwarted her woman's life so many times had been too **virulent** and too furious to die.

Vocabulary

circumvent (sur´ kəm vent´) *v.* prevent; get around

virulent (vir´ yoo lənt) *adj.* extremely hurtful or infectious

---

12. cabal (kə bäl´) *n.* small group of people joined in a secret plot.

When we next saw Miss Emily, she had grown fat and her hair was turning gray. During the next few years it grew grayer and grayer until it attained an even pepper-and-salt iron-gray, when it ceased turning. Up to the day of her death at seventy-four it was still that vigorous iron-gray, like the hair of an active man.

From that time on her front door remained closed, save for a period of six or seven years, when she was about forty, during which she gave lessons in china-painting. She fitted up a studio in one of the downstairs rooms, where the daughters and granddaughters of Colonel Sartoris' contemporaries were sent to her with the same regularity and in the same spirit that they were sent to church on Sundays with a twenty-five-cent piece for the collection plate. Meanwhile her taxes had been remitted.

Then the newer generation became the backbone and the spirit of the town, and the painting pupils grew up and fell away and did not send their children to her with boxes of color and tedious brushes and pictures cut from the ladies' magazines. The front door closed upon the last one and remained closed for good. When the town got free postal delivery, Miss Emily alone refused to let them fasten the metal numbers above her door and attach a mailbox to it. She would not listen to them.

Daily, monthly, yearly we watched the Negro grow grayer and more stooped, going in and out with the market basket. Each December we sent her a tax notice, which would be returned by the post office a week later, unclaimed. Now and then we would see her in one of the downstairs windows—she had evidently shut up the top

Comprehension
What items does Miss Emily order from the jeweler?

◀ **Critical Viewing**
What aspects of this image suggest the kind of refinement the townspeople attribute to Miss Emily? **ANALYZE**

floor of the house—like the carven torso of an idol in a niche, looking or not looking at us, we could never tell which. Thus she passed from generation to generation—dear, inescapable, impervious, tranquil, and perverse.[13]

And so she died. Fell ill in the house filled with dust and shadows, with only a doddering Negro man to wait on her. We did not even know she was sick; we had long since given up trying to get any information from the Negro. He talked to no one, probably not even to her, for his voice had grown harsh and rusty, as if from disuse.

She died in one of the downstairs rooms, in a heavy walnut bed with a curtain, her gray head propped on a pillow yellow and moldy with age and lack of sunlight.

V

The Negro met the first of the ladies at the front door and let them in, with their hushed, sibilant[14] voices and their quick, curious glances, and then he disappeared. He walked right through the house and out the back and was not seen again.

The two female cousins came at once. They held the funeral on the second day, with the town coming to look at Miss Emily beneath a mass of bought flowers, with the crayon face of her father musing profoundly above the bier[15] and the ladies sibilant and macabre[16]; and the very old men—some in their brushed Confederate uniforms—on the porch and the lawn, talking of Miss Emily as if she had been a contemporary of theirs, believing that they had danced with her and courted her perhaps, confusing time with its mathematical progression, as the old do, to whom all the past is not a diminishing road but, instead, a huge meadow which no winter ever quite touches, divided from them now by the narrow bottle-neck of the most recent decade of years.

Already we knew that there was one room in that region above stairs which no one had seen in forty years, and which would have to be forced. They waited until Miss Emily was decently in the ground before they opened it.

The violence of breaking down the door seemed to fill this room with pervading dust. A thin, acrid pall[17] as of the tomb seemed to lie everywhere upon this room decked and furnished as for a bridal: upon the valance curtains of faded rose color, upon the rose-shaded lights, upon the dressing

---

Conflict and Resolution

Is Miss Emily's death the resolution to the conflicts in this story? Explain.

---

13. **perverse** (pər vʉrs´) *adj.* stubbornly contrary or difficult.
14. **sibilant** (sib´ ə lənt) *adj.* making a hissing sound with *s* or *sh* sounds.
15. **bier** (bir) *n.* supporting platform for a coffin.
16. **macabre** (mə käb´ rə) *adj.* gruesome.
17. **acrid pall** (ak´ rid pôl) *n.* bitter and gloomy covering or atmosphere.

table, upon the delicate array of crystal and the man's toilet things backed with tarnished silver, silver so tarnished that the monogram was obscured. Among them lay a collar and tie, as if they had just been removed, which, lifted, left upon the surface a pale crescent in the dust. Upon a chair hung the suit, carefully folded; beneath it the two mute shoes and the discarded socks.

The man himself lay in the bed.

For a long while we just stood there, looking down at the profound and fleshless grin. The body had apparently once lain in the attitude of an embrace, but now the long sleep that outlasts love, that conquers even the grimace of love, had cuckolded[18] him. What was left of him, rotted beneath what was left of the nightshirt, had become **inextricable** from the bed in which he lay; and upon him and upon the pillow beside him lay that even coating of the patient and biding dust.

Then we noticed that in the second pillow was the indentation of a head. One of us lifted something from it, and leaning forward, that faint and invisible dust dry and acrid in the nostrils, we saw a long strand of iron-gray hair.

Vocabulary

inextricable (in eks´ tri kə bəl) *adj.* unable to be separated or freed from

---

18. cuckolded (kuk´ əld əd) *v.* betrayed by an unfaithful wife or lover.

Critical Reading

1. **Key Ideas and Details (a)** What happened when the judge tried to get Miss Emily to pay her taxes? **(b) Infer:** What does this incident reveal about her relationship to the town?

2. **Key Ideas and Details (a)** What had been the position of Miss Emily's family in Jefferson while her father was alive? **(b) Deduce:** How does her position change over time? **(c) Draw Conclusions:** What does she seem to feel about this change?

3. **Key Ideas and Details (a) Describe:** What happens when Emily buys arsenic? **(b) Summarize:** What problem do the townspeople notice shortly after that purchase? **(c) Speculate:** What do you think Emily did with the arsenic?

4. **Key Ideas and Details (a)** What does the story say about Homer Barron and his relationship with Emily? **(b) Infer:** What probably happened to Homer, and why?

5. **Integration of Knowledge and Ideas** In what ways does this story comment on discrepancies between society's ideas of class, privilege, and respectability and the darker sides of human nature? In your response, use at least two of these Essential Question words: *reputation, conventions, insight, respectability, ambition.* *[Connecting to the Essential Question: How does literature shape or reflect society?]*

Cite textual evidence to support your responses.

WILLIAM FAULKNER
Nobel Prize Acceptance Speech

BACKGROUND Swedish chemist Alfred Nobel earned fame as the inventor of dynamite. Nobel had intended dynamite to be used safely in mining and construction, but disasters often occurred, and his name became associated with tragedy. Nobel eventually succeeded in making dynamite safer. Later, he established a foundation to encourage achievement and diplomacy. The Nobel Prizes, the world's most prestigious awards, are the result of his efforts. When William Faulkner received the Nobel Prize for literature in 1950, he delivered a speech that is among the most moving examples of oratory in our literature.

Stockholm, Sweden
December 10, 1950

I feel that this award was not made to me as a man, but to my work—a life's work in the agony and sweat of the human spirit, not for glory and least of all for profit, but to create out of the materials of the human spirit something which did not exist before. So this award is only mine in trust. It will not be difficult to find a dedication for the money part of it commensurate with the purpose and significance of its origin. But I would like to do the same with the acclaim too, by using this moment as a pinnacle from which I might be listened to by the young men and women already dedicated to the same anguish and travail, among whom is already that one who will some day stand here where I am standing.

Our tragedy today is a general and universal physical fear so long sustained by now that we can even bear it. There are no longer problems of the spirit. There is only the question: When will I be blown up? Because of this, the young man or woman writing today has forgotten the problems of the human heart in conflict with itself which alone can make good writing because only that is worth writing about, worth the agony and the sweat.

He must learn them again. He must teach himself that the basest of all things is to be afraid; and, teaching himself that, forget it forever, leaving no room in his workshop for anything but the old verities and truths of the heart, the old universal truths lacking which any story is ephemeral and doomed—love and honor and pity and pride and compassion and sacrifice. Until he does so, he labors under a curse. He writes not of love but of lust, of defeats in which nobody loses anything of value, of victories without hope and, worst of all, without pity or compassion. His griefs grieve on no universal bones, leaving no scars. He writes not of the heart but of the glands.

Until he relearns these things, he will write as though he stood among and watched the end of man. I decline to accept the end of man. It is easy enough to say that man is immortal simply because he will endure: that when the last ding-dong of doom has clanged and faded from the last worthless rock hanging tideless in the last red and dying evening, that even then there will still be one more sound: that of his puny inexhaustible voice, still talking. I refuse to accept this. I believe that man will not merely endure: he will prevail. He is immortal, not because he alone among creatures has an inexhaustible voice, but because he has a soul, a spirit capable of compassion and sacrifice and endurance. The poet's, the writer's, duty is to write about these things. It is his privilege to help man endure by lifting his heart, by reminding him of the courage and honor and hope and pride and compassion and pity and sacrifice which have been the glory of his past. The poet's voice need not merely be the record of man, it can be one of the props, the pillars to help him endure and prevail.

> I decline
> to accept
> the end of
> man.

Critical Reading

1. **Key Ideas and Details (a)** According to Faulkner, why are there no longer problems of the spirit? **(b) Deduce:** What is the physical fear to which he refers?

2. **Key Ideas and Details (a)** What alone does Faulkner believe is the subject matter of good writing? **(b) Interpret:** Why does he view most modern literature as ephemeral?

3. **Key Ideas and Details (a)** According to Faulkner, will humanity endure or prevail? **(b) Define:** In what way does Faulkner define the difference between enduring and prevailing?

4. **Key Ideas and Details (a)** What does Faulkner say is a writer's "duty"? **(b) Interpret:** What distinction does he draw about the role of "the poet's voice"?

5. **Integration of Knowledge and Ideas (a) Extend:** What events not long before 1950 gave rise to the fear of which Faulkner speaks? **(b) Hypothesize:** If he were alive today, would he say we have lost or retained that fear? Explain.

Cite textual evidence to support your responses.

Close Reading Activities
A Rose for Emily • Nobel Prize Acceptance Speech

Literary Analysis

1. **Key Ideas and Details** Use a chart like the one shown to analyze the **internal** and **external conflicts** that affect Emily's life. **(a)** How is each conflict resolved, if at all? **(b)** What common thread runs through all the conflicts Emily faces?

Conflict	Who vs. Who/What?	Resolution
nonpayment of taxes	Emily vs. town	

Common Core State Standards

Writing
1. Write arguments to support claims in an analysis of substantive topics or texts, using valid reasoning and relevant and sufficient evidence.

Language
4.b. Identify and correctly use patterns of word changes that indicate different meanings or parts of speech.
5. Demonstrate understanding of word relationships.

2. **Key Ideas and Details (a)** What do Emily's external conflicts with the people of Jefferson reveal about her? **(b)** What do they reveal about the town? Explain.

3. **Key Ideas and Details (a)** Why are there no suitors available for Emily? **(b)** In what ways is this both an internal and an external conflict for Emily?

4. **Key Ideas and Details (a)** What conflict does Emily have with her father? **(b)** Does she ever find **resolution** for this conflict? Explain.

5. **Key Ideas and Details (a)** In his Nobel Prize acceptance speech, what conflicts does Faulkner seem to have with the era in which he lives? **(b)** What does he fear will happen to literature—and to humanity?

6. **Craft and Structure** The identity of the narrator in this story is uncertain and unspecified; therefore, it is ambiguous. **(a)** What clues help you **clarify ambiguity** about the narrator's identity? **(b)** Who do you think the narrator is? Explain your interpretation. **(c)** Why do you think Faulkner chose to leave the narrator's identity uncertain and open to interpretation?

7. **Integration of Knowledge and Ideas (a)** What event, character, or situation in the story do you find most ambiguous? **(b)** What possible interpretations would clarify that ambiguity? **(c)** Which of these interpretations do you think the text best supports? Explain.

8. **Integration of Knowledge and Ideas** In a 1955 interview, Faulkner explained the story's title: "The meaning was, here was a woman who had had a tragedy, an irrevocable tragedy and nothing could be done about it, and I pitied her and this [the story] was a salute . . . to a woman you would hand a rose." What is Emily's tragedy? Explain.

Vocabulary Acquisition and Use

Word Analysis: Latin Prefix *in-*

The Latin prefix *in-* has two basic meanings:

- a location or direction: "in," "into," "within," "on," or "toward," as in *insert, indent,* and *invade*

- a negative: "no," "not," or "without," as in *inextricable, inescapable,* and *inseparable*

When *in-* is used before a word beginning with *p*, the prefix becomes *im-*, as in *impossible*. Write the meaning of the following words, noting whether the prefix in each indicates location or negation.

1. indelible	**5.** impervious
2. impact	**6.** intention
3. insensible	**7.** impress
4. inundate	**8.** inexhaustible

Vocabulary: Analogies

Complete each analogy with a word from the vocabulary list. In each, your choice should make a word pair that matches the relationship between the first two words given. Explain your answers.

1. encroached : withdrew :: expanded :
   (a) inflated **(b)** collapsed **(c)** magnified

2. vanquished : strength :: comprehended :
   (a) intelligence **(b)** fear **(c)** mystery

3. vindicated : blame :: cured :
   (a) illness **(b)** medicine **(c)** physician

4. circumvent : avoid :: collect :
   (a) scatter **(b)** gather **(c)** repulse

5. virulent : disease :: nauseating :
   (a) weakness **(b)** discomfort **(c)** odor

6. inextricable : separate :: invisible :
   (a) see **(b)** hide **(c)** disappear

Writing to Sources

Argument In his Nobel Prize acceptance speech, Faulkner notes that the writer's duty is "to help man endure by lifting his heart, by reminding him of the courage and honor and hope and pride and compassion and pity and sacrifice which have been the glory of his past." Apply this criteria to a **critical review** of "A Rose for Emily." Consider whether Faulkner fulfills his ideal. Support your opinion with facts, details, quotations, or other information and examples from the story.

Prewriting Review the story, and make notes about whether the author has succeeded or failed, according to Faulkner's own standards.

Model: Elaborating to Explain an Idea Fully

In "A Rose for Emily," Faulkner fulfills his own criteria for writing about "truths of the heart." He accomplishes this by giving dignity to the story of a town recluse. His writing summons feelings of both pity and horror.

> Including specific information elaborates on a basic idea.

Drafting Introduce your review with a clear statement of your position. Then, elaborate through detailed and accurate references to the story.

Revising Reread your review to confirm that you have provided solid supporting evidence for your ideas.

Building Knowledge and Insight | *The Jilting of Granny Weatherall*

Connecting to the Essential Question In this story, Granny Weatherall remembers key moments from her life as it comes to a close. As you read, notice the judgments Granny makes about the life she has lived. Your observations will help you reflect on the Essential Question: **How does literature shape or reflect society?**

Close Reading Focus

Stream of Consciousness; Flashback

People's thoughts do not flow in neat patterns; they move unpredictably among perceptions, memories, and ideas. During the early 1900s, some writers began using a literary device called **stream of consciousness** to try to capture the natural flow of thought. These narratives usually

- present sequences of thought as if they were coming directly from a character's mind;
- leave out transitional words and phrases found in ordinary prose;
- connect details only through a character's associations.

Stream-of-consciousness narratives often include the use of **flashback,** an interruption in which earlier events are described. A flashback might take the form of a memory, a story told about a character, a dream or daydream, or a switch by the narrator to a time in the past. As you read, trace the path of Granny Weatherall's thoughts and note the details that trigger her memories and observations. Identify points at which a more traditional story would have provided transitions or other connections that smooth the reader's way. Finally, consider how these structural choices contribute both to the story's meaning and to its sense of artistry.

Preparing to Read Complex Texts In the present time of the story, Granny Weatherall is on her deathbed. However, events from her eighty years of life flow throughout the story and do not appear in chronological order. *Monitor your comprehension* of this complex narrative. At points where you are unclear about the relationships between details, **clarify the sequence of events.** Use a graphic organizer like the one shown to place the events of Granny's life in order.

Vocabulary

The words below are important to understanding the text that follows. Copy the words into your notebook, sorting them into words you know and words you do not know.

tactful **dyspepsia**

piety

© **Common Core State Standards**

Reading Literature
3. Analyze the impact of the author's choices regarding how to develop and relate elements of a story.
5. Analyze how an author's choices concerning how to structure specific parts of a text contribute to its overall structure and meaning as well as its aesthetic impact.

Ordering Events

— birth

— death

Katherine Anne Porter

(1890–1980)

Author of "The Jilting of Granny Weatherall"

Katherine Anne Porter's life spanned World War I, the Great Depression, World War II, and the rise of the nuclear age, making her deeply aware of what she called "the heavy threat of world catastrophe." For Porter, her fiction was an "effort to grasp the meaning of those threats, to trace them to their sources, and to understand the logic of this majestic and terrible failure of the life of man in the Western world." Her stories were often set in the South and featured characters at pivotal moments in their lives, faced with dramatic change, the constricting bonds of family, and the weight of the past.

A descendant of legendary pioneer Daniel Boone, Porter was born in Indian Creek, Texas. She was raised in poverty and haphazardly educated in convent schools. Porter claimed that her true education came by reading five writers—American authors Henry James, T. S. Eliot, and Ezra Pound, Irish writer James Joyce, and Irish poet W. B. Yeats.

Beginnings as a Writer Porter began writing at an early age, though she did not publish her first book until she was forty years old. As a young adult, she worked as a journalist. Her work took her to many places, including Mexico City, where she lived for eight years. While in Mexico, Porter developed an interest in writing fiction, and in 1922 she published her first story. Eight years later, she published her first book, *Flowering Judas*, a collection of short stories, which earned her critical praise and widespread recognition.

Literary Achievements Porter went on to produce several other major works, including *Noon Wine* (1937); *Pale Horse, Pale Rider* (1939); *The Leaning Tower and Other Stories* (1944); and *Ship of Fools* (1962)—her only novel. Although her body of work was relatively small, it consistently received high praise and earned her a place among the finest writers of the twentieth century. Her *Collected Stories* (1965) was awarded the Pulitzer Prize and the National Book Award.

A First-Rate Artist Critic Edmund Wilson once tried to account for the "elusive" quality that made Porter an "absolutely first-rate artist." He said, "What [these stories] show us are human relationships in their constantly shifting phases and in the moments of which their existence is made. There is no place for general reflections; you are to live through the experiences as the characters do."

"Now and again thousands of memories converge, harmonize, arrange themselves around a central idea in a coherent form, and I write a story."

THE JILTING OF GRANNY WEATHERALL

KATHERINE ANNE PORTER

Garden of Memories, (detail) 1917, Charles Burchfield, The Museum of Modern Art, New York

BACKGROUND Katherine Anne Porter's view of life and the fiction she wrote were shaped by a sense of disillusionment resulting from World War I, the despair of the Great Depression, and the World War II horrors of Nazism and nuclear warfare. Sometimes, as in the novel *Ship of Fools,* Porter focused on political issues such as Nazism. In contrast, works like "The Jilting of Granny Weatherall" pinpointed the dissolving families and communities of the modern age.

S he flicked her wrist neatly out of Doctor Harry's pudgy careful fingers and pulled the sheet up to her chin. The brat ought to be in knee breeches. Doctoring around the country with spectacles on his nose! "Get along now, take your schoolbooks and go. There's nothing wrong with me."

Doctor Harry spread a warm paw like a cushion on her forehead where the forked green vein danced and made her eyelids twitch. "Now, now, be a good girl, and we'll have you up in no time."

"That's no way to speak to a woman nearly eighty years old just because she's down. I'd have you respect your elders, young man."

"Well, Missy, excuse me," Doctor Harry patted her cheek. "But I've got to warn you, haven't I? You're a marvel, but you must be careful or you're going to be good and sorry."

"Don't tell me what I'm going to be. I'm on my feet now, morally speaking. It's Cornelia. I had to go to bed to get rid of her."

Her bones felt loose, and floated around in her skin, and Doctor Harry floated like a balloon around the foot of the bed. He floated and pulled down his waistcoat and swung his glasses on a cord. "Well, stay where you are, it certainly can't hurt you."

"Get along and doctor your sick," said Granny Weatherall. "Leave a well woman alone. I'll call for you when I want you. . . Where were you forty years ago when I pulled through milk leg[1] and double pneumonia? You weren't even born. Don't let Cornelia lead you on," she shouted, because Doctor Harry appeared to float up to the ceiling and out. "I pay my own bills, and I don't throw my money away on nonsense!"

She meant to wave good-bye, but it was too much trouble. Her eyes closed of themselves, it was like a dark curtain drawn around the bed. The pillow rose and floated under her, pleasant as a hammock in a light wind. She listened to the leaves rustling outside the window. No, somebody was swishing newspapers: no, Cornelia and Doctor Harry were whispering together. She leaped broad awake, thinking they whispered in her ear.

"She was never like this, never like this!" "Well, what can we expect?" "Yes, eighty years old. . . ."

Well, and what if she was? She still had ears. It was like Cornelia

1. **milk leg** painful swelling of the leg.

◀ **Critical Viewing**
Which elements of this surreal illustration of an old woman in her "garden of memories" might represent Granny Weatherall?
CONNECT

Stream of Consciousness
While Granny is rebuking the doctor, what is really happening in the room?

Comprehension
Where is Granny Weatherall as she speaks to the doctor?

Vocabulary

tactful (takt´ fəl)
adj. concerned about
upsetting or offending
others; diplomatic

to whisper around doors. She always kept things secret in such a public way. She was always being tactful and kind. Cornelia was dutiful; that was the trouble with her. Dutiful and good: "So good and dutiful," said Granny, "that I'd like to spank her." She saw herself spanking Cornelia and making a fine job of it.

"What'd you say, Mother?"

Granny felt her face tying up in hard knots.

"Can't a body think, I'd like to know?"

"I thought you might want something."

"I do. I want a lot of things. First off, go away and don't whisper."

She lay and drowsed, hoping in her sleep that the children would keep out and let her rest a minute. It had been a long day. Not that she was tired. It was always pleasant to snatch a minute now and then. There was always so much to be done, let me see: tomorrow.

Tomorrow was far away and there was nothing to trouble about. Things were finished somehow when the time came; thank God there was always a little margin over for peace: then a person could spread out the plan of life and tuck in the edges orderly. It was good to have everything clean and folded away, with the hair brushes and tonic bottles sitting straight on the white embroidered linen: the day started without fuss and the pantry shelves laid out with rows of jelly glasses and brown jugs and white stone-china jars with blue whirligigs and words painted on them: coffee, tea, sugar, ginger, cinnamon, allspice: and the bronze clock with the lion on top nicely dusted off. The dust that lion could collect in twenty-four hours! The box in the attic with all those letters tied up, well, she'd have to go through that tomorrow. All those letters—George's letters and John's letters and her letters to them both—lying around for the children to find afterwards made her uneasy. Yes, that would be tomorrow's business. No use to let them know how silly she had been once.

While she was rummaging around she found death in her mind and it felt clammy and unfamiliar. She had spent so much time preparing for death there was no need for bringing it up again. Let it take care of itself now. When she was sixty she had felt very old, finished, and went around making farewell trips to see her children and grandchildren, with a secret in her mind: This is the very last of your mother, children! Then she made her will and came down with a long fever. That was all just a notion like a lot of other things, but it was lucky too, for she had once for all got over the idea of dying for a long time. Now she couldn't be worried. She hoped she had better sense now. Her father had lived to be one hundred and two years old and had drunk a noggin of strong hot toddy on his last birthday. He told the reporters it was his daily habit, and he owed his

LITERATURE IN CONTEXT

History Connection

House Calls

In this story, eighty-year-old Ellen Weatherall dies at home, having been attended by the family doctor. Up until the 1930s, it was a common practice for doctors to deliver most of their services in the home. Medical technology was simple enough that home treatment was as good as—or better than—hospital treatment. However, after World War II, the field of medicine changed dramatically. New techniques for diagnosis and treatment required special technology and facilities. Economic factors also came into play; house calls were considered wasteful of the doctor's time. Today, except in some rural areas, the house call has faded into memory.

Connect to the Literature

How do you think Granny would react if she were moved to a hospital or nursing home? How would Cornelia feel?

long life to that. He had made quite a scandal and was very pleased about it. She believed she'd just plague Cornelia a little.

"Cornelia! Cornelia!" No footsteps, but a sudden hand on her cheek. "Bless you, where have you been?"

"Here, mother."

"Well, Cornelia, I want a noggin of hot toddy."

"Are you cold, darling?"

"I'm chilly, Cornelia. Lying in bed stops the circulation. I must have told you that a thousand times."

Well, she could just hear Cornelia telling her husband that Mother was getting a little childish and they'd have to humor her. The thing that most annoyed her was that Cornelia thought she was deaf, dumb, and blind. Little hasty glances and tiny gestures tossed around her and over her head saying, "Don't cross her, let her have her way, she's eighty years old," and she sitting there as if she lived in a thin glass cage. Sometimes Granny almost made up her mind to pack up and move back to her own house where nobody could remind her every minute that she was old. Wait, wait, Cornelia, till your own children whisper behind your back!

In her day she had kept a better house and had got more work done. She wasn't too old yet for Lydia to be driving eighty miles for advice when one of the children jumped the track, and Jimmy still dropped in and talked things over: "Now, Mammy, you've a good business head, I want to know what you think of this? . . ." Old. Cornelia couldn't change the furniture around without asking. Little things, little things! They had been so sweet when they were little. Granny wished the old days were back again with the children young and everything to be done over. It had been a hard pull, but not too much for her. When she thought of all the food she had cooked, and all the clothes she had cut and sewed, and all the gardens she had made— well, the children showed it. There they were, made out of her, and they couldn't get away from that. Sometimes she wanted to see John again and point to them and say, Well, I didn't do so badly, did I? But that would have to wait. That was for tomorrow. She used to think of him as a man, but now all the children were older than their father, and he would be a child beside her if she saw him now. It seemed strange and there was something wrong in the idea. Why, he couldn't possibly recognize her. She had fenced in a hundred acres once, digging the post holes herself and clamping the wires with just a negro boy to help. That changed a woman. John would be looking for a young woman with the peaked Spanish comb in her hair and the painted fan. Digging post holes changed a woman. Riding country roads in the winter when women had their babies was another thing: sitting up nights with sick horses and sick children and hardly ever losing one. John, I hardly ever lost one of them! John would see that in a minute, that would be something he could understand, she wouldn't have to explain anything!

She had fenced in a hundred acres once, digging the post holes herself. . .

Stream of Consciousness

Notice the path of Granny's thoughts. What are some topics she touches on, and how are they linked in her mind?

Comprehension

What journey did Granny Weatherall take when she was sixty years old? Why?

It made her feel like rolling up her sleeves and putting the whole place to rights again. No matter if Cornelia was determined to be everywhere at once, there were a great many things left undone on this place. She would start tomorrow and do them. It was good to be strong enough for everything, even if all you made melted and changed and slipped under your hands, so that by the time you finished you almost forgot what you were working for. *What was it I set out to do?* she asked herself intently, but she could not remember. A fog rose over the valley, she saw it marching across the creek swallowing the trees and moving up the hill like an army of ghosts. Soon it would be at the near edge of the orchard, and then it was time to go in and light the lamps. *Come in, children, don't stay out in the night air.*

Lighting the lamps had been beautiful. The children huddled up to her and breathed like little calves waiting at the bars in the twilight. Their eyes followed the match and watched the flame rise and settle in a blue curve, then they moved away from her. *The lamp was lit, they didn't have to be scared and hang on to mother any more. Never, never, never more. God, for all my life I thank Thee. Without Thee, my God, I could never have done it. Hail Mary, full of grace.*

I want you to pick all the fruit this year and see that nothing is wasted. There's always someone who can use it. Don't let good things rot for want of using. You waste life when you waste good food. Don't let things get lost. It's bitter to lose things. Now, don't let me get to thinking, not when I am tired and taking a little nap before supper. . . .

The pillow rose about her shoulders and pressed against her heart and the memory was being squeezed out of it: oh, push down the pillow, somebody: it would smother her if she tried to hold it. Such a fresh breeze blowing and such a green day with no threats in it. But he had not come, just the same. *What does a woman do when she has put on the white veil and set out the white cake for a man and he doesn't come?* She tried to remember. *No, I swear he never harmed me but in that. He never harmed me but in that . . . and what if he did? There was the day, the day,* but a whirl of dark smoke rose and covered it, crept up and over into the bright field where everything was planted so carefully in orderly rows. *That was hell,* she knew *hell* when she saw it. For sixty years she had prayed against remembering him and against losing her soul in the deep pit of hell, and now the two things were mingled in one and the thought of him was a smoky cloud from hell that moved and crept in her head when she had just got rid of Doctor Harry and was trying to rest a minute. *Wounded vanity, Ellen,* said a sharp voice in the top of her mind. *Don't let your wounded vanity get the upper hand of you. Plenty of girls get jilted. You were jilted, weren't you? Then stand up to it.* Her eyelids wavered and let in streamers of blue-gray light like tissue paper over her eyes. She must get up and pull the shades down or she'd never sleep. She was in bed again and the shades were not down. How could that happen? Better turn over, hide from the light, sleeping in the light

---

Flashback

What do you learn about Granny from this flashback to a time when her children were small?

Stream of Consciousness

What memory does Granny try to keep from surfacing? Why?

Don't let your wounded vanity get the upper hand of you. Plenty of girls get jilted.

◀ **Critical Viewing**
In what ways does the mood and subject of this painting reflect Granny's memories of being jilted at the altar? **INTERPRET**

gave you nightmares. "Mother, how do you feel now?" and a stinging wetness on her forehead. But I don't like having my face washed in cold water!

Hapsy? George? Lydia? Jimmy? No, Cornelia, and her features were swollen and full of little puddles. "They're coming, darling, they'll all be here soon." Go wash your face, child, you look funny.

Instead of obeying, Cornelia knelt down and put her head on the pillow. She seemed to be talking but there was no sound. "Well, are you tongue-tied? Whose birthday is it? Are you going to give a party?"

Cornelia's mouth moved urgently in strange shapes. "Don't do that, you bother me, daughter."

"Oh, no, Mother. Oh, no. . . ."

Comprehension
What happened to Granny sixty years ago?

Stream of Consciousness

What actual events are taking place in the room, and in what ways do they affect Granny's thoughts?

Nonsense. It was strange about children. They disputed your every word. "No what, Cornelia?"

"Here's Doctor Harry."

"I won't see that boy again. He just left five minutes ago."

"That was this morning, Mother. It's night now. Here's the nurse."

"This is Doctor Harry, Mrs. Weatherall. I never saw you look so young and happy!"

"Ah, I'll never be young again—but I'd be happy if they'd let me lie in peace and get rested."

She thought she spoke up loudly, but no one answered. A warm weight on her forehead, a warm bracelet on her wrist, and a breeze went on whispering, trying to tell her something. A shuffle of leaves in the everlasting hand of God, He blew on them and they danced and rattled. "Mother, don't mind, we're going to give you a little hypodermic." "Look here, daughter, how do ants get in this bed? I saw sugar ants yesterday." Did you send for Hapsy too?

It was Hapsy she really wanted. She had to go a long way back through a great many rooms to find Hapsy standing with a baby on her arm. She seemed to herself to be Hapsy also, and the baby on Hapsy's arm was Hapsy and himself and herself, all at once, and there was no surprise in the meeting. Then Hapsy melted from within and turned flimsy as gray gauze and the baby was a gauzy shadow, and Hapsy came up close and said, "I thought you'd never come," and looked at her very searchingly and said, "You haven't changed a bit!" They leaned forward to kiss, when Cornelia began whispering from a long way off, "Oh, is there anything you want to tell me? Is there anything I can do for you?"

Yes, she had changed her mind after sixty years and she would like to see George. I want you to find George. Find him and be sure to tell him I forgot him. I want him to know I had my husband just the same and my children and my house like any other woman. A good house too and a good husband that I loved and fine children out of him. Better than I hoped for even. Tell him I was given back everything he took away and more. Oh, no, oh, God, no, there was something else besides the house and the man and the children. Oh, surely they were not all? What was it? Something not given back. . . . Her breath crowded down under her ribs and grew into a monstrous frightening shape with cutting edges; it bored up into her head, and the agony was unbelievable: Yes, John, get the Doctor now, no more talk, my time has come.

When this one was born it should be the last. The last. It should have been born first, for it was the one she had truly wanted. Everything came in good time. Nothing left out, left over. She was strong, in three days she would be as well as ever. Better. A woman needed milk in her to have her full health.

"Mother, do you hear me?"

"I've been telling you—"

"Mother, Father Connolly's here."

"I went to Holy Communion only last week. Tell him I'm not so sinful as all that."

"Father just wants to speak to you."

He could speak as much as he pleased. It was like him to drop in and inquire about her soul as if it were a teething baby, and then stay on for a cup of tea and a round of cards and gossip. He always had a funny story of some sort, usually about an Irishman who made his little mistakes and confessed them, and the point lay in some absurd thing he would blurt out in the confessional showing his struggles between native **piety** and original sin. Granny felt easy about her soul. Cornelia, where are your manners? Give Father Connolly a chair. She had her secret comfortable understanding with a few favorite saints who cleared a straight road to God for her. All as surely signed and sealed as the papers for the new Forty Acres. Forever . . . heirs and assigns[2] forever. Since the day the wedding cake was not cut, but thrown out and wasted. The whole bottom dropped out of the world, and there she was blind and sweating with nothing under her feet and the walls falling away. His hand had caught her under the breast, she had not fallen, there was the freshly polished floor with the green rug on it, just as before. He had cursed like a sailor's parrot and said, "I'll kill him for you." Don't lay a hand on him, for my sake leave something to God. "Now, Ellen, you must believe what I tell you. . . ."

So there was nothing, nothing to worry about any more, except sometimes in the night one of the children screamed in a nightmare, and they both hustled out shaking and hunting for the matches and calling, "There, wait a minute, here we are!" John, get the doctor now, Hapsy's time has come. But there was Hapsy standing by the bed in a white cap. "Cornelia, tell Hapsy to take off her cap. I can't see her plain."

Her eyes opened very wide and the room stood out like a picture she had seen somewhere. Dark colors with the shadows rising towards the ceiling in long angles. The tall black dresser gleamed with nothing on it but John's picture, enlarged from a little one, with John's eyes very black when they should have been blue. You never saw him, so how do you know how he looked? But the man insisted the copy was perfect, it was very rich and handsome. For a picture, yes, but it's not my husband. The table by the bed had a linen cover and a candle and a crucifix. The light was blue from Cornelia's silk lampshades. No sort of light at all, just frippery. You had to live forty years with kerosene lamps to appreciate honest electricity. She felt very strong and she saw Doctor Harry with a rosy nimbus around him.

"You look like a saint, Doctor Harry, and I vow that's as near as

---

2. **assigns** persons to whom property is transferred.

... get the Doctor now, no more talk, my time has come.

Vocabulary

piety (pī´ ə tē) *n.* devotion to religion

Comprehension
What does Granny want George to know?

you'll ever come to it."

"She's saying something."

"I heard you, Cornelia. What's all this carrying on?"

"Father Connolly's saying—"

Cornelia's voice staggered and bumped like a cart in a bad road. It rounded corners and turned back again and arrived nowhere. Granny stepped up in the cart very lightly and reached for the reins, but a man sat beside her and she knew him by his hands, driving the cart. She did not look in his face, for she knew without seeing, but looked instead down the road where the trees leaned over and bowed to each other and a thousand birds were singing a Mass. She felt like singing too, but she put her hand in the bosom of her dress and pulled out a rosary, and Father Connolly murmured Latin in a very solemn voice and tickled her feet.[3] My God, will you stop that nonsense? I'm a married woman. What if he did run away and leave me to face the priest by myself? I found another a whole world better. I wouldn't have exchanged my husband for anybody except St. Michael[4] himself, and you may tell him that for me with a thank you in the bargain.

Light flashed on her closed eyelids, and a deep roaring shook her. Cornelia, is that lightning? I hear thunder. There's going to be a storm. Close all the windows. Call the children in. . . . "Mother, here we are, all of us." "Is that you, Hapsy?" "Oh, no, I'm Lydia. We drove as fast as we could." Their faces drifted above her, drifted away. The rosary fell out of her hands and Lydia put it back. Jimmy tried to help, their hands fumbled together, and Granny closed two fingers around Jimmy's thumb. Beads wouldn't do, it must be something alive. She was so amazed her thoughts ran round and round. So, my dear Lord, this is my death and I wasn't even thinking about it. My children have come to see me die. But I can't, it's not time. Oh, I always hated surprises. I wanted to give Cornelia the amethyst set— Cornelia, you're to have the amethyst set, but Hapsy's to wear it when she wants, and, Doctor Harry, do shut up. Nobody sent for you. Oh, my dear Lord, do wait a minute. I meant to do something about the Forty Acres, Jimmy doesn't need it and Lydia will later on, with that worthless husband of hers. I meant to finish the altar cloth and send six bottles of wine to Sister Borgia for her dyspepsia. I want to send six bottles of wine to Sister Borgia, Father Connolly, now don't let me forget.

Cornelia's voice made short turns and tilted over and crashed. "Oh, Mother, oh, Mother, oh Mother. . . ."

"I'm not going, Cornelia. I'm taken by surprise. I can't go."

You'll see Hapsy again. What about her? "I thought you'd never come." Granny made a long journey outward, looking for Hapsy. What if I don't find her? What then? Her heart sank down and down, there

Stream of Consciousness

What is the connecting link between Granny's thoughts about her amethyst set, the Forty acres, and the altar cloth?

Vocabulary

dyspepsia (dis pep′ shə) *n.* indigestion

---

3. murmured . . . feet administered the last rites of the Catholic Church.

4. St. Michael one of the archangels.

was no bottom to death, she couldn't come to the end of it. The blue light from Cornelia's lampshade drew into a tiny point in the center of her brain, it flickered and winked like an eye, quietly it fluttered and dwindled. Granny lay curled down within herself, amazed and watchful, staring at the point of light that was herself; her body was now only a deeper mass of shadow in an endless darkness and this darkness would curl around the light and swallow it up. God, give a sign!

For the second time there was no sign. Again no bridegroom and the priest in the house. She could not remember any other sorrow because this grief wiped them all away. Oh, no, there's nothing more cruel than this—I'll never forgive it. She stretched herself with a deep breath and blew out the light.

Critical Reading

> **Cite textual evidence to support your responses.**

1. **Key Ideas and Details (a)** Who sits with Granny during her final hours? **(b) Analyze:** What is Granny's attitude toward this person?

2. **Key Ideas and Details (a)** What are the names of Granny's children? **(b) Interpret:** Which of her children does Granny long to see? **(c) Deduce:** Why is she unable to see this child?

3. **Key Ideas and Details (a)** As she drifts in and out of consciousness, what memory is "squeezed out" of Granny's heart? **(b) Interpret:** How does Granny try to talk herself out of the pain of this memory?

4. **Key Ideas and Details (a) Interpret:** What memories and details suggest Granny's physical and emotional strength as a young woman? **(b) Analyze:** Why might the author have chosen "Weatherall" as an appropriate surname for Granny?

5. **Key Ideas and Details (a) Infer:** As she nears death, why does Granny say she "can't go"? **(b) Connect:** What is the connection between her experience of having been jilted and her experiences in the final paragraph?

6. **Craft and Structure Speculate:** In what ways might this story have been different if Granny had confronted George after he jilted her?

7. **Integration of Knowledge and Ideas** Whose criteria do you think Granny uses to judge her life? Is her assessment of her life accurate or fair? In your response, use at least three of these Essential Question words: *satisfying, fulfillment, judgment, critical, productive. [Connecting to the Essential Question: How does literature shape or reflect society?]*

Close Reading Activities

The Jilting of Granny Weatherall

Literary Analysis

1. **Craft and Structure** What impact does the use of **stream of consciousness** have on the reader's perceptions of Granny's children and of Doctor Harry?

2. **Key Ideas and Details** **Clarify the sequence of events** presented in this story by completing a timeline of Granny Weatherall's life.

3. **Craft and Structure** Use a chart like the one shown to analyze Granny's thoughts and their associations. **(a)** Identify two points at which Granny's thoughts drift from one subject to another without an obvious transition or connection. **(b)** What possible associations might connect her thoughts in each of these examples?

4. **Craft and Structure** Analyze three **flashbacks** in the story. **(a)** Identify the form each flashback takes (dream, memory, and so on). **(b)** Note what you learn from each flashback about Granny's life.

5. **Craft and Structure** **(a)** What details trigger Granny's flashback to lighting the lamps when her children were young? **(b)** What is the connection between this flashback and her experiences in the present?

6. **Craft and Structure** Describe a structure this story might have had if Porter had not used stream of consciousness and flashback. For example, how might Porter have introduced individual characters or narrated specific scenes?

7. **Craft and Structure** **(a)** Based on your response to question 6, what qualities does the use of stream of consciousness and flashback lend to the narrative? **(b)** Overall, do you think these techniques are effective for the telling of this particular tale? Explain.

8. **Integration of Knowledge and Ideas** Do you think Porter's use of stream of consciousness makes Granny's character more or less vivid to the reader? Explain.

9. **Integration of Knowledge and Ideas** Does the jumbled sequence of events as they appear in the story create a complete picture of Granny's life? Explain.

 Common Core State Standards

Writing

3. Write narratives to develop real or imagined experiences or events using effective technique, well-chosen details, and well-structured event sequences. *(p.845)*

3.b. Use narrative techniques, such as dialogue, pacing, description, reflection, and multiple plot lines, to develop experiences, events, and/or characters. *(p. 845)*

3.d. Use precise words and phrases, telling details, and sensory language to convey a vivid picture of the experiences, events, setting, and/or characters. *(p. 845)*

Language

4.b. Identify and correctly use patterns of word changes that indicate different meanings or parts of speech. *(p. 845)*

4.d. Verify the preliminary determination of the meaning of a word or phrase. *(p. 845)*

Vocabulary Acquisition and Use

Word Analysis: Greek Prefix *dys-*

The Greek prefix *dys-*, meaning "difficult" or "bad," can help you decipher many unfamiliar words. This prefix is often used in scientific terms involving medical or psychological diagnoses. Write a definition of each word below by combining the meaning of the prefix *dys-* with the clues in parentheses. After you have finished, use a dictionary to check your work and revise as necessary.

1. dysfunctional (*functional* = working properly)
2. dyslexia (*lexis* = word or speech)
3. dysentery (*entery* = intestine)
4. dyspepsia (*pepsis* = digestion)
5. dystopia (*topos* = place)

Vocabulary: Sentence Completions

Select the word from the vocabulary list on page 830 that best completes each sentence below. Then, explain your reasoning.

1. Kelly showed her _____ by attending religious services daily.
2. It is best to be _____ when discussing politics with people you do not know well.
3. I try to avoid eating pizza because it aggravates my _____.

Writing to Sources

Narrative Text A monologue is a dramatic form in which only one person speaks. A stream-of-consciousness monologue is a type of *interior monologue* in that it takes place within the mind of a character. Choose a character from the story or make up a new one. Write a **monologue** in which you use stream of consciousness to portray the character's thoughts.

Prewriting List concrete sensory details—words and phrases related to sight, sound, and smell. Think about gestures, actions, and feelings that come alive through these details. Organize the details into two categories: scenes in the present / scenes in the past.

Drafting Select several memories around which to organize the monologue. Add to the stream-of-consciousness effect by omitting transitions.

> **Model: Using Details to Create a Vivid Character**
>
> Here's the jetway, a chute, really. No going back now. *Fasten your seatbelts*. Night flight without my parents—was I nine, eleven?—daring myself to peek out the scratched plastic oval at the tiny lights below. *Ouch*. My stomach hurts because I buckled my belt so tight.

Using specific images emphasizes the character's feelings.

Revising Read your monologue aloud to make sure it sounds like a genuine, private voice. Add clues to help your audience follow the thought stream and clarify the ideas and memories expressed.

Building Knowledge and Insight | *A Worn Path*

Connecting to the Essential Question Phoenix Jackson, the main character in this story, addresses the natural world as if it were an old acquaintance. As you read, look for instances in which Phoenix relates to the landscape like another person. Doing so will help as you consider the Essential Question: **What is the relationship between literature and place?**

Close Reading Focus

Archetype; Hero's Quest

An **archetype** is a plot structure, character type, symbol, or idea that recurs in the literature or mythology of many different cultures across the world. The **hero's quest** is one archetypal plot structure. Classic quest tales—from ancient Egyptian myths to the modern-day *Star Wars* stories—typically follow a certain structure and share certain elements.

- The hero is on a journey to obtain something of great value.
- The hero encounters obstacles that test his or her character.
- The hero overcomes these obstacles, often with the aid of others, and often at great sacrifice.
- The hero receives a boon, or benefit, that is used to help others.
- The hero's quest symbolizes the larger journey of life.

As its title suggests, "A Worn Path" features a traveler on a familiar road. Phoenix Jackson, an elderly black woman in Depression-era Mississippi, faces a range of obstacles as she progresses through the landscape. Some of these obstacles are physical and some are societal. As you read, notice elements in the story that mirror the structure of the hero's quest archetype.

Preparing to Read Complex Texts The reason for Phoenix Jackson's journey remains a mystery for much of the story, although various details provide clues about the nature of her quest. As you read, **generate questions** about Phoenix's life and journey. Then, **make predictions** in response to the questions. As the story unfolds, use what you learn to *confirm* whether your predictions were correct. Use a chart like the one shown to generate questions, make predictions, and confirm them.

Vocabulary

The words below are important to understanding the text that follows. Copy the words into your notebook. What are some other forms of the word *persistent*?

grave

persistent

limber

obstinate

© Common Core State Standards

Reading Literature
3. Analyze the impact of the author's choices regarding how to develop and relate elements of a story or drama.
5. Analyze how an author's choices concerning how to structure specific parts of a text contribute to its overall structure and meaning as well as its aesthetic impact.

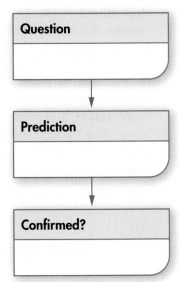

Question

Prediction

Confirmed?

Eudora Welty

(1909–2001)

Author of "A Worn Path"

Eudora Welty's stories and novels capture life in the deep South, creating images of the landscape and conveying the shared attitudes and values of the people. While she often confronts the hardships of life in poor rural areas and depicts people's suffering, her writing remains optimistic.

Welty was born in Jackson, Mississippi, where she spent most of her life. She attended Mississippi State College for Women before transferring to the University of Wisconsin, where she graduated in 1929. Hoping to pursue a career in advertising, she moved to New York City and enrolled at Columbia University's School of Business. However, because of the worsening economic depression, she was unable to find steady employment and returned to Jackson in 1931.

Traveling and Writing After accepting a job as a publicist for a government agency, Welty spent several years traveling throughout Mississippi, taking photographs and interviewing people. Her experiences inspired her to write, and in 1936 her first short story, "Death of a Traveling Salesman," was published.

In her fiction, Welty displays an acute sense of detail and a deep sense of compassion toward her characters. For example, in "A Worn Path," she paints a sympathetic portrait of an old woman whose feelings of love and sense of duty motivate her to make a long, painful journey through the countryside.

One of the leading American writers of the twentieth century, Welty published numerous collections of short stories and novels. In 1973, her novel *The Optimist's Daughter* won the Pulitzer Prize.

A Worn Path

EUDORA WELTY

Miz Emily, Joseph Holston, Courtesy of Joseph Holston

BACKGROUND This story is set in Mississippi during the Great Depression of the 1930s. Decades after the end of the Civil War and the emancipation of southern slaves, the people of Mississippi still suffered from the social and economic consequences of that war. Many whites continued to reject the idea of a biracial society, and most blacks, though "free," had become trapped in a tenant-farming system that kept them perpetually indebted to the white landowners. It was not a prosperous system for anyone, black or white. By the onset of the Depression in 1929, Mississippi was among the poorest states in the nation, with an average annual income of $287 per capita; by 1933, that average had fallen to $117. Families struggled to make ends meet in a state that could offer neither financial aid nor social services. This is the economic and social landscape through which Phoenix Jackson travels.

It was December — a bright frozen day in the early morning. Far out in the country there was an old Negro woman with her head tied in a red rag, coming along a path through the pinewoods. Her name was Phoenix Jackson. She was very old and small and she walked slowly in the dark pine shadows, moving a little from side to side in her steps, with the balanced heaviness and lightness of a pendulum in a grandfather clock. She carried a thin, small cane made from an umbrella, and with this she kept tapping the frozen earth in front of her. This made a grave and persistent noise in the still air, that seemed meditative like the chirping of a solitary little bird.

She wore a dark striped dress reaching down to her shoe tops, and an equally long apron of bleached sugar sacks, with a full pocket: all neat and tidy, but every time she took a step she might have fallen over her shoelaces, which dragged from her unlaced shoes. She looked straight ahead. Her eyes were blue with age. Her skin had a pattern all its own of numberless branching wrinkles and as though a whole little tree stood in the middle of her forehead, but a golden color ran underneath, and the two knobs of her cheeks were illumined by a yellow burning under the dark. Under the red rag her hair came down on her neck in the frailest of ringlets, still black, and with an odor like copper.

Now and then there was a quivering in the thicket. Old Phoenix said, "Out of my way, all you foxes, owls, beetles, jack rabbits, coons and wild animals! . . . Keep out from under these feet, little bob-whites[1]. . . . Keep the big wild hogs out of my path. Don't let none of

---

1. bob-whites *n.* partridges.

◄ **Critical Viewing** What details in this image suggest Phoenix's strong character? **CONNECT**

Vocabulary

grave (grāv) *adj.* serious; solemn

persistent (pər sist´ ənt) *adj.* repeated; continual

Comprehension

What are some of Phoenix Jackson's distinguishing features?

Vocabulary

limber (lim′ bər) *adj.*
flexible

Archetype of the Quest

What first obstacle does Phoenix encounter?

Generating Questions

What question about Phoenix might you ask based on her discussion with the thorns?

those come running my direction. I got a long way." Under her small black-freckled hand her cane, limber as a buggy whip, would switch at the brush as if to rouse up any hiding things.

On she went. The woods were deep and still. The sun made the pine needles almost too bright to look at, up where the wind rocked. The cones dropped as light as feathers. Down in the hollow was the mourning dove—it was not too late for him.

The path ran up a hill. "Seem like there is chains about my feet, time I get this far," she said, in the voice of argument old people keep to use with themselves. "Something always take a hold of me on this hill—pleads I should stay."

After she got to the top she turned and gave a full, severe look behind her where she had come. "Up through pines," she said at length. "Now down through oaks."

Her eyes opened their widest, and she started down gently. But before she got to the bottom of the hill a bush caught her dress.

Her fingers were busy and intent, but her skirts were full and long, so that before she could pull them free in one place they were caught in another. It was not possible to allow the dress to tear. "I in the thorny bush," she said. "Thorns, you doing your appointed work. Never want to let folks pass, no sir. Old eyes thought you was a pretty little *green* bush."

Finally, trembling all over, she stood free, and after a moment dared to stoop for her cane.

"Sun so high!" she cried, leaning back and looking, while the thick tears went over her eyes. "The time getting all gone here."

At the foot of this hill was a place where a log was laid across the creek.

"Now comes the trial," said Phoenix.

Putting her right foot out, she mounted the log and shut her eyes. Lifting her skirt, leveling her cane fiercely before her, like a festival figure in some parade, she began to march across. Then she opened her eyes and she was safe on the other side.

"I wasn't as old as I thought," she said.

But she sat down to rest. She spread her skirts on the bank around her and folded her hands over her knees. Up above her was a tree in a pearly cloud of mistletoe. She did not dare to close her eyes, and when a little boy brought her a plate with a slice of marble cake on it she spoke to him. "That would be acceptable," she said. But when she went to take it there was just her own hand in the air.

So she left that tree, and had to go through a barbed-wire fence. There she had to creep and crawl, spreading her knees and stretching her fingers like a baby trying to climb the steps. But she talked loudly to herself: she could not let her dress be torn now, so late in the day, and she could not pay for having her arm or her leg sawed off if she got caught fast where she was.

At last she was safe through the fence and risen up out in the clearing. Big dead trees, like black men with one arm, were standing in the purple stalks of the withered cotton field. There sat a buzzard.

"Who you watching?"

In the furrow she made her way along.

"Glad this not the season for bulls," she said, looking sideways, "and the good Lord made his snakes to curl up and sleep in the winter. A pleasure I don't see no two-headed snake coming around that tree, where it come once. It took a while to get by him, back in the summer."

She passed through the old cotton and went into a field of dead corn. It whispered and shook and was taller than her head. "Through the maze now," she said, for there was no path.

Then there was something tall, black, and skinny there, moving before her.

At first she took it for a man. It could have been a man dancing in the field. But she stood still and listened, and it did not make a sound. It was as silent as a ghost.

"Ghost," she said sharply, "who be you the ghost of? For I have heard of nary death close by."

But there was no answer—only the ragged dancing in the wind.

She shut her eyes, reached out her hand, and touched a sleeve. She found a coat and inside that an emptiness, cold as ice.

"You scarecrow," she said. Her face lighted. "I ought to be shut up for good," she said with laughter. "My senses is gone. I too old. I the oldest people I ever know. Dance, old scarecrow," she said, "while I dancing with you."

She kicked her foot over the furrow, and with mouth drawn down, shook her head once or twice in a little strutting way. Some husks blew down and whirled in streamers about her skirts.

Then she went on, parting her way from side to side with the cane, through the whispering field. At last she came to the end, to a wagon track where the silver grass blew between the red ruts. The quail were walking around like pullets, seeming all dainty and unseen.

"Walk pretty," she said. "This the easy place. This the easy going."

She followed the track, swaying through the quiet bare fields, through the little strings of trees silver in their dead leaves, past cabins silver from weather, with the doors and windows boarded shut, all like old women under a spell sitting there. "I walking in their sleep," she said, nodding her head vigorously.

In a ravine she went where a spring was silently flowing through a hollow log. Old Phoenix bent and drank. "Sweet-gum[2] makes the water sweet," she said, and drank more. "Nobody know who made this well, for it was here when I was born."

The track crossed a swampy part where the moss hung as white as lace from every limb. "Sleep on, alligators, and blow your bubbles." Then the track went into the road.

---

2. **sweet-gum** *a tree that produces a fragrant juice.*

A Worn Path **851**

WORLD LITERATURE CONNECTION

The Hero's Quest

"A Worn Path" tells of Phoenix Jackson's quest to get medicine for her grandson. One of the oldest archetypal forms, the quest plot appears in poetry and folk tales throughout the world. The *Odyssey*, an epic poem that was likely composed by the Greek poet Homer in the 8th century B.C., is one of the most famous examples of the quest plot.

The *Odyssey* tells of the voyage of the Greek warrior Odysseus. After the Trojan War, Odysseus loads his ship and sails for home, where his family awaits him on the island of Ithaca. The voyage turns out to be longer and harder than expected—ten years longer. Powerful winds blow the ship off course, and Odysseus lands on a series of islands, where he encounters frightening giants, monsters, cannibals, beautiful witches and seductive goddesses. These are the obstacles that Odysseus must overcome before reuniting with his family on Ithaca.

Connect to the Literature

Can the world of a rural, impoverished woman like Phoenix Jackson be as challenging as the world of a royal warrior like Odysseus? Why or why not?

Archetype of the Quest

What heroic trait does Phoenix display in her encounter with the "ghost"?

Comprehension

What is Phoenix Jackson's attitude as she walks?

Deep, deep the road went down between the high green-colored banks. Overhead the live-oaks met, and it was as dark as a cave.

A black dog with a lolling tongue came up out of the weeds by the ditch. She was meditating, and not ready, and when he came at her she only hit him a little with her cane. Over she went in the ditch, like a little puff of milkweed.[3]

Down there, her senses drifted away. A dream visited her, and she reached her hand up, but nothing reached down and gave her a pull.

▼ **Critical Viewing**
Does this image accurately represent the path Phoenix travels? Why or why not?
EVALUATE

3. **milkweed** *n.* a plant with pods that, when ripe, release feathery seeds.

So she lay there and presently went to talking. "Old woman," she said to herself, "that black dog come up out of the weeds to stall you off, and now there he sitting on his fine tail, smiling at you."

A white man finally came along and found her—a hunter, a young man, with his dog on a chain.

"Well, Granny!" he laughed. "What are you doing there?"

"Lying on my back like a June bug waiting to be turned over, mister," she said, reaching up her hand.

He lifted her up, gave her a swing in the air, and set her down. "Anything broken, Granny?"

"No sir, them old dead weeds is springy enough," said Phoenix, when she had got her breath. "I thank you for your trouble."

"Where do you live, Granny?" he asked, while the two dogs were growling at each other.

"Away back yonder, sir, behind the ridge. You can't even see it from here."

"On your way home?"

"No sir, I going to town."

"Why, that's too far! That's as far as I walk when I come out myself, and I get something for my trouble." He patted the stuffed bag he carried, and there hung down a little closed claw. It was one of the bob-whites, with its beak hooked bitterly to show it was dead. "Now you go on home, Granny!"

"I bound to go to town, mister," said Phoenix. "The time come around."

He gave another laugh, filling the whole landscape. "I know you old colored people! Wouldn't miss going to town to see Santa Claus!"

But something held old Phoenix very still. The deep lines in her face went into a fierce and different radiation. Without warning, she had seen with her own eyes a flashing nickel fall out of the man's pocket onto the ground.

"How old are you, Granny?" he was saying.

"There is no telling, mister," she said, "no telling."

Then she gave a little cry and clapped her hands and said, "Git on away from here, dog! Look! Look at that dog!" She laughed as if in admiration. "He ain't scared of nobody. He a big black dog." She whispered, "Sic him!"

"Watch me get rid of that cur," said the man. "Sic him, Pete! Sic him!"

Phoenix heard the dogs fighting, and heard the man running and throwing sticks. She even heard a gunshot. But she was slowly bending forward by that time, further and further forward, the lids stretched down over her eyes, as if she were doing this in her sleep. Her chin was lowered almost to her knees. The yellow palm of her hand came out from the fold of her apron. Her fingers slid down and along the ground under the piece of money with the grace and care they would have in lifting an egg from under a setting hen. Then she slowly straightened up, she stood erect, and the nickel was in her apron pocket. A bird flew by. Her lips moved. "God watching me the whole time. I come to stealing."

Georgia Red Clay, 1946, Nell Choate Jones, Morris Museum of Art, Augusta, Georgia

Archetype of the Quest

What element of the hero's quest might the hunter represent?

Generating Questions

What question might you ask about the nickel's importance in the story?

Comprehension

Who comes along to help Phoenix on her way?

The man came back, and his own dog panted about them. "Well, I scared him off that time," he said, and then he laughed and lifted his gun and pointed it at Phoenix.

She stood straight and faced him.

"Doesn't the gun scare you?" he said, still pointing it.

"No, sir, I seen plenty go off closer by, in my day, and for less than what I done," she said, holding utterly still.

He smiled, and shouldered the gun. "Well, Granny," he said, "you must be a hundred years old, and scared of nothing. I'd give you a dime if I had any money with me. But you take my advice and stay home, and nothing will happen to you."

"I bound to go on my way, mister," said Phoenix. She inclined her head in the red rag. Then they went in different directions, but she could hear the gun shooting again and again over the hill.

She walked on. The shadows hung from the oak trees to the road like curtains. Then she smelled wood-smoke, and smelled the river, and she saw a steeple and the cabins on their steep steps. Dozens of little black children whirled around her. There ahead was Natchez[4] shining. Bells were ringing. She walked on.

In the paved city it was Christmas time. There were red and green electric lights strung and crisscrossed everywhere, and all turned on in the daytime. Old Phoenix would have been lost if she had not distrusted her eyesight and depended on her feet to know where to take her.

She paused quietly on the sidewalk where people were passing by. A lady came along in the crowd, carrying an armful of red-, green- and silver-wrapped presents; she gave off perfume like the red roses in hot summer, and Phoenix stopped her.

"Please, missy, will you lace up my shoe?" She held up her foot.

"What do you want, Grandma?"

"See my shoe," said Phoenix. "Do all right for out in the country, but wouldn't look right to go in a big building."

"Stand still then, Grandma," said the lady. She put her packages down on the sidewalk beside her and laced and tied both shoes tightly.

"Can't lace 'em with a cane," said Phoenix. "Thank you, missy. I doesn't mind asking a nice lady to tie up my shoe, when I gets out on the street."

Moving slowly and from side to side, she went into the big building, and into a tower of steps, where she walked up and around and around until her feet knew to stop.

She entered a door, and there she saw nailed up on the wall the document that had been stamped with the gold seal and framed in the gold frame, which matched the dream that was hung up in her head.

"Here I be," she said. There was a fixed and ceremonial stiffness over her body.

"A charity case, I suppose," said an attendant who sat at the desk before her.

But Phoenix only looked above her head. There was sweat on her

Archetype of the Quest

Does Phoenix pass the "test" of the hunter? Explain.

Generating Questions

What questions might you ask about the big building and the goal of Phoenix's quest?

---

4. **Natchez** (nach´ iz) a town in southern Mississippi.

face, the wrinkles in her skin shone like a bright net.

"Speak up, Grandma," the woman said. "What's your name? We must have your history, you know. Have you been here before? What seems to be the trouble with you?"

Old Phoenix only gave a twitch to her face as if a fly were bothering her.

"Are you deaf?" cried the attendant.

But then the nurse came in.

"Oh, that's just old Aunt Phoenix," she said. "She doesn't come for herself—she has a little grandson. She makes these trips just as regular as clockwork. She lives away back off the Old Natchez Trace." She bent down. "Well, Aunt Phoenix, why don't you just take a seat? We won't keep you standing after your long trip." She pointed.

The old woman sat down, bolt upright in the chair.

"Now, how is the boy?" asked the nurse.

Old Phoenix did not speak.

"I said, how is the boy?"

But Phoenix only waited and stared straight ahead, her face very solemn and withdrawn into rigidity.

"Is his throat any better?" asked the nurse. "Aunt Phoenix, don't you hear me? Is your grandson's throat any better since the last time you came for the medicine?"

With her hands on her knees, the old woman waited, silent, erect and motionless, just as if she were in armor.

"You mustn't take up our time this way, Aunt Phoenix," the nurse said. "Tell us quickly about your grandson, and get it over. He isn't dead, is he?"

At last there came a flicker and then a flame of comprehension across her face, and she spoke.

"My grandson. It was my memory had left me. There I sat and forgot why I made my long trip."

"Forgot?" The nurse frowned. "After you came so far?"

Then Phoenix was like an old woman begging a dignified forgiveness for waking up frightened in the night. "I never did go to school. I was too old at the Surrender,"[5] she said in a soft voice. "I'm an old woman without an education. It was my memory fail me. My little grandson, he is just the same, and I forgot it in the coming."

"Throat never heals, does it?" said the nurse, speaking in a loud, sure voice to old Phoenix. By now she had a card with something written on it, a little list. "Yes. Swallowed lye. When was it?—January—two, three years ago—"

Phoenix spoke unasked now. "No, missy, he not dead, he just the same. Every little while his throat begin to close up again, and he not able to swallow. He not get his breath. He not able to help himself. So the time come around, and I go on another trip for the soothing medicine."

"All right. The doctor said as long as you came to get it, you could have it," said the nurse. "But it's an **obstinate** case."

---

5. the Surrender the surrender of the Confederate army, which ended the Civil War.

"There I sat and forgot why I made my long trip."

Vocabulary
obstinate (äb´ stə nət)
adj. stubborn

Comprehension
Why is Phoenix at the doctor's office?

"My little grandson, he sit up there in the house all wrapped up, waiting by himself," Phoenix went on. "We is the only two left in the world. He suffer and it don't seem to put him back at all. He got a sweet look. He going to last. He wear a little patch quilt and peep out holding his mouth open like a little bird. I remembers so plain now. I not going to forget him again, no, the whole enduring time. I could tell him from all the others in creation."

"All right." The nurse was trying to hush her now. She brought her a bottle of medicine. "Charity," she said, making a check mark in a book.

Old Phoenix held the bottle close to her eyes, and then carefully put it into her pocket.

"I thank you," she said.

"It's Christmas time, Grandma," said the attendant. "Could I give you a few pennies out of my purse?"

"Five pennies is a nickel," said Phoenix stiffly.

"Here's a nickel," said the attendant.

Phoenix rose carefully and held out her hand. She received the nickel and then fished the other nickel out of her pocket and laid it beside the new one. She stared at her palm closely, with her head on one side.

Then she gave a tap with her cane on the floor.

"This is what come to me to do," she said. "I going to the store and buy my child a little windmill they sells, made out of paper. He going to find it hard to believe there such a thing in the world. I'll march myself back where he is waiting, holding it straight up in this hand."

She lifted her free hand, gave a little nod, turned around, and walked out of the doctor's office. Then her slow step began on the stairs, going down.

> ## "We is the only two left in the world."

Critical Reading

Cite textual evidence to support your responses.

1. **Key Ideas and Details** **(a)** How does the young hunter address Phoenix? **(b) Analyze:** What contradictory attitudes toward Phoenix does the hunter express? Explain.

2. **Integration of Knowledge and Ideas** **Synthesize:** In mythology, the phoenix is a bird that rises from the ashes. Why do you think Welty named the main character of this story Phoenix?

3. **Integration of Knowledge and Ideas** **(a) Interpret:** At the end of the story, do you think Phoenix's grandson is alive? Explain. **(b) Assess:** Why do you think Welty does not clarify this ambiguity?

4. **Integration of Knowledge and Ideas** Does Phoenix seem more "at home" in the natural landscape or in the social landscape of Depression-era Mississippi? Explain. In your response, use at least two of these Essential Question words: *dignified, charity, perceptions, trials, status. [Connecting to the Essential Question: What is the relationship between literature and place?]*

Close Reading Activities   *A Worn Path*

Literary Analysis

1. **Key Ideas and Details (a)** What **prediction** did you make about the purpose of Phoenix's journey? **(b)** Was your prediction confirmed partly, fully, or not at all? Explain. **(c)** What unpredictable "gifts" does the end of the story offer?

2. **Craft and Structure** Use a chart like the one shown to analyze the obstacles Phoenix encounters on her **archetypal hero's quest.**

Obstacle	How Phoenix Responds

3. **Craft and Structure (a)** Which obstacles listed in your chart are physical? **(b)** Which are social? **(c)** In general, how does Phoenix deal differently with these two types of challenges? Consider her words, tone, and actions.

4. **Craft and Structure (a)** What object of great value does Phoenix seek? **(b)** What sacrifices must she make to obtain it?

5. **Craft and Structure (a)** What benefit, or boon, does Phoenix receive? **(b)** How is her use of this boon heroic?

6. **Integration of Knowledge and Ideas** In what ways does Phoenix's journey symbolize the journey of life?

Vocabulary Acquisition and Use

Context Clues Review the words from the list on page 846. Then, answer *yes* or *no* to each question below. Explain the context clues that help you.

1. Would someone bringing *grave* news be smiling?

2. If you heard a *persistent* noise, would you go investigate?

3. Would a gymnast need to be *limber* before performing?

4. Would you want to work on a project with an *obstinate* person?

Writing to Sources

Narrative Text Write a **sequel** to this story that describes what happens when Phoenix Jackson gets home. Use specific details and sensory language to create vivid pictures in your story. Use these questions to plan your sequel:

- Is Phoenix's grandson alive?
- What problem or problems does Phoenix face? What is/are its/their significance?
- What does Phoenix feel and do?
- How will your story end?

Common Core State Standards

Writing
3. Write narratives to develop real or imagined experiences or events using effective technique, well-chosen details, and well-structured event sequences.
3.a. Engage and orient the reader by setting out a problem and its significance, establishing one or multiple point(s) of view, and introducing a narrator and/or characters; create a smooth progression of experiences or events.

Language
4.a. Use context as a clue to the meaning of a word.

Connecting to the Essential Question James Thurber is a treasured humorist, known for a comic vision that has a decidedly American quality. As you read, notice elements that you find funny. Doing so will help you think about the Essential Question: **What makes American literature American?**

Close Reading Focus

Humorous Essay

Humor appears in all forms of literature, from drama to poetry to fiction. A **humorous essay** is a short, funny work of nonfiction. It requires literary skill and the use of specific strategies to translate the comedy of everyday life into an amusing work of writing. Humor writers use the following techniques to make written works funny:

- **hyperbole:** exaggeration or outrageous overstatement
- **understatement:** the opposite of hyperbole; downplaying a dramatic event, or saying less than what is meant
- **idioms:** expressions in which the literal meanings of the words do not add up to the actual meaning ("raining cats and dogs" = downpour)
- **dialect:** ways of speaking that are particular to a region or group

As you read, notice Thurber's use of these techniques and the ways in which they add to the essay's humor.

Preparing to Read Complex Texts A *cause* is the reason something happens; an *effect* is the result. Thurber structures this essay around cause and effect, or the idea that "one thing leads to another." He ratchets up the humor by making each successive moment sillier than the last. By **analyzing cause and effect** as you read, you can trace the flow of events and better appreciate the skill with which Thurber intensifies the humor. As you read, use a chart like the one shown to analyze causes and effects.

Vocabulary

You will encounter the words listed here in the text that follows. Copy the words into your notebook. Which words are adjectives? How can you tell?

despondent   reluctant

intervene   blaspheming

Common Core State Standards

Reading Informational Text

3. Analyze a complex set of ideas or sequence of events and explain how specific individuals, ideas, or events interact and develop over the course of the text.

4. Determine the meaning of words and phrases as they are used in the text, including figurative, connotative, and technical meanings.

Language

5.a. Interpret figures of speech in context and analyze their role in the text.

Cause
James and Herman hear footsteps on the stairs.

Effect/Cause
They slam doors in fear.

Effect
Their mother wakes up.

James Thurber

(1894–1961)

Author of **"The Night the Ghost Got In"**

James Thurber's essays, plays, sketches, cartoons, and short stories generally evolved from his own experiences. In his humorous sketches, Thurber embellishes facts and describes events in an amusing manner. In his short stories, Thurber's characters typically struggle against the unpleasant realities of modern life. In his pen-and-ink illustrations and cartoons, Thurber portrays men, women, and animals—especially dogs—facing the trials of everyday life.

The New Yorker Thurber was born in Columbus, Ohio. After attending Ohio State University, he joined *The New Yorker* magazine staff in 1927 as managing editor. From there, or so he claimed, he quickly worked his way down to writer. Until the end of his life, Thurber regularly contributed stories, essays, drawings, and cartoons to the magazine's pages. He also worked closely with the celebrated writer E. B. White, who wrote numerous essays for the magazine.

Comic Genius Thurber is one of the few humorists whose work is part of the American literary canon. About his comic genius, Thurber was quite modest:
"I write humor the way a surgeon operates, because it is a livelihood, because I have a great urge to do it, because many interesting challenges are set up, and because I have the hope it may do some good."
In much of his work, Thurber's humor reveals an edge of unhappiness, especially in his later years when his failing vision caused him much pain and bitterness. Thurber's many published works include *The Owl in the Attic and Other Perplexities* (1931), *The Seal in the Bedroom and Other Predicaments* (1932), *Fables for Our Time* (1940), and the bestselling *My World and Welcome to It* (1942).

> "The wit makes fun of other persons; the satirist makes fun of the world; the humorist makes fun of himself."

The Night the Ghost Got In

James Thurber

He always half suspected that something would get him. by James Thurber

▲ **Critical Viewing**

The humor in Thurber's drawing echoes the humor in his essay. What makes this sketch funny? **ANALYZE**

Humorous Essay

Which details in the first two paragraphs tell you that this essay is based on actual events from the author's life?

The ghost that got into our house on the night of November 17, 1915, raised such a hullabaloo of misunderstandings that I am sorry I didn't just let it keep on walking, and go to bed. Its advent caused my mother to throw a shoe through a window of the house next door and ended up with my grandfather shooting a patrolman. I am sorry, therefore, as I have said, that I ever paid any attention to the footsteps.

They began about a quarter past one o'clock in the morning, a rhythmic, quick-cadenced walking around the dining-room table. My mother was asleep in one room upstairs, my brother Herman in another; grandfather was in the attic, in the old walnut bed which, as you will remember, once fell on my father. I had just stepped out of the bathtub and was busily rubbing myself with a towel when I heard the steps. They were the steps of a man walking rapidly around the dining-room table downstairs. The light from the bathroom shone down the back steps, which dropped directly into the dining-room; I could see the faint shine of plates on the plate-rail; I couldn't see the table. The steps kept going round and round the table; at regular intervals a board creaked, when it was trod upon. I supposed at first that it was my father or my brother Roy, who had gone to Indianapolis but were expected home at any time. I suspected next that it was a burglar. It did not enter my mind until later that it was a ghost.

After the walking had gone on for perhaps three minutes, I tiptoed to Herman's room. "Psst!" I hissed, in the dark, shaking him. "Awp," he said, in the low, hopeless tone of a despondent beagle—he always half suspected that something would "get him" in the night. I told him who I was. "There's something downstairs!" I said. He got up and followed me to the head of the back staircase. We listened together. There was no sound. The steps had ceased. Herman looked at me in some alarm: I had only the bath towel around my waist. He wanted to go back to bed, but I gripped his arm. "There's something down there!" I said. Instantly the steps began again, circled the dining-room table like a man running, and started up the stairs toward us, heavily, two at a time. The light still shone palely down the stairs; we saw nothing coming; we only heard the steps. Herman rushed to his room and slammed the door. I slammed shut the door at the stairs top and held my knee against it. After a long minute, I slowly opened it again. There was nothing there. There was no sound. None of us ever heard the ghost again.

The slamming of the doors had aroused mother: she peered out of her room. "What on earth are you boys doing?" she demanded. Herman ventured out of his room. "Nothing," he said, gruffly, but he was, in color, a light green. "What was all that running around downstairs?" said mother. So she had heard the steps, too! We just looked at her. "Burglars!" she shouted intuitively. I tried to quiet her by starting lightly downstairs.

"Come on, Herman," I said.

"I'll stay with Mother," he said. "She's all excited."

I stepped back onto the landing.

"Don't either of you go a step," said mother. "We'll call the police." Since the phone was downstairs, I didn't see how we were going to call the police—nor did I want the police—but mother made one of her quick, incomparable decisions. She flung up a window of her bedroom which faced the bedroom windows of the house of a neighbor, picked up a shoe, and whammed it through a pane of glass across the narrow space that separated the two houses. Glass tinkled into the bedroom occupied by a retired engraver named Bodwell and his wife. Bodwell had been for some years in rather a bad way and was subject to mild "attacks." Most everybody we knew or lived near had some kind of attacks.

It was now about two o'clock of a moonless night; clouds hung black and low. Bodwell was at the window in a minute, shouting, frothing a little, shaking his fist. "We'll sell the house and go back to Peoria," we could hear Mrs. Bodwell saying. It was some time before mother "got through" to Bodwell. "Burglars!" she shouted. "Burglars in the house!" Herman and I hadn't dared to tell her that it was not burglars but ghosts, for she was even more afraid of ghosts than of burglars. Bodwell at first thought that she meant there were burglars in his house, but finally he quieted down and called the police for us over an extension phone by his bed. After he had disappeared from the window, mother suddenly made as if to throw another shoe, not because there was further need of it, but, as she later explained,

Vocabulary

despondent (di spän´ dənt) *adj.* without courage or hope

Analyzing Cause and Effect

Describe the chain of cause-and-effect that begins with the slamming doors and ends with a shattered window.

Comprehension

Who does Mother think the intruders are?

Some nights she threw them all. by James Thurber

▲ Critical Viewing

Thurber drew this cartoon to illustrate this essay. How does the illustration add to the essay's humor? **ASSESS**

because the thrill of heaving a shoe through a window glass had enormously taken her fancy. I prevented her.

The police were on hand in a commendably short time: a Ford sedan full of them, two on motorcycles, and a patrol wagon with about eight in it and a few reporters. They began banging at our front door. Flashlights shot streaks of gleam up and down the walls, across the yard, down the walk between our house and Bodwell's. "Open up!" cried a hoarse voice. "We're men from Headquarters!" I wanted to go down and let them in, since there they were, but mother wouldn't hear of it. "You haven't a stitch on," she pointed out. "You'd catch your death." I wound the towel around me again. Finally the cops put their shoulders to our big heavy front door with its thick beveled glass and broke it in: I could hear a rending of wood and a splash of glass on the floor of the hall. Their lights played all over the living-room and crisscrossed nervously in the dining-room, stabbed into hallways, shot up the front stairs and finally up the back. They caught me standing in my towel at the top. A heavy policeman bounded up the steps. "Who are you?" he demanded. "I live here," I said. "Well, whattsa matta, ya hot?" he asked. I was, as a matter of fact, cold; I went to my room and pulled on some trousers. On my way out, a cop stuck a gun into my ribs. "Whatta you doin' here?" he demanded. "I live here," I said.

The officer in charge reported to mother. "No sign of nobody, lady," he said. "Musta got away—whatt'd he look like?" "There were two or three of them," mother said, "whooping and carrying on and slamming doors." "Funny," said the cop. "All ya windows and doors was locked on the inside tight as a tick."

Downstairs, we could hear the tromping of the other police. Police were all over the place; doors were yanked open, drawers were yanked open, windows were shot up and pulled down, furniture fell with dull thumps. A half-dozen policemen emerged out of the darkness of the front hallway upstairs. They began to ransack the floor: pulled beds away from walls, tore clothes off hooks in the closets, pulled suitcases and boxes off shelves. One of them found an old zither[1] that Roy had won in a pool tournament. "Looky here, Joe," he said, strumming it with a big paw. The cop named Joe took it and turned it over. "What is it?" he asked me. "It's an old zither our guinea pig used to sleep on," I said. It was true that a pet guinea pig we once had would never sleep anywhere except on the zither, but I should never have said so. Joe and the other cop looked at me a long time. They put the zither back on a shelf.

---

1. zither (zith′ ər) *n.* musical instrument with thirty to forty strings stretched across a flat soundboard and played with the fingers.

"No sign o' nuthin'," said the cop who had first spoken to mother. "This guy," he explained to the others, jerking a thumb at me, "was nekked. The lady seems historical." They all nodded, but said nothing; just looked at me. In the small silence we all heard a creaking in the attic. Grandfather was turning over in bed. "What's 'at?" snapped Joe. Five or six cops sprang for the attic door before I could intervene or explain. I realized that it would be bad if they burst in on grandfather unannounced, or even announced. He was going through a phase in which he believed that General Meade's men, under steady hammering by Stonewall Jackson, were beginning to retreat and even desert.

When I got to the attic, things were pretty confused. Grandfather had evidently jumped to the conclusion that the police were deserters from Meade's army, trying to hide away in his attic. He bounded out of bed wearing a long flannel nightgown over long woolen underwear, a nightcap, and a leather jacket around his chest. The cops must have realized at once that the indignant white-haired old man belonged in the house, but they had no chance to say so. "Back, ye cowardly dogs!" roared grandfather. "Back t' the lines, ye yellow, lily-livered cattle!" With that, he fetched the officer who found the zither a flat-handed smack alongside his head that sent him sprawling. The others beat a retreat, but not fast enough; grandfather grabbed Zither's gun from its holster and let fly. The report seemed to crack the rafters; smoke filled the attic. A cop cursed and shot his hand to his shoulder. Somehow, we all finally got downstairs again and locked the door against the old gentleman. He fired once or twice more in the darkness and then went back to bed. "That was grandfather," I explained to Joe, out of breath. "He thinks you're deserters."

Vocabulary

intervene (in´ tər vēn´) *v.* take action in order to prevent something

Comprehension
What does grandfather think is happening?

Police were all over the place. by James Thurber

◄ **Critical Viewing**
Compare this illustration with Thurber's description of the police investigation. What makes each funny?
EVALUATE

Vocabulary

reluctant (re luk´ tənt) *adj.*
unwilling; disinclined

blaspheming (blas fēm´ iŋ)
v. cursing

"I'll say he does," said Joe.

The cops were **reluctant** to leave without getting their hands on somebody besides grandfather; the night had been distinctly a defeat for them. Furthermore, they obviously didn't like the "layout"; something looked—and I can see their viewpoint—phony. They began to poke into things again. A reporter, a thin-faced, wispy man, came up to me. I had put on one of mother's blouses, not being able to find anything else. The reporter looked at me with mingled suspicion and interest. "Just what the heck is the real lowdown here, Bud?" he asked. I decided to be frank with him. "We had ghosts," I said. He gazed at me a long time as if I were a slot machine into which he had, without results, dropped a nickel. Then he walked away. The cops followed him, the one grandfather shot holding his now-bandaged arm, cursing and **blaspheming**. "I'm gonna get my gun back from that old bird," said the zither-cop. "Yeh," said Joe. "You—and who else?" I told them I would bring it to the station house the next day.

"What was the matter with that one policeman?" mother asked, after they had gone. "Grandfather shot him," I said. "What for?" she demanded. I told her he was a deserter. "Of all things!" said mother. "He was such a nice-looking young man."

Grandfather was fresh as a daisy and full of jokes at breakfast next morning. We thought at first he had forgotten all about what had happened, but he hadn't. Over his third cup of coffee, he glared at Herman and me. "What was the idee of all them cops tarry-hootin' round the house last night?" he demanded. He had us there.

Critical Reading

Cite textual evidence to support your responses.

1. **Key Ideas and Details (a)** What event sets off the family's reactions? **(b) Classify:** Describe how each member of the family reacts. **(c) Distinguish:** In what way does Thurber's portrayal of himself in the situation differ from his portrayal of the other characters?

2. **Key Ideas and Details (a)** Why are the police summoned? **(b) Support:** How does this lack of communication contribute to the humor of the essay?

3. **Key Ideas and Details (a)** What does grandfather do when the police burst into his room? **(b) Infer:** Why do you think he does this?

4. **Integration of Knowledge and Ideas Evaluate:** Do you find the essay's conclusion fitting? Why?

5. **Integration of Knowledge and Ideas** This essay describes an event that took place in 1915. Has the American sense of humor changed since that time, or is this still funny? Explain. In your response, use at least two of these Essential Question words: *misunderstanding, slapstick, proportion, unconventional, exaggeration.* [Connecting to the Essential Question: What makes American literature American?]

Close Reading Activities — *The Night the Ghost Got In*

Literary Analysis

1. **Key Ideas and Details Analyze cause and effect** in this essay by tracing the final event back to the event that started the action.
2. **Key Ideas and Details** Are most of the effects reasonable reactions to the causes? Explain.
3. **Craft and Structure** Use a chart like the one shown to identify one example of each literary technique Thurber uses in this **humorous essay.**

Element of Humor	Example
Hyperbole	
Understatement	
Idiom	
Dialect	

4. **Craft and Structure (a)** How does the speech of the policemen contrast with the type of language Thurber uses as the narrator? **(b)** In what ways does the policemen's speech add to the essay's humor?
5. **Integration of Knowledge and Ideas** What human behaviors or weaknesses help to explain the escalation of the events to the fever pitch they reach?

Common Core State Standards

Writing
2. Write explanatory texts to examine and convey complex ideas, concepts, and information clearly and accurately through the effective selection, organization, and analysis of content.
2.b. Develop the topic thoroughly by selecting the most significant and relevant facts, extended definitions, concrete details, quotations, or other information and examples appropriate to the audience's knowledge of the topic.
2.f. Provide a concluding statement or section that follows from and supports the information or explanation presented.
Language
4.a. Use context as a clue to the meaning of a word or phrase.

Vocabulary Acquisition and Use

Context Clues Review the vocabulary list on page 858. Then, answer *yes* or *no* to each question. Explain the context clues that help you.

1. If someone were tired, is it likely she would be *reluctant* to sleep?
2. If someone won a contest, would he become *despondent*?
3. If a parent saw a child about to fall, would she *intervene*?

Writing to Sources

Explanatory Text Thurber once wrote that "the humorist makes fun of himself, but in so doing, he identifies himself with people—that is, people everywhere, not for the purpose of taking them apart, but simply revealing their true nature." Write an **essay** in which you apply Thurber's ideas to this selection. To begin, identify points in the essay at which Thurber pokes fun at himself. Then, discuss how these examples relate Thurber to all people. Finally, draw conclusions about human nature and the role of humor in revealing it.

Connecting to the Essential Question In these poems, work represents a source of strength and even redemption. As you read, look for details related to the value of labor and the vitality of workers. Doing so will help as you consider the Essential Question: **What makes American literature American?**

Close Reading Focus

Apostrophe
Apostrophe is a literary device in which a speaker directly addresses a thing, concept, or person who is dead or absent. In the poem "Chicago," the speaker uses apostrophe to address the city:

> *They tell me you are wicked and I believe them . . .*
> *And they tell me you are crooked and I answer: Yes . . .*

Comparing Literary Works Sandburg's portrayal of the city of Chicago relies on a figure of speech called **personification,** in which a nonhuman subject is given human qualities. Chicago is depicted as laughing, sweating, bareheaded, and alive. In "Grass," personification takes a different form. Instead of showing a person speaking to the grass, it shows the grass speaking to the reader. As you read these poems, compare Sandburg's use of personification. Note how the personification affects the meaning of each poem and evokes different emotions in you as you read.

Preparing to Read Complex Texts One way to *clarify meaning in poetry* is to identify ideas that the poet repeats. The structure of repetition may provide a gentle reminder of an idea already expressed or a forceful emphasis of an important point. When you **evaluate the effects of repetition,** you examine the feelings or ideas the repetition emphasizes. As you read, use a chart like the one shown to record repeated words, phrases, ideas, and grammatical forms in each poem and examine their effects on meaning.

Vocabulary

You will encounter the words listed here in the text that follows. Copy the words into your notebook. Decide whether each word has a positive or a negative connotation.

brutal   **cunning**

wanton

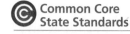

Common Core State Standards

Reading Literature
4. Determine the meaning of words and phrases as they are used in the text, including figurative and connotative meanings; analyze the impact of specific word choices on meaning and tone, including language that is particularly fresh, engaging, or beautiful.
5. Analyze how an author's choices concerning how to structure specific parts of a text contribute to its overall structure and meaning as well as its aesthetic impact.

Language
5.a. Interpret figures of speech in context and analyze their role in the text.

Repetition

Effect

Carl Sandburg

Author of **"Chicago"** and **"Grass"**

Carl Sandburg was an optimist who believed in the power of ordinary people to fulfill their dreams. His poems were concrete and direct, capturing the energy and enthusiasm of industrial America. His vivid portraits of the working class made Sandburg one of the most popular poets of his day.

The son of Swedish immigrants, Sandburg left school after eighth grade to help support his family. He found work as a laborer. When he was nineteen, however, he set out to see the country, hitching rides on freight trains and taking odd jobs wherever he landed. He completed a stint in the Army, then tried college for a few years before hitting the road again.

The Bard of Chicago In 1912, Sandburg settled in the dynamic industrial city of Chicago. He worked as a newspaper reporter and began to publish his poetry in literary magazines. His first book, *Chicago Poems*, gained recognition for both Sandburg and Chicago. Over the next ten years, he published three more successful poetry collections: *Cornhuskers* (1918), *Smoke and Steel* (1920), and *Slabs of the Sunburnt West* (1922).

Collecting Songs While continuing to write poetry, Sandburg started a career as a folk singer. He prepared an anthology of folk songs he collected from cowboys, lumberjacks, factory workers, and hobos as he toured the country. *The American Songbag* appeared in 1927.

Winning Awards During his tours of the country, Sandburg also delivered lectures on Walt Whitman and Abraham Lincoln and collected material for a biography of Lincoln. The resulting multi-volume work earned him a Pulitzer Prize in 1940. In 1951, Sandburg received a second Pulitzer Prize for his *Complete Poems*. He was also awarded the United States Presidential Medal in 1964.

Sandburg offered a variety of definitions of poetry, among them these two: "Poetry is a search for syllables to shoot at the barriers of the unknown and the unknowable" and "Poetry is the opening and closing of a door, leaving those who look through to guess about what is seen during a moment."

(1878–1967)

> "Nothing happens unless first we dream."

Chicago

Carl Sandburg

▼ **Critical Viewing**

In what ways does this bustling street scene of Chicago reflect Sandburg's poem? **CONNECT**

Hog Butcher for the World,
Tool Maker, Stacker of Wheat,
Player with Railroads and the Nation's Freight Handler;
Stormy, husky, brawling,
5   City of the Big Shoulders:

FRUITS & VEGETABLES
LA MANTIA BROS & ARRIGO

They tell me you are wicked and I believe them, for I have seen
    your painted women under the gas lamps luring the farm
    boys.
And they tell me you are crooked and I answer: Yes, it is true I
    have seen the gunman kill and go free to kill again.
And they tell me you are **brutal** and my reply is: On the faces of
    women and children I have seen the marks of **wanton** hunger.
And having answered so I turn once more to those who sneer at
    this my city, and I give them back the sneer and say to them:

10 Come and show me another city with lifted head singing so proud
    to be alive and coarse and strong and **cunning**.
Flinging magnetic curses amid the toil of piling job on job, here is
    a tall bold slugger set vivid against the little soft cities;
Fierce as a dog with tongue lapping for action, cunning as a
    savage pitted against the wilderness,
        Bareheaded,
        Shoveling,
15   Wrecking,
        Planning,
        Building, breaking, rebuilding,
Under the smoke, dust all over his mouth, laughing with
    white teeth,
Under the terrible burden of destiny laughing as a young man
    laughs,
20 Laughing even as an ignorant fighter laughs who has never lost
    a battle,
Bragging and laughing that under his wrist is the pulse, and
    under his ribs the heart of the people,
            Laughing!
Laughing the stormy, husky, brawling laughter of Youth, half-
    naked, sweating, proud to be a Hog Butcher, Tool Maker,
    Stacker of Wheat, Player with Railroads and Freight Handler
    to the Nation.

Vocabulary

brutal (broot′ əl) *adj.* cruel and without feeling; savage; violent

wanton (wän′ tən) *adj.* senseless; unjustified

cunning (kun′ iŋ) *adj.* skillful in deception; crafty; sly

Personification

In what way is the city like a "young man"?

Critical Reading

1. **Craft and Structure** **(a)** What names does the speaker use to address the city in the first stanza? **(b) Interpret:** What do the names tell you about the city's economy and atmosphere?

2. **Key Ideas and Details** **(a)** What are some of the city's faults? **(b) Interpret:** How do these faults affect the speaker's attitude toward the city?

3. **Key Ideas and Details** **(a) Summarize:** What overall sense of the city does Sandburg portray? **(b) Deduce:** Does Sandburg's portrayal reflect a larger sense of an American national character? Explain.

Cite textual evidence to support your responses.

GRASS

CARL SANDBURG

Evaluating Repetition

What idea does the poet emphasize through the repetition of the word "pile"?

Pile the bodies high at Austerlitz and Waterloo.[1]
Shovel them under and let me work—
    I am the grass; I cover all.

And pile them high at Gettysburg
5 And pile them high at Ypres and Verdun.[2]
Shovel them under and let me work.
Two years, ten years, and passengers ask the conductor:
    What place is this?
    Where are we now?

10   I am grass.
    Let me work.

---

1. **Austerlitz** (ôs′ tər lits′) **and Waterloo** sites of battles of the Napoleonic Wars.
2. **Ypres** (ē′ pr) **and Verdun** (vər dun′) sites of battles of World War I.

Critical Reading

Cite textual evidence to support your responses.

1. **Key Ideas and Details (a)** In the first stanza, what does the grass claim it is able to do? **(b) Interpret:** What does this claim mean? Support your answer.

2. **Key Ideas and Details (a)** What does each place name in the poem represent? **(b) Draw Conclusions:** By focusing on war, rather than death in general, what is Sandburg suggesting?

3. **Integration of Knowledge and Ideas** What do these poems suggest about the value of industry and labor to a society? In your response, use at least two of these Essential Question words: *ambition, magnitude, expansion, regional*. [Connecting to the Essential Question: How does literature shape or reflect society?]

Literary Analysis

1. **Craft and Structure (a)** In which lines of "Chicago" does Sandburg address the city directly? **(b)** What is the effect of this use of **apostrophe**?

2. **Craft and Structure (a)** Using a chart like the one shown, identify four examples of **personification** in the poem "Chicago." **(b)** For each example, identify the quality it communicates about the city.

Human Traits		City Traits
	→	

3. **Craft and Structure** **Evaluate the effect of repetition** on meaning in "Chicago." Why do you think "laughing" is repeated near the end of the poem?

4. **Craft and Structure** What entire line is repeated in "Grass" and to what effect?

5. **Comparing Literary Works (a)** How do Sandburg's uses of personification in "Chicago" and "Grass" differ? **(b)** In what ways do these different uses of personification serve the distinct goals of each poem?

Vocabulary Acquisition and Use

Context Clues Use a word from the vocabulary list on page 866 to complete each sentence below. Use each word only once. Explain the context clues that help you.

1. It was clear that the family had done nothing to deserve the _____ suffering that beset them.

2. That fox was a _____ creature, and the farmer could not figure out how to keep him from stealing eggs.

3. The winter storm was _____, and many members of the herd were lost in the snow.

Writing to Sources

Explanatory Text Review the chart of repeated words and phrases you made while you read these poems. Use those notes as the prewriting stage for an **essay** in which you analyze Sandburg's use of repetition in the poem "Chicago." In your essay, explain how the poet's repetition of words, phrases, sentence structures, and grammatical forms emphasizes particular ideas and heightens specific emotions. Support your ideas with relevant quotations from the poems.

Common Core State Standards

Writing

2. Write explanatory texts to examine and convey complex ideas, concepts, and information clearly and accurately through the effective selection, organization, and analysis of content.

2.b. Develop the topic thoroughly by selecting the most significant and relevant quotations.

9.a. Apply *grades 11–12 Reading standards* to literature.

Language

4.a. Use context as a clue to the meaning of a word or phrase.

Connecting to the Essential Question Many readers have learned about rural New England from Robert Frost's poetry. As you read, notice details that create a portrait of life in rural New England. This activity will help as you consider the Essential Question: **What is the relationship between literature and place?**

Close Reading Focus

Blank Verse; Pastorals

Robert Frost wove sound and sense into poems that are among the best loved in American literature. He often wrote in **blank verse,** or *unrhymed iambic pentameter,* which mimics the sound of natural speech:

- The basic unit of *meter* is a *foot*, which is usually one stressed syllable (ˊ) and one or more unstressed syllables (ˇ).

- The most common foot in English is the *iamb*, one unstressed syllable followed by a stressed syllable (ˇ ˊ).

- A line containing five iambs is written in *iambic pentameter.*

The use of iambic pentameter, blank verse, and other meters affects the sound and mood of a poem. Notice these effects as you read.

Many of Frost's poems, including five in this grouping, can be categorized as **pastorals,** or poems that deal with rural settings. Traditional pastorals present idealized views of rural life. In Frost's hands, however, rural life can be fraught with ethical lapses, accident, and conflict. As you read these poems, examine their portrayals of rural life, and notice the ways in which setting contributes to meaning.

Preparing to Read Complex Texts One way to *clarify the essential meaning* of poems is to **read poetry in sentences** rather than in poetic lines. Instead of pausing at the end of each line, follow the punctuation: pause briefly after commas, and pause longer after periods. Use the information in the chart shown here as a guide to your reading. However, as you apply this strategy, remain sensitive to the poem's pattern of organization, noticing how line breaks enrich and extend the meanings of individual sentences.

Vocabulary

The words below are important to understanding the text that follows. Copy the words into your notebook. Which word has a root that means "light"?

poise   luminary

rueful

**Common Core
State Standards**

Reading Literature
5. Analyze how an author's choices concerning how to structure specific parts of a text contribute to its overall structure and meaning as well as its aesthetic impact.

9. Demonstrate knowledge of early-twentieth-century foundational works of American literature, including how two or more texts from the same period treat similar themes or topics.

Sign	Means
→	No punctuation: Continue without pause.
↱	Pause for comma, dash, or semicolon and continue.
⬟	Full stop for period

Robert Frost *(1874–1963)*

In becoming one of America's most loved and respected poets, Robert Frost displayed the same persistence and determination exhibited by the rural New Englanders he depicted in his poems. Although he eventually received four Pulitzer Prizes and read at a presidential inauguration, Frost's success as a poet did not come overnight or easily. Only after years of rejection by publishers did he achieve the acceptance for which he had worked so hard.

Early Struggles Frost was born in San Francisco, California. His father died when Frost was eleven, and his mother moved the family to the textile city of Lawrence, Massachusetts. After graduating from high school, Frost briefly attended Dartmouth College. Disliking college life, he left school and spent time working as a farmer, mill hand, journalist, and schoolteacher. During his spare time, he wrote poetry and dreamed of someday being able to support himself solely by writing.

The English Years Frost married and spent ten years farming in New Hampshire. In 1912, unable to get his poems published, he moved his family to England. While living in England, Frost befriended a number of well-known poets, including Ezra Pound, and succeeded in publishing two collections of poetry, *A Boy's Will* (1913) and *North of Boston* (1914). When he returned to the United States in 1915, Frost found that his success in England had spread across the Atlantic, and he was on the road to fame.

Critical Acclaim Frost published several more volumes of poetry, for which he received many awards. He taught and lectured at dozens of schools and continued to farm in Vermont and New Hampshire. In 1960, at John F. Kennedy's invitation, Frost became the first poet to read his work at a presidential inauguration.

Deeper Meanings Frost's poetry was popular with both critics and the general public. He used traditional verse forms and conversational language to paint vivid portraits of New England. Despite their apparent simplicity, however, his poems are filled with profound meanings.

Like his poetry, Frost's personality also had multiple levels. In his public appearances, Frost presented himself as a folksy farmer who just happened to write poetry. In reality, however, Frost was a deep thinker whose darker, complicated personality sometimes mystified those who knew him.

> *"Like a piece of ice on a hot stove the poem must ride on its own melting."*

BIRCHES

ROBERT FROST

BACKGROUND Robert Frost spent most of his life in New Hampshire, Vermont, and Massachusetts—a heavily forested region of the United States. One of the most common trees of this region is the birch, a tall, slender tree with white bark and small, dainty leaves. Despite its graceful trunk, though, the birch is by no means delicate. Its wood is dense, hardy, and flexible, and its bark is practically waterproof (which made it a popular canoe covering among Native Americans). In this poem, Frost celebrates the birch's resilience and suggests that the human spirit shares this quality.

When I see birches bend to left and right
Across the lines of straighter darker trees,
I like to think some boy's been swinging them.
But swinging doesn't bend them down to stay

5 As ice storms do. Often you must have seen them
Loaded with ice a sunny winter morning
After a rain. They click upon themselves
As the breeze rises, and turn many-colored
As the stir cracks and crazes their enamel.

10 Soon the sun's warmth makes them shed crystal shells
Shattering and avalanching on the snow crust—
Such heaps of broken glass to sweep away
You'd think the inner dome of heaven had fallen.
They are dragged to the withered bracken by the load,

15 And they seem not to break; though once they are bowed
So low for long, they never right themselves:
You may see their trunks arching in the woods
Years afterwards, trailing their leaves on the ground
Like girls on hands and knees that throw their hair

20 Before them over their heads to dry in the sun.
But I was going to say when Truth broke in
With all her matter of fact about the ice storm,
I should prefer to have some boy bend them
As he went out and in to fetch the cows—

25 Some boy too far from town to learn baseball,
Whose only play was what he found himself,
Summer or winter, and could play alone.
One by one he subdued his father's trees
By riding them down over and over again

30 Until he took the stiffness out of them,
And not one but hung limp, not one was left
For him to conquer. He learned all there was
To learn about not launching out too soon
And so not carrying the tree away

35 Clear to the ground. He always kept his poise

◄ **Critical Viewing**

Frost's poem expresses the speaker's reaction to birch trees. What response does this photograph of birches evoke in you? **CONNECT**

Blank Verse

Does this poem sound like natural speech? Explain.

Vocabulary

poise (poiz) *n.* balance; stability

Comprehension

What does the speaker think of when he sees "birches bend to left and right"?

To the top branches, climbing carefully
With the same pains you use to fill a cup
Up to the brim, and even above the brim.
Then he flung outward, feet first, with a swish,
40 Kicking his way down through the air to the ground.
So was I once myself a swinger of birches.
And so I dream of going back to be.
It's when I'm weary of considerations,
And life is too much like a pathless wood
45 Where your face burns and tickles with the cobwebs
Broken across it, and one eye is weeping
From a twig's having lashed across it open.
I'd like to get away from earth awhile
And then come back to it and begin over.
50 May no fate willfully misunderstand me
And half grant what I wish and snatch me away
Not to return. Earth's the right place for love:
I don't know where it's likely to go better.
I'd like to go by climbing a birch tree,
55 And climb black branches up a snow-white trunk
Toward heaven, till the tree could bear no more,
But dipped its top and set me down again.
That would be good both going and coming back.
One could do worse than be a swinger of birches.

Reading Poetry in Sentences

How does reading lines 43–47 as a sentence help clarify its meaning?

Critical Reading

Cite textual evidence to support your responses.

1. **Key Ideas and Details (a)** What is the connection between the ice storm and the bent birches? **(b)** What does the speaker prefer to think when he sees birches "bend to left and right"? **(c) Interpret:** What does the speaker feel about the facts concerning the real causes of the bowed trees?

2. **Key Ideas and Details (a)** What is the connection between the "swinger of birches" and the speaker? **(b) Interpret:** What does the activity of swinging on birches come to symbolize for the speaker in the poem?

3. **Key Ideas and Details (a) Interpret:** What does the speaker say he would like to "begin over"? **(b) Analyze:** What aspects of this poem reflect the speaker's conflicting attitudes about life?

4. **Integration of Knowledge and Ideas Speculate:** What kinds of events, experiences, and feelings in his life might have caused the speaker to make the admission expressed in lines 48–49?

Stopping by Woods on a Snowy Evening

Robert Frost

Whose woods these are I think I know.
His house is in the village though;
He will not see me stopping here
To watch his woods fill up with snow.

5 My little horse must think it queer
To stop without a farmhouse near
Between the woods and frozen lake
The darkest evening of the year.

He gives his harness bells a shake
10 To ask if there is some mistake.
The only other sound's the sweep
Of easy wind and downy flake.

The woods are lovely, dark and deep,
But I have promises to keep,
15 And miles to go before I sleep,
And miles to go before I sleep.

▲ **Critical Viewing**
What elements of this scene differ from the one the speaker describes? What do the two scenes have in common? **COMPARE AND CONTRAST**

Blank Verse
Is this poem an example of blank verse? Explain.

Mending Wall

ROBERT FROST

BACKGROUND Much of Frost's poetry reflects not only the New England landscape, but also its distinctive personalities. Despite Frost's city roots, he was able to gain the acceptance of his country neighbors and to enter their world—a place that was usually closed to outsiders. In doing so, Frost gathered a wealth of material for his poetry.

Pastorals

What activities do lines 5–9 suggest are part of rural life?

Something there is that doesn't love a wall,
That sends the frozen-ground-swell under it
And spills the upper boulders in the sun,
And makes gaps even two can pass abreast.
5 The work of hunters is another thing:
I have come after them and made repair
Where they have left not one stone on a stone,
But they would have the rabbit out of hiding,
To please the yelping dogs. The gaps I mean,
10 No one has seen them made or heard them made,
But at spring mending-time we find them there.
I let my neighbor know beyond the hill;
And on a day we meet to walk the line
And set the wall between us once again.
15 We keep the wall between us as we go.

▼ Critical Viewing

What elements of this picture suggest that walls do not belong in the natural world?
ANALYZE

To each the boulders that have fallen to each.
And some are loaves and some so nearly balls
We have to use a spell to make them balance:
"Stay where you are until our backs are turned!"
20 We wear our fingers rough with handling them.
Oh, just another kind of outdoor game,
One on a side. It comes to little more:
There where it is we do not need the wall:
He is all pine and I am apple orchard.
25 My apple trees will never get across
And eat the cones under his pines, I tell him.
He only says, "Good fences make good neighbors."
Spring is the mischief in me, and I wonder
If I could put a notion in his head:
30 "*Why* do they make good neighbors? Isn't it
Where there are cows? But here there are no cows.
Before I built a wall I'd ask to know
What I was walling in or walling out,
And to whom I was like to give offense.
35 Something there is that doesn't love a wall,
That wants it down." I could say "Elves" to him,
But it's not elves exactly, and I'd rather
He said it for himself. I see him there,
Bringing a stone grasped firmly by the top
40 In each hand, like an old-stone savage armed.
He moves in darkness as it seems to me,
Not of woods only and the shade of trees.
He will not go behind his father's saying,
And he likes having thought of it so well
45 He says again, "Good fences make good neighbors."

Something there is that doesn't love a wall.

Reading Poetry in Sentences
Read lines 28–31 as sentences. In what ways are their meanings clarified?

Critical Reading

1. **Key Ideas and Details (a)** In the first stanza of "Stopping by Woods," what does the speaker do? **(b) Infer:** What internal conflict do these actions cause?

2. **Craft and Structure (a)** What phrase is repeated in the poem's last two lines? **(b) Analyze:** How does this repetition reinforce the poem's theme?

3. **Key Ideas and Details (a)** In "Mending Wall," what two causes of gaps in walls does the speaker identify? **(b) Speculate:** In what ways are these two causes expressions of a general force the speaker struggles to name?

Cite textual evidence to support your responses.

"Out, Out—"

ROBERT FROST

Blank Verse

Which words or phrases in lines 5–7 capture the rhythms of everyday speech?

The buzz saw snarled and rattled in the yard
And made dust and dropped stove-length sticks of wood,
Sweet-scented stuff when the breeze drew across it.
And from there those that lifted eyes could count
5 Five mountain ranges one behind the other
Under the sunset far into Vermont.
And the saw snarled and rattled, snarled and rattled,
As it ran light, or had to bear a load.
And nothing happened: day was all but done.

10   Call it a day, I wish they might have said
        To please the boy by giving him the half hour
        That a boy counts so much when saved from work.
        His sister stood beside them in her apron
        To tell them "Supper." At the word, the saw,
15   As if to prove saws knew what supper meant,
        Leaped out at the boy's hand, or seemed to leap—
        He must have given the hand. However it was,
        Neither refused the meeting. But the hand!
        The boy's first outcry was a rueful laugh,
20   As he swung toward them holding up the hand,
        Half in appeal, but half as if to keep
        The life from spilling. Then the boy saw all—
        Since he was old enough to know, big boy
        Doing a man's work, though a child at heart—
25   He saw all spoiled. "Don't let him cut my hand off—
        The doctor, when he comes. Don't let him, sister!"
        So. But the hand was gone already.
        The doctor put him in the dark of ether.[1]
        He lay and puffed his lips out with his breath.
30   And then—the watcher at his pulse took fright.
        No one believed. They listened at his heart.
        Little—less—nothing!—and that ended it.
        No more to build on there. And they, since they
        Were not the one dead, turned to their affairs.

---

1. ether (ē′ thər) *n.* chemical compound used as an anesthetic.

Vocabulary

rueful (rōō′ fəl) *adj.* feeling or showing someone sorrow or pity

Pastorals

In what ways do lines 19–34 portray a harsh view of rural life?

NO ONE BELIEVED. THEY LISTENED AT HIS HEART.

Critical Reading

1. **Key Ideas and Details (a)** At what time of day does the accident occur? **(b) Analyze:** What is ironic about the fact that the boy is cut at precisely that moment?

2. **Key Ideas and Details (a)** What are the boy's first and second responses to the accident? **(b) Interpret:** What does the speaker mean by the expression "the boy saw all" in line 22?

3. **Integration of Knowledge and Ideas Connect:** The title comes from a scene in Shakespeare's *Macbeth* in which Macbeth laments the death of his wife with these words: "Out, out, brief candle! / Life's but a walking shadow, a poor player, / That struts and frets his hour upon the stage, / And then is heard no more." What does this quotation reveal about the poem's theme?

Cite textual evidence to support your responses.

ACQUAINTED WITH THE Night.

ROBERT FROST

BACKGROUND: Frost wrote this poem in terza rima, a verse form invented by the Italian poet Dante (see sidebar below). The form is very challenging in English, and Frost's poem is one of only a few examples in American literature.

I have been one acquainted with the night.
I have walked out in rain—and back in rain.
I have outwalked the furthest city light.

I have looked down the saddest city lane.
5 I have passed by the watchman on his beat
And dropped my eyes, unwilling to explain.

I have stood still and stopped the sound of feet
When far away an interrupted cry
Came over houses from another street,

10 But not to call me back or say good-by;
And further still at an unearthly height
One luminary clock against the sky

Proclaimed the time was neither wrong nor right.
I have been one acquainted with the night.

Blank Verse
How do you know that this poem is not an example of blank verse?

Vocabulary
luminary (lo͞o´ mə ner´ ē)
adj. giving off light

WORLD LITERATURE CONNECTION

Terza Rima

Terza rima (Italian for "third rhyme") is a form of poetry consisting of three-line stanzas with the rhyme scheme *aba, bcb, cdc,* and so on. In other words, the first and third lines of each stanza rhyme with each other, and the second line rhymes with the first and third lines of the following stanza. The Italian poet Dante (ca. 1300) was the first to write a long epic poem—his masterpiece, *The Divine Comedy*—in terza rima. This choice was not accidental: in the Christian tradition, the number *3* is symbolic of the divine, and this number informs all levels of the poem's structure. The work is divided into three sections—the "Inferno," "Purgatorio," and "Paradisio"—each of which, in turn, is divided into 33 subsections called cantos. All together, the sections tell the story of the poet's imaginary journey through hell, purgatory, and finally into the light of heaven. In addition to its association with the number *3*, terza rima is a fitting verse structure for Dante's poem: the rhymes, echoing between stanzas and linking one to the next, draw the reader forward, just as the poet himself was compelled forward on his epic journey.

CONNECT TO THE LITERATURE

With its cycling rhyme scheme and reflections of a Christian worldview, terza rima was a meaningful verse form for Dante's epic. Explain how it fits the action and setting of Frost's twentieth-century poem.

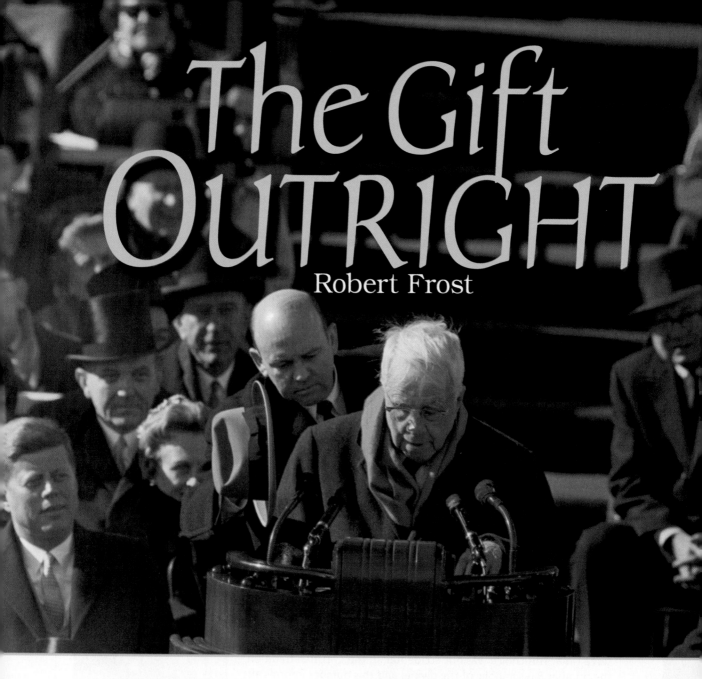

The Gift OUTRIGHT

Robert Frost

BACKGROUND During the planning stages of John F. Kennedy's presidential inauguration, his staff approached Robert Frost with a request: Would the poet write and recite a poem for the inauguration? Frost declined to write something new but agreed to recite "The Gift Outright." President Kennedy had a second request: Would Frost change the word "would" to "will" in the last line of the poem? The poet agreed. Shortly before the inauguration date, Frost was struck by inspiration and, despite his earlier refusal, drafted a forty-two-line poem, "Dedication," especially for the ceremony. The weather on inauguration day was windy, clear, and sunny. As Frost stood at the podium reading his new poem, the glare of the sun and the whipping wind made it almost impossible for him to see the words on the page. After struggling through the first half of "Dedication," he gave up the effort, and recited "The Gift Outright" from memory.

The land was ours before we were the land's.
She was our land more than a hundred years
Before we were her people. She was ours
In Massachusetts, in Virginia,

5   But we were England's, still colonials,
Possessing what we still were unpossessed by,
Possessed by what we now no more possessed.
Something we were withholding made us weak
Until we found out that it was ourselves

10   We were withholding from our land of living,
And forthwith found salvation in surrender.
Such as we were we gave ourselves outright
(The deed of gift was many deeds of war)
To the land vaguely realizing westward,

15   But still unstoried, artless, unenhanced,
Such as she was, such as she would become.

Reading Poetry in Sentences

In what ways does reading this poem in sentences help clarify its meaning?

Critical Reading

1. **Key Ideas and Details (a)** In "Acquainted with the Night," how does the speaker react to the watchman? **(b) Interpret:** What is the speaker "unwilling to explain"?

2. **Key Ideas and Details (a)** What does the speaker hear in the third stanza? **(b) Infer:** Based on line 10, what does it seem the speaker hoped?

3. **Key Ideas and Details (a)** In "The Gift Outright," what does the speaker say was the relationship between the land and the people in colonial America? **(b) Interpret:** What do you think the speaker means by the phrase "the land was ours"?

4. **Key Ideas and Details (a)** In what action did the early Americans find salvation? **(b) Connect:** What is the meaning of the poem's title?

5. **Integration of Knowledge and Ideas** What understanding of rural New England and America as a whole do these poems convey? Explain. In your response, use at least two of these Essential Question words: *industrious, self-determination, community, courage, severe.* *[Connecting to the Essential Question: What is the relationship between literature and place?]*

Cite textual evidence to support your responses.

Literary Analysis

1. **Key Ideas and Details** Explain how **reading poetry in sentences** clarified your understanding of **(a)** two specific lines; **(b)** the meaning of one poem as a whole.

2. **Craft and Structure** Traditional pastorals present nature and life itself as idyllic. In "Birches," however, nature gives rise to conflicting feelings. Use a chart like the one shown to provide evidence of the speaker's ambivalence.

3. **Key Ideas and Details** What ideas about land ownership and boundaries do "Stopping by Woods on a Snowy Evening" and "Mending Wall" express?

4. **Key Ideas and Details** Read "'Out, Out—,'" pausing at the end of each line. Then, read the poem as a series of sentences. How does each reading affect your understanding of the poem?

5. **Craft and Structure (a)** Find two instances in "'Out, Out—'" where Frost deviates from **blank verse. (b)** In what ways do these metrical variations emphasize a specific idea or image?

6. **Craft and Structure (a)** Rewrite "The Gift Outright" as five prose sentences. **(b)** What is the effect of this approach?

7. **Craft and Structure (a)** Which of the poems presented here are not written in blank verse? **(b)** What is one poetic device that distinguishes these poems from the ones written in blank verse? Explain.

8. **Craft and Structure** Which of the poems in this grouping would you classify as **pastorals**? Explain your choices.

9. **Integration of Knowledge and Ideas** Frost's poems often have simple surfaces—plain language and a conversational quality—but complex meanings. Choose one of these poems and explain how it combines apparent simplicity with deeper meanings.

10. **Analyzing Visual Information** Explain the humor in this cartoon.

Common Core State Standards

Writing
1. Write arguments to support claims in an analysis of substantive topics or texts, using valid reasoning and relevant and sufficient evidence. *(p. 887)*

Language
4.b. Identify and correctly use patterns of word changes that indicate different meanings or parts of speech. *(p. 887)*

5. Demonstrate understanding of word relationships. *(p. 887)*

© *The New Yorker* Collection 1993 Mick Stevens from cartoonbank.com. All Rights Reserved.

Vocabulary Acquisition and Use

Word Root: Latin Root -lum-

The word *luminary*, which means "giving off light," is based on the Latin root *-lum-*, meaning "light." The same root appears in the words *luminous* and *illuminate*. Complete each sentence with one of the words listed below. Use each word once. Explain each of your decisions.

luminous   illuminate   illumination

1. Is that small flashlight enough to _____ the entire campsite?

2. Cindy hoped to wear a _____ golden gown, but wound up in her sister's puffy, purple prom dress.

3. The teacher explained that students who are baffled may seek _____ in tutoring sessions.

Vocabulary: Analogies

Analogies show the relationships between pairs of words. Complete each analogy using a word from the vocabulary list on page 872. In each, your choice should create a word pair that matches the relationship between the first two words given. Then, explain your answers.

1. *Scorching* is to *fire* as _____ is to *moon*.

2. *Swiftness* is to *runner* as _____ is to *dancer*.

3. *Joyful* is to *celebrant* as _____ is to *mourner*.

Writing to Sources

Argument Robert Frost wrote during the early- to mid-20th century, an era that saw two world wars, growing industrialization, and increasing urbanization. Write a **critical essay** in which you explore this question: In the 20th and 21st centuries, how can poetry set in natural or rural settings be meaningful? In your essay, consider your own experiences in nature, whether good or bad, and draw conclusions about the relevance of pastoral poetry today.

Prewriting Reread Frost's poems, and make notes about how he describes the countryside. Then, decide whether your own experiences in nature have caused you to have similar or different feelings. Make notes explaining why.

Drafting Begin by stating your opinion on the relevance or importance of the pastoral in today's world. Then, support your opinion with examples from your own experience. In addition, use examples from Frost's poems to bolster your own views or to contrast his worldview with your own.

Revising As you review your work, make sure that you have clearly linked your ideas. Add transitions to introduce examples, where necessary.

Model: Revising to Smooth Transitions

In an age characterized by busyness, speed, and complexity, we sorely need real or imaginative escapes into nature. Robert Frost

    For example,

would agree. In "Birches," he admits that he would "like to get away…for awhile" when he is "weary of considerations."

> Phrases like *for example* provide transitions that improve clarity.

Trapped in a Comic Book

Cartoonist/Author

Cartooning as Literature

During the 1920s, James Thurber (p. 860) gave his comic stories an edge by illustrating them with his signature cartoons and drawings. These cartoons, witty, understated, and decidedly highbrow, were appreciated by a broad range of readers. In contrast, comic books, the action-packed, hero-driven tales that became wildly popular in the 1940s and 1950s, were not considered literature. They were frowned upon by many parents and educators. Today, looking at the many combinations of text and art available to readers—graphic novels of many genres, manga, collections of comic strips, and web comics—it becomes clear that the boundary between cartoon and serious literary art has blurred.

Cartoonist Jules Feiffer understands the nuance and power of comics, or "sequential art." He once said, "You can use cartoons to tell the truth about people." Perhaps this is where the connection between cartoons and literature lies. There is nothing more valuable about literature than the truth it contains.

About the Author

Jules Feiffer, born in 1929, is a big believer in pictures. As a lonely child, he filled his days reading the funnies and drawing his own. He worked on other artists' comic books in his early professional years, but he soon developed his distinctive personal style. His output has been exceptional. He drew cartoons for the alternative newspaper *The Village Voice* for decades; he wrote plays and screenplays. He won an Oscar in 1961 for the short animated film "Munro," about a 4-year-old boy drafted into the army. In 1986, Feiffer earned a Pulitzer Prize for editorial cartooning. As politically and socially acute as his creations tend to be, Feiffer also has a playful side and enjoys writing for young people. "Trapped in a Comic Book" shows his approach to a younger audience. Feiffer has thought a lot about what kids do and don't want. "What kids hate most," he insists, "is to be lectured at."

TRAPPED IN A COMIC BOOK

JULES FEIFFER

AND THIS IS WHAT I'M EXPLAINING TO THIS CARTOONIST IN HIS STUDIO WHERE I'M ON A SCHOOL VISIT WITH MY CLASS:

I'M ONLY TRYING TO HELP HIM, BECAUSE NORMAL KIDS LIKE ME ARE THE ONES WHO READ HIS STUFF, SO SHOULDN'T HE WANT TO KNOW WHAT I THINK?

SO I LOOK CLOSE.

OK, SO I LOOK CLOSER.

WHAT DOES HE WANT FROM ME?

OK, SO I LOOK CLOSER, AND EVEN CLOSER.

Critical Reading

1. **(a) Summarize:** Briefly summarize the superguys' actions. **(b) Interpret:** How does the boy react to these actions? **(c) Interpret:** What is Feiffer saying about comic books and the view of life they represent? Explain.

Use these questions to focus a discussion of the comic strip:

2. Why might Feiffer have chosen to write a comic—rather than a prose story—that makes fun of comics superheroes?

The Harlem Renaissance

Literary History: Langston Hughes and Harlem

Langston Hughes was a leading light of the Harlem Renaissance, an artistic movement in which the voices of African American artists rose to the forefront of American culture.

The Harlem Renaissance

Harlem in the 1920s: For some, it conjures images of jazz sessions at hot spots like the Cotton Club, of seedy speakeasies like the Clam Bake and the Hot Feet. For others, it brings to mind the artistic genius of writers like Langston Hughes and Zora Neale Hurston and painters like Aaron Douglas. In the 1920s, the New York City neighborhood of Harlem was home to an unprecedented flowering of African American talent that left an astonishing cultural legacy.

A Celebration of African American Life Known as the Harlem Renaissance, this remarkable period marked the first time that African American artists were taken seriously by the culture at large. "Negro life is seizing its first chances for group expression and self determination," wrote sociologist Alain Locke in 1926. Harlem became what Locke termed "the center of a spiritual coming of age," as its artists celebrated their culture and race.

The artists and writers of this renaissance did not share a style. Langston Hughes's realistic poems of downtrodden but determined people bear little resemblance to Countee Cullen's elegant sonnets. Instead, these artists shared the urgent need to document the experiences of their people.

The Center of the World In the early 1900s, hundreds of thousands of African Americans embarked on what has come to be called the Great Migration, moving from the rural South to the industrial cities of the North. As more and more African Americans settled in Harlem, it became a meeting ground for writers, musicians, and artists.

The work they produced was unique. Before the Harlem Renaissance, many African American writers had tried to emulate whites. By contrast, the Harlem writers celebrated their racial identity. The goal was to create, as Hughes put it, "an expression of our individual dark-skinned selves."

▲ **Critical Viewing**
What elements of the lives and works of Langston Hughes and Zora Neale Hurston are expressed in this image of the two writers? **INTERPRET**

An Outpouring of Expression From the 1920s through the mid-1930s, sixteen African American writers published more than fifty volumes of poetry and fiction—an astounding amount of work. Other African Americans made their marks in art, music, and theater. Aaron Douglas incorporated African images into his paintings. Blues singer Bessie Smith performed to packed houses. Musicians Jelly Roll Morton, Louis Armstrong, and Duke Ellington laid the foundations of jazz, a form of music that scholars argue is the only truly American art form.

The movement's most influential advocate may have been Langston Hughes, whose poems combined the rhythms of jazz and blues with stories of Harlem life. Other writers, such as Countee Cullen and Claude McKay, wrote in more classical forms. Novelist Zora Neale Hurston combined African folklore with realistic narratives.

A Powerful Legacy The impact of the Harlem Renaissance has been a subject of debate. Most scholars agree that it opened doors for the acceptance of art and writing by African Americans. However, some say that the Harlem Renaissance artists were too interested in seeking the approval of the white establishment. Even Langston Hughes admitted that few African Americans had read his work.

Still, the Harlem Renaissance gave Americans a language with which to begin a discussion of racism. It also broke ground for mid-century African American writers such as Richard Wright, Ralph Ellison, and James Baldwin. Today, Nobel Prize–winner Toni Morrison, novelist and poet Alice Walker, popular mystery writer Walter Mosley, and hundreds of other writers, painters, and musicians owe a debt to the artists of the Harlem Renaissance. For aspiring writers, artists, and musicians, the Harlem Renaissance was proof that art excludes no one.

Speaking and Listening: Group Discussion

Comprehension and Collaboration With a small group, discuss the influence of African Americans on contemporary art and culture.

- Research individual African Americans whose artistic accomplishments are helping to shape contemporary culture.
- Consider how our culture would be different without the contributions of African American artists and writers.
- Consider whether African Americans are fairly represented in all the arts. If not, what could be done to improve their representation?

Work together to establish rules for the discussion and to assign individual roles, such as note-taker and moderator. Respond respectfully to one another's insights and ask meaningful questions. Synthesize your ideas and choose a point person to share them with the class.

LANGSTON HUGHES (1902–1967)

HUMBLE BEGINNINGS Langston Hughes emerged from the Harlem Renaissance, a cultural movement of the 1920s, as one of the country's most successful African American writers and one of the major interpreters to the world of the African American experience. His work was anchored in a childhood that was not always easy. Shortly after his birth in Missouri, Hughes's parents separated, and Hughes was raised primarily by his grandmother. After his grandmother's death, he lived with his mother in half a dozen cities, finally settling in Cleveland, Ohio.

WRITING AND WANDERING

After graduating from high school in 1921, Hughes published his poem "The Negro Speaks of Rivers" in an African American magazine called *The Crisis*. He moved to New York, where he attended Columbia University and began to explore Harlem, forming a strong attachment to a place he would later help define. After a year, Hughes quit school to work as a steward on a freighter bound for Africa and then traveled in Europe.

Upon his return to the United States, Hughes took a job working in a hotel restaurant in Washington, D.C. One night in 1925, he put three of his poems beside the plate of poet Vachel Lindsay. The next day, newspapers trumpeted the news that Lindsay had discovered a new writer. Then, in 1926, Hughes's first collection of poetry, *The Weary Blues*, was published, earning him even more recognition. A scholarship followed, permitting Hughes to continue his education.

RENAISSANCE MAN

In 1926, Hughes also wrote an essay titled "The Negro Artist and the Racial Mountain." This work, which called for African American artists to "express our individual dark-skinned selves without fear or shame," helped define the spirit that motivated the Harlem Renaissance. Hughes became a major player in that movement, writing plays, fiction, musicals, autobiographies, and screenplays.

Over the course of his career, Hughes experimented with a variety of poetic forms and techniques. He often tried to recreate the rhythms of contemporary blues and jazz—two other major artistic expressions of the Harlem experience. However, just as he did not only write poetry, Hughes did not only live in Harlem. He traveled the world, and lived much of his life elsewhere. But Harlem was where he felt most welcome, nourished, and inspired. Today, Hughes is recognized as one of the most popular and enduring African American writers of the twentieth century.

> "I HAVE discovered in life that there are ways of getting almost anywhere you want to go, if you really want to go."

Hughes and the Blues

Langston Hughes made *beautiful music* with his words: what he, and others, called *jazz poetry.*

This poet of Harlem riffed with words much like a musician riffs with musical phrases, intentionally echoing the rhythms of American jazz and blues. Those rhythms could be traced back to the work songs and spirituals sung by slaves toiling in the fields of the South, and to older songs from West Africa. Classic blues songs are set to 12 bars of music in 4/4 time, using three simple chords. Hughes used this traditional structure in at least half of his poems.

- Hughes began his career in 1926 with a book of jazz poems, *The Weary Blues*, written to be performed to musical accompaniment.

- In his essay "Songs Called the Blues" (1941), Hughes wrote that the blues were sung by "black, beaten but unbeatable throats."

- A 1958 recording features Hughes reciting his poems to the accompaniment of the great jazz composer and musician Charles Mingus.

- The rhythms of jazz influenced Hughes's 1951 *Montage of a Dream Deferred*, a book-length poem depicting the African-American urban experience.

Building Knowledge and Insight	*The Negro Speaks of Rivers ▪ I, Too ▪ Dream Variations ▪ Refugee in America*

Connecting to the Essential Question These poems center on issues of racial identity and equality for African Americans. As you read, notice details that reflect pride, sorrow, and anger. This will help as you think about the Essential Question: **What makes American literature American?**

Close Reading Focus

Speaker; Multiple Themes

The **speaker** is the voice of a poem. Often, the speaker is the poet. However, a speaker may also be an imaginary person, a group of people, an animal, or an inanimate object. In some poems, such as many by Langston Hughes, the speaker is a voice that represents an entire people. As you read these poems, use a chart like the one shown to identify clues that suggest the identity of the speaker.

Comparing Literary Works These poems express **multiple themes,** or more than one essential meaning. While Hughes writes consistently about *cultural identity* and the status of African Americans within an oppressive society, his focus shifts from themes of suffering, injustice, and struggle to those of pride and beauty. As you read these poems, compare the images, memories, and attitudes Hughes expresses toward African American cultural identity. Look for clues in each poem that reveal the poem's themes.

Preparing to Read Complex Texts When you **apply a critical perspective** to literature, you read a selection through a particular lens or framing idea, such as the following:

- **Social or historical perspective:** viewing literature as it reflects issues in society at the time it was written
- **Archetypal perspective:** viewing literature as an expression of archetypes—characters, symbols, or patterns that cross cultures
- **Biographical perspective:** viewing literature as an expression of events and issues in a writer's personal life

As you read these poems, use a chart like the one shown to apply different critical perspectives and examine how varied lenses reveal different meanings.

Vocabulary

The words below are important to understanding the text that follows. Copy the words into your notebook. What are some other forms of the word *liberty*?

lulled   liberty

dusky

Ⓒ **Common Core State Standards**

Reading Literature
2. Determine two or more themes or central ideas of a text and analyze their development over the course of the text, including how they interact and build on one another to produce a complex account.

9. Demonstrate knowledge of early-twentieth-century foundational works of American literature, including how two or more texts from the same period treat similar themes or topics.

Speaking and Listening
SL.11–12.1.a, SL.11–12.1.b, SL.11–12.1.c, SL.11–12.1.d
(p. 897)
[For the full wording of the standards, see the standards chart in the front of your textbook.]

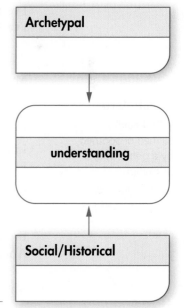

THE NEGRO SPEAKS OF RIVERS

Langston Hughes

BACKGROUND "The Negro Speaks of Rivers" was Langston Hughes's first great poem. He wrote it during the summer after he graduated from high school and it was published a short time later. Hughes considered Carl Sandburg and Walt Whitman to be the greatest American poets. In "The Negro Speaks of Rivers," Hughes follows the model of Whitman's "Song of Myself," using a first-person speaker to express the experience of an entire community.

Vocabulary

lulled (luld) *v.* calmed or soothed by a gentle sound or motion

dusky (dus′ kē) *adj.* dim; shadowy

I've known rivers:
I've known rivers ancient as the world and older than
    the flow of human blood in human veins.

My soul has grown deep like the rivers.

I bathed in the Euphrates when dawns were young.
5 I built my hut near the Congo and it lulled me to sleep.
I looked upon the Nile and raised the pyramids above it.
I heard the singing of the Mississippi when Abe Lincoln
    went down to New Orleans, and I've seen its muddy
    bosom turn all golden in the sunset.

I've known rivers:
Ancient, dusky rivers.

10 My soul has grown deep like the rivers.

Critical Viewing Which details in this painting, *Into Bondage*, by Harlem Renaissance painter Aaron Douglas, connect to Hughes's poem? **CONNECT ▶**

Into Bondage, Aaron Douglas, In the collection of the Corcoran Gallery of Art, Washington, D.C.

I, TOO

LANGSTON HUGHES

Nobody Around Here Calls Me Citizen, 1943, Robert Gwathmey, Collection Frederick R. Weisman Art Museum at the University of Minnesota, Minneapolis, © Estate of Robert Gwathmey/Licensed by VAGA, New York, NY

I, too, sing America.

I am the darker brother.
They send me to eat in the kitchen
When company comes,
5   But I laugh,
And eat well,
And grow strong.

Tomorrow,
I'll be at the table
10 When company comes.
Nobody'll dare
Say to me,
"Eat in the kitchen,"
Then.

15 Besides,
They'll see how beautiful I am
And be ashamed—

I, too, am America.

Applying Critical Perspectives

How does your understanding of this poem change when you read it with different critical perspectives?

◄ **Critical Viewing** Which image in this painting better illustrates the sentiments of this poem—the man or the lion? Explain. **MAKE A DECISION**

Critical Reading

1. **Key Ideas and Details (a)** In "The Negro Speaks of Rivers," which four rivers does the speaker mention? **(b) Deduce:** What does the age of these rivers imply about people of African ancestry?

2. **Key Ideas and Details (a) Infer:** Why does the speaker in "I, Too" have to eat in the kitchen when company comes? **(b) Interpret:** What does eating in the kitchen represent?

3. **Integration of Knowledge and Ideas (a) Interpret:** What does the speaker mean when he says "I, too, am America"? **(b) Synthesize:** Why do you think he refers so directly to Walt Whitman's poem?

Dream Variations
Langston Hughes

Girls Skipping, 1949, Hale Woodruff, Private Collection.
Courtesy of Michael Rosenfeld Gallery, New York

▲ **Critical Viewing**
How does the motion of
the figures in this painting
reflect the mood of the
poem? **CONNECT**

Speaker
Do you think the
speaker in this poem is
an individual or a group?

To fling my arms wide
In some place of the sun,
To whirl and to dance
Till the white day is done.
5   Then rest at cool evening
Beneath a tall tree
While night comes on gently,
    Dark like me—
That is my dream!

10 To fling my arms wide
In the face of the sun,
Dance! Whirl! Whirl!
Till the quick day is done.
Rest at pale evening . . .
15 A tall, slim tree . . .
Night coming tenderly
    Black like me.

REFUGEE IN AMERICA

LANGSTON HUGHES

There are words like *Freedom*
Sweet and wonderful to say.
On my heart-strings freedom sings
All day everyday.

5   There are words like Liberty
That almost make me cry.
If you had known what I knew
You would know why.

Vocabulary

liberty (lib´ ər tē) *n.*
condition of being free
from control by others

Critical Reading

1. **Key Ideas and Details** **(a)** In "Dream Variations," what does the speaker want to do till the "white" day is done? **(b) Analyze:** What double meaning can you identify in the phrase "white day"?

2. **Key Ideas and Details** **(a)** In "Refugee in America," what is the speaker's reaction to words like *freedom* and *liberty*? **(b) Interpret:** In what way does the title of the poem connect these words to the poem itself?

3. **Craft and Structure** **(a)** What words of emotion does the speaker use in "Refugee in America"? **(b) Evaluate:** In what way do these emotions contribute to the mood conveyed by the poem? Explain.

4. **Integration of Knowledge and Ideas** In what ways do these poems capture some of the complexities of the African American experience? In your response, use at least two of these Essential Question words: *perseverance, dignity, homeland, longing. [Connecting to the Essential Question: What makes American literature American?]*

Close Reading Activities

Literary Analysis

1. **Key Ideas and Details** **(a)** Who is the **speaker** in "The Negro Speaks of Rivers"? **(b)** How does the title help you identify the speaker? Explain.

2. **Key Ideas and Details** What can you infer about the identity and emotions of the speaker in "I, Too"?

3. **Craft and Structure** Walt Whitman, the author of "I Hear America Singing," was a great inspiration to Langston Hughes. How does this information about Hughes's biography affect your understanding of the poem "I, Too"?

4. **Key Ideas and Details** **(a)** Describe the speaker of "Dream Variations." **(b)** Which details in the poem support your description?

5. **Integration and Knowledge of Ideas** **(a)** What differences do you find between the speaker in "The Negro Speaks of Rivers" and the speaker in "Refugee in America"? **(b)** To what do you attribute those differences?

6. **Key Ideas and Details** Use a chart like the one shown to identify elements in the poems that reflect the **multiple themes** of racial identity, pride, and perseverance. Record words or phrases for each poem under the themes that they support. (Note: Not all poems have all three themes.)

	Racial Identity	**Pride**	**Perseverance**
Rivers			
I, Too			
Dream			
Refugee			

7. **Integration and Knowledge of Ideas** In what ways are the themes of racial identity, pride, and perseverance interconnected?

8. **Integration and Knowledge of Ideas** **(a)** When you read "Refugee in America" using a **social or historical critical perspective**, how do you understand the poem's last two lines? **(b)** What different interpretation of the poem might a **biographical perspective** provide?

9. **Integration and Knowledge of Ideas** **(a)** What aspects of "The Negro Speaks of Rivers" does an **archetypal critical perspective** help you interpret? Explain. **(b)** What other critical perspective might help you interpret this poem? Why?

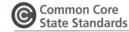

Common Core State Standards

Reading Literature
4. Determine the meaning of words and phrases as they are used in a text, including connotative meanings. *(p. 909)*

Writing
9.a. Apply *grades 11–12 Reading standards* to literature. *(p. 909)*

Language
4.b. Identify and correctly use patterns of word changes that indicate different meanings or parts of speech. *(p. 909)*
5. Demonstrate understanding of word relationships. *(p. 909)*
5.b. Analyze nuances in the meaning of words with similar denotations. *(p. 909)*

Vocabulary Acquisition and Use

Word Analysis: Latin Root *-liber-*

The word *liberty* contains the Latin root *-liber-* or *-liver-*, which means "free." The root is combined with the suffix *-ty,* which means "quality" or "condition." Thus, liberty is the quality or condition of being free. (Note: A different Latin word root that is spelled the same as *-liber-* contributes to the words *library* and *libretto.* Use context clues to confirm meanings when you see words that contain this root.)

Consider the meanings of the words below, that are based on *-liber-* or *-liver-*. Then, answer the questions.

liberate *v.* to release, to free

liberal *adj.* marked by generosity

deliverance *n.* the act of setting free or the state of being set free

1. *Simone was frustrated as she tried to liberate the coat lining from the zipper.* What has happened, and what is Simone trying to do?

2. *If the charity runs low on funds, the board will approach Mrs. Stephens, who has a liberal nature.* How do you think the charity hopes Mrs. Stephens will help? Explain.

3. *The soldiers hear gunfire and hope deliverance is near.* What are the soldiers hoping?

Vocabulary: Analogies

Analogies show the relationships between pairs of words. Complete each analogy using a word from the vocabulary list on page 901. In each, your choice should create a word pair that matches the relationship between the first two words given. Then, explain your answers.

1. *Deliverance* is to *bondage* as *capture* is to _____.

2. *Yellow* is to sunlight as *gray* is to _____.

3. *Dark* is to *light* as *stimulated* is to _____.

Using Resources to Build Vocabulary

Connotation and Denotation: Words for Freedom

Denotation is the direct meaning of a word. *Connotation* is an implied and often subjective meaning. For example, the denotative meaning of *license* is "freedom of action." The connotative meaning suggests a freedom that is used irresponsibly or without regard for rules.

Look up the words *freedom* and *liberty* in a thesaurus to find related words. Then, look up the new words in a dictionary. Make a chart or organize your notes to identify differences in connotation among all the words you find. Finally, rewrite "Refugee in America," with words other than *freedom* and *liberty.* Consider how the connotations of the substituted words alter the meaning of the poem.

Close Reading Activities Continued

Writing to Sources

Explanatory Text In a **multi-genre response** to literature you deliver an interpretation or critical assessment of a literary work in writing and in forms involving video, audio, performance, illustration, or other expressive media.

1. **Analytical Essay** Write an essay about "The Negro Speaks of Rivers" in which you apply historical and archetypal critical perspectives. Analyze Hughes's use of literary elements, such as simile, symbolism, and imagery, to advance meaning and evoke emotions. Follow the writing process instructions below to guide this part of your multi-genre response.

2. **Visual Elements** Add to your analysis of the poem with illustrations, a slide presentation, a series of photographs or drawings, or a poster.

3. **Audio Elements** Select music, spoken-word recordings, or other sound aids to accompany the visual element.

4. **Performance** Consider other ways to present your ideas. For example, you might interpret the poem in dance or set it to music.

To write your analytical essay, follow these steps:

Prewriting Reread the poem *applying a historical perspective*. To aid your work, consult an atlas or encyclopedia to find information about the rivers, objects, and time periods mentioned in the poem. Also, consider other issues in Hughes's era that may have inspired this poem.

Reread the poem again, *applying an archetypal perspective*. Consider what rivers mean to people across cultures. Note what the rivers in the poem symbolize and what their relationship is to the speaker. Identify similes or imagery that express those relationships. Write a clear thesis statement about the poem's meaning when viewed from two different perspectives.

Drafting In your introduction, state your main idea. In the body paragraphs, explain your interpretation. Clearly express the different understandings of the poem you gain from applying two critical perspectives. Use details from the poem and your research to support your ideas.

Revising Review your draft, paying particular attention to word choice. Replace vague or inappropriate words with more precise choices. In addition, make sure you use literary terms accurately.

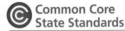

**Common Core
State Standards**

Writing
2. Write informative/ explanatory texts to examine and convey complex ideas, concepts, and information clearly and accurately through the effective selection, organization, and analysis of content.

2.d. Use precise language and domain-specific vocabulary to manage the complexity of the topic.

5. Develop and strengthen writing as needed by planning, revising, editing, rewriting, or trying a new approach, focusing on addressing what is most significant for a specific purpose and audience.

Speaking and Listening
5. Make strategic use of digital media in presentations to enhance understanding of findings, reasoning, and evidence and to add interest.

Language
1. Demonstrate command of the conventions of standard English grammar and usage when writing or speaking. *(p. 911)*

Model: Revising Word Choice

                                    most ancient civilizations
The Euphrates River was the site of some of the ~~oldest people~~ in
                                    thousands of years
history. Cities were being built on the shores of this river ~~long~~ ago.

Clear and specific language helps express ideas accurately.

Conventions and Style: Pronoun-Antecedent Agreement

Use correct pronoun-antecedent agreement to make your writing logical and clear. Remember that a **pronoun** stands for a noun, and the noun is its **antecedent**. The noun and pronoun should agree in person, number, and gender.

	Singular Pronouns	Plural Pronouns
First Person	I, me, my	we, us, our
Second Person	you, your	you, your
Third Person	he, she, it	they, them, their

The only pronouns that show gender are third-person singular pronouns.

Masculine	Feminine	Neuter
he, him, his	she, her, hers	it, its

Correcting Faulty Agreement

Unintended Shift in Person: Many *students* enjoy poems with images *you* can visualize.
Correct: Many *students* enjoy poems with images *they* can visualize.

Vague Reference: I liked "Dream Variations" because *they* helped me feel the dancing.
Correct: I liked "Dream Variations" because *the poet's words* helped me feel the dancing.

Unclear Reference: Bontemps and Hughes were friends, and after *his* death *he* compiled a book of Hughes's poetry.
Correct: After Hughes died, his friend *Bontemps* compiled a book of Hughes's poetry.

Practice Rewrite each sentence, correcting the problem in antecedent and pronoun agreement.

1. Langston Hughes wrote poetry to express pride in his heritage, which you see honored.
2. Countee Cullen and Claude McKay used images of fruit. That is in their poems.
3. Either Hughes or Cullen published their first poetry in 1925.
4. McKay sees fruit on a window ledge, and you feel like crying.
5. Bontemps and Cullen write poems of planting and reaping. They express despair.
6. Storms are dramatic and vivid. This makes them the subject of many poems and poets.
7. Poetry expresses feelings of sorrow, which not everyone likes.
8. Memories of dewy dawns and blue skies come back. They make the poet write.
9. Bontemps and Hughes corresponded. His letters were donated to a library.
10. The Harlem Renaissance poets celebrated freedom and their ancestors. They were oppressed.

Writing and Speaking Conventions

A. **Writing** Write a sentence for each noun below. Include one of the following pronouns to refer to the noun: *you, she, he, his, it, its, them, their,* or *they*. Make the pronoun and antecedent agree.

   1. rivers   2. brother   3. night   4. children   5. dream

   Example: company
   Sentence: If *company* comes, *they* will be welcome.

B. **Speaking** Present a review of a poem by Langston Hughes. Include at least two sentences that show correct pronoun-antecedent agreement.

POETRY OF IDENTITY

The Harlem Renaissance poets developed an artistic and cultural identity . . .

Claude McKay
Poet, journalist, activist

Arna Bontemps
Author of
A Black Man Talks of Reaping.

Countee Cullen
Poet and novelist

Langston Hughes
A leader of the
Harlem Renaissance

. . . that has grown through generations and will continue.

Colleen McElroy
Honors include
two Fulbright Fellowships

Lucille Clifton
National Book Award in 2000

Yusef Komunyakaa
Pulitzer Prize,
Ruth Lilly Poetry Prize

Nikki Giovanni
Honors include
Langston Hughes
Medal for poetry

Comparing Literary Works

The Poetry of Langston Hughes •
"study the masters" by Lucille Clifton •
"For My Children" by Colleen McElroy

Comparing Poetry of Cultural Identity

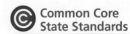

Common Core State Standards

Poetry of Cultural Identity Langston Hughes was famous before poets Colleen McElroy and Lucille Clifton were even born. Yet these three poets share a cultural identity that gives their work a "family resemblance." Cultural identity is a way of defining oneself as part of a culture or ethnic group. Culture, the way of life of a group of people, is expressed through manners, dress, language, rituals, beliefs, art, and food. The following are some of the cultural elements shared by African Americans, as expressed in these poems:

- **Roots and history:** from African origins through the era of slavery to freedom within a primarily white society
- **Values:** the importance of family, history, and cultural pride
- **Language:** the use of specific speech patterns and idioms

Other elements indicating a shared cultural identity include references to specific art forms, goals, beliefs, traditions, or social barriers—anything that establishes a community of common heritage.

In the mid- to late twentieth century, African American women writers sought to distinguish themselves from men because they often faced different problems. For example, women—both black and white—could not vote until long after African American men had won that right. As a result, female poets like McElroy and Clifton often emphasize women's views. Nevertheless, cultural identity is still paramount in their work. As you read these poems, use a chart like the one shown to compare elements in the poems that speak to cultural identity.

Reading Literature
2. Determine two or more themes or central ideas of a text and analyze their development over the course of the text, including how they interact and build on one another to produce a complex account.
4. Determine the meaning of words and phrases as they are used in the text; analyze the impact of specific word choices on meaning and tone, including language that is particularly fresh, engaging, or beautiful.

	Hughes	Clifton	McElroy
Roots/History	"I built my hut near the Congo…"		
Values	"On my heart-strings freedom sings/All day everyday."		
Goals	"Tomorrow, I'll be at the table"		

Gather Vocabulary Knowledge

Clifton and McElroy use related forms of the words *handiwork, heritage,* and *ritual.* Use a **dictionary** to find each word's part of speech and definition. Then, employ other references to further explore these words.

- **History of Language:** Use a history of English to research each word. Write a paragraph about each word's emergence in English.
- **Book of Quotations:** Use an online or print collection of quotations to find a passage containing one of the words. In a paragraph, explain subtleties in meaning that are evident from the context of the quotation.

Compare and contrast what you learn about the words from each reference.

The Poetry of Langston Hughes • study the masters • For My Children **913**

Lucille Clifton (1936–2010)

Author of "study the masters"

Lucille Clifton was born in New York. Her father, a steel worker, and her mother, a launderer and homemaker, were not formally educated, but had a love of books and language that they passed along to their daughter.

Lucille was only sixteen when she entered Howard University in Washington, D.C. There she met poets and writers (including Toni Morrison) who both influenced and encouraged her work. She later transferred to Fredonia State Teachers College, worked as an actor, and began to develop the style of poetry for which she would become known. A poet friend entered her work in a competition, which Clifton won. Part of the prize was the publication of her first volume of poems, *Good Times*. *The New York Times* called it one of the best books of 1969.

Clifton's work focuses largely on African American heritage and culture. In addition to her poetry, she has written a memoir and fourteen works of juvenile fiction, one of which received the Coretta Scott King Award in 1984. In 2007, Clifton became the first black woman to win the prestigious Ruth Lilly Poetry Prize.

Colleen McElroy (b. 1935)

Author of "For My Children"

An "army brat," McElroy spent much of her youth on the move, living in Missouri, Wyoming, and Germany—and she never seems to have stopped moving. She received her B.A. from Kansas State University, and then headed to Pennsylvania to study speech and language. Next, she headed west, receiving a Ph.D. in ethnolinguistics from the University of Washington. She stayed in Washington to teach English, but was still always on the move, traveling to Europe, South America, Japan, Africa, the South Pacific, and Southeast Asia.

McElroy began writing seriously when she was in her thirties. The many writers she knew encouraged her in her work. Her first collection of poems, *The Mules Done Long Since Gone*, was published in 1973. McElroy continued to both write and teach, and in 1983, she became the first black woman to be made a full professor at the University of Washington. In 1985, her collection *Queen of the Ebony Isles* received the American Book Award.

McElroy has also written short stories and plays, including a drama about Harriet Tubman, but is best known as a poet. She retired from teaching in 2006, but continues to write and travel.

STUDY THE MASTERS

Lucille Clifton

BACKGROUND The expression "study the masters" refers to the practice of looking at the work of great artists in order to learn an art form. In this poem, the master poet may be someone the speaker once studied, but just as she has abandoned the traditions of European poetry, she has also abandoned the idea that these were the only "masters" to be studied. Note that the title is really the first line of the poem. This is a common feature of Clifton's poems.

study the masters
like my aunt timmie.
it was her iron,
or one like hers,
5   that smoothed the sheets
the master poet slept on.
home or hotel, what matters is
he lay himself down on her handiwork
and dreamed. she dreamed too, words:
10   some cherokee¹, some masai² and some
huge and particular as hope.
if you had heard her
chanting as she ironed
you would understand form and line
15   and discipline and order and
america.

---

1. Cherokee (cher´ ə kē) a Native American people.
2. Masai (mä sī´) an African people.

▲ Critical Viewing

In what ways does this painting, like Aunt Timmie's words, say something about "form and line . . . and america"? **ANALYZE**

Vocabulary

handiwork (hand´ dē wʉrk´) *n.* work done by the hands; work done personally

The Madonna and Child (detail), 1990, Momodou Ceesay

▲ **Critical Viewing** In what ways does this painting reflect the heritage that the speaker in the poem seeks to hand on to her children? Explain. **ANALYZE**

BACKGROUND In societies without a written language, oral information that was passed down from one generaton to the next took the place of written historical accounts. The speaker of "For My Children" is a collector of the oral history of African American people. In telling this poem, the speaker sifts through facts, images, and other stories to pass on those with the greatest meaning. In doing so, the speaker connects the present to the past, the living to the dead, and North America to Africa.

I have stored up tales for you, my children
    My favorite children, my only children;
Of shackles and slaves and a bill of rights.
But skin of honey and beauty of ebony begins
5   In the land called Bilad as-Sudan,[1]
So I search for a heritage beyond St. Louis.

My memory floats down a long narrow hall,
    A calabash[2] of history.
Grandpa stood high in Watusi[3] shadows
10   In this land of yearly rituals for alabaster beauty;
Where effigies of my ancestors are captured
    In Beatle tunes,
And crowns never touch Bantu[4] heads.

My past is a slender dancer reflected briefly
15   Like a leopard in fingers of fire.
The future of Dahomey[5] is a house of 16 doors,
The totem of the Burundi[6] counts 17 warriors—
    In reverse generations.
While I cling to one stray Seminole.[7]
20 My thoughts grow thin in the urge to travel
    Beyond Grandma's tale
Of why cat fur is for kitten britches;[8]
Past the wrought-iron rail of first stairs
    In baby white shoes,
25 To Ashanti[9] mysteries and rituals.

---

1. **Bilad as-Sudan** (bē lād´ äs sōō dan´) "land of the blacks," an Arabic expression by which Arab geographers referred to the settled African countries north of the southern edge of the Sahara.
2. **calabash** (kal´ ə bash´) *n.* dried, hollow shell of a gourd, used as a bowl or a cup.
3. **Watusi** (wä tōō´ sē) a people of east-central Africa.
4. **Bantu** (ban´ tōō) Bantu-speaking peoples of Africa.
5. **Dahomey** (də hō´ mē) old name for Benin, in west-central Africa.
6. **Burundi** (boo roon´ dē) country in east-central Africa.
7. **Seminole** (sem´ ə nōl´) Native American people from Florida.
8. **Cat fur is for kitten britches** In the South, this was once a common saying used to correct those who pronounced "for" as "fur." If someone asked, "What's that fur?" rather than answering the intended question, the response of "Cat fur is for kitten britches" would remind the questioner to use standard English pronunciation.
9. **Ashanti** (ə shän´ tə) people of western Africa.

Comparing Poetry of Cultural Identity
Which details in the first stanza reflect the children's roots in Africa?

Vocabulary
heritage (her´ i tij´) *n.* something handed down from one's ancestors or from the past
rituals (rich´ ōō əlz´) *n.* established forms of ceremonies; ceremonial acts
effigies (ef´ i jēz) *n.* images or likenesses, especially of people

Comprehension
What has the speaker stored up for her children?

Back in the narrow hallway of my childhood.
    I cradled my knees
In limbs as smooth and long as the neck of a bud vase,
I began this ancestral search that you children yield now
30   In profile and bust
By common invention, in being and belonging.

The line of your cheeks recalls Ibo[10] melodies
    As surely as oboe and flute.
The sun dances a honey and cocoa duet on your faces.
35 I see smiles that mirror schoolboy smiles
    In the land called Bilad as-Sudan;
I see the link between the Mississippi and the Congo.

10. Ibo (ē′ bō′) a people of southeastern Nigeria.

Comparing Poetry of Cultural Identity

What physical connections to Africa does the speaker see in the children's faces?

Critical Reading

Cite textual evidence to support your responses.

1. **Key Ideas and Details (a)** In "study the masters," what is Aunt Timmie's occupation? **(b) Interpret:** What connection does the speaker make between Aunt Timmie's labor and the master poet?

2. **Key Ideas and Details (a)** What "huge and particular" word does the speaker say Aunt Timmie dreams? **(b) Analyze:** Why is this word so significant?

3. **Key Ideas and Details (a)** In "For My Children," for whom has the speaker "stored up tales"? **(b) Interpret:** Why has the speaker made this effort?

4. **Key Ideas and Details** Are the children solely the speaker's biological children? Explain.

5. **Key Ideas and Details (a)** Identify the cultures in which the speaker searches for evidence of her heritage. **(b) Analyze:** In the second and third stanzas, what impressions of her ancestors does the speaker convey? **(c) Analyze:** What images shape these impressions?

6. **Key Ideas and Details (a)** Which two rivers does the speaker mention in the last stanza? **(b) Interpret:** Why might these two rivers be important to the speaker and to her children?

7. **Integration of Knowledge and Ideas** In what specific ways might educating children about their heritage affect the choices they make in life?

Close Reading Activities

*The Poetry of Langston Hughes •
study the masters • For My Children*

Comparing Poetry of Cultural Identity

1. **Key Ideas and Details (a)** What rivers do both Hughes and McElroy mention? **(b)** What does the inclusion of these two rivers in the poems suggest about the shared cultural identities of the speakers?

2. **Integration and Knowledge of Ideas** What examples of pride in physical appearance do you find in "I, Too," "Dream Variations," and "For My Children"? Explain.

3. **Integration of Knowledge and Ideas** Both "I, Too" and "study the masters" end with the word "America." What does each speaker feel toward America? Explain.

Timed Writing

Explanatory Text: Essay

Langston Hughes and other artists of the Harlem Renaissance brought African American voices into the mainstream of American society. Today, issues of cultural identity still permeate American letters, as the poems by Clifton and McElroy demonstrate.

Assignment: Write an **analytical essay** in which you compare and contrast the explorations of cultural heritage in the poems by Hughes, Clifton, and McElroy. **[40 minutes]**

Use these questions to focus your analysis:

- What aspects of cultural identity are important in each poem?
- What is the message each speaker expresses?
- Based on these poems, in what ways is cultural identity both a private concern and one with meaning for an entire society?

As you write, incorporate these elements of a strong analytical essay:

- Craft effective introductory and concluding paragraphs, using a variety of sentence structures.
- Use a clear organizational scheme to compare the poems, either poem by poem or point by point.
- Include well-chosen details to support your statements.

5-Minute Planner

Complete these steps before you begin to write:

1. Read the assignment carefully. List key words and phrases.
2. Scan the poems for evidence that supports your ideas. **TIP** As you scan, jot down quotations for inclusion in your essay.
3. Create a rough outline for your essay.
4. Reread the prompt, and draft your essay.

**Common Core
State Standards**

Writing

2. Write explanatory texts to examine and convey complex ideas, concepts, and information clearly and accurately through the effective selection, organization, and analysis of content.

9. Draw evidence from literary or informational texts to support analysis, reflection, and research.

10. Write routinely over extended time frames and shorter time frames for a range of tasks, purposes, and audiences.

USE ACADEMIC VOCABULARY

As you write, use academic language, including the following words or their related forms:

comparison
reveal
categorize
discriminate

For more information about academic language, see the vocabulary charts in the introduction to this book.

Harlem Renaissance Poets

Claude McKay *(1890–1948)*

Author of "The Tropics in New York"

In some ways, poet and novelist Claude McKay seemed to be a man without roots. Once, while traveling overseas, he wrote to Langston Hughes, "I write of America as home [although] I am really a poet without a country." Born in Jamaica, he lived in numerous places in the United States and overseas. However, McKay considered Harlem his spiritual home, and it was to Harlem he returned in both his life and his work.

The son of Jamaican farm workers, McKay was able to emigrate to the United States when his first collection of poems, *Songs of Jamaica* (1912) won an award from the Institute of Arts and Letters. McKay moved to Harlem in 1914, after studying at Tuskegee Institute and Kansas State Teachers College. In 1917, McKay published two sonnets, "The Harlem Dancer" and "Invocation." McKay's poetry focused largely on the social injustices experienced by blacks in America. However, poems like "The Tropics in New York" are also marked by nostalgia for his homeland—a feeling echoed in the title of his autobiography, *A Long Way From Home* (1937).

Arna Bontemps *(1902–1973)*

Author of "A Black Man Talks of Reaping"

Arna Bontemps was one of the most scholarly figures of the Harlem Renaissance. Throughout his career as an editor, a novelist, a dramatist, and a poet, his commitment to social justice made him "the conscience of an era."

Born in Louisiana and raised in California, Bontemps came to New York during the height of the Harlem Renaissance. After teaching at several religious academies, he wrote *Black Thunder* (1936), a highly acclaimed novel about a Virginia slave revolt. In subsequent years, he published poems, biographies, dramas, and books for young readers. He also ran the library at Fisk University in Nashville, making it a major center for African American studies. In 1967, after the death of his friend Langston Hughes, Bontemps compiled *Hold Fast to Dreams* (1969), a poetry anthology. The bulk of the extensive correspondence between Hughes and Bontemps was donated to Yale University, where scholars can study this vivid chronicle of African American literary life.

Countee Cullen *(1903–1946)*

Author of **"From the Dark Tower"**

Unlike most other poets of his day, Countee Cullen used traditional forms and methods. Yet, no other poet expressed the sentiments of African Americans during the early 1900s more eloquently than did Cullen.

Cullen was born in Louisville, Kentucky, and raised by foster parents in New York. As a high-school student, Cullen's gift for poetry was recognized when he won a city-wide competition for his poem, "I Have a Rendevous With Life." An outstanding student, he also worked on his high-school newspaper and literary magazine. During his undergraduate career at New York University, Cullen's poetry was published in W.E.B. DuBois's magazine, *The Crisis.* Cullen later earned a master's degree in English and French from Harvard University. His first collection of poetry, *Color,* was published in 1925. That volume was followed by *Copper Sun* (1927), *The Ballad of the Brown Girl* (1927), and *The Black Christ* (1929). In 1932, he published *One Way to Heaven,* a satirical novel. In his later years, Cullen published two children's books, *The Lost Zoo* (1940) and *My Lives and How I Lost Them* (1942).

"Nations, like plants and human beings, grow. And if the development is thwarted they are dwarfed and overshadowed."

— Claude McKay

Connecting to the Essential Question These poems are filled with images of ripeness, but they focus on loss rather than bounty. As you read, look for details that express hope or despair. Doing so will help as you think about the Essential Question: **What is the relationship between literature and place?**

Close Reading Focus

Stanza; Stanza Structure; Imagery

A **stanza** is a group of lines that forms a division of a poem. Often, like paragraphs in prose, each stanza develops a single main idea that adds to a poem's overall meaning. **Stanza structure** refers to the way a poet organizes stanzas, which may vary in length or be evenly ordered. Types of stanzas are identified by the number of lines they contain:

two lines: *couplet*   **four lines**: *quatrain*
six lines: *sestet*   **eight lines**: *octave*

A **sonnet** is a fourteen-line lyric poem that follows one of two stanza structures. A *Petrarchan sonnet*, such as "From the Dark Tower," is divided into an opening octave followed by a sestet. A *Shakespearean sonnet* is divided into three quatrains and a final couplet. As you read these poems, notice how each poet uses stanza structure to develop his ideas.

Comparing Literary Works These poems contain similar types of **imagery,** or word pictures that appeal to the senses. As you read, compare each poet's use of imagery to express meaning and emotions.

Preparing to Read Complex Texts Literature can be read using a variety of critical approaches. These approaches are like spotlights that illuminate different aspects of a work. **Applying a political approach to literary criticism** allows a reader to interpret a work for its political content and themes. Writers may state political ideas directly or use symbols and other literary devices to suggest political meanings, as these poets do. You will understand these poems better if you read them for the political messages they express. As you read, use a chart like the one shown to note details that suggest political content.

Vocabulary

You will encounter the words listed here in the texts that follow. Copy the words into your notebook, sorting them into words you know and words you do not know.

benediction   countenance
increment   beguile

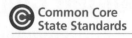

**Common Core
State Standards**

Reading Literature
5. Analyze how an author's choices concerning how to structure specific parts of a text contribute to its overall structure and meaning as well as its aesthetic impact.
9. Demonstrate knowledge of early-twentieth-century foundational works of American literature, including how two or more texts from the same period treat similar themes or topics.

Words/Phrases

Political Meaning

The TROPICS in New York

Claude McKay

BACKGROUND *This poem is marked by nostalgia for Jamaica, where the poet was born and raised.*

Bananas ripe and green, and ginger-root,
    Cocoa in pods and alligator pears,[1]
And tangerines and mangoes and grape fruit,
    Fit for the highest prize at parish fairs,

5 Set in the window, bringing memories
    Of fruit-trees laden by low-singing rills,[2]
And dewy dawns, and mystical blue skies
    In benediction over nun-like hills.

My eyes grew dim, and I could no more gaze;
10   A wave of longing through my body swept,
And, hungry for the old, familiar ways
    I turned aside and bowed my head and wept.

---

1. alligator pears avocados.
2. rills (rilz) *n.* little streams or brooks.

Stanza Structure
What type of stanza appears in this poem? Explain.

Vocabulary
benediction (ben e dik´ shen) *n.* prayer asking for God's blessing

A BLACK MAN
TALKS OF REAPING

Arna Bontemps

Hoeing, 1943, Robert Gwathmey, Carnegie Institute Museum of Art, Pittsburgh, Pennsylvania. © Estate of Robert Gwathmey/Licensed by VAGA, New York, NY

▲ **Critical Viewing**
What emotion does this image convey? In what way does it compare with the mood of the poem? **COMPARE AND CONTRAST**

BACKGROUND *In addition to poetry, Bontemps wrote num⸏
on African American history for younger readers. Planting ⸏
significant part of life for African Americans. In this poem, ⸏
uses this historic reality to explore the political realities of h⸏*

> I have sown beside all waters in my day.
> I planted deep, within my heart the fear
> that wind or fowl would take the grain awa⸏
> I planted safe against this stark, lean year⸏
>
> 5 I scattered seed enough to plant the land
> in rows from Canada to Mexico
> but for my reaping[1] only what the hand
> can hold at once is all that I can show.
>
> Yet what I sowed and what the orchard yields
> 10 my brother's sons are gathering stalk and root;
> small wonder then my children glean[2] in fields
> they have not sown, and feed on bitter fruit.

What political realities does the poet speak about symbolically in this stanza?

---

1. reaping (rēp´ iŋ) *v.* cutting or harvesting grain from a field.
2. glean (glēn) *v.* collect the remaining grain after reaping. Traditionally, the poor who did not own land gleaned the fields.

Critical Reading

1. **Key Ideas and Details (a)** In "The Tropics in New York," what memories does the fruit stir in the speaker? **(b) Infer:** Why do you think the speaker weeps?

2. **Key Ideas and Details Interpret:** What is ironic about the title as it relates to the message of the poem?

3. **Key Ideas and Details (a)** In "A Black Man Talks of Reaping," why does the speaker plant "deep"? **(b) Draw Conclusions:** What do you think is the meaning of the phrase "stark, lean year"?

4. **Key Ideas and Details (a)** How much of the seed does the speaker scatter? **(b) Infer:** Who reaps what the speaker has sown?

5. **Integration of Knowledge and Ideas Infer:** What does Bontemps suggest about what African Americans have received in exchange for their hard work?

Cite textual evidence to support your responses.

om The ARK TOWER

COUNTEE CULLEN (TO CHARLES S. JOHNSON)

BACKGROUND *Countee Cullen dedicated this poem to Charles S. Johnson, an African American sociologist, editor, and author of a landmark study of race relations in the 1920s.*

Vocabulary

increment (in´ crə mənt) *n.* increase, as in a series

countenance (koun´ tə nəns) *v.* approve; tolerate

beguile (bē gīl´) *v.* charm or delight

We shall not always plant while others reap
The golden increment of bursting fruit,
Not always countenance, abject and mute,
That lesser men should hold their brothers cheap;
5 Not everlastingly while others sleep
Shall we beguile their limbs with mellow flute,
Not always bend to some more subtle brute;
We were not made eternally to weep.

The night whose sable[1] breast relieves the stark,
10 White stars is no less lovely being dark,
And there are buds that cannot bloom at all
In light, but crumple, piteous, and fall;
So in the dark we hide the heart that bleeds,
And wait, and tend our agonizing seeds.

---

1. sable (sa´ bel) *adj.* black

Critical Reading

1. **Craft and Structure (a)** Which word is repeated five times in the first stanza? **(b) Analyze:** What is the effect of this repetition?

2. **Craft and Structure (a)** What contrast does the speaker set up in lines 9–10? **(b) Interpret:** What does Cullen mean by "no less lovely being dark?"

3. **Integration of Knowledge and Ideas** Are these poets hopeful or pessimistic about the future for African Americans? Explain. In your response, use at least two of these Essential Question words: *prospect, hurdle, expectation, overcome, surmount.* *[Connecting to the Essential Question: What is the relationship between literature and place?]*

Cite textual evidence to support your responses.

Literary Analysis

1. **Craft and Structure** What type of **stanza** does McKay use in "The Tropics in New York"?

2. **Integration of Knowledge and Ideas** How does a political reading clarify "A Black Man Talks of Reaping"?

3. **Craft and Structure** Using a chart like the one shown, identify the **stanza structure** of "A Black Man Talks of Reaping." Explain how each stanza works to develop the ideas expressed in the poem.

Stanza	Idea It Develops

4. **Integration of Knowledge and Ideas** **(a)** When you **apply a political approach** to "From the Dark Tower" how do you interpret the first stanza? **(b)** The last *couplet?*

5. **Craft and Structure** **(a)** Identify two stanza types in "From the Dark Tower." **(b)** How does the stanza structure of this *sonnet* help develop the poet's meaning?

6. **Comparing Literary Works** **(a)** For each poem, note examples of **imagery** related to planting and reaping. **(b)** Are the messages this imagery helps to express similar or different in each poem? Explain.

Vocabulary Acquisition and Use

Antonyms For each word, choose the letter of the correct antonym, or word of opposite meaning. Explain your choice.

1. benediction: **(a)** curse **(b)** talk **(c)** reap **(d)** bind

2. countenance: **(a)** face **(b)** remember **(c)** hope **(d)** disagree

3. beguile: **(a)** impress **(b)** disgust **(c)** steal **(d)** relate

4. increment: **(a)** tool **(b)** rapidity **(c)** decrease **(d)** multiplication

Writing to Sources

Explanatory Text Although Countee Cullen and Arna Bontemps were associated with the same literary movement, each had a distinct style. In an essay, **compare and contrast** "From the Dark Tower" and "A Black Man Talks of Reaping." Identify specific points of comparison, such as each poet's use of metaphor, and consider each poem's message and sound. Include vivid language and quote sufficiently from the poems to support your ideas.

Common Core State Standards

Writing
2. Write explanatory texts to examine and convey complex ideas, concepts, and information clearly and accurately through the effective selection, organization, and analysis of content.
2.b. Develop the topic thoroughly by selecting the most significant and relevant facts, extended definitions, concrete details, quotations, or other information and examples appropriate to the audience's knowledge of the topic.

Language
5. Demonstrate understanding of word relationships.
5.a. Interpret figures of speech in context and analyze their role in the text.

Connecting to the Essential Question Hurston writes of a time when she received encouragement from an unexpected source. As you read, look for details that reveal Hurston's self-confidence to help you think about the Essential Question: **How does literature shape or reflect society?**

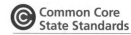
Common Core State Standards

Reading Informational Text
4. Determine the meaning of words and phrases as they are used in a text.

6. Determine an author's point of view or purpose in a text, analyzing how style and content contribute to the power, persuasiveness, or beauty of the text.

Close Reading Focus

Autobiography; Social Context; Dialogue; Dialect

Autobiography is a nonfiction account of a writer's life told in his or her own words. An autobiography documents the writer's feelings about key events and experiences. Because of this personal content, autobiographies often reveal **social context**—the attitudes, customs, and beliefs of the culture in which the writer lived. Hurston's autobiography provides a glimpse into the social context of her African American community in rural Florida during the early years of the twentieth century.

Hurston brings additional life to her characters and their social context by using two literary elements:

- **Dialogue:** the conversations among people
- **Dialect:** the form of a language spoken by people of a particular region or group

Hurston's use of dialogue allows her characters to speak for themselves. Her use of dialect allows them to speak with authenticity. As you read, notice the ways dialogue and dialect add nuance and depth to your understanding of Hurston's experience.

Preparing to Read Complex Texts Hurston's **purpose for writing**—to share her personal experience and show the vitality of the African American community—contributes to the decisions she makes about the events and thoughts to describe in her autobiography. The meaning of the piece is shaped by Hurston's purpose for writing it. As you read, **analyze the effect of the author's purpose** on meaning. Note words, details, characters, actions, and events in a chart like the one shown. Determine how each element helps Hurston meet her overall purpose for writing.

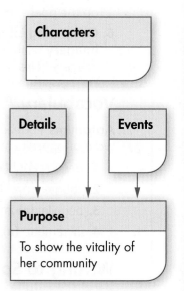

Vocabulary

You will encounter the words listed here in the text that follows. Copy the words into your notebook. What do the suffixes -*ness* and -*tion* tell you about the part of speech of two of the vocabulary words?

brazenness	duration
caper	exalted

Zora Neale Hurston *(1891–1960)*

Author of *Dust Tracks on a Road*

Zora Neale Hurston was an influential author and a pioneering force in African American culture. Yet, she died penniless and was buried in an unmarked grave in Fort Pierce, Florida. Hurston was almost entirely forgotten until author Alice Walker set out to locate and mark her grave, recording the experience in a 1975 *Ms.* magazine article. Walker's effort restored Hurston to her rightful place as "the dominant black woman writer" of her time.

Early Influences Hurston grew up in Eatonville, Florida, America's first fully incorporated African American township. One of eight children, she was, by her own account, a spirited, curious child who "always wanted to go." Hurston's childhood abruptly ended when her mother died. She then lived with a series of friends and relatives and, by age fourteen, was supporting herself.

Two Careers Hurston began writing while studying at Howard University. In 1925, she moved to New York City. She soon published a story and a play, firmly establishing herself as one of the bright new talents of the Harlem Renaissance. She attended Barnard College, where her work came to the attention of prominent anthropologist Franz Boas. He convinced Hurston to begin graduate studies in anthropology at Columbia University. With an academic grant, she began a second career as a folklorist.

Preserving a Culture Hurston was one of the first American writers to recognize that a cultural heritage was valuable in its own right. During the Great Migration, when African Americans from the South migrated by the hundreds of thousands to the North, Hurston moved against the tide. She returned to the South for six years to collect African American folk tales. In 1935, she published *Mules and Men*, the first volume of black American folklore compiled by an African American. Her work helped to document the African American connection to the stories, songs, and myths of Africa.

The Road to Obscurity Hurston achieved critical and popular success during the 1930s and 1940s with the novels *Jonah's Gourd Vine* (1934), *Their Eyes Were Watching God* (1937), *Moses, Man of the Mountain* (1939), and her prize-winning autobiography, *Dust Tracks on a Road* (1942).

> *"There are years that ask questions and years that answer."*

from

DUST TRACKS
ON A ROAD

Zora Neale Hurston

BACKGROUND In this excerpt from Zora Neale Hurston's autobiography, the young Zora experiences an event that opens her eyes to the world of literature and sets the stage for her career as a writer.

I used to take a seat on top of the gatepost and watch the world go by. One way to Orlando[1] ran past my house, so the carriages and cars would pass before me. The movement made me glad to see it. Often the white travelers would hail me, but more often I hailed them, and asked, "Don't you want me to go a piece of the way with you?"

They always did. I know now that I must have caused a great deal of amusement among them, but my self-assurance must have carried the point, for I was always invited to come along. I'd ride up the road for perhaps a half-mile, then walk back. I did not do this with the permission of my parents, nor with their foreknowledge.[2]

---

1. **Orlando** (ôr lan´ dō) city in central Florida, about five miles from Eatonville, Hurston's hometown.
2. **foreknowledge** (fôr´ näl´ ij) *n.* awareness of something before it happens or exists.

▲ **Critical Viewing** What elements of this photograph document the economic realities many of these children probably faced? **ANALYZE**

When they found out about it later, I usually got a whipping. My grandmother worried about my forward ways a great deal. She had known slavery and to her my brazenness was unthinkable.

"Git down offa dat gate-post! You li'l sow, you! Git down! Setting up dere looking dem white folks right in de face! They's gowine[3] to lynch you, yet. And don't stand in dat doorway gazing out at 'em neither. Youse too brazen to live long."[4]

Nevertheless, I kept right on gazing at them, and "going a piece of the way" whenever I could make it. The village seemed dull to me most of the time. If the village was singing a chorus, I must have missed the tune.

Perhaps a year before the old man[5] died, I came to know two other white people for myself. They were women.

It came about this way. The whites who came down from the North were often brought by their friends to visit the village school. A Negro school was something strange to them, and while they were always sympathetic and kind, curiosity must have been present, also. They came and went, came and went. Always, the room was hurriedly put in order, and we were threatened with a prompt and bloody death if we cut one caper while the visitors were present. We always sang a spiritual, led by Mr. Calhoun himself. Mrs. Calhoun always stood in the back, with a palmetto switch[6] in her hand as a

Vocabulary

brazenness (brā´ zən nəs) *n.* shamelessness; boldness; impudence

Vocabulary

caper (kā´ pər) *n.* prank

Comprehension

Why does her grandmother worry about Zora's sitting on the gatepost and accepting rides from strangers?

---

3. **gowine** "going."
4. **"Git down . . . live long"** Hurston's grandmother's fears reflect the belief of many people at the time that it was dangerous for African Americans to be assertive toward whites.
5. **the old man** white farmer who had developed a friendship with Hurston.
6. **palmetto** (pal met´ ō) **switch** whip made from the fan-shaped leaves of the palmetto, a type of palm tree.

squelcher. We were all little angels for the duration, because we'd better be. She would cut her eyes and give us a glare that meant trouble, then turn her face towards the visitors and beam as much as to say it was a great privilege and pleasure to teach lovely children like us. They couldn't see that palmetto hickory in her hand behind all those benches, but we knew where our angelic behavior was coming from.

Usually, the visitors gave warning a day ahead and we would be cautioned to put on shoes, comb our heads, and see to ears and fingernails. There was a close inspection of every one of us before we marched in that morning. Knotty heads, dirty ears and fingernails got hauled out of line, strapped and sent home to lick the calf over again.

This particular afternoon, the two young ladies just popped in. Mr. Calhoun was flustered, but he put on the best show he could. He dismissed the class that he was teaching up at the front of the room, then called the fifth grade in reading. That was my class.

So we took our readers and went up front. We stood up in the usual line, and opened to the lesson. It was the story of Pluto and Persephone. It was new and hard to the class in general, and Mr. Calhoun was very uncomfortable as the readers stumbled along, spelling out words with their lips, and in mumbling undertones before they exposed them experimentally to the teacher's ears.

Then it came to me. I was fifth or sixth down the line. The story was not new to me, because I had read my reader through from lid to lid, the first week that Papa had bought it for me.

That is how it was that my eyes were not in the book, working out the paragraph which I knew would be mine by counting the children ahead of me. I was observing our visitors, who held a book between them, following the lesson. They had shiny hair, mostly brownish. One had a looping gold chain around her neck. The other one was dressed all over in black and white with a pretty finger ring on her left hand. But the thing that held my eyes were their fingers. They were long and thin, and very white, except up near the tips. There they were baby pink. I had never seen such hands. It was a fascinating discovery for me. I wondered how they felt. I would have given those hands more attention, but the child before me was almost through. My turn next, so I got on my mark, bringing my eyes back to the book and made sure of my place. Some of the stories I had reread several times, and this Greco-Roman myth was one of my favorites. I was exalted by it, and that is the way I read my paragraph.

"Yes, Jupiter had seen her (Persephone). He had seen the maiden picking flowers in the field. He had seen the chariot of the dark monarch pause by the maiden's side. He had seen him when he seized Persephone. He had seen the black horses leap down Mount Aetna's fiery throat. Persephone was now in Pluto's dark realm and he had made her his wife."

The two women looked at each other and then back to me. Mr. Calhoun broke out with a proud smile beneath his bristly moustache, and instead of the next child taking up where I had ended, he nodded

Social Context

What concerns are revealed in this passage about preparation for visitors?

Vocabulary

duration (du ra′ shun) *n.* the time during which something continues or exists

exalted (eg zôlt′ id) *adj.* filled with joy or pride; elated

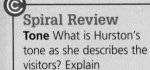

Spiral Review

Tone What is Hurston's tone as she describes the visitors? Explain to me to go on. So I read the story to the end, where flying Mercury, the messenger of the Gods, brought Persephone back to the sunlit earth and restored her to the arms of Dame Ceres, her mother, that the world might have springtime and summer flowers, autumn and harvest. But because she had bitten the pomegranate[7] while in Pluto's kingdom, she must return to him for three months of each year, and be his queen. Then the world had winter, until she returned to earth.

Mr. Calhoun broke out with a proud smile beneath his bristly moustache . . .

The class was dismissed, and the visitors smiled us away and went into a low-voiced conversation with Mr. Calhoun for a few minutes. They glanced my way once or twice and I began to worry. Not only was I barefooted, but my feet and legs were dusty. My hair was more uncombed than usual, and my nails were not shiny clean. Oh, I'm going to catch it now. Those ladies saw me, too. Mr. Calhoun is promising to 'tend to me. So I thought.

Then Mr. Calhoun called me. I went up thinking how awful it was to get a whipping before company. Furthermore, I heard a snicker run over the room. Hennie Clark and Stell Brazzle did it out loud, so I would be sure to hear them. The smart-aleck was going to get it. I slipped one hand behind me and switched my dress tail at them, indicating scorn.

"Come here, Zora Neale," Mr. Calhoun cooed as I reached the desk. He put his hand on my shoulder and gave me little pats. The ladies smiled and held out those flower-looking fingers towards me. I seized the opportunity for a good look.

Analyzing Effect of Author's Purpose
Why do you think Hurston includes this description of her response to taunting classmates?

"Shake hands with the ladies, Zora Neale," Mr. Calhoun prompted and they took my hand one after the other and smiled. They asked if I loved school, and I lied that I did. There was *some* truth in it, because I liked geography[8] and reading, and I liked to play at recess time. Who ever it was invented writing and arithmetic got no thanks from me. Neither did I like the arrangement where the teacher could sit up there with a palmetto stem and lick me whenever he saw fit. I hated things I couldn't do anything about. But I knew better than to bring that up right there, so I said yes, I *loved* school.

"I can tell you do," Brown Taffeta gleamed. She patted my head, and was lucky enough not to get sandspurs in her hand. Children who roll and tumble in the grass in Florida are apt to get sandspurs in their hair. They shook hands with me again and I went back to my seat.

When school let out at three o'clock, Mr. Calhoun told me to wait. When everybody had gone, he told me I was to go to the Park House,

Comprehension
Why is Zora afraid to approach her teacher after reading so well?

---

7. **pomegranate** (päm´ gran´ it) *n.* round, red-skinned fruit with many seeds.
8. **geography** (je äg´ rə fē) *n.* science that deals with the surface of the earth.

Analyzing Effect of Author's Purpose

Why do you think that Hurston includes this incident about her mother preparing her for her meeting with the women?

that was the hotel in Maitland,[9] the next afternoon to call upon Mrs. Johnstone and Miss Hurd. I must tell Mama to see that I was clean and brushed from head to feet, and I must wear shoes and stockings. The ladies liked me, he said, and I must be on my best behavior.

The next day I was let out of school an hour early, and went home to be stood up in a tub full of suds and be scrubbed and have my ears dug into. My sandy hair sported a red ribbon to match my red and white checked gingham dress, starched until it could stand alone. Mama saw to it that my shoes were on the right feet, since I was careless about left and right. Last thing, I was given a handkerchief to carry, warned again about my behavior, and sent off, with my big brother John to go as far as the hotel gate with me.

First thing, the ladies gave me strange things, like stuffed dates and preserved ginger, and encouraged me to eat all that I wanted. Then they showed me their Japanese dolls and just talked. I was then handed a copy of *Scribner's Magazine*,[10] and asked to read a place that was pointed out to me. After a paragraph or two, I was told with smiles, that that would do.

I was led out on the grounds and they took my picture under a palm tree. They handed me what was to me then a heavy cylinder done up in fancy paper, tied with a ribbon, and they told me goodbye, asking me not to open it until I got home.

My brother was waiting for me down by the lake, and we hurried home, eager to see what was in the thing. It was too heavy to be candy or anything like that. John insisted on toting it for me.

My mother made John give it back to me and let me open it. Perhaps, I shall never experience such joy again. The nearest thing to that moment was the telegram accepting my first book. One hundred goldy-new pennies rolled out of the cylinder. Their gleam lit up the world. It was not avarice[11] that moved me. It was the beauty of the thing. I stood on the mountain. Mama let me play with my pennies for a while, then put them away for me to keep.

That was only the beginning. The next day I received an Episcopal hymn-book bound in white leather with a golden cross stamped into the front cover, a copy of *The Swiss Family Robinson*, and a book of fairy tales.

Social Context

What does Zora's excitement about the books she receives reveal about the social context of her community?

I set about to commit the song words to memory. There was no music written there, just the words. But there was to my consciousness music in between them just the same. "When I Survey the Wondrous Cross" seemed the most beautiful to me, so I committed that to memory first of all. Some of them seemed dull and without life, and I pretended they were not there. If white people liked trashy singing like that, there must be something funny about them that I had not noticed before. I stuck to the pretty ones where the words marched to a throb I could feel.

---

9. Maitland (māt´ lənd) city in Florida, close to Eatonville.
10. *Scribner's Magazine* literary magazine no longer published.
11. avarice (av´ ə ris) *n.* extreme desire for wealth; greed.

A month or so after the young ladies returned to Minnesota, they sent me a huge box packed with clothes and books. The red coat with a wide circular collar and the red tam[12] pleased me more than any of the other things. My chums pretended not to like anything that I had, but even then I knew that they were jealous. Old Smarty had gotten by them again. The clothes were not new, but they were very good. I shone like the morning sun.

But the books gave me more pleasure than the clothes. I had never been too keen on dressing up. It called for hard scrubbings with Octagon soap suds getting in my eyes, and none too gentle fingers scrubbing my neck and gouging in my ears.

In that box were *Gulliver's Travels, Grimm's Fairy Tales, Dick Whittington, Greek and Roman Myths*, and best of all, *Norse Tales*. Why did the Norse tales strike so deeply into my soul? I do not know, but they did. I seemed to remember seeing Thor swing his mighty short-handled hammer as he sped across the sky in rumbling thunder, lightning flashing from the tread of his steeds and the wheels of his chariot. The great and good Odin, who went down to the well of knowledge to drink, and was told that the price of a drink from that fountain was an eye. Odin drank deeply, then plucked out one eye without a murmur and handed it to the grizzly keeper, and walked away. That held majesty for me.

Of the Greeks, Hercules moved me most. I followed him eagerly on his tasks. The story of the choice of Hercules as a boy when he met Pleasure and Duty, and put his hand in that of Duty and followed her steep way to the blue hills of fame and glory, which she pointed out at the end, moved me profoundly. I resolved to be like him. The tricks and turns of the other Gods and Goddesses left me cold. There were other thin books about this and that sweet and gentle little girl who gave up her heart to Christ and good works. Almost always they died from it, preaching as they passed. I was utterly indifferent to their deaths. In the first place I could not conceive of death, and in the next place they never had any funerals that amounted to a hill of beans, so I didn't care how soon they rolled up their big, soulful, blue eyes and kicked the bucket. They had no meat on their bones.

But I also met Hans Andersen and Robert Louis Stevenson. They seemed to know what I wanted to hear and said it in a way that tingled me. Just a little below these friends was Rudyard Kipling in his *Jungle Books*. I loved his talking snakes as much as I did the hero.

I came to start reading the Bible through my mother. She gave me a licking one afternoon for repeating something I had overheard a neighbor telling her. She locked me in her room after the whipping,

12. **tam** (tam) *n.* cap with a wide, round, flat top and sometimes a center pompom.

The American EXPERIENCE

Zora Neale Hurston Rediscovered
Although she died in a welfare home in 1960 penniless and unknown, the rediscovery of Zora Neale Hurston in the 1970s is among the most dramatic events in American literary history. Hurston became a subject of author Alice Walker's 1983 essay, "In Search of Our Mother's Gardens." Ten years earlier, Walker's article "Looking for Zora" described her 1973 search to find and mark Hurston's unknown grave.

In both of her writings, Walker speaks of the importance of recovering and remembering Hurston as one of the greatest African American folklorists of all time and a major American writer. Walker championed the cause to resurrect Hurston's literary reputation and, once again, give her a prominent place in our literary heritage.

Connect to the Literature

Think about the incident that Hurston describes in this excerpt from her autobiography. Why do you think she became a writer?

Comprehension

Of all the gifts she receives, which gives Zora the most pleasure? Explain.

and the Bible was the only thing in there for me to read. I happened to open to the place where David[13] was doing some mighty smiting, and I got interested. David went here and he went there, and no matter where he went, he smote 'em hip and thigh. Then he sung songs to his harp awhile, and went out and smote some more. Not one time did David stop and preach about sins and other things. All David wanted to know from God was who to kill and when. He took care of the other details himself. Never a quiet moment. I liked him a lot. So I read a great deal more in the Bible, hunting for some more active people like David. Except for the beautiful language of Luke and Paul,[14] the New Testament still plays a poor second to the Old Testament for me. The Jews had a God who laid about Him when they needed Him. I could see no use waiting until Judgment Day to see a man who was just crying for a good killing, to be told to go and roast. My idea was to give him a good killing first, and then if he got roasted later on, so much the better.

---

13. **David** in the Bible, the second king of Israel, the land of the Hebrews.
14. **Luke and Paul** two Christian Apostles who wrote parts of the New Testament.

Critical Reading

Cite textual evidence to support your responses.

1. **Key Ideas and Details (a)** What does Zora do when white travelers pass by her house? **(b) Infer:** What does this activity tell you about her?

2. **Key Ideas and Details (a)** Who are the two white women Zora meets, and why are they at her school? **(b) Support:** How can you tell that these two women made an impression on Hurston?

3. **Key Ideas and Details (a)** What does Zora find fascinating about the two visitors? **(b) Infer:** What does her fascination suggest about her life experiences so far?

4. **Key Ideas and Details (a)** Describe Zora's response to the gifts she receives. **(b) Infer:** What does her preference reveal about her?

5. **Integration of Knowledge and Ideas** What does this episode from Hurston's childhood suggest about the qualities that helped people of her era succeed despite social barriers, such as those of gender or race? In your response, use at least two of these Essential Question words: *self-reliance, individualism, persistence, dignity, creativity.* [**Connecting to the Essential Question:** *How does literature shape or reflect society?*]

Literary Analysis

1. **Key Ideas and Details** In this excerpt from her **autobiography,** Hurston describes her boldness as a child. **(a)** Why was Hurston's grandmother worried about her granddaughter's bold personality? **(b)** What do you understand about the **social context** from the grandmother's statements?

2. **Key Ideas and Details** What do you learn about the social context of Hurston's life from these details? **(a)** the schoolroom's being cleaned for visitors **(b)** students reading mythology **(c)** Hurston's going to school barefoot

3. **Key Ideas and Details** Find three more details that reveal the attitudes of Hurston's culture. Record them in a chart like the one shown.

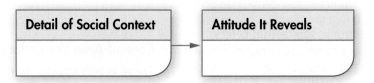

Detail of Social Context	Attitude It Reveals

4. **Craft and Structure (a)** What information about Hurston is revealed in the opening **dialogue** she has with her grandmother? **(b)** Why do you think Hurston included her grandmother's words in **dialect**?

5. **Key Ideas and Details (a)** What details does Hurston use to reveal her independence and passion for learning? **(b)** In what ways does her inclusion of details reflect her **purpose?**

6. **Integration and Knowledge of Ideas** Why do you think Hurston wrote about her experience with the Minnesotans?

Vocabulary Acquisition and Use

Write a sentence for each word pair, using the words correctly.

1. duration/exalted
2. brazenness/caper

Writing to Sources

Narrative Text Write a **reflective essay** that tells a story about a moment in your life that inspired you to pursue something you love. Develop a clear conflict or problem by describing obstacles you faced. Develop a clear resolution by showing the events that inspired you and the changes that occurred as a result. Enhance the plot and develop characters by using a range of literary strategies and devices, including dialogue.

Common Core State Standards

Writing

3. Write narratives to develop real or imagined experiences or events using effective technique, well-chosen details, and well-structured event sequences.

3.a. Engage and orient the reader by setting out a problem, situation, or observation and its significance.

3.b. Use narrative techniques, such as dialogue, to develop experiences, events, and/or characters.

3.e. Provide a conclusion that follows from and reflects on what is experienced, observed, or resolved over the course of the narrative.

Analyzing Functional and Expository Texts

Online Citation Organizer • Online Encyclopedia

About the Texts

An **online citation organizer** is a Web resource that provides correctly formatted citations to use in bibliographies. This service compiles the citation rules from many style books—MLA, APA, and others—and allows users to choose the style they prefer. Users input research source information and the site returns a citation correctly formatted to a specific style.

An **online encyclopedia** is an electronic source that offers articles on varied topics. Many traditional print encyclopedias now make their content available online; these sources maintain the same authority as their print versions. **Wikipedia** is an online encyclopedia written and edited by users, a practice that has led some to criticize its accuracy. Common features of online encyclopedias include a search engine that allows the user to locate articles, links to other Web pages with related information, and a list of references consulted by the writer or writers.

Preparing to Read Complex Texts

As you use a digital reference tool, it is important to ensure its truthfulness, or validity, and its accuracy, or reliability. To **evaluate validity and reliability,** follow these steps:

- Check references listed within or at the end of an article.
- Consult outside references that you know to be authoritative.
- Assess the authority of the writer or writers, if listed.

As you read, use a chart like the one shown to evaluate the validity and reliability of online reference sources.

Digital Resource _____			
Author or Creator _____			
Facts to Be Verified	**Sources**	**Discrepancies**	**Result**
1._____	_____	_____	_____
2._____	_____	_____	_____
3._____	_____	_____	_____

Common Core State Standards

Writing

8. Gather relevant information from multiple authoritative print and digital sources; assess the strengths and limitations of each source in terms of the task, purpose, and audience; integrate information, avoiding plagiarism and following a standard format for citation.

Content-Area Vocabulary

These words appear in the selections that follow. They may also appear in other content-area texts.

interactive (in´ tər ak´ tiv) *adj.* in computer technology, reacting or responding to the user

software (sôft wer´) *n.* the collection of electronic programming directions that controls a computer's functioning

wiki (wi´ kē) *n.* Web site that can be edited by any user

Q Citation Machine

Citation Machine™

CITATION MACHINE
Serving Students & Teachers
K-12, College, & University

▼ MLA

Print

- Book: One or More Authors
- Encyclopedia or other reference work
- Journal Article: One or More Authors
- Magazine Article: One or More Authors

Non-Print

- Internet Journal or Magazine Article: One or More Authors
- Web Page
- Online Encyclopedia
- Encyclopedia (CD-ROM)

▼ APA

▼ CHICAGO

▼ TURABIAN

Citation Machine™ is an **interactive** web tool designed to assist high school, college, and university students, their teachers, and independent researchers in their effort to respect other people's intellectual properties. To use Citation Machine™, simply ...

> Numbered items show how to use the organizer.

1. Click the citation format you need and then the type of resource you wish to cite.
2. Complete the Web form that appears with information from your source.
3. Click **Make Citations** to generate standard bibliographic and in-text citations.

The primary goal of this tool is to make it so easy for **high school**, **college**, and **university students** and other researchers to credit information sources that there is virtually no reason not to—because **SOMEDAY THE INFORMATION SOMEONE WANTS TO USE WILL BE YOURS.**

Warning: There are many nuances to how citations are formed, and this **software** may not pick up all of the circumstances that influence a citation's proper format. The Citation Machine™ cannot fully guarantee the accuracy of citations generated by this tool.

If you have questions about the proper citation of these or other source types, consult your local copy of:

> Bullets beneath each format or style of citation list additional resources.

- MLA Handbook for Writers of Research Papers: 6th Edition or
- Publication Manual of the American Psychological Association: 5th Edition.

There will be copies in your school or public libraries.

MLA

BOOK – TWO AUTHORS

Fewer Authors   More Authors

This input form is generated by clicking on the link for a book with two authors.

Last Name (Author 1)   The Freedom Writers
The first author appearing on the title page

First Name (Author 1)

First & Last Name (Author 2)   Erin Gruwell

Title of Work   The Freedom Writers Diary

Edition   2nd ed '1st ed', '2nd ed', etc.

Publishing City   New York, NY
Include state or country abbrev if not a commonly known publishing city

Publishing Company   Broadway Books

Publishing Date   1999
(YYYY)

submit

↑
Input Screen

Results screen →

Copy the citation below and paste it into your document.

The Freedom Writers, and Erin Gruwell. <u>The Freedom Writers Diary</u>, 2nd ed. New York, NY: Broadway Books, 1999.

Use your word processor to format your citations as illustrated below.
Do Not Copy this Citation.

The Freedom Writers, and Erin Gruwell. <u>The Freedom Writers Diary</u>, 2nd ed. New York, NY: Broadway Books, 1999.

Parenthetical in text citations. There are usually many variations for these. It may be wise to consult the Style Guide for clarification.

Return to Form to Correct any Mistakes

The organizer generates a citation based on the input information.

Citation Machine

Atlanta Braves

article | discussion | edit this page | history

Atlanta Braves

From **Wiki**pedia, the free encyclopedia

The **Atlanta Braves** are a National League Major League Baseball team based in Atlanta, Georgia since 1966, after having been located first in Boston (1871–1952) and then in Milwaukee (1953–1965). The franchise is one of the only two remaining National League charter members, along with the <u>Chicago Cubs</u>. The Braves compete in the NL East after being in the western division from 1969 to 1993.

> The first paragraph defines the topic, provides some history, and suggests other aspects of the topic the reader might explore.

For the last decade and a half, the Braves have been one of the most successful franchises in baseball, winning their division title an unprecedented 14 consecutive times from 1991 to 2005 (omitting the strike-shortened 1994 season in which there were no official division champions), and advancing to the <u>World Series</u> five times in that period, winning it in 1995. In their history, the Braves have won 16 divisional titles, nine <u>National League</u> pennants, and three World Series championships—in 1914 as the Boston Braves, in 1957 as the Milwaukee Braves, and in 1995 while in Atlanta. (The Braves are the only MLB franchise to have won the Series in three different home cities.)

> By clicking on a highlighted hyperlink (blue text), the user will be connected to other articles about baseball.

For current news on this topic, see
20--Atlanta Braves season

Atlanta Braves
Established 1871
Based in Atlanta since 1966

- **National League (1876–present)**
- **East Division (1994–present)**

Current uniform

Retired Numbers
3, 21, 35, 41, 42, 44

Name

- **Atlanta Braves (1966–present)**
- Milwaukee Braves (1953–1965)
- Boston Braves (1941–1952)
- Boston Bees (1936–1940)
- Boston Braves (1912–1935)
- Boston Rustlers (1911)
- Boston Doves (1907–1910)
- Boston Beaneaters (1883–1906)
- Boston Red Stockings (1871–1882)

Quick reference information is provided in a list format.

article | discussion | edit this page | history

Ballpark
- **Turner Field (1997–present)**
- Atlanta-Fulton County Stadium (1966–1976)
  - a.k.a. Atlanta Stadium (1966–1976)
- Milwaukee County Stadium (1953–1965)
- Braves Field (1915–1952)
  - a.k.a. National League Park (1936–1941)
- Fenway Park (1914–1915)
- South End Grounds (1894–1914)
- Congress Street Grounds (1894)
- South End Grounds (1871–1894)

NL Pennants (17)   1877 · 1878 · 1883 · 1891 · 1892 · 1893 · 1897 · 1898 · 1914 · 1948 · 1957 · 1958 · 1991 · 1992 · 1995 · 1996 · 1999
East Division titles (11)   1995 · 1996 · 1997 · 1998 · 1999 · 2000 · 2001 · 2002 · 2003 · 2004 · 2005
West Division titles (5)   1969 · 1982 · 1991 · 1992 · 1993

Quick Facts
- **Founded:** 1871 in Boston, Massachusetts as the Boston Red Stockings a charter member of the National Association. The club became a charter member of the National League in 1876 and has remained in the league without a break since then. The Braves are the oldest continuously operating sports franchise in North American sports. Arguably, they can trace their ancestry to the original Cincinnati Red Stockings of 1869–1870, baseball's first openly professional team. When the N.A. formed, Cincinnati's backers declined to field a team in the new league and Red Stockings player-manager Harry Wright along with three of the best players from that team moved collectively to Boston and took the nickname with them.

- **Formerly known as:** Boston Braves (1912–1952), and Milwaukee Braves (1953–1965). Prior to 1912, the Boston team had several unofficial nicknames: "Red Stockings" and "Red Caps" in the 1870s and 1880s; "Beaneaters" in the 1890s and early 1900s; "Doves" (when the Dovey family owned the franchise, 1907–1910) and "Rustlers" (when William Russell owned the franchise, 1911). Following the 1935 season, after enduring bankruptcy and a series of poor seasons, new owner Bob Quinn asked a team of sportswriters to choose a new nickname, to change the team luck. The sportswriters chose "Bees", which was adopted in 1936, though it never really caught on. The team dropped the nickname in 1941, using only the official name "Braves" from 1941 on.

- **Uniform colors:** Navy blue, garnet red, and white

- **Logo design:** The script word "Braves"

- **Team mottos:** "Atlanta's Pastime Since 1966" and "Welcome to the Bigs"

Critical Reading

1. Key Ideas and Details (a) Why might an online citation organizer be valuable to someone writing a research paper? **(b)** What advantages and disadvantages does it offer when compared to a traditional print resource?

2. Key Ideas and Details (a) What warning does the online citation organizer provide? **(b)** How does this warning help you evaluate the site's reliability and credibility?

3. Key Ideas and Details (a) CIte two facts presented in the Wikipedia article about the Atlanta Braves. **(b)** Explain two methods you could use to verify each fact and evaluate the overall reliability and credibility of the article.

4. Content-Area Vocabulary (a) Explain how the meaning of the Latin prefix *inter-* ("among or between") contributes to the meaning of *interactive*. **(b)** Determine the meaning of these words derived from the same Latin prefix: *intercom, interdict, intercept.* **(c)** Use a dictionary to verify your preliminary definitions.

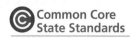

Common Core State Standards

Writing
10. Write routinely over extended time frames and shorter time frames for a range of tasks, purposes, and audiences.

Language
4.d. Verify the preliminary determination of the meaning of a word or phrase.

⏱ Timed Writing

Argument [40 minutes]

Format

An **argumentative essay** advances a thesis, or position supported by logical reasons. State your thesis in the introduction, support it in the body paragraphs, and restate it in your conclusion.

Write an **argumentative essay** in which you persuade readers that it is or is not a good idea to do important research using an online encyclopedia that is written and edited by its users. Consider both the benefits and **issues** such an online tool might present. Cite specific details, including your own observations, to support your argument.

Academic Vocabulary

Issues are the problems, concerns, or consequences created by a situation. Issues are often multifaceted, requiring you to discuss them from more than a single angle.

5-Minute Planner

Complete these steps before you begin to write:

1. Read the prompt carefully. Identify key words.

2. Make a list of varied types of evidence that support your thesis.

3. Sketch an outline of your essay.

4. Reread the prompt, and draft your essay. **TIP** Use transitional words and phrases such as *however* and *on the other hand* to distinguish ideas in your essay and convey your meaning more clearly.

Write a Multimedia Presentation of an Argument

Argumentative Text Today, electronic media dominates the communications landscape. The effect of the wide variety of media on an audience is very different from that of the printed word alone. By combining text, images, and sound in a multimedia presentation, you can bring ideas to life in new ways. For example, you can show video clips of an actual event or an interview with an expert as powerful evidence to support your argument. Follow the steps outlined in this workshop to write and deliver your own multimedia presentation of an argument.

Assignment Write and deliver a multimedia presentation in which you present a claim on a topic and support that claim.

What to Include Your multimedia presentation should feature the following elements:

- Integrated text, audio, and visual components
- The use of a wide range of media, including films, newspapers, magazines, online information, television, and videos
- Innovative use of media to convey concepts
- Reinforcement of key ideas with the use of an appropriate medium
- A scripted and logical organization to present a focused message

To preview the criteria on which your multimedia presentation may be assessed, see the rubric on page 951.

Common Core State Standards

Writing

1. Write arguments to support claims in an analysis of substantive topics or texts, using valid reasoning and relevant and sufficient evidence.

1.b. Develop claim(s) and counterclaims fairly and thoroughly, supplying the most relevant evidence for each while pointing out the strengths and limitations of both in a manner that anticipates the audience's knowledge level, concerns, values, and possible biases.

6. Use technology, including the Internet, to produce, publish, and update individual or shared writing products in response to ongoing feedback, including new arguments or information.

8. Gather relevant information from multiple authoritative print and digital sources, using advanced searches effectively.

Speaking and Listening

5. Make strategic use of digital media in presentations to enhance understanding of findings, reasoning, and evidence and to add interest.

	Sources of Existing Media	Hardware to Generate New Media	Software to Edit Media
Text	books, magazines, newspapers, Web sites, CD-ROMs, e-mails	keyboard; scanner	word processor; multimedia software
Photographs	books, magazines, newspapers, Web sites, CD-ROMs	digital camera; scanner	photo editing software
Illustrations	books, magazines, newspapers, Web sites, CD-ROMs	keyboard; graphics tablet; scanner	graphics programs
Movies	television, DVDs, videos, Web sites, CD-ROMs	digital video camera	digital editor; animation software
Sound	radio, CDs, Web sites, CD-ROMs	microphone; digital instruments	sound/music editor

Prewriting and Planning

Choosing Your Topic

To choose a subject for your multimedia presentation of an argument, use one of the following strategies:

- **List preferences.** Think about topics and local or global issues that you feel passionate about. What argument would you make to convince others to agree with you? What would your claim be? List your potential topics and choose your favorite.

- **Create a media checklist.** Using a chart like the one shown, list the various types of media that are available for several different topics. Note specific media that would best suit your topic in the left-hand column. Review your chart, and choose the topic that offers the richest possibilities.

Media Checklist	Animal Shelters
☑ Music	Sad or melancholy music
☑ Videos	Cats and dogs in cages
☑ Art	Sketches of cats and dogs
☑ Photographs	People adopting pets
☐ Web Pages	
☑ Interviews	Volunteer at the shelter

Narrowing Your Topic

Find a single example within a broad subject. The general topic you chose is probably too big to be manageable. For example, the topic of animal shelters is too broad to address effectively in an argument. However, volunteering at an animal shelter or adopting a pet is manageable. Be on the lookout for similar slices of a broad subject. Images and sounds can be more difficult to find than text, so continue to research varied material, and make sure you will have enough.

Gathering Materials

Research your topic. As you gather materials, note creative ways to involve viewers. Consult your library for audio or video clips of interviews, documentaries, music, and art resources. Search the Internet for photographs, recordings, cartoons, and archives of periodicals. Keep careful notes about your media sources so you can credit them accurately.

Develop your claim. Review your notes and research materials. Consider the most relevant, authoritative evidence from your research to develop your claim. Which evidence makes your claim the strongest and the most compelling?

Drafting

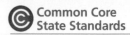

**Common Core
State Standards**

Writing

1.a. Introduce precise, knowledgeable claim(s), establish the significance of the claim(s), distinguish the claim(s) from alternate or opposing claims, and create an organization that logically sequences claim(s), counterclaims, reasons, and evidence.

Shaping Your Presentation

Sketch an outline. Your presentation needs the same solid structure as an argumentative essay or a research paper. Support your claim with a unified approach and a script that details the sequence of ideas. Your final script will orchestrate the presentation of multiple elements—as you draft, though, a breakdown of your presentation's major components will keep you focused and help you avoid oversights.

Opening Image	1
Audio: "Adagio for Strings" by Samuel Barber	
Photo: A sad-looking dog curled up in a blanket	

	2
Audio: (fade music level)	
Photo: Forlorn cat outside	
Narration: Animals need a home and someone to play with them.	

	3
Audio: (increase music level)	
Video: Cats and dogs peering out of their cages	

Plan your delivery. Remember that your delivery will require a script and format that allow you to use two or more different media at the same time. Consider a two- or three-column chart to diagram what will occur at any given moment. Add stage directions to your diagram as you include text, audio, and video. Also note any props or equipment you will need as you present your work.

2.a. Introduce a topic; organize complex ideas, concepts, and information so that each new element builds on that which precedes it to create a unified whole; include formatting, graphics, and multimedia when useful to aiding comprehension.

4. Produce clear and coherent writing in which the development, organization, and style are appropriate to task, purpose, and audience.

Providing Elaboration

Strike a balance. Too many stimuli will confuse viewers. Aim for a targeted interplay between two or three media at any one time. You want the viewer to be able to absorb primary materials along with any secondary elements, such as music. Consult the sample note cards on this page for guidance.

Keep your narration lively. Your text does more than anchor your presentation: it is an important part of the show. Avoid repeating in words what other media are already communicating to the viewer in sounds or visuals. Your writing should sparkle with lively language that presents your claim and evidence in an interesting way.

> **Model: Keep Narration Lively**
>
> Today,   yearn for
> there are millions of dogs and cats that ~~do not have~~ homes (pause for emphasis; cue video)…and someone needs to show compassion for them as they wait for a new home. (Pause as video plays.)

> Livelier words heighten the effect of pauses.

Writers on Writing

Tim O'Brien On Revision

Tim O'Brien is the author of "Ambush" (p. 811).

This is the opening to a novel called *The Things They Carried,* and it introduces the book's central motif: the physical and psychological burdens men carry through a war. I revised these sentences twenty or thirty times, sometimes deleting, sometimes adding bits of action to make the opening vivid and concrete.

I revised these sentences twenty or thirty times . . .

—Tim O'Brien

from *The Things They Carried*

First Lieutenant Jimmy Cross carried letters from a girl named Martha, a junior at Mount Sebastian College in New Jersey. They were not love letters, but Lieutenant Cross was hoping, so kept them folded in plastic at the bottom of his rucksack. In the late afternoon, after a day's march, he would dig his foxhole, wash his hands under a canteen, unwrap the letters, hold them with the tips of his fingers, and spend the last hour of light pretending. He would imagine romantic camping trips into the White Mountains in New Hampshire. He would sometimes taste the envelope flaps, knowing her tongue had been there. More than anything, he wanted Martha to love him as he loved her, but the letters were mostly chatty, elusive on the matter of love.... She was an English Major at Mount Sebastian, and she wrote beautifully about her professors and roommates and midterm exams, about her respect for Chaucer and her great affection for Virginia Woolf. She often quoted lines of poetry; she never mentioned the war, except to say, Jimmy, take care of yourself. The letters weighed 10 ounces. They were signed Love, Martha, but Lieutenant Cross understood that Love was only a way of signing and did not mean what he sometimes pretended it meant.

Instead of writing abstractly about Jimmy's love for Martha, I inserted this line. These actions, I hope, convey a sense of how precious the letters are to Jimmy Cross.

Although Martha isn't physically present in the scene, I wanted to hint at her character. I also wanted to suggest the vast emotional distance between college life and combat, how Jimmy and Martha are living in two different worlds.

By stating the precise weight of the letters, I hoped the reader might realize that some of the heaviest things we carry through life—letters, memories—can weigh almost nothing.

Revising

Revising Your Overall Structure

Improve your sequence. A seamless delivery is the goal of any presentation. Because your presentation may involve apparatus that requires time for setup, be organized. Practice in advance. Make sure that the room you will be using is properly lit and equipped for your presentation.

Peer Review: Hold a test run with a partner.

- Run through your presentation, incorporating all audiovisual elements.
- Ask your partner to comment on parts that lack clarity or seem unpolished.

If necessary, revise the sequence to clarify connections between ideas or to smooth awkward transitions. Consider eliminating elements that are distracting or overly complicated.

Common Core State Standards

Writing

1.c. Use words, phrases, and clauses as well as varied syntax to link the major sections of the text, create cohesion, and clarify the relationships between claim(s) and reasons, between reasons and evidence, and between claim(s) and counterclaims.

1.d. Establish and maintain a formal style and objective tone while attending to the norms and conventions of the discipline in which they are writing.

Speaking and Listening

2. Integrate multiple sources of information presented in diverse formats and media.

Model: Revising for Cohesion and Clarifying Relationships

(cue slide)

~~(cue video)~~ Shelter cats and dogs need to be
       often rely on donations and
groomed, fed, and loved. Many shelters barely
       Still,
survive on strict budgets. they need people to
care for and love the animals.

Video: cats and dogs in shelter cages or kennels

~~**Photo:** a cat outside looking for food~~

Revising Your Selection of Media

Use a variety of effects. By using a variety of media to enhance your narration, you will spice up your presentation and keep your audience's interest. Review your script for overuse of one form of media. If you decide that your presention lacks variation, replace repetitive elements with different media formats.

Without Variety	With Variety
• Audio interview of quarterback • Audio interview of ballerina • Recording of overture to ballet	• Video footage of quarterback • Audio interview of ballerina • Slides of ballet in performance

Developing Your Style

Integrating Media to Support Ideas

Choose different types of media. Your media must be appropriate for your argument. For example, you would render a serious, thoughtful claim or piece of evidence less effective if you introduced silly cartoons and other lighter fare. Use the following chart as you integrate your media.

Media Element	Claim It Expresses or Supports	Is the Idea Clear? (Include Strategy for Clarifying.)
Audio of interview with volunteer	Volunteering at the shelter is rewarding.	Clear
Video of cats and dogs in cages	Homeless cats and dogs are needy and helpless.	This is not very clear. Add a line of narration to explain the connection.
Sad music	Cats and dogs in a shelter are bored and lonely.	The music I selected may not be quiet enough. I need something that suggests dull days.

Find It in Your Reading

Read or review the Student Model on page 950.

1. Locate elements of the presentation that have been properly integrated. Note the ways in which different media work together.

2. In particular, consider how the audio and video work together toward an appropriate effect.

Apply It to Your Writing

Review the script for your multimedia presentation.

1. Evaluate the effect your media choices will have on the viewer. Consider each aspect separately, as well as its use with other media.

2. Circle each audio and video transition, as well as each stage direction, to make sure that all are working together. Look for ways to emphasize your claim, make your evidence convincing, and clearly show the connections to your argument.

3. Experiment with different combinations of images and music. Varying the content or the order might produce unexpectedly effective results. Add transitions as you try several options to improve the flow of your work. Once you have developed your script, confirm your choices by previewing the presentation.

Student Model: Afton Kapala, Ventura, CA

Wanted: Shelter Volunteers

Text	Video and Audio
(cue video and audio) Millions of homeless cats and dogs enter shelters each year across the nation. They are in need of care as they yearn for new homes.	**Video:** shots of cats and dogs in shelter cages or kennels **Audio:** slow melancholy music, somewhat quiet, even boring
According to the American Society for the Prevention of Cruelty to Animals (ASPCA), **(pause for emphasis; cue video)** . . . about half are euthanized each year. **(pause as video plays)**	**Video:** cats and dogs peering out of cages with zooms of their faces
(cue first slide) Shelter cats and dogs need to be groomed, fed, and loved. **(use pointer to highlight the cat searching for food)** Many shelters often rely on donations and barely survive on strict budgets. Still, they need people to care for and love the animals.	**Slide:** a forlorn cat looking for food outside
(cue audio and second slide) At an animal shelter, volunteers provide an essential service. **(cue third slide)** They clean, feed, and care for the animals. **(cue fourth slide)** They play with the animals, which can make the pets more attractive to potential adopters.	**Slide:** collage of photos showing a volunteer caring for a shelter dog (grooming, feeding, etc.) **Slide:** a volunteer using a toy to play with a puppy while a potential adoption family watches
(cue fifth slide) Volunteering at an animal shelter often may not provide a paycheck, but the rewards it brings are countless and last a lifetime. **(cue video)**	**Slide:** a group of teenagers walking together outside of school **Video interview clip with teenage shelter volunteer**
Volunteering at an animal shelter is a community service that will not only serve as a highlight on your resume but can also change your life and the lives of others.	**Video morphs to:** the volunteer handing a shelter cat to its new owner

> The claim has strong visual and audio elements, which fit a multimedia format.

> Afton uses a compelling image to develop his claim and appeal to his audience's values.

> The text, audio, and visual elements clarify the relationships between Afton's claims and reasons in a clear, cohesive way.

> This vivid image helps to support Afton's concluding statement and his argument that volunteering is needed and rewarding.

Editing and Proofreading

Review your script to eliminate errors in grammar, spelling, and punctuation.

Focus on punctuation and spelling. Make sure the text your audience will actually see—and not just hear—demonstrates correct punctuation and spelling.

Focus on sentence fragments. Look for sentence fragments in your text and fix them by adding the missing subjects or verbs.

>   **Fragment:** About half euthanized each year.

>   **Complete Sentence:** About half of that number are euthanized each year.

Spiral Review: Conventions Earlier in this unit you learned about subject-verb agreement (p. 755) and pronoun-antecedent agreement. Check your script to make sure you have used these conventions correctly.

Publishing, Presenting, and Reflecting

Share your multimedia presentation in one of the following ways, and reflect on the writing experience:

Stage a showing. Deliver your multimedia presentation to your class, followed by a question and discussion session.

Create a multimedia portfolio. Join with classmates to create a portfolio of multimedia presentations. Include a multimedia table of contents that uses catchy audio and visual components to summarize each presentation. If possible, post your portfolio to a classroom Web site or blog.

Reflect on your writing. Jot down your thoughts on the experience of creating a multimedia presentation. Answer these questions: What did you learn about focusing your presentation? How has creating a multimedia presentation changed the way you look at media? To what extent does media enhance argumentation?

Rubric for Self-Assessment

Evaluate your multimedia presentation using the following criteria and rating scale, or determine your own reasonable evaluation criteria.

Criteria	Rating Scale
	not very *very*
Purpose/Focus: How clearly do you present your argument?	1 2 3 4
Organization: How logical is the organization of your claim?	1 2 3 4
Development of Ideas/Elaboration: How well do your media elements express and support your claims and evidence?	1 2 3 4
Language: How effective are the words, phrases, and clauses that you use?	1 2 3 4
Conventions: How correct are the grammar, spelling, and punctuation in your presentation materials?	1 2 3 4

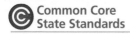

Common Core State Standards

Writing

1.a. Introduce precise, knowledgeable claim(s), establish the significance of the claim(s), distinguish the claim(s) from alternate or opposing claims, and create an organization that logically sequences claim(s), counterclaims, reasons, and evidence.

1.c. Use words, phrases, and clauses as well as varied syntax to link the major sections of the text, create cohesion, and clarify the relationships between claim(s) and reasons, between reasons and evidence, and between claim(s) and counterclaims.

5. Develop and strengthen writing as needed by editing, focusing on addressing what is most significant for a specific purpose and audience.

6. Use technology, including the Internet, to produce, publish, and update individual or shared writing products in response to ongoing feedback, including new arguments or information.

Language

1. Demonstrate command of the conventions of standard English grammar and usage when writing or speaking.

2.b. Spell correctly.

Analyze a Nonprint Political Advertisement

If you have turned on a TV or radio during an election cycle, you have surely observed messages explaining why you should vote for a particular candidate. These are **nonprint political advertisements**—a form of broadcast media designed to shape public opinion about candidates and issues. Airing on television and radio and streaming on the Internet, these ads rely on strong images and powerful language. Because they reach vast audiences, they often exert great influence on the outcomes of elections.

Identify Purpose of Political Advertising

At first glance, political ads might seem purely informational. However, like any ad, their purpose is to sell something—not soap or cars, but an issue or candidate. Political ads create name recognition for a candidate and transmit values to potential voters. These ads fall into two basic categories:

- *Issue-based ads* establish a candidate's position on a particular matter of public concern, such as health care, crime, or taxes.
- *Character-based ads* establish an image of the candidate as a person.

Identify Persuasive Techniques

Makers of nonprint political ads seek to convert viewers whose attitudes toward a candidate are neutral or hostile, as well as to reaffirm the opinions of supporters. To meet these goals, they use a number of visual and sound techniques to produce particular images of candidates.

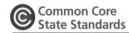

Common Core State Standards

Speaking and Listening
1. Initiate and participate effectively in a range of collaborative discussions with diverse partners on *grades 11–12 topics, texts, and issues,* building on others' ideas and expressing their own clearly and persuasively.

Language
1. Demonstrate command of the conventions of standard English grammar and usage when speaking. *(p. 953)*

Technique	Description	Effect
Editing	Arranging the sequence of images and sounds into a final product	An ad showing a candidate visiting young patients in a hospital with background music sung by children suggests that the candidate cares about children's health.
Camera Angles	Directions from which a camera operator shoots images	A high-angle shot can make a tall candidate look smaller and less imposing.
Camera Shots	The way in which the camera frames the subject; shot types include close-ups and long shots	A shot from the waist up allows the viewer to feel connected with the candidate.
Symbols	The association of a candidate with symbols that have positive associations	A candidate's ad including images of the American flag implies that he or she is patriotic.

Negative Techniques

Some political ads may use **propaganda,** or biased content, to damage an opponent's credibility or image. Such ads may also rely on **logical fallacies,** which are arguments that sound convincing at first but are based on faulty reasoning. Logical fallacies that may appear in political ads include the following:

- **Mud-slinging or *Ad Hominem* Attacks:** These criticize an opponent's character rather than addressing flaws in positions on issues.
- **Wrong or Incomplete Facts:** Hostile ads sometimes intentionally misrepresent candidates' positions or present only part of a story.
- **Generalizations:** Ads may include unfairly simplified descriptions of an opponent or his or her opinions.

As a citizen, it is your responsibility to understand how political messages are shaped and to determine the reliability of the claims they present.

Activities: Analyze Political Advertisements

Comprehension and Collaboration For both activities, use an evaluation form like the one shown below.

A. Watch a political ad on TV or the Internet and analyze the techniques the ad uses to sway viewers.

B. Research a national election from the past and the effect of advertising on the outcome. Locate an ad used in the campaign. (Organizations such as the American Museum of the Moving Image maintain archives of ads.) Watch the ad and evaluate it using the form shown here. Write a summary of your findings to share in a class discussion. Use the conventions of standard English in your summary.

Evaluation Form for a Political Ad

This ad was produced for _____
(name of candidate)

What type of voter is this ad targeting? ❏ *sympathetic* ❏ *undecided* ❏ *hostile*
Explain. _____

Identify the techniques used to convey the ad's message. Explain how each is used.
Visual and Sound Techniques: _____
Negative Techniques: _____

Are the claims made about the candidate truthful? (Check other sources if necessary.) _____

Would this ad help someone who wants to be informed about this candidate? Explain. _____

Etymology: Scientific, Medical, and Mathematical Terms

The European Renaissance saw renewed interest in the sciences and mathematics. English scholars turned to the works of the ancient Greeks, Romans, and Arabs to learn more about these subjects. As a result, many Greek and Latin words related to these fields entered the English language. The chart below lists some word parts from Greek, Latin, and Anglo-Saxon often used in scientific, medical, and mathematical matters. Understanding these word parts will help you decode the meanings of unfamiliar terms.

Prefixes	Roots	Suffixes
bi- (Latin): two *cardio-* (Greek): heart *centi-* (Latin): one-hundredth part; one hundred *micro-* (Greek): small *mono-* (Greek): single, one *pan-* (Greek): all *poly-* (Greek): many *psycho-* (Greek): mind	*-gno-* (Greek): know *-gon-* (Greek): angle *-oculus-* (Latin): eye *-path-* (Greek): feeling; disease; suffering *-ped-* (Latin): foot *-phon-* (Greek): sound; voice; speech	*-ar* (Latin): resembling *-graph* (Greek): something written or drawn *-iatry* (Greek): medical treatment *-ist* (Greek): one who specializes *-logy* (Greek): science, theory, study *-scope* (Greek): instrument for viewing *-teen* (Anglo-Saxon): ten

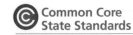

Common Core State Standards

Language

4.c. Consult general and specialized reference materials, both print and digital, to find the etymology of a word.

6. Acquire and use accurately general academic and domain-specific words and phrases, sufficient for reading, writing, speaking, and listening at the college and career readiness level; demonstrate independence in gathering vocabulary knowledge when considering a word important to comprehension or expression.

Practice

Directions: Choose the letter of the word that best fits each numbered definition. Explain your choice with reference to the chart above.

1. identification of a disease   a. psychologist   b. diagnosis
2. eye specialist   a. oculist   b. monocle
3. record of heart activity   a. seismograph   b. cardiograph
4. epidemic affecting a large area   a. pandemic   b. empathy
5. creature with two feet   a. biped   b. centipede
6. study of disease   a. biology   b. pathology
7. figure with many angles   a. polygon   b. polygraph
8. instrument for viewing small objects   a. microphone   b. microscope
9. treatment of mental disorders   a. prognosis   b. psychiatry

Directions: Use a dictionary to locate as many English words as you can that contain the following word parts: **(a)** Latin prefix *centi-*; **(b)** Latin word root *-ped-*; **(c)** Greek suffix *-scope*.

Vocabulary Acquisition and Use: Sentence Completions

Sentence Completion questions appear in most standardized tests. Sentence Completions test your vocabulary skills, as well as your ability to identify word/phrase relationships. In these types of questions you are given sentences with one or more missing words. Your task is to choose the correct word or words to complete each sentence logically.

Use this strategy to improve your results: **1.** Read the whole sentence, looking for signal words that suggest an attitude or emotion. **2.** Determine if the missing word will be positive or negative. **3.** Scan the answer choices for the ones that meet your criteria. Delete the ones that do not fit, and test the others in the sentence.

Practice

This exercise is modeled after the Sentence Completion exercises that appear in the Critical Reading section of the SAT.

Directions: Each of the following sentences is missing one or two words. Choose the word or set of words that best completes each sentence.

> **Test-Taking Tip**
> For sentences with two missing words, if one word in an answer choice does not fit, reject that choice.

1. The dire poverty and dislocation the dust storms caused created many __?__ scenes that moved readers of the photo magazines.
   A. poignant
   B. passionate
   C. mundane
   D. fortuitous
   E. obtuse

2. The migration of farmers from Oklahoma to California filled refugee camps with __?__ tents of starving, impoverished, and desperate people.
   A. insatiable
   B. palpable
   C. derivative
   D. voluminous
   E. detached

3. Many politicians blamed the farmers for poor land management, feeling they __?__ what they __?__ when they failed to rest fields between crops.
   A. disgraced . . . bequeathed
   B. reaped . . . sowed
   C. resigned . . . irrigated
   D. circumvented . . . extricated
   E. beguiled . . . endured

4. Black blizzards, as dust storms were called, brought __?__ destruction of farmlands, causing __?__ reactions from those who survived.
   A. sensible . . . preposterous
   B. virulent . . . inextricable
   C. despondent . . . indignant
   D. cunning . . . poised
   E. wanton . . . rueful

From Text to Understanding

You have studied each part of Unit 4 as a set of connected texts. In this workshop, you will have the chance to further explore the fundamental connections among these texts and to deepen your essential understanding of the literature and its social and historical context.

PART 1: Facing Troubled Times

Writing: Argumentative Essay As the Victorian era gave way to the modern world in the early twentieth century, values, art, and even global events began to change. Artists, inspired by changes in society, began to break the boundaries of form and content, which in turn contributed to further shifts in attitudes and behavior. Review the texts, especially F. Scott Fitzgerald's Anchor Text, "Winter Dreams," keeping in mind what each might tell us about social change.

Assignment: Develop a claim that addresses the social status of Dexter Green and Judy Jones in Fitzgerald's "Winter Dreams." Consider the perceived differences between wealth that comes from an individual's success and wealth that is inherited. What sort of impact did awareness of such differences have on the American experience? Consult other texts and background information in Part 1 to support and expand your claim.

> **Example:** America was built on the idea that people are free to make choices that hopefully lead to happiness and fulfillment. In the lives of characters in F. Scott Fitzgerald's "Winter Dreams," however, this concept takes on the taint of superficial striving and leads to disillusionment.

Identify character traits. Use a simple note-taking system like the one shown to identify character traits that can be considered "American."

Structure your essay. Explain your view of what defined social class as part of the American experience at the beginning of the twentieth century. Then identify and analyze characters as an expression of or departure from that view.

Demonstrate your familiarity. As you write, demonstrate your familiarity with the Anchor Text and any other works you engage. For example, identify literary elements that might reflect the nation's new Modernist outlook. Explain characters that might be used as metaphors for American ideals.

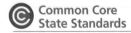

Common Core State Standards

Writing
1. Write arguments to support claims in an analysis of substantive topics or texts, using valid reasoning and relevant and sufficient evidence.

2. Write informative/explanatory texts to examine and convey complex ideas, concepts, and information clearly and accurately through the effective selection, organization, and analysis of content.

Speaking and Listening
4. Present information, findings, and supporting evidence, conveying a clear and distinct perspective, such that listeners can follow the line of reasoning, alternative or opposing perspectives are addressed, and the organization, development, substance, and style are appropriate to purpose, audience, and a range of formal and informal tasks.

Character Traits

"Winter Dreams":
Dexter Green: works hard, rises to higher social status; strives for better things but is often superficial

Judy Jones: beautiful; an unattainable ideal rather than a real person

---

PART 2: From Every Corner of the Land

Research: Magazine Articles Isolation was an undercurrent of American society and art in the early twentieth century. Review the background materials and selections in Part 2, considering how the forces of society and culture often sever people from a sense of belonging. Consider in particular, the Anchor Text—Ernest Hemingway's "In Another Country and the isolation caused by the pain of war.

Assignment: Working in a small group, design and create a series of magazine articles that examine the idea of isolation in early twentieth-century America. Each person should first choose a selection from Part 2 and think about the lack of social connection apparent in the text. Conduct research on the historical context of the text's setting—e.g. World War I, or the Great Depression—to help explain the factors that kept people from connecting with each other.

Include illustrations or photographs with each article, and model the layout on magazine pieces you have seen. Combine your group's articles into a magazine to share with the class.

PART 3: The Harlem Renaissance

Listening and Speaking: Oral Interpretation The writers of the Harlem Renaissance helped forge an artistic community that embraced a variety of styles but a singular purpose, to create art borne of their own experiences and culture.

Review the selections in Part 3, especially the Anchor Text, the excerpt from Zora Neale Hurston's autobiography, "Dust Tracks on a Road." Through their artistic expression, these writers create a cultural identity and define their own history.

Assignment: Listen as these writers speak for themselves. Select and read aloud an excerpt of Hurston's autobiography or one of the poems of a Harlem Renaissance writer. Include an introduction explaining why you chose the work, and conclude with a comment about why the work still matters. To prepare, read the selection aloud to become comfortable with speaking rate, volume, and enunciation. Encourage your audience to ask questions after your presentation.

Notes for Introduction:
Date selection was written/published: _____
Why I chose the selection: _____
What is powerful about the selection: _____
Impact of selection on literature and culture: _____

Notes for Conclusion:
Ideas from selection that are important today: _____
Feelings expressed in selection that are relevant today: _____

Production Checklist:

☐ **Thesis.** Include a clear statement of topic.

☐ **Title.** Create a concise, engaging title that captures the reader's attention.

☐ **Illustrations/Photographs.** Choose images that add meaning to your text.

☐ **Typeface.** Choose a typeface that is easy to read and does not distract the reader from your ideas.

☐ **Sources.** Include a list of sources at the end of your article.

Test-Taking Practice

Critical Reading Test: Long Reading Passage

Some critical reading tests present **long passages** that require extended concentration. Passages can be as long as 850 words and can present narrative, persuasive, and expository modes. You should spend more time answering the questions than reading the passage. This requires you to read purposefully to cover the material. If necessary, you can reread later for details.

 Common Core
State Standards

RL.11-12.1, RL.11-12.2, RL.11-12.3, RL.11-12.4, RL.11-12.5; L.11-12.1, L.11-12.2, L.11-12.4.a, L.11-12.5.b
[For the full wording of the standards, see the standards chart in the front of your textbook.]

Practice

The following exercise is modeled after the SAT Critical Reading section.

Directions: Read the following passage, taken from "Winter Dreams" by F. Scott Fitzgerald. Then, choose the best answer to each question.

He made money. It was rather amazing. After college he went to the city from which Black Bear Lake draws its wealthy patrons. When he was only twenty-three and had been there not quite two years, there were already people who liked to say: "Now *there's* a boy—" All about
5   him rich men's sons were peddling bonds precariously, or investing patrimonies precariously, or plodding through the two dozen volumes of the "George Washington Commercial Course," but Dexter borrowed a thousand dollars on his college degree and his confident mouth, and bought a partnership in a laundry.
10   It was a small laundry when he went into it, but Dexter made a specialty of learning how the English washed fine woolen golf stockings without shrinking them, and within a year he was catering to the trade that wore knickerbockers. Men were insisting that their Shetland hose and sweaters go to his laundry, just as they had insisted on a caddy who
15   could find golf balls. A little later he was doing their wives' lingerie as well—and running five branches in different parts of the city. Before he was twenty-seven he owned the largest string of laundries in his section of the country. It was then that he sold out and went to New York. But the part of this story that concerns us goes back to the days when he
20   was making his first big success.

Strategy

The content of a paragraph as a whole can be inferred from the first and last sentences.

- **First Sentence:** usually states the main idea of the paragraph

- **Last Sentence:** usually summarizes the major points of the paragraph and restates the main idea

- Scanning first and last sentences will help you identify paragraphs with information you need to answer given questions.

1. Which detail does the author include to show that Dexter was not like other men his age?
   A. investing money their fathers gave them
   B. borrowing money to start a business
   C. selling bonds in a dangerous manner
   D. reading books to learn how to make money
   E. returning to Black Bear Lake

2. One can infer from the mention of golfers wanting a caddy who could find golf balls that
   A. Dexter hired caddies who could find his lost golf balls.
   B. Dexter also could find lost golf balls when he wasn't at work.
   C. they frequently lost golf balls and needed a caddy to find them.
   D. they also wanted a laundry that washed their socks correctly.
   E. they wanted a laundry that could only wash socks and sweaters.

3. In line 5, the word *precariously* means
   A. dangerously
   B. aggressively
   C. illegally
   D. with a careful plan
   E. by instinct

4. What does the author suggest about the way men see Dexter in the mention from line 10, "A little later he was doing their wives' lingerie as well . . ."?
   A. Men thought that Dexter was their social equal.
   B. Men thought that he charged a low price for work.
   C. Men were embarrassed to discuss these matters.
   D. Dexter knew a great deal about women.
   E. Dexter had gained their trust.

5. What does the first sentence of the second paragraph convey to readers?
   A. It shows that Dexter got lucky in business.
   B. It tells the reader how to create a successful business.
   C. It defines the steps Dexter took in business.
   D. It explains how this information relates to his first success.
   E. It explains how he eventually owned five laundries.

6. Which excerpt from the passage best expresses the main idea of the passage?
   A. It was then that he sold out and went to New York.
   B. He made money. It was rather amazing.
   C. But the part of this story that concerns us goes back to the days when he was making his first big success.
   D. After college he went to the city from which Black Bear Lake draws its wealthy patrons.
   E. Men were insisting that their Shetland hose and sweaters go to his laundry.

7. What details about Dexter would the reader know from this passage?
   A. his age
   B. his size
   C. his background
   D. his beliefs
   E. his politics

8. What does the author infer about Dexter by mentioning "his confident mouth" in line 8?
   A. He talked his way through college to get ahead.
   B. He learned how to launder stockings a special way.
   C. He was a great salesman for a variety of products.
   D. He convinced people to lend him money.
   E. He did not doubt what other people said to him.

GO ON

Grammar and Writing: Improving Sentences

Improving sentences exercises often appear in the writing sections of standardized tests. The test items show five different versions of a sentence. Your job is to choose the most effective version. This type of exercise tests your ability to recognize and correct flaws in grammar, usage, and sentence structure.

Practice

This exercise is modeled after the Improving Sentences portion of the SAT Writing section. The full test has 25 such questions.

Directions: Part or all of each of the following sentences is underlined; beneath each sentence are five ways of phrasing the underlined portion. Choice A will always be the same as the original wording; B–E are different options. If you consider the original sentence to be the most effective sentence, select choice A; otherwise, select one of the other choices.

1. Many elderly town residents are entitled to property tax benefits <u>that you might consider</u> enviable.
   A. that you might consider
   B. that she might consider
   C. that he or she might consider
   D. which he or she might consider
   E. which you might consider

2. Faulkner and Hemingway were contemporaries, yet <u>while he won his Nobel Prize in 1950 he would not win</u> this prize for four more years.
   A. while he won his Nobel Prize in 1950 he would not win
   B. while he won his Nobel Prize in 1950 Hemingway would not win
   C. while Faulkner won his Nobel Prize in 1950, Hemingway would not win
   D. while Faulkner won his Nobel Prize in 1950 he would not win
   E. while they won a Nobel Prize in 1950 Hemingway would not win

3. Readers have long wondered about the basis for Faulkner's characters like Miss Grierson <u>because it is so real it had</u> to exist in his hometown.
   A. because it is so real it had
   B. because she is so real it had
   C. because she is so real they had
   D. because they are so real they had
   E. because it is so real they had

Strategy

Pinpoint the Confusion:
The majority of the sentence is correct and the error has to exist in the underlined portion. Usually one word or phrase is wrong while the rest may be misleading.

4. The men spread lime in the basement, <u>because they were doing their civic duty</u>.
   A. because they were doing their civic duty
   B. because it was its civic duty
   C. because he was doing their civic duty
   D. because they were doing our civic duty
   E. because he were doing his civic duty

5. Many elderly people hire an aide to help <u>them or else you would not be able</u> to manage.
   A. them or else you would not be able
   B. them or else they would not be able
   C. them or else she would not be able
   D. her or else she would not be able
   E. him or else it would not be able

6. Miss Emily, like Old Lady Wyatt, lived alone, so <u>when she died two younger cousins buried them</u>.
   A. when she died two younger cousins buried them
   B. when she died their young cousins buried her
   C. when Emily died two younger cousins buried them
   D. when it died two younger cousins buried of them
   E. when she died two younger cousins buried her

7. The druggist sold arsenic to <u>his customers, which you considered</u> dangerous.
   A. his customers, which you considered
   B. her customers, which he considered
   C. his customers, which he considered
   D. their customers, which they considered
   E. its customers, which it considered

8. The servant allowed the cousins into the house yet <u>they were upset by what they found</u> inside.
   A. they were upset by what they found
   B. he was upset by what they found
   C. they was upset by what they found
   D. they were upset by what he found
   E. they were upset by what they finds

9. <u>I love the short story form, although they are</u> often very intense and even eerie.
   A. I love the short story form, although they are
   B. I love the short story form, although it is
   C. You love the short story form, although you are
   D. I love the short story form, although characters are
   E. They love the short story form, although it are

 Timed Writing: Position Statement [25 minutes]

In his Nobel Prize acceptance speech of 1950, delivered at a time of world tension and fear, William Faulkner said, "I believe that man will not merely endure: he will prevail . . . because he has a soul, a spirit capable of compassion and sacrifice and endurance."

Would Faulkner express the same confident belief in humanity's future if he were to give his acceptance speech today? Write an essay in which you develop a point of view on this issue. Support your opinion with reasoning and evidence, and examples drawn either from your reading or experience. This assignment is similar to the Essay portion of the SAT Writing section.

> **Academic Vocabulary**
>
> To persuade your reader, you need to provide more than your **opinion**, or personal belief. Provide convincing **evidence** that supports your opinion.

Constructed Response

Follow the instructions to complete the tasks below as required by your teacher. As you work on each task, incorporate both general academic vocabulary and literary terms you learned in this unit.

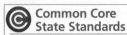

Common Core State Standards

RL.11-12.2, RL.11-12.3, RL.11-12.4, RL.11-12.5, RL.11-12.6, RI.11-12.6; W.11-12.2, W.11-12.5, W.11-12.9.a; SL.11-12.1, SL.11-12.2, SL.11-12.4, SL.11-12.6
[For the full wording of the standards, see the chart in the front of your textbook.]

Writing

Task 1: Literature [RL.11-12.2; W.11-12.2]
Analyze Development of Theme

*Write an **essay** in which you analyze the development of two themes in a work of literature from this unit.*

- Choose a literary work that clearly presents two themes.

- Introduce your essay with an objective summary of the work. Then, identify the two themes you will analyze.

- Identify whether the themes are implied or stated directly. If a theme is stated directly, indicate where this occurs in the text. If it is implied, describe how you inferred the theme based on imagery, events, dialogue, or the actions or interactions of characters in the work.

- Explain how each theme is developed over the course of the story.

- Analyze how the two themes are interconnected. How does this interaction of themes add depth and meaning to the story?

Task 2: Literature [RL.11-12.4; W.11-12.5]
Analyze the Impact of Word Choice

*Write an **essay** in which you analyze the impact of word choice in a poem from this unit.*

- Choose a poem from this unit that contains language that is fresh, engaging, or beautiful. Provide examples that show these qualities.

- Identify words and phrases that have interesting connotations. Interpret the meanings of these words and phrases as they are used in the poem.

- Identify figurative language in the poem. Name the specific type of language used, such as simile,

metaphor, or personification. Then, describe the impact of each use of figurative language on the overall meaning and tone of the poem.

- Finally, evaluate whether the poet's use of word choice was successful by giving your overall impression of the language in the work.

- When you are finished drafting your essay, review your work in order to strengthen the points that you think are most significant for your audience.

Task 3: Literature [RL.11-12.5; W.11-12.2, W.11-12.9.a]
Analyze Text Structure

*Write an **essay** in which you analyze how an author's choice of a particular structure adds to the overall meaning and impact of a story in this unit.*

- Choose a story from this unit that has a structure you find interesting. Explain your choice.

- Discuss the overall meaning of the story you have chosen. Explain how the story's structure supports this meaning.

- Analyze the author's choices concerning how to structure specific parts of the story. For example, where did the author choose to begin or end the story? What type of ending did the author choose and what was the impact of that decision?

- Explain how the author's choices concerning structure add to the meaning of the story. Consider how these choices create aesthetic effects, such as humor, horror, or beauty.

- Make sure to state your position clearly at the beginning of your essay in a thesis statement. Support your thesis with examples from the story and provide a concluding statement that follows naturally from the evidence you have provided.

Speaking and Listening

Task 4: Literature [RL.11-12.6; SL.11-12.6]
Analyze Point of View

*Deliver an **oral presentation** in which you analyze a work from this unit that uses satire, sarcasm, irony, or understatement to express point of view.*

- Choose a work that includes satire, sarcasm, irony, or understatement.
- Briefly summarize the work to begin your presentation. Explain how the writer uses the literary techniques of satire, sarcasm, irony, or understatement to express a particular perspective on a topic.
- Distinguish what is directly stated in the text from what is really meant. For example, if you are pointing out understatement, you might show how the writer deliberately shows a situation as better or worse than it actually is.
- Explain the underlying meaning or message the writer is attempting to convey through the use of satire, sarcasm, irony, or understatement.
- Rehearse your presentation and adapt word choice as needed to convey your intended tone.

Task 5: Literature [RL.11-12.3; SL.11-12.6]
Analyze Characterization in a Story

*Deliver an **analysis** of the impact of author's choices regarding characterization in a story from this unit.*

- Choose a story from this unit with interesting characters, and summarize it.
- Describe the individual characters in the story by identifying their main personality traits.
- Categorize the story's characters as either flat or round, and explain how you made this determination.
- Explain how the author uses direct or indirect characterization, or both, to establish character traits. Draw attention to story elements such as dialogue, plot events, and setting when discussing indirect characterization.
- Finally, describe how certain characters grow or change during the course of the story, and analyze which story elements help produce this change.
- As you present your analysis, be sure to use formal English and an appropriate tone.

Task 6: Literature/Informational Text [RL.11-12.4; RI.11-12.6; SL.11-12.1, SL.11-12.2]
Analyze Authors' Styles

Participate in a discussion group in which you compare and contrast authors' styles in a work of fiction and a work of nonfiction from this unit.

- Choose two works from this unit that provide interesting points to compare and contrast.
- Analyze the various elements that make up the author's style in each of the works. These include word choice, sentence structure, and tone.
- In your discussion, indicate specific examples from each of the texts to support your analysis of the author's style.
- Compare and contrast the two authors' styles by explaining how they create similar or different tones through the use of such devices as figurative language, humorous anecdotes, and lengthy sentences.
- Evaluate which author's style is more effective in achieving its purpose and producing an effect on the reader.
- Allow each person to state his or her view and support that view with evidence. Acknowledge new information by trying to connect it to earlier points or by modifying the group's position.
- Appoint a spokesperson from the group to present your findings to the rest of the class.

THE ESSENTIAL ? How does literature shape or reflect society?

The Modern Reader Modern writers, such as T. S. Eliot and William Faulkner, introduced new levels of innovation and experimentation into American literature. They presented new challenges for readers in their works, expecting more from their readers than did authors of previous eras.

Assignment Choose one Modernist work and one traditional work from this unit. Write a **comparison-and-contrast essay** about the challenges each work presents and the assumptions you feel each author makes about his or her readers.

Titles for Extended Reading

In this unit, you have read a variety of literature of the Modern Age. Continue to read works related to this era on your own. Select books that you enjoy, but challenge yourself to explore new topics, new authors, and works offering varied perspectives or approaches. The titles suggested below will help you get started.

LITERATURE

As I Lay Dying
William Faulkner

Modern Library, 2000   EXEMPLAR TEXT

 Novel This influential novel, told from the perspective of fifteen different narrators, is the story of the death of the matriarch of a poor Southern family and her family's journey to bury her.

[A short story and a speech by Faulkner begin on page 816 of this book. Build knowledge by reading a novel by this author.]

The Great Gatsby
F. Scott Fitzgerald

Scribner, 2004   EXEMPLAR TEXT

 Novel This tragic tale of grand dreams and ruined lives explores self-made millionaire Jay Gatsby's quest to win the love of the wealthy, beautiful—and married—Daisy Buchanan.

[Fitzgerald's short story "Winter Dreams" appears on page 730 of this book. Build knowledge by reading a novel by this author.]

A Farewell to Arms
Ernest Hemingway

Scribner, 1995   EXEMPLAR TEXT

 Novel This story of an American soldier and a British nurse in Italy during World War I is based largely on Hemingway's own experiences as an ambulance driver in the war. The story describes love and loss and the horror of war.

[Hemingway's short story "In Another Country" appears on page 800 of this book. Build knowledge by reading a novel by this author.]

The Complete Poems of Robert Frost
Robert Frost

Henry Holt and Company, 1969   EXEMPLAR TEXT

 Poetry All of poet laureate Robert Frost's books of poetry are collected in this one volume. Among the poems included is "Mending Wall."

[Seven of Frost's poems appear on pages 874–885 of this book. Build knowledge by reading the complete poems of this poet.]

INFORMATIONAL TEXTS

Historical Texts

Dust Tracks on a Road
Zora Neale Hurston

Harper Perennial Modern Classic, 2010

 Autobiography Hurston's autobiography tells the story of her childhood in the South and her rise to literary fame as a star of the Harlem Renaissance.

[An excerpt from Dust Tracks on a Road appears on page 930 of this book. Build knowledge by reading the full text.]

Contemporary Scholarship

The First World War
John Keegan

Vintage, 2000

 History Using diaries, letters, and action reports, historian John Keegan vividly describes the soldiers, leaders, and battles of what he believes was a tragic, preventable war.

Hard Times: An Oral History of the Great Depression
Studs Terkel

New Press, 2000

 Oral History For *Hard Times*, author Studs Terkel interviewed hundreds of people across America. Their stories describe in vivid detail what it was like to live in this difficult time.

The Reader's Companion to American History
edited by Eric Foner and John A. Garraty

Houghton Mifflin, 1991

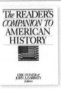 **Encyclopedia** This "readers' encyclopedia" contains almost 1,000 engaging articles about important events, people, and trends in American history. Included in the volume is Ellen Condliffe Lagemann's article "Education."

Preparing to Read Complex Texts

Reading for College and Career In both college and the workplace, readers must analyze texts independently, draw connections among works that offer varied perspectives, and develop their own ideas and informed opinions. The questions shown below, and others that you generate on your own, will help you more effectively read and analyze complex college-level texts.

**Common Core
State Standards**

**Reading Literature/Informational Text
10.** By the end of grade 11, read and comprehend literature, including stories, dramas, and poems, and literary nonfiction, in the grades 11-CCR text complexity band proficiently, with scaffolding as needed at the high end of the range.

When reading complex texts, ask yourself...

- What idea, experience, or story seems to have compelled the author to write? Has the author presented that idea, experience, or story in a way that I, too, find compelling?

- How might the author's era, social status, belief system, or personal experiences have affected the point of view he or she expresses in the text?

- How do my circumstances affect what I understand and feel about this text?

- What key idea does the author state explicitly? What key idea does he or she suggest or imply? Which details in the text help me to perceive implied ideas?

- Do I find multiple layers of meaning in the text? If so, what relationships do I see among these layers of meaning?

- How do details in the text connect or relate to one another? Do I find any details unconvincing, unrelated, or out of place?

- Do I find the text believable and convincing?

**Key Ideas
and Details**

- What patterns of organization or sequences do I find in the text? Do these patterns help me understand the ideas better?

- What do I notice about the author's style, including his or her diction, use of imagery and figurative language, and syntax?

- Do I like the author's style? Is the author's style memorable?

- What emotional attitude does the author express toward the topic, the story, or the characters? Does this attitude seem appropriate?

- What emotional attitude does the author express toward me, the reader? Does this attitude seem appropriate?

- What do I notice about the author's voice—his or her personality on the page? Do I like this voice? Does it make me want to read on?

**Craft and
Structure**

- Is the work fresh and original?

- Do I agree with the author's ideas entirely, or are there elements I find unconvincing?

- Do I disagree with the author's ideas entirely, or are there elements I can accept as true?

- Based on my knowledge of American literature, history, and culture, does this work reflect the American tradition? Why or why not?

**Integration
of Ideas**

Prosperity and Protest

Literature of the Post-War Era

1945–1970

Unit 5

"Sometimes I can see the future stretched out in front of me—just as plain as day. The future hanging over there at the edge of my days. Just waiting for me."

—Lorraine Hansberry

CLOSE READING TOOL

Use this tool to practice the close reading strategies you learn.

ONLINE WRITER'S NOTEBOOK

Easily capture notes and complete assignments online.

STUDENT eTEXT

Bring learning to life with audio, video, and interactive tools.

■ Find all Digital Resources at **pearsonrealize.com**.

Snapshot of the Period

The 1950s began with a booming consumer economy, the birth of American car culture, and the rise of suburbia as a new lifestyle norm. By the end of the decade, this apparent stability showed signs of strain. In 1957, the Soviet Union, America's cold-war opponent, launched the first earth-orbiting satellite and the United States entered the "Space Race" in dire earnestness. Unrest in the nation over Civil Rights issues led to protests— some organized and peaceful, some violent. The war in Vietnam, begun in 1954, did not end until 1975. It became a focal point of political and generational conflict. A period that began with complacency, ended with a spirit of revolution and the sense of a new age dawning.

A human footprint on the moon and *TIME* magazine's cover featuring Soviet cosmonaut Yuri Gagarin are two indelible images of the space race. ▶

O'Connor

Plath

Baldwin

Bishop

King

Miller

THE ESSENTIAL **?**

As you read the selections in this unit, you will be asked to think about them in view of three key questions:

How does literature shape or reflect *society?*

What makes American literature *American?*

What is the relationship between literature and *place?*

RIDING FOR FREEDOM

In 1961, a historic moment in the Civil Rights movement took place when a group of Freedom Riders challenged segregation codes in buses and bus terminals. They rode in integrated buses from Washington, D.C., to New Orleans. Along the way, buses were firebombed, riders were beaten, and finally Federal Marshals were called in.

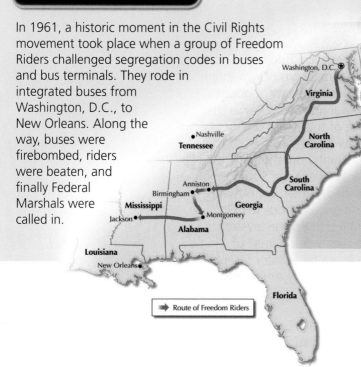

Route of Freedom Riders

Integration of Knowledge and Ideas What does the information contained in the map and graph, and expressed in the images on this page, suggest about political and social unrest during the mid-twentieth century? **[Synthesize]**

Buttons of the Era

A dove held by white and black hands symbolized racial harmony and world peace.

A march that took place in Jackson, Mississippi, was named for Civil Rights figure James Meredith.

President Kennedy dreamed of an international army of peace workers. This dream led to the creation of the Peace Corps.

The peace movement, lead by Hippies, used flowers as symbols for an alternative to war.

Many Americans believed in the Vietnam War and sought to support the troops overseas.

As the Vietnam War dragged on and more Americans died, support waned.

Vietnam War Approval Rates (1965–1971)

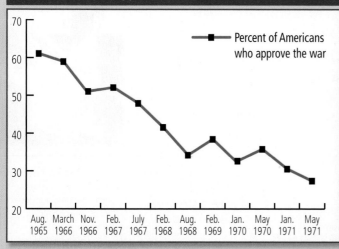

Percent of Americans who approve the war

Source: The Gallup Poll

Historical Background

The Post-War Era (1945–1970)

The United States emerged from World War II as the most powerful nation on Earth. Proud of their role in the Allied victory, Americans now wanted life to return to normal. Soldiers came home, rationing of scarce goods ended, and the nation prospered. Despite post-war jubilation, however, the dawn of the nuclear age and the dominance of the Soviet Union throughout Eastern Europe meant enormous new challenges.

In 1945, the United Nations was created amid high hopes that it would prevent future wars. Nonetheless, the Cold War between the Soviet Union and the West began as soon as World War II ended. Armed conflict arose in 1950 when President Harry S. Truman sent American troops to help anticommunist South Korean forces turn back a North Korean invasion. Within our borders, fear of communism fueled the "witch hunts" of the 1950s, unleashing investigations and accusations by Senator Joseph McCarthy that ruined the careers and reputations of many Americans.

The Complacent Fifties

Americans of the 1950s are sometimes called "the Silent Generation." Many of them had lived through both the Great Depression and World War II, and they were tired to the bone of sacrifice and conflict. When peace finally arrived, they were glad to adopt quiet ways of living. They wanted to stay at home, raise their families, and enjoy being consumers. They wanted to keep life the way it was for a while.

But the march of technology made complacency impossible. In October 1957, the Soviet Union launched Sputnik, the first artificial satellite to orbit Earth. The Space Age had begun, and the Soviet triumph spurred calls for changes in American education, especially in science and math. President John F. Kennedy, elected in 1960, promised to "get the nation moving again," and he set in motion an intense national effort to land an American on the moon.

TIMELINE

1945: The United Nations Charter is signed in San Francisco, California.

1945: The United States drops atomic bombs on Hiroshima and Nagasaki.

1947: Tennessee Williams's *A Streetcar Named Desire* premiers. ▶

1945

◀ **1945:** World War II ends as Germany and Japan surrender to Allies.

1947: The Cold War between the United States and the Soviet Union begins.

1947: India/Pakistan India and Pakistan granted independence from Great Britain.

968 Prosperity and Protest (1945–1970)

The Turbulent Sixties

The assassination of President Kennedy in 1963 was a deeply felt national tragedy. After the assassination came an escalating and increasingly unpopular war in Vietnam. Waves of protest disrupted the country's complacency. Gone were the calm of the 1950s and the high hopes of Kennedy's brief administration. In their place came idealistic but strident demands for an end to the war, progress on civil rights, and greater relevance in education. It was a time of crisis and confrontation, but it also brought genuine progress.

Lasting gains were made in civil rights during these years. In 1954, the Supreme Court had outlawed segregation in public schools, and the Sixties witnessed the continuing battle for racial equality. Tragedy struck again in 1968, however, when civil rights leader Martin Luther King, Jr., was assassinated. Riots broke out in many cities across the nation.

Culture and Counterculture

Through the Fifties and Sixties, television continued to spearhead a revolution in mass communication. By 1960, millions of Americans owned televisions, and masses of people shared common electronic experiences of news, entertainment, and advertising. At the same time, groups of Americans sought lifestyles that opposed the prevailing culture. In music, art, literature, occupations, speech, and dress, these Americans resisted the sameness and anonymity that seemed to be consuming the nation's personality.

Key Historical Theme: Recovery and Rebellion

- During the Fifties, many Americans who had lived through the Great Depression and World War II craved normalcy.
- During the Sixties, many Americans protested against the Vietnam War, racial injustice, and social conformity.

1948: Israel United Nations establishes state of Israel.

1949: The North Atlantic Treaty Organization (NATO) is founded to provide security for its member nations. ▶

1950

1948: Germany Soviet Union blockades Allied sectors of Berlin.

◀ **1949:** *Death of a Salesman* by Arthur Miller is produced.

Essential Questions Across Time

The Post-War Era (1945–1970)

How does literature shape or reflect *society?*

What social and political events affected Americans in the quarter-century after World War II?

The Holocaust and the Atomic Bomb As the war ended, concentration camps were liberated and journalists reported, in shocking words and images, the horrific facts of the Holocaust. In addition, the reality of the atomic bomb gave people all over the world a new fear and a new responsibility for managing international conflict.

Wars, Both Cold and Hot With the rise of the Soviet Union, the Cold War—competition between Eastern bloc countries and the West— became intense. Fear of unchecked Soviet aggression marked the period. Espionage, economic sanctions, treaties, defense measures, and diplomatic conflicts were constantly in the news. In Korea and in Vietnam, many Americans fought and died facing Communist forces.

Civil Rights Struggles and the Women's Movement During the Sixties, protests against racism gave way to riots. Many cities seethed as African Americans demanded change, and television brought the anguish into every living room. During these years, the assassinations of President John F. Kennedy, Malcolm X, Reverend Martin Luther King, Jr., and Senator Robert F. Kennedy underscored the violence of the decade. At the same time, women struggled for greater economic and social power, changing the American work force and the political landscape.

> **ESSENTIAL QUESTION VOCABULARY**
>
> These Essential Question words will help you think and write about literature and society:
>
> **international** (in´ tər nash´ ə nəl) *adj.* between or among countries
>
> **diplomacy** (də plō´ mə sē) *n.* the conducting of relations between nations
>
> **protest** (prō´ test) *n.* demonstration of disapproval; a gathering to voice dissent

TIMELINE

1950: Korea North Korean troops invade South Korea, marking the start of the Korean War.

1951: Julius and Ethel Rosenberg are sentenced to death for conspiracy to commit espionage. ▶

1950: Thousands are falsely accused of treason following McCarthy's claims of Communist spies infiltrating the government. ▶

1951: J.D. Salinger publishes *The Catcher in the Rye.*

— 1950

What values and attitudes grew from these events?

Age of Anxiety vs. Age of Aquarius The fear and violence of the postwar period characterized it as an Age of Anxiety. Americans seemed unable to stop thinking about terrible things that could or might happen. Schools regularly held air-raid drills, and Communists were hunted everywhere. By the late Sixties, however, some Americans put forth an alternative set of idealistic values that called for an "Age of Aquarius"—an era of universal peace and love.

Seeking Conformity During the 1950s, the nation enjoyed widespread prosperity, suburbs expanded, and the consumer society flourished. As a result, many Americans relished, and even demanded, social conformity. Beneath the surface, however, anxiety lurked. For example, in 1954, the United States Information Agency banned Henry David Thoreau's *Walden* from American embassy libraries for being "downright socialistic."

Protesting Conformity As the Sixties wore on, more and more Americans made strong assertions of their individuality. People resisted living with conformity and fear. This new spirit of independence energized the passions for justice and equality that swept the nation.

The American EXPERIENCE

ART IN THE HISTORICAL CONTEXT

The Landscapes of Richard Diebenkorn

After World War II, Abstract Expressionists like Jackson Pollock created paintings that drew attention to the process of how they were made. Their abstract forms emphasized a complex inner reality over a straightforward representation of the outer world. In the 1960s, however, Richard Diebenkorn combined the dynamic energy of abstract forms with shapes that evoked sunny California landscapes.

Diebenkorn captured vibrant West Coast color and light in his pictures. He was able to suggest the land, the sky, the ocean, and the buildings that fragment a scene into blocks of color and yet, at the same time, present a unified, humanized landscape. His 1963 painting *Cityscape I (Landscape No. 1)* fully achieves this blend of abstract thought and warm feeling.

Later in his career Diebenkorn shifted to an even more abstract approach. However, his long series of paintings called *Ocean Park* continued to suggest landscape-like images. Ocean Park is a community near Santa Monica, California, and this particular American place seems to have provided the artist with a firm ground for his stunning abstract visions.

◀ **1952:** Hollywood produces its first feature-length 3D movie to compete with the rising popularity of television.

1952: Ralph Ellison publishes *Invisible Man.*

1953: The heart-lung machine is invented, creating treatment options for patients with heart defects.

◀ **1953: England**
Francis Crick and James Watson discover DNA.

1954: Supreme Court rules public school segregation to be unconstitutional in *Brown v. Board of Education.*

1954: England
Lord of the Flies by William Golding is published.

1955

The American EXPERIENCE

CONTEMPORARY CONNECTION

Jack Kerouac: King of the Road Trip

Jack Kerouac was one of the original Beats—a group of cutting edge writers and artists that emerged during the 1950s. Daring, rebellious, intelligent, and mobile, the Beats gave voice to a new generation. Kerouac's best-known work is *On the Road,* a novel inspired by cross-country road-trips. The book was reputedly written in a full-throttle three-week creative frenzy. In fact, the original manuscript of *On the Road* is a continuous scroll made by taping tracing paper end to end. The scroll is typewritten, has no margins, no paragraph indents, and is single-spaced. It still exists; it was purchased by a private collector in 2001, and can be viewed by the public whenever it is on tour. It was displayed at the New York Public Library in 2007 and at the University of Texas at Austin in 2008.

Once Kerouac typed the scroll in 1951, it was not snapped up by publishers. That was not to happen until 1957. After it was published, though, *The New York Times* called *On the Road* "the most beautifully executed, the clearest and most important utterance" of Kerouac's generation.

On the fiftieth anniversary of *On the Road*'s publication, fellow Beat figure Lawrence Ferlinghetti said, "The road doesn't exist anymore in America; there is this huge nostalgia for it. That's one of the reasons *On the Road* is more popular than ever."

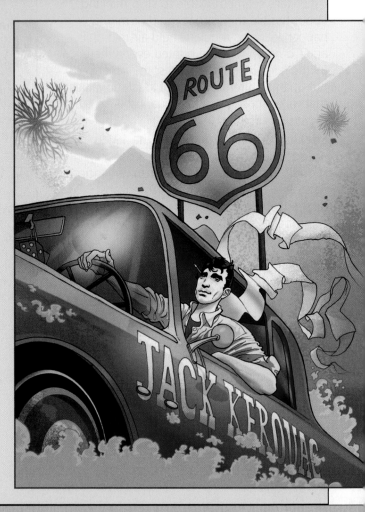

TIMELINE

1955: Flannery O'Connor publishes *A Good Man Is Hard to Find.*

1955: Argentina Jorge Luís Borges publishes *Extraordinary Tales.*

1955

1955: Rosa Parks is arrested, triggering the start of the Montgomery Bus Boycott. ▶

"We must learn to live together as brothers or perish together as fools."

— *Martin Luther King, Jr.*

How did these values and attitudes emerge in literature?

From Anxiety to Irony In the years just after World War II, literature dealt with the grief and shock of the conflict. Journalist John Hersey's *Hiroshima* appeared in 1946, graphically depicting the effects of the atomic bomb on the lives of ordinary Japanese citizens. In 1948, Randall Jarrell published *Losses*, intense poems that captured the feeling of postwar emptiness. By the 1960s, however, some writers were treating the war with tragicomic irony. Joseph Heller's *Catch-22* in 1961 and Kurt Vonnegut, Jr.'s, *Slaughterhouse-Five* in 1969 mixed bitterness with absurdity and fantasy that helped to distance readers from the mid-century violence.

Literature with Purpose The fight for racial equality generated powerful literary statements, including the autobiographical fiction of Ralph Ellison, James Baldwin, and Richard Wright; the poetry of Gwendolyn Brooks and Robert Hayden; the plays of Lorraine Hansberry; and the speeches and essays of Martin Luther King, Jr.

Equality for women was one of the purposes that drove the poems of Sylvia Plath, Adrienne Rich, and Denise Levertov. A general spirit of protest underlay the achievements of Beat poets Allen Ginsberg, Jack Kerouac, and Lawrence Ferlinghetti, while folk musician Bob Dylan produced lyrics that asked piercing social questions. Perhaps the finest socially purposeful literature of the time was Arthur Miller's *The Crucible*—the 1953 play that attacked the anti-Communist Congressional hearings chaired by Wisconsin Senator Joseph McCarthy.

Popular Culture Sails Along On a very different note, the two decades after World War II were high times for the Broadway musical. All over America people were humming tunes from *South Pacific*, *The King and I*, *The Music Man*, *Bye Bye Birdie*, *West Side Story*, *The Sound of Music*, and many other sparkling shows. Fans went crazy with Beatlemania, and families gathered every night around the electronic hearth—the television—to enjoy sitcoms like *I Love Lucy* and *Father Knows Best*, westerns like *Gunsmoke* and *Bonanza*, and the science fiction tales of *The Twilight Zone*.

◀ **1957: USSR** The first space satellite, *Sputnik 1*, is launched by the Soviet Union.

1957: Dr. Albert Sabin develops an oral vaccine for polio. ▶

1959: Lorraine Hansberry's *A Raisin in the Sun* is produced.

1960

1959: Alaska and Hawaii are admitted to the Union as the 49th and 50th states.

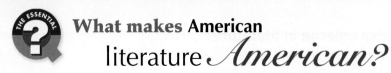

What makes American literature *American?*

What themes did American writers consider important?

Prosperity While the conspicuous consumption of consumer goods seemed to make people's lives easier, it also raised questions about the national character. Writers wondered about the realities of the American Dream. What did "the pursuit of happiness" really mean? The theme of success and its steep price was an important strand in postwar literature.

Rebellion During the 1960s, themes of rebellion ran through American writings. These were not the kinds of rebellious thoughts that Americans had expressed two hundred years earlier. Americans were not rebelling against a colonial government; they were rebelling against a culture they had themselves created. Counterculture movements gave rise to a variety of avant-garde artistic accomplishments with rebellion at their core.

Race After World War II, issues of race took on enormous urgency. When Martin Luther King, Jr., said "I have a dream," many Americans realized that the American Dream itself still needed work. This theme asserted itself in literature just as the civil rights struggle unfolded in American streets.

What roles did American writers play at this time?

The Witness In the literature that looked back at World War II, the writer's role was that of witness to history. Like Randall Jarrell, the writer was the one who had seen the horrors and lived to tell about them. Like John Hersey, the writer was the journalist or historian who could describe what had happened. The writer was also the witness to what was currently happening to the country. When Arthur Miller wrote *The Crucible*, he took on the role of witness to the effects of the rampant fear of Communism.

The Nonconformist Throughout history, writers have often set themselves apart from the mainstream of society. In the 1960s, however,

---

ESSENTIAL QUESTION VOCABULARY

These Essential Question words will help you think and write about American literature:

prosperity (präs per´ ə tē) *n.* good fortune, wealth

rebellion (ri bel´yən) *n.* defiance of or opposition to authority or control

avant-garde (ə vänt´ gärd´) *adj.* new, unconventional

TIMELINE

1961: Cuba The U.S.-supported Bay of Pigs Invasion fails at overthrowing Fidel Castro.

1961: Germany East Germany builds Berlin Wall. ▶

1962: Environmental protection movement is spurred by Rachel Carson's book *Silent Spring*.

1960

1961: Harper Lee wins the Pulitzer Prize for *To Kill a Mockingbird*. ▶

1961: The first American astronaut, Alan Shepard, is launched into space from Cape Canaveral Space Center in Florida. ▶

1962: USSR *One Day in the Life of Ivan Denisovich* by Alexander Solzhenitsyn is published.

they began to stand apart in greater numbers. These men and women were not "rebels without a cause." They had causes galore. They were anti-war, anti-racism, anti-sexism, anti-materialism, and anti-conformity. Earlier in the century, Modernists had usually confined their rebellions to *artistic* norms. By mid-century, many writers sought to alter *social* norms as well.

The Standard-Bearer Writers took on the vital task of articulating the principles that drove many social movements. They fulfilled this role directly in nonfiction and indirectly in fiction and poetry. Wielding the weapon of words, African American writers such as James Baldwin, Richard Wright, and Ralph Ellison gave definition to the Black experience, inspiring commitment and change. In the works of Sylvia Plath, Gwendolyn Brooks, Adrienne Rich, and many others, the women's movement in America found not only high literary art but also deep pride and energy.

At mid-century, how did writers build on the past?

Enlightening the Present American writers mined American history for parallels to their own era. In *The Crucible*, Arthur Miller shed light on the 1950s by examining a fearful incident of colonial history. In "Frederick Douglass," Robert Hayden looked back to the fight for freedom during the Civil War years to inspire the fight for freedom in the 1960s.

Continuing Forms and Styles Poets such as Robert Lowell, Elizabeth Bishop, and Richard Wilbur composed sonnets and sestinas, framing modern views in traditional forms. Novelists such as John Steinbeck continued to tell realistic stories, and the tradition of the Southern Gothic lived on in the work of William Faulkner, Carson McCullers, Flannery O'Connor, and others.

Keeping Modernism Alive The Modernist impulse that had revolutionized literature earlier in the century marched on into the 1950s. During these years, Modernist artists produced some of their greatest works, including William Carlos Williams's *Paterson*, Wallace Stevens's *The Auroras of Autumn*, and Ernest Hemingway's *The Old Man and the Sea*.

"We need men who can dream of things that never were."
— *John F. Kennedy*

1963: President John F. Kennedy is assassinated in Dallas. ▶

1964: South Africa
Anti-Apartheid leader Nelson Mandela is sentenced to life imprisonment.

1964: IBM produces OS-360, the first mass-produced computer operating system. ▶

◀ **1964:** 73 million people tune in to watch the Beatles perform on *The Ed Sullivan Show*.

1965

What is the **relationship** between literature and *place?*

How did World War II settings appear in American writing?

The battlefields of Europe, the jungles of the Pacific islands, and the devastated cities of Japan provided settings for great American writing after the war. Randall Jarrell's "The Death of the Ball Turret Gunner," Norman Mailer's novel *The Naked and the Dead*, and John Hersey's *Hiroshima* made readers feel they were standing amid the bloody landscapes. The tone of post–World War II writing, however, did not echo the despair of the literature that had emerged from World War I. War writing in the 1940s and 1950s was filled with pain, but still seemed to hold out the possibility of meaningful courage and even heroism.

How did urban life inspire post-war American literature?

Fiction and Drama In novels, stories, and plays, American writers used the lives of city-dwellers to explore a wide range of twentieth-century issues. The strivings of the middle-class for success, the struggles of immigrants to survive, the uncertainties of adolescents searching for love and independence—these themes and many more grew out of the modern cityscape. In the novels of Saul Bellow, Bernard Malamud, J. D. Salinger, James Agee, and Philip Roth, and in plays such as Arthur Miller's *Death of a Salesman* and Lorraine Hansberry's *A Raisin in the Sun*, urban life had powerful, even fatal, effects on characters.

Poetry The imagery of the city—its steel and glass beauties, its overarching bridges and underground tunnels, its smoke, speed, and noise—appeared often in poems. Brilliant collections by William Carlos Williams, Robert Lowell, Anne Sexton, Gwendolyn Brooks, and Allen Ginsberg define modern America as an increasingly urban place.

How did literature respond to the growth of suburbia?

Selling the American Dream After World War II, a "baby boom" created the need for more new homes. Developers across the nation

> ### ESSENTIAL QUESTION VOCABULARY
>
> These Essential Question words will help you think and write about literature and place.
>
> **cityscape** (sit´ē skāp´) *n.* urban scene or landscape
>
> **underground** (un´ dər ground´) *adj.* beneath the surface
>
> **suburbs** (sub´ ərbz) *n.* residential areas outside of cities

TIMELINE

1966: China Mao Zedong launches Cultural Revolution. ▶

1967: South Africa Christiaan Barnard performs the world's first heart transplant; the patient dies 18 days later.

1965

1966: *Ariel*, Sylvia Plath's last collection of poems, is published in the United States.

1967: Israel Israel gains territory from Arab states in Six-Day War.

1967: Thurgood Marshall becomes the first black U.S. Supreme Court justice. ▶

built new suburbs and expanded existing ones. Partly urban and partly pastoral, suburbs seemed to make the American Dream accessible for more people, at least for the middle class. Advertising, television, and movies sold the suburbs as the best chance for families to escape urban crowding and the pace and pressure of city life. Literature, however, explored both sides of the coin.

Dissecting the American Dream Many American writers recognized that, for some people, the dream could turn into a nightmare. A popular song of 1962 warned about what happens to people who all live in "little boxes" that "all look just the same." In 1845, Thoreau found peace by building his own house on the shore of a pond. What if, one hundred years later, thousands of people did the same thing, in the same place, at the same time?

Writers such as John Cheever and John Updike saw the dysfunction that could tear apart suburban families. In their novels and stories, they chronicled the symptoms of a new kind of alienation, brought on by too much sameness, too little genuine individuality, too much insistence on "keeping up with the Joneses." Issues that literature had once explored in small-town life in America now became transferred to suburban life.

The American EXPERIENCE

CLOSE-UP ON HISTORY

Rachel Carson and Environmental Writing

Today, most people are aware of the human impact on the environment. While people may disagree about the severity of environmental problems or how to address them, most feel these issues are important. Yet, even that understanding did not always exist. Americans were alerted to the problems facing the environment by a scientist named Rachel Carson.

In 1962, Carson published *Silent Spring*, the book that made millions of people conscious of the dangers of industrial pollution and of the damage it was doing throughout the natural world. In prose that is both scientifically accurate and passionate, Carson explained humanity's place in the world's ecosystem. She described the environmental consequences of technological progress, the chemical "rivers of death" that people allow to flow into the ocean.

Along with the naturalist Aldo Leopold, Rachel Carson sparked the modern environmental movement and also helped found a genre of literature that remains vital today. Writings about the environment—sometimes call eco-literature or green literature—continues to inform contemporary readers.

▲ **1968:** Martin Luther King, Jr., civil rights leader, murdered in Memphis.

▲ **1969:** Kurt Vonnegut publishes his novel *Slaughterhouse-Five.*

1969: Astronaut Neil Armstrong becomes the first person to set foot on the moon. ▶

1969: Northern Ireland
A long period of violence begins between Catholics and Protestants.

1969: Richard Nixon is sworn in as the 37th President of the United States.

1970

Recent Scholarship

The Purpose of THEATER

Arthur Miller

After a talk Arthur Miller gave at the University of Michigan, a member of the audience asked him: "What do you think the purpose, the ultimate purpose, of the theater is, really?" Miller responded: "I couldn't even speak in those terms because it's like asking, 'What is the ultimate purpose of the Universe?' To me the theater is not a disconnected entertainment, which it usually is to most people here. It's the sound and ring of the spirit of the people at any one time. It is where a collective mass of people, through the genius of some author, is able to project its terrors and its hopes and to symbolize them. Now how that's done—there are thousands of ways to do it of course. . . . I personally feel that the theater has to confront the basic themes always. And the faces change from generation to generation, but their roots are generally the same, and that is a question of man's increasing awareness of himself and his environment, his quest for justice and for the right to be human. That's a big order, but I don't know where else excepting a playhouse, where there's reasonable freedom, one should hope to see that."

Theater as a Bridge Between Cultures
Arthur Miller once wrote: "In a theater, people are themselves; they come of their own volition; they accept or reject, are moved or left cold not by virtue of reason alone or of emotion alone, but as whole human beings.

About the Author

Arthur Miller (1915–2005) is a legend of the twentieth-century American theater. He chronicled the dilemmas of common people pitted against powerful social forces. His most famous plays are *Death of a Salesman,* for which he won a Pulitzer Prize, and *The Crucible,* one of the most frequently performed plays in the world today.

Literature of the first rank is a kind of international signaling service . . .

▲ **Critical Viewing** What emotions do you think this theater audience is feeling? Explain. **SPECULATE**

"A communion through art is therefore unusually complete; it can be a most reliable indication of a fundamental unity; and an inability to commune through art is, I think, a stern indication that cultures have not yet arrived at a genuine common ground. Had there been no Flaubert, no Zola, no Proust, de Maupassant, Stendhal, Balzac, Dumas;[1] had there been no Mark Twain, or Poe, Hawthorne, Emerson, Hemingway, Steinbeck, Faulkner,[2] or the numerous other American artists of the first rank, our conviction of essential union with France and of France with us would rest upon the assurances of the two Departments of State and the impression of tourists. I think that had there been no Tolstoy, no Gogol, no Turgenev, no Chekov or Dostoyevsky,[3] we should have no assurance at all nor any faint hope that the Russian heart was even ultimately comprehensible to us.

---

1. **Flaubert . . . Dumas** influential French writers.
2. **Mark Twain . . . Faulkner** famous American writers.
3. **Tolstoy . . . Dostoyevsky** well-known Russian writers.

"Literature of the first rank is a kind of international signaling service, telling all who can read that wherever that distant blinker is shining live men of a common civilization."

Speaking and Listening: Collaboration

Arthur Miller's comments emphasize the unifying power of literature. Just as people are brought together in a theater, they are also brought together when they read. Drama, fiction, and poetry make people aware of each other and lead to "a communion through art."

With a partner, discuss Miller's comments and the implications they have for writers and for audiences. Do you agree or disagree with the comments? Why or why not? What responsibilities does Miller suggest writers have to bear? What responsibilities does he suggest lay with readers and audiences? Gather your ideas into a **written statement** to read for the class.

Integrate and Evaluate Information

1. Use a chart like the one shown to determine the key ideas expressed in the Essential Question essays on pages 970–977. Fill in two ideas related to each Essential Question and note the authors most closely associated with each concept. One example has been done for you.

Essential Question	Key Concept	Key Author
Literature and Place		
American Literature		
Literature and Society	Individuality and nonconformity	Lawrence Ferlinghetti

2. How do the visual sources in this section—map, graphs, timelines, paintings, photographs, and artifacts—add to your understanding of the ideas expressed in words? Cite specific examples.

3. During the 1950s, many Americans craved normalcy; but during the 1960s, many people rebelled against normalcy and conformity. Citing evidence from the multiple sources presented on pages 968–977, explain the underlying reasons for the mood of each decade. How were these moods made manifest in art and popular culture?

4. **Address a Question** Playwright Arthur Miller says that one purpose of theater is to ask and answer questions about "man's increasing aware-ness of himself and his environment, his quest for justice and for the right to be human." In your view, what other human activity or form of expression shares these purposes? In what other arenas can such goals be effectively pursued? Integrate information from this textbook and other sources to support your ideas.

Speaking and Listening: Interview

The 1960s were turbulent years in America. Conduct an **interview** with someone who lived through that decade. If possible, *use technology,* such as a digital camera or a video recorder, to capture the interview, and a computer to edit it. Present the edited interview to the class. Include a closing statement in which you summarize what you learned.

Solve a Research Problem To conduct an effective interview, you must ask thoughtful, informed questions. Create a research plan to educate yourself about the 1960s before conducting the interview. Use a variety of sources—print, digital, audio, and visual—to learn about this time period. Use the information you gather to write interview questions; for example:

- What were your reactions to the Kennedy and King assassinations?
- How did you feel about the Vietnam War?
- Were you a fan of the Beatles or other musical groups? Why?

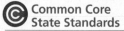

Common Core State Standards

Reading Informational Text
7. Integrate and evaluate multiple sources of information presented in different media or formats as well as in words in order to address a question or solve a problem.

Speaking and Listening
1.a. Come to discussions prepared, having read and researched material under study; explicitly draw on that preparation by referring to evidence from texts and other research on the topic or issue to stimulate a thoughtful, well-reasoned exchange of ideas.

1.c. Propel conversations by posing and responding to questions that probe reasoning and evidence; ensure a hearing for a full range of positions on a topic or issue; clarify, verify, or challenge ideas and conclusions; and promote divergent and creative perspectives.

ESSENTIAL QUESTION VOCABULARY

Use these words in your responses:

Literature and Place
cityscape
underground
suburbs

American Literature
prosperity
rebellion
avant-garde

Literature and Society
international
diplomacy
protest

War Shock

Connecting to the Essential Question These selections present unflinching portrayals of war. As you read, note details that emphasize the high costs of armed conflict. Doing so will help as you consider the Essential Question: **How does literature shape or reflect society?**

**Common Core
State Standards**

**Reading Literature/
Informational Text**
1. Cite strong and thorough textual evidence to support analysis of what the text says explicitly as well as inferences drawn from the text, including determining where the text leaves matters uncertain.

Close Reading Focus

Theme; Perspective

The **theme** is the central idea or insight in a work of literature. Many nonfiction works present explicitly stated central ideas, while most works of fiction, poetry, and drama express implied themes. The meaning is conveyed through details, characters, events, descriptions, and literary devices. However, some nonfiction works use the same literary techniques as fiction, including an implied or suggested theme. Both of these selections—one a work of journalism and the other a poem—express implied themes about war.

Comparing Literary Works An author's **perspective** is the point of view from which he or she writes. This perspective may be objective and impersonal, subjective and personal, or a mixture of both:

- With an *objective perspective,* the narrator reports events without obvious emotion or bias. *Hersey:* A hundred thousand people were killed by the atomic bomb.

- With a *subjective perspective,* the narrator expresses feelings about the events. *Jarrell:* I woke to black flak and the nightmare fighters.

As you read these selections about World War II, compare how the authors mix objectivity and subjectivity in surprising and effective ways.

Preparing to Read Complex Texts Both Hersey and Jarrell bring strong but unstated political beliefs to their writing. Because of this, **analyzing the writers' political assumptions** can lead you to a deeper understanding of their work. As you read, use a chart like the one shown to consider how key details express both the writers' political assumptions and deeper truths about human beings.

Key Details

Political Assumptions

Vocabulary

You will encounter the words listed here in the text that follows. Copy the words into your notebook, sorting them into words you know and words you do not know.

evacuated

volition

rendezvous

incessant

convivial

John Hersey *(1914–1993)*

Author of *Hiroshima*

John Hersey was born in China to American missionary parents. The family lived in China until Hersey was ten years old, when they returned to the United States. In 1936, Hersey graduated from Yale University and became a foreign correspondent in East Asia, Italy, and the Soviet Union. His experiences working as a journalist served as the premise for his twenty-five books and countless essays and articles.

Hersey combined a profound moral sensibility with the highest artistry. His novels and essays not only examine the moral implications of the major political and historical events of his day, they do so with high literary grace. In 1945, Hersey won a Pulitzer Prize for his novel *A Bell for Adano,* in which an American major discovers the human dignity of the Italian villagers who were his enemies in World War II.

The Atomic Bomb During the 1940s, Hersey traveled to China and Japan as a correspondent for *The New Yorker* and *Time* magazines. He also used these visits to gather material for his most famous and acclaimed book, *Hiroshima* (1946), a shocking, graphic depiction of the devastation caused by the atomic bomb that was dropped on the Japanese city of Hiroshima near the end of World War II. This remarkable report, which tells the vivid and detailed stories of victims of the bombing, was first published as a four-part article in *The New Yorker* on August 31, 1946. William Shawn, then editor of *The New Yorker,* made the unprecedented decision to bump all of the magazine's other editorial content in order to publish Hersey's article.

Stories of Inhumanity and Courage In 1950, Hersey published the novel *The Wall,* which tells of the extinction of the Warsaw ghetto by the Germans during World War II. Hersey's later works include *A Single Pebble* (1956), *The War Lover* (1959), *The Child Buyer* (1960), *The Algiers Motel Incident* (1968), *The Writer's Craft* (1974), *Blues* (1987), and *Fling and Other Stories* (1990).

> *"There is one sacred rule of journalism. The writer must not invent."*

from HIROSHIMA

John Hersey

BACKGROUND In August 1945, American President Harry Truman was faced with a terrible decision. The world had been at war for six years. Germany had surrendered in May, but Japan refused to give up. The United States had just finished developing an atomic bomb. President Truman had to decide whether or not to use this new technology to bring an end to the war. On August 6, Truman ordered that the atomic bomb be dropped on the Japanese city of Hiroshima. Three days later, another bomb was dropped on Nagasaki. These two bombs killed more than 200,000 people and forced the Japanese surrender. Like so many events of World War II, the atomic bomb gave the world a new horror, as John Hersey so carefully documents in this selection.

Exactly fifteen minutes past eight in the morning, on August 6, 1945, Japanese time, at the moment when the atomic bomb flashed above Hiroshima, Miss Toshiko Sasaki, a clerk in the personnel department of the East Asia Tin Works, had just sat down at her place in the plant office and was turning her head to speak to the girl at the next desk. At that same moment, Dr. Masakazu Fujii was settling down cross-legged to read the Osaka *Asahi* on the porch of his private hospital, overhanging one of the seven deltaic rivers which divide Hiroshima; Mrs. Hatsuyo Nakamura, a tailor's widow, stood by the window of her kitchen, watching a neighbor tearing down his house because it lay in the path of an air-raid-defense fire lane . . . and the Reverend Mr. Kiyoshi Tanimoto, pastor of the Hiroshima Methodist Church, paused at the door of a rich man's house in Koi, the city's western suburb, and prepared to unload a handcart full of things he had evacuated from town in fear of the massive B-29 raid which everyone expected Hiroshima to suffer. A hundred thousand people were killed by the atomic bomb, and these [four] were among the survivors. They still wonder why they lived when so many others died. Each of them counts many small items of chance or volition—a step taken in time, a decision to go indoors, catching one streetcar instead of the next—that spared him. And now each knows that in the act of survival he lived a dozen lives and saw more death than he ever thought he would see. At the time, none of them knew anything.

The Reverend Mr. Tanimoto got up at five o'clock that morning. He was alone in the parsonage, because for some time his wife had been commuting with their year-old baby to spend nights with a friend in Ushida, a suburb to the north. Of all the important cities of Japan, only two, Kyoto and Hiroshima, had not been visited

◀ **Critical Viewing** What do you find most disturbing about this photograph of the ruined city of Hiroshima? **TAKE A POSITION**

Vocabulary
evacuated (ē vak´ yōō āt´ id) v. made empty; withdrawn
volition (vō lish´ ən) n. act of using the will

Comprehension
What happened at exactly 8:15 in the morning on August 6, 1945?

in strength by *B-san,* or Mr. B, as the Japanese, with a mixture of respect and unhappy familiarity, called the B-29; and Mr. Tanimoto, like all his neighbors and friends, was almost sick with anxiety. He had heard uncomfortably detailed accounts of mass raids on Kure, Iwakuni, Tokuyama, and other nearby towns; he was sure Hiroshima's turn would come soon. He had slept badly the night before, because there had been several air-raid warnings. Hiroshima had been getting such warnings almost every night for weeks, for at that time the B-29s were using Lake Biwa, northeast of Hiroshima, as a rendezvous point, and no matter what city the Americans planned to hit, the Super-fortresses streamed in over the coast near Hiroshima. The frequency of the warning and the continued abstinence of Mr. B with respect to Hiroshima had made its citizens jittery; a rumor was going around that the Americans were saving something special for the city.

Mr. Tanimoto was a small man, quick to talk, laugh, and cry. He wore his black hair parted in the middle and rather long; the prominence of the frontal bones just above his eyebrows and the smallness of his mustache, mouth, and chin gave him a strange old-young look, boyish and yet wise, weak and yet fiery. He moved nervously and fast, but with a restraint which suggested that he is a cautious, thoughtful man. He showed, indeed, just those qualities in the uneasy days before the bomb fell. Mr. Tanimoto had been carrying all the portable things from his church, in the close-packed residential district called Nagaragawa, to a house that belonged to a rayon manufacturer in Koi, two miles from the center of town. The rayon man, a Mr. Matsui, had opened his then unoccupied estate to a large number of his friends and acquaintances, so that they might evacuate whatever they wished to a safe distance from the probable target area. Mr. Tanimoto had had no difficulty in moving chairs, hymnals, Bibles, altar gear, and church records by pushcart himself, but the organ console and an upright piano required some aid. A friend of his named Matsuo had, the day before, helped him get the piano out to Koi; in return, he had promised this day to assist Mr. Matsuo in hauling out a daughter's belongings. That is why he had risen so early.

Mr. Tanimoto cooked his own breakfast. He felt awfully tired. The effort of moving the piano the day before, a sleepless night, weeks of worry and unbalanced diet, the cares of his parish—all combined to make him feel hardly adequate to the new day's work. There was another thing, too: Mr. Tanimoto had studied theology at Emory College, in Atlanta, Georgia; he had graduated in 1940; he spoke excellent English; he dressed in American clothes; he had corresponded with many American friends right up to the time the war

Vocabulary
rendezvous (rän′dā voo′)
n. meeting place

LITERATURE IN CONTEXT

History Connection

B-29 Bombers

The Second World War saw major advances in the technology of mechanized warfare—warfare that relied heavily on machines. The B-29 Superfortress bomber that Hersey mentions was an aircraft capable of long-range, heavy bombing runs. It was used frequently against Japan during 1944 and 1945. Firebomb B-29 raids against industrial cities in Japan totaled nearly 7,000 flights and dropped 41,600 tons of bombs.

Connect to the Literature

In what way would having more information about the B-29 bomber increase Mr. Tanimoto's anxiety level?

began; and among a people obsessed with a fear of being spied upon—perhaps almost obsessed himself—he found himself growing increasingly uneasy. The police had questioned him several times, and just a few days before, he had heard that an influential acquaintance, a Mr. Tanaka, a retired officer of the Toyo Kisen Kaisha steamship line, an anti-Christian, a man famous in Hiroshima for his showy philanthropies and notorious for his personal tyrannies, had been telling people that Tanimoto should not be trusted. In compensation, to show himself publicly a good Japanese, Mr. Tanimoto had taken on the chairmanship of his local *tonarigumi,* or Neighborhood Association, and to his other duties and concerns this position had added the business of organizing air-raid defense for about twenty families.

Before six o'clock that morning, Mr. Tanimoto started for Mr. Matsuo's house. There he found that their burden was to be a *tansu,* a large Japanese cabinet, full of clothing and household goods. The two men set out. The morning was perfectly clear and so warm that the day promised to be uncomfortable. A few minutes after they started, the air-raid siren went off—a minute-long blast that warned of approaching planes but indicated to the people of Hiroshima only a slight degree of danger, since it sounded every morning at this time, when an American weather plane came over. The two men pulled and pushed the handcart through the city streets. Hiroshima was a fan-shaped city, lying mostly on the six islands formed by the seven estuarial rivers that branch out from the Ota River; its main commercial and residential districts, covering about four square miles in the center of the city, contained three-quarters of its population, which had been reduced by several evacuation programs from a wartime peak of 380,000 to about 245,000. Factories and other residential districts, or suburbs, lay compactly around the edges of the city. To the south were the docks, an airport, and the island-studded Inland Sea. A rim of mountains runs around the other three sides of the delta. Mr. Tanimoto and Mr. Matsuo took their way through the shopping center, already full of people, and across two of the rivers to the sloping streets of Koi, and up them to the outskirts and foothills. As they started up a valley away from the tight-ranked houses, the all-clear sounded. (The Japanese radar operators, detecting only three planes, supposed that they comprised a reconnaissance.) Pushing the handcart up to the rayon man's house was tiring, and the men, after they had maneuvered their load into the driveway and to the front steps, paused to rest awhile. They stood with a wing of the house between them and the city. Like most homes in this part of Japan, the house consisted of a wooden frame and wooden walls supporting a heavy tile roof. Its front hall, packed with rolls of bedding and clothing, looked like a cool cave full of fat cushions. Opposite the house, to the right of the front door, there was a large, finicky rock garden. There was no sound of planes. The morning was still; the place was cool and pleasant.

Implied Theme

In light of the bombing, what is ironic about an air-raid siren indicating only a "slight degree of danger"?

Comprehension

Why does Mr. Tanimoto move all the portable things in his church to a home farther from the town center?

▲ **Critical Viewing**

You may have seen photographs like this one of the aftermath of the Hiroshima bombing. Does Hersey's account change the way you view such pictures? Explain. **RELATE**

Then a tremendous flash of light cut across the sky. Mr. Tanimoto has a distinct recollection that it travelled from east to west, from the city toward the hills. It seemed a sheet of sun. Both he and Mr. Matsuo reacted in terror—and both had time to react (for they were 3,500 yards, or two miles, from the center of the explosion). Mr. Matsuo dashed up the front steps into the house and dived among the bedrolls and buried himself there. Mr. Tanimoto took four or five steps and threw himself between two big rocks in the garden. He bellied up very hard against one of them. As his face was against the stone, he did not see what happened. He felt a sudden pressure, and then splinters and pieces of board and fragments of tile fell on him. He heard no roar. (Almost no one in Hiroshima recalls hearing any noise of the bomb. But a fisherman in his sampan on the Inland Sea near Tsuzu, the man with whom Mr. Tanimoto's mother-in-law and sister-in-law were living, saw the flash and heard a tremendous explosion; he was nearly twenty miles from Hiroshima, but the thunder was greater than when the B-29s hit Iwakuni, only five miles away.)

When he dared, Mr. Tanimoto raised his head and saw that the rayon man's house had collapsed. He thought a bomb had fallen directly on it. Such clouds of dust had risen that there was a sort of twilight around. In panic, not thinking for the moment of Mr. Matsuo under the ruins, he dashed out into the street. He noticed as he ran that the concrete wall of the estate had fallen over—toward the house rather than away from it. In the street, the first thing he saw was a squad of soldiers who had been burrowing into the hillside opposite, making one of the thousands of dugouts in which the Japanese apparently intended to resist invasion, hill by hill, life for life; the soldiers were coming out of the hole, where they should have been safe, and blood was running from their heads, chests, and backs. They were silent and dazed.

Under what seemed to be a local dust cloud, the day grew darker and darker.

Nearly midnight, the night before the bomb was dropped, an announcer on the city's radio station said that about two hundred B-29s were approaching southern Honshu and advised the population of Hiroshima to evacuate to their designated "safe areas." Mrs. Hatsuyo Nakamura, the tailor's widow, who lived in the section called Nobori-cho and who had long had a habit of doing as she was told, got her three children—a ten-year-old boy, Toshio, an eight-year-old girl, Yaeko, and a five-year-old girl, Myeko—out of bed and dressed them and walked with them to the military area known as the East Parade Ground, on the northeast edge of the city. There she unrolled some mats and the children lay down on them. They slept until about two, when they were awakened by the roar of the planes going over Hiroshima.

As soon as the planes had passed, Mrs. Nakamura started back with her children. They reached home a little after two-thirty and she immediately turned on the radio, which, to her distress, was just then broadcasting a fresh warning. When she looked at the children and saw how tired they were, and when she thought of the number of trips they had made in past weeks, all to no purpose, to the East Parade Ground, she decided that in spite of the instructions on the radio, she simply could not face starting out all over again. She put the children in their bedrolls on the floor, lay down herself at three o'clock, and fell asleep at once, so soundly that when planes passed over later, she did not waken to their sound.

The siren jarred her awake at about seven. She arose, dressed quickly, and hurried to the house of Mr. Nakamoto, the head of her Neighborhood Association, and asked him what she should do. He said that she should remain at home unless an urgent warning—a series of intermittent blasts of the siren—was sounded. She returned home, lit the stove in the kitchen, set some rice to cook, and sat down to read that morning's Hiroshima *Chugoku*. To her relief, the all-clear

Spiral Review
Diction and Tone What do you notice about Hersey's diction and tone as he describes these awful scenes?

Author's Perspective
What do the details about Mrs. Nakamura's tired children suggest about the author's objectivity?

Comprehension
Why are Mrs. Nakamura's children so tired?

from Hiroshima **989**

sounded at eight o'clock. She heard the children stirring, so she went and gave each of them a handful of peanuts and told them to stay in their bedrolls, because they were tired from the night's walk. She had hoped that they would go back to sleep, but the man in the house directly to the south began to make a terrible hullabaloo of hammering, wedging, ripping, and splitting. The prefectural government,[1] convinced, as everyone in Hiroshima was, that the city would be attacked soon, had begun to press with threats and warnings for the completion of wide fire lanes, which, it was hoped, might act in conjunction with the rivers to localize any fires started by an incendiary[2] raid; and the neighbor was reluctantly sacrificing his home to the city's safety. Just the day before, the prefecture had ordered all able-bodied girls from the secondary schools to spend a few days helping to clear these lanes, and they started work soon after the all-clear sounded.

Implied Theme

Why do you think the author included information about the citizens' attempts to defend their city and its population?

---

1. **prefectural government** regional districts of Japan which are administered by a governor.
2. **incendiary** (in sen´ dē er´ ē) *adj.* designed to cause fires.

◄ **Critical Viewing**
There are no people shown in this photograph—nor in many others—depicting the devastation wrought by the Hiroshima bomb. Does the lack of humanity lessen or intensify the power of the image? Explain. **ASSESS**

Mrs. Nakamura went back to the kitchen, looked at the rice, and began watching the man next door. At first, she was annoyed with him for making so much noise, but then she was moved almost to tears by pity. Her emotion was specifically directed toward her neighbor, tearing down his home, board by board, at a time when there was so much unavoidable destruction, but undoubtedly she also felt a generalized, community pity, to say nothing of self-pity. She had not had an easy time. Her husband, Isawa, had gone into the Army just after Myeko was born, and she had heard nothing from or of him for a long time, until, on March 5, 1942, she received a seven-word telegram: "Isawa died an honorable death at Singapore." She learned later that he had died on February 15th, the day Singapore fell, and that he had been a corporal. Isawa had been a not particularly prosperous tailor, and his only capital was a Sankoku sewing machine. After his death, when his allotments stopped coming,

Comprehension
Why does the prefectural government call for the completion of fire lanes?

World War II

World War II began in September 1939, when German forces, following the orders of the dictator Adolf Hitler, invaded Poland. In response to this unprovoked invasion, France and Great Britain declared war on Germany. Just over two years later, the United States entered the war when Japan, a German ally, launched a surprise attack on an American naval base at Pearl Harbor in Hawaii. The war continued to escalate during the early 1940s. More than two dozen nations were eventually drawn into the conflict, and tens of millions of soldiers were killed. By 1945, the tide had turned strongly in favor of the United States and its allies. In early May 1945, the German forces surrendered. Fighting continued in the Pacific, however, as the Japanese refused to give up. The war finally ended in 1945 when the United States dropped two atomic bombs on the Japanese cities of Hiroshima and Nagasaki. The bombs killed more than 200,000 people and forced Japan's surrender.

Connect to the Literature

In what way does getting to know Dr. Fujii and the others affect your feelings about the dropping of the atom bombs on Hiroshima?

Vocabulary

incessant (in ses´ ent)
adj. constant; continuing in a way that seems endless

Mrs. Nakamura got out the machine and began to take in piecework herself, and since then had supported the children, but poorly, by sewing.

As Mrs. Nakamura stood watching her neighbor, everything flashed whiter than any white she had ever seen. She did not notice what happened to the man next door; the reflex of a mother set her in motion toward her children. She had taken a single step (the house was 1,350 yards, or three-quarters of a mile, from the center of the explosion) when something picked her up and she seemed to fly into the next room over the raised sleeping platform, pursued by parts of her house.

Timbers fell around her as she landed, and a shower of tiles pommelled her; everything became dark, for she was buried. The debris did not cover her deeply. She rose up and freed herself. She heard a child cry, "Mother, help me!" and saw her youngest—Myeko, the five-year-old—buried up to her breast and unable to move. As Mrs. Nakamura started frantically to claw her way toward the baby, she could see or hear nothing of her other children.

In the days right before the bombing, Dr. Masakazu Fujii, being prosperous, hedonistic,[3] and at the time not too busy, had been allowing himself the luxury of sleeping until nine or nine-thirty, but fortunately he had to get up early the morning the bomb was dropped to see a house guest off on a train. He rose at six, and half an hour later walked with his friend to the station, not far away, across two of the rivers. He was back home by seven, just as the siren sounded its sustained warning. He ate breakfast and then, because the morning was already hot, undressed down to his underwear and went out on the porch to read the paper. This porch—in fact, the whole building—was curiously constructed. Dr. Fujii was the proprietor of a peculiarly Japanese institution; a private, single-doctor hospital. This building, perched beside and over the water of the Kyo River, and next to the bridge of the same name, contained thirty rooms for thirty patients and their kinfolk—for, according to Japanese custom, when a person falls sick and goes to a hospital, one or more members of his family go and live there with him, to cook for him, bathe, massage, and read to him, and to offer incessant familial sympathy, without which a Japanese patient would be miserable indeed. Dr. Fujii had no beds—only straw mats—for his patients. He did, however, have all sorts of modern equipment: an X-ray machine, diathermy[4] apparatus, and a

---

3. hedonistic (he de nis´ tik) *adj.* indulgently seeking out pleasure.
4. diathermy (dī´ ə thur´ mē) *n.* medical treatment in which heat is produced beneath the skin to warm or destroy tissue.

fine tiled laboratory. The structure rested two-thirds on the land, one-third on piles over the tidal waters of the Kyo. This overhang, the part of the building where Dr. Fujii lived, was queer-looking, but it was cool in summer and from the porch, which faced away from the center of the city, the prospect of the river, with pleasure boats drifting up and down it, was always refreshing. Dr. Fujii had occasionally had anxious moments when the Ota and its mouth branches rose to flood, but the piling was apparently firm enough and the house had always held.

Dr. Fujii had been relatively idle for about a month because in July, as the number of untouched cities in Japan dwindled and as Hiroshima seemed more and more inevitably a target, he began turning patients away, on the ground that in case of a fire raid he would not be able to evacuate them. Now he had only two patients left—a woman from Yano, injured in the shoulder, and a young man of twenty-five recovering from burns he had suffered when the steel factory near Hiroshima in which he worked had been hit. Dr. Fujii had six nurses to tend his patients. His wife and children were safe; his wife and one son were living outside Osaka, and another son and two daughters were in the country on Kyushu. A niece was living with him, and a maid and a manservant. He had little to do and did not mind, for he had saved some money. At fifty, he was healthy, convivial, and calm, and he was pleased to pass the evenings drinking whiskey with friends, always sensibly and for the sake of conversation. Before the war, he had affected brands imported from Scotland and America; now he was perfectly satisfied with the best Japanese brand, Suntory.

Dr. Fujii sat down cross-legged in his underwear on the spotless matting of the porch, put on his glasses, and started reading the Osaka *Asahi*. He liked to read the Osaka news because his wife was there. He saw the flash. To him—faced away from the center and looking at his paper—it seemed a brilliant yellow. Startled, he began to rise to his feet. In that moment (he was 1,550 yards from the center), the hospital leaned behind his rising and, with a terrible ripping noise, toppled into the river. The Doctor, still in the act of getting to his feet, was thrown forward and around and over; he was buffeted and gripped; he lost track of everything, because things were so speeded up; he felt the water.

Dr. Fujii hardly had time to think that he was dying before he realized that he was alive, squeezed tightly by two long timbers in a V across his chest, like a morsel suspended between two huge chopsticks—held upright, so that he could not move, with his head miraculously above water and his torso and legs in it. The remains of his hospital were all around him in a mad assortment of splintered lumber and materials for the relief of pain. His left shoulder hurt terribly. His glasses were gone. . . .

> *Dr. Fujii hardly had time to think that he was dying before he realized that he was alive...*

Vocabulary
convivial (kən viv´ ē əl) *adj.* fond of good company; sociable

Author's Perspective
Is Hersey's description of Dr. Fujii objective or subjective? Explain.

Comprehension
Where is Dr. Fujii when the bomb hits?

▲ **Critical Viewing**

Based on this image, does survival in this setting seem possible? **ASSESS**

Miss Toshiko Sasaki, the East Asia Tin Works clerk, . . . got up at three o'clock in the morning on the day the bomb fell. There was extra housework to do. Her eleven-month-old brother, Akio, had come down the day before with a serious stomach upset; her mother had taken him to the Tamura Pediatric Hospital and was staying there with him. Miss Sasaki, who was about twenty, had to cook breakfast for her father, a brother, a sister, and herself, and—since the hospital, because of the war, was unable to provide food—to prepare a whole day's meals for her mother and the baby, in time for her father, who worked in a factory making rubber earplugs for artillery crews, to take the food by on his way to the plant. When she had finished and had cleaned and put away the cooking things, it was nearly seven. The family lived in Koi, and she had a forty-five-minute trip to the tin works, in the section of town called Kannonmachi. She was in charge of the personnel records in the factory. She left Koi at seven, and as soon as she reached the plant, she went with some of the other girls from the personnel department to the factory auditorium. A prominent local Navy man, a former employee, had committed suicide the day before by throwing himself under a train—a death considered honorable enough to warrant a memorial service, which was to be held at the tin works at ten o'clock that morning. In the large hall, Miss Sasaki and the others made suitable preparations for the meeting. This work took about twenty minutes.

Miss Sasaki went back to her office and sat down at her desk. She was quite far from the windows, which were off to her left, and behind her were a couple of tall bookcases containing all the books of the factory library, which the personnel department had organized. She settled herself at her desk, put some things in a drawer, and shifted papers. She thought that before she began to make entries in her lists of new employees, discharges, and departures for the Army, she would chat for a moment with the girl at her right. Just as she turned her head away from the windows, the room was filled with a blinding light. She was paralyzed by fear, fixed still in her chair for a long moment (the plant was 1,600 yards from the center).

Everything fell, and Miss Sasaki lost consciousness. The ceiling dropped suddenly and the wooden floor above collapsed in splinters and the people up there came down and the roof above them gave way; but principally and first of all, the bookcases right behind her swooped forward and the contents threw her down, with her left leg horribly twisted and breaking underneath her. There, in the tin factory, in the first moment of the atomic age, a human being was crushed by books.

Critical Reading

1. **Key Ideas and Details (a)** At what time and on what day was the bomb dropped on Hiroshima? **(b) Draw Conclusions:** Why do you think Hersey is so precise in noting the exact date and time?

2. **Key Ideas and Details (a)** In describing each individual's experience, which moment does Hersey refer to again and again? **(b) Interpret:** What is the effect of Hersey's returning to this moment repeatedly?

3. **Key Ideas and Details (a)** Note three details describing the city of Hiroshima in the hours preceding the bomb. **(b) Analyze:** Why does Hersey spend so much time describing the city before the blast?

4. **Key Ideas and Details (a)** By what is Miss Sasaki crushed? **(b) Infer:** What effect do you think Hersey intended when he described Miss Sasaki's experience?

5. **Key Ideas and Details (a) Classify:** Are the people Hersey portrays important decision makers or merely ordinary citizens? **(b) Draw Conclusions:** What is Hersey implying about the fates of individuals in the midst of war?

6. **Integration of Knowledge and Ideas Take a Position:** President Truman's hope that the atomic bomb would end the war proved true but at a great cost. Do you think he made the right decision? Why or why not?

Cite textual evidence to support your responses.

Randall Jarrell *(1914–1965)*

Author of "The Death of the Ball Turret Gunner"

Randall Jarrell was a gifted poet, literary critic, and teacher whose work was praised by both writers and critics. His literary essays, many of which appear in his book *Poetry and the Age* (1953), have been credited with changing the critical tastes and trends of his time.

Literary Ambitions Born in Nashville, Tennessee, Jarrell graduated from Vanderbilt University, where he studied under writers Robert Penn Warren, Allen Tate, and John Crowe Ransom. All of these men would prove helpful in promoting Jarrell's career. Warren and Tate published Jarrell's early poetry and criticism, and Tate helped land Jarrell his first teaching job at Kenyon College.

During World War II, Jarrell enlisted in the U.S. Air Force. He served only briefly as a pilot and spent the remaining war years as an aviation instructor, training pilots to fly the famed B-29 bombers that helped secure victory. Jarrell's war experiences provided him with the material for the poems in his books *Little Friend, Little Friend* (1945) and *Losses* (1948). These books rank among the finest literature to emerge from the war.

American Language Jarrell was a great admirer of the poetry of Robert Frost, and, like Frost, he wrote poems based on the sounds and rhythms of American speech. Jarrell's collections *The Seven-League Crutches* (1951) and *The Lost World* (1965) focus on childhood and innocence. *The Woman at the Washington Zoo* (1960), for which Jarrell won the National Book Award for poetry, deals with the themes of aging and loneliness. "The Death of the Ball Turret Gunner," a brief poem told in the first person of a soldier experiencing his last moments in a World War II bomber, is one of Jarrell's most famous works. American poet Robert Lowell said of Jarrell, "His gifts . . . were wit, pathos, and brilliance of intelligence. These qualities, in themselves, were often so well employed that he became, I think, the most heartbreaking English poet of his generation."

Photograph by Rollie McKenna

The Death of the Ball Turret Gunner

Randall Jarrell

Background A ball turret was a plexiglass sphere, or circular capsule, in the underside of certain World War II bombers; it held a small man and two machine guns. When the bomber was attacked by a plane below, the gunner, hunched in his little sphere, would revolve with the turret to fire his guns from an upside-down position.

> From my mother's sleep I fell into the State,
> And I hunched in its belly till my wet fur froze.
> Six miles from earth, loosed from its dream of life,
> I woke to black flak[1] and the nightmare fighters.
> 5 When I died they washed me out of the turret with a hose.

1. flak *n.* anti-aircraft fire.

Critical Reading

1. **Key Ideas and Details (a)** Which words does the gunner use to describe his view of life on Earth? **(b) Analyze:** In what way is this view of life related to the "nightmare" in the turret?

2. **Key Ideas and Details (a) Interpret:** To what does the word "State" refer? **(b) Draw Conclusions:** What is the poet suggesting about the relationship between a soldier in a war and the government?

3. **Integration of Knowledge and Ideas Take a Position:** Jarrell based his poem on observations of World War II, a war that has been called "the good war." Is there such a thing as a "good war"? Explain.

4. **Integration of Knowledge and Ideas** How do both the essay by Hersey and the poem by Jarrell create a societal memory of World War II? How important is that societal memory? Explain. In your response, use at least two of these Essential Question words: *encounter, information, repetition, ideals, confront.* *[Connecting to the Essential Question: How does literature shape or reflect society?]*

Cite textual evidence to support your responses.

Literary Analysis

1. **Key Ideas and Details (a)** Which details in *Hiroshima* provide clues to the **implied theme? (b)** What is that theme?

2. **Key Ideas and Details (a)** How and when is Mrs. Nakamura informed of her husband's death? **(b)** What political assumption about war does Hersey express through this detail?

3. **Key Ideas and Details** Of the survivors whose stories he documents, Hersey writes, "They still wonder why they lived when so many others died." What implied theme about war does Hersey express with this question?

4. **Key Ideas and Details** In "Death of the Ball Turret Gunner," what is the poet saying about the value of an individual human life during war?

5. **Key Ideas and Details** What political assumptions about the value of the individual underlie "The Death of the Ball Turret Gunner"? Explain.

6. **Craft and Structure (a)** Use a chart like the one shown to explore similarities and differences between Hersey's and Jarrell's portrayals of victims in war. **(b)** Do the two selections share a common theme? Explain.

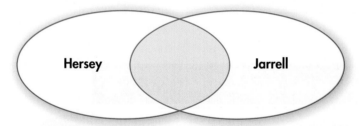

7. **Craft and Structure** In what ways does this quotation by Hersey speak to the implied theme of both selections? "It's a failure of national vision when you regard children as weapons, and talents as materials you can mine, assay, and fabricate for profit and defense."

8. **Integration of Knowledge and Ideas** **Analyze the political assumptions** Hersey expresses. **(a)** What political assumptions about the Japanese does Hersey challenge in *Hiroshima*? **(b)** How would you describe Hersey's political viewpoint? **(c)** Does Hersey present a consistent viewpoint on war throughout his account?

9. **Comparing Literary Works (a)** In *Hiroshima*, which descriptions evoke the strongest emotions in you? **(b)** Which lines in Jarrell's poem do you find most powerful? Explain. **(c)** For each work, would you characterize the writer's use of **perspective** as primarily objective or primarily subjective? Explain.

10. **Comparing Literary Works** Compare and contrast the effect of each author's use of the objective and subjective perspectives in these works.

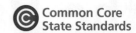 **Common Core State Standards**

Writing

2. Write explanatory texts to examine and convey complex ideas, concepts, and information clearly and accurately through the effective selection, organization, and analysis of content. *(p. 999)*

2.b. Develop the topic thoroughly by selecting the most significant and relevant facts, extended definitions, concrete details, quotations, or other information and examples appropriate to the audience's knowledge of the topic. *(p. 999)*

2.f. Provide a concluding statement that follows from and supports the information or explanation presented. *(p. 999)*

Language

4.c. Consult general reference materials, both print and digital, to determine or clarify the precise meaning of a word or its standard usage. *(p. 999)*

6. Acquire and use accurately general academic and domain-specific words and phrases, sufficient for reading, writing, speaking, and listening at the college and career readiness level. *(p. 999)*

Vocabulary Acquisition and Use

Military Words From Other Languages

A *rendezvous* was originally a place for the assembling of military troups. The word comes from the French words *rendez vous,* meaning "present yourself." Many English words related to the military and warfare have their origins in other languages. Match each word below with its origin. Then, provide the modern English definition of each word. Use a print or online dictionary to find or confirm the correct definitions.

1. *coup*	**a.** French for "barrel"
2. *barricade*	**b.** Urdu, Persian for "dusty"
3. *blitz*	**c.** French for "act of surveying"
4. *reconnaissance*	**d.** German for "lightning"
5. *khaki*	**e.** French for "blow" or "strike"

Vocabulary: Sentence Completions

Select the word from the vocabulary list on p. 982 that best completes each sentence below. Explain your choices.

1. She took on extra homework out of her own _____.

2. The birds _____ their nest and never returned to it.

3. The child's _____ whining bothered fellow train passengers on the long, slow trip.

4. We will have a _____ tomorrow at noon to compare our research notes.

5. Her _____ personality attracted many friends and admirers.

Writing to Sources

Explanatory Text Both Hersey and Jarrell present powerful themes about war. Write an **essay** to compare and contrast these themes as they are expressed in *Hiroshima* and "The Death of the Ball Turret Gunner."

Prewriting Review each selection and summarize the theme, or essential message about war that it presents. Jot down key similarities and differences between these messages, and note details from the selections that support these interpretations.

Drafting Begin with a vivid opening sentence. Then, summarize the similarities and differences you identified in the authors' themes. In the body of your essay, include detailed references to each selection to support your viewpoint. Restate your main points in a concluding paragraph.

Revising Review your work to make sure you have conveyed a clear sense of both literary works. Determine whether you have appropriately targeted the knowledge level of your expected audience, and revise as needed.

Model: Revising to Incorporate Quotations

Hersey's humane writing makes the city of Hiroshima very real for readers. He makes the day the atomic bomb exploded vivid by describing the lives of four survivors who still *"wonder why they lived when so many others died."* ~~think about what happened.~~

Adding quotations strengthens the connection between the writer's opinion and the text.

Primary Sources

Poster
Junk Rally Ad

Editorial Cartoon
The Battle of the Easy Chair

Editorial
Backing the Attack

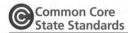 **Common Core State Standards**

Reading Informational Text
5. Analyze and evaluate the effectiveness of the structure an author uses in his or her exposition or argument, including whether the structure makes points clear, convincing, and engaging.

7. Integrate and evaluate multiple sources of information presented in different media or formats as well as in words in order to address a question or solve a problem.

About the Text Forms

All three of these selections are examples of persuasion—texts meant to convince an audience to take an action or think in a certain way. However, their approaches and structures are very different. An **editorial** is a persuasive essay that appears in a news publication and expresses the opinions of the publication's editor or editorial board. Its purpose is to affect readers' opinions on an issue of public concern. Most editorials are short and tightly structured. All include a clear *thesis*, or main idea, and several pieces of persuasive, high-interest support.

An **editorial cartoon** is a drawing that contains a message or opinion. It emphasizes visual elements such as oversimplified objects and caricatures. These combine with verbal elements, such as *captions* and embedded words, to express opinion, often in a humorous way.

An advertisement is a notice designed to attract customers or participation. Large, free-standing print ads, or **posters,** appear in every sort of public space. Poster ads typically include a heading, contact information or directions, visual elements, and one or more catchy phrases. As you read these texts, consider how their structural elements, both verbal and visual, help to convey the persuasive message.

Preparing to Read Complex Texts

Persuasive texts include many different types of techniques to sway readers or viewers. Among these is the use of visual symbols—pictures that carry strong meanings. For example, to evoke viewers' patriotism, a poster may use an image of the American flag, the bald eagle, or even just the colors red, white, and blue. Visual symbols have a variety of effects:

- They create immediate—and often strong—emotional associations.
- They may appeal to a viewers' sense of country, social group, or family.
- They may appeal to negative emotions, such as biases or fears.

As you review these documents, **evaluate the persuasive use of symbols** by identifying visual elements that are symbolic and assessing their effects on viewers.

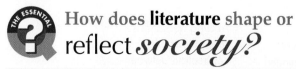

The makers of these documents were deeply concerned about national security during World War II. As you study the documents, identify the different goals each was designed to achieve. Ask what each document reveals about the forces that united and divided the country at war.

Note-Taking Guide

Primary source documents are a rich source of information for researchers. As you read these documents, use a note-taking guide like the one shown to organize relevant and accurate information.

1 Type of Primary Source (check one)
☐ E-mail ☐ Advertisement ☐ Letter ☐ Photograph
☐ Editorial ☐ Diary or Journal ☐ Map ☐ Cartoon

2 Date(s) of Document: _____

3 Are the messages in this source mainly visual, verbal, or both?

_____

Visual Elements

a Which visual elements are used in the piece?
☐ Objects ☐ People ☐ Colors
☐ Other Design Elements: _____

b Which of these elements are symbols, or stand for larger ideas? Explain. ◄······

Evaluating Symbols Images often do more than just decorate a text. They also convey meaning and may have symbolic value.

Verbal Elements

a Which verbal elements are used in the piece?
☐ Title: _____ ☐ Caption: _____
☐ Catchy Phrases: _____ ☐ Main Idea Statement: _____
☐ Other: _____

b Which of these verbal elements seem most important to you? Why?

_____
_____

4 Summarize the situation depicted in the primary source.

_____
_____

This guide was adapted from the **U.S. National Archives** poster and document analysis worksheets.

Vocabulary

civilian (sə vil´ yən) *n.* any person who is not a member of the armed forces (p. 1003)

license (lī´ səns) *n.* freedom from rules, appropriate behavior, or appropriate speech (p. 1005)

undertaking (un´ dər tā´ kiŋ) *n.* task or challenge (p. 1005)

canvass (kan´ vəs) *v.* to go through an area asking people for votes, orders, or participation (p. 1005)

collective (kə lek´ tiv) *adj.* gathered into a whole (p. 1005)

expenditures (ek spen´ di chərz) *n.* expenses; uses of money or resources (p. 1006)

estimates (es´ tə mits) *n.* general, careful calculations (p. 1006)

receipts (ri sēts´) *n.* amounts of money received (p. 1006)

THE STORY BEHIND THE DOCUMENTS

▲ World War II poster campaigns urged citizens to aid the war effort.

▲ Theodor Seuss Geisel, also known as Dr. Seuss

World War II began in Europe in 1939, with the Axis powers of Germany, Italy, and Japan opposing the Allied powers of France, Great Britain, and the Soviet Union. The United States, though sympathetic to the Allies, did not enter the war until December, 1941, after Japanese forces launched a surprise attack on the American naval base at Pearl Harbor, Hawaii.

Prior to the attack on Pearl Harbor, both the American government and the majority of its citizens had embraced a policy of isolationism, or neutrality. Still reeling from World War I and struggling to overcome the economic disaster of the Great Depression, Americans felt that they had few resources and little energy to offer the war effort. However, when 2,300 Americans were killed in the two-hour attack at Pearl Harbor, the mood changed dramatically. America entered the war—and it did so to win.

The United States and its allies fought on two main fronts: in Europe, against the totalitarian governments of Adolf Hitler in Germany and Benito Mussolini in Italy; and in the South Pacific, against fascist Japan. Throughout 1942, the Allies were on the defensive, but by 1943 the tide had turned. At home in the United States public optimism ran high. The war was surely near an end. Or was it?

The truth was that the war was more expensive than any conflict previously fought in American history. The United States government had to convert American optimism into action—and dollars. Appealing to the almost universal patriotism of its citizens, the government launched poster campaigns that urged citizens to support the war effort with their time, money, and even old junk. Efforts to rally the American public were also made by artists, celebrities, and high-profile journalists. The now-famous **Dr. Seuss** (Theodor Seuss Geisel, 1904–1991), for one, served as chief editorial cartoonist for the New York newspaper *PM* from 1941 to 1943. In that role he drew over 400 political cartoons condemning, among other things, isolationism, Hitler, the Japanese, and anti-war Americans. Meanwhile, in tandem with their political cartoonists, newspaper publishers printed editorials urging people not to grow complacent in their expectation of victory.

Americans responded. Families tightened their budgets and used the extra money to purchase war bonds, or government IOUs. Women tied kerchiefs in their hair and went to work in tank and airplane factories. Communities conserved resources by planting "victory gardens," and citizens of all ages hauled unused tires, appliances, and hardware to scrap drives. Participating in the drives made people feel useful, helped them express their patriotism, and boosted their morale.

Junk Rally
POSTER

The Winchester Salvage Committee

JUNK RALLY
For WINCHESTER

SATURDAY OCTOBER 3rd. at 2.30 P.M.
MANCHESTER FIELD

CIVILIAN DEFENSE DEMONSTRATION

Auxiliary Firemen
Auxiliary Police
Junior Police
Motor Corps
Medical Units
Canteen
Emergency Public Works Corps

St. Mary's Band Will Play

Junk helps make guns, tanks, ships for our fighting men . . . . Bring in anything made of metal . . .

If you cannot carry it
Call Winchester 0 2 0 7

Bring your family
Meet your friends

Throw YOUR scrap into the fight!

JUNK MAKES FIGHTING W

One old radiator will pr
scrap steel needed for s
teen .30 calibre rifle

One old lawn mower will
p make six 3-inch shells.

One useless old tire
will provide as much
rubber as is used in
12 gas masks.

One old shovel will
help make 4 hand
grenades.

Let's Jolt them with Junk from Winchester.

Salvage Committee, Defense Headquarters, 572 Main Street, Winchester 0207

Vocabulary
civilian (sə vil' yən) *n.* any person who is not a member of the armed forces

One old radiator will provide scrap steel needed for seventeen .30 calibre rifles.

One old lawn mower will help make six 3-inch shells.

One useless old tire will provide as much rubber as is used in 12 gas masks.

One old shovel will help make 4 hand grenades.

The Battle of the
EASY CHAIR

Dr. Seuss

This cartoon appeared in the newspaper *PM* on December 13, 1941, just five days after Japanese forces attacked the American base at Pearl Harbor, Hawaii. The setting is a members-only club where gentlemen could unwind, talk with friends, eat, and play games. Here, the club member relaxes in the company of his valet, or personal servant.

The Battle of the Easy Chair

"Wake me, Judkins, when the Victory Parade comes by!"

Dr. Seuss

BACKING THE ATTACK

The New York Times Editorial

On September 8, 1943, General Dwight D. Eisenhower, commander-in-chief of the Allied forces in the Mediterranean, announced that Italy had surrendered. This news followed closely on the heels of several successful Allied attacks in Japan. Suddenly, it seemed as if the war would come to a rapid end. However, in a radio address from the White House later that evening, President Franklin D. Roosevelt warned Americans that "The time for celebration is not yet . . . This war does not and must not stop for one single instant." Days later, *The New York Times* ran the following editorial. Its main subject is war bonds—certificates that promised a payback of the face value plus interest at a specified future date.

The New York Times

September 12, 1943

The great news you have heard today from General Eisenhower does not give you the **license** *to settle back in your rocking chairs and say "Well, that does it. We've got 'em on the run. Now we can start the celebration."*

With these words, President Roosevelt last Wednesday night warned Americans against over-optimism. He spoke on the eve of the Treasury Department's third campaign to sell $15,000,000,000 in war bonds. The next afternoon, to open the two-month drive, the greatest financial **undertaking** in the history of the world, 3,000 men and women of the armed forces, trained Army dogs, jeeps, trucks and war material paraded down New York's Fifth Avenue. There were similar celebrations across the United States. Half a million salesmen in New York City alone, millions more throughout the country, began a **canvass** of American citizens, who already are purchasing $4,600,000,000 in bonds by payroll savings deducted from their **collective** annual income of $140,000,000,000.

Vocabulary

license (lī′ səns) *n.* freedom from rules, appropriate behavior, or appropriate speech

undertaking (un′ dər tā′ kiŋ) *n.* task or challenge

canvass (kan′ vəs) *v.* to go through an area asking people for votes, orders, or participation

collective (kə lek′ tiv) *adj.* gathered into a whole

Comprehension
What enormous effort did the Treasury Department undertake?

Vocabulary

expenditures
(ek spen´ di chərz)
n. expenses; uses of
money or resources

estimates (es´ tə mits) *n.*
general, careful calculations

receipts (ri sēts´) *n.*
amounts of money received

The $15,000,000,000 bond issue will help finance the war. From July 1, 1940, to August 31, 1943, war expenditures totaled about $124,000,000,000. (Between 1789 and 1932, the Government spent $108,000,000,000.) The breakdown figure of $71,000,000,000 used for war in 1942 will be increased 80 per cent if estimates of $106,000,000,000 needed for military expenses during 1943 are correct.

The new estimate is three times the total cost of the World War, including loans to Allies. Taxes provide but 38 per cent of this. The first two War Bond drives added $31,500,000,000 to Government receipts. When the last War Bond is subscribed in this third campaign, the Government should have enough money to pay, at the present average spending rate, for two months of war.

The items of war which varying purchases of war bonds would buy were being listed by speakers at War Bond rallies in every State. The purchase of a hundred dollar bond would just about outfit a sailor. A $40,000,000 bond could build a cruiser; $150 would completely equip a soldier or marine or buy a parachute, $750 would build a bantam jeep, $1,500 would send up a barrage balloon, $3,000 would launch a marine landing barge. For $6,100, a bombsight would be made, for $125,000 a dive bomber. Medium bombers cost $175,000, and heavy bombers $300,000. It cost $436,000,000 to crush Hamburg. It will cost $2,076,000,000 to destroy Berlin.

Critical Reading

1. **Key Ideas and Details (a) Summarize:** Describe the event advertised in the poster. **(b) Connect:** How does the illustration at top right of the poster relate to the event? **(c) Analyze:** To what basic emotions or values does the illustration appeal?

2. **Key Ideas and Details (a) Infer:** What feelings or beliefs about the war does Dr. Seuss address in this editorial cartoon? Explain. **(b) Summarize:** How would you convey that same message in words?

3. **Integration of Knowledge and Ideas Evaluate:** Why do you think the editorial writer presented such a long list of specific items that could be purchased for the war effort?

Poster • Editorial Cartoon • Editorial

Comparing Primary Sources

Refer to your note-taking guide to complete these questions.

1. (a) Use a chart like the one shown to identify one strong visual element in the poster and in the editorial cartoon and one strong verbal element in the editorial. **(b)** Does each element you chose appeal to reason or to a particular emotion? Explain.

Document	Strong Verbal or Visual Element	What It Appeals To
Poster		
Cartoon		
Editorial		

2. (a) What does the junk rally poster reveal about small-town attitudes toward the war effort? **(b)** What does the poster reveal about American attitudes toward the enemy?

3. (a) Summarize the persuasive message of the editorial cartoon. **(b)** Summarize the message of the editorial. **(c)** How are these messages similar and different? Explain, identifying specific structural elements that contribute to the message of each text.

Vocabulary Acquisition and Use

Sentence Completions Use a word from the vocabulary list on page 1001 to fill in each blank, and explain your choice. Use each word only once.

1. This petition will be a big _____. First, let's _____ the neighborhood for signatures.

2. Winning the contest does not give you _____ to gloat.

Content-Area Vocabulary Answer each question. Then, explain your answer.

3. Should an elected official express the *collective* opinion of the voters?

4. To keep a budget balanced, should *expenditures* outweigh *receipts*?

5. How might population *estimates* help a city council?

6. When they are on the job, do *civilians* wear military uniforms?

Etymology Study The word *civilian* comes from the Latin word *civis*, which means "home" or "the place where one dwells." Use an online or print dictionary to locate four other words that come from this root. Explain how the meaning of each word relates to that of its Latin ancestor.

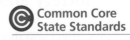
Common Core State Standards

Writing
6. Use technology, including the Internet, to produce individual writing products. *(p. 1008)*
7. Conduct short as well as more sustained research projects to answer a question or solve a problem; narrow or broaden the inquiry when appropriate; synthesize multiple sources on the subject, demonstrating understanding of the subject under investigation. *(p. 1008)*
8. Gather relevant information from multiple authoritative print and digital sources, using advanced searches effectively; integrate information into the text selectively to maintain the flow of ideas. *(p. 1008)*

Language
4.c. Consult general and specialized reference materials, both print and digital, to find the pronunciation of a word or determine or clarify its precise meaning, its part of speech, its etymology, or its standard usage.
6. Acquire and use accurately general academic and domain-specific words and phrases, sufficient for reading, writing, speaking, and listening at the college and career readiness level; demonstrate independence in gathering vocabulary knowledge when considering a word or phrase important to comprehension or expression.

Research Task

Topic: Society and Culture in the Media

Do images affect you more than words do? Politicians, business leaders, advertisers, cartoonists, and film directors all know that visual media may sway people more effectively than words or traditional texts on their own.

Assignment: Create a computer slide show or poster presentation in which you analyze several editorial cartoons. Use historical or contemporary cartoons, and evaluate how messages in the cartoons present social and cultural views differently than do traditional written texts.

Formulate your research plan. Editorial cartoons address almost every aspect of life, so you need to choose one area to research. Consider politics, sports, education, business, the arts, or an aspect of social life, such as dating. Then, formulate a limited and manageable research question, such as, "What attitudes do editorial cartoons express about schools in my city?"

Gather sources. Use online and library searches to examine editorial cartoons in historical collections or newspaper archives. Maintain accurate records of the source name, date, and page of each cartoon.

Synthesize information. Choose several cartoons to analyze. For each cartoon, use a graphic organizer like the one shown to identify the historical context, the intended audience, the social or cultural message, and the tone.

Model: Analyzing an Editorial Cartoon

Context	Historical: presidential election
Audience	Undecided voters
Message	Candidate does not inspire confidence
Tone	Ironic, humorous

Synthesize your findings about each cartoon into a single statement. Comment on how the use of visuals and humor makes the cartoon more or less effective than a traditional, written editorial. Consider this example:

> This cartoon uses exaggeration to persuade people that we should have a leader who inspires confidence. The cartoon format does this with no words at all, which is very different from a traditional, written text.

Organize and present your ideas. If possible, enlarge the cartoons and be sure all the text, including the captions and text in speech or thought "bubbles," is readable. Use typeface, layout, color, and graphics to make your presentation easy to follow.

▲ This editorial cartoon from 1942 indicates America's military might.

RESEARCH TIP

You might find ideas in the huge archive of categorized images available online through the Library of Congress American Memory collection.

Use a checklist like the one shown to evaluate your work.

Research Checklist

☐ Have I made my research question manageable?

☐ Have I answered my main research question?

☐ Have I identified and analyzed the individual elements of each cartoon?

☐ Have I synthesized my findings into clear and comprehensive statements?

Tradition and Rebellion

Connecting to the Essential Question This story paints a vivid picture of a rural community in the American South. As you read, notice how O'Connor depicts the setting and its influence on the characters. Your observations will help as you reflect on the Essential Question: **What is the relationship between literature and place?**

Close Reading Focus

Grotesque Character; Characterization

The word *grotesque* in literature does not mean "ugly" or "disgusting," as it sometimes does in popular speech. In literature, the **grotesque character** is one who has become bizarre or twisted, usually through some kind of obsession. Grotesque traits may be expressed in a character's physical appearance. Alternatively, they may be hidden, visible only in a character's actions and emotions.

O'Connor creates grotesques in this story through **characterization**—the revelation of personality. In **direct characterization,** the writer simply tells the reader what a character is like. With **indirect characterization,** traits are revealed through these elements:

- the character's words, thoughts, and actions
- descriptions of the character's appearance or background
- what other characters say about him or her
- how other characters react or respond

As you read, examine O'Connor's use of characterization, noting examples of extreme behavior, distortions, and striking oddities that make all three main characters grotesques.

Preparing to Read Complex Texts A *conclusion* is a decision or judgment you make after considering specific information. O'Connor writes with a sharp eye for meaningful details. As you read, **draw conclusions** from these details to deepen your understanding of the meaning of the story as a whole. Use a chart like the one shown to record details and the conclusions you draw from them.

Vocabulary

The words below are important to understanding the text that follows. Copy the words into your notebook. Which two words have the same suffix? What might that suffix indicate?

desolate	ravenous
listed	morose
ominous	

**Common Core
State Standards**

Reading Literature

1. Cite strong and thorough textual evidence to support analysis of what the text says explicitly as well as inferences drawn from the text, including determining where the text leaves matters uncertain.

3. Analyze the impact of the author's choices regarding how to develop and relate elements of a story or drama (e.g., how the characters are introduced and developed).

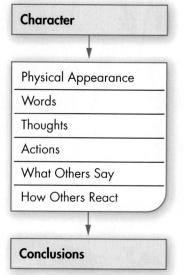

Flannery O'Connor
(1925–1964)

Author of **"The Life You Save May Be Your Own"**

Born in Savannah, Georgia, Flannery O'Connor was raised in the small Georgia town of Milledgeville. She earned her undergraduate degree from Georgia State College for Women and then attended the celebrated University of Iowa Writers' Workshop. While still in graduate school, she published her first short story, "Geranium."

Land of the Sick In 1950, O'Connor became ill with lupus, a serious disease that restricted her independence. She moved back to the family farm outside Milledgeville, where she lived with her mother. "I have never been anywhere but sick," she wrote. "In a sense, sickness is a place more instructive than a trip to Europe." Despite her illness, O'Connor committed herself not only to her writing but also to "the habit of art," an enlivened way of thinking and seeing. In 1952, she published her first novel, *Wise Blood*. She would ultimately publish a second novel and two story collections.

A Triumphant Spirit Throughout most of her adult life, O'Connor lived with pain and the awareness that she would probably die young. Despite her condition, she often seemed joyous, entertaining friends at home and painting watercolors of the peacocks that she and her mother raised. Still, her disease set her apart, and O'Connor felt a kinship with eccentrics and outsiders. Many of her characters are social misfits or people who are physically or mentally challenged. Although she paints these characters in an unsentimental way, O'Connor brings to their stories an underlying sense of sympathy, which reflects both her own physical problems and her Catholic faith.

Religious Faith O'Connor was raised as a devout Catholic in a region of the American South that was largely Protestant. She considered herself a religious writer in a world that had abandoned true values. In an effort to point out the spiritual failings of the modern world, she often highlights characters with dubious moral and intellectual capabilities. "The Life You Save May Be Your Own" is a typical O'Connor work. In its grim depiction of a group of outcasts, the story conveys shrewd insights, a powerful moral message, and an urgent sense of the tragic realities of modern life.

> "I am a writer because writing is the thing I do best."

Deep Fork Overlook, Joan Marron-LaRue

THE Life YOU Save MAY BE Your Own

Flannery O'Connor

Background Gothic literature, a genre of fiction that developed in Britain in the late 1700s, features horror and violence. Traditional gothic tales are often set against dramatic, gloomy backdrops—remote castles, deserted fortresses, and the like. Such literature acknowledges evil as a real force and ascribes to some characters a dark side that lures them to violent or wicked acts. Flannery O'Connor borrowed some devices from Gothic fiction, such as a foreboding atmosphere and grotesque characters, but she set her stories in an unremarkable American landscape. The story you are about to read is a perfect example of her exploration of the Gothic under the familiar sunlight of the American South.

The old woman and her daughter were sitting on their porch when Mr. Shiftlet came up their road for the first time. The old woman slid to the edge of her chair and leaned forward, shading her eyes from the piercing sunset with her hand. The daughter could not see far in front of her and continued to play with her fingers. Although the old woman lived in this desolate spot with only her daughter and she had never seen Mr. Shiftlet before, she could tell, even from a distance, that he was a tramp and no one to be afraid of. His left coat sleeve was folded up to show there was only half an arm in it and his gaunt figure listed slightly to the side as if the breeze were pushing him. He had on a black town suit and a brown felt hat that was turned up in the front and down in the back and he carried a tin tool box by a handle. He came on, at an amble, up her road, his face turned toward the sun which appeared to be balancing itself on the peak of a small mountain.

The old woman didn't change her position until he was almost into her yard; then she rose with one hand fisted on her hip. The daughter, a large girl in a short blue organdy dress, saw him all at once and jumped up and began to stamp and point and make excited speechless sounds.

◀ **Critical Viewing** Visually, what is the most important part of this setting—the chickens, the truck, or some other element? Explain. **ANALYZE**

Vocabulary

desolate (des´ ə lit) *adj.*
forlorn; wretched

listed (list´ id) *v.*
tilted; inclined

Comprehension

Who does the old woman notice coming up the road?

Mr. Shiftlet stopped just inside the yard and set his box on the ground and tipped his hat at her as if she were not in the least afflicted; then he turned toward the old woman and swung the hat all the way off. He had long black slick hair that hung flat from a part in the middle to beyond the tips of his ears on either side. His face descended in forehead for more than half its length and ended suddenly with his features just balanced over a jutting steel-trap jaw. He seemed to be a young man but he had a look of composed dissatisfaction as if he understood life thoroughly.

"Good evening," the old woman said. She was about the size of a cedar fence post and she had a man's gray hat pulled down low over her head.

The tramp stood looking at her and didn't answer. He turned his back and faced the sunset. He swung both his whole and his short arm up slowly so that they indicated an expanse of sky and his figure formed a crooked cross. The old woman watched him with her arms folded across her chest as if she were the owner of the sun, and the daughter watched, her head thrust forward and her fat helpless hands hanging at the wrists. She had long pink-gold hair and eyes as blue as a peacock's neck.

He held the pose for almost fifty seconds and then he picked up his box and came on to the porch and dropped down on the bottom step. "Lady," he said in a firm nasal voice, "I'd give a fortune to live where I could see me a sun do that every evening."

"Does it every evening," the old woman said and sat back down. The daughter sat down too and watched him with a cautious sly look as if he were a bird that had come up very close. He leaned to one side, rooting in his pants pocket, and in a second he brought out a package of chewing gum and offered her a piece. She took it and unpeeled it and began to chew without taking her eyes off him. He offered the old woman a piece but she only raised her upper lip to indicate she had no teeth.

Mr. Shiftlet's pale sharp glance had already passed over everything in the yard—the pump near the corner of the house and the big fig tree that three or four chickens were preparing to roost in—and had moved to a shed where he saw the square rusted back of an automobile. "You ladies drive?" he asked.

"That car ain't run in fifteen year," the old woman said. "The day my husband died, it quit running."

"Nothing is like it used to be, lady," he said. "The world is almost rotten."

"That's right," the old woman said. "You from around here?"

"Name Tom T. Shiftlet," he murmured, looking at the tires.

"I'm pleased to meet you," the old woman said. "Name Lucynell Crater and daughter Lucynell Crater. What you doing around here, Mr. Shiftlet?"

He judged the car to be about a 1928 or '29 Ford. "Lady," he said, and turned and gave her his full attention, "lemme tell you something.

Grotesque Characters and Characterization

What exaggerated traits do you perceive in this description of the three characters?

Grotesque Characters and Characterization

What personality traits are suggested by this description of Mr. Shiftlet's "pale sharp glance"?

There's one of these doctors in Atlanta that's taken a knife and cut the human heart—the human heart," he repeated, leaning forward, "out of a man's chest and held it in his hand," and he held his hand out, palm up, as if it were slightly weighted with the human heart, "and studied it like it was a day-old chicken, and lady," he said, allowing a long significant pause in which his head slid forward and his clay-colored eyes brightened, "he don't know no more about it than you or me."

"That's right," the old woman said.

"Why, if he was to take that knife and cut into every corner of it, he still wouldn't know no more than you or me. What you want to bet?"

"Nothing," the old woman said wisely. "Where you come from, Mr. Shiftlet?"

He didn't answer. He reached into his pocket and brought out a sack of tobacco and a package of cigarette papers and rolled himself a cigarette, expertly with one hand, and attached it in a hanging position to his upper lip. Then he took a box of wooden matches from his pocket and struck one on his shoe. He held the burning match as if he were studying the mystery of flame while it traveled dangerously toward his skin. The daughter began to make loud noises and to point to his hand and shake her finger at him, but when the flame was just before touching him, he leaned down with his hand cupped over it as if he were going to set fire to his nose and lit the cigarette.

He flipped away the dead match and blew a stream of gray into the evening. A sly look came over his face. "Lady," he said, "nowadays, people'll do anything anyways. I can tell you my name is Tom T. Shiftlet and I come from Tarwater, Tennessee, but you never have seen me before: how you know I ain't lying? How you know my name ain't Aaron Sparks, lady, and I come from Singleberry, Georgia, or how you know it's not George Speeds and I come from Lucy, Alabama, or how you know I ain't Thompson Bright from Toolafalls, Mississippi?"

"I don't know nothing about you," the old woman muttered, irked.

"Lady," he said, "people don't care how they lie. Maybe the best I can tell you is, I'm a man; but listen lady," he said and paused and made his tone more ominous still, "what is a man?"

The old woman began to gum a seed. "What you carry in that tin box, Mr. Shiftlet?" she asked.

"Tools," he said, put back. "I'm a carpenter."

"Well, if you come out here to work, I'll be able to feed you and give you a place to sleep but I can't pay. I'll tell you that before you begin," she said.

There was no answer at once and no particular expression on his face. He leaned back against the two-by-four that helped support the porch roof. "Lady," he said slowly, "there's some men that some things mean more to them than money." The old woman rocked without comment and the daughter watched the trigger that moved up and down in his neck. He told the old woman then that all most people

> "Lady," he said, "people don't care how they lie."

Drawing Conclusions
Why do you think Shiftlet is so concerned about lying?

Vocabulary
ominous (äm´ ə nəs)
adj. threatening; sinister

Comprehension
Can the young Lucynell speak?

were interested in was money, but he asked what a man was made for. He asked her if a man was made for money, or what. He asked her what she thought she was made for but she didn't answer, she only sat rocking and wondered if a one-armed man could put a new roof on her garden house. He asked a lot of questions that she didn't answer. He told her that he was twenty-eight years old and had lived a varied life. He had been a gospel singer, a foreman on the railroad, an assistant in an undertaking parlor, and he come over the radio for three months with Uncle Roy and his Red Creek Wranglers. He said he had fought and bled in the Arm Service of his country and visited every foreign land and that everywhere he had seen people that didn't care if they did a thing one way or another. He said he hadn't been raised thataway.

A fat yellow moon appeared in the branches of the fig tree as if it were going to roost there with the chickens. He said that a man had to escape to the country to see the world whole and that he wished he lived in a desolate place like this where he could see the sun go down every evening like God made it to do.

"Are you married or are you single?" the old woman asked.

There was a long silence. "Lady," he asked finally, "where would you find you an innocent woman today? I wouldn't have any of this trash I could just pick up."

The daughter was leaning very far down, hanging her head almost between her knees watching him through a triangular door she had made in her overturned hair; and she suddenly fell in a heap on the floor and began to whimper. Mr. Shiftlet straightened her out and helped her get back in the chair.

"Is she your baby girl?" he asked.

"My only," the old woman said "and she's the sweetest girl in the world. I would give her up for nothing on earth. She's smart too. She can sweep the floor, cook, wash, feed the chickens, and hoe. I wouldn't give her up for a casket of jewels."

"No," he said kindly, "don't ever let any man take her away from you."

"Any man come after her," the old woman said, "'ll have to stay around the place."

Mr. Shiftlet's eye in the darkness was focused on a part of the automobile bumper that glittered in the distance. "Lady," he said, jerking his short arm up as if he could point with it to her house and yard and pump, "there ain't a broken thing on this plantation that I couldn't fix for you, one-arm jackleg or not. I'm a man," he said with a sullen dignity, "even if I ain't a whole one. I got," he said, tapping his knuckles on the floor to emphasize the immensity of what he was going to say, "a moral intelligence!" and his face pierced out of the darkness into a shaft of doorlight and he stared at her as if he were astonished himself at this impossible truth.

Spiral Review
Personification Which words describe the moon as though it were a living creature? Explain.

Grotesque Characters and Characterization

What does this dialogue about her daughter reveal about the old woman?

Black Walnuts, 1945, Joseph Pollet, Oil on canvas, 30" × 40", Collection of Whitney Museum of American Art, Purchase, Gift of Gertrude Vanderbilt Whitney, by exchange

The old woman was not impressed with the phrase. "I told you you could hang around and work for food," she said, "if you don't mind sleeping in that car yonder."

"Why listen, lady," he said with a grin of delight, "the monks of old slept in their coffins!"

"They wasn't as advanced as we are," the old woman said.

The next morning he began on the roof of the garden house while Lucynell, the daughter, sat on a rock and watched him work. He had not been around a week before the change he had made in the place was apparent. He had patched the front and back steps, built a new hog pen, restored a fence, and taught Lucynell, who was completely deaf and had never said a word in her life, to say the word "bird." The big rosy-faced girl followed him everywhere, saying "Burrttddt ddb-irrrttdt," and clapping her hands. The old woman watched from a distance, secretly pleased. She was **ravenous** for a son-in-law.

Mr. Shiftlet slept on the hard narrow back seat of the car with his feet out the side window. He had his razor and a can of water on a crate that served him as a bedside table and he put up a piece of mirror against the back glass and kept his coat neatly on a hanger that he hung over one of the windows.

▲ **Critical Viewing**
Which aspects of the story are reflected in this painting? **CONNECT**

Vocabulary
ravenous (rav´ ə nəs)
adj. extremely eager

Comprehension
For what is the old woman "ravenous"?

> The girl
> was nearly
> thirty but
> because of her
> innocence it
> was impossible
> to guess.

In the evenings he sat on the steps and talked while the old woman and Lucynell rocked violently in their chairs on either side of him. The old woman's three mountains were black against the dark blue sky and were visited off and on by various planets and by the moon after it had left the chickens. Mr. Shiftlet pointed out that the reason he had improved this plantation was because he had taken a personal interest in it. He said he was even going to make the automobile run.

He had raised the hood and studied the mechanism and he said he could tell that the car had been built in the days when cars were really built. You take now, he said, one man puts in one bolt and another man puts in another bolt and another man puts in another bolt so that it's a man for a bolt. That's why you have to pay so much for a car: you're paying all those men. Now if you didn't have to pay but one man, you could get you a cheaper car and one that had had a personal interest taken in it, and it would be a better car. The old woman agreed with him that this was so.

Mr. Shiftlet said that the trouble with the world was that nobody cared, or stopped and took any trouble. He said he never would have been able to teach Lucynell to say a word if he hadn't cared and stopped long enough.

"Teach her to say something else," the old woman said.

"What you want her to say next?" Mr. Shiftlet asked.

The old woman's smile was broad and toothless and suggestive. "Teach her to say 'sugarpie,'" she said.

Mr. Shiftlet already knew what was on her mind.

The next day he began to tinker with the automobile and that evening he told her that if she would buy a fan belt, he would be able to make the car run.

The old woman said she would give him the money. "You see that girl yonder?" she asked, pointing to Lucynell who was sitting on the floor a foot away, watching him, her eyes blue even in the dark. "If it was ever a man wanted to take her away, I would say, 'No man on earth is going to take that sweet girl of mine away from me!' but if he was to say, 'Lady, I don't want to take her away, I want her right here,' I would say, 'Mister, I don't blame you none. I wouldn't pass up a chance to live in a permanent place and get the sweetest girl in the world myself. You ain't no fool,' I would say."

"How old is she?" Mr. Shiftlet asked casually.

"Fifteen, sixteen," the old woman said. The girl was nearly thirty but because of her innocence it was impossible to guess.

"It would be a good idea to paint it too," Mr. Shiftlet remarked. "You don't want it to rust out."

"We'll see about that later," the old woman said.

The next day he walked into town and returned with the parts he needed and a can of gasoline. Late in the afternoon, terrible noises issued from the shed and the old woman rushed out of the house,

Grotesque Characters and Characterization

What does Mr. Shiftlet's remark about the car reveal about his obsession?

thinking Lucynell was somewhere having a fit. Lucynell was sitting on a chicken crate, stamping her feet and screaming, "Burrdddtt! bddurrddtttt!" but her fuss was drowned out by the car. With a volley of blasts it emerged from the shed, moving in a fierce and stately way. Mr. Shiftlet was in the driver's seat, sitting very erect. He had an expression of serious modesty on his face as if he had just raised the dead.

That night, rocking on the porch, the old woman began her business, at once. "You want you an innocent woman, don't you?" she asked sympathetically. "You don't want none of this trash."

"No'm, I don't," Mr. Shiftlet said.

"One that can't talk," she continued, "can't sass you back or use foul language. That's the kind for you to have. Right there," and she pointed to Lucynell sitting crosslegged in her chair, holding both feet in her hands.

"That's right," he admitted. "She wouldn't give me any trouble."

"Saturday," the old woman said, "you and her and me can drive into town and get married."

Mr. Shiftlet eased his position on the steps.

"I can't get married right now," he said. "Everything you want to do takes money and I ain't got any."

"What you need with money?" she asked.

"It takes money," he said. "Some people'll do anything anyhow these days, but the way I think, I wouldn't marry no woman that I couldn't take on a trip like she was somebody. I mean take her to a hotel and treat her. I wouldn't marry the Duchesser Windsor," he said firmly, "unless I could take her to a hotel and giver something good to eat.

"I was raised thataway and there ain't a thing I can do about it. My old mother taught me how to do."

"Lucynell don't even know what a hotel is," the old woman muttered. "Listen here, Mr. Shiftlet," she said, sliding forward in her chair, "you'd be getting a permanent house and a deep well and the most innocent girl in the world. You don't need no money. Lemme tell you something: there ain't any place in the world for a poor disabled friendless drifting man."

The ugly words settled in Mr. Shiftlet's head like a group of buzzards in the top of a tree.

He didn't answer at once. He rolled himself a cigarette and lit it and then he said in an even voice, "Lady, a man is divided into two parts, body and spirit."

The old woman clamped her gums together.

"A body and a spirit," he repeated. "The body, lady, is like a house: it don't go anywhere; but the spirit, lady, is like a automobile: always on the move, always . . ."

"Listen, Mr. Shiftlet," she said, "my well never goes dry and my house is always warm in the winter and there's no mortgage on a thing about this place. You can go to the courthouse and see for

Grotesque Characters and Characterization

What is revealed about Mr. Shiftlet and the old woman in this exchange about marriage and money?

Comprehension

What does Mr. Shiftlet do with the old car?

> ...Mr. Shiftlet's smile stretched like a weary snake waking up by a fire.

Vocabulary

morose (mə rōs´) *adj.*
gloomy; sullen

Drawing Conclusions
Based on this speech about his dissatisfaction with the law, what conclusions can you draw about Shiftlet?

yourself. And yonder under that shed is a fine automobile." She laid the bait carefully. "You can have it painted by Saturday. I'll pay for the paint."

In the darkness, Mr. Shiftlet's smile stretched like a weary snake waking up by a fire. After a second he recalled himself and said, "I'm only saying a man's spirit means more to him than anything else. I would have to take my wife off for the weekend without no regards at all for cost. I got to follow where my spirit says to go."

"I'll give you fifteen dollars for a weekend trip," the old woman said in a crabbed voice. "That's the best I can do."

"That wouldn't hardly pay for more than the gas and the hotel," he said. "It wouldn't feed her."

"Seventeen-fifty," the old woman said. "That's all I got so it isn't any use you trying to milk me. You can take a lunch."

Mr. Shiftlet was deeply hurt by the word "milk." He didn't doubt that she had more money sewed up in her mattress but he had already told her he was not interested in her money. "I'll make that do," he said and rose and walked off without treating with her further.

On Saturday the three of them drove into town in the car that the paint had barely dried on and Mr. Shiftlet and Lucynell were married in the Ordinary's office while the old woman witnessed. As they came out of the courthouse, Mr. Shiftlet began twisting his neck in his collar. He looked morose and bitter as if he had been insulted while someone held him. "That didn't satisfy me none," he said. "That was just something a woman in an office did, nothing but paper work and blood tests. What do they know about my blood? If they was to take my heart and cut it out," he said, "they wouldn't know a thing about me. It didn't satisfy me at all."

"It satisfied the law," the old woman said sharply.

"The law," Mr. Shiftlet said and spit. "It's the law that don't satisfy me."

He had painted the car dark green with a yellow band around it just under the windows. The three of them climbed in the front seat and the old woman said, "Don't Lucynell look pretty? Looks like a baby doll." Lucynell was dressed up in a white dress that her mother had uprooted from a trunk and there was a Panama hat on her head with a bunch of red wooden cherries on the brim. Every now and then her placid expression was changed by a sly isolated little thought like a shoot of green in the desert.

"You got a prize!" the old woman said.

Mr. Shiftlet didn't even look at her. They drove back to the house to let the old woman off and pick up the lunch. When they were ready to leave, she stood staring in the window of the car, with her fingers clenched around the glass. Tears began to seep sideways out of her eyes and run along the dirty creases in her face. "I ain't ever been parted with her for two days before," she said.

Mr. Shiftlet started the motor.

"And I wouldn't let no man have her but you because I seen you would do right. Goodbye, Sugarbaby," she said, clutching at the sleeve of the white dress. Lucynell looked straight at her and didn't seem to see her there at all. Mr. Shiftlet eased the car forward so that she had to move her hands.

The early afternoon was clear and open and surrounded by pale blue sky. Although the car would go only thirty miles an hour, Mr. Shiftlet imagined a terrific climb and dip and swerve that went entirely to his head so that he forgot his morning bitterness. He had always wanted an automobile but he had never been able to afford one before. He drove very fast because he wanted to make Mobile by nightfall.

Occasionally he stopped his thoughts long enough to look at Lucynell in the seat beside him. She had eaten the lunch as soon as they were out of the yard and now she was pulling the cherries off the hat one by one and throwing them out the window. He became depressed in spite of the car. He had driven about a hundred miles when he decided that she must be hungry again and at the next small town they came to, he stopped in front of an aluminum-painted eating place called The Hot Spot and took her in and ordered her a plate of ham and grits. The ride had made her sleepy and as soon as she got up on the stool, she rested her head on the counter and shut her eyes. There was no one in The Hot Spot but Mr. Shiftlet and the boy behind the counter, a pale youth with a greasy rag hung over his shoulder. Before he could dish up the food, she was snoring gently.

"Give it to her when she wakes up," Mr. Shiftlet said. "I'll pay for it now." The boy bent over her and stared at the long pink-gold hair and the half-shut sleeping eyes. Then he looked up and stared at Mr. Shiftlet. "She looks like an angel of Gawd," he murmured.

"Hitchhiker," Mr. Shiftlet explained. "I can't wait. I got to make Tuscaloosa."

The boy bent over again and very carefully touched his finger to a strand of the golden hair and Mr. Shiftlet left.

He was more depressed than ever as he drove on by himself. The late afternoon had grown hot and sultry and the country had flattened out. Deep in the sky a storm was preparing very slowly and without thunder as if it meant to drain every drop of air from the earth before it broke. There were times when Mr. Shiftlet preferred not to be alone. He felt too that a man with a car had a responsibility to others and he kept his eye out for a hitchhiker. Occasionally he saw a sign that warned: "Drive carefully. The life you save may be your own."

The American EXPERIENCE

Southern Regionalism

While writers have the capacity to invent whole new worlds, they are human beings who are influenced by their environments. Regional writers are those who use specific geographical areas—usually their home turf—as settings. Yet, regionalists do more than simply set their fiction in familiar locales; they incorporate the distinct culture of an area, including characteristic speech patterns, customs, beliefs, history, and folklore into the very fabric of their stories. This marriage of place, sensibility, and style goes beyond mere reporting to present a sophisticated treatment of the culture of a region. With the best regional writers, local detail helps to create stories of universal impact. You need not be from the American South to appreciate the work of such great Southern regional writers as Flannery O'Connor, Truman Capote, Carson McCullers, Tennessee Williams, William Faulkner, Eudora Welty, or Robert Penn Warren.

Connect to the Literature

What details in this story reflect a Southern sensibility? Could this story be set in a different region? Explain.

Comprehension

What does Mr. Shiftlet do when Lucynell falls asleep at The Hot Spot?

▶ **Critical Viewing**

Does this painting reflect the mood of the story's closing scene? Explain. **EVALUATE**

The narrow road dropped off on either side into dry fields and here and there a shack or a filling station stood in a clearing. The sun began to set directly in front of the automobile. It was a reddening ball that through his windshield was slightly flat on the bottom and top. He saw a boy in overalls and a gray hat standing on the edge of the road and he slowed the car down and stopped in front of him. The boy didn't have his hand raised to thumb the ride, he was only standing there, but he had a small cardboard suitcase and his hat was set on his head in a way to indicate that he had left somewhere for good. "Son," Mr. Shiftlet said, "I see you want a ride."

The boy didn't say he did or he didn't but he opened the door of the car and got in, and Mr. Shiftlet started driving again. The child held the suitcase on his lap and folded his arms on top of it. He turned his head and looked out the window away from Shiftlet. Mr. Shiftlet felt oppressed. "Son," he said after a minute, "I got the best old mother in the world so I reckon you only got the second best."

The boy gave him a quick dark glance and then turned his face back out the window.

"It's nothing so sweet," Mr. Shiftlet continued, "as a boy's mother. She taught him his first prayers at her knee, she give him love when no other would, she told him what was right and what wasn't, and she seen that he done the right thing. Son," he said, "I never rued a day in my life like the one I rued when I left that old mother of mine."

The boy shifted in his seat but he didn't look at Mr. Shiftlet. He unfolded his arms and put one hand on the door handle.

"My mother was a angel of Gawd," Mr. Shiftlet said in a very strained voice. "He took her from heaven and giver to me and I left her." His eyes were instantly clouded over with a mist of tears. The car was barely moving.

The boy turned angrily in the seat. "You go to the devil!" he cried.

"My old woman is a flea bag and yours is a stinking pole cat!" and with that he flung the door open and jumped out with his suitcase into the ditch.

Mr. Shiftlet was so shocked that for about a hundred feet he drove along slowly with the door still open. A cloud, the exact color of the boy's hat and shaped like a turnip, had descended over the sun, and another, worse looking, crouched behind the car. Mr. Shiftlet felt that the rottenness of the world was about to engulf him. He raised his arm and let it fall again to his breast. "Oh Lord!" he prayed. "Break forth and wash the slime from this earth!"

The turnip continued slowly to descend. After a few minutes there was a guffawing peal of thunder from behind and fantastic raindrops, like tin-can tops, crashed over the rear of Mr. Shiftlet's car. Very quickly he stepped on the gas and with his stump sticking out the window he raced the galloping shower into Mobile.

Critical Reading

1. **Key Ideas and Details (a)** What is Mrs. Crater's first reaction to Shiftlet when she sees him from a distance as the story begins? **(b) Infer:** What object on the Crater farm does Mr. Shiftlet want? **(c) Analyze:** What clues about Mr. Shiftlet's true character does Mrs. Crater not seem to notice?

2. **Key Ideas and Details (a)** What arguments does Mrs. Crater use to persuade Shiftlet to marry Lucynell? **(b) Interpret:** What factors cause Shiftlet to agree?

3. **Key Ideas and Details (a)** What prayer does Shiftlet offer at the end of the story? **(b) Analyze:** What is ironic about the way in which his prayer is answered? **(c) Generalize:** What does this event suggest about those whose behavior contradicts their professed beliefs?

Cite textual evidence to support your responses.

4. **Integration of Knowledge and Ideas Make a Judgment:** When Mrs. Crater decides to marry Lucynell to Shiftlet, the girl seems to have no control over her fate. Do Mrs. Crater's actions have any moral justification? Explain.

5. **Integration of Knowledge and Ideas** Based on this story, a good example of regionalism, do you think there is a single, unified body of American literature? Explain. In your response, use at least two of these Essential Question words: *landscape, vision, commonplace, alienation, identity*. *[Connecting to the Essential Question: What makes American literature American?]*

Literary Analysis

1. **Key Ideas and Details** Use a chart like the one shown to examine Mrs. Crater and Mr. Shiftlet as **grotesque characters:**
   (a) What primary goal or obsession controls each character?
   (b) What actions does each undertake as a result of the obsession?

Character		Goal or Obsession	Actions Undertaken

2. **Craft and Structure** Note two examples of physical description that create an exaggerated, or grotesque, effect for **(a)** Mrs. Crater, **(b)** Mr. Shiftlet, and **(c)** Lucynell.

3. **Craft and Structure (a)** Shiftlet twice brings up the image of a human heart—the physical, beating heart of a person. Identify both references. **(b)** What idea does he express both times?

4. **Craft and Structure (a)** Note one example of **direct characterization** O'Connor uses to depict Lucynell. **(b)** Note at least two examples of **indirect characterization** that reveal Lucynell's innocence. Explain your choices.

5. **Craft and Structure** How important is the setting in shaping characters and determining their actions?

6. **Key Ideas and Details (a) Draw conclusions** about the meaning of Mr. Shiftlet's name by considering his interest in the automobile—a vehicle that allows for fast, ongoing motion. **(b)** In what ways is this meaning very different from that of Crater, the name O'Connor gives to the mother and daughter?

7. **Key Ideas and Details** When Mrs. Crater asks Shiftlet to marry Lucynell, he replies that a "man is divided into two parts, body and spirit." **(a)** According to Shiftlet, what does the spirit want? **(b)** What conclusion can you draw from this detail?

8. **Integration of Knowledge and Ideas (a)** What conclusion about his character can you draw from the description of Shiftlet forming "a crooked cross"? **(b)** What conclusions can you draw from the description of Lucynell as an "innocent" and "an angel of Gawd." **(c)** Knowing that O'Connor was a deeply religious writer, what overall conclusions about the story's meaning might you draw from these details?

@ **Common Core State Standards**

Writing
2. Write informative texts to examine and convey complex ideas, concepts, and information clearly and accurately through the effective selection, organization, and analysis of content. *(p. 1025)*

2.b. Develop the topic thoroughly by selecting the most significant and relevant facts, extended definitions, concrete details, quotations, or other information and examples appropriate to the audience's knowledge of the topic. *(p. 1025)*

2.c. Use appropriate and varied transitions and syntax to link the major sections of the text, create cohesion, and clarify the relationships among complex ideas and concepts. *(p. 1025)*

2.f. Provide a concluding statement that follows from and supports the information or explanation presented. *(p. 1025)*

Language
4.a. Use context as a clue to the meaning of a word or phrase. *(p. 1025)*

4.b. Identify and correctly use patterns of word changes that indicate different meanings or parts of speech. *(p. 1025)*

Vocabulary Acquisition and Use

Word Analysis: Latin Root -sol-

The Latin word root -sol-, meaning "alone," builds the meaning of these words:

a. desolate: uninhabited, deserted

b. solitary: alone, without company

c. soloist: one who performs by him- or herself

Use your knowledge of the Latin root -sol- to answer the following questions.

1. In a soliloquy, do two actors have an exchange or does one actor address the audience?

2. Would a pilot have a co-pilot on a solo flight?

3. Would a person who usually loves to take long walks alone enjoy the state of solitude?

4. How might you isolate a sick puppy?

5. If someone is the sole survivor, what has happened to the rest of the people?

Vocabulary: Context Clues

For each sentence below, indicate whether the word in italics is used correctly. Explain the context clues that help you decide. If the word is used incorrectly, write a new, correct sentence.

1. There were so many people at the town meeting that the atmosphere was utterly desolate.

2. The rickety fence listed in the strong winds.

3. In an ominous voice, the jury foreperson read the guilty verdict.

4. After the huge dinner, we were ravenous.

5. His morose reaction showed his delight with the entertainment.

Writing to Sources

Informative Text The title and ending of a story contain essential information that may help you interpret a story's meaning. Write an **essay** in which you explain the fate of each character in O'Connor's "The Life You Save May Be Your Own" and interpret the title.

Prewriting As you reread the story, use a chart like the one shown to analyze the relationships between the characters' fates and the meaning of the title. Jot down notes and look for connections among the ideas.

Drafting Present your interpretation of the story's title in your introduction. Then, write one paragraph about each of the three main characters. Explain how the final image of each character relates to the key idea of the title. Summarize and extend your analysis in your conclusion.

Model: Charting to Organize Ideas

	Mrs. Crater	Lucynell	Mr. Shiftlet
What happens to the character in the end?			
How does the character's fate connect to the title?			

Revising Review your essay, making sure you have presented a balanced, unified discussion. Clarify ideas that seem vague and develop incomplete thoughts more thoroughly. Consider adding transitional phrases, such as "in contrast," and "alternatively," to make comparisons easier to follow.

Connecting to the Essential Question In this story, a parent dreams of a better life for a child—a common theme in American literature. As you read, notice differences in the three main characters' aspirations and goals. Doing so will help you reflect on the Essential Question: **What makes American literature American?**

Close Reading Focus

Plot

A story follows a sequence of events called a **plot,** which is organized into distinct phases:

- The **exposition** introduces the setting, characters, and situation.
- An **inciting incident** establishes the central conflict.
- During the **development,** the conflict increases.
- The plot reaches a high point of interest or suspense at the **climax.**
- A **resolution** explains the end of the central conflict. Note that many modern stories, such as this one, have no resolution. Instead, a character may experience an **epiphany,** or moment of insight, that affects the conflict but does not resolve it.

The events that lead up to the climax make up the **rising action.** Those that follow make up the **falling action.** Along the way, writers may also use **foreshadowing,** or clues, to hint at what will happen next. Foreshadowing can increase suspense and help build toward the climax. It also creates a sense of unity in a story as hints planted early in the plot develop into meaningful moments later. As you read, notice how the author builds the conflict through the phases of the plot.

Preparing to Read Complex Texts All of the details in a story, including the events of the plot and the characters' reactions, add up to express deeper meanings, or **themes.** To better understand this process, **summarize** as you read. To summarize, briefly restate the main points in a passage. Pause after significant scenes and review which characters were involved and what happened. Use a chart like the one shown to identify key elements to note as you summarize.

Vocabulary

You will encounter the words listed here in the text that follows. Copy the words into your notebook. Which word is an antonym of *ethical*?

diligence   repugnant

illiterate   discern

unscrupulous

**Common Core
State Standards**

Reading Literature

2. Determine two or more themes or central ideas of a text and analyze their development over the course of the text; provide an objective summary of the text.

3. Analyze the impact of the author's choices regarding how to develop and relate elements of a story.

5. Analyze how an author's choices concerning how to structure specific parts of a text contribute to its overall structure and meaning as well as its aesthetic impact.

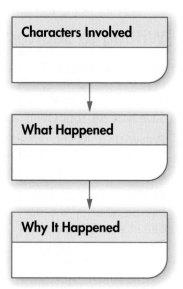

Bernard Malamud *(1914–1986)*

Author of **"The First Seven Years"**

Bernard Malamud was born in Brooklyn, New York, the son of Russian immigrants. His father ran a grocery store and worked hard to forge a better life for his family. According to his own account, Malamud's boyhood was "comparatively happy." He grew up hearing the constant mingling of Yiddish and English—an experience that contributed to his fine ear for the rhythms of spoken dialogue. A favored boyhood pastime was listening to his father recount tales of Jewish life in pre-Revolutionary Russia. Young Bernard began to display his father's gift for telling stories when, recovering from pneumonia at age nine, he spent hours in the back room of the family store writing down the stories he had composed to tell his friends.

> "LIFE IS A TRAGEDY FULL OF JOY."

A Literary Range Malamud attended City College of New York and Columbia University and began publishing stories in a number of well-known magazines. Despite the strong influence of Yiddish folk tales—many of Malamud's stories are drawn from this tradition—his work depicts a broad range of settings and characters. From the gifted baseball player in *The Natural* (1952), to the handyman living in czarist Russia in the Pulitzer Prize-winning *The Fixer* (1966), all of his characters come across as real and accessible, with universal hopes and concerns. Malamud's other novels include *The Assistant* (1957), *A New Life* (1961), *The Tenants* (1971), and *Dubin's Lives* (1979). He also wrote numerous short stories, many of which were published in *The Magic Barrel* (1958), which won the National Book Award.

A Touch of Magic Malamud tells his stories in spare, compressed prose, sprinkled with flashes of highly charged metaphorical language. He allows magical events to happen in gloomy city neighborhoods, and gives his hard-working characters unexpected flashes of passion. Some Malamud stories move readers to sadness as characters struggle courageously against tragedy. "The First Seven Years" depicts a Polish immigrant's desire to see his daughter achieve a better life. His notion of that life, however, is not the same as hers.

The First Seven Years

BERNARD MALAMUD

BACKGROUND During World War II, millions of Jews were murdered by the Nazis under the direction of German dictator Adolf Hitler. Many Jewish refugees immigrated to the United States, a pattern that continued after the end of the war. This story takes place in the 1950s, when many Holocaust survivors like Sobel, the shoemaker's assistant, struggled to establish new lives in the United States.

Feld, the shoemaker, was annoyed that his helper, Sobel, was so insensitive to his reverie that he wouldn't for a minute cease his fanatic pounding at the other bench. He gave him a look, but Sobel's bald head was bent over the last[1] as he worked he didn't notice. The shoemaker shrugged and continued to peer through the partly frosted window at the near-sighted haze of falling February snow. Neither the shifting white blur outside, nor the sudden deep remembrance of the snowy Polish village where he had wasted his youth could turn his thoughts from Max the college boy, (a constant visitor in the mind since early that morning when Feld saw him trudging through the snowdrifts on his way to school) whom he so much respected because of the sacrifices he had made throughout the years—in winter or direst heat—to further his education. An old wish returned

---

1. **last** *n.* block shaped like a person's foot, on which shoes are made or repaired.

to haunt the shoemaker: that he had had a son instead of a daughter, but this blew away in the snow for Feld, if anything, was a practical man. Yet he could not help but contrast the diligence of the boy, who was a peddler's son, with Miriam's unconcern for an education. True, she was always with a book in her hand, yet when the opportunity arose for a college education, she had said no she would rather find a job. He had begged her to go, pointing out how many fathers could not afford to send their children to college, but she said she wanted to be independent. As for education, what was it, she asked, but books, which Sobel, who diligently read the classics, would as usual advise her on. Her answer greatly grieved her father.

A figure emerged from the snow and the door opened. At the counter the man withdrew from a wet paper bag a pair of battered shoes for repair. Who he was the shoemaker for a moment had no idea, then his heart trembled as he realized, before he had thoroughly discerned the face, that Max himself was standing there, embarrassedly explaining what he wanted done to his old shoes. Though Feld listened eagerly, he couldn't hear a word, for the opportunity that had burst upon him was deafening.

He couldn't exactly recall when the thought had occurred to him, because it was clear he had more than once considered suggesting to the boy that he go out with Miriam. But he had not dared speak, for if Max said no, how would he face him again? Or suppose Miriam, who harped so often on independence, blew up in anger and shouted at him for his meddling? Still, the chance was too good to let by: all it meant was an introduction. They might long ago have become friends had they happened to meet somewhere, therefore was it not his duty—an obligation—to bring them together, nothing more, a harmless connivance to replace an accidental encounter in the subway, let's say, or a mutual friend's introduction in the street? Just let him once see and talk to her and he would for sure be interested. As for Miriam, what possible harm for a working girl in an office, who met only loud-mouthed salesmen and illiterate shipping clerks, to make the acquaintance of a fine scholarly boy? Maybe he would awaken in her a desire to go to college; if not—the shoemaker's mind at last came to grips with the truth—let her marry an educated man and live a better life.

When Max finished describing what he wanted done to his shoes, Feld marked them, both with enormous holes in the soles which he pretended not to notice, with large white-chalk x's, and the rubber heels, thinned to the nails, he marked with o's, though it troubled him he might have mixed up the letters. Max inquired the price, and the shoemaker cleared his throat and asked the boy, above Sobel's insistent hammering, would he please step through the side door there into the hall. Though surprised, Max did as the shoemaker requested, and Feld went in after him. For a minute they were both silent, because Sobel had stopped banging, and it seemed they understood neither was to say anything until the noise began again.

◀ **Critical Viewing** How does the young woman portrayed in this painting compare to your impression of Miriam? **COMPARE**

Vocabulary

diligence (dil′ ə jəns) *n* constant, careful effort; perseverance

Vocabulary

illiterate (i lit′ ər it) *adj.* unable to read or write

Comprehension

What hope does Feld hold for his daughter Miriam and the college boy Max?

When it did, loudly, the shoemaker quickly told Max why he had asked to talk to him.

"Ever since you went to high school," he said, in the dimly-lit hallway, "I watched you in the morning go to the subway to school, and I said always to myself, this is a fine boy that he wants so much an education."

"Thanks," Max said, nervously alert. He was tall and grotesquely thin, with sharply cut features, particularly a beak-like nose. He was wearing a loose, long slushy overcoat that hung down to his ankles, looking like a rug draped over his bony shoulders, and a soggy, old brown hat, as battered as the shoes he had brought in.

"I am a business man," the shoemaker abruptly said to conceal his embarrassment, "so I will explain you right away why I talk to you. I have a girl, my daughter Miriam—she is nineteen—a very nice girl and also so pretty that everybody looks on her when she passes by in the street. She is smart, always with a book, and I thought to myself that a boy like you, an educated boy—I thought maybe you will be interested sometime to meet a girl like this." He laughed a bit when he had finished and was tempted to say more but had the good sense not to.

Max stared down like a hawk. For an uncomfortable second he was silent, then he asked, "Did you say nineteen?"

"Yes."

"Would it be all right to inquire if you have a picture of her?"

"Just a minute." The shoemaker went into the store and hastily returned with a snapshot that Max held up to the light.

"She's all right," he said.

Feld waited.

"And is she sensible—not the flighty kind?"

"She is very sensible."

After another short pause, Max said it was okay with him if he met her.

"Here is my telephone," said the shoemaker, hurriedly handing him a slip of paper. "Call her up. She comes home from work six o'clock."

Max folded the paper and tucked it away into his worn leather wallet.

"About the shoes," he said. "How much did you say they will cost me?"

"Don't worry about the price."

"I just like to have an idea."

"A dollar—dollar fifty. A dollar fifty," the shoemaker said. At once he felt bad, for he usually charged two twenty-five for this kind of job. Either he should have asked the regular price or done the work for nothing.

Later, as he entered the store, he was startled by a violent clanging and looked up to see Sobel pounding with all his might upon the naked last. It broke, the iron striking the floor and jumping with a thump against the wall, but before the enraged shoemaker could cry out, the assistant had torn his hat

Summarizing

Briefly state what takes place in the conversation between Max and Feld.

and coat from the hook and rushed out into the snow.

So Feld, who had looked forward to anticipating how it would go with his daughter and Max, instead had a great worry on his mind. Without his temperamental helper he was a lost man, especially since it was years now that he had carried the store alone. The shoemaker had for an age suffered from a heart condition that threatened collapse if he dared exert himself. Five years ago, after an attack, it had appeared as though he would have either to sacrifice his business upon the auction block and live on a pittance thereafter, or put

Comprehension

What does Feld ask of Max?

Vocabulary
unscrupulous
(un skrōō´ pyə ləs)
adj. unethical; dishonest

BUT JUST AT THE MOMENT OF HIS DARKEST DESPAIR, THIS POLISH REFUGEE, SOBEL, APPEARED ONE NIGHT FROM THE STREET AND BEGGED FOR WORK.

Plot
What inciting incident creates a conflict between Feld and Sobel?

himself at the mercy of some unscrupulous employee who would in the end probably ruin him. But just at the moment of his darkest despair, this Polish refugee, Sobel, appeared one night from the street and begged for work. He was a stocky man, poorly dressed, with a bald head that had once been blond, a severely plain face and soft blue eyes prone to tears over the sad books he read, a young man but old—no one would have guessed thirty. Though he confessed he knew nothing of shoemaking, he said he was apt and would work for a very little if Feld taught him the trade. Thinking that with, after all, a landsman,[2] he would have less to fear than from a complete stranger, Feld took him on and within six weeks the refugee rebuilt as good a shoe as he, and not long thereafter expertly ran the business for the thoroughly relieved shoemaker.

Feld could trust him with anything and did, frequently going home after an hour or two at the store, leaving all the money in the till, knowing Sobel would guard every cent of it. The amazing thing was that he demanded so little. His wants were few; in money he wasn't interested—in nothing but books, it seemed—which he one by one lent to Miriam, together with his profuse, queer written comments, manufactured during his lonely rooming house evenings, thick pads of commentary which the shoemaker peered at and twitched his shoulders over as his daughter, from her fourteenth year, read page by sanctified page, as if the word of God were inscribed on them. To protect Sobel, Feld himself had to see that he received more than he asked for. Yet his conscience bothered him for not insisting that the assistant accept a better wage than he was getting, though Feld had honestly told him he could earn a handsome salary if he worked elsewhere, or maybe opened a place of his own. But the assistant answered, somewhat ungraciously, that he was not interested in going elsewhere, and though Feld frequently asked himself what keeps him here? why does he stay? he finally answered it that the man, no doubt because of his terrible experiences as a refugee, was afraid of the world.

After the incident with the broken last, angered by Sobel's behavior, the shoemaker decided to let him stew for a week in the rooming house, although his own strength was taxed dangerously and the business suffered. However, after several sharp nagging warnings from both his wife and daughter, he went finally in search of Sobel, as he had once before, quite recently, when over some fancied slight— Feld had merely asked him not to give Miriam so many books to read because her eyes were strained and red—the assistant had left the place in a huff, an incident which, as usual, came to nothing for he had returned after the shoemaker had talked to him, and taken

---

2. landsman *n.* fellow countryman.

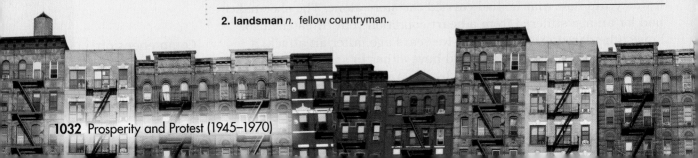

his seat at the bench. But this time, after Feld had plodded through the snow to Sobel's house—he had thought of sending Miriam but the idea became repugnant to him—the burly landlady at the door informed him in a nasal voice that Sobel was not at home, and though Feld knew this was a nasty lie, for where had the refugee to go? still for some reason he was not completely sure of—it may have been the cold and his fatigue—he decided not to insist on seeing him. Instead he went home and hired a new helper.

Having settled the matter, though not entirely to his satisfaction, for he had much more to do than before, and so, for example, could no longer lie late in bed mornings because he had to get up to open the store for the new assistant, a speechless, dark man with an irritating rasp as he worked, whom he would not trust with the key as he had Sobel. Furthermore, this one, though able to do a fair repair job, knew nothing of grades of leather or prices, so Feld had to make his own purchases: and every night at closing time it was necessary to count the money in the till and lock up. However, he was not dissatisfied, for he lived much in his thoughts of Max and Miriam. The college boy had called her, and they had arranged a meeting for this coming Friday night. The shoemaker would personally have preferred Saturday, which he felt would make it a date of the first magnitude, but he learned Friday was Miriam's choice, so he said nothing. The day of the week did not matter. What mattered was the aftermath. Would they like each other and want to be friends? He sighed at all the time that would have to go by before he knew for sure. Often he was tempted to talk to Miriam about the boy, to ask whether she thought she would like his type—he had told her only that he considered Max a nice boy and had suggested he call her—but the one time he tried she snapped at him—justly—how should she know?

At last Friday came. Feld was not feeling particularly well so he stayed in bed, and Mrs. Feld thought it better to remain in the bedroom with him when Max called. Miriam received the boy, and her parents could hear their voices, his throaty one, as they talked. Just before leaving, Miriam brought Max to the bedroom door and he stood there a minute, a tall, slightly hunched figure wearing a thick, droopy suit, and apparently at ease as he greeted the shoemaker and his wife, which was surely a good sign. And Miriam, although she had worked all day, looked fresh and pretty. She was a large-framed girl with a well-shaped body, and she had a fine open face and soft hair. They made, Feld thought, a first-class couple.

Miriam returned after 11:30. Her mother was already asleep, but the shoemaker got out of bed and after locating his bathrobe went into the kitchen, where Miriam, to his surprise, sat at the table, reading.

Vocabulary
repugnant (ri pug´ nənt) *adj.* offensive; disagreeable

Spiral Review
Context Clues
What can you conclude about the meaning of the word *magnitude* as it is used here?

Comprehension
To what extent does Feld trust Sobel?

Plot and Foreshadowing

What might Feld's conversation about Miriam's date with Max foreshadow?

"So where did you go?" Feld asked pleasantly.

"For a walk," she said, not looking up.

"I advised him," Feld said, clearing his throat, "he shouldn't spend so much money."

"I didn't care."

The shoemaker boiled up some water for tea and sat down at the table with a cupful and a thick slice of lemon.

"So how," he sighed after a sip, "did you enjoy?"

"It was all right."

He was silent. She must have sensed his disappointment, for she added, "You can't really tell much the first time."

"You will see him again?"

Turning a page, she said that Max had asked for another date.

"For when?"

"Saturday."

"So what did you say?"

"What did I say?" she asked, delaying for a moment—"I said yes."

Afterwards she inquired about Sobel, and Feld, without exactly knowing why, said the assistant had got another job. Miriam said nothing more and began to read. The shoemaker's conscience did not trouble him; he was satisfied with the Saturday date.

During the week, by placing here and there a deft question, he managed to get from Miriam some information about Max. It surprised him to learn that the boy was not studying to be either a doctor or lawyer but was taking a business course leading to a degree in accountancy. Feld was a little disappointed because he thought of accountants as bookkeepers and would have preferred "a higher profession." However, it was not long before he had investigated the subject and discovered that Certified Public Accountants were highly respected people, so he was thoroughly content as Saturday approached. But because Saturday was a busy day, he was much in the store and therefore did not see Max when he came to call for Miriam. From his wife he learned there had been nothing especially revealing about their meeting. Max had rung the bell and Miriam had got her coat and left with him—nothing more. Feld did not probe, for his wife was not particularly observant. Instead, he waited up for Miriam with a newspaper on his lap, which he scarcely looked at so lost was he in thinking of the future. He awoke to find her in the room with him, tiredly removing her hat. Greeting her, he was suddenly inexplicably afraid to ask anything about the evening. But since she volunteered nothing he was at last forced to inquire how she had enjoyed herself. Miriam began something noncommittal but apparently changed her mind, for she said after a minute, "I was bored."

When Feld had sufficiently recovered from his anguished disappointment to ask why, she answered without hesitation, "Because he's nothing more than a materialist."

"What means this word?"

"He has no soul. He's only interested in things."

He considered her statement for a long time but then asked, "Will you see him again?"

"He didn't ask."

"Suppose he will ask you?"

"I won't see him."

He did not argue: however, as the days went by he hoped increasingly she would change her mind. He wished the boy would telephone, because he was sure there was more to him than Miriam, with her inexperienced eye, could discern. But Max didn't call. As a matter of fact he took a different route to school, no longer passing the shoemaker's store, and Feld was deeply hurt.

Then one afternoon Max came in and asked for his shoes. The shoemaker took them down from the shelf where he had placed them, apart from the other pairs. He had done the work himself and the soles and heels were well built and firm. The shoes had been highly polished and somehow looked better than new. Max's Adam's apple went up once when he saw them, and his eyes had little lights in them.

"How much?" he asked, without directly looking at the shoemaker.

"Like I told you before," Feld answered sadly. "One dollar fifty cents."

Max handed him two crumpled bills and received in return a newly-minted silver half dollar.

He left. Miriam had not been mentioned. That night the shoemaker discovered that his new assistant had been all the while stealing from him, and he suffered a heart attack.

Though the attack was very mild, he lay in bed for three weeks. Miriam spoke of going for Sobel, but sick as he was Feld rose in wrath against the idea. Yet in his heart he knew there was no other way, and the first weary day back in the shop thoroughly convinced him, so that night after supper he dragged himself to Sobel's rooming house.

He toiled up the stairs, though he knew it was bad for him, and at the top knocked at the door. Sobel opened it and the shoemaker entered. The room was a small, poor one, with a single window facing the street. It contained a narrow cot, a low table and several stacks of books piled haphazardly around on the floor along the wall, which made him think how queer Sobel was, to be uneducated and read so much. He had once asked him, Sobel, why you read so much? and the assistant could not answer him. Did you ever study in a college someplace? he had asked but Sobel shook his head. He read, he said, to know. But to know what, the shoemaker demanded, and to know, why? Sobel never explained, which proved he read much because he was queer.

Feld sat down to recover his breath. The assistant was resting on his bed with his heavy back to the wall. His shirt and trousers were clean, and his stubby fingers, away from the shoemaker's bench, were strangely pallid. His face was thin and pale, as if he had been shut in this room since the day he had bolted from the store.

"So when you will come back to work?" Feld asked him.

Vocabulary
discern (di surn´) v. perceive or recognize.

Comprehension
Why is Miriam bored with Max?

To his surprise, Sobel burst out, "Never."

Jumping up, he strode over to the window that looked out upon the miserable street. "Why should I come back?" he cried.

"I will raise your wages."

"Who cares for your wages!"

The shoemaker, knowing he didn't care, was at a loss what else to say.

"What do you want from me, Sobel?"

"Nothing."

"I always treated you like you was my son."

Sobel vehemently denied it. "So why you look for strange boys in the street they should go out with Miriam? Why you don't think of me?"

The shoemaker's hands and feet turned freezing cold. His voice became so hoarse he couldn't speak. At last he cleared his throat and croaked, "So what has my daughter got to do with a shoemaker thirty-five years old who works for me?"

"Why do you think I worked so long for you?" Sobel cried out. "For the stingy wages I sacrificed five years of my life so you could have to eat and drink and where to sleep?"

"Then for what?" shouted the shoemaker.

"For Miriam," he blurted—"for her."

The shoemaker, after a time, managed to say, "I pay wages in cash, Sobel," and lapsed into silence. Though he was seething with excitement, his mind was coldly clear, and he had to admit to himself he had sensed all along that Sobel felt this way. He had never so much as thought it consciously, but he had felt it and was afraid.

"Miriam knows?" he muttered hoarsely.

"She knows."

"You told her?"

"No."

"Then how does she know?"

"How does she know?" Sobel said, "because she knows. She knows who I am and what is in my heart."

Feld had a sudden insight. In some devious way, with his books and commentary, Sobel had given Miriam to understand that he loved her. The shoemaker felt a terrible anger at him for his deceit.

"Sobel, you are crazy," he said bitterly. "She will never marry a man so old and ugly like you."

Sobel turned black with rage. He cursed the shoemaker, but then, though he trembled to hold it in, his eyes filled with tears and he broke into deep sobs. With his back to Feld, he stood at the window, fists clenched, and his shoulders shook with his choked sobbing.

Watching him, the shoemaker's anger diminished. His teeth were on edge with pity for the man, and his eyes grew moist. How strange and sad that a refugee, a grown man, bald and old with his miseries, who had by the skin of his teeth escaped Hitler's incinerators,[3] should fall in love, when he had got to America, with a girl less than half his

---

3. **Hitler's incinerators** The furnaces used in concentration camps to burn human bodies during Adolf Hitler's dictatorship.

age. Day after day, for five years he had sat at his bench, cutting and hammering away, waiting for the girl to become a woman, unable to ease his heart with speech, knowing no protest but desperation.

"Ugly I didn't mean," he said half aloud.

Then he realized that what he had called ugly was not Sobel but Miriam's life if she married him. He felt for his daughter a strange and gripping sorrow, as if she were already Sobel's bride, the wife, after all, of a shoemaker, and had in her life no more than her mother had had. And all his dreams for her—why he had slaved and destroyed his heart with anxiety and labor—all these dreams of a better life were dead.

The room was quiet. Sobel was standing by the window reading, and it was curious that when he read he looked young.

"She is only nineteen," Feld said brokenly. "This is too young yet to get married. Don't ask her for two years more, till she is twenty-one, then you can talk to her."

Sobel didn't answer. Feld rose and left. He went slowly down the stairs but once outside, though it was an icy night and the crisp falling snow whitened the street, he walked with a stronger stride.

But the next morning, when the shoemaker arrived, heavy-hearted, to open the store, he saw he needn't have come, for his assistant was already seated at the last, pounding leather for his love.

Plot and Epiphany
What does Feld suddenly understand about Sobel?

Critical Reading

1. **Key Ideas and Details (a)** Under what circumstances does Feld first notice Max? **(b) Interpret:** Why is Max so appealing to Feld?

2. **Key Ideas and Details (a)** To Feld, what values does Max seem to embody? **(b) Interpret:** Does Max really share Feld's values? Explain.

3. **Key Ideas and Details (a)** How does Miriam react to her second date with Max? **(b) Compare and Contrast:** Explain the differences between Miriam's feelings for Max and her feelings for Sobel.

4. **Key Ideas and Details (a)** What is Sobel's background? **(b) Speculate:** In what ways do the events of history that Sobel experienced add to his characterization?

5. **Key Ideas and Details (a) Interpret:** What does education represent to Feld and Max? **(b) Compare and Contrast:** How does Sobel's love of reading compare with both Feld's and Max's feelings about education?

6. **Integration of Knowledge and Ideas** In your view, is Feld's definition of a successful and meaningful life one many Americans share? Explain. In your response, use at least three of these Essential Question words: *prosperity, materialism, idealistic, realistic, independence. [Connecting to the Essential Question: What makes American literature American?]*

Cite textual evidence to support your responses.

Literary Analysis

1. **Craft and Structure** Use a chart like the one shown to outline key events in the **plot** of the story. **(a)** Explain the information contained in the story's **exposition. (b)** Identify the **inciting incident** that introduces the conflict. **(c)** Define the main conflict and explain how it develops to the **climax** and leads to the **resolution.**

Rising Action	Climax	Resolution
Exposition:		
Inciting Incident:		
Conflict:		

2. **Craft and Structure** Explain how the climax of this story is also an **epiphany** for Feld.

3. **Key Ideas and Details** What new ideas does Feld's epiphany introduce that challenge the values and assumptions about life he has always held?

4. **Key Ideas and Details (a)** How might Feld's epiphany affect his attitudes toward Miriam and Sobel in the future? **(b)** To what degree is the central conflict resolved at the end of the story? Explain.

5. **Key Ideas and Details (a) Summarize** what happens in the final scene between Feld and Sobel. **(b)** How does summarizing help you understand and interpret the meaning of the scene?

6. **Key Ideas and Details (a)** Summarize the entire story as briefly as possible. Carefully choose the information you feel is most important to understanding the story's essential meaning. **(b)** Compare your summary with another student's version. Identify elements that only one writer included. Decide whether or not each of these elements should be part of a useful summary.

7. **Craft and Structure** Early in the story, Feld asks to speak to Max privately. As they step into the side room, Sobel stops hammering. How is the detail about Sobel an example of **foreshadowing?**

8. **Craft and Structure (a)** Identify two other examples of foreshadowing in the story. **(b)** Explain how each is a clue for events that later unfold.

9. **Craft and Structure** Based on this story, explain how foreshadowing helps to give a story a sense of unity.

10. **Integration of Knowledge and Ideas (a)** What image of Sobel begins the story? **(b)** What image of Sobel ends it? **(c)** What meaning do you find in the relationship of the beginning of the story to its end?

**Common Core
State Standards**

Writing

2.a. Introduce a topic; organize complex ideas, concepts, and information so that each new element builds on that which precedes it to create a unified whole; include graphics when useful to aiding comprehension. *(p. 1039)*

2.b. Develop the topic thoroughly by selecting the most significant and relevant facts, extended definitions, concrete details, quotations, or other information and examples appropriate to the audience's knowledge of the topic. *(p. 1039)*

Language

4. Determine or clarify the meaning of unknown and multiple-meaning words and phrases based on *grades 11–12 reading and content,* choosing flexibly from a range of strategies. *(p. 1039)*

4.a. Use context as a clue to the meaning of a word or phrase. *(p. 1039)*

4.b. Identify and correctly use patterns of word changes that indicate different meanings or parts of speech. *(p. 1039)*

Vocabulary Acquisition and Use

Word Analysis: Latin Root *-litera-*

The root *-litera-* comes from the Latin word that means "letter." Words that derive from this root often relate to reading and language. Complete each sentence below with a *-litera-* word from the list. Then, explain the meaning of the word you used.

literary	illiteracy
literal	literati

1. He insists on a _____ interpretation of the law.
2. Improved education is one solution to the problem of _____.
3. Her _____ talents are obvious in her poetry.
4. All of the local _____ gathered at the book reading to meet the famous author.

Vocabulary: Context Clues

Review the vocabulary list on p. 1026. Then, select the word you would most likely find in each of these newspaper articles.

1. "Reading Rate Declines Among Adults"
2. "Residents Complain of Dump's Disagreeable Smell"
3. "Hard-Working Teens Turn Vacant Lot into Garden"
4. "Dishonorable Band of Thieves Gets Nabbed"
5. "Girl of Ten Recognizes Error in Mayor's Speech"

Writing to Sources

Informative Text Malamud creates believable and engaging characters in "The First Seven Years." Suppose you are developing a television show based on this story. Write a **personality profile** of one of the characters. The profile could be used by producers or the director to cast an appropriate actor.

Prewriting Your profile should include details about how the character looks, talks, and behaves. Use a cluster diagram like the one shown to jot down physical characteristics and personal qualities you observe in the character you are describing.

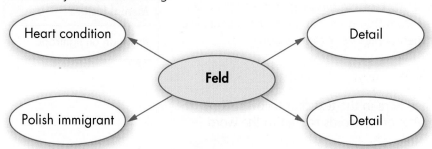

Drafting Begin with an informative detail or image of the character. Expand your profile in layers, referring to your cluster diagram as needed.

Revising Have a classmate create a new cluster diagram based on your profile. Compare it to your prewriting diagram to discover key information you may have omitted.

Connecting to the Essential Question In this poem, Ferlinghetti says that the poet risks seeming absurd. As you read, consider what types of activities, beliefs, or ideals are worth the risk of appearing absurd. Doing so will help you think about the Essential Question: **How does literature shape or reflect society?**

Close Reading Focus

Extended Metaphor; Puns

Ferlinghetti was a member of the "Beat Generation," a group of writers who rebelled against social, political, and literary norms. In an effort to free poetry from the hands of the elite and return it to "the streets," the Beats wrote poems that were playful, earthy, and defiant. Their guiding principle was "first thought, best thought"—the idea that an artist should not censor his or her immediate responses.

Ferlinghetti builds this poem as a single **extended metaphor,** or sustained comparison. In doing so, he demonstrates a poetic balance akin to the physical skills of the acrobat. To mimic the acrobat's agility, Ferlinghetti studs the poem with **puns**—words or phrases with double meanings:

- The acrobat/poet performs "above the heads" of his audience.
- The acrobat/poet climbs on "rime."
- The acrobat/poet balances on "eyebeams."

Puns can be amusing and clever. Under the guidance of a nimble poet, they also deepen the meaning and gravity of this poem.

Preparing to Read Complex Texts In this poem, Ferlinghetti uses phrases and line breaks rather than punctuation to signal units of meaning. As you read, *clarify your comprehension* by **visualizing or picturing the action** being described. If you lose track of the meaning, return to the last line you clearly pictured, and read from that point forward. Use a chart like the one shown to describe your mental pictures of the action.

Vocabulary

You will encounter the words listed here in the text that follows. Copy the words into your notebook. What other words related to the word *realist* can you list?

absurdity   **taut**

realist

© **Common Core State Standards**

Reading Literature
4. Determine the meaning of words and phrases as they are used in the text, including figurative and connotative meanings; analyze the impact of specific word choices on meaning and tone, including words with multiple meanings or language that is particularly fresh, engaging, or beautiful.

Language
5. Demonstrate understanding of figurative language, word relationships, and nuances in word meanings.
5.a. Interpret figures of speech in context and analyze their role in the text.

Line or Phrase

balancing on eyebeams

Mental Picture

tiny man on tightrope

LAWRENCE FERLINGHETTI (b. 1919)

Author of "Constantly Risking Absurdity"

Lawrence Ferlinghetti was born in Yonkers, New York, six months after the sudden death of his father. The loss left his mother helpless, and Ferlinghetti was raised by a series of relatives and foster parents.

After graduating from the University of North Carolina in 1941, Ferlinghetti joined the Navy and served as a ship's commander for the remainder of World War II. He stocked his ship with a set of small, inexpensive volumes of literature for his men to read. "We had all the classics stacked everywhere," he remembers. The horrors Ferlinghetti saw during the war made him a lifetime pacifist.

After the war, Ferlinghetti completed graduate degrees at Columbia University in New York and the Sorbonne in Paris. As a budding poet in France, Ferlinghetti was heavily influenced by the American expatriates T. S. Eliot and Ezra Pound. Fearful that he was merely imitating the greats, Ferlinghetti struck out in search of new models. He landed in San Francisco, California, the home of an edgy new literary scene that would later become known as the Beat movement.

In the Light Ferlinghetti launched the poetry magazine *City Lights* in 1953. Shortly thereafter, he opened a bookstore by the same name. It was the first store in the country to sell only paperbacks. Small, cheap, and transportable, this medium represented a democratic revolution in literature: Books could be owned, read, and shared by rich and poor alike.

Ferlinghetti also founded a paperback publishing house, City Lights Pocket Poets, in 1955. The fourth volume he produced was *Howl & Other Poems* by Allen Ginsberg, a raw and volatile work that was viewed by many conventional readers as immoral. The publication led to Ferlinghetti's arrest on charges of obscenity, although he was fully cleared in a landmark ruling in favor of free speech. The trial brought national attention to Beat movement writers, and City Lights Books instantly became the epicenter of a new intellectual movement.

> *"Poetry is more alive when it is about living things."*

A Poetry of Living Things In 1958 Ferlinghetti published his first poetry collection, *A Coney Island of the Mind*. Conversational, clear, and good-natured, his poems found a ready audience among those who were weary of the dense, subtle poetry of the Modernists. Ferlinghetti was named the first Poet Laureate of San Franciso in 1998 and received an Author's Guild Lifetime Achievement Award in 2003.

Constantly Risking Absurdity

Absurdity

Lawrence Ferlinghetti

Vocabulary

absurdity (ab sur′də tē) *n.*
nonsense; ridiculousness

Constantly risking absurdity
and death
whenever he performs
above the heads
5   of his audience
the poet like an acrobat
climbs on rime[1]
to a high wire of his own making
and balancing on eyebeams

---

1. rime An archaic spelling of the word *rhyme*; also, a thin coating of frost.

10 above a sea of faces
    paces his way
    to the other side of day
    performing entrechats[2]
    and sleight-of-foot tricks
15 and other high theatrics
    and all without mistaking
    any thing
    for what it may not be
    For he's the super **realist**
20 who must perforce perceive
    taut truth
    before the taking of each stance or step
    in his supposed advance
    toward that still higher perch
25 where Beauty stands and waits
    with gravity
    to start her death-defying leap
    And he
    a little charleychaplin man[3]
30 who may or may not catch
    her fair eternal form
    spreadeagled in the empty air
    of existence

Vocabulary

realist (rē´ ə list) *n.* a person or artist concerned with things as they are, rather than as they could or should be

taut (tôt) *adj.* tightly stretched

---

2. **entrechats** (än´ trə chä´) In ballet, leaps straight upward in which the dancer crosses and uncrosses the legs a number of times.
3. **charleychaplin man** Charlie Chaplin (1889–1977) was an English comedy actor famous for his character "the Little Tramp," who wore a tight coat, oversized pants and shoes, a derby hat, and a mustache.

Critical Reading

1. **Key Ideas and Details (a)** Who is waiting for the poet on the other side of the high wire? **(b) Interpret:** Why is the poet not certain he will catch this figure?

2. **Integration of Knowledge and Ideas Interpret:** In what ways is "truth" like a tightrope?

3. **Integration of Knowledge and Ideas** What does this poem suggest about the reasons poetry is important to a society? Explain. In your response, use at least two of these Essential Question words: *expression, unconventional, profound, authenticity, universal. [Connecting to the Essential Question: How does literature shape or reflect society?]*

Cite textual evidence to support your responses.

The BEATS

▲ Jack Kerouac

On an October evening in 1955, a crowd piled into San Francisco's Six Gallery to hear a group of poets read from their work. Poet and publisher Lawrence Ferlinghetti was among those in the audience. Halfway through the evening, a young man with intense brown eyes took the stage to perform a poem. When he ended, the room erupted into wild applause.

That night would go down in history as the debut of Beat literature. The young poet was Allen Ginsberg and his poem was "Howl." The next day, Ferlinghetti sent Ginsberg a telegram: "I greet you at the beginning of a great career." He published "Howl" the following year, and it is now considered one of the seminal works of the twentieth century.

The Beat movement had actually begun in New York City in the 1940s. It was not a formal movement, just a small group of writer friends that included Allen Ginsberg, Jack Kerouac, William Burroughs, and Gregory Corso. In the mid-fifties, Ginsberg and Kerouac traveled to California, where they connected with West Coast poets Kenneth Rexroth, Lawrence Ferlinghetti, and Gary Snyder, and received their first public attention.

▲ Bob Donlin, Neal Cassady, Allen Ginsberg, Robert LaVigne, and Lawrence Ferlinghetti (left to right) stand outside Ferlinghetti's City Lights Bookstore in San Francisco.

For their literary heroes, the Beats looked to figures as diverse as Walt Whitman, English poet William Blake, American novelist Thomas Wolfe, French poet Arthur Rimbaud, Spanish poet García Lorca, and Japanese writer Masaoki Shiki. The jazz riffs of musicians like Dizzy Gillespie and Charlie Parker inspired the rhythms of their poems, which they often performed to music. The Beats wrote about the perils of conformity, urging people to defy convention.

CONNECT TO THE LITERATURE

In what ways does "Constantly Risking Absurdity" express Beat ideas?

Allen Ginsberg ▶

Literary Analysis

1. **Key Ideas and Details (a)** As you **visualize or picture the action** of the poem, does your image of the acrobat change? Explain. **(b)** In what ways does picturing the action help you better understand the poem's meaning?

2. **Craft and Structure** Use a chart like the one shown to interpret the poem's **extended metaphor. (a)** List the acrobat's actions. **(b)** For each of the acrobat's actions, explain what corresponding task a poet must perform.

Acrobat's Action	Poet's Task

3. **Craft and Structure (a)** Identify and explain two **puns** used in the poem. **(b)** How does wordplay advance or illustrate the poem's underlying meaning?

4. **Craft and Structure** How does the poem's form, or look on the page, reflect the actions it describes?

5. **Integration of Knowledge and Ideas** The Beats believed that the poet should record without censoring his or her perception of the world. Does this poem affirm or challenge the idea of "first thought, best thought"? Explain.

Vocabulary Acquisition and Use

Use New Words For each word below, write a sentence that illustrates the word's meaning. Then, write one paragraph that uses all three words correctly.

    1. realist   **2.** taut   **3.** absurdity

Writing to Sources

Poem Using Ferlinghetti's poem as a model, write a **poem** using an extended metaphor. In your poem, compare an abstract idea to a concrete object or a physical activity. Before you begin, make a list of ways in which two things are alike. As you write, make sure to meet the following criteria:

- Clearly identify the two things that are being compared.

- Use strong, clear verbs to help your reader picture what is happening.

- Develop a form so that the look of the poem on the page mirrors or illustrates the action of the poem.

    Try to avoid revising too much. Instead, retain a sense of freshness and spontaneity, or "first thought" in your poem.

Common Core State Standards

Writing
4. Produce clear and coherent writing in which the development, organization, and style are appropriate to task, purpose, and audience.

Language
4. Determine or clarify the meaning of unknown and multiple-meaning words and phrases based on *grades 11–12 reading and content,* choosing flexibly from a range of strategies.

Artistic Upstarts Past and Present

On his social networking page, Charlie Todd describes himself this way: "In my free time, I'm a prankster." Todd is the founder of Improv Everywhere, a fluid mix of comedians, actors, and interested others. They travel around New York on self-described "missions," which appear to be free-form but are actually scripted and highly organized events.

Improv Everywhere missions are a modern equivalent of 1960s "happenings," artistic gatherings that included performance elements. They also have roots in the Beat Generation's rebelliousness toward set artistic modes. "We do what makes us laugh, but we're also interested in reclaiming public space," says Todd.

One public space perfect for an Improv Everywhere mission was the New York subway system, a setting not known to encourage eye contact or merriment. According to Todd, by staging a mock birthday on the No. 6 Lexington Line train, Improv "agents" hoped to "bring excitement to otherwise unexciting locales and give strangers a story they can tell for the rest of their lives."

CHARLIE TODD
Performance Artist

Charlie Todd graduated in 2001 from the University of North Carolina at Chapel Hill, where he majored in dramatic art. Todd decided that "if giant corporations can slap ads all over town, we should be able to blanket the city with comedy." The key to Improv Everywhere, Todd explained, is to make its stunts "somewhat plausible" and never to break character.

Subway BIRTHDAY

Charlie Todd

MISSION

February 2nd, 2002

Surprise!

Featuring: Kinney, Minton, White, Todd, Good, Rainswept, Lovejoy, Richardson, McKinley, Narasimhan, Ries, Boim

With our Subway Series, Improv Everywhere attempts to shatter the mundane and bring excitement and happiness to the underground. To us, the subway is a place where long lost brothers can meet, men can exchange outfits, and pants can be sold for $1.

With the goal of creating total fun, on February 2nd Improv Everywhere agents threw two surprise birthday parties on the 6 train. They came prepared with two 12-foot "Happy Birthday" banners, 24 party hats, and 20 "pin the tail on the donkey" games. IE Agents boarded the 6 train at Brooklyn Bridge. For the first party, agents White, Lovejoy, and Todd were throwing the birthday party for their friend Agent Good. Agent Rainswept, another friend of the birthday boy, was in charge of filming the party. The remaining seven IE Agents played strangers who did not know anyone else. They entered the train at various stops before the party (exiting an adjacent car and entering the party car when the train stopped).

As soon as they entered the train at Brooklyn Bridge, White, Lovejoy, and Todd ("The Party-throwers" from here on out) began decorating the car for the party. They casually mentioned what they were doing to those who asked. "We're throwing a surprise party. Our friend is boarding the train in a few stops." They began to solicit help from strangers to blow up balloons and tape them to the walls. As the IE Agent "strangers" agreed to help, real strangers began to help as well.

The Party-throwers began to raise their voices and explain to people on the train what was about to happen. "Hey everyone! We're throwing a surprise party and we need your help!" They passed out party hats and noisemakers, and the strangers (both real and planted) eagerly got ready for the party. "Our friend's name is Jesse! He's going to enter from the car over there at the Astor Place stop. One of our friends is with him to make sure he gets on this car." The Party-throwers had the undivided attention of everyone else in the smile-filled car.

As the train began to near the Astor Place stop, Agent Todd yelled out the final instructions, "I'll give everyone the signal when he enters the car! We'll yell surprise, and then as soon as the doors close, we'll all sing Happy Birthday together! Remember, his name is Jesse! Okay, here's Astor Place. Shhhh! Shhhhh!" Agent Todd quieted the entire train and the passengers sat in silent, giddy anticipation of Agent (Jesse) Good. At the stop agent Good and Minton (playing the role of Agent Good's friend) exited the adjacent car, walked down the platform, and entered the party car.

"Surprise!" In unison, the train full of strangers shouted out with smiles and laughs. Agent Good stood flabbergasted. Agent Todd counted down, "1, 2, 3, Everyone! Happy Birthday to you . . .", and the entire train sang Happy Birthday to dear Jesse. Everyone clapped and blew their noisemakers with joy. Agent White shouted, "Who wants cupcakes!?" and began to distribute the food to all the hungry passengers. Agent Lovejoy set up the "pin the tail on the donkey"

"We're throwing a surprise party. Our friend is boarding the train in a few stops."

▼ Strangers and Improv "agents" enjoy the party, complete with cupcakes and games.

games and a few undercover IE "strangers" began to play, as others looked on with glee. The party throwers began to shout for Agent Good to make a speech, and Jesse delivered a heartfelt thank you to everyone on the train for coming to his party.

On the return trip, the agents threw another surprise party, this time with Agent Richardson as the birthday boy. The results were the same. In a matter of minutes, the train went from quiet and dull, to loud and festive. For both parties, IE Agents had the participation of the entire train. People of all different ages and races joined together in the name of fun. Everyone from the three-year-old Chinese girl and her father to the 60-year-old tourist couple from Holland donned party hats, blew up balloons, and ate cupcakes together. We created a multicultural party for strangers of all ages, and man it was fun. We refer to those we don't know in this report as "strangers," but as these parties prove, there really are no strangers in this world, only potential friends. Sappy? Yeah. True? Absolutely.

Other Highlights

- Agent Richardson declares his birthday cupcake to be "communal," takes a bite out of it, and passes it on. Four strangers take a bite of the same cupcake.

- Woman leaves the train skipping.

- Woman declares, "I have the best story to tell, but none of my friends are ever going to believe this!"

- Before the second party begins, Agent Good gets the ENTIRE train to crouch to the ground for the surprise.

Critical Reading

1. **(a)** What did Improv Everywhere preplan for the "Surprise!" mission? **(b)** What was the mission's goal? **(c) Assess:** How did the preplanned activities help the group reach the mission's goal?

2. **(a) Summarize:** Briefly summarize the ways strangers participated in "Surprise!" **(b) Speculate:** Why do you think the strangers participated?

3. **(a) Describe:** Describe the effect Improv Everywhere's "Surprise!" mission had on its participants. **(b) Evaluate:** What might be the value of such an experience to participants? Explain.

Use these questions to focus a class discussion of "Surprise!":

4. By posting descriptions of missions like "Surprise!" on the Web, how does Improv Everywhere advance its goals?

5. Why do you think groups like Improv Everywhere strive to playfully disrupt people's ordinary routines? What value might exist in these types of activities?

Connecting to the Essential Question These poems focus on private emotions, yet reflect a broader social anxiety that was first felt during the 1950s. As you read, look for details that might refer both to an individual and to society at large. Doing so will help you consider the Essential Question: **How does literature shape or reflect society?**

Close Reading Focus

Figurative Language

Figurative language is language that is used imaginatively rather than literally. Two types of figurative language, simile and metaphor, compare seemingly dissimilar things:

- A **simile** is a comparison that uses a connecting word such as *like* or *as*: "love as simple as shaving soap."

- A **metaphor** is a comparison that does not use a connecting word. Instead, the comparison is either implied or directly stated: "Your courage was a small coal."

Comparisons such as these are especially useful for poets such as Plath and Sexton, who use language to capture and contain large, powerful, or painful emotions. As you read, notice how each poet uses simile and metaphor to define strong emotions and ideas.

Preparing to Read Complex Texts Poetry uses all the layers of meaning in words, from their *denotation*, or literal definitions, to their *connotations*, or associations. Gather clues to a poem's meaning by **interpreting the connotations** of individual words. To do so, consider the associations and feelings a word calls to mind. For example, Sexton compares being bullied to drinking *acid*—a strong and surprising word. To interpret its connotations, consider why she chose *acid* rather than another word, such as *venom* or *poison*. Consider the range of feelings and meanings the word *acid* carries that other words do not. Then, consider what such a word suggests about the poem's essential meaning, or theme. As you read, use a chart like the one shown to interpret the connotative meanings of individual words.

Attention-Grabbing Word	Associations and Feelings

Vocabulary

The words below are important to understanding the texts that follow. Copy the words into your notebook. Which two words have the same prefix?

preconceptions   transfusion

endured   transformed

Common Core State Standards

Reading Literature
4. Determine the meaning of words and phrases as they are used in the text, including figurative and connotative meanings; analyze the impact of specific word choices on meaning and tone, including words with multiple meanings or language that is particularly fresh, engaging, or beautiful.

Language
5. Demonstrate understanding of figurative language, word relationships, and nuances in word meanings.
5.a. Interpret figures of speech in context and analyze their role in the text.

Sylvia Plath *(1932–1963)*

Author of **"Mirror"**

Despite her success as a writer, Sylvia Plath lived a short, unhappy life. In many of her poems, she expresses intense feelings of despair and deep inner pain. Born in Boston, Plath wrote poetry and received scholastic and literary awards as a young woman. Her first national publication appeared in the *Christian Science Monitor* in 1950, just after she graduated from high school. Although she had emotional difficulties during her years at Smith College, she graduated with highest honors in 1955. She also studied at Cambridge University in England, where she met and married poet Ted Hughes. Her first book of verse, *The Colossus and Other Poems* (1960), was the only book published during her lifetime. Four more books of poetry and a novel, *The Bell Jar* (1963), were published posthumously. In 1982, Plath was awarded the Pulitzer Prize for her collected poems, making her the first poet to win a Pulitzer Prize after death.

Anne Sexton *(1928–1974)*

Author of **"Courage"**

Like her contemporary Sylvia Plath, Anne Sexton led a life marked by mental anguish and profound creativity. Born in Newton, Massachusetts, Sexton married at age nineteen, dabbled in modeling, then gave birth to two daughters. Suffering from severe postpartum depression, Sexton was admitted to a psychiatric hospital for the first of many times in her life. She was encouraged by a doctor to pursue an interest in poetry, and in 1957 enrolled in a local poetry workshop. The quality of her work earned Sexton a scholarship to study with Robert Lowell at Boston University, and by 1960 she had published her first collection, *To Bedlam and Part Way Back*. She won a Pulitzer Prize in 1967. Like other "confessional" poets of the time, Sexton's poems gave readers an intimate and sometimes uncomfortable look at the poet's own troubled psyche.

Mirror
❧ Sylvia Plath ❧

▶ **Critical Viewing**
The artist titled this painting *Mirror II*. What ideas are common to both the painting and Plath's poem? **CONNECT**

Mirror II, George Tooker, © Addison Gallery of American Art, Phillips Academy, Andover, Massachusetts

Vocabulary

preconceptions (prē′ kən sep′ shənz) *n.* ideas formed beforehand

I am silver and exact. I have no preconceptions.
Whatever I see I swallow immediately
Just as it is, unmisted by love or dislike.
I am not cruel, only truthful—
5   The eye of a little god, four-cornered.
Most of the time I meditate on the opposite wall.
It is pink, with speckles. I have looked at it so long
I think it is a part of my heart. But it flickers.
Faces and darkness separate us over and over.
10 Now I am a lake. A woman bends over me,
Searching my reaches for what she really is.
Then she turns to those liars, the candles or the moon.
I see her back, and reflect it faithfully.
She rewards me with tears and an agitation of hands.
15 I am important to her. She comes and goes.
Each morning it is her face that replaces the darkness.
In me she has drowned a young girl, and in me an old woman
Rises toward her day after day, like a terrible fish.

COURAGE

Anne Sexton

It is in the small things we see it.
The child's first step,
as awesome as an earthquake.
The first time you rode a bike,
5   wallowing up the sidewalk.
The first spanking when your heart
went on a journey all alone.
When they called you crybaby
or poor or fatty or crazy
10   and made you into an alien,
you drank their acid
and concealed it.
Later,
if you faced the death of bombs and bullets
15   you did not do it with a banner,
you did it with only a hat to
cover your heart.
You did not fondle the weakness inside you
though it was there.
20   Your courage was a small coal
that you kept swallowing.
If your buddy saved you
and died himself in so doing,
then his courage was not courage,
25   it was love; love as simple as shaving soap.
Later,
if you have endured a great despair,
then you did it alone,
getting a transfusion from the fire,

Vocabulary

endured (en dѹrd´) *v.* held up under; withstood

transfusion (trans fyo͞o´ zhən) *n.* the transferring of a life-giving substance from a source to a recipient

Comprehension

According to the speaker, which childhood events require courage?

30 picking the scabs off your heart,
    then wringing it out like a sock.
    Next, my kinsman, you powdered your sorrow,
    you gave it a back rub
    and then you covered it with a blanket
35 and after it had slept a while
    it woke to the wings of the roses
    and was transformed.
    Later,
    when you face old age and its natural conclusion
40 your courage will still be shown in the little ways,
    each spring will be a sword you'll sharpen,
    those you love will live in a fever of love,
    and you'll bargain with the calendar
    and at the last moment
45 when death opens the back door
    you'll put on your carpet slippers
    and stride out.

Vocabulary

transformed (trans fôrmd′)
adj. altered; changed

Critical Reading

1. **Key Ideas and Details (a)** In "Mirror", how does the woman "reward" the speaker? **(b) Interpret:** Why do you think she reacts this way?

2. **Key Ideas and Details (a)** To whom does the woman turn? **(b) Interpret:** Why are they called "liars"?

3. **Key Ideas and Details (a)** According to the speaker of "Courage," what happens to sorrow after it sleeps? **(b) Draw Conclusions:** What information does this give you about the speaker's own experience?

4. **Key Ideas and Details (a) Interpret:** What is the "natural conclusion" of old age? **(b) Analyze:** Do you find the response of "you" to this conclusion natural? Explain.

5. **Integration of Knowledge and Ideas** What do the private concerns expressed in these poems suggest about larger issues in society? Explain. In your response use at least two of these Essential Question words: *anxiety, sympathize, identity, collective.* *[Connecting to the Essential Question: How does literature shape or reflect society?]*

Literary Analysis

1. **Key Ideas and Details (a)** In "Mirror," what is the significance of the word *swallow* (line 2)? **(b)** In what ways does the word *swallow* add to the poem's meaning?

2. **Key Ideas and Details (a) Interpret the connotations** of the word *powdered* in "Courage" (line 32). What associations does the word carry? **(b)** What do these connotations suggest about the poem's essential meaning, or theme?

3. **Craft and Structure (a)** Identify three **metaphors** used in "Mirror." **(b)** What danger or threat does each of these metaphors suggest? **(c)** Which of these dangers comes to pass, and who is the victim?

4. **Craft and Structure (a)** With what **simile** does Plath conclude her poem? **(b)** What two dissimilar things are being compared? **(c)** Why do you think Plath chose to use a simile here—the only one in the poem—rather than a metaphor?

5. **Integration of Knowledge and Ideas (a)** Use a chart like the one shown to identify three metaphors in "Courage." **(b)** Taken together, what do these metaphors reveal about the life that "you" leads?

Metaphor	Things Compared	Significance

Common Core State Standards

Writing
2. Write informative texts to examine and convey complex ideas, concepts, and information clearly and accurately through the effective selection, organization, and analysis of content.

Language
4. Determine or clarify the meaning of unknown and multiple-meaning words and phrases based on *grades 11–12* reading and content, choosing flexibly from a range of strategies.

Vocabulary Acquisition and Use

Sentence Completions Use a vocabulary word to complete each sentence. Explain your choices.

1. The hikers _____ the rain for an hour, then sought shelter in a cave.

2. To keep the trial fair, only jurors with no _____ were chosen.

3. Many actors say that when they step onto the stage, they feel _____.

4. The doctors reported that only a blood _____ would save the patient's life.

Writing to Sources

Informative Text Both "Mirror" and "Courage" address the full sweep of a human life, from youth to adulthood to old age. However, the poets' portrayals of these stages of life are extremely different. Write an **essay** exploring how each speaker sees the process or progress of life. Consider these questions: What words describe each speaker's attitude toward aging? How are these attitudes depicted in the poem's images? Which portrayal is hopeful, and which is full of despair? Why?

Connecting to the Essential Question Some of Theodore Roethke's strongest images are drawn from childhood memories of his father's greenhouse. As you read, look for small-scale details with large-scale meaning. Doing so will contribute to your understanding of the Essential Question: **What is the relationship between literature and place?**

Close Reading Focus

Sound Devices

Roethke's poignant, imagistic poetry achieves some of its emotional effect and beauty through **sound devices,** such as the following:

- **Alliteration** is the repetition of a consonant sound at the beginnings of words: "What saint strained so much, / Rose on such lopped limbs to a new life?"

- **Assonance** is the repetition of a vowel sound in stressed syllables with dissimilar consonant sounds: "I quail, lean to beginnings, sheath-wet."

- **Consonance** is the repetition of consonant sounds in stressed syllables in the middle or at the end of words: "The small cells bulge."

In "Cuttings" and "Cuttings (later)," Roethke ponders the microscopic movements of a plant—movements so small in scale that their sounds are undetectable by the human ear. Through his use of sound devices, the poet gives these tiny movements a music all their own, and invites the reader to move in close to hear the delicate strains.

Preparing to Read Complex Texts Sometimes poets dive deep into the complexities of nature, producing images that help readers see both nature and themselves in a new light. In these cases, **using background knowledge** about nature and its processes can help you understand the nuances of a poem. For these poems, refer to the background note or use other resources about cuttings and propagation of plants to add to your understanding. Use a chart like the one shown to apply background knowledge and clarify meaning as you read.

Vocabulary

The words below are important to understanding the texts that follow. Copy the words into your notebook. Which word has multiple meanings?

intricate   quail

seeping

Common Core State Standards

Reading Literature
4. Analyze the impact of specific word choices on meaning and tone, including language that is particularly fresh, engaging, or beautiful.
5. Analyze how an author's choices concerning how to structure specific parts of a text contribute to its overall structure and meaning as well as its aesthetic impact.

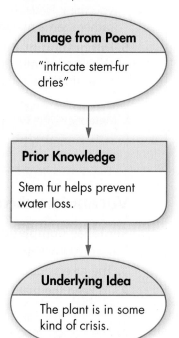

Image from Poem

"intricate stem-fur dries"

Prior Knowledge

Stem fur helps prevent water loss.

Underlying Idea

The plant is in some kind of crisis.

Theodore Roethke

(1908–1963)

Author of **"Cuttings"** and **"Cuttings (later)"**

Theodore Roethke (ret´ kē) was born and raised in Saginaw, Michigan, where his family owned several large commercial greenhouses. As a boy, Roethke was a passionate observer of the plants that grew in the greenhouses. He observed nature putting forth roots and blossoms, as well as falling into dormancy and death. These observations later provided him with ideas and inspiration for many of his poems. In 1923, Roethke's father lost his battle with cancer, an event that also heavily influenced Roethke's poetry.

Refuge in Writing Throughout his life, Roethke found it difficult to relate to other people. Poetry and nature gave him a refuge in which to explore various aspects of his own life. Although his style changed throughout his career, the impulse to explore the meaning of subjective, personal experience remained a constant.

First Successes After receiving his education at the University of Michigan and Harvard, Roethke taught writing at Bennington College, Pennsylvania State University, and the University of Washington. A slow, diligent writer, he spent many years assembling poems for his first book. At age thirty-three, he published his first volume, *Open House* (1941), launching a career as one of the most acclaimed poets of his day. He won the Pulitzer Prize for *The Waking* (1953) and the National Book Award for *The Far Field* (1964), which was published after his death. From short, witty poems to complex, philosophical free verse, Roethke's poetry reflects a wide range of feelings and poetic styles.

Roethke published several more books, including *The Lost Son* (1948) and *Words for the Wind* (1958).

A Lasting Influence Theodore Roethke's work was an inspiration both to his contemporaries and to writers today. Remarking on his place in American literature, renowned poet Stanley Kunitz said Roethke "was in possession of a dynasty of extraordinary gifts and powers."

"Art is the means we have of undoing the damage of haste. It's what everything else isn't."

BACKGROUND: When Theodore Roethke's grandparents immigrated to the United States in 1872, they settled in Saginaw, Michigan, where they earned a living by growing and selling plants. Roethke's father and uncle inherited this trade and would go on to own one of the largest greenhouses in the state. As a child, Roethke spent countless hours in this greenhouse, gaining an informal but extensive education in the art and science of gardening. One of the many gardening strategies he learned was how to grow a new plant from a cutting. A cutting—also known as a slip—is a twig, branch, or leaf cut from a mature plant and placed in water or wet sand. Water moves upward through the cutting from its base by a process called diffusion. Diffusion occurs when water molecules move from areas of high concentration to areas of low concentration by passing through the walls of cells. As more and more water enters the cells of the cutting, water pressure builds, which in turn causes the cutting to stand upright. Water pressure also stimulates cell growth, and soon, under the proper conditions, the cutting will sprout new roots and leaves. When the roots are strong enough, the cutting—now a plant—can be potted in soil.

Cuttings

Theodore Roethke

Sticks-in-a-drowse droop over sugary loam,
Their **intricate** stem-fur dries;
But still the delicate slips keep coaxing up water;
The small cells bulge;

5   One nub of growth
Nudges a sand-crumb loose,
Pokes through a musty sheath
Its pale tendrilous horn.

Vocabulary
intricate (in´ tri kit) *adj.* complex; having many small, interrelated parts

Cuttings (later)

Theodore Roethke

Vocabulary

seeping (sēp´ iŋ)
v. flowing slowly

quail (kwāl) *v.* draw
back in fear; lose heart

This urge, wrestle, resurrection of dry sticks,
Cut stems struggling to put down feet,
What saint strained so much,
Rose on such lopped limbs to a new life?

5   I can hear, underground, that sucking and sobbing,
In my veins, in my bones I feel it,—
The small waters **seeping** upward,
The tight grains parting at last.
When sprouts break out,

10 Slippery as fish,
I **quail**, lean to beginnings, sheath-wet.

Critical Reading

Cite textual evidence to support your responses.

1. **Key Ideas and Details** **(a)** In "Cuttings," what are the "delicate slips" doing? **(b) Analyze Cause and Effect:** What are two results of this action?

2. **Key Ideas and Details** **(a) Infer:** What seems to be happening inside the plant? **(b) Interpret:** What details in the poem confirm this observation?

3. **Craft and Structure** **(a)** In line 1 of "Cuttings (later)," what verbs does the poet use to describe what is happening? **(b) Distinguish:** How do these verbs suggest that the second poem is different from the first?

4. **Integration of Knowledge and Ideas** Do you think these poems document observed reality? Explain. In your response use at least two of these Essential Question words: *subjective, objective, scene, clarity, perceptions.* [Connecting to the Essential Question: *What is the relationship between literature and place?*]

Literary Analysis

Common Core State Standards

Language
3. Apply knowledge of language to understand how language functions in different contexts, to make effective choices for meaning or style, and to comprehend more fully when reading or listening.

1. **Key Ideas and Details** **(a) Apply background knowledge** to your reading of "Cuttings" to explain the natural processes indicated by the phrases "delicate slips keep coaxing up water" and "small cells bulge"? **(b)** In what way does this process reflect human growth or transformation?

2. **Craft and Structure** Use a chart like the one shown to analyze **sound devices** Roethke uses in these poems. **(a)** Identify one example of **alliteration, assonance,** and **consonance** from either poem. **(b)** Describe how each example brings an image to life or extends the poem's meaning.

	Example	Effect
alliteration		
assonance		
consonance		

3. **Craft and Structure** **(a)** In general, would you describe the sounds of "Cuttings" as easy and fluid or as mildly jarring? Explain. **(b)** How does this sound quality help convey the poem's central message?

4. **Integration of Knowledge and Ideas** Based on these poems, what do you think plant growth would sound like if human ears were sensitive enough to hear it?

Vocabulary Acquisition and Use

Revise for Logic Revise each sentence so that the underlined word is used logically.

1. The dance was so <u>intricate</u> even a beginner could perform it well.

2. If you <u>quail</u> at the mere thought of a horror film, then *Things That Go Bump in the Night* is the movie for you!

3. <u>Seeping</u> water is a sign that your roof is in fine shape.

Writing to Sources

Informative Text Research plant growth in a science book or on a science Web site. Compare and contrast the information in the science text with the depictions in Roethke's poems. Then, write an **essay** in which you evaluate each type of writing. Describe the types of language used in these different contexts as well as the authors' purposes and perspectives. Take a position about which presentation of plant growth is more engaging.

Connecting to the Essential Question These poems express longings for a life or a future that is different from the present. As you read, notice details that speak to longings and hopes. Doing so will help you consider the Essential Question: **How does literature shape or reflect society?**

Close Reading Focus

Repetition; Parallelism

Writers, including poets, use various *rhetorical devices* to emphasize messages or evoke emotions in their readers. Repetition and parallelism are two devices that often appear in poetry:

- **Repetition** is the repeating of key words or concepts: "Wee <u>griefs</u>, / Grand <u>griefs</u>. And <u>choices</u>. / He feared most of all the <u>choices</u>. . . ."
- **Parallelism** is the presentation of similar ideas using the same grammatical structures: "<u>When it</u> is finally ours. . . . / <u>when it</u> belongs at last to all, / <u>when it</u> is truly instinct. . . . "

In the first example above, the repetition of *griefs* and *choices* helps communicate the idea that one's grief is related to one's choices. In the second example, the repetition of the grammatical structure *when it* . . . builds a sense of urgency and expectation.

Comparing Literary Works As you read these poems, find examples of repetition and parallelism. Consider the specific purposes—emphasis or emotion—these devices help each poet achieve.

Preparing to Read Complex Texts When poets—and people—repeat words or phrases over and over, they are most likely trying to get your attention. When we read a text silently, though, it can be easy to gloss over repeated elements in order to get more quickly to "the point." As a result, we may miss the point altogether. To give these poems your full attention and to aid your comprehension, **read the poems aloud.** When you encounter repetition, slow down and emphasize it. Listen for the poet's use of repetition, parallelism, and other literary elements in these poems. Use a chart like the one shown to analyze the effects of reading passages aloud.

Vocabulary

The words below are important to understanding the texts that follow. Copy the words into your notebook. Which word could be an adjective or a verb?

frayed　　　　　**gaudy**

wily

**Common Core
State Standards**

Reading Literature
4. Analyze the impact of specific word choices on meaning and tone, including language that is particularly fresh, engaging, or beautiful.
5. Analyze how an author's choices concerning how to structure specific parts of a text contribute to its overall structure and meaning as well as its aesthetic impact.

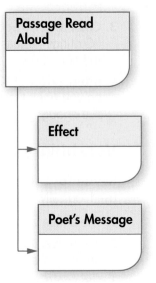

Gwendolyn Brooks

(1917–2000)

Author of "The Explorer"

Gwendolyn Brooks was raised in a Chicago neighborhood known as "Bronzeville"—the setting for her first book, *A Street in Bronzeville* (1945). Although her early poems focus on struggling urban blacks who feel uprooted and are unable to make a living, Brooks's own youth was quite different. Her home was warm and her family loving, supportive, and confident that Brooks would find success as a writer. Brooks began writing poetry at the age of seven. Her first published poem, "Eventide," appeared in *American Childhood* Magazine in 1930. When she was in high school, her mother took her to meet Harlem Renaissance poets Langston Hughes and James Weldon Johnson, who encouraged her interests.

Dedication and Recognition By the time she was sixteen, Brooks had published approximately seventy-five poems in local publications. She continued to study, write, and hone her craft. Her first book of poetry garnered critical acclaim. With the publication of her second book, *Annie Allen*, in 1950, she became the first African American writer to win a Pulitzer Prize. Honors and prizes followed throughout her career.

A New Generation Inspired by the civil rights movement of the 1960s—and its new generation of young black activists and artists—Brooks's works became increasingly political and experimental. As noted author Toni Cade Bambara remarked in the *New York Times Book Review*, Brooks's later works were marked by "a new movement and energy, intensity, richness, power of statement and a new stripped lean, compressed style. A change of style prompted by a change of mind."

By the time of her death at the turn of the twenty-first century, Brooks had become one of the most highly regarded poets of our time.

"I WANT THESE POEMS TO BE FREE."

THE EXPLORER

GWENDOLYN BROOKS

Vocabulary

frayed (frād) *adj.* tattered

wily (wī′ lē) *adj.* sly; cunning

Somehow to find a still spot in the noise
Was the frayed inner want, the winding, the frayed hope
Whose tatters he kept hunting through the din.
A satin peace somewhere.
5 A room of wily hush somewhere within.

So tipping down the scrambled halls he set
Vague hands on throbbing knobs. There were behind
Only spiraling, high human voices,
The scream of nervous affairs,
10 Wee griefs,
Grand griefs. And choices.

He feared most of all the choices, that cried to be taken.

There were no bourns.[1]
There were no quiet rooms.

_____

1. **bourns** (bōrnz) *n.* limits; boundaries.

Critical Reading

1. **Key Ideas and Details (a)** What is the "inner want" the speaker expresses? **(b) Interpret:** In what way does the title of the poem relate to the "inner want"?

2. **Craft and Structure (a)** What might the explorer's apartment building symbolize? **(b) Interpret:** What might the explorer's actions and feelings symbolize?

3. **Integration of Knowledge and Ideas** Why do you think people often fear making choices?

Robert Hayden *(1913–1980)*

Author of **"Frederick Douglass"**

Born in Detroit, Robert Hayden had a difficult childhood. He faced poverty, coped with the emotional difficulties of an unstable family, and struggled with extreme nearsightedness. Though his poor vision prevented him from playing sports, it did not stop him from reading. Hayden devoted his days to books, developing an appreciation for the transformative qualities of literature.

Experience, Research, and Art Hayden attended Detroit City College (now Wayne State University). In 1936, he joined the Federal Writers' Project, researching African American history and folk culture. The depth of historical awareness he gained from this research contributed to his poetry and artistry. As a young, politically active writer in the 1930s, he protested both the social and economic conditions of African Americans and what he saw as the nation's inadequate care of the poor.

Hayden was an extremely versatile writer who used a variety of poetic forms and techniques. While working toward his master's degree, he studied under W. H. Auden (p. 773), who influenced Hayden's choices of form and technique.

Publications and Honors During his career, Hayden published several collections of poetry, including *A Ballad of Remembrance* (1962), which won the Grand Prize for Poetry at the First World Festival for Negro Arts in 1966. From 1976 to 1978, Hayden served as Consultant in Poetry to the Library of Congress, a position later known as "Poet Laureate."

Although Hayden sought to undo racial stereotypes and to tell a truthful version of his people's history, he did not believe that race should define a poet. Instead, he believed that identity serves as a starting point from which to offer insights that transcend race and speak to all people.

> **"[My poetry is] a way of coming to grips with reality . . . a way of discovery and definition."**

The Life of Frederick Douglass, #30, Jacob Lawrence, The Jacob and Gwendolyn Lawrence Foundation, Artists Rights Society (ARS), New York

FREDERICK DOUGLASS

ROBERT HAYDEN

BACKGROUND Frederick Douglass (1817–1895) was a leading
abolitionist during the 19th century. (See the excerpt from Douglass's
autobiography on pages 520–527; see also "Douglass" by Paul
Laurence Dunbar on page 636.)

When it is finally ours, this freedom, this liberty,
   this beautiful
and terrible thing, needful to man as air,
usable as earth; when it belongs at last to all,
when it is truly instinct, brain matter, diastole, systole,[1]
5 reflex action; when it is finally won; when it is more
than the gaudy mumbo jumbo of politicians:
this man, this Douglass, this former slave, this Negro
beaten to his knees, exiled, visioning a world
where none is lonely, none hunted, alien,
10 this man, superb in love and logic, this man
shall be remembered. Oh, not with statues' rhetoric,
not with legends and poems and wreaths of bronze alone,
but with the lives grown out of his life, the lives
fleshing his dream of the beautiful, needful thing.

1. **diastole** (dī as′ tə lē′), **systole** (sis′ tə lē′) Diastole is the normal rhythmic dilation, or
opening, of the heart. Systole is the normal rhythmic closing of the heart.

◀ **Critical Viewing**
What impression of
Douglass does this
painting convey?
ANALYZE

Vocabulary
gaudy (gô′ dē)
adj. showy in a
tasteless way

Critical Reading

1. **Key Ideas and Details (a)** What is the "beautiful and terrible"
thing? **(b) Infer:** To whom does it not yet belong?
2. **Integration of Knowledge and Ideas Speculate:** How might
Frederick Douglass react to this poem? Explain.
3. **Integration of Knowledge and Ideas** What type of world do
the speakers in these poems hope to see realized? Explain. In
your response, use at least two of these Essential Question words:
*liberty, ambition, vision, lament, idealism. [Connecting to the
Essential Question: How does literature shape or reflect
society?]*

Cite textual
evidence to
support your
responses.

Literary Analysis

1. **Craft and Structure** **(a)** Identify an example of **repetition** in the first stanza of "The Explorer." **(b)** How does this repetition help the poet develop a particular idea?

2. **Craft and Structure** Use a chart like the one shown to identify examples of **parallelism** in each poem. **(a)** Note the example of **parallelism** in the last two lines of "The Explorer." **(b)** Identify an example of parallelism in lines 7–14 of "Frederick Douglass." **(c)** Explain how each example of parallelism heightens the emotional energy of the poem.

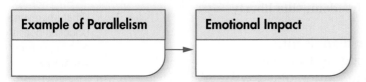

Example of Parallelism → Emotional Impact

3. **Craft and Structure** **(a)** What phrase is used to describe Douglass once in line 7 and twice in line 10? **(b)** Why do you think the poet chose to repeat this particular phrase?

4. **Craft and Structure** **(a)** List lines or phrases from each poem that are particularly striking when **read aloud. (b)** Then, explain how reading the passage aloud helps to clarify its meaning.

5. **Craft and Structure** **(a)** In what ways does reading aloud emphasize the poets' use of repetition? **(b)** From having read the poems aloud, do you better understand the poets' uses of parallelism? Explain.

6. **Craft and Structure** In your view, which poem lends itself more naturally to an oral reading? Why do you think this is?

7. **Integration of Knowledge and Ideas** Frederick Douglass was an orator, or public speaker, as well as an abolitionist. How does the form of Hayden's poem pay tribute to this aspect of Douglass's life?

8. **Integration of Knowledge and Ideas** **(a)** Which of the two poems do you find more emotionally moving? Explain. **(b)** Do you attribute this to its message or to the poet's uses of rhetorical devices, such as repetition and parallelism? Explain.

Common Core State Standards

Writing
2. Write explanatory texts to examine and convey complex ideas, concepts, and information clearly and accurately through the effective selection, organization, and analysis of content. *(p. 1069)*

2.b. Develop the topic thoroughly by selecting the most significant and relevant facts, extended definitions, concrete details, quotations, or other information and examples appropriate to the audience's knowledge of the topic. *(p. 1069)*

Language
4. Determine or clarify the meaning of unknown and multiple-meaning words and phrases based on *grades 11–12 reading and content,* choosing flexibly from a range of strategies. *(p. 1069)*

4.a. Use context as a clue to the meaning of a word or phrase. *(p. 1069)*

5. Demonstrate understanding of word relationships. *(p. 1069)*

Vocabulary Acquisition and Use

Word Analysis: Word/Phrase Relationships

The meaning of a descriptive word can change when it is connected to other words in a phrase. For example, the adjective *rigid* means "stiff" in the phrase *rigid posture*, but "harsh" or "severe" in the phrase *rigid rules*. Read each pair of sentences below. Explain how the meaning of the word differs in the context of each underlined phrase.

1. My <u>frayed shirt</u> is soft and comfortable.
   She expressed her <u>frayed emotions</u> in a long letter.

2. Lots of <u>gaudy jewelry</u> made the costume complete.
   The <u>gaudy compliment</u> fell on deaf ears.

3. The <u>wily fox</u> crept close to his prey.
   A <u>thin, wily moon</u> gave little guidance to the midnight travelers.

Vocabulary: Assessing Logic

Each sentence below features an underlined word from the vocabulary list on page 1062. For each item, explain whether the sentence makes sense, given the meaning of the underlined word. If it does not make sense, write a new sentence using the word correctly.

1. It is difficult to coax a <u>frayed</u> piece of thread through the narrow eye of a needle.

2. The <u>wily</u> behavior of the new mayor was reassuring to all those who had voted for him.

3. Our apartment complex has strict rules about holiday decorations: Only <u>gaudy</u> lights and plain green wreaths are allowed.

Writing to Sources

Explanatory Text In an **essay,** examine "The Explorer" and "Frederick Douglass" through two different critical lenses. First, *use a social perspective,* analyzing how each poem reflects the struggles of African Americans during the mid-twentieth century. Then, *use an archetypal perspective,* demonstrating how each poem expresses universal human longings.

Prewriting First, read each poem with the social perspective in mind. Jot down possible connections between details in the poem and issues in mid-1900s America. Then, read each poem from an archetypal perspective, making note of images and symbols with universal power and appeal.

Drafting Begin your essay with a general statement about the poem and the points you will cover. Then, present your material in an organized way: Discuss one poem from both perspectives, and then discuss the other poem from both perspectives; or, apply one perspective to both poems, and then apply the other perspective to both poems.

Revising Identify points in your draft at which you make important general statements about the poem. Strengthen your analysis by adding accurate quotations from the poems to support your interpretation.

> **Model: Using Quotations to Support Interpretation**
> The poet speaks to and about all humans when she
>   "wee griefs" and "grand griefs"   of
> acknowledges the ~~worries, large and small, that make up~~
> daily life.   ∧
>
> Using direct quotations supports the interpretation of the poem.

Connecting to the Essential Question In "One Art," the speaker explores the idea of losing objects, time, and—surprisingly—places. As you read these poems, look for places that have been lost and those that have been found. Doing so will help you consider the Essential Question: **What is the relationship between literature and place?**

Close Reading Focus

Diction; Rhetorical Devices

While Elizabeth Bishop's poems are elegant and carefully crafted, they create the feeling of a conversation between poet and reader. Several literary elements produce this double effect. The first is Bishop's **diction,** or word choice. For example, *master* and *disaster* are the rhyming words that cycle through the *villanelle* "One Art." These are ordinary words, yet their repetition invites readers to see them in new ways. Bishop also draws readers in through her use of **rhetorical devices**—word patterns that create emphasis and stir emotion:

- **Imperatives:** Mild commands invite readers to do or feel certain things. Example: "Lose something every day."

- **Exclamations:** Statements ending in an exclamation point inject an emotional intensity. Example: "Oh, but it is dirty!"

- **Questions:** Questions cast the reader in the role of the speaker's confidant. Example: "Why, oh why, the doily?"

As you read, use a chart like the one shown to note Bishop's use of rhetorical devices and the ways in which they involve the reader in the poems.

Preparing to Read Complex Texts Many poems—including "One Art" and "Filling Station"—are written in sentences and use the same punctuation marks that you find in prose. To *clarify the meaning of a poem,* **read according to punctuation.** As you read these poems, do not pause at line breaks. Instead, pause when you encounter a comma, a colon, a semicolon, a dash, or an end mark.

Vocabulary

You will encounter the words listed here in the texts that follow. Copy the words into your notebook. Which word can be used as either a verb or a noun?

master	permeated
intent	extraneous

Common Core
State Standards

Reading Literature
4. Analyze the impact of specific word choices on meaning and tone, including language that is particularly fresh, engaging, or beautiful.
5. Analyze how an author's choices concerning how to structure specific parts of a text contribute to its overall structure and meaning as well as its aesthetic impact.

Rhetorical Device

Imperative: "Accept the fluster/of lost door keys..."

↓

How It Involves the Reader

The reader is asked to adopt a new attitude toward minor disasters.

Elizabeth Bishop (1911–1979)

Author of "One Art" and "Filling Station"

Northern Roots The title of Elizabeth Bishop's first poetry collection, *North & South*, reflects the range of both her poetic skill and her world travels. These travels began in Worcester, Massachusetts, where Bishop was born. After the death of her father and the mental collapse of her mother, Bishop was raised by her grandparents. She attended Vassar College, where she founded a literary journal, *Con Spirito*, and began a lifelong friendship with fellow poet Marianne Moore.

Southern Sojourns After graduating from college, Bishop, who was independently wealthy, set out to see the world. She traveled first to France, where she spent a winter in Paris, and then south through the Mediterranean to North Africa. Her poetry from this period is filled with descriptions of sights from her travels—a subject to which she would return, exquisitely, throughout her career.

In 1938, Bishop bought an old house in Key West, Florida, and remained there for several years before heading even farther south. First, she visited Mexico, where she met the poet Pablo Neruda and learned Spanish. She then settled in Brazil, where she lived for almost twenty years. After the devastating loss of a close friend, Bishop returned to the United States, where she spent the rest of her life. She taught at Harvard University from 1970 to 1977.

Poet of Precision Bishop's poetry is celebrated for its precise, true-to-life images and for its polished and often witty language. Her belief that poetry should use the same sentence patterns as good prose gives her verse a conversational quality, though its subject matter is rarely personal. Instead, many of her poems focus on working-class settings such as factories and farms, or on universal human emotions such as grief and longing. Meticulous in the crafting of every line, Bishop wrote slowly and she published sparingly—nevertheless winning the Pulitzer Prize in poetry for *North and South* in 1956, and National Book Awards in 1965 and 1970. By the end of her life, the brilliance of her work had been fully appreciated, and she was hailed as one of the major American poets of the century.

ONE ART

ELIZABETH BISHOP

The art of losing isn't hard to master;
so many things seem filled with the intent
to be lost that their loss is no disaster.

Lose something every day. Accept the fluster
5 of lost door keys, the hour badly spent.
The art of losing isn't hard to master.

Then practice losing farther, losing faster:
places, and names, and where it was you meant
to travel. None of these will bring disaster.

10 I lost my mother's watch. And look! my last, or
next-to-last, of three loved houses went.
The art of losing isn't hard to master.

I lost two cities, lovely ones. And, vaster,
some realms I owned, two rivers, a continent.
15 I miss them, but it wasn't a disaster.

—Even losing you (the joking voice, a gesture
I love) I shan't have lied. It's evident
the art of losing's not too hard to master
though it may look like (*Write* it!) like disaster.

Vocabulary

master (mas´ tər) *v.*
become an expert in

intent (in tent´) *n.*
purpose or aim

LITERATURE IN CONTEXT

Poetic Structure

The Villanelle

"One Art" is a *villanelle,* a highly structured poem consisting of nineteen lines, two repeating end rhymes, and two refrains. These elements are arranged in a set way, as you can see in "One Art." Notice that the refrains—the first line of the first stanza, and the word *disaster* from the third line of the first stanza—are repeated alternately as the last lines of stanzas 2 through 5, and then repeated together at the end of stanza 6. Notice, too, that every first and third line ends with the *-aster* sound (or its near-rhyme *-uster*) and that every second line ends with the *-ent* sound. When the villanelle first appeared in sixteenth century France, it had a looser structure and focused on pastoral themes. Contemporary poets have used the villanelle to treat a broader range of themes, but within a tighter structure. The modern villanelle allows for slight changes in the refrains, which often signal an evolution in the speaker's thoughts.

Connect to the Literature

What evolution in the speaker's thoughts is evident from the changing refrain in "One Art"? Explain.

◀ **Critical Viewing** Elizabeth Bishop painted this landscape of a mountain valley in Brazil. In what ways does the painting echo the idea expressed in "One Art" of owning a realm? **INTERPRET**

Filling Station

Elizabeth Bishop

Oh, but it is dirty!
—this little filling station,
oil-soaked, oil-permeated
to a disturbing, over-all
5   black translucency.
Be careful with that match!

Father wears a dirty,
oil-soaked monkey suit
that cuts him under the arms,
10   and several quick and saucy
and greasy sons assist him
(it's a family filling station),
all quite thoroughly dirty.

Do they live in the station?
15   It has a cement porch
behind the pumps, and on it
a set of crushed and grease-
impregnated wickerwork;
on the wicker sofa
20   a dirty dog, quite comfy.

Some comic books provide
the only note of color—
of certain color. They lie
upon a big dim doily

Vocabulary
permeated (pʉr´ mē āt´ əd)
adj. soaked through with

Comprehension
What is the poet's first
impression of the filling
station?

◄ **Critical Viewing** Could the filling station shown in this
painting be the one the speaker describes in the poem? Explain.
MAKE A JUDGMENT

25   draping a taboret
   (part of the set), beside
   a big hirsute begonia.

   Why the extraneous plant?
   Why the taboret?
30   Why, oh why, the doily?
   (Embroidered in daisy stitch
   with marguerites, I think,
   and heavy with gray crochet.)

   Somebody embroidered the doily.
35   Somebody waters the plant,
   or oils it, maybe. Somebody
   arranges the rows of cans
   so that they softly say:
   ESSO—SO—SO—SO
40   to high-strung automobiles.
   Somebody loves us all.

Vocabulary

extraneous (ek strā´ nē əs)
adj. unrelated or unconnected

Critical Reading

Cite textual evidence to support your responses.

1. **Key Ideas and Details (a)** In "One Art," what are some things the speaker has lost? **(b) Interpret:** What do you think the speaker means by "practice losing farther, losing faster"? **(c) Make Inferences:** What does the speaker suggest will be the result of such practice?

2. **Key Ideas and Details (a)** According to the speaker, none of the losses has brought what? **(b) Assess:** Do you take this claim at face value, or do you suspect otherwise? Explain.

3. **Key Ideas and Details (a)** In line 14 of "Filling Station," what does the speaker wonder? **(b) Identify:** Cite three details that prompt the speaker to ask this question. Explain.

4. **Integration of Knowledge and Ideas Generalize:** Reread the poem's first and last lines. What might the poet be communicating about the world at large?

5. **Integration of Knowledge and Ideas** Are the places the speaker loses and finds in these poems parts of the actual, physical world, or parts of an emotional world? Explain. In your response, use at least two of these Essential Question words: *landscape, personal, lament, exile.* *[Connecting to the Essential Question: What is the relationship between literature and place?]*

Literary Analysis

1. **Craft and Structure** Read "One Art" aloud, pausing at the end of each line. Then, read it aloud according to punctuation. **(a)** What happens to the rhymes when you read the poem in sentences? **(b)** How does reading the poem according to punctuation help you better understand its meaning? Use a chart like the one below to analyze how different approaches to reading affect what you understand about each line.

Single Line	Complete Sentence	Meaning

2. **Craft and Structure** Because of its cycling, repeating form, the *villanelle* "One Art" highlights Bishop's **diction. (a)** What two words does the speaker repeat? **(b)** In what ways do these two words, taken together, capture an important part of the poem's overall meaning? **(c)** How does the repetition of these words subtly contradict this message?

3. **Craft and Structure (a)** Identify three **imperatives** in "One Art." **(b)** Why might the speaker urge the reader to do these things? **(c)** Why might the speaker need to address *herself* with these imperatives?

4. **Craft and Structure** Skim "Filling Station," **reading according to punctuation.** Compare the effects of this reading with one in which you follow the line breaks.

5. **Craft and Structure (a)** Identify three adjectives, nouns, or verbs that repeat in "Filling Station." **(b)** Do you consider these words particularly "poetic"? Explain. **(c)** Why do you think Bishop chose to repeat such words multiple times?

6. **Craft and Structure** How does Bishop's use of parentheses add to the intimate, conversational quality of her poems?

7. **Integration of Knowledge and Ideas (a)** Identify one **exclamation** and one **question** from either "One Art" or "Filling Station." **(b)** Rewrite each as a statement ending with a period. **(c)** Imagine that the poet had used the rewritten statements rather than the originals. How would this have changed the poem or your experience of the poem?

Common Core State Standards

Writing
5. Develop and strengthen writing as needed by planning, revising, editing, rewriting, or trying a new approach, focusing on addressing what is most significant for a specific purpose and audience. *(p. 1078)*

6. Use technology, including the Internet, to produce, publish, and update individual or shared writing products. *(p. 1078)*

Language
4.b. Identify and correctly use patterns of word changes that indicate different meanings or parts of speech. *(p. 1078)*

5. Demonstrate understanding of word relationships. *(p. 1078)*

Vocabulary Acquisition and Use

Word Analysis: Latin Word *extra*

The Latin word *extra* means "additional," "outside," or "beyond." In English, *extra* is sometimes used on its own; sometimes used as a root, as in *extraneous*; and often used as a prefix, as in *extraordinary*. For each of the words shown below, write a definition that includes either the word *additional, outside,* or *beyond*. Use a dictionary as necessary to aid your work.

1. extraordinary   **4.** extrasolar

2. extrasensory   **5.** extracranial

3. extraterrestrial   **6.** extracurricular

Vocabulary: Synonyms

Synonyms are words that share the same or similar meanings. Choose the best synonym for each vocabulary word below. Explain your choices.

1. permeated   **a.** stung   **b.** attached   **c.** soaked

2. extraneous   **a.** challenging   **b.** irrelevant   **c.** dense

3. master   **a.** learn   **b.** spend   **c.** choose

4. intent   **a.** goal   **b.** aversion   **c.** pretense

Writing to Sources

Explanatory Text Prepare a response to "One Art" and "Filling Station" in more than one genre, or form. Illustrate the poems with drawings, paintings, photographs, or a collage of images from other sources, including the Internet. Then, write an **explanation** of your choices. Finally, combine the images with the text in a poster to display in your classroom.

Prewriting Reread each poem, paying close attention to visual descriptions. Consider the images that form in your mind and how you will communicate themes in visual terms. Decide if your images will summarize the poem, draw conclusions about the poem, or depict your own personal reactions.

Model: Linking Images to Poem

Illustration	Connection to Poem
Photograph of dirt in a field	At first, the viewer of the filling station sees only dirt and grime.

Drafting As you draft your written explanation, refer to your illustration. Explain the thematic connections between the artwork and the poem.

Revising Reread your writing to make sure you have related your ideas to your illustration. Strengthen weak links by adding transitional words or quotations. Then, combine your writing and your illustration into a poster, making sure to observe the principles of design, such as effective use of fonts and white space.

Connecting to the Essential Question John, the main character in this story, is an outsider in almost all aspects of his life. As you read, look for details that reveal characters as insiders or outsiders. This will help you consider the Essential Question: **How does literature shape or reflect society?**

Close Reading Focus

Setting; Symbol

The **setting** of a story is the time and place in which it occurs; it may include details about the weather, physical features of the landscape, and other elements of an environment. "The Rockpile" is set in Harlem during the 1930s. Life in that time and place was influenced by the difficult economic and social realities that people faced.

A story's setting can also serve as a symbol. A **symbol** is a person, place, or object that has a meaning in itself but also suggests a larger meaning. While it is not the story's only symbol, the rockpile that dominates the setting is its most important one. Among other meanings, it can be interpreted as a symbol for violence and failure in the community:

> *They fought on the rockpile. Sure footed, dangerous, and reckless, they rushed each other and grappled on the heights . . .*

As you read, note how the narrator describes the rockpile, the characters that are associated with it, and the events that take place there. These details will help you interpret the symbolic meanings of the rockpile.

Preparing to Read Complex Texts A *cause* is the reason something happens. An *effect* is the result. Often, situations have multiple causes and multiple effects. You will understand the characters and events in a story better if you **identify cause-and-effect relationships** among them. For example, in this story, a child's disobedience results in a series of events that reveal a complicated family dynamic. As you read, use a chart like the one shown to record the reasons for characters' actions and their effects on others.

Vocabulary

You will encounter the words listed here in the text that follows. Copy the words into your notebook, sorting them into words you know and words you do not know.

latent   superficial

engrossed   perdition

jubilant

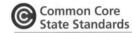

Common Core State Standards

Reading Literature

3. Analyze the impact of the author's choices regarding how to develop and relate elements of a story or drama (e.g., where a story is set).

5. Analyze how an author's choices concerning how to structure specific parts of a text contribute to its overall structure and meaning as well as its aesthetic impact.

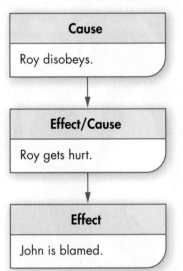

Cause
Roy disobeys.

Effect/Cause
Roy gets hurt.

Effect
John is blamed.

JAMES BALDWIN *(1924–1987)*

Author of **"The Rockpile"**

James Baldwin once told an interviewer that he "never had a childhood." Because his stepfather worked long hours as both a preacher and a factory hand, Baldwin was given much of the responsibility for raising his eight half brothers and half sisters. His main leisure activity was reading. He explained, "As [my half brothers and half sisters] were born, I took them over with one hand and held a book with the other . . . ; in this way, in fact, I read just about everything I could get my hands on." Baldwin's love for reading deepened his imagination, planting the seeds of inspiration for his later success as a writer.

A Harlem Childhood Baldwin was born in Harlem, the New York community that served as a cultural center for African Americans during the 1920s and 1930s. As a young boy, it was clear that he had a gift for words, but Baldwin's deeply religious parents disapproved of his interest in literature. At age fourteen, Baldwin followed their wishes and became a preacher. However, encouraged by poet Countee Cullen, who taught in Baldwin's junior high school, and inspired by author Richard Wright, Baldwin decided to devote his life to writing.

The Road to "Writer" For several years, Baldwin worked at odd jobs while writing in his spare time. When he was twenty-four, he won a fellowship that enabled him to live and write in Europe. For the next four years, he lived in Paris where he completed his first novel, *Go Tell It on the Mountain* (1953). The book marked the beginning of a distinguished career that included novels short stories, essays, and plays.

A Powerful Witness Baldwin once said, "One writes out of one thing only—one's own experience. Everything depends on how relentlessly one forces from this experience the last drop, sweet or bitter, it can possibly give." Baldwin's work bears powerful witness to his own experience as an African American. He expresses the need for social justice as well as the universal desire for love. Because his books dig deeply into contemporary life, they are sometimes painful to read, but the pain is always tempered by hope, and by Baldwin's magnificent language.

> *"It is certain, in any case, that ignorance, allied with power, is the most ferocious enemy justice can have."*

The Rockpile

James Baldwin

BACKGROUND Even though he spent most of his adult life in Europe, James Baldwin's impassioned voice is full of the rhythms and details of life in Harlem, the New York City neighborhood where he grew up. This story, about a struggling Harlem family, is a strong example of Baldwin's connection to the place that shaped him as both a writer and a person.

Across the street from their house, in an empty lot between two houses, stood the rockpile. It was a strange place to find a mass of natural rock jutting out of the ground; and someone, probably Aunt Florence, had once told them that the rock was there and could not be taken away because without it the subway cars underground would fly apart, killing all the people. This, touching on some natural mystery concerning the surface and the center of the earth, was far too intriguing an explanation to be challenged, and it invested the rockpile, moreover, with such mysterious importance that Roy felt it to be his right, not to say his duty, to play there.

Other boys were to be seen there each afternoon after school and all day Saturday and Sunday. They fought on the rockpile. Sure footed, dangerous, and reckless, they rushed each other and grappled on the heights, sometimes disappearing down the other side in a confusion of dust and screams and upended, flying feet. "It's a wonder they don't kill themselves," their mother said, watching sometimes from the fire escape. "You children stay away from there, you hear me?" Though she said "children" she was looking at Roy, where he sat beside John on the fire escape. "The good Lord knows," she continued, "I don't want you to come home bleeding like a hog every day the Lord sends." Roy shifted impatiently, and continued to stare at the street, as though in this gazing he might somehow acquire wings. John said nothing. He had not really been spoken to: he was afraid of the rockpile and of the boys who played there.

Each Saturday morning John and Roy sat on the fire escape and watched the forbidden street below. Sometimes their mother sat in the room behind them, sewing, or dressing their younger sister, or nursing the baby, Paul. The sun fell across them and across the fire escape with a high, benevolent indifference; below them, men and women, and boys and girls, sinners all, loitered; sometimes one of

Setting and Symbol
Which unique features of the rockpile are described in the opening paragraph?

Comprehension
Where is the rockpile located?

◄ **Critical Viewing** Which details shown in this painting connect to Baldwin's story?
CONNECT

The Rockpile **1083**

Vocabulary

latent (lāt´ əntd) *adj.*
present but invisible or
inactive

the church-members passed and saw them and waved. Then, for the moment that they waved decorously back, they were intimidated. They watched the saint, man or woman, until he or she had disappeared from sight. The passage of one of the redeemed made them consider, however vacantly, the wickedness of the street, their own latent wickedness in sitting where they sat; and made them think of their father, who came home early on Saturdays and who would soon be turning this corner and entering the dark hall below them.

But until he came to end their freedom, they sat, watching and longing above the street. At the end of the street nearest their house was the bridge which spanned the Harlem River[1] and led to a city called the Bronx; which was where Aunt Florence lived. Nevertheless, when they saw her coming, she did not come from the bridge, but from the opposite end of the street. This, weakly, to their minds, she explained by saying that she had taken the subway, not wishing to walk, and that, besides, she did not live in that section of the Bronx. Knowing that the Bronx was across the river, they did not believe this story ever, but, adopting toward her their father's attitude, assumed that she had just left some sinful place which she dared not name, as, for example, a movie palace.

Setting and Symbol

Can the tragedy of the boy's drowning in the river be seen as a symbol? If so, of what?

In the summertime boys swam in the river, diving off the wooden dock, or wading in from the garbage-heavy bank. Once a boy, whose name was Richard, drowned in the river. His mother had not known where he was; she had even come to their house, to ask if he was there. Then, in the evening, at six o'clock, they had heard from the street a woman screaming and wailing; and they ran to the windows and looked out. Down the street came the woman, Richard's mother, screaming, her face raised to the sky and tears running down her face. A woman walked beside her, trying to make her quiet and trying to hold her up. Behind them walked a man, Richard's father, with Richard's body in his arms. There were two white policemen walking in the gutter, who did not seem to know what should be done. Richard's father and Richard were wet, and Richard's body lay across his father's arms like a cotton baby. The woman's screaming filled all the street; cars slowed down and the people in the cars stared; people opened their windows and looked out and came rushing out of doors to stand in the gutter, watching. Then the small procession disappeared within the house which stood beside the rockpile. Then, *"Lord, Lord, Lord!"* cried Elizabeth, their mother, and slammed the window down.

One Saturday, an hour before his father would be coming home, Roy was wounded on the rockpile and brought screaming upstairs. He and John had been sitting on the fire escape and their mother had gone into the kitchen to sip tea with Sister McCandless. By and by Roy became bored and sat beside John in restless silence; and John began drawing into his schoolbook a newspaper advertisement

---

1. Harlem River river that separates Manhattan Island from the Bronx in New York City.

which featured a new electric locomotive. Some friends of Roy passed beneath the fire escape and called him. Roy began to fidget, yelling down to them through the bars. Then a silence fell. John looked up. Roy stood looking at him.

"I'm going downstairs," he said.

"You better stay where you is, boy. You know Mama don't want you going downstairs."

"I be right *back*. She won't even know I'm gone, less you run and tell her."

"I ain't *got* to tell her. What's going to stop her from coming in here and looking out the window?"

"She's talking," Roy said. He started into the house.

"But Daddy's going to be home soon!"

"I be back before *that*. What you all the time got to be so *scared* for?" He was already in the house and he now turned, leaning on the windowsill, to swear impatiently, "I be back in *five* minutes."

John watched him sourly as he carefully unlocked the door and disappeared. In a moment he saw him on the sidewalk with his friends. He did not dare to go and tell his mother that Roy had left the fire escape because he had practically promised not to.

He started to shout, *Remember, you said five minutes!* but one of Roy's friends was looking up at the fire escape. John looked down at his schoolbook: he became engrossed again in the problem of the locomotive.

When he looked up again he did not know how much time had passed, but now there was a gang fight on the rockpile. Dozens of boys fought each other in the harsh sun: clambering up the rocks and battling hand to hand, scuffed shoes sliding on the slippery rock; filling the bright air with curses and jubilant cries. They filled the air, too, with flying weapons: stones, sticks, tin cans, garbage, whatever could be picked up and thrown. John watched in a kind of absent amazement—until he remembered that Roy was still downstairs, and that he was one of the boys on the rockpile. Then he was afraid; he could not see his brother among the figures in the sun; and he stood up, leaning over the fire-escape railing. Then Roy appeared from the other side of the rocks; John saw that his shirt was torn; he was laughing. He moved until he stood at the very top of the rockpile. Then, something, an empty tin can, flew out of the air and hit him on the forehead, just above the eye. Immediately, one side of Roy's face ran with blood, he fell and rolled on his face down the rocks. Then for a moment there was no movement at all, no sound, the sun, arrested, lay on the street and the sidewalk and the arrested boys. Then someone screamed or shouted; boys began to run away, down the street, toward the bridge. The figure on the ground, having caught its breath and felt its own blood, began to shout. John cried, "Mama! Mama!" and ran inside.

"Don't fret, don't fret," panted Sister McCandless as they rushed down the dark, narrow, swaying stairs, "don't fret. Ain't a boy been

Identifying Cause and Effect
What causes Roy to go down to the street?

Vocabulary
engrossed (en grōst´) v. occupied wholly; absorbed
jubilant (jo͞o´ bə lənt) adj. joyful and triumphant

Comprehension
What happens to Roy on the rockpile?

> DOZENS OF BOYS FOUGHT EACH OTHER IN THE HARSH SUN: . . .

Setting

Which details of Roy's accident reflect the difficulties of life in this place?

Vocabulary

superficial (soō′ pər fish′ əl) *adj.* on the surface; shallow

Identifying Cause and Effect

What causes Elizabeth to look "with apprehension" toward the clock?

born don't get his knocks every now and again. *Lord!*" they hurried into the sun. A man had picked Roy up and now walked slowly toward them. One or two boys sat silent on their stoops; at either end of the street there was a group of boys watching. "He ain't hurt bad," the man said, "wouldn't be making this kind of noise if he was hurt real bad."

Elizabeth, trembling, reached out to take Roy, but Sister McCandless, bigger, calmer, took him from the man and threw him over her shoulder as she once might have handled a sack of cotton. "God bless you," she said to the man, "God bless you, son." Roy was still screaming. Elizabeth stood behind Sister McCandless to stare at his bloody face.

"It's just a flesh wound," the man kept saying, "just broke the skin, that's all." They were moving across the sidewalk, toward the house. John, not now afraid of the staring boys, looked toward the corner to see if his father was yet in sight.

Upstairs, they hushed Roy's crying. They bathed the blood away, to find, just above the left eyebrow, the jagged, superficial scar. "Lord, have mercy," murmured Elizabeth, "another inch and it would've been his eye." And she looked with apprehension toward the clock. "Ain't it the truth," said Sister McCandless, busy with bandages and iodine.

"When did he go downstairs?" his mother asked at last.

Sister McCandless now sat fanning herself in the easy chair, at the head of the sofa where Roy lay, bound and silent. She paused for a moment to look sharply at John. John stood near the window, holding the newspaper advertisement and the drawing he had done.

"We was sitting on the fire escape," he said. "Some boys he knew called him."

"When?"

"He said he'd be back in five minutes."

"Why didn't you tell me he was downstairs?"

He looked at his hands, clasping his notebook, and did not answer.

"Boy," said Sister McCandless, "you hear your mother a-talking to you?"

He looked at his mother. He repeated:

"He said he'd be back in five minutes."

"He said he'd be back in five minutes," said Sister McCandless with scorn, "don't look to me like that's no right answer. You's the man of the house, you supposed to look after your baby brothers and sisters—you ain't supposed to let them run off and get half-killed. But I expect," she added, rising from the chair, dropping the cardboard fan, "your Daddy'll make you tell the truth. Your Ma's way too soft with you."

He did not look at her, but at the fan where it lay in the dark red, depressed seat where she had been. The fan advertised a pomade[2] for the hair and showed a brown woman and her baby, both with glistening hair, smiling happily at each other.

---

2. **pomade** (päm ād′) *n.* perfumed ointment.

"Honey," said Sister McCandless, "I got to be moving along. Maybe I drop in later tonight. I don't reckon you going to be at Tarry Service tonight?"

Tarry Service was the prayer meeting held every Saturday night at church to strengthen believers and prepare the church for the coming of the Holy Ghost on Sunday.

"I don't reckon," said Elizabeth. She stood up; she and Sister McCandless kissed each other on the cheek. "But you be sure to remember me in your prayers."

"I surely will do that." She paused, with her hand on the door knob, and looked down at Roy and laughed. "Poor little man," she said, "reckon he'll be content to sit on the fire escape *now*."

Elizabeth laughed with her. "It sure ought to be a lesson to him. You don't reckon," she asked nervously, still smiling, "he going to keep that scar, do you?"

"Lord, no," said Sister McCandless, "ain't nothing but a scratch. I declare, Sister Grimes, you worse than a child. Another couple of weeks and you won't be able to *see* no scar. No, you go on about your housework, honey, and thank the Lord it weren't no worse." She opened the door; they heard the sound of feet on the stairs. "I expect that's the Reverend," said Sister McCandless, placidly, "I *bet* he going to raise cain."[3]

"Maybe it's Florence," Elizabeth said. "Sometimes she get here about this time." They stood in the doorway, staring, while the steps reached the landing below and began again climbing to their floor. "No," said Elizabeth then, "that ain't her walk. That's Gabriel."

"Well, I'll just go on," said Sister McCandless, "and kind of prepare his mind." She pressed Elizabeth's hand as she spoke and started

---

3. raise cain slang for "cause trouble."

▲ **Critical Viewing**

Which aspects of this painting are similar to the setting of this story? **ASSESS**

Comprehension

How does Sister McCandless criticize John?

Cultural Connection

James Baldwin and the Church

Baldwin's choice of words, and often the subject matter of his stories, was influenced by the evangelical church, of which his father was a minister. In this story, many details reflect this influence:

- references to "the good Lord" and "saints"
- reference to the father as "the Reverend"
- mention of prayer services
- the fact that the mother and her friend call each other "Sister"
- conflicts between the family's strict religious values and the temptations of the neighborhood

As a teenager, Baldwin earned renown for his gifts as a preacher. He brought those same gifts, including the use of impassioned, rhythmic language, to his writing, creating prose of great beauty and power.

Connect to the Literature

List two or three examples of Baldwin's rhythmic language in this story.

Identifying Cause and Effect

How does Gabriel react to Roy's tears?

into the hall, leaving the door behind her slightly ajar. Elizabeth turned slowly back into the room. Roy did not open his eyes, or move; but she knew that he was not sleeping; he wished to delay until the last possible moment any contact with his father. John put his newspaper and his notebook on the table and stood, leaning on the table, staring at her.

"It wasn't my fault," he said. "I couldn't stop him from going downstairs."

"No," she said, "you ain't got nothing to worry about. You just tell your Daddy the truth."

He looked directly at her, and she turned to the window, staring into the street. What was Sister McCandless saying? Then from her bedroom she heard Delilah's thin wail and she turned, frowning, looking toward the bedroom and toward the still open door. She knew that John was watching her. Delilah continued to wail, she thought, angrily, *Now that girl's getting too big for that,* but she feared that Delilah would awaken Paul and she hurried into the bedroom. She tried to soothe Delilah back to sleep. Then she heard the front door open and close—too loud, Delilah raised her voice, with an exasperated sigh Elizabeth picked the child up. Her child and Gabriel's, her children and Gabriel's: Roy, Delilah, Paul. Only John was nameless and a stranger, living, unalterable testimony to his mother's days in sin.

"What happened?" Gabriel demanded. He stood, enormous, in the center of the room, his black lunchbox dangling from his hand, staring at the sofa where Roy lay. John stood just before him, it seemed to her astonished vision just below him, beneath his fist, his heavy shoe.

The child stared at the man in fascination and terror—when a girl down home she had seen rabbits stand so paralyzed before the barking dog. She hurried past Gabriel to the sofa, feeling the weight of Delilah in her arms like the weight of a shield, and stood over Roy, saying:

"Now, ain't a thing to get upset about, Gabriel. This boy sneaked downstairs while I had my back turned and got hisself hurt a little. He's alright now."

Roy, as though in confirmation, now opened his eyes and looked gravely at his father. Gabriel dropped his lunchbox with a clatter and knelt by the sofa.

"How you feel, son? Tell your Daddy what happened?"

Roy opened his mouth to speak and then, relapsing into panic, began to cry. His father held him by the shoulder.

"You don't want to cry. You's Daddy's little man. Tell your Daddy what happened."

"He went downstairs," said Elizabeth, "where he didn't have no business to be, and got to fighting with them bad boys playing on the rockpile. That's what happened and it's a mercy it weren't nothing worse."

He looked up at her. "Can't you let this boy answer me for hisself?"

Ignoring this, she went on, more gently: "He got cut on the forehead, but it ain't nothing to worry about."

"You call a doctor? How you know it ain't nothing to worry about?"

"Is you got money to be throwing away on doctors? No, I ain't called no doctor. Ain't nothing wrong with my eyes that I can't tell whether he's hurt bad or not. He got a fright more'n anything else, and you ought to pray God it teaches him a lesson."

"You got a lot to say now," he said, "but I'll have *me* something to say in a minute. I'll be wanting to know when all this happened, what you was doing with your eyes *then*." He turned back to Roy, who had lain quietly sobbing eyes wide open and body held rigid: and who now, at his father's touch, remembered the height, the sharp, sliding rock beneath his feet, the sun, the explosion of the sun, his plunge into darkness and his salty blood; and recoiled, beginning to scream, as his father touched his forehead. "Hold still, hold still," crooned his father, shaking, "hold still. Don't cry. Daddy ain't going to hurt you, he just wants to see this bandage, see what they've done to his little man." But Roy continued to scream and would not be still and Gabriel dared not lift the bandage for fear of hurting him more. And he looked at Elizabeth in fury: "Can't you put that child down and help me with this boy? John, take your baby sister from your mother—don't look like neither of you got good sense."

John took Delilah and sat down with her in the easy chair. His mother bent over Roy, and held him still, while his father, carefully—but still Roy screamed—lifted the bandage and stared at the wound. Roy's sobs began to lessen. Gabriel readjusted the bandage. "You see," said Elizabeth, finally, "he ain't nowhere near dead."

"It sure ain't your fault that he ain't dead." He and Elizabeth considered each other for a moment in silence. "He came mightly close to losing an eye. Course, his eyes ain't as big as your'n, so I reckon you don't think it matters so much." At this her face hardened; he smiled. "Lord, have mercy," he said, "you think you ever going to learn to do right? Where was you when all this happened? Who let him go downstairs?"

"Ain't nobody let him go downstairs, he just went. He got a head just like his father, it got to be broken before it'll bow. I was in the kitchen."

"Where was Johnnie?"

"He was in here."

"Where?"

"He was on the fire escape."

"Didn't he know Roy was downstairs?"

"I reckon."

"What you mean, you reckon? He ain't got your big eyes for nothing, does he?" He looked over at John. "Boy, you see your brother go downstairs?"

> ROY OPENED HIS MOUTH TO SPEAK AND THEN, RELAPSING INTO PANIC, BEGAN TO CRY.

Comprehension
As John faces Gabriel, what sight does Elizabeth remember from her childhood?

"Gabriel, ain't no sense in trying to blame Johnnie. You know right well if you have trouble making Roy behave, he ain't going to listen to his brother. He don't hardly listen to me."

"How come you didn't tell your mother Roy was downstairs?"

John said nothing, staring at the blanket which covered Delilah.

"Boy, you hear me? You want me to take a strap to you?"

"No, you ain't," she said. "You ain't going to taken no strap to this boy, not today you ain't. Ain't a soul to blame for Roy's lying up there now but you—you because you done spoiled him so that he thinks he can do just anything and get away with it. I'm here to tell you that ain't no way to raise no child. You don't pray to the Lord to help you do better than you been doing, you going to live to shed bitter tears that the Lord didn't take his soul today." And she was trembling. She moved, unseeing, toward John and took Delilah from his arms. She looked back at Gabriel, who had risen, who stood near the sofa, staring at her. And she found in his face not fury alone, which would not have surprised her; but hatred so deep as to become insupportable in its lack of personality. His eyes were struck alive, unmoving, blind with malevolence—she felt, like the pull of the earth at her feet, his longing to witness her perdition. Again, as though it might be propitiation, she moved the child in her arms. And at this his eyes changed, he looked at Elizabeth, the mother of his children, the help-meet given by the Lord. Then her eyes clouded; she moved to leave the room; her foot struck the lunchbox lying on the floor.

"John," she said, "pick up your father's lunchbox like a good boy."

She heard, behind her, his scrambling movement as he left the easy chair, the scrape and jangle of the lunchbox as he picked it up, bending his dark head near the toe of his father's heavy shoe.

Vocabulary

perdition (pər dish′ ən) *n.* complete and irreparable loss; ruin

Critical Reading

Cite textual evidence to support your responses.

1. **Key Ideas and Details (a)** What do John and Roy do each Saturday morning? **(b) Deduce:** Why is the street "forbidden"?

2. **Key Ideas and Details (a)** How is John related to Gabriel? **(b) Support:** What evidence is there that Gabriel's relationship with John is different from his relationship with the other children?

3. **Integration of Knowledge and Ideas** In which aspects of their lives are the characters in this story insiders or outsiders? Explain. In your response, use at least two of these Essential Question words: *mainstream, identity, community, alienation, prejudice.* *[Connecting to the Essential Question: How does literature shape or reflect society?]*

Literary Analysis

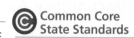 **Common Core State Standards**

Writing

3. Write narratives to develop real or imagined experiences or events using effective technique, well-chosen details, and well-structured event sequences. *(p. 1092)*

3.b. Use narrative techniques, such as dialogue, to develop experiences, events, and/or characters. *(p. 1092)*

3.d. Use precise words and phrases, telling details, and sensory language to convey a vivid picture of the experiences, events, setting, and/or characters. *(p. 1092)*

Language

1. Demonstrate command of the conventions of standard English grammar and usage when writing or speaking. *(p. 1093)*

4.b. Identify and correctly use patterns of word changes that indicate different meanings or parts of speech. *(p. 1092)*

4.d. Verify the preliminary determination of the meaning of a word or phrase. *(p. 1092)*

5. Demonstrate understanding of word relationships. *(p. 1092)*

1. **Key Ideas and Details** Find three details that describe physical aspects of the story's **setting**—the landmarks of the neighborhood.

2. **Key Ideas and Details** Find three details that describe the psychological aspects of the setting—the mood and atmosphere of the neighborhood.

3. **Key Ideas and Details (a)** What are some of the potential dangers the setting presents? **(b)** In what ways do you think this setting has influenced Gabriel and Elizabeth's decisions about how to raise their children?

4. **Key Ideas and Details (a) Identify cause and effect** in the events leading to Roy's injury. **(b)** What does Elizabeth say is the real cause of Roy's injury? **(c)** Do you agree with Elizabeth? Why or why not?

5. **Key Ideas and Details (a)** What are the causes of Elizabeth's protectiveness toward John? **(b)** What effect does Elizabeth's protectiveness toward John have on Gabriel?

6. **Key Ideas and Details (a)** How would you characterize Gabriel? **(b)** What are the similarities and differences between the effects of his presence on Roy, John, and Elizabeth?

7. **Key Ideas and Details (a)** How does Gabriel react to Roy's tears? **(b)** What does the effect of Roy's tears on Gabriel suggest about the family dynamic?

8. **Craft and Structure (a)** Use a chart like the one shown to analyze the rockpile as the main **symbol** in this story. **(b)** What does the rockpile represent?

The Rockpile			What It Represents
What People Say About It	Events Linked With It	Details Used To Describe It	

9. **Integration of Knowledge and Ideas (a)** How do the neighborhood children behave when playing on the rockpile? **(b)** How does this affect your understanding of the rockpile as both a setting and a symbol of problems within the community?

10. **Integration of Knowledge and Ideas (a)** What does "the toe of his father's heavy shoe," mentioned in the last line of the story, symbolize? **(b)** In what way does this symbol capture John's relationship to Gabriel? **(c)** How would you define their relationship at the end of the story?

Vocabulary Acquisition and Use

Word Analysis: Latin Prefix *super-*

The Latin prefix *super-* means "over," "above," or "beyond." English words with this prefix relate to the idea of surface, as in *superficial*, or the idea of extremity, as in *superhero*. Define each underlined word and explain if the prefix relates to surface or extremity. Use a dictionary to check your answers.

1. While <u>supersonic</u> travel is possible, it is not currently a commercial option.
2. The artist frequently <u>superimposes</u> an unusual image over a familiar one.
3. She is gifted with <u>superlative</u> athletic ability.
4. The global summit included leaders from five <u>superpowers</u>.

Vocabulary: Categorizing Vocabulary

For each numbered word, categorize the groups of words that follow as *synonyms, antonyms*, or a combination of both. Explain your choices.

1. **latent**   obvious; concealed; dormant
2. **engrossed**   distracted; captivated; detached
3. **jubilant**   exultant; elated; blissful
4. **perdition**   salvation; deliverance; reprieve
5. **superficial** external; profound; peripheral

Writing to Sources

Narrative Text A radio drama can capture the flow and feeling of a story while leaving listeners imaginative space in which to visualize the characters and settings. Adapt "The Rockpile" as a **radio play.** With a group, divide the story into scenes. Individually, choose a scene to develop into a script.

Prewriting Identify the characters from the story that will appear in your scene, and add a narrator to provide background information. Make an outline to list key events that occur in the scene.

Drafting Include stage directions to help actors reflect characters' emotions and to indicate sound effects. Pull dialogue directly from the story, and add description and other dialogue to smooth transitions.

Model: Using Stage Directions

[*From a distance, we hear the jubilant cries of kids playing.*]

JOHN: [*shouting out the window*] Roy, you said five minutes!

[*to himself*] I had enough. [*He slams the window. The sounds are muffled.*]

NARRATOR: John cannot see his brother among the figures in the sun. Then he appears on the other side of the rocks. His shirt is torn and he is laughing.

JOHN: [*opening the window*] Five minutes is up, Roy!

> Stage directions add detail to a scene.

Revising Read your draft aloud, listening for a smooth flow of events and clear presentation of characters. Rehearse the finished script with your group and perform it for the class. If possible, record the play, with sound effects, and arrange for it to air on your school or local public radio station.

Conventions and Style: Avoiding Shifts in Verb Tense

Verbs have different forms, called **tenses,** which indicate the time in which an action occurs. If you let verbs shift unnecessarily from one tense to another in your writing, readers will find it difficult to follow your meaning. Generally, use the same tense throughout a piece of writing.

Consistent Tense (past): James Baldwin *lived* in Europe, but he *wrote* about Harlem.

Consistent Tense (present): On Saturday mornings, Roy and John *sit* at the top of the fire escape and *watch* the people below.

Incorrect Verb Shift: On Saturday mornings, Roy and John *sat* at the top of the fire escape and *watch* the people below. (The action takes place at the same time but *sat* is in the past tense and *watch* is in the present.)

If you want to show a change in time, it is appropriate to shift tenses:

Appropriate Tense Shift: "The Rockpile" *is* an example of how Baldwin *used* his life experiences *to write* a story.

Practice In items 1–5, choose the verb that correctly completes each sentence. In items 6–10, correct unnecessary shifts in verb tense.

1. Roy's friends called to him, but John (warns, warned) him not to go.
2. Roy looks at his mother but (says, said) nothing.
3. Elizabeth hopes John (had not had, will not have) a scar.
4. Gabriel's expression (will change, changed) when he saw Delilah.
5. Elizabeth has been protecting John because she (is fearing, fears) Gabriel's anger.
6. Sister McCandless says the scar is gone in a few weeks' time.
7. Although the boys had been fighting a minute before, they disappear when Roy was hurt.
8. Before she left, Sister McCandless is stopping to talk to Gabriel.
9. John had not told his mother Roy is going to play in the street, and he felt guilty.
10. As John picked up the lunchbox, his head nearly touches his father's shoe.

Writing and Speaking Conventions

A. **Writing** Complete each sentence starter. Use a form of the verb in parentheses and appropriate verb tenses.

   Example: The boys played, _____. (fight)
   Sentence: The boys played, but then they fought.

   1. Roy watched the children play, _____. (join)
   2. The boys have been swimming, but _____. (dive)
   3. I will unlock _____. (call)
   4. Gabriel dropped _____. (kneel)
   5. Please turn _____. (look)

B. **Speaking** Write a brief account from Elizabeth's point of view, explaining what happened after Roy was hurt. Include at least one shift in verb tense to show a change in the time of the action.

Connecting to the Essential Question In this eulogy, one great writer describes her gratitude to another. As you read, decide whether Morrison speaks as a private individual, as the voice of a community, or both. Doing so will help you reflect on the Essential Question: **How does literature shape or reflect society?**

Close Reading Focus

Eulogy; Mood

A **eulogy** is a literary work written to pay tribute to someone who has died. Eulogies are defined less by their form, which may be a speech, essay, or poem, and more by the subject and occasion of the writing. Usually written shortly after the subject's death, they celebrate the person's strengths, virtues, and accomplishments:

> That is the astonishing gift of your art and your friendship. You gave us ourselves to think about, to cherish.

A eulogist creates a **mood,** or emotional quality, that expresses his or her feelings and captures qualities in the person being honored. Mood is evoked through *word choice, rhythms,* and *syntax,* or sentence structure. As you read, note the aspects of James Baldwin's life that Toni Morrison celebrates. Notice, too, the emotions she evokes and the literary devices that add to the feelings.

Preparing to Read Complex Texts One way to understand an essay or a eulogy is to **analyze patterns of organization,** the order and structure of ideas. In this eulogy, Toni Morrison follows a clear pattern when she discusses the "three gifts" that Baldwin gave to the world. The *pattern of threes* is an ancient narrative structure. Fairy tales, folk tales, and myths often tell of three siblings, three tests, and so on. The idea of the three gifts is a part of the Christmas story, to which Morrison alludes. In using this ancient, *archetypal structure,* Morrison both organizes her ideas and communicates a sense of Baldwin's depth as a literary artist. Use a chart like the one shown to analyze the effect of this organizational pattern on Morrison's message.

Vocabulary

The words below are important to understanding the text that follows. Copy the words into your notebook. Which word is very similar to the word *scene*?

summation   **platitudes**

scenario   **appropriate**

Common Core State Standards

Reading Informational Text
3. Analyze a complex set of ideas or sequence of events and explain how specific individuals, ideas, or events interact and develop over the course of the text.
5. Analyze and evaluate the effectiveness of the structure an author uses in his or her exposition or argument, including whether the structure makes points clear, convincing, and engaging.

Language
3.a. Apply an understanding of syntax to the study of complex texts when reading.

Gift
1
2
3

Morrison's Explanation
1
2
3

TONI MORRISON *(b. 1931)*

Author of "Life In His Language"

The first African-American woman to win the Nobel Prize in Literature, Toni Morrison is renowned for works that explore the experiences of black women and men, as well as the harsh realities of racism and sexism. She grew up in Lorain, Ohio, nurtured by her family's love of stories, songs, and folktales. These early experiences inspired her to study literature in college and become a professor herself. Later, she worked as an editor, preparing books by such well-known figures as the boxer Muhammad Ali, the writer Toni Cade Bambara, and the activist Angela Davis.

A Novelist's Eye Morrison's career as a writer was launched with the publication of her first novel, *The Bluest Eye* (1970), which depicts the struggle of a black girl who sees beauty as a trait held only by white people. She longs to have the blue eyes of her movie star idol, Shirley Temple. *Sula* (1973) focuses on a friendship that challenges the prejudices of a small community. *The Song of Solomon* (1977) presents a narrator's search for his own identity. *Beloved* (1987), a novel inspired by the true story of Margaret Garner, tells the tale of an escaped slave who was recaptured by her master. *Jazz* (1992) tells a sweeping tale of passion set against the backdrop of Harlem in the 1920s.

Honoring Legacies In addition to novels, Morrison has written literary criticism and children's books. Her writing reflects her deep respect for the wisdom of others, especially generations who have gone before her. She points out that "there is always an elder" in her writing. "These ancestors are not just parents, they are sort of timeless people whose relationships to the characters are benevolent, instructive, and protective, and they provide a certain kind of wisdom." In her essays and interviews, she often pays tributes to writers, like James Baldwin, who have inspired her.

> *"If there's a book you really want to read but it hasn't been written yet, then you must write it."*

LIFE IN HIS LANGUAGE

TONI MORRISON

BACKGROUND One of the great writers of the twentieth century, James Baldwin was an inspiration to many readers and writers. Toni Morrison wrote this essay to pay tribute to his influence on her and the entire literary community.

JIMMY.

There is too much to think about you, and too much to feel. The difficulty is your life refuses summation—it always did—and invites contemplation instead. Like many of us left here I thought I knew you. Now I discover that in your company it is myself I know. That is the astonishing gift of your art and your friendship. You gave us ourselves to think about, to cherish. We are like Hall Montana[1] watching "with new wonder" his brother saints, knowing the song he sang is us. "He is us."

I never heard a single command from you, yet the demands you made on me, the challenges you issued to me, were nevertheless unmistakable, even if unenforced: that I work and think at the top of my form, that I stand on moral ground but know that ground must be shored up by mercy, that "the world is before [me] and [I] need not take it or leave it as it was when [I] came in."

Well, the season was always Christmas with you there and, like one aspect of that scenario, you did not neglect to bring at least three gifts. You gave me a language to dwell in, a gift so perfect it seems my own invention. I have been thinking your spoken and written thoughts for so long I believed they were mine. I have been seeing the world through your eyes for so long, I believed that clear, clear view was my own. Even now, even here, I need you to tell me what I am feeling and how to articulate it. So I have pored again through the 6,895 pages of your published work to acknowledge the debt and thank you for the credit. No one possessed or inhabited language for me the way you did. You made American English honest—genuinely international. You exposed its secrets and reshaped it until it was truly modern, dialogic,[2] representative, humane. You stripped it of ease and false comfort and fake innocence and evasion and hypocrisy. And in place of deviousness was clarity. In place of soft, plump lies was lean, targeted power. In place of intellectual disingenuousness and what you called "exasperating egocentricity," you gave us undecorated truth.

---

1. **Hall Montana** The narrator of Baldwin's novel *Just Above My Head*, who describes the troubled life and death of his brother Arthur, a gospel singer.
2. **dialogic** (dī ə lä´ j ik) conversational.

Vocabulary

summation (sə mā´ shən)
n. details stated briefly

scenario (sə nar´ ē ō)
n. situation

Eulogy

Why do you think the gift of Baldwin's language is particularly important to Morrison?

Comprehension

According to Morrison, what was the first gift Baldwin gave her?

Vocabulary

platitudes (plaˊ tə tüdz)
n. tired expressions

appropriate (ə prōˊ prē āt)
v. to take or use without
permission

You replaced lumbering platitudes with an upright elegance. You went into that forbidden territory and decolonized it, "robbed it of the jewel of its naïveté," and un-gated it for black people so that in your wake we could enter it, occupy it, restructure it in order to accommodate our complicated passion—not our vanities but our intricate, difficult, demanding beauty, our tragic, insistent knowledge, our lived reality, our sleek classical imagination—all the while refusing "to be defined by a language that has never been able to recognize [us]." In your hands language was handsome again. In your hands we saw how it was meant to be: neither bloodless nor bloody, and yet alive.

It infuriated some people. Those who saw the paucity of their own imagination in the two-way mirror you held up to them attacked the mirror, tried to reduce it to fragments which they could then rank and grade, tried to dismiss the shards where your image and theirs remained—locked but ready to soar. You are an artist after all and an artist is forbidden a career in this place; an artist is permitted only a commercial hit. But for thousands and thousands of those who embraced your text and who gave themselves permission to hear your language, by that very gesture they ennobled themselves, became unshrouded, civilized.

The second gift was your courage, which you let us share: the courage of one who could go as a stranger in the village and transform the distances between people into intimacy with the whole world; courage to understand that experience in ways that made it a personal revelation for each of us. It was you who gave us the courage to appropriate an alien, hostile, all-white geography because you had discovered that "this world (meaning history) is white no longer and it will never be white again." Yours was the courage to live life in and from its belly as well as beyond its edges, to see and say what it was, to recognize and identify evil but never tear or stand in awe of it. It is a courage that came from a ruthless intelligence married to a pity so profound it could convince anyone who cared to know that those who despised us "need the moral authority of their former slaves, who are the only people in the world who know anything about them and who may be, indeed, the only people in the world who really care anything about them." When that unassailable combination of mind and heart, of intellect and passion was on display it guided us through treacherous landscape as it did when you wrote these words every rebel, every dissident, revolutionary, every practicing artist from Capetown to Poland from Waycross to Dublin memorized: "A person does not lightly elect to oppose his society. One would much rather be at home among one's compatriots than be mocked and detested by them. And there is a level on which the mockery of the people, even their hatred, is moving, because it is so blind: it is terrible to watch people cling to their captivity and insist on their own destruction."

Analyze Patterns of Organization

Is the second gift in any way related to the first? Explain.

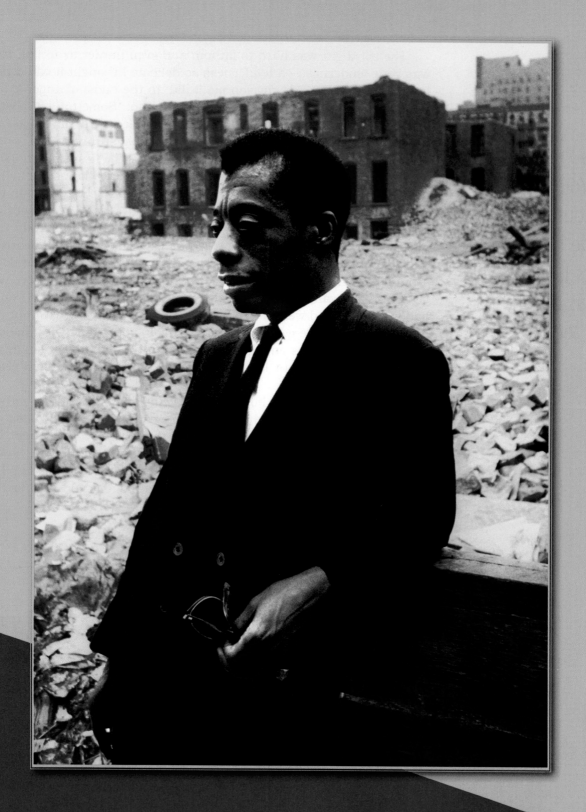

You gave me a language to dwell in, a gift
so perfect it seems my own invention.

> Yours was the courage to live life in and from its belly as well as beyond its edges . . .

The third gift was hard to fathom and even harder to accept. It was your tenderness—a tenderness so delicate I thought it could not last, but last it did and envelop me it did. In the midst of anger it tapped me lightly like the child in Tish's womb: "Something almost as hard to catch as a whisper in a crowded place, as light and as definite as a spider's web, strikes below my ribs, stunning and astonishing my heart . . . the baby, turning for the first time in its incredible veil of water, announces its presence and claims me; tells me, in that instant, that what can get worse can get better . . . in the meantime—forever—it is entirely up to me. Yours was a tenderness, a vulnerability, that asked everything, expected everything and, like the world's own Merlin,[3] provided us with the ways and means to deliver. I suppose that is why I was always a bit better behaved around you, smarter, more capable, wanting to be worth the love you lavished, and wanting to be steady enough to witness the pain you had witnessed and were tough enough to bear while it broke your heart, wanting to be generous enough to join your smile with one of my own, and reckless enough to jump on in that laugh you laughed. Because our joy and our laughter were not only all right, they were necessary.

You knew, didn't you, how I needed your language and the mind that formed it? How I relied on your fierce courage to tame wilderness for me? How strengthened I was by the certainty that came from knowing you would never hurt me? You knew, didn't you, how I loved your love? You knew. This then is no calamity. No. This is jubilee. "Our crown," you said, "has already been bought and paid for. All we have to do," you said, "is wear it."

And we do, Jimmy. You crowned us.

---

3. **Merlin** magician and wise counselor in the legends of King Arthur.

Critical Reading

Cite textual evidence to support your responses.

1. **Integration of Knowledge and Ideas Analyze:** Why do you think Morrison addresses her eulogy to Baldwin, rather than to an anonymous listener, or a third party?

2. **Integration of Knowledge and Ideas** American culture places a premium on newness. What does this essay suggest about the importance of past achievements to both individuals and society as a whole? In your response, use at least two of these Essential Question words: *innovation, contribute, legacy, generation.*
[*Connecting to the Essential Question: How does literature shape or reflect society?*]

Literary Analysis

Common Core State Standards

Writing
2. Write informative texts to examine and convey complex ideas, concepts, and information clearly and accurately through the effective selection, organization, and analysis of content.

2.a. Introduce a topic; organize complex ideas, concepts, and information so that each new element builds on that which precedes it to create a unified whole.

2.f. Provide a concluding statement or section that follows from and supports the information or explanation presented.

Language
4.a. Use context as a clue to the meaning of a word or phrase.

1. **Key Ideas and Details (a)** What do you learn about James Baldwin from Morrison's **eulogy**? **(b)** What personal qualities and values does Morrison see in Baldwin that she thinks are especially unique and valuable?

2. **Key Ideas and Details (a)** Use a chart like the one shown to analyze the **mood** Morrison creates in this eulogy. Identify four details that add to a particular feeling in the writing. **(b)** Then, list two or three adjectives you feel describe this mood.

3. **Craft and Structure (a)** Identify two examples of unusual *syntax*, or word order. **(b)** Rewrite each example in more common syntax. **(c)** Explain how Morrison's choice of syntax affects the meaning and mood of the writing.

4. **Integration of Knowledge and Ideas (a)** Analyze Morrison's **pattern of organization** by defining each of Baldwin's "three gifts." **(b)** Is one of these gifts more or less significant than the others? Explain.

Vocabulary Acquisition and Use

Sentence Completions Use a word from the vocabulary list to complete each sentence logically. Explain your choices.

1. An interesting <u>scenario</u> for a television series would be _____.

2. The <u>summation</u> of a book would include _____.

3. One example of a <u>platitude</u> is _____.

4. A poet might decide to <u>appropriate</u> _____.

Writing to Sources

Informative Text Write an **essay of tribute** to honor a person who has influenced you: someone you know or someone whose art has inspired you. *Organize your essay using a clear pattern of three.* Use Morrison's description of Baldwin's "three gifts" as your model. Include these elements:

- An introduction that identifies your subject and focus

- One paragraph for each of the three elements you will discuss

- A conclusion that summarizes and extends your view of this person

Connecting to the Essential Question Both President Kennedy and Dr. King refer to the protection of human rights as one of America's essential duties. As you read, notice specific actions the authors believe will protect or advance human rights. Doing so will enrich your consideration of the Essential Question: **What makes American literature American?**

Close Reading Focus

Rhetorical Devices; Argument/Support Structure

Persuasive writers, such as President Kennedy and Dr. King, use a variety of **rhetorical devices** to clarify and balance ideas and evoke emotions:

- **Parallelism** is the repetition of words, phrases, clauses, or sentences that have the same grammatical structure or the same meaning: "the torch has been passed to a new generation of Americans—<u>born</u> in this century, <u>tempered</u> by war, <u>disciplined</u> by a hard and bitter peace."

- **Antithesis** is a form of parallelism that emphasizes strong contrasts: "Now the trumpet summons us again—not as a <u>call to bear arms</u>, . . . not as a <u>call to battle</u> . . . but [as] a <u>call to bear the burden</u>."

The **organizational structure** of a text adds to its persuasive appeal. King uses an **argument/support** structure, which consists of a series of arguments supported with evidence. By contrast, Kennedy organizes his speech around two **lists**—one a series of pledges, and the other a series of directives, or requests.

Comparing Literary Works As you read, compare each writer's use of rhetorical devices and notice how the different organizational structures add to the power of both texts.

Preparing to Read Complex Texts The main, or central, ideas in a selection are the key points that the writer wants to express. The supporting details are the facts, examples, or reasons that explain or justify these ideas. Use a chart like the one shown to **identify two or more main ideas and supporting details** as you read these selections.

Vocabulary

The words below are important to understanding the texts that follow. Copy the words into your notebook. Which word is a synonym for *destroy*?

alliance	eradicate
invective	flagrant
adversary	profundity

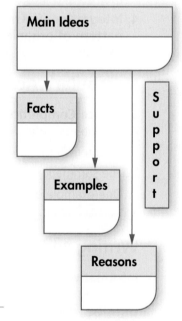

Common Core State Standards

Reading Informational Text

2. Determine two or more central ideas of a text and analyze their development over the course of the text, including how they interact and build on one another to provide a complex analysis.

5. Analyze and evaluate the effectiveness of the structure an author uses in his or her exposition or argument, including whether the structure makes points clear, convincing, and engaging.

Main Ideas

Facts

Examples

Support

Reasons

John Fitzgerald Kennedy *(1917–1963)*

Author of **Inaugural Address**

A Tradition of Service John Fitzgerald Kennedy was born into a family with a tradition of public service. His father Joseph served as U.S. Ambassador to Great Britain, and his maternal grandfather was elected mayor of Boston. After graduation from Harvard University, Kennedy served with distinction in the U.S. Navy during World War II. Having barely escaped death in battle, Kennedy returned home as a war hero, and in 1946 he easily won election to the House of Representatives. Kennedy served three terms in the House before he was elected senator from Massachusetts in 1952.

Thirty-Fifth President Eight years later, in 1960, Kennedy won a hard-fought contest for the presidency. At the age of forty-three, he became the youngest person ever to be elected to that office. While he was president, he witnessed events as diverse as the launch of the first communications satellite, *Telstar,* and the signing of the first nuclear nonproliferation treaty with the Soviet Union. The United States teetered on the brink of nuclear war during the Cuban missile crisis and put its first astronaut into orbit around the Earth.

Fallen Leader Tragically, Kennedy was assassinated on November 22, 1963, in Dallas, Texas. Two days after the president's murder, Lee Harvey Oswald, who had been arrested for the crime, was himself assassinated. In 1964, the Warren Commission, charged with investigating the circumstances of Kennedy's murder, ruled that Oswald had acted alone. Nevertheless, conspiracy theories have continued to swirl about the assassination.

"A man may die, nations may rise and fall, but an idea lives on."

INAUGURAL ADDRESS

JOHN F. KENNEDY

BACKGROUND When John F. Kennedy took office in 1961, the United States was locked in a potentially explosive stalemate with the then Soviet Union and its allies. Fierce adversaries in the Cold War, the United States and the Soviet Union were stockpiling nuclear weapons, creating the possibility of a disastrous war that could destroy the earth. In his now-famous inaugural address, Kennedy addressed our nation's fears and reached out to our adversaries, even as he reaffirmed our nation's strength and the ideals of freedom.

V*ice President Johnson, Mr. Speaker, Mr. Chief Justice, President Eisenhower, Vice President Nixon, President Truman,*[1] *reverend clergy, fellow citizens*, we observe today not a victory of party, but a celebration of freedom—symbolizing an end, as well as a beginning—signifying renewal, as well as change. For I have sworn before you and Almighty God the same solemn oath our forebears prescribed nearly a century and three quarters ago.

1. **Vice President . . . Truman** Present at Kennedy's inauguration were Lyndon B. Johnson, Kennedy's vice president; 34th president Dwight D. Eisenhower and his vice president, Richard M. Nixon; and 33rd president Harry S Truman.

Retroactive I, Robert Rauschenberg, 1964, Wadsworth Atheneum, Hartford, CT, ©Robert Rauschenberg/Licensed by VAGA, New York, NY

▲ **Critical Viewing** What do the images in this montage— and the unfinished quality of the upper right corner—suggest about Kennedy? **[Infer]**

The world is very different now. For man holds in his mortal hands the power to abolish all forms of human poverty and all forms of human life. And yet the same revolutionary beliefs for which our forebears fought are still at issue around the globe—the belief that the rights of man come not from the generosity of the state, but from the hand of God.

We dare not forget today that we are the heirs of that first revolution. Let the word go forth from this time and place, to friend and foe alike, that the torch has been passed to a new generation of Americans—born in this century, tempered by war, disciplined by a hard and bitter peace, proud of our ancient heritage—and unwilling to witness or permit the slow undoing of those human rights to which this Nation has always been committed, and to which we are committed today at home and around the world.

Let every nation know, whether it wishes us well or ill, that we shall pay any price, bear any burden, meet any hardship, support any friend, oppose any foe, to assure the survival and the success of liberty.

This much we pledge—and more.

To those old allies whose cultural and spiritual origins we share, we pledge the loyalty of faithful friends. United, there is little we cannot do in a host of cooperative ventures. Divided, there is little we can do—for we dare not meet a powerful challenge at odds and split asunder.[2]

Antithesis
What contrasting words and phrases does Kennedy use in this paragraph?

To those new States whom we welcome to the ranks of the free, we pledge our word that one form of colonial control shall not have passed away merely to be replaced by a far more iron tyranny. We shall not always expect to find them supporting our view. But we shall always hope to find them strongly supporting their own freedom—and to remember that, in the past, those who foolishly sought power by riding the back of the tiger ended up inside.

To those people in the huts and villages of half the globe struggling to break the bonds of mass misery, we pledge our best efforts to help them help themselves, for whatever period is required—not because the Communists may be doing it, not because we seek their votes, but because it is right. If a free society cannot help the many who are poor, it cannot save the few who are rich.

Vocabulary
alliance (ə li′ əns) n. union of nations for a specific purpose

To our sister republics south of our border, we offer a special pledge—to convert our good words into good deeds—in a new alliance for progress—to assist free men and free governments in casting off the chains of poverty. But this peaceful revolution of hope cannot become the prey of hostile powers. Let all our neighbors know that we shall join with them to oppose aggression or subversion anywhere in the Americas. And let every other power know that this Hemisphere intends to remain the master of its own house.

Comprehension
What does Kennedy say that Americans dare not forget?

---

2. United . . . Divided . . . split asunder Kennedy echoes the famous lines from Abraham Lincoln's second inaugural address: "United we stand . . . divided we fall."

Vocabulary

invective (in vek´ tiv) *n.*
verbal attack; strong
criticism

adversary (ad´ vər ser´ ē)
n. opponent; enemy

To that world assembly of sovereign states, the United Nations, our last best hope in an age where the instruments of war have far outpaced the instruments of peace, we renew our pledge of support—to prevent it from becoming merely a forum for invective—to strengthen its shield of the new and the weak—and to enlarge the area in which its writ may run.

Finally, to those nations who would make themselves our adversary, we offer not a pledge but a request: that both sides begin anew the quest for peace, before the dark powers of destruction[3] unleashed by science engulf all humanity in planned or accidental self-destruction.

We dare not tempt them with weakness. For only when our arms are sufficient beyond doubt can we be certain beyond doubt that they will never be employed.

But neither can two great and powerful groups of nations take comfort from our present course—both sides overburdened by the cost of modern weapons, both rightly alarmed by the steady spread of the deadly atom, yet both racing to alter that uncertain balance of terror that stays the hand of mankind's final war.

So let us begin anew—remembering on both sides that civility is not a sign of weakness, and sincerity is always subject to proof. Let us never negotiate out of fear. But let us never fear to negotiate.

Let both sides explore what problems unite us instead of belaboring those problems which divide us.

Let both sides, for the first time, formulate serious and precise proposals for the inspection and control of arms—and bring the absolute power to destroy other nations under the absolute control of all nations.

Rhetorical Devices

How does the list of directives in these four paragraphs add to the persuasive power of the speech?

Let both sides seek to invoke the wonders of science instead of its terrors. Together let us explore the stars, conquer the deserts, eradicate disease, tap the ocean depths, and encourage the arts and commerce.

Let both sides unite to heed in all corners of the earth the command of Isaiah—to "undo the heavy burdens . . . and let the oppressed go free."[4]

And if a beachhead of cooperation may push back the jungle of suspicion, let both sides join in creating a new endeavor, not a new balance of power, but a new world of law, where the strong are just and the weak secure and the peace preserved.

All this will not be finished in the first 100 days. Nor will it be finished in the first 1,000 days, nor in the life of this Administration, nor even perhaps in our lifetime on this planet. But let us begin.

In your hands, my fellow citizens, more than in mine, will rest the final success or failure of our course. Since this country was founded, each generation of Americans has been summoned to give testimony to

---

3. **dark powers of destruction** nuclear war.
4. **Isaiah . . . free** the quotation refers to the passage in Isaiah 58:6.

its national loyalty. The graves of young Americans who answered the call to service surround the globe.

Now the trumpet summons us again—not as a call to bear arms, though arms we need; not as a call to battle, though embattled we are—but a call to bear the burden of a long twilight struggle, year in and year out, "rejoicing in hope, patient in tribulation"[5]—a struggle against the common enemies of man: tyranny, poverty, disease, and war itself.

Can we forge against these enemies a grand and global alliance, North and South, East and West, that can assure a more fruitful life for all mankind? Will you join in that historic effort?

In the long history of the world, only a few generations have been granted the role of defending freedom in its hour of maximum danger. I do not shrink from this responsibility—I welcome it. I do not believe that any of us would exchange places with any other people or any other generation. The energy, the faith, the devotion which we bring to this endeavor will light our country and all who serve it—and the glow from that fire can truly light the world.

And so, my fellow Americans: ask not what your country can do for you—ask what you can do for your country.

My fellow citizens of the world: ask not what America will do for you, but what together we can do for the freedom of man.

Finally, whether you are citizens of America or citizens of the world, ask of us here the same high standards of strength and sacrifice which we ask of you. With a good conscience our only sure reward, with history the final judge of our deeds, let us go forth to lead the land we love, asking His blessing and His help, but knowing that here on earth God's work must truly be our own.

---

5. **"rejoicing . . . tribulation"** from Romans 12:12. In Paul's letter to the Romans, he calls people to work together in love and mutual respect.

Critical Reading

1. **Key Ideas and Details (a)** What difference does Kennedy stress between the world now and the world as it was during the American Revolution? **(b) Interpret:** How does Kennedy want his audience to respond to this difference?

2. **Integration of Knowledge and Ideas Evaluate:** How effective is the challenge that Kennedy offers in the final paragraphs of the speech? Explain your answer.

Cite textual evidence to support your responses.

Martin Luther King, Jr. *(1929–1968)*

Author of "Letter from Birmingham City Jail"

Martin Luther King, Jr., was born into a family of ministers: both his father and maternal grandfather were Baptist preachers. At Morehouse College in Atlanta, Georgia, King originally planned to study both medicine and law. However, under the influence of his mentor, the college president and eloquent orator Benjamin Mays, King committed himself to the ministry and to the struggle for racial equality.

Formative Years King prepared for the ministry at Crozer Theological Seminary in Chester, Pennsylvania. Here, the nonviolent philosophy of the Indian leader Mohandas K. ("Mahatma") Gandhi made a critical impression on him. At Boston University a few years later, King earned a doctorate in theology.

Civil Rights Leader King first gained prominence as the leader of the Montgomery Bus Boycott of 1955–1956. Convinced that political and social freedoms were attainable through nonviolence, he led boycotts, marches, and sit-ins to protest segregation, injustice, and the economic oppression of African Americans. A charismatic orator, King soon became known as the most eloquent and influential leader of the civil rights movement. In April 1963, he crystallized the movement's aims and methods in his "Letter from Birmingham City Jail." Four months later, he helped organize the March on Washington, where he delivered his memorable speech "I Have a Dream." Although King stressed nonviolence, he became a martyr for freedom when he was assassinated in Memphis, Tennessee, on April 4, 1968. Before her death in 2006, his widow, Coretta Scott King, worked to keep King's message and achievements alive. The King children continue to carry on their parents' work.

> "All labor that uplifts humanity has dignity and importance and should be undertaken with painstaking excellence."

from LETTER FROM BIRMINGHAM CITY JAIL

MARTIN LUTHER KING, JR.

▲ Martin Luther King, Jr., in a jail cell at the Jefferson County Courthouse in Birmingham, Alabama.

BACKGROUND By the late 1950s, Martin Luther King, Jr., had emerged as a key figure of the civil rights movement. During the Kennedy administration, King was arrested in April, 1963, for protesting racial segregation in Birmingham, Alabama. As he sat in jail, he read a newspaper article in which eight white clergymen criticized him for "unwise and untimely" demonstrations. Without proper writing paper, King drafted a response—this letter—in the cramped margins of that newspaper.

APRIL 16, 1963

I hope the church as a whole will meet the challenge of this decisive hour. But even if the church does not come to the aid of justice, I have no despair about the future. I have no fear about the outcome of our struggle in Birmingham, even if our motives are presently misunderstood. We will reach the goal of freedom in Birmingham and all over the nation, because the goal of America is freedom. Abused and scorned though we may be, our destiny is tied up with the destiny of America. Before the Pilgrims landed at Plymouth we were here. Before the pen of

▲ (left and center) Dr. King is arrested in Montgomery, Alabama (September 3, 1958). (right) Civil rights leaders James Meredith, Martin Luther King, Jr., Roy Wilkins, A. Phillip Randolph, and labor leader Walter Reuther lead a crowd at the March on Washington for Jobs and Freedom (August 28, 1963).

Identify Main Ideas and Supporting Details

What are two details King uses to support his main idea about police treatment of protesters?

Jefferson etched across the pages of history the majestic words of the Declaration of Independence, we were here. For more than two centuries our foreparents labored in this country without wages; they made cotton king; and they built the homes of their masters in the midst of brutal injustice and shameful humiliation—and yet out of a bottomless vitality they continued to thrive and develop. If the inexpressible cruelties of slavery could not stop us, the opposition we now face will surely fail. We will win our freedom because the sacred heritage of our nation and the eternal will of God are embodied in our echoing demands.

I must close now. But before closing I am impelled to mention one other point in your statement that troubled me profoundly. You warmly commended the Birmingham police force for keeping "order" and "preventing violence." I don't believe you would have so warmly commended the police force if you had seen its angry violent dogs literally biting six unarmed, nonviolent Negroes. I don't believe you would so quickly commend the policemen if you would observe their ugly and inhuman treatment of Negroes here in the city jail; if you would watch them push and curse old Negro women and young Negro girls; if you would see them slap and kick old Negro men and young Negro boys; if you will observe them, as they did on two occasions, refuse to give us food because we wanted to sing our grace together. I'm sorry that I can't join you in your praise for the police department.

It is true that they have been rather disciplined in their public handling of the demonstrators. In this sense they have been rather publicly "nonviolent." But for what purpose? To preserve the evil system of segregation. Over the last few years I have consistently preached that nonviolence demands that the means we use must be as pure as the ends we seek. So I have tried to make it clear that it is wrong to use immoral means to attain moral ends. But now I must affirm that it is just as wrong, or even more so, to use moral means to preserve immoral ends. Maybe Mr. Connor and his policemen have been rather publicly nonviolent, as Chief Pritchett was in Albany, Georgia, but they have used the moral means of nonviolence to maintain the immoral end of flagrant racial injustice. T. S. Eliot has said that there is no greater treason than to do the right deed for the wrong reason.

I wish you had commended the Negro sit-inners and demonstrators of Birmingham for their sublime courage, their willingness to suffer and their amazing discipline in the midst of the most inhuman provocation. One day the South will recognize its real heroes. They will be the James Merediths, courageously and with a majestic sense of purpose facing jeering and hostile mobs and the agonizing loneliness that characterizes the life of the pioneer. They will be old, oppressed, battered Negro women, symbolized in a seventy-two-year-old woman of Montgomery, Alabama, who rose up with a sense of dignity and with her people decided not to ride the segregated buses, and responded to one who inquired about her tiredness with ungrammatical profundity: "My feet is tired, but my soul is rested." They will be the young high school and college students, young ministers of the gospel and a host of their elders courageously and nonviolently sitting-in at lunch counters and willingly going to jail for conscience's sake. One day the South will know that when these disinherited

Vocabulary

flagrant (flā′ grənt) *adj.* glaring, outrageous

profundity (prō fun′ də tē) *n.* intellectual depth

Comprehension

According to King, who are the South's real heroes?

▼ Dr. King at the March on Washington (August 28, 1963)

children of God sat down at lunch counters they were in reality standing up for the best in the American dream and the most sacred values in our Judeo-Christian heritage, and thusly, carrying our whole nation back to those great wells of democracy which were dug deep by the Founding Fathers in the formulation of the Constitution and the Declaration of Independence.

Never before have I written a letter this long (or should I say a book?). I'm afraid that it is much too long to take your precious time. I can assure you that it would have been much shorter if I had been writing from a comfortable desk, but what else is there to do when you are alone for days in the dull monotony of a narrow jail cell other than write long letters, think strange thoughts, and pray long prayers?

If I have said anything in this letter that is an overstatement of the truth and is indicative of an unreasonable impatience, I beg you to forgive me. If I have said anything in this letter that is an understatement of the truth and is indicative of my having a patience that makes me patient with anything less than brotherhood, I beg God to forgive me.

I hope this letter finds you strong in the faith. I also hope that circumstances will soon make it possible for me to meet each of you, not as an integrationist or a civil rights leader, but as a fellow clergyman and a Christian brother. Let us all hope that the dark clouds of racial prejudice will soon pass away and the deep fog of misunderstanding will be lifted from our fear-drenched communities and in some not too distant tomorrow the radiant stars of love and brotherhood will shine over our great nation with all of their scintillating beauty.

Yours for the cause of Peace
and Brotherhood,
Martin Luther King, Jr.

Critical Reading

Cite textual evidence to support your responses.

1. **Key Ideas and Details (a)** In the first paragraph, what reasons does King give for his confidence in the outcome of the struggle? **(b) Infer:** Why do you think he emphasizes his attitude about the outcome?

2. **Key Ideas and Details Distinguish:** What two points does King make about the means by which a just goal should be reached? Explain.

3. **Integration of Knowledge and Ideas** What do both of these documents suggest are the privileges and obligations of freedom? In your response, use at least two of these Essential Question words: *democracy, liberty, criticize.* [*Connecting to the Essential Question: How does literature shape or reflect society?*]

Literary Analysis

**Common Core
State Standards**

Writing

1. Write arguments to support claims in an analysis of substantive topics or texts, using valid reasoning and relevant and sufficient evidence. *(p. 1114)*

1.d. Establish and maintain a formal style and objective tone while attending to the norms and conventions of the discipline in which they are writing. *(p. 1114)*

Language

3. Apply knowledge of language to understand how language functions in different contexts, to make effective choices for meaning or style, and to comprehend more fully when reading or listening. *(p. 1115)*

4.b. Identify and correctly use patterns of word changes that indicate different meanings or parts of speech. *(p. 1114)*

5. Demonstrate understanding of word relationships. *(p. 1114)*

1. **Key Ideas and Details** What details **support** Kennedy's **main idea** that the task of defending freedom should be welcomed? Explain.

2. **Craft and Structure (a)** Identify examples of **parallelism** in the sixth paragraph of Kennedy's inaugural address, beginning "To those old allies . . . ." **(b)** Which of these passages is also an example of **antithesis?** Explain.

3. **Craft and Structure (a)** Reread the paragraph on page 1106 in Kennedy's inaugural address that begins "And if a beachhead of cooperation. . . ." Using a chart like the one shown, identify the parallel words and phrases. **(b)** Choose the strongest example and explain your choice.

Parallel Words	Parallel Phrases

4. **Craft and Structure** Identify the two basic **lists** with which Kennedy organizes the majority of the speech.

5. **Craft and Structure** How does the passage that begins "Ask not what your country can do for you . . ." echo and reinforce the two lists Kennedy uses earlier in his speech?

6. **Key Ideas and Details** What supporting details does King give to support his central idea that "One day the South will recognize its real heroes"?

7. **Craft and Structure (a)** In King's letter, identify parallelism in the paragraph beginning "If I have said anything in this letter that is an overstatement . . . ." **(b)** What is the effect of this rhetorical device?

8. **Craft and Structure (a)** What underlying reason does King point out for the police department's "nonviolent" treatment of the demonstrators? **(b)** What **argument** does King make about this purpose? **(c)** How does he **support** this argument?

9. **Integration of Knowledge and Ideas (a)** What double audience, or group of readers, does King address in his letter? **(b)** Which details in the final paragraph show his awareness of both audiences? Explain.

10. **Comparing Literary Works (a)** Which text—Kennedy's speech or King's letter—makes more frequent use of parallelism and antithesis? **(b)** Explain why each author's use of these devices is appropriate to the kind of document he is writing and to its method of delivery.

Vocabulary Acquisition and Use

Word Analysis: Latin Root -vert- or -vers-

The word *adversary* contains the root *-vert-* or *-vers-*, meaning "to switch" or "to turn around." With this root in mind, you might define *adversary* as "a person who has turned against" someone or something. Other words that contain this root include *reverse,* which might be defined as "to turn around again," and *convert,* which might be defined as "to turn with." For each of the words below, write a definition that includes the word *switch* or *turn.* If you are unfamiliar with a word, refer to a dictionary before writing your own definition.

1. introvert   3. controversy   5. invert   7. revert
2. divert   4. vertigo   6. versatile   8. vertical

Vocabulary: Synonyms

For each item, choose the letter of its synonym, and explain your choice.

1. **flagrant: (a)** delicious **(b)** obvious **(c)** contorted
2. **alliance: (a)** contact **(b)** program **(c)** association
3. **profundity: (a)** exploration **(b)** wisdom **(c)** ambiguity
4. **eradicate: (a)** analyze **(b)** redefine **(c)** eliminate
5. **adversary: (a)** antagonist **(b)** friend **(c)** minister
6. **invective: (a)** insult **(b)** apology **(c)** rhetoric

Writing

Argument A letter to the editor is a *formal business letter* written by a member of a community and submitted to a newspaper or magazine for publication. Write a **letter to the editor** commenting on an issue about which you feel strongly. In your letter, keep in mind the needs, views, and prior knowledge of the audience you are addressing.

Prewriting Jot down a list of topics that matter to you. Use a chart like the one shown to list possible ideas and support.

Model: Listing to Generate Ideas

Issue: _____

Statement of Opinion: _____

Support (examples/reasons):

Drafting Craft your claim as a clear, concise statement about the issue that establishes a serious, formal tone. As you draft, support your claim with a variety of examples, reasons, and other details. In addition, use *parallelism* or *antithesis* to boost your letter's persuasive power. Follow correct *business letter format* with a formal inside address, salutation, and closing.

Revising Review your letter to be sure that you have maintained a formal tone while using strong, precise words, a variety of sentence structures, and a form of parallelism. Then, revise for coherence, adding transitional words and phrases as needed to present your argument smoothly and logically.

Conventions and Style: Using Active, Not Passive, Voice

A verb is in the **passive voice** if the action is done to the subject. A verb is in the **active voice** when the subject does the action. Use active voice in your writing whenever you can. It is more economical, forceful, and direct than the passive voice. For example, notice that the sentence using the active voice has two fewer words than the one using the passive voice:

Passive: Nuclear weapons were being stockpiled by the United States and the Soviet Union.

Active: The United States and the Soviet Union were stockpiling nuclear weapons.

Correct Use of Passive Voice

There are exceptions, of course. Some sentences correctly use passive voice verbs because the doer of the action is unknown or unimportant.

- John F. Kennedy was elected in 1960.
- Martin Luther King, Jr., was jailed.

Examples of Passive Voice Verbs	
Past	was held, had been held
Present	is held, has been held, is being held
Future	will be held, will have been held

Practice Identify each sentence as active or passive. If a sentence in the passive voice should be in the active voice, rewrite it.

1. Both groups of countries were being weighed down by the cost of weapons.
2. The torch of freedom was passed by the old generation to a new one.
3. A free society must help the poor.
4. A global alliance is needed to be formed by the nations of the world.
5. King wanted the struggle for civil rights to be won.
6. Oppressed women were symbolized by a seventy-two-year-old from Birmingham.
7. Democracy was established in America.
8. Sit-ins were supported by old and young.
9. The letter was not written by King from his comfortable desk but from jail.
10. King hoped the future would bring an end to racial prejudice.

Writing and Speaking Conventions

A. Writing Rewrite each passive sentence to make it active.

Example: People were called on by President Kennedy to celebrate freedom.

Rewritten Sentence: President Kennedy called on people to celebrate freedom.

1. Citizens were asked by President Kennedy to celebrate freedom.
2. Human life might have been destroyed by nuclear war.
3. King said that nonviolent protesters were mistreated by Birmingham police officers.
4. T. S. Eliot was quoted by Martin Luther King, Jr.

B. Speaking Deliver a formal response to Dr. King's "Letter from Birmingham City Jail." Include reasons for your opinion, and use active voice whenever possible.

*D*rama is life with the dull bits cut out.

–*Alfred Hitchcock*

Defining Drama

A **drama,** or **play,** is a story written to be performed by actors. Unlike a short story or novel, a drama presents action mainly through **dialogue,** the conversation and speeches of characters. A play typically includes several other key literary elements:

- **Plot** is the ordered sequence of events in a play. A play is often divided into large units called **acts,** which are then subdivided into smaller ones called **scenes.**
- **Characters** are the people who participate in the action of the play and are portrayed onstage or onscreen by **actors.**
- **Stage directions** are notes included in the play to describe sets, costumes, lighting, sound, props, and—in some cases—the ways in which actors should move and deliver their lines.

Types of Drama Ever since the development of Western drama in ancient Greece, plays have been divided into two broad categories.

- **Comedy** is drama that ends happily. Comedies may be funny, but humor is not their defining trait.
- **Tragedy** is drama that shows the downfall of a noble but flawed figure called the **tragic hero.**

Note that some plays, including several by Shakespeare, mix elements of both categories, or otherwise bend their definitions.

Modern Realistic Drama While some modern playwrights experiment with fantasy or absurdity, many more write realistic plays that feature recognizable settings and characters. For some modern playwrights, the realistic play is also a vehicle for social and political criticism.

Close Read: Modern Realistic Drama

These elements of modern realistic drama appear in the Model text at right.

Realistic Characters: authentic characters dealing with realistic, if heightened, conflicts *Example:* "LAURA: I don't do anything—much. Oh, please don't think I sit around doing nothing!" (Tennessee Williams)	**Realistic Settings:** the use of familiar, ordinary places, such as a family kitchen, as sites for the action *Example:* "[Mrs. Gibbs and Mrs. Webb enter their kitchens and start the day as in the first act.]" (Thornton Wilder)
Realistic Dialogue: the use of language that reflects how real people speak *Example:* "FRIENDLY: What say we grab a little dinner after the show? The 21 Club?" (Heslov and Clooney)	**Social and Political Criticism:** presentation, through the elements of the play, of the playwright's stand on social or political issues *Example:* "Long-held hatreds of neighbors could now be openly expressed, and vengeance taken..." (Arthur Miller)

EXEMPLAR TEXT

Model

About the Text Lorraine Hansberry (1930–1965) was the first African American woman dramatist to have a play produced on Broadway. *A Raisin in the Sun*, which premiered in New York City in 1959, tells the story of the Youngers, an African American family living in Chicago during the late 1940s or early 1950s. The family wants to buy a house in an all-white suburb. In the excerpt, Beneatha is angry at her brother because he has agreed to accept money in exchange for stopping the purchase.

from *A Raisin in the Sun*
by **Lorraine Hansberry**

BENEATHA: He's no brother of mine.

MAMA: What you say?

BENEATHA: I said that that individual in that room is no brother of mine.

MAMA: That's what I thought you said. You feeling like you better than he is today? [BENEATHA does not answer.] Yes? What you tell him a minute ago? That he wasn't a man? Yes? You give him up for me? You done wrote his epitaph too—like the rest of the world? Well, who give you the privilege?

BENEATHA: Be on my side for once! You saw what he just did, Mama! You saw him—down on his knees. Wasn't it you who taught me—to despise any man who would do that. Do what he's going to do.

MAMA: Yes—I taught you that. Me and your daddy. But I thought I taught you something else too…I thought I taught you to love him.

BENEATHA: Love him? There is nothing left to love.

MAMA: There is always something left to love. And if you ain't learned that, you ain't learned nothing. [looking at her] Have you cried for that boy today? I don't mean for yourself and for the family 'cause we lost the money. I mean for him; what he been through and what it done to him. Child, when do you think is the time to love somebody the most; when they done good and made things easy for everybody? Well then, you ain't through learning—because that ain't the time at all. It's when he's at his lowest and can't believe in hisself 'cause the world done whipped him so. When you starts measuring somebody, measure him right, child, measure him right. Make sure you done taken into account what hills and valleys he come through before he got to wherever he is.

Realistic Characters
The excerpt begins with a typical real-life situation: a sister angry at her brother.

Realistic Settings
The immediate physical setting is an ordinary family home. The realistic historical setting of post–World War II Chicago creates enormous conflicts for the Younger family.

Realistic Dialogue
The characters use informal, ordinary language. Mama, in particular, speaks expressive, non-standard English.

Social and Political Criticism
By simply telling the Youngers' story, the playwright is implicitly expressing social and political views. Specific speeches, such as Mama's statement that the "world done whipped him so," are more explicit critical statements.

Arthur Miller (1915–2005)

A legend of the modern American theater, Arthur Miller has chronicled the dilemmas of common people pitted against powerful and unyielding social forces. A native New Yorker, Miller lived through bad times as well as good. During the Depression, his family's business went bankrupt. Although Miller graduated from high school in 1932, he was forced to delay his enrollment at the University of Michigan for more than two years in order to raise money for tuition. He did so by working at a variety of jobs, including singing for a local radio station, driving a truck, and working as a stock clerk in an automobile parts warehouse.

Promising Playwright

Miller first began writing drama while still in college. In 1947, his play *All My Sons* opened on Broadway to immediate acclaim, establishing Miller as a bright new talent. Two years later, he won international fame and the Pulitzer Prize for *Death of a Salesman* (1949), which critics hailed as a modern American tragedy.

His next play, *The Crucible* (1953), was less warmly received because of its political content. Miller drew a parallel between the hysteria surrounding the witchcraft trials in Puritan New England and the postwar climate of McCarthyism—Senator Joseph McCarthy's obsessive quest to uncover Communist party infiltration of American institutions.

In the introduction to his *Collected Plays* (1957), Miller described his perceptions of the atmosphere during the McCarthy era and the way in which those perceptions influenced the writing of *The Crucible*. He said, "It was as though the whole country had been born anew, without a memory even of certain elemental decencies which a year or two earlier no one would have imagined could be altered, let alone forgotten. Astounded, I watched men pass me by without a nod whom I had known rather well for years; and again, the astonishment was produced by my knowledge, which I could not give up, that the terror in these people was being knowingly planned and consciously engineered, and yet that all they knew was terror. That so interior and subjective an emotion could have been so manifestly created from without was a marvel to me. It underlies every word in *The Crucible*."

In the Shadows of McCarthyism

During the two years following the publication and production of *The Crucible*, Miller was investigated for possible associations with the Communist party. In 1956, he was called to testify before the House Committee on Un-American Activities (HUAC). Although he had never joined the Communist party, Miller—and many of his contemporaries—had advocated principles of social justice and equality among the classes. He had become disillusioned, however, by the reality of communism as practiced in the Soviet Union. At the HUAC hearings, he testified about his own experiences, but he refused to discuss his colleagues and associates. He was found guilty of contempt of Congress for his silence. The sentence was later overturned.

Hollywood Glamour

In 1956, the spotlight focused on Miller's personal life when he married glamorous film star Marilyn Monroe. Although he wrote very little during their five-year marriage, he did pen the screenplay for a film, *The Misfits* (1961), in which Monroe starred. After the marriage ended, Miller wrote other noteworthy plays, including *After the Fall* (1964), *The Price* (1968), and *The Last Yankee* (1993).

A Voice of Conscience

Arthur Miller died in 2005 at the age of eighty-nine. Playwright Edward Albee said of him, "Arthur never compromised. He never sold out, he never did anything just for that awful word entertainment. . . . He was able to use art and his enormously important social and political points and make them so skillfully that people never thought they were being hit over the head."

Themes Across Time: Author's Insights
The Words of Arthur Miller on
The CRUCIBLE

The Historical Background of *The Crucible*

In *Echoes Down the Corridor*, published in 2000, Arthur Miller writes: "It would probably never have occurred to me to write a play about the Salem witch trials of 1692 had I not seen some astonishing correspondences with that calamity in the America of the late forties and early fifties. . . . my basic need was to respond to a phenomenon which, with only small exaggeration, one could say was paralyzing a whole generation and in an amazingly short time was drying up the habits of trust and toleration in public discourse.

"I refer, of course, to the anticommunist rage that threatened to reach hysterical proportions and sometimes did. I can't remember anyone calling it an ideological war, but I think now that that is what it amounted to. Looking back at the period, I suppose we very rapidly passed over anything like a discussion or debate and into something quite different, a hunt not alone for subversive people but ideas and even a suspect language."

The Writing of *The Crucible*

Miller explains where his ideas for *The Crucible* came from, saying, "On a lucky afternoon I happened upon a book, *The Devil in Massachusetts*, by Marion Starkey, a narrative of the Salem witch-hunt of 1692. I knew this story from my college reading more than a decade earlier, but now in this changed and darkened America it turned a wholly new aspect toward me, namely, the poetry of the hunt. Poetry may seem an odd word for a witch-hunt, but I saw now that there was something of the marvelous in the spectacle of the whole village, if not an entire province, whose imagination was literally captured by a vision of something that wasn't there. . . .

Meet the Author

Arthur Miller's *The Crucible* failed at the box office in its initial production in 1953, but it has since become one of the most popular American plays of the twentieth century.

"As I stood in the stillness of the Salem courthouse, surrounded by the miasmic swirl of the images of the 1950s but with my head in 1692, what the two eras had in common was gradually gaining definition. In both was the menace of concealed plots, but most startling were the similarities in the rituals of defense and the investigative routines. Three hundred years apart, both prosecutions were alleging membership in a secret, disloyal group; should the accused confess, his honesty could be proved only in precisely the same way—by naming former confederates, nothing less. Thus the informer became the very proof of the plot and the investigator's necessity."

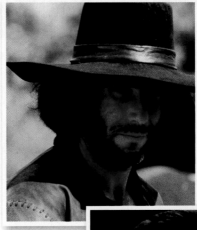

How the Play Has Lasted

Musing on the eventual popularity of *The Crucible*, Miller says, "*The Crucible* is my most-produced play, here and abroad. . . . And it is part of the play's history, I think, that to people in so many parts of the world its story seems so like their own. . . . In fact, I used to think, half seriously—although it was not far from the truth—that you could tell when a dictator was about to take power in a Latin American country or when one had just been overthrown, by whether *The Crucible* was suddenly being produced there."

▲ Daniel Day-Lewis as John Proctor and Winona Ryder as Abigail Williams in the 1996 film version of *The Crucible*

Critical Reading

> 1. **Key Ideas and Details (a)** What experience gave Miller the original idea for *The Crucible*? **(b) Infer:** What aspects of this experience helped Miller connect the Salem of 1692 with the United States of the late 1940s and 1950s?
>
> 2. **Key Ideas and Details (a)** What specific similarities does Miller see between the Salem witch trials of 1692 and the anticommunist hearings of the 1950s? **(b) Speculate:** Why do you think *The Crucible* is Miller's most-produced play?
>
> **As You Read *The Crucible* . . .**
>
> 3. Notice how the conflict in the play can represent a universal conflict.
>
> 4. Consider ways in which reading this commentary enhances your experience of the play.

Cite textual evidence to support your responses.

ARTHUR MILLER'S STARS

▶ Dustin Hoffman on the set of *Death of a Salesman* as Willy Loman.

Arthur Miller traveled in the circles of the rich, famous, and celebrated. He was at one time the husband of Marilyn Monroe. He became the father-in-law of Academy Award-winning actor Daniel Day-Lewis. Miller's works also drew actors with major star power, eager for the opportunity to be part of a Miller production.

▼ Arthur Miller and his wife, Marilyn Monroe

◀ George C. Scott and Arthur Miller

▶ Brian Dennehy and Arthur Miller accepting Tony awards for *Death of a Salesman*.

▲ John Malkovich played Biff Loman

▲ Clark Gable and Marilyn Monroe in Miller's film *The Misfits*.

Building Knowledge and Insight *The Crucible, Act I*

Connecting to the Essential Question In this tragic play, characters must decide what it means to do the right thing. As you read, look for moments when characters must choose between preserving themselves or their ideals. Doing so will help you think about the Essential Question: **How does literature shape or reflect society?**

Close Reading Focus

Plot; Dramatic Exposition
Plot is the sequence of events that happen in a story. Plots follow a series of phases that, taken together, are called the "dramatic arc." Plot is always driven by a *conflict*, or struggle, between opposing forces:

- **Rising Action:** The conflict is introduced and begins to build.
- **Climax:** The conflict reaches its moment of greatest intensity. This is the turning point, when an event signals the final outcome.
- **Falling Action:** The conflict diminishes and approaches resolution.
- **Resolution:** The conflict ends.

In a long, complex narrative such as this play, there may be multiple conflicts. In this play, Miller uses **dramatic exposition,** or prose commentaries, to provide background information about the characters and their world.

Preparing to Read Complex Texts Most plays are written to be performed, not read. When reading drama, it is important to **identify the text structures** that provide different kinds of information. Text structures include *dialogue*, the words spoken by the actors, and *stage directions*, details the playwright includes about the setting and action. Stage directions may be set in italic type or in brackets to distinguish them from dialogue. As you read Act I of *The Crucible*, use a chart like the one shown to examine how information from the two types of text structures contributes to your understanding of the characters.

Vocabulary

You will encounter the words listed here in the text that follows. Copy the words into your notebook. Which words have the same suffix and are nouns?

predilection	inculcation
ingratiating	propitiation
dissembling	evade
calumny	

Ⓒ **Common Core State Standards**

Reading Literature
3. Analyze the impact of the author's choices regarding how to develop and relate elements of a story or drama (e.g., how the action is ordered).

5. Analyze how an author's choices concerning how to structure specific parts of a text (e.g., the choice of where to begin or end a story, the choice to provide a comedic or tragic resolution) contribute to its overall structure and meaning as well as its aesthetic impact.

The CRUCIBLE [1]

Arthur Miller

Background In 1692, the British colony of Massachusetts was convulsed by a witchcraft hysteria that resulted in the execution of twenty people and the jailing of more than 100 others. The incident, though unprecedented for New England, was not unique. During the sixteenth and seventeenth centuries, witchhunts swept through Europe, resulting in tens of thousands of executions. Many of the accused were guilty only of practicing folk customs that had survived in Europe since pre-Christian times. In an era when religion and politics were intertwined, witch hunts were often politically motivated. England's James I, for example, wrote a treatise on witchcraft and sometimes accused his enemies of practicing the black arts. It was a cry that resonated well with a superstitious populace.

For the New England colonies, the witchcraft episode was perhaps inevitable. The colonists endured harsh conditions and punishing hardship from day to day. Finding themselves at the mercy of forces beyond their control—bitter weather, sickness and death, devastating fires, drought, and insect infestations that killed their crops—many colonists attributed their misfortunes to the powers of evil. They were fearful people and believed that witches, servants of the Devil, were real and dangerous. In the small parish of Salem Village, many were quick to blame witchcraft when the minister's daughter and several other girls were afflicted by seizures and lapsed into unconsciousness, especially after it was

---

1. crucible (kroo′ sə bel) *n.* heat resistant container in which metals are melted or fused at very high temperatures; a severe trial or test.

learned that the girls had been dabbling in fortunetelling with the minister's slave, Tituba. (They were not dancing in the woods, as portrayed in the play.) At first, only Tituba and two elderly women were called witches, but the hunt spread until some of the colony's most prominent citizens stood accused. Many historians have seen a pattern of social and economic animosity behind the accusations, but most scholars feel that mass hysteria was also a strong contributing factor.

A *crucible* is a heat-resistant container in which metals are melted or fused at very high temperatures. The word is used symbolically to suggest a severe trial or test. Miller chose this title well as the play depicts severely trying times. When *The Crucible* was first published, Arthur Miller added a note about the play's historical accuracy: "This play is not history in the sense in which the word is used by the academic historian. Dramatic purposes have sometimes required many characters to be fused into one; the number of girls involved in the 'crying-out' has been reduced; Abigail's age has been raised; while there were several judges of almost equal authority, I have symbolized them in Hathorne and Danforth. However, I believe that the reader will discover here the essential nature of one of the strangest and most awful chapters in human history. The fate of each character is exactly that of his historical model, and there is no one in the drama who did not play a similar—and in some cases exactly the same—role in history."

CHARACTERS

REVEREND PARRIS	MARTHA COREY
BETTY PARRIS	REVEREND JOHN HALE
TITUBA	ELIZABETH PROCTOR
ABIGAIL WILLIAMS	FRANCIS NURSE
SUSANNA WALCOTT	EZEKIEL CHEEVER
MRS. ANN PUTNAM	MARSHAL HERRICK
THOMAS PUTNAM	JUDGE HATHORNE
MERCY LEWIS	DEPUTY GOVERNOR DANFORTH
MARY WARREN	SARAH GOOD
JOHN PROCTOR	HOPKINS
REBECCA NURSE	GILES COREY

ACT 1

(An Overture)

A small upper bedroom in the home of REVEREND SAMUEL PARRIS, *Salem, Massachusetts, in the spring of the year 1692.*

There is a narrow window at the left. Through its leaded panes the morning sunlight streams. A candle still burns near the bed, which is at the right. A chest, a chair, and a small table are the other furnishings. At the back a door opens on the landing of the stairway to the ground floor. The room gives off an air of clean spareness. The roof rafters are exposed, and the wood colors are raw and unmellowed.

As the curtain rises, REVEREND PARRIS *is discovered kneeling beside the bed, evidently in prayer. His daughter,* BETTY PARRIS, *aged ten, is lying on the bed, inert.*

At the time of these events Parris was in his middle forties. In history he cut a villainous path, and there is very little good to be said for him. He believed he was being persecuted wherever he went, despite his best efforts to win people and God to his side. In meeting, he felt insulted if someone rose to shut the door without first asking his permission. He was a widower with no interest in children, or talent with them. He regarded them as young adults, and until this strange crisis he, like the rest of Salem, never conceived that the children were anything but thankful for being permitted to walk straight, eyes slightly lowered, arms at the sides, and mouths shut until bidden to speak.

His house stood in the "town"—but we today would hardly call it a village. The meeting house was nearby, and from this point outward—toward the bay or inland—there were a few small-windowed, dark houses snuggling against the raw Massachusetts winter. Salem had been established hardly forty years before. To the European world the whole province was a barbaric frontier inhabited by a sect of fanatics who, nevertheless, were shipping out products of slowly increasing quantity and value.

No one can really know what their lives were like. They had no novelists—and would not have permitted anyone to read a novel if one were handy. Their creed forbade anything resembling a theater or "vain enjoyment." They did not celebrate Christmas, and a holiday from work meant only that they must concentrate even more upon prayer.

Which is not to say that nothing broke into this strict and somber way of life. When a new farmhouse was built, friends assembled to "raise

Identifying Text Features

What important information is revealed in the third paragraph of the stage directions?

Arthur Miller
Author's Insight

Miller once speculated that *The Crucible*, with its large cast, would not be accepted by today's "commercialized" Broadway and was too large for off-Broadway theaters: ". . . what would one do with *The Crucible* on a shoebox stage [off-Broadway] with its twenty-one characters and several sets?"

the roof," and there would be special foods cooked and probably some potent cider passed around. There was a good supply of ne'er-do-wells in Salem, who dallied at the shovelboard[2] in Bridget Bishop's tavern. Probably more than the creed, hard work kept the morals of the place from spoiling, for the people were forced to fight the land like heroes for every grain of corn, and no man had very much time for fooling around.

That there were some jokers, however, is indicated by the practice of appointing a two-man patrol whose duty was to "walk forth in the time of God's worship to take notice of such as either lye about the meeting house, without attending to the word and ordinances, or that lye at home or in the fields without giving good account thereof, and to take the names of such persons, and to present them to the magistrates, whereby they may be accordingly proceeded against." This predilection for minding other people's business was time-honored among the people of Salem, and it undoubtedly created many of the suspicions which were to feed the coming madness. It was also, in my opinion, one of the things that a John Proctor would rebel against, for the time of the armed camp had almost passed, and since the country was reasonably—although not wholly—safe, the old disciplines were beginning to rankle. But, as in all such matters, the issue was not clear-cut, for danger was still a possibility, and in unity still lay the best promise of safety.

The edge of the wilderness was close by. The American continent stretched endlessly west, and it was full of mystery for them. It stood, dark and threatening, over their shoulders night and day, for out of it Indian tribes marauded from time to time, and Reverend Parris had parishioners who had lost relatives to these heathen.

The parochial snobbery of these people was partly responsible for their failure to convert the Indians. Probably they also preferred to take land from heathens rather than from fellow Christians. At any rate, very few Indians were converted, and the Salem folk believed that the virgin forest was the Devil's last preserve, his home base and the citadel of his final stand. To the best of their knowledge the American forest was the last place on earth that was not paying homage to God.

For these reasons, among others, they carried about an air of innate resistance, even of persecution. Their fathers had, of course, been persecuted in England. So now they and their church found it necessary to deny any other sect its freedom, lest their New Jerusalem[3] be defiled and corrupted by wrong ways and deceitful ideas.

They believed, in short, that they held in their steady hands the candle that would light the world. We have inherited this belief, and it has helped and hurt us. It helped them with the discipline it gave them. They were a dedicated folk, by and large, and they had to be to survive the life they had chosen or been born into in this country.

---

2. **shovelboard** game in which a coin or other disk is driven with the hand along a highly polished board, floor, or table marked with transverse lines.
3. **New Jerusalem** in the Bible, the holy city of heaven.

Dramatic Exposition
In what ways does this long exposition differ from a typical stage direction?

Vocabulary
predilection (pred´ ə lek´ shən) *n.* preexisting preference

Comprehension
What is a time-honored activity among the people of Salem?

The proof of their belief's value to them may be taken from the opposite character of the first Jamestown settlement, farther south, in Virginia. The Englishmen who landed there were motivated mainly by a hunt for profit. They had thought to pick off the wealth of the new country and then return rich to England. They were a band of individualists, and a much more ingratiating group than the Massachusetts men. But Virginia destroyed them. Massachusetts tried to kill off the Puritans, but they combined; they set up a communal society which, in the beginning, was little more than an armed camp with an autocratic and very devoted leadership. It was, however, an autocracy by consent, for they were united from top to bottom by a commonly held ideology whose perpetuation was the reason and justification for all their sufferings. So their self-denial, their purposefulness, their suspicion of all vain pursuits, their hard-handed justice, were altogether perfect instruments for the conquest of this space so antagonistic to man.

But the people of Salem in 1692 were not quite the dedicated folk that arrived on the *Mayflower*. A vast differentiation had taken place, and in their own time a revolution had unseated the royal government and substituted a junta[4] which was at this moment in power. The times, to their eyes, must have been out of joint, and to the common folk must have seemed as insoluble and complicated as do ours today. It is not hard to see how easily many could have been led to believe that the time of confusion had been brought upon them by deep and darkling forces. No hint of such speculation appears on the court record, but social disorder in any age breeds such mystical suspicions, and when, as in Salem, wonders are brought forth from below the social surface, it is too much to expect people to hold back very long from laying on the victims with all the force of their frustrations.

The Salem tragedy, which is about to begin in these pages, developed from a paradox. It is a paradox in whose grip we still live, and there is no prospect yet that we will discover its resolution. Simply, it was this: for good purposes, even high purposes, the people of Salem developed a theocracy, a combine of state and religious power whose function was to keep the community together, and to prevent any kind of disunity that might open it to destruction by material or ideological enemies. It was forged for a necessary purpose and accomplished that purpose. But all organization is and must be grounded on the idea of

Vocabulary

ingratiating (in grā´ shē āt´ iŋ) *adj.* charming; flattering

EXECUTION OF REV. STEPHEN BURROUGHS.

The Execution of Stephen Burroughs for Witchcraft at Salem, Massachusetts in 1692, 19th-Century Engraving

▲ **Critical Viewing**

This nineteenth-century engraving shows the hanging of the Reverend Stephen Burroughs during the Salem witchcraft trials. What does this image suggest about the condemned man's state of mind? **INFER**

4. **junta** (hōon´ tə) *assembly or council.*

exclusion and prohibition, just as two objects cannot occupy the same space. Evidently the time came in New England when the repressions of order were heavier than seemed warranted by the dangers against which the order was organized. The witch-hunt was a perverse manifestation of the panic which set in among all classes when the balance began to turn toward greater individual freedom.

When one rises above the individual villainy displayed, one can only pity them all, just as we shall be pitied someday. It is still impossible for man to organize his social life without repressions, and the balance has yet to be struck between order and freedom.

The witch-hunt was not, however, a mere repression. It was also, and as importantly, a long overdue opportunity for everyone so inclined to express publicly his guilt and sins, under the cover of accusations against the victims. It suddenly became possible—and patriotic and holy—for a man to say that Martha Corey had come into his bedroom at night, and that, while his wife was sleeping at his side, Martha laid herself down on his chest and "nearly suffocated him." Of course it was her spirit only, but his satisfaction at confessing himself was no lighter than if it had been Martha herself. One could not ordinarily speak such things in public.

Long-held hatreds of neighbors could now be openly expressed, and vengeance taken, despite the Bible's charitable injunctions. Land-lust which had been expressed before by constant bickering over boundaries and deeds, could now be elevated to the arena of morality; one could cry witch against one's neighbor and feel perfectly justified in the bargain. Old scores could be settled on a plane of heavenly combat between Lucifer[5] and the Lord; suspicions and the envy of the miserable toward the happy could and did burst out in the general revenge.

REVEREND PARRIS *is praying now, and, though we cannot hear his words, a sense of his confusion hangs about him. He mumbles, then seems about to weep; then he weeps, then prays again; but his daughter does not stir on the bed.*

The door opens, and his Negro slave enters. TITUBA *is in her forties.* PARRIS *brought her with him from Barbados, where he spent some years as a merchant before entering the ministry. She enters as one does who can no longer bear to be barred from the sight of her beloved, but she is also very frightened because her slave sense has warned her that, as always, trouble in this house eventually lands on her back.*

TITUBA, *already taking a step backward:* My Betty be hearty soon?

PARRIS: Out of here!

TITUBA, *backing to the door:* My Betty not goin' die . . .

PARRIS, *scrambling to his feet in a fury:* Out of my sight! *She is gone.* Out of my—*He is overcome with sobs. He clamps his teeth against them and closes the door and leans against it, exhausted.* Oh, my God! God

---

5. **Lucifer** (l$\overline{oo}$′ sə fər) the Devil.

Dramatic Exposition
Why is this background knowledge about Salem and the witch hunt important to your understanding of the play?

Plot
What conflict in the Parris household is introduced with Tituba's entrance?

Comprehension
What could now be openly expressed among the residents of Salem?

Vocabulary

dissembling (di sem′ blin)
n. concealment of one's real nature or motives

Identifying Text Features

Based on what stage directions have revealed about Abigail's personality, what can you conclude about her "worry" and "apprehension"?

Plot

What problem consumes Parris and a growing number of his neighbors?

help me! *Quaking with fear, mumbling to himself through his sobs, he goes to the bed and gently takes* BETTY's *hand.* Betty. Child. Dear child. Will you wake, will you open up your eyes! Betty, little one . . .

He is bending to kneel again when his niece, ABIGAIL WILLIAMS, *seventeen, enters—a strikingly beautiful girl, an orphan, with an endless capacity for dissembling. Now she is all worry and apprehension and propriety.*

ABIGAIL: Uncle? *He looks to her.* Susanna Walcott's here from Doctor Griggs.

PARRIS: Oh? Let her come, let her come.

ABIGAIL, *leaning out the door to call to Susanna, who is down the hall a few steps:* Come in, Susanna.

SUSANNA WALCOTT, *a little younger than Abigail, a nervous, hurried girl, enters.*

PARRIS, *eagerly:* What does the doctor say, child?

SUSANNA, *craning around* PARRIS *to get a look at* BETTY: He bid me come and tell you, reverend sir, that he cannot discover no medicine for it in his books.

PARRIS: Then he must search on.

SUSANNA: Aye, sir, he have been searchin' his books since he left you, sir. But he bid me tell you, that you might look to unnatural things for the cause of it.

PARRIS, *his eyes going wide:* No—no. There be no unnatural cause here. Tell him I have sent for Reverend Hale of Beverly, and Mr. Hale will surely confirm that. Let him look to medicine and put out all thought of unnatural causes here. There be none.

SUSANNA: Aye, sir. He bid me tell you. *She turns to go.*

ABIGAIL: Speak nothin' of it in the village, Susanna.

PARRIS: Go directly home and speak nothing of unnatural causes.

SUSANNA: Aye, sir. I pray for her. *She goes out.*

ABIGAIL: Uncle, the rumor of witchcraft is all about; I think you'd best go down and deny it yourself. The parlor's packed with people, sir. I'll sit with her.

PARRIS, *pressed, turns on her:* And what shall I say to them? That my daughter and my niece I discovered dancing like heathen in the forest?

ABIGAIL: Uncle, we did dance; let you tell them I confessed it—and I'll be whipped if I must be. But they're speakin' of witchcraft. Betty's not witched.

PARRIS: Abigail, I cannot go before the congregation when I know you have not opened with me. What did you do with her in the forest?

ABIGAIL: We did dance, uncle, and when you leaped out of the bush so suddenly, Betty was frightened and then she fainted. And there's the whole of it.

PARRIS: Child. Sit you down.

ABIGAIL, *quavering, as she sits:* I would never hurt Betty. I love her dearly.

PARRIS: Now look you, child, your punishment will come in its time.

But if you trafficked with spirits in the forest I must know it now, for surely my enemies will, and they will ruin me with it.

ABIGAIL: But we never conjured spirits.

PARRIS: Then why can she not move herself since midnight? This child is desperate! *Abigail lowers her eyes.* It must come out—my enemies will bring it out. Let me know what you done there. Abigail, do you understand that I have many enemies?

ABIGAIL: I have heard of it, uncle.

PARRIS: There is a faction that is sworn to drive me from my pulpit. Do you understand that?

ABIGAIL: I think so, sir.

PARRIS: Now then, in the midst of such disruption, my own household is discovered to be the very center of some obscene practice. Abominations are done in the forest—

ABIGAIL: It were sport, uncle!

PARRIS, *pointing at* BETTY: You call this sport? *She lowers her eyes. He pleads:* Abigail, if you know something that may help the doctor, for God's sake tell it to me. *She is silent.* I saw Tituba waving her arms over the fire when I came on you. Why was she doing that? And I heard a screeching and gibberish coming from her mouth. She were swaying like a dumb beast over that fire!

ABIGAIL: She always sings her Barbados songs, and we dance.

PARRIS: I cannot blink what I saw, Abigail, for my enemies will not blink it. I saw a dress lying on the grass.

ABIGAIL, *innocently:* A dress?

PARRIS—*it is very hard to say:* Aye, a dress. And I thought I saw—someone naked running through the trees!

ABIGAIL, *in terror:* No one was naked! You mistake yourself, uncle!

PARRIS, *with anger:* I saw it! *He moves from her. Then, resolved:* Now tell me true, Abigail. And I pray you feel the weight of truth upon you, for now my ministry's at stake, my ministry and perhaps your cousin's life. Whatever abomination you have done, give me all of it now, for I dare not be taken unaware when I go before them down there.

ABIGAIL: There is nothin' more. I swear it, uncle.

PARRIS, *studies her, then nods, half convinced:* Abigail, I have fought here three long years to bend these stiff-necked people to me, and now, just now when some good respect is rising for me in the parish, you compromise my very character. I have given you a home, child, I have put clothes upon your back—now give me upright answer. Your name in the

▼ **Critical Viewing**
Do you think that Abigail's expression in this image is genuine? **ASSESS**

Social Studies Connection

History Repeats Itself

The Crucible was written in the early 1950s when fear of communism swept America. The fears were understandable—eastern Europe and China had recently fallen to communism—but they were also exploited for political ends. In Congress, a Republican senator named Joseph McCarthy leapt into the limelight when he charged that the State Department had been infiltrated by more than two hundred communists.

Leading a Senate investigation, McCarthy repeatedly charged that those who opposed his hearings were themselves communists; then he investigated them. The parallels between events in Salem, as Miller depicts them, and ongoing events in Congress at the time Miller wrote the play are clear and deliberate.

Connect to the Literature

As you read, look for important parallels between the Senate investigation and the events in *The Crucible*.

town—it is entirely white, is it not?

ABIGAIL, *with an edge of resentment:* Why, I am sure it is, sir. There be no blush about my name.

PARRIS, *to the point:* Abigail, is there any other cause than you have told me, for your being discharged from Goody[6] Proctor's service? I have heard it said, and I tell you as I heard it, that she comes so rarely to the church this year for she will not sit so close to something soiled. What signified that remark?

ABIGAIL: She hates me, uncle, she must, for I would not be her slave. It's a bitter woman, a lying, cold, sniveling woman, and I will not work for such a woman!

PARRIS: She may be. And yet it has troubled me that you are now seven month out of their house, and in all this time no other family has ever called for your service.

ABIGAIL: They want slaves, not such as I. Let them send to Barbados for that. I will not black my face for any of them! *With ill-concealed resentment at him:* Do you begrudge my bed, uncle?

PARRIS: No—no.

ABIGAIL, *in a temper:* My name is good in the village! I will not have it said my name is soiled! Goody Proctor is a gossiping liar!

Enter MRS. ANN PUTNAM. *She is a twisted soul of forty-five, a death-ridden woman, haunted by dreams.*

PARRIS, *as soon as the door begins to open:* No—no, I cannot have anyone. *He sees her, and a certain deference springs into him, although his worry remains.* Why, Goody Putnam, come in.

MRS. PUTNAM, *full of breath, shiny-eyed:* It is a marvel. It is surely a stroke of hell upon you.

PARRIS: No, Goody Putnam, it is—

MRS. PUTNAM, *glancing at* BETTY: How high did she fly, how high?

PARRIS: No, no, she never flew—

MRS. PUTNAM, *very pleased with it:* Why, it's sure she did. Mr. Collins saw her goin' over Ingersoll's barn, and come down light as bird, he says!

PARRIS: Now, look you, Goody Putnam, she never—*Enter* THOMAS PUTNAM, *a well-to-do, hard-handed landowner, near fifty.* Oh, good morning, Mr. Putnam.

PUTNAM: It is a providence the thing is out now! It is a providence. *He goes directly to the bed.*

PARRIS: What's out, sir, what's—?

---

6. Goody title used for a married woman; short for Goodwife.

MRS. PUTNAM *goes to the bed.*

PUTNAM, *looking down at* BETTY: Why, *her* eyes is closed! Look you, Ann.

MRS. PUTNAM: Why, that's strange. *To* PARRIS: Ours is open.

PARRIS, *shocked:* Your Ruth is sick?

MRS. PUTNAM, *with vicious certainty:* I'd not call it sick; the Devil's touch is heavier than sick. It's death, y'know, it's death drivin' into them, forked and hoofed.

PARRIS: Oh, pray not! Why, how does Ruth ail?

MRS. PUTNAM: She ails as she must—she never waked this morning, but her eyes open and she walks, and hears naught, sees naught, and cannot eat. Her soul is taken, surely.

PARRIS *is struck.*

PUTNAM, *as though for further details:* They say you've sent for Reverend Hale of Beverly?

PARRIS, *with dwindling conviction now:* A precaution only. He has much experience in all demonic arts, and I—

MRS. PUTNAM: He has indeed; and found a witch in Beverly last year, and let you remember that.

PARRIS: Now, Goody Ann, they only thought that were a witch, and I am certain there be no element of witchcraft here.

PUTNAM: No witchcraft! Now look you, Mr. Parris—

PARRIS: Thomas, Thomas, I pray you, leap not to witchcraft. I know that you—you least of all, Thomas, would ever wish so disastrous a charge laid upon me. We cannot leap to witchcraft. They will howl me out of Salem for such corruption in my house.

A word about Thomas Putnam. He was a man with many grievances, at least one of which appears justified. Some time before, his wife's brother-in-law, James Bayley, had been turned down as minister at Salem. Bayley had all the qualifications, and a two-thirds vote into the bargain, but a faction stopped his acceptance, for reasons that are not clear.

Thomas Putnam was the eldest son of the richest man in the village. He had fought the Indians at Narragansett, and was deeply interested in parish affairs. He undoubtedly felt it poor payment that the village should so blatantly disregard his candidate for one of its more important offices, especially since he regarded himself as the intellectual superior of most of the people around him.

His vindictive nature was demonstrated long before the witchcraft began. Another former Salem minister, George Burroughs, had had to borrow money to pay for his wife's funeral, and, since the parish was remiss in his salary, he was soon bankrupt. Thomas and his brother John had Burroughs jailed for debts the man did not owe. The incident is important only in that Burroughs succeeded in becoming minister where Bayley, Thomas Putnam's brother-in-law, had been rejected; the motif of resentment is clear here. Thomas Putnam felt that his own name and the honor of his family had been smirched by

Plot

What conflict with the villagers is Parris desperately trying to avoid?

Comprehension

Why has Parris sent for Reverend Hale?

the village, and he meant to right matters however he could.

Another reason to believe him a deeply embittered man was his attempt to break his father's will, which left a disproportionate amount to a stepbrother. As with every other public cause in which he tried to force his way, he failed in this.

So it is not surprising to find that so many accusations against people are in the handwriting of Thomas Putnam, or that his name is so often found as a witness corroborating the supernatural testimony, or that his daughter led the crying-out at the most opportune junctures of the trials, especially when—But we'll speak of that when we come to it.

PUTNAM—*at the moment he is intent upon getting* PARRIS, *for whom he has only contempt, to move toward the abyss:*[7] Mr. Parris, I have taken your part in all contention here, and I would continue; but I cannot if you hold back in this. There are hurtful, vengeful spirits layin' hands on these children.

PARRIS: But, Thomas, you cannot—

PUTNAM: Ann! Tell Mr. Parris what you have done.

MRS. PUTNAM: Reverend Parris, I have laid seven babies unbaptized in the earth. Believe me, sir, you never saw more hearty babies born. And yet, each would wither in my arms the very night of their birth. I have spoke nothin', but my heart has clamored intimations. And now, this year, my Ruth, my only—I see her turning strange. A secret child she has become this year, and shrivels like a sucking mouth were pullin' on her life too. And so I thought to send her to your Tituba—

PARRIS: To Tituba! What may Tituba—?

MRS. PUTNAM: Tituba knows how to speak to the dead, Mr. Parris.

PARRIS: Goody Ann, it is a formidable sin to conjure up the dead!

MRS. PUTNAM: I take it on my soul, but who else may surely tell us what person murdered my babies?

PARRIS, *horrified:* Woman!

MRS. PUTNAM: They were murdered, Mr. Parris! And mark this proof! Mark it! Last night my Ruth were ever so close to their little spirits; I know it, sir. For how else is she struck dumb now except some power of darkness would stop her mouth? It is a marvelous sign, Mr. Parris!

PUTNAM: Don't you understand it, sir? There is a murdering witch among us, bound to keep herself in the dark. PARRIS *turns to* BETTY, *a frantic terror rising in him.* Let your enemies make of it

▼ **Critical Viewing**

Based on this image of Abigail, what role do you think she will play in the accusations of witchcraft in Salem? **SPECULATE**

---

7. **abyss** (ə bis´) *n.* deep crack in the Earth.

what they will, you cannot blink it more.

PARRIS, *to* ABIGAIL: Then you were conjuring spirits last night.

ABIGAIL, *whispering:* Not I, sir—Tituba and Ruth.

PARRIS *turns now, with new fear, and goes to* BETTY, *looks down at her, and then, gazing off:* Oh, Abigail, what proper payment for my charity! Now I am undone.

PUTNAM: You are not undone! Let you take hold here. Wait for no one to charge you—declare it yourself. You have discovered witchcraft—

PARRIS: In my house? In my house, Thomas? They will topple me with this! They will make of it a—

Enter MERCY LEWIS, *the Putnams' servant, a fat, sly, merciless girl of eighteen.*

MERCY: Your pardons. I only thought to see how Betty is.

PUTNAM: Why aren't you home? Who's with Ruth?

MERCY: Her grandma come. She's improved a little, I think—she give a powerful sneeze before.

MRS. PUTNAM: Ah, there's a sign of life!

MERCY: I'd fear no more, Goody Putnam. It were a grand sneeze; another like it will shake her wits together, I'm sure. *She goes to the bed to look.*

PARRIS: Will you leave me now, Thomas? I would pray a while alone.

ABIGAIL: Uncle, you've prayed since midnight. Why do you not go down and—

PARRIS: No—no. *To* PUTNAM: I have no answer for that crowd. I'll wait till Mr. Hale arrives. *To get* MRS. PUTNAM *to leave:* If you will, Goody Ann . . .

PUTNAM: Now look you, sir. Let you strike out against the Devil, and the village will bless you for it! Come down, speak to them—pray with them. They're thirsting for your word, Mister! Surely you'll pray with them.

PARRIS, *swayed:* I'll lead them in a psalm, but let you say nothing of witchcraft yet. I will not discuss it. The cause is yet unknown. I have had enough contention since I came; I want no more.

MRS. PUTNAM: Mercy, you go home to Ruth, d'y'hear?

MERCY: Aye, mum.

MRS. PUTNAM *goes out.*

PARRIS, *to* ABIGAIL: If she starts for the window, cry for me at once.

ABIGAIL: I will, uncle.

PARRIS, *to* PUTNAM: There is a terrible power in her arms today. *He goes out with* PUTNAM.

ABIGAIL, *with hushed trepidation:* How is Ruth sick?

MERCY: It's weirdish, I know not—she seems to walk like a dead one since last night.

> "There are hurtful, vengeful spirits layin' hands on these children."

Arthur Miller
Author's Insight
In *The Crucible*, Miller uses dialogue that sounds like the speech of New England Puritans. Commenting on the language of his plays, Miller wrote: "My own tendency has been to shift styles according to the nature of my subject. . . . I have done this in order to find speech that springs naturally out of the characters and their backgrounds. . . . "

Comprehension
What does Mrs. Putnam believe happened to her babies?

ABIGAIL, *turns at once and goes to* BETTY, *and now, with fear in her voice:* Betty? BETTY *doesn't move. She shakes her.* Now stop this! Betty! Sit up now!

BETTY *doesn't stir.* MERCY *comes over.*

MERCY: Have you tried beatin' her? I gave Ruth a good one and it waked her for a minute. Here, let me have her.

ABIGAIL, *holding* MERCY *back:* No, he'll be comin' up. Listen, now; if they be questioning us, tell them we danced—I told him as much already.

MERCY: Aye. And what more?

ABIGAIL: He knows Tituba conjured Ruth's sisters to come out of the grave.

MERCY: And what more?

ABIGAIL: He saw you naked.

MERCY: *clapping her hands together with a frightened laugh:* Oh, Jesus!

Enter MARY WARREN, *breathless. She is seventeen, a subservient, naive, lonely girl.*

MARY WARREN: What'll we do? The village is out! I just come from the farm; the whole country's talkin' witchcraft! They'll be callin' us witches, Abby!

▲ **Critical Viewing**

What emotion is conveyed in this image of Betty Parris's attempt to fly? Explain. **INTERPRET**

MERCY, *pointing and looking at* MARY WARREN: She means to tell, I know it.

MARY WARREN: Abby, we've got to tell. Witchery's a hangin' error, a hangin' like they done in Boston two year ago! We must tell the truth, Abby! You'll only be whipped for dancin', and the other things!

ABIGAIL: Oh, *we'll* be whipped!

MARY WARREN: I never done none of it, Abby. I only looked!

MERCY, *moving menacingly toward* MARY: Oh, you're a great one for lookin', aren't you, Mary Warren? What a grand peeping courage you have!

BETTY, *on the bed, whimpers.* ABIGAIL *turns to her at once.*

ABIGAIL: Betty? *She goes to* BETTY. Now, Betty, dear, wake up now. It's Abigail. *She sits* BETTY *up and furiously shakes her.* I'll beat you, Betty! BETTY *whimpers.* My, you seem improving.

I talked to your papa and I told him everything. So there's nothing to—

BETTY, *darts off the bed, frightened of* ABIGAIL, *and flattens herself against the wall:* I want my mama!

ABIGAIL, *with alarm, as she cautiously approaches* BETTY: What ails you, Betty? Your mama's dead and buried.

BETTY: I'll fly to Mama. Let me fly! *She raises her arms as though to fly, and streaks for the window, gets one leg out.*

ABIGAIL, *pulling her away from the window:* I told him everything; he knows now, he knows everything we—

BETTY: You drank blood, Abby! You didn't tell him that!

ABIGAIL: Betty, you never say that again! You will never—

BETTY: You did, you did! You drank a charm to kill John Proctor's wife! You drank a charm to kill Goody Proctor!

ABIGAIL, *smashes her across the face:* Shut it! Now shut it!

BETTY: *collapsing on the bed:* Mama, Mama! *She dissolves into sobs.*

ABIGAIL: Now look you. All of you. We danced. And Tituba conjured Ruth Putnam's dead sisters. And that is all. And mark this. Let either of you breathe a word, or the edge of a word, about the other things, and I will come to you in the black of some terrible night and I will bring a pointy reckoning that will shudder you. And you know I can do it; I saw Indians smash my dear parents' heads on the pillow next to mine, and I have seen some reddish work done at night, and I can make you wish you had never seen the sun go down! *She goes to* BETTY *and roughly sits her up.* Now, you—sit up and stop this!

But BETTY *collapses in her hands and lies inert on the bed.*

MARY WARREN, *with hysterical fright:* What's got her? ABIGAIL *stares in fright at* BETTY. Abby, she's going to die! It's a sin to conjure, and we—

ABIGAIL, *starting for* MARY: I say shut it, Mary Warren!

Enter JOHN PROCTOR. *On seeing him.* MARY WARREN *leaps in fright.*

Identifying Text Features

What do you learn about Abigail from this dialogue?

Comprehension

What does Mary Warren insist the girls do?

WORLD LITERATURE IN CONTEXT

POLITICAL DRAMA

MAXIM GORKY (1868–1936)

Writer Maxim Gorky grew up in Tsarist Russia at a time when millions of Russians lived in poverty. Gorky's parents died when he was young. When Maxim was ten, his grandfather turned him out of the house. Gorky spent his teenage years working at various jobs and tramping across Russia. During this time, he was often homeless but he began writing.

The Lower Depths, Gorky's most famous play, is set in a dark basement and its characters are modeled on the rootless, poverty-stricken people he met during his homeless years. He wrote it for the Moscow Art Theater, whose director, Constantin Stanislavski, was developing a new, realistic style of theater. When the play was first performed in 1902, it caused a sensation. Such an accurate portrayal of Russia's desperate underworld had never been seen on stage and it implicitly challenged the political system. The realistic drama that Gorky and Stanislavski pioneered gave birth to the style of acting that is used today. This style influenced theater around the world.

▲ Still from 1936 film version of *The Lower Depths.*

Connect to the Literature

Why would a realistic portrayal of poverty challenge a political system?

The Crucible, Act I **1137**

Proctor was a farmer in his middle thirties. He need not have been a partisan of any faction in the town, but there is evidence to suggest that he had a sharp and biting way with hypocrites. He was the kind of man—powerful of body, even-tempered, and not easily led—who cannot refuse support to partisans without drawing their deepest resentment. In Proctor's presence a fool felt his foolishness instantly—and a Proctor is always marked for calumny therefore.

But as we shall see, the steady manner he displays does not spring from an untroubled soul. He is a sinner, a sinner not only against the moral fashion of the time, but against his own vision of decent conduct. These people had no ritual for the washing away of sins. It is another trait we inherited from them, and it has helped to discipline us as well as to breed hypocrisy among us. Proctor, respected and even feared in Salem, has come to regard himself as a kind of fraud. But no hint of this has yet appeared on the surface, and as he enters from the crowded parlor below it is a man in his prime we see, with a quiet confidence and an unexpressed, hidden force. Mary Warren, his servant, can barely speak for embarrassment and fear.

MARY WARREN: Oh! I'm just going home, Mr. Proctor.

PROCTOR: Be you foolish, Mary Warren? Be you deaf? I forbid you leave the house, did I not? Why shall I pay you? I am looking for you more often than my cows!

MARY WARREN: I only come to see the great doings in the world.

Vocabulary

calumny (kal´ əm nē)
n. false accusation; slander

Dramatic Exposition

What important information does Miller reveal about Proctor through this dramatic exposition?

▼ Critical Viewing

Based on this movie still, do you think Proctor is expressing anger, fear, or another emotion?
INTERPRET

PROCTOR: I'll show you a great doin' on your arse one of these days. Now get you home; my wife is waitin' with your work! *Trying to retain a shred of dignity, she goes slowly out.*

MERCY LEWIS, *both afraid of him and strangely titillated:* I'd best be off. I have my Ruth to watch. Good morning, Mr. Proctor.

MERCY *sidles out. Since* PROCTOR's *entrance,* ABIGAIL *has stood as though on tiptoe, absorbing his presence, wide-eyed. He glances at her, then goes to* BETTY *on the bed.*

ABIGAIL: Gah! I'd almost forgot how strong you are, John Proctor!

PROCTOR, *looking at* ABIGAIL *now, the faintest suggestion of a knowing smile on his face:* What's this mischief here?

ABIGAIL, *with a nervous laugh:* Oh, she's only gone silly somehow.

PROCTOR: The road past my house is a pilgrimage to Salem all morning. The town's mumbling witchcraft.

ABIGAIL: Oh, posh! *Winningly she comes a little closer, with a confidential, wicked air.* We were dancin' in the woods last night, and my uncle leaped in on us. She took fright, is all.

PROCTOR, *his smile widening:* Ah, you're wicked yet, aren't y'! *A trill of expectant laughter escapes her, and she dares come closer, feverishly looking into his eyes.* You'll be clapped in the stocks before you're twenty.

He takes a step to go, and she springs into his path.

ABIGAIL: Give me a word, John. A soft word. *Her concentrated desire destroys his smile.*

PROCTOR: No, no, Abby. That's done with.

ABIGAIL, *tauntingly:* You come five mile to see a silly girl fly? I know you better.

PROCTOR, *setting her firmly out of his path:* I come to see what mischief your uncle's brewin' now. *With final emphasis:* Put it out of mind, Abby.

ABIGAIL, *grasping his hand before he can release her:* John—I am waitin' for you every night.

PROCTOR: Abby, I never give you hope to wait for me.

ABIGAIL, *now beginning to anger—she can't believe it:* I have something better than hope, I think!

PROCTOR: Abby, you'll put it out of mind. I'll not be comin' for you more.

ABIGAIL: You're surely sportin' with me.

PROCTOR: You know me better.

ABIGAIL: I know how you clutched my back behind your house and sweated like a stallion whenever I come near! Or did I dream that? It's she put me out, you cannot pretend it were you. I saw your face when she put me out, and you loved me then and you do now!

PROCTOR: Abby, that's a wild thing to say—

ABIGAIL: A wild thing may say wild things. But not so wild, I think. I have seen you since she put me out; I have seen you nights.

PROCTOR: I have hardly stepped off my farm this seven month.

Identifying Text Features

What important information about Abigail's behavior is conveyed through stage directions in this scene?

Plot

What conflict exists between Abigail and Proctor?

Comprehension

What does Abigail feel for Proctor?

ABIGAIL: I have a sense for heat, John, and yours has drawn me to my window, and I have seen you looking up, burning in your loneliness. Do you tell me you've never looked up at my window?

PROCTOR: I may have looked up.

ABIGAIL, *now softening:* And you must. You are no wintry man. I know you, John. I *know* you. *She is weeping.* I cannot sleep for dreamin'; I cannot dream but I wake and walk about the house as though I'd find you comin' through some door. *She clutches him desperately.*

PROCTOR, *gently pressing her from him, with great sympathy but firmly:* Child—

ABIGAIL, *with a flash of anger:* How do you call me child!

PROCTOR: Abby, I may think of you softly from time to time. But I will cut off my hand before I'll ever reach for you again. Wipe it out of mind. We never touched, Abby.

ABIGAIL: Aye, but we did.

PROCTOR: Aye, but we did not.

ABIGAIL, *with a bitter anger:* Oh, I marvel how such a strong man may let such a sickly wife be—

PROCTOR, *angered—at himself as well:* You'll speak nothin' of Elizabeth!

ABIGAIL: She is blackening my name in the village! She is telling lies about me! She is a cold, sniveling woman, and you bend to her! Let her turn you like a—

PROCTOR, *shaking her:* Do you look for whippin'?

A psalm is heard being sung below.

ABIGAIL, *in tears:* I look for John Proctor that took me from my sleep and put knowledge in my heart! I never knew what pretense Salem was, I never knew the lying lessons I was taught by all these Christian women and their covenanted men! And now you bid me tear the light out of my eyes? I will not, I cannot! You loved me, John Proctor, and whatever sin it is, you love me yet! *He turns abruptly to go out.* *She rushes to him.* John, pity me, pity me!

The words "going up to Jesus" are heard in the psalm, and BETTY *claps her ears suddenly and whines loudly.*

ABIGAIL: Betty? *She hurries to* BETTY, *who is now sitting up and screaming.* PROCTOR *goes to* BETTY *as* ABIGAIL *is trying to pull her hands down, calling "Betty!"*

PROCTOR, *growing unnerved:* What's she doing? Girl, what ails you? Stop that wailing!

The singing has stopped in the midst of this, and now PARRIS *rushes in.*

PARRIS: What happened? What are you doing to her? Betty! *He rushes to the bed, crying, "Betty, Betty!"* MRS. PUTNAM *enters, feverish with curiosity, and with her* THOMAS PUTNAM *and* MERCY LEWIS. PARRIS, *at the bed, keeps lightly slapping* BETTY'S *face, while she moans and tries to get up.*

ABIGAIL: She heard you singin' and suddenly she's up and screamin'.

Spiral Review
Context Clues
Use textual clues to define the word *sniveling* as it is used here.

MRS. PUTNAM: The psalm! The psalm! She cannot bear to hear the Lord's name!

PARRIS: No, God forbid. Mercy, run to the doctor! Tell him what's happened here! MERCY LEWIS *rushes out.*

MRS. PUTNAM: Mark it for a sign, mark it!

REBECCA NURSE, *seventy-two, enters. She is white-haired, leaning upon her walking-stick.*

PUTNAM, *pointing at the whimpering* BETTY: That is a notorious sign of witchcraft afoot, Goody Nurse, a prodigious sign!

MRS. PUTNAM: My mother told me that! When they cannot bear to hear the name of—

PARRIS, *trembling:* Rebecca, Rebecca, go to her, we're lost. She suddenly cannot bear to hear the Lord's—

GILES COREY, *eighty-three, enters. He is knotted with muscle, canny, inquisitive, and still powerful.*

REBECCA: There is hard sickness here, Giles Corey, so please to keep the quiet.

GILES: I've not said a word. No one here can testify I've said a word. Is she going to fly again?
I hear she flies.

PUTNAM: Man, be quiet now!

Everything is quiet. REBECCA *walks across the room to the bed. Gentleness exudes from her.* BETTY *is quietly whimpering, eyes shut.* REBECCA *simply stands over the child, who gradually quiets.*

And while they are so absorbed, we may put a word in for Rebecca. Rebecca was the wife of Francis Nurse, who, from all accounts, was one of those men for whom both sides of the argument had to have respect. He was called upon to arbitrate disputes as though he were an unofficial judge, and Rebecca also enjoyed the high opinion most people had for him. By the time of the delusion, they had three hundred acres, and their children were settled in separate homesteads within the same estate. However, Francis had originally rented the land, and one theory has it that, as he gradually paid for it and raised his social status, there were those who resented his rise.

Another suggestion to explain the systematic campaign against Rebecca, and inferentially against Francis, is the land war he fought with his neighbors, one of whom was a Putnam. This squabble grew to the proportions of a battle in the woods between partisans of both sides, and it is said to have lasted for two days. As for Rebecca herself, the general opinion of her character was so high that to explain how anyone dared cry her out for a witch—and more, how adults could bring themselves to lay hands on her—we must look to the fields and boundaries of that time.

As we have seen, Thomas Putnam's man for the Salem ministry was Bayley. The Nurse clan had been in the faction that prevented

---

Identifying Text Features

How does the combination of stage directions and dialogue reveal Mrs. Putnam's eagerness to see signs of witchcraft?

"I've not said a word. No one here can testify I've said a word."

Comprehension

What is Rebecca Nurse's effect on Betty?

Bayley's taking office. In addition, certain families allied to the Nurses by blood or friendship, and whose farms were contiguous with the Nurse farm or close to it, combined to break away from the Salem town authority and set up Topsfield, a new and independent entity whose existence was resented by old Salemites.

That the guiding hand behind the outcry was Putnam's is indicated by the fact that, as soon as it began, this Topsfield-Nurse faction absented themselves from church in protest and disbelief. It was Edward and Jonathan Putnam who signed the first complaint against Rebecca; and Thomas Putnam's little daughter was the one who fell into a fit at the hearing and pointed to Rebecca as her attacker. To top it all, Mrs. Putnam—who is now staring at the bewitched child on the bed—soon accused Rebecca's spirit of " tempting her to iniquity," a charge that had more truth in it than Mrs. Putnam could know.

MRS. PUTNAM, *astonished:* What have you done?

REBECCA, *in thought, now leaves the bedside and sits.*

PARRIS, *wondrous and relieved:* What do you make of it, Rebecca?

PUTNAM, *eagerly:* Goody Nurse, will you go to my Ruth and see if you can wake her?

REBECCA, *sitting:* I think she'll wake in time. Pray calm yourselves. I have eleven children, and I am twenty-six times a grandma, and I have seen them all through their silly seasons, and when it come on them they will run the Devil bowlegged keeping up with their mischief. I think she'll wake when she tires of it. A child's spirit is like a child, you can never catch it by running after it; you must stand still, and, for love, it will soon itself come back.

PROCTOR: Aye, that's the truth of it, Rebecca.

MRS. PUTNAM: This is no silly season, Rebecca. My Ruth is bewildered, Rebecca; she cannot eat.

REBECCA: Perhaps she is not hungered yet. *To* PARRIS: I hope you are not decided to go in search of loose spirits, Mr. Parris. I've heard promise of that outside.

PARRIS: A wide opinion's running in the parish that the Devil may be among us, and I would satisfy them that they are wrong.

PROCTOR: Then let you come out and call them wrong. Did you consult the wardens before you called this minister to look for devils?

PARRIS: He is not coming to look for devils!

PROCTOR: Then what's he coming for?

PUTNAM: There be children dyin' in the village, Mister!

PROCTOR: I seen none dyin'. This society will not be a bag to swing around your head, Mr. Putnam. *To* PARRIS: Did you call a meeting before you—?

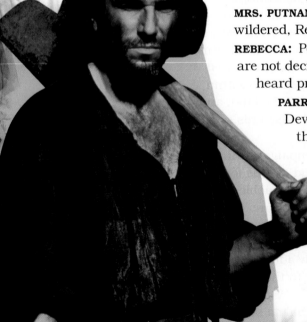

PUTNAM: I am sick of meetings; cannot the man turn his head without he have a meeting?

PROCTOR: He may turn his head, but not to Hell!

REBECCA: Pray, John, be calm. *Pause. He defers to her.* Mr. Parris, I think you'd best send Reverend Hale back as soon as he come. This will set us all to arguin' again in the society, and we thought to have peace this year. I think we ought rely on the doctor now, and good prayer.

MRS. PUTNAM: Rebecca, the doctor's baffled!

REBECCA: If so he is, then let us go to God for the cause of it. There is prodigious danger in the seeking of loose spirits. I fear it, I fear it. Let us rather blame ourselves and—

PUTNAM: How may we blame ourselves? I am one of nine sons; the Putnam seed have peopled this province. And yet I have but one child left of eight—and now she shrivels!

REBECCA: I cannot fathom that.

MRS. PUTNAM, *with a growing edge of sarcasm:* But I must! You think it God's work you should never lose a child, nor grandchild either, and I bury all but one? There are wheels within wheels in this village, and fires within fires!

PUTNAM, *to* PARRIS: When Reverend Hale comes, you will proceed to look for signs of witchcraft here.

PROCTOR, *to* PUTNAM: You cannot command Mr. Parris. We vote by name in this society, not by acreage.

PUTNAM: I never heard you worried so on this society, Mr. Proctor. I do not think I saw you at Sabbath meeting since snow flew.

PROCTOR: I have trouble enough without I come five mile to hear him preach only hellfire and bloody damnation. Take it to heart, Mr. Parris. There are many others who stay away from church these days because you hardly ever mention God any more.

PARRIS, *now aroused:* Why, that's a drastic charge!

REBECCA: It's somewhat true; there are many that quail to bring their children—

PARRIS: I do not preach for children, Rebecca. It is not the children who are unmindful of their obligations toward this ministry.

REBECCA: Are there really those unmindful?

PARRIS: I should say the better half of Salem village—

PUTNAM: And more than that!

PARRIS: Where is my wood? My contract provides I be supplied with all my firewood. I am waiting since November for a stick, and even in November I had to show my frostbitten hands like some London beggar!

GILES: You are allowed six pound a year to buy your wood, Mr. Parris.

PARRIS: I regard that six pound as part of my salary. I am paid little enough without I spend six pound on firewood.

Identifying Text Features

What punctuation marks show that Parris interrupts Rebecca?

Comprehension

What hardships does Parris complain of?

PROCTOR: Sixty, plus six for firewood—

PARRIS: The salary is sixty-six pound, Mr. Proctor! I am not some preaching farmer with a book under my arm; I am a graduate of Harvard College.

GILES: Aye, and well instructed in arithmetic!

PARRIS: Mr. Corey, you will look far for a man of my kind at sixty pound a year! I am not used to this poverty; I left a thrifty business in the Barbados to serve the Lord. I do not fathom it, why am I persecuted here? I cannot offer one proposition but there be a howling riot of argument. I have often wondered if the Devil be in it somewhere; I cannot understand you people otherwise.

PROCTOR: Mr. Parris, you are the first minister ever did demand the deed to this house—

PARRIS: Man! Don't a minister deserve a house to live in?

PROCTOR: To live in, yes. But to ask ownership is like you shall own the meeting house itself; the last meeting I were at you spoke so long on deeds and mortgages I thought it were an auction.

PARRIS: I want a mark of confidence, is all! I am your third preacher in seven years. I do not wish to be put out like the cat whenever some majority feels the whim. You people seem not to comprehend that a minister is the Lord's man in the parish; a minister is not to be so lightly crossed and contradicted—

PUTNAM: Aye!

PARRIS: There is either obedience or the church will burn like Hell is burning!

PROCTOR: Can you speak one minute without we land in Hell again? I am sick of Hell!

PARRIS: It is not for you to say what is good for you to hear!

PROCTOR: I may speak my heart, I think!

PARRIS, *in a fury:* What, are we Quakers?[8] We are not Quakers here yet, Mr. Proctor. And you may tell that to your followers!

PROCTOR: My followers!

PARRIS—*now he's out with it:* There is a party in this church. I am not blind; there is a faction and a party.

PROCTOR: Against you?

PUTNAM: Against him and all authority!

PROCTOR: Why, then I must find it and join it.

There is shock among the others.

REBECCA: He does not mean that.

PUTNAM: He confessed it now!

PROCTOR: I mean it solemnly, Rebecca; I like not the smell of this "authority."

Plot

How does Parris intensify his conflict with Proctor?

---

8. Quakers members of the Society of Friends, a Christian religious sect that was founded in the mid-17th century and has no formal creed, rites, or priesthood. Unlike the Quakers, the Puritans had a rigid code of conduct and were expected to heed the words of their ministers.

REBECCA: No, you cannot break charity with your minister. You are another kind, John. Clasp his hand, make your peace.

PROCTOR: I have a crop to sow and lumber to drag home. *He goes angrily to the door and turns to* COREY *with a smile.* What say you, Giles, let's find the party. He says there's a party.

GILES: I've changed my opinion of this man, John. Mr. Parris, I beg your pardon. I never thought you had so much iron in you.

PARRIS, *surprised:* Why, thank you, Giles!

GILES: It suggests to the mind what the trouble be among us all these years. *To all:* Think on it. Wherefore is everybody suing everybody else? Think on it now, it's a deep thing, and dark as a pit. I have been six time in court this year—

PROCTOR, *familiarly, with warmth, although he knows he is approaching the edge of Giles' tolerance with this:* Is it the Devil's fault that a man cannot say you good morning without you clap him for defamation? You're old, Giles, and you're not hearin' so well as you did.

GILES—*he cannot be crossed:* John Proctor, I have only last month collected four pound damages for you publicly sayin' I burned the roof off your house, and I—

PROCTOR, *laughing:* I never said no such thing, but I've paid you for it, so I hope I can call you deaf without charge. Now come along, Giles, and help me drag my lumber home.

PUTNAM: A moment, Mr. Proctor. What lumber is that you're draggin', if I may ask you?

PROCTOR: My lumber. From out my forest by the riverside.

PUTNAM: Why, we are surely gone wild this year. What anarchy is this? That tract is in my bounds, it's in my bounds, Mr. Proctor.

PROCTOR: In your bounds! *Indicating* REBECCA: I bought that tract from Goody Nurse's husband five months ago.

PUTNAM: He had no right to sell it. It stands clear in my grandfather's will that all the land between the river and—

PROCTOR: Your grandfather had a habit of willing land that never belonged to him, if I may say it plain.

GILES: That's God's truth; he nearly willed away my north pasture but he knew I'd break his fingers before he'd set his name to it. Let's get your lumber home, John. I feel a sudden will to work coming on.

PUTNAM: You load one oak of mine and you'll fight to drag it home!

GILES: Aye, and we'll win too, Putnam—this fool and I. Come on! *He turns to* PROCTOR *and starts out.*

LITERATURE IN CONTEXT

History Connection

The Inquisition

Miller alludes to the Inquisition, a "court of justice" established by the Catholic Church in the thirteenth century, but he does not describe it. The Inquisition bore some resemblance to the Salem witch hunts of the 1690s and to the Red Scare during the 1950s. In each case, a panel of judges decided allegations of heresy or treason. The Salem judges sentenced some to death, as had the Catholic judges of the Middle Ages. No one died in the 1950s as a result of Senator McCarthy's accusations, but many suffered damage to their personal and professional reputations.

Connect to the Literature

What else might the Salem trials have in common with the Inquisition?

Comprehension

What is a source of disagreement between Proctor and Putnam?

PUTNAM: I'll have my men on you, Corey! I'll clap a writ on you!

Enter REVEREND JOHN HALE *of Beverly.*

Dramatic Exposition

What important information does Miller provide about his view of the world?

Mr. Hale is nearing forty, a tight-skinned, eager-eyed intellectual. This is a beloved errand for him; on being called here to ascertain witchcraft he felt the pride of the specialist whose unique knowledge has at last been publicly called for. Like almost all men of learning, he spent a good deal of time pondering the invisible world, especially since he had himself encountered a witch in his parish not long before. That woman, however, turned into a mere pest under his searching scrutiny, and the child she had allegedly been afflicting recovered her normal behavior after Hale had given her his kindness and a few days of rest in his own house. However, that experience never raised a doubt in his mind as to the reality of the underworld or the existence of Lucifer's many-faced lieutenants. And his belief is not to his discredit. Better minds than Hale's were—and still are—convinced that there is a society of spirits beyond our ken. One cannot help noting that one of his lines has never yet raised a laugh in any audience that has seen this play; it is his assurance that "We cannot look to superstition in this. The Devil is precise." Evidently we are not quite certain even now whether diabolism is holy and not to be scoffed at. And it is no accident that we should be so bemused.

Like Reverend Hale and the others on this stage, we conceive the Devil as a necessary part of a respectable view of cosmology. Ours is a divided empire in which certain ideas and emotions and actions are of God, and their opposites are of Lucifer. It is as impossible for most men to conceive of a morality without sin as of an earth without "sky." Since 1692 a great but superficial change has wiped out God's beard and the Devil's horns, but the world is still gripped between two diametrically opposed absolutes. The concept of unity, in which positive and negative are attributes of the same force, in which good and evil are relative, ever-changing, and always joined to the same phenomenon—such a concept is still reserved to the physical sciences and to the few who have grasped the history of ideas. When it is recalled that until the Christian era the underworld was never regarded as a hostile area, that all gods were useful and essentially friendly to man despite occasional lapses; when we see the steady and methodical inculcation into humanity of the idea of man's worthlessness—until redeemed—the necessity of the Devil may become evident as a weapon, a weapon designed and used time and time again in every age to whip men into a surrender to a particular church or church-state.

Vocabulary

inculcation (in´ kul kā shən) *n.* teaching by repetition and urging

Our difficulty in believing the—for want of a better word—political inspiration of the Devil is due in great part to the fact that he is called up and damned not only by our social antagonists but by our own side, whatever it may be. The Catholic Church, through its Inquisition, is famous for cultivating Lucifer as the arch-fiend, but the Church's enemies relied no less upon the Old Boy to keep the human mind enthralled. Luther[9] was himself accused of alliance with Hell, and he in turn accused his enemies. To complicate matters further, he believed that he had had contact with the Devil and had argued theology with him. I am not surprised at this, for at my own university a professor of history—a Lutheran,[10] by the way—used to assemble his graduate students, draw the shades, and commune in the classroom with Erasmus.[11] He was never, to my knowledge, officially scoffed at for this, the reason being that the university officials, like most of us, are the children of a history which still sucks at the Devil's teats. At this writing, only England has held back before the temptations of contemporary diabolism. In the countries of the Communist ideology, all resistance of any import is linked to the totally malign capitalist succubi,[12] and in America any man who is not reactionary in his views is open to the charge of alliance with the Red hell. Political opposition, thereby, is given an inhumane overlay which then justifies the abrogation[13] of all normally applied customs of civilized intercourse. A political policy is equated with moral right, and opposition to it with diabolical malevolence. Once such an equation is effectively made, society becomes a congerie[14] of plots and counterplots, and the main role of government changes from that of the arbiter to that of the scourge of God.

The results of this process are no different now from what they ever were, except sometimes in the degree of cruelty inflicted, and not always even in that department. Normally, the actions and deeds of a man were all that society felt comfortable in judging. The secret intent of an action was left to the ministers, priests, and rabbis to deal with. When diabolism rises, however, actions are the least important manifests of the true nature of a man. The Devil, as Reverend Hale said, is a wily one, and, until an hour before he fell, even God thought him beautiful in Heaven.

The analogy, however, seems to falter when one considers that, while there were no witches then, there are Communists and capitalists now, and in each camp there is certain proof that spies of each side are at work undermining the other. But this is a snobbish

---

9. **Luther** Martin Luther (1483–1546), German theologian who led the Protestant Reformation.
10. **Lutheran** member of the Protestant denomination founded by Martin Luther.
11. **Erasmus** Erasmus Desiderius (1466?–1536), Dutch humanist, scholar, and theologian.
12. **succubi** (suk´ yoo bī) female demons thought to lie on sleeping men.
13. **abrogation** (ab´ rō gā´ shən) abolishment.
14. **congerie** (kän´ jə rē´) heap; pile.

Dramatic Exposition
How is Miller's view of the political uses of morality reflected in the play?

Comprehension
According to Miller, on what point does the analogy of the Salem witch hunts to the modern day seem to falter?

propitiation (prə pish′ ē
ā′ shən) *n.* action designed
to soothe

objection and not at all warranted by the facts. I have no doubt that
people *were* communing with, and even worshiping, the Devil in Salem,
and if the whole truth could be known in this case, as it is in others,
we should discover a regular and conventionalized propitiation of the
dark spirit. One certain evidence of this is the confession of Tituba, the
slave of Reverend Parris, and another is the behavior of the children
who were known to have indulged in sorceries with her.

There are accounts of similar *klatches*[15] in Europe, where the
daughters of the towns would assemble at night and, sometimes with
fetishes,[16] sometimes with a selected young man, give themselves to
love, with some bastardly results. The Church, sharp-eyed as it must
be when gods long dead are brought to life, condemned these orgies
as witchcraft and interpreted them, rightly, as a resurgence of the
Dionysiac[17] forces it had crushed long before. Sex, sin, and the Devil
were early linked, and so they continued to be in Salem, and are today.
From all accounts there are no more puritanical mores in the world
than those enforced by the Communists in Russia, where women's
fashions, for instance, are as prudent and all-covering as any American
Baptist would desire. The divorce laws lay a tremendous responsibility
on the father for the care of his children. Even the laxity of divorce regu-
lations in the early years of the revolution was undoubtedly a revulsion
from the nineteenth-century Victorian[18] immobility of marriage and the
consequent hypocrisy that developed from it. If for no other reasons, a
state so powerful, so jealous of the uniformity of its citizens, cannot long
tolerate the atomization of the family. And yet, in American eyes at least,
there remains the conviction that the Russian attitude toward women is
lascivious. It is the Devil working again, just as he is working within the
Slav who is shocked at the very idea of a woman's disrobing herself in a
burlesque show. Our opposites are always robed in sexual sin, and it is
from this unconscious conviction that demonology gains both its attractive sensuality and its capacity to infuriate and frighten.

Coming into Salem now, Reverend Hale conceives of himself much
as a young doctor on his first call. His painfully acquired armory of
symptoms, catchwords, and diagnostic procedures are now to be put
to use at last. The road from Beverly is unusually busy this morning,
and he has passed a hundred rumors that make him smile at the ignorance of the yeomanry in this most precise science. He feels himself
allied with the best minds of Europe—kings, philosophers, scientists,
and ecclesiasts of all churches. His goal is light, goodness and its preservation, and he knows the exaltation of the blessed whose intelligence,

---

15. klatches (klächz) informal gatherings.
16. fetishes (fet′ ish iz) objects believed to have magical power.
17. Dionysiac (dī′ ə nis′ ē ak′) characteristic of Dionysus, Greek god of wine and revelry; thus,
wild, frenzied, sensuous.
18. Victorian characteristic of the time when Victoria was queen of England (1837–1901), an
era associated with respectability, prudery, and hypocrisy.

sharpened by minute examinations of enormous tracts, is finally called upon to face what may be a bloody fight with the Fiend himself.

He appears loaded down with half a dozen heavy books.

HALE: Pray you, someone take these!

PARRIS, *delighted:* Mr. Hale! Oh! it's good to see you again! *Taking some books:* My, they're heavy!

HALE, *setting down his books:* They must be; they are weighted with authority.

PARRIS, *a little scared:* Well, you do come prepared!

HALE: We shall need hard study if it comes to tracking down the Old Boy. *Noticing* REBECCA: You cannot be Rebecca Nurse?

REBECCA: I am, sir. Do you know me?

HALE: It's strange how I knew you, but I suppose you look as such a good soul should. We have all heard of your great charities in Beverly.

PARRIS: Do you know this gentleman? Mr. Thomas Putnam. And his good wife Ann.

HALE: Putnam! I had not expected such distinguished company, sir.

PUTNAM, *pleased:* It does not seem to help us today, Mr. Hale. We look to you to come to our house and save our child.

HALE: Your child ails too?

MRS. PUTNAM: Her soul, her soul seems flown away. She sleeps and yet she walks . . .

PUTNAM: She cannot eat.

HALE: Cannot eat! *Thinks on it. Then, to* PROCTOR *and* GILES COREY: Do you men have afflicted children?

PARRIS: No, no, these are farmers. John Proctor—

GILES COREY: He don't believe in witches.

PROCTOR, *to* HALE: I never spoke on witches one way or the other. Will you come, Giles?

GILES: No—no, John, I think not. I have some few queer questions of my own to ask this fellow.

PROCTOR: I've heard you to be a sensible man, Mr. Hale. I hope you'll leave some of it in Salem.

PROCTOR *goes.* HALE *stands embarrassed for an instant.*

PARRIS, *quickly:* Will you look at my daughter, sir? *Leads* HALE *to the bed.* She has tried to leap out the window; we discovered her this morning on the highroad, waving her arms as though she'd fly.

HALE, *narrowing his eyes:* Tries to fly.

PUTNAM: She cannot bear to hear the Lord's name, Mr. Hale; that's a sure sign of witchcraft afloat.

HALE, *holding up his hands:* No, no. Now let me instruct you. We cannot look to superstition in this. The Devil is precise; the marks of his presence are definite as stone, and I must tell you all that I shall not proceed unless you are prepared to believe me if I should find no

Identifying Text Features

What is your impression of Hale based on the dramatic exposition, stage directions, and dialogue?

Comprehension

With what does Hale come prepared?

> "I cannot tell. If she is truly in the Devil's grip we may have to rip and tear to get her free."

Plot

How does Mrs. Putnam's confession add to the rising action?

bruise of hell upon her.

PARRIS: It is agreed, sir—it is agreed—we will abide by your judgment.

HALE: Good then. *He goes to the bed, looks down at* BETTY. *To* PARRIS: Now, sir, what were your first warning of this strangeness?

PARRIS: Why, sir—I discovered her—*indicating* ABIGAIL—and my niece and ten or twelve of the other girls, dancing in the forest last night.

HALE, *surprised:* You permit dancing?

PARRIS: No, no, it were secret—

MRS. PUTNAM, *unable to wait:* Mr. Parris's slave has knowledge of conjurin', sir.

PARRIS, *to* MRS. PUTNAM: We cannot be sure of that, Goody Ann—

MRS. PUTNAM, *frightened, very softly:* I know it, sir. I sent my child—she should learn from Tituba who murdered her sisters.

REBECCA, *horrified:* Goody Ann! You sent a child to conjure up the dead?

MRS. PUTNAM: Let God blame me, not you, not you, Rebecca! I'll not have you judging me any more! *To* HALE: Is it a natural work to lose seven children before they live a day?

PARRIS: Sssh!

REBECCA, *with great pain, turns her face away. There is a pause.*

HALE: Seven dead in childbirth.

MRS. PUTNAM, *softly:* Aye. *Her voice breaks; she looks up at him. Silence.* HALE *is impressed.* PARRIS *looks to him. He goes to his books, opens one, turns pages, then reads. All wait, avidly.*

PARRIS, *hushed:* What book is that?

MRS. PUTNAM: What's there, sir?

HALE, *with a tasty love of intellectual pursuit:* Here is all the invisible world, caught, defined, and calculated. In these books the Devil stands stripped of all his brute disguises. Here are all your familiar spirits—your incubi[19] and succubi, your witches that go by land, by air, and by sea; your wizards of the night and of the day. Have no fear now—we shall find him out if he has come among us, and I mean to crush him utterly if he has shown his face! *He starts for the bed.*

REBECCA: Will it hurt the child, sir?

HALE: I cannot tell. If she is truly in the Devil's grip we may have to rip and tear to get her free.

REBECCA: I think I'll go, then. I am too old for this. *She rises.*

PARRIS, *striving for conviction:* Why, Rebecca, we may open up the boil of all our troubles today!

REBECCA: Let us hope for that. I go to God for you, sir.

PARRIS, *with trepidation—and resentment:* I hope you do not mean we go to Satan here! *Slight pause.*

REBECCA: I wish I knew. *She goes out; they feel resentful of her note of*

---

19. incubi (in´ kyoo bī) spirits or demons thought to lie on sleeping women.

moral superiority.

PUTNAM, *abruptly:* Come, Mr. Hale, let's get on. Sit you here.

GILES: Mr. Hale, I have always wanted to ask a learned man—what signifies the readin' of strange books?

HALE: What books?

GILES: I cannot tell; she hides them.

HALE: Who does this?

GILES: Martha, my wife. I have waked at night many a time and found her in a corner, readin' of a book. Now what do you make of that?

HALE: Why, that's not necessarily—

GILES: It discomfits me! Last night—mark this—I tried and tried and could not say my prayers. And then she close her book and walks out of the house, and suddenly—mark this—I could pray again!

Old Giles must be spoken for, if only because his fate was to be so remarkable and so different from that of all the others. He was in his early eighties at this time, and was the most comical hero in the history. No man has ever been blamed for so much. If a cow was missed, the first thought was to look for her around Corey's house; a fire blazing up at night brought suspicion of arson to his door. He didn't give a hoot for public opinion, and only in his last years—after he had married Martha—did he bother much with the church. That she stopped his prayer is very probable, but he forgot to say that he'd only recently learned any prayers and it didn't take much to make him stumble over them. He was a crank and a nuisance, but withal a deeply innocent and brave man. In court, once, he was asked if it were true that he had been frightened by the strange behavior of a hog and had then said he knew it to be the Devil in an animal's shape. "What frighted you?" he was asked. He forgot everything but the word "frighted," and instantly replied, "I do not know that I ever spoke that word in my life."

HALE: Ah! The stoppage of prayer—that is strange. I'll speak further on that with you.

GILES: I'm not sayin' she's touched the Devil, now, but I'd admire to know what books she reads and why she hides them. She'll not answer me, y' see.

HALE: Aye, we'll discuss it. *To all:* Now mark me, if the Devil is in her you will witness some frightful wonders in this room, so please to keep your wits about you. Mr. Putnam, stand close in case she flies. Now, Betty, dear, will you sit up? PUTNAM *comes in closer, ready-handed.* HALE *sits* BETTY *up, but she hangs limp in his hands.* Hmmm. *He observes her carefully. The others watch breathlessly.* Can you hear me? I am John Hale, minister of Beverly. I have come to help you, dear. Do you remember my two little girls in Beverly? *She does not stir in his hands.*

PARRIS, *in fright:* How can it be the Devil? Why would he choose my house to strike? We have all manner of licentious people in the village!

Dramatic Exposition

Which details given in this background information explain Giles Corey's remarks about his wife, Martha?

Comprehension

What does Giles believe has made him unable to pray?

HALE: What victory would the Devil have to win a soul already bad? It is the best the Devil wants, and who is better than the minister?

GILES: That's deep, Mr. Parris, deep, deep!

PARRIS, *with resolution now:* Betty! Answer Mr. Hale! Betty!

HALE: Does someone afflict you, child? It need not be a woman, mind you, or a man. Perhaps some bird invisible to others comes to you—perhaps a pig, a mouse, or any beast at all. Is there some figure bids you fly? *The child remains limp in his hands. In silence he lays her back on the pillow. Now, holding out his hands toward her, he intones:* In nomine Domini Sabaoth sui filiique ite ad infernos.[20] *She does not stir. He turns to* ABIGAIL, *his eyes narrowing.* Abigail, what sort of dancing were you doing with her in the forest?

ABIGAIL: Why—common dancing is all.

PARRIS: I think I ought to say that I—I saw a kettle in the grass where they were dancing.

ABIGAIL: That were only soup.

HALE: What sort of soup were in this kettle, Abigail?

ABIGAIL: Why, it were beans—and lentils, I think, and—

HALE: Mr. Parris, you did not notice, did you, any living thing in the kettle? A mouse, perhaps, a spider, a frog—?

PARRIS, *fearfully:* I—do believe there were some movement—in the soup.

ABIGAIL: That jumped in, we never put it in!

HALE, *quickly:* What jumped in?

ABIGAIL: Why, a very little frog jumped—

PARRIS: A frog, Abby!

HALE, *grasping* ABIGAIL: Abigail, it may be your cousin is dying. Did you call the Devil last night?

ABIGAIL: I never called him! Tituba, Tituba . . .

PARRIS, *blanched:* She called the Devil?

HALE: I should like to speak with Tituba.

PARRIS: Goody Ann, will you bring her up? MRS. PUTNAM *exits.*

HALE: How did she call him?

ABIGAIL: I know not—she spoke Barbados.

HALE: Did you feel any strangeness when she called him? A sudden cold wind, perhaps? A trembling below the ground?

ABIGAIL: I didn't see no Devil! *Shaking* BETTY: Betty, wake up. Betty! Betty!

HALE: You cannot evade me, Abigail. Did your cousin drink any of the brew in that kettle?

ABIGAIL: She never drank it!

HALE: Did you drink it?

---

20. **In nomine Domini Sabaoth sui filiique ite ad infernos** (in nō′ mē nā dō′ mē nē sab′ ā äth sōō′ ē fē′ lē ē kwā ē′ tā äd in fur′ nōs) "In the name of the lord of hosts and his son, get thee to the lower world" (Latin).

▶ **Critical Viewing**
Based on this film still of Abigail, Tituba, and other girls of Salem, how would you describe what actually happened in the woods? **INTERPRET**

Vocabulary

evade (ē vād′) *v.* avoid and escape by deceit or cleverness

ABIGAIL: No, sir!

HALE: Did Tituba ask you to drink it?

ABIGAIL: She tried, but I refused.

HALE: Why are you concealing? Have you sold yourself to Lucifer?

ABIGAIL: I never sold myself! I'm a good girl! I'm a proper girl!

MRS. PUTNAM *enters with* TITUBA, *and instantly* ABIGAIL *points at* TITUBA.

ABIGAIL: She made me do it! She made Betty do it!

TITUBA, *shocked and angry:* Abby!

ABIGAIL: She makes me drink blood!

PARRIS: Blood!!

MRS. PUTNAM: My baby's blood?

TITUBA: No, no, chicken blood. I give she chicken blood!

HALE: Woman, have you enlisted these children for the Devil?

TITUBA: No, no, sir, I don't truck with no Devil!

HALE: Why can she not wake? Are you silencing this child?

TITUBA: I love me Betty!

HALE: You have sent your spirit out upon this child, have you not?
Are you gathering souls for the Devil?

▼ **Critical Viewing**

Abigail has accused Tituba of conjuring spirits. What can you infer about Tituba's reaction from her expression here? **INFER**

ABIGAIL: She sends her spirit on me in church; she makes me laugh at prayer!

PARRIS: She have often laughed at prayer!

ABIGAIL: She comes to me every night to go and drink blood!

TITUBA: You beg *me* to conjure! She beg *me* make charm—

ABIGAIL: Don't lie! *To* HALE: She comes to me while I sleep; she's always making me dream corruptions!

TITUBA: Why you say that, Abby?

ABIGAIL: Sometimes I wake and find myself standing in the open doorway and not a stitch on my body! I always hear her laughing in my sleep. I hear her singing her Barbados songs and tempting me with—

TITUBA: Mister Reverend, I never—

HALE, *resolved now:* Tituba, I want you to wake this child.

TITUBA: I have no power on this child, sir.

HALE: You most certainly do, and you will free her from it now! When did you compact with the Devil?

TITUBA: I don't compact with no Devil!

PARRIS: You will confess yourself or I will take you out and whip you to your death, Tituba!

PUTNAM: This woman must be hanged! She must be taken and hanged!

TITUBA, *terrified, falls to her knees:* No, no, don't hang Tituba! I tell him I don't desire to work for him, sir.

PARRIS: The Devil?

HALE: Then you saw him! TITUBA *weeps.* Now Tituba, I know that when we bind ourselves to Hell it is very hard to break with it. We are going to help you tear yourself free—

TITUBA, *frightened by the coming process:* Mister Reverend, I do believe somebody else be witchin' these children.

HALE: Who?

TITUBA: I don't know, sir, but the Devil got him numerous witches.

HALE: Does he! *It is a clue.* Tituba, look into my eyes. Come, look into me. *She raises her eyes to his fearfully.* You would be a good Christian woman, would you not, Tituba?

TITUBA: Aye, sir, a good Christian woman.

HALE: And you love these little children?

TITUBA: Oh, yes, sir, I don't desire to hurt little children.

HALE: And you love God, Tituba?

TITUBA: I love God with all my bein'.

HALE: Now, in God's holy name—

TITUBA: Bless Him. Bless Him. *She is rocking on her knees, sobbing in terror.*

HALE: And to His glory—

TITUBA: Eternal glory. Bless Him—bless God . . .

HALE: Open yourself, Tituba—open yourself and let God's holy light shine on you.

TITUBA: Oh, bless the Lord.

HALE: When the Devil come to you does he ever come—with another person? *She stares up into his face.* Perhaps another person in the village? Someone you know.

PARRIS: Who came with him?

PUTNAM: Sarah Good? Did you ever see Sarah Good with him? Or Osburn?

PARRIS: Was it man or woman came with him?

TITUBA: Man or woman. Was—was woman.

PARRIS: What woman? A woman, you said. What woman?

TITUBA: It was black dark, and I—

PARRIS: You could see him, why could you not see her?

TITUBA: Well, they was always talking; they was always runnin' round and carryin' on—

PARRIS: You mean out of Salem? Salem witches?

TITUBA: I believe so, yes, sir.

Now HALE *takes her hand. She is surprised.*

HALE: Tituba. You must have no fear to tell us who they are, do you understand? We will protect you. The Devil can never overcome a minister. You know that, do you not?

TITUBA, *kisses* HALE's *hand:* Aye, sir, oh, I do.

HALE: You have confessed yourself to witchcraft, and that speaks a

Identifying Text Features

In what way does the dialogue indicate that Tituba is making things up?

Comprehension

To what does Tituba confess?

The Crucible, Act I **1155**

Plot

How does Tituba's confirmation of Parris and Hale's suspicions add to the play's rising action?

wish to come to Heaven's side. And we will bless you, Tituba.

TITUBA, *deeply relieved:* Oh, God bless you, Mr. Hale!

HALE, *with rising exaltation:* You are God's instrument put in our hands to discover the Devil's agent among us. You are selected, Tituba, you are chosen to help us cleanse our village. So speak utterly, Tituba, turn your back on him and face God—face God, Tituba, and God will protect you.

TITUBA, *joining with him:* Oh, God, protect Tituba!

HALE, *kindly:* Who came to you with the Devil? Two? Three? Four? How many?

TITUBA *pants, and begins rocking back and forth again, staring ahead.*

TITUBA: There was four. There was four.

PARRIS, *pressing in on her:* Who? Who? Their names, their names!

TITUBA, *suddenly bursting out:* Oh, how many times he bid me kill you, Mr. Parris!

PARRIS: Kill me!

TITUBA, *in a fury:* He say Mr. Parris must be kill! Mr. Parris no goodly man, Mr. Parris mean man and no gentle man, and he bid me rise out of my bed and cut your throat! *They gasp.* But I tell him "No! I don't hate that man. I don't want kill that man." But he say, "You work for me, Tituba, and I make you free! I give you pretty dress to wear, and put you way high up in the air, and you gone fly back to Barbados!" And I say, "You lie, Devil, you lie!" And then he come one stormy night to me, and he say, "Look! I have *white* people belong to me." And I look—and there was Goody Good.

PARRIS: Sarah Good!

TITUBA, *rocking and weeping:* Aye, sir, and Goody Osburn.

MRS. PUTNAM: I knew it! Goody Osburn were midwife to me three times. I begged you, Thomas, did I not? I begged him not to call Osburn because I feared her. My babies always shriveled in her hands!

HALE: Take courage, you must give us all their names. How can you bear to see this child suffering? Look at her, Tituba. *He is indicating* BETTY *on the bed.* Look at her God-given innocence; her soul is so tender; we must protect her, Tituba; the Devil is out and preying on her like a beast upon the flesh of the pure lamb. God will bless you for your help.

ABIGAIL *rises, staring as though inspired, and cries out.*

ABIGAIL: I want to open myself! *They turn to her, startled. She is enraptured, as though in a pearly light.* I want the light of God, I want the sweet love of Jesus! I danced for the Devil; I saw him; I wrote in his book; I go back to Jesus; I kiss His hand. I saw Sarah Good with the Devil! I saw Goody Osburn with the Devil! I saw Bridget Bishop with the Devil!

As she is speaking, BETTY *is rising from the bed, a fever in her eyes, and*

Identifying Text Features

What do the dialogue and stage directions tell you about the atmosphere on the stage?

picks up the chant.

BETTY, *staring too:* I saw George Jacobs with the Devil! I saw Goody Howe with the Devil!

PARRIS: She speaks! *He rushes to embrace* BETTY. She speaks!

HALE: Glory to God! It is broken, they are free!

BETTY, *calling out hysterically and with great relief:* I saw Martha Bellows with the Devil!

ABIGAIL: I saw Goody Sibber with the Devil! *It is rising to a great glee.*

PUTNAM: The marshal, I'll call the marshal!

PARRIS *is shouting a prayer of thanksgiving.*

BETTY: I saw Alice Barrow with the Devil!

The curtain begins to fall.

HALE, *as* PUTNAM *goes out:* Let the marshal bring irons!

ABIGAIL: I saw Goody Hawkins with the Devil!

BETTY: I saw Goody Bibber with the Devil!

ABIGAIL: I saw Goody Booth with the Devil!

On their ecstatic cries—

THE CURTAIN FALLS

Critical Reading

1. **Key Ideas and Details (a)** What is Betty's condition when the play opens? **(b)** What does Abigail say she and Betty were doing in the forest? **(c) Infer:** What seems to be the main motivation for Reverend Parris's concern about the girls' behavior in the forest?

2. **Key Ideas and Details (a)** What do Abigail, Betty, Mercy, and Mary discuss after Reverend Parris leaves his daughter's room? **(b) Interpret:** What events does this scene suggest may occur later in the play?

3. **Key Ideas and Details (a)** Who is Reverend Hale? **(b)** Why is he contacted? **(c) Evaluate:** Do you think he is being fair and impartial so far? Why or why not?

4. **Key Ideas and Details (a) Summarize:** Summarize Abigail's prior relationship with the Proctors. **(b) Interpret:** What does Betty's revelation about Abigail's actions in the forest suggest about Abigail's feelings for Elizabeth Proctor?

5. **Key Ideas and Details (a) Support:** What evidence suggests that sharp divisions exist among the people of Salem Village? **(b) Apply:** Name two others who may be accused. Explain your choices.

Cite textual evidence to support your responses.

Close Reading Activities | *The Crucible, Act I*

Literary Analysis

1. **Key Ideas and Details** The **plot** of this play unfolds over four acts. Act I introduces the situation and initial conflicts. Describe the *conflicts* between **(a)** Reverend Parris and the village; **(b)** Abigail Williams and John Proctor.

2. **Key Ideas and Details** Explain how both of the conflicts you identified in response to question 1 contribute to the play's **rising action.**

3. **Key Ideas and Details** In Act I, what seeds of conflict exist among Rebecca Nurse, Reverend Parris, and the Putnams? Explain.

4. **Key Ideas and Details** Use a chart like the one shown to examine how two specific events or characters described in the play's opening **dramatic exposition** are carried through into the action of Act I.

5. **Key Ideas and Details** **(a)** According to the opening dramatic exposition, how did most of the members of Salem feel about the vast forest that surrounded them? **(b)** How do you think these feelings affected the girls' actions in the forest and Parris's reactions to what he saw there?

6. **Key Ideas and Details** **(a)** Reread the dramatic exposition on Thomas Putnam on pages 1133–1134. **(b)** Which details lead you to believe that Putnam will be a fierce figure as the plot unfolds? Explain.

7. **Key Ideas and Details** Explain how the closing scene, in which Abigail and Betty shout the names of the accused, serves as the **climax** of Act I.

8. **Craft and Structure (a)** Describe the character of Abigail Williams based on the information provided in Act I. **(b)** Identify which **text structures**—*dialogue* or *stage directions*—provide the meaningful information.

9. **Craft and Structure** What text features provide information about the relationship between Abigail and John Proctor?

10. **Integration of Knowledge and Ideas (a)** Which characters depart the Putnam house after Reverend Hale arrives? **(b)** Why do they leave? **(c)** What does this scene suggest about future plot developments?

Common Core State Standards

Writing

2. Write informative texts to examine and convey complex ideas, concepts, and information clearly and accurately through the effective selection, organization, and analysis of content. *(p. 1159)*

2.a. Introduce a topic; organize complex ideas, concepts, and information so that each new element builds on that which precedes it to create a unified whole; include formatting. *(p. 1159)*

2.b. Develop the topic thoroughly by selecting the most significant and relevant facts, extended definitions, concrete details, quotations, or other information and examples appropriate to the audience's knowledge of the topic. *(p. 1159)*

2.e. Establish and maintain a formal style and objective tone while attending to the norms and conventions of the discipline in which they are writing. *(p. 1159)*

Language

4.b. Identify and correctly use patterns of word changes that indicate different meanings or parts of speech. *(p. 1159)*

Vocabulary Acquisition and Use

Word Analysis: Latin Root -grat-

The Latin word *gratus,* which means "pleasing," is formed with the root *-grat-,* which means "pleasing" or "agreeable." An *ingratiating* attitude, for example, is one intended to please others. Similarly, a *gratuity* is a gift of money given for pleasing service, and *gratitude* is thankful appreciation for gifts received. Explain how the root *-grat-* contributes to the meaning of the following words:

1. congratulate

2. ingrate

3. gratify

4. grateful

Vocabulary: Sentence Completions

Complete each of the sentences below with the appropriate vocabulary word from page 1123. Explain your answers.

1. _____ can destroy a person's reputation.

2. Months of _____ helped me to learn.

3. He hid his true nature by _____.

4. She tried to _____ punishment by lying about her crime.

5. To soothe their gods, they made sacrifices as an act of _____.

6. Her _____ manner pleased the customers.

7. With my _____ for history, I knew I would enjoy *The Crucible.*

Writing to Sources

Informative Text In *The Crucible*, information about the young girls' mysterious ailments and the discovery of witches spreads through conversation and gossip. Stem the flow of misinformation by writing a **newspaper article** reporting on Betty's illness and the subsequent accusations of witchcraft.

Prewriting Review Act I to collect details to cite in your article. Use a chart like the one shown to organize the information.

Drafting Start with the most important information: the Who? What? and When? questions. Add details as you work your way through the article and quote from sources and eyewitnesses. *Maintain a journalistic distance and tone* by avoiding words that reveal your own emotions or attitudes. Finally, write a headline that summarizes the story in a few bold words.

Model: Using a Chart to Organize Ideas

Who is involved?	
What happened?	
When did it happen?	
Where did it happen?	
Why did it happen?	
How did it happen?	

Revising Review your work to make sure you have used correct proper names and accurately quoted witnesses and authorities. If necessary, return to the play to find additional supporting details.

Building Knowledge and Insight | *The Crucible, Act II*

Close Reading Focus

Conflict; Biblical Allusions

Conflict is a struggle between opposing forces. There are two broad categories of conflict. In a complex narrative like this play, there are often numerous conflicts, and most characters experience both types:

- An **external conflict** takes place between a character and an external force, such as society, nature, fate, or another person. In Act II, as accusations and hysteria mount in Salem, characters face increasingly dangerous external conflicts with their neighbors, Abigail and the other the accusing girls, and the authorities.

- An **internal conflict** takes place within a character who is torn by his or her own competing or contradictory values or desires. In Act II, deepening external threats create new internal conflicts for characters and magnify those that already exist.

Some of the conflicts in this play arise out of the stern religious world view that defines the Salem community. That world view is not only revealed through characters' actions and descriptions of their lifestyles. It is also revealed through **Biblical allusions,** or references to figures, stories, or settings from the Bible. These Biblical allusions remind characters—and readers—of the religious beliefs on which the Puritan community is based. As you read, notice the conflicts that intensify in Act II and the Biblical allusions that help characters to define, defend, and excuse their actions.

Preparing to Read Complex Texts As you read, help yourself stay alert to important details and changes in characters and situations by **making predictions** about what will happen next. Notice hints the author drops about what might occur and apply your own *background knowledge* and understanding of human nature. As you read, use a chart like the one shown to record and confirm the predictions you make.

Vocabulary

You will encounter the words listed here in the text that follows. Copy the words into your notebook, sorting them into words you know and words you do not know.

pallor   base

ameliorate   deference

avidly   theology

**Common Core
State Standards**

Reading Literature

3. Analyze the impact of the author's choices regarding how to develop and relate elements of a drama.

5. Analyze how an author's choices concerning how to structure specific parts of a text contribute to its overall structure and meaning as well as its aesthetic impact.

7. Analyze multiple interpretations of a drama, evaluating how each version interprets the source text. *(p. 1185)*

Speaking and Listening

1.d. Respond thoughtfully to diverse perspectives; synthesize comments, claims, and evidence made on all sides of an issue. *(p. 1185)*

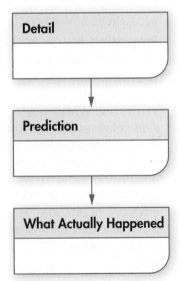

Review and Anticipate

As Act I draws to a close, Salem is in the grip of mounting hysteria. What had begun as concern over the strange behavior of Betty—a reaction that may have stemmed from guilty feelings about her activities in the woods the night before—had swelled by the act's end to a mass hysteria in which accusations of witchcraft were being made and accepted against a growing number of Salem's citizens. Which characters do you think will believe the accusations? Who do you think will be accused next?

The common room of PROCTOR's *house, eight days later.*

At the right is a door opening on the fields outside.
A fireplace is at the left, and behind it a stairway leading upstairs. It is the low, dark, and rather long living room of the time. As the curtain rises, the room is empty. From above, ELIZABETH *is heard softly singing to the children. Presently the door opens and* JOHN PROCTOR *enters, carrying his gun. He glances about the room as he comes toward the fireplace, then halts for an instant as he hears her singing. He continues on to the fireplace, leans the gun against the wall as he swings a pot out of the fire and smells it. Then he lifts out the ladle and tastes. He is not quite pleased. He reaches to a cupboard, takes a pinch of salt, and drops it into the pot. As he is tasting again, her footsteps are heard on the stair. He swings the pot into the fireplace and goes to a basin and washes his hands and face.* ELIZABETH *enters.*

ELIZABETH: What keeps you so late? It's almost dark.

PROCTOR: I were planting far out to the forest edge.

ELIZABETH: Oh, you're done then.

PROCTOR: Aye, the farm is seeded. The boys asleep?

ELIZABETH: They will be soon. *And she goes to the fireplace, proceeds to ladle up stew in a dish.*

PROCTOR: Pray now for a fair summer.

ELIZABETH: Aye.

PROCTOR: Are you well today?

ELIZABETH: I am. *She brings the plate to the table, and, indicating the food:* It is a rabbit.

PROCTOR, *going to the table:* Oh, is it! In Jonathan's trap?

ELIZABETH: No, she walked into the house this afternoon; I found her sittin' in the corner like she come to visit.

PROCTOR: Oh, that's a good sign walkin' in.

Comprehension
At what time of day does this scene take place?

ELIZABETH: Pray God. It hurt my heart to strip her, poor rabbit. *She sits and watches him taste it.*

PROCTOR: It's well seasoned.

ELIZABETH, *blushing with pleasure:* I took great care. She's tender?

PROCTOR: Aye. *He eats. She watches him.* I think we'll see green fields soon. It's warm as blood beneath the clods.

ELIZABETH: That's well.

PROCTOR *eats, then looks up.*

PROCTOR: If the crop is good I'll buy George Jacob's heifer. How would that please you?

ELIZABETH: Aye, it would.

PROCTOR, *with a grin:* I mean to please you, Elizabeth.

ELIZABETH—*it is hard to say:* I know it, John.

He gets up, goes to her, kisses her. She receives it. With a certain disappointment, he returns to the table.

PROCTOR, *as gently as he can:* Cider?

ELIZABETH, *with a sense of reprimanding herself for having forgot:* Aye! *She gets up and goes and pours a glass for him. He now arches his back.*

PROCTOR: This farm's a continent when you go foot by foot droppin' seeds in it.

ELIZABETH, *coming with the cider:* It must be.

PROCTOR, *drinks a long draught, then, putting the glass down:* You ought to bring some flowers in the house.

ELIZABETH: Oh! I forgot! I will tomorrow.

PROCTOR: It's winter in here yet. On Sunday let you come with me, and we'll walk the farm together; I never see such a load of flowers on the earth. *With good feeling he goes and looks up at the sky through the open doorway.* Lilacs have a purple smell. Lilac is the smell of nightfall, I think. Massachusetts is a beauty in the spring!

ELIZABETH: Aye, it is.

There is a pause. She is watching him from the table as he stands there absorbing the night. It is as though she would speak but cannot. Instead, now, she takes up his plate and glass and fork and goes with them to the basin. Her back is turned to him. He turns to her and watches her. A sense of their separation rises.

PROCTOR: I think you're sad again. Are you?

ELIZABETH—*she doesn't want friction, and yet she must:* You come so late I thought you'd gone to Salem this afternoon.

PROCTOR: Why? I have no business in Salem.

ELIZABETH: You did speak of going, earlier this week.

PROCTOR—*he knows what she means:* I thought better of it since.

ELIZABETH: Mary Warren's there today.

PROCTOR: Why'd you let her? You heard me forbid her go to Salem any more!

Conflict

As John eats his meal, which details suggest tension in the Proctors' relationship?

ELIZABETH: I couldn't stop her.

PROCTOR, *holding back a full condemnation of her:* It is a fault, it is a fault, Elizabeth—you're the mistress here, not Mary Warren.

ELIZABETH: She frightened all my strength away.

PROCTOR: How may that mouse frighten you, Elizabeth? You—

ELIZABETH: It is a mouse no more. I forbid her go, and she raises up her chin like the daughter of a prince and says to me, "I must go to Salem, Goody Proctor; I am an official of the court!"

PROCTOR: Court! What court?

ELIZABETH: Aye, it is a proper court they have now. They've sent four judges out of Boston, she says, weighty magistrates of the General Court, and at the head sits the Deputy Governor of the Province.

PROCTOR, *astonished:* Why, she's mad.

ELIZABETH: I would to God she were. There be fourteen people in the jail now, she says. PROCTOR *simply looks at her, unable to grasp it.* And they'll be tried, and the court have power to hang them too, she says.

PROCTOR, *scoffing but without conviction:* Ah, they'd never hang—

ELIZABETH: The Deputy Governor promise hangin' if they'll not confess, John. The town's gone wild, I think. She speak of Abigail, and I thought she were a saint, to hear her. Abigail brings the other girls into the court, and where she walks the crowd will part like the sea for Israel.[1] And folks are brought before them, and if they scream and howl and fall to the floor—the person's clapped in the jail for bewitchin' them.

PROCTOR, *wide-eyed:* Oh, it is a black mischief.

ELIZABETH: I think you must go to Salem, John. *He turns to her.* I think so. You must tell them it is a fraud.

PROCTOR, *thinking beyond this:* Aye, it is, it is surely.

ELIZABETH: Let you go to Ezekiel Cheever—he knows you well. And tell him what she said to you last week in her uncle's house. She said it had naught to do with witchcraft, did she not?

PROCTOR, *in thought:* Aye, she did, she did. *Now, a pause.*

ELIZABETH, *quietly, fearing to anger him by prodding:* God forbid you keep that from the court, John. I think they must be told.

PROCTOR, *quietly, struggling with his thought:* Aye, they must, they must. It is a wonder they do believe her.

ELIZABETH: I would go to Salem now, John—let you go tonight.

PROCTOR: I'll think on it.

ELIZABETH, *with her courage now:* You cannot keep it, John.

PROCTOR, *angering:* I know I cannot keep it. I say I will think on it!

ELIZABETH, *hurt, and very coldly:* Good, then, let you think on it. *She stands and starts to walk out of the room.*

PROCTOR: I am only wondering how I may prove what she told me,

---

1. **part like . . . Israel** In the Bible, God commanded Moses, the leader of the Jews, to part the Red Sea to enable the Jews to escape from the Egyptians into Canaan.

Biblical Allusion

What does Elizabeth's allusion to Moses' parting of the Red Sea reveal about Abigail's new standing in the community?

Making Predictions

Do you think Proctor will go before the court and denounce Abigail? Explain.

Comprehension

According to Elizabeth, how has Mary Warren changed?

Elizabeth. If the girl's a saint now, I think it is not easy to prove she's fraud, and the town gone so silly. She told it to me in a room alone—I have no proof for it.

ELIZABETH: You were alone with her?

PROCTOR, *stubbornly:* For a moment alone, aye.

ELIZABETH: Why, then, it is not as you told me.

PROCTOR, *his anger rising:* For a moment, I say. The others come in soon after.

ELIZABETH, *quietly—she has suddenly lost all faith in him:* Do as you wish, then. *She starts to turn.*

PROCTOR: Woman. *She turns to him.* I'll not have your suspicion any more.

ELIZABETH, *a little loftily:* I have no—

PROCTOR: I'll not have it!

ELIZABETH: Then let you not earn it.

PROCTOR, *with a violent undertone:* You doubt me yet?

ELIZABETH, *with a smile, to keep her dignity:* John, if it were not Abigail that you must go to hurt, would you falter now? I think not.

PROCTOR: Now look you—

ELIZABETH: I see what I see, John.

PROCTOR, *with solemn warning:* You will not judge me more, Elizabeth. I have good reason to think before I charge fraud on Abigail, and I will think on it. Let you look to your own improvement before you go to judge your husband any more. I have forgot Abigail, and—

ELIZABETH: And I.

PROCTOR: Spare me! You forget nothin' and forgive nothin'. Learn charity, woman. I have gone tiptoe in this house all seven month since she is gone. I have not moved from there to there without I think to please you, and still an everlasting funeral marches round your heart. I cannot speak but I am doubted, every moment judged for lies, as though I come into a court when I come into this house!

ELIZABETH: John, you are not open with me. You saw her with a crowd, you said. Now you—

PROCTOR: I'll plead my honesty no more, Elizabeth.

ELIZABETH—*now she would justify herself:* John, I am only—

PROCTOR: No more! I should have roared you down when first you told me your suspicion. But I wilted, and, like a Christian, I confessed. Confessed! Some dream I had must have mistaken you for God that day. But you're not, you're not, and let you remember it! Let you look sometimes for the goodness in me, and judge me not.

ELIZABETH: I do not judge you. The magistrate sits in your heart that judges you. I never thought you but a good man, John—*with a smile*—only somewhat bewildered.

Conflict

What is the source of conflict between Proctor and Elizabeth?

PROCTOR, *laughing bitterly:* Oh, Elizabeth, your justice would freeze beer! *He turns suddenly toward a sound outside. He starts for the door as* MARY WARREN *enters. As soon as he sees her, he goes directly to her and grabs her by the cloak, furious.* How do you go to Salem when I forbid it? Do you mock me? *Shaking her.* I'll whip you if you dare leave this house again!

Strangely, she doesn't resist him, but hangs limply by his grip.

MARY WARREN: I am sick, I am sick, Mr. Proctor. Pray, pray, hurt me not. *Her strangeness throws him off, and her evident* pallor *and weakness. He frees her.* My insides are all shuddery; I am in the proceedings all day, sir.

PROCTOR, *with draining anger—his curiosity is draining it:* And what of these proceedings here? When will you proceed to keep this house, as you are paid nine pound a year to do—and my wife not wholly well?

As though to compensate, MARY WARREN *goes to* ELIZABETH *with a small rag doll.*

MARY WARREN: I made a gift for you today, Goody Proctor. I had to sit long hours in a chair, and passed the time with sewing.

ELIZABETH, *perplexed, looking at the doll:* Why, thank you, it's a fair poppet.[2]

MARY WARREN, *with a trembling, decayed voice:* We must all love each other now, Goody Proctor.

ELIZABETH, *amazed at her strangeness:* Aye, indeed we must.

MARY WARREN, *glancing at the room:* I'll get up early in the morning and clean the house. I must sleep now. *She turns and starts off.*

PROCTOR: Mary. *She halts.* Is it true? There be fourteen women arrested?

MARY WARREN: No, sir. There be thirty-nine now— *She suddenly breaks off and sobs and sits down, exhausted.*

ELIZABETH: Why, she's weepin'! What ails you, child?

MARY WARREN: Goody Osburn—will hang!

There is a shocked pause, while she sobs.

PROCTOR: Hang! *He calls into her face.* Hang, y'say?

MARY WARREN, *through her weeping:* Aye.

PROCTOR: The Deputy Governor will permit it?

MARY WARREN: He sentenced her. He must. To ameliorate it: But not Sarah Good. For Sarah Good confessed, y'see.

PROCTOR: Confessed! To what?

MARY WARREN: That she—*in horror at the memory*—she sometimes made a compact with Lucifer, and wrote her name in his black book— with her blood—and bound herself to torment Christians till God's thrown down—and we all must worship Hell forevermore.

Pause.

---

2. **poppet** doll.

Vocabulary

pallor (pal′ ər) *n.* paleness

ameliorate (ə mēl′ yə rāt′) *v.* make better

Arthur Miller
Author's Insight
Miller was fully aware that those who participated in the trials had no perspective on their beliefs or actions. He once wrote: "I spent some ten days in the Salem courthouse reading the crudely recorded trials of the 1692 outbreak, and it was striking how totally absent was the least sense of irony, let alone humor."

Comprehension
What gift does Mary Warren give Elizabeth?

Arthur Miller and the Blacklist

In the late 1940s, the House Un-American Activities Committee developed a "blacklist" of Hollywood screenwriters suspected of being Communists. For many years, film producers used this list to deny employment to these writers.

Arthur Miller himself was called before the House Un-American Activities Committee and asked to name people he had met at a meeting of alleged Communist writers. After refusing, Miller was convicted of contempt; later, he appealed and the contempt charge was overturned.

In 1999, Arthur Miller commented on the relationship between the "Red Scare" and the Salem witch trials. Miller said there were startling similarities in both the rituals of defense and the investigative routines. Three hundred years apart, both prosecutions were alleging membership in a secret, disloyal group.

Connect to the Literature

Which characters in his play resemble Miller in his refusal to answer questions?

Vocabulary
avidly (av´ id lē) *adv.* eagerly

PROCTOR: But—surely you know what a jabberer she is. Did you tell them that?

MARY WARREN: Mr. Proctor, in open court she near to choked us all to death.

PROCTOR: How, choked you?

MARY WARREN: She sent her spirit out.

ELIZABETH: Oh, Mary, Mary, surely you—

MARY WARREN, *with an indignant edge:* She tried to kill me many times, Goody Proctor!

ELIZABETH: Why, I never heard you mention that before.

MARY WARREN: I never knew it before. I never knew anything before. When she come into the court I say to myself, I must not accuse this woman, for she sleep in ditches, and so very old and poor. But then—then she sit there, denying and denying, and I feel a misty coldness climbin' up my back, and the skin on my skull begin to creep, and I feel a clamp around my neck and I cannot breathe air; and then—*entranced*—I hear a voice, a screamin' voice, and it were my voice—and all at once I remembered everything she done to me!

PROCTOR: Why? What did she do to you?

MARY WARREN, *like one awakened to a marvelous secret insight:* So many time, Mr. Proctor, she come to this very door, beggin' bread and a cup of cider—and mark this: whenever I turned her away empty, she *mumbled*.

ELIZABETH: Mumbled! She may mumble if she's hungry.

MARY WARREN: But *what* does she mumble? You must remember, Goody Proctor. Last month—a Monday, I think—she walked away, and I thought my guts would burst for two days after. Do you remember it?

ELIZABETH: Why—I do, I think, but—

MARY WARREN: And so I told that to Judge Hathorne, and he asks her so. "Goody Osburn," says he, "what curse do you mumble that this girl must fall sick after turning you away?" And then she replies—*mimicking an old crone*—"Why, your excellence, no curse at all. I only say my commandments; I hope I may say my commandments," says she!

ELIZABETH: And that's an upright answer.

MARY WARREN: Aye, but then Judge Hathorne say, "Recite for us your commandments!"—*leaning avidly toward them*—and of all the ten she could not say a single one. She never knew no commandments, and they had her in a flat lie!

PROCTOR: And so condemned her?

MARY WARREN, *now a little strained, seeing his stubborn doubt:* Why, they must when she condemned herself.

PROCTOR: But the proof, the proof!

MARY WARREN, *with greater impatience with him:* I told you the proof. It's hard proof, hard as rock, the judges said.

PROCTOR, *pauses an instant, then:* You will not go to court again, Mary Warren.

MARY WARREN: I must tell you, sir, I will be gone every day now. I am amazed you do not see what weighty work we do.

PROCTOR: What work you do! It's strange work for a Christian girl to hang old women!

MARY WARREN: But, Mr. Proctor, they will not hang them if they confess. Sarah Good will only sit in jail some time—*recalling*—and here's a wonder for you; think on this. Goody Good is pregnant!

ELIZABETH: Pregnant! Are they mad? The woman's near to sixty!

MARY WARREN: They had Doctor Griggs examine her, and she's full to the brim. And smokin' a pipe all these years, and no husband either! But she's safe, thank God, for they'll not hurt the innocent child. But be that not a marvel? You must see it, sir, it's God's work we do. So I'll be gone every day for some time. I'm—I am an official of the court, they say, and I—*She has been edging toward offstage.*

PROCTOR: I'll official you! *He strides to the mantel, takes down the whip hanging there.*

MARY WARREN, *terrified, but coming erect, striving for her authority:* I'll not stand whipping any more!

ELIZABETH, *hurriedly, as* PROCTOR *approaches:* Mary, promise now you'll stay at home—

MARY WARREN, *backing from him, but keeping her erect posture, striving, striving for her way:* The Devil's loose in Salem, Mr. Proctor; we must discover where he's hiding!

PROCTOR: I'll whip the Devil out of you! *With whip raised he reaches out for her, and she streaks away and yells.*

MARY WARREN, *pointing at* ELIZABETH: I saved her life today!

Silence. His whip comes down.

ELIZABETH, *softly:* I am accused?

MARY WARREN, *quaking:* Somewhat mentioned. But I said I never see no sign you ever sent your spirit out to hurt no one, and seeing I do live so closely with you, they dismissed it.

ELIZABETH: Who accused me?

MARY WARREN: I am bound by law, I cannot tell it. *To* PROCTOR: I only hope you'll not be so sarcastical no more. Four judges and the King's deputy sat to dinner with us but an hour ago. I—I would have you speak civilly to me, from this out.

PROCTOR, *in horror, muttering in disgust at her:* Go to bed.

MARY WARREN, *with a stamp of her foot:* I'll not be ordered to bed no more, Mr. Proctor! I am eighteen and a woman, however single!

PROCTOR: Do you wish to sit up? Then sit up.

MARY WARREN: I wish to go to bed!

Conflict

What conflict is developing between the Proctors and their community?

Spiral Review

Text Sructures How do the stage directions here both describe the action and develop the characters?

Comprehension

What evidence does Mary Warren use to prove that Goody Osburn is a witch?

PROCTOR, *in anger:* Good night, then!

MARY WARREN: Good night. *Dissatisfied, uncertain of herself, she goes out. Wide-eyed, both* PROCTOR *and* ELIZABETH *stand staring.*

ELIZABETH, *quietly:* Oh, the noose, the noose is up!

PROCTOR: There'll be no noose.

ELIZABETH: She wants me dead. I knew all week it would come to this!

PROCTOR, *without conviction:* They dismissed it. You heard her say—

ELIZABETH: And what of tomorrow? She will cry me out until they take me!

PROCTOR: Sit you down.

ELIZABETH: She wants me dead, John, you know it!

PROCTOR: I say sit down! *She sits, trembling. He speaks quietly, trying to keep his wits.* Now we must be wise, Elizabeth.

ELIZABETH, *with sarcasm, and a sense of being lost:* Oh, indeed, indeed!

PROCTOR: Fear nothing. I'll find Ezekiel Cheever. I'll tell him she said it were all sport.

ELIZABETH: John, with so many in the jail, more than Cheever's help is needed now, I think. Would you favor me with this? Go to Abigail.

PROCTOR, *his soul hardening as he senses . . .:* What have I to say to Abigail?

ELIZABETH, *delicately:* John—grant me this. You have a faulty understanding of young girls. There is a promise made in any bed—

PROCTOR, *striving against his anger:* What promise!

ELIZABETH: Spoke or silent, a promise is surely made. And she may dote on it now—I am sure she does—and thinks to kill me, then to take my place.

PROCTOR'S *anger is rising; he cannot speak.*

ELIZABETH: It is her dearest hope, John, I know it. There be a thousand names; why does she call mine? There be a certain danger in calling such a name—I am no Goody Good that sleeps in ditches, nor Osburn, drunk and half-witted. She'd dare not call out such a farmer's wife but there be monstrous profit in it. She thinks to take my place, John.

PROCTOR: She cannot think it! *He knows it is true.*

ELIZABETH, *"reasonably":* John, have you ever shown her somewhat of contempt? She cannot pass you in the church but you will blush—

PROCTOR: I may blush for my sin.

ELIZABETH: I think she sees another meaning in that blush.

PROCTOR: And what see you? What see you, Elizabeth?

ELIZABETH, *"conceding":* I think you be somewhat ashamed, for I am there, and she so close.

PROCTOR: When will you know me, woman? Were I stone I would have cracked for shame this seven month!

ELIZABETH: Then go and tell her she's a whore. Whatever promise she may sense—break it, John, break it.

PROCTOR, *between his teeth:* Good, then. I'll go. *He starts for his rifle.*

Making Predictions

Do you think the authorities are more likely to believe Proctor or Abigail? Explain.

"I think you be somewhat ashamed, for I am there, and she so close."

ELIZABETH, *trembling, fearfully:* Oh, how unwillingly!

PROCTOR, *turning on her, rifle in hand:* I will curse her hotter than the oldest cinder in hell. But pray, begrudge me not my anger!

ELIZABETH: Your anger! I only ask you—

PROCTOR: Woman, am I so base? Do you truly think me base?

ELIZABETH: I never called you base.

PROCTOR: Then how do you charge me with such a promise? The promise that a stallion gives a mare I gave that girl!

ELIZABETH: Then why do you anger with me when I bid you break it?

PROCTOR: Because it speaks deceit, and I am honest! But I'll plead no more! I see now your spirit twists around the single error of my life, and I will never tear it free!

ELIZABETH, *crying out:* You'll tear it free—when you come to know that I will be your only wife, or no wife at all! She has an arrow in you yet, John Proctor, and you know it well!

Quite suddenly, as though from the air, a figure appears in the doorway. They start slightly. It is MR. HALE. *He is different now—drawn a little, and there is a quality of deference, even of guilt, about his manner now.*

HALE: Good evening.

PROCTOR, *still in his shock:* Why, Mr. Hale! Good evening to you, sir. Come in, come in.

HALE, *to Elizabeth:* I hope I do not startle you.

ELIZABETH: No, no, it's only that I heard no horse—

HALE: You are Goodwife Proctor.

PROCTOR: Aye; Elizabeth.

HALE, *nods, then:* I hope you're not off to bed yet.

PROCTOR, *setting down his gun:* No, no. HALE *comes further into the room. And* PROCTOR, *to explain his nervousness:* We are not used to visitors after dark, but you're welcome here. Will you sit you down, sir?

HALE: I will. *He sits.* Let you sit, Goodwife Proctor.

She does, never letting him out of her sight. There is a pause as HALE *looks about the room.*

PROCTOR, *to break the silence:* Will you drink cider, Mr. Hale?

HALE: No, it rebels my stomach; I have some further traveling yet tonight. Sit you down, sir. PROCTOR *sits.* I will not keep you long, but I have some business with you.

PROCTOR: Business of the court?

HALE: No—no, I come of my own, without the court's authority. Hear me. *He wets his lips.* I know not if you are aware, but your wife's name is—mentioned in the court.

PROCTOR: We know it, sir. Our Mary Warren told us. We are entirely amazed.

HALE: I am a stranger here, as you know. And in my ignorance I find it hard to draw a clear opinion of them that come accused before the court. And so this afternoon, and now tonight, I go from house to

Vocabulary
base (bās) *adj.* low; mean

Vocabulary
deference (def′ ər əns) *n.* courteous regard or respect

Comprehension
What does Elizabeth fear that Abigail will do to her?

The Crucible, Act II **1169**

house—I come now from Rebecca Nurse's house and—

ELIZABETH, *shocked:* Rebecca's charged!

HALE: God forbid such a one be charged. She is, however—mentioned somewhat.

ELIZABETH, *with an attempt at a laugh:* You will never believe, I hope, that Rebecca trafficked with the Devil.

HALE: Woman, it is possible.

PROCTOR, *taken aback:* Surely you cannot think so.

HALE: This is a strange time, Mister. No man may longer doubt the powers of the dark are gathered in monstrous attack upon this village. There is too much evidence now to deny it. You will agree, sir?

PROCTOR, *evading:* I—have no knowledge in that line. But it's hard to think so pious a woman be secretly a Devil's bitch after seventy year of such good prayer.

HALE: Aye. But the Devil is a wily one, you cannot deny it. However, she is far from accused, and I know she will not be. *Pause.* I thought, sir, to put some questions as to the Christian character of this house, if you'll permit me.

PROCTOR, *coldly, resentful:* Why, we—have no fear of questions, sir.

HALE: Good, then. *He makes himself more comfortable.* In the book of record that Mr. Parris keeps, I note that you are rarely in the church on Sabbath Day.

PROCTOR: No, sir, you are mistaken.

HALE: Twenty-six time in seventeen month, sir. I must call that rare. Will you tell me why you are so absent?

PROCTOR: Mr. Hale, I never knew I must account to that man for I come to church or stay at home. My wife were sick this winter.

HALE: So I am told. But you, Mister, why could you not come alone?

PROCTOR: I surely did come when I could, and when I could not I prayed in this house.

HALE: Mr. Proctor, your house is not a church; your theology must tell you that.

PROCTOR: It does, sir, it does; and it tells me that a minister may pray to God without he have golden candlesticks upon the altar.

HALE: What golden candlesticks?

PROCTOR: Since we built the church there were pewter candlesticks upon the altar; Francis Nurse made them y'know, and a sweeter hand never touched the metal. But Parris came, and for twenty week he preach nothin' but golden candlesticks until he had them. I labor the earth from dawn of day to blink of night, and I tell you true, when I look to heaven and see my money glaring at his elbows—it hurt my prayer, sir, it hurt my prayer.

Vocabulary

theology (thē äl′ ə jē) *n*
the study of religion

▼ Critical Viewing

Does Hale, as pictured here, seem sincere? Explain.
MAKE A JUDGMENT

I think, sometimes, the man dreams cathedrals, not clapboard meetin' houses.

HALE, *thinks, then:* And yet, Mister, a Christian on Sabbath Day must be in church. *Pause.* Tell me—you have three children?

PROCTOR: Aye. Boys.

HALE: How comes it that only two are baptized?

PROCTOR, *starts to speak, then stops, then, as though unable to restrain this:* I like it not that Mr. Parris should lay his hand upon my baby. I see no light of God in that man. I'll not conceal it.

HALE: I must say it, Mr. Proctor; that is not for you to decide. The man's ordained, therefore the light of God is in him.

PROCTOR, *flushed with resentment but trying to smile:* What's your suspicion, Mr. Hale?

HALE: No, no, I have no—

PROCTOR: I nailed the roof upon the church, I hung the door—

HALE: Oh, did you! That's a good sign, then.

PROCTOR: It may be I have been too quick to bring the man to book, but you cannot think we ever desired the destruction of religion. I think that's in your mind, is it not?

HALE, *not altogether giving way:* I—have—there is a softness in your record, sir, a softness.

Comprehension

Why has Proctor avoided attending the church?

WORLD LITERATURE IN CONTEXT

POLITICAL DRAMA

BERTOLT BRECHT (1898-1956)

German playwright and poet Bertolt Brecht began writing in the chaotic years after World War I. Hyperinflation in Germany had severely reduced the value of German money and unemployment had climbed to thirty percent. Brecht pondered how to address the reality of the times. "Can we speak of money in the poetry of iambs?" he asked.

Brecht came to believe an artist's job is to wake people up. He rejected traditional theater where the audience loses itself in the drama. Brecht organized a group of artists who developed a new style of theater. Actors sometimes broke out of character to speak to the audience.

During the early 1930s, Brecht watched with dismay as the Nazis rose to power. In 1933, he and his family fled Germany. While in exile, Brecht completed some of his most important works, including "Mother Courage," a play about the horrors of war.

Connect to the Literature

In what ways can art challenge people to think differently? Explain.

▲ Production of *Mother Courage*

ELIZABETH: I think, maybe, we have been too hard with Mr. Parris. I think so. But sure we never loved the Devil here.

HALE, *nods, deliberating this. Then, with the voice of one administering a secret test:* Do you know your Commandments, Elizabeth?

ELIZABETH, *without hesitation, even eagerly:* I surely do. There be no mark of blame upon my life, Mr. Hale. I am a covenanted Christian woman.

HALE: And you, Mister?

PROCTOR, *a trifle unsteadily:* I—am sure I do, sir.

HALE, *glances at her open face, then at* JOHN, *then:* Let you repeat them, if you will.

PROCTOR: The Commandments.

HALE: Aye.

PROCTOR, *looking off, beginning to sweat:* Thou shalt not kill.

HALE: Aye.

PROCTOR, *counting on his fingers:* Thou shalt not steal. Thou shalt not covet thy neighbor's goods, nor make unto thee any graven image. Thou shalt not take the name of the Lord in vain; thou shalt have no other gods before me. *With some hesitation:* Thou shalt remember the Sabbath Day and keep it holy. *Pause. Then:* Thou shalt honor thy father and mother. Thou shalt not bear false witness. *He is stuck. He counts back on his fingers, knowing one is missing.* Thou shalt not make unto thee any graven image.

HALE: You have said that twice, sir.

PROCTOR, *lost:* Aye. *He is flailing for it.*

ELIZABETH, *delicately:* Adultery, John.

PROCTOR, *as though a secret arrow had pained his heart:* Aye. *Trying to grin it away—to* HALE: You see, sir, between the two of us we do know them all. HALE *only looks at* PROCTOR, *deep in his attempt to define this man.* PROCTOR *grows more uneasy.* I think it be a small fault.

HALE: Theology, sir, is a fortress; no crack in a fortress may be accounted small. *He rises; he seems worried now. He paces a little, in deep thought.*

PROCTOR: There be no love for Satan in this house, Mister.

HALE: I pray it, I pray it dearly. *He looks to both of them, an attempt at a smile on his face, but his misgivings are clear.* Well, then—I'll bid you good night.

ELIZABETH, *unable to restrain herself:* Mr. Hale. *He turns.* I do think you are suspecting me somewhat? Are you not?

HALE, *obviously disturbed—and evasive:* Goody Proctor, I do not judge you. My duty is to add

▼ **Critical Viewing**

Does this image reflect the qualities you have noticed in Elizabeth up to this point in the play? Explain. **CONNECT** what I may to the godly wisdom of the court. I pray you both good health and good fortune. *To* JOHN: Good night, sir. *He starts out.*

ELIZABETH, *with a note of desperation:* I think you must tell him, John.

HALE: What's that?

ELIZABETH, *restraining a call:* Will you tell him?

Slight pause. HALE *looks questioningly at* JOHN.

PROCTOR, *with difficulty:* I—I have no witness and cannot prove it, except my word be taken. But I know the children's sickness had naught to do with witchcraft.

HALE, *stopped, struck:* Naught to do—?

PROCTOR: Mr. Parris discovered them sportin' in the woods. They were startled and took sick.

Pause.

HALE: Who told you this?

PROCTOR, *hesitates, then:* Abigail Williams.

HALE: Abigail.

PROCTOR: Aye.

HALE, *his eyes wide:* Abigail Williams told you it had naught to do with witchcraft!

PROCTOR: She told me the day you came, sir.

HALE, *suspiciously:* Why—why did you keep this?

PROCTOR: I never knew until tonight that the world is gone daft with this nonsense.

HALE: Nonsense! Mister, I have myself examined Tituba, Sarah Good, and numerous others that have confessed to dealing with the Devil. They have *confessed* it.

PROCTOR: And why not, if they must hang for denyin' it? There are them that will swear to anything before they'll hang; have you never thought of that?

HALE: I have. I—I have indeed. *It is his own suspicion, but he resists it. He glances at* ELIZABETH, *then at* JOHN. And you—would you testify to this in court?

PROCTOR: I—had not reckoned with goin' into court. But if I must I will.

HALE: Do you falter here?

PROCTOR: I falter nothing, but I may wonder if my story will be credited in such a court. I do wonder on it, when such a steady-minded minister as you will suspicion such a woman that never lied, and cannot, and the world knows she cannot! I may falter somewhat, Mister; I am no fool.

HALE, *quietly—it has impressed him:* Proctor, let you open with me now, for I have a rumor that troubles me. It's said you hold no belief that there may even be witches in the world. Is that true, sir?

PROCTOR—*he knows this is critical, and is striving against his disgust with* HALE *and with himself for even answering:* I know not what I have said, I may have said it. I have wondered if there be witches in the

Conflict
What internal conflict do these stage directions suggest Hale experiences?

Comprehension
What does John Proctor tell Reverend Hale about Abigail Williams?

world—although I cannot believe they come among us now.

HALE: Then you do not believe—

PROCTOR: I have no knowledge of it; the Bible speaks of witches, and I will not deny them.

HALE: And you, woman?

ELIZABETH: I—I cannot believe it.

HALE, *shocked:* You cannot!

PROCTOR: Elizabeth, you bewilder him!

ELIZABETH, *to* HALE: I cannot think the Devil may own a woman's soul, Mr. Hale, when she keeps an upright way, as I have. I am a good woman, I know it; and if you believe I may do only good work in the world, and yet be secretly bound to Satan, then I must tell you, sir, I do not believe it.

HALE: But, woman, you do believe there are witches in—

ELIZABETH: If you think that I am one, then I say there are none.

HALE: You surely do not fly against the Gospel, the Gospel—

PROCTOR: She believe in the Gospel, every word!

ELIZABETH: Question Abigail Williams about the Gospel, not myself!

HALE *stares at her.*

PROCTOR: She do not mean to doubt the Gospel, sir, you cannot think it. This be a Christian house, sir, a Christian house.

HALE: God keep you both; let the third child be quickly baptized, and go you without fail each Sunday to Sabbath prayer; and keep a solemn, quiet way among you. I think—

GILES COREY *appears in doorway.*

GILES: John!

PROCTOR: Giles! What's the matter?

GILES: They take my wife.

FRANCIS NURSE *enters.*

GILES: And his Rebecca!

PROCTOR, *to* FRANCIS: Rebecca's in the *jail!*

FRANCIS: Aye, Cheever come and take her in his wagon. We've only now come from the jail, and they'll not even let us in to see them.

ELIZABETH: They've surely gone wild now, Mr. Hale!

FRANCIS, *going to* HALE: Reverend Hale! Can you not speak to the Deputy Governor? I'm sure he mistakes these people—

HALE: Pray calm yourself, Mr. Nurse.

FRANCIS: My wife is the very brick and mortar of the church, Mr. Hale—*indicating* GILES—and Martha Corey, there cannot be a woman closer yet to God than Martha.

"They've surely gone wild now, Mr. Hale!"

HALE: How is Rebecca charged, Mr. Nurse?

FRANCIS, *with a mocking, half-hearted laugh:* For murder, she's charged! *Mockingly quoting the warrant:* "For the marvelous and supernatural murder of Goody Putnam's babies." What am I to do, Mr. Hale?

HALE, *turns from* FRANCIS, *deeply troubled, then:* Believe me, Mr. Nurse, if Rebecca Nurse be tainted, then nothing's left to stop the whole green world from burning. Let you rest upon the justice of the court; the court will send her home. I know it.

FRANCIS: You cannot mean she will be tried in court!

HALE, *pleading:* Nurse, though our hearts break, we cannot flinch; these are new times, sir. There is a misty plot afoot so subtle we should be criminal to cling to old respects and ancient friendships. I have seen too many frightful proofs in court—the Devil is alive in Salem, and we dare not quail to follow wherever the accusing finger points!

PROCTOR, *angered:* How may such a woman murder children?

HALE, *in great pain:* Man, remember, until an hour before the Devil fell, God thought him beautiful in Heaven.

GILES: I never said my wife were a witch, Mr. Hale; I only said she were reading books!

HALE: Mr. Corey, exactly what complaint were made on your wife?

GILES: That bloody mongrel Walcott charge her. Y'see, he buy a pig of my wife four or five year ago, and the pig died soon after. So he come dancin' in for his money back. So my Martha, she says to him, "Walcott, if you haven't the wit to feed a pig properly, you'll not live to own many," she says. Now he goes to court and claims that from that day to this he cannot keep a pig alive for more than four weeks because my Martha bewitch them with her books!

Enter EZEKIEL CHEEVER. *A shocked silence.*

CHEEVER: Good evening to you, Proctor.

PROCTOR: Why, Mr. Cheever. Good evening.

CHEEVER: Good evening, all. Good evening, Mr. Hale.

PROCTOR: I hope you come not on business of the court.

CHEEVER: I do, Proctor, aye. I am clerk of the court now, y'know.

Enter MARSHAL HERRICK, *a man in his early thirties, who is somewhat shamefaced at the moment.*

GILES: It's a pity, Ezekiel, that an honest tailor might have gone to Heaven must burn in Hell. You'll burn for this, do you know it?

CHEEVER: You know yourself I must do as I'm told. You surely know that, Giles. And I'd as lief[3] you'd not be sending me to Hell. I like not the sound of it, I tell you; I like not the sound of it. *He fears* PROCTOR, *but starts to reach inside his coat.* Now believe me, Proctor, how heavy be the law, all its tonnage I do carry on my back tonight. *He takes out a warrant.* I have a warrant for your wife.

---

3. as lief (as lēf) *adv.* rather.

Biblical Allusion

How does Hale use this allusion to the Devil to justify the accusation against Rebecca Nurse?

Comprehension

With what crime is Rebecca Nurse charged?

PROCTOR, *to* HALE: You said she were not charged!

HALE: I know nothin' of it. *To* CHEEVER: When were she charged?

CHEEVER: I am given sixteen warrant tonight, sir, and she is one.

PROCTOR: Who charged her?

CHEEVER: Why, Abigail Williams charge her.

PROCTOR: On what proof, what proof?

CHEEVER, *looking about the room:* Mr. Proctor, I have little time. The court bid me search your house, but I like not to search a house. So will you hand me any poppets that your wife may keep here?

PROCTOR: Poppets?

ELIZABETH: I never kept no poppets, not since I were a girl.

CHEEVER, *embarrassed, glancing toward the mantel where sits* MARY WARREN'S *poppet:* I spy a poppet, Goody Proctor.

ELIZABETH: Oh! *Going for it:* Why, this is Mary's.

CHEEVER, *shyly:* Would you please to give it to me?

ELIZABETH, *handing it to him, asks* HALE: Has the court discovered a text in poppets now?

CHEEVER, *carefully holding the poppet:* Do you keep any others in this house?

PROCTOR: No, nor this one either till tonight. What signifies a poppet?

CHEEVER: Why, a poppet—*he gingerly turns the poppet over*—a poppet may signify—Now, woman, will you please to come with me?

PROCTOR: She will not! *To* ELIZABETH: Fetch Mary here.

CHEEVER, *ineptly reaching toward* ELIZABETH: No, no, I am forbid to leave her from my sight.

PROCTOR, *pushing his arm away:* You'll leave her out of sight and out of mind, Mister. Fetch Mary, Elizabeth. ELIZABETH *goes upstairs.*

HALE: What signifies a poppet, Mr. Cheever?

CHEEVER, *turning the poppet over in his hands:* Why, they say it may signify that she—*he has lifted the poppet's skirt, and his eyes widen in astonished fear.* Why, this, this—

PROCTOR, *reaching for the poppet:* What's there?

CHEEVER: Why—*He draws out a long needle from the poppet*—it is a needle! Herrick, Herrick, it is a needle!

HERRICK *comes toward him.*

PROCTOR, *angrily, bewildered:* And what signifies a needle!

CHEEVER, *his hands shaking:* Why, this go hard with her, Proctor, this—I had my doubts, Proctor, I had my doubts, but here's calamity. *To* HALE, *showing the needle:* You see it, sir, it is a needle!

HALE: Why? What meanin' has it?

CHEEVER, *wide-eyed, trembling:* The girl, the Williams girl, Abigail Williams, sir. She sat to dinner in Reverend Parris's house tonight, and without word nor warnin' she falls to the floor. Like a struck beast, he says, and screamed a scream that a bull would weep to hear. And

Making Predictions

How do you think the poppet will affect Elizabeth's fate?

he goes to save her, and, stuck two inches in the flesh of her belly, he draw a needle out. And demandin' of her how she come to be so stabbed, she—*to* PROCTOR *now*—testify it were your wife's familiar spirit pushed it in.

PROCTOR: Why, she done it herself! *To* HALE: I hope you're not takin' this for proof, Mister!

HALE, *struck by the proof, is silent.*

CHEEVER: 'Tis hard proof! *To* HALE: I find here a poppet Goody Proctor keeps. I have found it, sir. And in the belly of the poppet a needle's stuck. I tell you true, Proctor, I never warranted to see such proof of Hell, and I bid you obstruct me not, for I—

Enter ELIZABETH *with* MARY WARREN. PROCTOR, *seeing* MARY WARREN, *draws her by the arm to* HALE.

PROCTOR: Here now! Mary, how did this poppet come into my house?

MARY WARREN, *frightened for herself, her voice very small:* What poppet's that, sir?

PROCTOR, *impatiently, points at the doll in* CHEEVER'S *hand:* This poppet, this poppet.

MARY WARREN, *evasively, looking at it:* Why, I—I think it is mine.

PROCTOR: It is your poppet, is it not?

MARY WARREN, *not understanding the direction of this:* It—is, sir.

PROCTOR: And how did it come into this house?

MARY WARREN, *glancing about at the avid faces:* Why—I made it in the court, sir, and—give it to Goody Proctor tonight.

PROCTOR, *to* HALE: Now, sir—do you have it?

HALE: Mary Warren, a needle have been found inside this poppet.

MARY WARREN, *bewildered:* Why, I meant no harm by it, sir.

PROCTOR, *quickly:* You stuck that needle in yourself?

MARY WARREN: I—I believe I did, sir, I—

PROCTOR, *to* HALE: What say you now?

HALE, *watching* MARY WARREN *closely:* Child, you are certain this be your natural memory? May it be, perhaps that someone conjures you even now to say this?

MARY WARREN: Conjures me? Why, no, sir, I am entirely myself, I think. Let you ask Susanna Walcott—she saw me sewin' it in court. *Or better still:* Ask Abby, Abby sat beside me when I made it.

PROCTOR, *to* HALE, *of* CHEEVER: Bid him begone. Your mind is surely settled now. Bid him out, Mr. Hale.

ELIZABETH: What signifies a needle?

HALE: Mary—you charge a cold and cruel murder on Abigail.

MARY WARREN: Murder! I charge no—

HALE: Abigail were stabbed tonight; a needle were found stuck into her belly—

ELIZABETH: And she charges me?

Making Predictions

Based on Hale's reaction to Mary Warren's testimony, what do you think will be the fate of those accused?

Comprehension

Who put the needle in the poppet?

HALE: Aye.

ELIZABETH, *her breath knocked out:* Why—! The girl is murder! She must be ripped out of the world!

CHEEVER, *pointing at* ELIZABETH: You've heard that, sir! Ripped out of the world! Herrick, you heard it!

PROCTOR, *suddenly snatching the warrant out of* CHEEVER'S *hands:* Out with you.

CHEEVER: Proctor, you dare not touch the warrant.

PROCTOR, ripping the warrant: Out with you!

CHEEVER: You've ripped the Deputy Governor's warrant, man!

PROCTOR: Damn the Deputy Governor! Out of my house!

HALE: Now, Proctor, Proctor!

▼ **Critical Viewing**

What thoughts or feelings do the facial expressions of Elizabeth Proctor, the deputy, and Parris convey in this photo? **INTERPRET**

PROCTOR: Get y'gone with them! You are a broken minister.

HALE: Proctor, if she is innocent, the court—

PROCTOR: If *she* is innocent! Why do you never wonder if Parris be innocent, or Abigail? Is the accuser always holy now? Were they born this morning as clean as God's fingers? I'll tell you what's walking Salem—vengeance is walking Salem. We are what we always were in Salem, but now the little crazy children are jangling the keys of the kingdom, and common vengeance writes the law! This warrant's vengeance! I'll not give my wife to vengeance!

ELIZABETH: I'll go, John—

PROCTOR: You will not go!

HERRICK: I have nine men outside. You cannot keep her. The law binds me, John, I cannot budge.

PROCTOR, *to* HALE, *ready to break him:* Will you see her taken?

HALE: Proctor, the court is just—

PROCTOR: Pontius Pilate![4] God will not let you wash your hands of this!

ELIZABETH: John—I think I must go with them. *He cannot bear to look at her.* Mary, there is bread enough for the morning; you will bake, in the afternoon. Help Mr. Proctor as you were his daughter—you owe me that, and much more. *She is fighting her weeping. To* PROCTOR: When the children wake, speak nothing of witchcraft—it will frighten them. *She cannot go on.*

PROCTOR: I will bring you home. I will bring you soon.

ELIZABETH: Oh, John, bring me soon!

PROCTOR: I will fall like an ocean on that court! Fear nothing, Elizabeth.

ELIZABETH, *with great fear:* I will fear nothing. *She looks about the room, as though to fix it in her mind.* Tell the children I have gone to visit someone sick.

She walks out the door, HERRICK *and* CHEEVER *behind her. For a moment,* PROCTOR *watches from the doorway. The clank of chain is heard.*

PROCTOR: Herrick! Herrick, don't chain her! *He rushes out the door. From outside:* Damn you, man, you will not chain her! Off with them! I'll not have it! I will not have her chained!

There are other men's voices against his. HALE, *in a fever of guilt and uncertainty, turns from the door to avoid the sight:* MARY WARREN *bursts into tears and sits weeping.* GILES COREY *calls to* HALE.

GILES: And yet silent, minister? It is fraud, you know it is fraud! What keeps you, man?

PROCTOR *is half braced, half pushed into the room by two deputies and* HERRICK.

PROCTOR: I'll pay you, Herrick, I will surely pay you!

HERRICK, *panting:* In God's name, John, I cannot help myself. I must

---

4. **Pontius** (pän´ shəs) **Pilate** (pī´ lət) Roman leader who condemned Jesus to be crucified.

> "Get y'gone with them! You are a broken minister."

Biblical Allusion
How is Proctor's allusion to Pontius Pilate an insult to Hale?

Comprehension
What happens to Elizabeth Proctor?

The Crucible, Act II **1179**

chain them all. Now let you keep inside this house till I am gone! *He goes out with his deputies.*

PROCTOR *stands there, gulping air. Horses and a wagon creaking are heard.*

HALE, *in great uncertainty:* Mr. Proctor—

PROCTOR: Out of my sight!

HALE: Charity, Proctor, charity. What I have heard in her favor, I will not fear to testify in court. God help me, I cannot judge her guilty or innocent—I know not. Only this consider: the world goes mad, and it profit nothing you should lay the cause to the vengeance of a little girl.

PROCTOR: You are a coward! Though you be ordained in God's own tears, you are a coward now!

HALE: Proctor, I cannot think God be provoked so grandly by such a petty cause. The jails are packed—our greatest judges sit in Salem now—and hangin's promised. Man, we must look to cause proportionate. Were there murder done, perhaps, and never brought to light? Abomination? Some secret blasphemy that stinks to Heaven? Think on cause, man, and let you help me to discover it. For there's your way, believe it, there is your only way, when such confusion strikes upon the world. *He goes to* GILES *and* FRANCIS. Let you counsel among yourselves; think on your village and what may have drawn from heaven such thundering wrath upon you all. I shall pray God open up our eyes.

HALE *goes out.*

FRANCIS, *struck by* HALE'S *mood:* I never heard no murder done in Salem.

PROCTOR—*he has been reached by* HALE'S *words:* Leave me, Francis, leave me.

GILES, *shaken:* John—tell me, are we lost?

PROCTOR: Go home now, Giles. We'll speak on it tomorrow.

GILES: Let you think on it. We'll come early, eh?

PROCTOR: Aye. Go now, Giles.

GILES: Good night, then.

GILES COREY *goes out. After a moment:*

MARY WARREN, *in a fearful squeak of a voice:* Mr. Proctor, very likely they'll let her come home once they're given proper evidence.

PROCTOR: You're coming to the court with me, Mary. You will tell it in the court.

MARY WARREN: I cannot charge murder on Abigail.

PROCTOR, *moving menacingly toward her:* You will tell the court how that poppet come here and who stuck the needle in.

MARY WARREN: She'll kill me for sayin' that! PROCTOR *continues toward her.* Abby'll charge lechery[5] on you, Mr. Proctor!

Making Predictions

What impact do you think the charge of lechery would have on Proctor and his family?

---

5. **lechery** (lech′ ər ē) *n.* lust; adultery—a charge almost as serious as witchcraft in this Puritan community.

PROCTOR, *halting:* She's told you!

MARY WARREN: I have known it, sir. She'll ruin you with it, I know she will.

PROCTOR, *hesitating, and with deep hatred of himself:* Good. Then her saintliness is done with. MARY *backs from him.* We will slide together into our pit; you will tell the court what you know.

MARY WARREN, *in terror:* I cannot, they'll turn on me—

PROCTOR *strides and catches her, and she is repeating, "I cannot, I cannot!"*

PROCTOR: My wife will never die for me! I will bring your guts into your mouth but that goodness will not die for me!

MARY WARREN, *struggling to escape him:* I cannot do it. I cannot!

PROCTOR, *grasping her by the throat as though he would strangle her:* Make your peace with it! Now Hell and Heaven grapple on our backs, and all our old pretense is ripped away—make your peace! *He throws her to the floor, where she sobs, "I cannot, I cannot . . ." And now, half to himself, staring, and turning to the open door:* Peace. It is a providence, and no great change; we are only what we always were, but naked now. *He walks as though toward a great horror, facing the open sky.* Aye, naked! And the wind, God's icy wind, will blow!

And she is over and over again sobbing, "I cannot, I cannot, I cannot," as

THE CURTAIN FALLS

Critical Reading

1. **Key Ideas and Details (a)** What does Mary Warren bring home to Elizabeth Proctor? **(b) Interpret:** What is the significance of this gift?

2. **Key Ideas and Details (a)** What evidence is used to support Abigail Williams's assertion that Elizabeth Proctor is guilty of witchcraft? **(b) Assess:** Do you think the evidence is compelling? Why or why not?

3. **Key Ideas and Details (a)** What does Sarah Good do to save herself from hanging? **(b) Draw Conclusions:** Why would such an action save her?

4. **Key Ideas and Details (a)** According to John Proctor, what is "walking Salem" and writing the law in the community? **(b) Support:** What evidence would support Proctor's assertion?

5. **Key Ideas and Details (a)** Who says the witchcraft trials are "a black mischief"? **(b) Analyze:** What is ironic about that remark?

6. **Key Ideas and Details Analyze:** Why is it surprising that Rebecca Nurse is charged with witchcraft?

7. **Integration of Knowledge and Ideas Evaluate:** Do you find any irony in the fact that Ezekiel Cheever is the one who arrests Elizabeth Proctor? Why or why not?

> Cite textual evidence to support your responses.

Close Reading Activities   *The Crucible, Act II*

Literary Analysis

1. **Key Ideas and Details (a)** What **external conflict** confronts those convicted of witchcraft? **(b)** What **internal conflict** do they face?

2. **Key Ideas and Details (a)** What conflicts do Elizabeth and John Proctor struggle with in their relationship? **(b)** Which of these are internal conflicts each character faces alone, and which are external?

3. **Key Ideas and Details** Is it an internal or external conflict, or some combination, that causes Elizabeth's awkward reaction to Proctor's kiss on page 1162? Explain.

4. **Key Ideas and Details** What profound conflict does Proctor note when he confronts Hale with the following words?

   "I'll tell you what's walking Salem—vengeance is walking Salem. We are what we always were . . . but now the little crazy children are jangling the keys of the kingdom . . ."

5. **Key Ideas and Details** What is the nature of the conflict suggested by Proctor's last lines and the last stage directions describing him in Act II?

6. **Key Ideas and Details (a)** Note three **predictions** you made about John Proctor in Act II. **(b)** What details led you to make those predictions? **(c)** Were your predictions confirmed by the end of the act? Explain.

7. **Key Ideas and Details (a)** What predictions did you make about Elizabeth in Act II? **(b)** What details or events suggested those predictions?

8. **Key Ideas and Details (a)** What predictions can you make based on Mary Warren's information about the convictions of Sarah Good and Goody Osburn? **(b)** Is that prediction proved accurate or inaccurate by the arrest of Elizabeth? **(c)** Based on both pieces of information, what predictions can you make about other accusations to come? Explain.

9. **Craft and Structure** Use a chart like the one shown to examine the meanings of **Biblical allusions** in Act II. **(a)** Identify the allusion. **(b)** Determine what the allusion means. **(c)** Explain what it reveals about the character or situation in which it is used.

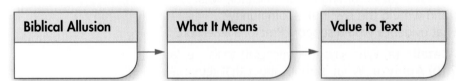

| Biblical Allusion | What It Means | Value to Text |

10. **Integration of Knowledge and Ideas** Based on *background knowledge* you acquired in Act I and earlier in Act II, what chance do you think Elizabeth stands in defending herself against Abigail's accusations? Explain, providing supporting evidence.

Common Core State Standards

Writing
1. Write arguments to support claims in an analysis of substantive topics or texts, using valid reasoning and relevant and sufficient evidence. *(p. 1183)*

Language
4.a. Use context as a clue to the meaning of a word or phrase. *(p. 1183)*
4.b. Identify and correctly use patterns of word changes that indicate different meanings or parts of speech. *(p. 1183)*

Vocabulary Acquisition and Use

Word Analysis: Greek Suffix -logy

The Greek suffix -*logy* means "the science, theory, or study of." When combined with the Greek root -*theo*-, meaning "god," the word *theology* means "the study of religion." Add the prefixes noted below to the suffix -*logy* to generate five science-related terms. Write definitions for all five new words. Use a dictionary if necessary.

1. psych-: *mind*
2. bio-: *life*
3. cardio-: *heart*
4. geo-: *environment or habitat*
5. zoo-: *animals*

Vocabulary: True or False?

Answer each question based on your knowledge of the italicized words. Then, explain your answer.

1. Lying is *base* behavior.
2. If she watches soccer *avidly,* she probably knows very little about it.
3. Rude youngsters show *deference* to elders.
4. A blushing person exhibits a *pallor.*
5. Puritans, in general, analyzed and questioned their *theology.*
6. When you *ameliorate* a situation, you make it better.

Writing to Sources

Argumentative Text Effective persuasive writing in Salem could have saved lives or even more effectively condemned the accused. Assume the persona of a character in the play and write a **persuasive letter** urging another character to take a particular course of action.

Prewriting Review the first two acts of the play, and choose the character and position you will represent. Then, use a chart like the one shown to gather support. Note facts, examples, and personal experiences that will support your persuasive points.

Model: Gathering Evidence

Facts	Examples	Personal Experiences
1.		
2.		
3.		

Drafting Organize your letter using one piece of evidence from the chart in each paragraph. Add to the persuasive effect by using *rhetorical devices*, such as *repetition, parallel structures,* and *analogies.*

Revising Reread your letter and assess its effectiveness. Strengthen sections with more specific, emotional language, or with more precise use of rhetorical devices.

Literary History: Drama

Twentieth-Century Drama: America Takes the Stage

It is opening night at the theater. As the curtain rises, you are filled with the anticipation of seeing an exciting new play. No, it is not a big-budget musical with elaborate sets and costumes. It is a night of talk—sometimes loud and angry, sometimes hushed and mournful, but always riveting.

For much of the twentieth century, the theater was the center of American intellectual life. Great plays offered thrilling stories, crackling dialogue, and philosophical truth. The best American playwrights of the twentieth century chronicled different aspects of the American experience.

- **Thornton Wilder** (1897–1975), best known for *Our Town* (1938), revealed the secrets of small-town America.

- **Arthur Miller** (1915–2005) combined politics and realism to give America some of its most moving plays, including *Death of a Salesman* (1949) and *The Crucible* (1953) (see p. 1118).

- **Lorraine Hansberry** (1930–1965) dramatized the lives of African Americans. Her play *A Raisin in the Sun* (1959) was the first drama by a black woman to be produced on Broadway.

- **Edward Albee** (b. 1928) shocked audiences with his psychological dramas, including the harsh and powerful *Who's Afraid of Virginia Woolf?* (1962).

America's First Great Playwright "I want to be an artist or nothing," Eugene O'Neill said at the age of twenty-five. When he died forty years later, he had written more than fifty plays and won the Nobel Prize and four Pulitzer Prizes.

O'Neill's work reflects his troubled childhood and rough-and-tumble youth. He was born in New York City in 1888. In his mid-twenties, hard living landed O'Neill in the hospital, where he pondered his life for the first time: "It was in this enforced period of reflection that the urge to write first came to me," he said.

▲ **Critical Viewing**
This photograph shows a scene from Tennessee Williams's *A Streetcar Named Desire*. In what ways does this scene depict the "raw power of human emotion"? **INTERPRET**

O'Neill experimented with different styles: realistic, symbolic, and political. *Beyond the Horizon* (1920), his first Broadway play, was a smash hit. *The Iceman Cometh* (1946) tells the stories of dreamers and losers who frequent a waterfront bar. *Long Day's Journey Into Night* (1956), O'Neill's masterpiece, recounts his troubled childhood.

A Woman's Voice Born in 1905 in New Orleans, Lillian Hellman became the most influential female playwright of the twentieth century. Her first play, *The Children's Hour* (1934), is the tale of two teachers whose lives are ruined by malicious accusations. Her best-known work, *The Little Foxes* (1939), takes a harsh look at a rich and powerful southern family. Her political drama *Watch on the Rhine* (1941) warned the world of the dangers of Nazism. By the time of her death in 1984, Hellman had helped shape a golden age in American theater and paved the way for women playwrights to exert influence and express powerful views.

The Raw Power of Human Emotion Born in 1911 in rural Mississippi, Tennessee Williams decided to become a writer while he was still a teenager. His first major play, *The Glass Menagerie* (1945), moved audiences with its compassion for a mother and sister who cling to their ever-fading dreams. In 1947, Williams shocked audiences with *A Streetcar Named Desire,* a hard-hitting story filled with both cruelty and beauty. Its effect on audiences was so great that it inspired dozens of imitations. By the time Williams died in 1983, he had written more than 60 plays and become one of the most important dramatists of all time.

Speaking and Listening: Group Discussion

Comprehension and Collaboration **Analyzing Interpretations** With your class, view two or more productions of *The Crucible.* Consider the 1996 film starring Daniel Day Lewis and Winona Ryder, and the 1967 TV adaptation starring George C. Scott and Colleen Dewhurst. If possible, also view a live stage production. In a small group, discuss the interpretation of the play each version presents. Use questions such as these to focus your discussion:

- Does each production faithfully interpret the play? If so, which elements bring Miller's vision to life? If not, how does the interpretation fail?
- How does each production present the setting? Does it depart in any way from the source material? If so, to what effect?
- Do the actors effectively portray the characters? Are any portrayals misguided? If so, why?
- Do the themes of the play emerge clearly in each adaptation? If not, why not?
- Is one interpretation much better or much worse than the others? If so, why?

Take notes as you converse and work to synthesize, or pull together, the opinions and ideas. Then, prepare a summary of the discussion and share the group's ideas with the class.

Building Knowledge and Insight

The Crucible, Act III

Close Reading Focus

Characterization; Irony

Characterization is the art of revealing characters' personalities. In **direct characterization,** the author simply tells the reader what a character is like. A playwright may use direct characterization in stage directions, but most dramatic literature requires **indirect characterization** in which characters' traits are revealed through

- the character's words, actions, and appearance;
- other characters' comments;
- other characters' reactions.

Like people in real life, characters in plays are not always what they seem. Fear, greed, guilt, love, loyalty, pride, and revenge are some of the forces that drive human behavior, but they may be masked or hidden. *Characters' motives*—the reasons for their behavior—may be stated directly or suggested through indirect characterization.

Like characters, situations are also not always what they seem. When there is a contrast between expectation and reality, **irony** is at work. With **dramatic irony,** there is a contradiction between what a character thinks and what the audience knows. With **verbal irony,** there is a contrast between what a character says and what is really meant. As you read, notice how you learn about characters. Assess their motivations, and identify the many ironies that swirl around them as dangers in Salem mount.

Preparing to Read Complex Texts In this act, the court proceedings become the focus of attention. As they do, the faulty logic supporting accusations of witchcraft becomes more formalized. The justifications accusers use are examples of *logical fallacy,* arguments that may seem reasonable but are founded on a wrong premise. As you read, **evaluate arguments** used to bring accusations and condemn the innocent. Determine the premise that underlies the accusations and trace the logic that supports the argument. As you read, use a chart like the one shown to assess the arguments presented in Act III.

Vocabulary

The words below are important to understanding the text that follows. Copy the words into your notebook. What other words do you know that are related to the word *imperceptible*?

contentious	anonymity
deposition	effrontery
imperceptible	incredulously

**Common Core
State Standards**

Reading Literature
3. Analyze the impact of the author's choices regarding how to develop and relate elements of a story or drama (e.g., how the characters are introduced and developed).
6. Analyze a case in which grasping a point of view requires distinguishing what is directly stated in a text from what is really meant.

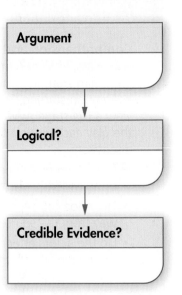

Review and Anticipate

Act II ends as Elizabeth Proctor is accused of witchcraft and carted off to jail as a result of the connivance of Abigail Williams. John Proctor demands that Mary Warren tell the court the truth; Mary, though aware of Abigail's ploys, is terrified of exposing her. Do you think John will convince Mary to overcome her fears and testify against Abigail? If he does convince her, how will the judges receive Mary Warren's testimony? Read Act III to see what happens in the Salem courtroom.

ACT 3

The vestry room of the Salem meeting house, now serving as the anteroom of the General Court.

As the curtain rises, the room is empty, but for sunlight pouring through two high windows in the back wall. The room is solemn, even forbidding. Heavy beams jut out, boards of random widths make up the walls. At the right are two doors leading into the meeting house proper, where the court is being held. At the left another door leads outside.

There is a plain bench at the left, and another at the right. In the center a rather long meeting table, with stools and a considerable armchair snugged up to it.

Through the partitioning wall at the right we hear a prosecutor's voice, JUDGE HATHORNE'S, *asking a question; then a woman's voice,* MARTHA COREY'S, *replying.*

HATHORNE'S VOICE: Now, Martha Corey, there is abundant evidence in our hands to show that you have given yourself to the reading of fortunes. Do you deny it?

MARTHA COREY'S VOICE: I am innocent to a witch. I know not what a witch is.

HATHORNE'S VOICE: How do you know, then, that you are not a witch?

MARTHA COREY'S VOICE: If I were, I would know it.

HATHORNE'S VOICE: Why do you hurt these children?

MARTHA COREY'S VOICE: I do not hurt them. I scorn it!

GILES'S VOICE, *roaring:* I have evidence for the court!

Voices of townspeople rise in excitement.

DANFORTH'S VOICE: You will keep your seat!

GILES' VOICE: Thomas Putnam is reaching out for land!

DANFORTH'S VOICE: Remove that man, Marshal!

Comprehension

What accusation does Hathorne make of Martha Corey?

Characterization
What is Giles's motivation for interrupting the court?

GILES' VOICE: You're hearing lies, lies!

A roaring goes up from the people.

HATHORNE'S VOICE: Arrest him, excellency!

GILES' VOICE: I have evidence. Why will you not hear my evidence?

The door opens and GILES *is half carried into the vestry room by* HERRICK.

GILES: Hands off, damn you, let me go!

HERRICK: Giles, Giles!

GILES: Out of my way, Herrick! I bring evidence—

HERRICK: You cannot go in there, Giles; it's a court!

Enter HALE *from the court.*

HALE: Pray be calm a moment.

GILES: You, Mr. Hale, go in there and demand I speak.

HALE: A moment, sir, a moment.

GILES: They'll be hangin' my wife!

JUDGE HATHORNE *enters. He is in his sixties, a bitter, remorseless Salem judge.*

▼ Critical Viewing
Which aspects of the judges' appearance and demeanor, as shown here, would instill fear in the people of Salem?
ASSESS

HATHORNE: How do you dare come roarin' into this court! Are you gone daft, Corey?

GILES: You're not a Boston judge yet, Hathorne. You'll not call me daft!

Enter DEPUTY GOVERNOR DANFORTH *and, behind him,* EZEKIEL CHEEVER *and* PARRIS. *On his appearance, silence falls.* DANFORTH *is a grave man in his sixties, of some humor and sophistication that does not, however, interfere with an exact loyalty to his position and his cause. He comes down to* GILES, *who awaits his wrath.*

DANFORTH, *looking directly at* GILES: Who is this man?

PARRIS: Giles Corey, sir, and a more contentious—

GILES, *to* PARRIS: I am asked the question, and I am old enough to answer it! *To* DANFORTH, *who impresses him and to whom he smiles through his strain:* My name is Corey, sir, Giles Corey. I have six hundred acres, and timber in addition. It is my wife you be condemning now. *He indicates the courtroom.*

DANFORTH: And how do you imagine to help her cause with such contemptuous riot? Now be gone. Your old age alone keeps you out of jail for this.

GILES, *beginning to plead:* They be tellin' lies about my wife, sir, I—

DANFORTH: Do you take it upon yourself to determine what this court shall believe and what it shall set aside?

GILES: Your Excellency, we mean no disrespect for—

DANFORTH: Disrespect indeed! It is disruption, Mister. This is the highest court of the supreme government of this province, do you know it?

GILES, *beginning to weep:* Your Excellency, I only said she were readin' books, sir, and they come and take her out of my house for—

DANFORTH, *mystified:* Books! What books?

GILES, *through helpless sobs:* It is my third wife, sir; I never had no wife that be so taken with books, and I thought to find the cause of it, d'y'see, but it were no witch I blamed her for. *He is openly weeping.* I have broke charity with the woman, I have broke charity with her. *He covers his face, ashamed.* DANFORTH *is respectfully silent.*

HALE: Excellency, he claims hard evidence for his wife's defense. I think that in all justice you must—

DANFORTH: Then let him submit his evidence in proper affidavit.[1] You are certainly aware of our procedure here, Mr. Hale. *To* HERRICK: Clear this room.

HERRICK: Come now, Giles. *He gently pushes* COREY *out.*

FRANCIS: We are desperate, sir; we come here three days now and cannot be heard.

DANFORTH: Who is this man?

FRANCIS: Francis Nurse, Your Excellency.

HALE: His wife's Rebecca that were condemned this morning.

---

1. **affidavit** (af′ ə dā′ vit) *n.* written statement made under oath.

Characterization
What do you learn about Danforth through direct characterization in these stage directions?

Vocabulary
contentious (kən ten′ shəs) *adj.* argumentative

Comprehension
Why does Giles smile at Danforth?

DANFORTH: Indeed! I am amazed to find you in such uproar. I have only good report of your character, Mr. Nurse.

HATHORNE: I think they must both be arrested in contempt, sir.

DANFORTH, *to* FRANCIS: Let you write your plea, and in due time I will—

FRANCIS: Excellency, we have proof for your eyes; God forbid you shut them to it. The girls, sir, the girls are frauds.

DANFORTH: What's that?

FRANCIS: We have proof of it, sir. They are all deceiving you.

DANFORTH *is shocked, but studying* FRANCIS.

HATHORNE: This is contempt, sir, contempt!

DANFORTH: Peace, Judge Hathorne. Do you know who I am, Mr. Nurse?

FRANCIS: I surely do, sir, and I think you must be a wise judge to be what you are.

DANFORTH: And do you know that near to four hundred are in the jails from Marblehead to Lynn, and upon my signature?

FRANCIS: I—

DANFORTH: And seventy-two condemned to hang by that signature?

FRANCIS: Excellency, I never thought to say it to such a weighty judge, but you are deceived.

Enter GILES COREY *from left. All turn to see as he beckons in* MARY WARREN *with* PROCTOR. MARY *is keeping her eyes to the ground;* PROCTOR *has her elbow as though she were near collapse.*

PARRIS, *on seeing her, in shock:* Mary Warren! *He goes directly to bend close to her face.* What are you about here?

PROCTOR, *pressing* PARRIS *away from her with a gentle but firm motion of protectiveness:* She would speak with the Deputy Governor.

DANFORTH, *shocked by this, turns to* HERRICK: Did you not tell me Mary Warren were sick in bed?

HERRICK: She were, Your Honor. When I go to fetch her to the court last week, she said she were sick.

GILES: She has been strivin' with her soul all week, Your Honor; she comes now to tell the truth of this to you.

DANFORTH: Who is this?

PROCTOR: John Proctor, sir. Elizabeth Proctor is my wife.

PARRIS: Beware this man, Your Excellency, this man is mischief.

HALE, *excitedly:* I think you must hear the girl, sir, she—

DANFORTH, *who has become very interested in* MARY WARREN *and only raises a hand toward* HALE: Peace. What would you tell us, Mary Warren?

PROCTOR *looks at her, but she cannot speak.*

PROCTOR: She never saw no spirits, sir.

DANFORTH, *with great alarm and surprise, to* MARY: Never saw no spirits!

GILES, *eagerly:* Never.

PROCTOR, *reaching into his jacket:* She has signed a deposition, sir—

DANFORTH, *instantly:* No, no, I accept no depositions. *He is rapidly calculating this; he turns from her to* PROCTOR. Tell me, Mr. Proctor, have you given out this story in the village?

PROCTOR: We have not.

PARRIS: They've come to overthrow the court, sir! This man is—

DANFORTH: I pray you, Mr. Parris. Do you know, Mr. Proctor that the entire contention of the state in these trials is that the voice of Heaven is speaking through the children?

PROCTOR: I know that, sir.

DANFORTH, *thinks, staring at* PROCTOR, *then turns to* MARY WARREN: And you, Mary Warren, how come you to cry out people for sending their spirits, against you?

MARY WARREN: It were pretense, sir.

DANFORTH: I cannot hear you.

PROCTOR: It were pretense, she says.

DANFORTH: Ah? And the other girls? Susanna Walcott, and—the others? They are also pretending?

MARY WARREN: Aye, sir.

DANFORTH, *wide-eyed:* Indeed. *Pause. He is baffled by this. He turns to study* PROCTOR'S *face.*

PARRIS, *in a sweat:* Excellency, you surely cannot think to let so vile a lie be spread in open court!

DANFORTH: Indeed not, but it strike hard upon me that she will dare come here with such a tale. Now, Mr. Proctor, before I decide whether I shall hear you or not, it is my duty to tell you this. We burn a hot fire here; it melts down all concealment.

PROCTOR: I know that, sir.

DANFORTH: Let me continue. I understand well, a husband's tenderness may drive him to extravagance in defense of a wife. Are you certain in your conscience, Mister, that your evidence is the truth?

PROCTOR: It is. And you will surely know it.

DANFORTH: And you thought to declare this revelation in the open court before the public?

PROCTOR: I thought I would, aye—with your permission.

DANFORTH, *his eyes narrowing:* Now, sir, what is your purpose in so doing?

PROCTOR: Why, I—I would free my wife, sir.

DANFORTH: There lurks nowhere in your heart, nor hidden in your spirit, any desire to undermine this court?

PROCTOR, *with the faintest faltering:* Why, no, sir.

CHEEVER, *clears his throat, awakening:* I—Your Excellency.

DANFORTH: Mr. Cheever.

CHEEVER: I think it be my duty, sir—*Kindly, to* PROCTOR: You'll not deny it, John. *To* DANFORTH: When we come to

Characterization

What is Parris's motive for discrediting Mary Warren in court?

Comprehension

What new testimony does Mary Warren give?

take his wife, he damned the court and ripped your warrant.

PARRIS: Now you have it!

DANFORTH: He did that, Mr. Hale?

HALE, *takes a breath:* Aye, he did.

PROCTOR: It were a temper, sir. I knew not what I did.

DANFORTH, *studying him:* Mr. Proctor.

PROCTOR: Aye, sir.

DANFORTH, *straight into his eyes:* Have you ever seen the Devil?

PROCTOR: No, sir.

DANFORTH: You are in all respects a Gospel Christian?

PROCTOR: I am, sir.

PARRIS: Such a Christian that will not come to church but once in a month!

DANFORTH, *restrained—he is curious:* Not come to church?

PROCTOR: I—I have no love for Mr. Parris. It is no secret. But God I surely love.

CHEEVER: He plow on Sunday, sir.

DANFORTH: Plow on Sunday!

CHEEVER, *apologetically:* I think it be evidence, John. I am an official of the court, I cannot keep it.

PROCTOR: I—I have once or twice plowed on Sunday. I have three children, sir, and until last year my land give little.

GILES: You'll find other Christians that do plow on Sunday if the truth be known.

HALE: Your Honor, I cannot think you may judge the man on such evidence.

Evaluating Arguments

In what way does Danforth's statement represent a logical fallacy?

DANFORTH: I judge nothing. *Pause. He keeps watching* PROCTOR, *who tries to meet his gaze.* I tell you straight, Mister—I have seen marvels in this court. I have seen people choked before my eyes by spirits; I have seen them stuck by pins and slashed by daggers. I have until this moment not the slightest reason to suspect that the children may be deceiving me. Do you understand my meaning?

PROCTOR: Excellency, does it not strike upon you that so many of these women have lived so long with such upright reputation, and—

PARRIS: Do you read the Gospel, Mr. Proctor?

PROCTOR: I read the Gospel.

PARRIS: I think not, or you should surely know that Cain were an upright man, and yet he did kill Abel.[2]

PROCTOR: Aye, God tells us that. *To* DANFORTH: But who tells us Rebecca Nurse murdered seven babies by sending out her spirit on them? It is the children only, and this one will swear she lied to you.

DANFORTH *considers, then beckons* HATHORNE *to him.* HATHORNE *leans in, and he speaks in his ear.* HATHORNE *nods.*

---

2. **Cain . . . Abel** In the Bible, Cain, the oldest son of Adam and Eve, killed his brother Abel.

HATHORNE: Aye, she's the one.

DANFORTH: Mr. Proctor , this morning, your wife send me a claim in which she states that she is pregnant now.

PROCTOR: My wife pregnant!

DANFORTH: There be no sign of it—we have examined her body.

PROCTOR: But if she say she is pregnant, then she must be! That woman will never lie, Mr. Danforth.

DANFORTH: She will not?

PROCTOR: Never, sir, never.

DANFORTH: We have thought it too convenient to be credited. However, if I should tell you now that I will let her be kept another month; and if she begin to show her natural signs, you shall have her living yet another year until she is delivered—what say you to that? JOHN PROCTOR *is struck silent.* Come now. You say your only purpose is to save your wife. Good, then, she is saved at least this year, and a year is long. What say you, sir? It is done now. *In conflict,* PROCTOR *glances at* FRANCIS *and* GILES. Will you drop this charge?

PROCTOR: I—I think I cannot.

DANFORTH, *now an almost imperceptible hardness in his voice:* Then your purpose is somewhat larger.

PARRIS: He's come to overthrow this court, Your Honor!

PROCTOR: These are my friends. Their wives are also accused—

DANFORTH, *with a sudden briskness of manner:* I judge you not, sir. I am ready to hear your evidence.

PROCTOR: I come not to hurt the court; I only—

DANFORTH, *cutting him off:* Marshal, go into the court and bid Judge Stoughton and Judge Sewall declare recess for one hour. And let them go to the tavern, if they will. All witnesses and prisoners are to be kept in the building.

HERRICK: Aye, sir. *Very deferentially:* If I may say it, sir. I know this man all my life. It is a good man, sir.

DANFORTH —*it is the reflection on himself he resents:* I am sure of it, Marshal. HERRICK *nods, then goes out.* Now, what deposition do you have for us, Mr. Proctor? And I beg you be clear, open as the sky, and honest.

PROCTOR, *as he takes out several papers:* I am no lawyer, so I'll—

DANFORTH: The pure in heart need no lawyers. Proceed as you will.

PROCTOR, *handing* DANFORTH *a paper:* Will you read this first, sir? It's a sort of testament. The people signing it declare their good opinion of Rebecca, and my wife, and Martha Corey.

DANFORTH *looks down at the paper.*

PARRIS, *to enlist* DANFORTH'S *sarcasm:* Their good opinion! *But* DANFORTH *goes on reading, and* PROCTOR *is heartened.*

PROCTOR: These are all landholding farmers, members of the church. *Delicately, trying to point out a paragraph:* If you'll notice, sir—they've

---

I tell you straight, Mister—I have seen marvels in this court.

Vocabulary

imperceptible
(im′ pər sep′ tə bəl)
adj. barely noticeable

Verbal Irony

What makes Danforth's statement about the "pure in heart" an example of verbal irony?

Comprehension

What document does Proctor present to the court?

known the women many years and never saw no sign they had dealings with the Devil.

PARRIS *nervously moves over and reads over* DANFORTH'S *shoulder.*

DANFORTH, *glancing down a long list:* How many names are here?

FRANCIS: Ninety-one, Your Excellency.

PARRIS, *sweating:* These people should be summoned. DANFORTH *looks up at him questioningly.* For questioning.

FRANCIS. *trembling with anger:* Mr. Danforth, I gave them all my word no harm would come to them for signing this.

PARRIS: This is a clear attack upon the court!

HALE, *to* PARRIS, *trying to contain himself:* Is every defense an attack upon the court? Can no one—?

PARRIS: All innocent and Christian people are happy for the courts in Salem! These people are gloomy for it. *To* DANFORTH *directly:* And I think you will want to know, from each and every one of them, what discontents them with you!

HATHORNE: I think they ought to be examined, sir.

DANFORTH: It is not necessarily an attack, I think. Yet—

FRANCIS: These are all covenanted Christians, sir.

DANFORTH: Then I am sure they may have nothing to fear. *Hands* CHEEVER *the paper.* Mr. Cheever, have warrants drawn for all of these—arrest for examination. *To* PROCTOR: Now, Mister, what other information do you have for us? FRANCIS *is still standing, horrified.* You may sit, Mr. Nurse.

FRANCIS: I have brought trouble on these people: I have—

DANFORTH: No, old man, you have not hurt these people if they are of good conscience. But you must understand, sir, that a person is either with this court or he must be counted against it, there be no road between. This is a sharp time, now, a precise time—we live no longer in the dusky afternoon when evil mixed itself with good and befuddled the world. Now, by God's grace, the shining sun is up, and them that fear not light will surely praise it. I hope you will be one of those. MARY WARREN *suddenly sobs.* She's not hearty, I see.

PROCTOR: No, she's not, sir. *To* MARY, *bending to her, holding her hand, quietly:* Now remember what the angel Raphael said to the boy Tobias.[3] Remember it.

MARY WARREN, *hardly audible:* Aye.

PROCTOR: "Do that which is good, and no harm shall come to thee."

MARY WARREN: Aye.

Evaluating Arguments

What is faulty about Parris's claim that "all innocent and Christian people are happy for the courts in Salem"?

Verbal Irony

In what sense is Proctor's quotation from the Bible ironic?

---

3. **Raphael . . . Tobias** In the Bible, Tobias is guided by the archangel Raphael to save two people who have prayed for their deaths. One of the two is Tobias's father, Tobit, who has prayed for his death because he has lost his sight. The other is Sara, a woman who is afflicted by a demon and has killed her seven husbands on their wedding day. With Raphael's assistance, Tobias exorcises the devil from Sara and cures his father of blindness.

DANFORTH: Come, man, we wait you.

MARSHAL HERRICK *returns, and takes his post at the door.*

GILES: John, my deposition, give him mine.

PROCTOR: Aye. *He hands* DANFORTH *another paper.* This is Mr. Corey's deposition.

DANFORTH: Oh? *He looks down at it. Now* HATHORNE *comes behind him and reads with him.*

HATHORNE, *suspiciously:* What lawyer drew this, Corey?

GILES: You know I never hired a lawyer in my life, Hathorne.

DANFORTH, *finishing the reading:* It is very well phrased. My compliments. Mr. Parris, if Mr. Putnam is in the court, will you bring him in? HATHORNE *takes the deposition, and walks to the window with it.* PARRIS *goes into the court.* You have no legal training, Mr. Corey?

GILES, *very pleased:* I have the best, sir—I am thirty-three time in court in my life. And always plaintiff, too.

DANFORTH: Oh, then you're much put-upon.

GILES: I am never put-upon; I know my rights, sir, and I will have them. You know, your father tried a case of mine—might be thirty-five year ago, I think.

DANFORTH: Indeed.

GILES: He never spoke to you of it?

DANFORTH: No, I cannot recall it.

GILES: That's strange, he gave me nine pound damages. He were a fair judge, your father. Y'see, I had a white mare that time, and this fellow come to borrow the mare—*Enter* PARRIS *with* THOMAS PUTNAM. *When he sees* PUTNAM, GILES' *ease goes; he is hard.* Aye, there he is.

DANFORTH: Mr. Putnam, I have here an accusation by Mr. Corey against you. He states that you coldly prompted your daughter to cry witchery upon George Jacobs that is now in jail.

PUTNAM: It is a lie.

DANFORTH, *turning to* GILES: Mr. Putnam states your charge is a lie. What say you to that?

GILES, *furious, his fists clenched:* A fart on Thomas Putnam, that is what I say to that!

DANFORTH: What proof do you submit for your charge, sir?

GILES: My proof is there! *Pointing to the paper.* If Jacobs hangs for a witch he forfeit up his property—that's law! And there is none but Putnam with the coin to buy so great a piece. This man is killing his neighbors for their land!

DANFORTH: But proof, sir, proof.

GILES, *pointing at his deposition:* The proof is there! I have it from an honest man who heard Putnam say it! The day his daughter cried out on Jacobs, he said she'd given him a fair gift of land.

HATHORNE: And the name of this man?

> This is a clear attack upon the court!

Verbal Irony

What is ironic about Danforth's request for proof from Giles?

Comprehension

What is Giles Corey's defense? Explain.

Arthur Miller
Author's Insight
During the Cultural Revolution in China (1966–1976), Communist party true-believers persecuted intellectuals and artists. Miller wrote how a young Chinese author thought that the courtroom scenes in *The Crucible* were all too familiar: "As she listened to [a production of the play] . . . the interrogations sounded . . . precisely the same as the ones she and others had been subjected to by the Cultural Revolutionaries. . . ."

Vocabulary

anonymity (an´ ə nim´ ə tē) *n.* the condition of being unknown

GILES, *taken aback:* What name?

HATHORNE: The man that give you this information.

GILES, *hesitates, then:* Why, I—I cannot give you his name.

HATHORNE: And why not?

GILES, *hesitates, then bursts out:* You know well why not! He'll lay in jail if I give his name!

HATHORNE: This is contempt of the court, Mr. Danforth!

DANFORTH, *to avoid that:* You will surely tell us the name.

GILES: I will not give you no name. I mentioned my wife's name once and I'll burn in hell long enough for that. I stand mute.

DANFORTH: In that case, I have no choice but to arrest you for contempt of this court, do you know that?

GILES: This is a hearing; you cannot clap me for contempt of a hearing.

DANFORTH: Oh, it is a proper lawyer! Do you wish me to declare the court in full session here? Or will you give me good reply?

GILES, *faltering:* I cannot give you no name, sir, I cannot.

DANFORTH: You are a foolish old man. Mr. Cheever, begin the record. The court is now in session. I ask you, Mr. Corey—

PROCTOR, *breaking in:* Your Honor—he has the story in confidence, sir, and he—

PARRIS: The Devil lives on such confidences! *To* DANFORTH: Without confidences there could be no conspiracy, Your Honor!

HATHORNE: I think it must be broken, sir.

DANFORTH, *to* GILES: Old man, if your informant tells the truth let him come here openly like a decent man. But if he hide in anonymity I must know why. Now sir, the government and central church demand of you the name of him who reported Mr. Thomas Putnam a common murderer.

HALE: Excellency—

DANFORTH: Mr. Hale.

HALE: We cannot blink it more. There is a prodigious fear of this court in the country—

DANFORTH: Then there is a prodigious guilt in the country. Are you afraid to be questioned here?

HALE: I may only fear the Lord, sir, but there is fear in the country nevertheless.

DANFORTH, *angered now:* Reproach me not with the fear in the country; there is fear in the country because there is a moving plot to topple Christ in the country!

HALE: But it does not follow that everyone accused is part of it.

DANFORTH: No uncorrupted man may fear this court, Mr. Hale! None! *To* GILES: You are under arrest in contempt of this court. Now sit you down and take counsel with yourself, or you will be set in the jail until you decide to answer all questions.

GILES COREY *makes a rush for* PUTNAM. PROCTOR *lunges and holds him.*

PROCTOR: No, Giles!

GILES, *over Proctor's shoulder at* PUTNAM: I'll cut your throat, Putnam, I'll kill you yet!

PROCTOR, *forcing him into a chair:* Peace, Giles, peace. *Releasing him.* We'll prove ourselves. Now we will. *He starts to turn to* DANFORTH.

GILES: Say nothin' more, John. *Pointing at* DANFORTH: He's only playin' you! He means to hang us all!

MARY WARREN *bursts into sobs.*

DANFORTH: This is a court of law, Mister. I'll have no effrontery here!

PROCTOR: Forgive him, sir, for his old age. Peace, Giles, we'll prove it all now. *He lifts up* MARY's *chin.* You cannot weep, Mary. Remember the angel, what he say to the boy. Hold to it, now; there is your rock. MARY *quiets. He takes out a paper, and turns to* DANFORTH. This is Mary Warren's deposition. I—I would ask you remember, sir, while you read it, that until two week ago she were no different than the other children are today. *He is speaking reasonably, restraining all his fears, his anger, his anxiety.* You saw her scream, she howled, she swore familiar spirits choked her; she even testified that Satan, in the form of women now in jail, tried to win her soul away, and then when she refused—

DANFORTH: We know all this.

PROCTOR: Aye, sir. She swears now that she never saw Satan; nor any spirit, vague or clear, that Satan may have sent to hurt her. And she declares her friends are lying now.

PROCTOR *starts to hand* DANFORTH *the deposition, and* HALE *comes up to* DANFORTH *in a trembling state.*

HALE: Excellency, a moment. I think this goes to the heart of the matter.

DANFORTH, *with deep misgivings:* It surely does.

HALE: I cannot say he is an honest man; I know him little. But in all justice, sir, a claim so weighty cannot be argued by a farmer. In God's name, sir, stop here; send him home and let him come again with a lawyer—

DANFORTH, *patiently:* Now look you, Mr. Hale—

HALE: Excellency, I have signed seventy-two death warrants; I am a minister of the Lord, and I dare not take a life without there be a proof so immaculate no slightest qualm of conscience may doubt it.

DANFORTH: Mr. Hale, you surely do not doubt my justice.

HALE: I have this morning signed away the soul of Rebecca Nurse, Your Honor. I'll not conceal it, my hand shakes yet as with a wound! I pray you, sir, *this* argument let lawyers present to you.

DANFORTH: Mr. Hale, believe me; for a man of such terrible learning you are most bewildered—I hope you will forgive me. I have been thirty-two year at the bar, sir, and I should be confounded were I called upon to defend these people. Let you consider, now—*To* PROCTOR *and the others:*

Vocabulary

effrontery (e frunt′ ər ē) *n.* shameless boldness

Comprehension

According to Danforth, why do people in Salem fear the court?

The Crucible, Act III **1197**

Evaluating Arguments

In what ways is Danforth's entire argument based on a faulty premise?

▼ **Critical Viewing**

In this movie still, Danforth conveys a feeling of sympathy, or understanding, for Mary Warren. Compare this portrayal with your own image of Danforth. **COMPARE/CONTRAST**

And I bid you all do likewise. In an ordinary crime, how does one defend the accused? One calls up witnesses to prove his innocence. But witchcraft is *ipso facto*,[4] on its face and by its nature, an invisible crime, is it not? Therefore, who may possibly be witness to it? The witch and the victim. None other. Now we cannot hope the witch will accuse herself; granted? Therefore, we must rely upon her victims—and they do testify, the children certainly do testify. As for the witches, none will deny that we are most eager for all their confessions. Therefore, what is left for a lawyer to bring out? I think I have made my point. Have I not?

HALE: But this child claims the girls are not truthful, and if they are not—

DANFORTH: That is precisely what I am about to consider, sir. What more may you ask of me? Unless you doubt my probity?[5]

HALE, *defeated:* I surely do not, sir. Let you consider it, then.

DANFORTH: And let you put your heart to rest. Her deposition, Mr. Proctor.

PROCTOR *hands it to him.* HATHORNE *rises, goes beside* DANFORTH, *and starts reading.* PARRIS *comes to his other side.* DANFORTH *looks at* JOHN

---

4. *ipso facto* (ip′ sō fak′ tō) "by that very fact"; "therefore" (Latin).
5. probity (prō′ bə tē) *n.* complete honesty; integrity.

PROCTOR, *then proceeds to read.* HALE *gets up, finds position near the judge, reads too.* PROCTOR *glances at* GILES. FRANCIS *prays silently, hands pressed together.* CHEEVER *waits placidly, the sublime official, dutiful.* MARY WARREN *sobs once.* JOHN PROCTOR *touches her head reassuringly. Presently* DANFORTH *lifts his eyes, stands up, takes out a kerchief and blows his nose. The others stand aside as he moves in thought toward the window.*

PARRIS, *hardly able to contain his anger and fear:* I should like to question—

DANFORTH *—his first real outburst, in which his contempt for* PARRIS *is clear:* Mr. Parris, I bid you be silent! *He stands in silence, looking out the window. Now, having established that he will set the gait:* Mr. Cheever, will you go into the court and bring the children here? CHEEVER *gets up and goes out upstage.* DANFORTH *now turns to* MARY. Mary Warren, how came you to this turnabout? Has Mr. Proctor threatened you for this deposition?

MARY WARREN: No, sir.

DANFORTH: Has he ever threatened you?

MARY WARREN, *weaker:* No, sir.

Comprehension
sWhat document does Danforth read?

WORLD LITERATURE CONNECTION

POLITICAL DRAMA

FEDERICO GARCÍA LORCA (1898–1936)

Playwright and poet Federico García Lorca was born in a village in southern Spain, a region that had changed little since the Middle Ages. For centuries, the land had been owned by the wealthy and tilled by peasants. As a child, Lorca entertained his family by performing puppet shows. He grew up to write plays that were unique in the Spanish tradition. They were simple and elemental, poetic, and powerful. They spoke of the suffering of people who were not free to express themselves.

In 1931, Spain elected a democratic government and it seemed a freer era had dawned. However, Spain was fiercely divided. In May of 1936, Lorca completed his last play, *The House of Bernarda Alba*, about a tyrannical widow who keeps her five daughters locked in the house. Two months later, before the play could be performed, civil war erupted. Lorca, along with thousands of others, was murdered by fascists. His plays were banned in Spain for many years.

▲ The National Theatre's production of *The House of Bernarda Alba* at the National Theatre, London.

CONNECT TO THE LITERATURE

Speculate about why a government might prevent the performance of a play.

Characterization

What do you think motivates Danforth's repeated questioning of Mary Warren?

DANFORTH, *sensing a weakening:* Has he threatened you?

MARY WARREN: No, sir.

DANFORTH: Then you tell me that you sat in my court, callously lying, when you knew that people would hang by your evidence? *She does not answer.* Answer me!

MARY WARREN, *almost inaudibly:* I did, sir.

DANFORTH: How were you instructed in your life? Do you not know that God damns all liars? *She cannot speak.* Or is it now that you lie?

MARY WARREN: No, sir—I am with God now.

DANFORTH: You are with God now.

MARY WARREN: Aye, sir.

DANFORTH, *containing himself:* I will tell you this—you are either lying now, or you were lying in the court, and in either case you have committed perjury and you will go to jail for it. You cannot lightly say you lied, Mary. Do you know that?

MARY WARREN: I cannot lie no more. I am with God, I am with God.

But she breaks into sobs at the thought of it, and the right door opens, and enter SUSANNA WALCOTT, MERCY LEWIS, BETTY PARRIS, *and finally* ABIGAIL. CHEEVER *comes to* DANFORTH.

CHEEVER: Ruth Putnam's not in the court, sir, nor the other children.

DANFORTH: These will be sufficient. Sit you down, children. *Silently they sit.* Your friend, Mary Warren, has given us a deposition. In which she swears that she never saw familiar spirits, apparitions, nor any manifest of the Devil. She claims as well that none of you have seen these things either. *Slight pause.* Now, children, this is a court of law. The law, based upon the Bible, and the Bible, writ by Almighty God, forbid the practice of witchcraft, and describe death as the penalty thereof. But likewise, children, the law and Bible damn all bearers of false witness. *Slight pause.* Now then. It does not escape me that this deposition may be devised to blind us; it may well be that Mary Warren has been conquered by Satan, who sends her here to distract our sacred purpose. If so, her neck will break for it. But if she speak true, I bid you now drop your guile and confess your pretense, for a quick confession will go easier with you. *Pause.* Abigail Williams, rise. ABIGAIL *slowly rises.* Is there any truth in this?

Dramatic Irony

In what ways do Danforth's statements create dramatic irony?

ABIGAIL: No, sir.

DANFORTH, *thinks, glances at* MARY *then back to* ABIGAIL: Children, a very augur bit[6] will now be turned into your souls until your honesty is proved. Will either of you change your positions now, or do you force me to hard questioning?

ABIGAIL: I have naught to change, sir. She lies.

DANFORTH, *to* MARY: You would still go on with this?

---

6. augur bit sharp point of an augur, a tool used for boring holes.

MARY WARREN, *faintly:* Aye, sir.

DANFORTH, *turning to* ABIGAIL: A poppet were discovered in Mr. Proctor's house, stabbed by a needle. Mary Warren claims that you sat beside her in the court when she made it, and that you saw her make it and witnessed how she herself stuck her needle into it for safe-keeping. What say you to that?

ABIGAIL, *with a slight note of indignation:* It is a lie, sir.

DANFORTH, *after a slight pause:* While you worked for Mr. Proctor, did you see poppets in that house?

ABIGAIL: Goody Proctor always kept poppets.

PROCTOR: Your Honor, my wife never kept no poppets. Mary Warren confesses it was her poppet.

CHEEVER: Your Excellency.

DANFORTH: Mr. Cheever.

CHEEVER: When I spoke with Goody Proctor in that house, she said she never kept no poppets. But she said she did keep poppets when she were a girl.

PROCTOR: She has not been a girl these fifteen years, Your Honor.

HATHORNE: But a poppet will keep fifteen years, will it not?

PROCTOR: It will keep if it is kept, but Mary Warren swears she never saw no poppets in my house, nor anyone else.

PARRIS: Why could there not have been poppets hid where no one ever saw them?

PROCTOR, *furious:* There might also be a dragon with five legs in my house, but no one has ever seen it.

PARRIS: We are here, Your Honor, precisely to discover what no one has ever seen.

PROCTOR: Mr. Danforth, what profit this girl to turn herself about? What may Mary Warren gain but hard questioning and worse?

DANFORTH: You are charging Abigail Williams with a marvelous cool plot to murder, do you understand that?

PROCTOR: I do, sir. I believe she means to murder.

DANFORTH, *pointing at* ABIGAIL, *incredulously:* This child would murder your wife?

PROCTOR: It is not a child. Now hear me, sir. In the sight of the congregation she were twice this year put out of this meetin' house for laughter during prayer.

DANFORTH, *shocked, turning to* ABIGAIL: What's this? Laughter during—!

PARRIS: Excellency, she were under Tituba's power at that time, but she is solemn now.

GILES: Aye, now she is solemn and goes to hang people!

DANFORTH: Quiet, man.

HATHORNE: Surely it have no bearing on the question, sir. He charges contemplation of murder.

Evaluating Arguments
On what faulty premise is this argument against Elizabeth based?

Vocabulary
incredulously
(in krej′ o͞o ləs lē) *adv.* skeptically

Characterization
How does Proctor try to shift Danforth's understanding of Abigail?

Comprehension
Of what serious charge do Proctor and Giles accuse Abigail?

DANFORTH: Aye. *He studies* ABIGAIL *for a moment, then:* Continue, Mr. Proctor.

PROCTOR: Mary. Now tell the Governor how you danced in the woods.

PARRIS, *instantly:* Excellency, since I come to Salem this man is blackening my name. He—

DANFORTH: In a moment, sir. *To* MARY WARREN, *sternly, and surprised.* What is this dancing?

MARY WARREN: I—*She glances at* ABIGAIL, *who is staring down at her remorselessly. Then, appealing to* PROCTOR: Mr. Proctor—

PROCTOR, *taking it right up:* Abigail leads the girls to the woods, Your Honor, and they have danced there naked—

PARRIS: Your Honor, this—

PROCTOR, *at once:* Mr. Parris discovered them himself in the dead of night! There's the "child" she is!

DANFORTH— *it is growing into a nightmare, and he turns, astonished, to* PARRIS: Mr. Parris—

PARRIS: I can only say, sir, that I never found any of them naked, and this man is—

DANFORTH: But you discovered them dancing in the woods? *Eyes on* PARRIS, *he points at* ABIGAIL. Abigail?

HALE: Excellency, when I first arrived from Beverly, Mr. Parris told me that.

DANFORTH: Do you deny it, Mr. Parris?

PARRIS: I do not, sir, but I never saw any of them naked.

▼ **Critical Viewing**

In this scene, Parris and Danforth order Mary to pretend to faint. Analyze this movie still and describe the emotions conveyed by Parris, Danforth, Mary, and the girls. **ANALYZE**

DANFORTH: But she have *danced?*

PARRIS, *unwillingly:* Aye, sir.

DANFORTH, *as though with new eyes, looks at* ABIGAIL.

HATHORNE: Excellency, will you permit me? *He points at* MARY WARREN.

DANFORTH, *with great worry:* Pray, proceed.

HATHORNE: You say you never saw no spirits, Mary, were never threatened or afflicted by any manifest of the Devil or the Devil's agents.

MARY WARREN, *very faintly:* No, sir.

HATHORNE, *with a gleam of victory:* And yet, when people accused of witchery confronted you in court, you would faint, saying their spirits came out of their bodies and choked you—

MARY WARREN: That were pretense, sir.

DANFORTH: I cannot hear you.

MARY WARREN: Pretense, sir.

PARRIS: But you did turn cold, did you not? I myself picked you up many times, and your skin were icy. Mr. Danforth, you—

DANFORTH: I saw that many times.

PROCTOR: She only pretended to faint, Your Excellency. They're all marvelous pretenders.

HATHORNE: Then can she pretend to faint now?

PROCTOR: Now?

PARRIS: Why not? Now there are no spirits attacking her, for none in this room is accused of witchcraft. So let her turn herself cold now, let her pretend she is attacked now, let her faint. *He turns to* MARY WARREN. Faint!

MARY WARREN: Faint?

PARRIS: Aye, faint. Prove to us how you pretended in the court so many times.

MARY WARREN, *looking to* PROCTOR: I—cannot faint now, sir.

PROCTOR, *alarmed, quietly:* Can you not pretend it?

MARY WARREN: I—*She looks about as though searching for the passion to faint.* I—have no *sense* of it now, I—

DANFORTH: Why? What is lacking now?

MARY WARREN: I—cannot tell, sir, I—

DANFORTH: Might it be that here we have no afflicting spirit loose, but in the court there were some?

MARY WARREN: I never saw no spirits.

PARRIS: Then see no spirits now, and prove to us that you can faint by your own will, as you claim.

MARY WARREN, *stares, searching for the emotion of it, and then shakes her head:* I—cannot do it.

PARRIS: Then you will confess, will you not? It were attacking spirits made you faint!

MARY WARREN: No, sir, I—

> "... let her pretend she is attacked now, let her faint."

Evaluating Arguments

In what sense does Danforth's question express a logical fallacy?

Comprehension

What do Parris and Hathorne ask Mary Warren to do?

PARRIS: Your Excellency, this is a trick to blind the court!

MARY WARREN: It's not a trick! *She stands.* I—I used to faint because I—I thought I saw spirits.

DANFORTH: *Thought* you saw them!

MARY WARREN: But I did not, Your Honor.

HATHORNE: How could you think you saw them unless you saw them?

MARY WARREN: I—I cannot tell how, but I did. I—I heard the other girls screaming, and you, Your Honor, you seemed to believe them, and I—It were only sport in the beginning, sir, but then the whole world cried spirits, spirits, and I—I promise you, Mr. Danforth, I only thought I saw them but I did not.

DANFORTH *peers at her.*

PARRIS, *smiling, but nervous because* DANFORTH *seems to be struck by* MARY WARREN'S *story:* Surely Your Excellency is not taken by this simple lie.

DANFORTH, *turning worriedly to* ABIGAIL: Abigail. I bid you now search your heart and tell me this—and beware of it, child, to God every soul is precious and His vengeance is terrible on them that take life without cause. Is it possible, child, that the spirits you have seen are illusion only, some deception that may cross your mind when—

ABIGAIL: Why, this—this—is a base question, sir.

DANFORTH: Child, I would have you consider it—

ABIGAIL: I have been hurt, Mr. Danforth; I have seen my blood runnin' out! I have been near to murdered every day because I done my duty pointing out the Devil's people—and this is my reward? To be mistrusted, denied, questioned like a—

DANFORTH, *weakening:* Child, I do not mistrust you—

ABIGAIL, *in an open threat:* Let *you* beware, Mr. Danforth. Think you to be so mighty that the power of Hell may not turn *your* wits? Beware of it! There is—*Suddenly, from an accusatory attitude, her face turns, looking into the air above—it is truly frightened.*

DANFORTH, *apprehensively:* What is it, child?

ABIGAIL, *looking about in the air, clasping her arms about her as though cold:* I—I know not. A wind, a cold wind, has come. *Her eyes fall on* MARY WARREN.

MARY WARREN, *terrified, pleading:* Abby!

MERCY LEWIS, *shivering:* Your Honor, I freeze!

PROCTOR: They're pretending!

HATHORNE, *touching* ABIGAIL'S *hand:* She is cold, Your Honor, touch her!

MERCY LEWIS, *through chattering teeth:* Mary, do you send this shadow on me?

MARY WARREN: Lord, save me!

SUSANNA WALCOTT: I freeze, I freeze!

ABIGAIL, *shivering, visibly:* It is a wind, a wind!

◄ **Critical Viewing**
Abigail pretends to be under the control of spirits. Does this scene from the movie effectively portray the scene in the play? Explain. **EVALUATE**

Spiral Review
Conflict What conflicts, both internal and external, might Danforth be experiencing in this scene? Explain.

Comprehension
How does Abigail threaten Danforth?

MARY WARREN: Abby, don't do that!

DANFORTH, *himself engaged and entered by* ABIGAIL: Mary Warren, do you witch her? I say to you, do you send your spirit out?

With a hysterical cry MARY WARREN *starts to run.* PROCTOR *catches her.*

MARY WARREN, *almost collapsing:* Let me go, Mr. Proctor, I cannot, I cannot—

ABIGAIL, *crying to Heaven:* Oh, Heavenly Father, take away this shadow!

Without warning or hesitation, PROCTOR *leaps at* ABIGAIL *and, grabbing her by the hair, pulls her to her feet. She screams in pain.* DANFORTH, *astonished, cries,* "What are you about?" *and* HATHORNE *and* PARRIS *call,* "Take your hands off her!" *and out of it all comes* PROCTOR'S *roaring voice.*

PROCTOR: How do you call Heaven! Whore! Whore!

HERRICK *breaks* PROCTOR *from her.*

HERRICK: John!

DANFORTH: Man! Man, what do you—

PROCTOR, *breathless and in agony:* It is a whore!

DANFORTH, *dumfounded:* You charge—?

ABIGAIL: Mr. Danforth, he is lying!

PROCTOR: Mark her! Now she'll suck a scream to stab me with, but—

DANFORTH: You will prove this! This will not pass!

PROCTOR, *trembling, his life collapsing about him:* I have known her, sir. I have known her.

DANFORTH: You—you are a lecher?

FRANCIS, *horrified:* John, you cannot say such a—

PROCTOR: Oh, Francis, I wish you had some evil in you that you might know me! *To* DANFORTH: A man will not cast away his good name. You surely know that.

DANFORTH, *dumfounded:* In—in what time? In what place?

PROCTOR, *his voice about to break, and his shame great:* In the proper place—where my beasts are bedded. On the last night of my joy, some eight months past. She used to serve me in my house, sir. *He has to clamp his jaw to keep from weeping.* A man may think God sleeps, but God sees everything. I know it now. I beg you, sir, I beg you—see her what she is. My wife, my dear good wife, took this girl soon after, sir, and put her out on the highroad. And being what she is, a lump of vanity, sir—*He is being overcome.* Excellency, forgive me, forgive me. *Angrily against himself, he turns away from the* GOVERNOR *for a moment. Then, as though to cry out is his only means of speech left:* She thinks to dance with me on my wife's grave! And well she might, for I thought of her softly. God help me, I lusted, and there *is* a promise in such sweat. But it is a whore's vengeance, and you must see it; I set myself entirely in your hands. I know you must see it now.

DANFORTH, *blanched, in horror, turning to* ABIGAIL: You deny every scrap and tittle of this?

Characterization

What motivates Proctor to make his confession?

ABIGAIL: If I must answer that, I will leave and I will not come back again! DANFORTH *seems unsteady.*

PROCTOR: I have made a bell of my honor! I have rung the doom of my good name—you will believe me, Mr. Danforth! My wife is innocent, except she knew a whore when she saw one!

ABIGAIL, *stepping up to* DANFORTH: What look do you give me? DANFORTH *cannot speak.* I'll not have such looks! *She turns and starts for the door.*

DANFORTH: You will remain where you are! HERRICK *steps into her path. She comes up short, fire in her eyes.* Mr. Parris, go into the court and bring Goodwife Proctor out.

PARRIS, *objecting:* Your Honor, this is all a—

DANFORTH, *sharply to* PARRIS: Bring her out! And tell her not one word of what's been spoken here. And let you knock before you enter. PARRIS *goes out.* Now we shall touch the bottom of this swamp. *To* PROCTOR: Your wife, you say, is an honest woman.

PROCTOR: In her life, sir, she have never lied. There are them that cannot sing, and them that cannot weep—my wife cannot lie. I have paid much to learn it, sir.

DANFORTH: And when she put this girl out of your house, she put her out for a harlot?

PROCTOR: Aye, sir.

DANFORTH: And knew her for a harlot?

PROCTOR: Aye, sir, she knew her for a harlot.

DANFORTH: Good then. *To* ABIGAIL: And if she tell me, child, it were for harlotry, may God spread His mercy on you! *There is a knock. He calls to the door.* Hold! *To* ABIGAIL: Turn your back. Turn your back. *To* PROCTOR: Do likewise. *Both turn their backs*—ABIGAIL *with indignant slowness.* Now let neither of you turn to face Goody Proctor. No one in this room is to speak one word, or raise a gesture aye or nay. *He turns toward the door, calls:* Enter! *The door opens.* ELIZABETH *enters with* PARRIS. PARRIS *leaves her. She stands alone, her eyes looking for* PROCTOR. Mr. Cheever, report this testimony in all exactness. Are you ready?

CHEEVER: Ready, sir.

DANFORTH: Come here, woman. ELIZABETH *comes to him, glancing at* PROCTOR'S *back.* Look at me only, not at your husband. In my eyes only.

ELIZABETH, *faintly:* Good, sir.

DANFORTH: We are given to understand that at one time you dismissed your servant, Abigail Williams.

ELIZABETH: That is true, sir.

DANFORTH: For what cause did you dismiss her? *Slight pause. Then* ELIZABETH *tries to glance at* PROCTOR. You will look in my eyes only and not at your husband. The answer is in your memory and you need no help to give it to me. Why did you dismiss Abigail Williams?

ELIZABETH, *not knowing what to say, sensing a situation, wetting her*

Evaluating Arguments
Why does Proctor insist that the court must believe his argument?

Dramatic Irony
Which details in Elizabeth's exchange with Danforth reveal the dramatic irony at work in this scene?

Comprehension
What does Proctor reveal about Abigail?

History Connection

Puritans and Nathaniel Hawthorne

One of the many characters in *The Crucible* who have real historical counterparts is John Hathorne, a judge who takes part in the Salem witchcraft trials. The real Hathorne's most famous descendant was the writer Nathaniel Hawthorne (see p. 271), who lived in Salem during the nineteenth century. Hawthorne used the Puritan colonies of his ancestors as the settings for much of his work. In Puritan rigidity and repression he found an expression for his dark vision of the human soul.

Hawthorne's best-known novel, *The Scarlet Letter*, examines the repressive side of Puritanism and the hypocrisy and pain that such an atmosphere produced. His short stories "Young Goodman Brown" and "The Minister's Black Veil" also focus on New England's Puritan communities.

Connect to the Literature

What inspiration for Hawthorne's dark vision may have come from his Salem ancestor?

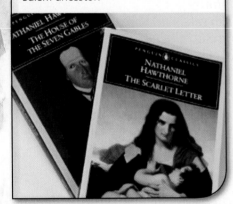

lips to stall for time: She—dissatisfied me. *Pause.* And my husband.

DANFORTH: In what way dissatisfied you?

ELIZABETH: She were—*She glances at* PROCTOR *for a cue.*

DANFORTH: Woman, look at me? ELIZABETH *does.* Were she slovenly? Lazy? What disturbance did she cause?

ELIZABETH: Your Honor, I—in that time I were sick. And I—My husband is a good and righteous man. He is never drunk as some are, nor wastin' his time at the shovelboard, but always at his work. But in my sickness—you see, sir, I were a long time sick after my last baby, and I thought I saw my husband somewhat turning from me. And this girl—*She turns to* ABIGAIL.

DANFORTH: Look at me.

ELIZABETH: Aye, sir. Abigail Williams—*She breaks off.*

DANFORTH: What of Abigail Williams?

ELIZABETH: I came to think he fancied her. And so one night I lost my wits, I think, and put her out on the highroad.

DANFORTH: Your husband—did he indeed turn from you?

ELIZABETH, *in agony:* My husband—is a goodly man, sir.

DANFORTH: Then he did not turn from you.

ELIZABETH, *starting to glance at* PROCTOR: He—

DANFORTH, *reaches out and holds her face, then:* Look at me! To your own knowledge, has John Proctor ever committed the crime of lechery? *In a crisis of indecision she cannot speak.* Answer my question! Is your husband a lecher!

ELIZABETH, *faintly:* No, sir.

DANFORTH: Remove her, Marshal.

PROCTOR: Elizabeth, tell the truth!

DANFORTH: She has spoken. Remove her!

PROCTOR, *crying out:* Elizabeth, I have confessed it!

ELIZABETH: Oh, God! *The door closes behind her.*

PROCTOR: She only thought to save my name!

HALE: Excellency, it is a natural lie to tell; I beg you, stop now before another is condemned! I may shut my conscience to it no more—private vengeance is working through this testimony! From the beginning this man has struck me true. By my oath to Heaven, I believe him now, and I pray you call back his wife before we—

DANFORTH: She spoke nothing of lechery, and this man has lied!

HALE: I believe him! *Pointing at* ABIGAIL: This girl has always struck me false! She has—

ABIGAIL, *with a weird, wild, chilling cry, screams up to the ceiling.*

ABIGAIL: You will not! Begone! Begone, I say!

DANFORTH: What is it, child? *But* ABIGAIL, *pointing with fear, is now raising up her frightened eyes, her awed face, toward the ceiling—the girls are doing the same—and now* HATHORNE, HALE, PUTNAM, CHEEVER, HERRICK, *and* DANFORTH *do the same.* What's there? *He lowers his eyes from the ceiling, and now he is frightened; there is real tension in his voice.* Child! *She is transfixed—with all the girls, she is whimpering, open-mouthed, agape at the ceiling.* Girls! Why do you—?

MERCY LEWIS, *pointing:* It's on the beam! Behind the rafter!

DANFORTH, *looking up:* Where!

ABIGAIL: Why—? *She gulps.* Why do you come, yellow bird?

PROCTOR: Where's a bird? I see no bird!

ABIGAIL, *to the ceiling:* My face? My face?

PROCTOR: Mr. Hale—

DANFORTH: Be quiet!

PROCTOR, *to* HALE: Do you see a bird?

DANFORTH: Be quiet!!

ABIGAIL, *to the ceiling, in a genuine conversation with the "bird," as though trying to talk it out of attacking her:* But God made my face; you cannot want to tear my face. Envy is a deadly sin, Mary.

MARY WARREN, *on her feet with a spring, and horrified, pleading:* Abby!

ABIGAIL, *unperturbed, continuing to the "bird":* Oh, Mary, this is a black art to change your shape. No, I cannot, I cannot stop my mouth; it's God's work I do.

MARY WARREN: Abby, I'm *here!*

PROCTOR, *frantically:* They're pretending, Mr. Danforth!

ABIGAIL —*now she takes a backward step, as though in fear the bird will swoop down momentarily:* Oh, please, Mary! Don't come down.

SUSANNA WALCOTT: Her claws, she's stretching her claws!

PROCTOR: Lies, lies.

ABIGAIL, *backing further, eyes still fixed above:* Mary, please don't hurt me!

MARY WARREN, *to* DANFORTH: I'm not hurting her!

DANFORTH, *to* MARY WARREN: Why does she see this vision?

MARY WARREN: She sees nothin'!

ABIGAIL, *now staring full front as though hypnotized, and mimicking the exact tone of* MARY WARREN'S *cry:* She sees nothin'!

MARY WARREN, *pleading:* Abby, you mustn't!

ABIGAIL AND ALL THE GIRLS, *all transfixed:* Abby, you mustn't!

MARY WARREN, *to all the girls:* I'm here, I'm here!

Comprehension

In what way does Elizabeth's testimony differ from John's?

GIRLS: I'm here, I'm here!

DANFORTH, *horrified:* Mary Warren! Draw back your spirit out of them!

MARY WARREN: Mr. Danforth!

GIRLS, *cutting her off:* Mr. Danforth!

DANFORTH: Have you compacted with the Devil? Have you?

MARY WARREN: Never, never!

GIRLS: Never, never!

DANFORTH, *growing hysterical:* Why can they only repeat you?

PROCTOR: Give me a whip—I'll stop it!

MARY WARREN: They're sporting. They—!

GIRLS: They're sporting!

MARY WARREN, *turning on them all hysterically and stamping her feet:* Abby, stop it!

GIRLS, *stamping their feet:* Abby, stop it!

MARY WARREN: Stop it!

GIRLS: Stop it!

MARY WARREN, *screaming it out at the top of her lungs, and raising her fists:* Stop it!!

GIRLS, *raising their fists:* Stop it!!

MARY WARREN, *utterly confounded, and becoming overwhelmed by* ABIGAIL'S—*and the girls'—utter conviction, starts to whimper, hands half raised, powerless, and all the girls begin whimpering exactly as she does.*

DANFORTH: A little while ago you were afflicted. Now it seems you afflict others; where did you find this power?

MARY WARREN, *staring at* ABIGAIL: I—have no power.

GIRLS: I have no power.

PROCTOR: They're gulling[7] you, Mister!

DANFORTH: Why did you turn about this past two weeks? You have seen the Devil, have you not?

HALE, *indicating* ABIGAIL *and the* GIRLS: You cannot believe them!

MARY WARREN: I—

PROCTOR, *sensing her weakening:* Mary, God damns all liars!

DANFORTH, *pounding it into her:* You have seen the Devil, you have made compact with Lucifer, have you not?

PROCTOR: God damns liars, Mary!

MARY *utters something unintelligible, staring at* ABIGAIL, *who keeps watching the "bird" above.*

DANFORTH: I cannot hear you. What do you say? MARY *utters again unintelligibly.* You will confess yourself or you will hang! *He turns her roughly to face him.* Do you know who I am? I say you will hang if you do not open with me!

---

7. **gulling** fooling.

"You have seen the Devil... have you not?"

PROCTOR: Mary, remember the angel Raphael—do that which is good and—

ABIGAIL, *pointing upward:* The wings! Her wings are spreading! Mary, please, don't, don't—!

HALE: I see nothing, Your Honor!

DANFORTH: Do you confess this power! *He is an inch from her face.* Speak!

ABIGAIL: She's going to come down! She's walking the beam!

DANFORTH: Will you speak!

MARY WARREN, *staring in horror:* I cannot!

GIRLS: I cannot!

PARRIS: Cast the Devil out! Look him in the face! Trample him! We'll save you, Mary, only stand fast against him and—

ABIGAIL, *looking up:* Look out! She's coming down!

She and all the girls run to one wall, shielding their eyes. And now, as though cornered, they let out a gigantic scream, and MARY, *as though infected, opens her mouth and screams with them. Gradually* ABIGAIL *and the girls leave off, until only* MARY *is left there, staring up at the "bird," screaming madly. All watch her, horrified by this evident fit.* PROCTOR *strides to her.*

▼ **Critical Viewing**
Examine the girls' expressions in this movie still. What dominant emotions do you think they feel as they follow Abigail's lead? **ASSESS**

Comprehension
What do the girls do to undermine Mary Warren's testimony?

PROCTOR: Mary, tell the Governor what they—*He has hardly got a word out, when, seeing him coming for her, she rushes out of his reach, screaming in horror.*

MARY WARREN: Don't touch me—don't touch me! *At which the girls halt at the door.*

PROCTOR, *astonished:* Mary!

MARY WARREN, *pointing at* PROCTOR: You're the Devil's man!

He is stopped in his tracks.

PARRIS: Praise God!

GIRLS: Praise God!

PROCTOR, *numbed:* Mary, how—?

MARY WARREN: I'll not hang with you! I love God, I love God.

DANFORTH, *to* MARY: He bid you do the Devil's work?

MARY WARREN, *hysterically, indicating* PROCTOR: He come at me by night and every day to sign, to sign, to—

DANFORTH: Sign what?

PARRIS: The Devil's book? He come with a book?

MARY WARREN, *hysterically, pointing at* PROCTOR, *fearful of him:* My name, he want my name. "I'll murder you," he says, "if my wife hangs! We must go and overthrow the court," he says!

DANFORTH'S *head jerks toward* PROCTOR, *shock and horror in his face.*

PROCTOR, *turning, appealing to* HALE: Mr. Hale!

MARY WARREN, *her sobs beginning:* He wake me every night, his eyes were like coals and his fingers claw my neck, and I sign, I sign . . .

HALE: Excellency, this child's gone wild!

PROCTOR, *as* DANFORTH'S *wide eyes pour on him:* Mary, Mary!

MARY WARREN, *screaming at him:* No, I love God; I go your way no more. I love God, I bless God. *Sobbing, she rushes to* ABIGAIL. Abby, Abby, I'll never hurt you more! *They all watch, as* ABIGAIL, *out of her infinite charity, reaches out and draws the sobbing* MARY *to her, and then looks up to* DANFORTH.

DANFORTH, *to* PROCTOR: What are you? PROCTOR *is beyond speech in his anger.* You are combined with anti-Christ,[8] are you not? I have seen your power; you will not deny it! What say you, Mister?

HALE: Excellency—

DANFORTH: I will have nothing from you, Mr. Hale! *To* PROCTOR: Will you confess yourself befouled with Hell, or do you keep that black allegiance yet? What say you?

PROCTOR, *his mind wild, breathless:* I say—I say—God is dead!

PARRIS: Hear it, hear it!

PROCTOR, *laughs insanely, then:* A fire, a fire is burning! I hear the boot

Verbal Irony

Which two words in these stage directions are an example of verbal irony? Explain.

---

8. **anti-Christ** In the Bible, the great antagonist of Christ expected to spread universal evil.

of Lucifer, I see his filthy face! And it is my face, and yours, Danforth! For them that quail to bring men out of ignorance, as I have quailed, and as you quail now when you know in all your black hearts that this be fraud—God damns our kind especially, and we will burn, we will burn together.

DANFORTH: Marshal! Take him and Corey with him to the jail!

HALE, *staring across to the door:* I denounce these proceedings!

PROCTOR: You are pulling Heaven down and raising up a whore!

HALE: I denounce these proceedings, I quit this court! *He slams the door to the outside behind him.*

DANFORTH, *calling to him in a fury:* Mr. Hale! Mr. Hale!

THE CURTAIN FALLS

Critical Reading

1. **Key Ideas and Details (a)** Which three depositions are presented to the judges and on whose behalf? **(b) Analyze:** How do the judges discourage defenses of the accused?

2. **Key Ideas and Details (a)** What does John Proctor confess to Danforth? **(b) Interpret:** Why does Proctor make this confession? **(c) Infer:** What does his confession reveal about his character?

3. **Key Ideas and Details (a)** What is the lie Elizabeth Proctor tells Danforth? **(b) Analyze:** What are the consequences of her lie?

4. **Key Ideas and Details (a)** What truth does Mary Warren reveal about her involvement with "spirits"? **(b) Analyze:** Why does she change her testimony and turn on John Proctor?

5. **Key Ideas and Details (a)** What does Hale denounce at the end of Act III? **(b) Evaluate:** Do you find Hale sympathetic? Why or why not?

6. **Integration of Knowledge and Ideas Apply:** Imagine that Elizabeth Proctor had told Danforth the truth. In what way might the outcome of the trials have been different?

7. **Integration of Knowledge and Ideas Assess:** Who bears the most guilt for the fate of those hanged in the Salem witch trials—the girls who accused innocent people or the judges who sentenced them to death?

Cite textual evidence to support your responses.

Close Reading Activities

The Crucible, Act III

Literary Analysis

1. **Craft and Structure (a)** Identify two examples of **direct characterization** Miller uses to describe Giles Corey in stage directions. **(b)** Identify two examples of **indirect characterization**—dialogue or action—that supports this description. Explain your choices.

2. **Craft and Structure (a)** Identify three examples of **indirect characterization** that reveal Mary Warren's personality. **(b)** For each example, explain what you learn about her.

3. **Key Ideas and Details (a)** What is Elizabeth's *motive* for evading Danforth's questions about Abigail's dismissal from the Proctor household? **(b)** Considering Elizabeth's belief that lying is a sin, what does her evasion suggest about her character, her feelings for her husband, and her understanding of the court proceedings?

4. **Key Ideas and Details (a)** What motivates Hale to denounce the proceedings and quit the court? **(b)** How do Hale's character and motivations change from when he first arrives in Salem? Explain.

5. **Craft and Structure (a)** Using a chart like the one shown below question 6, list two examples of **dramatic irony** in Act III. **(b)** For each, explain what the audience understands or knows that the characters themselves do not.

6. **Craft and Structure (a)** Using the same type of chart, identify two examples of **verbal irony** in Act III. **(b)** Explain what each speaker really means.

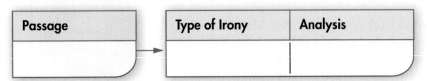

Passage		Type of Irony	Analysis

7. **Craft and Structure** In what ways is the effect of Elizabeth's testimony ironic?

8. **Craft and Structure** What is ironic about Mary Warren's statement, "I—have no power," when she is being interrogated in front of Abigail Williams?

9. **Integration of Knowledge and Ideas (a) Evaluate the argument** Judge Danforth uses in the dramatic exchange with Reverend Hale by identifying the erroneous idea that underlies his reasoning about the legal proceedings. **(b)** Is Danforth's argument credible?

10. **Integration of Knowledge and Ideas** In what sense does Danforth's *logical fallacy* have ramifications far beyond the conviction of John Proctor?

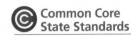
Common Core State Standards

Writing
1. Write arguments to support claims in an analysis of substantive topics or texts, using valid reasoning and relevant and sufficient evidence. *(p. 1215)*

1.a. Introduce precise, knowledgeable claim(s), establish the significance of the claim(s), distinguish the claim(s) from alternate or opposing claims, and create an organization that logically sequences claim(s), counterclaims, reasons, and evidence. *(p. 1215)*

1.b. Develop claim(s) and counterclaims fairly and thoroughly, supplying the most relevant evidence for each while pointing out the strengths and limitations of both in a manner that anticipates the audience's knowledge level, concerns, values, and possible biases. *(p. 1215)*

1.e. Provide a concluding statement or section that follows from and supports the argument presented. *(p. 1215)*

Language
5. Demonstrate understanding of word relationships. *(p. 1215)*

6. Acquire and use accurately general academic and domain-specific words and phrases, sufficient for reading, writing, speaking, and listening at the college and career readiness level; demonstrate independence in gathering vocabulary knowledge when considering a word or phrase important to comprehension or expression. *(p. 1215)*

Vocabulary Acquisition and Use

Word Analysis: Legal Terms

The Crucible contains numerous legal terms, specifically words referring to sworn speech. The following Latin roots often form the basis of such words:

-fid- (faith, trust) *-pos-* (to place)

-testis- (a witness) *-jurare-* (to swear)

Use your knowledge of these roots to explain how they contribute to the meaning of the following words. If necessary, use a dictionary to determine the meanings of prefixes or suffixes.

1. affidavit 3. testimony
2. deposition 4. perjury

Then, use a dictionary to find one word containing each of these roots: *-fid-, -testis-, -pos-, -jurare-*. Write a sentence for each new word.

Vocabulary: Synonyms or Antonyms

Review the vocabulary list on page 1186. Then, for each item below, indicate whether the paired words are synonyms or antonyms. Explain your answers.

1. contentious, combative
2. deposition, testimony
3. imperceptible, obvious
4. anonymity, notoriety
5. effrontery, timidity
6. incredulously, disbelievingly

Writing to Sources

Argument A brief is a legal document that contains information about the facts of a case, the legal issues to be decided, and the law the Court ought to apply. An *amicus curiae*—or "friend of the court"—brief is a persuasive document submitted by individuals who are not themselves party to a case. Such briefs are offered in the hope that the court will take their advice. Write a **"friend of the court" brief** as if you were a respected official of a Puritan community near Salem.

Prewriting Review the court scene in Act III from the perspective of someone who shares the Puritan worldview but has no personal involvement in the trial. Use a chart like the one shown to outline your position, evidence, and counterarguments.

Drafting In the first paragraph, explain your position. Then, present arguments and supporting evidence, followed by counterarguments and evidence. Conclude by restating your position and making a final claim.

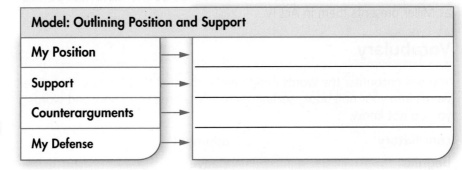

Model: Outlining Position and Support

My Position	
My Support	
Counterarguments	
My Defense	

Revising Reread your brief and make sure your word choices are accurate, precise, and vivid. Replace details or words that are inaccurate or vague with better choices.

Building Knowledge and Insight | *The Crucible, Act IV*

Close Reading Focus

Tragedy; Allegory

Tragedy is a dramatic form that was first developed in ancient Greece. A tragedy usually has these characteristics:

- The main character is involved in a struggle that ends in disaster. This character, often called the **tragic hero,** is a person of high rank who has the respect of the community.
- The tragic hero's downfall is usually the result of some combination of fate, an error in judgment, and a personality weakness often called a **tragic flaw.**
- Once the tragedy is in motion, the downfall is usually inevitable.
- The tragic hero gains wisdom or insight by the play's end.

Tragedy arouses feelings of pity and fear in the audience. Spectators pity the plight of the main character and fear that a similar fate might befall them. A tragic drama may also suggest that the human spirit is capable of remarkable nobility even in the midst of great suffering.

An **allegory** is a story with more than one layer of meaning: a literal meaning and one or more symbolic meanings. The characters, settings, and themes in an allegory are symbols of ideas and qualities that exist outside the story. *The Crucible* is an allegory, because Miller uses one historical period and setting (seventeenth-century New England) to comment on another (1950s America). The tragedy that occurs in Salem is an allegory for the anti-Communist hysteria that gripped the United States during the 1950s. As you read, notice how the events in Salem echo the events surrounding the McCarthy hearings to tragic effect.

Preparing to Read Complex Texts Arthur Miller brings many areas of Puritan thought to bear on the story of *The Crucible.* These philosophical, political, religious, ethical, and social influences shape the characters, setting, actions, and ultimate meaning of the play. As you read, use a chart like the one shown to **evaluate the influences of the historical period** as Miller presents them in Act IV.

Vocabulary

You will encounter the words listed here in the text that follows. Copy the words into your notebook, sorting them into words you know and words you do not know.

conciliatory	adamant
beguile	cleave
retaliation	tantalized

 Common Core
State Standards

Reading Literature
3. Analyze the impact of the author's choices regarding how to develop and relate elements of a drama.
6. Analyze a case in which grasping a point of view requires distinguishing what is directly stated in a text from what is really meant.

Philosophical Idea

Characters

Settings

Events

Review and Anticipate

"Is every defense an attack upon the court?" Hale asks in Act III. Danforth observes, "A person is either with this court or he must be counted against it." Such remarks stress the powerlessness of people like John Proctor and Giles Corey against the mounting injustices in Salem. In pursuing justice, their efforts backfire, and their own names join the list of those accused. What do you think the final outcome will be? Who will survive, and who will perish? Read the final act to see if your predictions are correct.

ACT 4

A cell in Salem jail, that fall.

At the back is a high barred window; near it, a great, heavy door. Along the walls are two benches.

The place is in darkness but for the moonlight seeping through the bars. It appears empty. Presently footsteps are heard coming down a corridor beyond the wall, keys rattle, and the door swings open. MARSHAL HERRICK *enters with a lantern.*

He is nearly drunk, and heavy-footed. He goes to a bench and nudges a bundle of rags lying on it.

HERRICK: Sarah, wake up! Sarah Good! *He then crosses to the other benches.*

SARAH GOOD, *rising in her rags:* Oh, Majesty! Comin', comin'! Tituba, he's here, His Majesty's come!

HERRICK: Go to the north cell; this place is wanted now. *He hangs his lantern on the wall.* TITUBA *sits up.*

TITUBA: That don't look to me like His Majesty; look to me like the marshal.

HERRICK, *taking out a flask:* Get along with you now, clear this place. *He drinks, and* SARAH GOOD *comes and peers up into his face.*

SARAH GOOD: Oh, is it you, Marshal! I thought sure you be the devil comin' for us. Could I have a sip of cider for me goin'-away?

HERRICK, *handing her the flask:* And where are you off to, Sarah?

TITUBA, *as* SARAH *drinks:* We goin' to Barbados, soon the Devil gits here with the feathers and the wings.

HERRICK: Oh? A happy voyage to you.

SARAH GOOD: A pair of bluebirds wingin' southerly, the two of us! Oh, it be a grand transformation, Marshal! *She raises the flask to drink again.*

Comprehension

For whom does Sarah Good mistake Herrick?

HERRICK, *taking the flask from her lips:* You'd best give me that or you'll never rise off the ground. Come along now.

TITUBA: I'll speak to him for you, if you desires to come along, Marshal.

HERRICK: I'd not refuse it, Tituba; it's the proper morning to fly into Hell.

TITUBA: Oh, it be no Hell in Barbados. Devil, him be pleasure man in Barbados, him be singin' and dancin' in Barbados. It's you folks—you riles him up 'round here; it be too cold 'round here for that Old Boy. He freeze his soul in Massachusetts, but in Barbados he just as sweet and—*A bellowing cow is heard, and* TITUBA *leaps up and calls to the window:* Aye, sir! That's him, Sarah!

SARAH GOOD: I'm here, Majesty! *They hurriedly pick up their rags as* HOPKINS, *a guard, enters.*

HOPKINS: The Deputy Governor's arrived.

HERRICK, *grabbing* TITUBA: Come along, come along.

TITUBA, *resisting him:* No, he comin' for me. I goin' home!

HERRICK, *pulling her to the door:* That's not Satan, just a poor old cow with a hatful of milk. Come along now, out with you!

TITUBA, *calling to the window:* Take me home, Devil! Take me home!

SARAH GOOD, *following the shouting* TITUBA *out:* Tell him I'm goin', Tituba! Now you tell him Sarah Good is goin' too!

In the corridor outside TITUBA *calls on—"Take me home, Devil; Devil take me home!" and* HOPKINS' *voice orders her to move on.* HERRICK *returns and begins to push old rags and straw into a corner. Hearing footsteps, he turns, and enter* DANFORTH *and* JUDGE HATHORNE. *They are in greatcoats and wear hats against the bitter cold. They are followed in by* CHEEVER, *who carries a dispatch case and a flat wooden box containing his writing materials.*

HERRICK: Good morning, Excellency.

DANFORTH: Where is Mr. Parris?

HERRICK: I'll fetch him. *He starts for the door.*

DANFORTH: Marshal. HERRICK *stops.* When did Reverend Hale arrive?

HERRICK: It were toward midnight, I think.

DANFORTH, *suspiciously:* What is he about here?

HERRICK: He goes among them that will hang, sir. And he prays with them. He sits with Goody Nurse now. And Mr. Parris with him.

DANFORTH: Indeed. That man have no authority to enter here, Marshal. Why have you let him in?

HERRICK: Why, Mr. Parris command me, sir. I cannot deny him.

DANFORTH: Are you drunk, Marshal?

HERRICK: No, sir; it is a bitter night, and I have no fire here.

DANFORTH, *containing his anger:* Fetch Mr. Parris.

HERRICK: Aye, sir.

DANFORTH: There is a prodigious stench in this place.

HERRICK: I have only now cleared the people out for you.

Evaluating the Influences of the Historical Period

How does Tituba's desire for home reflect historical realities?

DANFORTH: Beware hard drink, Marshal.

HERRICK: Aye, sir. *He waits an instant for further orders. But* DANFORTH, *in dissatisfaction, turns his back on him, and* HERRICK *goes out. There is a pause.* DANFORTH *stands in thought.*

HATHORNE: Let you question Hale, Excellency; I should not be surprised he have been preaching in Andover[1] lately.

DANFORTH: We'll come to that; speak nothing of Andover. Parris prays with him. That's strange. *He blows on his hands, moves toward the window, and looks out.*

HATHORNE: Excellency, I wonder if it be wise to let Mr. Parris so continuously with the prisoners. DANFORTH *turns to him, interested.* I think, sometimes, the man has a mad look these days.

DANFORTH: Mad?

HATHORNE: I met him yesterday coming out of his house, and I bid him good morning—and he wept and went his way. I think it is not well the village sees him so unsteady.

DANFORTH: Perhaps he have some sorrow.

CHEEVER, *stamping his feet against the cold:* I think it be the cows, sir.

DANFORTH: Cows?

CHEEVER: There be so many cows wanderin' the highroads, now their masters are in the jails, and much disagreement who they will belong to now. I know Mr. Parris be arguin' with farmers all yesterday—there is great contention, sir, about the cows. Contention make him weep, sir; it were always a man that weep for contention. *He turns, as do* HATHORNE *and* DANFORTH *hearing someone coming up the corridor.* DANFORTH *raises his head as* PARRIS *enters. He is gaunt, frightened, and sweating in his greatcoat.*

PARRIS, *to* DANFORTH, *instantly:* Oh, good morning, sir, thank you for coming. I beg your pardon wakin' you so early. Good morning, Judge Hathorne.

DANFORTH: Reverend Hale have no right to enter this—

PARRIS: Excellency, a moment. *He hurries back and shuts the door.*

HATHORNE: Do you leave him alone with the prisoners?

DANFORTH: What's his business here?

PARRIS, *prayerfully holding up his hands:* Excellency, hear me. It is a providence. Reverend Hale has returned to bring Rebecca Nurse to God.

DANFORTH, *surprised:* He bids her confess?

PARRIS, *sitting:* Hear me. Rebecca have not given me a word this three month since she came. Now she sits with him, and her sister and Martha Corey and two or three others, and he pleads with them,

Allegory

How might this description of Salem in chaos warn against anti-communist fear and suspicion in Miller's time?

Comprehension

Why are so many cows wandering the roads?

---

1. **Andover** During the height of the terror in Salem Village, a similar hysteria broke out in the nearby town of Andover. There, many respected people were accused of practicing witchcraft and confessed to escape death. However, in Andover people soon began questioning the reality of the situation and the hysteria quickly subsided.

confess their crimes and save their lives.

DANFORTH: Why—this is indeed a providence. And they soften, they soften?

PARRIS: Not yet, not yet. But I thought to summon you, sir, that we might think on whether it be not wise, to—*He dares not say it.* I had thought to put a question, sir, and I hope you will not—

DANFORTH: Mr. Parris, be plain, what troubles you?

PARRIS: There is news, sir, that the court—the court must reckon with. My niece, sir, my niece—I believe she has vanished.

DANFORTH: Vanished!

PARRIS: I had thought to advise you of it earlier in the week, but—

DANFORTH: Why? How long is she gone?

PARRIS: This be the third night. You see, sir, she told me she would stay a night with Mercy Lewis. And next day, when she does not return, I send to Mr. Lewis to inquire. Mercy told him she would sleep in *my* house for a night.

DANFORTH: They are both gone?!

PARRIS, *in fear of him:* They are, sir.

DANFORTH, *alarmed:* I will send a party for them. Where may they be?

PARRIS: Excellency, I think they be aboard a ship. DANFORTH *stands* agape. My daughter tells me how she heard them speaking of ships last week, and tonight I discover my—my strongbox is broke into. *He presses his fingers against his eyes to keep back tears.*

HATHORNE, *astonished:* She have robbed you?

PARRIS: Thirty-one pound is gone. I am penniless. *He covers his face and sobs.*

DANFORTH: Mr. Parris, you are a brainless man! *He walks in thought, deeply worried.*

PARRIS: Excellency, it profit nothing you should blame me. I cannot think they would run off except they fear to keep in Salem any more. *He is pleading.* Mark it, sir, Abigail had close knowledge of the town, and since the news of Andover has broken here—

DANFORTH: Andover is remedied. The court returns there on Friday, and will resume examinations.

PARRIS: I am sure of it, sir. But the rumor here speaks rebellion in Andover, and it—

DANFORTH: There is no rebellion in Andover!

PARRIS: I tell you what is said here, sir. Andover have thrown out the court, they say, and will have no part of witchcraft. There be a faction here, feeding on that news, and I tell you true, sir, I fear there will be riot here.

HATHORNE: Riot! Why at every execution I have seen naught but high satisfaction in the town.

PARRIS: Judge Hathorne—it were another sort that hanged till now. Rebecca Nurse is no Bridget that lived three year with Bishop before

▶ **Critical Viewing**

What might Parris be saying to Judge Danforth in this court scene from execution day? **SPECULATE** she married him. John Proctor is not Isaac Ward that drank his family to ruin. *To* DANFORTH: I would to God it were not so, Excellency, but these people have great weight yet in the town. Let Rebecca stand upon the gibbet[2] and send up some righteous prayer, and I fear she'll wake a vengeance on you.

HATHORNE: Excellency, she is condemned a witch. The court have—

DANFORTH, *in deep concern, raising a hand to* HATHORNE: Pray you. *To* PARRIS: How do you propose, then?

PARRIS: Excellency, I would postpone these hangin's for a time.

DANFORTH: There will be no postponement.

PARRIS: Now Mr. Hale's returned, there is hope, I think—for if he bring even one of these to God, that confession surely damns the others in the public eye, and none may doubt more that they are all linked to Hell. This way, unconfessed and claiming innocence, doubts are multiplied, many honest people will weep for them, and our good purpose is lost in their tears.

DANFORTH, *after thinking a moment, then going to* CHEEVER: Give me the list.

CHEEVER *opens the dispatch case, searches.*

PARRIS: It cannot be forgot, sir, that when I summoned the congregation for John Proctor's excommunication there were hardly thirty people come to hear it. That speak a discontent, I think, and—

DANFORTH, *studying the list:* There will be no postponement.

PARRIS: Excellency—

DANFORTH: Now, sir—which of these in your opinion may be brought to God? I will myself strive with him till dawn. *He hands the list to* PARRIS, *who merely glances at it.*

---

2. **gibbet** (jib′ it) *n.* gallows.

Tragedy

How does Parris's description of Proctor suggest some of the qualities of a tragic hero?

Comprehension

What has happened to Abigail?

PARRIS: There is not sufficient time till dawn.

DANFORTH: I shall do my utmost. Which of them do you have hope for?

PARRIS, *not even glancing at the list now, and in a quavering voice, quietly:* Excellency—a dagger—*He chokes up.*

DANFORTH: What do you say?

PARRIS: Tonight, when I open my door to leave my house—a dagger clattered to the ground. *Silence.* DANFORTH *absorbs this. Now* PARRIS *cries out:* You cannot hang this sort. There is danger for me. I dare not step outside at night!

REVEREND HALE *enters. They look at him for an instant in silence. He is steeped in sorrow, exhausted, and more direct than he ever was.*

DANFORTH: Accept my congratulations, Reverend Hale; we are gladdened to see you returned to your good work.

HALE, *coming to* DANFORTH *now:* You must pardon them. They will not budge.

HERRICK *enters, waits.*

DANFORTH, *conciliatory:* You misunderstand, sir; I cannot pardon these when twelve are already hanged for the same crime. It is not just.

PARRIS, *with failing heart:* Rebecca will not confess?

HALE: The sun will rise in a few minutes. Excellency, I must have more time.

DANFORTH: Now hear me, and beguile yourselves no more. I will not receive a single plea for pardon or postponement. Them that will not confess will hang. Twelve are already executed; the names of these seven are given out, and the village expects to see them die this morning. Postponement now speaks a floundering on my part; reprieve or pardon must cast doubt upon the guilt of them that died till now. While I speak God's law, I will not crack its voice with whimpering. If retaliation is your fear, know this—I should hang ten thousand that dared to rise against the law, and an ocean of salt tears could not melt the resolution of the statutes. Now draw yourselves up like men and help me, as you are bound by Heaven to do. Have you spoken with them all, Mr. Hale?

HALE: All but Proctor. He is in the dungeon.

DANFORTH, *to* HERRICK: What's Proctor's way now?

HERRICK: He sits like some great bird; you'd not know he lived except he will take food from time to time.

DANFORTH, *after thinking a moment:* His wife—his wife must be well on with child now.

HERRICK: She is, sir.

DANFORTH: What think you, Mr. Parris? You have closer knowledge of this man; might her presence soften him?

PARRIS: It is possible, sir. He have not laid eyes on her these three months. I should summon her.

DANFORTH, *to* HERRICK: Is he yet adamant? Has he struck at you again?

Vocabulary

conciliatory (kən sil′ ē ə toʊr′ ē) *adj.* tending to soothe anger

beguile (bē gīl′) *v.* trick

retaliation (ri tal′ ē ā′ shən) *n.* act of returning an injury or wrong

adamant (ad′ ə mənt) *adj.* firm; unyielding

HERRICK: He cannot, sir, he is chained to the wall now.

DANFORTH, *after thinking on it:* Fetch Goody Proctor to me. Then let you bring him up.

HERRICK: Aye, sir. HERRICK *goes. There is silence.*

HALE: Excellency, if you postpone a week and publish to the town that you are striving for their confessions, that speak mercy on your part, not faltering.

DANFORTH: Mr. Hale, as God have not empowered me like Joshua to stop this sun from rising,[3] so I cannot withhold from them the perfection of their punishment.

HALE, *harder now:* If you think God wills you to raise rebellion, Mr. Danforth, you are mistaken!

DANFORTH, *instantly:* You have heard rebellion spoken in the town?

HALE: Excellency, there are orphans wandering from house to house; abandoned cattle bellow on the highroads, the stink of rotting crops hangs everywhere, and no man knows when the harlots' cry will end his life—and you wonder yet if rebellion's spoke? Better you should

---

3. **Joshua . . . rising** In the Bible, Joshua, leader of the Jews after the death of Moses, asks God to make the sun and the moon stand still during a battle, and his request is granted.

Tragedy

According to Danforth, are the events taking place in Salem inevitable? Explain.

Comprehension

Why has Hale returned to Salem?

WORLD LITERATURE IN CONTEXT

POLITICAL DRAMA

WOLE SOYINKA (b. 1934)

Playwright Wole Soyinka grew up in Nigeria, immersed in two cultures. His parents were English-speaking Christians, while his grandparents followed the local Yoruba religion. After attending college in Britain, Soyinka returned to Nigeria, organized a theater troupe, and wrote plays that combine elements of European drama with African folk culture. In 1960, Nigeria won its independence from Britain. Years of political violence followed and a succession of dictators took control of the country. Soyinka wrote political satires that skewered the government, making him powerful enemies. During the 1960s, he was arrested twice and thrown into jail.

Although he has spent much of the last 40 years living in exile, Soyinka has continued writing about Africa. In 1984, he directed the world premiere of *A Play of Giants*, a dark satire about four African dictators visiting New York City. Two years later, Soyinka won the Nobel Prize for Literature.

Connect to the Literature

Why might a playwright choose satire as a form for political commentary?

marvel how they do not burn your province!

DANFORTH: Mr. Hale, have you preached in Andover this month?

HALE: Thank God they have no need of me in Andover.

DANFORTH: You baffle me, sir. Why have you returned here?

HALE: Why, it is all simple. I come to do the Devil's work. I come to counsel Christians they should belie themselves. *His sarcasm collapses.* There is blood on my head! Can you not see the blood on my head!!

PARRIS: Hush! *For he has heard footsteps. They all face the door.* HERRICK *enters with* ELIZABETH. *Her wrists are linked by heavy chain, which* HERRICK *now removes. Her clothes are dirty; her face is pale and gaunt.* HERRICK *goes out.*

DANFORTH, *very politely:* Goody Proctor. *She is silent.* I hope you are hearty?

ELIZABETH, *as a warning reminder:* I am yet six month before my time.

DANFORTH: Pray be at your ease, we come not for your life. We— *uncertain how to plead, for he is not accustomed to it.* Mr. Hale, will you speak with the woman?

HALE: Goody Proctor, your husband is marked to hang this morning *Pause.*

ELIZABETH, *quietly:* I have heard it.

HALE: You know, do you not, that I have no connection with the court? *She seems to doubt it.* I come of my own, Goody Proctor. I would save your husband's life, for if he is taken I count myself his murderer. Do you understand me?

ELIZABETH: What do you want of me?

HALE: Goody Proctor, I have gone this three month like our Lord into the wilderness. I have sought a Christian way, for damnation's doubled on a minister who counsels men to lie.

HATHORNE: It is no lie, you cannot speak of lies.

HALE: It is a lie! They are innocent!

DANFORTH: I'll hear no more of that!

HALE, *continuing to* ELIZABETH: Let you not mistake your duty as I mistook my own. I came into this village like a bridegroom to his beloved, bearing gifts of high religion; the very crowns of holy law I brought, and what I touched with my bright confidence, it died; and where I turned the eye of my great faith, blood

▼ **Critical Viewing**

From this movie still, what emotions do you imagine John and Elizabeth Proctor are experiencing at this point? **INFER**

flowed up. Beware, Goody Proctor— cleave to no faith when faith brings blood. It is mistaken law that leads you to sacrifice. Life, woman, life is God's most precious gift; no principle, however glorious, may justify the taking of it. I beg you, woman, prevail upon your husband to confess. Let him give his lie. Quail not before God's judgment in this, for it may well be God damns a liar less than he that throws his life away for pride. Will you plead with him? I cannot think he will listen to another.

ELIZABETH, *quietly:* I think that be the Devil's argument.

HALE, *with a climactic desperation:* Woman, before the laws of God we are as swine! We cannot read His will!

ELIZABETH: I cannot dispute with you, sir; I lack learning for it.

DANFORTH, *going to her:* Goody Proctor, you are not summoned here for disputation. Be there no wifely tenderness within you? He will die with the sunrise. Your husband. Do you understand it? *She only looks at him.* What say you? Will you contend with him? *She is silent.* Are you stone? I tell you true, woman, had I no other proof of your unnatural life, your dry eyes now would be sufficient evidence that you delivered up your soul to Hell! A very ape would weep at such calamity! Have the devil dried up any tear of pity in you? *She is silent.* Take her out. It profit nothing she should speak to him!

ELIZABETH, *quietly:* Let me speak with him, Excellency.

PARRIS, *with hope:* You'll strive with him? *She hesitates.*

DANFORTH: Will you plead for his confession or will you not?

ELIZABETH: I promise nothing. Let me speak with him.

A sound—the sibilance of dragging feet on stone. They turn. A pause. HERRICK enters with JOHN PROCTOR. His wrists are chained. He is another man, bearded, filthy, his eyes misty as though webs had overgrown them. He halts inside the doorway, his eyes caught by the sight of ELIZABETH. The emotion flowing between them prevents anyone from speaking for an instant. Now HALE, visibly affected, goes to DANFORTH and speaks quietly.

HALE: Pray, leave them Excellency.

DANFORTH, *pressing HALE impatiently aside:* Mr. Proctor, you have been notified, have you not? PROCTOR *is silent, staring at* ELIZABETH. I see light in the sky, Mister; let you counsel with your wife, and may God help you turn your back on Hell. PROCTOR *is silent, staring at* ELIZABETH.

HALE, *quietly:* Excellency, let—

DANFORTH *brushes past HALE and walks out. HALE follows. CHEEVER stands and follows,* HATHORNE *behind.* HERRICK *goes.* PARRIS, *from a safe distance, offers:*

PARRIS: If you desire a cup of cider, Mr. Proctor, I am sure I—PROCTOR *turns an icy stare at him, and he breaks off.* PARRIS *raises his palms toward* PROCTOR. God lead you now. PARRIS *goes out.*

Vocabulary

cleave (klēv) *v.* adhere; cling

Comprehension

What does Hale urge Elizabeth Proctor to do?

Media Connection

Being Abigail Williams

For more than four decades, no American film director chose to tackle Arthur Miller's challenging stage drama *The Crucible*. Finally, in 1996, Nicholas Hytner enlisted actors including Winona Ryder, Daniel Day-Lewis, and Joan Allen to star in a film based on a screenplay by Miller himself.

Ryder found playing Abigail Williams engrossing and disturbing. "I've heard Abigail called the villain of the piece, but I'm not so sure," she says. "She's never been given any power. . . . Abigail understands that she could get attention and power, so she goes with it. There's always a part of her that knows she is fooling, but I think she was convinced that spirits were attacking her. I see her as insane in a way, but so is the whole town. It's like a disease."

Connect to the Literature

Do you agree with Ryder's assessment of Abigail? Explain.

Alone, PROCTOR *walks to her, halts. It is as though they stood in a spinning world. It is beyond sorrow, above it. He reaches out his hand as though toward an embodiment not quite real, and as he touches her, a strange soft sound, half laughter, half amazement, comes from his throat. He pats her hand. She covers his hand with hers. And then, weak, he sits. Then she sits, facing him.*

PROCTOR: The child?

ELIZABETH: It grows.

PROCTOR: There is no word of the boys?

ELIZABETH: They're well. Rebecca's Samuel keeps them.

PROCTOR: You have not seen them?

ELIZABETH: I have not. *She catches a weakening in herself and downs it.*

PROCTOR: You are a—marvel, Elizabeth.

ELIZABETH: You—have been tortured?

PROCTOR: Aye. *Pause. She will not let herself be drowned in the sea that threatens her.* They come for my life now.

ELIZABETH: I know it.

Pause.

PROCTOR: None—have yet confessed?

ELIZABETH: There be many confessed.

PROCTOR: Who are they?

ELIZABETH: There be a hundred or more, they say. Goody Ballard is one; Isaiah Goodkind is one. There be many.

PROCTOR: Rebecca?

ELIZABETH: Not Rebecca. She is one foot in Heaven now; naught may hurt her more.

PROCTOR: And Giles?

ELIZABETH: You have not heard of it?

PROCTOR: I hear nothin', where I am kept.

ELIZABETH: Giles is dead.

He looks at her incredulously.

PROCTOR: When were he hanged?

ELIZABETH, *quietly, factually:* He were not hanged. He would not answer aye or nay to his indictment; for if he denied the charge they'd hang him surely, and auction out his property. So he stand mute, and died Christian under the law. And so his sons will have his farm. It is the law, for he could not be condemned a wizard without he answer the indictment, aye or nay.

PROCTOR: Then how does he die?

ELIZABETH, *gently:* They press him, John.

PROCTOR: Press?

ELIZABETH: Great stones they lay upon his chest until he plead aye or nay. *With a tender smile for the old man:* They say he give them but two words. "More weight," he says. And died.

PROCTOR, *numbed—a thread to weave into his agony:* "More weight."

ELIZABETH: Aye. It were a fearsome man, Giles Corey.

Pause.

PROCTOR, *with great force of will, but not quite looking at her:* I have been thinking I would confess to them, Elizabeth. *She shows nothing.* What say you? If I give them that?

ELIZABETH: I cannot judge you, John.

Pause.

PROCTOR, *simply—a pure question:* What would you have me do?

ELIZABETH: As you will, I would have it. *Slight pause:* I want you living, John. That's sure.

PROCTOR, *pauses, then with a flailing of hope:* Giles' wife? Have she confessed?

ELIZABETH: She will not.

Pause.

PROCTOR: It is a pretense, Elizabeth.

ELIZABETH: What is?

PROCTOR: I cannot mount the gibbet like a saint. It is a fraud. I am not that man. *She is silent.* My honesty is broke, Elizabeth; I am no good man. Nothing's spoiled by giving them this lie that were not rotten long before.

ELIZABETH: And yet you've not confessed till now. That speak goodness in you.

PROCTOR: Spite only keeps me silent. It is hard to give a lie to dogs. *Pause, for the first time he turns directly to her.* I would have your forgiveness, Elizabeth.

ELIZABETH: It is not for me to give, John, I am—

PROCTOR: I'd have you see some honesty in it. Let them that never lied die now to keep their souls. It is pretense for me, a vanity that will not blind God nor keep my children out of the wind. *Pause.* What say you?

ELIZABETH, *upon a heaving sob that always threatens:* John, it come to naught that I should forgive you, if you'll not forgive yourself. *Now he turns away a little, in great agony.* It is not my soul, John, it is yours. *He stands, as though in physical pain, slowly rising to his feet with a great immortal longing to find his answer. It is difficult to say, and she is on the verge of tears.* Only be sure of this, for I know it now: Whatever you will do, it is a good man does it. *He turns his doubting, searching gaze upon her.* I have read my heart this three month, John. *Pause.* I have sins of my own to count. It needs a cold wife to prompt lechery.

PROCTOR, *in great pain:* Enough, enough—

ELIZABETH, *now pouring out her heart:* Better you should know me!

Tragedy

At this point in the play, how does Proctor view himself? Explain.

Comprehension

Why does Proctor say that he "cannot mount the gibbet like a saint"?

PROCTOR: I will not hear it! I know you!

ELIZABETH: You take my sins upon you, John—

PROCTOR, *in agony:* No, I take my own, my own!

ELIZABETH: John, I counted myself so plain, so poorly made, no honest love could come to me! Suspicion kissed you when I did; I never knew how I should say my love. It were a cold house I kept! *In fright, she swerves, as* HATHORNE *enters.*

HATHORNE: What say you Proctor? The sun is soon up.

PROCTOR, *his chest heaving, stares, turns to* ELIZABETH. *She comes to him as though to plead, her voice quaking.*

ELIZABETH: Do what you will. But let none be your judge. There be no higher judge under Heaven than Proctor is! Forgive me, forgive me, John—I never knew such goodness in the world! *She covers her face, weeping.*

PROCTOR *turns from her to* HATHORNE; *he is off the earth, his voice hollow.*

PROCTOR: I want my life.

HATHORNE *electrified, surprised:* You'll confess yourself?

PROCTOR: I will have my life.

HATHORNE, *with a mystical tone:* God be praised! It is a providence! *He rushes out the door, and his voice is heard calling down the corridor:* He will confess! Proctor will confess!

PROCTOR, *with a cry, as he strides to the door:* Why do you cry it? *In great pain he turns back to her.* It is evil, is it not? It is evil.

ELIZABETH, *in terror, weeping:* I cannot judge you, John, I cannot!

PROCTOR: Then who will judge me? *Suddenly clasping his hands:* God in Heaven, what is John Proctor, what is John Proctor? *He moves as an animal, and a fury is riding in him, a* tantalized *search.* I think it is honest, I think so; I am no saint. *As though she had denied this he calls angrily at her:* Let Rebecca go like a saint; for me it is fraud! *Voices are heard in the hall, speaking together in suppressed excitement.*

ELIZABETH: I am not your judge, I cannot be. *As though giving him release:* Do as you will, do as you will!

PROCTOR: Would you give them such a lie? Say it. Would you ever give them this? *She cannot answer.* You would not; if tongs of fire were singeing you you would not! It is evil. Good, then—it is evil, and I do it!

HATHORNE *enters with* DANFORTH, *and, with them,* CHEEVER, PARRIS, *and* HALE. *It is a businesslike, rapid entrance, as though the ice had been broken.*

DANFORTH, *with great relief and gratitude:* Praise to God, man, praise to God; you shall be blessed in Heaven for this. CHEEVER *has hurried to the bench with pen, ink, and paper.* PROCTOR *watches him.* Now then, let us have it. Are you ready, Mr. Cheever?

PROCTOR , *with a cold, cold horror at their efficiency:* Why must it be written?

DANFORTH: Why, for the good instruction of the village, Mister; this

Vocabulary

tantalized (tan´ tə līzd)
adj. tormented; frustrated

we shall post upon the church door! *To* PARRIS, *urgently:* Where is the marshal?

PARRIS, *runs to the door and calls down the corridor:* Marshal! Hurry!

DANFORTH: Now, then, Mister, will you speak slowly, and directly to the point, for Mr. Cheever's sake. *He is on record now, and is really dictating to* CHEEVER, *who writes.* Mr. Proctor, have you seen the Devil in your life? PROCTOR'S *jaws lock.* Come, man, there is light in the sky; the town waits at the scaffold; I would give out this news. Did you see the Devil?

PROCTOR: I did.

PARRIS: Praise God!

DANFORTH: And when he come to you, what were his demand?

PROCTOR *is silent.* DANFORTH *helps.* Did he bid you to do his work upon the earth?

PROCTOR: He did.

DANFORTH: And you bound yourself to his service? DANFORTH *turns, as* REBECCA *Nurse enters, with* HERRICK *helping to support her. She is barely able to walk.* Come in, come in, woman!

REBECCA, *brightening as she sees* PROCTOR: Ah, John! You are well, then, eh?

PROCTOR *turns his face to the wall.*

DANFORTH: Courage, man, courage—let her witness your good example that she may come to God herself. Now hear it, Goody Nurse! Say on, Mr. Proctor. Did you bind yourself to the Devil's service?

REBECCA, *astonished:* Why, John!

PROCTOR, *through his teeth, his face turned from* REBECCA: I did.

DANFORTH: Now, woman, you surely see it profit nothin' to keep this conspiracy any further. Will you confess yourself with him?

REBECCA: Oh, John—God send his mercy on you!

DANFORTH: I say, will you confess yourself, Goody Nurse?

REBECCA: Why, it is a lie, it is a lie; how may I damn myself? I cannot, I cannot.

DANFORTH: Mr. Proctor. When the Devil came to you did you see Rebecca Nurse in his company? PROCTOR *is silent.* Come, man, take courage—did you ever see her with the Devil?

▲ Critical Viewing

Judge Danforth says, "He who weeps for these weeps for corruption." What do you think the people surrounding the condemned are thinking? **ANALYZE**

Comprehension

What sins does Elizabeth think she has committed?

Allegory

How might Proctor's refusal to incriminate others relate to the McCarthy hearings of the 1950s?

PROCTOR, *almost inaudibly:* No.

DANFORTH, *now sensing trouble, glances at* JOHN *and goes to the table, and picks up a sheet—the list of condemned.*

DANFORTH: Did you ever see her sister, Mary Easty, with the Devil?

PROCTOR: No, I did not.

DANFORTH, *his eyes narrow on* PROCTOR: Did you ever see Martha Corey with the Devil?

PROCTOR: I did not.

DANFORTH, *realizing, slowly putting the sheet down:* Did you ever see anyone with the Devil?

PROCTOR: I did not.

DANFORTH: Proctor, you mistake me. I am not empowered to trade your life for a lie. You have most certainly seen some person with the Devil. PROCTOR *is silent.* Mr. Proctor, a score of people have already testified they saw this woman with the Devil.

PROCTOR: Then it is proved. Why must I say it?

DANFORTH: Why "must" you say it! Why, you should rejoice to say it if your soul is truly purged of any love for Hell!

PROCTOR: They think to go like saints. I like not to spoil their names.

DANFORTH, *inquiring, incredulous:* Mr. Proctor, do you think they go like saints?

PROCTOR, *evading:* This woman never thought she done the Devil's work.

DANFORTH: Look you, sir. I think you mistake your duty here. It matter nothing what she thought—she is convicted of the unnatural murder of children, and you for sending your spirit out upon Mary Warren. Your soul alone is the issue here, Mister, and you will prove its whiteness or you cannot live in a Christian country. Will you tell me now what persons conspired with you in the Devil's company? PROCTOR *is silent.* To your knowledge was Rebecca Nurse ever—

PROCTOR: I speak my own sins; I cannot judge another. *Crying out, with hatred:* I have no tongue for it.

HALE, *quickly to* DANFORTH: Excellency, it is enough he confess himself. Let him sign it, let him sign it.

PARRIS, *feverishly:* It is a great service, sir. It is a weighty name; it will strike the village that Proctor confess. I beg you, let him sign it. The sun is up, Excellency!

DANFORTH, *considers; then with dissatisfaction:* Come, then, sign your testimony. *To* CHEEVER: Give it to him. CHEEVER *goes to* PROCTOR, *the confession and a pen in hand.* PROCTOR *does not look at it.* Come, man, sign it.

PROCTOR, *after glancing at the confession:* You have all witnessed it—it is enough.

DANFORTH: You will not sign it?

PROCTOR: You have all witnessed it; what more is needed?

> "I speak my own sins; I cannot judge another."

DANFORTH: Do you sport with me? You will sign your name or it is no confession, Mister! *His breast heaving with agonized breathing,* PROCTOR *now lays the paper down and signs his name.*

PARRIS: Praise be to the Lord!

PROCTOR *has just finished signing when* DANFORTH *reaches for the paper. But* PROCTOR *snatches it up, and now a wild terror is rising in him, and a boundless anger.*

DANFORTH, *perplexed, but politely extending his hand:* If you please, sir.

PROCTOR: No.

DANFORTH, *as though* PROCTOR *did not understand:* Mr. Proctor, I must have—

PROCTOR: No, no. I have signed it. You have seen me. It is done! You have no need for this.

PARRIS: Proctor, the village must have proof that—

PROCTOR: Damn the village! I confess to God, and God has seen my name on this! It is enough!

DANFORTH: No, sir, it is—

PROCTOR: You came to save my soul, did you not? Here! I have confessed myself; it is enough!

DANFORTH: You have not con—

PROCTOR: I have confessed myself! Is there no good penitence but it be public? God does not need my name nailed upon the church! God sees my name; God knows how black my sins are! It is enough!

DANFORTH: Mr. Proctor—

PROCTOR: You will not use me! I am no Sarah Good or Tituba, I am John Proctor! You will not use me! It is no part of salvation that you should use me!

DANFORTH: I do not wish to—

PROCTOR: I have three children—how may I teach them to walk like men in the world, and I sold my friends?

DANFORTH: You have not sold your friends—

PROCTOR: Beguile me not! I blacken all of them when this is nailed to the church the very day they hang for silence!

DANFORTH: Mr. Proctor, I must have good and legal proof that you—

PROCTOR: You are the high court, your word is good enough! Tell them I confessed myself; say Proctor broke his knees and wept like a woman; say what you will, but my name cannot—

DANFORTH, *with suspicion:* It is the same, is it not? If I report it or you sign to it?

PROCTOR —*he knows it is insane:* No, it is not the same! What others say and what I sign to is not the same!

DANFORTH: Why? Do you mean to deny this confession when you are free?

PROCTOR: I mean to deny nothing!

DANFORTH: Then explain to me, Mr. Proctor, why you will not let—

Tragedy

In what ways do Proctor's statements here reflect those of a tragic hero?

Comprehension

What does Danforth want Proctor to do?

PROCTOR, *with a cry of his whole soul:* Because it is my name! Because I cannot have another in my life! Because I lie and sign myself to lies! Because I am not worth the dust on the feet of them that hang! How may I live without my name? I have given you my soul; leave me my name!

DANFORTH, *pointing at the confession in* PROCTOR'S *hand:* Is that document a lie? If it is a lie I will not accept it! What say you? I will not deal in lies, Mister! PROCTOR *is motionless.* You will give me your honest confession in my hand, or I cannot keep you from the rope. PROCTOR *does not reply.* What way do you go, Mister?

His breast heaving, his eyes staring, PROCTOR *tears the paper and crumples it, and he is weeping in fury, but erect.*

DANFORTH: Marshal!

PARRIS, *hysterically, as though the tearing paper were his life:* Proctor, Proctor!

HALE: Man, you will hang! You cannot!

PROCTOR, *his eyes full of tears:* I can. And there's your first marvel, that I can. You have made your magic now, for now I do think I see some shred of goodness in John Proctor. Not enough to weave a banner with, but white enough to keep it from such dogs. ELIZABETH, *in a burst of terror, rushes to him and weeps against his hand.* Give them no tear! Tears pleasure them! Show honor now, show a stony heart and sink them with it! *He has lifted her, and kisses her now with great passion.*

REBECCA: Let you fear nothing! Another judgment waits us all!

DANFORTH: Hang them high over the town! Who weeps for these, weeps for corruption! *He sweeps out past them.* HERRICK *starts to lead* REBECCA, *who almost collapses, but* PROCTOR *catches her, and she glances up at him apologetically.*

REBECCA: I've had no breakfast.

HERRICK: Come, man.

HERRICK *escorts them out,* HATHORNE *and* CHEEVER *behind them.* ELIZABETH *stands staring at the empty doorway.*

PARRIS, *in deadly fear, to* ELIZABETH: Go to him, Goody Proctor! There is yet time!

From outside a drumroll strikes the air. PARRIS *is startled.* ELIZABETH *jerks about toward the window.*

PARRIS: Go to him! *He rushes out the door, as though to hold back his fate.* Proctor! Proctor!

Again, a short burst of drums.

HALE: Woman, plead with him! *He starts to rush out the door, and then goes back to her.* Woman! It is pride, it is vanity. *She avoids his eyes, and moves to the window. He drops to his knees.* Be his helper!—What profit him to bleed? Shall the dust praise him? Shall the worms declare his truth? Go to him, take his shame away!

Tragedy
What insight does Proctor express?

Spiral Review
Biblical Allusion To what does Rebecca Nurse allude in saying, "Another judgment waits us all"?

ELIZABETH, *supporting herself against collapse, grips the bars of the window, and with a cry:* He have his goodness now. God forbid I take it from him!

The final drumroll crashes, then heightens violently. HALE *weeps in frantic prayer, and the new sun is pouring in upon her face, and the drums rattle like bones in the morning air.*

THE CURTAIN FALLS

Critical Reading

1. **Key Ideas and Details (a)** Who seeks confessions from Rebecca Nurse and other condemned prisoners? **(b) Infer:** What motivates this person—or people—to seek these confessions?

2. **Key Ideas and Details (a)** What unexpected action does Abigail take in this act? **(b) Draw Conclusions:** Why do you think she does this?

3. **Key Ideas and Details (a)** What decision torments John Proctor? **(b) Interpret:** What conflict does Elizabeth experience as her husband seeks her guidance?

4. **Key Ideas and Details (a)** What does John Proctor have "no tongue for"? **(b) Analyze:** Why does Proctor confess and then retract his confession?

5. **Key Ideas and Details Interpret:** Why does Elizabeth say her husband has "his goodness" as he is about to be hanged?

6. **Integration of Knowledge and Ideas** In the world of the play, are the sacrifices of characters like John Proctor and Rebecca Nurse meaningful and important? If so, to whom? How would you answer this question for the real world? In your response, use at least two Essential Question words: *nobility, lament, idealism, profound, humility.* *[Connecting to the Essential Question: How does literature shape or reflect society?]*

Cite textual evidence to support your responses.

Close Reading Activities ‖ *The Crucible, Act IV*

Literary Analysis

1. **Key Ideas and Details** **Evaluate the influence of the historical period** on characters by examining the role of the Puritans' religious views. In what ways do Proctor's religious convictions affect his choice of death over a false confession?

2. **Key Ideas and Details** In what ways do Hale's changing views of the trials reflect influences of the historical period?

3. **Craft and Structure** In what ways is *The Crucible* a **tragedy**? Explain, citing specific traits a dramatic tragedy contains and the effects it has on an audience.

4. **Craft and Structure** **(a)** Who is the **tragic hero** in *The Crucible*? **(b)** Why would this character be considered a tragic hero? **(c)** What other characters in the play could be considered tragic heroes?

5. **Craft and Structure** How is Proctor's downfall in *The Crucible* a combination of **(a)** fate; **(b)** a mistake in judgment; **(c)** a personality flaw?

6. **Craft and Structure** In many ancient tragedies, once the story is under way, the hero's downfall is inevitable. Are the downfalls of John Proctor, Rebecca Nurse, or any of the other characters in this drama inevitable? Explain.

7. **Craft and Structure** Using a chart like the one shown, cite examples from the play that show how ideas such as witchcraft and "the work of the Devil" function in *The Crucible* as an **allegory** for Communism.

Passage From the Text	How It Relates to Communism

8. **Integration of Knowledge and Ideas** **(a)** What does the ending of the play suggest about the value of integrity? **(b)** How might this idea relate to the McCarthy era?

9. **Integration of Knowledge and Ideas** Miller uses the proceedings of the Salem court as an allegory for the hearings conducted by Congress during the late 1940s to mid-1950s. Based on the play's details, what criticisms is Miller making about the way these congressional committees dealt with those it questioned and those who criticized it?

10. **Analyze Visual Information** Explain the dark humor in this cartoon.

Common Core State Standards

Language

4. Determine or clarify the meaning of unknown and multiple-meaning words and phrases based on *grades 11–12 reading and content,* choosing flexibly from a range of strategies. *(p. 1235)*

4.c. Consult general and specialized reference materials, both print and digital, to find the pronunciation of a word or determine or clarify its precise meaning, its part of speech, its etymology, or its standard usage. *(p. 1235)*

5. Demonstrate understanding of word relationships. *(p. 1235)*

▲ "It's Okay—We're Hunting Communists"

From "Herblock Special Report" (W.W. Norton, 1974). Reprinted by permission of the Herb Block Foundation.

Vocabulary Acquisition and Use

Word Analysis: Words from Myths

The word *tantalize* comes from the Greek myth about Tantalus, a man tormented by the gods. Likewise, the word *siren* comes from the myth about the Greek sea nymphs called Sirens, whose sweet singing lured sailors off course. Review the list of mythological characters below. Write a sentence using the word in parentheses that is derived from each character's name.

1. Ceres: Goddess of the harvest (cereal)
2. Titan: A race of giants with brute strength (titanic)
3. Narcissus: A boy punished by the gods for vanity (narcissistic)
4. Mars: God of war (martial)
5. Pan: God who caused fear in herds and crowds (panic)

Vocabulary: Synonyms

Synonyms are words that have the same, or nearly the same, meaning. Review the vocabulary list on page 1216. Then, for each item, select the letter of the word that is the closest in meaning to the first word.

1. **conciliatory: (a)** soothing, **(b)** rude, **(c)** vengeful
2. **beguile: (a)** plead, **(b)** fool, **(c)** straighten
3. **retaliation: (a)** narration, **(b)** restatement, **(c)** revenge
4. **adamant: (a)** calm, **(b)** first, **(c)** stubborn
5. **cleave: (a)** depart, **(b)** grow, **(c)** adhere
6. **tantalized: (a)** freed, **(b)** tempted, **(c)** danced

Using Resources to Build Vocabulary

Theatrical Words: Words for Cueing Actors

In the stage directions, Miller includes modifiers to describe the way he envisions actors speaking, reacting, and moving on the stage. Here are a few of them:

suspiciously (p. 1218)	politely (p. 1224)
instantly (p. 1219)	feverishly (p. 1230)
prayerfully (p. 1219)	hysterically (p. 1232)

Review these words by rereading the relevant lines in the play. Then, use a print or electronic thesaurus to find a synonym for each word. For example, a synonym for *politely* might be *courteously*. On your own paper, rewrite the stage directions in which the word appears, replacing the word with your synonym. Reread the stage directions. In a few sentences, explain why Miller would choose vivid words to direct the speech and movement of actors.

Close Reading Activities Continued

Writing to Sources

Explanatory Text Although Miller wrote *The Crucible* in response to the hysteria caused by the anti-Communist hearings of the late 1940s to 1950s, the themes of the play have endured. Indeed, *The Crucible* remains one of the most-performed plays worldwide. Write an **essay** in which you interpret the play's primary themes and explain how they reflect both the play's historical context and universal human issues.

Prewriting Review the play and briefly summarize the action of each act. Then, generate a list of the themes, or essential ideas, you think are most important. Use a chart like the one shown to examine ideas that reflect the play's historical period and also have a universal application. List characters and situations in the play that exemplify the themes you identify. Then, list events from the world at large that reflect a more expansive, timeless version of the themes.

Model: Identifying Universal Themes

Drafting Organize your essay by focusing on one theme at a time.

- Clearly state the first theme.
- Next, identify the historical context in which the theme is presented. Discuss how the theme has meaning within that context.
- Explain that a universal theme is meaningful to all people in all times and places. Discuss how the theme you chose is relevant to people regardless of where—or when—they happen to live.
- Draw details that illustrate universal thematic appeal from your own experiences and knowledge.

Continue this pattern of organization with the remaining themes. End your essay with a strong conclusion that reviews the themes you discussed, along with your explanations of their universality. To end on a compelling note, suggest current issues or situations that you think might become the next best expression of the play's themes.

Revising As you review your draft, note places where you could clarify the connection between the historical and universal meanings of a theme. Add strong, clear transitions to help guide the reader through your ideas.

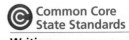

Common Core State Standards

Writing

2. Write explanatory texts to examine and convey complex ideas, concepts, and information clearly and accurately through the effective selection, organization, and analysis of content.

2.a. Introduce a topic; organize complex ideas, concepts, and information so that each new element builds on that which precedes it to create a unified whole.

2.b. Develop the topic thoroughly by selecting the most significant and relevant facts, extended definitions, concrete details, quotations, or other information and examples appropriate to the audience's knowledge of the topic.

2.f. Provide a concluding statement or section that follows from and supports the information or explanation presented.

9.a. Apply *grades 11–12 Reading standards* to literature. [RL.11-12.2]

Language

1. Demonstrate command of the conventions of standard English grammar and usage when writing or speaking. *(p. 1237)*

Conventions and Style: Avoiding Sentence Fragments and Run-ons

A **sentence fragment** is a group of words with end punctuation that is missing a subject, a verb, or both. A **run-on sentence** is two or more sentences punctuated as one. Work to avoid these two common errors in your writing.

Correcting Fragments

Fragment: *The Crucible*, a play by Arthur Miller.

Add to another sentence: I enjoyed the production of *The Crucible,* a play by Arthur Miller.

Add a subject or verb: *The Crucible* is a play by Arthur Miller.

Correcting Run-Ons

Run-on sentence: The setting was Salem in 1692 young girls caused much suffering.

1. Add punctuation: The setting was Salem in 1692. Young girls caused much suffering.

2. Add a comma and conjunction: The setting was Salem in 1692, and young girls caused much suffering.

3. Add a semicolon: The setting was Salem in 1692; young girls caused much suffering.

Practice Rewrite each item as a sentence. If an item is a complete sentence, write "Correct."

1. John Proctor, a respected, hard-working farmer, known to be strong and steady.
2. Rebecca Nurse accused one reason may have been resentment against her husband.
3. The Putnams were bitter because they had had eight children yet only one survived birth.
4. The Devil was used as a weapon to control people make them obey out of fear.
5. Reverend Parris believed there were much more sinful households in Salem than his.
6. Giles Corey, at age eighty. Both a nuisance and a brave man.
7. Reverend John Hale arrived in Salem armed with books, he came to fight the Devil.
8. John Proctor appeared. With a testament signed by ninety-one people.
9. Giles refused to name those who gave him information was arrested.
10. John Proctor confessed his own sin. Refused to judge others.

Writing and Speaking Conventions

A. Writing Rewrite the paragraph below, eliminating any fragments and run-ons. You may combine two sentences or break one item into more than one sentence.

Reverend Parris was a straitlaced man. Often felt persecuted by others. His daughter, Betty, lay in bed as if dead then she sat up screaming. After Abigail made accusations. Betty said she saw townspeople with the Devil. Hysteria seemed to spread like a virus through Salem neighboring villages were not affected.

Example: His daughter, Betty, lay in bed as if dead then she sat up screaming.

Rewritten Sentence: His daughter, Betty, lay in bed as if dead; then she sat up screaming.

B. Speaking Deliver testimony from the point of view of one of the characters in the play. Briefly tell what you did and why. Avoid sentence fragments and run-ons as you speak.

POLITICAL DRAMA AROUND THE WORLD

Dramatists around the world and throughout history have used the power of the stage to communicate their ideas about social and political situations.

Arthur Miller
The Crucible
United States

Bertolt Brecht
Mother Courage
Germany

Maxim Gorky
Lower Depths
Russia

Federico Garcia Lorca
The House of Bernarda Alba
Spain

Aristophanes
Lysistrata
Ancient Greece

Wole Soyinka
A Play of Giants
Nigeria

Athol Fugard
The Township Plays
South Africa

Comparing Literary Works

The Crucible • from *Good Night, and Good Luck*

Comparing Political Drama Past and Present

The Crucible is part of a tradition of political drama begun by the first Western dramatists, the ancient Greeks. Greek playwrights such as Aristophanes and Sophocles in the fifth century B.C. wrote and staged plays about the politics of war, gender, and politics itself. From the Greeks to Arthur Miller, political drama exhibits the following qualities:

- It reflects the author's political opinions.
- It characterizes a politician or describes a series of political events.
- It questions inequities or injustices in society.
- It examines a political issue from the past or present, or uses past events to comment on current problems.

Today, political drama appears in movies and television programs, as well as stage plays. In their screenplay for the movie *Good Night, and Good Luck* (2005), George Clooney and Grant Heslov, like Arthur Miller before them, focus on the "red scare" of the 1950s. They do so, however, from a very different angle. As you read the excerpt, use a chart like the one shown to compare how Miller and Clooney and Heslov represent political ideas in dramatic form.

Common Core State Standards

Reading Literature
1. Cite strong and thorough textual evidence to support analysis of what the text says explicitly as well as inferences drawn from the text, including determining where the text leaves matters uncertain.

Language
4.c. Consult general and specialized reference materials, both print and digital, to find the pronunciation of a word or determine or clarify its precise meaning, its part of speech, its etymology, or its standard usage.

	Miller	Clooney and Heslov
Specific Political Figures	• Puritan leaders of Salem • Senator Joseph McCarthy	
Specific Events	• Salem witch trials • Senate hearings	
Opinion (stated or implied)	Those instigating both events were blameworthy.	
Critique of Society (stated or implied)	Miller critiques both the individuals who create mass hysteria and the communities that submit to it.	

Gather Vocabulary Knowledge

These selections include forms of *vulnerable, acknowledge, statute,* and *disregard.* Use the following references to explore these words.

- **Book of Quotations:** Use a print or online collection to find a quotation containing one of the words. Explain the meaning of the quotation.
- **Other Related References:** Use resources, such as a visual thesaurus or a vocabulary builder, to learn more about each word's meanings. Create a word map for one of the words, including three synonyms, three antonyms, and a sentence in which you use the word correctly.

George Clooney (born 1961)
Grant Heslov (born 1963)

Co-Authors of *Good Night, and Good Luck*

GEORGE CLOONEY, born in Lexington, Kentucky, has been surrounded by acting, television, and politics all his life. His father, Nick Clooney, was a long-time television newscaster and ran for Congress as a representative from Kentucky in 2004. Clooney had a famous aunt, uncle, and cousin in the film industry. In 1994, he gained national recognition as Dr. Doug Ross on the television drama *ER*.

Acting and Directing Clooney followed his successful television career with critically acclaimed work as a film actor and director. *Good Night, and Good Luck* (2005), about broadcast journalist Edward R. Murrow and his battle against Senator Joseph McCarthy, brings all of Clooney's familial influences together: television, journalism, and politics.

GRANT HESLOV, born in Pittsburgh, Pennsylvania, is an actor, director, and producer who has often worked with George Clooney. Heslov's commitment to producing political drama continues with Clooney. Together, they started Smoke House productions to make smaller films, one of which will tell the story of a man unjustly sent to prison for a murder he did not commit.

▲ George Clooney and Grant Heslov

GOOD NIGHT, AND GOOD LUCK
Cast of Characters

Good Night, and Good Luck features a clash between two high-profile personalities: Edward R. Murrow, the pioneering 1950s broadcast journalist, and Senator Joseph McCarthy, who pursued an obsessive search for communists in positions of power.

Edward R. Murrow	Journalist, star of television news show *See It Now*
Don Hewitt	Television news executive; director of *See It Now*
Joe Wershba	Television journalist; colleague of Murrow's
Shirley Wershba	Television journalist; colleague of Murrow's
Fred Friendly	Television journalist; colleague of Murrow's
Joseph McCarthy	Senator from Wisconsin who instigated "Red Scare" with his pursuit of supposed communists in the U.S.
William Paley	Chairman of the Board of the CBS television network

from good night, and good luck

George Clooney
Grant Heslov

▲ David Strathairn as
Edward R. Murrow

BACKGROUND As this excerpt begins, Murrow's newsroom staff is preparing to air McCarthy's rebuttal to a story Murrow had run about the senator. The story was true and dangerous, for it showed McCarthy to be using unfair, unethical methods. Interestingly, the movie includes historical footage of that rebuttal. Woven into this section of the screenplay is a a verbatim transcript of McCarthy's speech as it aired on Murrow's CBS news show *See It Now* in 1954.

INT.¹ CONTROL ROOM—SHOW NIGHT

This scene will be built with a lot of very tight close ups of crew and reporters. Everyone is very aware of their vulnerability. Cameramen glancing at one another. Stage Manager focusing on the monitor.

Right now it's silent as they wait for MURROW to arrive.

We pull Ed in a close up as he enters into the room and sees the film canisters.

> **HEWITT.** Ed, it's twenty eight minutes. I could clip a little off the end for you to have time to . . .

> **MURROW.** I think we have to leave it alone, Don.

He starts tearing out pages.

---

1. INT interior.

Vocabulary
vulnerability (vəln ə rə bil′ ət ē) *n.* state of being open to attack, criticism, or temptation

Comprehension
What is the setting of this scene?

MURROW (CONT'D)

> Very smart, no time for comment . . .
> when did it come in?

HEWITT. Ten minutes ago. We put it up, I saw the first couple of minutes, you're right.

MURROW. Coming after me?

HEWITT nods.

MURROW (CONT'D)

> Joe, have you seen the latest polls? . . . The most trustworthy man in America is Milton Berle.[2]

WERSHBA. Maybe he should do the story.

MURROW. Get him on the line, will ya?

MURROW walks onto the stage. FRIENDLY'S there. Against the back wall are Murrow's team.

MURROW (CONT'D)

> Fred.

FRIENDLY. What say we grab a little dinner after the show? The 21 Club?

MURROW. Sure.

He sits noticing The Boys. They give little waves, MURROW acknowledges them.

MURROW (CONT'D)

> What're they here for? "The Monkey and the Bell" show is on stage three.

FRIENDLY. They changed the title. "Goin' Ape."

MURROW. Who's their first guest?

The loudspeaker—"Thirty seconds to Air"

FRIENDLY. After tonight, I hear it's you.

They smile.

FRIENDLY (CONT'D)

> Look, there's nothing fun about this one. You've just gotta put your gloves down, stick your chin out and just take it for a whole round. Next week's our round.

MURROW. If I make it up off the mat.

MURROW takes out a cigarette, FRIENDLY lights it.

Loudspeaker—"Twenty seconds to air"

Vocabulary

acknowledges (ak näl´ ij əz) *v.* to admit the existence, reality, or truth of something

▲ George Clooney directing actors Frank Langella and David Strathairn

---

2. **Milton Berle** (1908–2002) Comedian and first major star of television.

▲ David Strathairn as Edward R. Murrow on the set of *See it Now*

FRIENDLY. You will.

MURROW. Did you see the latest polls, Milton Berle's the most trusted man in America . . .

FRIENDLY. You already did this joke for me . . .

They look at each other.

FRIENDLY (CONT'D)

I'll get Berle on the line.

Loudspeaker—"Ten seconds"

MURROW sits there again in silence. The weight of the world sitting there with him.

STAGE MANAGER. In five, four, three, two . . .

He points to MURROW.

We come up on the monitor as MURROW speaks directly at us.

MURROW. One month ago tonight we presented a report on Senator Joseph R. McCarthy. We labeled it as controversial. Most of that report consisted of words and pictures of the Senator. At that time, we said if the Senator believes we have done violence to his words or pictures, if he desires to speak, to answer himself, an opportunity would be afforded him on this program. The Senator sought the opportunity, asked for a delay of three weeks because he said he was very busy and he wished adequate time to prepare his reply. We agreed. We placed no restrictions on the manner or method of the presentation of his reply and we suggested that we would not take time to comment on this program. Here now is Senator Joseph R. McCarthy, Junior Senator from Wisconsin.

McCarthy begins. As he delivers his rebuttal we will cut to various places that it is airing. For the moment we're right on MURROW as he watches.

Comprehension
What is McCarthy's reason for being on Murrow's show?

The Crucible • *from* Good Night, and Good Luck 1243

▲ Patricia Clarkson as Shirley Wershba and Robert Downey, Jr. as Joe Wershba

Comparing Literary Works

Political Drama

Why do you think the screenwriters chose to include actual footage of McCarthy's rebuttal?

MCCARTHY. Good evening. Mr. Edward R. Murrow, Educational Director of the Columbia Broadcasting System, devoted his program to an attack on the work of the United States Senate investigating committee and on me personally as its Chairman. Now, over the past four years, he has made repeated attacks upon me and those fighting communists. Now, of course, neither Joe McCarthy nor Edward R. Murrow is of any great importance as individuals. We are only important in our relations to the great struggle to preserve our American liberties.

CUT TO:[3]

INT. PALEY'S OFFICE

PALEY watches in silence.

Now ordinarily, I wouldn't take time out of the important work at hand to answer Murrow. However in this case I felt justified in doing so because Murrow is a symbol, the leader and the cleverest of the jackal pack which is always found at the throat of anyone who dares expose individual communists and traitors.

CUT TO:

INT. JOE & SHIRLEY WERSHBA'S NY APT.

Shirley watches.

I am compelled by the fact to say to you that Mr. Edward R. Murrow, as far back as twenty years ago was engaged in propaganda for communist causes. For example, the Institute for International Education of which he was the Acting Director, was chosen to act as a representative by a Soviet agency to do a job which would normally be done by the Russian Secret Police.

---

3. **CUT TO** Screenwriter's shorthand to indicate a change of scene; the camera "cuts to" a new location.

Back to MURROW on the set.

Mr. Murrow sponsored a communist school in Moscow . . .

This speech will continue but we'll hear MURROW and FRIENDLY talking.

>   **MURROW.** When the politicians complain that TV turns the proceedings into a circus, it should be clear that the circus was already there, and that TV has only demonstrated that not all the performers are well trained.

>   **FRIENDLY.** We've got him, Ed.

>   **MURROW.** If he led with his best.

>   **FRIENDLY.** He led with his best.

CUT TO:

INT. PALEY'S OFFICE

>   **MCCARTHY.** Now, Mr. Murrow, by his own admission, was a member of the IWW, that's the Industrial Workers of the World, a terrorist organization cited by an Attorney General of the United States . . .

CUT TO:

INT. HALLWAY CBS

It's empty. McCarthy's voice echoing.

>   **MCCARTHY.** Now, Mr. Murrow said on this program and I quote, he said, "The actions of the Junior Senator from Wisconsin have given considerable comfort to the enemy."

MURROW walks into the hall followed by FRIENDLY, WERSHBA, MACK; they walk toward us as the speech continues.

MCCARTHY (CONT'D)

>   That is the language of our statute of treason. If I am giving comfort to our enemies, I ought not to be in the Senate. If on the other hand, Mr. Murrow is giving comfort to the enemies, he ought not to be brought into the homes of Americans by the Columbia Broadcasting System.

As they exit we stay on the empty hallway. We fade to black as McCarthy drones on. WE'LL PLAY AN ALCOA COMMERCIAL HERE

INT. SEE IT NOW SET

We are on the set of *See it Now* as MURROW addresses us directly.

>   **MURROW.** Last week, Senator McCarthy appeared on this program to correct any errors he might have thought we made in our report of March 9th. Since he made no reference to

▼ Director George Clooney behind the camera

Vocabulary

statute (stach´ o͞ot) *n.* document in which a standard, rule, or law is expressed

Comprehension

What organization does McCarthy say Murrow once joined?

any statements of fact that we made, we must conclude that he found no errors of fact. He proved again that anyone who exposes him, anyone who does not share his hysterical disregard to decency and human dignity and the rights guaranteed by the Constitution must be either a Communist or a fellow traveler. I fully expected this treatment. The Senator added this reporter's name to a long list of individuals and institutions he has accused of serving the communist cause. His proposition is very simple: Anyone who criticizes or opposes McCarthy's methods must be a Communist. And if that be true, there are an awful lot of Communists in this country. For the record, let's consider briefly some of the Senator's charges.

(MORE)

MURROW (CONT'D)

He claimed but offered no proof that I had been a member of the Industrial Workers of the World. That is false. I was never a member of the IWW, never applied for membership.

CUT TO:

INT. CONTROL BOOTH

We cut to the control booth, PALMER WILLIAMS and company watch on as the broadcast continues.

WILLIAMS. Ready two . . . hold it . . . hold . . . take two . . . tell 'em Ed.

MURROW. The Senator charged that Professor Harold Laski, a British scholar and politician dedicated a book to me. That's true. He is dead. He was a Socialist, I am not. He was one of those civilized individuals who did not insist upon agreement with his political principles as a pre-condition for conversation or friendship. I do not agree with his political ideas. Laski, as he makes clear in the introduction, dedicated the book to me not because of political agreement but because he held my war-time broadcast from London in high regard; and the dedication so reads.

WILLIAMS. Ready on one . . . closer, Charlie . . . take one . . .

CUT TO:

INT. SEE IT NOW SET

Again MURROW addresses us directly.

MURROW. I believed twenty years ago and I believe today that mature Americans can engage in conversation and controversy, the clash of ideas, with Communists anywhere in the world without becoming contaminated or converted. I believe that our faith, our conviction, our determination are stronger than

Vocabulary
disregard (dis ri gärd´) *v.* to pay no attention to; ignore

▲ Grant Heslov as Don Hewitt

theirs and that we can compete and successfully, not only in the area of bombs but in the area of ideas.

CUT TO:

INT. PALEY'S OFFICE

As PALEY watches on a television.

> I have worked for CBS for more than nineteen years. The company has subscribed fully to my integrity and responsibility as a broadcaster and as a loyal American. I require no lectures from the junior Senator from Wisconsin as to the dangers or terrors of Communism—having watched the aggressive forces at work in Western Europe.

CUT TO:

INT. SEE IT NOW SET

> Having had friends in Eastern Europe butchered and driven in exile, having broadcast from London in 1943 that the Russians were responsible for the Katyn Massacre—having told the story of the Russian refusal to allow allied aircraft to land on Russian fields after dropping supplies to those who rose in Warsaw and then were betrayed by the Russians.

CUT TO:

INT. BULLPEN

Murrow's team watch.

> **WERSHBA.** (Quietly)
> Go Ed.

> **MURROW.** And having been denounced by the Russian radio for

▲ George Clooney as Fred Friendly and David Strathairn as Edward R. Murrow behind the scenes of *See it Now*

Comprehension
What personal beliefs does Murrow express?

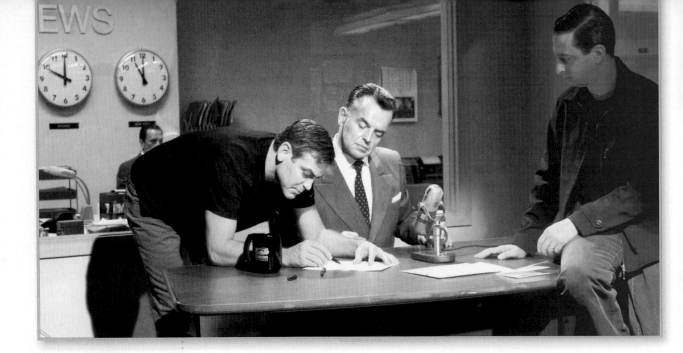

▲ Director Clooney
with actor Ray Wise and
producer/co-writer Grant
Heslov on set

these reports. I cannot feel that I require instruction from the
Senator on the evils of Communism.

CUT TO:

INT. SEE IT NOW SET

MURROW addresses us directly.

Having searched my conscience and my files, I cannot contend that
I have always been right or wise but, I have attempted to pursue the
truth with some diligence and to report it, even though as in this case
I had been warned in advance that I would be subjected to the atten-
tions of Senator McCarthy. We shall hope to deal with matters of more
vital interest to the country next week. Good night. And, good luck.

We go to a commercial. As we hear it play, we see Murrow stand
up. He shakes people's hands, there are some pats on the back
. . . not victorious . . . not afraid . . . simply a job well done.

Critical Reading

Cite textual
evidence to
support your
responses.

1. **Key Ideas and Details (a)** Why was McCarthy invited to speak
   on Murrow's program? **(b) Draw Conclusions:** What use does
   McCarthy make of his time on Murrow's program?

2. **Key Ideas and Details (a)** What charges does McCarthy make
   against Murrow, and what is Murrow's response? **(b) Interpret:**
   Why would McCarthy make such claims against Murrow?

After You Read

The Crucible ▪ from *Good Night, and Good Luck*

Comparing Political Drama Past and Present

1. Integration of Knowledge and Ideas (a) Explain Miller's opinion regarding the hysteria surrounding the witch hunt in *The Crucible*. **(b)** What opinions do you think Clooney and Heslov hold about Murrow and McCarthy? Explain. **(c)** Are the authors' views in the two works similar? Explain.

2. Integration of Knowledge and Ideas (a) The events portrayed in *The Crucible* occurred in the 1600s. What modern political event underlies the play? **(b)** How are aspects of that political struggle dramatized in the screenplay?

3. Integration of Knowledge and Ideas (a) Does *The Crucible* engage politics of the distant past, the modern era, or both? **(b)** Does the political story in *Good Night, and Good Luck* reflect distant history, modern times, or both? Explain.

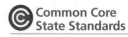
Common Core State Standards

Writing
2. Write explanatory texts to examine and convey complex ideas, concepts, and information clearly and accurately through the effective selection, organization, and analysis of content.
10. Write routinely over shorter time frames for a range of tasks, purposes, and audiences.

Timed Writing

Explanatory Text: Essay

Political playwrights like Miller, Clooney, and Heslov present their own opinions and perspectives through the characters and events of their stories.

Assignment: Write an **essay** in which you analyze the author's political opinions as they are expressed through the two works. Identify the characters in each work that most clearly articulate the political viewpoints of the author or authors. Determine whether those characters are effective or ineffective as the voice of the authors' political views. **[40 minutes]**

Use these questions to focus your analysis.
- Which specific actions or dialogue suggest that a character speaks for the author?
- How do other characters help define these opinions?
- Is drama an effective form for the expression of political views? Explain, citing details of your analysis as support.

As you write, follow the conventions of a strong analytical essay:
- Advance a clear thesis statement.
- Follow a clear organizational plan. Arrange the body of your essay either point by point, or in two sections, one for each play.

5-Minute Planner

Complete these steps before you begin to write:

1. Read the assignment carefully. Jot down key words and phrases.
2. Scan the selections, looking for details that illustrate the points you want to make. **TIP** As you jot down details from the selections, put points you want to compare or contrast side by side.
3. Decide whether to use point-by-point or two-section organization.
4. Reread the prompt, and draft your essay.

> **USE ACADEMIC VOCABULARY**
>
> As you write, use academic language, including the following words or their related forms:
>
> illustrate
> convey
> contrast
> protest
>
> For more information about academic language, see the vocabulary charts in the introduction to this book.

Analyzing Argumentative and Expository Texts

Theater/Film Review • Feature Article

Common Core State Standards

Reading Informational Text
5. Analyze and evaluate the effectiveness of the structure an author uses in his or her exposition or argument, including whether the structure makes points clear, convincing, and engaging.

About the Texts

A **review** is a persuasive nonfiction article in which a writer states an opinion about a work of art. Books, movies, museum exhibitions, plays, concerts, and other artworks or performances are the usual topics of reviews. Reviews usually include a summary of a work; a clear statement of opinion about the work's quality; a quick review device, such as numbered stars; and ticket or contact information.

A **feature article** is a work of nonfiction about a general-interest topic. Unlike news articles that focus on current events, feature articles explore trends, events, or personalities. The basic structure of a feature article includes an attention-grabbing lead, or opening that establishes a theme; a body of facts, anecdotes, quotes, and details; and photos or illustrations of the article's subject.

Preparing to Read Complex Texts

In feature articles—and especially reviews—a writer builds meaning and a sense of knowledgeable insight by weaving fact and opinion together in an authoritative way. As you read reviews and feature articles, **distinguish between fact and opinion** and assess how the writer applies different types of information to build and support his or her ideas:

- **Facts:** hard data, such as statistics, dates, and events, that can be proved true and do not change with the context
- **Opinions:** statements of belief that cannot be proved true or false; may use language that is evaluative ("too much"; "genuine contribution") or emotional ("powerful"; "silly")

As you read, use a chart like the one shown to identify fact and opinion in the reviews and article.

Facts	Opinions
Summaries:	Evaluative Language:
Dates/Events/People:	Emotional Language:

Content-Area Vocabulary

These words appear in the selections that follow. They may also appear in other content-area texts.

trials (trī´ əlz) *n.* in law, examinations of evidence and charges to determine claims or punishments

accusation (ak´ yoo zā´ shən) *n.* act of charging someone with an error

tribunal (trī byoo´ nəl) *n.* court of justice

adaptation (a dap tā´ shən) *n.* modification of a work for production in another medium

This classic review is by a famous theater critic whose approval or disapproval often determined a play's success.

The New York Times

January 23, 1953

The Crucible
By Brooks Atkinson

The reviewer begins with a general assessment of the play and then follows with a brief summary.

Arthur Miller has written another powerful play. *The Crucible*, it is called, and it opened at the Martin Beck last evening in an equally powerful performance. Riffling back the pages of American history, he has written the drama of the witch trials and hangings in Salem in 1692. Neither Mr. Miller nor his audiences are unaware of certain similarities between the perversions of justice then and today.

But Mr. Miller is not pleading a cause in dramatic form. For *The Crucible*, despite its current implications, is a self-contained play about a terrible period in American history. Silly accusations of witchcraft by some mischievous girls in Puritan dress gradually take possession of Salem. Before the play is over good people of pious nature and responsible temper are condemning other good people to the gallows.

Having a sure instinct for dramatic form, Mr. Miller goes bluntly to essential situations. John Proctor and his wife, farm people, are the central characters of the play. At first the idea that Goodie Proctor is a witch is only an absurd rumor. But *The Crucible* carries the Proctors through the whole ordeal—first vague suspicion, then the arrest, the implacable, highly wrought trial in the church vestry, the final opportunity for John Proctor to save his neck by confessing to something he knows is a lie, and finally the baleful roll of the drums at the foot of the gallows.

Although *The Crucible* is a powerful drama, it stands second to *Death of a Salesman* as a work of art. Mr. Miller has had more trouble with this one, perhaps because he is too conscious of its implications. The literary style is cruder. . . .

It may be that Mr. Miller . . . has permitted himself to be concerned more with the technique of the witch hunt than with its humanity. For all its power generated on the surface, *The Crucible* is most moving in the simple, quiet scenes between John Proctor and his wife. By the standards of *Death of a Salesman*, there is too much excitement and not enough emotion in *The Crucible*.

As the director, Jed Harris has given it a driving performance in which the clashes are fierce and clamorous. Inside Boris Aronson's gaunt, pitiless sets of rude buildings, the acting is at a high pitch of bitterness, anger and fear. As the patriarchal deputy Governor, Walter Hampden gives one of his most vivid performances in which righteousness and ferocity are unctuously mated. Fred Stewart as a vindictive parson, E. G. Marshall as a parson who finally rebels at the indiscriminate ruthlessness of the trial, Jean Adair as an aging woman of God . . . all give able performances.

As John Proctor and his wife, Arthur Kennedy and Beatrice Straight have the most attractive roles in the drama. . . . They are superb—Mr. Kennedy clear and resolute, full of fire, searching his own mind; Miss Straight, reserved, detached, above and beyond the contention. Like all the members of the cast, they are dressed in the chaste and lovely costumes Edith Lutyens has designed from old prints of early Massachusetts.

After the experience of *Death of a Salesman* we probably expect Mr. Miller to write a Masterpiece every time. *The Crucible* is not of that stature and it lacks that universality. On a lower level of dramatic history with considerable pertinence for today, it is a powerful play and a genuine contribution to the season.

Los Angeles Times

Dec. 13, 1996

Hysteria Resides at Heart of Frantic 'Crucible'

> The title identifies the topic of the review and suggests the writer's opinion.

KENNETH TURAN

The Crucible, Arthur Miller's play about fear of the devil on the loose in colonial Massachusetts, comes to the screen with powerful credentials: high-profile stars Daniel Day-Lewis and Winona Ryder, the impressive Paul Scofield and Joan Allen in supporting roles, Miller himself doing the screenplay and director Nicholas Hytner in his first film since *The Madness of King George.*

And the play itself, which debuted in 1953, has manifested a powerful durability, selling 6 million copies in paperback in this country alone and allowing Miller to recently claim, "I don't think there has been a week in the past 40-odd years when it hasn't been on the stage somewhere in the world."

But whenever a film has hysteria as its subject, as this one does, the danger exists that it will become hysterical itself, and *The Crucible,* all its promise notwithstanding, falls into that trap with a demoralizing thud. Rife with screaming fits and wild-eyed rantings, this film is too frantic to be involving, too much an outpost of bedlam to be believable.

Part of the difficulty may be inherent in adapting a theater piece to the movies, with Miller himself noting in the introduction to his published screenplay that "the play wants to tell, the movie to show . . . the stage scene is written to be vocally projected onto an audience, a movie scene wants to be overheard." Which makes hysteria on film considerably harder to tolerate than in the stage version.

And, especially in its second half, when Lewis gets warmed up and Scofield and Allen do the brunt of their impeccable work, the film is not without its quietly effective moments. But they are too few and too late to make sufficient headway against the rampant tide of frenzy that is the film's signature emotion.

The madness starts early, as Abigail Williams (Ryder) and her cousin Betty sneak out of their Salem house one night in 1692 and join other young girls for a fairly innocent gathering headed by the slave Tituba (Charlayne Woodard).

While most of the girls are content to wish for help with the boys they have crushes on. Abigail has darker thoughts in mind. But before it's clear what they are, Betty's father, the fatuous Rev. Parris (Bruce Davison) stumbles on their group and Betty is so traumatized at being caught she goes into a trance.

As modern Americans prefer to blame "the government" for all ills, their colonial counterparts put everything on "the devil," and little Betty's spell brings to Salem the respected Rev. Hale (Rob Campbell), a specialist in Satan and all his black arts.

Fearful of being found out. Abigail and her teenage friends raise the stakes by insisting the evil one made them do it. The new sense of empowerment they feel in suddenly being taken seriously encourages them to scream and scream again. Soon the town is rife with accusation and counter-accusation, as the high-decibel charge of witchcraft is manipulated by adults as well as children for their own power and property aims. . . .

Though Ryder's performance is fatally hampered by the one-note nature of her part, her co-star does somewhat better. Always adept at suffering and looking here like the brooding hero of "Mohicans II: The Colonial Years," Day-Lewis gets to fully inhabit his part only in the film's later stages when he attempts to be the community's voice of sanity.

It is no coincidence that both Day-Lewis and Allen, finely drawn as the wife uncertain of her husband's love, flourish in their scenes with Scofield as Judge Danforth, the somber leader of a tribunal sent to investigate the witchcraft allegations.

Using his celebrated presence and commanding voice, Scofield emphasizes the sincerity in the judge and makes him a figure of formidable dignity and power, able to wring everything there is out of Miller's artificial lines. Only in Scofield's scenes can director Hytner, whose penchant for high emotion served him better in "King George," be persuaded to pitch things at a human level.

Despite these involving moments, *The Crucible* finally seems too schematic, more useful as an allegory than as drama, and possibly owing that undoubted popularity to its simplistic qualities as much as its insights into group psychology.

It's also interesting to note that many of the original stage reviewers had similar reservations about the play. *The New York Times* said, "There is too much excitement and not enough emotion in *The Crucible,* and the *Herald Tribune's* Walter Kerr called it "a step backward into mechanical parable." Those seeing the new film version will appreciate the wisdom of those words as much as Miller's.

> The reviewer quotes historical reviews of the play to support his opinion.

The New York Times

A Rock of the Modern Age, Arthur Miller is Everywhere
By Mel Gussow

The title clearly shows the reader this profile is about Arthur Miller.

When Arthur Miller was in Alaska to receive an award this year, he and a local environmental official went fishing for salmon in Prince William Sound. As they passed an iceberg, Mr. Miller's companion leaned over the side of the boat, chopped off pieces of blue glacial ice and threw them into the bucket with the fish. "That ice is probably millennia old," the playwright said in a recent interview. "Eight-million-year-old ice! It doesn't melt."

If ice can last that long, perhaps that says something about the survival of civilization—and art. Mr. Miller, who has never been known to sidestep a metaphor, smiled and said, "You hang around long enough . . . you don't melt."

In his 60-year career, Mr. Miller has been impervious to winds of fashion and periods of critical neglect. Even when receptivity for his work waned on Broadway, he found an audience in other countries, particularly in England, where he has been honored for his plays and also for his political consciousness.

The writer draws connections between various moments in Miller's career.

Just turned 81, he finds himself in the middle of one of his busiest seasons. Nicholas Hytner's passionate film version of *The Crucible,* starring Daniel Day-Lewis and Winona Ryder, opened this week to generally favorable reviews. In *The New York Times,* Janet Maslin called it a "vibrant" and "beautifully acted" **adaptation** of Mr. Miller's 1953 play about witch hunts and marital betrayal in 17th-century Salem, Mass. Davis Thacker's television film of *Broken Glass* was shown last month on Masterpiece Theater, and his revival of *Death of a Salesman* recently opened at the Royal National Theater in London.

With both the film of *The Crucible* and the television production of *Broken Glass,* there is a trans-Atlantic creative alliance. Each is directed by an Englishman and has a British and American cast. Although Mr. Miller's work has been closely identified with American actors (from Lee J. Cobb to Dustin Hoffman in *Death of a Salesman*), certain English actors have also expressed a natural affinity for his work, including Mr. Day-Lewis and Paul Scofield in *The Crucible* and Michael Gambon, who gave a galvanizing performance in *A View From the Bridge* several years ago at the Royal National Theater.

Analyzing his English connection, Mr. Miller said, "Maybe because of the large amounts of work they do on classical plays, there's an assumption there that fundamentally a play is a metaphor, not simply a series of actions by characters."

From his perspective, his work is not basically naturalistic. With his assent, foreign productions often emphasize the symbolic aspects, as in a Swedish version of *The Last Yankee,* which had a six-foot rose as a life-enhancing emblem at the center of the production. There is no such flower in the text.

In the National Theater production of *Death of a Salesman,* Mr. Thacker has unmoored the play from its realistic roots. On an open turntable stage are aligned artifacts of Willy Loman's life: his old car and refrigerator and beds from Brooklyn to Boston. In a surprising, perhaps temporary turnabout for the playwright, the play and production received mixed reviews from London critics.

With the film of *The Crucible,* Mr. Hytner has made the drama more tangible and believable. The film was shot on rugged Hog Island, near Salem, where witch trials took place in the 17th century. Mr. Miller said the location was an asset, counteracting the "tendency to make it a static, photographed stage play." On Hog Island, "the environment kept moving in on you." . . .

Over the years, *The Crucible* has become his most produced play, seemingly transferrable to any country. No matter where it has been done—and he remembered one fanciful production in Georgia in the Soviet Union in which John Proctor was chased by a mob wearing balloon trousers and carrying scimitars—the most important thing is that Proctor is not meant to be heroic. He is "a damaged man" who rises against injustice.

In a recent speech, Robert Brustein said, "I defy you to name a single work of art that has ever changed anything." In response, Mr. Miller said, "I think works of art change the consciousness of people and their estimate of who they are and what they stand for." He pointed to John Steinbeck's *Grapes of Wrath* and to Mark Twain, "who gave America an image of itself, the idea of the innocent American, with his simple-minded appreciation of reality as against the complications of life." . . .

Speaking about his body of work, he said, "I have a feeling my plays are my character, and your character is your fate." Asked if he regretted any of his plays, he said, "That would be like regretting you lost your hair. They're part of my life. Each was terribly important to me at that moment."

As always, he works every day. He is writing a new play and he is revising *The Ride Down Mount Morgan* for its first New York production. And next season there will be a cycle of his plays in New York when he is playwright in residence Off Broadway with the Signature Theater Company.

Suddenly, he repeated his old refrain: "I never had a critic in my corner in this country." When it was pointed out that few playwrights have ever had critical champions, he readily agreed, adding, "As I look back, I honestly feel I have nothing to complain about." But still he keeps complaining.

"Well, yeah," he admitted, with a shrug. "You've got to keep the ball in the air."

> The writer is even-handed and fair, presenting both positive and negative reactions to Miller's work.

> The writer includes telling details that are not general knowledge.

Critical Reading

1. (a) What is Brooks Atkinson's overall **opinion** of the first production of *The Crucible*? **(b)** Cite one element in the play that Atkinson found effective and one he found ineffective. **(c)** For each, identify one piece of evidence Atkinson uses to support his opinion. Explain whether that evidence is a **fact** or another opinion.

2. (a) Identify three facts Kenneth Turan presents in the first three paragraphs of his review. **(b)** At what point does he first state an opinion? **(c)** What is that opinion?

3. (a) Distinguish between fact and opinion in the feature article by citing two opinions and two facts it presents. **(b)** Overall, does the article rely more heavily on fact or on opinion? Explain.

4. Content-Area Vocabulary (a) Explain how the meaning of the Latin word *adaptare* ("fit, adjust") contributes to the meaning of the English word *adaptation*. **(b)** Determine the meaning and parts of speech of the following words derived from the same linguistic source: *adaptable, adaptive, adaptivity.* **(c)** Use a dictionary to verify your preliminary definitions.

 ## Timed Writing

Argument [40 minutes]

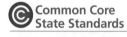 **Common Core State Standards**

Writing

1. Write arguments to support claims in an analysis of substantive topics or texts, using valid reasoning and relevant and sufficient evidence.

10. Write routinely over shorter time frames for a range of tasks, purposes, and audiences.

Language

4.b. Identify and correctly use patterns of word changes that indicate different meanings or parts of speech.

4.d. Verify the preliminary determination of the meaning of a word or phrase.

Format

An **argumentative essay** is not a piece of writing in which you start a fight. An argument is a well-reasoned position or opinion. In an essay, you must explain and support your argument.

In 1953, when *The Crucible* premiered, critics had the power to make or break a Broadway play. Today, with the rise of the Internet, social networking sites, and numerous forms of publishing, can any one critic still be as important or as powerful in any art form? Write an **argumentative essay** in which you express and **defend** your opinion on this topic. **Support** your claims with details from the feature article and theater reviews as well as your own observations and experience.

Academic Vocabulary

The prompt does not simply require you to express your personal opinions. Instead, it asks you to **defend** and **support** your views. To do so, cite convincing and varied evidence.

5-Minute Planner

Complete these steps before you begin to write.

1. Read the prompt carefully. List key words.

2. Draft a thesis that clearly responds to the prompt.

3. Skim the text for details you can use as evidence. **TIP** Topic sentences or key ideas are usually stated in either the first or last sentence of a paragraph. Locate details quickly by reading those sentences first.

4. Reread the prompt, and draft your essay.

Write an Argumentative Essay

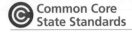 **Common Core State Standards**

Writing
1. Write arguments to support claims in an analysis of substantive topics or texts, using valid reasoning and relevant and sufficient evidence.
1.a. Distinguish the claim(s) from alternate or opposing claims.
7. Conduct short research projects to answer a question or solve a problem; narrow or broaden the inquiry when appropriate; synthesize multiple sources on the subject, demonstrating understanding of the subject under investigation.

Argument John F. Kennedy and Martin Luther King, Jr., wrote argumentative pieces to convince others to accept their views. Argumentative writing can take many forms, such as speeches, letters, articles, and essays. Argumentative essays are prose works that argue for a claim, using valid reasoning and sufficient, relevant evidence. Follow the steps outlined in this workshop to write an argumentative essay.

Assignment Write an argumentative essay that urges readers to accept your viewpoint on and claims about an issue.

What to Include Your argumentative essay should have these elements:

- A claim that clearly states your position
- Well-organized evidence that supports your argument, such as facts, examples, statistics, and personal experience
- Discussion that defuses or refutes counterclaims and their supporting evidence
- Language that is compelling and convincing
- A concluding statement that follows from and supports your ideas

To preview the criteria on which your argumentative essay may be assessed, see the rubric on page 1263.

Focus on Research

When you write argumentative essays, you should conduct research to locate the following information:

- Evidence to support your claims
- Information to refute or defuse counterclaims

The best evidence will come from valid sources such as reputable, authoritative organizations, books, and websites. Be sure to note all sources you use in your research, and credit appropriately. Refer to the Conducting Research pages in the Introductory Unit as well as the Citing Sources and Preparing Manuscript pages in the Resource section (R21–R23) for information on citation.

Prewriting and Planning

Choosing Your Topic

A good topic for an argumentative essay is an issue that you feel strongly about and that might even affect you personally. It should also be an issue that provokes disagreement. To choose a topic for your argumentative essay, try this strategy:

Make a "news" notebook. Find topics by reading newspapers and maga-zine editorials, letters to the editor, and op-ed pages. Watch television news-casts and listen to radio talk shows, particularly those that feature experts on both sides of an issue. Record interesting opinions in a news notebook and note your response. Then, review your list, and choose an issue that you find compelling. As you learn more about the topic, your opinion may change.

Source	Topic	Opinion	My Response
Nightly News (7:30 PM)	Community volunteering	PTA leaders believe volunteering should be a requirement for graduation.	It is not volunteering if you have to do it. On the other hand, it could help the community a lot.

Narrowing Your Topic

Focus by looping. Once you have chosen a general topic, a strategy called looping can help you narrow your focus. Freewrite about your broad topic for five minutes. Read what you have written, and then circle the idea that you find most compelling. Then, freewrite for another five minutes about the idea you circled. Repeat the process until you arrive at a manageable topic.

Gathering Details

Compile your evidence. Review the position you stated in your news notebook. Gather evidence to support the position. Use books, newspapers, magazines, Internet sources, and other resources. Look for facts and well-argued opinions.

- A **fact** is a statement that can be proved true. (More than 78% of students were late to school at least once last year.)

- An **opinion** is a judgment or belief that can-not be proved, although it can be supported by facts and arguments. (Students should not have to wake up before 6:00 A.M.)

Analyze both sides of the issue. Use a T-chart to record facts and arguments for and against your position. Prepare counterclaims that will address opinions that contradict yours.

High school should start later in the morning.

Pro	Con
Teenagers are half-asleep at school because they are biologically wired to fall asleep late and wake up late.	Starting school later will create problems for students who do extracurriculars, play sports, or have jobs.

Drafting

Shaping Your Writing

Follow an effective organization. Review your notes. Rank your reasons from most to least convincing. Choose an organization that will highlight your strongest reasons and evidence. This chart shows two structures you might follow.

Introduction:

Include a strong **claim** that identifies the issue and clearly states your position.

Body: Organization A

- Begin with your second strongest reason and evidence.
- Present other reasons and evidence in descending order of strength.
- Present and refute opposing claims, or counterclaims.
- End with your strongest reason and evidence.

Body: Organization B

- Begin with your strongest reason and evidence.
- State and refute the strongest opposing claims, or counterclaims.
- Present other reasons and evidence in increasing order of strength.
- End with your second strongest reason and evidence.

Conclusion:

End with a memorable paragraph that restates your claim and sums up your strongest supporting evidence.

Include sufficient, relevant supporting evidence. Convince readers by making sure you have enough evidence, that it supports your claim, and that it comes from reliable sources.
Maintain a formal style and tone. A calm, formal tone, or attitude, is more persuasive than a reactive emotional one. Maintain a formal style and tone as you draft.

Providing Elaboration

Use effective arguing techniques. You can use these types of reasoning to build a strong case for your claim.

Type of Reasoning	Definition	Example
Inductive Reasoning	Specific facts used to lead to a general truth	Bicycle injury rates in Oaktown decreased when a helmet law was passed. Therefore, a helmet law will help our community prevent bicycle injuries.
Deductive Reasoning	A general truth applied to a specific case	Helmet laws have been shown to reduce accidents. If we had a stronger helmet law, Alicia Martinez would not have been injured last month.

Common Core State Standards

Writing
1.a. Introduce precise, knowledgeable claim(s), establish the significance of the claim(s), distinguish the claim(s) from alternate or opposing claims, and create an organization that logically sequences claim(s), counterclaims, reasons, and evidence.
1.b. Develop claim(s) and counterclaims fairly and thoroughly, supplying the most relevant evidence for each while pointing out the strengths and limitations of both in a manner that anticipates the audience's knowledge level, concerns, values, and possible biases.
1.d. Establish and maintain a formal style and objective tone while attending to the norms and conventions of the discipline in which they are writing.
1.e. Provide a concluding statement or section that follows from and supports the argument presented.

Writers on Writing

Arthur Miller On Using Historical Facts

Arthur Miller is the author of *The Crucible* (p. 1124).

In reading the record [of the Salem witchcraft trials], which was taken down verbatim at the trial, I found one recurring note which had a growing effect upon my concept, not only of the phenomenon itself, but of our modern way of thinking about people, and especially of the treatment of evil in contemporary drama. Some critics have taken exception, for instance, to the unrelieved badness of the prosecution in the play [*The Crucible*]. I understand how this is possible, and I plead no mitigation, but I was up against historical facts which were immutable.

". . . I could not imagine a theatre worth my time that did not want to change the world."
—Arthur Miller

from *The Crucible*

HALE: Man, you will hang! You cannot!

PROCTOR, *his eyes full of tears*: I can. And there's your first marvel, that I can. You have made your magic now, for now I do think I see some shed of goodness in John Proctor. Not enough to weave a banner with, but white enough to keep it from such dogs.

ELIZABETH, *in a burst of terror, rushes to him and weeps against his hand*: Give them no tear! Tears pleasure them! Show honor now, show a stony heart and sink them with it! *He has lifted her, and kisses her now with great passion.*

REBECCA: Let you fear nothing! Another judgment awaits us all!

DANFORTH: Hang them high over the town! Who weeps for these, weeps for corruption! *He sweeps out past them.*

I do not think that either the record itself or the numerous commentaries upon it reveal any mitigation of the unrelieved, straightforward, and absolute dedication to evil displayed by the judges of these trials and the prosecutors. After days of study it became quite incredible how perfect they were in this respect....

No human weakness could be displayed without the prosecution's stabbing into the greater fury. The most patent contradictions, almost laughable even in that day, were overridden with warnings not to repeat their mention.

Revising

Revising Your Overall Structure

Eliminate faulty logic and weak reasoning. When you write argumentatively, you can get carried away with your passionate convictions. Make sure your writing will persuade your reader with careful logical thinking. Review your draft for these common mistakes:

Faulty Logic and Weak Reasoning		
Type	**Definition**	**Example**
circular reasoning	Supporting a point by simply stating it in other words	"The law *should be amended* because it needs *changing*."
post hoc argument	Assuming that because one event occurs after another, the first event causes the second	"Since she became principal, our school ranking has fallen drastically. She must resign now."
bandwagon appeal	Urging readers to adopt a course of action because "everybody is doing it"	"Every other high school in the county has a soccer team; we need one too."
loaded language	Using words with strong negative or positive connotations to hide weak arguments	"The *ridiculous* new uniforms look *terrible*, so they won't help discipline at all."

Revising Your Sentences

Strengthen your transitions. In argumentative writing, good transitions highlight the logic of an extended argument. Both between paragraphs and within them, transitions can make your reasoning more obvious.

Examples:

Transitions that show contrast: *however, although, despite*

Transitions that point to a reason: *since, because, if*

Transitions that signal a conclusion: *therefore, consequently, so, then*

Color-code to check transitions. Circle transitions in your draft. Then, read each paragraph of your essay. Underline in green the places where you set up contrasts, underline in blue where you provide reasons, and underline in red where you have drawn conclusions. In each case, decide whether the transition you have used is effective. Revise or add transitions as needed.

Peer Review: Ask a group of three or four classmates to read your draft and identify places where you might improve your transitions. Make revisions as needed. Then, explain to the group how each of your revisions clarifies your logic or improves the connection between ideas.

Common Core State Standards

Writing
1.b. Develop claim(s) and counterclaims fairly and thoroughly, supplying the most relevant evidence for each while pointing out the strengths and limitations of both in a manner that anticipates the audience's knowledge level, concerns, values, and possible biases.
1.c. Use words, phrases, and clauses as well as varied syntax to link the major sections of the text, create cohesion, and clarify the relationships between claim(s) and reasons, between reasons and evidence, and between claim(s) and counterclaims.

Language
3.a. Vary syntax for effect.

Developing Your Style

Using Parallelism

Parallel structure is the repeated use of related ideas in a similar grammatical form. Parallel expressions emphasize your arguments and create a compelling rhythm. If the parallel ideas are in the same sentence, they must have the same grammatical form. Mixing forms is a grammatical error called "faulty parallelism."

Faulty Parallelism	Correct Parallelism
Philadelphia is famous for <u>the First Continental Congress</u>, <u>housing the Liberty Bell</u>, and <u>publishing the country's first newspaper.</u> (one noun and two gerund phrases)	Philadelphia is famous for <u>hosting the First Continental Congress</u>, <u>housing the Liberty Bell</u>, and <u>publishing the country's first newspaper.</u> (three gerund phrases)

Review your draft to identify similar or contrasting concepts. Consider expressing these concepts in parallel form. Phrase the ideas with the same grammatical structure, using similar words, phrases, clauses, or sentences.

Find It in Your Reading

Read or review the Inaugural Address by John F. Kennedy on page 1104.

1. Identify three sentences that use parallelism.

2. Write out the sentences, and underline the parallel elements.

3. Explain the way each sentence uses the same grammatical structure.

Apply It in Your Writing

For each paragraph in your essay, follow these steps:

1. Identify writing that expresses related or contrasting concepts.

2. If these concepts are in different sentences, use parallelism to combine them.

3. If the concepts are in the same sentence, make sure they have the same grammatical structure, as shown:

Faulty Parallelism: *We rowed <u>past the boathouse, under the bridge,</u> and <u>the boat crossed the finish line.</u> (two prepositional phrases and one independent clause)*

Correct Parallelism: *We rowed <u>past the boathouse, under the bridge,</u> and <u>across the finish line.</u> (three prepositional phrases)*

Student Model: Steven Waldorf, Fort Myers, FL

The Internet: Positives Outweigh Negatives

Throughout the course of modern history, technological innovations have revolutionized the world. Of these, few have altered everyday life like the Internet has. From purchasing products to researching information, there is little that cannot be accomplished over the World Wide Web. By making research more convenient and enhancing the speed of communication, the Internet has had an overwhelmingly positive effect on society.

When it comes to writing a research paper or creating a scholastic presentation, the Internet is a tool that puts millions of resources from around the world at your fingertips. With the mere click of a mouse, a researcher can access information on topics ranging from organic chemistry to the American Civil War. Research that once required driving to the library and rifling through hundreds of books can now be conducted in one's own home, and in a fraction of the time. This convenience and ease of use also carries an important implication. Students who live in rural parts of the country, many of whom have traditionally not had as many resources as those who live in suburban or metropolitan areas, can now access the same quality research information. Therefore, students who have previously been at an academic disadvantage now have at their disposal a tool that helps to level the playing field between students from all areas of the country. Overall, the Internet is of tremendous assistance to students everywhere looking for information on scholastic subjects.

Some are quick to point out, however, that the use of the Internet for academic pursuits also has some negative consequences. Research purists often say that information obtained over the Internet is not as accurate as that found in books. This is occasionally the case, but if a researcher uses discretion in the sites from which he or she harvests information, this argument becomes irrelevant. For instance, what difference does it make whether a student uses facts from the Encyclopedia Britannica or from the book's virtual counterpart? Critics also say that information from the Internet is more likely to be plagiarized than material extracted from books. In reality, though, a student who is willing to plagiarize information from the Internet would be just as likely to pass ideas from a book off as his or her own. Furthermore, it is not more difficult to properly cite sources from Web sites than from books or articles. When all the facts are considered, these counterarguments do not hold up to close scrutiny.

Aside from research, the Internet has also revolutionized the way in which people communicate. No longer is it necessary to wait days, even weeks, for letters to travel through the postal system. Now, in literally an instant, written communication can be sent across the country. E-mail can be used to chat with a close relative or to file a complaint with a major corporation. Again, some may claim that this detracts from human-to-human contact. However, there is little empirical evidence to suggest that this impacts society in a harmful way. On the contrary, the Web has opened up a whole new medium by which individuals can correspond with others.

The Internet has had an enormously beneficial impact on the way we conduct research and communicate with one another. Few can argue against the fact that it has made life much easier, particularly for students. Because of this, the Internet has definitely exerted a positive influence on society.

Steven presents a claim that states the opinion that he wants to persuade readers to accept.

Steven gives evidence to support his opinion about the benefits of the Internet.

The writer elaborates on his argument by anticipating counterclaims and answering these in his writing.

Steven appeals to his audience by citing evidence that they are familiar with.

In his conclusion, Steven strengthens his essay by restating his claim and the main points of his argument.

Editing and Proofreading

Check your essay for errors in grammar, usage, punctuation, and spelling.

Focus on punctuation. Make sure you have used commas to separate three or more parallel words, phrases, or clauses in a series.

> **Words:** *The train was crowded, noisy, and slow.*
> **Phrases:** *We toured the town by bus, by car, and by train.*
> **Clauses:** *The survey revealed that most residents support the mayor, oppose the new highway, and plan to vote for the upcoming bond issue.*

Focus on spelling. The sound of *sh* is sometimes spelled *ci*, as in *gracious*, or *ti*, as in *cautious*. Read your essay aloud, listening for words with the *sh* sound. Make sure your spelling of these words is correct.

Publishing, Presenting, and Reflecting

Consider one of the following ways to share and think further about your writing.

Publish in a newspaper. Find out the length requirements for an opinion piece for your local or school newspaper. Modify your essay to meet those requirements and submit it for publication.

Deliver a speech. Use your argumentative essay as the basis for a speech to your classmates or to another audience. Make adjustments to the text to ensure that your audience can follow your line of reasoning and that your content and language are appropriate for the situation. Use eye contact and gestures to add impact to your presentation.

Reflect on your writng. In a writer's journal, jot down your thoughts on the experience of writing an argumentative essay. Begin by answering these questions: How did writing an argumentative essay reinforce or change your opinion? Has any action been taken as a result of your essay? Explain.

Rubric for Self-Assessment

Evaluate your argumentative essay using the following criteria and rating scale.

Criteria	Rating Scale
	not very *very*
Purpose/Focus: How clear is your claim?	1 2 3 4
Organization: How effectively do you organize your arguments?	1 2 3 4
Development of Ideas/Elaboration: How well do you use a variety of reasons and evidence to support your position?	1 2 3 4
Language: How well do you use parallel structure?	1 2 3 4
Conventions: How correct is your grammar, especially your use of commas?	1 2 3 4

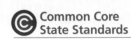
Common Core State Standards

Writing
4. Produce clear and coherent writing in which the development, organization, and style are appropriate to task, purpose, and audience.
5. Develop and strengthen writing as needed by planning, revising, editing, rewriting, or trying a new approach, focusing on addressing what is most significant for a specific purpose and audience.

Language
2.b. Spell correctly.

Speaking and Listening
4. Present information, findings, and supporting evidence, conveying a clear and distinct perspective, such that listeners can follow the line of reasoning, alternative or opposing perspectives are addressed, and the organization, development, substance, and style are appropriate to purpose, audience, and a range of formal and informal tasks.

Analyze and Evaluate Entertainment Media

Television shows, movies, music videos, podcasts, and radio broadcasts have become constants in American life. All of these broadcast forms present different types of entertainment media—programming explicitly designed for enjoyment rather than for instruction or information. While entertainment media draws people in for fun and leisure, it also conveys powerful messages and can be highly influential in transmitting cultural values.

Types of Entertainment Media

While people may sometimes dismiss entertainment media as frivolous, it is very powerful and can affect how people see the world. You can enjoy a film or a television show but at the same time understand that you are receiving the mediamaker's ideas, values, and perspectives. Just as you think critically when you read a novel, so should you view critically when you watch a movie.

Media Effects The main purpose of nearly all entertainment media is to give viewers an interesting viewing experience; however, these media forms also have profound effects on individuals and the culture. These effects fall into three main categories:

- *To interpret facts.* Movies or TV shows may give viewers new understandings of past or current events. Sometimes, these new understandings are accurate; often, they are not, as media makers emphasize or even distort specific elements for dramatic effect. It is important to know the facts, or use resources to check them, before accepting a view of history or of a current issue as it is presented in entertainment media.

- *To persuade.* Media makers may embed opinions within the elements of an entertainment product. They may depict groups of people in negative ways, fail to provide multiple points of view on a complex problem, or otherwise skew an issue. It is important to be alert to the use of *stereotypes*, *bias*, and other unfair or misleading depictions.

- *To transmit culture and values.* Various forms of entertainment media reflect and shape cultural values and norms. Television sitcoms with morals at the end of each episode or talk radio shows that examine social dynamics are examples of media that reflect and influence cultural values. These media forms can have clear effects on society. For example, in the 1960s and 1970s, television reflected the changing roles of women and minorities in society. These depictions also allowed the culture to arrive at a new understanding of what is "normal." As you watch entertainment media, be alert to portrayals of people that do not reflect the realities in the world around you.

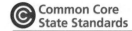

Common Core State Standards

Language
1. Demonstrate command of the conventions of standard English grammar and usage when speaking.

Speaking and Listening
2. Integrate multiple sources of information presented in diverse formats and media in order to make informed decisions and solve problems, evaluating the credibility and accuracy of each source and noting any discrepancies among the data.

Media Tools and Techniques

Entertainment media use numerous techniques, including those listed here, to make representations more effective or dramatic:

Technique	Description	Example
Special Effects	Visual and audio illusions	Firefighters run in slow motion away from a collapsing building.
Camera Angles	Directions from which a camera operator shoots images	A scene is shot from above to give a bird's-eye view.
Reaction Shots	Shots that show a character's responses	As a girl falls from her horse, the camera pans to her mother's face.
Sequencing	Events arranged in a specific order to tell a story	A flashback interrupts the chronological presentation of events to give the audience background information.
Music	Music used to create a desired mood	As a father and son reunite, soft piano music plays in the background.

Activities: Analyze a Movie, TV Episode, or Skit

Comprehension and Collaboration For Activity A, use an evaluation form like the one below.

A. Choose an example of visual entertainment media, such as a movie or television show, that you enjoy. Examine how the director uses different tools and techniques to shape the content. Present your conclusions to the class, using standard English grammar and usage as you speak.

B. A **parody** is a comic imitation of a serious form. Its purpose is to poke fun at the form itself or the ideas it represents. Locate and watch a parody of a particular type of entertainment media. As you watch, consider the following questions: What qualities in the original are being parodied? How do the media makers create the parody—through visual effects, story line, exaggerated characters, or another element?

Evaluation Form for Entertainment Media

Type of Entertainment Media: _____

Name of Movie, Show, or Skit: _____

Write a summary of the plot: _____

What cultural values are represented in the plot? _____

How are certain groups of people represented? _____

Identify and describe the technical elements used in the film.

☐ special effects _____   ☐ camera angles _____

☐ reaction shots _____   ☐ sequencing _____

☐ music _____

Which of these technical elements is the most significant? Explain.

_____

Idioms and Idiomatic Expressions

© Common Core
State Standards

Language
4. Determine or clarify the meaning of unknown and multiple-meaning words and phrases based on *grades 11–12 reading and content,* choosing flexibly from a range of strategies.
4.a. Use context as a clue to the meaning of a word or phrase.
5. Demonstrate understanding of figurative language, word relationships, and nuances in word meanings.

Idioms are figurative expressions commonly used in conversation and informal writing. Idiomatic expressions do not literally mean what they say. For example, if you *burned the midnight oil,* you stayed up late to work on something. You probably did not not actually rise at midnight to burn oil. To define idioms, look at context clues, or the words and phrases around them. These will help you infer the meanings of unfamiliar expressions.

Consider these examples:

Example	Context Clues
Claire volunteered to be on three committees. Later, she felt that she had bitten off more than she could chew.	The idea that Claire is on three committees helps you understand that the idiom means she had agreed to do too much.
My philosophy is to let sleeping dogs lie rather than to constantly bring up problems.	The words "rather than" set up a contrast. Therefore, you know that *let sleeping dogs lie* means the opposite of "bring up problems."

Practice

Directions: Identify the idiom in each sentence. Then, use context clues to define it.

1. After winning the hot dog–eating contest, Jamal felt under the weather for a day or two.

2. She knew she would have to hit the books tonight if she wanted to do well on the test tomorrow.

3. The instructions made putting the bookcase together seem like a piece of cake, but I knew better from past experience.

4. The ninth-graders are wet behind the ears at first, but they soon get older and wiser.

5. Maria bent over backward to make sure the party was a success.

6. After six days of rainy, cold weather, I felt blue.

7. Sam is too forthright to beat around the bush.

Directions: Complete each **analogy** below. Then, write an explanation of the idiomatic expression and word relationships in each pairing.

1. pouring : "raining cats and dogs" :: _____ : "safe and sound"
   a. loud   **b.** secure   **c.** wet   **d.** friendly

2. "out of hand" : _____ :: "the eleventh hour" : in advance
   a. done with skill   **b.** running late   **c.** wild   **d.** under control

Vocabulary Acquisition and Use:
Sentence Completions

Sentence Completion questions appear in most standardized tests. They test not only vocabulary skills but also knowledge of sentence structure. Each item is a sentence with one or more missing words. Your task is to choose the correct word or words to complete each sentence logically.

Practice

This exercise is modeled after the Sentence Completion exercises that appear in the Critical Reading section of the SAT.

Directions: Each of the following sentences is missing one or two words. Choose the word or set of words that best completes each sentence.

Test-Taking Tip
Eliminate any words with similar meanings, because a single correct answer choice should be obvious.

1. Some ___?___ opportunists deprived rural landowners of their legal rights.
   A. illiterate
   B. rueful
   C. unscrupulous
   D. convivial
   E. morose

2. A lonely countryside can appear to be either beautiful or ___?___.
   A. desolate
   B. punitive
   C. repugnant
   D. intricate
   E. frayed

3. A newcomer would be ___?___ by our peculiar local customs and habits.
   A. blanched
   B. confounded
   C. exalted
   D. dissuaded
   E. permeated

4. If poverty and malnutrition exist, society should attempt ___?___ restructuring to solve these problems.
   A. contiguous
   B. systemic
   C. punitive
   D. mundane
   E. virulent

5. Some downtrodden people ___?___ a difficult life of their own   .
   A. impelled . . . profundity
   B. endured . . . volition
   C. appeased . . . collusion
   D. maneuvered . . . disillusions
   E. concocted . . . brazenness

6. Those who did escape poverty proved to be ___?___ survivors who shook off the effects of the ___?___ surrounding them.
   A. intriguing . . . perdition
   B. exalted . . . avarice
   C. vanquished . . . geography
   D. wily . . . malevolence
   E. gaudy . . . diligence

From Text to Understanding

You have studied each part of Unit 5 as a set of connected texts. In this workshop, you will have the chance to further explore the fundamental connections among these texts and to deepen your essential understanding of the literature and its social and historical context.

PART 1: War Shock

Writing: Argumentative Essay The selections in Part 1 show different intersections between people's lives and World War II. Although the actual field of battle was vast, these texts focus on smaller spaces— ordinary places upon which the war encroached. As you review the Part 1 selections, focusing on the Anchor Text, the excerpt from John Hersey's *Hiroshima*, think about how the settings are tied to the works' themes.

Assignment: Develop a claim that analyzes the use of setting in Hersey's *Hiroshima* and one other selection in Part 1. Why are the settings so important in these works? In what ways do the places themselves inspire the writers? Background material and other Part 1 texts can help you develop your claim, which might resemble the following:

> **Example:** In times of war, all space has the potential to become part of the conflict. Focusing on everyday locations, like Dr. Seuss's easy chair and those painfully detailed in John Hersey's *Hiroshima*, show how writers use setting to illustrate the reach of war.

Read closely. Make a list of guided questions related to the settings of the works. Then, take notes as you review the selections using your questions as a framework.

Evaluate the methods. Notice how authors use adjectives and figurative language to describe concrete physical details. Identify how the description of setting connects to the theme of the work in a clear and significant way.

Show your reasoning. As you write, develop your argument in an organized, methodical way. State your claim, then support it with details and evidence. The structure of your essay should show your thinking in a progression from introduction through development to conclusion.

Focus on word choice. As you write, choose your words with precision. Words specific to war, such as *destruction*, *innocence*, and *inescapable*, can add power to your writing.

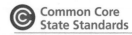

Common Core State Standards

Writing

1. Write arguments to support claims in an analysis of substantive topics or texts, using valid reasoning and relevant and sufficient evidence.

7. Conduct short as well as more sustained research projects to answer a question (including a self-generated question) or solve a problem; narrow or broaden the inquiry when appropriate; synthesize multiple sources on that subject, demonstrating understanding of the subject under investigation.

Speaking and Listening

1. Initiate and participate effectively in a range of collaborative discussions (one-on-one, in groups, and teacher-led) with diverse partners on *grades 11–12 topics, texts, and issues*, building on others' ideas and expressing their own clearly and persuasively.

Writing Checklist

☐ Clear claim

Identify: _____

☐ References to and thoughtful commentary on quotations from the texts

Examples: _____

☐ Clear discussion of the author's use of language and style for specific effects

Examples: _____

PART 2: Tradition and Rebellion

Research: Documentary Slide Show The selections in Part 2 resonate with the play between expectation and disappointment. Review the Part 2 texts, focusing on the Anchor Text poems, "Mirror" by Sylvia Plath and "Courage" by Anne Sexton, and consider the individual experiences and versions of reality they offer.

Assignment: Work with a partner to create documentary slide shows that present multimedia interpretations of literary works. Develop one presentation about one of the Anchor Text poems, and one about a Part 2 selection that you see as thematically related.

Conduct research and analyze the texts to answer questions such as:

- What is the history of each work?

- What does a close reading of each work reveal about its meaning?

Gather video clips and images such as photographs, paintings, and illustrations. Use sound when possible. Embed the video files or links to videos in your slide show. Share your documentaries with your classmates.

PART 3: Literature of Protest

Listening and Speaking: Roundtable Discussion Review the selections in Part 3, paying special attention to the Anchor Texts, the "Inaugural Address" by John F. Kennedy and "Letter from Birmingham City Jail" by Martin Luther King, Jr. These texts are a clear call to people's better instincts, a call to join the fight against injustice, a call infused with hope even in the face of alarming struggle. These and other Part 3 selections show that acts of protest include speaking and writing, as well as physical resistance.

Assignment: Work with a small group and lead a discussion about how the fight against injustice is engaged in the Anchor Texts by President Kennedy and Dr. King, as well as by a third writer, such as Arthur Miller, author of *The Crucible*. Choose someone to moderate the discussion. Invite classmates to join in with thoughts and questions. You may base your discussion on questions such as the following:

- What is the specific problem?
- How does the writer propose to address the problem?
- How convincing is the writer's approach?
- Is one method of protest more effective than another?
- How is the idea of hope present in these works?

Documentary Production Plan:

- ☐ **Choose the selections.** Choose texts that speak most powerfully to you.

- ☐ **Research the texts' backgrounds.** Find out when they were written and any interesting information about their publication history.

- ☐ **Analyze the texts.** Close-read the texts, drawing parallels between them and making observations about author's style, meaning, and theme.

- ☐ **Research images.** Use the library and the Internet to locate images that reflect the texts' meaning. Include images of the authors.

- ☐ **Choose your format.** Combine video and photographs; create a computer-generated slide show; or make posters.

- ☐ **Put it all together.** Assemble your research, literary analysis, and images, and write a script that tells the story of the works you chose. Read the script aloud while you display images on a computer or posters.

Test-Taking Practice

Reading Test: Prose Fiction

Standardized tests often include **prose fiction** reading selections, passages drawn from novels and short stories. You will be tested on your comprehension of the text as well as your literary analysis skills. Questions will focus on topics such as main ideas, significant details, causes and effects, and author's perspective, as well as theme and underlying meaning.

 Common Core State Standards

RL.11-12.1, RL.11-12.4, RL.11-12.5; L.11-12.1, L.11-12.4, L.11-12.4.a; W.11-12.2, W.11-12.5.
[For the full wording of the standards, see the standards chart in the front of your textbook.]

Practice

The following exercise is modeled after the ACT Reading Test, Prose Fiction section. The full test has 40 questions.

Directions: Read the following passage from *The First Seven Years,* by Bernard Malamud. Then, choose the best answer to each question.

During the week, by placing here and there a deft question, he managed to get from Miriam some information about Max. It surprised him to learn that the boy was not studying to be either a doctor or a lawyer but was taking a business course leading to a degree in
5   accountancy. Feld was a little disappointed because he thought of accountants as bookkeepers and would have preferred "a higher profession." However, it was not long before he had investigated the subject and discovered that Certified Public Accountants were highly respected people, so he was thoroughly content as Saturday
10 approached. But because Saturday was a busy day, he was much in the store and therefore did not see Max when he came to call for Miriam. From his wife he learned there had been nothing especially revealing about their meeting. Max had rung the bell and Miriam had got her coat and left with him—nothing more. Feld did not probe, for his wife
15 was not particularly observant. Instead, he waited up for Miriam with a newspaper on his lap, which he scarcely looked at so lost was he in thinking of the future. He awoke to find her in the room with him, tiredly removing her hat. Greeting her, he was suddenly inexplicably afraid to ask anything about the evening. But since she volunteered
20 nothing he was at last forced to inquire how she had enjoyed herself. Miriam began something noncommittal but apparently changed her mind, for she said after a minute, "I was bored."

Strategy

Focus on sequence.

- **Underline time words** like dates and time of day, to understand the flow of events.

- **Look for transition words,** such as "then" and "as a result," to further link events together.

- Before answering the questions, reread any section in which you are unsure of the story's progression.

1. Which part of Feld's thinking foreshadows the disappointing results of his daughter's date?
   - **A.** his surprise that the boy would not become a doctor or a lawyer
   - **B.** his contentment as Saturday approached
   - **C.** his preoccupation being busy in the store that day
   - **D.** his wife's lack of observance

2. Considering the events of the entire passage, it is most reasonable to infer that Miriam hesitated to say anything about the date after it was over because:
   - **F.** she was reluctant to dash her father's hopes.
   - **G.** she was too tired after work to speak.
   - **H.** the date had been so fulfilling she could not speak.
   - **J.** the date had left her without any opinion of it.

3. As it is used in line 18, the word *inexplicably* most nearly means:
   - **A.** overly exhausted.
   - **B.** unreasonably frightened.
   - **C.** without any motivation.
   - **D.** unable to be explained.

4. Which of the following would be included in a summary of this selection?
   - **I.** Feld had tried to learn more about the boy who was dating his daughter.
   - **II.** Feld did not see his daughter and the boy when they first met.
   - **III.** Feld waited up to find out how the date he arranged had gone.
   - **F.** II only
   - **G.** III only
   - **H.** I and III only
   - **J.** I, II, and III

5. The author provides a visual image to increase the reader's understanding of his characters' motivations by:
   - **A.** describing the differences between professions.
   - **B.** revealing what happened at work that day.
   - **C.** mentioning that Feld's wife was not observant.
   - **D.** describing how Miriam removes her hat when she comes home.

6. According to the narrator, Feld was first upset and then later relieved that Max was an accountant because:
   - **F.** he always wanted his daughter to marry a doctor.
   - **G.** he wanted his daughter to marry someone famous.
   - **H.** he finally learned that accountants were highly respected.
   - **J.** he had hoped his daughter would date someone with his profession.

7. Which element of the author's style helps describe the character of Feld?
   - **A.** a long paragraph of connected thoughts
   - **B.** the character's use of a personal "I"
   - **C.** a disjointed stop/start self-argument
   - **D.** revealing snippets of conversation

8. The details and events in the passage suggest that the friendship between Miriam and her father would most accurately be described as:
   - **F.** tender.
   - **G.** competitive.
   - **H.** intense.
   - **J.** distant.

9. According to the narrator, Feld learned about Max's course of study by:
   - **A.** questioning his daughter.
   - **B.** asking Max directly.
   - **C.** diligent research.
   - **D.** consulting with his wife.

GO ON

Grammar and Writing: Editing in Context

Editing-in-context segments often appear in the English sections of standard-ized testing. They are made up of a reading passage with highlighted and numbered areas, some of which contain errors in grammar, style, and usage. For each question, you must choose the best way to correct a given sentence.

Practice

This exercise is modeled after the ACT English Test.

Directions: For each underlined sentence or portion of a sentence, choose the best alternative. If an item asks a question about a numbered portion of the essay, choose the best answer to the question.

[1]

Flannery O'Connor is perhaps the equal of her contemporary, William Faulkner, but her far smaller output has made her less well known. She wrote in a Southern Gothic style and <u>relies</u> on colorful regional characters and customs. <u>**Characters with deformities of body or spirit were often**</u> <u>**described by O'Connor.**</u> This type of character is referred to as a Grotesque character. Ms. O'Connor herself was afflicted with a long-term illness, which made her feel like an outsider, perhaps even an outcast. <u>**Like many of her**</u> <u>**characters.**</u> She knew well of what she wrote.

[2]

Though her characters are often misfits, Flannery O'Connor has an underlying sympathy for them. In an effort to point out the spiritual failings of the mod-ern world, O'Connor created characters with dubious moral capacities, <u>**not**</u> <u>**with clear values**</u>. She had a strong sense of spirituality due to her deeply religious upbringing. She never wrote cloyingly optimistic stories, for her sen-sibilities <u>runs</u> deeper than a happy surface.

[3]

Ms. O'Connor contracted lupus in 1951. Lupus is a serious and often deadly disease. 6 She died in 1964 at the age of 39, leaving a literary legacy of two novels and 31 short stories. 7

Strategy

What is different?
Examine the answer choices with an eye to what makes them differ-ent. Various aspects of writing can vary in mul-tiple answers. Make sure each part is effective.

1. **A.** NO CHANGE
   B. relied
   C. has relied
   D. was relying

2. The writer is considering changing this sentence to make a more active statement. Which of the following sentences would do that best?
   F. Were characters with deformities of mind or body often described by O'Connor?
   G. Characters often described by O'Connor had deformities of mind or body.
   H. O'Connor's characters were often described as Grotesque.
   J. O'Connor often described characters with deformities of body or spirit.

3. **A.** NO CHANGE
   B. attach it to previous sentence
   C. attach it to next sentence
   D. OMIT

4. **F.** NO CHANGE
   G. OMIT
   H. not having clear values
   J. not possessing clear values

5. **A.** NO CHANGE
   B. will run
   C. ran
   D. will always run

6. Where in Paragraph 3 would the following best be placed?
   Not long after being accepted into the prestigious Iowa Writer's Workshop,
   A. before the previous sentence
   B. before the first sentence
   C. as part of the previous sentence
   D. after the sentence that follows

7. In reviewing paragraph 3, the writer decides to add more information. What would most benefit the paragraph?
   F. more details about O'Connor's lifetime
   G. more details about O'Connor's published works
   H. more details about O'Connor's mother
   J. more details about O'Connor's love of birds

8. This question refers to the essay as a whole. This short essay would be most accurately categorized as which mode of writing?
   A. informational essay
   B. autobiography
   C. literary criticism
   D. reflective essay

 ## Timed Writing: Position Statement [30 minutes]

Feld, the hard-working shoemaker in *The First Seven Years*, wants his daughter to marry a highly respected professional. He thinks it is important to move up in society. Others might say that honest work and pride in one's work are more important than social status.

Write an **essay** in which you discuss the ideas of work, career, and status and which is most important in one's life. Back up your opinions with sound reasoning. Remember that there is no right or wrong answer but that your opinion should be clearly stated and supported. This exercise is similar to the optional ACT Writing Test.

Academic Vocabulary

An essay often argues with itself by first presenting one way of looking at an issue, and then refuting that argument with another viewpoint.

Constructed Response

 **Common Core
State Standards**

RL.11-12.1, RL.11-12.2; RL.11-12.3;
RL.11-12.4, RL.11-12.5; RL.11-12.6;
RI.11-12.4; W.11-12.2; W.11-12.4;
W.11-12.9a, W.11-12.9b; SL.11-12.4;
SL.11-12.6
[For the full wording of the standards,
see the standards chart in the front of
your textbook.]

Directions: *Follow the instructions to complete the tasks below as required by your teacher. As you work on each task, incorporate both general academic vocabulary and literary terms you learned in this unit.*

Writing

Task 1: Literature [RL.11-12.4, W.11-12.2]
Analyze Word Choice

*Write an **essay** in which you analyze the figurative and connotative language in a story or poem from this unit.*

- Choose a poem or story from this unit that uses figurative and connotative language in a way that is unique and memorable.
- For figurative language, first categorize the type of language used. For example, identify similes, metaphors, idioms, extended metaphors, or personification. Determine the meaning of all examples you cite and offer explanations.
- For connotative language, describe the associations, positive and negative, that a reader would bring to certain words. Then, analyze why the author chose each word or phrase for that particular context.
- Finally, for both types of language, evaluate the effect of word choice on the overall meaning and tone of the work.

Task 2: Literature [RL.11-12.3; W.11-12.2]
Analyze Story Elements

*Write an **essay** in which you analyze the role that setting and character play in driving the plot events in a story from this unit.*

- Choose a story with elements that are clearly or strongly related. For example, you might choose a story with a plot in which the setting is crucial.
- Summarize the story, describing the setting(s) and the major characters.
- Analyze the ways in which setting is essential to the plot of the story. For example, in an adventure story the plot events might hinge on severe weather conditions, high altitude, or heavy snowfall.
- Analyze the ways in which the main characters are crucial to the arc of the story. For example, a reckless climber might take a risk that becomes an inciting event that drives the entire story's action.
- In your conclusion, summarize how the author's choices in creating and developing characters and establishing setting impact the sequence of events in the story.

Task 3: Literature [RL.11-12.5, W.11-12.4]
Analyze Text Structure

*Write an **essay** in which you analyze how an author's choice of structure adds to the overall meaning and impact of a story in this unit.*

- Select a story from this unit in which the choice of structure affects the work's impact and meaning.
- Analyze the author's choices concerning how to structure specific parts of the story. Does the author choose to begin the story in the middle of exciting events or in a more quiet way? Does the author choose a resolution that ties up all loose ends or a resolution that leaves readers guessing? Does the ending emphasize comedic or tragic events?
- Consider how these choices add to the story's meaning and beauty.
- Describe the overall structure of the story. Identify the specific parts of the story you will analyze in depth.
- Evaluate what the specific parts of the story add to the story as a whole.
- Use academic vocabulary, such as *introduction, exposition, rising action, climax,* or *denouement,* in your explanation of structure.
- Organize and develop your ideas logically to produce a clear and coherent essay.

Speaking and Listening

Task 4: Informational Text [RI.11-12.4, SL.11-12.6]
Analyze Word Choice in a Work of Nonfiction

*Deliver an **oral presentation** in which you analyze word choice in a nonfiction work in this unit.*

- Choose a nonfiction work that includes diction you find interesting or challenging.

- Explain the meanings of key words and phrases as they are used in the work. Include explanations of figurative, connotative, and technical meanings.

- Analyze how word choice develops the central ideas of the work in a way that impacts or influences a reader. Include a discussion of specific rhetorical devices that an author uses in the piece, such as parallelism, imperatives, repetition, antithesis, and rhetorical questions.

- To provide support for your analysis, read key passages from the text aloud, stopping to point out examples of interesting word choices, figurative language, and rhetorical devices.

- Draw your audience's attention especially to words and phrases whose meaning the author explores and develops over the course of the work. Then, show how that exploration is connected to the overall meaning of the work. Keep your audience's prior knowledge and understanding of vocabulary in mind as you present.

Task 5: Literature [RL.11-12.4, SL.11-12.4]
Analyze Sound Devices

*In an **oral presentation,** analyze the effect of sound devices in a poem from this unit.*

- Choose a poem in which sound devices play a prominent role in creating an overall effect on the reader.

- Introduce the poem by explaining what sound devices you have found in the poem.

- Recite the poem aloud, emphasizing sound devices, such as alliteration, in your reading.

- Identify the various types of sound devices in the poem, provide examples of each, and explain the overall effect they create for the reader.

- Connect the poet's use of sound devices to the overall mood and meaning of the poem.

Task 6: Literature [RL.11-12.1, RL.11-12.2; SL.11-12.6]
Analyze Theme

*Prepare and present an **analysis** of two themes and their development over the course of a story from this unit.*

- Choose a story from this unit with multiple themes.

- Summarize the story. Then identify at least two of its themes or central ideas.

- Describe whether the themes you have identified are directly stated or implied. If they are directly stated, indicate where in the text this occurs. If they are implicit, indicate the clues that contribute to the theme you inferred. These clues might take the form of lines of dialogue or characters' reactions to events.

- Analyze how the author develops the themes throughout the story using dialogue, characters' actions, or story events. Discuss how the themes interact and build on one another as the story progresses.

- Cite the most significant and relevant quotations from the story to support your analysis.

- Use formal English as you deliver your presentation.

What is the relationship between place and literature?

The Point of a Place The writers in this unit describe a variety of places— a ruined twentieth-century city, a fragile Puritan village, an ordinary gas station, a greenhouse. Why are settings so critical in literature? In what ways does place itself inspire literary works and contribute to an author's theme or message?

Assignment Choose two descriptions of settings by two different authors from this unit. Write a **comparison-and-contrast essay** in which you analyze each description and compare what the setting adds to each work's overall meaning.

Titles for Extended Reading

In this unit, you have read a variety of literature of the post-war era. Continue to read works related to this era on your own. Select books that you enjoy, but challenge yourself to explore new topics, new authors, and works offering varied perspectives or approaches. The titles suggested below will help you get started.

LITERATURE

Baldwin: Early Stories and Novels
James Baldwin

Fiction James Baldwin is known today as one of the greatest and most influential African American writers, as well as a dedicated civil rights activist. Baldwin's early works reflect the reality of coming of age as an African American in Harlem in the 1950s. Included in this collection is Baldwin's first novel, *Go Tell It on the Mountain.* Largely autobiographical, it reveals many of the author's own feelings and experiences as a teenager.

[Baldwin's short story "The Rockpile" appears on page 1082 of this book. Build knowledge by reading other fiction by this author.]

Anthology of Modern American Poetry
edited by Cary Nelson
Oxford University Press, 2000   **EXEMPLAR TEXT**

 Poetry This collection includes poems by 161 different poets—including poems such as Ezra Pound's "The River Merchant's Wife: A Letter," and selections by newer poets such as Yusef Komunyakaa and Sherman Alexie.

The Adventures of Augie March
Saul Bellow   **EXEMPLAR TEXT**

 Novel Growing up poor in Chicago during the Great Depression, Augie March leaves home to try his hand at many different occupations, including dog groomer, shoplifter, and boxing coach. This is the story of Augie's attempt to create a great life for himself.

Death of a Salesman
Arthur Miller   **EXEMPLAR TEXT**

 Drama This play relates the end of the life of Willy Loman, an aging salesman who fails to achieve the greatness in life he so longs for.

[Miller's play The Crucible *begins on page 1124 of this book. Build knowledge by reading another play by this playwright.]*

A Raisin in the Sun
Lorraine Hansberry   **EXEMPLAR TEXT**

 Drama The Youngers family must decide how to spend a $10,000 insurance check in this play, often recognized as the first American drama to realistically portray an African American family.

INFORMATIONAL TEXTS

Historical Texts

A Call to Conscience: The Landmark Speeches of Dr. Martin Luther King, Jr.
Dr. Martin Luther King, Jr.

 Speech This collection includes twelve of King's most famous orations, including "I Have a Dream" and "I've Been to the Mountaintop" (delivered the night before his assassination).

Contemporary Scholarship

Patriots: The Vietnam War Remembered from All Sides
Christian G. Appy

 Primary Source The story of the longest military conflict in United States history comes alive through the candid and emotional testimonies of veterans, peace activists, former Vietcong fighters, and others affected by the war.

A Man on the Moon: The Voyages of the Apollo Astronauts
Andrew Chaikin (with a foreword by Tom Hanks)

 History Through interviews with astronauts and those who supported them from Earth, science writer Andrew Chaikin brings these missions to life, setting them against the backdrop of the war in Vietnam and social unrest in America.

Preparing to Read Complex Texts

Reading for College and Career In both college and the workplace, readers must analyze texts independently, draw connections among works that offer varied perspectives, and develop their own ideas and informed opinions. The questions shown below, and others that you generate on your own, will help you more effectively read and analyze complex college-level texts.

Common Core State Standards

Reading Literature/Informational Text
10. By the end of grade 11, read and comprehend literature, including stories, dramas, and poems, and literary nonfiction, in the grades 11-CCR text complexity band proficiently, with scaffolding as needed at the high end of the range.

When reading analytically, ask yourself...

- What idea, experience, or story seems to have compelled the author to write? Has the author presented that idea, experience, or story in a way that I, too, find compelling?

- How might the author's era, social status, belief system, or personal experiences have affected the point of view he or she expresses in the text?

- How do my circumstances affect what I understand and feel about this text?

- What key idea does the author state explicitly? What key idea does he or she suggest or imply? Which details in the text help me to perceive implied ideas?

- Do I find multiple layers of meaning in the text? If so, what relationships do I see among these layers of meaning?

- Do I find the text believable and convincing? Why or why not?

© Key Ideas and Details

- What patterns of organization or sequences do I find in the text? Do these patterns help me understand the ideas better? If so, how?

- What do I notice about the author's style, including his or her diction, use of imagery and figurative language, and syntax?

- Do I like the author's style? Is the author's style memorable? Why or why not?

- What emotional attitude does the author express toward the topic, the story, or the characters? Does this attitude seem appropriate? Why or why not?

- What emotional attitude does the author express toward me, the reader? Does this attitude seem appropriate? Why or why not?

- What do I notice about the author's voice—his or her personality on the page? Do I like this voice? Does it make me want to read on?

© Craft and Structure

- Is the work fresh and original? How do I know?

- Do I agree with the author's ideas entirely, or are there elements I find unconvincing?

- Do I disagree with the author's ideas entirely, or are there elements I can accept as true?

- Based on my knowledge of American literature, history, and culture, does this work reflect the American tradition? Why or why not?

 Integration of Ideas

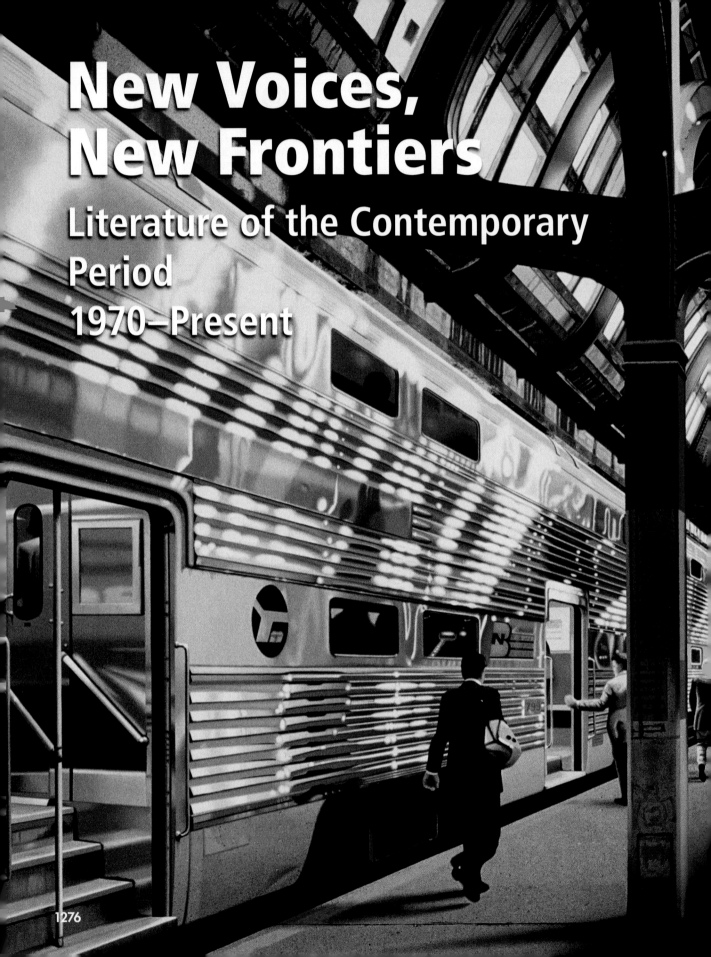

New Voices, New Frontiers

Literature of the Contemporary Period
1970–Present

Unit 6

CLOSE READING TOOL

Use this tool to practice
the close reading strategies
you learn.

**ONLINE WRITER'S
NOTEBOOK**

Easily capture notes and
complete assignments online.

STUDENT eTEXT

Bring learning to life with audio,
video, and interactive tools.

▪ Find all Digital Resources at
pearsonrealize.com.

"... Perhaps this is our strange
and haunting paradox here in
America—that we are fixed and
certain only when we are in
movement."

— *Tom Wolfe*

Snapshot of the Period

America emerged from the Cold War period as the sole superpower in a dramatically changing world. While national boundaries are still critical, globalization is the new model as the countries of the world become ever more interconnected economically, environmentally, and culturally.

Increasing globalization is due, in large part, to the dawning of the "Information Age" during the second half of the twentieth century. Computers, the Internet, cell phones, and other new technologies change the way people around the world work, play, and communicate. The world has become—simultaneously—more accessible and more complex.

Despite this new global energy, the new millennium opened with shock and sadness for Americans. The terrorist attacks of September 11, 2001, damaged the sense of security that Americans had always enjoyed. Though the world in the twenty-first century offers opportunities, beauty, and inspiration, it also presents individuals with complex questions and uncertainties.

▲ ▶ (top) Firemen raise the American flag over the rubble of the World Trade Center. (right) The Security Advisory System categorizes the level of terrorist risk.

Alvarez

Kunitz

Walker

Carver

Momaday

Tan

 As you read the selections in this unit, you will be asked to think about them in view of three key questions:

What is the **relationship** between literature and *place?*

How does **literature** shape or reflect *society?*

What makes **American** literature *American?*

Globalization in the Marketplace

Minneapolis, MN **1**

Los Angeles, CA **4**

Stockholm, Sweden **3**

Shanghai, China **5**

Bangalore, India **2**

1. A woman in Minneapolis shops for a pair of snowshoes online. She calls a toll-free number on the Web site with questions.

2. A customer-service agent in Bangalore, India answers her questions.

3. The customer's order is received and processed by a computer at the sporting goods company in Stockholm, Sweden. Messages are sent to two locations.

4. A message to the Swedish company's warehouse in Los Angeles tells workers to ship the snowshoes.

5. Another message to a factory in Shanghai, China tells workers to produce more snowshoes and ship them to Los Angeles.

© Integration of Knowledge and Ideas What does the information presented in the charts and graphs on this page suggest about changing relationships among countries and individuals in the contemporary period? **[Connect]**

The United States Online

Popular Online Activities

E-mail
News and weather
Shopping
Travel planning
Medical advice
Personal finances
Playing games
Instant messaging
Online auctions
Video webcasts
Download music

0   20   40   60   80   100
Percentage of Internet Users by Activity

(Sample Year: 2005)

Holiday Online Sales

Estimate of Weekly Sales by Billions

$5.0
$4.5
$4.0
$3.5
$3.0
$2.5
$2.0
$1.5
$1.0
$0.5
$0

Week 1 (11/4)   Week 3 (11/18)   Week 5 (12/2)   Week 7 (12/16)   Week 9 (12/30)

Source: comScore, Inc.   ■ 2003   ■ 2007

Environmental Movement 1970 – Present

1970: The first Earth Day is celebrated on April 22.

1971: Greenpeace Foundation protests U.S. nuclear testing off the coast of Alaska.

1977: Negotiations on the Kyoto Protocol are finalized on December 11. The goal is to reduce greenhouse gases.

1999: For the first time, a mass-produced hybrid vehicle is available in the United States.

2007: The Live Earth concert on July 7 gathers a global audience in support of a campaign to solve the climate crisis.

2007: Al Gore and the Intergovernmental Panel on Climate Change share the Nobel Peace Prize for their roles in climate change education.

Historical Background

The Contemporary Period (1970–Present)

When they created the United States, the American founders set out to build a democratic republic in a natural paradise. They established a great nation, and they foresaw its leadership role, but they could hardly have imagined how interconnected and interdependent all the nations of the world would become by the twenty-first century. At the nation's beginning, Americans celebrated the New World. Now, as part of the global community, Americans are shaping a *new* New World.

Politics and Space The bicentennial of the United States in 1976 highlighted pride in the American accomplishment. Even though the nation was still recovering from the traumas of the Vietnam War and the Watergate affair—the burglary of Democratic Party headquarters that forced the resignation of President Richard Nixon in 1974—Americans celebrated the nation's 200th birthday with great pride. Space exploration, especially the triumph of the space shuttle, offered an escape from politics. The first American woman in space, Sally Ride, was part of the crew of the space shuttle *Challenger* in 1983.

Leadership and Conflict Voters sent Ronald Reagan, the popular governor of California, to the White House in 1980 and again in 1984 with a landslide victory. George Bush, Reagan's vice president, was elected to the presidency in 1988. Seeking reelection in 1992, Bush faced a tough fight against high unemployment, a recession, and growing dissatisfaction with government. Democrat Bill Clinton and his running mate Al Gore—the youngest ticket in American history—won the election. Clinton won reelection in 1996, but in 2000 Al Gore lost to George Bush's son, George W. Bush. In the wake of the terrorist attacks of September 11, 2001, Bush was reelected in 2004. The elections of 2008 resulted in a historic victory with the election of Barack Obama, the nation's first African American president.

TIMELINE

1970

◀ **1970:** Walt Disney World opens in Florida, becoming one of the top travel destinations in the world.

1972: China President Nixon makes a historic visit to China.

1970: At Kent State University, four students are killed by the National Guard while protesting the Vietnam War.

1971: Chile Poet Pablo Neruda wins the Nobel Prize for Literature.

▼ **1972:** Last U.S. combat troops leave Vietnam.

The Computer Age With the introduction of the microprocessor in the 1970s, American life shifted. Computers that began as military and business tools soon became personal companions. The Internet has made information and entertainment available at any time to anyone with a desktop computer, a laptop, or a cellphone. Ever smaller, faster, and easier, technology can now connect anyone with everyone electronically, raising new questions of privacy and personal relations. "Mail" has a new meaning and "text" has become a verb. Workers "telecommute" and fans "download" their favorites. From how your government runs to how you gossip with your friends, computers have transformed virtually every aspect of life in America.

The New Millennium Despite the speed of technological change, however, some of the oldest issues still dominate human affairs. What is our relationship to the natural world? How can people of different cultures live together peacefully? How can people build a better future? One thing is certain: As the new millennium moves forward, America will continue to change and Americans will continue to explore new aspects of life, liberty, and the pursuit of happiness.

Key Historical Theme: Creating the Future

- Americans celebrated two hundred years of progress and democracy during the 1976 bicentennial.
- Americans struggle with political and economic problems at home while dealing with intense international conflicts.
- Americans live in a time of accelerated technological change that makes life easier and raises new questions.
- Americans work toward creating the future while facing persistent issues, such as care of the natural world.

◀ **1973:** The Sears Tower is built in Chicago, becoming the world's tallest building.

◀ **1974:** Nixon resigns as president following exposure of his involvement in the Watergate scandals.

1978

1970: Africa A seven-year drought results in the starvation of 100,000 people.

1975: Francisco Franco dies, ending his dictatorship that began with the Spanish Civil War.

Essential Questions Across Time

The Contemporary Period (1970–Present)

How does **literature** shape or reflect *society?*

What social and political events have had the greatest impact on Americans since 1970?

Advance of the Computer Age Digital libraries, electronic voting, global positioning, virtual communities—Americans work, play, think, and even feel differently than did earlier generations. In an increasingly wireless and paperless world, Americans express themselves differently. Change is constant and quick, and many Americans are eager to live on the edge of the latest electronic moment.

Cultural Diversity The 2010 census reported nearly 309 million people in the United States, encompassing a wide spectrum of races and cultural origins. Americans have grown closely attuned to cultural difference and diversity. Historians have revised views of the contributions of individuals once thought to be marginal, and virtually every cultural group has entered into the mainstream of American political, business, and artistic life.

Terrorism The terrorist attacks of September 11, 2001, had an enormous impact on the American consciousness. Americans reacted with anger, fear, appeals for calm, and calls for retaliation. The first decade of the millennium was characterized by an increased sense of vulnerability, more active participation in international affairs, and heightened awareness of the need to resolve the complex situation.

TIMELINE

1979: Trinidad V. S. Naipaul publishes *A Bend in the River.*

1979: England Margaret Thatcher becomes British prime minister. ▶

1978

1978: The Supreme Court upholds affirmative action in *Regents of the University of California v. Bakke.*

1979: Vietnam Hundreds of thousands of "boat people" flee Vietnam.

What values and attitudes have grown out of these events?

Personality vs. Anonymity "On the Internet, nobody knows you're a dog." So goes the caption of a cartoon showing a canine computer user. The cartoon highlights a great advance and a great drawback of the Computer Age. People may express themselves more fully than ever before, but they may also remain, or become, anonymous. Computers have made trust, authenticity, and accuracy major social and cultural concerns.

Materialism and Commercialism While aiding many countries around the world and dealing with economic problems at home, the United States still revels in material progress. Despite ups and downs, commerce fueled by advertising provides most Americans with a high standard of living compared to that of most other nations.

Multiculturalism Once, the "melting pot" image described American life: Immigrants were expected to become indistinguishable from the mass of other Americans. Now, Americans recognize the value of maintaining and savoring the cultural identities of people who are, at the same time, American. Global awareness, too, has made the achievements of cultures around the world not merely exotic but celebrated.

Security Attacked on its own soil in 2001, the nation guards itself with vigilance. Individuals, too, protect themselves from the new computer-assisted crime of identity theft.

The American EXPERIENCE

DAILY LIFE

Blogs: Democratizing the Writing World

The Life You Blog May Be Your Own—in fact, it probably is. Born of the word Weblog—a log or record of activities, thoughts, and comments that anyone may post on the World Wide Web—blogging has become a significant cultural enterprise. Contemporary technology has made it possible for anyone to be published, and millions of people turn themselves into authors every day.

Entering the blogosphere is like having a diary of the world available, the private made public. Want to know what someone in another part of the country had for breakfast? You can certainly find a blog that lets you know. Want to tell the world what you thought of the latest movie? Someone somewhere wants your opinion.

In an age dominated by visual media—movies, television, video, Webcasts—blogging reminds us of the central role that writing still plays in our culture. Of course (like all writing) blogs may be trivial, tedious, self-serving, stupid, or even cruel. They can also be intelligent, incisive, entertaining, and even beautiful.

Political candidates explain themselves in blogs. Teachers expand their lessons in blogs. Artists experiment in blogs, and critics share their insights in blogs. It is even possible to become a professional and blog for a living.

There is a world of words out there in the blogosphere. So blog away!

1981: IBM makes "PC" a household term in America with the release of its first personal computer. ▶

1982: Colombian novelist Gabriel Garcia Márquez wins the Nobel Prize for Literature.

1982: Alice Walker publishes *The Color Purple.*

1984

◀ **1981:** Sandra Day O'Connor becomes the first woman appointed to the U.S. Supreme Court.

▶ **1982:** Vietnam Veterans Memorial is dedicated in Washington, D.C.

How are these values and attitudes expressed in American literature?

Diversity Perhaps nothing characterizes contemporary American literature more clearly than the range of its writers. Authors of every race, age, religion, nationality, culture, occupation, political affiliation, economic class, and level of talent express themselves.

Nonfiction Although fiction continues as a vital literary mode, contemporary readers have a strong appetite for reality-based tales and nonfiction. Autobiography, biography, history, true-life adventures, and stories of ordeals and practical accomplishments fill the bookstores.

Technology New modes of delivery, made possible by computer technology, enable people to read in new ways. Books and periodicals can be read on computer screens, cell phones, and electronic readers. Books, or parts of books, can be ordered and printed on demand.

Themes While American writers continue to explore the fundamental themes that literature has always addressed, some themes have a special appeal in our time:

- **Identity** Personal identity and cultural identity—who we are as individuals and who we are as Americans—are often profound concerns for writers of contemporary fiction and nonfiction.

- **Truth and Illusion** What is true, and how do we know it? In an age when "special effects" can manipulate almost anything, contemporary literature explores what it means to merge reality and imagination.

- **Success** Success—whether material, political, or spiritual—has always been an American preoccupation. Writers are now taking another hard look at it: What makes a person genuinely happy? How do ideas of success affect individuals, communities, or the planet as a whole?

- **Family** Contemporary society is redefining the family, creating the future with new social units. American literature is playing a vital role in examining what a family is and what it can be.

ESSENTIAL QUESTION VOCABULARY

These Essential Question words will help you think and write about literature and society:

virtual (vur´chŏŏ əl) *adj.* of, pertaining to, or taking place in cyberspace

diversity (də vur´sə tē) *n.* quality of being varied, not homogenous

spectrum (spek´trəm) *n.* wide range; complete extent

TIMELINE

1986: USSR Chernobyl nuclear disaster spreads a radioactive cloud across Eastern Europe.

1988: George Bush is elected president. ▼

1984

1986: The Space Shuttle *Challenger* explodes 73 seconds after launching, killing all seven crew members.

▲ **1987:** President Reagan and Soviet leader Mikhail Gorbachev sign the INF treaty, agreeing to ban short-range and medium-range nuclear missiles.

What is the **relationship** between literature and *place?*

What kinds of places do contemporary Americans write about?

Ordinary Places Of course Americans still write about cities and towns, homes and schools, streets and malls. Readers find realistic life in the works of such writers as John Updike, Anne Tyler, Richard Russo, Richard Ford, Edward P. Jones, Michael Chabon, Jhumpa Lahiri, and Annie Proulx.

Ordinary Places Transformed Some writers set their stories in what-if places that have been dramatically, even fantastically, transformed. In Philip Roth's *The Plot Against America* (2004), prejudice and chaos rule the nation. In *The Road* (2006), Cormac McCarthy tracks a grim journey through a post-apocalyptic American landscape.

How does a global awareness show up in American literature?

Green Literature A literary sub-genre emphasizes the relationship of people to the planet as a whole, tackling such topics as pollution and ecoterrorism. "Ecofiction" includes Barbara Kingsolver's *Prodigal Summer* (2000) and T. C. Boyle's *A Friend of the Earth* (2000). In nonfiction, essays by Annie Dillard and John McPhee build on the legacy of Henry David Thoreau. In poetry, natural imagery is at the heart of the verse of Gary Snyder, W. S. Merwin, and A. R. Ammons.

The American EXPERIENCE

A LIVING TRADITION

A. R. Ammons, Emersonian Postmodernist

A. R. Ammons, a North Carolinian, looked at an unusual aspect of the American place. In a long poem called *Garbage* (1993), Ammons takes trash—and the reprocessing of it—as a symbol of our times. Unlike Modernists who strove to create poems that were well-constructed artifacts, Ammons, in good Postmodernist style, creates a talky, sprawling, shifting poem that is itself like a trash heap and that considers, among so many other things, its own making.

Emerson might have blinked and rubbed his eyes if he could have read this poem. However, he might also have recognized in it his own, distinctly American belief in newness.

from "Garbage" by A. R. Ammons

garbage has to be the poem of our time because
garbage is spiritual, believable enough

to get our attention, getting in the way, piling
up, stinking, turning brooks brownish and

creamy white: what else deflects us from the
errors of our illusionary ways . . .

•   •   •

here is the gateway to beginning, here the portal
of renewing change . . .

1989: China Pro-democracy demonstrations are violently suppressed at Tiananmen Square. ▶

1991: USSR The Soviet Union is dissolved, resulting in the formation of fifteen independent nations.

1991: Middle East Unified forces led by U.S. defeat Iraq in Persian Gulf War.

◀ **1989: Germany** The Berlin Wall comes down.

1990: Congress passes the Americans with Disabilities Act, prohibiting discrimination against people with disabilities.

1991: South Africa Apartheid—the system of racial segregation—is repealed.

1992

How has electronic technology, by changing our surroundings, also changed our literature?

Communication Technology that has made communication faster and easier has altered the limitations of physical space and place.

- *Character to character:* Fictional characters frequently communicate by cell phone, and e-mail is a common plot device.
- *Author to reader:* Authors now use Web sites to explain, expand, and discuss their works with their audiences.
- *Reader to reader:* Readers meet online to discuss books and authors, sharing ideas and opinions.
- *Reader to author:* Readers ask questions, respond, criticize, and make suggestions. This greater interactivity even turns some readers into authors themselves when fans write their own prequels and sequels to their favorite books.

Cultural References Similes, metaphors, allusions, and references of all kinds now often stem from television, movies, and the world of computers. Electronic media have centered themselves in the cultural mainstream, sometimes overshadowing traditional literary sources. Contemporary readers are just as likely to meet a reference to the Starship *Enterprise* as they are to Captain Ahab's *Pequod*. Cultural merging is taking place: In 2007, MtvU, part of the popular MTV Network, chose the renowned postmodern poet John Ashbery to be its first poet laureate.

Cyberliterature Cyberliterature, including hyperfiction and electronic poetry, is literature that is composed and experienced on computers. Hyperfiction offers nonlinear, multi-path, open-ended narratives that enable readers to "travel" around within a story, choosing where they want to go, deciding which characters and themes they want to follow. Electronic poetry uses the visual and aural capabilities of the computer to unfold new and colorful poetic experiences right before the reader's eyes.

> **ESSENTIAL QUESTION VOCABULARY**
>
> These Essential Question words will help you think and write about literature and place:
>
> **transform** (trans fôrm´) *v.* change the condition, nature, or function of
>
> **interactive** (in´tər ak´tiv) *adj.* reciprocally active; involving communication between technology and users or among people
>
> **global** (glō´bəl) *adj.* affecting or including the whole world

TIMELINE

1992: Bill Clinton is elected president. ▶

1994: Rwanda Hundreds of thousands of ethnic Tutsis are killed in the Rwandan Genocide. ●

1994: England/France The Channel Tunnel that crosses the English Channel opens.

 1992

1993: Toni Morrison wins the Nobel Prize for Literature. ▶

1994: South Africa Nelson Mandela becomes the first democratically elected president. ▶

What makes American literature *American?*

What qualities distinguish American literature today?

Cultural Diversity Just as American identity is a unique combination of the nation's mix of people, so is American literature a unique product of that mix. Cross-cultural contributions in subjects, forms, styles, and languages keep American writing alive, open, and adaptable.

Expanding Definition of Literature The definition of literature itself is changing. Just as nonfiction and fiction are merging, so are the "popular" and the "literary." Walk into a bookstore to find a novel that includes recipes, a poem that accompanies a photo essay, a romance that is "based on a true story," a graphic novel that is based on a movie, or a "nonfiction novel" based on a current event. All of it is literature.

Traditional and Postmodern Despite all that is changing, however, the American literary tradition continues to flourish. Writers still produce literature in time-tested forms and styles. Hawthorne would recognize a story by Joyce Carol Oates, and Whitman would celebrate a poem by A. R. Ammons. The co-existence of the traditional and the new has spurred a new vibrancy in American literary life.

The **American** EXPERIENCE

DEVELOPING AMERICAN ENGLISH

Brave New Words
by Richard Lederer

The history of a living language like English is a history of constant change. Language is like a tree that sheds its leaves and grows new ones so that it may live on. New words, like new leaves, are essential to a living, healthy vocabulary.

Throughout history, as English speakers and writers have met with new objects, experiences, and ideas, they have needed new words to describe them. Nowadays, an average of 5,000 new words enter our language each year! The Anglo-Saxons used a vivid term to describe the great wealth of English—the *word-hoard*.

We needed a name for the system that connects computers around the world. So we combined the Latin prefix *inter*, "together," with the Anglo-Saxon word for a mesh fabric, and—presto!—we came up with the *Internet*.

The study of life on other worlds we have labeled *astrobiology*, from the Greek word parts *astro* ("star") + *bio* ("life") + *logy* ("study of").

The entire chromosomal makeup of an organism we now call the *genome*—a blend of two Greek words, *gene(e)* and *(chromos)ome*.

The brave new worlds of the arts and sciences, technology and medicine make headlines every day, but our English "word-hoard" will never run out of prefixes, suffixes, and roots to identify new concepts.

1996: Summer Olympic Games are held in Atlanta, Georgia.

1997: A lamb is cloned from a single cell of an adult sheep.

1999: Conflict between Albanians and Serbs in Kosovo leads to a war between Serbia and NATO forces.

2000

1995: Amy Tan publishes her third novel, *The Hundred Secret Senses*.

1997: China Hong Kong returns to Chinese rule, ending British rule. ▶

1287

The American EXPERIENCE

CONTEMPORARY CONNECTION

Stephanie Strickland:
Hypertext Poetry Pioneer

Take the power of poetry to evoke emotion and charge the imagination and combine it with the power of new media and you get what some are calling a new literary genre: hypertext, or electronic poetry. Hypertext poetry presents text with graphics, images, sound, and live links to other texts. By choosing particular links, the reader shapes his or her own reading experience.

Poet Stephanie Strickland is a hypertext pioneer whose works live on the Web. Words dance on the screen, images shimmer, colors swirl. The reader becomes a viewer, a listener, and a participant. An artfully lettered phrase drifts across the screen and turns like a falling leaf while a wave crashes behind it, then more phrases follow.

On the one hand, Strickland simply does what poets have always done, which is engage readers' senses and emotions. However, she uses more than words in her creation of poetry. Readers might wonder, then: Is this a new generation of poetry or a different art form entirely? Just because it is easy to enjoy, is it easy to understand? In an interview in the *Iowa Web Review*, Strickland offers some insight. "My poetry wants to move from static moment to dynamic movement because that is the way the world feels to me."

TIMELINE

2000

▲ **2000:** George W. Bush defeats Al Gore in an extremely close and controversial presidential election.

2001: Hijacked planes crash into the World Trade Center in New York, the Pentagon in Washington, D.C., and a field in Pennsylvania on the same day. Thousands of lives are lost.

2002: The computer industry sells its 1 billionth personal computer, according to a study of worldwide sales.

◀ **2002: Europe** The Euro becomes the official currency of the European Union.

What is "postmodern" in American literature?

"Postmodern" signals works created after Modernism. Here are some of the qualities that help to define postmodern literature:

- **Awareness of Itself** A postmodern work is self-conscious. A postmodern character might refer to the novel he lives in, and a postmodern writer might comment on the story or poem the reader is reading.

- **Release from Meaning** World War II, the atomic bomb, and the Holocaust undercut reliance on rational meaning and the assumption that a work of art could, or needed to, mean anything at all.

- **Interest in Process** A postmodern work is recognized as an ongoing experience. Some works offer alternative versions of themselves.

- **Desire to Revise the Past** A postmodern work does not hesitate to use the past extensively, even re-seeing and rewriting it.

- **Desire to Have Fun** A postmodern work does not take itself so seriously. It may merge "high" and "low" culture. It may feel like a game.

Which American writers are pointing us toward the future?

American writing of extraordinary beauty, passion, imagination, and zest continues to tell us who we are and who we can become:

- Toni Morrison's *Beloved* (1987), an acclaimed narrative of slavery and sacrifice told in a challenging mosaic style

- Andrea Barrett's *Ship Fever* (1996), gripping stories that interweave fiction, history, and science

- Dave Eggers's *A Heartbreaking Work of Staggering Genius* (2000), a postmodern family memoir of profound compassion

Contemporary American poets such as Louise Glück, Ann Lauterbach, Yusef Komunyakaa, and Li-Young Lee provide the verbal soundtrack that will accompany us through the twenty-first century.

> **ESSENTIAL QUESTION VOCABULARY**
>
> These Essential Question words will help you think and write about American literature:
>
> **cross-cultural** (krôs-kul′chər əl) *adj.* of or relating to different cultures and nations
>
> **vibrancy** (vī′ brən sē) *n.* radiance, energy, vigor
>
> **self-conscious** (self-kän′shəs) *adj.* state of being aware of oneself

◄ 2004: The National Museum of the American Indian opens in Washington, D.C.

◄ 2008: Barack Obama is elected the first African American president of the United States.

Present

▼ 2003: 43,435 hybrid electrical vehicles are registered in the United States, a 25.8% increase over the previous year.

2004: Indonesia An earthquake in the Indian Ocean causes a tsunami that claims 186,000 lives.

2005: Hurricane Katrina results in a severe loss of life and property in Louisiana, Mississippi, and Alabama.

Recent Scholarship

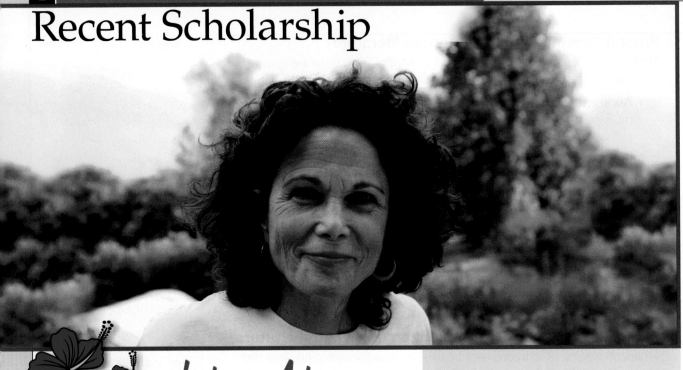

Julia Alvarez
All-American Writer

People often ask me how come I became an American writer. Often there is a tone of surprise. For although I was born in New York City, my Dominican parents returned "home" when I was a month old. I grew up in another culture and language.

I like to respond to the question by saying, I am an all-American writer. My love of stories and many of my characters and even the cadences of my English sentences come from the southern Americas and the musical, rococo extravagances of Spanish; whereas the language I've learned to craft and the literary tradition I've studied comes from the northern part of the Americas. I truly am an all-American writer, in the more expansive, hemispheric sense.

I grew up in a culture, steeped in the oral tradition of story-telling. Stories were shared within a community or family gathering, not through the solitary act of reading. In part, we were living in a repressive dictatorship, where books marked you as an intellectual and a troublemaker. People relied on "Radio Bemba": Radio Big Mouth. Stories were passed on from one teller to another, keeping the love of freedom alive. When we escaped in 1960 leaving everything behind, I carried with me this love and respect for the power of stories.

About the Author

Shortly after her birth, Julia Alvarez moved from New York City to the Dominican Republic with her family. When Alvarez was ten, however, her family was forced to return to the United States because her father was involved in a rebellion against the country's dictator. The sudden change of home and culture was a shock to Alvarez, but she found solace in reading and writing. *In the Time of the Butterflies* and *How the Garcia Girls Lost Their Accents* are among Alvarez's acclaimed novels that reflect these early experiences.

We arrived in a United States that was not very welcoming to foreigners who looked and acted different, who spoke English with an accent. I felt homesick and lost until I discovered the world of written-down stories where everyone was welcomed. I became a reader and again realized the power of stories. Reading, I could become a Danish prince or a young Greek girl wanting to bury her dead brother or an old man on a boat trying to catch a fish. I no longer felt so lonely or lost. The more I read, the more I wanted to contribute to this great circle of storytellers. I had stories to tell and by writing them down I could share them with an invisible community of readers that were to become my new native country.

But I had entered a United States where the civil rights movement was just getting under way. The women's movement, multiculturalism, Native American rights—all these awakenings were still to come. Literature itself reflected these biases. There wasn't a diversity of authors of different traditions and backgrounds in our anthologies and in the curriculum in our classrooms. Since none of the classics we were studying were written by people like me, I began to doubt that I could become an American writer.

But then in one of those anthologies among absent voices and missing stories, I found the Langston Hughes poem, "I, too, Sing America." It was music to my ears. I understood what Mr. Hughes was saying: he was claiming his place in the chorus of American song, an America that was still not listening to him, still treating him as a second-class literary citizen, sent to the kitchen of minor writers, instead of allowing him a place at the table of American literature. But no matter. Mr. Hughes knew that tomorrow he'd be at the table. The fact that Mr. Hughes' poem was in my textbook meant his dream had come true. This was an important voice for a young girl of another culture and language and background with her heart full of dreams to hear.

In my lifetime, I've been lucky enough to experience a sea change in what is considered American literature. When I started writing in the late 60s, the work of my fellow Latina/o writers and other so-called ethnic writers was still considered the province of sociol-ogy. But in the late seventies and early eighties, influenced by the opening up of the canon to Afro-American and women's literature, writers of other traditions within the United States were suddenly "discovered." Just as Columbus "discovered" an America that was already home to old cultures and traditions, we who had been writing for several decades began to be welcome at Mr. Hughes' table.

It's an expansion that has enriched American literature—all these varied cadences and stories from so many different traditions. It's a richness that is truly at the heart of America, as Walt Whitman, the quintessential "American" poet, knew way back when he wrote, "I hear America singing, the varied carols I hear." This has always been a country made up of people who came from somewhere else encountering the people who preceded them here. Out of this encounter can come silencing and segregation but also—and this can be our greatness: a more inclusive and astonishingly diverse country and culture. Literature has always been about this multiculturalism, about becoming each other and realizing that we share the same human experience. Stories have always known that the table is wide enough for all of us, Langston Hughes and Walt Whitman and Raymond Carver and Maxine Hong Kingston, and even an all-American writer born in New York City but raised in the Dominican Republic, Julia Alvarez.

There's also room for you. So, pull up a chair because if you want to be a writer, you have to become a reader first.

Collaboration: Speaking and Listening

In her celebration of multiculturalism, Julia Alvarez asserts that "becoming each other" has always been part of the American experience. At the same time, American identity has also been defined by individuality and independence. In a **small group discussion,** examine these two aspects of American life. As a group, choose a moderator to help keep your discussion going and to be sure all opinions are heard. Encourage diverse perspectives from all participants.

Integrate and Evaluate Information

1. Use a chart like the one shown to determine the key ideas expressed in the Essential Question essays on pages 1282–1289. Fill in two ideas related to each Essential Question and note an author closely associated with each concept. One example has been done for you.

Essential Question	Key Concept	Key Author
Literature and Place		
American Literature	Environmental Concerns	Annie Dillard
Literature and Society		

2. How do the visual sources in this section—maps, graphs, timelines, photographs, and artifacts—add to your understanding of the ideas expressed in words? Cite specific examples.

3. Throughout our history as a nation, Americans have valued innovation and progress. Are those values as important in contemporary America as they were in, for example, the nineteenth century? Have other values, such as those involving respect for traditions or a wish to slow the pace of change, arisen to modify the national character? Cite evidence from the multiple sources presented on pages 1278–1289, as well as other materials provided throughout this textbook, in your answer.

4. **Solve a Research Problem** Julia Alvarez explains, "I am an all-American writer, in the ... hemispheric sense." Her complex cultural perspective is part of a broader development in American letters. Research another contemporary author who writes from a similar dual perspective. Write a report of your findings. Integrate information from this textbook and other sources to support your ideas.

Speaking and Listening: Presentation and Discussion

Almost anyone can now shop, meet friends, and pay bills on the Web. Is cyberspace a new place, equal to the real world? Explore this question in an **oral presentation and discussion.**

Answer a Question As the basis for your presentation, create two sets of **travel directions** and maps. For the first set, pick a destination on the Web. Write directions that explain how to get there from a home page. Illustrate the directions with a "map." Then, choose a real-world place. Write directions, with a map, that explain how to get there from school. During your presentation, compare and contrast the sets of directions and maps. Then, conduct a class discussion. As a group, decide whether the virtual world of the Internet is a place equal in any way to the real world.

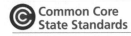

Common Core State Standards

Reading Informational Text
7. Integrate and evaluate multiple sources of information presented in different media or formats as well as in words in order to address a question or solve a problem.

Speaking and Listening
1. Initiate and participate effectively in a range of collaborative discussions with diverse partners on grade 11 topics, texts, and issues.
1.a. Come to discussions prepared, having read and researched material under study; explicitly draw on that preparation by referring to evidence from texts and other research on the topic or issue to stimulate a thoughtful, well-reasoned exchange of ideas.
1.b. Work with peers to promote civil, democratic discussions and decision-making and establish individual roles as needed. *(p. 1291)*
1.c. Ensure a hearing for a full range of positions on a topic or issue; promote divergent and creative perspectives. *(p. 1291)*

ESSENTIAL QUESTION VOCABULARY

Use these words in your responses:

Literature and Place
transform
interactive
global

American Literature
cross-cultural
vibrancy
self-conscious

Literature and Society
virtual
diversity
spectrum

Contemporary Fiction

Julia Alvarez Introduces

Antojos

Little did I know when I was writing my short story, "Antojos," that some day it would become the opening chapter of my first novel, *How the García Girls Lost Their Accents.* It makes sense though, that I would begin small— after all, I was an immigrant kid, daring to join my voice to the literature of my new country. As I gained confidence, I would inch forward, chapter by chapter, towards a larger, book-length form, a novel.

I often advise young writers who feel overwhelmed when they begin their first novels to think of each chapter as a short story with a beginning, a middle, and an end. When you finally put all those stories together, you will, of course, have to revise the whole from the perspective of a novel. But you will have written your first draft! This is another version of the writing advice that goes, write your essay, story, poem, word by word, page by page. That assures that each paragraph is beautifully and carefully crafted. Each word counts! Emily Dickinson, one of my favorite writers, once noted that there are "no approximate words in a poem." Now that's a high standard for prose, but a passionate writer doesn't mind a challenge!

But when I began writing "Antojos," I was not plotting a novel. I had been writing many short stories about being an immigrant and arriving in a new country. At some point, I wondered what would it be like for my characters to go back to where they came from? In one of my English classes, we had read a short story by Thomas Wolfe, whose bio mentioned that he'd written a novel titled *You Can't Go Home Again.* Often, in my own return trips to visit family in the Dominican Republic, I had found myself feeling the same thing!

Now I could have written an essay addressing why exactly you can never go back to where you came from. Elaborating central issues. Citing research on returning exiles. Maybe including certain personal experiences that supported my thesis. But that's not how a short story works. You actually play out a situation through characters and actions and see where it takes you! It's like life, you live through an

About the Author

Julia Alvarez is an award-winning and commercially successful novelist, poet, and nonfiction writer.

For more information about her, see page 1297.

experience and when you come out the other end and think about it, you go, wow, Better to have loved and lost than never to have loved at all! But that lived experience (that leads to that insight) is what stories are interested in. And that experience, of course, happens to a character. In your life, it's you; in a story, it's someone you make up who might have a lot of you in him or her.

Another way a story speaks is through details and little scenes of dialogue and interaction. In my story, I didn't know why I tacked that Palmolive poster on the cantina post. Sure, I had seen such posters when I traveled in the D.R. (A writer is always "doing research"!) When I was describing the setting in my story, I pulled that little detail from past experience. Once it was in the story, I realized I had one of those "loaded details" that teachers sometimes call "symbols." Just a way of saying, pay attention to this detail. It has something to tell you. But it's never a set meaning. It's rich and ambiguous and shifts with each reading.

Which leads to a final point about stories. They say what can't be put in easy capsule form. They don't have messages. They are luminous and mysterious. You can go home in some ways, and in other ways you can't. But only a story can include all these nuances and feelings and insights in a way that gives us pleasure and deepens our understanding of our lives. You can't sum up a story. You have to be there. And a good writer puts you there, word by word, page by page.

Critical Reading

1. **Key Ideas and Details (a)** According to Alvarez, how do essays and short stories differ? **(b) Speculate:** What kind of understanding might a short story provide about an experience that an essay could not, and vice versa?

2. **Key Ideas and Details (a) Interpret:** What does Alvarez suggest about the connection between authors and their characters? **(b) Speculate:** Do you think most stories contain insights into the lives of their authors? Explain.

   As You Read "Antojos" . . .

3. Notice ways in which Alvarez's story speaks through "details and little scenes of dialogue and interaction."

4. Think about ways in which Alvarez's fictional story is reminiscent of her own real life experiences.

Cite textual evidence to support your responses.

Connecting to the Essential Question In this story, a young woman returns to her native country after many years away. As you read, notice details that suggest the people, places, sounds, sights, and tastes Yolanda misses about her homeland. Doing so will help you think about the Essential Question: **What is the relationship between literature and place?**

Close Reading Focus

Plot Devices

While many stories begin at the start of a series of events, some begin *in medias res,* which is Latin for "in the middle of things." Alvarez begins this story with her main character well on her way into the mountains:

> *For the first time since Yolanda had reached the hills, there was a shoulder on the left side of the narrow road.*

In medias res is a **plot device** writers use to grab readers' interest. Other plot devices are **flashback,** in which a scene from the past interrupts the action, and **foreshadowing,** the dropping of clues to suggest events that have yet to occur. As you read "Antojos," notice how Alvarez uses all of these plot devices to fill in background information, heighten suspense, and add interest and excitement.

Preparing to Read Complex Texts **Making predictions,** or anticipating events, is a useful way to engage with a story and better understand its meaning. To make predictions, consider what you know about the characters and setting and apply your understanding of human nature. In this story, you may also consider background information about the Dominican Republic. As you read, use a chart like the one shown to track and confirm the predictions you make.

Vocabulary

The words below are important to understanding the text that follows. Copy the words into your notebook. Which part of speech is the word *collusion*? How can you tell?

dissuade	machetes
maneuver	collusion
appease	docile

**Common Core
State Standards**

Reading Literature
3. Analyze the impact of the author's choices regarding how to develop and relate elements of a story or drama (e.g., how the action is ordered).
5. Analyze how an author's choices concerning how to structure specific parts of a text contribute to its overall structure and meaning as well as its aesthetic impact.

Background Knowledge

+

Clues Within the Text

=

Prediction

JULIA ALVAREZ (b. 1950)

Author of "Antojos"

Poet and fiction writer Julia Alvarez was
born in New York City but raised in the
Dominican Republic until she was ten years
old. When her father's involvement in a plot
to overthrow that country's dictator, Rafael
Trujillo, was uncovered, the family fled to
the United States. "I came into English as a
ten-year-old from the Dominican Republic,
and I consider this radical uprooting
from my culture, my native language,
my country, the reason I began writing,"
Alvarez once explained.

Writing to Ease the Pain While moving
to a new country changed her life, Alvarez
quickly found her voice as a writer. She
said, "I landed, not in the United States,
but in the English language. That became
my new home . . . ." As a young adult,
Alvarez found that writing helped her
deal with the pain of adjustment to a new
culture and language. After graduating from
college, Alvarez earned a masters degree in creative writing at Syracuse
University. She went on to join the Kentucky Arts Commission's poetry-
in-the-schools program. For two years, she traveled around Kentucky
teaching poetry.

> "*The point is not to
> pay back kindness
> but to pass it on.*"

Writing to Understand For Alvarez, writing "is a way to understand
yourself. You learn how you feel about things, but you're also making
your little statement about things, and that makes you feel a little bit
more powerful." Alvarez's poetry often focuses on her personal experiences as well as her Caribbean heritage. She has published three
volumes of poetry: *Homecoming* (1984), *The Other Side* (1995), and *The
Woman I Kept to Myself* (2004).

A Storytelling Tradition After *Homecoming* was published, Alvarez
began to focus on a new area of writing: fiction. "My own island
background was steeped in a tradition of storytelling that I wanted to
explore in prose," Alvarez explained. The move to prose proved fruitful,
for Alvarez has won fame for four novels rooted in Hispanic American
tradition: *How the Garcia Girls Lost Their Accents* (1991), *In the Time of the
Butterflies* (1994), *¡Yo!* (1997), and *In the Name of Salomé* (2000). Her fiction,
like her poetry, deals with both the immigrant experience and her own
bicultural identity.

Antojos[1]

JULIA ALVAREZ

---

1. Antojos (än tō´ hōs) Spanish for "cravings." The story explores additional connotations of the word.

BACKGROUND Alvarez's homeland, the Dominican Republic, won independence in 1844 after a rebellion against Haitian rule. Since then, the country has suffered through dictatorships and foreign domination. One of the most ruthless dictators was Rafael Trujillo, who ruled from 1930 until he was assassinated in 1961. Alvarez's father was part of an underground movement against Trujillo and it was this involvement that forced the Alvarez family to flee the country.

For the first time since Yolanda had reached the hills, there was a shoulder on the left side of the narrow road. She pulled the car over out of a sense of homecoming: every other visit she had stayed with her family in the capital.

Once her own engine was off, she heard the sound of another motor, approaching, a pained roar as if the engine were falling apart. She made out an undertow of men's voices. Quickly, she got back into the car, locked the door, and pulled off the shoulder, hugging her right side of the road.

—Just in time too. A bus came lurching around the curve, obscuring her view with a belching of exhaust, the driver saluting or warning with a series of blasts on his horn. It was an old army bus, the official name brushed over with paint that didn't quite match the regulation gray. The passengers saw her only at the last moment, and all up and down her side of the bus, men poked out of the windows, hooting and yelling, waving purple party flags, holding out bottles and beckoning to her. She speeded up and left them behind, the small compact climbing easily up the snakey highway, its well-oiled hum a gratifying sound after the hullabaloo of the bus.

She tried the radio again, but all she could tune to was static even here on the summit hills. She would have to wait until she got to the coast to hear news of the hunger march in the capital. Her family had been worried that trouble would break out, for the march had been scheduled on the anniversary of the failed revolution nineteen years ago today. A huge turnout was expected. She bet that bus she had just passed had been delayed by breakdowns on its way to the capital. In fact, earlier on the road when she had first set out, Yolanda had passed buses and truckloads of men, drinking and shouting slogans. It crossed her mind that her family had finally agreed to loan her a car because they knew she'd be far safer on the north coast than in the capital city where revolutions always broke out.

The hills began to plane out into a high plateau, the road widening. Left and right, roadside stands began appearing. Yolanda slowed down and kept an eye out for guavas, supposedly in season this far north. Piled high on wooden stands were fruits she hadn't seen in so many years: pinkish-yellow mangoes, and tamarind pods oozing their rich sap, and small cashew fruits strung on a rope to keep them from bruising each other. There were little brown packets of roasted

◄ **Critical Viewing**
What elements of this artist's portrayal of fruit mirror Yolanda's feelings about guavas? **COMPARE**

Plot Devices
How do the opening paragraphs pull readers into the story?

Comprehension
What political event is occurring in the city as Yolanda drives into the hills?

cashews and bars of milk fudge wrapped in waxed paper and tied with a string, the color of which told what filling was inside the bar. Strips of meat, buzzing with flies, hung from the windows of butcher stalls. An occasional display of straw hats and baskets and hammocks told that tourists sometimes did pass by here. Looking at the stores spread before her, it was hard to believe the poverty the organizers of the march kept discussing on the radio. There seemed to be plenty here to eat—except for guavas.

In the capital, her aunts had plied her with what she most craved after so many years away. "Any little *antojo,* you must tell us!" They wanted to spoil her, so she'd stay on in her nativeland before she forgot where she had come from. "What exactly does it mean, *antojo?*" Yolanda asked. Her aunts were proven right: After so many years away, their niece was losing her Spanish.

"An *antojo*—" The aunts exchanged quizzical looks. "How to put it? An *antojo* is like a craving for something you have to eat."

A cousin blew out her cheeks. "Calories."

An *antojo,* one of the older aunts continued, was a very old Spanish word from before "your United States was thought of," she added tartly. In the countryside some *campesinos*[2] still used the word to mean possession by an island spirit demanding its due.

Her island spirit certainly was a patient soul, Yolanda joked. She hadn't had her favorite *antojo,* guavas, since her last trip seven years ago. Well, on this trip, her aunts promised, Yoyo could eat guavas to her heart's content. But when the gardener was summoned, he wasn't so sure. Guavas were no longer in season, at least not in the hotter lowlands of the south. Maybe up north, the chauffeur could pick her up some on his way back from some errand. Yolanda took this opportunity to inform her aunts of her plans: she could pick the guavas herself when she went up north in a few days.

—She was going up north? By herself? A woman alone on the road! "This is not the States." Her old aunts had tried to dissuade her. "Anything can happen." When Yolanda challenged them, "What?" they came up with boogeymen stories that made her feel as if she were talking to china dolls.[3] Haitian hougans[4] and Communist kidnappers. "And Martians?" Yolanda wanted to tease them. They had led such sheltered lives, riding from one safe place to another in their air-conditioned cars.

She had left the fruit stands behind her and was approaching a compound very much like her family's in the capital. The underbrush stopped abruptly at a high concrete wall, topped with broken bottle glass. Parked at the door was a chocolate brown Mercedes. Perhaps the owners had come up to their country home for the weekend to

Plot Devices

What information about Yolanda and her family is conveyed in this flashback?

Vocabulary

dissuade (di swād´) *v.* convince someone not to do something

Plot Devices

What do the warnings of Yolanda's aunts suggest about future events in the story?

---

2. *campesinos* (käm´ pe sē´ nōs) "poor farmers; simple rural dwellers" (Spanish).
3. **china dolls** old-fashioned, delicate dolls made of fragile high-quality porcelain or ceramic ware.
4. **Haitian hougans** (o͞o gänz´) voodoo priests or cult leaders.

avoid the troubles in the capital?

Just beyond the estate, Yolanda came upon a small village—ALTAMIRA in rippling letters on the corrugated tin roof of the first house. It was a little cluster of houses on either side of the road, a good place to stretch her legs before what she'd heard was a steep and slightly (her aunts had warned "very") dangerous descent to the coast. Yolanda pulled up at a cantina, the thatched roof held up by several posts. Instead of a menu, there was a yellowing, grimy poster for Palmolive soap tacked on one of the posts with a picture of a blonde woman under a spraying shower, her head thrown back in seeming ecstasy, her mouth opened in a wordless cry. ("Palmolive"? Yolanda wondered.) She felt even thirstier and grimier looking at this lathered beauty after her hot day on the road.

An old woman emerged at last from a shack behind the cabana, buttoning up a torn housedress, and followed closely by a little boy, who kept ducking behind her whenever Yolanda smiled at him. Asking him his name just drove him further into the folds of the old woman's skirt.

"You must excuse him, Doña,"[5] she apologized. "He's not used to being among people." But Yolanda knew the old woman meant, not the people in the village, but the people with money who drove through Altamira to the beaches on the coast. "Your name," the old woman repeated, as if Yolanda hadn't asked him in Spanish. The little boy mumbled at the ground. "Speak up!" the old woman scolded, but her voice betrayed pride when she spoke up for him. "This little know-nothing is Jose Duarte Sanchez y Mella Garcia."

Yolanda laughed. Not only were those a lot of names for such a little boy, but they certainly were momentous: the surnames of the three liberators of the country!

"Can I serve the Doña in any way?" the woman asked. Yolanda gave the tree line beyond the woman's shack a glance. "You think you might have some guavas around?"

The old woman's face scrunched up. "Guavas?" she murmured and thought to herself a second. "Why, they're all around, Doña. But I can't say as I've seen any."

"With your permission—" Jose Duarte had joined a group of little boys who had come out of nowhere and were milling around the car, boasting how many automobiles they had ridden in. At Yolanda's mention of guavas, he sprung forward, pointing across the road

5. **Doña** (dō′ nyä) "Madam" (Spanish).

LITERATURE IN CONTEXT

Geography Connection

The Dominican Republic
Located in the West Indies, the Dominican Republic takes up the eastern two thirds of the island of Hispaniola. The country is bounded on the north by the Atlantic Ocean; on the east by the Mona Passage, which separates it from Puerto Rico; on the south by the Caribbean Sea; and on the west by Haiti.

In Alvarez's story, Yolanda begins her journey in Santo Domingo, the capital city, which is located on the country's southern coast. Yolanda's journey takes her into the Cordillera Central Range, which includes Pico Duarte, the highest mountain in the Caribbean. The slopes of many of these mountains are covered with dense semi-tropical forests, like those in which Yolanda searches for guavas.

Connect to the Literature

In what ways does the story's setting—both geographical and cultural—contribute to Yolanda's conflict?

Comprehension
Who does Yolanda meet at the roadside cantina?

Antojos **1301**

towards the summit of the western hills. "I know where there's a whole grove of them." Behind him, his little companions nodded.

"Go on, then!" His grandmother stamped her foot as if she were scatting a little animal. "Get the Doña some."

A few boys dashed across the road and disappeared up a steep path on the hillside, but before Jose could follow, Yolanda called him back. She wanted to go along too. The little boy looked towards his grandmother, unsure of what to think. The old woman shook her head. The Doña would get hot, her nice clothes would get all dirty. Jose would get the Doña as many guavas as she was wanting.

"But they taste so much better when you've picked them yourself," Yolanda's voice had an edge, for suddenly, it was as if the woman had turned into the long arm of her family, keeping her away from seeing her country on her own.

The few boys who had stayed behind with Jose had congregated around the car. Each one claimed to be guarding it for the Doña. It occurred to Yolanda that there was a way to make this a treat all the way around. "What do you say we take the car?"

"*Sí, Sí, Sí*,"[6] the boys screamed in a riot of excitement.

The old woman hushed them but agreed that was not a bad idea if the Doña insisted on going. There was a dirt road up ahead she could follow a ways and then cross over onto the road that was paved all the way to the coffee barns. The woman pointed south in the direction of the big house. Many workers took that short cut to work.

They piled into the car, half a dozen boys in the back, and Jose

▼ **Critical Viewing**

Do you think the people in this picture have more in common with Yolanda and her family or with the people she meets in the mountains? Explain. **COMPARE**

6. *Sí, Sí, Sí* (sē) "Yes, Yes, Yes" (Spanish).

as co-pilot in the passenger seat beside Yolanda. They turned onto a bumpy road off the highway, which got bumpier and bumpier, and climbed up into wilder, more desolate country. Branches scraped the sides and pebbles pelted the underside of the car. Yolanda wanted to turn back, but there was no room to maneuver the car around. Finally, with a great snapping of twigs and thrashing of branches across the windshield, as if the countryside were loath to release them, the car burst forth onto smooth pavement and the light of day. On either side of the road were groves of guava trees. Among them, the boys who had gone ahead on foot were already pulling down branches and shaking loose a rain of guavas. The fruit was definitely in season.

For the next hour or so, Yolanda and her crew scavenged the grove, the best of the pick going into the beach basket Yolanda had gotten out of the trunk, with the exception of the ones she ate right on the spot, relishing the slightly bumpy feel of the skin in her hand, devouring the crunchy, sweet, white meat. The boys watched her, surprised by her odd hunger.

Yolanda and Jose, partners, wandered far from the path that cut through the grove. Soon they were bent double to avoid getting entangled in the thick canopy of branches overhead. Each addition to the basket caused a spill from the stash already piled high above the brim. Finally, it was a case of abandoning the treasure in order to cart some of it home. With Jose hugging the basket to himself and Yolanda parting the wayward branches in front of them, they headed back toward the car.

When they cleared the thicket of guava branches, the sun was low on the western horizon. There was no sign of the other boys. "They must have gone to round up the goats," Jose observed.

Yolanda glanced at her watch: it was past six o'clock. She'd never make the north coast by nightfall, but at least she could get off the dangerous mountain roads while it was still light. She hurried Jose back to the car, where they found a heap of guavas the other boys had left behind on the shoulder of the road. Enough guavas to appease even the greediest island spirit for life!

They packed the guavas in the trunk quickly and climbed in, but the car had not gone a foot before it lurched forward with a horrible hobble. Yolanda closed her eyes and laid her head down on the wheel, then glanced over at Jose. The way his eyes were searching the inside of the car for a clue as to what could have happened, she could tell he didn't know how to change a flat tire either.

It was no use regretting having brought the car up that bad stretch of road. The thing to do now was to act quickly. Soon the sun would set and night would fall swiftly, no lingering dusk as in the States. She explained to Jose that they had a flat tire and had to hike back to town and send for help down the road to the big house. Whoever tended to the brown Mercedes would know how to change the tire on her car.

Vocabulary

maneuver (mə noo′ vər) *v.* move something by some plan or scheme

appease (ə pēz′) *v.* satisfy

Spiral Review

Characterization Which details here help you understand how Yolanda and Jose look, behave, feel, and think? Explain.

Plot Devices

How might Yolanda's thoughts about the dangerous mountain roads be a clue to later events?

Comprehension

As Yolanda and Jose start to leave, what happens to the car?

"With your permission," Jose offered meekly. He pointed down the paved road. "This goes directly to the big house." The Doña could just wait in the car and he would be back in no time with someone from the Miranda place.

She did not like the idea of staying behind in the car, but Jose could probably go and come back much quicker without her. "All right," she said to the boy. "I'll tell you what." She pointed to her watch. It was almost six thirty. "If you're back by the time this hand is over here, I'll give you"—she held up one finger "a dollar." The boy's mouth fell open. In no time, he had shot out of his side of the car and was headed at a run toward the Miranda place. Yolanda climbed out as well and walked down a pace, until the boy had disappeared in one of the turnings of the road.

Suddenly, the countryside was so very quiet. She looked up at the purple sky. A breeze was blowing through the grove, rustling the leaves, so they whispered like voices, something indistinct. Here and there a light flickered on the hills, a *campesino* living out his solitary life. This was what she had been missing without really knowing that she was missing it all these years. She had never felt at home in the States, never, though she knew she was lucky to have a job, so she could afford her own life and not be run by her family. But independence didn't have to be exile. She could come home, home to places like these very hills, and live here on her own terms.

Heading back to the car, Yolanda stopped. She had heard footsteps in the grove. Could Jose be back already? Branches were being thrust aside, twigs snapped. Suddenly, a short, dark man, and then a slender, light-skin man emerged from a footpath on the opposite side of the grove from the one she and Jose had scavenged. They wore ragged work clothes stained with patches of sweat; their faces were drawn and tired. Yolanda's glance fell on the machetes that hung from their belts.

The men's faces snapped awake from their stupor at the sight of her. They looked beyond her at the car. "Yours?" the darker man spoke first. It struck her, even then, as an absurd question. Who else's would it be here in the middle of nowhere?

"Is there some problem?" the darker man spoke up again. The taller one was looking her up and down with interest. They were now both in front of her on the road, blocking her escape. Both—she had looked them up and down as well—were strong and quite capable of catching her if she made a run for the Miranda's. Not that she could have moved, for her legs seemed suddenly to have been hammered into the ground beneath her. She thought of explaining that she was just out for a drive before dinner at the big house, so that these men would think someone knew where she was, someone would come looking for her if they tried to carry her off. But she found she could not speak. Her tongue felt as if it'd been stuffed in her mouth like a rag to keep her quiet.

Vocabulary

machetes (mə shet′ ēz) *n.* large knives with broad blades

Making Predictions

Based on the description of the men, how do you predict they will respond to Yolanda?

The men exchanged a look—it seemed to Yolanda of collusion. Then the shorter, darker one spoke up again, "Señorita,[7] are you all right?" He peered at her. The darkness of his complexion in the growing darkness of the evening made it difficult to distinguish an expression. He was no taller than Yolanda, but he gave the impression of being quite large, for he was broad and solid, like something not yet completely carved out of a piece of wood. His companion was tall and of a rich honey-brown color that matched his honey-brown eyes. Anywhere else, Yolanda would have found him extremely attractive, but here on a lonely road, with the sky growing darker by seconds, his good looks seemed dangerous, a lure to catch her off her guard.

"Can we help you?" the shorter man repeated.

The handsome one smiled knowingly. Two long, deep dimples appeared like gashes on either side of his mouth. "*Americana,*" he said to the other in Spanish, pointing to the car. "She doesn't understand."

The darker man narrowed his eyes and studied Yolanda a moment. "*Americana?*" he asked her as if not quite sure what to make of her.

She had been too frightened to carry out any strategy, but now a road was opening before her. She laid her hand on her chest—she could feel her pounding heart—and nodded. Then, as if the admission itself loosened her tongue, she explained in English how it came that she was on a back road by herself, her craving for guavas, her never having learned to change a flat. The two men stared at her, uncomprehendingly, rendered docile by her gibberish. Strangely enough, it soothed her to hear herself speaking something they could not understand. She thought of something her teacher used to say to her when as a young immigrant girl she was learning English, "Language is power." It was her only defense now.

Yolanda made the motions of pumping. The darker man looked at the other, who had shown better luck at understanding the foreign lady. But his companion shrugged, baffled as well. "I'll show you," Yolanda waved for them to follow her. And suddenly, as if after pulling and pulling at roots, she had finally managed to yank them free of the soil they had clung to, she found she could move her own feet forward to the car.

The small group stood staring at the sagging tire a moment, the two men kicking at it as if punishing it for having failed the Señorita. They squatted by the passenger's side, conversing in low tones. Yolanda led them to the rear of the car, where the men lifted the spare out of its sunken nest—then set to work, fitting the interlocking pieces of the jack, unpacking the tools from the deeper hollows of the trunk. They laid their machetes down on the side of the road, out of the way. Yolanda turned on the headlights to help them see in the growing darkness. Above the small group, the sky was purple with twilight.

There was a problem with the jack. It squeaked and labored, but the car would not rise. The shorter man squirmed his way underneath

---

7. Señorita (se′ nyō rē′ tä) "Miss" (Spanish).

Vocabulary

collusion (kə lōō′ zhən) *n.* secret agreement; conspiracy

docile (däs′ əl) *adj.* easy to direct or manage; obedient

She laid her hand on her chest—she could feel her pounding heart...

Comprehension

What does Yolanda pretend when she is approached by the two men?

and placed the mechanism deeper under the bowels of the car. There, he pumped vigorously, his friend bracing him by holding him down by the ankles. Slowly, the car rose until the wheel hung suspended. When the man came out from under the car, his hand was bloody where his knuckles had scraped against the pavement.

Yolanda pointed to the man's hand. She had been sure that if any blood were going to be spilled tonight, it would be hers. She offered him the towel she kept draped on her car seat to absorb her perspiration. But he waved it away and sucked his knuckles to make the bleeding stop.

Once the flat had been replaced with the spare, the two men lifted the deflated tire into the trunk and put away the tools. They handed Yolanda her keys. There was still no sign of Jose and the Miranda's. Yolanda was relieved. As she had waited, watching the two men hard at work, she had begun to dread the boy's return with help. The two men would realize she spoke Spanish. It was too late to admit that she had tricked them, to explain she had done so only because she thought her survival was on the line. The least she could do now was to try and repay them, handsomely, for their trouble.

"I'd like to give you something," she began reaching for the purse she'd retrieved from the trunk. The English words sounded hollow on her tongue. She rolled up a couple of American bills and offered them to the men. The shorter man held up his hand. Yolanda could see where the blood had dried dark streaks on his palm. "No, no, Señorita. *Nuestro placer.*"[8] Our pleasure.

Yolanda turned to the other man, who had struck her as more pliant than his sterner companion. "Please," she urged the bills on him. But he too looked down at the ground with the bashfulness she had observed in Jose of country people not wanting to offend. She felt the poverty of her response and stuffed the bills quickly into his pocket.

The two men picked up their machetes and raised them to their shoulders like soldiers their guns. The tall man motioned towards the big house. "*Directo, directo,*"[9] he enunciated the words carefully. Yolanda looked in the direction of his hand. In the faint light of what was left of day, she could barely make out the road ahead. It was as if the guava grove had overgrown into the road and woven its mat of branches so securely and tightly in all directions, she would not be able to escape.

But finally, she was off! While the two men waited a moment on the shoulder to see if the tire would hold, Yolanda drove a few yards, poking her head out the window before speeding up. "*Gracias!*"[10] she called, and they waved, appreciatively, at the foreign lady making an effort in their native tongue. When she looked for them in her rear-view mirror, they had disappeared into the darkness of the guava grove.

---

8. *Nuestro placer* (nōō es′ trō plä ser′) "Our pleasure" (Spanish).
9. *Directo, directo* (dē rek′ tō) "Straight, straight" (Spanish).
10. *Gracias* (grä′ sē äs) "Thank you" (Spanish).

Just ahead, her lights described the figure of a small boy: Jose was walking alone, listlessly, as if he did not particularly want to get to where he was going.

Yolanda leaned over and opened the door for him. The small overhead light came on; she saw that the boy's face was streaked with tears.

"Why, what's wrong, Jose?"

The boy swallowed hard. "They would not come. They didn't believe me." He took little breaths between words to keep his tears at bay. He had lost his chance at a whole dollar. "And the guard, he said if I didn't stop telling stories, he was going to whip me."

"What did you tell him, Jose?"

"I told him you had broken your car and you needed help fixing it."

She should have gone along with Jose to the Miranda's. Given all the trouble in the country, they would be suspicious of a boy coming to their door at nightfall with some story about a lady on a back road with a broken car. "Don't you worry, Jose," Yolanda patted the boy. She could feel the bony shoulder through the thin fabric of his worn shirt. "You can still have your dollar. You did your part."

But the shame of being suspected of lying seemed to have obscured any immediate pleasure he might feel in her offer. Yolanda tried to distract him by asking what he would buy with his money, what he most craved, thinking that on a subsequent trip, she might bring him his little *antojo*. But Jose Duarte Sanchez y Mella said nothing, except a bashful thank you when she left him off at the cantina with his promised dollar. In the glow of the headlights, Yolanda made out the figure of the old woman in the black square of her doorway, waving good-bye. Above the picnic table on a near post, the Palmolive woman's skin shone; her head was thrown back, her mouth opened as if she were calling someone over a great distance.

Making Predictions

Based on your knowledge of the Dominican Republic's economic and political situation, why do you think Jose looks so forlorn?

Critical Reading

1. **Key Ideas and Details (a)** What are *antojos*? **(b) Connect:** What theme does the title of the story stress?

2. **Key Ideas and Details (a) Infer:** What is suggested about the country's political situation by the idea of a "hunger march" taking place in the capital? **(b) Analyze:** What role do economic issues play in this story?

3. **Key Ideas and Details (a) Interpret:** When Yolanda first sees the two men, what does she feel? **(b) Analyze:** Why does she pretend not to speak Spanish?

4. **Integration of Knowledge and Ideas** What details suggest that Yolanda longs for a deeper connection to her homeland? Use at least two of these Essential Question words: *influence, longing, nurture, transformation.* [*Connecting to the Essential Question: What is the relationship between literature and place?*]

Cite textual evidence to support your responses.

Literary Analysis

1. **Key Ideas and Details** **(a)** What **prediction** did you make about Yolanda's trip to the north coast? **(b)** What actually happened?

2. **Key Ideas and Details** **(a)** What prediction did you make about the strangers who emerge from the grove? **(b)** Was your prediction confirmed? Explain.

3. **Craft and Structure** **(a)** Make a list of the events in this story as they occur in chronological order. **(b)** At what point in that sequence does Alvarez begin the narration? **(c)** What effect does this use of *in medias res* create?

4. **Craft and Structure** **(a)** What does the **flashback** to Yolanda's visit with her aunts reveal about Yolanda's reasons for traveling north? **(b)** Is the author's use of flashback effective? Explain.

5. **Craft and Structure** What does the flashback to Yolanda's visit with the aunts reveal about the family's social and economic circumstances? Explain.

6. **Craft and Structure** **(a)** How else might Alvarez have conveyed the information given in the flashback? **(b)** Is her use of flashback more or less effective than another technique might be? Explain.

7. **Craft and Structure** **(a)** What future event do Yolanda's thoughts about the dangerous mountain roads **foreshadow? (b)** In what ways does the author's use of foreshadowing add suspense to this scene?

8. **Craft and Structure** **(a)** Using a chart like the one shown, find two other examples of foreshadowing in the story. List the clues Alvarez provides and the events they hint will happen. **(b)** Do the events unfold exactly as one might expect from the clues? Explain.

Clues from Foreshadowing	Event

9. **Integration of Knowledge and Ideas** Explain how the author's use of **plot devices** serves two purposes: **(a)** to engage readers; and **(b)** to create a sense of unity and logic in the story.

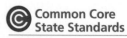

**Common Core
State Standards**

Writing

3. Write narratives to develop real or imagined experiences or events using effective technique, well-chosen details, and well-structured event sequences. *(p. 1309)*

3.b. Use narrative techniques, such as dialogue, to develop experiences, events, and/or characters. *(p. 1309)*

3.c. Use a variety of techniques to sequence events so that they build on one another to create a coherent whole and build toward a particular tone and outcome. *(p. 1309)*

3.d. Use precise words and phrases, telling details, and sensory language to convey a vivid picture of the experiences, events, setting, and/or characters. *(p. 1309)*

Language

4.a. Use context as a clue to the meaning of a word or phrase. *(p. 1309)*

4.c. Consult general and specialized reference materials, both print and digital, to clarify the precise meaning of a word, its etymology, or its standard usage. *(p. 1309)*

5. Demonstrate understanding of word relationships. *(p. 1309)*

Vocabulary Acquisition and Use

Words from Other Languages: Spanish

Many words, such as *machete, tortilla,* and *sombrero,* come to English directly from Spanish. Use the story context to help you answer these questions about five other Spanish words. Consult a dictionary to check your work.

1. Which English word used in the story probably comes from *guayaba,* the Spanish name for the same tropical fruit?

2. *Cantina,* from the Spanish for "bar" or "tavern," is related to an Italian word for "wine cellar." Which English word probably has a similar origin?

3. In English, a *cabana* or *cabaña* is a small building at a pool or beach. Is that the word's meaning on page 1301? Explain.

4. *Gracias,* the Spanish word for "thank you," comes from the Latin word *gratia,* meaning "pleasing quality, favor, thanks." Which English words probably have a similar origin?

Vocabulary: Synonyms or Antonyms

Categorize each of the following pairs of words as either synonyms or antonyms. Explain your thinking.

1. dissuade, discourage
2. maneuver, reposition
3. appease, arouse
4. machetes, knives
5. collusion, plotting
6. docile, cantankerous

Writing to Sources

Narrative Text In both literature and life, stories are shaped by the points of view of those who tell them. Write a new version of the **story** from the point of view of one of the men who changes Yolanda's tire.

Prewriting Choose the character whose point of view you will use and reread the story considering that perspective. Note details to incorporate and develop. Then, write a brief outline of your new version.

Drafting Write the story from the new point of view. Use sensory details, flashbacks, internal monologue, and dialogue to provide background and flesh out the character's world.

Revising Reread your story, and look for points where you may have strayed from the perspective you have chosen. Delete details the character might not know, and add information to strengthen your use of point of view.

> **Model: Using Details to Create a Vivid Portrayal**
> Paulo saw a small white car stuck in the foliage. The tire was busted, and a lady stood there. Her eyes were nervous and black. She reminded Paulo of a cornered chihuahua, and he thought she might bite. He laughed at the thought. "How can we help you, Doña?" he asked.

The inclusion of dialogue and a character's inner thoughts add to the vividness of a narrative.

Connecting to the Essential Question In this story, distance and the passage of time lead a mother and daughter to two very different views of the world. Notice details in the story that suggest how personal relationships reflect social changes. Doing so will help you think about the Essential Question: **How does literature shape or reflect society?**

Close Reading Focus

Characterization; Dialect

Varied types of language are key to the **characterization,** or *development of characters*, in this story. The narrator uses standard English to express her internal thoughts:

> *I will wait for her in the yard that Maggie and I made so clean and wavy yesterday afternoon.*

However, when she speaks aloud, the narrator uses **dialect,** a language variation specific to the region in which she lives and the ethnic group of which she is a part. The narrator's spoken language also reflects her level of education and other aspects of her character:

> *"You know as well as me you was named after your aunt Dicie,"* I said.

As you read, consider how this duality of language allows readers to develop different perceptions of the narrator than those held by other characters in the story, especially the narrator's oldest daughter.

Preparing to Read Complex Texts As this story opens, you learn that two sisters and their life experiences are quite different. By **comparing and contrasting characters,** or identifying the ways in which they are alike and different, you can uncover the major conflict in the story. Use a Venn diagram like the one shown to note the character traits, such as details in behavior and speech, that separate Dee from Maggie. Consider the ways in which their experiences have shaped their differences.

Vocabulary

You will encounter the words listed here in the text that follows. Copy the words into your notebook. Which word is a verb? How can you tell?

homely	cowering
furtive	doctrines

Ⓒ **Common Core State Standards**

Reading Literature
3. Analyze the impact of the author's choices regarding how to develop and relate elements of a story or drama (e.g., how the characters are introduced and developed).

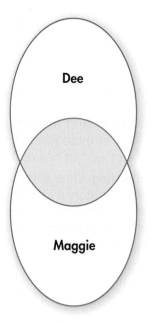

Dee

Maggie

Alice Walker *(b. 1944)*

Author of **"Everyday Use"**

Born in Eatonton, Georgia, Alice Walker was the eighth and youngest child in a family of sharecroppers. Of her childhood, Walker writes, "It was great fun being cute. But then, one day, it ended."

The security of her childhood was challenged by an accident with a BB gun that scarred and nearly blinded her. Eight years old when the accident happened, Walker reports that she did not lift her head for six years. It was not until the family could afford surgery that Walker finally had the scar tissue on her eye removed. With that surgery, her confidence returned.

Civil Rights Walker graduated from high school as both class valedictorian and prom queen. She attended Spelman College, an elite Atlanta school for African American women. While at Spelman, Walker became deeply involved in the civil rights movement. In August 1963, she traveled to Washington, D.C., to take part in the March on Washington for Jobs and Freedom. The guest speaker that day was Dr. Martin Luther King, Jr. Unable to see him through the crowd, Walker perched in a tree to get a better view. From there, she heard Dr. King deliver his famous "I Have a Dream" address.

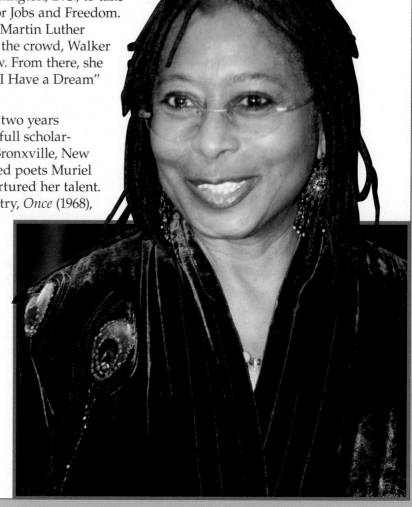

From Prom Queen to Poet After two years at Spelman, Walker was awarded a full scholarship to Sarah Lawrence College in Bronxville, New York. There, she studied under famed poets Muriel Rukeyser and Jane Cooper, who nurtured her talent. She wrote her first collection of poetry, *Once* (1968), while a student at Sarah Lawrence.

The Color Purple With the publication of her novel *The Color Purple* in 1982, Walker shot to international fame. The novel portrays women who are oppressed by the men in their lives, but go on to find inner strength and personal dignity. Awarded both the Pulitzer Prize and a National Book Award, the book was later adapted into a successful film.

"Everyday Use" explores Walker's maternal heritage, describing the creative legacy of "ordinary" black southern women.

Everyday Use

Alice Walker

BACKGROUND In this story, the narrator's oldest daughter wants an antique butter churn and two quilts—artifacts of her family's history—that she finds in her mother's house. The quilts are especially important items. Like most folk art, quilts serve both practical and aesthetic purposes: keeping people warm, recycling old clothing, providing a focal point for the social gathering of women, preserving precious bits of family history, and adding color and beauty to a home. In this story, the characters' differing attitudes toward the quilts and other objects in the household become critical points of conflict.

I will wait for her in the yard that Maggie and I made so clean and wavy yesterday afternoon. A yard like this is more comfortable than most people know. It is not just a yard. It is like an extended living room. When the hard clay is swept clean as a floor and the fine sand around the edges lined with tiny, irregular grooves, anyone can come and sit and look up into the elm tree and wait for the breezes that never come inside the house.

Maggie will be nervous until after her sister goes: she will stand hopelessly in corners, homely and ashamed of the burn scars down her arms and legs, eyeing her sister with a mixture of envy and awe. She thinks her sister has held life always in the palm of one hand, that "no" is a word the world never learned to say to her.

You've no doubt seen those TV shows where the child who has

Vocabulary

homely (hōm′ lē) *adj.* not elegant or polished; crude

"made it" is confronted, as a surprise, by her own mother and father, tottering in weakly from backstage. (A pleasant surprise, of course: What would they do if parent and child came on the show only to curse out and insult each other?) On TV mother and child embrace and smile into each other's faces. Sometimes the mother and father weep, the child wraps them in her arms and leans across the table to tell how she would not have made it without their help. I have seen these programs.

Sometimes I dream a dream in which Dee and I are suddenly brought together on a TV program of this sort. Out of a dark and soft-seated limousine I am ushered into a bright room filled with many people. There I meet a smiling, gray, sporty man like Johnny Carson who shakes my hand and tells me what a fine girl I have. Then we are on the stage and Dee is embracing me with tears in her eyes. She pins on my dress a large orchid, even though she has told me once that she thinks orchids are tacky flowers.

In real life I am a large, big-boned woman with rough, man-working hands. In the winter I wear flannel nightgowns to bed and overalls during the day. I can kill and clean a hog as mercilessly as a man. My fat keeps me hot in zero weather. I can work outside all day, breaking ice to get water for washing; I can eat pork liver cooked over the open fire minutes after it comes steaming from the hog. One winter I knocked a bull calf straight in the brain between the eyes with a sledge hammer and had the meat hung up to chill before nightfall. But of course all of this does not show on television. I am the way my daughter would want me to be: a hundred pounds lighter, my skin like an uncooked barley pancake. My hair glistens in the hot bright lights. Johnny Carson has much to do to keep up with my quick and witty tongue.

But that is a mistake. I know even before I wake up. Who ever knew a Johnson with a quick tongue? Who can even imagine me looking a strange white man in the eye? It seems to me I have talked to them always with one foot raised in flight, with my head turned in whichever way is farthest from them. Dee, though. She would always look anyone in the eye. Hesitation was no part of her nature.

"How do I look, Mama?" Maggie says, showing just enough of her thin body enveloped in pink skirt and red blouse for me to know she's there, almost hidden by the door.

"Come out into the yard," I say.

Have you ever seen a lame animal, perhaps a dog run over by some careless person rich enough to own a car, sidle up to someone

Characterization

What do the details in these paragraphs reveal about the narrator?

Comprehension

Who are Maggie and her mother waiting to welcome?

who is ignorant enough to be kind to him? That is the way my Maggie walks. She has been like this, chin on chest, eyes on ground, feet in shuffle, ever since the fire that burned the other house to the ground.

Dee is lighter than Maggie, with nicer hair and a fuller figure. She's a woman now, though sometimes I forget. How long ago was it that the other house burned? Ten, twelve years? Sometimes I can still hear the flames and feel Maggie's arms sticking to me, her hair smoking and her dress falling off her in little black papery flakes. Her eyes seemed stretched open, blazed open by the flames reflected in them. And Dee. I see her standing off under the sweet gum tree she used to dig gum out of; a look of concentration on her face as she watched the last dingy gray board of the house fall in toward the red-hot brick chimney. Why don't you do a dance around the ashes? I'd want to ask her. She had hated the house that much.

I used to think she hated Maggie, too. But that was before we raised the money, the church and me, to send her to Augusta to school. She used to read to us without pity; forcing words, lies, other folks' habits, whole lives upon us two, sitting trapped and ignorant underneath her voice. She washed us in a river of make-believe, burned us with a lot of knowledge we didn't necessarily need to know. Pressed us to her with the serious way she read, to shove us away at just the moment, like dimwits, we seemed about to understand.

Dee wanted nice things. A yellow organdy dress to wear to her graduation from high school; black pumps to match a green suit she'd made from an old suit somebody gave me. She was determined to stare down any disaster in her efforts. Her eyelids would not flicker for minutes at a time. Often I fought off the temptation to shake her. At sixteen she had a style of her own, and knew what style was.

I never had an education myself. After second grade the school was closed down. Don't ask me why: in 1927 colored asked fewer questions than they do now. Sometimes Maggie reads to me. She stumbles along good-naturedly but can't see well. She knows she is not bright. Like good looks and money, quickness passed her by. She will marry John Thomas (who has mossy teeth in an earnest face) and then I'll be free to sit here and I guess just sing church songs to myself. Although I never was a good singer. Never could carry a tune. I was always better at a man's job. I used to love to milk till I was hooved in the side in '49. Cows are soothing and slow and don't bother you, unless you try to milk them the wrong way.

> *Why don't you do a dance around the ashes? I'd want to ask her.*

Contrasting Characters

What contrasts between herself and Dee does the narrator describe?

I have deliberately turned my back on the house. It is three rooms, just like the one that burned, except the roof is tin; they don't make shingle roofs any more. There are no real windows, just some holes cut in the sides, like the portholes in a ship, but not round and not square, with rawhide holding the shutters up on the outside. This house is in a pasture, too, like the other one. No doubt when Dee sees it she will want to tear it down. She wrote me once that no matter where we "choose" to live, she will manage to come see us. But she will never bring her friends. Maggie and I thought about this and Maggie asked me, "Mama, when did Dee ever *have* any friends?"

She had a few. Furtive boys in pink shirts hanging about on washday after school. Nervous girls who never laughed. Impressed with her they worshiped the well-turned phrase, the cute shape, the scalding humor that erupted like bubbles in lye.[1] She read to them.

When she was courting Jimmy T she didn't have much time to pay to us, but turned all her faultfinding power on him. He *flew* to marry a cheap city girl from a family of ignorant flashy people. She hardly had time to recompose herself.

When she comes I will meet—but there they are!

Maggie attempts to make a dash for the house, in her shuffling way, but I stay her with my hand. "Come back here," I say. And she stops and tries to dig a well in the sand with her toe.

It is hard to see them clearly through the strong sun. But even the first glimpse of leg out of the car tells me it is Dee. Her feet were always neat-looking, as if God himself had shaped them with a certain style. From the other side of the car comes a short, stocky man. Hair is all over his head a foot long and hanging from his chin like a kinky mule tail. I hear Maggie suck in her breath. "Uhnnnh," is what it sounds like. Like when you see the wriggling end of a snake just in front of your foot on the road. "Uhnnnh."

Dee next. A dress down to the ground, in this hot weather. A dress so loud it hurts my eyes. There are yellows and oranges enough to throw back the light of the sun. I feel my whole face warming from the heat waves it throws out. Earrings gold, too, and hanging down to her shoulders. Bracelets dangling and making noises when she moves her arm up to shake the folds of the dress out of her armpits. The dress is loose and flows, and as she walks closer, I like it. I hear Maggie go "Uhnnnh" again. It is her sister's hair. It stands straight up like the wool on a sheep. It is black as night and around the edges are two long

Vocabulary
furtive (fur´ tiv) *adj.* sneaky

Comprehension
What traumatic event occurred in the lives of the mother and her daughters?

1. **lye** (lī) *n.* strong alkaline solution used in cleaning and making soap.

pigtails that rope about like small lizards disappearing behind her ears.

"Wa-su-zo-Tean-o!"[2] she says, coming on in that gliding way the dress makes her move. The short stocky fellow with the hair to his navel is all grinning and he follows up with "Asalamalakim,[3] my mother and sister!" He moves to hug Maggie but she falls back, right up against the back of my chair. I feel her trembling there and when I look up I see the perspiration falling off her chin.

"Don't get up," says Dee. Since I am stout it takes something of a push. You can see me trying to move a second or two before I make it. She turns, showing white heels through her sandals, and goes back to the car. Out she peeks next with a Polaroid. She stoops down quickly and lines up picture after picture of me sitting there in front of the house with Maggie **cowering** behind me. She never takes a shot without making sure the house is included. When a cow comes nibbling around the edge of the yard she snaps it and me and Maggie and the house. Then she puts the Polaroid in the back seat of the car, and comes up and kisses me on the forehead.

Meanwhile Asalamalakim is going through motions with Maggie's hand. Maggie's hand is as limp as a fish, and probably as cold, despite the sweat, and she keeps trying to pull it back. It looks like Asalamalakim wants to shake hands but wants to do it fancy. Or maybe he don't know how people shake hands. Anyhow, he soon gives up on Maggie.

"Well," I say. "Dee."

"No, Mama," she says. "Not 'Dee,' Wangero Leewanika Kemanjo!"

"What happened to 'Dee'?" I wanted to know.

"She's dead," Wangero said. "I couldn't bear it any longer, being named after the people who oppress me."

"You know as well as me you was named after your aunt Dicie," I said. Dicie is my sister. She named Dee. We called her "Big Dee" after Dee was born.

"But who was *she* named after?" asked Wangero.

"I guess after Grandma Dee," I said.

"And who was she named after?" asked Wangero.

"Her mother," I said, and saw Wangero was getting tired. "That's about as far back as I can trace it," I said. Though, in fact, I probably could have carried it back beyond the Civil War through the branches.

"Well," said Asalamalakim, "there you are."

"Uhnnnh," I heard Maggie say.

2. Wa-su-zo-Tean-o (wä sōō zō tēn´ ō) African greeting.

3. Asalamalakim *Salaam aleikhim* (sə läm´ ä lī´ kēm´) Islamic greeting meaning "Peace be with you."

Vocabulary

cowering (kou´ ər iŋ) *v.* trembling or cringing, as with fear

Dialect

How does the narrator's spoken language differ from her narrative voice?

"There I was not," I said, "before 'Dicie' cropped up in our family, so why should I try to trace it that far back?"

He just stood there grinning, looking down on me like somebody inspecting a Model A car. Every once in a while he and Wangero sent eye signals over my head.

"How do you pronounce this name?" I asked.

"You don't have to call me by it if you don't want to," said Wangero.

"Why shouldn't I?" I asked. "If that's what you want us to call you, we'll call you."

"I know it might sound awkward at first," said Wangero.

"I'll get used to it," I said. "Ream it out again."

Well, soon we got the name out of the way. Asalamalakim had a name twice as long and three times as hard. After I tripped over it two or three times he told me to just call him Hakim-a-barber. I wanted to ask him was he a barber, but I didn't really think he was, so I didn't ask.

"You must belong to those beef-cattle people down the road," I said. They said "Asalamalakim" when they met you, too, but they didn't shake hands. Always too busy: feeding the cattle, fixing the fences, putting up salt-lick shelters, throwing down hay. When the white folks poisoned some of the herd the men stayed up all night with rifles in their hands. I walked a mile and a half just to see the sight.

Hakim-a-barber said, "I accept some of their doctrines, but farming and raising cattle is not my style." (They didn't tell me, and I didn't ask, whether Wangero (Dee) had really gone and married him.)

We sat down to eat and right away he said he didn't eat collards[4] and pork was unclean. Wangero, though, went on through the chitlins[5] and corn bread, the greens and everything else. She talked a blue streak over the sweet potatoes. Everything delighted her. Even the fact that we still used the benches her daddy made for the table when we couldn't afford to buy chairs.

"Oh, Mama!" she cried. Then turned to Hakim-a-barber. "I never knew how lovely these benches are. You can feel the rump prints," she said, running her hands underneath her and along the bench. Then she gave a sigh and her hand closed over Grandma Dee's butter dish. "That's it!" she said. "I knew there was something I wanted to ask you if I could have." She jumped up from the table and went over in the corner where the churn stood, the milk in it clabber by now. She

Vocabulary
doctrines (däk´ trinz) *n.* religious beliefs or principles

Comprehension
Why has Dee changed her name?

---

4. collards (käl´ ərdz) *n.* leaves of the collard plant, often referred to as "collard greens."
5. chitlins (chit´ lənz) *n.* chitterlings, a pork dish popular among southern African Americans.

looked at the churn and looked at it.

"This churn top is what I need," she said. "Didn't Uncle Buddy whittle it out of a tree you all used to have?"

"Yes," I said.

"Uh huh," she said happily. "And I want the dasher, too."

"Uncle Buddy whittle that, too?" asked the barber.

Dee (Wangero) looked up at me.

"Aunt Dee's first husband whittled the dash," said Maggie so low you almost couldn't hear her. "His name was Henry, but they called him Stash."

"Maggie's brain is like an elephant's," Wangero said, laughing. "I can use the churn top as a centerpiece for the alcove table," she said, sliding a plate over the churn, "and I'll think of something artistic to do with the dasher."

When she finished wrapping the dasher the handle stuck out. I took it for a moment in my hands. You didn't even have to look close to see where hands pushing the dasher up and down to make butter had left a kind of sink in the wood. In fact, there were a lot of small sinks; you could see where thumbs and fingers had sunk into the wood. It was beautiful light yellow wood, from a tree that grew in the yard where Big Dee and Stash had lived.

After dinner Dee (Wangero) went to the trunk at the foot of my bed and started rifling through it. Maggie hung back in the kitchen over the dishpan. Out came Wangero with two quilts. They had been pieced by Grandma Dee and then Big Dee and me had hung them on the quilt frames on the front porch and quilted them. One was in the Lone Star pattern. The other was Walk Around the Mountain. In both of them were scraps of dresses Grandma Dee had worn fifty and more years ago. Bits and pieces of Grandpa Jarrell's Paisley shirts. And one teeny faded blue piece, about the size of a penny matchbox, that was from Great Grandpa Ezra's uniform that he wore in the Civil War.

"Mama," Wangero said sweet as a bird. "Can I have these old quilts?"

I heard something fall in the kitchen, and a minute later the kitchen door slammed.

"Why don't you take one or two of the others?" I asked. "These old things was just done by me and Big Dee from some tops your grandma pieced before she died."

"No," said Wangero. "I don't want those. They are stitched around the borders by machine."

"That'll make them last better," I said.

"That's not the point," said Wangero. "These are all pieces of dresses Grandma used to wear. She did all this stitching by hand. Imagine!" She held the quilts securely in her arms, stroking them.

"Some of the pieces, like those lavender ones, come from old clothes her mother handed down to her," I said, moving up to touch the quilts. Dee (Wangero) moved back just enough so that I couldn't reach the quilts. They already belonged to her.

"Imagine!" she breathed again, clutching them closely to her bosom.

"The truth is," I said, "I promised to give them quilts to Maggie, for when she marries John Thomas."

She gasped like a bee had stung her.

"Maggie can't appreciate these quilts!" she said. "She'd probably be backward enough to put them to everyday use."

"I reckon she would," I said. "God knows I been saving 'em for long enough with nobody using 'em. I hope she will!" I didn't want to bring up how I had offered Dee (Wangero) a quilt when she went away to college. Then she had told me they were old-fashioned, out of style.

"But they're *priceless*!" she was saying now, furiously; for she has a temper. "Maggie would put them on the bed and in five years they'd be in rags. Less than that!"

"She can always make some more," I said. "Maggie knows how to quilt."

Dee (Wangero) looked at me with hatred. "You just will not understand. The point is these quilts, *these quilts*!"

"Well," I said, stumped. "What would *you* do with them?"

"Hang them," she said. As if that was the only thing you *could* do with quilts.

Maggie by now was standing in the door. I could almost hear the sound her feet made as they scraped over each other.

"She can have them, Mama," she said, like somebody used to never winning anything, or having anything reserved for her.

"I can 'member Grandma Dee without the quilts."

I looked at her hard. She had filled her bottom lip with checkerberry snuff and it gave her face a kind of dopey, hangdog look. It was Grandma Dee and Big Dee who taught her how to quilt herself. She stood there with her scarred hands hidden in the folds of her skirt. She looked at her sister with something like fear but she wasn't mad at her. This was Maggie's portion. This was the way she knew God to work.

When I looked at her like that something hit me in the top of my head and ran down to the soles of my feet. Just like when I'm in church and the spirit of God touches me and I get happy and

Dialect
How does the narrator's speech affect Dee's perception of her?

Contrasting Characters
In what way does the dispute over the quilts reveal the differences between the two sisters?

Comprehension
Why does Dee think Maggie should not have the quilts?

shout. I did something I never had done before: hugged Maggie to me, then dragged her on into the room, snatched the quilts out of Miss Wangero's hands and dumped them into Maggie's lap. Maggie just sat there on my bed with her mouth open.

"Take one or two of the others," I said to Dee.

But she turned without a word and went out to Hakim-a-barber.

"You just don't understand," she said, as Maggie and I came out to the car.

"What don't I understand?" I wanted to know.

"Your heritage," she said. And then she turned to Maggie, kissed her, and said, "You ought to try to make something of yourself, too, Maggie. It's really a new day for us. But from the way you and Mama still live you'd never know it."

She put on some sunglasses that hid everything above the tip of her nose and her chin.

Maggie smiled; maybe at the sunglasses. But a real smile, not scared. After we watched the car dust settle I asked Maggie to bring me a dip of snuff. And then the two of us sat there just enjoying, until it was time to go in the house and go to bed.

Cite textual evidence to support your responses.

Critical Reading

1. **Key Ideas and Details (a)** What objects does Dee ask to have? **(b)** What does Dee plan to do with the items? **(c) Evaluate:** What is ironic about her request for these objects and her professed interest in her heritage?

2. **Key Ideas and Details (a) Interpret:** What do the quilts symbolize? **(b) Compare and Contrast:** In what ways do the quilts hold different meanings for Dee and for Maggie?

3. **Integration of Knowledge and Ideas** Does this story suggest that there is a personal price for social change—even change for the better? Explain. In your response, use at least two of these Essential Question words: *communication, perspective, compromise, understanding. [Connecting to the Essential Question: How does literature shape or reflect society?]*

Literary Analysis

1. **Key Ideas and Details (a)** What sort of awareness does each sister have about her heritage? **(b)** To what extent does each sister think it is important to incorporate knowledge of her African heritage into her daily life?

2. **Key Ideas and Details** How would you describe the narrator's relationship with **(a)** Maggie and **(b)** Dee? Use examples from the text to support your answers.

3. **Craft and Structure** Explain how the narrator's internal narrative voice differs from her spoken, external voice.

4. **Craft and Structure** Use a chart like the one shown to identify specific details that portray the narrator. **(a)** Identify each detail you chose as either an example of the narrator's internal voice, using standard English, or an example of her spoken voice, using **dialect. (b)** What do you learn about the narrator through each of these examples?

5. **Craft and Structure** How does her use of these different types of language add to Walker's **characterization** of the narrator?

6. **Craft and Structure** What does the reader learn about Dee through **(a)** the narrator's internal voice and **(b)** spoken dialogue?

7. **Craft and Structure** What does the author reveal about Maggie through **(a)** the narrator's internal voice and **(b)** spoken dialogue?

8. **Integration of Knowledge and Ideas (a)** Does Dee/Wangero truly know her mother? Explain. **(b)** How does the duality between the narrator's internal and external expression create different portraits of the narrator for the reader and for Dee?

9. **Integration of Knowledge and Ideas Compare and contrast the characters** of Maggie and Dee **(a)** physically, **(b)** intellectually, and **(c)** emotionally.

10. **Integration of Knowledge and Ideas (a)** How are Dee and the narrator different from one another? **(b)** How are they alike?

Common Core State Standards

Writing
1. Write arguments to support claims in an analysis of substantive topics or texts, using valid reasoning and relevant and sufficient evidence. *(p. 1322)*

5. Develop and strengthen writing as needed by planning, revising, editing, rewriting, or trying a new approach, focusing on addressing what is most significant for a specific purpose and audience. *(p. 1322)*

Language
1. Demonstrate command of the conventions of standard English grammar and usage when writing or speaking. *(p. 1323)*

4.b. Identify and correctly use patterns of word changes that indicate different meanings or parts of speech. *(p. 1322)*

5. Demonstrate understanding of word relationships. *(p. 1322)*

Vocabulary Acquisition and Use

Word Analysis: Latin Root -doc- / -doct-

The word *doctrines*, meaning "teachings, ideas, or beliefs," includes the Latin root -doc- / -doct-, meaning "teach." Combine this information with context clues to choose the best word to complete each sentence. Explain your choices.

documents   indoctrinate   docile   documentary

1. We watched a _____ on the history of quilt-making in America.

2. A _____ learner is one who accepts without question anything he or she is taught.

3. The political leader worked to _____ his followers by repeating his ideology at every opportunity.

4. Immigrants were asked to show _____ to prove their citizenship in their original country.

Vocabulary: Analogies

Analogies show the relationships between pairs of words. Complete each analogy using a word from the vocabulary list on page 1310. In each, your choice should create a word pair that matches the relationship between the first two words given. Then, explain your answers.

1. *Laughing* is to *amused* as _____ is to *frightened*.

2. *Comely* is to *stunning* as _____ is to *unattractive*.

3. *Competitive* is to *athlete* as _____ is to *prowler*.

4. *Morals* is to *lessons* as _____ is to *beliefs*.

Writing to Sources

Argument Write a **critical review** of "Everyday Use," explaining whether you think the story is effective. Note your reactions to the story and explain whether the characters are believable and interesting. Consider the story's message, and express your opinion about its importance.

Prewriting Review the story and list your responses, both positive and negative. Beside each item, note the page numbers of appropriate examples. Review your chart, and summarize your opinion in a sentence or two.

Drafting Begin by stating your overall opinion of the story. Then, present a series of paragraphs in which you support your ideas with details.

Revising Evaluate your draft to replace weak modifiers with precise adjectives and adverbs. If necessary, use a print or online thesaurus to locate words that vividly and precisely express your meaning.

Model: Revising to Add Precise Details

genuine

Dee, as Wangero, appears ∧nice, but she is really quite

her heritage

insincere. She is not at all interested in∧ the things, but rather in appearances.

Replacing weak modifiers with specific words makes writing more precise and interesting. Words like *really* do not add meaning to the work.

Conventions and Style: Using Transitional Expressions

To connect ideas in your writing, join one independent clause to another with a **transitional expression.** Transitional expressions are words and phrases that help define specific relationships among ideas. The chart shown here lists common transitional expressions:

Common Transitional Expressions

Intended Meaning	Sample Words or Phrases
Cause-effect	therefore; consequently; as a result
Time	the next step; subsequently
Illustrate	in fact; that is; for example; indeed
Sum up	in conclusion; in summary
Compare	similarly; in the same way
Contrast	however; conversely; on the other hand

Punctuation Tip When you use a transitional expression to join two independent clauses, precede the transition with a semicolon and follow it with a comma.

Connecting Ideas With Transitions

Choppy: Maggie was caught in a fire. She has scars.

Revision with Transition: Maggie was caught in a fire; *consequently*, she has scars.

Choppy: Dee couldn't wait to leave. Maggie likes living with Mama.

Revision with Transition: Dee couldn't wait to leave; *in contrast*, Maggie likes living with Mama.

Practice Rewrite each item using a transitional expression. Punctuate the new sentence correctly.

1. The church raised money. Dee was able to get an education.

2. Maggie was shy. She shuffled when she walked, her head down.

3. Dee liked to read aloud. Maggie read hesitantly, though cheerfully.

4. Dee changed her name. She felt weighed down by her family ancestry.

5. Mama had trouble pronouncing the man's name. Dee said to call him Hakim-a-barber.

Writing and Speaking Conventions

A. Writing Complete each sentence starter. Remember to use a comma after a transitional expression.

1. Maggie is upset by the visit; clearly _____.
2. Dee was not alarmed when the house burned; to be sure _____.
3. Dee insisted she would not bring friends to visit; in fact _____.
4. Dee criticized Jimmy T.; as a result _____.
5. Dee left; after a while _____.

> **Example:** Maggie is upset by Dee's visit; clearly _____.
> **Complete Sentence:** Maggie is upset by the visit; clearly, she feels inferior.

B. Speaking When Dee asked for the quilts, Mama heard something drop. Explain to a partner what happened and why you think the author included this detail. Include at least two transitional expressions in your explanation.

Connecting to the Essential Question In this story, an adult daughter struggles to make an emotional connection with her father. As you read, notice how the characters in the story speak—what they say and how they say it. Doing so will help you think about the Essential Question: **What makes American literature American?**

Close Reading Focus

Author's Style

All writers use language and may even explore similar themes or events. What distinguishes one writer from another is the **author's style**—*how* he or she uses language. Many literary elements, including word choice, sentence length and complexity, types of images, and types of subject matter, contribute to style. Raymond Carver's style, which is one of the most influential in contemporary literature, is marked by certain traits:

- He favors an economy of words and suggests more than he states.
- His restrained use of language creates a distant, almost subdued emotional attitude, or tone.
- He focuses on the lives of the working poor, a recurring theme.
- His characters often seem to struggle, unsuccessfully, to find words to express what they see and feel. They persist in a quiet isolation.

As you read, look for these elements of Carver's intense, pared-down style and think about how they affect the meaning, mood, and power of the story.

Preparing to Read Complex Texts When reading fiction, **asking questions** can clarify your understanding of passages, relationships, or events that may at first seem unclear. For example, in this story, the time frame moves back and forth between an outer story, or *frame story*, narrated by the author, to an inner story narrated by one of the main characters. Clarify your understanding by asking questions about the characters and events. Then, look for details or clues in the writing that help you reach a logical conclusion. As you read, use a chart like the one shown to aid your understanding.

Vocabulary

The words below are important to understanding the text that follows. Copy the words into your notebook. Which one of the words is a multiple-meaning word? Jot down at least two meanings for that word.

coincide   striking

ambitions   fitfully

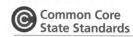

**Common Core
State Standards**

Reading Literature
4. Determine the meaning of words and phrases as they are used in the text, including figurative and connotative meanings; analyze the impact of specific word choices on meaning and tone, including words with multiple meanings or language that is particularly fresh, engaging, or beautiful.
5. Analyze how an author's choices concerning how to structure specific parts of a text contribute to its overall structure and meaning as well as its aesthetic impact.

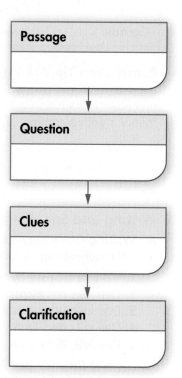

RAYMOND CARVER *(1938–1988)*

Author of **"Everything Stuck to Him"**

Raymond Carver is one of a handful of authors said to have revitalized the art of short-story writing in the late 1900s. Born in a small Oregon logging town to a mill worker and a waitress, Carver grew up penniless in Washington State. As an adult, he drew heavily from his life in his writings about the hardships of the working poor.

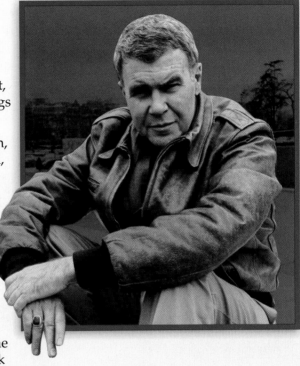

Inauspicious Beginnings At age nineteen, one year after graduating from high school, Carver married his sixteen-year-old sweetheart. By age twenty, he had fathered two children. Struggling to support his family, Carver took on a series of jobs, including work as a janitor, a sawmill worker, and a gas-station attendant.

After moving his family to California in 1958, Carver began studying at Chico State College. There he took a creative writing course taught by the acclaimed novelist John Gardner, who quickly became his mentor. Carver worked nights and took classes during the day. He later attended the prestigious Iowa Writer's Workshop and in 1967 received critical praise for his story "Will You Please Be Quiet, Please?"

A Turning Point In 1971, Carver began publishing his work in *Esquire* magazine, where he began a decade-long partnership with editor Gordon Lish. Lish encouraged a "less-is-more" approach to writing. As a result, Carver's writing became lean and sparse, earning him a reputation as a minimalist. A few years later, Carver published his short-story collection *Will You Please Be Quiet, Please?* and his career took off.

Opening Up In the 1980s, Carver parted ways with Lish, and his work grew more expansive. Then, in 1983, Carver won an award that changed his life. The Mildred and Harold Strauss Livings award brought with it five years of tax-free income and gave Carver financial independence. He earned celebrity treatment, with profiles in the *New York Times Magazine*, *Vanity Fair*, and *People* magazine. In 1984, his short story collection *Cathedral* was nominated for the Pulitzer Prize.

Carver divorced his first wife in 1982, and in 1988 he married the poet Tess Gallagher. That same year, Carver published his final collection of stories and was inducted into the American Academy and Institute of Arts and Letters. A few months later, at age fifty, Carver succumbed to lung cancer. He is remembered as one of the greatest storytellers of his time.

EVERYTHING STUCK TO HIM

—RAYMOND CARVER—

BACKGROUND This is a **frame story**, or a story within a story. There are many frame narratives in world literature, including the *Arabian Nights* and *The Canterbury Tales*. "The Notorious Jumping Frog of Calaveras County" (p. 576) by Mark Twain is an American example. To be a genuine frame narrative, the introductory story must be of secondary importance to the internal one. Consider whether this is true of Carver's tale.

◄ **Critical Viewing**
How does the setting of the frame story as shown here differ from the setting of the internal story? **COMPARE AND CONTRAST**

She's in Milan for Christmas and wants to know what it was like when she was a kid.

Tell me, she says. Tell me what it was like when I was a kid. She sips Strega,[1] waits, eyes him closely.

She is a cool, slim, attractive girl, a survivor from top to bottom.

That was a long time ago. That was twenty years ago, he says.

You can remember, she says. Go on.

What do you want to hear? he says. What else can I tell you? I could tell you about something that happened when you were a baby. It involves you, he says. But only in a minor way.

Tell me, she says. But first fix us another so you won't have to stop in the middle.

He comes back from the kitchen with drinks, settles into his chair, begins.

They were kids themselves, but they were crazy in love, this eighteen-year-old boy and this seventeen-year-old girl when they married. Not all that long afterwards they had a daughter.

The baby came along in late November during a cold spell that just happened to coincide with the peak of the waterfowl season. The boy loved to hunt, you see. That's part of it.

The boy and girl, husband and wife, father and mother, they lived in a little apartment under a dentist's office. Each night they cleaned the dentist's place upstairs in exchange for rent and utilities. In summer they were expected to maintain the lawn and the flowers. In winter the boy shoveled snow and spread rock salt on the walks. Are you still with me? Are you getting the picture?

I am, she says.

That's good, he says. So one day the dentist finds out they were using his letterhead for their personal correspondence. But that's another story.

He gets up from his chair and looks out the window. He sees the tile rooftops and the snow that is falling steadily on them.

Tell the story, she says.

The two kids were very much in love. On top of this they had great ambitions. They were always talking about the things they were going to do and the places they were going to go.

Vocabulary
coincide (kō´ in sīd´) *v.* to happen at the same time
ambitions (am bish´ ənz) *n.* strongly desired goals

Comprehension
How old were the boy and the girl when they married?

---

1. Strega *n.* an Italian herbal liqueur.

Author's Style

Why do you think Carver chooses to name minor characters, while leaving the main characters nameless?

Now the boy and girl slept in the bedroom, and the baby slept in the living room. Let's say the baby was about three months old and had only just begun to sleep through the night.

On this one Saturday night after finishing his work upstairs, the boy stayed in the dentist's office and called an old hunting friend of his father's.

Carl, he said when the man picked up the receiver, believe it or not, I'm a father.

Congratulations, Carl said. How is the wife?

She's fine, Carl. Everybody's fine.

That's good, Carl said, I'm glad to hear it. But if you called about going hunting, I'll tell you something. The geese are flying to beat the band. I don't think I've ever seen so many. Got five today. Going back in the morning, so come along if you want to.

I want to, the boy said.

The boy hung up the telephone and went downstairs to tell the girl. She watched while he laid out his things. Hunting coat, shell bag, boots, socks, hunting cap, long underwear, pump gun.

What time will you be back? the girl said.

Probably around noon, the boy said. But maybe as late as six o'clock. Would that be too late?

It's fine, she said. The baby and I will get along fine. You go and have some fun. When you get back, we'll dress the baby up and go visit Sally.

The boy said, Sounds like a good idea.

Sally was the girl's sister. She was striking. I don't know if you've seen pictures of her. The boy was a little in love with Sally, just as he was a little in love with Betsy, who was another sister the girl had. The boy used to say to the girl, If we weren't married, I could go for Sally.

What about Betsy? the girl used to say. I hate to admit it, but I truly feel she's better looking than Sally and me. What about Betsy?

Betsy too, the boy used to say.

Vocabulary

striking (strī′ kin) *adj.* very noticeable or impressive

After dinner he turned up the furnace and helped her bathe the baby. He marveled again at the infant who had half his features and half the girl's. He powdered the tiny body. He powdered between fingers and toes.

He emptied the bath into the sink and went upstairs to check the air. It was overcast and cold. The grass, what there was of it, looked like canvas, stiff and gray under the street light.

Snow lay in piles beside the walk. A car went by. He heard sand under the tires. He let himself imagine what it might be like tomorrow, geese beating the air over his head, shotgun plunging against his shoulder.

Then he locked the door and went downstairs.

In bed they tried to read. But both of them fell asleep, she first, letting the magazine sink to the quilt.

It was the baby's cries that woke him up.

The light was on out there, and the girl was standing next to the crib rocking the baby in her arms. She put the baby down, turned out the light, and came back to the bed.

He heard the baby cry. This time the girl stayed where she was. The baby cried fitfully and stopped. The boy listened, then dozed. But the baby's cries woke him again. The living room light was burning. He sat up and turned on the lamp.

I don't know what's wrong, the girl said, walking back and forth with the baby. I've changed her and fed her, but she keeps on crying. I'm so tired I'm afraid I might drop her.

You come back to bed, the boy said. I'll hold her for a while.

He got up and took the baby, and the girl went to lie down again.

Just rock her for a few minutes, the girl said from the bedroom. Maybe she'll go back to sleep.

The boy sat on the sofa and held the baby. He jiggled it in his lap until he got its eyes to close, his own eyes closing right along. He rose carefully and put the baby back in the crib.

It was a quarter to four, which gave him forty-five minutes. He crawled into bed and dropped off. But a few minutes later the baby was crying again, and this time they both got up.

The boy did a terrible thing. He swore.

For God's sake, what's the matter with you? the girl said to the boy. Maybe she's sick or something. Maybe we shouldn't have given her the bath.

The boy picked up the baby. The baby kicked its feet and smiled.

Look, the boy said, I really don't think there's anything wrong with her.

How do you know that? the girl said. Here, let me have her. I know I ought to give her something, but I don't know what it's supposed to be.

The girl put the baby down again. The boy and the girl looked at the baby, and the baby began to cry.

The girl took the baby. Baby, baby, the girl said with tears in her eyes.

Probably it's something on her stomach, the boy said.

The girl didn't answer. She went on rocking the baby, paying no attention to the boy.

The boy waited. He went to the kitchen and put on water for coffee. He drew his woolen underwear on over his shorts and T-shirt, buttoned up, then got into his clothes.

What are you doing? the girl said.

Going hunting, the boy said.

I don't think you should, she said. I don't want to be left alone with her like this.

Vocabulary

fitfully (fit´ fəl ē) *adv.*
without regularity; restlessly

> Baby, baby, the girl said with tears in her eyes.

Comprehension

What "terrible thing" does the boy do?

Carl's planning on me going, the boy said. We've planned it.

I don't care about what you and Carl planned, she said. And I don't care about Carl, either. I don't even know Carl.

You've met Carl before. You know him, the boy said. What do you mean you don't know him?

That's not the point and you know it, the girl said.

What is the point? the boy said. The point is we planned it.

The girl said, I'm your wife. This is your baby. She's sick or something. Look at her. Why else is she crying?

I know you're my wife, the boy said.

The girl began to cry. She put the baby back in the crib. But the baby started up again. The girl dried her eyes on the sleeve of her nightgown and picked the baby up.

The boy laced up his boots. He put on his shirt, his sweater, his coat. The kettle whistled on the stove in the kitchen.

You're going to have to choose, the girl said. Carl or us. I mean it.

What do you mean? the boy said.

You heard what I said, the girl said. If you want a family, you're going to have to choose.

They stared at each other. Then the boy took up his hunting gear and went outside. He started the car. He went around to the car windows and, making a job of it, scraped away the ice.

He turned off the motor and sat awhile. And then he got out and went back inside.

The living-room light was on. The girl was asleep on the bed. The baby was asleep beside her.

The boy took off his boots. Then he took off everything else. In his socks and his long underwear, he sat on the sofa and read the Sunday paper.

The girl and the baby slept on. After a while, the boy went to the kitchen and started frying bacon.

The girl came out in her robe and put her arms around the boy.

Hey, the boy said.

I'm sorry, the girl said.

It's all right, the boy said.

I didn't mean to snap like that.

It was my fault, he said.

You sit down, the girl said. How does a waffle sound with bacon?

Sounds great, the boy said.

She took the bacon out of the pan and made waffle batter. He sat at the table and watched her move around the kitchen.

She put a plate in front of him with bacon, a waffle. He spread butter and poured syrup. But when he started to cut, he turned the plate into his lap.

I don't believe it, he said, jumping up from the table.

If you could see yourself, the girl said.

Author's Style

How does this exchange between the boy and the girl reflect the author's unadorned style?

The boy looked down at himself, at everything stuck to his underwear.

I was starved, he said, shaking his head.

You were starved, she said, laughing.

He peeled off the woolen underwear and threw it at the bathroom door. Then he opened his arms and the girl moved into them.

We won't fight anymore, she said.

The boy said, We won't.

He gets up from his chair and refills their glasses.

That's it, he says. End of story. I admit it's not much of a story.

I was interested, she says.

He shrugs and carries his drink over to the window. It's dark now but still snowing.

Things change, he says. I don't know how they do. But they do without your realizing it or wanting them to.

Yes, that's true, only—But she does not finish what she started.

She drops the subject. In the window's reflection he sees her study her nails. Then she raises her head. Speaking brightly, she asks if he is going to show her the city, after all.

He says, Put your boots on and let's go.

But he stays by the window, remembering. They had laughed. They had leaned on each other and laughed until the tears had come, while everything else—the cold, and where he'd go in it—was outside, for a while anyway.

Author's Style

Carver is known for his use of "silence." Why do you think the girl does not finish her sentence?

Critical Reading

1. **Key Ideas and Details** **(a)** What is the internal story about? **(b) Draw Conclusions:** Why does the man refer to himself and his family members as "the boy," "the girl," and "the baby"?

2. **Key Ideas and Details** **(a)** To what incident does the title of the story refer? **(b) Infer:** What other significance might the title have?

3. **Integration of Knowledge and Ideas** **(a) Speculate:** What might the young woman have said to her father if she had finished her sentence at the end of the story? **(b) Evaluate:** Do you feel hopeful about the future of the father and daughter's relationship? Why or why not?

4. **Integration of Knowledge and Ideas** Although the frame story is set in Italy, the characters are from the United States. What aspects of their speech strike you as distinctly American? Explain. In your response, use at least two of these Essential Question words: *ornate, vernacular, direct, realistic, regional.* *[Connecting to the Essential Question: What makes American literature American?]*

Cite textual evidence to support your responses.

Literary Analysis

1. **Key Ideas and Details (a)** What **questions** did you ask to clarify connections between the characters in the external, or *frame*, and internal stories? **(b)** Which details helped you clarify that relationship?

2. **Key Ideas and Details** Note another question you asked about the story, and list the details that answered it.

3. **Craft and Structure** Using a chart like the one shown, describe elements of Carver's **style** and cite examples from the story.

Element	Description	Example
Word Choice		
Sentences		
Details and Images		
Thematic Events		

4. **Integration of Knowledge and Ideas (a)** Explain how Carver suggests more than he states in this story. **(b)** What mood does Carver's pared-down style help create?

Vocabulary Acquisition and Use

Use New Words Write a sentence for each word pair in which you use both words correctly.

1. striking / ambitions

2. fitfully / coincide

Writing to Sources

Explanatory Text Write an **analytical essay** in which you examine the story's ending. Consider the following questions as you draft: In what ways does the story end happily? What note of discord is introduced? How is that note introduced? What do you understand about the father and daughter's relationship from earlier details? How is your sense of the ending affected by that understanding?

Begin your essay by stating your position. Then, defend your position with details from the story.

Common Core State Standards

Writing
2. Write explanatory texts to examine and convey complex ideas, concepts, and information clearly and accurately through the effective selection, organization, and analysis of content.
9.a. Apply grades 11–12 Reading standards to literature. [RL.11-12.5]

Language
4. Determine or clarify the meaning of unknown and multiple-meaning words and phrases based on *grades 11–12 reading and content,* choosing flexibly from a range of strategies.

Contemporary Poetry

Connecting to the Essential Question These poems focus on moments of unexpected connections or perceptions. As you read, notice details that express a new understanding. Doing so will help you consider the Essential Question: **How does literature shape or reflect society?**

Close Reading Focus

Lyric Poem; Epiphany

The literary works presented here are lyric poems. A **lyric poem** expresses the thoughts and feelings of a single speaker and often has a lilting, musical quality, as in these lines from Li-Young Lee's "The Gift":

> *I can't remember the tale,*
> *but hear his voice still, a well*
> *of dark water, a prayer.*

Lyric poems are usually relatively short but have great depth. The **theme,** or essential meaning, of such a poem is often multifaceted. The precise, nuanced language of many lyric poems may even help to express multiple themes. In most lyric poems, the theme emerges as a flash of insight or understanding. Although this flash—also known as an **epiphany**—may seem sudden, the details of the poem lead the reader gradually and steadily toward this new understanding. The epiphany is usually accompanied by a shift in perspective: the speaker may face up to a loss, make a decision, or simply see something in a new light. The reader, too, experiences the epiphany alongside the speaker, and comes away from the lyric poem feeling as if he or she has been on a small but meaningful journey.

Preparing to Read Complex Texts Poets rarely spell out their exact meaning in a lyric poem. Instead, it is up to the reader to interpret the poem by noting details and considering the message they collectively present. When **interpreting** lyric poetry, look for a central image or idea that is introduced and revisited throughout the poem. Consider new information about the image that emerges over the course of the poem. As you read, use a chart like the one shown to interpret how key details contribute to the ultimate meaning in each poem.

Vocabulary

The words below are important to understanding the texts that follow. Copy the words into your notebook, sorting them into words you know and words you do not know.

swerve   shard

exhaust

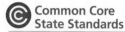

Common Core State Standards

Reading Literature
1. Cite strong and thorough textual evidence to support analysis of what the text says explicitly as well as inferences drawn from the text, including determining where the text leaves matters uncertain.
2. Determine two or more themes or central ideas of a text and analyze their development over the course of the text, including how they interact and build on one another to produce a complex account.

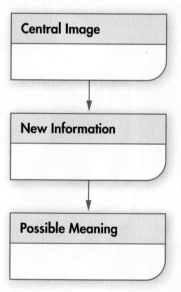

Central Image

New Information

Possible Meaning

William Stafford

(1914–1993)

> *"I have woven a parachute out of everything broken."*

Author of **"Traveling Through the Dark"**

William Stafford grew up in Kansas. When the Great Depression struck, he traveled with his family from town to town selling newspapers, working in the fields, and finding whatever work they could. These childhood experiences would greatly influence Stafford's poetry, both in its themes and its use of unadorned language.

Conscientious Objector A believer in the sanctity of life, Stafford served in World War II as a conscientious objector. In this role, he performed tasks such as fighting fires, building roads, and cultivating crops. Stafford's experiences during this time are described in his memoir, *Down in My Heart*, published in 1947.

After years of working for the U.S. Forest Service, Stafford published his first volume of poetry, *West of Your City* in 1960. He was forty-six years old at the time. In that book and others, Stafford's poems focus on a range of subjects, including the threat of nuclear war and the beauty of nature. His accessible, conversational style invites readers to appreciate the simple elegance of the everyday while considering deeper issues. Writing about Stafford in *Babel to Byzantium,* a book of critical essays, poet James Dickey described Stafford's work as "mystical, half-mocking and highly personal daydreaming about the western United States."

Stafford's other poetry collections include *The Rescued Year* (1966) and *Stories That Could Be True: New and Collected Poems* (1977). In 1970, he was appointed Consultant of Poetry to the Library of Congress, a position now known as Poet Laureate of the United States.

TRAVELING THROUGH THE DARK

William Stafford

Traveling through the dark I found a deer
dead on the edge of the Wilson River road.
It is usually best to roll them into the canyon:
that road is narrow; to **swerve** might make more dead.

5 By glow of the tail-light I stumbled back of the car
and stood by the heap, a doe, a recent killing;
she had stiffened already, almost cold.
I dragged her off; she was large in the belly.

My fingers touching her side brought me the reason—
10 her side was warm; her fawn lay there waiting,
alive, still, never to be born.
Beside that mountain road I hesitated.

The car aimed ahead its lowered parking lights;
under the hood purred the steady engine.
15 I stood in the glare of the warm **exhaust** turning red;
around our group I could hear the wilderness listen.

I thought hard for us all—my only swerving—,
then pushed her over the edge into the river.

Vocabulary

swerve (swurv) *v.*
turn aside sharply and
suddenly

Vocabulary

exhaust (eg zôst')
n. discharge of used
steam or gas from an
engine

Critical Reading

1. **Key Ideas and Details (a)** What discovery does the speaker make when he examines the deer? **(b) Infer:** Why does the speaker hesitate upon making this discovery?

2. **Key Ideas and Details (a) Interpret:** In the fourth stanza, what details make the car seem alive? **(b) Connect:** In what ways does this description echo the speaker's discovery about the deer?

3. **Key Ideas and Details (a) Deduce:** What factors does the speaker weigh in his decision about what to do with the deer? **(b) Analyze:** How does the title reflect the speaker's moral dilemma?

Cite textual evidence to support your responses.

Denise Levertov

(1923–1997)

Author of **"The Secret"**

Born in England, Denise Levertov grew up wandering the parks and museums of London and reveling in her family's private library. By the age of five, she had decided to become a writer, and by seventeen she had published her first poem. Her collection *The Double Image* appeared in 1946, earning the poet recognition in both England and the United States.

Becoming American After serving as a civilian nurse in London during World War II, Levertov married an American writer and moved to the United States. There, she developed a close friendship with the poet William Carlos Williams and studied the works of Emerson and Thoreau. From these writers Levertov learned to pay deep attention to the realities of life, both large and small.

When she came to the United States, Levertov became part of a loosely-organized group known as "The Black Mountain Poets." These writers rejected poetic tradition and embraced a conversational style of writing. In her poem, "The Man," Levertov expresses the force of individualism the Black Mountain poets sought: "you pick out / your own song from the uproar / line by line, / and at last throw back / your head and sing it."

Although her poems cover a broad range of topics—from love to art to politics and war—they are all characterized by a clear, direct voice and a profound reverence for the mystery at the heart of existence. Levertov published more than twenty volumes of poetry during her lifetime, including the award-winning *The Freeing of the Dust*.

"... celebration of mystery probably constitutes the most consistent theme of my poetry..."

THE SECRET

Denise Levertov

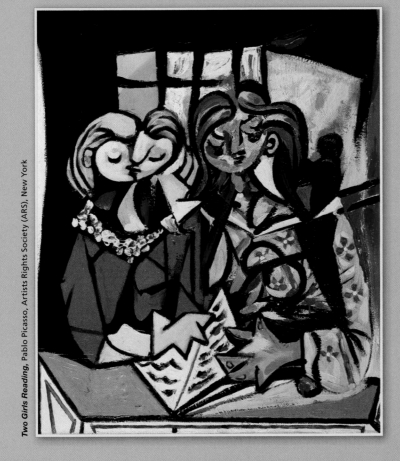

Two Girls Reading, Pablo Picasso, Artists Rights Society (ARS), New York

◀ **Critical Viewing**
This painting by Pablo Picasso is entitled "Two Girls Reading." Does this painting suggest a moment of discovery that is in any way similar to the one described in the poem? **ASSESS**

Two girls discover
the secret of life
in a sudden line of
poetry.

5   I who don't know the
secret wrote
the line. They
told me

(through a third person)
10   they had found it

Comprehension
What do two girls discover in a poem?

but not what it was
not even

what line it was. No doubt
by now, more than a week
15 later, they have forgotten
the secret,

the line, the name of
the poem. I love them
for finding what
20 I can't find,

and for loving me
for the line I wrote,
and for forgetting it
so that

25 a thousand times, till death
finds them, they may
discover it again, in other
lines

in other
30 happenings. And for
wanting to know it,
for

assuming there is
such a secret, yes,
35 for that
most of all.

**Lyric Poem
and Epiphany**

What sudden understanding
does the speaker have about
the nature of "the secret
of life"?

Critical Reading

Cite textual
evidence to
support your
responses.

1. **Key Ideas and Details (a)** Who discovers "the secret" of life,
and where? **(b) Assess:** In lines 1–16, how does the speaker seem
to feel about this discovery?

2. **Key Ideas and Details (a)** For what does the speaker love the
secret-finders most of all? **(b) Interpret:** Why does the speaker
love the idea that the secret-finders have already lost the secret?
(c) Infer: Based on this evidence, do you think the speaker herself
believes there is a secret?

3. **Integration of Knowledge and Ideas Synthesize:** Do you
believe there is a secret of life that can be discovered in a sudden
moment? Explain.

Li-Young Lee (b. 1957)

Author of "The Gift"

Li-Young Lee was born in Indonesia after his parents were exiled from China. Indonesia proved equally unwelcoming to Lee's father—who was both Christian and pro-Western—and he was imprisoned for nineteen months. After his release, the family moved first to Hong Kong, and then traveled through Macau and Japan. Finally, in 1964, Lee and his family moved to the United States.

Landing in America After a childhood of constant motion, Lee adjusted to a calm life in Pittsburgh, Pennsylvania. As an 11-year-old boy, he met a young woman who would later become his wife and the inspiration for many of his poems. Although Lee's transition to life in the United States was smooth, he still says that he is unable to decide if he should consider himself Chinese, Chinese-American, Asian-American, or American. The search for identity is a recurring theme throughout his work.

Although his father often read poetry aloud, Lee did not begin writing poetry until he was a student at the University of Pittsburgh. After further studies in Arizona and New York, Lee settled in Chicago, where he continues to live and work as a full-time poet. Over the years he has published a number of poetry collections and other works.

Story-Poems Lee's poems are known for their meandering, free-verse style and for the complex web of memories they present. Many of his "story-poems" focus on his childhood experiences as an immigrant and the son of exiles, often recalling, with affection, the strength and gentleness of his father. Influenced by both the Bible and classic Chinese poets, Lee's works have a silent, reverent quality that gives even his most personal subject matter a universal appeal. His many awards include a Lannan Literary Award, a Whiting Writer's Award, three Pushcart Prizes, and a Guggenheim Foundation fellowship.

> "The knowledge that it takes to write a poem gets burnt up in the writing of the poem."

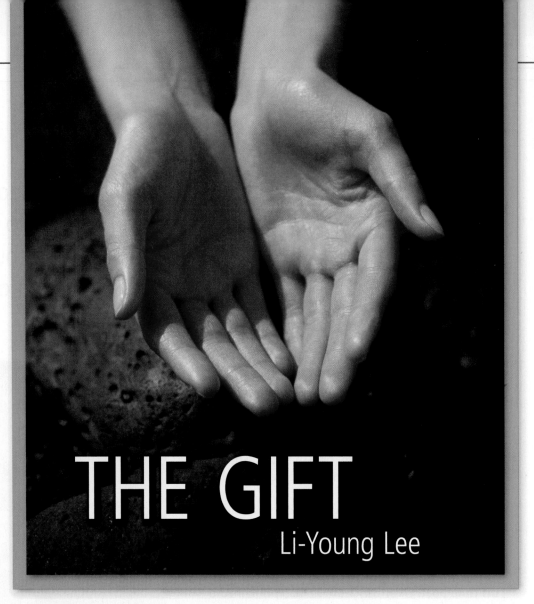

THE GIFT

Li-Young Lee

Interpreting

What central image is presented in the first line of the poem?

To pull the metal splinter from my palm
my father recited a story in a low voice.
I watched his lovely face and not the blade.
Before the story ended, he'd removed
5   the iron sliver I thought I'd die from.

I can't remember the tale,
but hear his voice still, a well
of dark water, a prayer.
And I recall his hands,
10   two measures of tenderness
he laid against my face,
the flames of discipline
he raised above my head.

Had you entered that afternoon

15 you would have thought you saw a man
planting something in a boy's palm,
a silver tear, a tiny flame.
Had you followed that boy
you would have arrived here,
20 where I bend over my wife's right hand.

Look how I shave her thumbnail down
so carefully she feels no pain.
Watch as I lift the splinter out.
I was seven when my father
25 took my hand like this,
and I did not hold that shard
between my fingers and think,
Metal that will bury me,
christen it Little Assassin,
30 Ore Going Deep for My Heart.
And I did not lift up my wound and cry,
Death visited here!
I did what a child does
when he's given something to keep.
35 I kissed my father.

Vocabulary

shard (shärd) *n.* a sharp fragment of glass or metal

Critical Reading

1. **Key Ideas and Details (a)** What does the father do as he removes the boy's splinter? **(b) Analyze:** How does the poem itself mirror this detail?

2. **Key Ideas and Details (a)** How does the boy view the splinter when it is set in his hand? **(b) Infer:** Why does the grown speaker refer to the splinter as "Little Assassin" and "Ore Going Deep for My Heart"? **(c) Interpret:** What makes the memory of the splinter meaningful for the speaker?

3. **Integration of Knowledge and Ideas** What do each of these poems suggest about the connections between small events and larger meanings? In your response, use at least two of these Essential Question words: *transform, vision, identity, ambiguity, landscape.* [*Connecting to the Essential Question: How does literature shape or reflect society?*]

Cite textual evidence to support your responses.

Literary Analysis

1. **Key Ideas and Details (a)** In "Traveling Through the Dark," what is the speaker's moral dilemma? **(b)** In line 16, the speaker can "hear the wilderness listen." What is it listening for? **(c)** How does the speaker "answer"?

2. **Key Ideas and Details** In "Traveling Through the Dark," the speaker refers to his hard thought as his "only swerving." Explain the sudden insight, or **epiphany,** the speaker experiences after this "swerving."

3. **Key Ideas and Details (a)** What new understanding does the speaker arrive at in "The Secret"? **(b)** Would you say the theme of this poem centers on a thing, or on a process? Explain.

4. **Key Ideas and Details (a)** "The Gift" tells two mini-stories. What are they? **(b)** Identify two ways in which the speaker is like his father.

5. **Key Ideas and Details (a)** In "The Gift," what paradoxical realization does the speaker make about the removal of splinters? **(b)** How does this realization apply to memories, as well?

6. **Craft and Structure** A **lyric poem** can be thought of as a journey in which the speaker travels through a landscape of nature, memory, spirit, or morality, and returns to the starting point with a new understanding. Using a chart like the one shown, choose one of the poems in this grouping and analyze it from this perspective.

Poem:			
Type of Journey	**Starting Point**	**Events of Journey**	**How Speaker Changes**

7. **Integration of Knowledge and Ideas** Follow these steps to **interpret** each of these lyric poems:
   a. Identify the the central image or event in each poem.
   b. List two pieces of new information you learn about this image over the course of the poem.
   c. Explain how your understanding of the image changes.
   d. Interpret the poem by telling what you think each central image means to the speaker.

Common Core State Standards

Writing
2. Write explanatory texts to examine and convey complex ideas, concepts, and information clearly and accurately through the effective selection, organization, and analysis of content. *(p. 1345)*
2.c. Use appropriate and varied transitions and syntax to link the major sections of the text, create cohesion, and clarify the relationships among complex ideas and concepts. *(p. 1345)*

Language
4.b. Identify and correctly use patterns of word changes that indicate different meanings or parts of speech. *(p. 1345)*

Vocabulary Aquisition and Use

Related Words: *Exhaust*

The word *exhaust* derives from the Latin word *exhaustus* meaning "to draw off or out" or "to use up completely." As a noun, the word *exhaust* means "the discharge of used steam or gas from an engine." However, the word may also function as a verb meaning "to empty completely" or "to tire out." Complete each of the sentences below with one of the related words from the list. Explain your choices.

inexhaustible   exhausted   exhaustion

1. The _____ I felt was due to lack of sleep.

2. By the race's end, the runner was _____.

3. The strength of a fit athlete can seem _____.

Vocabulary: Repairing Logic

Revise each sentence so that the underlined vocabulary word is used logically. Do not change the vocabulary word.

1. If you <u>swerve</u> your car on an icy road, you will most likely get where you are going slowly but surely.

2. After a car has had a tune-up, it should produce a steady stream of black <u>exhaust</u>.

3. Stepping on a <u>shard</u> of glass can be a soothing experience.

Writing to Sources

Informative Text The title of each of these poems has a direct relationship to the poem's meaning. Choose two of the poems, and write an **essay** in which you first **analyze** the relationship between each poem and its title, and then compare and contrast the two title/poem relationships with each other.

Prewriting First, review each poem and decide what you think each title means. Consider whether it has more than one meaning. Use a diagram like the one shown to record your ideas.

Model: Comparing and Contrasting Titles

Consider turning each part of the diagram into a section of the essay.

Drafting As you draft, use a logical method of organization. You might discuss the significance of each title in turn and then ways in which the titles are similar and different. Alternatively, you might discuss each key similarity or difference and then draw conclusions about each title.

Revising Clarify the logic of your ideas by adding transitions such as *similarly, equally, to compare, in contrast, in one case,* and *in the other case.*

Building Knowledge and Insight

Connecting to the Essential Question These poets express ideas about important issues that may prompt readers to think twice about their own views. As you read, look for details that reveal the speaker's beliefs. Doing so will help you consider the Essential Question: **How does literature shape or reflect society?**

Close Reading Focus

Voice; Social Commentary

Just as each person has a distinctive way of speaking, every poet has a unique **voice,** or literary personality. A poet's voice is based on word choice, tone, sound devices, rhyme (or its absence), pace, attitude, and even the patterns of vowels and consonants. Consider these examples:

- *Espada:* No gloves: fingertips required / for the perfection of paper . . .
- *Komunyakaa:* We hugged bamboo & leaned / against a breeze off the river . . .
- *Nye:* . . . the sky which sews and sews, tirelessly sewing, / drops her purple hem. . . .

As you read these poems, note the distinctive voice each one reveals.

Comparing Literary Works Each of these poets uses personal experience as a springboard for **social commentary,** a reflection on a public or political concern. In "Who Burns for the Perfection of Paper," for example, Martín Espada describes an experience from his youth to call attention to a social problem. In "Streets," Naomi Shihab Nye sets her own beliefs about loss and death beside the very different beliefs of others. As you read these poems, identify the particular brand of social commentary each poet offers.

Preparing to Read Complex Texts Poems are almost always subjective—that is, they express the poet's experiences, opinions, and beliefs. While a poet may not always state beliefs directly, those beliefs shape a poem's meaning and are revealed in images and details. Therefore, **drawing inferences about the poet's beliefs** will help you better understand poetry. As you read, use a chart like the one shown to identify details and draw inferences about the implicit beliefs they suggest.

Vocabulary

You will encounter the words listed here in the texts that follow. Copy the words into your notebook, sorting them into words you know and words you do not know.

crevices   refuge

terrain

Common Core State Standards

Reading Literature

1. Cite strong and thorough textual evidence to support analysis of what the text says explicitly as well as inferences drawn from the text, including determining where the text leaves matters uncertain.

4. Determine the meaning of words and phrases as they are used in the text, including figurative and connotative meanings; analyze the impact of specific word choices on meaning and tone, including words with multiple meanings or language that is particularly fresh, engaging, or beautiful.

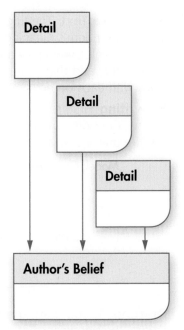

Martín Espada (b. 1957)

Author of "Who Burns for the Perfection of Paper"

Not many lawyers pursue simultaneous careers as poets, but, until 1993, Martín Espada was an exception. Espada was inspired by his father Frank Espada, a photographer based in the New York City borough of Brooklyn. Father and son worked together on a 1981 photo documentary called *The Puerto Rican Diaspora Documentary Project*. A year later, Espada published his first volume of poetry, *The Immigrant Iceboy's Bolero*, which was enhanced by his father's photographs.

Politics and Art A poet of deep social and political consciousness, Espada draws on his Puerto Rican heritage in his work, as well as his experiences as a legal-aid lawyer and activist. His poems celebrate and often lament the experiences of working-class people, especially those of Hispanic descent. He has been acclaimed as "*the* Latino poet of his generation."

To date, Espada has published thirteen books as a poet, essayist, editor, and translator. His many honors include the Paterson Award for Sustained Literary Achievement, the American Book Award, as well as numerous awards and fellowships, including the Robert Creeley Award, the Paterson Poetry Prize, the PEN/Revson Fellowship, and two NEA Fellowships. Espada received the Guggenheim Memorial Foundation Fellowship in 2006. He is a professor of creative writing at the University of Massachusetts at Amherst, where he also teaches the work of Chilean poet Pablo Neruda.

"No change for the good ever happens without being imagined first."

Who Burns for the Perfection of Paper

Martín Espada

At sixteen, I worked after high school hours
at a printing plant
that manufactured legal pads:
Yellow paper
5 stacked seven feet high
and leaning
as I slipped cardboard
between the pages,
then brushed red glue
10 up and down the stack.
No gloves: fingertips required
for the perfection of paper,
smoothing the exact rectangle.
Sluggish by 9 PM, the hands
15 would slide along suddenly sharp paper,
and gather slits thinner than the crevices
of the skin, hidden.
Then the glue would sting,
hands oozing
20 till both palms burned
at the punchclock.

Ten years later, in law school,
I knew that every legal pad
was glued with the sting of hidden cuts,
25 that every open lawbook
was a pair of hands
upturned and burning.

Vocabulary
crevices (krev´ is iz) *n.*
narrow cracks or splits

Yusef Komunyakaa

(b. 1947)

Author of **"Camouflaging the Chimera"**

Yusef Komunyakaa (yōō′ sef kō mun yä′ kä) was born in Bogalusa, Louisiana. In 1965, he joined the army and was sent to Vietnam. He served there as an "information specialist," reporting from the front lines, and editing a military newspaper called the *Southern Cross*. He also earned a Bronze Star. After the war, Komunyakaa pursued his education, earning a B.A. at the University of Colorado, an M.A. at Colorado State University, and an M.F.A. at the University of California, Irvine. In 1977, he published his first collection of poetry, and he has been publishing his poems ever since.

Poet of the Vietnam War Komunyakaa achieved his true breakthrough moment in literature with the 1988 publication of *Dien Cai Dau (Vietnamese for "this crazy head")*, in which he took on the subject of his experiences in Vietnam. "It took me fourteen years to write poems about Vietnam," said Yusef Komunyakaa in 1994, shortly after winning the Pulitzer Prize for *Neon Vernacular*, another poetry collection. "I had never thought about writing about it, and in a way I had been systematically writing around it."

About Komunyakaa's work, the poet Toi Derricotte has written, "He takes on the most complex moral issues . . . His voice, whether it embodies the specific experiences of a black man, a soldier in Vietnam, or a child in Bogalusa, Louisiana, is universal. It shows us in ever deeper ways what it is to be human."

BACKGROUND: THE VIETNAM WAR American involvement in the Vietnam War lasted from 1961 to 1973. The war presented American military forces with the frustrating and terrifying problem of how to fight in dense jungle against the Viet Cong (or VC), an enemy capable of magically "merging" with the landscape. As "Camouflaging the Chimera" demonstrates, part of the answer to this problem involved sending small groups of American soldiers into the jungle to wait in ambush for the elusive enemy.

"Each poem relates to a place—the internal terrain as well as the external terrain..."

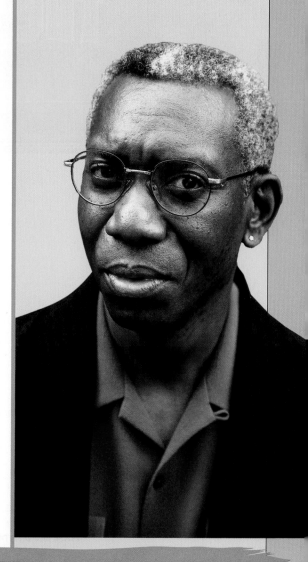

Camouflaging the Chimera [1]

Yusef Komunyakaa

We tied branches to our helmets.
We painted our faces & rifles
with mud from a riverbank,

blades of grass hung from the pockets
5   of our tiger suits. We wove
ourselves into the terrain,
content to be a hummingbird's target.

We hugged bamboo & leaned
against a breeze off the river,
10 slow-dragging with ghosts

from Saigon to Bangkok,
with women left in doorways
reaching in from America.
We aimed at dark-hearted songbirds.

Vocabulary

terrain (tə rān´) *n.* an area of ground and its features

---

1. Chimera (kī mir´ ə) from Greek mythology, a firebreathing monster with a lion's head, a goat's body, and a serpent's tail.

15 In our way station of shadows
    rock apes tried to blow our cover,
    throwing stones at the sunset. Chameleons

    crawled our spines, changing from day
    to night: green to gold,
20 gold to black. But we waited
    till the moon touched metal,

    till something almost broke
    inside us. VC struggled
    with the hillside, like black silk

25 wrestling iron through grass.
    We weren't there. The river ran
    through our bones. Small animals took refuge
    against our bodies; we held our breath,

    ready to spring the L-shaped
30 ambush, as a world revolved
    under each man's eyelid.

▲ **Critical Viewing**
How does this photograph
reflect the image of soldiers
who "wove ourselves into
the terrain"? **CONNECT**

Vocabulary
refuge (ref´ yōōj) *n.*
shelter or protection
from danger

Naomi Shihab Nye (b. 1952)

Author of "Streets"

Arab American poet Naomi Shihab Nye spent her teenage years in Jerusalem, far from the cities of St. Louis, Missouri, and San Antonio, Texas, where she had been a child. Her father had emigrated from Palestine and settled in St. Louis, where he and his wife operated stores specializing in imported goods. When Naomi was fourteen, the family moved back to Jerusalem to be near her father's Arab relatives. Nye says the family's years in Jerusalem enabled her to discover her heritage.

Poetry of the Everyday In addition to publishing award-winning volumes of poetry, Nye has also written picture books for children. This versatile writer, whose work is built on the sturdy foundation of everyday experiences, believes that "the primary source of poetry has always been local life, random characters met on the streets, our own ancestry sifting down to us through small essential daily tasks."

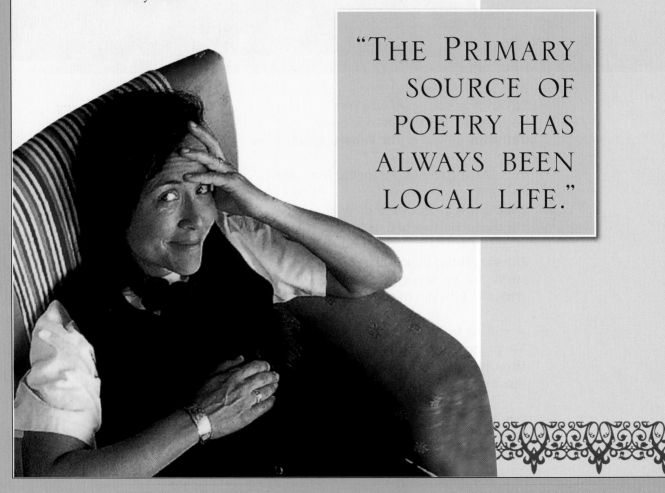

"THE PRIMARY SOURCE OF POETRY HAS ALWAYS BEEN LOCAL LIFE."

STREETS

Naomi Shihab Nye

A man leaves the world
and the streets he lived on
grow a little shorter.
One more window dark
5   in this city, the figs on his branches
will soften for birds.
If we stand quietly enough evenings
there grows a whole company of us
standing quietly together.
10   Overhead loud grackles are claiming
     their trees
and the sky which sews and sews,
     tirelessly sewing,
drops her purple hem.

Comprehension

According to the speaker, what happens when a man leaves the world?

Each thing in its time, in its place,
it would be nice to think the same about people.
15 Some people do. They sleep completely,
waking refreshed. Others live in two worlds,
the lost and remembered.
They sleep twice, once for the one who is gone,
once for themselves. They dream thickly,
20 dream double, they wake from a dream
into another one, they walk the short streets
calling out names, and then they answer.

Social Commentary

Does the speaker belong to the group of "some people," or to the group of "others"?

Critical Reading

Cite textual evidence to support your responses.

1. **Key Ideas and Details (a)** In "Who Burns for the Perfection of Paper," what was the speaker's first experience with legal pads? **(b)** What was the speaker's later job with legal pads? **(c) Interpret:** What did the speaker learn from the first job?

2. **Key Ideas and Details (a)** What word does the speaker use twice to describe cuts on the hands? **(b) Interpret:** What are two possible meanings of this word?

3. **Key Ideas and Details (a)** Where does "Camouflaging the Chimera" take place? **(b) Analyze:** What obstacles and burdens does the speaker face?

4. **Key Ideas and Details (a)** What runs through the soldiers' bones? **(b) Support:** What other images suggest that the speaker is merging with his surroundings? **(c) Interpret:** What does the speaker mean by his observation that "We weren't there"?

5. **Key Ideas and Details (a)** In "Streets," what happens when a man "leaves the world"? **(b) Interpret:** What might these events symbolize?

6. **Key Ideas and Details (a)** What do the people who "sleep completely" believe? **(b) Compare:** What do those who "sleep twice" experience? **(c) Speculate:** Who might "they" refer to in line 22?

7. **Integration of Knowledge and Ideas** What do these poems suggest about the power of poetry to convey experience that is both private and public? Explain. In your response, use at least two of these Essential Question words: *transform, alienation, global, awareness, understanding.* **[Connecting to the Essential Question: How does literature shape or reflect society?]**

Literary Analysis

1. **Craft and Structure (a)** Use a chart like the one shown to select the adjective that best describes each poet's **voice. (b)** Then, choose additional adjectives that accurately characterize each voice. Explain your choices.

> **Adjectives:** haunting, meditative, mournful, yearning, reverent, pained

Poet	Voice	Evidence		Additional Adjectives
			→	

2. **Integration of Knowledge and Ideas Draw inferences about the poet's beliefs** as they are expressed in these poems. **(a)** In "Camouflaging . . . ," what do you think the speaker feels about the enemy? Explain. **(b)** Do the images suggest that the speaker is opposed to the war? Explain.

3. **Integration of Knowledge and Ideas (a)** Cite two details in "Who Burns . . ." that show the speaker's diligence. **(b)** Based on these details, what beliefs about consumer society do you think the poet holds?

4. **Comparing Literary Works (a)** What "invisible" members of society are brought into focus in each poem? **(b)** Compare and contrast the **social commentary** each poet makes about that group of people.

Vocabulary Acquisition and Use

Synonyms Use a dictionary or thesaurus to choose a synonym for each word below. Then, explain how the synonym suggests different *connotative meanings*, or associations, from those of the original word.

   1. crevices   **2.** terrain   **3.** refuge

Writing to Sources

Informative Text Each of these poems expresses a belief about an aspect of life as it affects a specific group of people. In an **essay,** analyze the way in which each poem's *theme*, or central meaning, is also a comment on life for all people. In your essay, consider the following questions:

- What insights or experiences are described in each poem?
- How do these experiences relate to all people?
- What wish for humanity does each poem express?

Common Core State Standards

Writing
2. Write informative texts to examine and convey complex ideas, concepts, and information clearly and accurately through the effective selection, organization, and analysis of content.
9.a. Apply grades 11–12 Reading standards to literature. [RL.11-12.2]

Language
5. Demonstrate understanding of word relationships and nuances in word meanings.
5.b. Analyze nuances in the meaning of words with similar denotations.

Connecting to the Essential Question In this poem, the speaker revisits a moment from his childhood. As you read, look for specific places that the speaker visits in memory. Doing so will help you think about the Essential Question: **What is the relationship between literature and place?**

Close Reading Focus

Free Verse

Free verse is poetry without regular meter or rhyme. Nevertheless, free verse does contain many formal elements. In this poem, the poet uses carefully crafted lines to recreate the rhythms of natural speech or to emphasize meaning. The lines are shaped in one of two ways:

- **End-stopped lines** are lines that complete a grammatical unit, often (although not always) with a punctuation mark at the end. Such lines create a storytelling quality:

  > *"Repent, ye sinners!" he shouted,*
  > *waving his hand-lettered sign.*

- **Enjambed** lines are those that do not end with a grammatical break and do not make full sense without the line that follows:

  > *. . . They never heard me steal*
  > *into the stairwell hall and climb*
  > *the ladder to the fresh night air.*

Enjambed lines help the poet emphasize important words and hint at double meanings. As you read, notice how the lines give shape to the poem and help convey nuances in the poet's meaning.

Preparing to Read Complex Texts Poets writing in free verse often use subtle techniques to emphasize important details. As you read "Halley's Comet," **identify key details,** especially changes in verb tenses and *tone*, or emotional attitude. Consider whether these changes signal a shift in meaning, a shift in point of view, or both. Use a chart like the one shown to record your observations.

Vocabulary

You will encounter the words listed here in the text that follows. Copy the words into your notebook. What other forms of the vocabulary words do you know?

proclaiming   **steal**

repent

Common Core State Standards

Reading Literature

1. Cite strong and thorough textual evidence to support analysis of what the text says explicitly as well as inferences drawn from the text, including determining where the text leaves matters uncertain.

5. Analyze how an author's choices concerning how to structure specific parts of a text contribute to its overall structure and meaning as well as its aesthetic impact.

6. Analyze a case in which grasping a point of view requires distinguishing what is directly stated in a text from what is really meant.

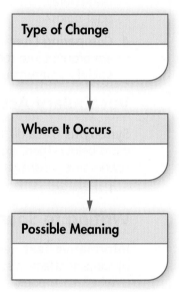

Type of Change

Where It Occurs

Possible Meaning

Stanley Kunitz (1905–2006)

Author of "Halley's Comet"

Lonely Youth "The deepest thing I know is that I am living and dying at once," Stanley Kunitz once wrote. Indeed, the poet's life was shadowed by death from the beginning as his father died shortly before Kunitz was born. This loss would haunt the poet for nearly a century.

Kunitz was born in Worcester, Massachusetts, where he spent a lonely childhood in a household where birthdays were not celebrated and talk of his father's death not allowed. Kunitz excelled at school, however, and became valedictorian of his class. He attended Harvard University, graduating with highest honors in English.

Poetic Evolution After completing his master's degree at Harvard, Kunitz worked as a newspaper journalist and later moved to a farmhouse in Connecticut. There, he wrote poems and edited reference books. At the age of twenty-five, he published *Intellectual Things,* a volume of poems abstract in theme and formal in style. His next collection, *Passport to the War,* represented his attempt to work out, in verse, the trauma of his childhood. The collection earned high critical praise and paved the way for his third book, *Selected Poems,* which would earn the Pulitzer Prize in 1959.

During his career as a poet, Kunitz taught at a series of prestigious schools, including Yale, Columbia, and Princeton. He was also an avid gardener—"I am never closer to the miraculous as when I am grubbing in the soil," he observed—and a lifelong patron of the visual arts.

As the poet aged, his poetry changed. Kunitz abandoned the distant tone of his early work and adopted a clear, spare style—"almost nonpoetic on the surface," he once described it, but with "reverberations within that keep it intense and alive." His form became freer and looser, his lines shorter, and his subjects more human.

Gifts of Conscience A conscientious objector to World War II, Kunitz was nevertheless drafted and served in the army for several years. Later, during the Vietnam War, Kunitz would become loudly critical of the U. S. government. His commitment to high moral standards and to his own inner truth, however, would lead this same government to name him Consultant in Poetry to the Library of Congress in 1974, and, at the age of ninety-five, the tenth Poet Laureate of the United States.

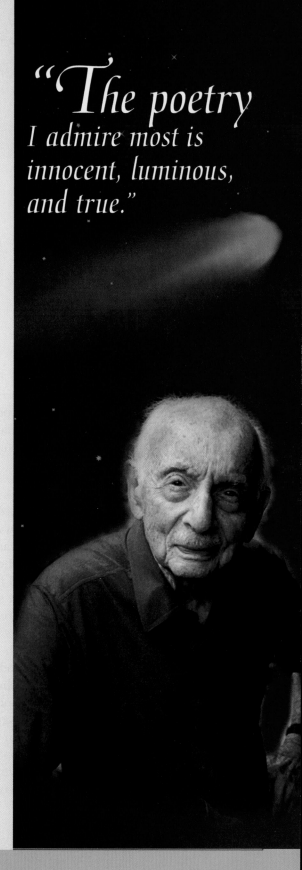

"The poetry I admire most is innocent, luminous, and true."

Halley's Comet

Stanley Kunitz

BACKGROUND Halley's Comet is the most famous of the periodic comets, appearing in Earth's skies every 75-76 years. This poem centers on its arrival in 1910, when the poet was five years old. The poem also reflects the poet's loss of his father, who died shortly before Kunitz was born. Like much of Kunitz's work, the mood is simultaneously one of darkest doom and brightest hope.

Miss Murphy in first grade
wrote its name in chalk
across the board and told us
it was roaring down the stormtracks
5   of the Milky Way at frightful speed
and if it wandered off its course
and smashed into the earth
there'd be no school tomorrow.
A red-bearded preacher from the hills
10   with a wild look in his eyes
stood in the public square
at the playground's edge
proclaiming he was sent by God
to save everyone of us,
15   even the little children.
"Repent, ye sinners!" he shouted,
waving his hand-lettered sign.
At supper I felt sad to think

Vocabulary

proclaiming (prō klām´ iŋ) *v.* announcing

repent (ri pent´) *v.* feel sorry for what one has done and vow to change one's behavior

that it was probably
20 the last meal I'd share
with my mother and sisters;
but I felt excited too
and scarcely touched my plate.
So mother scolded me
25 and sent me early to my room.
The whole family's asleep
except for me. They never heard me steal
into the stairwell hall and climb
the ladder to the fresh night air.

30 Look for me, Father, on the roof
of the red brick building
at the foot of Green Street—
that's where we live, you know, on the top floor.
I'm the boy in the white flannel gown
35 sprawled on this coarse gravel bed
searching the starry sky,
waiting for the world to end.

Vocabulary
steal (stēl) *v.* creep

Critical Reading

1. **Key Ideas and Details (a)** What is the "wild-eyed" preacher doing in the public square? **(b) Infer:** Why might he be doing this? **(c) Assess:** What effect does the preacher have on the mood of the poem?

2. **Craft and Structure (a) Distinguish:** What makes line 27 different from every other line in the poem? **(b) Interpret:** What break or shift in the action of the poem does this mirror?

3. **Key Ideas and Details (a) Draw Conclusions:** At the end of the poem, what is the speaker waiting for? Name two possibilities. **(b) Speculate:** Do you think either desire will be fulfilled? Explain.

4. **Integration of Knowledge and Ideas** How does the "place" described in the last seven lines differ from the places mentioned in lines 1–29? Why might the poet have wanted to revisit this particular spot in the landscape of his memories? In your response, use at least two of these Essential Question words: *transformation, awe, lament, personal, fantastic. [Connecting to the Essential Question: What is the relationship between literature and place?]*

Cite textual evidence to support your responses.

Literary Analysis

1. **Key Ideas and Details (a) Identify a key detail**—a change in verb tense—that occurs in line 26. **(b)** How does this change affect your sense of the poem's action?

2. **Craft and Structure** In what ways does the poet's use of **enjambment** in line 4 after the word *stormtracks* add to the meaning of the sentence?

3. **Craft and Structure (a)** What does the teacher tell the class in lines 6–8? **(b)** How is the poet's use of **end-stopped lines** at that point appropriate for the moment being described? **(c)** Explain how those lines are both reassuring and alarming at the same time.

4. **Craft and Structure (a)** What is happening in lines 34–37? **(b)** Why do you think the poet uses end-stopped lines here?

5. **Craft and Structure** Using a chart like the one shown, write three lines from the poem that seem to break in an unusual place. Then, explain how each line break affects the poem's mood or extends its meaning.

Line	Effect

6. **Craft and Structure (a)** Whom does the speaker seem to address in lines 1–29? **(b)** Whom does he address in lines 30–37? **(c)** How does this change affect the *tone* of the poem? **(d)** How does this change affect its meaning?

7. **Craft and Structure (a)** What are the speaker's two primary emotions in the poem? **(b)** How does **free verse** help the poet convey these emotions?

8. **Craft and Structure** Because free-verse poetry does not have a set meter or rhyme, its patterns are sometimes unpredictable. How is the form of "Halley's Comet" related to its content?

9. **Integration of Knowledge and Ideas** This poem moves from a public situation—a classroom—to a private, solitary one. **(a)** Identify a line or a phrase that reflects each situation. **(b)** Identify at least one key detail in each line that clearly expresses the difference in both subject matter and mood.

10. **Analyze Visual Information** Explain the humor in this cartoon.

Common Core State Standards

Writing

3. Write narratives to develop real or imagined experiences or events using effective technique, well-chosen details, and well-structured event sequences. *(p. 1361)*

3.e. Provide a conclusion that follows from and reflects on what is experienced, observed, or resolved over the course of the narrative. *(p. 1361)*

Language

4.b. Identify and correctly use patterns of word changes that indicate different meanings or parts of speech. *(p. 1361)*

5. Demonstrate understanding of word relationships. *(p. 1361)*

©2008 Bob Eckstein from cartoonbank.com. All Rights Reserved.

HECKLERS ON POETRY NIGHT

(left) "Great poem . . . if you're in a coma."

(middle) "You call that a metaphor?!?"

(right) "One word for you, pal: metre!"

Vocabulary Acquisition and Use

Word Analysis: Latin Prefix *pro-*

The Latin prefix *pro-* means "before" or "forward." It can refer to either place or time. The word *proclaim* literally means "to claim or announce before a group"; the word *protract* means "to draw forward in time." For each of the words below, write a definition that includes either the word *before* or *forward*. Then, explain whether the word relates to space, time, or both.

1. protrude

2. provide

3. prospect

4. propose

5. propel

6. prologue

7. promenade

8. prolong

Vocabulary: Word Mapping

Study the word map for the vocabulary word *proclaiming* below. Then, create similar word maps for the words *repent* and *steal*.

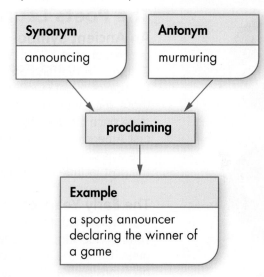

Writing

Narrative Text Children often have their own unique—and inaccurate—interpretations of things. Write an **autobiographical essay** about something you misunderstood or misinterpreted when you were a kid. Try to capture the mix of feelings the misunderstanding evoked or represented at the time, as well as how you feel about it today.

Prewriting For several minutes, write quickly and freely about innocent misunderstandings you held as a child and the incidents that happened to teach you they were incorrect. Choose one to focus on in your essay.

Drafting Organize your essay in chronological order, using a consistent verb tense. After describing your misunderstanding and the related incident, consider how the experience contributed to who you are today.

Revising Share your essay with a classmate

> **Model: Using Details to Create a Vivid Portrayal**
> I was five years old when my father took me to the planetarium. Terror struck me as we entered the enormous domed structure. I looked around, wondering where the spaceship was going to launch and when I would get my helmet. There were hundreds of people sitting in the dim light. Were all these people going to the moon, too?

Adjectives like *enormous* and *dim* portray the speaker's feeling of foreboding.

to see if he or she can identify with your experience. Elaborate or eliminate details in response to his or her comments.

Brooks

Kunitz

Collins

Glück

Warren

Dove

Being poet laureate made me realize I was capable of a larger voice. There is a more public utterance I can make *as a poet.*

—*Rita Dove*

The Poets Laureate

An Ancient Symbol The ancient Greeks adorned their heroes—whether athletes or poets—with wreaths made of laurel leaves. Today, the Library of Congress in Washington, D.C., honors one American poet each year with the title of "poet laureate consultant in poetry." The word "laureate" invokes those ancient wreaths of laurels. Although Britain has been naming poets laureate since the year 1630, the United States did not name one until 1937. The first American poet laureate was Joseph Auslander—though at first the official title was simply "consultant in poetry." Famous American poets who have held the post include Robert Frost, Gwendolyn Brooks, and Stanley Kunitz.

The Early Years of the Poetry Consultancy When the position was first established, the consultant was not expected to perform many duties beyond overseeing, in a general way, the poetry collection at the Library of Congress. Unlike the British poet laureate, who is required to write poems for state occasions such as the Queen's birthday, the American laureate has never been asked to write official poetry or preside over events of state. In the beginning, the position was largely honorary.

Over time, some of the appointed poets began to make a larger role for themselves. In 1945, **Louise Bogan,** the first woman named to the post, made audio recordings of poets reading from their work for the Library's poetry archives. She convinced W. H. Auden and T. S. Eliot to record some of their poems and she also recorded her own. **Léonie Adams,** in 1948, was the first to establish the tradition of having a public poetry reading early in the year. When **Robert Frost** was appointed in 1958, he took a more public stance, calling press conferences and speaking with the attorney general on behalf of poet Ezra Pound, who was incarcerated at the time. Shortly after his term expired, Frost read a poem at the inauguration of President John F. Kennedy (see p. 884), thereby bringing poetry into the homes of television viewers across the nation. **Maxine Kumin,** who served in 1981, started a series of women's poetry workshops at the Poetry and Literature Center. **Gwendolyn Brooks,** who, in 1985, became the first black woman to serve in the post, arranged for poetry-reading luncheons and brought poems into elementary schools.

◀ A sampling of poets who have held the post of poet laureate, from top, Gwendolyn Brooks, Stanley Kunitz, Billy Collins, Louise Glück, Robert Penn Warren, and Rita Dove.

The Laureate's Changing Role The poet laureate's job is to promote the enjoyment of poetry throughout America by encouraging people to read and write poetry. Each laureate has interpreted the job in a different way. In 1991, concerned that only a small number of Americans were reading poetry, laureate **Joseph Brodsky** started a program to distribute free poetry books to motels and schools. **Robert Hass** was dubbed the first "activist" laureate in 1995 when he traveled across the country, speaking to civic groups and visiting businesses to raise money for literacy programs.

Two years later, laureate **Robert Pinsky** invited Americans to share their favorite poems by recording them on tape and video. He published them in *An Invitation to Poetry*, a book packaged with a DVD. **Rita Dove,** in 1999, brought children to the Library of Congress to read and record their poems for the archives.

Ted Kooser launched the American Life in Poetry project, which made a poem available every week for newspapers to print, while **Billy Collins** created a Web site where high school students could find a new poem every day of the school year.

Common Core State Standards

W.11-12.1; SL.11-12.5
[For the full wording of the standards, see the standards chart in the front of your textbook.]

Speaking and Listening: Advertising Campaign

Comprehension and Collaboration Imagine that the office of the poet laureate—the client—has asked your advertising agency to write and design an ad campaign. The goal is to show that poetry is relevant to people's daily lives. With a small group, develop a strategy and materials for an **ad campaign.**

- Advertising is a form of persuasion. Decide how you will use *appeals to logic, emotion, and authority* to develop your content.

- Choose the media you will use: print, radio, television, the Internet, or some combination.

- Consider the populations, or demographics, you will target: students, adults, children, or older people.

- Think about the situations in which people will experience the ads. For example, will they encounter ads on their way to school or work, as they make dinner, or during entertainment or sporting events?

- Design the message and write a slogan to use in a variety of media.

  Create preliminary designs for print advertisements and scripts for radio commercials. For television or Web-based videos, make storyboards, or scene-by-scene sketches. Organize your materials and deliver a presentation that will convince the client to hire your agency.

Connecting to the Essential Question This poem is a reflection on homesickness, not simply for a prized neighborhood or a person, but for a culture. As you read, note details that reflect different cultures. Doing so will help as you consider the Essential Question: **What is the relationship between literature and place?**

Close Reading Focus

Imagery

Imagery is descriptive language that uses *images*—combinations of words that appeal to the senses and create pictures in the reader's mind. Images draw readers into a literary work by recreating the sensations of actual experience:

> . . . they walk down the narrow aisles of her store
> reading the labels of packages aloud, as if
> they were the names of lost lovers: *Suspiros,*
> *Merengues,* the stale candy of everyone's childhood.

Images invite the reader into the world of the poem: to walk down the narrow aisle, to scan the shelves of packages, and to murmur the names on the labels. They are the tools by which the poet builds meaning and emotion. As you read, notice how the images accumulate to paint a portrait of a place and a group of people and to, ultimately, convey the poem's essential message.

Preparing to Read Complex Texts Sensory details are words or phrases that appeal to the senses and are the building blocks of images. You will add to your appreciation of poetry if you pay attention to the specific words a poet uses to spark readers' associations of sight, touch, taste, smell, and sound. **Analyze sensory details** by following these steps:

- First, picture in your mind each separate detail.
- Second, consider the details as a group, asking yourself what they have in common and what overall feeling or idea they express.

As you read, use a chart like the one shown to analyze sensory details.

Vocabulary

The words below are important to understanding the text that follows. Copy the words into your notebook. Decide whether all three words have a positive or a negative connotation.

heady   **divine**

ample

Common Core State Standards

Reading Literature
4. Determine the meaning of words and phrases as they are used in the text, including figurative and connotative meanings; analyze the impact of specific word choices on meaning and tone, including words with multiple meanings or language that is particularly fresh, engaging, or beautiful.

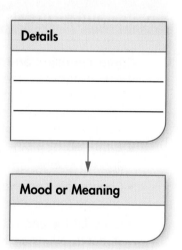

Details

Mood or Meaning

Judith Ortiz Cofer (b. 1952)

Author of "The Latin Deli: An Ars Poetica"

Nomadic Youth Judith Ortiz Cofer was born in Puerto Rico to young parents. To provide for his family, her father gave up his dream of a college education and joined first the United States Army and then the Navy. When he was assigned to the Brooklyn Navy Yard in 1955, the Ortiz family moved to Paterson, New Jersey.

Ortiz Cofer's father spent long stretches of time in Europe. During his absences, her mother would pack up the family and return to Puerto Rico. The constant shuffling made Ortiz Cofer feel like a permanent "new girl." When in the United States, she attended public school, spoke English, and behaved according to the strict social customs of the American Northeast. When in Puerto Rico, she attended a Catholic school and was immersed in a relaxed and colorful Latino culture. This geographically divided life left Ortiz Cofer with a sense of homelessness that would eventually fuel her creativity as a writer.

Putting Down Roots After graduating from Augusta College in 1974, Ortiz Cofer moved to Florida with her husband, Charles Cofer, whom she had married in 1971. She spent the next ten years teaching, earning a master's degree, and discovering poetry. Within several years, she had published three small books of poetry.

In 1984, Ortiz Cofer and her family moved to Georgia, where she continues to live, teach, and write. She is the author of several volumes of poetry, a memoir, a short-story collection, and a collection of essays. She has also published two novels. The second of these, *The Line of the Sun*, was nominated for a Pulitzer Prize in 1989.

Though she writes in all genres, Ortiz Cofer holds poetry especially dear. "It taught me how to write," she says. "Poetry contains the essence of language. Every word weighs a ton."

> "I speak English with a Spanish accent and Spanish with an American accent . . . I am a composite of two worlds."

THE LATIN DELI:
An Ars Poetica

Judith Ortiz Cofer

BACKGROUND Beginning in the mid-1900s, a stream of immigrants from the Spanish-speaking countries of Latin America and the Caribbean have sought sanctuary of various kinds in the United States. Some flee economic hardship or deprivation; others, political oppression. Still others seek a better education or job training. This *ars poetica*, or poem about the "art of poetry," combines the circumstances of these immigrants with the idea of poetry itself serving as a kind of home. (For more about the literary tradition of the *ars poetica*, see page 1368.)

Vocabulary
heady (hed´ ē) *adj.* strongly affecting the senses; intense

> Presiding over a formica counter,
> plastic Mother and Child magnetized
> to the top of an ancient register,
> the heady mix of smells from the open bins
> 5 of dried codfish, the green plantains[1]
> hanging in stalks like votive offerings,
> she is the Patroness of Exiles,

---

1. plantains (plan´ tinz) a banana-like fruit used as a cooking staple in tropical regions.

a woman of no-age who was never pretty,
who spends her days selling canned memories
10 while listening to the Puerto Ricans complain
that it would be cheaper to fly to San Juan[2]
than to buy a pound of Bustelo coffee[3] here,
and to Cubans perfecting their speech
of a "glorious return" to Havana[4]—where no one
15 has been allowed to die and nothing to change until then;
to Mexicans who pass through, talking lyrically
of *dólares* to be made in El Norte[5]—

                     all wanting the comfort
of spoken Spanish, to gaze upon the family portrait
20 of her plain wide face, her ample bosom
resting on her plump arms, her look of maternal interest
as they speak to her and each other
of their dreams and their disillusions—
how she smiles understanding,
25 when they walk down the narrow aisles of her store
reading the labels of packages aloud, as if
they were the names of lost lovers: *Suspiros*,[6]
Merengues,[7] the stale candy of everyone's childhood.

                         She spends her days
30 slicing *jamón y queso*[8] and wrapping it in wax paper
tied with string: plain ham and cheese
that would cost less at the A&P, but it would not satisfy
the hunger of the fragile old man lost in the folds
of his winter coat, who brings her lists of items
35 that he reads to her like poetry, or the others,
whose needs she must divine, conjuring up products
from places that now exist only in their hearts—
closed ports she must trade with.

Vocabulary

ample (am´ pəl) *adj.* large

Imagery

To what senses do the images in lines 25–29 appeal?

Vocabulary

divine (də vīn´) *v.* make a guess based on intuition

---

2. **San Juan** capital of Puerto Rico.
3. **Bustelo coffee** (bōō stē´ lo) a brand of strong, inexpensive Cuban coffee.
4. **Cubans . . . Havana** Cuba is the westernmost island in the Caribbean Sea; Havana is its capital. When Fidel Castro overthrew the government in 1959, the island's close ties to the United States were severed, and Cuba became a communist state with strong links to the Soviet Union. Since the revolution, thousands of Cubans have emigrated from the country to escape Castro's harsh regime.
5. **El Norte** (el nôr´ tā) "the north" (Spanish); commonly used in Mexico to refer to the United States and Canada.
6. **Suspiros** (sōō spē´ rōs) "sighs" (Spanish); also, a light, sugary cookie.
7. **Merengues** (me reŋ´ ges) "meringues" (Spanish); sweets made of egg whites and sugar.
8. **jamón y queso** (häm ōn´ ē kä´ sō) "ham and cheese" (Spanish).

Ars Poetica

The term *ars poetica* comes from Latin and means "the art of poetry." Today, the phrase describes a statement about what poetry should be. The earliest and most famous *ars poetica* was "Poetics," written by the Greek philosopher Aristotle in 335 B.C. Aristotle laid out his ideas about what makes good art and especially good literature. Writing a century after Sophocles and Euripides had composed their famous tragedies, Aristotle analyzed their plays to derive the "rules"of great drama. He argued art should be an imitation of reality and he judged the quality of art on the basis of that idea.

Three centuries after Aristotle, the Roman poet Horace wrote his own statement on literature. Written in verse, his "Ars Poetica" stressed the importance of harmony and balance in art. Horace said the job of the writer is to delight and instruct at the same time.

▲ Roman poet Horace (65 B.C.– 8 B.C.)

Connect to the Literature

Why does Ortiz Cofer call this poem an *ars poetica*? In what ways does it define poetry?

Critical Reading

Cite textual evidence to support your responses.

1. **Key Ideas and Details (a)** What objects are arranged on and around the deli's counter? **(b)** What title is given to the woman who "presides" over the counter? **(c) Interpret:** What do the objects, the title, and the verb "presides" tell you about the woman?

2. **Key Ideas and Details (a)** What does the old man read to the woman "like poetry"? **(b) Compare:** How is this object like the poem itself?

3. **Key Ideas and Details** Is this *ars poetica* solely about the art of poetry? Explain.

4. **Integration of Knowledge and Ideas** What geographical, cultural, and emotional boundaries does the poet explore or even merge in this poem? In your response, use at least two of these Essential Question words: *diversity, innovation, transform, global, landscape. [Connecting to the Essential Question: What is the relationship between literature and place?]*

Literary Analysis

1. **Key Ideas and Details (a)** Identify two words or phrases in the poem that relate to each of the five senses—sight, smell, touch, sound, and taste. **(b)** To which sense would you say most of the **sensory details** in the poem appeal? Explain.

2. **Key Ideas and Details** Choose one word to describe the deli in this poem. Explain your choice.

3. **Craft and Structure (a)** Use a chart like the one shown to note five examples of **imagery** in the poem. **(b)** Use the details you have noted to explain the word picture each image creates in your mind.

Image that appeals to . . .				
Sight	**Smell**	**Touch**	**Sound**	**Taste**

4. **Integration of Knowledge and Ideas (a)** Identify three images in the poem that have religious overtones. **(b)** How do these images suggest a similarity between the store owner and a religious figure? **(c)** Why is the use of imagery more effective than an outright explanation of such content?

Vocabulary Acquisition and Use

Sentence Completions Use a word from the vocabulary list on page 1364 to complete each item below. Use each word only once. Explain your choices.

1. The _____ amount of food Betsy prepared would satisfy everyone.

2. The _____ aroma of cooking from the kitchen was wonderful.

3. Based on the smells alone, Maya tried to _____ the ingredients.

Writing to Sources

Informative Text A person who is in exile has been forced by circumstances to leave his or her home. The *connotative meanings* of exile suggest sadness and a longing for the land of origin. Write an **essay** in which you explore the ideas of exile and home in this poem. In your essay, answer the following questions:

• Who is exiled in this poem? From where? Why?

• Which does the deli represent—exile, home, or both?

• What does the poem suggest about language as a kind of home?

Common Core State Standards

Writing

2. Write informative texts to examine and convey complex ideas, concepts, and information clearly and accurately through the effective selection, organization, and analysis of content.

9.a. Apply grades 11–12 Reading standards to literature. [RL.11-12.4]

Language

4. Determine or clarify the meaning of unknown and multiple-meaning words and phrases based on *grades 11–12 reading and content,* choosing flexibly from a range of strategies.

POETRY AND NUMBERS: THE FIBONACCI SEQUENCE

Late in the 12th century, an Italian mathematician named Leonardo of Pisa, also known as Fibonacci (fib ə nä´chē), journeyed throughout the Mediterranean to study with the leading mathematicians of the day, especially the Persians al-Karaji and al-Khwarizmi. Fibonacci became convinced that the numeral system the Arab mathematicians were using was far better than the Roman numerals then popular in Europe. Upon his return to Italy, Fibonacci wrote *Liber Abaci*, or *Book of Calculation*, in which he explained the Hindu-Arabic numeral system he had learned from his Persian mentors. The book also included a number sequence that would come to bear Fibonacci's name.

In *Liber Abaci*, Fibonacci proposed a method of calculating the number of rabbits that might result from one set of parents and each subsequent generation in a single year. Although he did not discover this solution, it became known as the Fibonacci sequence. In this sequence, each number after the starting values of 0 and 1 is the sum of the previous two numbers:

0, 1, 1, 2, 3, 5, 8, 13, 21, 34, 55, 89, 144, 233, 377...

The Fibonacci sequence is evident in such marvels of nature as the spiral patterns of nautilus shells, pinecones, and flower petals. It also provides the basis for some traditional poetry, particularly some Sanskrit forms. In recent years, new interest in poetry based on Fibonacci numbers has arisen. In 2006, Gregory Pincus, a writer and librarian from Los Angeles, published a six-line, 20-syllable poem on his blog. He coined his work the "fib."

THE FIB

One
Small,
Precise,
Poetic,
Spiraling mixture:
Math plus poetry yields the Fib.
—*Gregory Pincus*

In Pincus's fib, the number of syllables in each line equals the sum of syllables in the preceding two lines. On his blog, Pincus invited others to write and share their fibs and soon these precise little poems were popping up all over the Internet. Several examples of Fibonacci poems appear on the next page.

◀ The Fibonacci Sequence is visible in the spirals of the nautilus shell.

While the numbers of lines and stanzas may vary from fib to fib, all are based on Fibonacci's sequence.

(Ø)

Rain
So
Thick this
Summer day
I can barely see
Ginkgo offer small umbrellas.
—*Patricia Lee Lewis*

Dig
deep
enough
and you'll find
proof of something said
that must have meant more than it seems,
must have meant something like 'Love' or 'Come back' or 'Yes, now.'
—*Athena Kildegaard*

Book
Waits
Unread
Paper sits
No words to be found
You left me alone with no Muse
—*Patricia Vogel*

Critical Reading

1. Take a Position: Some readers see similarities between fibs and haiku. Do you agree with this comparison? Explain.

Use these questions to focus a group discussion:

2. Could these writers have expressed the same ideas through another type of writing, or is the form essential to their meaning? Explain.

3. Why do you think a poet, or any artist, might choose to impose constraints, such as a mathematical sequence, on his or her work?

4. In what ways do these poems affect your view of math, poetry, or both? Explain.

Contemporary Nonfiction

The essay
is a literary device for almost everything about almost anything.

— ALDOUS HUXLEY

Defining Essays

An **essay** is a brief nonfiction work about a specific subject. The term was first used in 1580 by the French philosopher Michel de Montaigne, who published a collection of short prose pieces entitled *Essais*. The French word means "attempts" or "tries," and Montaigne used the title to suggest that his discussions were casual explorations of a subject, rather than thorough interpretations. That quality of inquisitive exploration remains a defining feature of the essay form.

Types of Essays Essays are often divided into two main categories, according to the writer's overall approach.

- **Formal essays** are serious explorations of important public topics, such as political, social, or cultural issues.

- **Informal essays,** also called **personal essays,** explore everyday topics in a conversational style. They may also employ a loose structure, circling around a topic and developing ideas in an indirect way.

Within these two broad categories, essays can be further classified according to the **author's purpose:** to inform, to persuade, to tell a story, to convey a sense of place, or to analyze an idea.

- In a **persuasive essay,** the writer tries to convince readers to accept his or her opinion or to take a course of action.

- In a **descriptive essay,** the writer uses sensory details to present a portrait of a person, a place, or an object.

- In an **expository essay,** the writer explains an issue or process.

Close Read: The Essay
These elements of essays appear in the Model Text at right.

Thesis/Central Idea: the author's main idea or essential point *Example: "Trust thyself: every heart vibrates to that iron string." (Ralph Waldo Emerson)*	**Diction and Syntax:** the types of words (diction) and sentence structures (syntax) an author favors *Example: "Reaching for an alliterative onomatope, the poet Milton chose 'melodious murmurs'..." (William Safire)*
Evidence: facts, quotations, data, personal observations, anecdotes, and other details that help to develop and support the author's thesis *Example: "She reads the Forbes report, listens to Wall Street Week, converses daily with her stockbroker..." (Amy Tan)*	**Tone:** the writer's attitude toward the topic or audience *Example: "...before closing I am impelled to mention one other point in your statement that troubled me profoundly." (Dr. Martin Luther King, Jr.)*

EXEMPLAR TEXT

Model

About the Text H. L. Mencken (1880–1956) began his career with a Baltimore newspaper at the age of eighteen and went on to become one of America's legendary journalists. He was especially celebrated for his acute ear for language and his satirical—often biting—commentaries on American cultural life. Mencken's book *The American Language* is now regarded as a classic.

"American Slang," from *The American Language* by H. L. Mencken

What chiefly lies behind [slang] is simply a kind of linguistic exuberance, an excess of word-making energy. It relates itself to the standard language a great deal as dancing relates itself to music. But there is also something else. The best slang is not only ingenious and amusing; it also embodies a kind of social criticism. It not only provides new names for a series of everyday concepts, some new and some old; it also says something about them. "Words which produce the slang effect," observes Frank K. Sechrist, "arouse associations which are incongruous or incompatible with those of customary thinking."

Everyone, including even the metaphysician in his study and the eremite[1] in his cell, has a large vocabulary of slang, but the vocabulary of the vulgar is likely to be larger than that of the cultured, and it is harder worked. Its content may be divided into two categories: (a) old words, whether used singly or in combination, that have been put to new uses, usually metaphorical, and (b) new words that have not yet been admitted to the standard vocabulary. Examples of the first type are *rubberneck,* for a gaping and prying person, and *iceberg,* for a cold woman; examples of the second are *hoosegow, flim-flam, blurb, bazoo* and *blah.* There is a constant movement of slang terms into accepted usage. *Nice,* as an adjective of all work, signifying anything satisfactory, was once in slang use only, and the purists denounced it, but today no one would question "a *nice* day," "a *nice* time," or "a *nice* hotel."…The verb-phrase *to hold up* is now perfectly good American, but so recently as 1901 the late Brander Matthews was sneering at it as slang. In the same way many other verb-phrases, e.g., *to cave in, to fill the bill* and *to fly off the handle,* once viewed askance, have gradually worked their way to a relatively high level of the standard speech. On some indeterminate tomorrow *to stick up* and *to take for a ride* may follow them.

Thesis The author presents a two-part thesis: (a) that slang is a type of linguistic play, and (b) that the best slang carries a distinct note of social criticism.

Evidence Although Mencken is himself an expert on his topic, he uses a quotation from another expert to support his point.

Diction and Syntax Mencken chooses sophisticated words and writes elegant, long sentences. However, he will modify both diction and syntax for effect. (See the short sentence in the first paragraph: "But there is also something else.")

Tone Mencken was famous for his tone, which often combines sharp humor and a sense of intellectual command and boldness.

---

1. **metaphysician ... eremite** A metaphysician is a type of philosopher; an eremite is a hermit or recluse.

Building Knowledge and Insight *Onomatopoeia*

Connecting to the Essential Question: In this essay, the author explores the connections between the sounds of certain words and their meanings. As you read, notice details that show the author's fascination with words of all kinds. Doing so will help you think about the Essential Question: **What makes American literature American?**

Close Reading Focus

Expository Essay; Diction

In an **expository essay,** a writer explains a topic or process, or discusses ideas. In this expository essay, William Safire explains the origin, meaning, and uses of *onomatopoeia*—words like *hiss* or *buzz* that sound like what they mean. Expository essays may use other modes, such as persuasion, description, or narration. However, the main emphasis is on explanation. Therefore, when reading expository works, you will find more facts than opinions, as well as definitions, data, and other informative content.

Safire takes a lighthearted approach to his topic. His **diction,** or word choice, combines scholarly and folksy elements, including idioms. **Idioms** are common expressions that have acquired figurative and connotative meanings that differ from their literal meanings:

- **Scholarly, or technical, diction:** "rhetorical bestiary"
- **Folksy, or familiar, diction:** "it had better be spelled right"
- **Idiom:** "slammed the vocabulary <u>right in the kisser</u>"

As you read, notice how Safire's mix of diction allows him to treat his subject with authority, while simultaneously amusing and surprising the reader. Consider how his uses of diction both clarify and serve as examples for the ideas he presents throughout the essay.

Preparing to Read Complex Texts To clarify the main ideas in an expository essay, take time to **paraphrase** any passages that challenge your understanding. When you paraphrase, you restate the author's ideas in your own words. As you read this essay, use a chart like the one shown to paraphrase unfamiliar phrases or whole passages, and track how doing so aids your understanding.

Vocabulary

You will encounter the words listed here in the text that follows. Copy the words into your notebook. Which of the words is a verb? How can you tell?

synonymous   speculation

derive   coinage

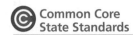

**Common Core
State Standards**

Reading Informational Text
3. Analyze a complex set of ideas or sequence of events and explain how specific ideas, individuals, or events interact and develop over the course of the text.
4. Determine the meaning of words and phrases as they are used in a text, including figurative, connotative, and technical meanings; analyze how an author uses and refines the meaning of a key term or terms over the course of a text.

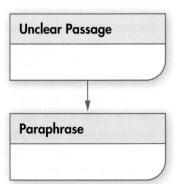

Unclear Passage

Paraphrase

WILLIAM SAFIRE *(1929–2009)*

Author of **"Onomatopoeia"**

When it comes to questions about the use—and misuse—of
the English language, few people have more answers or
observations than William Safire. A political columnist for the
New York Times until his retirement in 2005, Safire continues to
write the *New York Times Magazine*'s "On Language" column.
The column has generated ten books and made Safire the
world's most widely read author on the English language.

Safire is a graduate of the Bronx High School of Science, an
elite public school in New York City. He attended Syracuse
University but dropped out after two years. A generation later,
he delivered the commencement address at Syracuse and also
became a trustee of the university.

A Career in Writing The 1978 Pulitzer Prize winner for
Distinguished Commentary, Safire worked in public rela-
tions and television before becoming involved in politics.
He worked for Richard Nixon's presidential campaign in
1960 and again in 1968. When Nixon was elected in 1968,
Safire became the senior White House speechwriter.

In addition to his writings on language, Safire is
the author of three novels, a political dictionary,
several anthologies, and other works. In 2006, he
was awarded the Presidential Medal of Freedom
by George W. Bush.

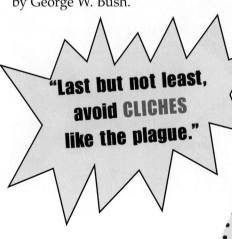

"Last but not least,
avoid CLICHES
like the plague."

Blam, 1962, Roy Lichtenstein

▲ **Critical Viewing** What meaning does the onomatopoeia *Blam* convey in this image? **ANALYZE**

ONOMATOPOEIA

William Safire

Background The vocabulary of English is the largest of any language in the world. English readily incorporates new words from a wide variety of sources, including borrowing them from other languages. William Safire, a former presidential speechwriter, describes another way in which English evolves. According to Safire, when we consider onomatopoeia—the figure of speech in which a word sounds like what it means—we discover that new words are not just based on what we experience, but on what we merely imagine.

The word *onomatopoeia* was used above, and it had better be spelled right or one usage dictator and six copy editors will get zapped. That word is based on the Greek for "word making"—the *poe* is the same as in *poetry,* "something made"—and is synonymous with *imitative* and *echoic,* denoting words that are made by people making sounds like the action to be described. (The *poe* in *onomatopoeia* has its own rule for pronunciation. Whenever a vowel follows *poe,* the *oe* combination is pronounced as a long *e: onomato-PEE-ia.* Whenever a consonant follows, as in *poetry* and *onomatopo-etic,* pronounce the long *o* of Edgar Allan's name.)

Henry Peacham, in his 1577 book on grammar and rhetoric called *The Garden of Eloquence,* first used *onomatopoeia* and defined it as "when we invent, devise, fayne, and make a name intimating the sound of that it signifieth, as *hurlyburly,* for an uprore and tumultuous stirre." He also gave *flibergib* to "a gossip," from which we derive *flibbertigibbet,* and the long-lost *clapperclaw* and *kickle-kackle.*

Since Willard Espy borrowed the title of Peacham's work for his rhetorical bestiary in 1983, the author went beyond the usual examples of *buzz, hiss, bobwhite* and *babble.* He pointed out that one speculation about the origin of language was the *bow-wow theory,* holding that words originated in imitation of natural sounds of animals and thunder. (Proponents of the *pooh-pooh theory* argued that interjections like *ow!* and *oof!* started us all yakking toward language. Other theories—*arrgh!*—abound.)

Reaching for an alliterative onomatope, the poet Milton chose "melodious *murmurs;*" Edgar Allan Poe one-upped him with "the *tin-tinnabulation* of the bells." When carried too far, an obsession with

Vocabulary
synonymous
(si nän´ ə məs) *adj.* of the same or almost the same meaning

Vocabulary
derive (di rīv´) *v.* get or receive from a source

speculation (spek´ yə lā´ shən) *n.* a conjecture; a guess

Comprehension
What is the Greek origin of *onomatopoeia?*

Vocabulary

coinage (koi′ nij) *n.* a word or expression that has been made up or invented

words is called *onomatomania;* in the crunch (a word imitating the sound of an icebreaker breaking through ice) Gertrude Stein turned into an *onomatomaniac.*

What makes a word like *zap* of particular interest is that it imitates an imaginary noise—the sound of a paralyzing ray gun. Thus we can see another way that the human mind creates new words: imitating what can be heard only in the mind's ear. The **coinage** filled a need for an unheard sound and—*pow!*—slammed the vocabulary right in the kisser. Steadily, surely, under the watchful eye of great lexicographers and with the encouragement of columnists and writers who ache for color in verbs, the creation of Buck Rogers's creator has blasted its way into the dictionaries. The verb will live long after superpowers agree to ban ray guns; no sound thunders or crackles like an imaginary sound turned into a new word.

Took me a while to get to the point today, but that is because I did not know what the point was when I started.

"I now zap all the commercials," says the merry Ellen Goodman. "I zap to the memory of white tornadoes past. I zap headaches, arthritis, bad breath and laundry detergent. I zap diet-drink maidens and hand-lotion mavens . . . Wiping out commercials could entirely and joyfully upend the TV industry. Take the word of The Boston Zapper."

Critical Reading

Cite textual evidence to support your responses.

1. **Key Ideas and Details** **(a)** What is the *bow-wow theory* concerning the origin of language? **(b) Compare and Contrast:** Compare and contrast that theory with the *pooh-pooh theory* of language. **(c) Make a Judgment:** Do you think either of these terms is actually used by linguists? Explain.

2. **Key Ideas and Details** **(a)** What does Safire find so interesting about the word *zap*? **(b) Analyze:** Why does he believe that this word will "live long after superpowers agree to ban ray guns"?

3. **Craft and Structure** **Evaluate:** Do you think Safire's humorous style is more or less effective than a more somber explanation would be? Explain.

4. **Integration of Knowledge and Ideas** When someone celebrates language, what other aspects of a culture are they implicitly celebrating? In your response, use at least two of these Essential Question words: *resilience, invention, innovation, diversity, interpretation.* [*Connecting to the Essential Question: What makes American literature American?*]

Close Reading Activities   *Onomatopoeia*

Literary Analysis

1. **Key Ideas and Details (a)** Identify four important pieces of information Safire includes in this **expository essay. (b)** Classify each item you chose: Is it a fact, a definition, an example, or another form of information?

2. **Craft and Structure (a)** Locate two examples of scholarly **diction** Safire uses. **(b)** Locate two examples of folksy, or familiar, diction. **(c)** In what ways does this mix of diction add to the effectiveness of the essay?

3. **Craft and Structure (a)** In a chart like the one shown, list two examples of idioms Safire uses in this essay. **(b)** For each, explain its literal and acquired meanings.

Idiom	Literal Meaning	Acquired Meaning

4. **Integration of Knowledge and Ideas Paraphrase** the following passages from "Onomatopoeia" as though you are explaining their meaning to a friend: **(a)** "The coinage filled a need . . . right in the kisser"; **(b)** "The verb will live long after . . . imaginary sound turned into a new word."

5. **Integration of Knowledge and Ideas** Choose one paraphrase you wrote and explain how it might help readers understand an idea that was previously unclear.

Vocabulary Acquisition and Use

Sentence Completions Select the word from the list on page 1376 that best completes each sentence. Explain the context clues that support your choice.

1. Hannah _____ great pleasure from her getaways to the mountains.

2. *Supercalifragilisticexpialidocious* is a _____ made popular by a movie.

3. On election night, there was much _____ about the voting results.

4. *Boisterous* is _____ with *rowdy,* which means "loud and unruly."

Writing to Sources

Informative Text Choose a word or phrase in English that you find interesting, odd, or funny. Research the history of the word: its first appearance in the language and changes in its meaning. In an **informative essay,** explain your research. Use a mixture of scholarly diction, familiar diction, and idiomatic expressions.

© **Common Core State Standards**

Writing
2. Write informative texts to examine and convey complex ideas, concepts, and information clearly and accurately through the effective selection, organization, and analysis of content.
7. Conduct short research projects to answer a question or solve a problem.

Language
4.a. Use context as a clue to the meaning of a word or phrase.

Building Knowledge and Insight | *Coyote v. Acme*

Connecting to the Essential Question In this humorous essay, the author uses events in a popular 1950s TV cartoon to make a point about the American legal system. As you read, notice details that mock the legal system. Doing so will help you think about the Essential Question: **How does literature shape or reflect society?**

Close Reading Focus

Parody; Satire

A **parody** is a comic piece of writing that mocks the characteristics of a literary form, a specific work, or the style of a certain writer. Through the use of exaggeration, a parody calls attention to ridiculous aspects of the original. This essay parodies legal language and argument:

> *My client, Mr. Wile E. Coyote, a resident of Arizona and contiguous states, does hereby bring suit for damages against the Acme Company . . .*

The purpose of this parody is to create **satire,** writing that ridicules the faults of individuals, groups, institutions, or humanity in general. Although satire can be funny, its purpose is not simply to make readers laugh but also to correct the shortcomings that it addresses. As you read, think about the serious point Frazier makes in this parody of a legal document and whether the form and language of satire bring out Frazier's main point effectively.

Preparing to Read Complex Texts This essay is organized using a *cause-and-effect text structure*. The lawyer for Mr. Coyote must prove that the poor design of Acme products (cause) results in injury to Mr. Coyote (effect). To **analyze cause and effect,** look for words and phrases such as *subsequently* and *resulted in* that signal those relationships. Consider how these structural elements help to clarify the comic sequences of events the essay describes and the ideas it expresses. As you read, use a chart like the one shown to outline cause and effect in this essay.

Vocabulary

The words below are important to understanding the text that follows. Copy the words into your notebook. Which word is a synonym for *forcefully*?

contiguous	systemic
incorporated	emit
vigorously	punitive

Common Core State Standards

Reading Informational Text
5. Analyze and evaluate the effectiveness of the structure an author uses in his or her exposition or argument, including whether the structure makes points clear, convincing, and engaging.
6. Determine an author's point of view or purpose in a text in which the rhetoric is particularly effective, analyzing how style and content contribute to the power, persuasiveness or beauty of the text.

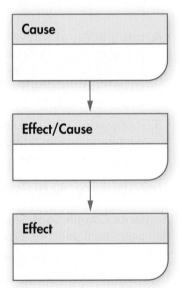

IAN FRAZIER *(b. 1951)*

Author of **"Coyote v. Acme"**

Humorist Ian Frazier was born in Cleveland, Ohio. He is a 1973 graduate of Harvard University, where he wrote for the Harvard *Lampoon,* a humor magazine. After graduating, Frazier joined the staff of *The New Yorker* magazine. He worked there for two decades as a staff writer. His work has also appeared in many other publications, including the *Atlantic,* the *Washington Post Magazine,* and *Outside* magazine.

A Comic Sense Known for both humorous essays and affectionate descriptions of rural and urban America, Frazier brings an irreverent sense of fun to much of his work. "Coyote v. Acme" is typical of his writing: a ludicrous premise packaged in serious style.

Frazier has received many honors for his writing, including the Thurber Prize for American Humor and a 1990 Spur Award for Best Nonfiction from the Western Writers of America. He also has appeared on the National Public Radio program *A Prairie Home Companion* and has acted in two movies, *Smoke* and *Blue in the Face.* His books include *Dating Your Mom* (1986), *Nobody Better, Better Than Nobody* (1987), *Family* (1994), *Coyote v. Acme* (1996), *On the Rez* (2000), *The Fish's Eye* (2002), and *Gone to New York: Adventures in the City* (2005).

"I really like pieces where you start at the beginning, and as you get farther and farther you realize this person has no idea what he's talking about."

COYOTE V. ACME

IAN FRAZIER

BEEP! BEEP!

BACKGROUND This essay is the fictional opening statement of a lawsuit by Mr. Wile E. Coyote, charging the Acme Company with the sale of defective merchandise. If these names sound familiar, you may remember watching Wile E. Coyote chase the Road Runner around the desert. The Warner Brothers cartoon "Road Runner and Coyote" was popular in the 1950s; more than half a century later, both the coyote and the elusive bird are still going strong. As you read the essay, consider what Frazier is really satirizing—the cartoon character who is his subject or the legal profession.

> **In the United States District Court,**
> **Southwestern District,**
> **Tempe, Arizona**
> **Case No. B19294,**
> **Judge Joan Kujava, Presiding**
>
> WILE E. COYOTE, Plaintiff
> —v.—
> ACME COMPANY, Defendant

Vocabulary

contiguous (kən tig´ yō̄ əs)
adj. bordering; adjacent

incorporated
(in kôr´ pə rāt´ id) *v.* united
or combined to function
legally as a business

Opening Statement of Mr. Harold Schoff, attorney for Mr. Coyote: My client, Mr. Wile E. Coyote, a resident of Arizona and contiguous states, does hereby bring suit for damages against the Acme Company, manufacturer and retail distributor of assorted merchandise, incorporated in Delaware and doing business in every state, district, and territory. Mr. Coyote seeks compensation for personal injuries, loss of business income, and mental suffering caused as a direct result of the actions and/or gross negligence of said company, under Title 15 of the United States Code, Chapter 47, section 2072, subsection (a), relating to product liability.

Mr. Coyote states that on eighty-five separate occasions he has purchased of the Acme Company (hereinafter, "Defendant"), through that company's mail-order department, certain products which did cause him bodily injury due to defects in manufacture or improper cautionary labeling. Sales slips made out to Mr. Coyote as proof of purchase are at present in the possession of the Court, marked Exhibit A. Such injuries sustained by Mr. Coyote have temporarily restricted his ability to make a living in his profession of predator. Mr. Coyote is self-employed and thus not eligible for Workmen's Compensation.[1]

Mr. Coyote states that on December 13th he received of Defendant via parcel post one Acme Rocket Sled. The intention of Mr. Coyote was to use the Rocket Sled to aid him in pursuit of his prey. Upon receipt of the Rocket Sled Mr. Coyote removed it from its wooden shipping crate and, sighting his prey in the distance, activated the ignition. As Mr. Coyote gripped the handlebars, the Rocket Sled accelerated with such sudden and precipitate force as to stretch Mr. Coyote's forelimbs to a length of fifty feet. Subsequently, the rest of Mr. Coyote's body shot forward with a violent jolt, causing severe strain to his back and neck and placing him unexpectedly astride the Rocket Sled. Disappearing over the horizon at such speed as to leave a diminishing jet trail along its path, the Rocket Sled soon brought Mr. Coyote abreast of his prey. At that moment the animal he was pursuing veered sharply to the right. Mr. Coyote vigorously attempted to follow this maneuver but was unable to, due to poorly designed steering on the Rocket Sled and a faulty or nonexistent braking system. Shortly thereafter, the unchecked progress of the Rocket Sled brought it and Mr. Coyote into collision with the side of a mesa.[2]

Paragraph One of the Report of Attending Physician (Exhibit B), prepared by Dr. Ernest Grosscup, M.D., D.O., details the multiple fractures, contusions, and tissue damage suffered by Mr. Coyote as

---

1. **Workmen's Compensation** form of disability insurance that provides income to workers who are unable to work due to injuries sustained on the job.
2. **mesa** (mā´ sə) *n.* small, high plateau with steep sides.

Vocabulary

vigorously (vig´ ər əs lē) *adv.* forcefully or powerfully

▼ Critical Viewing

Based on this single frame of a cartoon, is Mr. Coyote's claim valid? Explain. **MAKE A JUDGMENT**

Comprehension

For what three reasons does Mr. Coyote seek compensation from the Acme Company?

Literature Connection

Parodies in American Culture

There are many famous parodies in American literature, film, and music. Mark Twain's novel *A Connecticut Yankee in King Arthur's Court* parodies the chivalric romance. Stephen Crane's story "The Bride Comes to Yellow Sky" parodies the western.

Popular culture is full of parodies, as well. The films of Mel Brooks satirize absurd aspects of other movies. "Canadian Idiot," a 2006 spoof of the band Green Day's song "American Idiot," is only one of musician "Weird Al" Yankovic's many parodies. "Mockumentaries" such as *Best in Show* and *A Mighty Wind* mimic the documentaries they parody by including fake "confessionals" and pretending to capture actual events.

Connect to the Literature

Parodies are modeled on the pieces they satirize. Which conventions of legal writing does Frazier imitate?

Parody

How does this list of injuries make fun of personal injury claims?

---

a result of this collision. Repair of the injuries required a full bandage around the head (excluding the ears), a neck brace, and full or partial casts on all four legs.

Hampered by these injuries, Mr. Coyote was nevertheless obliged to support himself. With this in mind, he purchased of Defendant as an aid to mobility one pair of Acme Rocket Skates. When he attempted to use this product, however, he became involved in an accident remarkably similar to that which occurred with the Rocket Sled. Again, Defendant sold over the counter, without caveat, a product which attached powerful jet engines (in this case, two) to inadequate vehicles, with little or no provision for passenger safety. Encumbered by his heavy casts, Mr. Coyote lost control of the Rocket Skates soon after strapping them on, and collided with a roadside billboard so violently as to leave a hole in the shape of his full silhouette.

Mr. Coyote states that on occasions too numerous to list in this document he has suffered mishaps with explosives purchased of Defendant: the Acme "Little Giant" Firecracker, the Acme Self-Guided Aerial Bomb, etc. (For a full listing, see the Acme Mail Order Explosives Catalogue and attached deposition,[3] entered in evidence as Exhibit C.) Indeed, it is safe to say that not once has an explosive purchased of Defendant by Mr. Coyote performed in an expected manner. To cite just one example: At the expense of much time and personal effort, Mr. Coyote constructed around the outer rim of a butte[4] a wooden trough beginning at the top of the butte and spiraling downward around it to some few feet above a black X painted on the desert floor. The trough was designed in such a way that a spherical explosive of the type sold by Defendant would roll easily and swiftly down to the point of detonation indicated by the X. Mr. Coyote placed a generous pile of birdseed directly on the X, and then, carrying the spherical Acme Bomb (Catalogue #78–832), climbed to the top of the butte. Mr. Coyote's prey, seeing the birdseed, approached, and Mr. Coyote proceeded to light the fuse. In an instant, the fuse burned down to the stem, causing the bomb to detonate.

In addition to reducing all Mr. Coyote's careful preparations to naught, the premature detonation of Defendant's product resulted in the following disfigurements to Mr. Coyote:

1. Severe singeing of the hair on the head, neck, and muzzle.

2. Sooty discoloration.

---

3. **deposition** (dep´ ə zish´ ən) *n.* legal term for the written testimony of a witness.
4. **butte** (byoot) *n.* steep hill standing alone in a plain.

3. Fracture of the left ear at the stem, causing the ear to dangle in the aftershock with a creaking noise.

4. Full or partial combustion of whiskers producing kinking, frazzling, and ashy disintegration.

5. Radical widening of the eyes, due to brow and lid charring.

We come now to the Acme Spring-Powered Shoes. The remains of a pair of these purchased by Mr. Coyote on June 23rd are Plaintiff's Exhibit D. Selected fragments have been shipped to the metallurgical laboratories of the University of California at Santa Barbara for analysis, but to date no explanation has been found for this product's sudden and extreme malfunction. As advertised by Defendant, this product is simplicity itself: two wood-and-metal sandals, each attached to milled-steel springs of high tensile strength and compressed in a tightly coiled position by a cocking device with a lanyard release. Mr. Coyote believed that this product would enable him to pounce upon his prey in the initial moments of the chase, when swift reflexes are at a premium.

To increase the shoes' thrusting still further, Mr. Coyote affixed them by their bottoms to the side of a large boulder. Adjacent to the boulder was a path which Mr. Coyote's prey was known to frequent. Mr. Coyote put his hind feet in the wood-and-metal sandals and crouched in readiness, his right forepaw holding firmly to the lanyard release. Within a short time Mr. Coyote's prey did indeed appear on the path coming toward him. Unsuspecting, the prey stopped near Mr. Coyote, well within range of the springs at full extension. Mr. Coyote gauged the distance with care and proceeded to pull the lanyard release.

▲ **Critical Viewing**
Describe Mr. Coyote's injuries as shown in this cartoon frame. Use an approach similar to Frazier's. **DESCRIBE**

 Spiral Review
Diction Describe the diction used in this essay.

Comprehension
Have Acme products performed well for Mr. Coyote? Explain.

Analyzing Cause and Effect

Trace the sequence of cause and effect that results from Mr. Coyote's use of the thrusting shoes.

Vocabulary

systemic (sis tem´ ik) *adj.* of or affecting the entire bodily system

emit (i mit´) *v.* send out or give forth

▼ Critical Viewing

Based on this cartoon frame, how worried does Road Runner seem about being Mr. Coyote's "prey"?
DEDUCE

At this point, Defendant's product should have thrust Mr. Coyote forward and away from the boulder. Instead, for reasons yet unknown, the Acme Spring-Powered Shoes thrust the boulder away from Mr. Coyote. As the intended prey looked on unharmed, Mr. Coyote hung suspended in air. Then the twin springs recoiled, bringing Mr. Coyote to a violent feet-first collision with the boulder, the full weight of his head and forequarters falling upon his lower extremities.

The force of this impact then caused the springs to rebound, whereupon Mr. Coyote was thrust skyward. A second recoil and collision followed. The boulder, meanwhile, which was roughly ovoid in shape, had begun to bounce down a hillside, the coiling and recoiling of the springs adding to its velocity. At each bounce, Mr. Coyote came into contact with the boulder, or the boulder came into contact with Mr. Coyote, or both came into contact with the ground. As the grade was a long one, this process continued for some time.

The sequence of collisions resulted in systemic physical damage to Mr. Coyote, viz., flattening of the cranium, sideways displacement of the tongue, reduction of length of legs and upper body, and compression of vertebrae from base of tail to head. Repetition of blows along a vertical axis produced a series of regular horizontal folds in Mr. Coyote's body tissues—a rare and painful condition which caused Mr. Coyote to expand upward and contract downward alternately as he walked, and to emit an off-key accordion-like wheezing with every step. The distracting and embarrassing nature of this symptom has been a major impediment to Mr. Coyote's pursuit of a normal social life.

As the Court is no doubt aware, Defendant has a virtual monopoly of manufacture and sale of goods required by Mr. Coyote's work. It is our contention that Defendant has used its market advantage to the detriment of the consumer of such specialized products as itching powder, giant kites, Burmese tiger traps, anvils, and two-hundred-foot-long rubber bands. Much as he has come to mistrust Defendant's products, Mr. Coyote has no other domestic source of supply to which to turn. One can only wonder what our trading partners in Western Europe and Japan would make of such a situation, where a giant company is allowed to victimize the consumer in the most reckless and wrongful manner over and over again.

Mr. Coyote respectfully requests that the Court regard these larger economic implications and assess punitive damages in the amount of seventeen million dollars. In addition, Mr. Coyote seeks actual damages (missed meals, medical expenses, days lost from professional occupation) of one million dollars; general damages (mental suffering, injury to reputation) of twenty million dollars; and attorney's fees of seven hundred and fifty thousand dollars. Total damages: thirty-eight million seven hundred and fifty thousand dollars. By awarding Mr. Coyote the full amount, this Court will censure Defendant, its directors, officers, shareholders, successors, and assigns, in the only language they understand, and reaffirm the right of the individual predator to equal protection under the law.

Vocabulary

punitive (pyoo′ nə tiv)
adj. punishing or having to do with punishment

Critical Reading

Cite textual evidence to support your responses.

1. **Key Ideas and Details (a)** What happens to Wile E. Coyote's forelimbs when he uses the Rocket Sled? **(b) Support:** What details in this essay suggest that Wile E. Coyote is a cartoon character?

2. **Key Ideas and Details (a)** How often does Wile E. Coyote buy products from the Acme Company? **(b) Support:** Find evidence to explain why he maintains this relationship with Acme, despite the outcomes he has faced with their products.

3. **Key Ideas and Details (a)** What action is Wile E. Coyote seeking from the court? **(b) Make a Judgment:** If you were a member of the jury in this case, what would your verdict be? Explain.

4. **Integration of Knowledge and Ideas** Based on this essay, do you think humorous exaggeration is an effective way to make a serious point? Why or why not? In your response, use at least three of these Essential Question words: *communication, evaluation, perception, transformation, understanding. [Connecting to the Essential Question: How does literature shape or reflect society?]*

Close Reading Activities | *Coyote v. Acme*

Literary Analysis

1. **Key Ideas and Details (a)** Summarize the first paragraph of the attorney's opening statement. **(b)** What circumstances caused Wile E. Coyote to sue the Acme Company? **(c)** What words or phrases establish this **cause-and-effect** relationship?

2. **Key Ideas and Details (a)** What specific products caused Mr. Coyote's injuries? **(b)** According to the attorney, how do these injuries affect Mr. Coyote's health and livelihood?

3. **Key Ideas and Details (a)** According to the attorney, what effect will a judgment in favor of his client have on the defendant? **(b)** What larger effect does he believe it will it have on society?

4. **Key Ideas and Details (a)** In "Coyote v. Acme" what type of text does Frazier **parody? (b)** What specific characteristics of the original form's language and types of reasoning does the essay exaggerate?

5. **Key Ideas and Details** How does the topic of this parody—a lawsuit brought by a cartoon character—in and of itself mock the original?

6. **Craft and Structure** Using a graphic organizer like the one shown, list three examples of exaggeration in the essay.

7. **Craft and Structure** In what way is this parody also an example of **satire**—what serious point does Frazier convey through his use of humor?

8. **Key Ideas and Details (a)** Who is the defendant and who is the plaintiff described in this essay? **(b)** Why do you think Frazier chose to parody the opening statement for the plaintiff rather than for the defense?

9. **Integration of Knowledge and Ideas** Americans have been criticized for being excessively "litigious," which means bringing many frivolous or unfounded lawsuits. Based on "Coyote v. Acme," do you think Frazier would agree with that assessment? Explain.

10. **Integration of Knowledge and Ideas (a)** Based on "Coyote v. Acme," what values do you think Frazier considers important? **(b)** What type of society would he support? Defend your answer with details from the text.

**Common Core
State Standards**

Writing
1. Write arguments to support claims in an analysis of substantive topics or texts, using valid reasoning and relevant and sufficient evidence. *(p. 1391)*

1.a. Introduce precise, knowledgeable claim(s), establish the significance of the claim(s), distinguish the claim(s) from alternate or opposing claims, and create an organization that logically sequences claim(s), counterclaims, reasons, and evidence. *(p. 1391)*

1.c. Use phrases to link the major sections of the text, create cohesion, and clarify the relationships between claim(s) and reasons, between reasons and evidence, and between claim(s) and counterclaims. *(p. 1391)*

Language
4.b. Identify and correctly use patterns of word changes that indicate different meanings or parts of speech. *(p. 1391)*

Vocabulary Acquisition and Use

Word Analysis: Latin Root -corpus-

The word *incorporated* includes the Latin root corpus, which means "body." A company that is incorporated is "granted, as a body, certain of the legal powers, rights, privileges, and liabilities of an individual." The root -*corpus*- is often featured in scientific and medical terms. Combine this infor- mation about the root -*corpus*- with context clues to choose the best word to complete each sen- tence below.

corpuscles   corpulent   incorporeal

1. The ____ man began an exercise program to help him lose weight.

2. We learned about the two types of ____ in human blood.

3. In the movie, the woman stared in shock as an ____ figure appeared before her eyes.

Vocabulary: Definitions

Review the vocabulary list on page 1382. Then, choose the definition from the right column that best fits the word in the left column. Explain your choices.

1. systemic   a. share a common border
2. incorporated   b. inflicting punishment
3. punitive   c. spread throughout the body
4. contiguous   d. performed with great power
5. emit   e. formed into a legal business
6. vigorously   f. give off, discharge

Writing to Sources

Argument In his satirical essay "Coyote v. Acme," Frazier parodies aspects of the legal system. Working in groups as teams of attorneys defending the Acme Company, develop a **response to the arguments** presented by the plaintiff's lawyer in "Coyote v. Acme."

Prewriting Work together to develop effective responses to the main arguments presented in the essay. Use cluster diagrams like the one shown to organize your thoughts.

Drafting As you draft, use legal language and present your arguments logically and persuasively. Clearly establish cause-and-effect relationships and refute those presented by the plaintiff. Your arguments should appeal primarily to logic, but you can also work in some emotional appeals.

Main Argument
The plaintiff did not use the Acme Rocket Sled properly.

Did not properly follow assembly instructions

Revising Review your open- ing statement to make sure that you have clearly answered each of the plaintiff's main arguments. Clarify cause and effect by adding transitional phrases, such as "resulted in" or "due to."

Building Knowledge and Insight

Connecting to the Essential Question In this essay, the writer reflects on the tragic events of September 11, 2001, when the United States suffered terrorist attacks on its own soil. As you read, consider how writings about such public trauma affect individuals and communities. Doing so will help you think about the Essential Question: **How does literature shape or reflect society?**

Close Reading Focus

Comparison-and-Contrast Essay

In a **comparison-and-contrast** essay, a writer analyzes similarities and differences between two or more people, topics, or events. Effective comparison-and-contrast essays have the following qualities:

- The discussion is not arbitrary; the two topics genuinely shed light on each other.
- The discussion is balanced; the topics are of equal importance.
- The essay follows an effective organizational structure; the author may alternate between the two topics in a point-by-point organization, or consider each topic as a whole in a block organization.

In this essay, the author compares perceptions of America in the days just after the events of September 11, 2001 and again one year later. As you read, use a chart like the one shown to note the similarities and differences Quindlen discusses. Then, consider whether the comparison-and-contrast structure adds to the essay's clarity and power.

Preparing to Read Complex Texts Many documents that become primary sources begin as private communications in which the writer shares his or her perceptions of historical events. When you read literature about those same events, it can be useful to **relate the literary work to primary sources.** For example, eyewitness accounts of an event may offer useful insights into a literary work about the same topic. As you read, consider how primary source documents, such as those on pages 1401 and 1403, add to your understanding of the ideas Quindlen presents in her essay.

Vocabulary

The words below are important to understanding the text that follows. Copy the words into your notebook and note which words are nouns.

mundane   revelations

induce   prosperity

savagery

Common Core State Standards

Reading Informational Text
3. Analyze a complex set of ideas or sequence of events and explain how specific individuals, ideas, or events interact and develop over the course of the text.
5. Analyze and evaluate the effectiveness of the structure an author uses in his or her exposition or argument, including whether the structure makes points clear, convincing, and engaging.

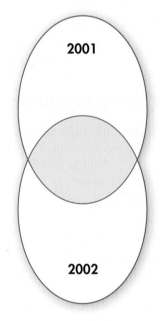

Anna Quindlen (b. 1953)

Author of "One Day, Now Broken in Two"

"I show up. I listen. I try to laugh."

Young Reporter As a junior at Barnard College, Anna Quindlen already had a passion for words and an interest in journalism. When her writing professor walked into class with a stack of manila envelopes and encouraged his students to submit their stories for publication, Quindlen did just that. The piece she sent was published soon after in *Seventeen* magazine. This first step launched Quindlen on a successful career as a reporter, columnist, and novelist.

Before she finished college, Quindlen started working part time at the *New York Post*. She took a full-time position at the paper after graduation, and within a few years landed a job at *The New York Times*. In 1986, the *Times* asked Quindlen to write a weekly column.

Life in the 30s Quindlen's column, "Life in the '30s," ran for more than two years. Quindlen's discussions of politics and global issues showed a deep level of insight, but what most attracted critics (and her growing fan base) was her ability to discuss these topics with a personal touch. Her next *Times* column, "Public and Private," won the Pulitzer Prize for Commentary in 1992.

Life as a Novelist In 1995, Quindlen left journalism to devote her time to writing fiction. She went on to publish four bestselling novels: *Object Lessons*, *Black and Blue*, *One True Thing*, and *Blessings*. Quindlen's fiction often centers on the dynamics of family relationships, a subject she finds especially compelling.

Today, Quindlen is again an active journalist. She currently writes a column for *Newsweek* magazine entitled "The Last Word" in which she expresses opinions in her distinctive, personal style. "One Day, Now Broken in Two," appeared in *Newsweek* in 2002.

ONE DAY, NOW BROKEN IN TWO

Anna Quindlen

▲ **Critical Viewing**
In what ways do the two scenes within this image echo Quindlen's ideas in this essay? **ANALYZE**

BACKGROUND This essay was published in *Newsweek* magazine one year after the September 11, 2001, terrorist attacks on the World Trade Center in New York City and the Pentagon building in Washington, D.C. Quindlen's column was part of a commemorative edition of the magazine entitled *America: A Year After.*

Vocabulary
mundane (mun dān´) *adj.* commonplace, everyday

September 11 is my eldest child's birthday. When he drove cross-country this spring and got pulled over for pushing the pedal on a couple of stretches of monotonous highway, two cops in two different states said more or less the same thing as they looked down at his license: aw, man, you were really born on 9-11? Maybe it was coincidence, but in both cases he got a warning instead of a ticket.

Who are we now? A people who manage to get by with the help of the everyday, the ordinary, the mundane, the old familiar life muting the terror of the new reality. The day approaching will always be bifurcated[1] for me: part September 11, the anniversary of one of the happiest days of my life, and part 9-11, the day America's mind reeled, its spine stiffened, and its heart broke.

That is how the country is now, split in two. The American people used their own simple routines to muffle the horror they felt looking at that indelible loop of tape—the plane, the flames, the plane, the fire, the falling bodies, the falling buildings. Amid the fear and the shock there were babies to be fed, dogs to be walked, jobs to be done.

---

1. bifurcated (bi´ fər kā təd) *adj.* divided into two parts.

After the first months almost no one bought gas masks anymore; fewer people than expected in New York City asked for the counseling that had been provided as part of the official response. Slowly the planes filled up again. A kind of self-hypnosis prevailed, and these were the words used to induce the happy trance: life goes on.

Who are we now? We are better people than we were before. That's what the optimists say, soothed by the vision of those standing in line to give blood and money and time at the outset, vowing to stop and smell the flowers as the weeks ticked by. We are people living in a world of unimaginable cruelty and savagery. So say the pessimists. The realists insist that both are right, and, as always, they are correct.

We are people whose powers of imagination have been challenged by the revelations of the careful planning, the hidden leaders, the machinations[2] from within a country of rubble and caves and desperate want, the willingness to slam headlong into one great technological achievement while piloting another as a way of despising modernity. Why do they hate us, some asked afterward, and many Americans were outraged at the question, confusing the search for motivation with mitigation.[3] But quietly, as routine returned, a new routine based on a new bedrock of loss of innocence and loss of life, a new question crept almost undetected into the national psyche: did we like ourselves? Had we become a people who confused prosperity with probity,[4] whose culture had become personified by oversize sneakers and KFC? Our own individual transformations made each of us wonder what our legacy would be if we left the world on a sunny September day with a "to do" list floating down eighty stories to the street below.

So we looked at our lives a little harder, called our friends a little more often, hugged our kids a little tighter. And then we complained about the long lines at the airport and obsessed about the stock market in lieu of soul-searching. Time passed. The blade dulled. The edges softened. Except, of course, for those who lived through birthdays, anniversaries, holidays, without someone lost in the cloud of silvery dust, those families the living embodiment of what the whole

▲ (left) Firefighters mourn victims of the World Trade Center attack; (center) an impromptu memorial; (right) a firefighter at Ground Zero

Vocabulary

induce (in do͞os´) v. cause; bring on

savagery (sav´ ij rē) n. the condition of being savage or brutal

revelations (rev´ ə lā´ shəns) n. things revealed or made known

prosperity (präs per´ ə tē) n. the condition of being prosperous, wealthy

Comprehension

In what way will the date of September 11 always be "bifurcated" for Quindlen?

---

2. **machinations** (mak´ ə nā´ shənz) n. secret schemes.
3. **mitigation** (mit´ ə gā´ shən) n. relief; moderation; lessening of severity.
4. **probity** (prō´ bə tē) n. integrity; moral uprightness.

One Day, Now Broken in Two **1395**

nation had first felt and then learned not to feel.

We are people of two minds now, the one that looks forward and the one that unwillingly and unexpectedly flashes back. Flying over lower Manhattan, the passengers reflexively lean toward the skyline below, looking for ghost buildings. "Is everything back to normal?" someone asked me in another country not long ago, and I said yes. And no. The closest I could come to describing what I felt was to describe a bowl I had broken in two and beautifully mended. It holds everything it once did; the crack is scarcely visible. But I always know it's there. My eye worries it without even meaning to.

On September 10 of last year my daughter and I went to the funeral of a neighbor we both loved greatly. We rushed home so I could go to the hospital, where my closest friend had just had serious surgery. Someone else took the cat to the vet after we discovered that he was poisoned and was near death. That night, as my daughter got ready for bed, I said to her, without the slightest hint of hyperbole,[5] "Don't worry, honey. We'll never again have a day as bad as this one."

Who are we now? We are people who know that we never understood what "bad day" meant until that morning that cracked our world cleanly in two, that day that made two days, September 11 and 9-11. The mundane and the monstrous. "Tell me how do you live brokenhearted?" Bruce Springsteen sings on his new album about the aftermath. September 11 is my boy's birthday; 9-11 is something else. That is the way we have to live, or we cannot really go on living at all.

▲ The "Tribute in Light" is an annual remembrance of the 9/11 attacks.

---

5. hyperbole (hī pʉr´ bə lē) *n.* exaggeration.

Critical Reading

Cite textual evidence to support your responses.

1. **Key Ideas and Details (a)** According to Quindlen, what is the optimists' view of who Americans have become as a result of 9/11? **(b) Compare and Contrast:** What is the pessimists' answer to the same question? **(c) Analyze:** In Quindlen's opinion, which view is correct? Explain.

2. **Key Ideas and Details (a)** According to Quindlen, what two questions have Americans asked themselves as a result of 9/11? **(b) Interpret:** Why does she believe it is a mistake to be outraged by the first question?

3. **Integration of Knowledge and Ideas** In the wake of a traumatic event like 9-11, is literature important? Explain. In your response, use at least two of these Essential Question words: *community, insight, perspective, profound.* *[Connecting to the Essential Question: How does literature shape or reflect society?]*

Close Reading Activities

One Day, Now Broken in Two

Literary Analysis

1. **Craft and Structure (a)** What two perspectives or concepts does Quindlen explore in this **comparison-and-contrast essay? (b)** Does Quindlen's use of comparison-and-contrast text structure genuinely illuminate each perspective? Explain.

2. **Craft and Structure (a)** To what object does Quindlen compare life in post 9/11 America? **(b)** In that context, does her use of the word *worries* have more than one meaning? Explain.

3. **Craft and Structure (a)** Is the phrase Quindlen uses in her final paragraph—"the mundane and the monstrous"—a useful summary of the comparison and contrast she describes in the essay? Explain. **(b)** Why do you think she leaves that phrase as its own sentence fragment?

4. **Integration of Knowledge and Ideas Relate primary sources to a literary work** by listing details from 9/11 primary source documents that offer insight into the outpouring of grief and solicitude that Quindlen refers to in her essay. Read the two primary source articles on pages 1401–1405. Then, use a chart like the one shown to record your observations.

One Day...	Urban Renewal	Playing for the Fighting Sixty-Ninth

Vocabulary Acquisition and Use

Use New Words For each item below, write a sentence in which you use the word or word pair correctly.

   1. mundane   **2.** induce / savagery   **3.** revelation / prosperity

Writing to Sources

Explanatory Text Write a **letter** to Anna Quindlen in which you share your thoughts about her essay. Add to the discussion by answering the following questions:

• What is the situation now as Americans look back to 2001 and 2002?

• How might we answer the question "Is everything back to normal?"

As you draft, maintain a formal, objective, and respectful tone in keeping with your audience and purpose.

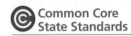

Common Core State Standards

Writing

2. Write informative texts to examine and convey complex ideas, concepts, and information clearly and accurately through the effective selection, organization, and analysis of content.

2.e. Establish and maintain a formal style and objective tone while attending to the norms and conventions of the discipline in which they are writing.

Language

4. Determine or clarify the meaning of unknown and multiple-meaning words and phrases based on *grades 11–12 reading and content,* choosing flexibly from a range of strategies.

Primary Sources

Oral History Transcript
Urban Renewal

E-mail
Playing for the Fighting Sixty-Ninth

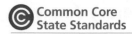
Common Core State Standards

Reading Informational Text
1. Cite strong and thorough textual evidence to support analysis of what the text says explicitly as well as inferences drawn from the text, including determining where the text leaves matters uncertain.

About the Text Forms

An **oral history** is a spoken account of an event by an eyewitness. Oral histories are usually unrehearsed and combine facts with impressions and memories. It was only in the 1900s—with the development of audio recording technologies—that oral histories were first collected and treated as historical records.

An **e-mail** (short for "electronic mail") is a typed message sent through a computer network. E-mails are delivered and received almost instantaneously and can be sent to multiple recipients at once. Because of these two qualities, e-mails can be powerful historical records of dramatic events.

Preparing to Read Complex Texts

Most Americans are aware of the terrorist attacks that took place in New York City and Washington, D.C., on September 11, 2001. Issues that arose as a result of the attacks are still in the news. These texts express the responses of two ordinary people who witnessed some of the events of that day and its aftermath. Their observations suggest, but do not always explicitly state, larger meanings. To gain a deeper understanding, **apply your background knowledge to make inferences and draw conclusions,** interpreting stated details to derive unstated meanings.

- First, take note of incidental details. Consider why the writer or speaker included these details.

- Next, ask yourself what you already know that relates to each detail.

- Finally, apply your background knowledge to each detail to make inferences about the speakers, their connections to larger events, and the extent to which their feelings and experiences represent those of other people across the city, country, and world.

As you read these primary source documents, consider what they illuminate about these dramatic events in America's recent history.

How does **literature** shape or reflect *society?*

The events described in these documents took place in New York City in the days that followed September 11, 2001. These accounts describe a new and different world. As you read, notice details that tell how both the physical and emotional terrain of New York City changed. Notice, too, how these changes trigger deep feelings in the storytellers.

Note-Taking Guide

Primary source documents are a rich source of information for researchers. As you read these documents, use a note-taking guide like the one shown to organize relevant and accurate information.

1 Type of Document
  ☐ Newspaper ☐ Transcript ☐ Telegram ☐ Advertisement
  ☐ Press Release ☐ Journal Entry ☐ E-mail ☐ Editorial

2 Date(s) of Document _____

3 Writer or Speaker _____

4 Note important details in the text. Then, identify any related background knowledge you already have.

  a Important Details _____
  _____

  b Related Background Knowledge _____
  _____

◄ •••••••••••••••••••••••••••••••••• **Using Background Knowledge to Make Inferences and Draw Conclusions** For each detail, think about related information you might have gathered from TV reports, newspaper articles, or conversations.

5 What broad conclusions can you draw about the speaker, his experiences, or the larger historical event?
  _____
  _____
  _____
  _____

This guide was adapted from the **U.S. National Archives** document analysis worksheet.

Vocabulary

memorials (mə môr´ ē əlz) *n.* objects displayed in memory of a person or event (p. 1401)

homages (äm´ ij əz) *n.* acts showing honor and reverence (p. 1402)

intently (in tent´ lē) *adv.* in a focused, purposeful manner (p. 1402)

fatigues (fə tēgz´) *n.* sturdy clothing worn by soldiers (p. 1403)

intonation (in´ tō nā´ shən) *n.* the quality of playing musical notes in or out of tune (p. 1404)

regiment (rej´ ə mənt) *n.* a military unit (p. 1404)

casualties (kazh´ ool tēz) *n.* members of the armed forces who die in combat (p. 1405)

cadence (kād´ ns) *n.* series of notes or chords near the end of a musical work (p. 1405)

THE STORY BEHIND THE DOCUMENTS

Sean Ramsay

William Harvey

On the morning of September 11, 2001, nineteen members of the extremist group al-Qaeda, based in Afghanistan, boarded and hijacked four American jetliners. They flew two of the planes into the north and south towers of the World Trade Center in New York City; another struck the Pentagon, the U.S. Department of Defense headquarters in Washington, D.C. The fourth crashed in the Pennsylvania countryside after its passengers mounted a defense against the terrorists.

By 10:30 A.M., both Trade Center towers had collapsed, and Americans began their journey through shock, disbelief, horror, anger, and grief. While millions of people sat stunned before TV sets, thousands more sprang into action at the attack sites. In New York City, fire-fighters, police officers, soldiers, doctors, nurses, emergency medical technicians, and counselors worked tirelessly to rescue victims and treat the injured. College students handed out water and food to the exhausted workers. People collected and delivered boxes of supplies to work stations. Once rescue efforts ceased, the emergency crews, along with scores of skilled volunteers began the grueling work of clearing the smoldering rubble of "Ground Zero," the 16 acres on which the 110-story towers had stood. Behind the scenes, volunteers such as **William Harvey** continued to offer what they could, from massages to music, to soothe the weary bodies and souls of those who labored. William, a freshman at Juilliard Conservatory of Music, offered his musical gifts, and e-mailed home about his experiences. E-mails flew across the country, delivering to distant friends and relatives millions of first-hand accounts of events both horrifying and poignant.

Meanwhile, impromptu memorials in honor of lost loved ones sprang up across the city. These were outward, collective expressions of profound grief. Downtown parks such as Union Square and Washington Square became oceans of flowers, letters, photos, candles, and other mementos. **Sean Ramsay,** a Brooklyn resident and museum exhibit designer, witnessed a remarkable scene at one of these memorials, which he recounts in his oral history.

By now, many of the questions about 9/11 have been answered. We know, for example, that close to 3,000 people from thirteen countries died in the attacks, that more than 400 of these victims were fire-fighters and police officers, and that forty percent of the victims remain either unfound or unidentified. These answers and numbers provide little consolation, though. More comforting are the stories people continue to tell and remember—stories of quiet heroism, tender gestures, and intangible gifts.

URBAN RENEWAL

Sean Ramsay

This story was first told at a storytelling "slam" in New York City, shortly after September 11, 2001. The storyteller, Sean Ramsay, won the contest, and was invited to appear on the public radio show Studio 360. *Following is a transcript of the version of the story he told on the November 3, 2001 episode of that show.*

▼ In the days after the attack, people expressed their grief and sympathy in makeshift memorials.

Sean Ramsay: So, it had been ten days since the tragedy had happened and again I found myself walking towards the promenade on Brooklyn Heights. The Promenade is a walkway on the western edge of Brooklyn that has these sweeping views of the financial district and the Brooklyn Bridge. That is where I had watched events unfold on September 11th. This morning I had gotten there early, and there were a few people sitting on the benches, looking at the skyline, and I was surprised to see that the Promenade was covered with memorials. I had seen on television that there were large displays in Washington Square Park and Union Square, but I guess I just didn't expect to see them here. So, I walked along the walkway and there were these forests of half-melted candles and objects strewn about the ground; there was a plastic child's fireman's helmet with the word "Bravest" written across the front; there were flags strewn up along the railing and there was a small framed quote on the ground by Martin Luther King decrying violence; there were flowers, a fresh vase of white roses, and all sorts of photographs and pictures and children's drawings of the Twin Towers themselves. And as I walked along I noticed there were signs posted along the railing as well, and these signs came in two varieties: one was the quick posters that were obviously put together in the days right after the tragedy—they had a photograph of the person, maybe the first one that could be found, and a quick description of their physical characteristics and

Vocabulary

memorials (mə môr´ ē əlz) *n.* objects displayed in memory of a person or event

Comprehension

What does Ramsay notice on the Promenade?

▲ People posted photos and pleas for the safe return of loved ones.

Vocabulary

homages (äm´ ij əz) *n.* acts showing honor and reverence

a phone number. And there were other signs that you saw that were obviously hung up several days later, and they were more like homages. They would have three or four photographs of the loved one that had been lost, with family members or on vacation at the beach, and they were accompanied by messages like, "Katie always had such a great smile. We miss her so." And, "Davey, now you will have to look after us."

I walked along reading these messages and looking at these photographs and I felt an immense sense of loss. You could feel the vacuum of the towers across the water, there on the edge [pause. speaker's voice breaks]. I felt connected to these faces and to these families in a way I hadn't through all the news coverage and all the intellectualizing and all the discussions of war and revenge and vengeance. [speaker's voice trails off]

And as I walked along having this experience, I noticed that up ahead of me there was a sanitation truck, a small garbage truck, and some sanitation workers along the walkway. They were holding these large plastic bags and then beyond them the walkway was clear, everything had been stripped, no flowers, candles, objects, everything was gone. Obviously they were cleaning things up and I became very angry. I thought, "But it's too soon! We need these things, we need to understand what has happened to us, we need to remember what happened that day." We weren't finished grieving yet, and I wasn't finished grieving yet. And I thought I should say something. I mean I didn't know what to do, I thought that it just . . . it wasn't right that this was happening. I walked over to them not knowing what I would say, I mean I knew these were just people doing their job, but I had to say something . . . as I got close, I realized that they weren't taking the things down.

As I watched, they were taking the plastic bags and one by one they were taking out the photographs and the letters and the signs and they were carefully repairing the torn edges with cellophane tape and attaching them to the railing. Then I watched as they took out the candles and made small groupings. They put toy firetrucks on the ground; they put down the framed photographs; and they hung up the flowers upside down so that they would last longer. And as I watched this I realized that it had rained heavily the night before. Apparently what had happened was the sanitation department had come out and collected all these objects and stored them safely from the rain and this morning was intently and carefully replacing every single one.

Thank you.

Vocabulary

intently (in tent´ lē) *adv.* in a focused, purposeful manner

Playing for the
FIGHTING SIXTY-NINTH

William Harvey

William Harvey was a freshman at Juilliard, a New York City music conservatory, in September, 2001. After the 9/11 attacks, he e-mailed this firsthand account of his experiences to his family in Indianapolis, Indiana. He describes his encounter with members of the "Fighting Sixty-Ninth," the 69th Infantry Regiment of the New York Army National Guard. This regiment—one of the most celebrated in all of American history—was the first military force to secure Ground Zero.

On September 16, 2001, I had probably the most incredible and moving experience of my life. Juilliard organized a quartet to go play at the Armory. The Armory is a huge military building where families of people missing from Tuesday's disaster go to wait for news of their loved ones. Entering the building was very difficult emotionally because the entire building (the size of a city block) was covered with missing posters. Thousands of posters, spread out up to eight feet above the ground, each featuring a different smiling face. I made my way into the huge central room and found my Juilliard buddies.

For two hours we sight-read quartets (with only three people!), and I don't think I will soon forget the grief counselor from the Connecticut State Police who listened the entire time, or the woman who listened only to "Memory" from *Cats*, crying the whole time. At 7:00 P.M., the other two players had to leave; they had been playing at the Armory since 1:00 P.M. and simply couldn't play anymore. I volunteered to stay and play solo, since I had just got there.

I soon realized that the evening had just begun for me: a man in fatigues who introduced himself as Sergeant Major asked me if I'd mind playing for his soldiers as they came back from digging through the rubble at Ground Zero. Masseuses had volunteered to give his men massages, he said, and he didn't think anything would be more soothing than getting a massage and listening to violin music at the same time. So at 9:00 P.M., I headed up to the second floor as the first men were arriving.

From then until 11:30 P.M., I played everything I could do from memory: Bach's *B Minor Partita*, Tchaikovsky's *Concerto*, Dvorak's *Concerto*, Paganini's *Caprices 1* and *17*, Vivaldi's *Winter* and *Spring*, "Theme from *Schindler's List*," Tchaikovsky's *Melodie*, "Meditation"

Vocabulary
fatigues (fə tēgz´) *n.* sturdy clothing worn by soldiers

Comprehension
What event did Juilliard organize?

▶ Rescue workers at Ground Zero

Vocabulary

intonation (in´ tō nā´ shən) *n.* the quality of playing musical notes in or out of tune

from *Thais,* "Amazing Grace," "My Country 'Tis of Thee," "Turkey in the Straw," "Bile Them Cabbages Down." Never have I played for a more grateful audience. Somehow it didn't matter that by the end, my intonation was shot and I had no bow control. I would have lost any competition I was playing in, but it didn't matter. The men would come up the stairs in full gear, remove their helmets, look at me, and smile.

At 11:20 P.M., I was introduced to Col. Slack, head of the regiment. After thanking me, he said to his friends, "Boy, today was the toughest day yet. I made the mistake of going back into the pit, and I'll never do that again."

Eager to hear a firsthand account, I asked, "What did you see?"

He stopped, swallowed hard, and said, "What you'd expect to see."

The Colonel stood there as I played a lengthy rendition of "Amazing Grace," which he claimed was the best he'd ever heard. By this time it was 11:30 P.M., and I didn't think I could play anymore. I asked Sergeant Major if it would be appropriate if I played the National Anthem. He shouted above the chaos of the milling soldiers to call them to attention, and I played the National Anthem as the 300 men of the 69th Regiment saluted an invisible flag.

After shaking a few hands and packing up, I was prepared to leave when one of the privates accosted me and told me the Colonel wanted to see me again. He took me down to the War Room, but we couldn't find the Colonel, so he gave me a tour of the War Room. It turns out that the division I played for is the Famous Fighting Sixty-Ninth, the most decorated regiment in the U.S. Army. He pointed out a letter from Abraham Lincoln offering his condolences after the

Vocabulary

regiment (rej´ ə mənt) *n.* a military unit

Battle of Antietam . . . the 69th suffered the most casualties of any regiment at that historic battle.

Finally, we located the Colonel. After thanking me again, he presented me with the coin of the regiment. "We only give these to someone who's done something special for the 69th," he informed me. He called over the division's historian to tell me the significance of all the symbols on the coin.

As I rode the taxi back to Juilliard—free, of course, since taxi service is free in New York right now—I was numb. Not only was this evening the proudest I've ever felt to be an American, it was my most meaningful as a musician and a person as well.

At Juilliard, kids can be critical of each other and competitive. Teachers expect, and in many cases get, technical perfection. But this wasn't about that. The soldiers didn't care that I had so many memory slips I lost count. They didn't care that when I forgot how the second movement of the Tchaikovsky went, I had to come up with my own insipid improvisation until I somehow (and I still don't know how) got to a cadence. I've never seen a more appreciative audience, and I've never understood so fully what it means to communicate music to other people.

And how did it change me as a person? Let's just say that, next time I want to get into a petty argument about whether Richter or Horowitz was better, I'll remember that when I asked the Colonel to describe the pit formed by the tumbling of the Towers, he couldn't. Words only go so far, and even music can only go a little further from there.

Vocabulary

casualties (kazh´ ō̅o̅l tēz) *n.* members of the armed forces who die in combat

cadence (kād´ ns) *n.* series of notes or chords near the end of a musical work.

Critical Reading

1. **Key Ideas and Details (a) Identify:** What unusual text feature appears in the second paragraph of Ramsay's story? **(b) Analyze:** How does this feature add to your experience of reading the transcript?

2. **Key Ideas and Details (a)** Name three objects Ramsay sees on the walkway. **(b) Evaluate:** Which object has the greatest emotional impact on you? Why do you think this is so?

3. **Key Ideas and Details (a)** In the e-mail, why does Harvey say he has trouble entering the Armory? **(b) Draw Conclusions:** What does this detail tell you about the situation in New York?

4. **Key Ideas and Details (a)** In what tangible way is Harvey rewarded for his efforts? **(b) Infer:** What intangible gifts does he receive that evening?

Cite textual evidence to support your responses.

Oral History Transcript • E-mail

Comparing Primary Sources

Refer to your Note-Taking Guide to complete these questions.

1. (a) Find two details that suggest Ramsay told his story aloud.
(b) How is the language in Harvey's e-mail similar to and different from Ramsay's?

2. (a) Record the final image from each document in a chart like the one shown. Add a note about the background knowledge you bring to the image that helps you understand it. **(b)** Based on the image and on the larger historical event, draw a conclusion about the speaker's experience of events in New York City after 9/11.

	Visual Image	Background Knowledge	Conclusion
Urban Renewal			
Fighting 69th			

3. (a) In several paragraphs, explain inferences you drew from each document about the days immediately following 9/11. **(b)** In what ways is the information you derive from these documents similar and different? **(c)** Explain the reasons for these similarities and differences.

Vocabulary Acquisition and Use

Synonyms Replace each italicized word below with a synonym from the vocabulary list on page 1399. Use each word only once.

1. Tribute concerts might be *acts of respect* to great musicians.
2. Someone must *carefully* plan every detail of such an event.
3. Statues of heroes are fine *commemorations* of great achievements.

Content-Area Vocabulary Match each word on the left with a set of words on the right. Explain why the word belongs to that set.

4. fatigues   **a.** pitch, melody, tempo, dynamics
5. intonation   **b.** active duty, company, defense
6. casualties
7. regiment
8. cadence

Etymology Study The word *fatigues* comes from the Latin word *fatigare* meaning "to make weary." Use a reference source, such as an etymology dictionary, to explain how the word *fatigues* evolved from its Latin origin. Then, locate another word based on the same root and explain how its meaning is related to that of *fatigues*.

Common Core State Standards

Writing
1. Write arguments to support claims in an analysis of substantive topics or texts, using valid reasoning and relevant and sufficient evidence. *(p. 1407)*

7. Conduct sustained research projects to answer a question or solve a problem; narrow or broaden the inquiry when appropriate; synthesize multiple sources on the subject, demonstrating understanding of the subject under investigation. *(p. 1407)*
8. Gather relevant information from multiple authoritative print and digital sources. *(p. 1407)*

Language
4.c. Consult general and specialized reference materials, both print and digital, to find the etymology of a word.
5. Demonstrate understanding of word relationships.
6. Acquire and use accurately general academic and domain-specific words and phrases, sufficient for reading, writing, speaking, and listening at the college and career readiness level.

Research Task

Topic: The Value and Values of Memorials

The impromptu memorials described by Sean Ramsay and William Harvey embodied a wide range of human values. Throughout history, people have created memorials, whether local or national, spontaneous or planned, temporary or permanent. Why?

Assignment: Write a **persuasive article** that takes a stand on the value of a memorial. Conduct research that will allow you to provide an authoritative analysis of this subject. Use a variety of strategies to develop and support your opinion.

Formulate your research plan. To focus your research, pinpoint a specific type of memorial, recalling

- a battle or a war;
- a natural catastrophe or local disaster;
- a landmark event, such as a city founding;
- a heroic individual.

Formulate a meaningful research question. The answer to your research question will be your thesis, or controlling idea.

Gather sources. Use online and library searches to explore multiple sources and perspectives about existing and proposed memorials. Pay special attention to arguments *against* memorials, such as "Money could be better spent." This will help you better anticipate and refute counterarguments when drafting.

Synthesize information. Develop and support your opinion, as opposed to simply restating existing information. To do this, draw inferences from your research:

- What can you infer about people from memorials they create?
- What can you infer about people from their responses when they visit memorials?
- What can you infer about universal human values from the values exhibited or celebrated in memorials?

Organize and present your ideas. Use a variety of formats, including visual elements and rhetorical strategies, to argue for your thesis. For example, graphic organizers may be useful in compiling and presenting responses to counterarguments.

Model: Refuting Counterarguments

Counter-argument	My Response	My Support
Merely another sad reminder of violence	Reminder of the heroism needed to face violence	• Basic emotional need • Shouldn't ignore history • Prevent reoccurrence

▲ A detail of the Vietnam Veterans Memorial in Washington, D.C., designed by Maya Lin

RESEARCH TIP

Information from multiple sources may reveal discrepancies. Use asterisks or colored markers to note information from one source—such as a date, name, or cost—that is contradicted in another source.

Use a checklist like the one shown to ensure that your persuasive article is well-researched and well-argued.

Research Checklist

☐ Have I answered my main research question?

☐ Have I presented adequate support for my opinion?

☐ Have I used a variety of formats and rhetorical strategies to argue for my thesis?

☐ Have I addressed discrepancies and refuted counterarguments?

Connecting to the Essential Question The following essays by Amy Tan and Rita Dove explore the idea that the language we grow up with helps shape who we are. As you read, notice details that describe how relationships are strengthened—or weakened—through words. Doing so will help as you consider the Essential Question: **What makes American literature American?**

Close Reading Focus

Reflective Essay

An essay is a short piece of nonfiction in which a writer explores his or her view of a topic. In a **reflective essay,** the writer describes a personal experience, condition, or event and reflects on its larger meanings. For example, Rita Dove focuses on the love of reading she has had since she was a child:

> . . . *always, I have been passionate about books. . . . I loved to feel their heft in my hand . . .*

In most reflective essays, the writer makes connections between personal experience and a larger or more universal idea about life.

Comparing Literary Works These two writers address the same central idea, or **theme:** the struggle to create a true sense of identity. As you read, examine how each writer describes the role played by other people in her creation of a genuine sense of self. Determine if a true sense of identity is to be discovered among our companions, in the recesses of our own privacy, or in some combination of the two.

Preparing to Read Complex Texts Regardless of its specific organizational structure, an effective essay presents ideas in a logical order. To better appreciate this logic and to clarify the meaning of an essay, **outline** the text as you read. Use a simple numbered list like the one shown to identify the central idea of each paragraph. Then, review the outline to trace how the writer sequences two or more central ideas to build meaning. Analyze ways in which these central ideas interact and build upon one another.

Vocabulary

You will encounter the words listed here in the texts that follow. Copy the words into your notebook. Circle the word that is an antonym for *malignant*.

transcribed   daunting

benign   aspirations

ecstasy

Common Core State Standards

Reading Informational Text

1. Cite strong and thorough textual evidence to support analysis of what the text says explicitly as well as inferences drawn from the text, including determining where the text leaves matters uncertain.

2. Determine two or more central ideas of a text and analyze their development over the course of the text, including how they interact and build on one another to provide a complex analysis; provide an objective summary of the text.

5. Analyze and evaluate the effectiveness of the structure an author uses in his or her exposition or argument, including whether the structure makes points clear, convincing, and engaging.

Main Ideas
Mother Tongue
1.
2.
3.
Love of Books
1.
2.
3.

Amy Tan *(b. 1952)*

Author of **"Mother Tongue"**

As a child, Amy Tan—the daughter of Chinese immigrants—answered her mother's Chinese questions in English. Growing up in Oakland, California, Tan continued to embrace typical American values, which she assumed defined her identity.

Early Years Tan's parents both came to America in search of a more peaceful life. Her father left his home to avoid the Chinese Civil War, while her mother found passage to America on the last boat to leave Shanghai before the Communist takeover of 1949. Her parents married and settled in Northern California, where they raised Amy and her two brothers.

Moving Abroad While still in her teens, tragedy struck Tan's family. Within a year, Amy's father and oldest brother both died of brain tumors. Mrs. Tan moved her surviving children to Switzerland, where Amy finished high school.

Changing Careers After graduating from college in America, Tan began a successful business writing career. Though she prospered financially, Tan found her work unfulfilling, and sought relief by playing piano and writing fiction. After publishing several short stories, Tan found an agent, who encouraged her to write full-time.

A Rich Background A trip to China with her mother kindled in Tan an appreciation of her Chinese roots. At the time, she was leaving a successful career as a business writer to become a fiction writer. When she returned to the United States, she began *The Joy Luck Club* (1989), a novel about four Chinese American women and their mothers. The book made Tan a celebrity and was followed by more novels, including *The Kitchen God's Wife* (1991), *The Hundred Secret Senses* (1995), and *The Bonesetter's Daughter* (2001).

*"*I have a writer's memory which makes everything worse than maybe it actually was.*"*

Mother Tongue

Amy Tan

I am not a scholar of English or literature. I cannot give you much more than personal opinions on the English language and its variations in this country or others.

I am a writer. And by that definition, I am someone who has always loved language. I am fascinated by language in daily life. I spend a great deal of my time thinking about the power of language—the way it can evoke an emotion, a visual image, a complex idea, or a simple truth. Language is the tool of my trade. And I use them all—all the Englishes I grew up with.

Recently, I was made keenly aware of the different Englishes I do use. I was giving a talk to a large group of people, the same talk I had already given to half a dozen other groups. The nature of the talk was about my writing, my life, and my book, *The Joy Luck Club.* The talk was going along well enough, until I remembered one major difference that made the whole talk sound wrong. My mother was in the room. And it was perhaps the first time she had heard me give a lengthy speech, using the kind of English I have never used with her. I was saying things like, "The intersection of memory upon imagination" and "There is an aspect of my fiction that relates to thus-and-thus"—a speech filled with carefully wrought grammatical phrases, burdened, it suddenly seemed to me, with nominalized forms, past perfect tenses, conditional phrases, all the forms of standard English that I had learned in school and through books, the forms of English I did not use at home with my mother.

Just last week, I was walking down the street with my mother, and I again found myself conscious of the English I was using, the English I do use with her. We were talking about the price of new and used furniture and I heard myself saying this: "Not waste money that way." My husband was with us as well, and he didn't notice any switch in my English. And then I realized why. It's because over the twenty years we've been together I've often used the same kind of English with him, and sometimes he even uses it with me. It has become our language of intimacy, a different sort of English that relates to family talk, the language I grew up with.

So you'll have some idea of what this family talk I heard sounds like, I'll quote what my mother said during a recent conversation which I videotaped and then transcribed.

During this conversation, my mother was talking about a political gangster in Shanghai[1] who had the same last name as her family's,

---

1. **Shanghai** (shaŋˊ hĭˊ) seaport city in eastern China.

◀ **Critical Viewing**
Based on this photograph of Amy Tan and her mother, what kind of a relationship do you think they share? Explain. **INFER**

Theme
What theme do you see developing through Tan's thoughts about the use of language?

Vocabulary
transcribed (tran skrībdˊ) *v.* wrote or typed a copy

Comprehension
How does Tan's language change when she gives her speech?

Du, and how the gangster in his early years wanted to be adopted by her family, which was rich by comparison. Later, the gangster became more powerful, far richer than my mother's family, and one day showed up at my mother's wedding to pay his respects. Here's what she said in part:

"Du Yusong having business like fruit stand. Like off the street kind. He is Du like Du Zong—but not Tsung-ming Island people. The local people call putong, the river east side, he belong to that side local people. That man want to ask Du Zong father take him in like become own family. Du Zong father wasn't look down on him, but didn't take seriously, until that man big like become a mafia. Now important person, very hard to inviting him. Chinese way, come only to show respect, don't stay for dinner. Respect for making big celebration, he shows up. Mean gives lots of respect. Chinese custom. Chinese social life that way. If too important won't have to stay too long. He come to my wedding. I didn't see, I heard it. I gone to boy's side, they have YMCA[2] dinner. Chinese age I was nineteen."

You should know that my mother's expressive command of English belies how much she actually understands. She reads the *Forbes*[3] report, listens to *Wall Street Week*,[4] converses daily with her stockbroker, reads all of Shirley MacLaine's[5] books with ease—all kinds of things I can't begin to understand. Yet some of my friends tell me they understand 50 percent of what my mother says. Some say they understand 80 to 90 percent. Some say they understand none of it, as if she were speaking pure Chinese. But to me, my

2. **YMCA** Young Men's Christian Association.
3. *Forbes* magazine of business and finance.
4. *Wall Street Week* weekly television program that reports business and investment news.
5. **Shirley MacLaine's** (mək lānz´) Shirley MacLaine is an American actress who has written several books.

▼ **Critical Viewing**
What do these signs in San Francisco's Chinatown district suggest about the multiple "Englishes" spoken there?
DISTINGUISH

mother's English is perfectly clear, perfectly natural. It's my mother tongue. Her language, as I hear it, is vivid, direct, full of observation and imagery. That was the language that helped shape the way I saw things, expressed things, made sense of the world.

Lately, I've been giving more thought to the kind of English my mother speaks. Like others, I have described it to people as "broken," or "fractured" English. But I wince when I say that. It has always bothered me that I can think of no way to describe it other than "broken," as if it were damaged and needed to be fixed, as if it lacked a certain wholeness and soundness. I've heard other terms used, "limited English," for example. But they seem just as bad, as if everything is limited, including people's perceptions of the limited English speaker.

I know this for a fact, because when I was growing up, my mother's "limited" English limited my perception of her. I was ashamed of her English. I believed that her English reflected the quality of what she had to say. That is, because she expressed them imperfectly her thoughts were imperfect. And I had plenty of empirical evidence to support me: the fact that people in department stores, at banks, and at restaurants did not take her seriously, did not give her good service, pretended not to understand her, or even acted as if they did not hear her.

My mother has long realized the limitations of her English as well. When I was fifteen, she used to have me call people on the phone to pretend I was she. In this guise, I was forced to ask for information or even to complain and yell at people who had been rude to her. One time it was a call to her stockbroker in New York. She had cashed out her small portfolio and it just so happened we were going to go to New York the next week, our very first trip outside California. I had to get on the phone and say in an adolescent voice that was not very convincing, "This is Mrs. Tan."

And my mother was standing in the back whispering loudly, "Why he don't send me check, already two weeks late. So mad he lie to me, losing me money."

And then I said in perfect English, "Yes, I'm getting rather concerned. You had agreed to send the check two weeks ago, but it hasn't arrived."

Then she began to talk more loudly. "What he want, I come to New York tell him front of his boss, you cheating me?" And I was trying to calm her down, make her be quiet, while telling the stockbroker, "I can't tolerate any more excuses. If I don't receive the check immediately, I am going to have to speak to your manager when I'm in New York next week." And sure enough, the following week there we were in front of this astonished stockbroker, and I was sitting there red-faced and quiet, and my mother, the real Mrs. Tan, was shouting at his boss in her impeccable broken English.

We used a similar routine just five days ago, for a situation that was far less humorous. My mother had gone to the hospital for an

Reflective Essay
What specific words in this paragraph reinforce the idea that the essay is reflective?

Comprehension
How does Mrs. Tan's spoken English compare to her understanding of the language?

appointment, to find out about a benign brain tumor a CAT scan[6] had revealed a month ago. She said she had spoken very good English, her best English, no mistakes. Still, she said, the hospital did not apologize when they said they had lost the CAT scan and she had come for nothing. She said they did not seem to have any sympathy when she told them she was anxious to know the exact diagnosis, since her husband and son had both died of brain tumors. She said they would not give her any more information until the next time and she would have to make another appointment for that. So she said she would not leave until the doctor called her daughter. She wouldn't budge. And when the doctor finally called her daughter, me, who spoke in perfect English—lo and behold—we had assurances the CAT scan would be found, promises that a conference call on Monday would be held, and apologies for any suffering my mother had gone through for a most regrettable mistake.

I think my mother's English almost had an effect on limiting my possibilities in life as well. Sociologists and linguists probably will tell you that a person's developing language skills are more influenced by peers. But I do think that the language spoken in the family, especially in immigrant families which are more insular, plays a large role in shaping the language of the child. And I believe that it affected my results on achievement tests, IQ tests, and the SAT.[7] While my English skills were never judged as poor, compared to math, English could not be considered my strong suit. In grade school I did moderately well, getting perhaps B's, sometimes B-pluses, in English and scoring perhaps in the sixtieth or seventieth percentile on achievement tests. But those scores were not good enough to override the opinion that my true abilities lay in math and science, because in those areas I achieved A's and scored in the ninetieth percentile or higher.

> *I think my mother's English almost had an effect on limiting my possibilities in life as well.*

This was understandable. Math is precise; there is only one correct answer. Whereas, for me at least, the answers on English tests were always a judgment call, a matter of opinion and personal experience. Those tests were constructed around items like fill-in-the-blank sentence completion, such as, "Even though Tom was _____, Mary thought he was _____." And the correct answer always seemed to be the most bland combinations of thoughts, for example, "Even though Tom was shy, Mary thought he was charming," with the grammatical structure "even though" limiting the correct answer to some sort of semantic opposites, so you wouldn't get answers like, "Even though Tom was foolish, Mary thought he was ridiculous." Well, according to my mother, there were very few limi-

Reflective Essay

What conflict between her personal sensibilities and the values of society does Tan highlight in this discussion of her English classes?

---

6. **CAT scan** method used by doctors to diagnose brain disorders.
7. **SAT** Scholastic Aptitude Test; national college entrance exam.

tations as to what Tom could have been and what Mary might have thought of him. So I never did well on tests like that.

The same was true with word analogies, pairs of words in which you were supposed to find some sort of logical, semantic relationship — for example, "*Sunset* is to *nightfall* as _____ is to _____." And here you would be presented with a list of four possible pairs, one of which showed the same kind of relationship: *red* is to *stoplight*, *bus* is to *arrival*, *chills* is to *fever*, *yawn* is to *boring*. Well, I could never think that way. I knew what the tests were asking, but I could not block out of my mind the images already created by the first pair, "*sunset* is to *nightfall*"—and I would see a burst of colors against a darkening sky, the moon rising, the lowering of a curtain of stars. And all the other pairs of words—red, bus, stoplight, boring—just threw up a mass of confusing images, making it impossible for me to sort out something as logical as saying: "A sunset precedes nightfall" is the same as "a chill precedes a fever." The only way I would have gotten that answer right would have been to imagine an associative situation, for example, my being disobedient and staying out past sunset, catching a chill at night, which turns into feverish pneumonia as punishment, which indeed did happen to me.

I have been thinking about all this lately, about my mother's English, about achievement tests. Because lately I've been asked, as a writer, why there are not more Asian Americans represented in American literature. Why are there few Asian Americans enrolled in creative writing programs? Why do so many Chinese students go into engineering? Well, these are broad sociological questions I can't begin to answer. But I have noticed in surveys—in fact, just last week—that Asian students, as a whole, always do significantly better on math achievement tests than in English. And this makes me think that there are other Asian-American students whose English spoken in the home might also be described as "broken" or "limited." And perhaps they also have teachers who are steering them away from writing and into math and science, which is what happened to me.

Fortunately, I happen to be rebellious in nature and enjoy the challenge of disproving assumptions made about me. I became an English major my first year in college, after being enrolled as pre-med. I started writing nonfiction as a freelancer the week after I was told by my former boss that writing was my worst skill and I should hone my talents toward account management.

But it wasn't until 1985 that I finally began to write fiction. And at first I wrote using what I thought to be wittily crafted sentences, sentences that would finally prove I had mastery over the English language. Here's an example from the first draft of a story that later made its way into *The Joy Luck Club*, but without this line: "That was my mental quandary in its nascent state." A terrible line, which I can barely pronounce.

Fortunately, for reasons I won't get into today, I later decided I

Spiral Review
Rhetorical Devices Note two rhetorical techniques Tan uses in this paragraph.

Comprehension
What did Tan's "rebellious" nature move her to do?

should envision a reader for the stories I would write. And the reader I decided upon was my mother, because these were stories about mothers. So with this reader in mind—and in fact she did read my early drafts—I began to write stories using all the Englishes I grew up with: the English I spoke to my mother, which for lack of a better term might be described as "simple"; the English she used with me, which for lack of a better term might be described as "broken"; my translation of her Chinese, which could certainly be described as "watered down"; and what I imagined to be her translation of her Chinese if she could speak in perfect English, her internal language, and for that I sought to preserve the essence, but neither an English nor a Chinese structure. I wanted to capture what language ability tests can never reveal: her intent, her passion, her imagery, the rhythms of her speech and the nature of her thoughts.

Apart from what any critic had to say about my writing, I knew I had succeeded where it counted when my mother finished reading my book and gave me her verdict: "So easy to read."

Critical Reading

Cite textual evidence to support your responses.

1. **Key Ideas and Details** **(a)** What does Tan realize while speaking to an audience that includes her mother? **(b) Infer:** What circumstances account for Tan's having developed more than one "English"?

2. **Key Ideas and Details** **(a)** According to Tan, in what ways do math skills differ from language skills? **(b) Interpret:** In what ways did Tan's sense of different "Englishes" prevent her from answering correctly on grammar and standardized tests?

3. **Key Ideas and Details** **(a) Summarize:** Summarize one experience Tan had involving her mother's difficulty with Standard English. **(b) Compare and Contrast:** In what ways does Tan's sense of her mother's English differ from the perceptions of strangers?

4. **Key Ideas and Details** **Evaluate:** What influence has Tan's mother had on her daughter's writing? Support your answer.

Rita Dove *(b. 1952)*

Author of **"For the Love of Books"**

Education Rita Dove was born in Akron, Ohio, to highly educated parents. Encouraged to read from an early age, Dove excelled in school. Upon graduating from high school, she was invited to the White House as a Presidential scholar. Although her first writing efforts—at the age of nine or ten—had been comic books with female superheroes, she turned to poetry in college. Dove attended Miami University in Oxford, Ohio, and graduated with highest honors, winning a Fulbright Scholarship to study in Germany. From there, she continued her education at the famous Writers' Workshop at the University of Iowa.

Teacher and Poet Laureate While teaching creative writing at Arizona State University, Dove gained critical acclaim with several volumes of poetry. In 1987, she won the Pulitzer Prize for *Thomas and Beulah,* a collection of poems based on the lives of her grandparents. In 1993, she was appointed Poet Laureate of the United States, becoming the youngest person ever to hold that position. She has published many volumes of poetry since, including *On the Bus with Rosa Parks* (1999), and *American Smooth* (2004). Dove has also written a play, a novel, and a collection of short stories. "Every time I write a poem," Dove has said, "I try to imagine the reader— the reader that I was—curled up on the couch, at the moment of opening a book and absolutely having my world fall away and entering into another one."

> "Poetry is language at its most distilled and most powerful."

For the
Love OF
Books

Rita Dove

▲ **Critical Viewing**
Do you think this image
expresses the same love of
books Dove felt as a child?
CONNECT

Vocabulary
ecstasy (ek´ stə sē) *n.*
a feeling of overpowering
joy; great delight

Reflective Essay
Which elements in these
first two paragraphs
identify this work as a
personal essay?

When I am asked: "What made you want to be a writer?" my answer has always been: "Books." First and foremost, now, then, and always, I have been passionate about books. From the time I began to read, as a child, I loved to feel their heft in my hand and the warm spot caused by their intimate weight in my lap; I loved the crisp whisper of a page turning, the musky odor of old paper and the sharp inky whiff of new pages. Leather bindings sent me into ecstasy. I even loved to gaze at a closed book and daydream about the possibilities inside—it was like contemplating a genie's lamp. Of course, my favorite fairy tale was *A Thousand and One Nights*—imagine buying your life with stories!—and my favorite cartoons were those where animated characters popped out of books and partied while the unsuspecting humans slept. In books, I could travel anywhere, be anybody, understand worlds long past and imaginary colonies in the future. My idea of a bargain was to go to the public library, wander along the bookshelves, and emerge with a chin-high stack of books that were mine, all mine, for two weeks—free of charge!

What I remember most about long summer days is browsing the bookshelves in our solarium to see if there were any new additions. I grew up with those rows of books; I knew where each one was shelved and immediately spotted newcomers. And after months had gone by and there'd be no new books, I would think: Okay, I guess I'll try this one—and then discover that the very book I had been avoiding because of a drab cover or small print was actually a wonderful read. Louis Untermeyer's *Treasury of Best Loved Poems* had a sickeningly sweet lilac and gold cover and was forbiddingly thick, but I finally pulled it off the shelf and discovered a cornucopia of emotional and linguistic delights, from "The Ballad of Barbara Fritchie," which I adored for its sheer length and rather numbing rhymes, to Langston Hughes's dazzlingly syncopated "Dream Boogie." Then there was Shakespeare—daunting for many years because it was his entire oeuvre,[1] in matching wine-red volumes that were so thick they looked more like over-sized bouillon cubes than books, and yet it was that ponderous title—*The Complete Works of William Shakespeare*—that enticed me, because here was a lifetime's work—a lifetime!—in two compact, dense packages. I began with the long poem "The Rape of Lucrece" . . . I sampled a few sonnets, which I found beautiful but rather adult; and finally wandered into the plays—first *Romeo and Juliet*, then *Macbeth, Julius Caesar, A Midsummer Night's Dream, Twelfth Night*—enthralled by the language, by the fact that poetry was spinning the story. Of course I did not understand every single word, but I was too young to know that this was supposed to be difficult; besides, no one was waiting to test me on anything, so, free from pressure, I dove in.

At the same time, my brother, two years my senior, had become a science fiction buff, so I'd read his *Analog* and *Fantasy* and Science Fiction magazines after he was finished with them. One story particularly fascinated me: A retarded boy in a small town begins building a sculpture in his backyard, using old and discarded materials —coke bottles, scrap iron, string, and bottle caps. Everyone laughs at him, but he continues building. Then one day he disappears. And when the neighbors investigate, they discover that the sculpture has been dragged onto the back porch and that the screen door is open. Somehow the narrator of the story figures out how to switch on the sculpture: The back door frame begins to glow, and when he steps through it, he's in an alternate universe, a town the mirror image of his own—even down to the colors, with green roses and an orange sky. And he walks through this town until he comes to the main square, where there is a statue erected to—who else?—the village idiot.

I loved this story, the idea that the dreamy, mild, scatter-brained boy of one world could be the hero of another. And in a way, I identified with that village idiot because in real life I was painfully shy and awkward; the place where I felt most alive was between the pages of a book.

Although I loved books, for a long time I had no aspirations to be a writer. The possibility was beyond my imagination. I liked to write, however—and on long summer days when I ran out of reading material or my legs had fallen asleep because I had been curled up

---

1. **oeuvre** (ĕ´ vrə) *n.* all the works, usually of a lifetime, of a particular writer, artist, or composer.

Vocabulary
daunting (dônt´ iŋ) *adj.* intimidating

Vocabulary
aspirations (as´ pə rā´ shənz) *n.* strong desires or ambitions

Comprehension
What made Dove want to be a writer?

on the couch for hours on end, I made up my own stories. Most were abandoned midway. Those that I did bring to a conclusion I neither showed to others nor considered saving.

My first piece of writing I thought enough of to keep was a novel called *Chaos*, which was about robots taking over the earth. I had just entered third or fourth grade; the novel had forty-three chapters, and each chapter was twenty lines or less because I used each week's spelling list as the basis for each chapter, and there were twenty words per list. In the course of the year I wrote one installment per week, and I never knew what was going to happen next—the words led me, not the other way around.

At that time I didn't think of writing as an activity people admitted doing. I had no living role models—a "real" writer was a long-dead white male, usually with a white beard to match. Much later, when I was in eleventh grade, my English teacher, Miss Oechsner, took me to a book-signing in a downtown hotel. She didn't ask me if I'd like to go—she asked my parents instead, signed me and a classmate (who is now a professor of literature) out of school one day, and took us to meet a writer. The writer was John Ciardi, a poet who also had translated Dante's *Divine Comedy*, which I had heard of, vaguely. At that moment I realized that writers were real people and how it was possible to write down a poem or story in the intimate sphere of one's own room and then share it with the world.

> . . . I never knew what was going to happen next— the words led me, not the other way around.

Critical Reading

Cite textual evidence to support your responses.

1. **Key Ideas and Details (a)** Which emotion did Dove feel in the presence of an unopened book? **(b) Interpret:** For Dove, what traits did an unopened book and a genie's lamp share? **(c) Analyze:** What attitude toward the imagination is suggested by this simile?

2. **Key Ideas and Details (a)** What happens in the science fiction story that Dove enjoys so much? **(b) Connect:** Why is the story especially meaningful to Dove?

3. **Key Ideas and Details (a)** Which experience made Dove realize that she could be a "real" writer? **(b) Speculate:** Do you think Dove would have gone on to become a writer if she had not had that experience? Why or why not?

4. **Integration of Knowledge and Ideas** What do these essays suggest about the ways language itself makes or breaks connections among people, both within families and communities? In your response, use at least two of these Essential Question words: *alienation, transformation, community, identity, self-reliance. [Connecting to the Essential Question: What makes American literature American?]*

Literary Analysis

1. **Key Ideas and Details** Consult the **outline** you made as you read Amy Tan's essay. **(a)** What central idea does Tan introduce in her first paragraph? **(b)** How does she develop or extend that idea in paragraphs 2 through 4? **(c)** How does Tan's inclusion of her mother's story about the Chinese gangster relate to the ideas with which she introduces the essay?

2. **Craft and Structure (a)** In this **reflective essay,** how does Tan describe her changing attitudes toward her mother? **(b)** What role does language play in shaping those attitudes?

3. **Key Ideas and Details (a)** What books does Dove say most delighted her as a child? **(b)** What point is Dove making about the imaginative life of a child through this catalog of her favorite literature?

4. **Key Ideas and Details (a)** What general question does Dove address in this essay? **(b)** What ultimate insight does Dove state in her final paragraph?

5. **Integration of Knowledge and Ideas** Based on these two examples, why might an author write a reflective essay rather than fiction or poetry to explore a specific subject?

6. **Comparing Literary Works** Compare and contrast the ways in which Tan's and Dove's relationships to words and books shaped their careers as writers. Use a chart like the one shown to organize your thinking.

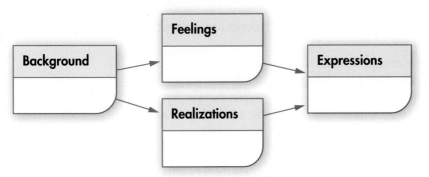

7. **Comparing Literary Works (a)** What evidence do you find in these reflective essays related to the **theme** that one must struggle or sacrifice to create a true sense of identity? **(b)** Explain why a reflective essay is a particularly suitable literary form to explore this theme.

8. **Comparing Literary Works (a)** In what ways do these authors' inner lives contrast—or conflict—with the outside world? **(b)** What role does writing play in the relationship between each writer's inner and outer life?

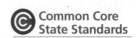
Common Core State Standards

Writing
2. Write informative texts to examine and convey complex ideas, concepts, and information clearly and accurately through the effective selection, organization, and analysis of content. *(p. 1422)*

2.d Use precise language and techniques such as metaphor, simile, and analogy to manage the complexity of the topic. *(p. 1422)*

Language
3. Apply knowledge of language to understand how language functions in different contexts, to make effective choices for meaning or style, and to comprehend more fully when reading or listening. *(p. 1423)*

4.b. Identify and correctly use patterns of word changes that indicate different meanings or parts of speech. *(p. 1422)*

Vocabulary Acquisition and Use

Word Analysis: Latin Root *-scrib-*, *-script-*

The word *transcribe,* which means "write out or type out in full," is formed from the Latin root *-scrib-*, which means "write." Using each pair of words below, write a sentence that demonstrates the meaning of this root. If necessary, use a dictionary to aid your work.

1. scribble, child
2. prescription, doctor
3. inscription, trophy
4. author, manuscript
5. playwright, script
6. proscription, legislator

Vocabulary: Sentence Completions

Complete each sentence by filling in each blank with a vocabulary word from the list on page 1408. Explain your choices.

1. The idea of speaking in front of so many highly qualified colleagues is _____.
2. The huge hot fudge sundaes sent the children into a state of _____.
3. The kindly old woman had a _____ influence on her children.
4. One of his many _____ is traveling to all seven continents before turning forty.
5. The archaeologist _____ the message that was carved on the wall of the tomb.

Writing to Sources

Informative Text Write a **letter to the author** of the essay you found most interesting. Explain what you liked, what you did not like, and ask any questions you might have.

Prewriting Choose the essay you wish to discuss and reread it. Take notes about the author's message and style. List statements and images that you like, or that disturb you in some way.

Drafting In your opening paragraph, state how much you enjoyed the essay and why. In the body paragraphs, go into greater detail, and ask any relevant questions. Consider drawing parallels to your own life. Include figurative language, such as similes and metaphors, to make your ideas clearer and more interesting. For example, consider modeling a simile after Tan's description of books "so thick they looked more like over-sized bouillon cubes . . ."

Revising Review your letter, and determine whether or not you have used the best language to communicate your thoughts. Replace any vague words with more specific ones.

> **Model: Revising to Include Precise Language**
>
>   *captured*
> I enjoyed the way you ~~stated~~ your mother's English in
>   *This example of her speech*
> the anecdote of the Shanghai gangster. ~~It~~ helped me to
>   *incident described*
> see my own prejudices. The ~~point you~~ added with the
> stockbroker made your mother's struggle very clear.

Replacing vague references with precise words and phrases more accurately conveys ideas.

Conventions and Style: Using Parallel Structure

In your writing, work to express equal ideas using the same grammatical structures. This creates **parallel structure,** the use of similar patterns of words to show that two or more ideas have a close relationship and level of importance. Below are some examples of sentences rewritten to make nouns, phrases, and clauses parallel. Notice that the coordinating conjunction *and* is a clue to the presence of similar ideas in sentences.

Non-Parallel	Parallel
She spoke about her writing, life, and her book.	She spoke about her writing, her life, and her book.
Reading developed her imagination, and it inspired her to become a writer.	Reading developed her imagination and inspired her to become a writer.
She loved reading books, smelled their musky odor, and hearing their crisp pages turn.	She loved reading books, smelling their musky odor, and hearing their crisp pages turn.

Practice Rewrite each item to correct the non-parallel structure.

1. Reading as a child influenced her life and being a writer.
2. Good writers create stories that are believable, vivid, and to be enjoyed.
3. She writes easily, steadily, and in a clear way.
4. Words call up emotions, ideas, and helps to see images.
5. The writer videotaped and then wrote a transcription of the conversation.
6. Having a rebellious nature and adventurous can lead to success.
7. She read books as a child, and wrote them when she was an adult.
8. The teacher says that I have writing ability but I need to follow the rules.
9. She enjoys reading Shakespeare as much as reading science fiction pleases her brother.
10. She was Chinese, a woman, and living in a family as the only daughter.

Writing and Speaking Conventions

A. Writing Use the following items to write sentences with parallel structure.

1. English, Chinese
2. in math, in science, in English
3. judgment, opinion, experience
4. read, listen, talk
5. grades, tests, scores

    Example: English, Chinese
    Sentence: Mrs. Tan understands English as well as she speaks Chinese.

B. Speaking Deliver an explanation of something you did that you never thought possible, such as writing a prize-winning story or doing well on an achievement test. Use at least two examples of parallel structure.

Connecting to the Essential Question These selections explore the relationship between heritage and homeland. As you read, look for details that reveal the writers' feelings about the settings. Doing so will help you think about the Essential Question: **What is the relationship between literature and place?**

Close Reading Focus

Memoir

Memoirs are nonfiction narratives that recount events in which the writer was a participant or eyewitness. Memoirs are, by definition, acts of memory shaped by literary skill. Often, the memoirist sets personal reflections against historical or cultural landscapes. For example, these lines from Kingston's memoir weave the personal and the historical:

> *These new immigrants had it easy. On Ellis Island*
> *the people were thin after forty days at sea . . .*

Both Kingston and Momaday skillfully incorporate details of culture, place, and history into their recollections of events from their lives.

Comparing Literary Works These selections are now classic works of American memoir, noteworthy in many ways. As you read, consider how the two works are similar and different. For example, the two writers use language very differently. In addition, Momaday relates his experiences from the **first-person point of view.** Kingston, however, uses the **limited third-person point of view,** referring to both herself and her own mother, Brave Orchid, as *she.* As you read these memoirs, examine how the authors' uses of language and choices of point of view help to shape the meaning and power of their work.

Preparing to Read Complex Texts If you have ever loved a pet or listened to relatives tell stories, you can relate to these memoirs. To appreciate these memoirs more deeply, **relate them to your own experience.** As you read, use a chart like the one shown to record the connections you make between the writers' experiences and your own life.

Vocabulary

The words below are important to understanding the texts that follow. Copy the words into your notebook, sorting them into words you know and words you do not know.

inaudibly	pastoral
gravity	supple
oblivious	

Common Core State Standards

**Reading Informational Text
6.** Determine an author's point of view or purpose in a text in which the rhetoric is particularly effective, analyzing how style and content contribute to the power, persuasiveness or beauty of the text.

Experience in Memoir

My Own Experience

Insight Gained

Maxine Hong Kingston

(b. 1940)

Author of *The Woman Warrior*

"I was born to be a writer," Maxine Hong Kingston once told an interviewer. "In the midst of any adventure, a born writer has a desire to hurry home and put it into words."

Crossing Cultures Although Kingston was born in America, she did not begin describing her adventures in English until she was nearly ten because the language her family spoke at home was Say Yup, a Chinese dialect spoken around Canton, now known as Guangzhou, China. Kingston's parents came from a village near Guangzhou. Her father left first for "the Golden Mountain" of America and settled in New York City. His training as a poet and calligrapher was unmarketable in the United States, so he earned a living working in the laundry business. Kingston's mother, who was trained as a midwife, used the money her husband sent home to run a clinic in their native village. She did so until 1939, when she escaped war-torn China and joined her husband. Not long afterward, the couple resettled in Stockton, California, where Maxine Hong was born.

Building a Love for Story Young Maxine, whose Chinese name is Ting Ting, was a shy and quiet girl who repeated kindergarten because she spoke very little English. While at home, however, she listened intently to the stories told by family members and friends; this love of storytelling later influenced her writing style as Kingston developed her own "talk stories." By the time she was nine years old, she had mastered English and begun writing poetry. Soon, she began to earn straight A's in school.

A Bestseller Kingston shot to success with her first and best-known book, *The Woman Warrior: Memoirs of a Girlhood Among Ghosts*. The subtitle refers to the pale "ghosts" of white America, as well as the ghosts of the narrator's ancestors in China. *The Woman Warrior*, a unique blend of folklore, myth, feminism, and autobiography, won a National Book Critics' Circle Award in 1976.

Kingston earned a National Book Critics' Circle Award a second time, in 1980, for *China Men*, which chronicles the lives of three generations of Chinese men in America. A methodical writer, Kingston labors over numerous revisions to her books. Her latest book is *Veterans of War, Veterans of Peace* (2006), which transforms the horrors experienced by veterans of World War II, Vietnam, and Iraq into words and stories from which they can draw strength.

from The Woman Warrior

Maxine Hong Kingston

▲ **Critical Viewing**

What is your impression of the relationship between the mother and daughter in this photograph? Explain. **INFER**

BACKGROUND *The Woman Warrior* is an innovative memoir that attempts to capture the experience of growing up in a bicultural world—part Chinese, part American. To accomplish her purpose, Kingston mingles the narrative with "talk stories," tales full of magical events that she heard as a girl from her mother, Brave Orchid. The subtitle of the book, *Memoir of a Girlhood Among Ghosts*, refers both to white America, whose pale inhabitants remind Brave Orchid of ghosts, and to the family's ancestors in China. In this excerpt, Brave Orchid reunites with her sister, one of the ghosts of her past.

When she was about sixty-eight years old, Brave Orchid took a day off to wait at San Francisco International Airport for the plane that was bringing her sister to the United States. She had not seen Moon Orchid for thirty years. She had begun this waiting at home, getting up a half-hour before Moon Orchid's plane took off in Hong Kong.[1] Brave Orchid would add her will power to the forces that keep an airplane up. Her head hurt with the concentration. The plane had to be light, so no matter how tired she felt, she dared not rest her spirit on a wing but continuously and gently pushed up on the plane's belly. She had already been waiting at the airport for nine hours. She was wakeful.

Next to Brave Orchid sat Moon Orchid's only daughter, who was helping her aunt wait. Brave Orchid had made two of her own children come too because they could drive, but they had been lured away by the magazine racks and the gift shops and coffee shops. Her American children could not sit for very long. They did not understand sitting; they had wandering feet. She hoped they would get back from the pay TV's or the pay toilets or wherever they were spending their money before the plane arrived. If they did not come back soon, she would go look for them. If her son thought he could hide in the men's room, he was wrong.

"Are you all right, Aunt?" asked her niece.

"No, this chair hurts me. Help me pull some chairs together so I can put my feet up."

She unbundled a blanket and spread it out to make a bed for herself. On the floor she had two shopping bags full of canned peaches, real peaches, beans wrapped in taro leaves,[2] cookies, Thermos bottles,[3] enough food for everybody, though only her niece would eat with her. Her bad boy and bad girl were probably sneaking hamburgers, wasting their money. She would scold them.

Many soldiers and sailors sat about, oddly calm, like little boys in cowboy uniforms. (She thought "cowboy" was what you would call a Boy Scout.) They should have been crying hysterically on their way to Vietnam.[4] "If I see one that looks Chinese," she thought, "I'll go over and give him some advice." She sat up suddenly; she had forgotten about her own son, who was even now in Vietnam. Carefully she split her attention, beaming half of it to the ocean, into the water to keep him afloat. He was on a ship. He was in Vietnamese waters. She was sure of it. He and the other children were lying to her. They had said he was in Japan, and then they said he was in the Philippines. But

Memoirs

Whose impressions are described in this passage about "her American children"?

Comprehension

Who is Brave Orchid waiting to meet?

---

1. **took off in Hong Kong** After mainland China fell to the Communists in the late 1940s, many native Chinese fled first to Hong Kong (a British colony until 1997) before immigrating to the United States.
2. **taro** (te′ rō) **leaves** leaves of an edible tuberous plant widely eaten in Asia.
3. **Thermos** (thʉr′ məs) **bottles** insulated containers for holding liquids and keeping them warm or cold.
4. **Vietnam** southeast Asian nation where, in the late 1960s when this selection takes place, the U.S. had joined the conflict known as the Vietnam War (1954–1975).

Relating to Your Own Experiences

Can you relate to Brave Orchid's feeling that her family is keeping something from her?

Memoirs

What historical detail does Kingston include in this passage?

when she sent him her help, she could feel that he was on a ship in Da Nang.[5] Also she had seen the children hide the envelopes that his letters came in.

"Do you think my son is in Vietnam?" she asked her niece, who was dutifully eating.

"No. Didn't your children say he was in the Philippines?"

"Have you ever seen any of his letters with Philippine stamps on them?"

"Oh, yes. Your children showed me one."

"I wouldn't put it past them to send the letters to some Filipino they know. He puts Manila[6] postmarks on them to fool me."

"Yes, I can imagine them doing that. But don't worry. Your son can take care of himself. All your children can take care of themselves."

"Not him. He's not like other people. Not normal at all. He sticks erasers in his ears, and the erasers are still attached to the pencil stubs. The captain will say, 'Abandon ship,' or 'Watch out for bombs,' and he won't hear. He doesn't listen to orders. I told him to flee to Canada,[7] but he wouldn't go."

She closed her eyes. After a short while, plane and ship under control, she looked again at the children in uniforms. Some of the blond ones looked like baby chicks, their crew cuts like the downy yellow on baby chicks. You had to feel sorry for them even though they were Army and Navy Ghosts.

Suddenly her son and daughter came running. "Come, Mother. The plane's landed early. She's here already." They hurried, folding up their mother's encampment. She was glad her children were not useless. They must have known what this trip to San Francisco was about then. "It's a good thing I made you come early," she said.

Brave Orchid pushed to the front of the crowd. She had to be in front. The passengers were separated from the people waiting for them by glass doors and walls. Immigration Ghosts were stamping papers. The travellers crowded along some conveyor belts to have their luggage searched. Brave Orchid did not see her sister anywhere. She stood watching for four hours. Her children left and came back. "Why don't you sit down?" they asked.

"The chairs are too far away," she said.

"Why don't you sit on the floor then?"

No, she would stand, as her sister was probably standing in a line she could not see from here. Her American children had no feelings and no memory.

To while away time, she and her niece talked about the Chinese

---

5. **Da Nang** (dä näŋ) city in central Vietnam that was the site of an important U.S. military base during the Vietnam War; also spelled Danang.
6. **Manila** (mə nil′ ə) capital of the Philippines.
7. **flee to Canada** During the Vietnam War era, thousands of Americans fled to Canada to escape the military draft, even though such draft dodgers were subject to prosecution upon returning to the U.S.

passengers. These new immigrants had it easy. On Ellis Island[8] the people were thin after forty days at sea and had no fancy luggage.

"That one looks like her," Brave Orchid would say.

"No, that's not her."

Ellis Island had been made out of wood and iron. Here everything was new plastic, a ghost trick to lure immigrants into feeling safe and spilling their secrets. Then the Alien Office could send them right back. Otherwise, why did they lock her out, not letting her help her sister answer questions and spell her name? At Ellis Island when the ghost asked Brave Orchid what year her husband had cut off his pigtail, a Chinese who was crouching on the floor motioned her not to talk. "I don't know," she had said. If it weren't for that Chinese man, she might not be here today, or her husband either. She hoped some Chinese, a janitor or a clerk, would look out for Moon Orchid. Luggage conveyors fooled immigrants into thinking the Gold Mountain was going to be easy.

Brave Orchid felt her heart jump—Moon Orchid. "There she is," she shouted. But her niece saw it was not her mother at all. And it shocked her to discover the woman her aunt was pointing out. This was a young woman, younger than herself, no older than Moon Orchid the day the sisters parted. "Moon Orchid will have changed a little, of course," Brave Orchid was saying. "She will have learned to wear western clothes." The woman wore a navy blue suit with a bunch of dark cherries at the shoulder.

"No, Aunt," said the niece. "That's not my mother."

"Perhaps not. It's been so many years. Yes, it is your mother. It must be. Let her come closer, and we can tell. Do you think she's too far away for me to tell, or is it my eyes getting bad?"

"It's too many years gone by," said the niece.

Brave Orchid turned suddenly—another Moon Orchid, this one a neat little woman with a bun. She was laughing at something the person ahead of her in line said. Moon Orchid was just like that, laughing at nothing. "I would be able to tell the difference if one of them would only come closer," Brave Orchid said with tears, which she did not wipe. Two children met the woman with the cherries, and she shook their hands. The other woman was met by a young man. They looked at each other gladly, then walked away side by side.

Up close neither one of those women looked like Moon Orchid at all. "Don't worry, Aunt," said the niece. "I'll know her."

"I'll know her too. I knew her before you did."

The niece said nothing, although she had seen her mother only five years ago. Her aunt liked having the last word.

Finally Brave Orchid's children quit wandering and drooped on a railing. Who knew what they were thinking? At last the niece called out, "I see her! I see her! Mother! Mother!" Whenever the doors parted,

Memoirs

How does Brave Orchid's memory of Ellis Island convey the challenges experienced by immigrants at that place and time?

"Moon Orchid will have changed a little, of course."

Comprehension

Why does Brave Orchid worry about her son?

---

8. **Ellis Island** island in the harbor off New York City that was the chief U.S. immigration station from 1892 to 1943.

she shouted, probably embarrassing the American cousins, but she didn't care. She called out, "Mama! Mama!" until the crack in the sliding doors became too small to let in her voice. "Mama!" What a strange word in an adult voice. Many people turned to see what adult was calling, "Mama!" like a child. Brave Orchid saw an old, old woman jerk her head up, her little eyes blinking confusedly, a woman whose nerves leapt toward the sound anytime she heard "Mama!" Then she relaxed to her own business again. She was a tiny, tiny lady, very thin, with little fluttering hands, and her hair was in a gray knot. She was dressed in a gray wool suit; she wore pearls around her neck and in her earlobes. Moon Orchid *would* travel with her jewels showing. Brave Orchid momentarily saw, like a larger, younger outline around this old woman, the sister she had been waiting for. The familiar dim halo faded, leaving the woman so old, so gray. So old. Brave Orchid pressed against the glass. *That* old lady? Yes, that old lady facing the ghost who stamped her papers without questioning her was her sister. Then, without noticing her family, Moon Orchid walked smiling over to the Suitcase Inspector Ghost, who took her boxes apart, pulling out puffs of tissue. From where she was, Brave Orchid could not see what her sister had chosen to carry across the ocean. She wished her sister would look her way. Brave Orchid thought that if she were entering a new country, she would be at the windows. Instead Moon Orchid

▼ **Critical Viewing**

How might life in the city of San Francisco, shown in this image, compare with life in Hong Kong, from where Moon Orchid has just arrived? **COMPARE AND CONTRAST**

hovered over the unwrapping, surprised at each reappearance as if she were opening presents after a birthday party.

"Mama!" Moon Orchid's daughter kept calling. Brave Orchid said to her children, "Why don't you call your aunt too? Maybe she'll hear us if all of you call out together." But her children slunk away. Maybe that shame-face they so often wore was American politeness.

"Mama!" Moon Orchid's daughter called again, and this time her mother looked right at her. She left her bundles in a heap and came running. "Hey!" the Customs Ghost yelled at her. She went back to clear up her mess, talking inaudibly to her daughter all the while. Her daughter pointed toward Brave Orchid. And at last Moon Orchid looked at her—two old women with faces like mirrors.

Their hands reached out as if to touch the other's face, then returned to their own, the fingers checking the grooves in the forehead and along the sides of the mouth. Moon Orchid, who never understood the gravity of things, started smiling and laughing, pointing at Brave Orchid. Finally Moon Orchid gathered up her stuff, strings hanging and papers loose, and met her sister at the door, where they shook hands, oblivious to blocking the way.

"You're an old woman," said Brave Orchid.

"Aiaa. *You're* an old woman."

Vocabulary

inaudibly (in ôd´ə blē) *adv.* in a manner that cannot be heard

gravity (grav´ i tē) *n.* seriousness

oblivious (ə bliv´ ē əs) *adj.* lacking all awareness

Comprehension

What aspect of Moon Orchid's appearance most surprises Brave Orchid?

"You're so old . . . How did you get so old?"

"But *you* are really old. Surely, you can't say that about me. I'm not old the way you're old."

"But you really are old. You're one year older than I am."

"Your hair is white and your face all wrinkled."

"You're so skinny."

"You're so fat."

"Fat women are more beautiful than skinny women."

The children pulled them out of the door-way. One of Brave Orchid's children brought the car from the parking lot, and the other heaved the luggage into the trunk. They put the two old ladies and the niece in the back seat. All the way home—across the Bay Bridge,[9] over the Diablo hills,[10] across the San Joaquin River[11] to the valley, the valley moon so white at dusk—all the way home, the two sisters exclaimed every time they turned to look at each other, "Aiaa! How old!"

Brave Orchid forgot that she got sick in cars, that all vehicles but palanquins[12] made her dizzy. "You're so old," she kept saying. "How did you get so old?"

Brave Orchid had tears in her eyes. But Moon Orchid said, "You look older than I. You *are* older than I," and again she'd laugh. "You're wearing an old mask to tease me." It surprised Brave Orchid that after thirty years she could still get annoyed at her sister's silliness.

---

9. **Bay Bridge** one of the bridges across San Francisco Bay.
10. **Diablo** (dë äb´ lö) **hills** hills outside San Francisco.
11. **San Joaquin** (wô kēn´) **River** river of central California; its valley is one of the state's richest agricultural areas.
12. **palanquins** (pal´ ən kēnz´) hand-carried covered litters once widely used to transport people in China and elsewhere in eastern Asia.

Critical Reading

Cite textual evidence to support your responses.

1. **Key Ideas and Details (a)** Identify the family members waiting for Moon Orchid at the airport, and briefly describe each one's behavior. **(b) Interpret:** What do Brave Orchid's thoughts about her children's behavior reveal about her?

2. **Key Ideas and Details (a)** How does Brave Orchid try to keep both her sister's plane and her son's ship safe? **(b) Connect:** What does this behavior reveal about Brave Orchid's view of the world?

3. **Key Ideas and Details (a) Interpret:** What is Brave Orchid's main impression when she finally sees Moon Orchid? **(b) Draw Conclusions:** When the two sisters finally meet, why do they speak to each other as they do?

4. **Key Ideas and Details (a) Infer:** What seems to be Brave Orchid's attitude toward America and American culture? **(b) Apply:** What does this selection suggest about the conflicts that face immigrants and the children of immigrants in America?

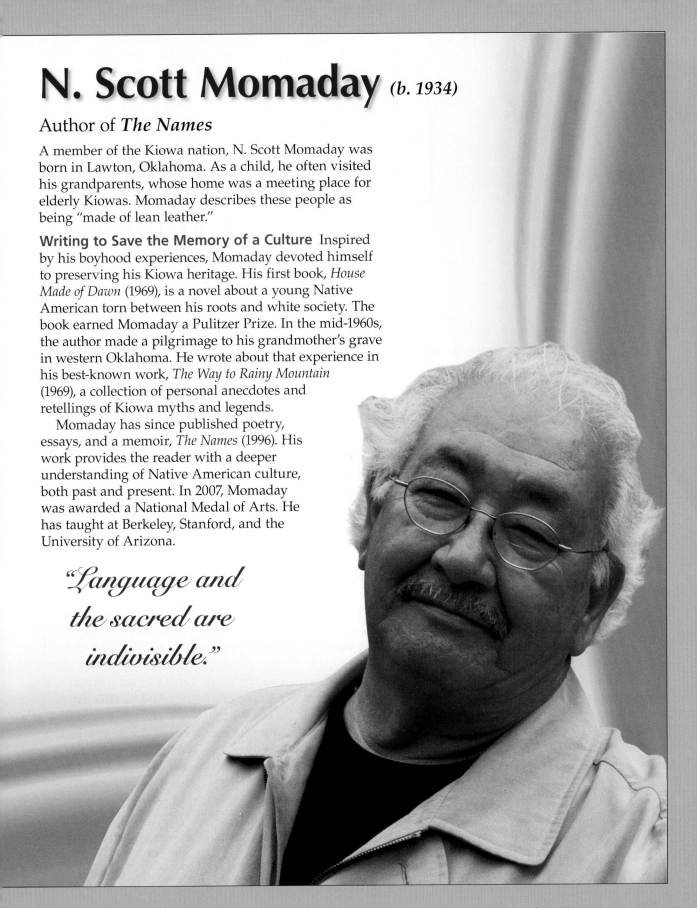

N. Scott Momaday *(b. 1934)*

Author of *The Names*

A member of the Kiowa nation, N. Scott Momaday was born in Lawton, Oklahoma. As a child, he often visited his grandparents, whose home was a meeting place for elderly Kiowas. Momaday describes these people as being "made of lean leather."

Writing to Save the Memory of a Culture Inspired by his boyhood experiences, Momaday devoted himself to preserving his Kiowa heritage. His first book, *House Made of Dawn* (1969), is a novel about a young Native American torn between his roots and white society. The book earned Momaday a Pulitzer Prize. In the mid-1960s, the author made a pilgrimage to his grandmother's grave in western Oklahoma. He wrote about that experience in his best-known work, *The Way to Rainy Mountain* (1969), a collection of personal anecdotes and retellings of Kiowa myths and legends.

Momaday has since published poetry, essays, and a memoir, *The Names* (1996). His work provides the reader with a deeper understanding of Native American culture, both past and present. In 2007, Momaday was awarded a National Medal of Arts. He has taught at Berkeley, Stanford, and the University of Arizona.

"Language and the sacred are indivisible."

from

The NAMES

N. Scott Momaday

BACKGROUND In the book-length memoir from which this excerpt is taken, N. Scott Momaday weaves together poetry, prose, photographs, and drawings, to describe his childhood, his family, and his ancestors. As Momaday explains, Kiowa society is a "horse culture." In this section, Momaday focuses on the story of a favorite horse and the beginnings of his own independent journey through life.

I sometimes think of what it means that in their heyday—in 1830, say—the Kiowas owned more horses *per capita* than any other tribe on the Great Plains, that the Plains Indian culture, the last culture to evolve in North America, is also known as "the horse culture" and "the centaur[1] culture," that the Kiowas tell the story of a horse that died of shame after its owner committed an act of cowardice, that I am a Kiowa, that therefore there is in me, as there is in the Tartars,[2] an old, sacred notion of the horse. I believe that at some point in my racial life, this notion must needs be expressed in order that I may be true to my nature.

It happened so: I was thirteen years old, and my parents gave me a horse. It was a small nine-year-old gelding of that rare, soft color that is called strawberry roan. This my horse and I came to be, in the course of our life together, in good understanding, of one mind, a true story and history of that large landscape in which we made the one entity of whole motion, one and the same center of an intricate, pastoral composition, evanescent,[3] ever changing. And to this my horse I gave the name Pecos.

On the back of my horse I had a different view of the world. I could see more of it, how it reached away beyond all the horizons I had ever seen; and yet it was more concentrated in its appearance,

Vocabulary

pastoral (pas´ tər əl) *adj.* characteristic of rural life; idealized as peaceful, simple, and natural

---

1. **centaur** (sen´ tôr) *adj.* pertaining to a mythical creature with the head and upper body of a man and the lower body of a horse.
2. **Tartars** (tär´ tərz) *n.* nomadic Turkish peoples who took part in the invasions of Eastern Europe during the Middle Ages.
3. **evanescent** (ev´ ə nes´ ənt) *adj.* transient; tending to fade from sight.

too, and more accessible to my mind, my imagination. My mind loomed upon the farthest edges of the earth, where I could feel the full force of the planet whirling into space. There was nothing of the air and light that was not pure exhilaration, and nothing of time and eternity. Oh, Pecos, *un poquito mas!* Oh, my hunting horse! Bear me away, bear me away!

It was appropriate that I should make a long journey. Accordingly I set out one early morning, traveling light. Such a journey must begin in the nick of time, on the spur of the moment, and one must say to himself at the outset: Let there be wonderful things along the way; let me hold to the way and be thoughtful in my going; let this journey be made in beauty and belief.

I sang in the sunshine and heard the birds call out on either side. Bits of down from the cottonwoods drifted across the air, and butterflies fluttered in the sage. I could feel my horse under me, rocking at my legs, the bobbing of the reins to my hand; I could feel the sun on my face and the stirring of a little wind at my hair. And through the hard hooves, the slender limbs, the supple shoulders, the fluent back of my horse I felt the earth under me. Everything was under me, buoying me up; I rode across the top of the world. My mind soared; time and again I saw the fleeting shadow of my mind moving about me as it went winding upon the sun.

When the song, which was a song of riding, was finished, I had Pecos pick up the pace. Far down on the road to San Ysidro I overtook my friend Pasqual Fragua. He was riding a rangy, stiff-legged black and white stallion, half wild, which horse he was breaking for the

▲ Critical Viewing
Using the third paragraph of the essay as a guide, how do you think Momaday would describe this photograph?
HYPOTHESIZE

Vocabulary
supple (sup´ əl) *adj.* able to bend and move easily; nimble

Comprehension
What is Momaday's idea of a great journey?

The thing was this: that the stallion was half wild, and I came to wonder about the wild half of it...

Memoir

What significant event does Momaday recount in this passage?

rancher Cass Goodner. The horse skittered and blew as I drew up beside him. Pecos began to prance, as he did always in the company of another horse. "Where are you going?" I asked in the Jemez language. And he replied, "I am going down the road." The stallion was hard to manage, and Pasqual had to keep his mind upon it; I saw that I had taken him by surprise. "You know," he said after a moment, "when you rode up just now I did not know who you were." We rode on for a time in silence, and our horses got used to each other, but still they wanted their heads.[4] The longer I looked at the stallion the more I admired it, and I suppose that Pasqual knew this, for he began to say good things about it: that it was a thing of good blood, that it was very strong and fast, that it felt very good to ride it. The thing was this: that the stallion was half wild, and I came to wonder about the wild half of it; I wanted to know what its wildness was worth in the riding. "Let us trade horses for a while," I said, and, well, all right, he agreed. At first it was exciting to ride the stallion, for every once in a while it pitched and bucked and wanted to run. But it was heavy and raw-boned and full of resistance, and every step was a jolt that I could feel deep down in my bones. I saw soon enough that I had made a bad bargain, and I wanted my horse back, but I was ashamed to admit it. There came a time in the late afternoon, in the vast plain far south of San Ysidro, after thirty miles, perhaps, when I no longer knew whether it was I who was riding the stallion or the stallion who was riding me. "Well, let us go back now," said Pasqual at last. "No. I am going on; and I will have my horse back, please," I said, and he was surprised and sorry to hear it, and we said goodbye. "If you are going south or east," he said, "look out for the sun, and keep your face in the shadow of your hat. *Vaya con Dios.*"[5] And I went on my way alone then, wiser and better mounted, and thereafter I held on to my horse. I saw no one for a long time, but I saw four falling stars and any number of jackrabbits, roadrunners, and coyotes, and once, across a distance, I saw a bear, small and black, lumbering in the ravine. The mountains drew close and withdrew and drew close again, and after several days I swung east.

Now and then I came upon settlements. For the most part they were dry, burnt places with Spanish names: Arroyo Seco, Las Piedras, Tres Casas. In one of these I found myself in a narrow street between high adobe walls. Just ahead, on my left, was a door in the wall. As I approached the door was flung open, and a small boy came running out, rolling a hoop. This happened so suddenly that Pecos shied very sharply, and I fell to the ground, jamming the thumb of my left hand. The little boy looked very worried and said that he was sorry to have caused such an accident. I waved the matter off, as if it were nothing; but as a matter of fact my hand hurt so much that tears welled up in my eyes. And the pain lasted for many days. I have fallen many times

---

4. **... they wanted their heads** The horses wanted to be free of the control of the reins.
5. **Vaya con Dios** (vī yə kən dē′ ōs) "Go with God" (Spanish).

from a horse, both before and after that, and a few times I fell from a running horse on dangerous ground, but that was the most painful of them all.

In another settlement there were some boys who were interested in racing. They had good horses, some of them, but their horses were not so good as mine, and I won easily. After that, I began to think of ways in which I might even the odds a little, might give some advantage to my competitors. Once or twice I gave them a head start, a reasonable head start of, say, five or ten yards to the hundred, but that was too simple, and I won anyway. Then it came to me that I might try this: we should all line up in the usual way, side by side, but my competitors should be mounted and I should not. When the signal was given I should then have to get up on my horse while the others were breaking away; I should have to mount my horse during the race. This idea appealed to me greatly, for it was both imaginative and difficult, not to mention dangerous; Pecos and I should have to work very closely together. The first few times we tried this I had little success, and over a course of a hundred yards I lost four races out of five. The principal problem was that Pecos simply could not hold still among the other horses. Even before they broke away he was hard to manage, and when they were set running nothing could hold him back, even for an instant. I could not get my foot in the stirrup, but I had to throw myself up across the saddle on my stomach, hold on as best I could, and twist myself into position, and all this while racing at full speed. I could ride well enough to accomplish this feat, but it was a very awkward and inefficient business. I had to find some way to use the whole energy of my horse, to get it all into the race. Thus far I had managed only to break his motion, to divert him from his purpose and mine. To correct this I took Pecos away and worked with him through the better part of a long afternoon on a broad reach of level ground beside an irrigation ditch. And it was hot, hard work. I began by teaching him to run straight away while I ran beside him a few steps, holding on to the saddle horn, with no pressure on the reins. Then, when we had mastered this trick, we proceeded to the next one, which was this: I placed my weight on my arms, hanging from the saddle horn, threw my feet out in front of me, struck them to the ground, and sprang up against the saddle. This I did again and again, until Pecos came to expect it and did not flinch or lose his stride. I sprang a little higher each time. It was in all a slow process of trial and error, and after two or three hours both Pecos and I were covered with bruises

LITERATURE IN CONTEXT

Mythology Connection

The Centaur

In his first paragraph, N. Scott Momaday refers to the Plains Indian culture as "the centaur culture." In alluding to that mythical creature with the upper body of a man and the lower body of a horse, Momaday indirectly places his discussion within the larger context of cultural history. According to Greek myth, centaurs like the one shown below were a race of wild, inhospitable beings who dwelled in the mountains of northern Greece. However, one centaur, Chiron, taught many Greek heroes and was well-known for his wisdom and knowledge of medicine.

Connect to the Literature

Why do you think Momaday calls the Plains Indian culture a "centaur culture" rather than a "horse culture"?

Comprehension

Why were Momaday and Pecos training together?

I vaulted all the way over my horse…

and soaked through with perspiration. But we had much to show for our efforts, and at last the moment came when we must put the whole performance together. I had not yet leaped into the saddle, but I was quite confident that I could now do so; only I must be sure to get high enough. We began this dress rehearsal then from a standing position. At my signal Pecos lurched and was running at once, straight away and smoothly. And at the same time I sprinted forward two steps and gathered myself up, placing my weight precisely at my wrists, throwing my feet out and together, perfectly. I brought my feet down sharply to the ground and sprang up hard, as hard as I could, bringing my legs astraddle of my horse—and everything was just right, except that I sprang too high. I vaulted all the way over my horse, clearing the saddle by a considerable margin, and came down into the irrigation ditch. It was a good trick, but it was not the one I had in mind, and I wonder what Pecos thought of it after all. Anyway, after a while I could mount my horse in this way and so well that there was no challenge in it, and I went on winning race after race.

I went on, farther and farther into the wide world. Many things happened. And in all this I knew one thing: I knew where the journey was begun, that it was itself a learning of the beginning, that the beginning was infinitely worth the learning. The journey was well undertaken, and somewhere in it I sold my horse to an old Spanish man of Vallecitos. I do not know how long Pecos lived. I had used him hard and well, and it may be that in his last days an image of me like thought shimmered in his brain.

Critical Reading

Cite textual evidence to support your responses.

1. **Key Ideas and Details (a)** What inspires Momaday's decision to take a journey? **(b) Draw Conclusions:** What do you think such a journey meant to him, and how did it make him feel?

2. **Key Ideas and Details (a)** What does Momaday trade with Pasqual? **(b) Analyze:** What motivates him to make this trade?

3. **Key Ideas and Details (a) Support:** Provide one detail that shows that Pecos was an extremely good horse. **(b) Infer:** What does the writer mean when he says that he "had used him hard and well"? **(c) Draw Conclusions:** Why do you think Momaday sold Pecos?

4. **Integration of Knowledge and Ideas** Based on these two memoirs, what does the idea of homeland mean? Use at least two of these Essential Question words: *global, natural, formative, environment, exile.* [*Connecting to the Essential Question: What is the relationship between literature and place?*]

Literary Analysis

1. **Craft and Structure** Using a chart like the one shown, list at least two examples that show how each **memoir** combines historical or cultural elements with personal details from the writer's life.

Historical Details	Personal Details

2. **Craft and Structure** **(a)** Cite two memories Brave Orchid has while waiting at the airport. **(b)** Are these memories typical features of a memoir? Why or why not?

3. **Craft and Structure** **(a)** Whose impressions provide the **limited third-person point of view** in the excerpt from *The Woman Warrior?* **(b)** Explain why this choice of point of view is unusual for any autobiographical work.

4. **Craft and Structure** Brave Orchid is Kingston's mother. What techniques more commonly found in fiction does Kingston use to portray her mother as a literary character?

5. **Craft and Structure** How might Brave Orchid's story have been different if the narrative had been written in her voice, using *I* instead of *she*? Explain.

6. **Key Ideas and Details** **(a)** Identify two events that Momaday describes in this excerpt. **(b)** What connects these events to the cultural theme he introduces in the opening paragraph?

7. **Integration of Knowledge and Ideas** In what specific ways does **relating to your own experiences** help you better understand the feelings and thoughts the writers express in these memoirs? In your answer, mention specific examples from the text.

8. **Integration of Knowledge and Ideas** What similarities or differences did you find between the selections and your own experiences?

9. **Comparing Literary Works** Compare and contrast the effects of each writer's choice of point of view in these memoirs, using these questions to guide you: **(a)** Does the **first-person point of view** bring the reader closer to the narrator than third-person point of view allows? Explain. **(b)** Does the limited third-person point of view allow the writer greater freedom of expression? Explain. **(c)** In which essay do stye and content most effectively communicate the author's purpose? Explain.

Common Core State Standards

Writing
3. Write narratives to develop real experiences or events using effective technique, well-chosen details, and well-structured event sequences. *(p. 1440)*

3.d. Use precise words and phrases, telling details, and sensory language to convey a vivid picture of the experiences, events, setting, and/or characters. *(p. 1440)*

Language
3.a. Vary syntax for effect; apply an understanding of syntax to the study of complex texts when reading. *(p. 1441)*

4.b. Identify and correctly use patterns of word changes that indicate different meanings or parts of speech. *(p. 1440)*

4.d. Verify the preliminary determination of the meaning of a word or phrase. *(p. 1440)*

Vocabulary Acquisition and Use

Word Analysis: Latin Root -aud-

The word *inaudibly* is based on the Latin word root -aud-, which means "hear." Words that share this root relate to hearing or sound. For example, *inaudibly* means "in a tone too low to be heard." Apply your knowledge of the root -aud- to write definitions for each word listed below. Check your work in a dictionary as needed.

1. audiotape
2. auditory
3. auditorium
4. audition
5. auditor
6. audiology
7. audiophile

Vocabulary: Sentence Completions

Review the vocabulary list on page 1424. Then, complete each sentence with an appropriate word from the list. Explain your choices.

1. The dancer's _____ legs carried her across the stage.

2. _____ to passage of time, she worked on into the night.

3. When David replied _____, I asked him to speak up.

4. The _____ of the situation silenced all petty bickering.

5. The _____ scene in the painting reminded me of a simpler time.

Writing

Narrative Text Both of these writers share an experience from the past. Choose a significant event that you have experienced and write a brief **memoir** exploring its meaning.

Prewriting Brainstorm for a list of events that affected you earlier in life. For each, write two or three reasons why the event was significant. Decide which event you will write about.

Drafting After describing the event or experience, provide the insight to explain its effect on you. Include details that build the emotional impact of your insight.

Model: Elaborating to Add Emotional Depth

It was during my aunt's visit in the summer of 1996 that I discovered my pride in my Native American heritage. Through her stories about my grandparents and their struggles, I finally learned to celebrate what makes my life different instead of trying to hide it.

Words like *pride*, *finally*, and *celebrate* relate to the symbolic meaning of the event.

Revising Ask a classmate to read your draft to see if he or she can identify with your experience. Based on the feedback you receive, revise your draft, adding elaboration to ensure that readers will understand the importance of the event and the feelings it inspired in you.

Conventions and Style: Varying Sentences

In both your personal and academic writing, avoid using the same types of sentences repeatedly. Repetition of the same sentence types diminishes the flow of your ideas and is monotonous for the reader. Instead, work to achieve sentence variety in your writing.

One effective way to add sentence variety is to **vary your sentences' beginnings.** Start by reviewing a draft of your own writing. Examine one paragraph, and bracket the first words of each sentence. Make a list of those words. If you see the same types of words over and over—all nouns or all adverbs, for example—work to break that pattern. The sample sentences below show different types of sentence beginnings:

Types of Sentence Beginnings

Adverb: <u>Suddenly,</u> I realized that my mistake was not that serious.

Direct Object: <u>My mistake,</u> I suddenly realized, was not that serious.

Prepositional Phrase: <u>Above the city lights,</u> we could barely see the silver moon.

Participial Phrase: <u>Working late into the night,</u> I found the solution.

Inverted Subject-Predicate Order: <u>On the table sat</u> a book, a pen, and a rose in a vase.

Practice Revise the following sentences to begin with the part of speech in parentheses, or invert the subject and verb if so indicated.

1. The boy saw his journey would lead him deeper into the desert. (direct object)

2. Pasqual, riding a stallion, was breaking in the horse. (participle)

3. The narrator, wiser, went on alone riding his own horse. (participle)

4. Rolling a hoop, a boy came out of the door. (noun)

5. Mounting a horse during a race wasn't easy. (prepositional phrase)

6. Moon Orchid had shopping bags filled with food on the floor next to her. (prepositional phrase)

7. At the airport were Brave Orchid, Moon Orchid's niece, and Brave Orchid's children. (put subject before predicate)

8. Crowding along the conveyer belts, passengers waited to have their luggage searched. (noun)

9. The sisters stood in the doorway and greeted each other, blocking the way. (participle)

10. Each sister looked surprisingly old to the other one. (adverb)

Writing and Speaking Conventions

A. Writing Write sentences beginning with the following items. Use the item as the part of speech given in parentheses.

1. Silently (adverb)

2. At (prepositional phrase)

3. The settlements (noun)

4. Bruised (participle)

5. Waiting (participle)

Example: Silently

Sentence: Silently, the narrator and his friend rode on together.

B. Speaking Tell a partner or a small group a brief story about a journey. You may use an experience you have had or one you have read about. As you speak, make sure to vary your sentence beginnings.

Analyzing Functional and Expository Texts

Technical Report • Mission Statement

About the Texts

A **technical report** is a document that provides an in-depth explanation of a topic or process related to science or technology. Technical reports are usually written for knowledgeable readers, so they tend to contain advanced language and technical terms. These documents often include

- an introduction;
- a list of numbered parts or sections;
- procedural elements or a description of a process;
- graphics, charts, and other visual presentations of information.

A **mission statement** is a document that expresses in a concise way an organization's purpose, direction, and goals. A mission statement may appear with a brief history of the organization.

Preparing to Read Complex Texts

Documents about scientific or technical topics may contain advanced, specialized concepts with which you are not familiar. Use the following approaches to **clarify** unfamiliar material:

- *Reread* to isolate unfamiliar elements. Focus on elements you do understand, from which you can gather a general meaning.
- Identify familiar words and phrases that serve as *context clues* to help you define unfamiliar terms.

You may also check print or online dictionaries or other sources to define technical terms. As you read, use a chart like the one shown to help as you apply these clarifying strategies.

Strategy	Unfamiliar	Familiar	Clarification
Reread	concatenation of multiple name parts (e.g., first and initial) on a single line.	multiple; first and initial; single line	The names might be combined on a single line.
Use context clues	For purposes of these tabulations; a captured name is considered to be "valid" if . . .	name; valid	Only some names are valid for this study.

Common Core State Standards

Reading Informational Text
4. Determine the meaning of words and phrases as they are used in a text, including technical meanings

Language
4.a. Use context as a clue to the meaning of a word or phrase.
6. Acquire and use accurately general academic and domain-specific words and phrases, sufficient for reading at the college and career readiness level; demonstrate independence in gathering vocabulary knowledge when considering a word or phrase important to comprehension or expression.

Content-Area Vocabulary

These words appear in the selections that follow. They may also appear in other content-area texts.

demographic (dem ə graf´ ik) *adj.* relating to the science of analyzing human populations

aggregates (ag´ rə gits) *n.* groups of distinct things considered together as a whole

cumulative (kyoo´ myə lə tiv) *adj.* accumulated; adding up

assimilation (ə sim´ ə la´ sh ə n) *n.* in sociology, the merging of a minority group into mainstream culture

U.S. Census Bureau

Demographic Aspects of Surnames from Census 2000

David L. Word, Charles D. Coleman, Robert Nunziata and Robert Kominski

> The introduction gives an overview of the information contained in the report and also focuses on some technical aspects of the research.

> This report was issued by the United States Census Bureau, an arm of the federal government that researches and distributes data about the nation's people. The full report is twenty-one pages long.

1. Introduction

This report documents both the overall frequency of surnames (last names), as well as some of the basic demographic characteristics that are associated with surnames. **The presentation of data in this report focuses on summarized aggregates of counts and characteristics associated with surnames, and, as such, do not in any way identify any specific individuals. . . .**

3. Characteristics of Surnames

3.1 How many names are there?

> The report is organized into numbered and titled sections, making it simpler for readers to navigate the material.

Even after applying various edits and acceptance criteria to the names, there are a sizable number of unique names in the population. Over 6 million last names were identified. Many of these names were either unique (occurred once) or nearly so (occurred 2-4 times) raising questions about the actual validity of the name. Cursory examination of the data indicates that many of these unique names were probably the entire name of the person (first and last, or first, middle initial and last) concatenated into a single continuous string, with some other information. . . .

Table 1 shows the frequency of last names and the numbers of people who are defined by them. Seven last names are held by a million or more people. The most common last name reported was SMITH, held by about 2.3 million people, or about 9 percent of the population. Another 6 names with over a million respondents (JOHNSON, WILLIAMS, BROWN, JONES, MILLER and DAVIS), along with SMITH, account for about 4 percent of the population, or one in every 25 people. There are another 268 last names each occurring at least 100,000 times, but less than 1 million times. Together, these 275 last names, just 4/100,000 of all reported last names, account together for 26 percent of the population, or about one of every four people. On the flip side of this distribution, about 65 percent (or 4 million) of all captured last names were held by just one person, and about 80 percent (or 5 million) were held by no more than 4 people.

> The authors provide help in interpreting the chart on the next page.

A discussion of the numerical data presented in this chart appears on the preceding page.

Table 1

Last Names by Frequency of Occurrence and Number of People: 2000

Frequency of Occurrence	Last Names				People with these Names		
	Number	Cumulative Number	Cumulative Proportion (percent)	Number	Cumulative Number	Cumulative Proportion (percent)
1,000,000+	7	7	0.0	10,710,446	10,710,446	4.0
100,000-999,999	268	275	0.0	60,091,601	70,802,047	26.2
10,000-99,999	3,012	3,287	0.1	77,657,334	148,459,381	55.0
1,000-9,999	20,369	23,656	0.4	58,264,607	206,723,988	76.6
100-999	128,015	151,671	2.4	35,397,085	242,121,073	89.8
50-99	105,609	257,280	4.1	7,358,924	249,479,997	92.5
25-49	166,059	423,339	6.8	5,772,510	255,252,507	94.6
10-24	331,518	754,857	12.1	5,092,320	260,344,827	96.5
5-9	395,600	1,150,457	18.4	2,568,209	262,913,036	97.5
2-4	1,056,992	2,207,449	35.3	2,808,085	265,721,121	98.5
1	4,040,966	6,248,415	100.0	4,040,966	269,762,087	100.0

4. Methodology of Measuring Names

4.1 Turning names into data

Turning a written name on a census form into usable data for tabulation purposes is a task which involves a number of assumptions and decision rules. This section describes both the operational and logical decision rules used to turn 'names into data'.

The data for this research comes from the written-in names persons provided when they filled out their census form. . . . Obviously, many factors enter into the process of turning a written response on paper into a numerically-coded value. For instance, alternate spellings, including incorrect spellings, random marks on the paper, abbreviations, etc., must all have decision rules associated with them, in order to code them. . . . Transformation of names into data [is] complex, engaging a larger set of rules and procedures. In addition to the possible sources of error already mentioned, a number of other issues relevant to the character strings defining names come into play. This includes things such as: 1) scanning or reading errors by the OCR [Optical Character Recognition] software, 2) mis-keying, 3) respondents entering data into incorrect locations in questionnaires, 4) respondents entering no name or an invalid name, and 5) concatenation of multiple name parts (e.g, first and initial) when they are written in the space for a single name. Each of these problems must be addressed

The authors provide information on research challenges and solutions. This information is helpful to readers who are assessing the data.

either with some kind of editing or resolution rule, or the name must be left as is. It is due to many of these issues that there are a large number of 'names' which occur only once or twice – many of these 'unique' names are variants of more common names which short of inspection on a one-by-one basis, cannot be "corrected" to the character string they actually are supposed to represent.

4.2 Definition of a name

For purposes of these tabulations, a captured name from Census 2000 is considered to be "valid" if it satisfies the following two criteria:

1. Both the first and last names must have at least two alphabetic characters.

2. A first or last name may also be considered valid if it has support in the Social Security Administration's 1998 NUMIDENT file. The NUMIDENT file used in this research is a 5 percent sample of all people who had been issued Social Security numbers as of November 1998. The advantage of using the NUMIDENT file as a benchmark is that individuals receive Social Security cards with the names they provide on their applications. If an individual receives a card with an error in their name, they have an incentive to report the error and have it corrected. Thus, it is assumed that the NUMIDENT file is the most current and correct source for validating names. . . .

> The authors do not assume readers' knowledge but provide more information about specialized content.

Records with names that did not satisfy the two criteria were deleted for purposes of these tabulations. For example, names such as A LINCOLN or MISTER T would be ruled invalid because neither the first name A nor the last name T contains two letters, thus violating criterion 1. . . .

Examples of invalid names under criterion 2 are strings such as PERSON (as a first name), ADULT, BABY, HOUSEHOLDER, or SPOUSE. Thus, a census record with the name BABY MILLER would have been dropped from the analysis, because BABY is not supported as a valid name in the NUMIDENT file.

As names become less frequent, the possibility that a string of letters is not a valid name increases. As has been noted, this is due to many factors – misplaced or misscanned letter(s), bad spelling, and a variety of other causes. All names occurring 300 or more times were reviewed for validity, using a series of rules described in section 4.4.5, although certainly this process did not delete or modify all invalid names. However, names occurring fewer than 300 times were not examined at all, because of their large relative volume.

The initial data file used for this report contains 279,132,770 data-defined person records (census records with at least two data fields with valid responses) from an intermediate file created during the processing for Census 2000. After applying the criteria and the edits we developed for improving names, the final number of records for analysis comprises 269,762,087 people, or approximately 96 percent of all people counted in Census 2000.

The Statue of Liberty-Ellis Island Foundation, Inc.

Mission and Background

Mission: To restore and preserve the Statue of Liberty National Monument, which includes, in addition to the Statue itself, Ellis Island and its Museum of Immigration; Custody and control of records, relics and other things of historic interest related to the Statue of Liberty and the millions of immigrants who entered the United States via Ellis Island; To foster, promote and stimulate public knowledge of and interest in the history of the Statue of Liberty and Ellis Island.

> This mission statement includes the full range of goals of the foundation.

The National Park Service (NPS), a unit of the United States Department of the Interior, operates both the Statue of Liberty and Ellis Island (the "Monument") and has accepted grants pursuant to an agreement dated October 14, 1983 and subsequent agreements with the Foundation for the restoration and preservation of the Monument.

Background: The first projects of the Foundation from 1982 until 1992 included the restoration of the Statue of Liberty, upgrade of Liberty Island, the preservation of the main building on Ellis Island, upgrading Castle Clinton, and establishment of the Statue of Liberty Museum and the 220,000 square foot Ellis Island Immigration Museum (which has had 25 million visitors since opening). . . .

In 1992 the Foundation launched a project campaign for the restoration and adaptation of the "kitchen and laundry" building, the "bakery and carpentry" building and the "shop" building on Ellis Island. This allowed the museum to expand and establish the Oral History Studio, the Library, Living Theater, Children's Orientation Center and the changing Exhibition Center. It also established new offices for the employees of the NPS.

During 1995 to 2001 the Foundation stepped forward to create the American Family Immigration History Center on Ellis Island and the Internet. The Center contains computerized immigration records (manifests) of 25 million people who arrived in America through the Port of New York between 1892 and 1924. . . . In 2004 the Foundation spearheaded a campaign to make critical safety upgrades to the Statue of Liberty, which was closed to the public after 9/11/01. The Foundation successfully raised the necessary funds and managed the construction work so that the National Park Service/U.S. Department of the Interior could reopen Lady Liberty's doors to the public on August 3, 2004.

In 2007, the Foundation initiated a campaign for The Peopling of America Center (the "Center"). The Center will expand upon the story currently told of the Ellis Island Years (1892-1954) by including the story of those who arrived before Ellis Island and after, right up to the present, becoming citizens, and altering the demographic landscape of America. The Center will follow the arc of the American experience: from immigration, to assimilation, to citizenship, played out in every generation, past, present and future.

> The background highlights past achievements and shows how the foundation has grown.

Critical Reading

1. **Key Ideas and Details (a)** Summarize the criteria the Census Bureau used to determine the validity of a name. **(b)** According to the report, what might cause a name to be omitted as invalid? **(c)** Given this criteria, why is it likely that "unique" names are not valid?

2. **Key Ideas and Details (a)** Based on context clues in the report, explain what a "decision rule" is. **(b)** Identify two decision rules the scientists used to turn written responses into quantifiable data.

3. **Key Ideas and Details (a)** In your own words, explain the mission of The Statue of Liberty-Ellis Island Foundation, Inc. **(b)** Identify two details from the "Background" section that best express that mission. Explain your choices.

4. **Content-Area Vocabulary (a)** How do the meanings of the Greek word *demos* ("people") and root *-graph-* ("writing") contribute to the meaning of *demographic*? **(b)** How do the meanings of *demos* and the combining form *-cracy* ("power, might") contribute to the meaning of *democracy*?

Common Core State Standards

Writing

1. Write arguments to support claims in an analysis of substantive topics or texts, using valid reasoning and relevant and sufficient evidence.

10. Write routinely over shorter time frames for a range of tasks, purposes, and audiences.

⏱ Timed Writing

Argument [40 minutes]

Format

In a strong **argumentative essay,** the writer states a position and supports it with evidence. In a Timed Writing sitation, the strongest evidence will be quotations from the texts under discussion.

Both the Technical Report and Mission Statement touch on the idea of heritage. Names represent the heritage of families and ethnic groups, while museums preserve our shared historical and cultural heritage. Write an **argumentative essay** in which you discuss who should bear the most **responsibility** for preserving heritage sites. Consider the government, the general public, non-profit organizations, or another institution. Cite information from the Technical Report and Mission Statement to support your ideas.

Academic Vocabulary

The prompt asks you to discuss issues of **responsibility,** which can mean many different things. In your essay include a brief discussion of how you are applying that term to this topic.

5-Minute Planner

Complete these steps before you begin to write.

1. Read the prompt carefully. Identify key words.

2. Take notes that relate to the prompt. **TIP** Sketch a quick chart to categorize notes that apply to different aspects of the prompt.

3. Reread the prompt, and draft your essay.

4. Before you hand in your essay, check for correct use of the conventions of punctuation and capitalization.

Write a Short Story

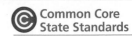
Common Core
State Standards

Writing

3. Write narratives to develop real or imagined experiences or events using effective technique, well-chosen details, and well-structured event sequences.

3.a. Engage and orient the reader by setting out a problem, situation, or observation and its significance, establishing one or multiple point(s) of view, and introducing a narrator and/or characters; create a smooth progression of experiences or events.

3.b. Use narrative techniques, such as dialogue, pacing, description, reflection, and multiple plot lines, to develop experiences, events, and/or characters.

3.c. Use a variety of techniques to sequence events so that they build on one another to create a coherent whole and build toward a particular tone and outcome.

Fictional Narrative Writers create short stories to tell about events that never happened. They use the tools of narrative writing to invent stories that can be exciting, inspiring, or moving. Many short stories focus on a single incident that reveals an insight about a main character. Those insights can give the short story form a surprising depth and relevance. Even though the events are made up, the feelings they generate are real. A good short story can leave a powerful and lasting impression.

Assignment Write a short story that tells about a fictional event in which a central conflict is—or is not—resolved.

What to Include Your short story should have these elements:

- a setting that presents a time and place using concrete sensory details
- a main character who is involved in a conflict or has a problem to be resolved
- a plot that includes a clear sequence of events related to the conflict
- dialogue between characters that moves the plot forward and develops characters' personalities
- effective pacing and plot strategies, such as flashback and foreshadowing

To preview the criteria on which your short story may be assessed, see the rubric on page 1455.

Focus on Research

Research can enrich short stories in the following ways:

- by ensuring historical accuracy in a story that is set in a particular time and place
- by adding credible details to descriptions of clothing, scenery, weather, architecture, and food
- by leading to new story ideas

Keep records of your sources when researching for fiction. If you use a direct quote from another source, credit it. However, most of the time your research will be with the aim of gaining general knowledge about a topic so that you can write about it convincingly or accurately in a fictional context.

Prewriting and Planning

Choosing Your Topic

To choose a topic for your short story, use one of these strategies:

- **Make a blueprint.** Sketch a possible setting—anything from a shopping mall to a space station. As you draw, think about events that might unfold there. List three or four ideas and choose one to develop.

- **Focus on a conflict.** Like all writers, you will be influenced by your own life. Make a list about conflicts you have experienced, witnessed, or studied. Consider conflicts between people, between a person and nature, or within a single person. Choose a conflict from your list that you think will make an interesting story.

Narrowing Your Topic

Create a story chart. While anything can happen in fiction, you need to narrow your choices as you organize your story. Make a story chart like the one shown to plan the four stages of your narrative. After you have identified the basic plot events, decide whether you will **foreshadow,** or give hints about what will happen. You might also decide to use **flashbacks,** which give readers information about events that happened before the beginning of the story.

Using a Story Chart			
Exposition: Establish the setting, main characters, and set up the conflict.	**Rising Action:** Describe the events that increase the conflict and tension.	**Climax:** Identify the point of greatest tension.	**Resolution:** Tell how the conflict is or is not resolved.
Omar wants to go on a trip. His father will not allow him to go, but he does not explain why.	*Omar wages an all-out campaign at home.*	*Omar's father finally explains his reasoning.*	*Omar respects his father's opinion and decides to wait a year.*

Gathering Details

Interview your characters. The more unique and detailed your characters are, the more interesting they will be for your readers. Conduct an interview with each of your main characters. You might ask a partner to ask you questions while you play the role of each character. Your answers will help you generate specific information. Here are some starter questions:

- Where do you live?
- What is a typical day like for you? What would be a perfect day?
- How would you describe yourself?
- What are your main goals and obstacles?

Drafting

Shaping Your Writing

Establish a tense and a point of view. Decide if you will use the past or present tense when you write your story. Also, choose the point of view from which your story will be told. This chart shows three options.

Common Core State Standards

Writing
3.a. Engage and orient the reader by setting out a problem, situation, or observation and its significance, establishing one or multiple point(s) of view, and introducing a narrator and/or characters; create a smooth progression of experiences or events.

Narrator	Description	Example
First-person	The narrator is a character in the story.	*I knew what I had to do. I had to tell Shana the truth.*
Third-person omniscient	The narrator is outside the story and knows everything that happens.	*Julia was finally ready to tell Shana the truth, but Shana didn't want to hear it.*
Third-person limited	The narrator is outside the story, but only knows what one character does and thinks.	*Julia was finally ready to tell Shana the truth. But would Shana listen?*

3.b. Use narrative techniques, such as dialogue, pacing, description, reflection, and multiple plot lines, to develop experiences, events, and/or characters.

Remember your audience. Keep your readers in mind as you draft your story. Ask yourself these questions:

- Is the opening of my story intriguing enough to grab readers' attention?
- What does my audience need to know to follow the story?
- Have I included enough information to make the setting clear? Do readers need more details about time or place?
- Am I explaining my characters' motivations clearly; can readers understand why characters do what they do?
- Does the action make sense? Do I need to include more information or explanation?

Providing Elaboration

Use dialogue or interior monologue. Incorporating a character's own thoughts and words can add to the portrayal of your characters and make a story more entertaining. Use dialogue between two characters to establish tension and relate plot events. If you are using the first-person point of view, write an interior monologue to share the narrator's private thoughts and feelings about events.

Dialogue	Interior Monologue
"Yeah, right," I laughed. "There's no way I'm going to jump off this cliff." *"I wish we had a choice," said the guide, "but we don't."*	*I looked at the sharp, long drop and the tiny pool of water at the bottom. The guide gave me a vaguely encouraging nod. No way. No way could I jump.*

Writers on Writing

Julia Alvarez On Flashback and Exposition

Julia Alvarez is the author of "Antojos" (p. 1298).

I knew when I titled the story "Antojos" that somewhere in the story I was going to have to give my reader some idea of what the word meant. But where and when? A story doesn't come with footnotes, so anything you want your reader to know you've got to put in a story. The opportunity came when Yolanda is driving in the mountains. We all daydream when we're stuck in a car. So, I have Yolanda flash back to a scene with her aunts in the capital where the Spanish word was explained to her.

from *"Antojos"*

Left and right, roadside stands began appearing. Yolanda slowed down and kept an eye out for guavas . . .

In the capital, her aunts had plied her with what she most craved after so many years away. "Any little *antojo*, you must tell us!" They wanted to spoil her, so she'd stay on in her nativeland before she forgot where she had come from. "What exactly does it mean, *antojo*?" Yolanda asked. Her aunts were proven right: After so many years away, their niece was losing her Spanish.

"An *antojo*—" The aunts exchanged quizzical looks. "How to put it? An *antojo* is like a craving for something you have to eat."

A cousin blew out her cheeks. "Calories."

An *antojo*, one of the older aunts continued, was a very old Spanish word from before "your United States was thought of," she added tartly. In the countryside some *campesinos* still used the word to mean possession by an island spirit demanding its due.

Her island spirit certainly was a patient soul, Yolanda joked. She hadn't had her favorite *antojo*, guavas, since her last trip seven years ago. Well, on this trip, her aunts promised, Yoyo could eat guavas to her heart's content.

> Memories often come as little scenes. It's a good way to give readers background they need. They feel they've been there, too.

> How to show a character's character? There's language (dialogue) but also body language. Instead of a speech tag ("she said"), describe a little gesture that "speaks volumes."

> At issue in the story is what language Yolanda speaks. This scene, in which a Spanish word has to be explained, "foreshadows"/hints at what's coming.

Revising

Revising Your Overall Structure

Show instead of tell. Stories are more engaging when the writer shows what is happening rather than simply telling one event after another.

> **Telling:** *Then we had a big argument and got very angry.*
>
> **Showing:** *He raised his voice, so I raised mine. Soon, we were shouting so loudly our neighbors probably had to turn up the volume on their televisions.*

Follow this strategy to determine if you are showing more than telling:

☆ Place a star next to events in which you show what is happening.

X Place an X next to events that you tell, rather than show.

When you find several Xs in a row, revise to bring your story to life. You might use any of the following techniques:

- Add dialogue to show what people say.
- Use figurative language, including *similes, metaphors,* or *personification,* to heighten descriptions of events, people, or settings.
- Describe specific actions and reactions rather than general emotions.

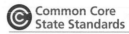

Common Core State Standards

Writing

3.b. Use narrative techniques, such as dialogue, pacing, description, reflection, and multiple plot lines, to develop experiences, events, and/or characters.

3.d. Use precise words and phrases, telling details, and sensory language to convey a vivid picture of the experiences, events, setting, and/or characters.

5. Develop and strengthen writing as needed by planning, revising, editing, rewriting, or trying a new approach, focusing on addressing what is most significant for a specific purpose and audience.

Language

2. Demonstrate command of the conventions of standard English punctuation.

Model: Revising to Make Writing More Interesting

,as if he expected someone to snatch it
away from him at any moment
X Mark ate his dinner rapidly.
"You must have grown up in a big family," she remarked.
Mark looked up, a noodle dangling from his pursed lips.
He slurped, and it disappeared. "Yup," he said.
Kim watched with amusement.

> Adding dialogue and descriptive language makes the story livelier.

Peer Review: Exchange drafts with a partner. Identify two or three sections in your partner's story that could be strengthened by showing rather than telling. Provide clear suggestions for improvement strategies.

Revising Your Word Choice

Replace ineffective words. The words in your story work together to create an overall effect. Review your word choices to make sure that each word is pulling its weight. Replace flat or vague words with words that reflect the senses of sight, hearing, touch, smell, or taste.

Revising to Add Sensory Language

Dull: The fire burns at night.
Lively: The crackling fire sprays hot red sparks into the eerie darkness.

| Sentence Fluency | Voice | Organization | Word Choice | Ideas | Conventions |

Developing Your Style

Using Punctuation in Dialogue

Dialogue conveys the way characters speak. Punctuation can help readers "hear" dialogue. End punctuation—periods, question marks, and exclamation points—affects the tone of a sentence. Other forms of punctuation can also indicate how a character says something.

Rule	Example
Use commas to indicate short pauses.	"Yeah, well, I don't think so."
Use ellipses to show a longer pause or hesitation. Ellipses can also suggest a voice trailing off.	"Well…I guess so." "I suppose we could…"
Use a dash to indicate a sudden stop, such as an interruption.	"Hey—" "Hurry up, we've got to—"
Use italics to emphasize a word.	"What is *she* doing here?" "What is she doing *here*?"
Use apostrophes to show dropped letters in dialect.	"You're kiddin' me, right?"

Find It in Your Reading

Review the dialogue in "Everyday Use" by Alice Walker.

1. Look for examples of dialogue that are especially vivid or effective.

2. **Discuss:** With a partner, read your favorite examples aloud. Discuss how punctuation contributes to the effect of each example.

Apply It to Your Writing

To improve the dialogue in your story, follow these steps:

1. Read each line aloud. Listen to decide whether it sounds natural. Consider adding punctuation to indicate natural pauses in your character's voice.

2. Decide if there is more than one possible reading for the line. For important lines, consider using italics to show which word the character emphasizes.

3. Be careful not to overuse special punctuation, such as ellipses, dashes, and italics. Limit exclamation points, as well; they are more effective when used sparingly. Reread all of the dialogue in your story, paying attention to the balance of punctuation.

Hallway

Walking through the dimly red corridor in the complex, Gerald found himself surrounded by the uniform shuffling of countless pairs of brown work shoes. Looking down, he saw that his shoes were actually of the same stuff as everyone else's, yet they simply refused to blend in to their surroundings. The rhythmic *THUMP, THUMP, THUMP* was not soothing at all to Gerald, who preferred his own little *tap* interspersed between the monotonous beat.

Gazing down the seemingly endless straight hallway, he could see the doors, measured off oh so carefully, exactly at ten feet apart. Every so often, as if on cue, a body would turn, leave the line, and meander his way into one of these rooms. As Gerald inched past, pushed along at a pace unbearably slow, he glanced in each room only to see the blank expression on each man's face as he sat down with his wife, son, and daughter. Sometimes there was a dog, sometimes two sons, sometimes even a grandmother. All trifling differences, he thought. But such thoughts are unnecessary, not becoming of oneself. Another person turned in, and another, and another.

He wondered why the hallway had to be so perfectly, boringly straight. Couldn't they make it curved a little, or have a turn here or there? As he looked behind all he could see was the red hallway filled with pale faces, blank as canvas. He couldn't help but wonder if anyone else thought like he did. I talk to myself in my head, is this normal?

He managed to catch himself considering the silly notion of running, just running to the end of the hallway. He continued walking. The line made a turn at the end of the hallway, seemingly because it had purpose, going up the stairs on the left, but the fact was that there was no other option. It was how it always has been and how it always shall remain, he thought, smiling at himself, smiling at his childishness in thinking he'd break the line. He made the sharp left up the stairs, thinking, as he often did, "A circular staircase would really save space, and be more interesting anyway." But that idea was preposterous, and he soon rid himself of it, as always. Turning into his room, he sat and ate with his family, not speaking a word. "Really, there's nothing to speak about. It's all been said before," he sighed into his food.

Suddenly, he realized himself in the concave reflection of the spoon. Suddenly, all he could see was the upside-down reflection of himself. Suddenly, I realized myself in the concave reflection of that spoon. Suddenly, all I could focus on was the blurry, upside-down ME in that spoon.

For the complete story, visit www.PHLITonline.com.

Michael immediately establishes a clear point of view—limited third person.

Michael uses internal monologue to develop character.

Michael provides vivid details that help readers visualize the scene.

A shift to first-person point of view signals a turning point in the plot.

Editing and Proofreading

Check your story to eliminate errors in grammar, spelling, or punctuation. Also, be sure that your story is neatly presented and legible.

Focus on punctuation in dialogue. Check that you have punctuated dialogue correctly. Remember to use quotation marks only for direct quotations. Check that you have used commas and capital letters correctly.

> *Direct Quotation: "We'd better keep practicing," he said.*
> *Indirect Quotation: He said we need a lot more rehearsal.*

Focus on spelling. For words ending in silent *-e,* drop the e before adding a suffix beginning with a vowel, such as *-ing, -ed,* or *-es.* For example: *communicate* becomes *communicated, communicating, communicates.* Double-check verbs in the past tense to be sure you have applied this spelling rule.

Spiral Review: Transitional Expressions Earlier in this unit you learned how transitional expressions (page 1323) help connect ideas and reduce choppiness in your writing. Check your story to make sure that you connected ideas correctly with transitional expressions.

Publishing, Presenting, and Reflecting

Consider the following ways to share and reflect on your writing:

Recite your story. Read your story aloud, using appropriate expressions, gestures, pauses, pacing, volume, and body language.

Illustrate and design your story. Use desktop publishing software to create a layout for your story that includes one or more illustrations, as well as an effective type design for the title and text.

Reflect on your writing. Jot down your thoughts about the experience of writing a short story. Begin by answering these questions: Did you always feel in control of the writing process, or did you sometimes feel as if the story took over? Did writing a short story change the way you feel about reading them?

Rubric for Self-Assessment

Evaluate your short story using the following criteria and rating scale:

Criteria	Rating Scale			
	not very			*very*
Purpose/Focus: How clearly do you describe the setting and events in the story?	1	2	3	4
Organization: How effectively do the events and conflict in your story build up to a strong climax and a satisfying resolution?	1	2	3	4
Development of Ideas/Elaboration: How well do you use dialogue to reveal actions and personalities of the characters?	1	2	3	4
Language: How effective are your sentences and their punctuation, both in dialogue and narration?	1	2	3	4
Conventions: How correct is your use of grammar in punctuating dialogue?	1	2	3	4

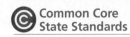

Common Core State Standards

Writing

5. Develop and strengthen writing as needed by planning, revising, editing, rewriting, or trying a new approach, focusing on addressing what is most significant for a specific purpose and audience.

6. Use technology, including the Internet, to produce, publish, and update individual or shared writing products in response to ongoing feedback, including new arguments or information.

Language

2. Demonstrate command of the conventions of standard English capitalization, punctuation, and spelling when writing.

2.b. Spell correctly.

Compare Print News Coverage

Our world is saturated with broadcast news and information. Television, radio, the Internet, and even cell phones are now vehicles for the delivery of news. However, print media—newspapers and magazines—are still important sources of information, and their online versions extend their reach into the world of electronic media. The ways in which print media cover news stories has significant effects on how the public understands current events.

Print Media Genres

There are two main forms of print news media:

Types of Print Media

Newspapers	Magazines
• Daily newspapers present timely coverage of events; many update stories online. • Articles include basic facts and information. • News articles aim to be unbiased. • Photos and captions supplement stories.	• Weekly and monthly magazines target specific topics. • Articles provide in-depth analysis of an event or one aspect of a news story. • Articles include commentary and opinions. • Images provide additional content.

Factors that Shape Print News Coverage

The same news event can be described in many ways, resulting in different messages. The following factors affect the way writers, editors, and news directors shape a story for publication:

- **Purpose:** Most news articles are written to inform, but some media makers may also want to influence opinion or entertain. The purpose of a story will affect the information the reporter writes and the editors include.

- **Author's Perspective:** News articles are meant to be objective. Sometimes, however, a writer may omit certain facts or emphasize others that implicitly express an opinion or shape a particular perception.

- **Audience:** Some publications target specific populations and cater to the interests, needs, or even the biases of those groups. Understanding the target audience can help you identify possible slants in the presentation of a news story.

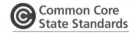

Common Core State Standards

Reading Informational Text

7. Integrate and evaluate multiple sources of information presented in different media or formats as well as in words in order to address a question or solve a problem.

Speaking and Listening

1. Initiate and participate effectively in a range of collaborative discussions with diverse partners on grades 11–12 topics, texts, and issues, building on others' ideas and expressing their own clearly and persuasively.

1.a. Come to discussions prepared, having read and researched material under study; explicitly draw on that preparation by referring to evidence from texts and other research on the topic or issue to stimulate a thoughtful, well-reasoned exchange of ideas.

2. Integrate multiple sources of information presented in diverse formats and media in order to make informed decisions and solve problems, evaluating the credibility and accuracy of each source and noting any discrepancies among the data.

Aspects of Print News Presentation

News editors organize stories to meet a variety of purposes. As you read, notice how the treatment of the following elements affects your understanding of a news story:

- **Headlines:** The people or groups mentioned in a headline and the use of active or passive voice can affect the meaning. Notice the difference between "President Signs Important War Veterans Bill" and "Key War Veterans Bill Finally Signed into Law."
- **Story Placement:** Placing a story on the front page or burying it in the middle of a paper reflects the level of attention editors think a story deserves.
- **Duration of Coverage:** The length of time a story is covered—a day, a week, a month—also indicates an assessment of its importance.
- **Visual Elements:** Photos shape readers' understanding. The quality of images (flattering, embarrassing, etc.) also has an effect.

Activities: Compare Print Coverage of Same Event

Comprehension and Collaboration For both activities, use an evaluation form like the one shown below.

A. Select a news event and examine its coverage in three different newspapers or magazines. Look for similarities and differences in the ways each publication approaches its coverage, and examine how the coverage emphasizes different elements, including facts. Conduct a group discussion in which members exchange and discuss what they have learned and what ideas they have developed in their own media examinations. Use the Evaluation form below as a guide.

B. Find coverage of the same event in broadcast media (television or radio). Compare the broadcast coverage to the print media versions of the story. Determine if specific information was added or omitted. Write a paragraph explaining your findings.

Evaluation Form for Print Media Coverage

News Event: _____

Three Sources in Which It Is Covered: _____

Intended Audience of Each Publication: _____

How are the headlines different? _____

Are the stories placed differently? Explain: _____

Do any of the stories seem to favor one side? Explain. _____

What information is the same? What is different? _____

How does each story provide a different understanding of the event? _____
_____

Language Study

Cognates

Cognates are words that are essentially the same in different languages. They share origins and meanings and sound and look similar. For example, many English words are rooted in Latin, the same language from which Spanish evolved. Therefore, many English and Spanish words have similar spellings and definitions. You will be better equipped to infer the meaning of a word in one language if you know its definition in another. Study the chart of Spanish words and their meanings shown below.

Spanish Word	Definition
arduo	hard; difficult
beneficio	performing acts of kindness or charity
estudioso	attentive; serious about studying
florido	flushed with rosy color
grave	dignified and serious
indignación	anger caused by something unjust, mean, or unworthy
pedante	someone concerned with formal rules and book learning
perspicaz	shrewd, keen
ubicuidad	appearing to be everywhere at the same time

Practice

Directions: Replace the cognate in each sentence below with a synonym. Explain your answer.

1. Training for the marathon was a highly <u>arduous</u> project.

2. Samara <u>studiously</u> examined the menu before she chose her meal.

3. The judge <u>gravely</u> considered the matter before him.

4. Thanks to the woman's <u>beneficence,</u> the library built its new wing.

5. In the hot room, everyone's cheeks gradually took on a <u>florid</u> hue.

Directions: Evaluate each sentence below and indicate whether the use of the italicized word is logical. If it is logical, explain why. If it is not, rewrite the sentence so that it makes sense.

6. Everywhere I look, that *ubiquitous* weed is flourishing.

7. Dora was easy to trick because she was so *perspicacious*.

8. His *pedantic* approach to playing the game added spontaneity.

9. The injustice of the comment made her *indignant*.

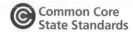

Common Core State Standards

Language

4. Determine or clarify the meaning of unknown and multiple-meaning words and phrases based on *grades 11–12 reading and content,* choosing flexibly from a range of strategies.

4.a. Use context as a clue to the meaning of a word or phrase.

5. Demonstrate understanding of word relationships.

Vocabulary Acquisition and Use:
Sentence Completions

Sentence Completion questions appear in most standardized tests. Sentence Completions test your vocabulary skills as well as your understanding of sentence structure. In these types of questions you are given sentences with one or more missing words. Your task is to choose the correct word or words to complete each sentence logically. One method for choosing the correct word involves three steps: (1) Read the whole sentence carefully and identify the idea the missing word should have; (2) Think of a word or words that would have that meaning; (3) Look for those words or synonyms among the answer choices.

Practice

This exercise is modeled after the Sentence Completion exercises that appear in the Critical Reading section of the SAT.

Directions: Each of the following sentences is missing one or two words. Choose the word or set of words that best completes each sentence.

> **Test-Taking Tip**
> Monitor your timing. Leave problem questions blank and return to them after you have answered the other questions.

1. Naomi Shihab Nye often writes about people who have been ___?___ by the cultures that surround them.
   A. dissuaded
   B. oppressed
   C. maneuvered
   D. swerved
   E. exhausted

2. Martín Espada writes about the revolutionary struggle in ___?___ and moving images.
   A. ample
   B. heady
   C. contiguous
   D. mundane
   E. striking

3. The life of a poet may often be inspiring, but is sometimes a ___?___ struggle.
   A. supple
   B. pugilistic
   C. daunting
   D. oblivious
   E. synonymous

4. Nye's work has often ___?___ the ordinary activities of life and the shared experiences of different cultures.
   A. precipitated
   B. emitted
   C. induced
   D. incorporated
   E. appeased

5. Are the ideas that form ___?___ in our minds the organized sentences of prose or the ___?___ of impressions of poetry?
   A. benignly . . . aspirations
   B. virulently . . . revelations
   C. furtively . . . prosperity
   D. inaudibly . . . shards
   E. ambitiously . . . ecstasy

From Text to Understanding

You have studied each part of Unit 6 as a set of connected texts. In this workshop, you will have the chance to further explore the fundamental connections among these texts and to deepen your essential understanding of the literature and its social and historical context.

PART 1: Contemporary Fiction

Writing: Argumentative Essay A commonplace object or event can take on deep significance as part of a person's history or heritage. Used as symbols or as elements of characterization, everyday objects have a powerful presence in the works in Part 1. Review the texts in Part 1, paying special attention to the Anchor Text, "Everyday Use," by Alice Walker. Think about how ordinary items or experiences are valued differently by different people.

Assignment: Develop and defend a claim about the ways in which one or more characters in this text set, particularly the Anchor Text, use the past to create a sense of identity. As a way of exploring this idea, consider how an everyday item, experience, or encounter connects a person to his or her heritage. Use textual evidence and background information to support your claim, which might look like the following:

> **Example:** Yolanda's craving for guavas in "Antojos" and Dee's yearning to have Grandma Dee's quilts in "Everyday Use" symbolize two different senses of heritage and identity.

Identify the past and present. Pay attention to the characters' past, as well as present, circumstances.

Identify the ordinary. Read the selections carefully. Look for what the text says about the value of ordinary things.

Craft your claim. Decide what you have concluded about characters, heritage, values, and ordinary things. State your idea in an interesting way.

Structure your writing. As you present and defend your claim, be logical and thorough. Present your thinking in an organized way. Make sure you include all the information your reader will need to understand your argument.

Use new words. As you write, experiment with a broader academic vocabulary. Use thematic words, such as *diversity*, *heritage*, and *assumptions*.

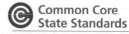

Common Core State Standards

Writing

1. Write arguments to support claims in an analysis of substantive topics or texts, using valid reasoning and relevant and sufficient evidence.

7. Conduct short as well as more sustained research projects to answer a question (including a self-generated question) or solve a problem; narrow or broaden the inquiry when appropriate; synthesize multiple sources on that subject, demonstrating understanding of the subject under investigation.

Speaking and Listening

1. Initiate and participate effectively in a range of collaborative discussions (one-on-one, in groups, and teacher-led) with diverse partners on *grades 11–12 topics, texts, and issues*, building on others' ideas and expressing their own clearly and persuasively.

Model: Taking Notes About Passages

Topic: Past and Present

Character name and story: Dee (Wangero) from "Everyday Use"

Past: Grew up in the rural South; ambitious and intelligent; wished for more in life

Present: Politically and racially aware; adopting new cultural values

PART 2: Contemporary Poetry

Research: Culture Fair Multiculturalism is one of the hallmarks of American literature. The Anchor Text, Yosef Komunyakaa's "Camouflaging the Chimera," is about Vietnam, written by a poet of Trinidadian descent who grew up in Louisiana. Other Part 2 poets are Americans with roots in Indonesia, China, Puerto Rico, England, and Israel.

Review the selections in Part 2, especially the Anchor Text by Komunyakaa. Think about how writers focus on local places and individual experience, yet also manage to speak with a voice that is universal.

Assignment: With a partner, research the literary history, major writers, and important works of two specific American cultural groups represented by the writers in Part 2. Include Yosef Komunyakaa's group as one of your choices. Discuss the similarities and differences between the two groups. Present your research in a display for a Literary Culture Fair, a celebration of American multicultural writing. Use a checklist like the one shown to help organize your research and your presentation.

PART 3: Contemporary Nonfiction

Listening and Speaking: Nonfiction Book Club Proposal

The writers in Part 3 share a passion for language. Some are devoted to words, both written and spoken. Others express their thoughts about non-verbal forms of communication, such as music or the power of a kind gesture, in eloquent prose. Language becomes a path to identity, humor, and healing, a path that can span cultural divides.

Review the texts in Part 3, especially the Anchor Text by Anna Quindlen, "One Day, Now Broken in Two." Consider how the selections reflect one of the most basic needs of a writer: to make sense of the world through language.

Assignment: Create a proposal for a nonfiction book club. Select several selections from Part 3, including the Anchor Text, as the first works you will read and study. Choose texts that you think will make an interesting grouping. Explain what is important and engaging about these works and why you will read them together. Prepare a list of sample discussion questions that you would use in your first meeting. Present your completed proposal aloud to the class to convince them to join your group. Encourage classmates' questions and comments about your choices.

Outline for Nonfiction Book Club Presentation

- Which selections did you choose?
- What are your reasons for grouping these texts together?
- What is compelling or interesting about each selection?
- What questions will be used to begin our book discussion?

Literary Culture Fair Checklist

☐ **Choose the cultural or ethnic groups.** Choose two heritages represented by the Part 2 writers, including Yusef Komunyakaa. You and your partner may decide that together you will work on both cultural groups, or you may each focus on one.

☐ **Make an annotated bibliography.** Conduct research to identify the major writers of that cultural group, both past and present. Create an annotated bibliography in which you list important works and briefly explain their contributions to the American literary scene.

☐ **Identify themes, problems, and issues.** Consider the themes that have been particularly important to this group. For example, are these writers concerned with issues of assimilation, racism, family, education, personal happiness, or the American Dream? Describe the stances writers take on these issues.

☐ **Research the selection in detail.** Find out more about the writers' selections included in Part 2 as examples of work from their respective groups. Find out more about the style of the poem and the circumstances under which it was written. Devote part of your display to this work.

☐ **Research images.** Use the library and the Internet to locate photographs, paintings, and illustrations to enliven your display. You may also include music that is representative of the cultural group you have chosen.

Test-Taking Practice

Critical Reading: Short Reading Passage

The **short reading passages** of standardized tests require you to read selections that may only be a paragraph or two in length, or about 100 words. They may be poetry or fiction selections, or readings from natural science, social studies, or the humanities. They may include narrative, expository, or persuasive (argumentative) elements. The majority of the questions require extended reasoning in which you analyze and synthesize information. You may also be required to comment on the author's assumptions and style.

 Common Core State Standards

RL.11-12.4; RI.11-12.5, RI.11-12.2.c; L.11-12.3; W.11-12.1, W.11-12.5
[For the full wording of the standards, see the standards chart in the front of your textbook.]

Practice

The following exercise is modeled after the SAT Short Passage Critical Reading section. This section usually includes 48 questions.

Directions: Read the following passage from "The Gift" by Li-Young Lee. Then, choose the best answer to each question.

> To pull the metal splinter from my palm
> my father recited a story in a low voice.
> I watched his lovely face and not the blade.
> Before the story ended, he'd removed
> 5 the iron sliver I thought I'd die from.
> I can't remember the tale,
> but hear his voice still, a well
> of dark water, a prayer.
> And I recall his hands,
> 10 two measures of tenderness
> he laid against my face,
> the flames of discipline
> he raised above my head.
> Had you entered that afternoon
> 15 you would have thought you saw a man
> planting something in a boy's palm,
> a silver tear, a tiny flame.

Strategy

- **Read carefully** to find text directly related to the question.
- **Avoid being misled** by an answer that looks correct but is not supported by information directly stated.
- **Prove your answer** by matching specific details in the text to what a question is asking.

1. What literary device does this part of the poem employ?
   A. flashback
   B. in medias res
   C. foreshadowing
   D. hyperbole
   E. chronological order

2. What detail does the poet use to convey his father's character?
   A. his accomplishments
   B. his support of the family
   C. his voice and hands
   D. his face and head
   E. the story he told

3. In line 10 the word "measures" most nearly means
   A. musical divisions
   B. cups or pounds
   C. courses of action
   D. amounts
   E. rulers

4. It can be inferred that the poet's father told him a story to
   A. describe what happened when he put something in his son's palm
   B. tell him about how other men had died from metal splinters
   C. distract him from the pain and worry of the metal splinter
   D. help him remember how his voice was like a deep well
   E. explain how the boy got the metal splinter in his palm in the first place

5. What action would inspire the image of "a man planting" in lines 14–17?
   A. arms held above the boy's head in a gesture of working
   B. someone pushing a tiller through a garden
   C. a quick pulling action
   D. heads leaning together in quiet conversation
   E. the father gently touching the boy's palm

6. How are "a well" and "a prayer" in lines 7–8 related to the father's voice?
   A. They are sacred and inspiring.
   B. They are threatening and desperate.

C. They are nourishing and appealing.
D. They are deep and solemn.
E. They are dark, invisible, and mysterious.

7. Which of these moments could be described as an epiphany for the speaker?
   A. when he realizes he has a metal splinter in the palm of his hand
   B. when he realizes removing something can add something
   C. when he understands that the splinter is finally out of his hand
   D. when he remembers the voice but cannot recall the story
   E. when he thinks about his father's hands beside his face

8. What are "the flames of discipline" mentioned in line 12?
   A. the metal splinters he fears will kill him
   B. his father's strict self-control
   C. his father's words that have scolded him
   D. his father's hands that may have punished him
   E. the dark well water and the prayer his father says

9. What formal element does this poem contain?
   A. The verses are shaped like a sliver.
   B. It has internal rhymes.
   C. It is structured in quatrains.
   D. It is a villanelle.
   E. It contains epic qualities.

10. Which choice best analyzes the poet's use of metal and flame imagery?
    A. He connects the iron splinter to his father's passion and caring.
    B. He links the blade that removes the splinter to the planting of ideas.
    C. He suggests his father's story is about precious metals in a flame.
    D. He indicates that one needs to be hard like metal to endure the heat.
    E. He contrasts tenderness, hardness, and deep emotion.

GO ON ⟶

Grammar and Writing: Improving Paragraphs

Improving paragraphs exercises may appear in the writing sections of standardized tests. They are made up of a reading passage with numbered sentences. The passages are usually drafts of student essays containing errors in grammar, style, and usage. For each question, you must decide which of five possible answers will best correct the given sentence.

Practice

This exercise is modeled after the Improving Paragraphs portion of the SAT Writing Test.

Directions: Questions 1-8 refer to the following draft of a student essay.

[1] Naomi Shihab Nye was born in 1952 in St. Louis, Missouri, published her first poem at age seven, and moved to Jerusalem with her family at age fourteen. **[2]** She ended up in San Antonio, Texas where she lives today. **[3]** Her writing echoes the voices of the Mexican-Americans in her neighborhood. **[4]** It also presents the perspectives of Arab-Americans like herself. **[5]** Her father was a Palestinian and her mother an American citizen. **[6]** Her background gives her a unique perspective on the cultural richness of America.

[7] Nye's career as a writer began with her becoming a speaker, freelancer, and editor after she graduated from Trinity University in 1974. **[8]** Her first collection of poetry explored the differences between cultures. **[9]** Her second collection concerns itself with what is shared between cultures. **[10]** <u>More poems she collected</u> explored the more mature themes of political struggle in the Mideast and the suffering there.

[11] Recently, Nye has expanded beyond writing her own poetry. **[12]** She has written a young adult novel, penned a collection of essays, and a poetry anthology she edited that won many awards.

> ### Strategy
>
> ***Focus only on the answers provided.***
> As you read the essay, you will notice errors. Do not take time to edit these errors on your own. Select the best version of the answer choices only.

1. Which revision is most needed in sentence 1?

   (A) (As it is now)

   (B) Naomi Shihab Nye was born in 1952 in St. Louis, published her first poem at age seven and moved to Jerusalem with her family at age fourteen.

   (C) Naomi Shihab Nye, born in 1952 in St. Louis, Missouri, then published a poem when she was seven, and moved to Jerusalem with her family at age fourteen.

   (D) Naomi Shihab Nye as born in 1952 in St. Louis, Missouri, publishes her first poem at age seven, and moves to Jerusalem with her family at age fourteen.

   (E) Naomi Shihab Nye, born in 1952 in St. Louis, Missouri, then published her first poem at age seven.

2. Which sentence would provide the best transition between the first and second paragraphs?

(A) She has won many awards, including the Pushcart Prize.

(B) Nye believes that the source of her poetry is the voice of the people combined with her broader background as a professional writer.

(C) Nye listens to the people around her and tries to incorporate their concerns into her work.

(D) Moving around a lot has sometimes made Nye feel rootless, which is reflected in her poetry.

(E) Nye has had many jobs and a good education.

3. In context, which of the following revisions to sentence 7 is most needed to provide variety?

(A) Delete "with her becoming a speaker, freelancer, and editor."

(B) Change "her" to "she."

(C) Add at the end "and she also won the Jane Patterson Award for Poetry."

(D) Move "after she graduated from Trinity University in 1974" to the start of the sentence.

(E) Add a semicolon after "editor."

4. Which transition would show the relationship between sentences 8 and 9 while uniting them?

(A) similarly
(B) therefore
(C) for example
(D) in conclusion
(E) in contrast

5. Which is the best version of the underlined portion of sentence 10?

(A) More poems in a collection
(B) Her third collection
(C) More collected poems
(D) Nye's next poems
(E) More poems in her third book

6. Which grammatical or stylistic error is exhibited in sentence 12?

(A) run-on sentence
(B) faulty parallelism
(C) unjustified use of fragments
(D) misplaced modifier
(E) use of passive voice

 Timed Writing: Position Statement [25 minutes]

Naomi Shihab Nye has said, "Anyone who feels poetry is an alien or ominous force should consider the style in which human beings think. 'How do you think?' I ask my students. 'Do you think in complete, elaborate sentences? . . . Or in flashes and bursts of images, snatches of lines leaping one to the next?' We think in poetry. But some people pretend poetry is far away."

Write an essay in which you agree or disagree with Nye's **perspective** on poetry. Provide reasons for your opinions based on the poetry you have read and your own ideas about the relationship between poetry and life. Use handwriting that is fluent and legible. This assignment is similar to the essay portion of the SAT Writing Section.

> **Academic Vocabulary**
>
> **Perspective** is both a way of looking at things and a personal definition. In your essay, discuss the author's perspective before stating your opinion.

Constructed Response

Directions: *Follow the instructions to complete the tasks below as required by your teacher. As you work on each task, incorporate both general academic vocabulary and literary terms you learned in this unit.*

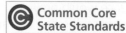

> **Common Core State Standards**
>
> **RL.11-12.3, RL.11-12.4, RL.11-12.5, RL.11-12.6; RI.11-12.4, RI.11-12.6; W.11-12.1, W.11-12.2, W.11-12.9.a, W.11-12.9.b; SL.11-12.4, SL.11-12.6**
> [For the full wording of the standards, see the standards chart in the front of your textbook.]

Writing

Task 1: Literature [RL.11-12.6; W.11-12.2, W.11-12.9.a]
Analyze Point of View

Write an **essay** *in which you analyze the author's point of view as expressed in a literary work from this unit.*

- Identify the story you will discuss and explain why you chose it.

- Express a clear central idea, or thesis.

- Consider the author's diction and tone, as well as his or her use of literary devices, such as hyperbole, understatement, satire, or irony. In all such cases, clearly analyze the relationship between direct statements and their actual meanings. Explain how the true meaning suggests the author's point of view.

- Cite evidence from the story to support your interpretation of meaning and your determination of point of view.

- In your conclusion, restate your central idea.

Task 2: Literature [RL.11-12.4; W.11-12.2]
Analyze Word Choice and Tone

Write an **essay** *in which you analyze the word choice and tone in a literary work from this unit.*

- Identify the literary work you will discuss and explain why you chose it.

- Summarize the work and explain the various types of diction it employs, including figurative or technical language.

- Provide examples from the work of each type of diction you identified. Then, discuss each example in turn. Consider denotative and connotative meanings; figurative meanings; and the impact of each example on the author's overall meaning and tone.

- Conclude with a paragraph or section in which you explain in broader terms the role word choice plays in an author's craft.

Task 3: Informational Text [RI.11-12.6; W.11-12.1, W.11-12.9.b]
Analyze and Evaluate Rhetoric

Write an **essay** *in which you analyze and evaluate the author's rhetoric in a nonfiction work from this unit.*

- Choose a nonfiction work in which the rhetoric is particularly effective. State which work you chose and your reasons for choosing it.

- Include a clear statement of your position—your claim or thesis.

- Discuss the author's purpose for writing the work. Also, explain the author's perspective or point of view on the topic.

- Discuss how the author's rhetoric advances his or her purpose and perspective. Include illustrative examples of specific types of rhetorical devices, such as parallelism, restatement, anaphora, or other rhetorical figures.

- Organize your essay logically, so that the introduction provides information and establishes the reader's expectations, the body paragraphs progress in a clear order, and the conclusion supports the ideas presented earlier.

Speaking and Listening

Task 4: Literature [RL.11-12.3; SL.11-12.4]
Analyze Story Elements

*Deliver an **oral presentation** in which you analyze the development of and relationship among elements of a work of fiction from this unit.*

- Identify the work of fiction from this unit you will discuss. Explain why you chose it.

- Identify three story elements, such as setting, character, and conflict, that you will use as a focus for your presentation. Dicsuss why you chose the three elements rather than other aspects of the story.

- Explain the choices the author made concerning each element. For example, discuss the choice of setting, the order of the action, or the methods by which characters are introduced and developed.

- Explain how the elements you chose combine to create an effective work of fiction.

- Keep your audience in mind as you make your presentation. Provide background information that will help your audience comprehend your analysis.

Task 5: Informational Text [RI.11-12.4; SL.11-12.6]
Analyze Word Choice

*In an **oral presentation,** analyze word choice and meaning in a nonfiction work from this unit.*

- Choose a nonfiction work from this unit that you feel uses noteworthy diction. Identify the work you chose and briefly explain why you chose it.

- Identify three examples of word choice that you feel are particularly effective or critical to the meaning of the work as a whole.

- Cite your choices in context, and then discuss each one separately. Consider their figurative, connotative, or technical meanings.

- Discuss whether the author's use or definition of a key word changes over the course of the work. Explain the effect of any such refinements on the meaning of the work as a whole.

- Use formal English as you deliver your presentation.

Task 6: Literature [RL.11-12.5; SL.11-12.4]
Analyze and Assess Structure

*Prepare and present an **analysis and assessment** of the structure of a literary work from this unit.*

- Choose a literary work with a structure that you feel is closely connected to or helps to convey its meaning. Explain which work you chose and why you chose it.

- Provide a detailed description of the author's structural choices. Use slides, a whiteboard, or hand-outs to present this information clearly and concisely. Discuss how the structural choices of passages or sections contribute to the work's overall structure.

- Discuss how structural choices affect meaning. For example, consider whether structural elements add to a character's complexity or heighten suspense.

- Express your ideas logically so that listeners can easily follow your reasoning.

? THE ESSENTIAL

What makes American literature American?

Everyday Life A conversation, a journey, a meal, a sunrise—literary versions of such common experiences reveal a great deal about American identity now and throughout history. Does the sight of a bird have a different meaning for a Puritan, a Romantic, a Realist, a contemporary? Are Americans' values different today from what they were in the past?

Assignment Choose an everyday event described in this unit and find a similar event in a previous unit. Write a **comparison-and-contrast essay** in which you discuss the similarities and differences of the passages and explain what each suggests about American identity.

Titles for Extended Reading

In this unit, you have read a variety of literature of the contemporary period. Continue to read works related to this era on your own. Select books that you enjoy, but challenge yourself to explore new topics, new authors, and works offering varied perspectives or approaches. The titles suggested below will help you get started.

LITERATURE

Sailing Alone Around the Room
Billy Collins
Random House, 2001 **EXEMPLAR TEXT**

 Poetry Billy Collins was the U.S. poet laureate from 2001 to 2003. This collection of poems by Collins, which includes "Man Listening to Disc," covers topics ranging from insomnia to snow days with wit, freshness, and vivid imagery.

The Bluest Eye
Toni Morrison
Vintage, 1970 **EXEMPLAR TEXT**

 Novel This powerful, disturbing novel explores themes of abuse and the destruction of self-esteem caused by racism. Pecola, a young African American girl during the Great Depression, believes all her troubles would be solved if she only had blue eyes.

Dreaming in Cuban
Cristina Garcia
One World Books, 1992 **EXEMPLAR TEXT**

 Novel Three generations of Cuban woman from the del Pino family tell their stories of life in Cuba and in exile. Using narratives, love letters, and memories, Garcia brings these troubled but passionate women to life.

The Namesake
Jhumpa Lahiri
First Mariner Books, 2003 **EXEMPLAR TEXT**

 Novel *The Namesake* explores the life of Gogol Ganguli, a second-generation Indian immigrant who struggles to find his place in his family and in American culture.

Death and the King's Horseman
Wole Soyinka
W. W. Norton, 2002 **EXEMPLAR TEXT**

 Drama When the king dies in this Nigerian play, his horseman is expected to follow tradition and kill himself. What will happen when the horseman's son arrives from London and a colonial district officer decides to intervene?

Mother Love: Poems
Rita Dove
W. W. Norton, 1996 **EXEMPLAR TEXT**

 Poetry In this collection, former U.S. poet laureate Rita Dove uses the mythical Greek figures Demeter and Persephone to explore themes of love between mothers and daughters. Included in the collection is "Demeter's Prayer to Hades."

INFORMATIONAL TEXTS

Nonfiction Readings Across the Curriculum
Pearson Prentice Hall

 Nonfiction Football great Joe Namath gives players a pep talk. Beverly Cleary tells how she got her start as an author. These and other essays by famous people provide new perspectives on subjects ranging from arts and literature to science, social studies, and sports.

On Nature: Great Writers on the Great Outdoors
edited by Lee Gutkind
Putnam, 2002

 Nonfiction This book of contemporary nature essays by some of America's best contemporary authors will appeal to those who love outdoor activities as well as those who prefer getting their [mental] exercise in an armchair with a good book. It features nonfiction by Joyce Carol Oates, Barry Lopez, Mark Doty, Diane Ackerman, John McPhee, and Bill Bryson, among others.

The Tipping Point: How Little Things Can Make a Big Difference
Malcolm Gladwell
Back Bay Books, 2002 **EXEMPLAR TEXT**

 Nonfiction Gladwell suggests that "ideas, messages, and behaviors spread just like viruses," and then uses engaging examples to show how small changes can bring us to the "tipping point," where they transform the world.

Preparing to Read Complex Texts

Reading for College and Career In both college and the workplace, readers must analyze texts independently, draw connections among works that offer varied perspectives, and develop their own ideas and informed opinions. The questions shown below, and others that you generate on your own, will help you more effectively read and analyze complex college-level texts.

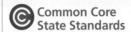

Common Core State Standards

Reading Literature/Informational Text
10. By the end of grade 11, read and comprehend literature, including stories, dramas, and poems, and literary nonfiction, in the grades 11-CCR text complexity band proficiently, with scaffolding as needed at the high end of the range.

While reading analytically, ask yourself…

- What idea, experience, or story seems to have compelled the author to write? Has the author presented that idea, experience, or story in a way that I, too, find compelling?

- How might the author's era, social status, belief system, or personal experiences have affected the point of view he or she expresses in the text?

- How do my circumstances affect what I understand and feel about this text?

- What key idea does the author state explicitly? What key idea does he or she suggest or imply? Which details in the text help me to perceive implied ideas?

- Do I find multiple layers of meaning in the text? If so, what relationships do I see among these layers of meaning?

- How do details in the text connect or relate to one another? Do I find any details unconvincing, unrelated, or out of place?

- Do I find the text believable and convincing?

© Key Ideas and Details

- What patterns of organization or sequences do I find in the text? Do these patterns help me understand the ideas better?

- What do I notice about the author's style, including his or her diction, uses of imagery and figurative language, and syntax?

- Do I like the author's style? Is the author's style memorable?

- What emotional attitude does the author express toward the topic, the story, or the characters? Does this attitude seem appropriate?

- What emotional attitude does the author express toward me, the reader? Does this attitude seem appropriate?

- What do I notice about the author's voice—his or her personality on the page? Do I like this voice? Does it make me want to read on?

© Craft and Structure

- Is the work fresh and original?

- Do I agree with the author's ideas entirely, or are there elements I find unconvincing?

- Do I disagree with the author's ideas entirely, or are there elements I can accept as true?

- Based on my knowledge of American literature, history, and culture, does this work reflect the American tradition? Why or why not?

© Integration of Ideas

Resources

English Glossary

Essential Question vocabulary appears in **blue type**. High-Utility Academic Vocabulary is <u>underlined</u>.

A

abeyance (uh BAY uhns) *n.* temporary suspension

absolve (ab ZOLV) *v.* pardon; free from guilt

absurdity (ab SUR duh tee) *n.* nonsense; ridiculousness

accosted (uh KAWST uhd) *v.* approached and spoke to in an eager way

account (uh KOWNT) *n.* a report or description

acknowledges (ak NOL ihj) *v.* to admit the existence, reality, or truth of

acquiesce (AK wee EHS) *v.* agree without protest

adamant (AD uh mant) *adj.* firm; unyielding

adjourned (uh JURND) *v.* closed for a time

advantageous (ad vuhn TAY juhs) *adj.* favorable; beneficial

adversary (AD vuhr sehr ee) *n.* opponent; enemy

adversity (ad VUR suh tee) *n.* hardship; difficulty

affections (uh FEHK shuhnz) *n.* emotions

affliction (uh FLIHK shuhn) *n.* anything causing pain or distress

agape (uh GAYP) *adj.* in surprise; wonder

aggregation (ag ruh GAY shuhn) *n.* group of distinct objects or individuals

agricultural (ag ruh KUHL chuhr uhl) *adj.* with farming as the main way of life

alacrity (uh LAK ruh tee) *n.* speed

alienation (AY lee uh NAY shuhn) *n.* a withdrawing or separation of feeling or affection

alliance (uh LY uhns) *n.* union of nations for a specific purpose

ambiguity (AM buh GYOO uh tee) *n.* state of having two or more possible meanings

ambition (am BIHSH uhn) *n.* strong desire to gain a particular objective; drive to succeed

ameliorate (uh MEEL yuh rayt) *v.* make better

ample (AM puhl) *adj.* large in size; more than enough

<u>**analyze**</u> (AN uh lyz) *v.* break down a topic into parts and explain them

anarchy (AN uhr kee) *n.* absence of government

ancestor (AN sehs tuhr) *n.* person from whom other people descend

anonymity (an uh NIHM uh tee) *n.* the condition of being unknown

<u>**anticipate**</u> (an TIHS uh payt) *v.* prepare for or signal something

anxiety (ang ZY uh tee) *n.* state of being uneasy, apprehensive, or worried about what may happen.

apparel (uh PAR uhl) *n.* clothing

apparition (ap uh RIHSH uhn) *n.* act of appearing or becoming visible

appease (uh PEEZ) *v.* satisfy

appendage (uh PEHN dihj) *n.* external part of a plant or animal, such as a tail or a limb

<u>**appraise**</u> (uh PRAYZ) *v.* evaluate something's worth, significance, or status

apprehension (ap rih HEHN shuhn) *n.* an anxious feeling of foreboding; dread

appropriate (uh PROH pree ayt) *v.* to take or use something without permission

arduous (AHR joo uhs) *adj.* difficult

<u>**argue**</u> (AHR gyoo) *v.* give reasons for or against; prove by giving reasons

<u>**arrange**</u> (uh RAYNJ) *v.* put into order or sequence

ascended (uh SEHND uhd) *v.* climbed up

aspirations (as puh RAY shuhnz) *n.* strong desires or ambitions

assault (uh SAWLT) *n.* violent attack

assent (uh SEHNT) *n.* agreement

<u>**assess**</u> (uh SEHS) *v.* determine importance, size, or value

austerity (aw STEHR uh tee) *n.* sternness in manner or appearance; harshness; severity

auxiliary (awg ZIHL yuhr ee) *adj.* giving help or support

avarice (AV uhr ihs) *n.* greed

aversion (uh VUR zhuhn) *n.* object arousing an intense dislike

avidly (AV ihd lee) *adv.* eagerly

awe (aw) *n.* mixed feelings of fear and wonder

B

base (bays) *adj.* low; mean

beguile (bih GYL) *v.* charm or delight

benediction (behn uh DIHK shuhn) *n.* prayer asking for God's blessing

benevolent (buh NEHV uh luhnt) *adj.* kindly; charitable

benign (bih NYN) *adj.* not injurious or malignant; not cancerous

bequeath (bih KWEETH) *v.* hand down; pass on

blaspheming (BLAS feem ihng) *v.* cursing

brazenness (BRAY zuhn nehs) n. shamelessness; boldness; impudence

brigade (brih GAYD) n. a unit of soldiers

brutal (BROO tuhl) adj. cruel and without feeling; savage; violent

C

cadence (KAY duhns) *n.* a series of notes or chords near the end of a musical work

calamity (kuh LAM uh tee) *n.* disaster; catastrophe

calumny (KAL uhm nee) *n.* false accusation; slander

candid (KAN dihd) *adj.* straightforward

canvass (KAN vuhs) *v.* go through an area asking people for votes, orders, or participation

capable (KAY puh buhl) *adj.* having the skills needed to do something

caper (KAY puhr) *n.* prank

casualties (KAZH oo uhl teez) *n.* members of the armed forces who die in combat

<u>**categorize**</u> (KAT uh guh ryz) *v.* place in related groups

cavernous (KAV uhr nuhs) *adj.* cavelike; vast

celestial (suh LEHS chuhl) *adj.* of or in the sky, as planets or stars

chaos (KAY os) *n.* disorder of matter and space, supposed to have existed before the ordered universe

chronicles (KRON uh kuhlz) *n.* stories; histories

circumvent (sur kuhm VEHNT) *v.* prevent; get around

civilian (suh VIHL yuhn) *n.* any person who is not a member of the armed forces

<u>**classify**</u> (KLAS uh fy) *v.* assign to a category

cleave (kleev) *v.* adhere; cling

coinage (KOY nihj) *n.* an invented word or expression

coincide (koh ihn SYD) *v.* to occur at the same time

collective (kuh LEHK tihv) *n.* gathered into a whole

collusion (kuh LOO zhuhn) *n.* secret agreement; conspiracy

commercial (kuh MUR shuhl) *adj.* connected with trade or business

commissioners (kuh MIHSH uh nuhrz) *n.* government officials

commonplace (KOM uhn PLAYS) *adj.* everyday; ordinary

commotion (kuh MOH shuhn) *n.* noisy confusion

community (kuh MYOO nuh tee) *n.* all the people living a particular district, city, or area

<u>**compare**</u> (kuhm PAIR) *v.* point out similarities or differences

conciliatory (kuhn SIHL ee uh tawr ee) *adj.* intended to make peace or to reconcile; friendly

conclude (kuhn KLOOD) *v.* reach as a logically necessary end by reasoning

condolences (kuhn DOH luhns ez) *n.* expressions of sympathy

conduct (KON duhkt) *n.* behavior

conflagration (kon fluh GRAY shuhn) *n.* big, destructive fire

conformity (kuhn FAWR muh tee) *n.* action in agreement with generally accepted standards

confounded (kon FOWN dihd) *adj.* confused; dismayed

conjectural (kuhn JEHK chuhr uhl) *adj.* based on guesswork

conjectured (kuhn JEHK chuhrd) *v.* guessed

conjuring (KON juhr ihng) *v.* causing to be; appearing as by magic

consecrate (KON suh krayt) *v.* cause to be revered or honored

conspicuous (kuhn SPIHK yoo uhs) *adj.* obvious; easy to see or perceive

consternation (kon stuhr NAY shuhn) *n.* great fear or shock that makes one feel helpless or bewildered

constitute (KON stuh toot) *v.* serve as the parts or basis of; form; comprise

constitution (kon stuh TOO shuhn) *n.* physical makeup of a person

contentious (kuhn TEHN shuhs) *adj.* argumentative

contiguous (kuhn TIHG yoo uhs) *adj.* bordering; adjacent

contract (KON trakt) *n.* written agreement

contrast (KON trast) *v.* examine to discover differences

convention (kuhn VEHN shuhn) *n.* a meeting attended by members or delegates

conviction (kuhn VIHK shuhn) *n.* strong belief

convivial (kuhn VIHV ee uhl) *adj.* fond of good company; sociable

copious (KOH pee uhs) *adj.* plentiful; abundant

correspond (KAWR uh SPOND) *v.* be in agreement; relate to

countenance (KOWN tuh nuhns) *v.* approve; tolerate

cowering (KOW uhr ihng) *v.* trembling or cringing, as with fear

create (kree AYT) *v.* produce through imaginative skill

crevices (KREHV ihs iz) *n.* narrow openings caused by cracks or splits

critic (KRIHT ihk) *n.* person who disapproves or finds fault

critique (krih TEEK) *v.* examine critically; review

cunning (KUHN ihng) *adj.* skillful in deception; crafty; sly

cyberspace (SY buhr SPAYS) *n.* online world of computer networks

D

daunting (DAWNT ihng) *adj.* intimidating

decorum (dih KAWR uhm) *n.* rightness; suitability

deduce (dih DOOS) *v.* infer from a general principle

defend (dih FEHND) *v.* maintain or support in the face of argument

deference (DEHF uhr uhns) *n.* courteous regard or respect

deficient (dih FIHSH uhnt) *adj.* lacking; not having something needed

define (dih FYN) *v.* tell the qualities that make something what it is

degenerate (dih JEHN uh ruht) *adj.* morally corrupt

dejected (dih JEHK tihd) *v.* in low spirits; downcast; depressed

deliberation (dih lihb uh RAY shuhn) *n.* careful consideration

deposition (dehp uh ZIHSH uhn) *n.* testimony of a witness made under oath but not in open court

depths (dehpths) *n.* deepest areas

derivative (dih RIHV uh tihv) *adj.* not original; based on something else

derive (dih RYV) *v.* trace to or from a source; get by reasoning

describe (dih SKRYB) *v.* represent in words

design (dih ZYN) *v.* create, fashion, execute, or construct according to plan

desolate (DEHS uh liht) *adj.* deserted; isolated

despondent (dih SPON duhnt) *adj.* without courage or hope

despotism (DEHS puh tihz uhm) *n.* absolute rule; tyranny

destitute (DEHS tuh toot) *adj.* living in complete poverty

destruction (dih STRUHK shuhn) *n.* act of demolishing or defeating

detached (dih TACHT) *adj.* not emotionally involved

devise (dih VYZ) *v.* form in the mind by new combinations of ideas; invent

dictum (DIHK tuhm) *n.* formal statement of fact or opinion

differentiate (DIHF uh REHN shee ayt) *v.* recognize a dissimilarity

digress (duh GREHS) *v.* depart temporarily from the main subject

dilapidated (duh LAP uh day tuhd) *adj.* in disrepair

diligence (DIHL uh juhns) *n.* constant, careful effort; perseverance

discern (duh SURN) *v.* perceive or recognize; make out clearly

discord (DIHS kawrd) *n.* difference of opinion; disputing

discretion (dihs KREHSH uhn) *n.* judgment

discriminate (dihs KRIHM uh nayt) *v.* recognize differences between or among things

disdainfully (dihs DAYN fuhl ee) *adv.* showing scorn or contempt

disgrace (dihs GRAYS) *n.* something that brings shame or dishonor

disillusion (DIHS ih LOO zhuhn) *n.* freedom from a false idea; disenchantment

dispatched (dihs PACHT) *v.* sent off, usually on official business

dispersal (dihs PUR suhl) *n.* distribution

disposition (dihs puh ZIHSH uhn) *n.* inclination; tendency

disregard (dihs rih GAHRD) *v.* to pay no attention to; leave out of consideration; ignore

dissembling (dih SEHM buhl ihng) *v.* disguising one's real nature or motives

dissention (dih SEHN shuhn) *n.* disagreement; discord as expressed in intense quarreling

dissuade (dih SWAYD) *v.* convince someone not to do something

distinguish (dihs TIHNG gwihsh) *v.* mark as separate or different

diversity (duh VUR suh tee) *n.* variety; point of unlikeness

divine (duh VYN) *v.* find out by intuition

docile (DOS uhl) *adj.* easy to direct or manage; obedient

doctrine (DOK truhn) *n.* what is taught

dogma (DAWG muh) *n.* authoritative doctrines or beliefs

dubious (DOO bee uhs) *adj.* questionable; suspicious

duplicate (DOO pluh kayht) *v.* make a copy

duration (du RAY shuhn) *n.* the time during which something continues or exists

dusky (DUHS kee) *adj.* dark; dim; shadowy

dyspepsia (dihs PEHP see uh) *n.* indigestion

E

ecstasy (EHKS tuh see) *n.* a feeling of overpowering joy; great delight

efface (uh FAYS) *v.* erase; wipe out

effigies (eh FIHJ eez) *n.* images or likenesses, especially of people

effrontery (uh FRUHN tuhr ee) *n.* shameless boldness

effuse (ih FYOOZ) *v.* pour out; gush

eloquence (EHL uh kwuhns) *n.* talent for vivid, forceful speech

elusive (ih LOO sihv) *adj.* hard to grasp

embankment (ehm BANGK muhnt) *n.* mound of earth or stone built to hold back water or support or a roadway

embark (ehm BAHRK) *v.* to begin a venture, project, or activity

emigrants (EHM uh gruhnts) *n.* people who leave one place to settle in another

eminence (EHM uh nuhns) *n.* greatness; celebrity

emit (ih MIHT) *v.* utter words or sounds

enamored (ehn AM uhrd) *adj.* charmed; captivated

encroached (ehn KROHCHT) *v.* intruded

endured (ehn DURD) *v.* held up under

engrossed (ehn GROHST) *v.* occupied wholly; absorbed

entreated (ehn TREET uhd) *v.* begged; pleaded

entrenchments (ehn TREHNCH muhnts) *n.* long deep holes with steep sides, used as defense against enemy fire

environment (ehn VY ruhn muhnt) *n.* the surrounding objects or conditions

epitaph (EHP uh taf) *n.* inscription on a tombstone or grave marker

equivocal (ih KWIHV uh kuhl) *adj.* having more than one possible interpretation

eradicate (ih RAD uh kayt) *v.* wipe out; destroy

establishment (ehs TAB lihsh muhnt) *n.* household or business

estimates (EHS tuh mihts) *n.* general, careful calculations

etiquette (EHT uh keht) *n.* appropriate behavior and ceremonies

evacuated (ih VAK yu ayt uhd) *v.* emptied; withdrawn

evade (ih VAYD) *v.* avoid or escape from by deceit or cleverness

evaluate (ih VAL yu ayt) *v.* determine something's significance, worth, or condition through careful study

exalted (ehg ZAWL tihd) *adj.* filled with joy or pride; elated

examine (ehg ZAM uhn) *v.* carefully inquire into a topic

exasperation (ehg zas puh RAY shuhn) *n.* annoyance; frustration

exhaust (ehg ZAWST) *n.* discharge of used steam or gas from an engine

exile (EHG zyl) *n.* the state or period of being banished

expansion (ehk SPAN shuhn) *n.* act or process of increasing in extent, size, or volume

expedient (ehk SPEE dee uhnt) *n.* method used to achieve a goal quickly

expenditures (ehk SPEHN duh churz) *n.* expenses; uses of money or resources

exposures (ehk SPOH zhuhrz) *n.* sections of film on which light falls when a photograph is taken

extort (ehk STAWRT) *v.* obtain by threat or violence

extraneous (ehk STRAY nee uhs) *adj.* unrelated; unconnected

F

fallowness (FAL oh nuhs) *n.* inactivity

fantastic (fan TAS tihk) *adj.* excellent; unbelievable

fastidious (fas TIHD ee uhs) *adj.* careful; meticulous

fatigues (fuh TEEGZ) *n.* sturdy clothing worn by soldiers doing hard work

feigned (faynd) *v.* pretended

fervent (FUR vuhnt) *adj.* extremely passionate; very enthusiastic

finite (FY nyt) *adj.* having measurable or definable limits

fitfully (FIHT fuhl ee) *adv.* characterized by irregular or intermittent activity

flagrant (FLAY gruhnt) *adj.* glaring; outrageous

flourished (FLUR ihsht) *v.* grew strong, healthy, and happy; prospered

fluctuation (fluhk chu AY shuhn) *n.* a change in level or intensity

foothold (FUT hohld) *n.* secure position from which further actions can be taken

forded (FAWRD uhd) *v.* crossed a river at a low point

forestall (fawr STAWL) *v.* prevent by acting ahead of time

formulate (FAWR myuh layt) *v.* express fully and clearly

fortuitous (fawr TOO uh tuhs) *adj.* fortunate

fortune (FAWR chuhn) *n.* wealth; luck

fragmentation (frag muhn TAY shuhn) *n.* act or process of breaking up into parts

frantic (FRAN tihk) *adj.* marked by frenzy

frayed (frayd) *adj.* tattered

freedom (FREE duhm) *n.* not being under another's control

frontier (fruhn TIHR) *n.* border between inhabited regions; a developing region of field of thought

furtive (FUR tihv) *adj.* sneaky

G

garrulous (GAR uh luhs) *adj.* talking too much

gaudy (GAW dee) *adj.* showy in a tasteless way

generalize (JEHN uhr uh lyz) *v.* draw a larger principle from details

genial (JEEN yuhl) *adj.* cheerful; friendly

genre (zhahn ruh) *n.* catagory, or style

global (GLOH buhl) *adj.* spread throughout the world

govern (GUHV uhrn) *v.* to rule; control; manage

grandeur (GRAN juhr) *n.* greatness

grave (grayv) *adj.* serious; solemn

gravity (GRAV uh tee) *n.* seriousness

guile (gyl) *n.* craftiness

H

habitation (hab uh TAY shuhn) *n.* place to live; group of homes or dwellings

hallow (HAL oh) *v.* honor as sacred

handiwork (HAN dee wurk) *n.* work done by the hands; work done personally

harass (HUH ras) *v.* attack; bother

heady (HEHD ee) *adj.* intoxicating

heightened (HY tuhnd) *v.* raised the level of

heritage (HEHR uh tihj) *n.* traits, beliefs, or customs passed on from one's ancestors

homages (HOM ihj uhz) *n.* acts showing honor and reverence

homely (HOHM lee) *adj.* not elegant or polished; crude

huddled (HUHD uhld) *v.* gathered closely; nestled

humor (HYOO muhr) *n.* funny or amusing quality

hypothesize (hy POTH uh syz) *v.* develop a theory about

I

idealism (y DEE uh lihz uhm) *n.* thought based on following standards of perfection or beauty

identify (y DEHN tuh fy) *v.* establish the identity of something

identity (y DEHN tuh tee) *n.* who a person is

illiterate (ih LIHT uhr iht) *adj.* unable to read or write

illustrate (IHL uh strayt) *v.* give examples that support an idea

immigration (ihm uh GRAY shuhn) *n.* act of coming into a foreign country or region to live

imperceptible (ihm puhr SEHP tuh buhl) *adj.* not easy to perceive; unnoticeable

impertinent (ihm PUR tuh nuhnt) *adj.* not showing proper respect; saucy

implore (ihm PLAWR) *v.* ask or beg earnestly; plead

imply (ihm PLY) *v.* hint or suggest

impulsive (ihm PUHL sihv) *adj.* done without thinking

impulsively (ihm PUHL sihv lee) *adv.* spontaneously; suddenly

inanimate (ihn AN uh miht) *adj.* not alive; lifeless

inarticulate (ihn ahr TIHK yuh liht) *adj.* unclearly spoken or expressed

inaudibly (ihn AW duh blee) *adv.* in a manner that cannot be heard

incessant (ihn SEHS uhnt) *adj.* constant; seemingly endless

incorporated (ihn KAWR puh rayt uhd) *v.* organized as a legal corporation

incorrigible (ihn KAWR uh juh buhl) *adj.* impossible to correct; incurable

incredulously (ihn KREHD juh luhs lee) *adv.* skeptically

increment (IHN kruh muhnt) *n.* increase, as in a series

indelible (ihn DEHL uh buhl) *adj.* permanent; that cannot be erased

independence (IHN dih PEHN duhns) *n.* freedom from the control of others

individualism (IHN duh VIHJ u uh LIHZ uhm) *n.* belief that personal freedom is most important

induce (ihn DOOS) *v.* cause; bring about

industry (IHN duh stree) *n.* any branch of business, trade, or manufacturing

ineffable (ihn EHF uh buhl) *adj.* too overwhelming to be spoken

inert (ihn URT) *adj.* motionless

inextricable (ihn EHK struh kuh buhl) *adj.* unable to be separated or freed from

infer (ihn FUR) *v.* derive a conclusion from facts or premises

infinity (ihn FIHN uh tee) *n.* endless or unlimited space, time, or distance

ingratiating (ihn GRAY shee ay tihng) *adj.* charming or flattering

innovation (ihn uh VAY shuhn) *n.* a new idea, method, or device

innumerable (ih NOO muhr uh buhl) *adj.* too many to count

insatiable (ihn SAY shuh buhl) *adj.* constantly wanting more

inscrutable (ihn SKROO tuh buhl) *adj.* not able to be easily understood

inseparable (ihn SEHP uhr uh buhl) *adj.* not able to be divided; linked

insidious (ihn SIHD ee uhs) *adj.* deceitful; treacherous

inspection (ihn SPEHK shuhn) *n.* examination

intent (ihn TEHNT) *n.* purpose or aim

intently (ihn TEHNT lee) *adv.* in a focused, purposeful manner

intercepted (ihn tuhr SEHPT uhd) *v.* seized or stopped something on its way from one place to another

interminable (ihn TUR muh nuh buhl) *adj.* seeming to last forever

interposed (ihn tuhr POHZD) *v.* came between

interspersed (ihn tuhr SPURSD) *v.* placed here and there

intervene (ihn tuhr VEEN) *v.* take action in order to prevent something

intolerable (ihn TOL uhr uh buhl) *adj.* difficult or painful that it cannot be endured; unbearable

intonation (ihn toh NAY shuhn) *n.* the quality of playing musical notes in or out of tune

intricate (IHN truh kiht) *adj.* complex; having many small, interrelated parts

intuitively (ihn TOO uh tihv lee) *adv.* without having to be taught; instinctively

invective (ihn VEHK tihv) *n.* verbal attack; strong criticism

invent (ihn VEHNT) *v.* devise by thinking

investigate (ihn VEHS tuh gayt) *v.* make a systematic examination

J

jocularity (jok yuh LAR uh tee) *n.* joking good humor

jubilant (JOO buh luhnt) *adj.* joyful and triumphant

judge (juhj) *v.* form an estimate or evaluation of something

judgment (JUHJ muhnt) *n.* power to form an opinion well; good sense

justify (JUHS tuh fy) *v.* prove or show to be just, right, or reasonable

L

label (LAY buhl) *v.* describe or designate

lament (luh MEHNT) *v.* to express sorrow for; mourn aloud for

landscape (LAND skayp) *n.* an area that can be seen at one time from one place

latent (LAY tuhnt) *adj.* present but invisible or inactive

latitude (LAT uh tood) *n.* distance north or south from the equator

levee (LEHV ee) *n.* embankment built along the side of a river to prevent flooding

liberty (LIHB uhr tee) *n.* freedom

license (LY suhns) *n.* freedom from appropriate behavior or speech

licentious (ly SEHN shuhs) *adj.* lacking moral restraint

limber (LIHM buhr) *adj.* flexible

list (lihst) *v.* make a list; enumerate

listed (LIHST uhd) *v.* tilted; inclined

locate (LOH kayt) *v.* find the place of something

longitude (LON juh tood) *n.* distance east or west on the earth's surface

lulled (luhld) *v.* calmed or soothed by a gentle sound or motion

luminary (LOO muh nehr ee) *adj.* giving off light

M

machetes (muh SHEHT eez) *n.* large heavy knives with broad blades

magnanimity (mag nuh NIHM uh tee) *n.* generosity

magnitude (MAG nuh tood) *n.* greatness of size

maledictions (mal uh DIHK shuhnz) *n.* curses

malign (muh LYN) *adj.* malicious; very harmful

malingers (muh LIHNG guhrz) *v.* pretends to be ill

maneuver (muh NOO vuhr) *v.* to move something by some plan or scheme

manifold (MAN uh fohld) *adj.* in many ways

martial (MAHR shuhl) *adj.* relating to war

marvel (MAHR vuhl) *n.* wonderful or astonishing thing

master (MAS tuhr) *v.* become an expert in

media (MEE dee uh) *n.* systems of communication designed to reach the masses

mediator (MEE dee ay tuhr) *n.* one who reconciles opposing groups

melancholy (MEHL uhn kol ee) *adj.* sad and depressed; gloomy

membrane (MEHM brayn) *n.* thin, soft layer serving as a covering or lining

memorials (muh MAWR ee uhlz) *n.* objects displayed in memory of a person or event

meticulous (muh TIHK yuh luhs) *adj.* extremely careful about details

metropolis (muh TROP uh lihs) *n.* large city

migrant (MY gruhnt) *adj.* moving from place to place

monotonous (muh NOT uh nuhs) *adj.* tiresome because unvarying

morose (muh ROHS) *adj.* gloomy; sullen

mundane (muhn DAYN) *adj.* commonplace, everyday, ordinary

munificent (myoo NIHF uh suhnt) *adj.* generous

myriad (MIHR ee uhd) *adj.* countless

N

native (NAY tihv) *adj.* belonging to a place by birth

natural (NACH uhr uhl) *adj.* not man-made or artificial

nostalgia (nos TAL juh) *n.* a longing for something

nuance (NOO ahns) *n.* a slight or delicate variation in tone, color, meaning

O

oblivion (uh BLIHV ee uhn) *n.* condition of being completely forgotten

oblivious (uh BLIHV ee uhs) *adj.* lacking all awareness

obstinacy (OB stuh nuh see) *n.* stubbornness

obstinate (OB stuh niht) *adj.* stubborn

obtuse (uhb TOOS) *adj.* slow to understand or perceive

offensive (uh FEHN sihv) *n.* an attitude or position of attack

ominous (OM uh nuhs) *adj.* threatening; sinister

omnipotent (om NIHP uh tuhnt) *adj.* all-powerful

opposition (op uh ZIHSH uhn) *n.* hostile or resistant attitude toward something

oppressed (uh PREHST) *v.* kept down by cruel or unjust power

optimism (OP tuh mihz uhm) *n.* tendency to be positive

order (AWR duhr) *v.* arrange

ordinances (AWR duh nuhns uhz) *n.* sacraments or religious rites

ostentation (os tehn TAY shuhn) *n.* boastful display

P

pacify (PAS uh fy) *v.* to calm or soothe

pallor (PAL uhr) *n.* paleness

palpable (PAL puh buhl) *adj.* able to be touched, felt, or handled

parsimony (PAHR suh moh nee) *n.* stinginess

pastoral (PAS tuhr uhl) *adj.* characteristic of rural life; idealized as peaceful, simple, and natural

pathos (PAY thohs) *n.* quality that arouses pity, sorrow, or sympathy in others

pedestrian (puh DEHS tree uhn) *adj.* going on foot; walking

pensive (PEHN sihv) *adj.* thinking earnestly; plead

perdition (puhr DIHSH uhn) *n.* complete and irreparable loss; ruin

peremptorily (puh REHMP tuhr uh lee) *adv.* decisively; commandingly

peril (PEHR uhl) *n.* danger

permeated (PUR mee ayt uhd) *v.* soaked through with

perpetual (puhr PEHCH oo uhl) *adj.* lasting forever

persevere (pur suh VIHR) *v.* continue despite hardship; persist

persistent (puhr SIHS tuhnt) *adj.* repeated; continual

personal (PUR suh nuhl) *adj.* belonging to an individual; private

pessimism (PEHS uh mihz uhm) *n.* tendency to be negative

piety (PY uh tee) *n.* devotion to religion

platitudes (PLAT uh toodz) *n.* empty statements; tired expressions

plodding (PLOD ihng) *v.* walking or moving heavily and laboriously; trudging

poignant (POY nuhnt) *adj.* sharply painful to the feelings

poise (poyz) *n.* balance; stability

posterity (pos TEHR uh tee) *n.* all future generations

practicable (PRAK tuh kuh buhl) *adj.* practical, possible

prairie (PRAIR ee) *n.* a treeless, grass-covered plain

precipitate (prih SIHP uh tayt) *v.* cause to happen before expected or desired

preconceptions (prih kuhn SEHP shuhnz) *n.* ideas formed beforehand

predict (prih DIHKT) *v.* foretell on the basis of observation, experience, or reason

predilection (pree duh LEHK shuhn) *n.* preexisting preference

prelude (PREHL yood) *n.* introductory section or movement of a work of music

prescient (PREE shee uhnt) *adj.* having foreknowledge

pervading (puhr VAYD ihng) *v.* spreading throughout

prevalent (PREHV uh lehnt) *adj.* widely existing or occurring

privileges (PRIHV uh lihj uhz) *n.* special rights; advantages

proclaiming (pruh KLAYM ihng) *v.* announcing

procure (pruh KYUR) *v.* bring about through some effort

prodigious (pruh DIHJ uhs) *adj.* of great power or size

profundity (pruh FUHN duh tee) *n.* intellectual depth

profusion (pruh FYOO zhuhn) *n.* abundance; rich supply

propitiation (pruh pihsh ee AY shuhn) *n.* action designed to soothe or satisfy a person, a cause, etc.

propitious (pruh PIHSH uhs) *adj.* favorably inclined or disposed

prospect (PROS pehkt) *n.* something hoped for or expected

prosperity (pros PEHR uh tee) *n.* condition of being successful; wealth

protruded (proh TROOD uhd) *v.* stuck out

prudence (PROO duhns) *n.* carefulness; caution

prudent (PROO duhnt) *adj.* sensible; careful

psychology (sy KOL uh jee) *n.* science dealing with the mind and with mental and emotional processes

punitive (PYOO nuh tihv) *adj.* concerned with punishment

purged (purjd) *v.* cleansed

Q

quail (kwayl) *v.* draw back in fear; lose heart

quench (kwehnch) *v.* satisfy a thirst

quote (kwoht) *v.* speak or write a passage by someone else

R

range (raynj) *n.* distance between certain limits; extent

ravenous (RAV uh nuhs) *adj.* extremely hungry for something

ravine (ruh VEEN) *n.* long, deep hollow in the ground; a gully

realist (REE uh lihst) *n.* person or artist concerned with things as they are, rather than as they could or should be

realistic (REE uh LIHS tihk) *adj.* based on facts; practical

reaped (reept) *v.* gathered; brought in

receipts (rih SEETS) *n.* amounts of money received

recognize (REHK uhg nyz) *v.* perceive clearly

recompense (REHK uhm pehns) *n.* something given or done in return for something else; repayment

recourse (REE kawrs) *n.* access to a form of help or aid

recruits (rih KROOTS) *n.* newly drafted soldiers

rectitude (REHK tuh tood) *n.* correctness; righteousness

redress (rih DREHS) *n.* compensation for a wrong done

refuge (REHF yooj) *n.* shelter or protection from danger

regiment (REHJ uh muhnt) *n.* military unit

regional (REE juh nuhl) *adj.* of or in a particular localized area

regionalism (REE juh nuh LIHZ uhm) *n.* strong or loyal attachment to a certain region or area

relent (rih LEHNT) *v.* become less harsh; be more merciful

reluctant (rih LUHK tuhnt) *adj.* unwilling; disinclined

rendezvous (RAHN duh voo) *n.* meeting place

repeat (rih PEET) *v.* say or state again

repent (rih PEHNT) *v.* feel sorry for what one has done and vow to change one's behavior

repose (rih POHZ) *n.* state of being at rest

repression (rih PREHSH uhn) *n.* restraint

reproduce (REE pruh DOOS) *v.* imitate closely

repugnant (rih PUHG nuhnt) *adj.* offensive; disagreeable

resign (rih ZYN) *v.* accept something as unavoidable; submit oneself to a something negative

resources (rih SAWR sihz) *n.* supplies

retaliation (rih tal ee AY shuhn) *n.* act of returning an injury or wrong

revelations (rehv uh LAY shuhnz) *n.* newly revealed information; disclosures

reverential (rehv uh REHN shuhl) *adj.* showing deep respect and love

revise (rih VYZ) *v.* make a new, improved version

rights (ryts) *n.* that which a person has claim to

rituals (RIHCH oo uhlz) *n.* established forms of ceremonies; ceremonial acts

robust (roh BUHST) *adj.* strong and healthy; full of life

rueful (ROO fuhl) *adj.* feeling or showing someone sorrow or pity

rural (RUR uhl) *adj.* of or relating to the country or agriculture

S

salient (SAY lee uhnt) *adj.* standing out from the rest

salutary (SAL yuh tehr ee) *adj.* beneficial; promoting a good purpose

salvage (SAL vihj) *v.* the saving of goods or materials from waste

satire (SAT yr) *n.* literary work mocking human vices or mistakes

saunter (SAWN tuhr) *n.* a slow, leisurely gait

savagery (SAV ihj ree) *n.* barbarity

scale (skayl) *n.* the extent or size of something

scenario (sih NAIR ee oh) *n.* situation

sediment (SEHD uh muhnt) *n.* material that settles to the bottom of a liquid

seeping (SEEP ihng) *v.* flowing slowly

self-conscious (SEHLF KON shuhs) *adj.* uncomfortable, especially by the presence or the thought of other people

self-reliance (SEHLF rih LY uhns) *n.* dependence on one's own acts

self-reliant (SEHLF rih LY uhnt) *adj.* dependent on one's own acts

sensible (SEHN suh buhl) *adj.* emotionally or intellectually aware

sentience (SEHN shuhns) *n.* capacity for feeling

separate (SEHP uh rayt) *v.* make a distinction between

shard (shahrd) *n.* a fragment or broken piece

shares (shairz) *n.* portions of ownership of a company or a piece of property

sinister (SIHN uh stuhr) *adj.* threatening harm, evil or misfortune

sinuous (SIHN yoo uhs) *adj.* moving in and out; wavy

skyscraper (SKY SKRAY puhr) *n.* very tall building

smite (smyt) *v.* kill by a powerful blow

solemn (SOL uhm) *adj.* serious or grave

somnolent (SOM nuh luhnt) *adj.* sleepy; drowsy

sort (sawrt) *v.* put in place according to kind, class, or nature

sowed (sohd) *v.* scattered; planted

specious (SPEE shuhs) *adj.* seeming to be good or sound without actually being so

spectator (SPEHK tay tuhr) *n.* a person who watches something without taking part in it

speculate (SPEHK yuh layt) *v.* use evidence to guess what might happen

splendor (SPLEHN duhr) *n.* great display of riches; great brightness

squander (SKWON duhr) *v.* spend or use wastefully

stark (stahrk) *adj.* stiff; rigid

state (stayt) *v.* express in words

statute (STACH oot) *n.* the document in which such an enactment is expressed

steal (steel) *v.* creep

stealthily (STEHLTH uh lee) *adv.* slyly or secretively

stirring (STUR ihng) *adj.* busy; full of energy

storytelling (STAWR ee TEHL ihng) *n.* act or art of telling tales or anecdotes

striking (STRYK ihng) *adj.* very noticeable or impressive

structure (STRUHK chuhr) *v.* create a general plot or outline

subject to (SUHB jihkt too) *adj.* likely to be affected by something

sublime (suh BLYM) *adj.* noble; majestic

subsisted (suhb SIHST uhd) *v.* remained alive; were sustained

suburbia (suh BUR bee uh) *n.* region outside of a major city

successive (suhk SEHS ihv) *adj.* following one after another

suffice (suh FYS) *v.* be adequate; meet the needs of

summarily (SUHM uhr uh lee) *adv.* promptly and without formality

summarize (SUHM uh ryz) *v.* briefly state the most important ideas and details

summation (suh MAY shuhn) *n.* summing up; giving all the key details of in a brief form

superficial (SOO puhr FIHSH uhl) *adj.* on the surface; shallow

superfluous (su PUR floo uhs) *adj.* strong belief

supple (SUHP uhl) *adj.* able to bend and move easily and nimbly

surmised (suhr MYZD) *v.* guessed; concluded

surveyed (suhr VAYD) *v.* measured and marked to show boundaries

swerve (swurv) *v.* to turn aside sharply or suddenly from a straight course

synonymous (sih NON uh muhs) *adj.* equivalent or similar in meaning

systemic (sihs TEHM ihk) *adj.* affecting the entire organism or bodily system

T

taboo (tuh BOO) *n.* something forbidden within a particular society or culture

tactful (TAKT fuhl) *adj.* concerned about upsetting or offending others

tantalized (TAN tuh lyzd) *v.* tormented; frustrated

taut (tawt) *adj.* tightly stretched

technology (tehk NOL uh jee) *n.* science of the mechanical and industrial arts

tedious (TEE dee uhs) *adj.* long or verbose and wearisome

tempered (TEHM puhrd) *v.* treated to achieve just the right strength or balance

tempest (TEHM pihst) *n.* violent storm with high winds

terrain (teh RAYN) *n.* ground or track of ground, especially with regard to its natural features

terrors (TEHR uhrz) *n.* great fears

theology (thee OL uh jee) *n.* the study of religion

tranquil (TRANG kwuhl) *adj.* calm; quiet; still

transcribed (tran SKRYBD) *v.* wrote or typed a copy

transformed (trans FAWRMD) *adj.* altered; changed

transfusion (trans FYOO zhuhn) *n.* the act of transference or transmission

transient (TRAN shuhnt) *adj.* not permanent

transition (tran ZIHSH uhn) *n.* change or passing from one condition to another

traversed (trav UHRST) *v.* moved over, across, or through

treacherous (TREHCH uhr uhs) *adj.* giving a false appearance of security; dangerous

tremulously (TREHM yuh luhs lee) *adv.* fearfully; timidly

tumultuously (too MUHL choo uhs lee) *adv.* in an agitated way

tyranny (TIHR uh nee) *n.* oppressive power

U

unabated (uhn uh BAY tihd) *adj.* not lessened or reduced

unanimity (yoo nuh NIHM uh tee) *n.* complete agreement

unconscious (uhn KON shuhs) *adj.* having temporarily lost awareness; in a faint

undertaking (UHN duhr tay kihng) *n.* task or challenge

unscrupulous (uhn SKROO pyuh luhs) *adj.* unethical; dishonest

unwonted (uhn WOHN tihd) *adj.* unusual; unfamiliar

urban (UR buhn) *adj.* characteristic of a city

V

<u>**validate**</u> (VAL uh dayt) *v.* prove to be factual or effective

vanquished (VAN kwihsht) *v.* thoroughly defeated

venerable (VEHN uhr uh buhl) *adj.* commanding respect

<u>**verify**</u> (VEHR uh fy) *v.* prove to be true by evidence

vernacular (vuhr NAK yuh luhr) *n.* native language

vigilance (VIHJ uh luhns) *n.* watchfulness

vigilant (VIHJ uh luhnt) *adj.* alert to danger

vigorously (VIHG uhr uhs lee) *adv.* forcefully or powerfully

vindicated (VIHN duh kayt ihd) *v.* cleared from blame

virtuous (VUR choo uhs) *adj.* characterized by moral virtue; righteous

virulent (VIHR yuh luhnt) *adj.* extremely hurtful or infectious

vision (VIHZH uhn) *n.* sense of sight; something seen in a dream or the imagination

volition (voh LIHSH uhn) *n.* act of using the will; decision

voluminous (vuh LOO muh nuhs) *adj.* of enough material to fill volumes

votive (VOH tihv) *adj.* designed to accomplish or fulfill a special intention

vulnerability (vuhl nuhr uh BIHL uh tee) *n.* open to moral attack, criticism, temptation, etc

W

wanton (WON tuhn) *adj.* senseless; unjustified

wasteland (WAYST LAND) *n.* land that is uncultivated or barren

wilderness (WIHL duhr nihs) *n.* region with no people living in it

wily (WY lee) *adj.* sly; cunning

wretched (REHCH uhd) *adj.* deeply distressed; miserable

Spanish Glossary

El vocabulario de Pregunta Esencial aparece en **azul**. El vocabulario académico de alta utilidad está <u>subrayado</u>.

A

abeyance / suspensión *s.* cesación temporal

absolve / absolver *v.* perdonar; liberar de culpa

absurdity / absurdo *s.* disparate; irracionalidad

accosted / abordó *v.* se dirigió a o habló con alguien de manera vehemente

account / cuenta *s.* informe o detalle

acknowledges / reconoce *v.* acepta la existencia, realidad o verdad de algo

acquiesce / asentir *v.* aceptar sin protesta

adamant / obstinado *adj.* firme; inflexible

adjourned / suspendió *v.* clausuró temporalmente

advantageous / ventajoso *adj.* provechoso; beneficioso

adversary / adversario *s.* opositor; enemigo

adversity / adversidad *s.* desgracia, calamidad

affections / afectos *s.* emociones

affliction / aflicción *s.* algo que causa dolor o angustia

agape / boquiabierto *adj.* con sorpresa; con asombro

aggregation / conjunto *s.* agrupación de objetos o individuos distintos

agricultural / agrícola *adj.* donde la agricultura es el principal medio de vida

alacrity / alacridad *s.* velocidad

alienation / enajenación *s.* distanciamiento o separación de sentimiento o afecto

alliance / alianza *s.* unión de naciones para un fin específico

ambiguity / ambigüedad *s.* estado de tener dos o más significados posibles

ambition / ambición *s.* deseo vehemente de lograr un objetivo específico; ímpetu por triunfar

ameliorate / mejorar *v.* hacer mejor

ample / amplio *adj.* de gran tamaño; más que suficiente

<u>**analyze / analizar**</u> *v.* descomponer un tema en partes y explicarlas

anarchy / anarquía *s.* ausencia de gobierno

ancestor / antepasado *s.* persona de la que descienden otras personas

anonymity / anonimato *s.* la condición de ser desconocido

<u>**anticipate / prever**</u> *v.* prepararse para algo o indicar algo

anxiety / ansiedad *s.* estado de sentirse intranquilo, aprehensivo o preocupado por lo que pudiera ocurrir

apparel / vestido *s.* ropa

apparition / aparición *s.* acto de aparecer o hacerse visible

appease / saciar *v.* satisfacer

appendage / apéndice *s.* parte externa de una planta o animal, como una rama o cola

<u>**appraise / evaluar**</u> *v.* calcular el valor, la importancia o el estatus de algo

apprehension / aprensión *s.* inquietante sensación de premonición; pavor

appropriate / apropiar *v.* tomar o usar algo sin permiso

arduous / arduo *adj.* difícil

<u>**argue / argumentar**</u> *v.* expresar razones a favor o en contra; comprobar expresando razones

<u>**arrange / acomodar**</u> *v.* poner en orden o en secuencia

ascended / ascendió *v.* subió

aspirations / aspiraciones *s.* fuertes deseos o ambiciones

assault / asalto *s.* ataque violento

assent / asentir *v.* acordar

<u>**assess / evaluar**</u> *v.* determinar la importancia, el tamaño o el valor de algo

austerity / austeridad *s.* adustez en la conducta o la apariencia; dureza; severidad

auxiliary / auxiliar *adj.* que brinda ayuda o apoyo

avarice / avaricia *s.* codicia

aversion / aversión *s.* objeto que provoca una fuerte antipatía

avidly / ávidamente *adv.* ansiosamente

awe / asombro *s.* sentimientos encontrados de temor y admiración

B

base / bajo *adj.* ruin; vil

beguile / cautivar *v.* encantar o deleitar

benediction / bendición *s.* plegaria que invoca la gracia de Dios

benevolent / benévolo *adj.* bondadoso; caritativo

benign / benigno *adj.* no injurioso ni maligno; no canceroso

bequeath / legar *v.* transmitir; pasar a otro

brazenness / descaro *s.* desfachatez; atrevimiento; insolencia

brigade / brigada *s.* unidad de soldados

brutal / brutal *adj.* cruel y sin sentimientos; salvaje; violento

C

cadence / cadencia *s.* serie de notas o acordes hacia el final de una obra musical

calamity / calamidad *s.* desastre; catástrofe

calumny / calumnia *s.* falsa acusación; difamación

candid / franco *adj.* sincero

canvass / solicitar *v.* recorrer cierta área solicitando los votos, mandatos o participación de la gente

capable / capaz *adj.* poseer las destrezas necesarias para realizar algo

caper / travesura *s.* picardía

casualties / bajas *s.* miembros de las fuerzas armadas que mueren en combate

categorize / categorizar *v.* colocar en grupos relacionados

cavernous / cavernoso *adj.* que se asemeja a una caverna; vasto

celestial / celestial *adj.* que pertenece o está en el cielo, como los planetas o las estrellas

chaos / caos *s.* desorden de la materia y el espacio, que presuntamente existió antes del universo ordenado

chronicles / crónicas *s.* cuentos; historias

circumvent / circundar *v.* evitar; rodear

civilian / civil *s.* cualquier persona que no es miembro de las fuerzas armadas

classify / clasificar *v.* asignar a una categoría

cleave / asir *v.* adherirse; pegarse

coinage / invención *s.* palabra o expresión inventada

coincide / coincidir *v.* que sucede al mismo tiempo

collective / colectividad *s.* acto de agrupar en un todo

collusion / confabulación *s.* acuerdo secreto; conspiración

commercial / comercial *adj.* relacionado con el comercio o los negocios

commissioners / comisionados *s.* funcionarios de gobierno

commonplace / común *adj.* habitual; ordinario

commotion / conmoción *s.* confusión ruidosa

community / comunidad *s.* todas las personas que viven en un distrito, ciudad o área específica

compare / comparar *v.* señalar las similitudes o las diferencias

conciliatory / conciliatorio *adj.* que busca la paz o la conciliación; amistoso

conclude / concluir *v.* llegar a un fin lógicamente necesario por medio de razonamiento

condolences / condolencias *s.* expresiones de pesar

conduct / conducta *v.* comportamiento

conflagration / conflagración *s.* incendio extenso y destructivo

conformity / conformidad *s.* acción que concuerda con las normas generalmente aceptadas

confounded / confundido *adj.* confuso; consternado

conjectural / conjetural *adj.* basado en la suposición

conjectured / conjeturó *v.* supuso

conjuring / conjurando *v.* invocando; apareciendo como por arte de magia

consecrate / consagrar *v.* motivo para ser venerado u honrado

conspicuous / conspicuo *adj.* obvio; fácilmente visible o perceptible

consternation / consternación *s.* gran temor o conmoción que provoca sentimientos de impotencia e incertidumbre

constitute / constituir *v.* servir de base o parte de algo; formar; abarcar

constitution / constitución *s.* composición física de una persona

contentious / contencioso *adj.* disputable

contiguous / contiguo *adj.* lindante; adyacente

contract / contrato *s.* acuerdo escrito

contrast / contrastar *v.* inspeccionar para descubrir las diferencias

convention / convención *s.* reunión a la que asisten miembros o delegados

conviction / convicción *s.* creencia profunda

convivial / jovial *adj.* que goza de la buena compañía; sociable

copious / copioso *adj.* cuantioso; abundante

correspond / corresponder *v.* concordar; relacionarse con

countenance / aprobar *v.* sancionar; tolerar

cowering / encogiendo *v.* temblando o agachándose, como con miedo

create / crear *v.* producir por medio de habilidad imaginativa

crevices / grietas *s.* estrechas aberturas causadas por resquebraduras o fisuras

critic / crítico *s.* persona que desaprueba o detecta fallas

critique / criticar *v.* examinar críticamente; reseñar

cunning / astuto *adj.* hábil para el engaño; artificioso; taimado

cyberspace / ciberespacio *s.* mundo en línea de redes informáticas

D

daunting / atemorizante *adj.* intimidante

decorum / decoro *s.* rectitud; idoneidad

deduce / deducir *v.* inferir a partir de un principio general

defend / defender *v.* mantener o apoyar en vista de un argumento

deference / deferencia *s.* estimación o respeto cortés

deficient / deficiente *adj.* con falta de; que carece de algo necesario

define / definir *v.* expresar las cualidades que hacen de algo lo que es

degenerate / degenerado *adj.* moralmente corrupto

dejected / abatido *v.* desanimado; cabizbajo; deprimido

deliberation / deliberación *s.* consideración meticulosa

deposition / deposición *s.* declaración de un testigo bajo juramento, aunque no en un tribunal en pleno

depths / profundidades *s.* áreas más profundas

derivative / derivado *adj.* que no es original; que se basa en otra cosa

derive / derivar *v.* rastrear hasta o desde una fuente; obtener por medio de razonamiento

describe / describir *v.* representar en palabras

design / diseñar *v.* crear, elaborar, ejecutar o construir según un plan

desolate / desolado *adj.* abandonado; aislado

despondent / desalentado *adj.* sin valor ni esperanza

despotism / despotismo *s.* dominio absoluto; tiranía

destitute / indigente *adj.* que vive en abyecta pobreza

destruction / destrucción *s.* acto de demoler o abatir

detached / indiferente *adj.* no involucrado emocionalmente

devise / idear *v.* formar en la mente por medio de nuevas combinaciones de ideas; inventar

dictum / dictamen *s.* declaración formal de hecho u opinión

differentiate / diferenciar *v.* reconocer una disparidad

digress / divagar *v.* alejarse temporalmente del tema principal

dilapidated / dilapidado *adj.* ruinoso

diligence / diligencia *s.* esfuerzo constante y minucioso; perseverancia

discern / discernir *v.* percibir o reconocer; distinguir claramente

discord / desacuerdo *s.* diferencia de opinión; disputa

discretion / discreción *s.* Prudencia

discriminate / discriminar *v.* reconocer diferencias entre elementos

disdainfully / desdeñosamente *adv.* que muestra desdén o desprecio

disgrace / ignominia *s.* algo que genera vergüenza o deshonra

disillusion / desengaño *s.* libertad de una idea falsa; desencanto

dispatched / despachó *v.* envió, generalmente en asuntos oficiales

dispersal / dispersión *s.* distribución

disposition / disposición *s.* inclinación; tendencia

disregard / desatender *v.* no prestar atención a; hacer caso omiso de; ignorar

dissembling / disimulando *v.* encubriendo la verdadera naturaleza o los motivos propios

dissention / disensión *s.* desacuerdo; discordia expresada mediante fuertes discusiones

dissuade / disuadir *v.* convencer a alguien de no hacer algo

distinguish / distinguir *v.* marcar como independiente o diferente

diversity / diversidad *s.* variedad; punto de disimilitud

divine / adivinar *v.* averiguar mediante la intuición

docile / dócil *adj.* fácil de dirigir o manejar; obediente

doctrine / doctrina *s.* lo que se enseña

dogma / dogma *s.* doctrinas o credos autorizados

dubious / dudoso *adj.* cuestionable; sospechoso

duplicate / duplicar *v.* hacer una copia

duration / duración *s.* tiempo durante el cual algo continúa o existe

dusky / obscuro *adj.* poco claro; sombrío; tenebroso

dyspepsia / dispepsia *s.* indigestión

E

ecstasy / éxtasis *s.* sentimiento de alegría abrumadora; enorme deleite

efface / tachar *v.* borrar; eliminar

effigies / efigies *s.* imágenes o retratos, especialmente de personas

effrontery / desvergüenza *s.* audacia descarada

effuse / derramar *v.* verter; brotar

eloquence / elocuencia *s.* talento para la oratoria vívida y enérgica

elusive / evasivo *adj.* difícil de comprender

embankment / dique *s.* montículo de tierra o piedra construido para retener agua, o como soporte para una carretera

embark / embarcar *v.* iniciar una empresa, proyecto o actividad

emigrants / emigrantes *s.* personas que abandonan un sitio para establecerse en otro

eminence / eminencia *s.* grandeza; celebridad

emit / emitir *v.* articular palabras o sonidos

enamored / enamorado *adj.* encantado; cautivado

encroached / usurpó *v.* invadió

endured / soportó *v.* aguantó

engrossed / absorto *adj.* completamente ocupado; enfrascado

entreated / suplicó *v.* rogó; imploró

entrenchments / trincheras *s.* zanjas profundas y extensas con paredes empinadas, utilizadas para defenderse del fuego enemigo

environment / entorno *s.* objetos o condiciones circundantes

epitaph / epitafio *s.* inscripción en una lápida o piedra sepulcral

equivocal / ambiguo *adj.* que se puede interpretar de más de una manera

eradicate / erradicar *v.* eliminar; destruir

establishment / establecimiento *s.* casa o negocio

estimates / estimaciones *s.* cálculos generales minuciosos

etiquette / etiqueta *s.* comportamiento correcto y formal

evacuated / evacuó *v.* desalojó; retiró

evade / evadir *v.* eludir o escapar mediante el engaño o ingenio

evaluate / evaluar *v.* determinar la importancia, el valor o la condición de algo estudiándolo detalladamente

exalted / exaltado *adj.* lleno de júbilo u orgullo; regocijado

examine / examinar *v.* indagar detalladamente sobre un tema

exasperation / exasperación *s.* enojo; frustración

exhaust / escape *s.* descarga de vapor o gas ya usado de un motor

exile / exilio *s.* estado o período de destierro

expansion / expansión *s.* acto o proceso de aumentar la amplitud, el tamaño o el volumen

expedient / recurso *s.* método utilizado para alcanzar un objetivo rápidamente

expenditures / desembolsos *s.* gastos; usos del dinero o recursos

exposures / exposiciones *s.* secciones de una película donde se refleja la luz al tomar una fotografía

extort / extorsionar *v.* obtener mediante amenaza o violencia

extraneous / extraño *adj.* no relacionado; desvinculado

F

fallowness / ociosidad *s.* inactividad

fantastic / fantástico *adj.* excelente; increíble

fastidious / exigente *adj.* cuidadoso; meticuloso

fatigues / trajes de fatiga *s.* ropa resistente que usan los soldados para trabajos pesados

feigned / fingió *v.* simuló

fervent / ferviente *adj.* extremadamente apasionado; muy entusiasta

finite / finito *adj.* que tiene límites mensurables o definibles

fitfully / irregularmente *adv.* se distingue por actividad interrumpida o intermitente

flagrant / flagrante *adj.* deslumbrante; escandaloso

flourished / floreció *v.* creció fuerte, saludable y feliz; prosperó

fluctuation / fluctuación *s.* cambio de nivel o intensidad

foothold / asidero *s.* posición estable para emprender acciones subsiguientes

forded / vadeó *v.* cruzó el río en el punto menos profundo

forestall / impedir *v.* prevenir mediante una acción anticipada

formulate / formular *v.* expresar plena y claramente

fortuitous / fortuito *adj.* que ocurre por suerte

fortune / fortuna *s.* riqueza; suerte

fragmentation / fragmentación *s.* acto o proceso de descomponer en partes

frantic / frenético *adj.* marcado por el frenesí

frayed / raído *adj.* andrajoso

freedom / libertad *s.* no estar bajo el control de otros

frontier / frontera *s.* frontera entre regiones deshabitadas; región en desarrollo de un campo de conocimiento

furtive / furtivo *adj.* sigiloso

G

garrulous / gárrulo *adj.* que habla demasiado

gaudy / llamativo *adj.* que llama la atención con mal gusto

generalize / generalizar *v.* llegar a un principio más amplio a partir de detalles

genial / afable *adj.* jovial; cordial

genre / género *s.* categoría o estilo

global / global *adj.* extendido por todo el mundo

govern / gobernar *v.* regir; controlar; manejar

grandeur / grandiosidad *s.* grandeza

grave / grave *adj.* serio; solemne

gravity / gravedad *s.* seriedad

guile / maña *s.* astucia

H

habitation / morada *s.* lugar para vivir; conjunto de casas o viviendas

hallow / venerar *v.* honrar como sagrado

handiwork / manualidad *s.* trabajo hecho a mano; obra hecha con las propias manos

harass / hostigar *v.* acosar; molestar

heady / embriagante *adj.* intoxicante

heightened / enalteció *v.* elevó el nivel de

heritage / patrimonio *s.* rasgos, creencias o costumbres transmitidos de una generación a otra

homages / homenaje *s.* actos que expresan honor y reverencia

homely / sencillo *adj.* que no es elegante ni refinado; tosco

huddled / amontonó *v.* apiñó; acurrucó

humor / humor *s.* cualidad de ser gracioso o divertido

hypothesize / hipotetizar *v.* desarrollar una teoría acerca de algo

I

idealism / idealismo *s.* pensamiento basado en seguir las normas de perfección o belleza

identify / identificar *v.* establecer la identidad de algo

identity / identidad *s.* lo que caracteriza a una persona

illiterate / analfabeto *adj.* incapaz de leer o escribir

illustrate / ilustrar *v.* dar ejemplos para apoyar una idea

immigration / inmigración *s.* acto de llegar a otro país o región para vivir ahí

imperceptible / imperceptible *adj.* difícil de distinguir; desapercibido

impertinent / impertinente *adj.* que no muestra el respeto apropiado; insolente

implore / implorar *v.* pedir o suplicar con devoción; rogar

imply / insinuar *v.* dar a entender o sugerir

impulsive / impulsivo *adj.* que se realiza sin pensar

impulsively / impulsivamente *adv.* espontáneamente; repentinamente

inanimate / inanimado *adj.* sin vida; muerto

inarticulate / inarticulado *adj.* pronunciado o expresado sin claridad

inaudibly / imperceptiblemente *adv.* que no puede ser escuchado

incessant / incesante *adj.* constante; aparentemente interminable

incorporated / constituido *adj.* establecido legalmente como corporación

incorrigible / incorregible *adj.* imposible de corregir; irremediable

incredulously / incrédulamente *adv.* escépticamente

increment / incrementar *v.* aumentar, como en serie

indelible / indeleble *adj.* permanente; que no se puede borrar

independence / independencia *s.* libertad del control de otros

individualism / individualismo *s.* creencia de que la libertad personal es lo más importante

induce / inducir *v.* causar; provocar

industry / industria *s.* cualquier ramo de negocios, comercio o manufactura

ineffable / inefable *adj.* demasiado abrumador para ser expresado

inert / inerte *adj.* sin movimiento

inextricable / inextricable *adj.* que no puede separarse o liberarse de

infer / inferir *v.* derivar una conclusión a partir de hechos o premisas

infinity / infinito *s.* espacio, tiempo o distancia interminable o ilimitado

ingratiating / congraciador *adj.* encantador o halagador

innovation / innovación *s.* una nueva idea, método o dispositivo

innumerable / innumerable *adj.* son tantos que no se pueden contar

insatiable / insaciable *adj.* que constantemente desea más

inscrutable / inescrutable *adj.* que no puede comprenderse fácilmente

inseparable / inseparable *adj.* que no puede dividirse; enlazados

insidious / insidioso *adj.* engañoso; traicionero

inspection / inspección *s.* examen

intent / intención *s.* propósito u objetivo

intently / asiduamente *adv.* de manera concentrada y con un propósito determinado

intercepted / interceptó *v.* capturó o detuvo a algo o a alguien en su trayecto de un lugar a otro

interminable / interminable *adj.* que parece perdurar para siempre

interposed / interpuso *v.* intermedió

interspersed / esparció *v.* colocó por doquier

intervene / intervenir *v.* tomar medidas con el fin de prevenir algo

intolerable / intolerable *adj.* tan difícil o doloroso que resulta insoportable; inaguantable

intonation / entonación *s.* la capacidad de tocar notas musicales de manera afinada o desafinada

intricate / intrincado *adj.* complicado; que tiene muchas partes pequeñas correlacionadas

intuitively / intuitivamente *adv.* que no hace falta aprenderlo; instintivamente

invective / invectiva *s.* ataque verbal; crítica violenta

invent / inventar *v.* crear pensando

investigate / investigar *v.* realizar una inspección sistemática

J

jocularity / jocosidad *s.* buen humor chistoso

jubilant / jubiloso *adj.* alegre y triunfante

judge / juzgar *v.* formar una estimación o evaluación de algo

judgment / juicio *s.* capacidad de formar una opinión apropiadamente; buen razonamiento

justify / justificar *v.* comprobar o demostrar que algo es justo, correcto o razonable

L

label / etiquetar v. describir o designar

lament / lamentar v. expresar pesar por algo; sufrir en voz alta

landscape / paisaje s. área que puede verse a la vez desde un lugar

latent / latente adj. presente pero invisible o inactivo

latitude / latitud s. distancia al norte o al sur del ecuador

levee / dique s. muro construido en las márgenes de un río para detener las inundaciones

liberty / libertad s. autonomía

license / libertad de acción s. exención de una conducta o lenguaje correcto

licentious / licencioso adj. sin refrenamiento moral

limber / flexible adj. elástico

list / enumerar v. hacer una lista; incluir

listed / inclinado adj. ladeado; en declive

locate / ubicar v. hallar el lugar de algo

longitude / longitud s. distancia este u oeste en la superficie de la Tierra

lulled / arrulló v. calmó o sosegó mediante un sonido o movimiento suave

luminary / luminaria adj. que irradia luz

M

machetes / machetes s. cuchillos grandes y pesados de hoja ancha

magnanimity / magnanimidad s. generosidad

magnitude / magnitud s. grandeza de tamaño

maledictions / maldiciones s. maleficios

malign / maligno adj. maléfico; muy dañino

malingers / fingirse enfermo v. simular una enfermedad

maneuver / maniobrar v. mover algo utilizando un plan o conspiración

manifold / múltiple adj. de muchas maneras

martial / marcial adj. relativo a la guerra

marvel / maravilla s. cosa maravillosa o sorprendente

master / dominar v. volverse experto en

media / medios s. sistemas de comunicación diseñados para llegar a las masas

mediator / mediador s. aquél que reconcilia grupos opositores

melancholy / melancólico adj. triste y deprimido; lúgubre

membrane / membrana s. capa delgada y suave que sirve de cubierta o forro

memorials / monumentos s. objetos que se exhiben en memoria de una persona o suceso

meticulous / meticuloso adj. extremadamente cuidadoso de los detalles

metropolis / metrópolis s. ciudad grande

migrant / migrante adj. que se traslada de un lugar a otro

monotonous / monótono adj. tedioso porque no varía

morose / esquivo adj. melancólico; retraído

mundane / mundano adj. común, cotidiano, ordinario

munificent / munificente adj. generoso

myriad / innumerable adj. incontable

N

native / nativo adj. que pertenece a un lugar por nacimiento

natural / natural adj. que no ha sido elaborado por el hombre ni es artificial

nostalgia / nostalgia s. sentimiento de añoranza por algo

nuance / matiz s. una pequeña o sutil variación en tono, color o significado

O

oblivion / olvido s. condición de ser totalmente olvidado

oblivious / abstraído adj. falto de todo conocimiento

obstinacy / obstinación s. terquedad

obstinate / obstinado adj. terco

obtuse / obtuso adj. lento para comprender o percibir

offensive / ofensiva s. actitud o posición de ataque

ominous / ominoso adj. amenazador; siniestro

omnipotent / omnipotente adj. todopoderoso

opposition / oposición s. actitud hostil o resistente hacia algo

oppressed / oprimió v. reprimió mediante un poder injusto o cruel

optimism / optimismo s. tendencia a ser positivo

order / ordenar v. acomodar

ordinances / ordenanzas s. sacramentos o ritos religiosos

ostentation / ostentación s. exhibición jactanciosa

P

pacify / pacificar v. calmar o apaciguar

pallor / palor s. palidez

palpable / palpable adj. que puede ser tocado, sentido o manipulado

parsimony / parsimonia s. tacañería

pastoral / pastoril adj. característico de la vida rural; idealizado como pacífico, sencillo y natural

pathos / pathos s. cualidad que inspira lástima, pena o compasión en otros

pedestrian / peatonal adj. a pie; caminando

pensive / pensativo adj. que piensa intensamente; que suplica

perdition / perdición s. pérdida total e irreparable; ruina

peremptorily / perentoriamente adv. terminantemente; autoritariamente

peril / peligro s. riesgo

permeated / permeó v. impregnó

perpetual / perpetuo adj. que dura para siempre

persevere / perseverar v. continuar a pesar de las penurias; persistir

persistent / persistente adj. recurrente; constante

personal / personal adj. que pertenece a una persona; privado

pessimism / pesimismo s. tendencia a ser negativo

piety / piedad s. devoción a la religión

platitudes / trivialidades s. declaraciones sin sentido; expresiones desgastadas

plodding / caminar pausadamente v. avanzar o moverse pesadamente y con dificultad; recorrer penosamente

poignant / conmovedor adj. que hiere profundamente los sentimientos

poise / equilibrio s. balance; estabilidad

posterity / posteridad s. todas las futuras generaciones

practicable / practicable adj. factible, posible

prairie / llanura s. planicie cubierta de pasto sin árboles

precipitate / precipitar v. provocar que ocurra antes de lo esperado o deseado

preconceptions / preconcepciones s. ideas preconcebidas

predict / predecir v. vaticinar basándose en observación, experiencia o raciocinio

predilection / predilección s. preferencia preexistente

prelude / preludio s. parte o movimiento preliminar de una obra musical

prescient / presciente adj. que se conoce de antemano

pervading / difundirse v. que se esparce a través de

prevalent / extendido adj. que existe u ocurre abundantemente

privileges / privilegios s. derechos especiales; ventajas

proclaiming / proclamar v. anunciar

procure / procurar *v.* llevar a cabo con cierto esfuerzo

prodigious / prodigioso *adj.* de enorme poder o tamaño

profundity / profundidad *s.* profundidad intelectual

profusion / profusión *s.* abundancia; provisión cuantiosa

propitiation / apaciguamiento *s.* acción que busca aquietar o satisfacer a una persona, causa, etc.

propitious / propicio *adj.* favorablemente inclinado hacia o dispuesto a

prospect / prospecto *s.* algo deseado o esperado

prosperity / prosperidad *s.* condición de tener éxito; riqueza

protruded / sobresalió *v.* destacó

prudence / prudencia *s.* cuidado; cautela

prudent / prudente *adj.* perceptible; cauteloso

psychology / psicología *s.* la ciencia que estudia la mente y los procesos mentales y emocionales

punitive / punitivo *adj.* relativo al castigo

purged / purgó *v.* limpió

Q

quail / acobardar *v.* amedrentarse; descorazonarse

quench / aplacar *v.* calmar la sed

quote / citar *v.* decir o escribir un pasaje de la autoría de otra persona

R

range / rango *s.* distancia entre ciertos límites; alcance

ravenous / voraz *adj.* extremadamente hambriento

ravine / cañada *s.* zanja larga y profunda en la tierra; hondonada

realist / realista *s.* persona o artista que se interesa en las cosas como son y no como podrían o deberían ser

realistic / realista *adj.* basado en hechos; práctico

reaped / recolectó *v.* recogió; cosechó

receipts / ingresos *s.* cantidades de dinero recibidas

recognize / reconocer *v.* percibir claramente

recompense / recompensa *s.* algo que se da o se hace como retribución por otra cosa; compensación

recourse / recurso *s.* acceso a cierta forma de ayuda o asistencia

recruits / reclutas *s.* soldados recién alistados

rectitude / rectitud *s.* corrección; probidad

redress / resarcimiento *s.* compensación por un mal cometido

refuge / refugio *s.* amparo o protección del peligro

regiment / regimiento *s.* unidad militar

regional / regional *adj.* de o en un área específica

regionalism / regionalismo *s.* apego intenso o leal a cierta región o área

relent / aplacar *v.* hacerse menos tosco; ser más compasivo

reluctant / reacio *adj.* renuente; maldispuesto

rendezvous / punto de reunión *s.* sitio de encuentro

repeat / repetir *v.* decir o expresar de nuevo

repent / arrepentir *v.* sentir remordimiento por una mala acción y prometer cambiar su comportamiento

repose / reposo *s.* estado de descanso

repression / represión *s.* restricción

reproduce / reproducir *v.* imitar con detalle

repugnant / repugnante *adj.* ofensivo; desagradable

resign / resignar *v.* aceptar que algo es inevitable; someterse a algo negativo

resources / recursos *s.* suministros

retaliation / represalia *s.* acto de desquitarse por un perjuicio o mal

revelations / revelaciones *s.* información recientemente revelada; divulgaciones

reverential / reverencial *adj.* que muestra gran respeto y devoción

revise / revisar *v.* hacer una versión nueva y mejorada

rights / derechos *s.* aquello que una persona puede exigir

rituals / rituales *s.* formas establecidas de ceremonias; actos ceremoniales

robust / robusto *adj.* fuerte y saludable; vigoroso

rueful / desconsolado *adj.* sentir o mostrarle pena o lástima a alguien

rural / rural *adj.* relacionado con el campo o la agricultura

S

salient / sobresaliente *adj.* que se destaca entre los demás

salutary / saludable *adj.* benéfico; que promueve una buena causa

salvage / recuperar *v.* rescatar bienes o materiales de los desechos

satire / sátira *s.* obra literaria que se burla de los vicios o errores humanos

saunter / deambular *s.* paso lento y sin prisa

savagery / salvajismo *s.* barbarie

scale / escala *s.* el alcance o tamaño de algo

scenario / circunstancias *s.* situación

sediment / sedimento *s.* material que se deposita en el fondo de un líquido

seeping / filtrando *v.* fluyendo lentamente

self-conscious / cohibido *adj.* incómodo, especialmente por la presencia de otras personas o lo que ellas piensan

self-reliance / autosuficiencia *s.* dependencia únicamente en los actos propios

self-reliant / autosuficiente *adj.* dependiente únicamente de los actos propios

sensible / sensato *adj.* emocional o intelectualmente razonable

sentience / sensible *s.* que responde a o es conciente de las sensaciones

separate / separar *v.* hacer distinción entre

shard / fragmento *s.* pequeña parte o pedazo roto

shares / acciones *s.* porciones de participación en una compañía o propiedad

sinister / siniestro *adj.* que amenaza con perjuicio, maldad o infortunio

sinuous / sinuoso *adj.* con movimiento serpenteante; ondulante

skyscraper / rascacielos *s.* edificio de gran altura

smite / aniquilar *v.* matar de un fuerte golpe

solemn / solemne *adj.* serio o grave

somnolent / soñoliento *adj.* adormecido; amodorrado

sort / clasificar *v.* ordenar por tipo, clase o calidad

sowed / sembrado *adj.* esparcido; plantado

specious / especioso *adj.* que aparenta estar bueno o sano sin estarlo realmente

spectator / espectador *s.* persona que observa algo sin tomar parte

speculate / especular *v.* usar evidencia para predecir lo que puede ocurrir

speculation / especulación *s.* idea; conjetura

splendor / esplendor *s.* gran exhibición de riqueza; gran brillo

squander / despilfarrar *v.* gastar o derrochar

stark / rígido *adj.* tieso; inflexible

state / establecer *v.* expresar en palabras

statute / estatuto *s.* documento en el cual se expresa la promulgación, aprobación y sanción del mismo

steal / arrastrar *s.* reptar

stealthily / furtivamente *adv.* astuta o disimuladamente

stirring / incitante *adj.* activo; lleno de energía

storytelling / contar cuentos *s.* acto o arte de narrar cuentos o anécdotas

striking / impresionante *adj.* excesivamente llamativo o impactante

structure / estructurar *v.* crear una trama o un esquema general

subject / propenso *adj.* que puede ser afectado por algo

sublime / sublime *adj.* noble; majestuoso

subsisted / subsistieron *v.* permanecieron con vida; soportaron

suburbia / suburbio *s.* región fuera de una ciudad principal

successive / sucesivo *adj.* uno tras otro

suffice / bastar *v.* ser idóneo; satisfacer las necesidades de

summarily / sumariamente *adv.* brevemente y sin formalidades

summarize / resumir *v.* expresar brevemente las ideas y detalles más importantes

summation / recapitulación *s.* compendio; acto de dar todos los detalles principales en forma sucinta

superficial / superficial *adj.* en la superficie; poco profundo

superfluous / superfluo *adj.* innecesario

supple / flexible *adj.* capaz de doblarse y moverse fácil y ágilmente

surmised / conjeturó *v.* adivinó; dedujo

surveyed / deslindó *v.* midió y marcó para mostrar los linderos

swerve / desviar *v.* virar hacia un lado brusca o repentinamente y salirse del rumbo fijo

synonymous / sinónimo *adj.* con significado igual o similar

systemic / sistémico *adj.* que afecta el organismo o sistema físico completo

T

taboo / tabú *adj.* algo prohibido dentro de una sociedad o cultura en particular

tactful / discreto *adj.* que se preocupa por no enfadar u ofender a otros

tantalized / exasperó *v.* atormentó; frustró

taut / tirante *adj.* muy estirado

technology / tecnología *s.* ciencia de las artes mecánicas e industriales

tedious / tedioso *adj.* extenso o verboso y fastidioso

tempered / temperado *adj.* tratado para alcanzar exactamente la fuerza o equilibrio correcto

tempest / tempestad *s.* poderosa tormenta con fuertes vientos

terrain / terreno *s.* tierra o trocha de tierra, principalmente en lo relativo a sus características naturales

terrors / terrores *s.* grandes temores

theology / teología *s.* el estudio de la religión

tranquil / tranquilo *adj.* calmado; quieto; sosegado

transcribed / transcribió *v.* escribió o mecanografió una copia

transform / transformar *v.* cambiar en forma o apariencia

transformed / transformó *v.* cambió la condición o naturaleza de

transfusion / transfusión *s.* acto de transferencia o transmisión

transient / transitorio *adj.* no permanente

transition / transición *s.* cambiar o pasar de una condición a otra

traversed / atravesó *v.* cruzó sobre, a través de, o de un extremo a otro

treacherous / traicionero *adj.* que da una falsa apariencia de seguridad; peligroso

tremulously / trémulamente *adv.* con temor; tímidamente

tumultuously / tumultuosamente *adv.* de forma agitada

tyranny / tiranía *s.* poder opresor

U

unabated / cabal *adj.* no disminuido ni reducido

unanimity / unanimidad *s.* acuerdo total

unconscious / inconsciente *adj.* temporalmente sin conocimiento; desmayado

undertaking / empresa *s.* tarea o desafío

unscrupulous / inescrupuloso *adj.* poco ético; deshonesto

unwonted / inusitado *adj.* inusual; poco familiar

urban / urbano *adj.* característico de una ciudad

V

validate / validar *v.* demostrar que algo se basa en hechos o es efectivo

vanquished / venció *v.* derrotó completamente

venerable / venerable *adj.* que inspira respeto imponente

verify / verificar *v.* demostrar que algo es cierto con evidencia

vernacular / lengua vernácula *s.* idioma nativo

vigilance / vigilancia *s.* cuidado

vigilant / vigilante *adj.* alerta al peligro

vigorously / vigorosamente *adv.* enérgicamente o poderosamente

vindicated / vindicado *adj.* liberado de culpa

virtuous / virtuoso *adj.* que se distingue por sus virtudes morales; con rectitud

virulent / virulento *adj.* extremadamente doloroso o infeccioso

vision / visión *s.* sentido de la vista; algo que se ve en un sueño o en la imaginación

volition / volición *s.* acto de usar la voluntad; determinación

voluminous / voluminoso *adj.* con suficiente material como para llenar volúmenes

votive / votivo *adj.* diseñado para lograr o cumplir una intención especial

vulnerability / vulnerabilidad *s.* exposición a ataques morales, críticas, tentaciones, etc.

W

wanton / displicente *adj.* insensible; injustificable

wasteland / tierra baldía *s.* tierra en su estado natural, sin cultivar

wilderness / tierra salvaje *s.* región en la que no habitan personas

wily / artero *adj.* solapado; astuto

wretched / miserable *adj.* profundamente atormentado; desdichado

Life of the English Language

The life of every language depends on the people who use it. Whenever you use English by asking a question, talking on the phone, going to a movie, reading a magazine, or writing an e-mail, you keep it healthy and valuable.

Using a Dictionary

Use a **dictionary** to find the meaning, the pronunciation, and the part of speech of a word. Consult a dictionary also to trace the word's *etymology*, or its origin. Etymology explains how words change, how they are borrowed from other languages, and how new words are invented, or "coined."

Here is an entry from a dictionary. Notice what it tells about the word *anthology*.

> **anthology** (an thäl′ə jè) *n., pl.* —gies [Gr. anthologia, a garland, collection of short poems < *anthologos*, gathering flowers < *anthos*, flower + *legein*, to gather] a collection of poems, stories, songs, excerpts, etc., chosen by the compiler.

Dictionaries provide the *denotation* of each word, or its objective meaning. The symbol < means "comes from" or "is derived from." In this case, the Greek words for "flower" and "gather" combined to form a Greek word that meant a garland, and then that word became an English word that means a collection of literary flowers—a collection of literature like the one you are reading now.

Using a Thesaurus

Use a **thesaurus** to increase your vocabulary. In a thesaurus, you will find synonyms, or words that have similar meanings, for most words. Follow these guidelines to use a thesaurus:

- Do not choose a word just because it sounds interesting or educated. Choose the word that expresses exactly the meaning you intend.
- To avoid errors, look up the word in a dictionary to check its precise meaning and to make sure you are using it properly.

Here is an entry from a thesaurus. Notice what it tells about the word *book*.

> **book** *noun* A printed and bound work: tome, volume. See WORDS.
> **book** *verb* **1.** To register in or as if in a book: catalog, enroll, inscribe, list, set down, write down. *See* REMEMBER. **2.** To cause to be set aside, as for one's use, in advance: bespeak, engage, reserve. *See* GET.

If the word can be used as different parts of speech, as *book* can, the thesaurus entry provides synonyms for the word as each part of speech. Many words also have connotations, or emotional associations that the word calls to mind. A thesaurus entry also gives specific synonyms for each connotation of the word.

Activity Look up the words *knight* and *chivalry* in a dictionary. **(a)** What are their etymologies? **(b)** Explain what their etymologies reveal about the development of English. Then, check the word *chivalry* in a thesaurus. **(c)** What are two synonyms for this word? **(d)** In what way do the connotations of the synonyms differ?

The Origin and Development of English

Old Engish English began about the year 500 when Germanic tribes settled in Britain. The language of these peoples—the Angles, Saxons, and Jutes—combined with Danish and Norse when Vikings attacked Britain and added some Latin elements when Christian missionaries arrived. The result was Old English, which looked like this:

> Hwaet! We Gar-Dena   in gear-dagum,
> peod-cyninga,   prym gefrunon,
> hu da aepelingas   ellen fremedon!

These words are the opening lines of the Old English epic poem *Beowulf*, probably composed in the eighth century. In modern English, they mean: "Listen! We know the ancient glory of the Spear-Danes, and the heroic deeds of those noble kings!"

Middle English The biggest change in English took place after the Norman Conquest of Britain in 1066. The Normans spoke a dialect of Old French, and Old English changed dramatically when the Normans became the new aristocracy. From about 1100 to 1500, the people of Britain spoke what we now call Middle English.

> A Knyght ther was, and that a worthy man,
> That fro the tyme that he first bigan
> To riden out, he loved chivalrie,
> Trouthe and honour, fredom and curtesie.

These lines from the opening section of Chaucer's *Canterbury Tales* (c. 1400) are much easier for us to understand than the lines from *Beowulf*. They mean: "There was a knight, a worthy man who, from the time he began to ride, loved chivalry, truth, honor, freedom, and courtesy."

Modern English During the Renaissance, with its emphasis on reviving classical culture, Greek and Latin languages exerted a strong influence on the English language. In addition, Shakespeare added about two thousand words to the language. Grammar, spelling, and pronunciation continued to change. Modern English was born.

> *But soft! What light through yonder window breaks?*
> *It is the East, and Juliet is the sun!*

These lines from Shakespeare's *Romeo and Juliet* (c. 1600) need no translation, although it is helpful to know that "soft" means "speak softly." Since Shakespeare's day, conventions of usage and grammar have continued to change. For example, the *th* at the ends of many verbs has become s. In Shakespeare's time, it was correct to say "Romeo *hath* fallen in love." In our time, it is right to say "he *has* fallen in love." However, the changes of the past five hundred years are not nearly as drastic as the changes from Old English to Middle English, or from Middle English to Modern English. We still speak Modern English.

Old Words, New Words

Modern English has a larger vocabulary than any other language in the world. The *Oxford English Dictionary* contains about a half million words, and it is estimated that another half million scientific and technical terms do not appear in the dictionary. Here are the main ways that new words enter the language:

- **War**—Conquerors introduce new terms and ideas—and new vocabulary, such as anger, from Old Norse.

- **Immigration**—When large groups of people move from one country to another, they bring their languages with them, such as *boycott*, from Ireland.

- **Travel and Trade**—Those who travel to foreign lands and those who do business in faraway places bring new words back with them, such as *shampoo*, from Hindi.

- **Science and Technology**—In our time, the amazing growth of science and technology adds multitudes of new words to English, such as *Internet*.

English is also filled with **borrowings,** words taken directly from other languages. Sometimes borrowed words keep basically the same meanings they have in their original languages: *pajamas* (Hindi), *sauna* (Finnish), *camouflage* (French), *plaza* (Spanish). Sometimes borrowed words take on new meanings. *Sleuth,* for example, an Old Norse word for trail, has come to mean the person who follows a *trail*—a detective.

Mythology contributed to our language too. Some of the days of the week are named after Norse gods—Wednesday was Woden's Day, Thursday was Thor's Day. Greek and Roman myths have given us many words, such as jovial (from Jove), *martial* (from Mars), *mercurial* (from Mercury), and *herculean* (from Hercules).

Americanisms are words, phrases, usages, or idioms that originated in American English or that are unique to the way Americans speak. They are expressions of our national character in all its variety: *easy as pie, prairie dog, bamboozle, panhandle, halftime, fringe benefit, bookmobile, jackhammer, southpaw, lickety split.*

Activity Look up the following words in a dictionary. Describe the ways in which you think these words entered American English.

> *sabotage   burrito   moccasin   mecca   megabyte*

The Influence of English

English continues to have an effect on world cultures and literature. There are about three hundred million native English speakers, and about the same number who speak English as a second language. Although more people speak Mandarin Chinese, English is the dominant language of trade, tourism, international diplomacy, science, and technology.

Language is a vehicle of both communication and culture, and the cultural influence of English in the twenty-first century is unprecedented in the history of the world's languages. Beyond business and science, English spreads through sports, pop music, Hollywood movies, television, and journalism. A book that is translated into English reaches many more people than it would in its native language alone. Perhaps most significantly, English dominates the Internet. The next time you log on, notice how many Web sites from around the world also have an English version. The global use of English is the closest the world has ever come to speaking an international language.

Activity Choose one area of culture—such as sports, fashion, the arts, or technology—and identify three new words that English has recently added to the *world's* vocabulary.
(a) How do you think non-English speakers feel about the spread of English? **(b)** Do you think English helps to bring people together? Why or why not?

Tips for Improving Fluency

When you were younger, you learned to read. Then, you read to expand your experiences or for pure enjoyment. Now, you are expected to read to learn. As you progress in school, you are given more and more material to read. The tips on these pages will help you improve your reading fluency, or your ability to read easily, smoothly, and expressively. Use these tips as you read daily.

Keeping Your Concentration

One common problem that readers face is the loss of concentration. When you are reading an assignment, you might find yourself rereading the same sentence several times without really understanding it. The first step in changing this behavior is to notice that you do it. Becoming an active, aware reader will help you get the most from your assignments. Practice using these strategies:

- Cover what you have already read with a note card as you go along. Then, you will not be able to reread without noticing that you are doing it.

- Set a purpose for reading beyond just completing the assignment. Then, read actively by pausing to ask yourself questions about the material as you read. Check the accuracy of your answers as you continue to read.

- Use the Reading Strategy instruction and notes that appear with each selection in this textbook.

- Look at any art or illustrations that accompany the reading and use picture clues to help your comprehension.

- Stop reading after a specified period of time (for example, 5 minutes) and summarize what you have read. To help you with this strategy, use the Reading Check questions that appear with each selection in this textbook. Reread to find any answers you do not know.

Reading Phrases

Fluent readers read phrases rather than individual words. Reading this way will speed up your reading and improve your comprehension. Here are some useful ideas:

- Experts recommend rereading as a strategy to increase fluency. Choose a passage of text that is neither too hard nor too easy. Read the same passage aloud several times until you can read it smoothly. When you can read the passage fluently, pick another passage and keep practicing.

- Read aloud into a tape recorder. Then, listen to the recording, noting your accuracy, pacing, and expression. You can also read aloud and share feedback with a partner.

- Use the *Prentice Hall Audio Program Literature Hear It!* to hear the selections read aloud. Read along silently in your textbook, noticing how the reader uses his or her voice and emphasizes certain words and phrases.

- Set a target reading rate. Time yourself as you read and work to increase your speed without sacrificing the level of your comprehension.

Understanding Key Vocabulary

If you do not understand some of the words in an assignment, you may miss out on important concepts. Therefore, it is helpful to keep a dictionary nearby when you are reading. Follow these steps:

- Before you begin reading, scan the text for unfamiliar words or terms. Find out what those words mean before you begin reading.
- Use context—the surrounding words, phrases, and sentences—to help you determine the meanings of unfamiliar words.
- If you are unable to understand the meaning through context, refer to the dictionary.

Paying Attention to Punctuation

When you read, pay attention to punctuation. Commas, periods, exclamation points, semicolons, and colons tell you when to pause or stop. They also indicate relationships between groups of words. When you recognize these relationships you will read with greater understanding and expression. Look at the chart below.

Punctuation Mark	Meaning
comma	brief pause
period	pause at the end of a thought
exclamation point	pause that indicates emphasis
semicolon	pause between related but distinct thoughts
colon	pause before giving explanation or examples

Using the Reading Fluency Checklist

Use the checklist below each time you read a selection in this textbook. In your Language Arts journal or notebook, note which skills you need to work on and chart your progress each week.

Reading Fluency Checklist
☐ Preview the text to check for difficult or unfamiliar words.
☐ Practice reading aloud.
☐ Read according to punctuation.
☐ Break down long sentences into the subject and its meaning.
☐ Read groups of words for meaning rather than reading single words.
☐ Read with expression (change your tone of voice to add meaning to the word).

Reading is a skill that can be improved with practice. The key to improving your fluency is to read. The more you read, the better your reading will become.

Approaches to Criticism

By writing **criticism**—writing that analyzes literature—readers share their responses to a written work. Criticism is also a way for a reader to deepen his or her own understanding and appreciation of the work, and to help others to deepen theirs.

The information in this handbook will guide you through the process of writing criticism. In addition, it will help you to refine your critical perceptions to ensure that you are ready to produce work at the college level.

Understanding Criticism

There are a few different types of criticism. Each can enhance understanding and deepen appreciation of literature in a distinctive way. All types share similar functions.

The Types of Criticism

Analysis Students are frequently asked to analyze, or break into parts and examine, a passage or a work. When you write an analysis, you must support your ideas with references to the text.

Archetypal Criticism Archetypal criticism evaluates works of literature by identifying and analyzing the archetypes contained within them. An archetype, sometimes called a "universal symbol," is a plot, character, symbol, image, setting, or idea that recurs in the literature of many different cultures. Archetypes and patterns of archetypes can be seen as representing common patterns of human life and experience.

Biographical Criticism Biographical criticism uses information about a writer's life to shed light on his or her work.

Historical Criticism Historical criticism traces connections between an author's work and the events, circumstances, or ideas that shaped the writer's historical era.

Political Criticism Political criticism involves viewing an author's work with a focus on political assumptions and content—whether explicit or implicit—and, possibly, assessing the political impact of the work. Similar to historical criticism, political criticism draws connections between an author's work and the political issues and assumptions of the times.

Philosophical Criticism In philosophical criticism, the elements of a literary work such as plot, characters, conflict, and motivations are examined through the lens of the author's philosophical arguments and stances. The critic taking a philosophical approach will analyze philosophical arguments presented in a literary work and determine how those arguments have molded the work.

The Functions of Criticism

Critical writing serves a variety of important functions:

Making Connections All criticism makes connections between two or more things. For instance, an analysis of a poem may show similarities among different images.

Making Distinctions Criticism must make distinctions as well as connections. In an analysis of a poem, a critic may distinguish between two possible purposes for poetry: first, to create an enduring image and, second, to present a deeper meaning.

Achieving Insight By making connections and distinctions, criticism achieves insight. An analysis of a poem may reach the insight that the poem stands on its own as a work of beauty apart from any deeper meaning.

Making a Judgment Assessing the value of a work is an important function of criticism. A critic may assess a work by comparing it with other works and by using a standard such as enjoyment, insight, or beauty.

"Placing" the Work Critics guide readers not by telling them *what* to think but by giving them *terms in which to think.* Critical writing may help readers apply varied perspectives to illuminate different aspects of a work.

Writing Criticism

Like all solid writing, a work of criticism presents a thesis (a central idea) and supports it with arguments and evidence. Follow the strategies below to develop a critical thesis and gather support for it.

Formulate a Working Thesis

Once you have chosen a work or works on which to write, formulate a working thesis. First, ask yourself questions like these:

- What strikes you most about the work or the writer that your paper will address? What puzzles you most?

- In what ways is the work unlike others you have read?

- What makes the techniques used by the writer so well-suited to (or so poorly chosen for) conveying the theme of the work?

Jot down notes answering your questions. Then, reread passages that illustrate your answers, jotting down notes about what each passage contributes to the work. Review your notes, and write a sentence that draws a conclusion about the work.

Gather Support

Taking Notes From the Work

Once you have a working thesis, take notes on passages in the work that confirm it. To aid your search for support, consider the type of support suited to your thesis, as in the chart.

Conducting Additional Research
If you are writing biographical or historical criticism, you will need to consult sources on the writer's life and era. Even if you are writing a close analysis of a poem, you should consider consulting the works of critics to benefit from their insights and understanding.

If your thesis concerns . . .	look for support in the form of . . .
Character	• dialogue • character's actions • writer's descriptions of the character • other characters' reactions to the character
Theme	• fate of characters • patterns and contrasts of imagery, character, or events • mood • writer's attitude toward the action
Style	• memorable descriptions, observations • passages that "sound like" the writer • examples of rhetorical devices, such as exaggeration and irony
Historical Context	• references to historical events and personalities • evidence of social or political pressures on characters • socially significant contrasts between characters (for example, between the rich and the poor)
Literary Influences	• writer's chosen form or genre • passages that "sound like" another writer • events or situations that resemble those in other works • evidence of an outlook similar to that of another writer

Take Notes

Consider recording notes from the works you are analyzing, as well as from any critical works you consult, on a set of note cards. A good set of note cards enables you to recall details accurately, to organize your ideas effectively, and to see connections between ideas.

One Card, One Idea If you use note cards while researching, record each key passage, theme, critical opinion, or fact on a separate note card. A good note card includes a brief quotation or summary of an idea and a record of the source, including the page number, in which you found the information. When copying a sentence from a work, use quotation marks and check to make sure you have copied it correctly.

Coding Sources Keep a working bibliography, a list of all works you consult, as you conduct research. Assign a code, such as a letter, to each work on the list. For each note you take, include the code for the source.

Coding Cards Organize your note cards by labeling each with the subtopic it concerns.

Present Support Appropriately

As you draft, consider how much support you need for each point and the form that support should take. You can provide support in the following forms:

- **Summaries** are short accounts in your own words of important elements of the work, such as events, a character's traits, or the writer's ideas. They are appropriate for background information.

- **Paraphrases** are restatements of passages from a work in your own words. They are appropriate for background and for information incidental to your main point.

- **Quotations of key passages** are direct transcriptions of the writer's words, enclosed in quotation marks or, if longer than three lines, set as indented text. If a passage is crucial to your thesis, you should quote it directly and at whatever length is necessary.

Quotations of multiple examples are required to support claims about general features of a work, such as a claim about the writer's ironic style or use of cartoonlike characters.

DOs and DON'Ts of Academic Writing

Avoid gender and cultural bias. Certain terms and usages reflect the bias of past generations. To eliminate bias in any academic work you do, edit with the following rules in mind:

- **Pronoun usage** When referring to an unspecified individual in a case in which his or her gender is irrelevant, use forms of the pronoun phrase he or she. Example: "A lawyer is trained to use his or her mind."

- **"Culture-centric" terms** Replace terms that reflect a bias toward one culture with more generally accepted synonyms. For instance, replace terms such as primitive (used of hunting-gathering peoples), the Orient (used to refer to Asia), and Indians (used of Native Americans), all of which suggest a view of the world centered in Western European culture.

Avoid plagiarism. Presenting someone else's ideas, research, or exact words as your own is plagiarism, the equivalent of stealing or fraud. Laws protect the rights of writers and researchers in cases of commercial plagiarism. Academic standards protect their rights in cases of academic plagiarism.

To avoid plagiarism, follow these practices:

- Read from several sources.

- Synthesize what you learn.

- Let the ideas of experts help you draw your own conclusions.

- Always credit your sources properly when using someone else's ideas to support your view.

By following these guidelines, you will also push yourself to think independently.

Forming Your Critical Vocabulary

To enhance your critical perceptions—the connections you find and the distinctions you make—improve your critical vocabulary. The High-Utility Academic Words that appear in this textbook and are underlined in the Glossary (pp. R1–R13) are useful in critical writing.

Citing Sources and Preparing Manuscript

In research writing, cite your sources. In the body of your paper, provide a footnote, an endnote, or an internal citation, identifying the sources of facts, opinions, or quotations. At the end of your paper, provide a bibliography or a Works Cited list, a list of all the sources you cite. Follow an established format, such as Modern Language Association (MLA) Style or American Psychological Association (APA) Style.

Works Cited List (MLA Style)

A Works Cited list must contain accurate information sufficient to enable a reader to locate each source you cite. The basic components of an entry are as follows:

- Name of the author, editor, translator, or group responsible for the work
- Title
- Place and date of publication
- Publisher

For print materials, the information required for a citation generally appears on the copyright and title pages of a work. For the format of Works Cited list entries, consult the examples at right and in the chart on page R22.

Parenthetical Citations (MLA Style)

A parenthetical citation briefly identifies the source from which you have taken a specific quotation, factual claim, or opinion. It refers the reader to one of the entries on your Works Cited list. A parenthetical citation has the following features:

- It appears in parentheses.
- It identifies the source by the last name of the author, editor, or translator.
- It gives a page reference, identifying the page of the source on which the information cited can be found.

Punctuation A parenthetical citation generally falls outside a closing quotation mark but within the final punctuation of a clause or sentence. For a long quotation set off from the rest of your text, place the citation at the end of the excerpt without any punctuation following.

Special Cases

- If the author is an organization, use the organization's name, in a shortened version if necessary.
- If you cite more than one work by the same author, add the title or a shortened version of the title.

Sample Works-Cited Lists (MLA 7th Edition)

Carwardine, Mark, Erich Hoyt, R. Ewan Fordyce, and Peter Gill. *The Nature Company Guides: Whales, Dolphins, and Porpoises*. New York: Time-Life, 1998. Print.

"Discovering Whales." *Whales on the Net*. 1998. Whales in Danger Information Service. Web. 18 Oct. 1999.

Neruda, Pablo. "Ode to Spring." *Odes to Opposites*. Trans. Ken Krabbenhoft. Ed. and illus. Ferris Cook. Boston: Little, 1995. Print.

The Saga of the Volsungs. Trans. Jesse L. Byock. London: Penguin, 1990. Print.

List an anonymous work by title.

List both the title of the work and the collection in which it is found.

Sample Parenthetical Citations

It makes sense that baleen whales such as the blue whale, the bowhead whale, the humpback whale, and the sei whale (to name just a few) grow to immense sizes (Carwardine, Hoyt, and Fordyce 19–21). The blue whale has grooves running from under its chin to partway along the length of its underbelly. As in some other whales, these grooves expand and allow even more food and water to be taken in (Ellis 18–21).

Author's last name

Page numbers where information can be found

MLA Style for Listing Sources

Book with one author	Pyles, Thomas. *The Origins and Development of the English Language.* 2nd ed. New York: Harcourt, 1971. Print.
Book with two or three authors	McCrum, Robert, William Cran, and Robert MacNeil. *The Story of English.* New York: Penguin, 1987. Print.
Book with an editor	Truth, Sojourner. *Narrative of Sojourner Truth.* Ed. Margaret Washington. New York: Vintage, 1993. Print.
Book with more than three authors or editors	Donald, Robert B., et al. *Writing Clear Essays.* Upper Saddle River: Prentice, 1996. Print.
Single work in an anthology	Hawthorne, Nathaniel. "Young Goodman Brown." *Literature: An Introduction to Reading and Writing.* Ed. Edgar V. Roberts and H. E. Jacobs. Upper Saddle River: Prentice, 1998. 376–385. Print. [Indicate pages for the entire selection.]
Introduction to a work in a published edition	Washington, Margaret. Introduction. *Narrative of Sojourner Truth.* By Sojourner Truth. Ed. Washington. New York: Vintage, 1993. v–xi. Print.
Signed article from an encyclopedia	Askeland, Donald R. "Welding." *World Book Encyclopedia.* 1991 ed. Print.
Signed article in a weekly magazine	Wallace, Charles. "A Vodacious Deal." *Time* 14 Feb. 2000: 63. Print.
Signed article in a monthly magazine	Gustaitis, Joseph. "The Sticky History of Chewing Gum." *American History* Oct. 1998: 30–38. Print.
Newspaper	Thurow, Roger. "South Africans Who Fought for Sanctions Now Scrap for Investors." *Wall Street Journal* 11 Feb. 2000: A1+. Print. [For a multipage article that does not appear on consecutive pages, write only the first page number on which it appears, followed by the plus sign.]
Unsigned editorial or story	"Selective Silence." Editorial. *Wall Street Journal* 11 Feb. 2000: A14. Print. [If the editorial or story is signed, begin with the author's name.]
Signed pamphlet or brochure	[Treat the pamphlet as though it were a book.]
Work from a library subscription service	Ertman, Earl L. "Nefertiti's Eyes." *Archaeology* Mar.–Apr. 2008: 28–32. *Kids Search.* EBSCO. New York Public Library. Web. 18 June 2008 [Indicate the date you accessed the information.]
Filmstrips, slide programs, videocassettes, DVDs, and other audiovisual media	*The Diary of Anne Frank.* Dir. George Stevens. Perf. Millie Perkins, Shelley Winters, Joseph Schildkraut, Lou Jacobi, and Richard Beymer. 1959. Twentieth Century Fox, 2004. DVD.
CD-ROM (with multiple publishers)	Simms, James, ed. *Romeo and Juliet.* By William Shakespeare. Oxford: Attica Cybernetics; London: BBC Education; London: Harper, 1995. CD-ROM.
Radio or television program transcript	"Washington's Crossing of the Delaware." *Weekend Edition Sunday.* Natl. Public Radio. WNYC, New York. 23 Dec. 2003. Television transcript.
Internet Web page	"Fun Facts About Gum." NACGM site. 1999. National Association of Chewing Gum Manufacturers. Web. 19 Dec. 1999 [Indicate the date you accessed the information.]
Personal interview	Smith, Jane. Personal interview. 10 Feb. 2000.

All examples follow the style given in the *MLA Handbook for Writers of Research Papers,* seventh edition, by Joseph Gibaldi.

APA Style for Listing Sources

Book with one author	Pyles, T. (1971). *The origins and development of the English language* (2nd ed.). New York: Harcourt Brace Jovanovich.
Book with two or three authors	McCrum, R., Cran, W., & MacNeil, R. (1987). *The story of English.* New York: Penguin Books.
Book with an editor	Truth, S. (1993). *Narrative of Sojourner Truth* (M. Washington, Ed.). New York: Vintage Books.
Book with more than three authors or editors	Donald, R. B., Morrow, B. R., Wargetz, L. G., & Werner, K. (1996). *Writing clear essays.* Upper Saddle River, NJ: Prentice Hall. [With eight or more authors, abbreviate all authors after the sixth as "et al."]
Single work from an anthology	Hawthorne, N. (1998). Young Goodman Brown. In E. V. Roberts, & H. E. Jacobs (Eds.), *Literature: An introduction to reading and writing* (pp. 376–385). Upper Saddle River, NJ: Prentice Hall.
Introduction in a published edition	Washington, M. (1993). Introduction. In M. Washington (Ed.), S. Truth, *Narrative of Sojourner Truth* (pp. v–xi). New York: Vintage Books.
Signed article from an encyclopedia	Askeland, D. R. (1991). Welding. In *World Book Encyclopedia.* (Vol. 21. pp. 190–191). Chicago: World Book.
Signed article in a weekly magazine	Wallace, C. (2000, February 14). A vodacious deal. *Time, 155,* 63. [The volume number appears in italics before the page number.]
Signed article in a monthly magazine	Gustaitis, J. (1998, October). The sticky history of chewing gum. *American History, 33,* 30–38.
Newspaper	Thurow, R. (2000, February 11). South Africans who fought for sanctions now scrap for investors. *Wall Street Journal,* pp. A1, A4. [If an article appears on discontinuous pages, give all page numbers and separate the numbers with a comma.]
Unsigned editorial or story	Selective silence [Editorial]. (2000, February 11). *Wall Street Journal,* p. A14.
Signed pamphlet	Pearson Education. (2000). *LifeCare* (2nd ed.) [Pamphlet]. New York: Smith, John: Author.
Filmstrips, slide programs, videocassettes, DVDs, and other audiovisual media	Wallis, H. B. (Producer), & Curtiz, M. (Director). (1942). *Casablanca* [Motion Picture]. United States: Warner.
Radio or television program transcript	Hackett Fischer, D. (Guest), & Hansen, L. (Host). (2003, December 23). Washington's crossing of the Delaware. [Radio series installment]. *Weekend Edition Sunday.* New York: National Public Radio. Retrieved March 6, 2008 from http://www.npr.org/templates/story/story.php?storyId=1573202
Internet	National Association of Chewing Gum Manufacturers. (1999). Retrieved December 19, 1999, from http://www.nacgm.org/consumer/funfacts.html [References to Websites should begin with the author's last name, if available. Indicate the site name and the available path or URL address.]
Work from a library subscription service	Ertman, E. L. (2008 March–April). Nefertiti's eyes. *Archaeology, 61,* 28–32. Retrieved June 18, 2008, from EBSCO Science Reference Center database.
CD	Shakespeare, W. (1995). *Romeo and Juliet.* (J. Simms, Ed.) [CD-ROM]. Oxford: Attica Cybernetics.
Personal interview	[APA states that, since interviews (and other personal communications) do not provide "recoverable data," they should only be cited in text.]

Literary Terms

ALLEGORY An *allegory* is a story or tale with two or more levels of meaning—a literal level and one or more symbolic levels. The events, setting, and characters in an allegory are symbols for ideas or qualities. Arthur Miller's play *The Crucible* (p. 1124) is an allegory.

ALLITERATION *Alliteration* is the repetition of consonant sounds at the beginning of words or accented syllables. Sara Teasdale uses alliteration in these lines from her poem "Understanding":

> Your spirit's secret hides like gold
>
> Sunk in a Spanish galleon

ALLUSION An *allusion* is a reference to a well-known person, place, event, literary work, or work of art. Writers often make allusions to stories from the Bible, to Greek and Roman myths, to plays by Shakespeare, to political and historical events, and to other materials with which they can expect their readers to be familiar. In "The Love Song of J. Alfred Prufrock" (p. 708), T. S. Eliot alludes to, among other things, Dante's *Inferno*, Italian artist Michelangelo, Shakespeare's *Hamlet*, and the Bible. By using allusions, writers can suggest complex ideas simply and easily.

AMBIGUITY *Ambiguity* is the effect created when words suggest and support two or more divergent interpretations. Ambiguity may be used in literature to express experiences or truths that are complex or contradictory. Ambiguity often derives from the fact that words have multiple meanings.

See also *Irony.*

ANALOGY An *analogy* is an extended comparison of relationships. It is based on the idea that the relationship between one pair of things is like the relationship between another pair. Unlike a metaphor, an analogy involves an explicit comparison, often using the words *like* or *as*.

See also *Metaphor* and *Simile.*

ANECDOTE An *anecdote* is a brief story about an interesting, amusing, or strange event. An anecdote is told to entertain or to make a point. In the excerpt from *Life on the Mississippi* (p. 570), Mark Twain tells several anecdotes about his experiences on the Mississippi River.

ANTAGONIST An *antagonist* is a character or force in conflict with a main character, or protagonist. In Jack London's "To Build a Fire" (p. 596), the antagonist is neither a person nor an animal but rather the extreme cold. In many stories, the conflict between the antagonist and the protagonist is the basis for the plot.

See also *Conflict, Plot,* and *Protagonist.*

APHORISM An *aphorism* is a general truth or observation about life, usually stated concisely. Often witty and wise, aphorisms appear in many kinds of works. An essay writer may have an aphoristic style, making many such statements. Ralph Waldo Emerson was famous for his aphoristic style. His essay entitled "Fate" contains the following aphorisms:

> Nature is what you may do.
>
> So far as a man thinks, he is free.
>
> A man's fortunes are the fruit of his character.

Used in an essay, an aphorism can be a memorable way to sum up or to reinforce a point or an argument.

APOSTROPHE An *apostrophe* is a figure of speech in which a speaker directly addresses an absent person or a personified quality, object, or idea. Phillis Wheatley uses apostrophe in this line from "To the University of Cambridge, in New England":

> Students, to you 'tis given to scan the heights

See also *Figurative Language.*

ARCHETYPAL LITERARY ELEMENTS

Archetypal literary elements are patterns in literature found around the world. For instance, the occurrence of events in threes is an archetypal element of fairy tales. Certain character types, such as mysterious guides, are also archetypal elements of such traditional stories. Archetypal elements make stories easier to remember and retell. In **Moby-Dick** (p. 336), Melville uses the archetype of a whale—like the biblical mammal in conflict with Jonah—to address man's conflict with nature.

ARGUMENT See *Persuasion.*

ASSONANCE *Assonance* is the repetition of vowel sounds in conjunction with dissimilar consonant sounds. Emily Dickinson uses assonance in the line "The mountain at a given distance." The *i* sound is repeated in *given* and *distance*, in the context of the dissimilar consonant sounds *g–v* and *d–s*.

ATMOSPHERE See *Mood.*

AUTOBIOGRAPHY An *autobiography* is a form of nonfiction in which a person tells his or her own life story. Notable examples of autobiographies include those by Benjamin Franklin and Frederick Douglass. *Memoirs,* first-person accounts of personally or historically significant events in which the writer was a participant or an eyewitness, are a form of autobiographical writing.

See also *Biography* and *Journal.*

BALLAD A *ballad* is a songlike poem that tells a story, often one dealing with adventure and romance. Most ballads include simple language, four- or six-line stanzas, rhyme, and regular meter.

BIOGRAPHY A *biography* is a form of nonfiction in which a writer tells the life story of another person. Carl Sandburg's *Abe Lincoln Grows Up* is a biography of President Lincoln.

See also *Autobiography.*

BLANK VERSE *Blank verse* is poetry written in unrhymed iambic pentameter. An iamb is a poetic foot consisting of one weak stress followed by one strong stress. A pentameter line has five poetic feet. Robert Frost's "Birches" (p. 874) is written in blank verse.

CHARACTER A *character* is a person or an animal that takes part in the action of a literary work. The following are some terms used to describe various types of characters:

The *main character* in a literary work is the one on whom the work focuses. *Major characters* in a literary work include the main character and any other characters who play significant roles. A *minor character* is one who does not play a significant role. A *round character* is one who is complex and multifaceted, like a real person. A *flat character* is one who is one-dimensional. A *dynamic character* is one who changes in the course of a work. A *static character* is one who does not change in the course of a work.

See also *Characterization* and *Motivation.*

CHARACTERIZATION *Characterization* is the act of creating and developing a character. In *direct characterization,* a writer simply states a character's traits, as when F. Scott Fitzgerald writes of the main character in his story "Winter Dreams" (p. 730), "He wanted not association with glittering things and glittering people—he wanted the glittering things themselves." In *indirect characterization,* character is revealed through one of the following means:

1. words, thoughts, or actions of the character
2. descriptions of the character's appearance or background
3. what other characters say about the character
4. the ways in which other characters react to the character

See also *Character.*

CINQUAIN See *Stanza.*

CLASSICISM *Classicism* is an approach to literature and the other arts that stresses reason, balance, clarity, ideal beauty, and orderly form in imitation of the arts of ancient Greece and Rome. Classicism is often contrasted with *Romanticism,* which stresses imagination, emotion, and individualism. *Classicism* also differs from *Realism,* which stresses the actual rather than the ideal.

See also *Realism* and *Romanticism.*

CLIMAX The *climax* is the high point of interest or suspense in a literary work. For example, Jack London's "To Build a Fire" (p. 596) reaches its climax when the man realizes that he is going to freeze to death. The climax generally appears near the end of a story, play, or narrative poem.

See also *Plot.*

COMEDY A *comedy* is a literary work, especially a play, that has a happy ending.

CONFLICT A *conflict* is a struggle between opposing forces. Sometimes this struggle is internal, or within a character, as in Bernard Malamud's "The First Seven Years" (p. 1028). At other times, this struggle is external, or between a character and an outside force, as in Jack London's "To Build a Fire" (p. 596). Conflict is one of the primary elements of narrative literature because most plots develop from conflicts.

See also *Antagonist, Plot,* and *Protagonist.*

CONNOTATION A *connotation* is an association that a word calls to mind in addition to the dictionary meaning of the word. Many words that are similar in their dictionary meanings, or denotations, are quite different in their connotations. Consider, for example, José García Villa's line, "Be beautiful, noble, like the antique ant." This line would have a very different effect if it were "Be pretty, classy, like the old ant." Poets and other writers choose their words carefully so that the connotations of those words will be appropriate.

See also *Denotation.*

CONSONANCE *Consonance* is the repetition of similar final consonant sounds at the ends of words or accented syllables. Emily Dickinson uses consonance in these lines:

> But if he ask where you are hid
>
> Until to-morrow,—happy letter!
>
> Gesture, coquette, and shake your head!

COUPLET See *Stanza.*

CRISIS In the plot of a narrative, the *crisis* is the turning point for the protagonist—the point at which the protagonist's situation or understanding changes dramatically. In Bernard Malamud's "The First Seven Years" (p. 1028), the crisis occurs when Feld recognizes that Sobel loves Miriam.

DENOTATION The *denotation* of a word is its objective meaning, independent of other associations that the word brings to mind.

See also *Connotation.*

DENOUEMENT See *Plot.*

DESCRIPTION A *description* is a portrayal, in words, of something that can be perceived by the senses. Writers create descriptions by using images, as John Wesley Powell does in this passage from "The Most Sublime Spectacle on Earth," his description of the Grand Canyon:

> Clouds creep out of canyons and wind into other canyons. The heavens seem to be alive, not moving as move the heavens over a plain, in one direction with the wind, but following the multiplied courses of these gorges.

See also *Image.*

DEVELOPMENT See *Plot.*

DIALECT A *dialect* is the form of a language spoken by people in a particular region or group. Writers often use dialect to make their characters seem realistic and to create local color. See, for example, Mark Twain's "The Notorious Jumping Frog of Calaveras County" (p. 576).

See also *Local Color.*

DIALOGUE A *dialogue* is a conversation between characters. Writers use dialogue to reveal character, to present events, to add variety to narratives, and to arouse their readers' interest.

See also *Drama.*

DICTION *Diction* is a writer's or speaker's word choice. Diction is part of a writer's style and may be described as formal or informal, plain or ornate, common or technical, abstract or concrete.

See also *Style.*

DRAMA A *drama* is a story written to be performed by actors. The playwright supplies dialogue for the characters to speak, as well as stage directions that give information about costumes, lighting, scenery, properties, the setting, and the characters' movements and ways of speaking. Dramatic conventions include soliloquies, asides, or the passage of time between acts or scenes.

See also *Genre.*

DRAMATIC MONOLOGUE A *dramatic monologue* is a poem or speech in which an imaginary character speaks to a silent listener. T. S. Eliot's "The Love Song of J. Alfred Prufrock" (p. 708) is a dramatic monologue.

See also *Dramatic Poem* and *Monologue.*

DRAMATIC POEM A *dramatic poem* is one that makes use of the conventions of drama. Such poems may be monologues or dialogues or may present the speech of many characters. Robert Frost's "The Death of the Hired Man" is a famous example of a dramatic poem.

See also *Dramatic Monologue.*

DYNAMIC CHARACTER See *Character.*

EPIGRAM An *epigram* is a brief, pointed statement, in prose or in verse. Benjamin Franklin was famous for his epigrams, which include "Fools make feasts, and wise men eat them," and "A plowman on his legs is higher than a gentleman on his knees."

EPIPHANY An *epiphany* is a sudden revelation or flash of insight. The shoemaker in Bernard Malamud's "The First Seven Years" (p. 1028) experiences an epiphany when he suddenly and thoroughly comprehends that the actions of his apprentice, Sobel, are motivated by his secret love for Miriam.

ESSAY An *essay* is a short nonfiction work about a particular subject. Essays can be classified as *formal* or *informal*, *personal* or *impersonal*. They can also be classified according to purpose, such as *cause-and-effect* (see the excerpt from "One Day, Now Broken in Two" on p. 1404), *satirical* (see "Coyote v. Acme" on p. 1384), or *reflective* (see Amy Tan's "Mother Tongue" on p. 1410). Modes of discourse, such as *expository*, *descriptive*, *persuasive*, or *narrative*, are other means of classifying essays.

See also *Satire, Exposition, Description, Persuasion,* and *Narration.*

EXPOSITION *Exposition* is writing or speech that explains, informs, or presents information. The main techniques of expository writing include analysis, classification, comparison and contrast, definition, and exemplification, or illustration. An essay may be primarily expository, as is William Safire's "Onomatopoeia" (p. 1378), or it may use exposition to support another purpose, such as persuasion or argumentation, as in Ian Frazier's satirical essay "Coyote v. Acme" (p. 1384).

In a story or play, the exposition is that part of the plot that introduces the characters, the setting, and the basic situation.

See also *Plot.*

FALLING ACTION See *Plot.*

FICTION *Fiction* is prose writing that tells about imaginary characters and events. Short stories and novels are works of fiction.

See also *Genre, Narrative, Nonfiction,* and *Prose.*

FIGURATIVE LANGUAGE *Figurative language* is writing or speech not meant to be taken literally. Writers use figurative language to express ideas in vivid and imaginative ways. For example, Emily Dickinson begins one poem with the following description of snow:

> It sifts from leaden sieves, / It powders all the wood

> By describing the snow as if it were flour, Dickinson renders a precise and compelling picture of it.

See also *Figure of Speech.*

FIGURE OF SPEECH A *figure of speech* is an expression or a word used imaginatively rather than literally.

See also *Figurative Language.*

FLASHBACK A *flashback* is a section of a literary work that interrupts the chronological presentation of events to relate an event from an earlier time. A writer may present a flashback as a character's memory or recollection, as part of an account or story told by a character, as a dream or a daydream, or simply by having the narrator switch to a time in the past.

FLAT CHARACTER See *Character.*

FOIL A *foil* is a character who provides a contrast to another character. In F. Scott Fitzgerald's "Winter Dreams" (p. 730), Irene Scheerer is a foil for the tantalizing Judy Jones.

FOLK LITERATURE *Folk literature* is the body of stories, legends, myths, ballads, songs, riddles, sayings, and other works arising out of the oral traditions of peoples around the globe. The folk literature traditions of the United States, including those of Native Americans and of the American pioneers, are especially rich.

FOOT See *Meter.*

FORESHADOWING *Foreshadowing* in a literary work is the use of clues to suggest events that have yet to occur.

FREE VERSE *Free verse* is poetry that lacks a regular rhythmical pattern, or meter. A writer of free verse is at liberty to use any rhythms that are appropriate to what he or she is saying. Free verse has been widely used by twentieth-century poets such as Leslie Marmon Silko, who begins "Where Mountain Lion Lay Down With Deer" with these lines:

> I climb the black rock mountain
>
> stepping from day to day
>
> silently.

See also *Meter.*

GENRE A *genre* is a division, or type, of literature. Literature is commonly divided into three major genres: poetry, prose, and drama. Each major genre can in turn be divided into smaller genres. Poetry can be divided into lyric, concrete, dramatic, narrative, and epic poetry. Prose can be divided into fiction and nonfiction. Drama can be divided into serious drama, tragedy, comic drama, melodrama, and farce.

See also *Drama, Poetry,* and *Prose.*

GOTHIC *Gothic* refers to the use of primitive, medieval, wild, or mysterious elements in literature. Gothic novels feature places like mysterious and gloomy castles, where horrifying, supernatural events take place. Their influence on Edgar Allan Poe is evident in "The Fall of the House of Usher" (p. 292).

GROTESQUE *Grotesque* refers to the use of bizarre, absurd, or fantastic elements in literature. The grotesque is generally characterized by distortions or striking incongruities. *Grotesque characters*, like those in Flannery O'Connor's "The Life You Save May Be Your Own" (p. 1012), are characters who have become bizarre through their obsession with an idea or a value or as a result of an emotional problem.

HARLEM RENAISSANCE The *Harlem Renaissance,* which occurred during the 1920s, was a time of African American artistic creativity centered in Harlem, in New York City. Writers of the Harlem Renaissance include Countee Cullen, Claude McKay, Jean Toomer, and Langston Hughes.

HYPERBOLE *Hyperbole* is a deliberate exaggeration or overstatement, often used for comic effect. In Mark Twain's "The Notorious Jumping Frog of Calaveras County" (p. 576), the claim that Jim Smiley would follow a bug as far as Mexico to win a bet is hyperbole.

IAMBIC PENTAMETER *Iambic pentameter* is a line of poetry with five iambic feet, each containing one unstressed syllable followed by one stressed syllable (˘ ´). Iambic pentameter may be rhymed or unrhymed. Unrhymed iambic pentameter is called blank verse. These lines from Anne Bradstreet's "The Author to Her Book" are in iambic pentameter:

> And fŏr thў, Móthĕr, shĕ ălás ĭs póor,
>
> Whĭch caŭséd hĕr thús tŏ sénd thĕe oút ŏf dóor.

See also *Blank Verse* and *Meter.*

IDYLL An *idyll* is a poem or part of a poem that describes and idealizes country life. John Greenleaf Whittier's "Snowbound" is an idyll.

IMAGE An *image* is a word or phrase that appeals to one or more of the five senses—sight, hearing, touch, taste, or smell.

See also *Imagery.*

IMAGERY *Imagery* is the descriptive or figurative language used in literature to create word pictures for the reader. These pictures, or images, are created by details of sight, sound, taste, touch, smell, or movement.

IMAGISM *Imagism* was a literary movement that flourished between 1912 and 1927. Led by Ezra Pound and Amy Lowell, the Imagist poets rejected nineteenth-century poetic forms and language. Instead, they wrote short poems that used ordinary language and free verse to create sharp, exact, concentrated pictures. Pound's poetry (p. 722) provides examples of Imagism.

IRONY *Irony* is a contrast between what is stated and what is meant, or between what is expected to happen and what actually happens. In *verbal irony*, a word or a phrase is used to suggest the opposite of its usual meaning. In *dramatic irony*, there is a contradiction between what a character thinks and what the reader or audience knows. In *irony of situation*, an event occurs that contradicts the expectations of the characters, of the reader, or of the audience.

JOURNAL A *journal* is a daily autobiographical account of events and personal reactions. For example, Mary Chesnut's journal (p. 495) records events during the Civil War.

LEGEND A *legend* is a traditional story. Usually a legend deals with a particular person—a hero, a saint, or a national leader. Often legends reflect a people's cultural values. American legends include those of the early Native Americans and those about folk heroes such as Davy Crockett.

See also *Myth.*

LETTER A *letter* is a written message or communication addressed to a reader or readers and is generally sent by mail. Letters may be *private* or *public*, depending on their intended audience. A public letter, also called a *literary letter* or *epistle*, is a work of literature written in the form of a personal letter but created for publication. Michel-Guillaume Jean de Crèvecoeur's "Letters From an American Farmer" are public letters.

LOCAL COLOR *Local color* is the use in a literary work of characters and details unique to a particular geographic area. It can be created by the use of dialect and by descriptions of customs, clothing, manners, attitudes, and landscape. Local-color stories were especially popular after the Civil War, bringing readers the West of Bret Harte and the Mississippi River of Mark Twain.

See also *Realism* and *Regionalism.*

LYRIC POEM A *lyric poem* is a melodic poem that expresses the observations and feelings of a single speaker. Unlike a narrative poem, a lyric poem focuses on producing a single, unified effect. Types of lyric poems include the *elegy*, the *ode*, and the *sonnet*. Among contemporary American poets, the lyric is the most common poetic form.

MAIN CHARACTER See *Character.*

MEMOIR A *memoir* is a type of nonfiction autobiographical writing that tells about a person's own life, usually focusing on the writer's involvement in historically or culturally significant events—either as a participant or an eyewitness.

METAPHOR A *metaphor* is a figure of speech in which one thing is spoken of as though it were something else. The identification suggests a comparison between the two things that are identified, as in "death is a long sleep."

A *mixed metaphor* occurs when two metaphors are jumbled together. For example, thorns and rain are illogically mixed in "the thorns of life rained down on him." A *dead metaphor* is one that has been overused and has become a common expression, such as "the arm of the chair" or "nightfall."

METER The *meter* of a poem is its rhythmical pattern. This pattern is determined by the number and types of stresses, or beats, in each line. To describe the meter of a poem, you must scan its lines. *Scanning* involves marking the stressed and unstressed syllables, as follows:

Soon ăs | thĕ sún | forsŏok | thĕ eăs|tĕrn máin

Thĕ peăl | ĭng thŭn | dĕr shŏok | thĕ heăv´n | lў pláin;

　　　　　—"An Hymn to the Evening," Phillis Wheatley

As the example shows, each strong stress is marked with a slanted line (´) and each weak stress with a horseshoe symbol (˘). The weak and strong stresses are then divided by vertical lines (|) into groups called feet. The following types of feet are common in poetry written in English:

1. *Iamb:* a foot with one unstressed syllable followed by one stressed syllable, as in the word "around"

2. *Trochee:* a foot with one stressed syllable followed by one unstressed syllable, as in the word "broken"

3. *Anapest:* a foot with two unstressed syllables followed by one stressed syllable, as in the phrase "in a flash"

4. *Dactyl:* a foot with one stressed syllable followed by two unstressed syllables, as in the word "argument"

5. *Spondee:* a foot with two stressed syllables, as in the word "airship"

6. *Pyrrhic:* a foot with two unstressed syllables, as in the last foot of the word "imag|ining"

Lines of poetry are often described as iambic, trochaic, anapestic, or dactylic. Lines are also described in terms of the number of feet that occur in them, as follows:

1. *Monometer:* verse written in one-foot lines

　　Év|ĭl
　　Bég|ĕts
　　Év|ĭl
　　　　　　—Anonymous

2. *Dimeter:* verse written in two-foot lines
　　Thĭs ís | thĕ tíme
　　ŏf thĕ trág|ĭc mán
　　　　　—"Visits to St. Elizabeth's," Elizabeth Bishop

3. *Trimeter:* verse written in three-foot lines:
　　Over | the win|ter glaciers
　　I see | the sum|mer glow,
　　And through | the wild-|piled snowdrift
　　The warm | rosebuds | below.
　　　　　—"Beyond Winter," Ralph Waldo Emerson

4. *Tetrameter:* verse written in four-foot lines:
　　The sun | that brief | Decem|ber day
　　Rose cheer|less ov|er hills | of gray
　　　　　—"Snowbound," John Greenleaf Whittier

5. **Pentameter:** verse written in five-foot lines:

Ĭ doúbt | nŏt Gód | ĭs goód, | wĕll-meán|ĭng, kínd,

Ănd díd | Hĕ stoóp | tŏ quíb|blĕ coúld | tĕll whý

Thĕ lít|tlĕ búr|ĭed móle | cŏntín|ŭes blínd

—"Yet Do I Marvel," Countee Cullen

A complete description of the meter of a line tells both how many feet there are in the line and what kind of foot is most common. Thus, the lines from Countee Cullen's poem would be described as *iambic pentameter.* *Blank verse* is poetry written in unrhymed iambic pentameter. Poetry that does not have a regular meter is called *free verse.*

MONOLOGUE A *monologue* is a speech delivered entirely by one person or character.

See also *Dramatic Monologue.*

MOOD *Mood*, or atmosphere, is the feeling created in the reader by a literary work or passage. Elements that can influence the mood of a work include its setting, tone, and events.

See also *Setting* and *Tone.*

MOTIVATION A *motivation* is a reason that explains a character's thoughts, feelings, actions, or speech. Characters are motivated by their values and by their wants, desires, dreams, wishes, and needs. Sometimes the reasons for a character's actions are stated directly, as in Willa Cather's "A Wagner Matinée" (p. 652), when Clark explains his reception of his aunt by saying, "I owed to this woman most of the good that ever came my way in my boyhood." At other times, the writer will just suggest a character's motivation.

MYTH A *myth* is a fictional tale that explains the actions of gods or heroes or the causes of natural phenomena. Myths that explain the origins of earthly life, as do the Onondaga, Navajo, and Modoc myths in this text, are known as origin myths. Other myths express the central values of the people who created them.

NARRATION *Narration* is writing that tells a story. The act of telling a story is also called *narration*. The *narrative*, or story, is told by a storyteller called the *narrator*. A story is usually told chronologically, in the order in which events take place in time, though it may include flashbacks and foreshadowing. Narratives may be true, like the events recorded in Mary Chesnut's journal (p. 495), or fictional, like the events in Flannery O'Connor's "The Life You Save May Be Your Own" (p. 1012). Narration is one of the forms of discourse and is used in novels, short stories, plays, narrative poems, anecdotes, autobiographies, biographies, and reports.

See also *Narrative Poem* and *Narrator.*

NARRATIVE A *narrative* is a story told in fiction, nonfiction, poetry, or drama. Narratives are often classified by their content or purpose. An *exploration narrative* is a firsthand account of an explorer's travels in a new land. Alvar Núñez Cabeza de Vaca's account of his exploration of the wilderness that is now Texas, "A Journey Through Texas," appears on page 48. "The Interesting Narrative of the Life of Olaudah Equiano" (excerpt on p. 170) is a *slave narrative*, an account of the experiences of an enslaved person. A *historical narrative* is a narrative account of significant historical events, such as William Bradford's *Of Plymouth Plantation.* (p. 58).

See also *Narration.*

NARRATIVE POEM A *narrative* poem tells a story in verse. Three traditional types of narrative verse are *ballads*, songlike poems that tell stories; *epics*, long poems about the deeds of gods or heroes; and *metrical romances*, poems that tell tales of love and chivalry.

See also *Ballad.*

NARRATOR A *narrator* is a speaker or character who tells a story. A story or novel may be narrated by a main character, by a minor character, or by someone uninvolved in the story. The narrator may speak in the first person or in the third person. An *omniscient narrator* is all-knowing, while a *limited narrator* knows only what one character does.

See also *Point of View.*

NATURALISM *Naturalism* was a literary movement among novelists at the end of the nineteenth century and during the early decades of the twentieth century. The Naturalists tended to view people as hapless victims of immutable natural laws. Early exponents of Naturalism included Stephen Crane, Jack London, and Theodore Dreiser.

See also *Realism.*

NONFICTION *Nonfiction* is prose writing that presents and explains ideas or that tells about real people, places, objects, or events. Essays, biographies, autobiographies, journals, and reports are all examples of nonfiction.

See also *Fiction* and *Genre.*

NOVEL A *novel* is a long work of fiction. A novel often has a complicated plot, many major and minor characters, a significant theme, and several varied settings. Novels can be classified in many ways, based on the historical periods in which they are written, the subjects and themes that they treat, the techniques that are used in them, and the literary movements that inspired them. Classic nineteenth-century novels include Herman Melville's *Moby-Dick* (p. 336) and Nathaniel Hawthorne's *The Scarlet Letter* (an extended reading suggestion). Well-known twentieth-century novels include F. Scott Fitzgerald's *The Great Gatsby* and Edith Wharton's *Ethan Frome* (recommended selections for extended reading). A *novella* is not as long as a novel but is longer than a short story. Ernest Hemingway's *The Old Man and the Sea* is a novella.

ODE An *ode* is a long, formal lyric poem with a serious theme that may have a traditional stanza structure. Odes often honor people, commemorate events, respond to natural scenes, or consider serious human problems.

See also *Lyric Poem*.

OMNISCIENT NARRATOR See *Narrator* and *Point of View*.

ONOMATOPOEIA *Onomatopoeia* is the use of words that imitate sounds. Examples of such words are *buzz*, *hiss*, *murmur*, and *rustle*.

ORAL TRADITION *Oral tradition* is the passing of songs, stories, and poems from generation to generation by word of mouth. The oral tradition in America has preserved Native American myths and legends, spirituals, folk ballads, and other works originally heard and memorized rather than written down.

See also *Ballad, Folk Literature, Legend, Myth,* and *Spiritual*.

ORATORY *Oratory* is public speaking that is formal, persuasive, and emotionally appealing. Patrick Henry's "Speech in the Virginia Convention" (p. 100) is an example of oratory.

OXYMORON An *oxymoron* is a figure of speech that combines two opposing or contradictory ideas. An oxymoron, such as "freezing fire," suggests a paradox in just a few words.

See also *Figurative Language* and *Paradox*.

PARADOX A *paradox* is a statement that seems to be contradictory but that actually presents a truth. Marianne Moore uses paradox in "Nevertheless" when she says, "Victory won't come / to me unless I go / to it." Because a paradox is surprising, it draws the reader's attention to what is being said.

See also *Figurative Language* and *Oxymoron*.

PARALLELISM *Parallelism* is the repetition of a grammatical structure. Robert Hayden concludes his poem "Astronauts" with these questions in parallel form:

> What do we want of these men?

> What do we want of ourselves?

Parallelism is used in poetry and in other writing to emphasize and to link related ideas.

PARODY A *parody* is a humorous imitation of a literary work, one that exaggerates or distorts the characteristic features of the original.

PASTORAL *Pastoral* poems deal with rural settings, including shepherds and rustic life. Traditionally, pastoral poems have presented idealized views of rural life. In twentieth-century pastorals, however, poets like Robert Frost introduced ethical complexity into an otherwise simple landscape.

PERSONIFICATION *Personification* is a figure of speech in which a nonhuman subject is given human characteristics. In "April Rain Song," Langston Hughes personifies the rain:

> Let the rain sing you a lullaby.

Effective personification of things or ideas makes them seem vital and alive, as if they were human.

See also *Figurative Language*.

PERSUASION *Persuasion* is writing or speech that attempts to convince a reader to think or act in a particular way. During the Revolutionary War period, leaders such as Patrick Henry, Thomas Paine, and Thomas Jefferson used persuasion in their political arguments. Persuasion is also used in advertising, in editorials, in sermons, and in political speeches. An *argument* is a logical way of presenting a belief, conclusion, or stance. A good argument is supported with reasoning and evidence.

PLAIN STYLE *Plain style* is a type of writing in which uncomplicated sentences and ordinary words are used to make simple, direct statements. This style was favored by those Puritans who wanted to express themselves clearly, in accordance with their religious beliefs. In the twentieth century, Ernest Hemingway was a master of plain style.

See also *Style*.

PLOT *Plot* is the sequence of events in a literary work. In most fiction, the plot involves both characters and a central conflict. The plot usually begins with an *exposition* that introduces the setting, the characters, and the basic situation. This is followed by the *inciting incident*, which introduces the central conflict. The conflict then increases during the *development* until it reaches a high point of interest or suspense, the *climax*. The climax is followed by the end, or resolution, of the central conflict. Any events that occur after the *resolution* make up the *denouement*. The events that lead up to the climax make up the *rising action*. The events that follow the climax make up the *falling action*.

See also *Conflict*.

POETRY *Poetry* is one of the three major types of literature. In poetry, form and content are closely connected, like the two faces of a single coin. Poems are often divided into lines and stanzas and often employ regular rhythmical patterns, or meters. Most poems use highly concise, musical, and emotionally charged language. Many also make use of imagery, figurative language, and special devices such as rhyme.

See also *Genre*.

POINT OF VIEW *Point of view* is the perspective, or vantage point, from which a story is told. Three commonly used points of view are first person, omniscient third person, and limited third person.

In the *first-person point of view*, the narrator is a character in the story and refers to himself or herself with the first-person pronoun "I." "The Fall of the House of Usher" (p. 292) is told by a first-person narrator.

The two kinds of third-person point of view, limited and omniscient, are called "third person" because the narrator uses third-person pronouns such as "he" and "she" to refer to the characters. There is no "I" telling the story.

In stories told from the **omniscient third-person point of view**, the narrator knows and tells about what each character feels and thinks. "The Devil and Tom Walker" (p. 228) is written from the omniscient third-person point of view.

In stories told from the **limited third-person point of view**, the narrator relates the inner thoughts and feelings of only one character, and everything is viewed from this character's perspective. "An Occurrence at Owl Creek Bridge" (p. 480) is written from the limited third-person point of view.

See also **Narrator.**

PROSE **Prose** is the ordinary form of written language. Most writing that is not poetry, drama, or song is considered prose. Prose is one of the major genres of literature. It occurs in two forms: fiction and nonfiction.

See also **Fiction, Genre,** and **Nonfiction.**

PROTAGONIST The **protagonist** is the main character in a literary work. In "The Jilting of Granny Weatherall" (p. 834), the protagonist is the dying grandmother.

See also **Antagonist.**

QUATRAIN See **Stanza.**

REALISM **Realism** is the presentation in art of the details of actual life. Realism was also a literary movement that began during the nineteenth century and stressed the actual as opposed to the imagined or the fanciful. The Realists tried to write objectively about ordinary characters in ordinary situations. They reacted against Romanticism, rejecting heroic, adventurous, or unfamiliar subjects. Naturalists, who followed the Realists, traced the effects of heredity and environment on people helpless to change their situations.

See also **Local Color, Naturalism,** and **Romanticism.**

REFRAIN A **refrain** is a repeated line or group of lines in a poem or song. Most refrains end stanzas, as does "And the tide rises, the tide falls," the refrain in Henry Wadsworth Longfellow's poem (p. 260), or "Coming for to carry me home," the refrain in "Swing Low, Sweet Chariot" (p. 534). Although some refrains are nonsense lines, many increase suspense or emphasize character and theme.

REGIONALISM **Regionalism** in literature is the tendency among certain authors to write about specific geographical areas. Regional writers, like Willa Cather and William Faulkner, present the distinct culture of an area, including its speech, customs, beliefs, and history. Local-color writing may be considered a type of Regionalism, but Regionalists, like the Southern writers of the 1920s, usually go beyond mere presentation of cultural idiosyncrasies and attempt, instead, a sophisticated sociological or anthropological treatment of the culture of a region.

See also **Local Color** and **Setting.**

RESOLUTION See **Plot.**

RHYME **Rhyme** is the repetition of sounds at the ends of words. Rhyming words have identical vowel sounds in their final accented syllables. The consonants before the vowels may be different, but any consonants occurring after these vowels are the same, as in *frog* and *bog* or *willow* and *pillow*. End rhyme occurs when rhyming words are repeated at the ends of lines. Internal rhyme occurs when rhyming words fall within a line. **Approximate**, or **slant**, **rhyme** occurs when the rhyming sounds are similar, but not exact, as in *prove* and *glove*.

See also **Rhyme Scheme.**

RHYME SCHEME A **rhyme scheme** is a regular pattern of rhyming words in a poem. To describe a rhyme scheme, one uses a letter of the alphabet to represent each rhyming sound in a poem or stanza. Consider how letters are used to represent the *abab* rhyme scheme rhymes in the following example:

With innocent wide penguin eyes, three	**a**
large fledgling mocking-birds below	**b**
the pussywillow tree,	**a**
stand in a row	**b**

—"Bird-Witted," Marianne Moore

See also **Rhyme.**

RHYTHM **Rhythm** is the pattern of beats, or stresses, in spoken or written language. Prose and free verse are written in the irregular rhythmical patterns of everyday speech. Consider, for example, the rhythmical pattern in the following free-verse lines by Gwendolyn Brooks:

Life for my child is simple, and is good.

He knows his wish. Yes, but that is not all.

Because I know mine too.

Traditional poetry often follows a regular rhythmical pattern, as in the following lines by America's first great female poet, Anne Bradstreet:

In critic's hands beware thou dost not come,

And take thy way where yet thou art not known

—"The Author to Her Book"

See also **Meter.**

RISING ACTION See **Plot.**

ROMANTICISM *Romanticism* was a literary and artistic movement of the nineteenth century that arose in reaction against eighteenth-century Neoclassicism and placed a premium on imagination, emotion, nature, individuality, and exotica. Romantic elements can be found in the works of American writers as diverse as Cooper, Poe, Thoreau, Emerson, Dickinson, Hawthorne, and Melville. Romanticism is particularly evident in the works of the Transcendentalists.

See also *Classicism* and *Transcendentalism.*

ROUND CHARACTER See *Character.*

SATIRE *Satire* is writing that ridicules or criticizes individuals, ideas, institutions, social conventions, or other works of art or literature. The writer of a satire, the satirist, may use a tolerant, sympathetic tone or an angry, bitter tone. Some satire is written in prose and some, in poetry. Examples of satire in this text include W. H. Auden's "The Unknown Citizen" (p. 774) and Ian Frazier's "Coyote v. Acme" (p. 1384).

SCANSION *Scansion* is the process of analyzing a poem's metrical pattern. When a poem is scanned, its stressed and unstressed syllables are marked to show what poetic feet are used and how many feet appear in each line. The last two lines of Edna St. Vincent Millay's "I Shall Go Back Again to the Bleak Shore" may be scanned as follows:

> But I | shall find | the sul|len rocks | and skies
>
> Unchanged | from what | they were | when I | was young.

See also *Meter.*

SENSORY LANGUAGE *Sensory language* is writing or speech that appeals to one or more of the five senses.

See also *Image.*

SETTING The *setting* of a literary work is the time and place of the action. A setting may serve any of a number of functions. It may provide a background for the action. It may be a crucial element in the plot or central conflict. It may also create a certain emotional atmosphere, or mood.

SHORT STORY A *short story* is a brief work of fiction. The short story resembles the novel but generally has a simpler plot and setting. In addition, the short story tends to reveal character at a crucial moment rather than developing it through many incidents. For example, Thomas Wolfe's "The Far and the Near" concentrates on what happens to a train engineer when he visits people who had waved to him every day.

See also *Fiction* and *Genre.*

SIMILE A *simile* is a figure of speech that makes a direct comparison between two subjects, using either *like* or *as*. Here are two examples of similes:

> The trees looked like pitch forks against the sullen sky.
>
> Her hair was as red as a robin's breast.

See also *Figurative Language.*

SLANT RHYME See *Rhyme.*

SONNET A *sonnet* is a fourteen-line lyric poem focused on a single theme. Sonnets have many variations but are usually written in iambic pentameter, following one of two traditional patterns: the *Petrarchan*, or *Italian*, *sonnet*, which is divided into two parts, the eight-line octave and the six-line sestet; and the *Shakespearean*, or *English*, *sonnet*, which consists of three quatrains and a concluding couplet.

See also *Lyric Poem.*

SPEAKER The *speaker* is the voice of a poem. Although the speaker is often the poet, the speaker may also be a fictional character or even an inanimate object or another type of nonhuman entity. Interpreting a poem often depends upon recognizing who the speaker is, whom the speaker is addressing, and what the speaker's attitude, or tone, is.

See also *Point of View.*

SPIRITUAL A *spiritual* is a type of African American folk song dating from the period of slavery and Reconstruction. A typical spiritual deals both with religious freedom and, on an allegorical level, with political and economic freedom. In some spirituals the biblical river Jordan was used as a symbol for the Ohio River, which separated slave states from free states; and the biblical promised land, Canaan, was used as a symbol for the free northern United States. Most spirituals made use of repetition, parallelism, and rhyme. See "Go Down Moses" (p. 532) and "Swing Low, Sweet Chariot" (p. 534).

STAGE DIRECTIONS See *Drama.*

STANZA A *stanza* is a group of lines in a poem that are considered to be a unit. Many poems are divided into stanzas that are separated by spaces. Stanzas often function just like paragraphs in prose. Each stanza states and develops a single main idea.

Stanzas are commonly named according to the number of lines found in them, as follows:

1. Couplet: a two-line stanza
2. Tercet: a three-line stanza
3. Quatrain: a four-line stanza
4. Cinquain: a five-line stanza
5. Sestet: a six-line stanza
6. Heptastich: a seven-line stanza
7. Octave: an eight-line stanza

STATIC CHARACTER See *Character.*

STREAM OF CONSCIOUSNESS *Stream of conscious-ness* is a narrative technique that presents thoughts as if they were coming directly from a character's mind. Instead of being arranged in chronological order, the events are presented from the character's point of view, mixed in with the character's thoughts just as they might spontaneously occur. Katherine Anne Porter uses this technique in "The Jilting of Granny Weatherall" (p. 834) to capture Granny's dying thoughts and feelings. Ambrose Bierce also uses the stream of consciousness technique in "An Occurrence at Owl Creek Bridge" (p. 480).

See also *Point of View.*

STYLE A writer's *style* includes word choice, tone, degree of formality, figurative language, rhythm, grammatical structure, sentence length, organization—in short, every feature of a writer's use of language. Ernest Hemingway, for example, is noted for a simple prose style that contrasts with Thomas Paine's aphoristic style and with N. Scott Momaday's reflective style.

See also *Diction* and *Plain Style.*

SUSPENSE *Suspense* is a feeling of growing uncertainty about the outcome of events. Writers create suspense by raising questions in the minds of their readers. Suspense builds until the climax of the plot, at which point the suspense reaches its peak.

See also *Climax* and *Plot.*

SYMBOL A *symbol* is anything that stands for or represents something else. A *conventional symbol* is one that is widely known and accepted, such as a voyage symbolizing life or a skull symbolizing death. A *personal symbol* is one developed for a particular work by a particular author. Examples in this textbook include Hawthorne's black veil and Melville's white whale.

SYMBOLISM *Symbolism* was a literary movement during the nineteenth century that influenced poets, including the Imagists and T. S. Eliot. Symbolists turned away from everyday, realistic details to express emotions by using a pattern of symbols.

See also *Imagism* and *Realism.*

THEME A *theme* is a central message or insight into life revealed by a literary work. An essay's theme is often directly stated in its thesis statement. In most works of fiction, the theme is only indirectly stated: A story, poem, or play most often has an *implied theme*. For example, in "A Worn Path" (p. 848), Eudora Welty does not directly say that Phoenix Jackson's difficult journey shows the power of love, but readers learn this indirectly by the end of the story.

TONE The *tone* of a literary work is the writer's attitude toward his or her subject, characters, or audience. A writer's tone may be formal or informal, friendly or distant, personal or pompous. For example, William Faulkner's tone in his "Nobel Prize Acceptance Speech" (p. 828) is earnest and serious, whereas James Thurber's tone in "The Night the Ghost Got In" (p. 860) is humorous and ironic.

See also *Mood.*

TRAGEDY A *tragedy* is a work of literature, especially a play, that shows the downfall or death of the main character, or *tragic hero*.

TRANSCENDENTALISM *Transcendentalism* was an American literary and philosophical movement of the nineteenth century. The Transcendentalists, who were based in New England, believed that intuition and the individual conscience "transcend" experience and thus are better guides to truth than are the senses and logical reason. Influenced by Romanticism, the Transcendentalists respected the individual spirit and the natural world, believing that divinity was present everywhere, in nature and in each person. The Transcendentalists included Ralph Waldo Emerson, Henry David Thoreau, Bronson Alcott, W. H. Channing, Margaret Fuller, and Elizabeth Peabody.

See also *Romanticism.*

College Application Essay

If you are applying for admission to a college, you will probably need to submit an essay as part of your application. This essay will help admissions committee members get a sense of you as a person and as a student. Review the chart at right for general strategies, and follow the guidelines below to produce an effective college application essay.

Selecting a Topic

Read the essay question on the application form with care. Mark key criteria and direction words such as *describe* and *explain*. After you have written a first draft, check to make sure you have met all of the requirements of the question. Your essay has a better chance of succeeding if it meets the requirements exactly.

General Questions About You

The essay question on a college application may be as general as "Describe a significant experience or event in your life and explain its consequences for you." To choose the right topic for such a question, think of an event or experience that truly is meaningful to you—a camping trip, a volunteer event, a family reunion. Test the subject by drafting a letter about it to a good friend or relative. If you find that your enthusiasm for the subject grows as you write, and if your discussion reveals something about your growth or your outlook on life, the topic may be the right one for your essay.

Directed Questions

The essay question on an application may be a directed question, rather than a general question. For instance, you may be asked to select three figures from history you would like to meet and to explain your choices.

In such cases, do not give an answer just because you think it will please reviewers. Rely on your own interests and instincts. Your most convincing writing will come from genuine interest in the subject.

Strategies for Writing an Effective College Application Essay
• **Choose the right topic**. If you have a choice of essay topics, choose one that truly interests you.
• **Organize.** Use a strong organization that carries the reader from introduction to conclusion.
• **Begin Strongly.** Open with an introduction that has a good chance of sparking the reader's interest.
• **Elaborate.** Be sure to explain why the experiences you discuss are important to you or what you learned from them.
• **Show style.** Bring life to your essay through vivid descriptions, precise word choice, and sophisticated sentence structure, such as parallelism. Consider including dialogue where appropriate.
• **Close with a clincher.** Write a conclusion that effectively sums up your ideas.
• **Do a clean job**. Proofread your essay carefully. It should be error-free.

Style

Remember that an essay is a formal document addressed to strangers. Use a formal to semiformal style. Avoid incomplete sentences and slang unless you are using them for clear stylistic effect. Use words with precision, selecting one or two accurate words to express your meaning. Do not use a word if you are unsure of its meaning.

Format

Most applications limit the length of essays. Do not exceed the allowed space or word count. Your college application essay should be neatly typed or printed, using adequate margins. Proofread your final draft carefully. If you submit a separate copy of the essay (rather than writing on the application form), number the pages and include your name and contact information on each page.

Reusing Your Essay

Most students apply to a number of different colleges. Once you have written a strong essay for one application, you may adapt it for others. However, do not submit a single essay to several schools blindly. Always read the application essay question carefully to insure that the essay you submit fulfills all of its requirements.

Workplace Writing

Job Search Document: Cover Letter

A cover letter is a formal letter in which the writer asks to be considered for a job. It usually accompanies, or "covers," a completed job application, a résumé, or both. A good cover letter relates specifically to the job for which the writer is applying.

Write a Cover Letter

Consider a part-time job or a summer job you would like to have. Then, write a cover letter to accompany a job application. Include a header, an inside address, an introductory paragraph, one or two body paragraphs, a closing paragraph, and a signature. Mention your main qualifications, and explain how they make you a good fit for the job.

000 Park Avenue
San Marcos, Texas 00000
512-000-0000
emailaddress@theinternet.com

January 15, 20—

Barbara Jones, Director
River Place Day Camp
500 S. Camp Street
Austin, TX 00000

Dear Ms. Jones:

    I am writing to apply for the position of Activities Coordinator for your summer camp. The job description posted on the Texas Summer Camps job board perfectly parallels my own interests and experience.

    As noted on the enclosed résumé, I have four years' experience as a camp counselor, including one as Lead Counselor and one as Assistant Activities Director. In these roles, I learned not only to work as a team leader, but also to help tailor a camp's programs to the needs of its campers. As an education student at Texas State University, I have completed basic education courses as well as electives in counseling, recreational learning, and youth leadership. These courses, along with my volunteer work as an after-school mentor, have sparked my interest in non-classroom education. In fact, I plan to base my entire career on the idea that learning can be fun—and can happen anywhere.

    I hope to help make River Place Day Camp a fun, educational, and well-organized experience for both its campers and its staff. I look forward to meeting with you and discussing my qualifications in more detail.

Sincerely,

Cesar Moreno

The heading should include the writer's name, address, phone number, e-mail address, and the date of the letter.

The inside address includes the name, title, and address of the recipient.

The body paragraph describes how the writer's experiences relate specifically to the job responsibilities.

Job Search Document: Résumé

A **résumé** is a written summary or outline of a person's job qualifications. It plays a key part in most career or job searches. An effective résumé has the following elements:

- candidate's name, current address, phone number, and e-mail address;
- educational background, work experience, and other relevant life experiences;
- logical organization;
- clearly labeled sections.

Compile a Résumé

Write a résumé to use in a job search. Consider a specific job you would like to pursue. Then, brainstorm for relevant information in your schooling or work experience. Include important details and maintain a professional tone.
As you develop your document, experiment with different fonts to create a professional-looking, readable document.

CESAR MORENO
000 Park Avenue
San Marcos, Texas 00000
512-000-0000 • emailaddress@theinternet.com

> Place contact information at the top of the résumé.

EDUCATION
- **Texas State University**, San Marcos, TX
  Bachelor of Science in Education
  Expected: May, 20—
- **Austin High School**, Austin, TX
  Graduated with honors, May, 20—

> The headings *Education, Work Experience*, and so on indicate that this résumé is organized by topic.

WORK EXPERIENCE
- **Summer 2008–Summer 2010**
  Camp Lazy J, Fredericksburg, TX
  Camp Counselor: Supervised groups of campers aged 8–12. Served as Lead Counselor in 20– and as Assistant Activities Director in 20–.
- **2009–2010**
  YMCA, Austin, Texas
  Life Guard and Swim Instructor: Guarded weekend free-swim sessions and taught beginning and intermediate youth swim classes.

> The items under each topic are bulleted and arranged from most to least recent.

VOLUNTEER EXPERIENCE
- **2009–present**
  San Marcos Community Center, San Marcos, TX
  After-School Mentor: Help elementary and middle school students organize and complete schoolwork, develop skills and interests, and resolve personal issues.
- **2008–2009**
  Stepping Up Preschool, Austin, TX
  Teacher's Aide: Assisted in the 3- and 4-year-old classroom; helped plan and execute special summer programs.

ADDITIONAL SKILLS AND CERTIFICATIONS
- CPR certified, 2007 to the present
- Fluent in Spanish
- Proficient in water sports, including rowing, kayaking, and rafting
- Proficient in Microsoft Word, Excel, and PowerPoint
- Completed childcare training course, YMCA, 2007

> A résumé should be no longer than a single page.

REFERENCES
Furnished on request.

Job Search Document: Job Application

Many employers require job applicants to complete a **job application.** A job application is a standard form that asks for particular kinds of information, including the candidate's contact information, education, and work experience.

Complete a Job Application

Consider a part-time job you would like to have. Then, copy and complete the job application shown here using your own information.

Employment Application

PERSONAL INFORMATION
Full Name: Cesar Moreno
Address: 000 Park Ave., San Marcos, TX, 00000
Phone Number: (512) 000-0000
E-mail Address: emailaddress@theinternet.com

POSITION AND AVAILABILITY
Position Applied For: Activities Coordinator

EDUCATION

School	Degree/Diploma	Graduation Date
Texas State University Austin High School	B.S./Education diploma	expected 5/20— May, 20—

Additional Skills, Qualifications, Licenses, Training, Awards
CPR and childcare certified, 2007–present Fluent in Spanish

EMPLOYMENT HISTORY
Present/Last Position and Dates: Camp Counselor, Summer 2006–Summer 2009
Employer: Camp Lazy J
Responsibilities: supervised campers aged 8–12
Supervisor: Mr. Smith
May we contact Supervisor? If so, phone number: yes; (512) 000-0000

Previous Position: Lifeguard and Swim Instructor, 2007–2008
Employer: Austin YMCA
Responsibilities: Guarded free-swim sessions; taught youth swim classes
Supervisor: Mrs. Smith
May we contact Supervisor? If so, phone number: yes; (512) 000-0000

Please list additional employment information on a separate sheet of paper.

I certify that the information contained in this application is true and complete. I authorize the verification of any or all information listed above.

Signature: Cesar Moreno
Date: January 15, 20—

> Include only relevant information, and condense it to fit the space available.

> Get your former supervisor's permission before responding "yes" to this item.

> The applicant's signature gives the employer permission to check the information provided.

Business Communications: Business Letter

Business letters are formal letters in which the content is other than personal. Whatever the subject, an effective business letter has the following elements:

- a heading, inside address, salutation or greeting, body, closing, and signature
- one of several acceptable formats, including *block format,* in which each part of the letter begins at the left margin, and *modified block format,* in which the heading, closing, and signature are indented to the center of the page
- formal and courteous language

Write a Business Letter

Choose one of the following purposes and write a business letter to accomplish it. Include heading, inside address, salutation, body, closing, and signature. Use polite and formal language.

- complain about poor service in a restaurant
- accompany a short story you hope to have published
- praise the work of an artist or musician
- gain support for a beautification plan in your community

Bright Orange Lodge
000 Orange Dr.
Orchard, FL 00000

May 1, 20—

Tom Manager, Business Manager
Universal Bank, Inc.
00000 Adams Park Drive
Miami, FL 00000

Dear Mr. Manager:

I am writing to confirm the reservation you have made for your organization's annual corporate retreat.

Per our phone conversation of April 28, you requested that the Bright Orange Lodge facilities be reserved for Universal Bank, Inc. from Friday, June 10, at 6:00 p.m. to Sunday, June 12, at 3:00 p.m. Facilities are to include the large meeting room, the kitchen, and a block of between 20 and 30 double-occupancy rooms. As we discussed, I anticipate a firm room count from you by the end of this month.

Per the same conversation, I understand that Universal Bank is planning to use its own caterers for all meals. Should this change, Bright Orange can provide food services in its main dining hall, but we will need advance notice.

A bill for the above-specified services will be sent to your attention under separate cover.

Thank you for choosing Bright Orange for your corporate retreat. If I can be of any further assistance, or if you have any questions, please contact me directly at (352) 000-0000.

Sincerely,
Pat Brown

Pat Brown
Event Coordinator

> The heading shows the writer's address, organization, and date.

> The inside address includes the name, title, company, and address of the recipient.

> This letter is organized in block format.

> Business letters end with formal closings, such as *Sincerely* or *Respectfully yours,* followed by the writer's signature and typed name.

Business Communications: Memo

A **memo**—short for *memorandum*—is a brief printed message between co-workers. It usually focuses on information necessary for the completion of a particular task or project. An effective memo has the following elements:

- block organization, with each new element beginning at the left margin
- sender's name, intended audience, date, and topic
- clear and brief description, including statement of actions required

MEMO

TO: Members of the Corporate Retreat Staff
FROM: Ann Smith, Vice President
DATE: May 11, 20—
RE: PLANNING SESSION

Our annual corporate retreat is fast approaching. To ensure that all aspects of the retreat are coordinated, let's meet this Friday, May 14, at 9:00 a.m. in the second-floor conference room.

We will discuss the following topics, so please be prepared to report the status of your assigned area of responsibility.

- finalized dates, times, and location of the retreat (Tom)
- schedule of sessions and events (Bruno)
- presenters and topics (Yolanda)
- caterers and pricing (Barry)
- employee communications — invitations, RSVPs, etc. (DeShon)

I appreciate the many hours you have already invested in the planning process, and hope that our meeting on Friday will be brief and productive.

AS

> Most memos follow this format: To, From, Date, and Re (Regarding). The word *re* is Latin for "about." It introduces the subject of the memo.

> The body of a memo is brief and informative, and should clearly state a course of action.

> Memos are often initialed (either at the conclusion or next to the "FROM" line) in order to indicate that the contents have been approved by the sender.

Business Communications: E-Mail

An **e-mail** is a message sent through an electronic communication system such as a computer network or the Internet. Like a memo, an e-mail may be sent to many recipients at once; however, an e-mail has the added benefit of traveling instantaneously. It can also be used to send an attachment—a file that travels with the e-mail but that must be opened using a separate application. While e-mail messages are often more casual than memos, a workplace e-mail (unlike a personal e-mail) should maintain an appropriately formal tone.

Write a Memo and an E-mail

Choose one of the topics below and write a memo that states the message quickly and efficiently. Then, recast the memo as an e-mail.

- announcement of an upcoming event to members of a club or organization
- reminder to fellow workers in a gift shop about store procedures
- information about a surprise party for a teacher
- details about about transportation to a sports competition

The header of an e-mail is arranged into fields. CC stands for "Carbon Copy." A copy of the e-mail will be sent to the address listed in the CC field.

To see the attached document, recipients can double-click on this icon. The file will then open into the word-processing application.

Business Communications: Meeting Minutes

Meeting minutes are notes that tell what transpired at a meeting: what was said, what was decided, and what was left unresolved. Often, the person taking the minutes will jot down abbreviated notes during the meeting, and then rewrite the minutes afterward to distribute to meeting participants.

Write Meeting Minutes

In a small group, conduct a business meeting. Take notes during the meeting. Afterward, write a set of minutes to distribute to your fellow group members.

Meeting to Finalize Corporate Retreat Plans
Friday, May 14, 20–
Main Office, 2nd Floor Conference Room, 9:00 a.m.

Committee Members Present: Ann Smith, Tom Bernard, Yolanda Valois, DeShon Allen
Committee Members Absent: Bruno Jones
Others Present: Sara Hayes, assistant to Ann Smith

Proceedings:
Meeting called to order at 9:00 a.m. by Ann Smith.
Agenda was distributed by Sara Hayes.

First Agenda Item: Retreat dates, times, and location, presented by Tom Bernard.
  Tom reported that he has received a letter from Bright Orange Lodge that confirms reservation of their retreat facilities for Universal Bank, Inc. from Friday, June 10, at 6:00 p.m. through Sunday, June 12, at 3:00 p.m. A copy of this letter is attached to the minutes.

Second Agenda Item: Schedule of sessions and events, presented by Ann Smith for Bruno Jones.
  Bruno is out of the office today, but e-mailed Ann the finalized retreat schedule. Ann distributed copies of the schedule to all members. MOTION to approve schedule; passed unanimously.

Assessment of the meeting: Members agreed that the retreat promises to be very successful. Jeff congratulated committee members on a job well done.

Meeting adjourned at 10:05 a.m.
Meeting minutes compiled by Sarah Hayes.

The header should include the name of the meeting and its date, location, and time.

These minutes are formatted to show that the meeting followed an agenda.

A *motion* is a proposal to vote on something. All motions and their results should be carefully noted in meeting minutes.

Business Communications: Technical Writing

Technical writing refers to any kind of writing that presents specialized information to help someone perform a task. Scientific reports, troubleshooting guides, assembly instructions, and school handbooks are all examples of technical writing. Although the format varies with the purpose, all technical writing must be clear and easy to use—in other words, "user friendly." It must also be absolutely precise.

Write a Section of a Technical Document

Think of something you know how to do well and write a set of procedures for completing the task. Remember to use specific language that accurately describes the details of the task.

Porterdale Community Library rev. 7/09
Policies and Procedures
Section IV: Collection Maintenance

> A page header identifies the publication title, the section, and the revision date.

IV.D. PROCESSING NEW MATERIALS

When new items are delivered to the library, they must be processed, or prepared for use by patrons. The steps for processing a new shipment of items are as follows.

> A brief introduction tells the reader what is included in this section.

1. **Before unpacking the items:**
   a. Remove the packing slip from the box.
   b. Find the matching order form in the main filing cabinet. Order forms are filed alphabetically by vendor.

2. **Unpacking the items:**
   a. Check each item against both the order form and the packing slip.
   b. Place a checkmark on each document next to the title of the item.
   c. If all items in the shipment correspond with those on the order form, send the order form and invoice to the business office for payment. The invoice is usually inside the shipment or affixed to the outside in an envelope.
   d. If an item is missing or damaged, make a note and/or set the item aside. (See section IV.B. for Ordering and Returning procedures.)

(To process books, see item 3, below. To process other media items, proceed to item 4 on the following page.)

> Cross-references and navigational guides are included to help the reader find additional needed information with ease.

3. **Processing books:**
   a. Attach a bar code label to the upper left-hand corner of the front cover.
   b. Stamp books with the library name on the front inside cover and back inside cover.
   c. Prepare a spine label for books. (See section II.A. for call number designation.) Affix the label to the spine with a label protector.
   d. Enter information for the new item into the library catalog database. (See section III.B. for cataloging procedures.)

Tips for Discussing Literature

As you read and study literature, discussions with other readers can help you understand, enjoy, and develop interpretations of what you read. Use the following tips to practice good speaking and listening skills in group discussions of literature.

- ## Understand the purpose of your discussion.

  Your purpose when you discuss literature is to broaden your understanding and appreciation of a work by testing your own ideas and hearing the ideas of others. Be sure to stay focused on the literature you are discussing and to keep your comments relevant to that literature. Starting with one focus question will help to keep your discussion on track.

- ## Communicate effectively.

  Effective communication requires thinking before speaking. Plan the points that you want to make and decide how you will express them. Organize these points in logical order and cite details from the work to support your ideas. Jot down informal notes to help keep your ideas focused.

  Remember to speak clearly, pronouncing words slowly and carefully so that your listeners will understand your ideas. Also, keep in mind that some literature touches readers deeply—be aware of the possibility of counterproductive emotional responses and work to control them.

- ## Make relevant contributions.

  Especially when responding to a short story or a novel, avoid simply summarizing the plot. Instead, consider *what* you think might happen next, *why* events take place as they do, or *how* a writer provokes a response in you. Let your ideas inspire deeper thought or discussion about the literature.

- ## Consider other ideas and interpretations.

  A work of literature can generate a wide variety of responses in different readers—and that can make your discussions really exciting. Be open to the idea that many interpretations can be valid. To support your own ideas, point to the events, descriptions, characters, or other literary elements in the work that led to your interpretation. To consider someone else's ideas, decide whether details in the work support the interpretation he or she presents. Be sure to convey your criticism of the ideas of others in a respectful and supportive manner.

- ## Ask questions and extend the contributions of others.

  Get in the habit of asking questions to help you clarify your understanding of another reader's ideas. You can also use questions to call attention to possible areas of confusion, to points that are open to debate, or to errors in the speaker's points.

  In addition, offer elaboration of the points that others make by providing examples and illustrations from the literature. To move a discussion forward, summarize and evaluate tentative conclusions reached by the group members.

Oral and Visual Communication

You use speaking and listening skills every day. When you talk with your friends, teachers, or parents, or when you interact with store clerks, you are communicating orally. In addition to everyday conversation, oral communication includes class discussions, speeches, interviews, presentations, debates, and performances. The following terms will give you a better understanding of the many elements that are part of communication and help you eliminate barriers to listening by managing any distractions:

Body language refers to the use of facial expressions, eye contact, gestures, posture, and movement to communicate a feeling or an idea.

Connotation is the set of associations a word calls to mind. The connotations of the words you choose influence the message you send. For example, most people respond more favorably to being described as "slim" rather than as "skinny." The connotation of *slim* is more appealing than that of *skinny*.

Eye contact is direct visual contact with another person's eyes.

Feedback is the set of verbal and nonverbal reactions that indicate to a speaker that a message has been received and understood.

Gestures are the movements made with arms, hands, face and fingers to communicate.

Listening is understanding and interpreting sound in a meaningful way. You listen differently for different purposes.

> **Listening for key information:** For example, when a teacher gives an assignment, or when someone gives you directions to a place, you listen for key information.

> **Listening for main points:** In a classroom exchange of ideas or information, or while watching a television documentary, you listen for main points.

> **Listening critically:** When you evaluate a performance, song, or a persuasive or political speech, you listen critically, questioning and judging the speaker's message.

Medium is the material or technique used to present a visual image. Common media include paint, clay, and film.

Nonverbal communication is communication without the use of words. People communicate nonverbally through gestures, facial expressions, posture, and body movements. Sign language is an entire language based on nonverbal communication. Be aware of your nonverbal communication and make sure that your gestures and facial expressions do not conflict with your words.

Projection is speaking in such a way that the voice carries clearly to an audience. It's important to project your voice when speaking in a large space like a classroom or an auditorium.

Viewing is observing, understanding, analyzing, and evaluating information presented through visual means. You might use the following questions to help you interpret what you view:

- What subject is presented?
- What is communicated about the subject?
- Which parts are factual? Which are opinion?
- What mood, attitude, or opinion is conveyed?
- What is your emotional response?

Vocal delivery is the way in which you present a message. Your vocal delivery involves all of the following elements:

> *Volume:* the loudness or quietness of your voice

> *Pitch:* the high or low quality of your voice

> *Rate:* the speed at which you speak; also called pace

> *Stress:* the amount of emphasis placed on different syllables in a word or on different words in a sentence

All of these elements individually, and the way in which they are combined, contribute to the meaning of a spoken message.

Speaking, Listening, and Viewing Situations

Here are some of the many types of situations in which you apply speaking, listening, and viewing skills:

Audience Your audience in any situation refers to the person or people to whom you direct your message. An audience can be a group of people observing a performance or just one person. When preparing for any speaking situation, it's useful to analyze your audience, so that you can tailor your message to them.

Charts and graphs are visual representations of statistical information. For example, a pie chart might indicate how the average dollar is spent by government, and a bar graph might compare populations in cities over time.

Debate A debate is a formal public-speaking situation in which participants prepare and present arguments on opposing sides of a question, stated as a **proposition.**

The two sides in a debate are the *affirmative* (pro) and the *negative* (con). The affirmative side argues in favor of the proposition, while the negative side argues against it. Each side has an opportunity for *rebuttal,* in which they may challenge or question the other side's argument.

Documentaries are nonfiction films that analyze news events or other focused subjects. You can watch a documentary for the information on its subject.

Graphic organizers summarize and present information in ways that can help you understand the information. Graphic organizers include charts, outlines, webs, maps, lists, and diagrams. For example, a graphic organizer for a history chapter might be an outline. A Venn diagram is intersecting circles that display information showing how concepts are alike and different.

Group discussion results when three or more people meet to solve a common problem, arrive at a decision, or answer a question of mutual interest. Group discussion is one of the most widely used forms or interpersonal communication in modern society.

Interview An interview is a form of interaction in which one person, the interviewer, asks questions of another person, the interviewee. Interviews may take place for many purposes: to obtain information, to discover a person's suitability for a job or a college, or to inform the public of a notable person's opinions.

Maps are visual representations of Earth's surface. Maps may show political boundaries and physical features and provide information on a variety of other topics. A map's titles and its key identify the content of the map.

Oral interpretation is the reading or speaking of a work of literature aloud for an audience. Oral interpretation involves giving expression to the ideas, meaning, or even the structure of a work of literature. The speaker interprets the work through his or her vocal delivery. **Storytelling,** in which a speaker reads or tells a story expressively, is a form of oral interpretation.

Panel discussion is a group discussion on a topic of interest common to all members of a panel and to a listening audience. A panel is usually composed of four to six experts on a particular topic who are brought together to share information and opinions.

Pantomime is a form of nonverbal communication in which an idea or a story is communicated completely through the use of gesture, body language, and facial expressions, without any words at all.

Political cartoons are drawings that comment on important political or social issues. Often, these cartoons use humor to convey a message about their subject. Viewers use their own knowledge of events to evaluate the cartoonist's opinion.

Readers theatre is a dramatic reading of a work of literature in which participants take parts from a story or play and read them aloud in expressive voices. Unlike a play, however, sets and costumes are not part of the performance, and the participants remain seated as they deliver their lines.

Role play To role-play is to take the role of a person or character and act out a given situation, speaking, acting, and responding in the manner of the character.

Speech A speech is a talk or address given to an audience. A speech may be **impromptu** or **extemporaneous**—delivered on the spur of the moment with no preparation—or formally prepared and delivered for a specific purpose or occasion.

- *Purposes:* the most common purposes of speeches are to persuade, to entertain, to explain, and to inform.

- *Occasions:* Different occasions call for different types of speeches. Speeches given on these occasions could be persuasive, entertaining, or informative, as appropriate.

Visual representation refers to informative texts, such as newspapers and advertisements, and entertaining texts, such as magazines. Visual representations use elements of design—such as texture and color, shapes, drawings, and photographs—to convey the meaning, message, or theme.

Grammar, Usage, and Mechanics Handbook

Parts of Speech

Every English word, depending on its meaning and its use in a sentence, can be identified as one of the eight parts of speech. These are nouns, pronouns, verbs, adjectives, adverbs, prepositions, conjunctions, and interjections.

Understanding the parts of speech will help you learn the rules of English grammar and usage.

Part of Speech	Definition	Examples
Noun	**Names a person, place, or thing**	
Common	• Names any one of a class of persons, places, or things	writer, country, novel
Proper	• Names a specific person, place or thing	Charles Dickens, Great Britain, *Hard Times*
Pronoun	**Stands for a noun or for a word that takes the place of a noun**	
Personal	• Refers to the person speaking (first person); the person spoken to (second person); or the person, place, or thing spoken about (third person)	I, me, my, mine, we, us, our, ours, you, our, yours, he, him, his, she, her, hers, it, its, they, them, their, theirs, myself, ourselves, yourself, yourselves, himself, herself, itself, themselves
Reflexive	• Names the person or thing receiving an action when that person or thing is the same as the one performing the action	"They click upon *themselves/* As the breeze rises,…" –Robert Frost
Intensive	• Adds emphasis to a noun or pronoun	"The United States *themselves* are essentially the greatest poem…" –Walt Whitman
Demonstrative	• Singles out specific person(s), place(s), or thing(s)	this, that, these, those
Relative	• Begins a subordinate clause and connects it to another idea in the sentence	that, which, who, whom, whose
Interrogative	• Begins a question	what, which, who, whom, whose
Indefinite	• Refers to a person, place, or thing that may or may not be specifically named	another, everyone, nobody, one, both, few, all, most, none

(Parts of Speech continues)

(continued)

Part of Speech	Definition	Examples
Verb	**Expresses time while showing an action, condition, or the fact that something exists**	
Action	• Tells what action someone or something is performing	gather, read, work, jump, imagine, analyze, conclude
Linking	• Connects the subject with another word that identifies or describes the subject	appear, be, become, feel, look, remain, sound, stay, taste
Helping	• Added to another verb to make a verb phrase	be, do, have, should, can, could, may
Adjective	**Used to describe a noun or pronoun or give it a more specific meaning**	*purple* hat, *happy* face, *this* bowl, *three* cars, *enough* food, *a loud* sound
Adverb	**Modifies a verb, an adjective, or another adverb by telling *where, when, how* or *to what extent***	will answer *soon, extremely* sad, calls *more* often
Preposition	**Relates a noun or pronoun that appears with it to another word in the sentence**	Dad made a meal *for* us. We talked *till* dusk. Bo missed school *because of* his illness.
Conjunction	**Connects words or groups of words**	
Coordinating	• Connects equal words or word groups	bread *and* cheese, brief *but* powerful
Correlative	• Used in pairs to connect equal words or word groups	*both* Luis *and* Rosa, neither you nor I
Subordinating	• Indicates the connection between two ideas by placing one below the other in rank or importance	We will miss her *if* she leaves. Hank shrieked *when* he slipped on the ice.
Interjection	**Expresses feeling or emotion**	ah, hey, ouch, well, yippee

Phrases and Clauses

Phrases A **phrase** is a group of words that does not have a subject and verb and that functions as one part of speech.

Prepositional Phrases A **prepositional phrase** is a group of words that includes a preposition and a noun or pronoun.

   beyond the horizon   **according to** the manager

An **adjective phrase** is a prepositional phrase that modifies a noun or pronoun.

   The works **of Benjamin Franklin** appeal to me.

An **adverb phrase** is a prepositional phrase that modifies a verb, an adjective, or an adverb.

   I often read **about early American writers.**

Appositive Phrases An **appositive phrase** is a noun or pronoun with modifiers, placed next to a noun or pronoun to add information.

   Tamika, **one of my best friends,** is moving away.

Verbal Phrases A **participial phrase** is a participle that is modified by an adverb or an adverb phrase or that has a complement. The entire phase acts as an adjective.

   Be alert for snakes **sunning themselves on the rocks.**

A **gerund** is a noun formed from the present participle of a verb (ending in *–ing*). A **gerund phrase** is a gerund with modifiers or a complement, all acting together as a noun.

Her favorite pastime is **hiking in the mountains.**

An **infinitive phrase** is an infinitive with modifiers, complements, or a subject, all acting together as a single part of speech.

I would like **to learn about wilderness survival.**

Clauses A **clause** is a group of words with its own subject and verb.

Independent Clauses An independent clause can stand by itself as a complete sentence.

Henry David Thoreau was considered an eccentric.

Subordinate Clauses A subordinate clause cannot stand by itself as a complete sentence.

Henry David Thoreau, **who did not follow society's rules,** was considered an eccentric.

An **adjective clause** is a subordinate clause that modifies a noun or pronoun by telling what kind or which one.

The journey **that Lewis undertook** was dangerous.

An **adverb clause** is a subordinate clause that modifies a verb, an adjective, an adverb, or a verbal by telling *where, when, in what way, to what extent, under what condition,* or *why.*

As I read the poem, I pictured the Grand Canyon.

A **noun clause** is a subordinate clause that acts as a noun.

Whoever visits the Grand Canyon should remember John Wesley Powell's contributions.

Sentence Structure

Subject and Predicate A **sentence** is a group of words with two main parts: a *subject* and a *predicate.* Together, these parts express a complete thought.

The **complete subject** tells *whom* or *what* the sentence is about. The **complete predicate** tells what the complete subject of the sentence does or is.

Complete Subject	Complete Predicate
One of those poems	was written by Claude McKay.

The **simple subject** is the essential noun, pronoun, or group of words acting as a noun that cannot be left out of the complete subject. The **simple predicate** is the essential verb or verb phrase that cannot be left out of the complete predicate.

Simple Subject	Simple Predicate
One of those poems	**was written** by Claude McKay.

Complements A **complement** is a word or word group that completes the meaning of the predicate. There are five kinds of complements: *direct objects, indirect objects, objective complements, predicate nominatives,* and *predicate adjectives.*

A **direct object** is a noun, a pronoun, or a group of words acting as a noun that receives the action of a transitive verb.

Washington Irving used several **pseudonyms.**

An **indirect object** is a noun or pronoun that appears with a direct object and names the person or thing that something is given to or done for.

Folk tales gave **Irving** inspiration for his stories. [The direct object is *inspiration.*]

An **objective complement** is an adjective or noun that appears with a direct object and describes or renames it.

Ms. Gates considers Phillis Wheatley a brilliant **poet.** [The direct object is *Phillis Wheatley.*]

A **predicate nominative** is a noun or pronoun that appears with a linking verb and tells something about the subject.

John Smith became a famous **explorer.**

A **predicate adjective** is an adjective that appears with a linking verb and describes the subject of the sentence.

Smith was **adventurous** and **daring**.

Classifying Sentences by Structure

Sentences are often classified according to the kind and number of clauses they contain. The four basic sentence structures are *simple, compound, complex,* and *compound-complex.*

A **simple sentence** consists of one independent clause.

Alisa enjoys contemporary American poetry.

A **compound sentence** consists or two or more independent clauses.

Alisa enjoys contemporary American poetry, but Joyce prefers earlier works.

A **complex sentence** consists of one independent clause and one or more subordinate clauses.

Alisa, who likes all things modern, enjoys contemporary American poetry.

A **compound-complex sentence** consists of two or more independent clauses and one or more subordinate clauses.

Alisa, who likes all things modern, enjoys contemporary American poetry, but Joyce prefers earlier works.

Paragraph Structure

An effective paragraph is organized around one **main idea,** which is often stated in a topic sentence. The other sentences support the main idea. To give the paragraph unity, make sure the connection between each sentence and the main idea is clear.

Usage

Lessons throughout your literature book will help you with many usage problems. See Unit 1 for help with **using coordinating conjunctions** (p. 31), **using correlative conjunctions** (p. 94), and **using subordinating conjunctions** (p. 155). See Unit 2 for help with **using adjective and adverb clauses** (p. 287), **comparative and superlative adjectives and adverbs** (p. 321), and **using participles, gerunds, and infinitives** (p. 358). In Unit 3 you will find lessons on **misplaced and dangling modifiers** (p. 585) and **introductory phrases and clauses** (p. 613). See Unit 4 for help with **subject-verb agreement problems** (p. 755) and **pronoun-antecedent agreement problems** (p. 911). In Unit 5 you will find lessons on **avoiding shifts in verb tense** (p. 1093), **using active, not passive, voice** (p. 1115), and **sentence fragments and run-ons** (p. 1237). Go to Unit 6 for lessons on **transitional expressions** (p. 1323), using **parallel structure** (p. 1423), and **creating sentence variety** (p. 1441).

Unintended Shift in Person

Do not change needlessly from one person to another. Keep the person consistent in your sentences.

> **Tara** is a good babysitter, but **you** have to pay her well. [shift from third person to second person]

> **Tara** is a good babysitter, but **she** charges high rates. [consistent]

Modifier Placement

To avoid confusion, a modifying word, phrase, or clause should be placed as close as possible to the word or words it is supposed to modify.

> We saw a large swan **rowing the boat near the shore.** [misplaced modifier]

> **Rowing the boat near the shore,** we saw a large swan. [correct placement]

Agreement

Subject and Verb Agreement

A singular subject must have a singular verb. A plural subject must have a plural verb.

> **Daniel cooks** chicken tortilla soup to perfection.

> The **boys cook** several different casseroles.

A phrase or clause that comes between a subject and verb does not affect subject-verb agreement.

> My **sister**, along with her friends, **plays** softball.

Two subjects joined by *and* usually take a plural verb.

> The **players** and the **coach take** the game seriously.

Two singular subject joined by *or* or *nor* must have a singular verb.

> Neither the **coach** nor the **player is** ready.

Two plural subjects joined by *or* or *nor* must have a plural verb.

> The **players** or the **coaches suggest** special plays.

Pronoun and Antecedent Agreement

Pronouns must agree with their antecedents in number and gender. Use singular pronouns with singular antecedents and plural pronouns with plural antecedents.

> **Kate Chopin** became a bold and controversial writer in spite of **her** conservative upbringing.

> **Writers** must be courageous in facing **their** critics.

Use a singular pronoun when the antecedent is a singular indefinite pronoun such as *anybody, each, either, everybody, neither, no one, one,* or *someone.*

> **Anybody** can offer **his or her** help with the report.

Use a plural pronoun when the antecedent is a plural indefinite pronoun (*both, few, many,* or *several.*)

> **Few** of the students offered **their** help.

The indefinite pronouns *all, any, more, most, none,* and *some* can be singular or plural depending on the number of the word to which they refer.

> **All** of the *books* are missing **their** covers.

> **All** of the *book* is ready for **its** final edit.

Using Verbs

Principal Parts of Regular and Irregular Verbs

A verb has four principal parts:

Present	Present Participle	Past	Past Participle
learn	learning	learned	learned
discuss	discussing	discussed	discussed
stand	standing	stood	stood
begin	beginning	began	begun

Regular verbs such as *talk* and *maintain* form the past and past participle by adding *–ed* to the present form. **Irregular verbs** such as *keep* and *give* form the past and past participle in other ways. If you are in doubt about the principal parts of an irregular verb, check a dictionary.

The Tenses of Verbs

The different tenses of verbs indicate the time an action or condition occurred.

The **present tense** is most often used to show one of the following:

Present action or condition:	Jamal **hikes** to the lake. The sky **is** clear.
Regularly occurring action or condition:	Tourists **flock** to the site yearly. **I am** usually tired by 9:00.
Constant action or condition:	The earth **orbits** the sun. Pets **are** good for our health.

The **past tense** is used to express a completed action or condition.

The dog **grabbed** the bone and **ran** away.

The **present perfect tense** is used to express (1) an action or condition that happened at an indefinite time in the past or (2) an action or condition from the past that is continuing into the present.

The mayor **has made** changes in the city code.

My clothes **have been** in the dryer all day.

The **past perfect tense** shows an action or condition completed before another past action or condition.

Micah **had hidden** the gift before he left the house.

The **future tense** is used to show a future action or condition.

The Garcias **will travel** to Rome this summer.

The future perfect tense is used to show a future action or condition that is completed before another future action or condition.

Jess **will have washed** the dishes by the time we return.

Using Modifiers

Degrees of Comparison

Adjectives and adverbs take different forms to show the three degrees of comparison: the *positive*, the *comparative*, and the *superlative.*

Positive	Comparative	Superlative
fast	faster	fastest
crafty	craftier	craftiest
abruptly	more abruptly	most abruptly
bad	worse	worst
much	more	most

Using Comparative and Superlative Adjectives and Adverbs

Use comparative adjectives and adverbs to compare two things. Use superlative adjectives and adverbs to compare three or more things.

The bread is fresher than the rolls.

Of all the foods here, this bread is the freshest.

Using Pronouns

Pronoun Case

The **case** of a pronoun is the form it takes to show its use in a sentence. There are three pronoun cases: *nominative, objective,* and *possessive.*

Nominative	Objective	Possessive
I, you, he, she, it, we, you, they	me, you, him, her, it, us, you, them	my, your, his, her, its, our, their, mine, yours, his, hers, its, ours, theirs

Use the **nominative case** for the *subject* or for a *predicate nominative.*

They worked together to write the play. [subject]

The biggest theater fan is **he.** [predicate nominative]

Use the **objective case** for a *direct object,* an *indirect object,* or the *object of a preposition.*

Jamal drove **me** to the game. [direct object]

Aunt Lil bought **us** the tickets. [indirect object]

The fans cheered for **her.** [object of preposition]

The **possessive case** is used to show ownership.

I think the blue jacket is **his.**

Commonly Confused Words

Diction refers to word choice. The words you choose contribute to the overall effectiveness of your writing. One aspect of diction has to do with choosing between commonly confused words, such as the pairs listed below.

affect, effect

Affect is almost always a verb meaning "to influence." *Effect* is usually a noun meaning "result." Effect can also be a verb meaning "to bring about" or "to cause."

An understanding of T.S. Eliot's multiple allusions can *affect* one's appreciation of his poetry.

In Cather's story, the concert has a profound *effect* on Aunt Georgina.

The aim of persuasive writing is often to *effect* a change in the attitudes of the audience.

farther, further

Use *farther* when you refer to distance. Use *further* when you mean "to a greater degree."

In "A Worn Path," the *farther* Phoenix Jackson travels, the more her determination grows.

In his speech, Patrick Henry urges his countrymen to trust the British no *further*.

good, well

Use the predicate adjective *good* after linking verbs such as *feel, look, smell, taste,* and *seem.* Use *well* whenever you need an adverb.

At the end of "Winter Dreams," Devon implies that Judy does not look as *good* as she used to.

Anne Tyler writes especially *well* about ordinary people and family relationships.

its, it's

Do not confuse the possessive pronoun its with the contraction it's, which stands for "it is" or "it has."

One memorable line in Emerson's poem "The Rhodera" is "Beauty is *its* own excuse for being."

Wallace Stevens's "Anecdote of the Jar" suggests that *it's* impossible to mediate completely between the wilderness and the world of civilization.

set, sit

Set is a transitive verb meaning "to put (something) in a certain place." Its principal parts are *set, setting, set, set. Sit* is an intransitive verb meaning "to be seated." Its principal parts are *sit, sitting, sat, sat.*

Phillis Wheatley's poem is so complimentary to Washington that it seems to *set* him on a pedestal.

As Mrs. Mallard *sits* upstairs alone, she contemplates the death of her husband.

Editing For English Language Conventions

Capitalization

First Words

Capitalize the first word of a sentence.

Compare and contrast the works of Poe and Emerson.

Capitalize the first word of a direct quotation.

Bill asked, "**W**hat are the similarities?"

Proper Nouns and Proper Adjectives

Capitalize all proper nouns.

Carl **S**andburg   **N**ovember   **H**arvard **U**niversity

Capitalize all proper adjectives.

Turkish heritage   **P**uerto **R**ican writers

Academic Course Names

Capitalize course names only if they are language courses, are followed by a number, or are preceded by a proper noun or adjective.

German	**S**ocial **S**cience 101	**H**onors **E**nglish
geometry	**p**hysics	**l**anguage **a**rts

Titles

Capitalize titles showing family relationships when they refer to a specific person unless they are preceded by a possessive noun or pronoun.

Granny Weatherall my **g**randfather Mammedaty

Capitalize the first word and all other key words in the titles of books, stories, songs, and other works of art.

The Crucible   "**M**ending **W**all"

Punctuation

End Marks

Use a **period** to end a declarative sentence or an imperative sentence.

War literature can be quite powerful**.**

Discuss the historical context of Hemingway's story**.**

Use periods with abbreviations.

T.**S.** Eliot   Mr**.** Shiftlet

Use a **question mark** to end an interrogative sentence.

Why did Mr. Hooper wear the black veil**?**

Use an **exclamation mark** after an exclamatory sentence or a forceful imperative sentence.

Our team won in overtime**!**Come here now**!**

Commas

Use a **comma** before the conjunction to separate two independent clauses in a compound sentence.

I read a story by Eudora Welty**,** and I liked it.

Use commas to separate three or more words, phrases, or clauses in a series.

Benjamin Franklin was a statesman**,** a scientist**,** and a journalist.

Use a comma after an introductory word, phrase, or clause.

When the crew heard Ahab's plan**,** they were stunned.

Use commas to set of nonessential expressions.

Captain Ahab**,** as you know**,** was seeking revenge.

Use commas with places and dates.

Boston**,** Massachusetts   November 17**,** 1915

Semicolons

Use a **semicolon** to join closely related independent clauses that are not already joined by a conjunction.

Byron is a point guard; Mick usually plays center.

Use semicolons to avoid confusion when items in a series contain commas.

Kevin, the team captain; Mr. Reece, the coach; and Mr. Jenkins, the assistant coach, had a long talk.

Colons

Use a **colon** before a list of items following an independent clause.

Great literature provides us with many things: entertainment, enrichment, and inspiration.

Use a colon to introduce an independent clause that summarizes or explains the sentence before it.

Joleen left for a walk: She wanted to clear her mind.

Quotation Marks

Use **quotation marks** to enclose a direct quotation.

"A good poet," Mr. Charles said, "uses words skillfully and carefully."

An **indirect quotation** does not require quotation marks.

Mr. Charles said that good poets use words skillfully and carefully.

Use quotation marks around the titles of short written works, episodes in a series, songs, and titles of works mentioned as parts of collections.

"Winter Dreams"   "Go Down, Moses"

Italics

Italicize the titles of long written works, movies, television and radio shows, lengthy works of music, paintings, and sculptures.

Mary Poppins   *House by the Railroad*

For handwritten material, you can use underlining instead of italics.

The Great Gatsby   Aida

Dashes

Use **dashes** to indicate an abrupt change of thought, a dramatic interrupting idea, or a summary statement.

I told my teacher—and I was being entirely sincere—that I loved studying American drama.

Parentheses

Use **parentheses** to set off asides and explanations when the material is not essential or when it consists of one or more sentences.

The chair of the city council (she also happens to be our neighbor) explained the new ordinance to us.

In the example above, the sentence in parentheses interrupts the larger sentence, so it does not have a capital letter and a period. When a sentence in parentheses falls between two other complete sentences, it should start with a capital letter and end with a period.

My family often travels to El Paso. (It is the nearest large city.) We like to shop there.

Apostrophes

Add an **apostrophe** and an *s* to show the possessive case of most singular nouns and of plural nouns that do not end in –s or –es.

Taylor's poetry   women's hats

Names ending in s form their possessives in the same way, except for classical and biblical names, which add only an apostrophe to form the possessive.

Adams's letter   Achilles' death

Add an apostrophe to show the possessive case of plural nouns ending in –s and –es.

the boys' ambition   the Cruzes' house

Use an apostrophe in a contraction to indicate the position of the missing letter or letters.

We've been studying the works of Edgar Allan Poe.

Brackets

Use **brackets** to enclose a word or words you insert in a quotation when you are quoting someone else.

Columbus's journal entry from October 21, 1492, begins as follows: "At 10 o'clock, we arrived at a cape of the island [San Salvador], and anchored, the other vessels in company."

Ellipses

Use three **ellipses** to indicate where you have omitted words from quoted material.

It was Thoreau who wrote, " . . . if one advances confidently in the direction of his dreams, . . . he will meet with a success unexpected . . . ."

In the example above, the four dots at the end of the sentence are the three ellipses plus the period from the original sentence.

Spelling

Spelling Rules

Learning the rules of English spelling will help you make **generalizations** about how to spell words.

Rules for Spelling with Word Parts

The three word parts that can combine to form a word are roots, prefixes, and suffixes. Many of these word parts come from the Greek, Latin, and Anglo-Saxon languages.

The **root word** carries a word's basic meaning.

Root and Origin	Meaning	Examples
-ject- [L.]	to throw	re*ject*
-leg- (-log-) [Gr.]	to say, speak	*leg*al, *log*ic

A **prefix** is one or more syllables at the beginning of a word. A prefix adds to the meaning of the root.

Prefix and Origin	Meaning	Examples
in- (il-, im-, ir-) [L.]	not	*in*human, *il*legal
mono- [Gr.]	alone, one	*mono*poly
over- [A.S.]	above, in excess	*over*flow

A **suffix** is added to the end of a root word and can change the word's meaning or part of speech.

Suffix and Origin	Meaning	Part of Speech
-fy [L.]	to cause to become: clari*fy*	verb
-ish [A.S.]	of, tending to: fool*ish*	adjective
-ism [Gr.]	act, practice, or result of: tru*ism*	noun
-ly [A.S.]	in a manner: quick*ly*	adverb

Rules for Adding Suffixes to Root Words

When adding a suffix to a root word ending in *y* preceded by a consonant, change *y* to *i* unless the suffix begins with *i*.

funny + -est = funniest   silly + -ness = silliness
modify + -ing = modifying   cry + -ing = crying

For a root word ending in *e*, drop the *e* when adding a suffix beginning with a vowel.

nature + -al = natural   seize + -ure = seizure
SOME EXCEPTIONS: courageous, mileage, dyeing

For root words ending with a consonant + vowel + consonant in a stressed syllable, double the final consonant when adding a suffix that begins with a vowel.

slim + -er = slimmer   permit + -ed = permitted
SOME EXCEPTIONS: rowing, conference

Rules for Adding Prefixes to Root Words

When a prefix is added to a root word, the spelling of the root remains the same.

in- + sincere = insincere   over- + eat = overeat

With some prefixes, the spelling of the prefix changes when joined to the root to make the pronunciation easier.

in- + pact = impact   com- + found = confound

Orthographic Patterns

Certain letter combinations in English make certain sounds. For instance, *ph* sounds like *f, eigh* usually makes a long *a* sound, and the *k* before an *n* is often silent.

phase   w**eigh**t   **kn**eeling

Understanding orthographic patterns such as these can help you improve your spelling.

Forming Plurals

The plural form of most nouns is formed by adding *–s* or *–es* to the singular.

merit**s** sparrow**s**   American**s**

For words ending in *s, ss, x, z, sh, ch*, add *–es*.

dress**es**   waltz**es**   pouch**es**

For words ending in *y* or *o* preceded by a vowel, add *–s*.

way**s**   rodeo**s**   buoy**s**

For words ending in *y* preceded by a consonant, change the *y* to an *i* and add *–es*.

quer**ies**   cemeter**ies**   luxur**ies**

For most words ending in *o* preceded by a consonant, add *–es*.

potato**es**   echo**es**

Some words form the plural in irregular ways.

mice   alumni   women   crises

Foreign Words Used in English

Some words used in English are actually foreign words we have adopted. Learning to spell these words requires memorization. When in doubt, check a dictionary.

origami   desperado   protégé
laissez faire   croissant

Note: Page numbers in *italics* refer to biographical information for authors, or commentary for titles; nonfiction and informational text appears in red.

Index of Skills

Boldface numbers indicate pages where terms are defined.

Trochee, **256**, **R28**
Understatement, **858**
Values, **196**, **913**, 1264
Visual representation, **R43**
Voice, **445**, **1346**, 1355
Word choice, **425**, 438, **448**, **796**, 797
Workplace writing, **R35**, **R36**, **R37**, **R38**, **R39**, **R40**, **R41**, **R42**
Works cited list (MLA style), **671**
Writer's style. *See* Author's style

Comprehension Skills

READING FOR INFORMATION

Analyzing Functional and Expository Text
Assessment, 133, 397, 562, 943, 1255, 1447
Consumer guide, 393
Government form, 561
Government report, 395
Manual, 129
Mission statement, 1446
Newspaper feature article, 1253
Online citation organizer, 939
Online encyclopedia, 941
Periodical abstract, 559
Public service advertisement (PSA), 132
Technical report, 1443
Theater/film review, 1251, 1252

Primary Sources
Art, 246, 250, 252, 253, 496, 500, 503
Assessment, 187, 255, 505, 624, 764, 1008, 1398
Ballad, 768
Cartoon, editorial, 1004
Commission, 245
Comparing, 186, 254, 504, 623, 770, 1007, 1406
Diaries (personal history), 495, 502, 617
Editorial, 1005
E-mail, 1403
Field report, 250
Floor plan, 185
Journals, 500
Letters, 181
Note-taking guides, 179, 243, 493, 615, 765, 1001, 1399
Oral history transcript, 1401
Photographs, 617, 767
Poster, 1003
Speeches, 622

READING STRATEGIES
Action, visualize/picture, **1040**, 1045
Ambiguity, clarify, **814**, 830

Anecdotal scripting, **558**
Annotated bibliography, make, **558**
Aphorisms, compare, 139, 152
Appeal to audience, critique, **98**, 105, 108
Archetypal perspective, apply, **901**, 908
Archetypes, compare and contrast, 18, 29
Arguments, evaluate, **1186**, 1190, 1192, 1194, 1198, 1201, 1203, 1207, 1214
Audience, shape message for, 110, 120
Author's perspective. *See* Writer's perspective
Author's purpose. *See* Writer's purpose
Autobiographies, compare, **157**, 160, 162, 165
Background knowledge, use, **506**, 510, 514, 536, 542, 543, **1056**, 1061, **1160**, **1398**, 1399, 1407
Biographical perspective, apply, **901**, 908
Cause and effect, analyze/identify, **139**, 152, **858**, 861, 865, **1080**, 1085, 1086, 1088, 1091, **1382**, 1388, 1390
Challenge the text, **364**, 372
Characters
compare and contrast, **1310**, 1314, 1319, 1321
draw inferences about, **728**, 737, 739, 745, 747, 750, 753
identify with, **798**, 802, 807
Compare and contrast Sample Test Item, 454
Comprehension, monitor, 80
Concentration, keep, **R16**
Concept mapping, **558**
Conclusions, draw, **1010**, 1015, 1020, 1024, **1398**, 1407
Conflict, identify/analyze, **796**
Connotations, interpret, **1050**, 1055
Context clues, use, **84**, 90, 92, **1442**
Contrast, relate, 46
Critical perspectives, apply, **901**, 905, 908
Cultural identity, compare, 917, 918, 919
Details
analyze sensory, **1364**, 1369
identify key, **1356**, 1360
identify relevant, **334**, 342, 349, 356, **552**, 557
identify supporting, **1102**, 1110, 1113
Details chart, use, 18
Dictionary, use, 74
Drama, reading, **1116**
Essays, reading, **1374**
Essential message
determine, **334**, 342, 349, 356, **552**, 557
paraphrase to understand, **74**
summarize to identify, **168**
Fact and opinion, distinguish between, **1250**
Fluency, improve, **R16**
Fluency checklist, use, **R17**
Footnotes, integrate, 83

Gothic literature, comparing, 323, 326, 327, 328, 330, 333
Historical period, evaluate influences of, **226**, 229, 231, 237, 240, **634**, 639, **1216**, 1218, 1234
Historical perspective, apply, **901**, 908
Humor, comparing past/present, **587**, 593
Imagery, compare, **922**, 927, 1462
Images, compare, **718**, 726
Inference, draw
about poet's beliefs, **1346**, 1355
informational texts, **764**, 765, 769
to interpret meaning, **270**, 275, 277, 279, 285
Test Practice, 771
Information, organize/record, **558**
Integrate and evaluate information, 16, 224, 476, 704, 980, 1292
Interpret, **1334**, 1342, 1344
Listening to lyrics, **530**, 534
Literary criticism, apply political approach to, 922
Main idea, **1102**
identify support of, 1110, 1113
summarize to identify, **168**
Meaning, clarify, 56, **650**, 659, 660, 662
Moods, compare, **256**, 268
Multiple themes, compare, **901**, 908
Narrative accounts, reading, **516**
Note-taking, **558**
Online source, evaluate, **938**
Organizational patterns, analyze, **128**, **478**, 484, 490, **1094**, 1098, 1101
Outline, **558**, **1408**, 1421
Parallelism, find, 1062, 1068
Paraphrase to determine meaning, **74**, 76, 79, **778**, 781, 783, **1376**, 1381
Performance, visualize action in, **1117**
Personification, compare use of, **866**, 871
Perspectives, compare, **982**, 998
Persuasive techniques, identify, **97**
Philosophical argument, analyze, **626**, 633, **784**, 793
Philosophical assumptions, analyze, **40**, 43, 45, **376**, 381, 386, 390, **614**, 615, 619, 620, 624
Plot turning points, Sample Test to identify, 1270
Poems, compare and contrast, **640**, 648
Poetry, reading/responding to, **403**
Poetry of cultural identity, compare, **913**
Points of view, compare, **1424**, 1439
Political approach, apply, 922, 925
Political assumptions, analyze, **98**, 108, **982**, 998
Political drama, compare past/present, **1239**, 1244, 1249

LANGUAGE STUDY WORKSHOPS

Writing/Writing to Sources

WRITING APPLICATIONS

Listening and Speaking

Assessment

Test-Taking Practice

Reading for Information

Recent Scholarship

Speaking and Listening

Test-Taking Practice

Themes Across Centuries

Text Set Workshop

Unit Introduction

Writing Workshop

Acknowledgments

Acknowledgments continued from copyright page.

William Harvey "Playing for the Fighting Sixty-Ninth" by William Harvey from *Playing for the Fighting Sixty-Ninth*. Copyright © 2001 by William Harvey. Used by permission.

Historical Museum of Southern Florida "Museum Mission/History" from *http://www.hmsf.org*. Copyright © Historical Museum of Southern Florida. Used by permission.

The Barbara Hogenson Agency, Inc. "The Night the Ghost Got In" by James Thurber. Copyright © 1933, 1961 by James Thurber, © Rosemary Thurber. Used by permission.

Henry Holt and Company, Inc. "Acquainted with the Night" by Robert Frost from *The Poetry of Robert Frost* edited by Edward Connery Latham. Copyright © 1956 by Robert Frost. Copyright 1928, © 1969 by Henry Holt and Co. "The Gift Outright" by Robert Frost from *The Poetry of Robert Frost*. Copyright 1942 by Robert Frost, © 1970 by Lesley Frost Ballantine, © 1969 by Henry Holt & Company. "Stopping By Woods on a Snowy Evening" by Robert Frost from *The Poetry of Robert Frost*, edited by Edward Connery Lathem. Copyright 1951 by Robert Frost, © 1923, 1969 by Henry Holt and Company. Used by permission of Henry Holt and Company, LLC.

Houghton Mifflin Company, Inc. "Ambush" from *The Things They Carried* by Tim O'Brien. Copyright © 1990 by Tim O'Brien. "Ars Poetica" by Archibald MacLeish from *Collected Poems, 1917–1982* by Archibald MacLeish. Copyright © 1985 by The Estate of Archibald MacLeish. "Courage" by Anne Sexton from *The Awful Rowing Toward God* by Anne Sexton. Copyright © 1975 by Loring Conant, Jr., Executor of the Estate of Anne Sexton. Used by permission of Houghton Mifflin Company. All rights reserved.

Hyperion From *Cold Mountain: The Screenplay* by Anthony Minghella, based on a novel by Charles Frazier. Copyright © 2003 by Anthony Minghellla. Used by permission of Hyperion. All rights reserved.

International Creative Management, Inc. "One Day, Now Broken in Two" by Anna Quindlen from *Newsweek*. Copyright © 2002 by Anna Quindlen. First appeared in *Newsweek*. "Life in His Language" by Toni Morrison from *James Baldwin*. Copyright © 1989 by Toni Morrison. Published in James Baldwin: The Legacy (Quincy Troupe, ed.), Simon & Schuster, 1989. Copyright © 1989 by Simon & Schuster. Used by permission of International Creative Management, Inc.

Athena Kildegaard "untitled" poem by Athena Kildegaard used from *Rare Momentum*, Red Dragonfly Press, 2006, by permission of the author.

The Estate of Dr. Martin Luther King, Jr. c/o Writer's House LLC From "Letter from Birmingham Jail" by Dr. Martin Luther King, Jr. from *A Testament of Hope:The Essential Writings of Martin Luther King, Jr*. Used by arrangement with the Heirs to the Estate of Martin Luther King, Jr. c/o Writers House as agent for the proprietor. Copyright 1963 Martin Luther King, Jr.; renewed 1991 Coretta Scott King.

Galway Kinnell "Reckless Genius" by Galway Kinnell from *http://www.salon.com*. Used by permission.

Alfred A. Knopf, Inc. "Dream Variations" by Langston Hughes from *The Selected Poems of Langston Hughes*. Copyright © 1926 by Alfred A. Knopf, Inc. and renewed 1954 by Langston Hughes. "I, Too" by Langston Hughes from *The Selected Poems of Langston Hughes*. Copyright © 1994 by the Estate of Langston Hughes. "Refugee in America" by Langston Hughes from *The Selected Poems of Langston Hughes*. Copyright © 1943 by The Curtis Publishing Company. "The Negro Speaks of Rivers" by Langston Hughes from *Selected Poems of Langston Hughes*. Copyright © 1926 by Alfred A. Knopf, Inc. and renewed 1954 by Langston Hughes. From "The Woman Warrior" by Maxine Hong Kingston from *The Woman Warrior*. Copyright © 1975, 1976 by Maxine Hong Kingston. "Of Modern Poetry" by Wallace Stevens from *The Collected Poems of Wallace Stevens*. Copyright 1942 by Wallace Stevens and renewed 1970 by Holly Stevens from by Wallace Stevens. "Of Plymouth Plantation" by William Bradford from Of Plymouth Plantation 1620–1647 by William Bradford, edited by Samuel Eliot Morison, copyright 1952 by Samuel Eliot Morison and renewed 1980 by Emily M. Beck. From "Hiroshima" by John Hersey. Copyright 1946 and renewed 1974 by John Hersey. Used by permission of Alfred A. Knopf, a division of Random House, Inc. Excerpt from *The American Language*, 4th Edition by H.L. Mencken. Copyright © 1919, 1921, 1923, 1936 by Alfred A. Knopf, Inc. All rights reserved.

The Landmark Project "Son of Citation Machine and Landmarks Son of Citation Machine Masthead" from *http://citationmachine.net*. Copyright © 2006 by David Warlick & The Landmark Project. Used by permission of The Landmark Project.

League of Women Voters "How to Watch a Debate" from *www.lwv.org*. The material in this publication on "How to Watch a Debate" was excerpted from a League of Women Voters of the United States (LWVUS) online document of the same title, located at www.lwv.org, with express permission of the LWVUS for this one-time use in Pearson Prentice Hall Literature 8e Program. Secondary users must request permission directly from the LWVUS, the copyright owner. Copyright © 2007 League of Women Voters. All rights reserved. Used by permission.

Patricia Lee Lewis "(0)" by Patricia Lee Lewis.

Liveright Publishing Corporation "anyone lived in a pretty how town" by E. E. Cummings from *Complete Poems, 1904–1962*. Copyright 1940, © 1968, 1991 by the Trustees for the E.E. Cummings Trust. "old age sticks" by E. E. Cummings. Copyright 1958 © 1986, 1991 by the Trustees for the E. E. Cummings Trust, from *Complete Poems: 1904–1962* by E. E. Cummings, edited by George J. Firmage. "Frederick Douglass" by Robert Hayden. Copyright © 1966 by Robert Hayden, from *Collected Poems of Rober Hayden* by Robert Hayden, edited by Frederick Glaysher. "Runagate Runagate" by Robert Hayden from *The Collected Poems of Robert Hayden* by Robert Hayden, edited by Frederick Glaysher. Copyright © 1966 by Robert Hayden. "Storm Ending" by Jean Toomer from Cane. Copyright 1923 by Boni & Liveright, renewed 1951 by Jean Toomer. Used by permission of Liveright Publishing Corporation.

Los Angeles Times Syndicate "Hysteria Resides at Heart of the Frantic Crucible" by Kenneth Turan from Los Angeles Times, 12/13/96. Copyright © 1996 The Times Mirror Company, Los Angeles Times. Used by permission.

Ludlow Music c/o The Richmond Organization (TRO) "Dust Bowl Blues" Words and Music by Woody Guthrie TRO-© Copyright 1964 (Renewed) 1977 Ludlow Music, Inc., New York, NY Used by permission.

The Estate of Edgar Lee Masters "Lucinda Matlock" by Edgar Lee Masters from *The Spoon River Anthology*. Permission by Hilary Masters.

The Miami Herald "Crucible Casts a Newly Contempo rary Spell/Free from Chains of McCarthyism, Arthur Miller's Classic Soars" by Rene Rodriguez from *The Miami Herald*, 12/20/96. Copyright © 1996 The Miami Herald. Used by permission.

Milkweed Editions "Museum Indians" by Susan Power from *Roofwalker* (Minneapolis: Milkweed Editions, 2002). Copyright © 2002 by Susan Power. Used with permission from Milkweek Editions.

Navarre Scott Momaday From "The Names" by N. Scott Momaday. Copyright © by N. Scott Momaday. Used by permission.

New Directions Publishing Corporation From "A Retrospect: Few Don'ts By an Imagiste" by Ezra Pound, from *The Literary Essays of Ezra Pound*, copyright © 1935 by Ezra Pound. "Constantly Risking Absurdity" by Lawrence Ferlinghetti from *These Are My Rivers: New and Selected Poems 1955–1993*. Copyright © 1955, 1958, 1959, 1960, 1961, 1964, 1966, 1967, 1968, 1969, 1971, 1972, 1975, 1976, 1977, 1978, 1979, 1981, 1984, 1988, 1993 by Lawrence Ferlinghetti. All rights reserved. "The Great Figure" by William Carlos Williams from *Collected Poems: 1909–1939, Volume I*, copyright © 1938 by New Directions Publishing Corp. "Heat" by H. D. from *Collected Poems, 1912–1944*, copyright © 1982 by The Estate of Hilda Doolittle. "In a Station of the Metro" by Ezra Pound from *Personae*, copyright © 1926 by Ezra Pound. "Pear Tree" by H. D. from *Collected Poems, 1912–1944*, copyright © 1982 by The Estate of Hilda Doolittle. "The Red Wheelbarrow" by William Carlos Williams from *Collected Poems: 1909–1939, Volume 1*, copyright © 1938 by New Directions Publishing Corp. "The Secret" by Denise Levertov from *Poems 1960–1967*. Copyright © 1964 by Denise Levertov Goodman. "This is Just to Say" by William Carlos Williams from *Collected Poems 1909–1939, Volume I*, copyright © 1938 by New Directions Publishing Corp. Used by permission of New Directions Publishing Corp.

New York Times Agency "At the Theater/The Crucible" by Brooks Atkinson from *The New York Times*, January 23, 1953. Copyright © 1953 by the New York Times Co. "Onomatopoeia" originally titled "Zapmanship" by William Safire from *You Could Look It Up*. Copyright 1984, The New York Times. "The Nation: Backing the Attack" from *The New York Times*, September 12, 1943. Copyright © The New York Times. "Rock of the Modern Age, Arthur Miller is Everywhere" by Mel Gussow from *diversityjobmarket.com*. Used by permission and protected by the copyright Laws of the United States. The printing, copying, redistribution, or retransmission of the material without express written permission is prohibited.

Newmarket Press From "Good Night, and Good Luck: The Screenplay and History behind the Landmark Movie". Screenplay by George Clooney and Grant Heslov. Copyright © 2005 by Section Eight Production. Used by permission of Newmarket Press, 18 East 48th Street, New York, New York 10017. www.newmarketpress.com.

Naomi Shihab Nye "Streets" by Naomi Shihab Nye from *Words Under the Words: Selected Poems*. Copyright © Naomi Shihab Nye. Used by permission.

Harold Ober Associates, Inc. "A Black Man Talks of Reaping" by Arna Bontemps from *American Negro Poetry*. Copyright © 1963 by Arna Bontemps. Used by permission of Harold Ober Associates Incorporated.

Gregory K. Pincus "Fib" by Gregory K. Pincus, originally posted online at *http://gottabook.blogspot.com/2006/04/fib.html*. Used by permission of the author.

Popular Photography Magazine From "The Assignment I'll Never Forget" by Dorothea Lange from *Popular Photography*, February 1960, Vol. 46, No. 2. Copyright © Popular Photography, 1960.

Princeton University Press From "Walden" by Henry David Thoreau. Copyright © 1971 by Princeton University Press, 1999 renewed PUP, 1989 paperback edition. Used by permission of Princeton University Press.

Sean Ramsay "Urban Renewal" by Sean Ramsay. Copyright © 2001 by Sean Ramsay. Used by permission.

Random House, Inc. "A Rose for Emily" by William Faulkner from *Collected Stories of William Faulkner* copyright © 1930 and renewed © 1958 by William Faulkner. "The Unknown Citizen", copyright 1940 & copyright renewed 1968 by W.H. Auden from Collected Poems by W.H. Auden. Used by permission of Random House, Inc. "A Raisin in the Sun" by Lorraine Hansberry. Copyright © 1958 by Robert Nemiroff, as an unpublished work. Copyright © 1959, 1966, 1984, by Robert Nemiroff.

Random House, Inc. & Sterling Lord Literistic, Inc. "Man Listening to Disc" by Billy Collins from Random House Trade Paperbacks. Copyright © 2001 by Billy Collins. Used by permission.

Schomburg Center for Research in Black Culture "The Tropics in New York" by Claude McKay from *The Poems of Claude McKay*. Courtesy of the Literary Representative for the Works of Claude McKay, Schomburg Center for Research in Black Culture, The New York Public Library, Astor, Lenox and Tilden Foundations. Used by permission.

Scribner, an imprint of Simon & Schuster "In Another Country" by Ernest Hemingway from *Men Without Woman*. Copyright 1927 by Charles Scribner's Sons. Copyright renewed 1955 by Ernest Hemingway. Used by permission of Scribner, an imprint of Simon & Schuster Adult Publishing Group. "Poetry" by Marianne Moore from *The Collected Poems of Marianne Moore*. Copyright © 1935 by Marianne Moore, copyright renewed © 1963 by Marianne Moore and T.S. Eliot. Used with the permission of Scribner, an imprint of Simon & Schuster Adult Publishing Group.

Simon & Schuster, Inc. "1776" by David McCullough from Chapter 3, "Dorchester Heights." New York: Simon & Schuster, 2005. All rights reserved.

South Florida Water Management District "Kissimmee River Restoration and Upper Basin Initiatives" by Staff from *2007 South Florida Environmental Report*. Copyright © 2007 South Florida Water Management District. Courtesy of South Florida Water Management District. Used by permission.

Donald D. Stanford "Huswifery" from *The Poems of Edward Taylor* ed. by Donald E. Stanford, University of North Carolina Press, 1989. Copyright © 1960, renewed 1988 by Donald E. Stanford.

State of California—Dept. of Parks and Recreation "Archaeological Site Record" from *http://ohp.parks.ca.gov*. Used by permission.

The Statue of Liberty-Ellis Island Foundation, Inc. "Statue of Liberty-Ellis Island Foundation Mission and Background" from *www.statueofliberty.org*. Copyright © The Statue of Liberty-Ellis Island Foundation, Inc. www.ellisisland.org. Used by permission.

Sterling Lord Literistic, Inc. "Mission Update blog" by Steve Squyres from *http://athena.cornell.edu/news/mubss/*. Used by permission of SLL/Sterling Lord Literistic, Inc. Copyright by Steven Squyres.

Syracuse University Press "The Iroquois Constitution" from *Arthur C. Parker on the Iroquois: Iroquois Uses of Maize and Other Food Plants, The Code of Handsome Lake; The Seneca Prophet; The Constitution of the Five Nations* by Arthur C. Parker, edited by William N. Fenton (Syracuse University Press, Syracuse, NY, 1981). Copyright © 1968 by Syracuse University Press.

Thompson and Thompson From "The Dark Tower" by Countee Cullen. Published in *Copper Sun* © 1927 Harper & Bros, NY. Renewed 1954 by Ida M. Cullen. Copyrights held by Amistad Research Center, Tulane University. Administered by Thompson and Thompson, New York, NY. Used by permission.

Anthony Thwaite "When I went to visit" by Ki no Tsurayuki translated by Geoffrey Bownas and Anthony Thwaite from *The Penguin Book of Japanese Verse*. Penguin Books copyright © 1964, revised edition 1998. Translation copyright © Geoffrey Bownas and Anthony Thwaite, 1964, 1998. Used by permission.

Charlie Todd "Surprise! Subway Birthday" by Charlie Todd and improve everywhere.com Copyright © 2002. Used by permission of Charlie Todd.

The University of Chicago Press "America's Epic" by James Miller, Jr. from *Whitman: A Collection of Critical Essays*. Copyright © 1957 by The University of Chicago. © 1962 by Prentice Hall, Inc.

University of Nebraska Press "Crossing the Great Divide" by Meriweather Lewis from *The Journals of the Lewis and Clark Expedition, volume 5*. Edited by Gary E. Moulton, used by permission of the University of Nebraska Press. Copyright © 1988 by the University of Nebraska Press.

University of North Carolina Press "To His Excellency, General Washington" by Phillis Wheatley from *The Poems of Phillis Wheatley*. Edited and with an introduction by Julian D. Mason Jr. Copyright © 1966 by the University of North Carolina Press, renewed 1989. Used by permission of the publisher. www.uncpress.unc.edu.

University of North Texas "Help North Texas Vote" from *http://www.eac.gov*.

Viking Penguin, Inc. "The Turtle (Chapter 3)" by John Steinbeck from *The Grapes of Wrath*. Copyright © 1939, renewed copyright © 1967 by John Steinbeck. "The Crucible" by Arthur Miller from *The Crucible*. Copyright 1952, 1953, 1954, renewed © 1980, 1981, 1982 by Arthur Miller. Used by permission of Viking Penguin, a division of Penguin Books USA Inc. CAUTION: Professionals and amateurs are hereby warned that "The Crucible" being fully protected under the copyright laws of the United States of America, the British Commonwealth countries, including the Dominion of Canada, and the other countries of the Universal Copyright and Berne Conventions, are subject to royalty. All rights, including professional, amateur, motion picture, recitation, lecturing, public reading, radio, television and cable broadcasting, and the rights of translation into foreign languages, are strictly reserved. Particular emphasis is laid on the question of readings, permission for which must be secured in writing. Any inquiries for The Crucible should be addressed to Viking Penguin, 375 Hudson Street, NY, NY 10014.

Virginia Department of Historic Resources "Virginia Department of Historic Resources Archaeological Site Inventory Form" from Virginia Department of Historic Resources. Used by permission.

Patricia Vogel "untitled" (Fibonacci poem) by Patricia Vogel. Used by permission of the author.

W. W. Norton & Company, Inc. "Halley's Comet" by Stanley Kunitz from *Passing Through: The Later Poems*, New and Selected. Copyright © 1985 by Stanley Kunitz. Used by permission of W.W. Norton & Company, Inc. Copyright © 1985 by Stanley Kunitz. "Who Burns for the Perfection of Paper" by Martin Espada from *City of Coughing and Dead Radiators*. Copyright © 1993 by Martin Espada. Used by permission of W. W. Norton & Company, Inc.

Wesleyan University Press "Camouflaging the Chimera" by Yusef Komunyakaa from *Neon Vernacular*. From Dien Cai Dau (Wesleyan University Press, 1988). Used by permission of Wesleyan University Press.

Wikipedia.org "Kennedy Space Center" from *http://en.wikipedia.org/wiki/Kennedy_Space_Center*; retrieved from http://en.wikpedia.org accessed on 07/06/07. "Atlanta Braves" from *http://en.wikipedia.org/wiki/Atlanta_Braves*; retrieved from http://en.wikipedia.org accessed on 07/06/07. "Mojave Desert" from *http://en.wikipedia.org/wiki/Mojave_desert*; retrieved from http://en.wikipedia.org accessed on 07/06/07.

The Wylie Agency, Inc. "Everything Stuck to Him" by Raymond Carver from *What We Talk About When We Talk About Love*. Copyright © 1981 by Tess Gallagher, used with the permission of the the Wylie Agency. "Journey to the Crucible" by Arthur Miller, first published in *The New York Times*, February 8, 1953 © 1953 by Arthur Miller. Copyright renewed 2008 by The Arthur Miller Estate, used with the permission of The Wylie Agency Inc.

Yale University Press From "Sinners in the Hands of an Angry God" by Jonathan Edwards from *The Sermons of Jonathan Edwards: A Reader* published by Yale University Press. Copyright © 1999 by Yale University Press. From "Mary Chesnut's Civil War" by Mary Chesnut edited by C. Vann Woodward. Copyright © 1981 by C. Vann Woodward, Sally Bland Metts, Barbara G. Carpenter, Sally Bland Johnson, and Katherine W. Herbert. All rights reserved. Used by permission of the publisher, Yale University Press.

Note: Every effort has been made to locate the copyright owner of material reproduced on this component. Omissions brought to our attention will be corrected in subsequent editions.

Credits

Photo Credits

F & B cover Alan Copson/JAI/Corbis

Lxxii, Universal/Photofest; **lxxiii** TR Universal/Marvel Entertainment/The Kobal Collection/Art Resource; **lxxiii** L Universal/Photofest; **lxxii** Michel Setboun/CORBIS; **lxxv** Paul Knight, Trevillion Images; **lxxvi** Bettmann/Corbis; **lxxvii** TL Time Life Pictures/Time Magazine/Getty Images Inc.; **lxxviii** BR Bettmann/Corbis; **lxxxii** Joseph Sohm/Visions of America/Corbis; **lxxxiii** Lewis H. Hine/George Eastman House/Getty Images, Inc.; **lxxxiv** The Granger Collection, NYC; **lxxxv** Stephen Pierce; **lxxxvii, xi, xii** The Art Archive/Gift of Mrs. Karl Frank/Buffalo Bill Historical Center, Cody, Wyoming/14.86/Art Resource, NY; **xiv–xv** Geoffrey Clements/Corbis; **xlvi–xlvii** gallimaufry/Shutterstock; **xvii–xviii** Bettmann/Corbis; **xxiv–xxv** The Museum of Modern Art/Licensed by SCALA/Art Resource, NY; **xxi–xxii** Drought Stricken Area, 1934 (oil on canvas), Hogue, Alexandre (1898–1994)/Dallas Museum of Art, Texas, USA/The Bridgeman Art Library; **xxvii** Louis K. Meisel Gallery, Inc./Corbis; **0001** The Art Archive/Gift of Mrs. Karl Frank/Buffalo Bill Historical Center, Cody, Wyoming/14.86/Art Resource, NY; **2** TCR Library of Congress; **2** L Buffalo Bill Historical Center/The Art Archive at Art Resource, NY; **2** RCR Portrait of an African, c.1757–60 (oil on canvas), Ramsay, Allan (1713–84) (attr. to)/Royal Albert Memorial Museum, Exeter, Devon, UK/The Bridgeman Art Library; **2** CL Bettmann/Corbis; **2** CR The Granger Collection, NYC; **2** LCL The Granger Collection, NY; **2** TR Courtesy of The Historical Society of Pennsylvania Collection, Atwater Kent Museum of Philadelphia; **2** R Photo by Michael J. Deas/Time Magazine/Time & Life Pictures/Getty Images; **4** R Bettmann/CORBIS; **4** L Bettmann/CORBIS; **5** R Blue Lantern Studio/CORBIS; **5** L The Gallery Collection/CORBIS; **6** L Lee Snider/Photo Images/CORBIS; **6** R The Granger Collection, NYC; **7** T topora/Shutterstock; **7** R Scala/Art Resource, NY; **7** L Bettmann/CORBIS; **8** R istockphoto.com; **8** L Burstein Collection/CORBIS; **9** T istockphoto.com; **9** BR Chris Hillier/CORBIS; **9** BL The Granger Collection, NY; **10** R Blue Lantern Studio/CORBIS; **10** L Bettmann/CORBIS; **10** C Bettmann/CORBIS; **11** L istockphoto.com; **11** R The Granger Collection, NY; **12** T; **12** BR Cynthia Hart Designer/CORBIS; **12** BC The Gallery Collection/CORBIS; **12** BL The Granger Collection, NY; **13** R Francis G. Mayer/CORBIS; **13** L Gerrit Greve/CORBIS; **1** R Prentice Hall; **15** Library of Congress; **17** Smithsonian American Art Museum, Washington, DC/Art Resource, NY; **19** Buffalo Bill Historical Center/The Art Archive at Art Resource, NY; **21** Mary Ann McDonald/Corbis; **23** istockphoto.com; **24** bkgd istockphoto.com; **26** bkgd istockphoto.com; **27** kstudija/Fotolia; **32** BL The Roofwalker, Susan Power. Milkweed Editions. ç 22, Text by Susan Power. Cover and Interior design by Dale Cooney. Cover painting, "Migrations", oil, 1996 by Ojibwe artist Jim Denomie; **32** BR The Grass Dancer, Susan Power. Penguin Putnam, Inc. Copyright ©1994 by Susan Power; **32** T Photo by Rebecca Dallinger; Courtesy of Susan Power; **34** Brooklyn Museum/Corbis; **35** istockphoto.com; **37**; The Old Guitarist, 193, Pablo Picasso, Spanish, 1881–1973, oil on panel 122.9 x 82.6 cm, Helen Birch Bartlett Memorial Collection, 1926.253. Reproduction, The Art Institute of Chicago, ©24Estate of Pablo Picasso/Artists Rights Society (ARS), New York; **38** Buffalo Bill Historical Center; Cody, Wyoming; Gift of Hon. and Mrs. William Henry Harrison; NA.

22.70; 39 DLILLC/Corbis; **41** John Kahionhes Fadden; **42** bkgd istockphoto.com; **42** Corbis; **43** W. Perry Conway/Corbis; **48** Jeremy Woodhouse/Masterfile; **50** Courtesy Catholic Archives of Texas, Austin; **52** Daryl Benson/Masterfile; **53** Jay Krishnan/Shutterstock; **57** T Bettmann/Corbis; **58** Bettmann/Corbis; **60** Bettmann/Corbis; **61** istockphoto.com; **63** The Granger Collection, NY; **68** Ric Francis/epa/Corbis; **69** Denis Scott/Corbis; **70–71** bkgd NASA/Handout/Getty Images; **71** R AP/Wide World Photos; **72** bkgd FILATOV ALEXEY/Shutterstock; **73** Pilgrims Going to Church, George Henry Boughton, Collection of The New-York Historical Society; **75** The Granger Collection, NY; **76** istockphoto.com; **77** Anne Bradstreet, The Tenth Muse Lately Sprung Up in America, Ladonna Gulley Warrick, Courtesy of the artist; **78** BR Dance of Apollo with the Nine Muses (tempera on panel), Peruzzi, Baldassarre (1481–1536)/Palazzo Pitti, Florence, Italy, Alinari/The Bridgeman Art Library; **78** ML Mimmo Jodice/Corbis; **78** T The Granger Collection, NY; **78** BL Demetrio Carrasco CONACULTA-INAH-MEX. Authorized by the Instituto Nacional de Antropologia e Historia; **85** Corbis; **86** Johnson B. Curtis; **87** B istockphoto.com; **87** T istockphoto.com; **89** North Wind Picture Archives; **95** George Washington (1732–99) (colour litho) by John Trumbull (1756–1843) (after) Private Collection/Peter Newark American Pictures/The Bridgeman Art Library; **96** The Granger Collection, NYC; **99** B istockphoto.com; **99** National Portrait Gallery, Smithsonian Institution/Art Resource, NY; **10** Superstock; **14** Bettmann/Corbis; **106** Swim Ink 2, LLC/CORBIS; **18** The New Yorker Collection 200 Frank Cotham from cartoonbank.com; **111** The Granger Collection, NYC; **112** istockphoto.com; **112** bkgd National Archives and Records Administisration; **116** The Granger Collection, NYC; **117** The Granger Collection, New York; **118** The Granger Collection, New York; **123** Bettmann/Corbis; **124** New York State Historical Association, Cooperstown, New York; **129** ©ZUMA Press, Inc. / Alamy; **131** ©Bob Daemmrich / Alamy; **132** TL istockphoto.com; **132** Bkgrd; **134** The Granger Collection, NYC; **135** L The Granger Collection, NYC; **135** C The Granger Collection, NYC; **135** R The Granger Collection, NYC; **136** R The Granger Collection, NYC; **136** Photo by Michael J. Deas/Time Magazine/Time & Life Pictures/Getty Images; **137** R The Granger Collection, NYC; **137** C The Granger Collection, NYC; **137** L The Granger Collection, NYC; **138** TL The Granger Collection, New York; **138** TC The Granger Collection, NYC; **138** TR The Granger Collection, NYC; **138** BL Judith Miller/Dorling Kindersley; **138** BR Courtesy of the Bakken Library, Minneapolis; **140** Christie's Images/SuperStock; **142** ©British Museum; **144**; **146** BC istockphoto.com; **146** T ©Richard Cummings/Corbis; **146** BL Accoutrements LLC; **146** BR Liberty Kids is a registered trademark of DIC Entertainment Corp. Used under license. All rights reserved; **148** The Granger Collection, NYC; **149** The Granger Collection, NYC; **151** TL The Granger Collection, NYC; **151** bkgd Seattle Art Museum, Gift of Katherine White and the Boeing Company. Photo by Paul Macapia; **151** BR Seattle Art Museum, Gift of Katherine White and the Boeing Company. Photo by Paul Macapia; **152** The New Yorker Collection 1965 William Hamiliton from cartoonbank.com. All Rights Reserved; **153** Hulton-Deutsch Collection/Corbis; **156** BCR AP Photo/Eric Risberg; **156** BR AP Photo/Eric Gay; **156** BCL Bassouls

Sophie/Corbis; **156 BL** ©Rune Hellestad/Corbis; **156 CL** Bettmann/Corbis; **156 TL** Bettmann/Corbis; **156 TR** Bettmann/Corbis; **156 CR** Getty Images; **156 CCR** Hulton Archive/Getty Images; **156 CCL** The Granger Collection, New York; **158** AP Photo/Eric Gay; **159** DK Limited/Corbis; **160–161** Michael Storrings; **161** Rivera, Diego (1886–1957). The grinder (La molendera). 1926. Oil on canvas, 35 7/16 x 46 1/16 in. Museo Nacional de Arte Moderno, Instituto Nacional de Bellas Artes, Mexico City, D.F., Mexico. (c)Banco de Mexico Diego Rivera & Frida Kahlo Museums Trust. **A 162** ©JUPITERIMAGES/ PHOTOS.COM / Alamy; **162–163** Michael Storrings; **164** ©Imagebroker/Alamy; **166 T** Pearson; **166 B** From To Tell a Free Story: The First Century of Afro-American Autobiography, 1760–1865. ©1986 by the Board of Trustees of the University of Illinois. Used with permission of the author and the University of Illinois Press.; **167** Courtesy of the Library of Congress; **169** Portrait of an African, c.1757-60 (oil on canvas), Ramsay, Allan (1713–84) (attr. to)/Royal Albert Memorial Museum, Exeter, Devon, UK/The Bridgeman Art Library; **170** The Art Archive/Maritime Museum Kronborg Castle Denmark/Dagli Orti/Art Resource, NY; **171** /©Dorling Kindersley, Courtesy of the Wilberforce House Museum; **171** bkgd From THE WAY WE LIVED IN NORTH CAROLINA edited by Joe A. Mobley. Maps by Mark Anderson Moore. Copyright ©23 by the University of North Carolina Press. Published in association with the North Carolina Department of Cultural Resources, Office of Archives; **172** The Granger Collection, NYC; **175** istockphoto.com; **180 T** Bettmann/Corbis; **180 C** The Granger Collection, NYC; **180 B** The Granger Collection, NYC; **181 T** Judith Miller/Dorling Kindersley/Dreweatt Neate; **181 B** Profiles in History/Corbis; **183** The Granger Collection, NYC; **184** Library of Congress; **185** Library of Congress; **187** William Manning/Corbis; **191** Photo by Rebecca Dallinger; Courtesy of Susan Power; **206 BR** AP Images; **28–29** ©Geoffrey Clements/Corbis; **210 LCL** Library of Congress; **210 CL** ©Stefano Bianchetti/Corbis; **210 L** Smithsonian Institution/Corbis; **210 CR** ©adoc-photos/Corbis; **210 CR** Bettmann/Corbis; **210 RB** The Granger Collection, NYC; **210 TR** The Granger Collection, NYC; **210 RCR** Amherst College Archives and Special Collections, by permission of the Trustees of Amherst College; **210 TC** Cover of Democracy in American by Alexis De Tocqueville, ©1965 by Harper & Row. Publishers, Inc. Reprinted by permission of HarperColins Publishers; **211 RB** Bettmann/Corbis; **211 TL** Bettmann/Corbis; **211 BL** National Museum of American History, Smithsonian Institution; **211 TCR** National Museum of American History, Smithsonian Institution; **211 TR** Old Sturbridge Village; **211 BCR** Science Museum; **211 BC** Science Museum; **212** The Granger Collection, NYC; **213 R** The Granger Collection, New York; **213 L** The Art Archive/Musée du Château de Versailles/Gianni Dagli Orti/Art Resource, NY; **214 R** Bettmann/Corbis; **215 R** Bettmann/Corbis; **215 L** The Granger Collection, NYC; **216 R** Bettmann/Corbis; **216 L** The Granger Collection, NYC; **217 R** Image Source/Corbis; **217 L** ©Stefano Bianchetti/Corbis; **217 C** The Granger Collection, NYC; **218 T**; **218 BR** ©Frank Lukasseck/Corbis; **218 BL** The Granger Collection, New York; **218 BC** The Granger Collection, NYC; **219 L** The Granger Collection, NYC; **219 C** The Granger Collection, NYC; **219 R** The Granger Collection, NYC; **220 L** Bettmann/Corbis; **220 R** The Granger Collection, NYC; **221 L** Bettmann/Corbis; **221 C** ©Joseph Sohm/Visions of America/Corbis; **221** North Wind Picture Archives; **222** Aurora/Getty Images; **223** Aurora/Getty Images; **225** ©Private Collection/Photo ©Christie's Images/The Bridgeman Art Library; **227** Bettmann/Corbis; **228** Richard Bowden/Shutterstock; **229** ©Dorling Kindersley; **230** ©Corbis; **233** ©johannesspreter/Fotolia; **234** ©Paul Souders/Corbis; **235** Bettmann/Corbis; **236** ©Phil Schermeister/Corbis; **238** ©Lothar Lenz/zefa/Corbis; **239** ©Zack Seckler/Corbis; **244 B** National Portrait Gallery, Smithsonian Institution/Art Resource, NY; **244 T** The Granger Collection, NYC; **245** Smithsonian Institution, 95-3550; **246** North Wind Picture Archives; **247** Missouri Historical Society Museum Collections. Photograph and scan ©1998-21, Missouri Historical Society; **248** Library of Congress; **250 T** Missouri Historical Society, St. Louis, David Schultz; **250 B** The Thomas Gilcrease Institute of Art, Tulsa, Oklahoma; **251** North Wind Picture Archives; **252 R** North Wind Picture Archives; **252 L** Missouri Historical Society; **253 B** Library of Congress; **253 T** North Wind Picture Archives; **255** Connie Ricca/Corbis; **257** Corbis; **258** The Art Archive/Whitney Purchase Fund/Buffalo Bill Historical Center, Cody, Wyoming/19.61; **260** ©Craig Tuttle/Corbis; **261** The Granger Collection, NYC; **262** Image copyright ©The Metropolitan Museum of Art/Art Resource, NY; **265** The Granger Collection, NYC; **266** ©Ira Wyman/Sygma/Corbis; **269** Mary Evans Picture Library; **271** Smithsonian Institution/Corbis; **272; 276** Louis R. Linscott and S.B. Goddard & Son Co.; **278; 280** Fenimore Art Museum, Cooperstown, New York; **282** The Puritan, c. 1898, Frank E. Schoonover, Oil on canvas, Collection of The Brandywine River Museum, Gift of Mr. and Mrs. Jacob J. Foster, 1981. ©22 Brandywine Conservancy; **288** Bettmann/Corbis; **289** ©Classic Image/Alamy; **290 BL**; **290** bkgd Steven Bourelle/Shutterstock, Inc.; **290 C** AIP/The Kobal Collection/Art Resource; **290 BR** Accoutrements LLC; **292** Royal Photographic Society/Science & Society Picture Library; **295**; Mary Evans Picture Library; **297; 298; 300; 311** iStockphoto.com; **311 R** Adam Woolfitt/Corbis; **312–313** ©Patrick Coughlin/Getty Images; **316** University of Delaware Library, Newark, Delaware; **318** ©The New Yorker Collection 1990 Ed Frascino from cartoonbank.com. All Rights Reserved; **319** Bettmann/Corbis; **322** bkgd ©Aaron/Horowitz/Corbis; **322 BL** Bettmann/Corbis; **322 R** ©Susan Shacter/Corbis; **324** ©Peter Freed/Corbis; **325** Paul Knight, Trevillion Images; **326** Yolande de Kort, Trevillion Images; **329** Geoff Eley, Trevillion Images; **331** Gaetan Charbonneau/Getty Images; **335 B** Bettmann/Corbis; **335 T** Bettmann/Corbis; **336** ©1998 Kinuko Y. Craft All Rights Reserved; **338** Bettmann/Corbis; **340** Private Collection/©Bonhams, London, UK/The Bridgeman Art Library; **344 T** Frank Greenaway ©Dorling Kindersley, Courtesy of the Town Docks Museum, Hull; **344 BCR** Frank Greenaway ©Dorling Kindersley, Courtesy of the Town Docks Museum, Hull; **344 BL** Frank Greenaway ©Dorling Kindersley, Courtesy of the Town Docks Museum, Hull; **344 BL** David Lyons ©Dorling Kindersley, Courtesy of the Courtesy of the New Bedford Whaling Museum, Massachusetts; **344 TCR** Frank

Greenaway ©Dorling Kindersley, Courtesy of the Town Docks Museum, Hull; **344 BCR** Frank Greenaway ©Dorling Kindersley, Courtesy of the Town Docks Museum, Hull; **344 BR** Christian Darkin/Photo Researchers, Inc.; **344 C** Courtesy of the New Bedford Whaling Museum; **346** National Maritime Museum; **348** Bettmann/Corbis; **350** Bettmann/Corbis; **352** The Granger Collection, NYC; **356** ©The New Yorker Collection 1998 Arnie Levinfrom cartoonbank.com. All Rights Reserved; **359** ©Mark Karrass/Corbis; **360** ©Lee Snider/Corbis; **362 B**; **362 T** ©Elisheba Johnson; **363** Bettmann/Corbis; **365** Bettmann/Corbis; **366–368** sanderstock/fotolia; **371** ©Christian Delbert/Fotolia; **371** Leonard Harris/Stock Boston; **374 T** Pearson; **375** Courtesy Concord Free Public Library, Concord Massachusetts; **377** The Granger Collection, NYC; **378** Curtis Hamilton (c) Rough Guides; **382 BR** Bildarchiv Preussischer Kulturbesitz/Art Resource, NY; **382 BC** ©Araldo de Luca/Corbis; **382 BL** Pat O'Hara/Corbis; **382–383** TOP BORDER; Curtis Hamilton (c) Rough Guides; **384** MyLoupeRF\UIG/AGE Fotostock America; **388** istockphoto.com; **388** istockphoto.com; **389** bkgd Mitchell, S. Augustus 1792–1868/Library of Congress; **389** Bettmann/CORBIS; **390** The New Yorker Collection 1988 J.B. Handelsman from cartoonbank.com. All Rights Reserved; **393 BL** istockphoto.com; **393** bkgd istockphoto.com; **395** istockphoto.com; **396** istockphoto.com; **398–399** Bridget Besaw/Aurora Photos; **40** Bridget Besaw/Aurora Photos; **401** Christie's Images/Corbis; **404 T** istockphoto.com; **404 B** ©James Marshall/Corbis; **404 T** The Granger Collection, NYC; **405 T** Property of the Amherst Historical Society.Photo by J.K. Tuthill; **405 B** Courtesy of the Emily Dickinson Museum, Amherst, Massachusetts; **406** Amherst College Archives and Special Collections, by permission of the Trustees of Amherst College; **406** Bettmann/Corbis; **48; 410** BPK Berlin/Nationalgalerie, Staatliche Museen/Joerg P. Anders/Art Resource, NY.; **412** istockphoto.com; **413** Heibonsha/Pacific Press Service; **413** Heibonsha/Pacific Press Service; **415** istockphoto.com; **416–417** istockphoto.com; **418** Photo by Maud Kinnell; **422** Library of Congress; **426–427** Janina Dierks/Fotolia; **428** Courtesy of the Library of Congress; **432** The Lawrence Tree,1929, Georgia O'Keeffe, Wadsworth Atheneum, Hartford, CT. The Ella Gallup Sumner and Mary Catlin SumnerCollection; ©1998 The Georgia O'Keeffe Foundation/Artists Rights Society (ARS), New York; **434–435**; Haystack, 1938 (tempera with oil glaze on linen on panel), Benton, Thomas Hart (1889–1975)/Museum of Fine Arts, Houston, Texas, USA, ©DACS/Gift of Mr. Frank J. Hevrdejs/The Bridgeman Art Library International/ ©T.H. Benton and R.P. Benton Testamentar; **436** istockphoto.com; **443** Pearson; **460–461** Bettmann/Corbis; **462 LCL** Bettmann/Corbis; **462 T** Bettmann/Corbis; **462 CR** Bettmann/Corbis; **462 RCR** New York Times Co./Getty Images, Inc.; **462 TR** The Granger Collection, NYC; **462 L** The Granger Collection, NYC; **462 CL** Missouri Historical Society; **462 R** National Anthropological Archives, Smithsonian Institute, NAA INV 94200; **463** Chas Howson ©Dorling Kindersley; **463** Dave King ©Dorling Kindersley; **463** The Granger Collection, NYC; **463** The British Museum/HIP/The Image Works; **463** Detail from the original painting,The Museum of the Confederacy, Richmond, Virginia, Photography by Katharine Wetzel; **464 L** The Art Archive/Bibliothèque des Arts Décoratifs Paris/Gianni Dagli Orti; **464 R** Corbis; **465 R** The Gallery Collection/Corbis; **465 C** Bettmann/Corbis; **465 L** Archive Photos/Getty Images; **466 R** pinky/Shutterstock; **466 L** The Granger Collection, NYC; **467 L** The Art Archive/ Art Resource, NY; **467 BR** The Gallery Collection/Corbis; **467 CR** Six O'Clock, Winter, 1912, John Sloan, The Phillips Collection; **468** istockphoto.com; **468 T; 468 BL** Museum of the City of New York/Corbis; **468** The Granger Collection, NYC; **469 L** ©Jose Fuste Raga/Corbis; **469 R** Columbia Pictures/Photofest; **470** L H. Armstrong Roberts/Corbis; **470 R** Underwood & Underwood/Corbis; **471 L** Bettmann/Corbis; **471 R** The Old Guitarist, 193, Pablo Picasso, Spanish, 1881–1973, oil on panel 122.9 x 82.6 cm, Helen Birch Bartlett Memorial Collection, 1926.253.Reproduction, The Art Institute of Chicago, ©24Estate of Pablo Picasso/Artists Rights Society (ARS), New York; **472 L** ©Deborah Betz Collection/Corbis; **472 C** ©Ted Streshinsky/Corbis; **472 R** Science Museum/Science & Society Picture Library; **473 R** Bettmann/Corbis; **473 L** Rue des Archives/The Granger Collection, NYC; **475** Pearson; **476** Bettmann/Corbis; **477** Adoc-photos/Art Resource, NY; **479** Bettmann/CORBIS; **480; 482; 486; 487; 494 B** Getty Images; **494 T** Mulberry Plantation, Camden, S.C.; **496** Courtesy of the Library of Congress; **50; 53** The Granger Collection, NYC; **55** AP/Wide World Photos; **57** Bettmann/Corbis; **58** Bettmann/Corbis; **59** Bettmann/Corbis; **511** Bettmann/Corbis; **512** Courtesy of the National Museum of the U.S. Army, Army Art Collection; **513** Museum of the Confederacy, Richmond, Virginia; **519** The National Portrait Gallery, Smithsonian Institution, Washington, D.C./Art Resource, NY; **520** Smithsonian American Art Museum, Washington, DC/Art Resource, NY; **522** The Granger Collection, NYC; **525** A Home on the Mississippi, 1871, Currier & Ives, The Museum of the City of New York, Harry T. Peters Collection; **526** Bettmann/Corbis; **532** Layne Kennedy/Corbis; **533** Corbis; **537** Bettmann/Corbis; **538** Bettmann/Corbis; **540** Corbis; **541** The Granger Collection, NYC; **544 L** Shaun Curry/AFP/Getty Images; **544 R** Cover design by John Gall. Cover photograph courtesy of National Geographic. Grove Press and imprint of Grove Atlantic, Inc. Distributed by Publishers Group West; **545** Miramax/Photofest; **546** Miramax/Photofest; **546–547** bkgd Purestock/Getty Images; **547** Miramax/Photofest; **548–549** Purestock/Getty Images; **550 T** Pearson; **550 B** Cover design by Francine Kass.Cover photograph courtesy of the National Portrait Gallery, Smithsonian Institution.W.W. Norton; **553** Hulton Archive/Getty Images; **554** Bettmann/Corbis; **555–556** istockphoto.com; **559** National Portrait Gallery, Smithsonian Institution/Art Resource, NY; **560 T** Samir S. Patel; **560 B** Samir S. Patel; **563** North Wind Picture Archives; **564 B** Corel Professional Photos CD-ROM™; **564 T** Courtesy National Archives; **566** Bettmann/Corbis; **566–567** bkgd ©Joseph Sohm/Visions of America/Corbis; **567** The Granger Collection, NYC; **568** bkgd istockphoto.com; **568** Bettmann/Corbis; **570** Minnesota Historical Society/Corbis; **572** Historical Picture Archive/Corbis; **577** The Granger Collection, NYC; **579** The Granger Collection, NYC; **582; 583** istockphoto.com; **586 T; 588** Rick Friedman/Corbis; **589 T** Tom Kelley/Retrofile/Getty Images;

589 B ClassicStock/Fotosearch; 590 T Image of The Advertising Archive; 590 B Image of The Advertising Archive; 592 WALTER SANDERS/Time & Life Pictures/Getty Images; 595; Corbis; 596 bkgd Hans Blohm/Masterfile; 596 Peter Lilja/The Image Bank/Getty Images; 598 istockphoto.com; 600 Shutterstock.com; 602 Paul A. Souders/Corbis; 604 Jeff Curtes/Corbis; 610 Will Datene/Alamy; 616 National Anthropological Archives, Smithsonian Institute, NAA INV 94200; 617 Kansas State Historical Society; 619 Connie Ricca/Corbis; 620 Courtesy of the Lane County Historical Museum; 622 National Portrait Gallery, Smithsonian Institution/Art Resource, NY; 624 Library of Congress; 625 Channel to the Mills, 1913, Edwin M. Dawes, oil on canvas, 51 x 39 1/2 in. Minneapolis Institute of Arts, anonymous gift.; 627 Missouri Historical Society; 629 Afternoon in Piedmont, (Elsie at the Window), c.1911, Xavier Martínez, Collection of The Oakland Museum of California, Gift of Dr. William S. Porter; 631 Hulton-Deutsch Collection/Corbis; 632 Corel Professional Photos CD-ROM™; 635 The Granger Collection, NYC; 636 Bettmann/Corbis; 638 istockphoto.com; 641 Colby College Special Collections, Waterville, ME; 642 Paul Knight, Trevillion Images; 643 istockphoto.com; 644 Photo ©The Metropolitan Museum of Art/Art Resource, NY; 645 National Portrait Gallery, Smithsonian Institution, Washington, D.C./Art Resource, NY; 646 Christie's Images/Corbis; 647 Joel Greenstein/Omni-Photo Communications, Inc.; 651 New York Times Co./Getty Images, Inc.; 652 George Schreiber (194–1977), From Arkansas, 1939, oil on canvas, Sheldon Swope Art Museum, Terre Haute, Indiana; 653 The Granger Collection, NYC; 654–655 The Granger Collection, NYC; 656 Beatriz Schiller/Time & Life Pictures/Getty Images; 656–657 The Granger Collection, NYC; 658 ARS,NYC/photo ©Erich Lessing/Art Resource, NY; 659 The Granger Collection, NYC; 660–661 The Granger Collection, NYC; 669 Pearson; 688–689 Drought Stricken Area, 1934 (oil on canvas), Hogue, Alexandre (1898–1994)/Dallas Museum of Art, Texas, USA/The Bridgeman Art Library; 690 R Library of Congress; 690 C Bettmann/Corbis; 690 L Bettmann/Corbis; 690 T Underwood & Underwood/Corbis; 690 CL Corbis; 690 RCR Corbis; 690 LCL Bettmann/Corbis; 690 CR Hulton Archive/Getty Images; 691 BCB Henry Guttmann/Moviepix/Getty Images; 691 T Chaplin/Photofest; 691 B Warner Bros. Pictures/Photofest; 691 CT United Artists/Photofest; 691 CB MGM/Photofest; 691 TCT; 692 L Bettmann/Corbis; 692 R Hulton Archive/Getty Images; 693 C Bettmann/Corbis; 693 L Corbis; 693 R Mansell/Time & Life Pictures/Getty Images; 694 L Hulton Archive/Getty Images; 694 R FRAN CAFFREY/AFP/Getty Images; 695 L AP Photo; 695 R JazzSign/Lebrecht Music & Arts/Corbis; 696 L Bettmann/Corbis; 696 R Lipnitzki/Roger Viollet/Getty Images; 697 TR Bettmann/Corbis; ©Salvador Dali, Gala-Salvador Dali Foundation/Artists Rights Society (ARS), New York; 697 BR Bettmann/Corbis; 697 TL Bettmann/Corbis; 697 BL Icon Communications/Archive Photos/Getty Images; 698 T; 698 RT AP Photo; 698 RB Bettmann/Corbis; 698 L Hulton Archive/Getty Images; 699 L Bettmann/Corbis; 699 R The Granger Collection, NYC; 700 R The Granger Collection, NYC; 700 L The Granger Collection, NYC; 701 Radius Images/Alamy; 701 B Richard Peter Snr/Archive Photos/Getty Images; 703 Pearson; 704 Jason Hetherington/Stone/Getty Images; 705 Corbis; 707 Hulton-Deutsch Collection/Corbis; 78 Erich Lessing/Art Resource, NY; 713 T CNAC/MNAM/Dist. Réunion des Musées Nationaux/Art Resource, NY; 713 C The Metropolitan Museum of Art/Art Resource, NY; 713 B Jerry Cooke/Pix Inc./Time Life Pictures/Getty Image; 714 The New Yorker Collection 1994 Bruce Eric Kaplanfrom cartoonbank.com. All Rights Reserved.; 716 Corbis; 717 B Bettmann/Corbis; 717 T Bettmann/Corbis; 719 istockphoto.com/stephen mulcahey; 720 The Granger Collection, NYC; 722 Paul Seheult/Eye Ubiquitous/Corbis; 723 B istockphoto.com/James Pauls; 723 T istockphoto.com/Branko Miokovic; 724 The Metropolitan Museum of Art/Art Resource, NY; 725 age fotostock/SuperStock; 729 Bettmann/Corbis; 730 Mary Evans Picture Library; 731 istockphoto.com/Gary Godby; 732 L istockphoto.com/Vincent Giordano; 732 R C Squared Studios/Photodisc/Getty Images; 733 Mary Evans Picture Library; 735 Mary Evans Picture Library; 736 Mary Evans Picture Library; 738 Mary Evans Picture Library; 740 Mary Evans Picture Library; 742 Underwood & Underwood/Corbis; 747 Mary Evans Picture Library; 751 istockphoto.com; 752 Mary Evans Picture Library; 757 L Bettmann/Corbis; 757 R SuperStock, Inc; 758–759 David Lee/Shutterstock; 760–761 SuperStock, Inc; 766 T Library of Congress; 766 B Corbis; 766 C John Springer Collection/Corbis; 767 Library of Congress; 767 Library of Congress; 767 L Library of Congress; 768 Library of Congress; 771 Sandy Feisenthal/Corbis; 773 Bettmann/Corbis; 774 The Turret Lathe Operator (J.G. Cherry series), 1925, Grant Wood, oil on canvas18" x 24" Cedar Rapids Museum of Art, Cedar Rapids, Iowa,Gift of the Cherry Burrell Charitable Foundation Collection. 75.5.8, ©Estate of Grant Wood/Figge Ar Museum, success; 779 Bettmann/Corbis; 780 Hood Museum of Art, Dartmouth College, Hanover, New Hampshire; gift of Frank L. Harrington, Class of 1924; 785 Bettmann/Corbis; 786 istockphoto.com/Dmytro Konstantynov; 788 B Bettmann/Corbis; 788 T Oscar White/Corbis; 789 istockphoto.com; 791 Untitled, 1964,Alexander Calder, (one of seven lithographs in series), 19 1/2 x 25 1/2" Solomon R. Guggenheim Museum, New York, Gift of the artist, 1965, 65.1736.7. Photo by David Heald, ©The Solomon R. Guggenheim Foundation, New York, ©1998 Estate of; 795 Columbus Museum of Art, Ohio: Gift of Ferdinand Howald 1931.146; 799 Bettmann/Corbis; 800 Military Ambulance, First World War (bodycolour on paper), Simpson, Charles Walter (1885–1971)/Private Collection, ©Chris Beetles, London, U.K./The Bridgeman Art Library; 803 Corbis; 804 Corbis; 805 Corbis; 808 T Pearson; 808 B Random House Inc.; 89 AP Photo; 810 Mary Evans Picture Library; 812 Philip Jones Griffiths/Magnum Photos; 815 Corbis; 816 Snark/Art Resource, NY; 818 San Francisco Museum of Modern Art, Collection of the Sack Photographic Trust; 819 istockphoto.com; 823 Réunion des Musées Nationaux/Art Resource, NY; 824 Markus Amon/The Image Bank/Getty Images; 825 Pierre Vauthey/Sygma/Corbis; 826 age fotostock/SuperStock; 828 ANSA/Corbis; 833 istockphoto.com; 833 Hulton Archive/Getty Images; 834 bkgd istockphoto.com; 834; The Museum of Modern Art/Licensed by SCALA/Art Resource, NY; 839 The Bride, 1886 (w/c on paper), Zorn, Anders Leonard

(1860–1920)/©Nationalmuseum, Stockholm, Sweden,/The Bridgeman Art Library International; 840 J. Fishkin/Custom Medical Stock Photo; 847 Philip Gould/Corbis; 848 Miz Emily, Joseph Holston, 24" x 16", Courtesy of Joseph Holston; 852 Georgia Red Clay, 1946, Nell Choate Jones, oil on canvas, 25 x 30 inches, 1989.1.94, Morris Museum of Art, Augusta, Georgia; 859 istockphoto.com; 859 Bettmann/Corbis; 860 My Life and Hard Times Copyright ©1933 by James Thurber. Copyright ©renewed 1961 by James Thurber. Reprinted by arrangement with Rosemary A. Thurber and The Barbara Hogenson Agency.; 862 My Life and Hard Times Copyright ©1933 by James Thurber. Copyright ©renewed 1961 by James Thurber. Reprinted by arrangement with Rosemary A. Thurber and The Barbara Hogenson Agency.; 863 My Life and Hard Times Copyright ©1933 by James Thurber. Reprinted by arrangement with Rosemary A. Thurber and The Barbara Hogenson Agency.; 867 Bettmann/Corbis; 867 bkgd Stock Montage, Inc.; 868 Stock Montage, Inc.; 870 istockphoto.com; 873 Bettmann/Corbis; 874 Exactostock/SuperStock; 877 istockphoto.com; 878–879 Destinations/Corbis; 880 Corel Professional Photos CD-ROM™; 882 Fine Art Photographic Library/Corbis; 883 Dante reading from the 'Divine Comedy', detail of Dante Alighieri (1265–1321), 1465 (panel) (detail of 42355), Domenico di Michelino, (1417–91)/Duomo, Florence, Italy/The Bridgeman Art Library; 884 Bettmann/Corbis; 886 The New Yorker Collection 1993 Mick Stevens from cartoonbank.com.All Rights Reserved.; 888 Walter Weissman/Corbis; 889 Jules Feiffer; 890 Jules Feiffer; 891 Jules Feiffer; 892 Jules Feiffer; 893 Jules Feiffer; 894 Jules Feiffer; 895 Aspiration, Aaron Douglas, Fine Arts Museums of San Francisco, Museum purchase; 896 ©Phoebe Beasley; 898 Corbis; 899 Atlantide Phototravel/Corbis; 900 T istockphoto.com; 900 B National Portrait Gallery, Smithsonian Institution/Art Resource, NY; 903 Aaron Douglas, Into Bondage, 1936,60 3/8 x 60 1/2, oil on canvas.In the collection of the Corcoran Gallery of Art, Washington, DC. Museum Purchaseand Partial Gift of Thurlow Tibbs Jr., The Evans-Tibbs Collection. 1996.9; 904 Nobody Around Here Calls Me Citizen, 1943, Robert Gwathmey, oil on canvas. H. 14-1/4" x W. 17" Collection Frederick R. Weisman Art Museum at the University of Minnesota; 906 Girls Skipping, 1949, Hale Woodruff, oil on canvas, 24" x 32", Private Collection. ©Estate of Hale Woodruff/Elnora, Inc.; Courtesy of Michael Rosenfeld Gallery, New York; 912; 912 bkgd age fotostock/SuperStock; 912; 912 title/author/Dover Publication, Inc.; 912 Hill and Wang; 912; 912; 912 Vintage Books; 912; 914 T Christopher Felver/Corbis; 914 B Miriam Berkley/Authorpix; 915 Smithsonian American Art Museum, Washington, DC/Art Resource, NY; 916 The Madonna and Child (detail), 1990, ©Momodou Ceesay; 920 B National Portrait Gallery, Smithsonian Institution/Art Resource, NY; 920 T Corbis; 921 Bettmann/Corbis; 923 B; 923 T Dave G. Houser/Corbis; 924 Hoeing, 1934, Robert Gwathmey, Oil on canvas, 40 by 60 1/4 (11.6 by 153),Carnegie Institute Museum of Art, Pittsburgh, Pennsylvania, Patrons Art Fund, 44.3.Photograph by Richard Stoner, ©Estate of Robert Gwathmey/Licensed by VAGA, New York, NY; 924–925 istockphoto.com; 926 istockphoto.com; 929 Library of Congress; 930 The Granger Collection, NYC; 930–931 bkgd Lake County Museum/Corbis; 931 Hulton Archive/Getty Images; 932–933 Lake County Museum/Corbis; 934–935 Lake County Museum/Corbis; 936 Lake County Museum/Corbis; 941 L Joe Robbins/Getty Images; 941 R The Atlanta Braves/MLB Photos via Getty Images; 947 Pearson; 964–965 The Museum of Modern Art/Licensed by SCALA/Art Resource, NY; 966 L AP/Wide World Photos; 966 CR Everett Collection Inc/Alamy; 966 R Deborah Feingold/Corbis; 966 RCR Flip Schulke/Corbis; 966 CL Peter Turnley/Corbis; 966 LCL Bettmann/Corbis; 966 TL NASA/Photo Researchers, Inc.; 966 TR Time Life Pictures/Time Magazine/Getty Images Inc.; 967 TCT David J. and Janice L. Frent/Corbis; 967 BCB David J. and Janice L. Frent/Corbis; 967 B Hulton Archives/Getty Images Inc.; 967 RC Herbert Orth/Time Life Pictures/Getty Imagess, Inc.; 967 T Herbert Orth/Time Life Pictures/Getty Imagess, Inc.; 967 TC Courtesy of The Peace Corps; 968 R John Springer Collection/Corbis; 968 L Bettmann/Corbis; 969 R Image Source/Getty Images; 969 L Bettmann/Corbis; 970 R Bettmann/Corbis; 970 L Michael Rougier/Time & Life Pictures/Getty Images; 971 L Bettmann/Corbis; 971 R Alfred Pasieka/Photo Researchers, Inc.; 972 T; 972 B Bettmann/Corbis; 973 R Bettmann/Corbis; 973 L Novosti/Photo Researchers, Inc.; 974 L Judith Miller/Dorling Kindersley/Bauman Rare Books; 974 T Bettmann/Corbis; 974 R Hulton Archives/Getty Images; 975 L Bettmann/Corbis; 975 R Charles E. Rotkin/Corbis; 975 C Bettmann/Corbis; 976 R Bettmann/Corbis; 976 L Bettmann/Corbis; 977 C Judith Miller/Dorling Kindersley/Bauman Rare Books; 977 L Bettmann/Corbis; 977 R Bettmann/Corbis; 979 T Sophie Bassouls/Sygma/Corbis; 979 B Playbill, is a registered trademark of Playbill, Inc. All rights reserved. Used by permission.; 980 Adam Woolfitt/Corbis; 981 MPI/Getty Images; 983 Bettmann/Corbis; 984 AP Photo/Stanley Troutman; 986 Corbis; 988 The Granger Collection, NYC; 990–991 The Granger Collection, NYC; 994 The Granger Collection, NYC; 996 Rollie McKenna; 997 Nik Keevil/Alamy; 1002 B Bettmann/Corbis; 1002 T Bettmann/Corbis; 1003 Courtesy Harry S. Truman Library 1004; 1008 Library of Congress; 1009 Choke, 1964, Robert Rauschenberg, Oil and screenprint on canvas, 60" x 48", Washington University Gallery of Art, St. Louis, Gift of Mr. and Mrs. Richard K. Weil, 1972, ©Robert Rauschenberg/Licensed by VAGA, New York, NY; 1011 AP/Wide World Photos; 1012 Deep Fork Overlook, Joan Marron-LaRue, Courtesy of the artist. Gallery is Nedra Matteucci Fine Art, 555 Canyon Rd., Santa Fe, New Mex.55-983-2731; 1017 Black Walnuts, Joseph Pollet, Collection of Whitney Museum of American Art.Purchase and gift of Gertrude Vanderbilt Whitney, by exchange (52.30).Photograph Copyright ©200: Whitney Museum of American Art; 1022 Vlaminck, Maurice de (1876–1958) ARS, NY Banque d'Images, ADAGP/Art Resource, NY; 1027 David Lees/Corbis; 1028 bkgd Shutterstock.com; 1028 Reading by the Oven, 1961 (oil on canvas), Sokolovskaya, Oksana Dmitrievna (fl.1961)/Springville Museum of Art, Utah, USA,/The Bridgeman Art Library; 1029 Shutterstock.com; 1030 istockphoto.com/Robyn Mackenzie; 1032–1033 istockphoto.com; 1034 istockphoto.com/Roel Smart; 1036; 1041 Sean Gallup/Getty Images; 1042 images.com/Corbis; 1044 BC ©Allen Ginsberg/Corbis;

1044 T Bettmann/Corbis; 1044 B Bettmann/Corbis; 1044 TC Timothy Clary/AFP/ Getty Images; 1046 Improv Everywhere Productions, Inc.; 1047 Improv Everywhere Productions, Inc.; 1048 Improv Everywhere Productions, Inc.; 1048 Improv Everywhere Productions, Inc.; 1048 Improv Everywhere Productions, Inc.; 1049 Improv Everywhere Productions, Inc.; 1051 T Bettmann/ Corbis; 1051 B Ian Cook/Time Life Pictures/Getty Images; 1052 Mirror II, George Tooker, (1920–1938), Egg tempera on gesso panel, 20 x 20 in., 1968.4, Gift of R. H. Donnelley Erdman (PA 1956), ©Addison Gallery of American Art, Phillips Academy, Andover, Massachusetts.All Rights Reserved; 1053 Sunny Forest/ Shutterstock; 1054 Sunny Forest/Shutterstock; 1057 Bettmann/Corbis; 1058 28 Masterfile Corporation; 1059 istockphoto.com/Dar Yang Yan; 1063 Bettmann/ Corbis; 1064 istockphoto.com/Valerie Loiseleux; 1065 Pach Brothers/Corbis; 1066; The Jacob and Gwendolyn Lawrence Foundation/Art Resource, NY Image; 1071 Everett Collection Inc/Alamy; 1072 Smithsonian American Art Museum, Washington, DC/Art Resource, NY; 1074–1075 Smithsonian American Art Museum, Washington, DC/Art Resource, NY; 1079 Bettmann/Corbis; 1081 Peter Turnley/Corbis; 1082 Push to Walk, collage 48" x 48" ©Phoebe Beasley; 1087 Patti Mollica/SuperStock; 1095 Katy Winn/Corbis; 1096 Bettmann/ Corbis; 1099 Walter Daran/Hulton Archive/Getty Images; 1113 Corbis; 1114 Retroactive I,Robert Rauschenberg, 1964, Wadsworth Atheneum, Hartford, CT, Gift of Susan Morse Hilles, ©Robert Rauschenberg/Licensed by VAGA, New York, NY; 1117 Paul Schutzer/Time & Life Pictures/Getty Images; 1118 Flip Schulke/Corbis; 1119 Bettmann/Corbis; 1110 L Bettmann/Corbis; 1110 R Express Newspapers/Staff/Hulton Archive/Getty Images; 1110 C Charles Moore/Black Star/stockphoto.com; 1111 Hulton-Deutsch Collection/Corbis; 1116 Boden/ Ledingham/Masterfile; 1118 B Courtesy Everett Collection; 1118 BC Photofest; 1118 TC The Granger Collection, New York; 1118 T Playbill, is a registered trademark of Playbill, Inc. All rights reserved. Used by permission.; 1119 Deborah Feingold/Corbis; 1120 T ©Deborah Feingold/Corbis; 1120 B; 1121 20th Century Fox, The Kobal Collection/Art Resource, NY; 1121 20th Century Fox, The Kobal Collection/Art Resource, NY; 1122 RT Punch/Roxbury/Bioskop Film/ The Kobal Collection/Art Resource, NY; 1122 BR Dave Allocca/DMI/Time Life Pictures/Getty Images; 1122 LT Paul Schutzer/Time & Life Pictures/Getty Images; 1122 RC Ron Galella/Wireimage/Getty Images; 1122 BL Jason Merritt/ FilmMagic/Getty Images; 1122 BC Popperfoto/Getty Images; 1124 20th Century Fox/Photofest; 1128 The Granger Collection, NYC; 1131 Twentieth Century Fox Film Corporation/Photofest; 1132 AP/Wide World Photos; 1134 20th Century Fox/The Kobal Collection/Art Resource; 1136 Twentieth Century Fox Film Corporation/Photofest; 1137 L Bettmann/Corbis; 1137 R Pathe Contemporary/ Photofest; 1138 Getty Images; 1142 Twentieth Century Fox Film Corporation/ Photofest; 1145 Musee Conde, Chantilly, France/Bridgeman Art Library, London/New York; 1146 Steve Cole/Photodisc/Getty Images; 1153 Twentieth Century Fox Film Corporation/Photofest; 1154 20th Century-Fox/Photofest; 1170 Twentieth Century Fox Film Corporation/Photofest; 1171 R Robbie Jack/ Corbis; 1171 L Alfredo Dagli Orti/The Art Archive/Corbis; 1172 Twentieth Century Fox Film Corporation/Photofest; 1174 Pocumtuck Valley Memorial Association, Memorial Hall Museum, Deerfield, Massachusetts; 1178 Twentieth Century Fox Film Corporation/Photofest; 1184 Bettmann/Corbis; 1188 Twentieth Century Fox Film Corporation/Photofest; 1198 Twentieth Century Fox Film Corporation/Photofest; 1199 R Robbie Jack/Corbis; 1199 L Archivo Iconografico, S.A./Corbis; 122 Twentieth Century Fox Film Corporation/Photofest; 124 Twentieth Century Fox Film Corporation/Photofest; 129 The Granger Collection, NYC; 1211 Twentieth Century Fox Film Corporation/Photofest; 1221 20th Century-Fox/Photofest; 1223 Micheline Pelletier/Sygma/Corbis; 1224 Twentieth Century Fox Film Corporation/Photofest; 1226 Reuters/Brad Rickerby; 1229 20th Century Fox/The Kobal Collection/Art Resource; 1234 "It's Okay-We're Hunting Communists". From "Herblock Special Report (W.W. Norton, 1974). Reprinted by permission of the Herb Block Foundation. 1238; 1240 Fred Prouser/Reuters/Corbis; 1241 Warner Independent/2929 Productions/ The Kobal Collection/Melinda Sue Gordon/Art Resource, NY; 1242 Warner Independent/2929 Productions/The Kobal Collection/Melinda Sue Gordon/Art Resource, NY; 1243 Warner Independent/2929 Productions/The Kobal Collection/Melinda Sue Gordon/Art Resource, NY; 1244 Warner Independent/2929 Productions/The Kobal Collection/Melinda Sue Gordon/Art Resource, NY; 1245 Warner Independent/2929 Productions/ The Kobal Collection/Melinda Sue Gordon/Art Resource, NY; 1246 Warner Independent/2929 Productions/The Kobal Collection/Melinda Sue Gordon/Art Resource, NY; 1247 Warner Independent/2929 Productions/The Kobal Collection/Melinda Sue Gordon/Art Resource, NY; 1248 Warner Independent/2929 Productions/The Kobal Collection/Melinda Sue Gordon/Art Resource, NY; 1259 Deborah Feingold/Corbis; 1274 TCR Time& Life Pictures/ Getty Images Inc.; 1276–1277 Louis K. Meisel, Inc./Corbis; 1278 L Pearson; 1278 B U.S. Department of Defense; 1278 CR Sophie Bassouls/Sygma/ Corbis; 1278 CL Keith Bedford/Reuters/Corbis; 1278 R Todd France/Corbis; 1278 LCL Stephen Rose/Liaison/Getty Images; 1278 T Ricky Flores/The Journal News/Corbis; 1279 T istockphoto.com; 1279 B Bob Rowan/ Progressive Image/ Corbis; 1280 R Bettmann/Corbis; 1280 L; 1281 Lrudi1976/Fotolia; 1281 R Bettmann/ Corbis; 1282 Tim Graham/Corbis; 1283 L Bettmann/Corbis; 1283 C Courtesy of International Business Machines Corporation, International Business Machines Corporation; 1283 R PhotoEdit Inc.; 1284 L Corbis; 1284 R Wally McNamee/Corbis; 1285 R AP Photo/Jeff Widener; 1285 L Peter Turnley/Corbis; 1286 C AP Photo; 1286 L Reuters/Corbis; 1286 R Reuters/Corbis; 1287 Reuters/ Corbis; 1288 L AP Photo/The Express-Times, Joe Gill 1288 T; 1288 Andrew Brookes/Corbis; 1289 Car Culture/Corbis; 1289 C Molly Riley/Reuters/Corbis; 1289 R Newscom; 1291 Pearson; 1293 Do It Yourself Landscape (detail), 1962, Andy Warhol. photo: The Andy Warhol Foundation, Inc./Art Resource, NY. ©210 Andy Warhol Foundation for the Visual Arts/ARS, New York; 1294 Daniel Cima; 1295 Leslie Hinrichs/SuperStock; 1297 Pearson; 1298 Will & Deni McIntyre/Getty Images, Inc.; 1298–1299 istockphoto.com/Teresa Hurst; 132 Catherine Karnow/Corbis; 1311 Keith Bedford/Reuters/Corbis; 1312 istockphoto.com/Maksim Sokolov; 1312 istockphoto.com; 1312 istockphoto. com/Emilia Kun; 1318 Erich Lessing/Art Resource, NY; 1325 Sophie Bassouls/ Sygma/Corbis; 1326 David Lees/Corbis; 1333 Louis K. Meisel Gallery, Inc./ Corbis; 1335 Kit Stafford; 1336–1337 Punchstock; 1338 Christopher Felver/ Corbis; 1339 Art Resource, NY; 1341 Donna Lee, courtesy of BOA Editions, Ltd.; 1342 Daniel Aeschlimann/zefa/Corbis; 1347 Shelley Rotner/Omni-Photo Communications, Inc.; 1349 Miriam Berkley/Authorpix; 1350–1351 AP Photo; 1351 istockphoto.com; 1352 James McGoon Photography; 1353–1354 istockphoto.com; 1353–1354 Christie's Images/Corbis; 1357 Stephen Rose/ Liaison/Getty Images; 1358–1359 Shutterstock; 1360 28 Bob Eckstein from cartoonbank.com.All Rights Reserved; 1362 T Library of Congress; 1362 CB AP Photo/TobyTalbot; 1362 CT Christopher Felver/Corbis; 1362 B Christopher Felver/Corbis; 1362 BCB Bettmann/Corbis; 1362 TCT Bettmann/Corbis; 1365 Miriam Berkley/Authorpix; 1366 Jack Gunter/Corbis; 1368 The Granger Collection, NYC; 1370 barneyboogles/fotolia; 1371 B istockphoto.com; 1371 T The Granger Collection, NYC; 1372 C istockphoto.com; 1372 T istockphoto. com; 1372 B Martin Cerny/Fotolia; 1373 Anna Hymas/Science Source/Photo Researchers, Inc; 1377 Alex Gotfryd/Corbis; 1378 Lichtenstein, Roy (1923–1997) ©Copyright Blam, 1962. Oil on canvas, 68 x 80 in. (172.7 x 23.2 cm). Gift of Richard Brown Baker, B.A. 1935. 1995.32.9. Yale University Art Gallery/ Art Resource, NY; 1383 James Keyser/Time & Life Pictures/Getty Images; 1384 Warner Bros./Photofest; 1385 Warner Bros./Photofest; 1387 Warner Bros./ Photofest; 1388 Warner Bros./Photofest; 1393 AP Photo/STR; 1394 David Butow/ CORBIS SABA; 1395 R US Navy Photo/Alamy; 1395 L vario images GmbH & Co.KG/Alamy; 1395 C Reuters/CORBIS; 1396 istockphoto.com; 140 T Delta Hunter; 140 B William Harvey; 141 Michel Setboun/CORBIS; 142 Peter Turnley/ Corbis; 143 istockphoto.com/Tomaz Levstek; 144 Peter Turnley/Corbis; 147 James Leynse/Corbis; 149 Todd France/Corbis; 1410 istockphoto.com; 1410 Jim McHugh; 1412 Andrew Gunners/Photodisc/Getty Images; 1415 Rudy Sulgan/Corbis; 1416 Andrew Gunners/Photodisc/Getty Images; 1417 Tim Wright/Corbis; 1418 Morning, 24 (oil on linen), Clarke, Daniel (Contemporary Artist)/Private Collection/The Bridgeman Art Library; 1425 Doug Menuez/ Corbis; 1426 Redchopsticks/Photolibrary; 1430–1431 Matt Lambert/Stone/Getty Images; 1433 RCR Sophie Bassouls/Sygma/Corbis; 1433 Sophie Bassouls/ Sygma/Corbis; 1434 istockphoto.com; 1435 istockphoto.com; 1437 Museo de Santa Cruz/Bridgeman Art Library, London/New York; 1446 TL istockphoto. com; 1446 TR istockphoto.com; 1451 Daniel Cima

Staff Credits

Dori Amtmann, Tricia Battipede, Rachel Beckman, Nancy Bolsover, Laura Brancky, Odette Calderon, Pam Carey, Kelly Casanova, Geoff Cassar, Jessica Cohn, Kyle Cooper, Sarah Cunningham, Anthony DeSacia, Kim Doster, Irene Ehrmann, Andy Ekedahl, Sandy Engleman, Samantha Fahy, Janet Fauser, Amy Fleming, Pam Gallo, Mark Gangi, Nicole Gee, Susan Graef, Leslie Griffin, Elaine Goldman, Brian Hawkes, Steve Hernacki, Martha Heller, Amanda House, Rick Hickox, Patricia Isaza, Etta Jacobs, Blair Jones, Jim Kelly, Nathan Kinney, Sarah Kraus, Gregory Lynch, Nancy Mace, Jim McPherson, Charles Morris, Pa Moua, Elizabeth Nielsen, Kim Ortell, Kathleen Pagliaro, Jennie Rakos, Sheila Nealon Ramsay, Karen Randazzo, Julianne Regnier, Christopher Richardson, Melissa Schreiner, Hillary Schwei, Jeff Shagawat, Susan Sheehan, Charlene Smith, DeAnn Smith, Sheila Smith, Cynthia Summers, Morgan Taylor, Brian Thomas, Lucia Tirondola, Karen Tully, Merle Uuesoo, Kristen Varina, Jackie Westbrook, Jessica White

70235001197240